MANAGEMENT ACCOUNTING

Text, Problems and Cases

Seventh Edition

MANAGEMENT ACCOUNTING

Text, Problems and Cases

Seventh Edition

M Y KHAN

Formerly Professor of Finance and
Dean, Faculty of Business and
Head, Department of Financial Studies
University of Delhi
Delhi

P K JAIN

Emeritus Professor of Finance
Department of Management Studies
Indian Institute of Technology Delhi

McGraw Hill Education (India) Private Limited

Published by McGraw Hill Education (India) Private Limited,
444/1, Sri Ekambara Naicker Industrial Estate, Alapakkam, Porur, Chennai 600116, Tamil Nadu, India.

Management Accounting: Text, Problems and Cases, 7/e

Second reprint 2019
RQQZCDDTDCLQR

Print Edition
ISBN (13 digits): 978-93-5260-678-8
ISBN (10 digits): 93-5260-678-7

E-Book Edition
ISBN (13 digits): 978-93-5260-687-0
ISBN (10 digits): 93-5260-687-6

03 04 05 06 07 RAJ 23 22 21 20 19

Managing Director: *Lalit Singh*
Senior Portfolio Manager: *Nikhil Wadhera*
Portfolio Manager: *Shivkant Singhal*
Senior Manager: Content Development & Production Services: *Shalini Jha*
Head—Production Services: *Satinder S Baveja*
Assistant Manager—Production: *Atul Gupta*
General Manager—Production: *Rajender P Ghansela*
Manager—Production: *Reji Kumar*

Typeset at The Composers, 260, C.A Apt., Paschim Vihar, New Delhi 110063, and,
Printed and Bound in India at Rajkamal Electric Press, Plot No. 2, Phase – IV, Kundli, Sonepat, Haryana.

Visit us at: www.mheducation.co.in ; (Toll free in India): **1800 103 5875**
Write to us at: info.india@mheducation.com

CIN: U80302TN2010PTC111532

Preface to the Seventh Edition

We are pleased to place in the hands of the readers this thoroughly revised edition of our highly successful reference-cum-textbook **MANAGEMENT ACCOUNTING: Text, Problems and Cases.** The main focus continues to be on providing to the readers an in-depth analysis of how to use accounting information for financial analysis, profit planning, cost control and decision-making. It is primarily designed for teachers and students of management and finance. It should also be useful to students and teachers of commerce and accounting and related professional disciplines. Practitioners in these fields would also find it useful.

Changes in the Seventh Edition

Apart from updating the contents of various chapters, the outstanding features of the revised edition are the inclusion of:

Chapter 2: Completely rewritten incorporating Indian Accounting Standards, 2016 in place of the existing Accounting Standards.

Chapter 4: Updated Indian Accounting Standards relevant to the preparation of Corporate Reports.

Chapter 5: Updated (2015-16) Cash Flow Statement of Reliance Industries Ltd.

Chapter 6: (i) Updated (2015-16) Financial Statement Analysis of Reliance Industries Ltd.
(ii) Inclusion of two cases (a) Tata Motors Ltd. and (b) ITC Limited on Ratio Analysis.

Chapter 7: Inclusion of Appendix 7A on Cost Ascertainment/Product Costing.

Chapter 19: Addition of a case on Material Cost Variance.

Chapter 24: Inclusion of Appendix 24A on Time Value of Money.

Pedagogical Features

In addition to the time tested pedagogical features in terms of organisation, solved problems, review questions and support items, the new edition retains the new features of the sixth edition listed below:

Learning Objectives Each chapter begins with a number of learning objectives to ensure broad understanding of the concepts, theories and techniques of management accounting.

Margin Notes Throughout the text, margin notes in side bars define the important concepts and key terms when they are first introduced. They would enable the readers to re-inforce their learning.

Rearrangement of Solved Problems / Review Questions have been rearranged in order of level of difficulty, namely, easy, medium and difficult.

Comprehensive Summaries Chapter-end comprehensive summaries would provide a bird's eye view of the main points by way of recapitulation.

Cases Yet another distinct feature is the inclusion of numerous additional cases to portray the emerging managerial accounting practices in the country. The chapter-end cases can be used by the readers to synthesise and apply related concepts, theories and techniques.

Solution Manual The revised edition continues to have the solution manual on the accompanying website: **(http://www.mhhe.com/khan_jain_ma7e)** covering all the chapter-end numerical review questions in the text.

Financial Tables and Bibliography A set of financial tables is included as a ready reckoner. A select bibliography should be of special interest to teachers/senior-level students of the subject.

Acknowledgements

We would like to express our intellectual debt of gratitude to the numerous authors who have enriched the stream of literature in management accounting on which we have liberally drawn. Some of the more specific references are indicated in the text itself. The authors also record a word of appreciation for Professor Surendra S Yadav's contribution.

We have a word of appreciation for the excellent support from Ms Laxmi Singh and Mr Atul Gupta of McGraw-Hill Education for the speedy and excellent publication of the book.

M Y KHAN
P K JAIN

Preface to the First Edition

Management Accounting is a complementary volume to our earlier work, *Financial Management.* It addresses itself to the use of accounting information for planning, control and decision-making. Management accounting, as a system of accounting, focuses on *how to use* as distinct from *how to prepare* accounts of business firms. The *use* of the information contained in the accounts of business enterprises can be made by outsiders such as creditors, shareholders, prospective investors, government, and so on for decision-making regarding a firm. Such information can also be used for decision-making by a firm itself. Thus, the uses to which accounting information can be put may be either *external* or *internal.* The present volume describes in depth both types of *uses* of accounting information.

A distinct feature of this book is that it provides a penetrating and comprehensive analysis of the concepts, theories and techniques in a simple, lucid style in the framework of the Indian business environment. It also contains a variety of real-life solved problems/illustrations to explain the intricacies of the theories/concepts/techniques. Yet another feature of this book is that it contains a comprehensive list of problems/exercises at the end of each chapter to help the readers test their understanding of the subject. A fairly exhaustive bibliography is also given at the end of the book.

Management Accounting, we hope, will be found useful by a wide section of readers, particularly teachers and advanced students of Commerce, Business Management, Chartered and Cost Accountancy. Those appearing in the civil services examination and the examination conducted by the Indian Institute of Bankers would also find it a satisfying text. Practising accountants/managers would find it no less useful.

The subject matter of this volume is woven round the application of accounting information for decision-making both *about* a firm as well as *by* a firm. It is divided into six parts consisting of 19 chapters.

Part I consists of one chapter which presents an overview of management accounting in terms of its relationship with financial accounting—the second element of the accounting system of a business firm—and the main contents of management accounting information. This obviously serves as a background to the detailed discussions in chapters that follow.

Parts II, comprising 3 chapters, relates to decision-making *about* a firm by outside parties. Chapter 5 provides an insight into the nature and type of information contained in the two conventional financial statements, namely the balance sheet and the profit and loss account (income statement). The main elements of the third financial statement, i.e., statement of changes in financial position are covered in Chapter 6. Chapters 5 and 6 are very useful and important in analysing the financial statements for decision-making purposes. It is against this background that Chapter 6 dwells on the analysis and interpretation of the financial statements.

The preparation of the conventional financial statements involves certain problems in terms of policy alternatives to management. Part II is concerned with three such policy issues. The first aspect relates to the alternative methods and pricing of inventory which is examined in Chapter 2. Chapter 3 addresses itself to the choice of an appropriate method of depreciation of fixed assets. Price level adjusted financial statements is the theme of Chapter 4.

Parts IV through VI deal with decision-making *by* a firm. Budgeting, as tool of profit planning and control, is explained in Part IV. The first chapter of this part (Chapter 8) provides an overview of budgeting and illustrates the operating and financial budgets.

Long-term budgeting is elaborated upon in Chapters 9 and 10. While Chapter 9 deals with the generation of data, Chapter 10 outlines the methods/techniques for capital budgeting.

Part V consists of seven chapters. The theme of this section is the use of cost data for planning and control. Chapter 11 highlights the different types of cost data as related to varying managerial needs. The subsequent chapters of this section dwell on the various techniques relevant to cost/profit planning and control (Chapter 12); standard costs (Chapter 13); variance analysis (Chapters 14 and 15); variable costing and absorption costing (Chapter 16); and cost-volume-profit analysis (Chapter 17).

Finally, the two chapters of Part VI cover the special short-term non-recurring decisions. While Chapter 18 relates to pricing and product decisions, Chapter 19 illustrates resource decisions.

In the preparation of this book we have received help and encouragement from different sources. In particular, Mr H C Jain, Librarian, Delhi University South Campus Library deserves our gratitude for the prompt and generous help in supplying the books and journals but for which our efforts would not have succeeded.

Professor Abad Ahmed, Director, Delhi University South Campus, has been a source of constant encouragement and help. Our colleagues Prof. R S Nigam, Head of the Department of Commerce, Delhi School of Economics, Delhi University, Prof. L S Porwal, Prof. P K Ghosh, Dr H M Mathur, Principal, Shri Ram Collage of Commerce, University of Delhi, Dr R N Goyale, Dr R A Sharma have assisted us in several ways.

We also thank the Yarmouk University, Jordan particularly, Dr. Hisham Gharaibeh, Dean, Faculty of Economics and Administrative Sciences, where a part of the book was written.

We would be failing in our duty if we did not put on record our deep sense of obligation to our families who provided an environment conductive to hardwork. Finally, Mr P L Kadalbaju, Deputy Registrar, Delhi University South Campus, deserves our thanks for the diverse assistance he provided.

Complete solutions to all exercises given at the end of various chapters of this book is available in the authors book entitled *Management Accounting and Financial Management—Problems and solutions.*

M Y KHAN
P K JAIN

Contents

PART 4
COST ACCUMULATION

PART 6
COST CONTROL

PART 1

BACKGROUND

This part dwells on the nature of management accounting. It describes the relationship between financial accounting, cost accounting and management accounting. The uses of management accounting information are also discussed here. These discussions form a background for a detailed account of management accounting in the subsequent parts of this book.

Nature of Management Accounting

1

LEARNING OBJECTIVES

After reading this chapter you will be able to:

LO 1.1 Identify management accounting information
LO 1.2 Understand the functions of controller vis-a-vis treasurer
LO 1.3 Compare management accounting information with information used for financial reporting/accounting
LO 1.4 Show the relationship between cost accounting and management accounting
LO 1.5 Describe the main uses of management accounting information
LO 1.6 Summarize overall contents of the book

INTRODUCTION

LO 1.1 Identify management accounting information

This chapter focuses on the nature of management accounting information. It compares and contrasts management accounting information with information used for financial reporting/accounting. It also compares management accounting information with cost accountancy information. The main uses of management accounting information are also described in the chapter. The main points are summarised by way of recapitulation.

Accounting is the process of identifying, measuring and communicating information to permit informed judgements and decisions by users of information.

Accounting is the process of identifying, measuring and communicating economic information to permit informed judgements and decisions by users of information. The business accounting system consists of three parts: **(i)** Financial accounting, **(ii)** Cost accounting and **(iii)** Management accounting. The accounting information specifically prepared to aid managers is called **management accounting information**. This information is used in three managerial functions: **(i)** planning, **(ii)** implementation and **(iii)** control.

Management accounting information is the accounting information specifically prepared to aid managers.

Planning is the process of deciding what action should be taken in the future.

Planning is the process of deciding what action should be taken in the future. A plan may be made for any segment or for the organisation as a whole. An important form of planning is **budgeting**. Budgeting is the process of planning the overall activities of an organisation for a specified period of time, usually an year. The primary objective of budgeting is to coordinate the separate plans for various segments of the organisation so as to harmonise them with one another. Planning involves making decisions. Accounting information is useful in analysing the consequences of each alternative in the decision-making process.

Budgeting is the process of planning the overall activities of an organisation for a year.

Implementation involves specific actions planned in advance to fulfill the budgets. It requires supervision on the part of the managers. A key managerial responsibility is to change previous plans appropriately to adjust for new conditions.

Implementation involves specific actions planned in advance to fulfil the budgets.

Control is the process to ensure that employees perform properly. Accounting information is used in the control process as a means for communication, motivation, getting attention and for appraisal.

Control is the process to ensure that employees perform properly.

The information that managers use is quite varied. Operating information provides most of the raw data for management accounting but much of this information is not of direct interest to managers. The manager is interested in summarises drawn from the detail records rather than in the underlying details. Therefore, management accounting information is **summary** information.[1]

FUNCTIONS OF CONTROLLER VIS-A-VIS TREASURER

LO 1.2 Understand the functions of controller vis-a-vis treasurer

Management accountants are responsible for the design and operation of the management accounting system.

The members of an organisation who are responsible for the design and operation of the management accounting system are called **management accountants**. The highest level management accountant is called the **controller.** He typically reports to the chief financial offer (CFO) who in turn reports to the chief executive officer/managing director. The role and status of management accountants have increased in recent years. Once viewed primarily as cost accountants, controllers have become key members of the top management and some have become even members of the Board of Directors of large Indian companies. The organisation of a controllers' department is depicted in Exhibit 1.2.

Controller is the highest level management accountant.

The distinction between the functions of corporate controllers and treasurers are depicted in Exhibit 1.1.[2]

EXHIBIT 1.1 Distinction between Controller and Treasurer

Controllership	*Treasurership*
1 Planning for control	1 Provision of capital
2 Reporting and interpreting	2 Investor relations
3 Evaluating and consulting	3 Short-term financing
4 Tax administration	4 Banking and custody
5 Government reporting	5 Credits and collections
6 Protection of assets	6 Investments
7 Economic appraisal	7 Risk management

Exhibit 1.2 Organisation Chart of a Controller's Department

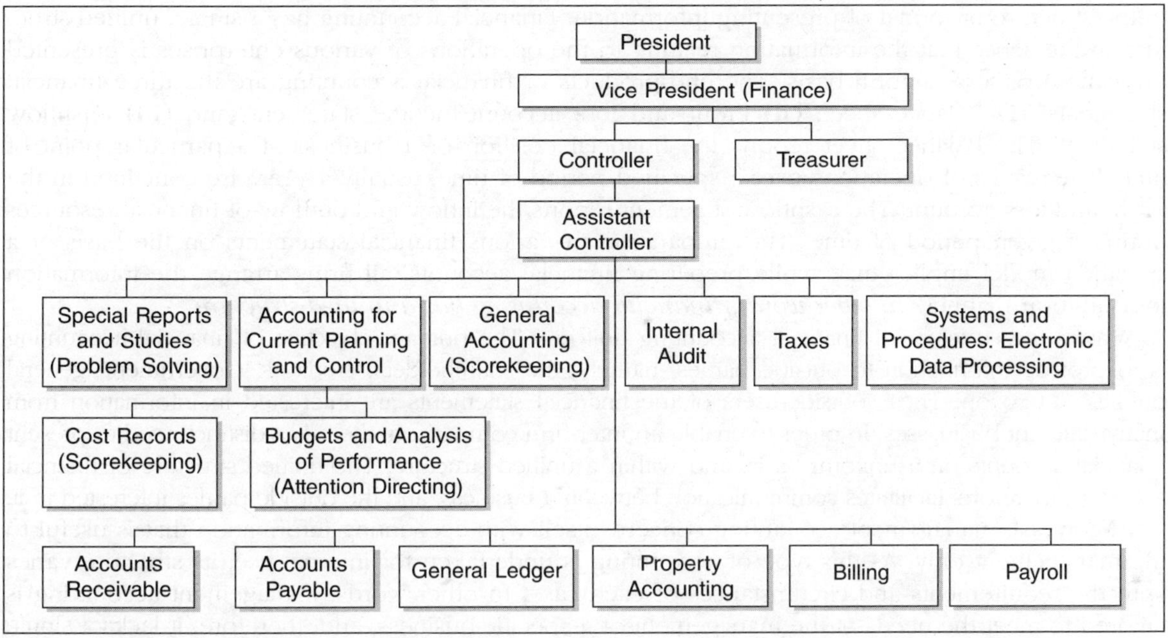

Management Accounting and Financial Accounting

Management accounting differs in several ways from financial accounting/reporting process. There are also some important similarities between financial and management accounting.

LO 1.3 Compare management accounting information with information used for financial reporting/accounting

Differences The important differences between management accounting and financial accounting/reporting are summarised in Exhibit 1.3.

Exhibit 1.3 Management Accounting vs. Financial Accounting

Dimension	*Management Accounting*	*Financial Accounting*
1 Structure	Varies according to use of the information	Unified structure
2 Sources of principles	Whatever is useful to management	Generally accepted accounting principles (GAAPs)
3 Need	Optional	Statutory obligation
4 Time-orientation	Historical and estimates of the future	Historical
5 Report entity	Responsibility centers	Overall organisation
6 Purpose	A means to the end of assisting management	External reporting/ statements for outside users
7 Users[3]	Relatively small group: known identity	Relatively large group: mostly unknown
8 Information content[3]	Monetary and non-monetary	Primarily monetary
9 Information precision[3]	Many approximations	Few approximations
10 Report frequency[3]	Varies with purpose; monthly and weekly common	Quarterly and annual
11 Report timeliness[3]	Reports issued promptly after end of period covered	Delay of weeks or even months
12 liability potential[3]	Virtually none	Few lawsuits but threat is always present

Structure One basic difference between financial accounting and management accounting relates to the structure or format of presenting information. Financial accounting has a single, unified structure in the sense that the information relating to the operations of various enterprises is presented on a more or less uniform basis. The end-products of financial accounting are the three financial statements: **(i)** Balance sheet, **(ii)** Profit and loss account/Income statement, and **(iii)** Cashflow statement. The balance sheet reports the financial position of a business at a particular point of time. The results of operations over a specified period of time, usually a year, are contained in the profit and loss account. The cashflow statement reports the inflow and outflow of financial resources during a given period of time. The preparation of various financial statements on the basis of a specified model implies that, while preparing financial accounts, all firms arrange the information in a uniform manner. *In other words, financial accounting has a unified structure.*

Why is the structure of financial accounting uniform? The primary objective of financial accounting is to provide information to outside parties, namely, the shareholders, creditors, Government, general public, and so on. These outside-users of the financial statements are interested in information from many different businesses. In order to enable an inter-firm comparison, there is a distinct need to present financial accounts on a uniform basis, and within a unified structure. The unified structure of financial accounts, therefore, facilitates communication between a business, and the outside parties interested in it.

In contrast, management accounting concerns itself with accounting information that is useful to the management only. As this type of accounting is undertaken for internal use, its structure varies with the requirements and circumstances of each case. In other words, management accounting is tailored to meet the needs of the management of a specific business, and, therefore, it lacks a single unified structure.

Sources of Principles A related aspect is the impact of the **GAAPs** (Generally Accepted Accounting Principles) on the preparation of the two types of accounting. Financial accounting is prepared in accordance with the **GAAPs**. Accounting is the 'language of business' as it is the principal means by which information about a business is communicated to those interested in it. If, therefore, the information is to be communicated effectively and understood properly, it should be prepared in accordance with a mutually understood set of rules. These ground rules are referred to as **GAAPs**. They represent laws or rules to be used as a guideline in the preparation of financial accounts. In other words, **GAAPs** provide a specified framework for the preparation of financial accounts which have evolved over the years and are based on experience, reason, usage, convention and necessity. Thus, **GAAPs** ensure that financial accounts are prepared in accordance with certain norms and standards for better comprehension and reliability. On the other hand, management accounting is for the exclusive use of the management of a firm. Outsiders do not need such accounts and have no access to them. Therefore, there is scope for flexibility in their preparation. They can be tailored to the specified needs of the management. The criteria for inclusion of any information in management accounting is ***utility***. In short, financial accounting, which essentially caters to the needs of outsiders, is prepared according to the norms set by the **GAAPs**, whereas management accounting, as an aid to managerial decision-making, is dependent on, and largely influenced by, the internal requirements of the management.

> **GAAPs** represent laws/rules to be used as a guideline in the preparation of the financial statements.

Need Another difference between financial accounting and management accounting relates to the need for preparing such accounts. The preparation of financial accounts is a **statutory obligation**. In fact, the corporate laws and regulations that govern the functioning of corporate enterprises not only make it mandatory to prepare such accounts but also lay the model/format in which such accounts are to be prepared. Corporate laws also prescribe independent audit by professional auditors to ensure that the accounts reflect *a true and fair view* of the firm's affairs. Apart from this, tax regulations also require the maintenance of records by business establishments. In sharp contrast, management accounting is entirely ***optional***. It is prepared only if it is deemed useful to the management. There are no external compulsions for its preparation. The format, as also the items to be included, are exclusively dependent on the management's discretion.

Time Orientation The end-products of financial accounting are the three financial statements, namely, the balance sheet, profit and loss account, and cashflow statement. These are essentially records of what has happened in the past. Therefore, these are aptly called ***historical accounts***. On the other hand, management accounting does not record the financial history of an enterprise. Though past data is included in management accounting, a major part of its contents is related to the future plans. It is, therefore, ***future-oriented***. It aims at providing data for budgeting, planning, and so on. Thus, management accounting lays more emphasis on the future.

Report Entity Financial accounting relates to the business as a ***whole***. While there is no doubt that some firms prepare financial accounts on a segmented basis for the main lines of business, the fact remains that, the emphasis is on the entire business. Management accounting focuses on ***parts*** of the business. In management accounting, the business is divided into different responsibility centres—cost, profit and investment. The term **responsibility centre** refers to the division of an enterprise into sections, departments, products, individual activities, and so on. In brief, financial accounting deals with the business as a whole, whereas management accounting focuses on its different parts.

Responsibility centre refers to the division of an enterprise into sections, departments, products, individual activities, and so on.

Purpose Financial accounting and management accounting also differ in relation to their ultimate objectives. Financial accounting is prepared to serve the purpose of external reporting. Therefore, from the viewpoint of the management, the purpose of financial accounting is accomplished when it is reflected in the three financial statements, that is, the balance sheet, profit and loss account and cashflow statement. In a way, it is an *end* in itself whereas management accounting is only a *means to an end.* In other words, management accounting is designed to serve as an aid to managerial decision making. With the help of management accounting, the management can discharge its planning, directing and controlling functions. In planning, the manger decides what actions should be taken to help the *organisation achieve its goals.* In directing, the manager oversees the conduct of *day-to-day* operations. And in controlling, steps are taken to ensure that the responsibility centers are operating in the best possible manner.

Users The users of financial accounting information (other than management itself) often are essentially a faceless group. The managers of most companies do not personally know many shareholders, creditors, or others who use the information in the financial statements. Moreover, the information needs of most of these external users must be presumed; most external users do not individually request the information they would like to receive. By contrast, the users of management accounting information are known managers plus the people who help these managers analyse the information. Internal users' information needs are relatively well known because the controller's office solicits these needs in designing or revising the management accounting system.

Information Content Financial accounting systems capture only a few characteristics (i.e., date, account, and amount) about only a subset of organisational events, those defined by financial accountants to be "**accounting transactions**." Financial accounting reports summarise the effects of these events in primarily monetary form. Management accounting reports, on the other hand, summarise many different kinds of information that is useful for decision-makers. They include nonmonetary as well as monetary information. They show quantities of material as well as monetary cost, number of employees and hours worked as well as labour costs, units of products sold as well as the amounts of revenue, defect rates as well as scrap costs, and so on. Some of the information is strictly nonmonetary; examples include new product development times, production yields, percentage of shipments made on time, product failure rates, numbers of customer complaints received, and competitors' estimated market shares.

Information Precision Management needs information rapidly and is often willing to sacrifice some precision to gain speed in reporting. Thus, in management accounting approximations are often as useful as, or even more useful than, numbers that are more precise. Although financial accounting cannot be absolutely precise either, the approximations used in management accounting are broader than those in financial accounting.

Report Frequency Corporates issue detailed financial statements only annually and less detailed interim reports quarterly. By contrast, fairly detailed management accounting reports are issued monthly in most larger organisations, and reports on certain activities may be prepared weekly, daily, or even more frequently. Some management accounting information must even be constantly updated and made available to managers on an instant access (real-time) basis.

Report Timeliness Because of the need for precision and a review by outside auditors, plus the time requirements of printing and distribution, financial accounting reports are distributed several weeks after the close of the accounting period. Larger corporates' annual reports for a fiscal year ending March 31 are often not received by shareholders until June or July. By contrast, because management accounting reports may contain information on which management needs to take prompt action, these reports are usually issued within a few days of the end of the month (or the next morning for a daily report).

Liability Potential Although it happens infrequently, a company may be sued by its shareholders or creditors for allegedly reporting misleading financial information in its annual report. By contrast, as previously stated, management accounting reports need not be in accord with **GAAP** and are not public documents. Although a manager may be held liable for some illegal or unethical action and management accounting information conceivably may have played some role in his or her taking that action, it is the action itself, not the management accounting documents, that gives rise to the liability.

Similarities Some important similarities between financial and management accounting do exist. Most elements of financial accounting are also found in management accounting. There are two reasons for this. First, the same considerations that make **GAAP** sensible for purposes of financial accounting are likely to be relevant for purposes of management accounting. For example, management cannot base its reporting system on unverifiable, subjective estimates of profits submitted by lower echelons; for the same reason, financial accounting adheres to the cost and realisation concepts.

Second, summaries of the documents or computer records of operating results, such as of orders placed, filled and shipped, customer billings, warranties made, customer payments received, invoices received, cheques written, labour used, amounts borrowed, and payments due and made on borrowings, provide much of the raw material used in both financial reporting and management accounting. There is a presumption, therefore, that the basic data will be collected in accordance with generally accepted financial accounting principles. To do otherwise would require duplication of data collection activities.

Perhaps the most important similarity between financial and management accounting information is that both are used in decision making. Financial accounting information assists investors in evaluating companies' prospects so that decisions can be made about supplying debt or equity funds to these companies. Management accounting information is used in a wider array of decisions made by managers, including (but by no means limited to) decision about product pricing, raw material sourcing, personnel staffing, investing in long-lived assets, and evaluating performances of individual entities and managers.[4]

COST AND MANAGEMENT ACCOUNTING

LO 1.4 Show the relationship between cost accounting and management accounting

Cost accounting is that branch of the accounting information system, which records, measures and reports information about costs. A cost is a ***sacrifice of resources***. Costs are reflected in the accounting system by outlays of cash, promises to pay cash at a future date, and the expiration of the value of an asset. The primary purpose of cost accounting is cost ascertainment and its use in decision-making and performance evaluation. A cost accounting system provides data for both financial accounting and management accounting. When costs are used by outsiders, such as shareholders or creditors, to evaluate the performance of the management and make investment decisions, they are said to be used for financial accounting purposes. On the other hand, when cost data are used inside the organisation to evaluate the performance of operations, activities, personnel, and so on, as the basis of decision-making, they are said to be used for management accounting purposes. For instance, in a manufacturing business, the costs of products sold, and on hand, include the total expenditure on materials, labour and all the other production costs. Each of these costs must first be measured, then accumulated, and finally, distributed to the work-in-process, finished goods and cost of goods sold. Consequently, the amount of profit reported by a manufacturing company depends on the *accuracy of it cost calculations.* Thus, cost accounting is useful for performance appraisal.

Cost accounting is that branch of accounting information system which records, measures and reports information about costs.

Cost is a sacrifice of resources.

Cost accounting also helps in planning. Planning is a process of setting goals and allocating resources to achieve these goals. The expected financial outcome of planning is expressed in terms of budgets. A firm can increase its profits in two ways: **(i)** by increasing unit sale price/sales volume and **(ii)** by reducing costs.

While the first cannot always be under the control of the management, the second falls well within the managerial domain. A detailed cost accounting system is an important requirement for a systematic cost control. For this reason, the management must understand the nature and behaviour of different elements of cost, know when and where they are incurred and who is responsible for them. The actual cost should be compared with the planned estimates. The differences between these should be analysed to identify the reasons for deviations, and corrective action should be taken to eliminate them. Thus, cost accounting is very useful to management for profit planning.

Cost accounting is also useful for the purpose of control. **Control** comprises managerial action to correct conditions that cause deviation between the actual and planned performance. Comparison between the actual and budgeted cost will highlight a poor or good performance, as well as the operations that have gone out of control and warrant corrective action. Thus, cost accounting provides the basis for managerial control.

Control comprises managerial action to correct conditions that cause deviation between the actual and planned performance.

MAIN USES OF MANAGEMENT ACCOUNTING INFORMATION

LO 1.5 Describe the main uses of management accounting information

While outlining the differences between financial accounting and management accounting, it was pointed out that management accounting does not have a unified structure.

The format in which it is prepared varies widely according to the circumstances in reach case and the purpose for which the information is being summarised. The information in the management accounting system is used for three different purposes: **(i)** measurement, **(ii)** control and **(iii)** decision-making (alternative choice problems). For each of the three management accounting purposes, there is a set of principles and generalisations applicable to the use of information for that purpose but not necessarily for other purposes. The uses of information for each of the three purposes of management accounting is summarised in Exhibit 1.4.

EXHIBIT 1.4 Purposes and Uses of Management Accounting Information[5]

Purposes	*Uses* — *Historical data*	*Uses* — *Future estimates*
1. Measurement	Basis for external reporting Analysing economic performance Cost-plus contract payments	Normal pricing decisions
2. Control	Analysing managerial performance	Strategic planning Budgeting
3. Alternative choices	None	Capital budgeting Short-run decisions

Measurement

> **Full cost accounting** measures the resources used in performing some activity. It is the sum of direct and indirect costs.

> **Direct costs** are costs directly traced to goods/services.

> **Indirect costs** are a fair share of costs incurred jointly in producing goods/services.

For the measurement purpose the management accounting system focuses on the measurement of ***full costs***. Full cost accounting measures the resources used in performing some activity. The full cost of producing goods or providing services is the sum of **(1)** the costs directly traced to the goods or services, called **direct costs**, plus **(2)** a fair share of costs incurred jointly in producing these and other goods or services, called **indirect costs**. Full cost accounting measures not only the direct and indirect costs of producing goods or providing services but also the direct and indirect costs of any other activity of interest to management, such performing a research project or operating an employees cafeteria. Thus, full cost accounting is not restricted solely to measuring the costs of manufactured goods.

To illustrate full costing, assume that the direct cost of manufacturing an item of machinery is ₹5,00,000. And the indirect cost associated with it is ₹1,00,000. Assuming a 10 per cent profit, the full cost and sole price of the machine would be ₹6,00,000 and ₹6,60,000 respectively. Historical full costs are used in financial reporting/ accounting. **We have discussed this use, particularly in Chapters 2-3** which gives the journal entries that accumulated materials costs, direct labour costs, and other production costs for good as these goods moved through the production process.

In many sales contracts the buyer agrees to pay the seller the cost of the goods produced or of the services rendered, plus a profit margin. Cost, in this context, usually means full cost. Similarly, in deciding what price to charge for its goods or services, a company often uses estimates of full costs plus a profit margin as a guide.

Finally, estimates of full costs are used in some types of planning activities, particularly in the type of long-range planning called *strategic planning*.

In Chapters 7–15 we describe the measurement of full cost information and its uses.

Control

> **Responsibility centre** is an organisation unit headed by a manager who is responsible for its operations and performance.

The management accounting system is structured so that it measures costs by responsibility centers. **A responsibility center is an organisation unit headed by a manager who is responsible for its operations and performance**. Such a structure is necessary because control can be exercised only through people.

Estimates of future responsibility costs are used in the planning process, particularly in the annual planning process called budgeting. Historical records of actual costs incurred in responsibility centers are used in reporting and analysing their performance. Such reports are useful because they are aligned with the organisational structure of managers who are responsible for performance. Corrective action can be taken only by individuals; so if performance is unsatisfactory, the person responsible must be identified before corrective action can be taken.

A simplified view of the responsibility accounting is given in Table 1.1.

TABLE 1.1 Responsibility Accounting

(Amount in ₹ lakh)

Product	*Responsibility (Expense) Centres*					
	X			Y		
	Budget	*Actual*	*Difference*	*Budget*	*Actual*	*Difference*
(1)	*(2)*	*(3)*	*(4)*	*(5)*	*(6)*	*(7)*
A	₹1,000	₹1,100	₹(100)	₹500	₹450	₹50
B	500	600	(100)	300	280	20
C	1,500	1,700	(200)	200	190	10
Total cost by responsibility centres	3,000	3,400	(400)	1,000	920	80

Chapters 16–22 describe the uses of cost information structured by responsibility centres.

Alternative Choice Decisions

Many decisions involve the comparison of the estimated costs to be incurred (and also the revenues to be realised and/or assets to be employed) for each of the alternatives being considered. This information cannot be obtained directly from the management accounting system because the relevant costs are specific to the alternatives being considered.

These costs are always estimates of future costs. As with estimates of all types, they are sometimes derived from historical cost records. Because these estimates describe how costs would be different in the alternative being considered, they are often called **differential costs**.

> **Differential costs** are costs which would be different in the alternatives being considered.

To illustrate differential accounting, assume that the management of a firm is considering the acquisition of a component to be used in its final product. The firm has a choice between buying it from an outside supplier, or producing it. Assume the price at which the component can be purchased, ₹5 per unit and let its annual requirement be 10,000 units. The cost of manufacturing 10,000 units by the firm is calculated as follows: material cost, ₹2 per unit; direct labour cost, Re 1 per unit and additional fixed cost, ₹10,000; thus, total cost amounts to ₹40,000. Since the total cost involved in buying the component is ₹50,000 (10,000 units x ₹5), the differential cost is ₹10,000. Obviously, it is preferable to make the component rather than buy it.

Many alternative choice decisions involve short-run problems that relate only to a specific part of the business. For these decisions only estimated direct costs are relevant. These problems are described in Chapter 23. Other decisions are longer range and involve the whole business or a major segment of it. For these decisions full costs are relevant. They are discussed in Chapter 24.

An Overview of the Book

This book addresses itself to the use of accounting information for planning, control and decision-making. It focuses on **how to use** as distinct from **how to prepare** accounts of a business firm. The use of the information contained in the accounts of business enterprises is made by **outsiders** such as creditors, shareholders, prospective investors, government and so on. Such information is also used for decision-making by the **firm itself**. The book describes in depth both the **external** (by outsiders) and **internal** (by management) uses of accounting information. It provides a comprehensive analysis of the concepts, theories and techniques of management accounting in the framework of indian business environment/practices. Each chapter begins with a number of **learning objectives** to ensure broad understanding of the theories, concepts and techniques. Throughout the text, the **margin notes/margin glossary** in shaded sidebars define the important concepts and key terms when they are first introduced. They would enable the readers to reinforce their learning. At the end of each chapter, there are **chapter summaries**, **review questions**, **solved problems** and **self-test problems** that can be used to test the readers understanding of the subject. The **chapter-end cases** can be used to synthesise and apply related concepts and techniques. The theme of the book is described in seven separate but related parts and 24 chapters which are briefly outlined below.

Part 1 BACKGROUND **Chapter 1** outlines the nature of management accounting. It compares and contrasts management accounting information with formation used for financial accounting and cost accounting purposes. It also describes the main uses of management accounting information.

Part 2 FINANCIAL ACCOUNTING **Chapter 2** describes the basic accounting concepts, principles and the accounting standards issued by the Institute of Chartered Accountants of India (ICAI) which have a bearing on the preparation and presentation of financial statements. The chapter also contains the present status of International Financial Reporting Standards (IFRS) in India. **Chapter 3** dwells on the accounting cycle and preparation of financial statements. The preparation and presentation of financial statements and reports by indian companies is illustrated in **Chapter 4**.

Part 3 FINANCIAL ANALYSIS **Chapter 5** explains preparation and analysis of cashflows statements and focuses on the as-3: cashflow statement issued by the icai. The technique of analysing and interpreting balance sheet and income statement is covered in **Chapter 6**.

Part 4 COST ACCUMULATION **Chapter 7** treats the cost concepts in relation to managerial needs. **Chapters 8-11** describe cost elements of material, labour, factory overheads and selling, distribution and administrative overheads respectively. **Chapter 12** analyses activity-based costing system. **Chapters 13-14** discuss the cost accumulation process in job-order, batch and service costing, and process, by-product and joint costing respectively. The income determination in full costing and variable costing is shown in **Chapter 15**.

Part 5 PROFIT PLANNING The volume-cost-profit analysis is presented in **Chapter 16** and **Chapter 17** explains the various tools of budgeting.

Part 6 COST CONTROL The discussions in **Chapter 18** relate to standard costs and quality costs. **Chapters 19-20** discuss cost efficiencies/control through standard costs in terms of variance analysis. While **Chapter 19** deals with cost variances analysis, **Chapter 20** analyses profit and revenue variances. Responsibility accounting as a measure of divisional performance, is examined in **Chapter 21**. Balanced scorecard as a measure of performance has been explained in Chapter 22.

Part 7 DECISION-MAKING Short-term decisions relating to pricing and product are discussed in **Chapter 23**. **Chapter 24** covers long-term decision-making.

SUMMARY

- Accounting is the process of identifying, measuring and communicating economic information to permit informed judgements and decisions by users of information. The accounting system of a business firm companies of **(1)** Financial accounting, **(2)** Cost accounting and **(3)** Management Accounting.
- The accounting information specifically prepared to aid managers is called management accounting information.
- The information managers use is quite varied. Operating information provides most of the raw data for management accounting but much of this information is not of direct interest to managers. The manager is interested in summaries drawn from the detailed records rather than in the underlying details. Therefore, management accounting information is summary information.

LO 1.2

- Management accounting differs in several ways from financial accounting. The important differences between them relate to: **(i)** structure, **(ii)** sources of principles, **(iii)** need, **(iv)** time-orientation, **(v)** report entity, **(vi)** purpose, **(vii)** users, **(viii)** information control, **(ix)** information precision, **(x)** report frequency, **(xi)** report timeliness and **(xii)** liability potential.
- Some important similarities between financial and management accounting are: **(i)** most elements of financial accounting are also found in management accounting, **(ii)** basic data collected for both are in accordance with the generally accepted financial accounting principles to avoid duplication and **(iii)** both are used in decision making.

LO 1.3

- Management accounting information is used for three distinct purposes: **(a)** measurement, **(b)** control and **(c)** alternative choices.
- For measurement purposes the management accounting system focuses on the measurement of full cost. Full cost accounting includes direct and indirect costs of both manufacturing goods and other related activities. Full costs are used in **(i)** financial reporting, **(ii)** analysing economic performance and **(iii)** cost-plus contracts.
- For control purposes, management accounting measures costs by responsibility centres. A responsibility centre is an organisation unit headed by a manager who is responsible for its operations and performance.
- The alternative decisions use differential costs. Differential costs are costs which differ according to the alternatives. For short-run decisions only direct costs are relevant. For long-range decisions full costs are relevant.

LO 1.5

REFERENCES

1. Anthony, R.N., Hawkins, D.F. and Merchant, K., *Accounting: Text and Cases*, Tata McGraw-Hill Publishing Company Ltd (New Delhi; 2005), p.495.
2. Horngren, Sundem and Stratton, *Introduction to Managerial Accounting* (Pearson Education, 2004), p.18.
3. Anthony, *op.cit*, p.497.
4. *Ibid*, p.499.
5. *Ibid*, p.501.

REVIEW QUESTIONS

LOD: Easy

RQ.1.1 Indicate whether the followings statements are 'True' or 'False'. LO 1.1,3,4,5

(a) **(i)** It is optional for a company to have financial accounting.

(ii) Generally accepted accounting principles constitute the basis for the preparation of management accounting reports.

(iii) Like financial accounting, management accounting is also concerned only with information which is amenable of being expressed in monetary terms.

(iv) Management accounting lacks a single unified structure.

(v) Financial accounting is tailored to the specific needs of the management.

(vi) Management accounting caters internal requirements of the management.

(vii) Financial accounting lays more emphasis on the future.

(viii) Management accounting reports are public documents.

[Answers: (i) False, (ii) False, (iii) False, (iv) True, (v) False, (vi) True, (vii) False, (viii) False]

(b) Fill in the following blanks

(i) The accounting information specifically prepared to aid managers is called ____________ information.

(ii) ____________ is the process to ensure that employees perform properly.

(iii) The highest level management accountant is called the ____________.

(iv) Management accounting is ____________ (optional/statuary obligation).

(v) Financial accounting has a ____________ structure.

(vi) While financial accounting relates to the business as a ____________, management accounting focuses on ____________ of business.

(vii) ____________ provides data both for both financial accounting and management accounting.

(viii) Historical costs are used in ____________ accounting.

[Answers: (i) management accounting, (ii) Control, (iii) controller, (iv) optional, (v) unified, (vi) whole, Part, (vii) Cost accounting, (viii) financial]

RQ.1.2 "There are no externally imposed "Generally Accepted Accounting Principles' for Management Accounting." In the light of the above statement, discuss, giving illustrations, the nature and scope of management accounting. LO 1.1,3,5

RQ.1.3 "The emphasis of financial accounting is different from that of cost accounting." Comment. LO 1.4

RQ.1.4 In what essential respects is management accounting different from financial accounting? LO 1.3

RQ.1.5 Discuss the three managerial functions in which management accounting information can be used. LO 1.5

LOD: Medium

RQ.1.6 "Management accounting is a mid-way between financial accounting and cost accounting." Elucidate. LO 1.3,4

RQ.1.7 Explain the following:

(a) "Management accounting is an extension of financial accounting." LO 1.3

(b) "Management accounting assists in corporate planning process." LO 1.1

RQ.1.8 **(a)** "There is no single, unified management accounting system, rather there are three different types of information, each used for different purposes." Elaborate. LO 1.5

(b) Mention the differences which exist between financial accounting and management accounting. Also point out the similarities, if any, between the two. LO 1.3

LOD: Difficult

RQ.1.9 "Management accounting is the presentation of accounting information in such a way as to assist the management in the creation of policy, and in the day-to-day operation of an undertaking." Elucidate. LO 1.1,5

PART 2

FINANCIAL ACCOUNTING

One use of accounting information is decision-making about a firm by outsiders such as shareholders, creditors and prospective investors. Part two, devoted to a discussion of financial accounting as a source of information to outsiders, is divided into three chapters. Chapter 2 dwells on generally accepted accounting principles and accounting standards. The accounting cycle and statements of financial information are illustrated in Chapter 3. Finally, corporate financial statements and reports are explained and illustrated with actual case of Reliance Industries Ltd in Chapter 4.

Generally Accepted Accounting Principles and Accounting Standards

2

Learning Objectives

After reading this chapter you will be able to:

LO 2.1 Understand the generally accepted accounting principles (GAPPs), and the broad contents of balance sheet as well as of profit and loss account/income statement

LO 2.2 Explain significant accounting standards issued by the ICAI along with their usefulness in formulating accounting policies and practices

Introduction

The financial accounting profession, over the years, has evolved accounting principles and standards which are generally accepted and universally practised. Since these form the basis of accounting records, the financial statements (namely, balance sheet, income statement and cash flow statement) indicating the financial health of a business enterprise can be relied upon and, hence the importance of knowing these principles and standards. The chapter explains the GAAPs which are also known as basic accounting concepts, assumptions and conventions. Select accounting standards formulated by the Institute of Chartered Accountants of India (ICAI) are also briefly described. The main points are summarised by way of recapitulation.

Generally Accepted Accounting Principles

LO 2.1 Understand the generally accepted accounting principles (GAPPs), and the broad contents of balance sheet as well as of profit and loss account/income statement

The GAAPs which form the basis of accounting records are depicted in Exhibit 2.1.

EXHIBIT 2.1 Generally Accepted Accounting Principles

• Money Measurement Concept	• Conservative Principle Concept
• Separate Entity Concept	• Realisation Concept
• Duality Concept	• Accrual Concept
• Going Concern Concept	• Matching Concept
• Cost Concept	• Consistency Concept
• Accounting Period Concept	• Materiality Concept

Money Measurement Concept

Money measurement concept stipulates recording of only those transactions which can be expressed in monetary terms. It provides a homogeneous measuring yardstick for heterogeneous items.

Financial accounting should record only that information about a business enterprise which can be expressed in monetary terms. In other words, business events which cannot be quantified in monetary terms are outside the purview of accounting records, irrespective of their significance. For example, the emergence of a substitute product (better in quality and at a lower price) in the market, low morale of work force working in factory, demise of the chief executive officer, senior general managers of marketing and production leaving the firm and joining the competing firms, switching over of key customers, and so on, are important business events likely to affect the profitability of the firm at least in the immediate future. Nevertheless, their record is outside the scope of financial accounts as they are not amenable to expression in monetary terms. Thus, **financial accounting is incapable of providing all information about the operations of a business.** In operational terms, it implies that the readers of an accounting report (say, investors, lenders and creditors) should not expect to find therein all the facts or perhaps even the most important ones, about an organisation.[1]

A related aspect of the money measurement concept is that transactions should be recorded in monetary values at the time they take place. Subsequent changes in the purchasing power of money (due to changes in prices) have no effect on the financial accounts. Thus, a piece of land purchased in 2016 for ₹20 crore and another of a similar size (at the same place) purchased 25 years earlier for ₹2 crore are both recorded in 2016 accounting records at their respective acquisition prices (that is, ₹2 crore and ₹20 crore respectively and shown at total sum of ₹22 crore), although the current market value of the land is ₹40 crore. An important implication is that the reader of an accounting report should be aware that the change in purchasing power of the rupee is not recognised by financial accounting records.

The rationale for the use of money measurement concept in financial accounting is that it has the virtue of providing a common measuring yardstick (in the form of money) which enables *heterogeneous* facts (expressed in different units) to be expressed as *homogeneous* numbers which then can easily be added or subtracted. For instance, raw materials may be expressed in terms of numbers or weights; consumption of electricity is expressed in KWs, labour time spent on job is measured in terms of hours, and so on. Obviously, addition of these items is not possible. To compute the total cost of product, all items, say, raw materials, electricity and labour are expressed in terms of their respective monetary values.

Separate Entity Concept

Separate entity concept A firm has entity separate from its owners.

For accounting records, a business firm should be considered a *separate* entity from its owners. Accordingly, every business transaction should be viewed from the perspective of the firm and not form the viewpoint of owner(s) of the business entity. It is for this reason that the capital provided by the owner(s) is reckoned liability of the firm. Likewise, profits (retained/undrawn) are shown as liabilities of the firm as they are payable to the owners. For the same reason, the withdrawals (from the firm) made by the owner(s) to meet their household/personal expenses and losses are reckoned assets of the firm as they are recoverable from the owner(s).

Why is such a distinction made between the firm and owner when everything, in effect, belongs to the latter? The reason is that it enables the business enterprise to determine correctly the income/profits from operating business. Assume that Sohan commences business with ₹20 lakh on 1st April, 2015. During the year (ending 31st March 2016), he withdraws ₹25,000 per month to meet household expenses, the aggregate sum being ₹3,00,000. Assume further that no record has been made of these withdrawals/drawings during 2015–16, (by not taking cognizance of separate entity concept). Suppose, the firm's accounts show capital balance (31.3.2016) of ₹19 lakh. It would mistakenly imply that there is loss of ₹1 lakh (₹20 lakh – ₹19 lakh). On the contrary, the firm has actually earned profits of ₹2 lakh as shown in Format 2.1.

FORMAT 2.1 Computation of Profits (Reckoning Withdrawals)

1. Initial capital (1.4.2015)	₹20,00,000
2. Less withdrawals during the year (2015–16)]	(3,00,000)
3. Effective capital retained in business (1 – 2)	17,00,000
4. Ending capital balance as on (31.3.2016)	19,00,000
5. Profit earned during the year (4 – 3)	2,00,000

Likewise, the firm would have an erroneous impression of earning profit of ₹1 lakh assuming it does not record additional capital contribution of ₹2 lakh made during the year and it has closing balance of ₹21 lakh (with zero withdrawals made during the period under reference). The fact, on the other hand, is that the firm has incurred a loss of ₹1 lakh as shown in Format 2.2.

FORMAT 2.2 Computation of Loss (Considering Additional Contribution)

1. Initial capital (1.4.2015)	₹20,00,000
2. Additional capital introduced during the year (2015–16)]	2,00,000
3. Effective capital provided (1 + 2)	22,00,000
4. Ending capital balance	21,00,000
5. Loss suffered during the period (4 – 3)	(1,00,000)

Thus, accounting records are to be considered from the *view point of the firm only* to determine true profit and loss from business unit. It is for this reason that the transactions between the owner and the firm are not omitted but recorded (keeping in mind their impact on the firm). For the purpose of accounting records, the owner is assumed as an *outside* entity dealing with the firm.

Duality Concept

Dualty concept means that every transaction affects two accounts.

Accounting records should be based on the double entry system/duality concept in that there are two aspects/impacts of each accounting transaction. Transactions are the economic events of an enterprise that are recorded.[2] Every business transaction has its effect on two items as is illustrated in Example 2.1 The example also helps to understand the balance sheet which has to sides—assets owned and liabilities owned/payable—and why its two sides always tally.

Example 2.1

Transaction (1) Investment by Shareholders: Let us assume that a group of 5 friends form the Attractive Toy Company Private Limited (ATCPL) to market toys (each contributing ₹2 lakh in cash) on 1st January, 2016. The effect of this transaction is two fold: first, the ATCPL has ₹10 lakh cash (i.e. asset) and, second, the company has ₹10 lakh capital. Capital represents liability for the company as per the separate-entity concept (explained earlier). Accordingly, the company's balance sheet would appear as follows:

Balance Sheet of ATCPL *as on January 1, 2016*

Liabilities	*Amount (₹lakh)*	*Amount*	*Amount (₹lakh)*
Capital	10	Cash	10
	10		10

The two sides of balance sheet are tallying. This parity would always be maintained (as shown in subsequent transactions). The equal and simultaneous effect on the sides of balance sheet is referred to as the *duality concept.*

Transaction (2) Deposit in Bank: Let us assume further that out of ₹10 lakh, ₹7 lakh is deposited in a bank on January 2 by ATCPL. As a result of this transaction, cash balance would come down to ₹3 lakh (₹10 lakh – ₹7 lakh) and new item ₹7 lakh shown as cash at bank on asset side. Observe that the composition of assets has changed, liability in terms of capital remains unchanged and two sides of the balance sheet tally (totalling ₹10 lakh).

Balance Sheet of ATCPL *as on January 2, 2016*

Liabilities	*Amount (₹lakh)*	*Assets*	*Amount (₹lakh)*
Capital	10	Cash	3
		Cash at bank	7
	10		10

Transaction (3) Purchase of Toys for Cash: Assume further that ATPCL purchases toys/goods for ₹2 lakh against cash payment on January 4. As a result, cash balance declines to ₹1 lakh (₹3 lakh - ₹2 lakh) and a new asset in the form of inventory of finished goods appears on the assets side. The two sides of balance sheet again tally as shown below:

Balance Sheet of ATCPL *as on January 4, 2016*

Liabilities	*Amount (₹lakh)*	*Assets*	*Amount (₹lakh)*
Capital	10	Cash	1
		Cash at bank	7
		Inventory of finished goods	2
	10		10

Transaction (4) Sales of Toys for Cash: Assume further that ATCPL sells the toys for ₹1.25 lakh (on cash basis) during 5–10 January. As a result of this transaction, its cash balance goes up by the amount of cash sales (₹1.25 lakh). However, the value of inventory *falls by ₹1 lakh only* (i.e. cost of toys sold). The difference of ₹25,000 between sale amount and cost is profit earned. Since the company is a custodian of the promoters/owners funds, profit earned belongs to them. In other words, profit are payable to owners as per separate entity concept and, therefore, shown on the liabilities side of the balance sheet.

Balance Sheets of ATCPL *as on January 10, 2016*

Liabilities	*Amount (₹lakh)*	*Assets*	*Amount (₹lakh)*
Capital	10.00	Cash	2.25
	0.25	Cash at bank	7.00
		Inventory of finished goods	1.00
	10.25		10.25

It may be observed that the composition of balance sheet changes with each accounting transaction. For this reason, the balance sheet is aptly referred to as a *snapshot of financial position* (in terms of asses owned and liabilities payable) *of a firm at a particular point in time*, say, as on January 10, 2016. The position holds true for the specified reference date only; it changes on the following date if a new business transaction takes place (as shown below).

Transaction (5) Raising Loan: Gradually, the ATCPL establishes itself and decides to venture into manufacturing of toys. Its credibility helps in raising a 5-year loan of ₹8 lakh from State Industrial Development Corporation (SIDC) at 12 per cent rate of interest (payable annually) on January, 15. This results in higher bank balance at ₹15 lakh (₹7 lakh + ₹8 lakh) on assets side and a new item of 12 per cent loan appears on liability side. There is an increase of ₹8 lakh on both sides of balance sheet; the new total would be ₹18.25 lakh. (Attempt to prepare balance sheet on your own.)

Transactions (6 and 7) Purchase of Small Industrial Shed and Machinery: For expansion, the company buys a small industrial shed for ₹5 lakh and machinery for ₹7 lakh on January 21. This time, the vendors accept the cheque and the payment is made through the bank. The bank balance would decline to ₹3 lakh (₹15 lakh – ₹5 lakh – ₹7 lakh) and building/shed and machinery as two new items of assets would respectively appear at ₹5 lakh and at ₹7 lakh in balance sheet as shown below:

Balance Sheet of ATCPL *as on January 21, 2016*

Liabilities	*Amount (₹lakh)*	*Assets*	*Amount (₹lakh)*
Capital	10.00	Cash	2.25
Profit	0.25	Cash at bank	3.00
12% Loan	8.00	Stock of finished goods	1.00
		Building/shed	5.00
		Machinery	7.00
	18.25		18.25

Transaction (8) Purchase of Raw-materials on Credit: By now the ATCPL is fairly well known and the suppliers are willing to transact business on credit basis. It acquires raw material worth ₹1 lakh from Supreme Plastics Limited on credit on January 22. As a result, raw material is recorded on the assets side. Since the supplier is yet to be paid, Supreme Plastic Limited appears as *creditor* on liabilities side. The two sides of the balance sheet tally at higher total of ₹19.25 lakh (₹18.25 lakh + ₹1 lakh) (Attempt to prepare the balance sheet on your own).

Transaction (9) Sale of Toys on Credit: Assume the ATCPL sells the whole stock of finished goods on credit to Reliable Sound Buyers Company for ₹1.27 lakh (on January 24). As a result of this transaction, profits would increase by ₹27,000 (₹1,27,000 – ₹1,00,000) to ₹52,000 (Existing, ₹25,000 + Additional, ₹27,000). On assets side, the inventory of finished goods (toys) would disappear and a new item accounts receivable/debtors (₹1,27,000) would appear. Observe, there is a net increase of ₹27,000 on the assets side as well as on the liabilities side and the balance sheet matches.

Transaction (10) Payment of Expenses in Cash: During 28–31st January 2016, the company incurred total operating expenses of ₹32,000 (on salaries, rent of the shop, electricity, telephone, refreshments, cartage, courier, postage, stationery, etc) and paid in cash. As a result of this transaction, there is a decrease in profit to ₹20,000 (₹52,000 – ₹32,000). The sum of ₹52,000 is termed as *gross profit* (sales revenue, ₹2,52,000 – cost of goods/toys sold, ₹2,00,000). Obviously, expenses reduce profit of the company. Ignoring taxes for the time being, the firm has net profit (Gross profit, ₹52,000 – Total expenses, ₹32,000 of ₹20,000). Since expenses have been paid in cash, cash balance is reduced to ₹1,93,000 (₹2,25,000 – ₹32,000). The balance sheet on January 31, 2016 would appear as shown below.

Balance Sheet of ATCPL *as on January 31, 2016*

Liabilities	*Amount (₹lakh)*	*Assets*	*Amount (₹lakh)*
Capital	10.00	Cash	1.93
Profit	0.20	Cash at bank	3.00
12% Loan	8.00	Building/shed	5.00
Creditors@	1.00	Machinery	7.00
		Inventory of raw materials	1.00
		Debtors@@	1.27
	19.20		19.20

@As the sum is payable, Supreme Plastic Limited is creditor. In practice, the name of creditor is not mentioned.
@@As the sum is receivable, Reliable Sound Buyers Company is debtor.

The last balance sheet drawn is the most comprehensive. It shows that ATCPL owns assets worth ₹19.20 lakh. These assets are financed from two major sources, namely, owners [₹10.2 lakh (i.e., ₹10 lakh capital + ₹0.2 lakh net profit)] and outsiders [(₹9 lakh (i.e., lenders money, ₹8 lakh and creditors ₹1 lakh)]. Viewed from this new perspective, the balance sheet is a statement of sources of funds (listing sources from where funds/finances have been obtained) and resources/uses of funds (listing items in which funds have been invested). Sources represent liabilities as they are payable and resources in which funds have been invested are assets.

According to the duality concept, the two sides (liabilities and assets/sources and resources) of balance sheet always tally. If the firm has ₹100 lakh resources/assets, there must be corresponding sources/liabilities of ₹100 lakh to finance these assets. This equality

$$\text{Liabilities} = \text{Assets} \quad \textbf{(2.1)}$$

is the genesis of accounting equation. This fundamental accounting equation is the formal expression of the duality concept.[3]

Liabilities can be segregated into two categories: (i) Owners' funds (also referred to as *owner's equity*) implying owners contribution in financing assets/stake or claim of owners in assets. They are designated as *internal liabilities* (being internal to the firm). In the case of companies, they are *shareholders' equity*; and (ii) External liabilities are the claims of outsiders (lenders and other creditors) on the assets of the firm. Accordingly, the expanded version of accounting equation 2.1 can be written as

$$\text{Owners' equity} + \text{External liabilities} = \text{Assets} \quad \textbf{(2.2)}$$

The accounting equation indicates that a business transaction can assume any *one* of the following *four* forms (possible concrete transaction is shown in brackets):

(i) Increase in asset followed by increase in liability (e.g. purchase of raw materials on credit)
(ii) Decrease in asset followed by decrease in liability (e.g. payment to creditors)
(iii) Increase in one asset followed by decrease in another asset (e.g. deposit in bank).
(iv) Increase in one liability followed by decrease in another liability (e.g. payment to creditors by taking bank overdraft).

Going Concern Concept

The going concern concept assumes that the entity is a *going concern*, that is, it will continue to operate for an indefinitely long period in future. In other words, it will not cease doing business, sell its assets and make final payment to its lenders, creditors and owners. The operational significance of this assumption is that the assets (say, plant and machinery, office equipment, land and building etc.) are not shown in the balance sheet at the value at which they can be sold in the market. Instead, these assets are valued considering their likely contribution to the value of goods produced/services rendered by their use in future years.

Going Concern Concept assumes that the business entity would continue to operate indefinitely.

Assume the ATCPL purchases machine for ₹50 lakh on April 1, 2016 with expected economic useful life of 5 years, with no salvage value. Assume further that the machine's efficiency/productivity is likely to be the same for all its 5-year useful life. Accordingly, ₹10 lakh would be charged as depreciation as an expense for its use in year 2016–17. On 31st March 2017, it would be shown at ₹40 lakh (₹50 lakh – ₹10 lakh) as asset in balance sheet. Obviously, ₹40 lakh does not represent sale/market value of the assets. Since the assumption is going concern, the current resale value of the machine is irrelevant.

In valuing assets, therefore, current resale value (of assets shown in balance sheet) is irrelevant as they will not be sold as such, but rather they will be used in the creation of future output values. In other words, the going concern value is an antithesis of the liquidation value.

Cost Concept

Another fundamental accounting concept closely related to the going concern concept is the cost concept. According to this concept, assets/resources owned by the firm should be ordinarily/normally shown at their acquisition cost (and not at their current market value/sale value). The cost basis has two merits. First, it provides a relatively *objective* basis for accounting records; estimating current market value of assets is not only difficult but also is subjective. Secondly, the market value/current value concept is difficult to apply. The difficulty arises from the fact that those responsible for preparing accounts would be compelled to keep a track of the changes in the market price; the exercise may not only be time consuming but also, sometimes, may be fairly expensive. Market valuation is not required, in particular, for the long-term assets (say, plant and machinery, office equipments etc.) as they are acquired to be used in business and not for sale.

Cost concept Closely related to the going concern postulate, it implies that assets/resources owned by a firm should be shown at acquisition cost in contrast to their current market value.

The operational implication of the cost concept is that most of the assets (the notable exceptions being cash, bank balance, marketable securities) shown in the balance sheet (more often) do not reflect their current market worth. In general, while some assets (say, plant and machinery, office furniture and equipments) may tend to have lower market value than shown in books (i.e. book value), assets like land and buildings may have higher market value than their book values.

Accounting Period Concept

The accounting period concept requires *notional or artificial pause* for the going concern concept with the intent to prepare income statement for a specific period of time. Conventionally, it is normal to have a one year period as accounting period for reporting to shareholders/stakeholders and determining taxes payable to the government. In the majority of business firms, the accounting period chosen is April 1–March 31 so that it matches with the fiscal year of the government.

Accounting period concept requires notional/artificial pause to prepare financial statements, normally one-year period.

The rationale of the accounting period concept is that it enables the management of the firm to assess its financial performance in terms of profit earned or loss suffered at periodic intervals. In the event of the low/inadequate profits or losses, it provides the opportunity for the managers to initiate remedial measures to improve the performance before it goes out of hand. It is for this reason, though one year time span is the usual accounting period, it is not uncommon for the vast majority of business firms to prepare income statement on monthly or quarterly basis for internal purposes of performance evaluation. In fact, it is mandatory under Clause 41 of listing agreement for listed companies in India to publish financial results (i.e. income statement) on quarterly basis. Its preparation requires computation of revenues earned and expenses incurred during the period under reference. This exercise is based on concepts such as conservatism, realisation, accrual, matching and consistency (discussed below).

Conservatism Principle

Conservative principle postulates recognition of income only on actual realisation but actual as well as anticipated expenses should be accounted for.

Be conservative in determining profits/income of a business firms is the requirement of conservatism concept. In operational terms, the dictum is "*anticipate no profit and provide for all possible losses*". Thus, the concept leads to a prudent/safe/sound policy which recognises profits/income only when actually realised but account is/must to be taken of all expenses—actual as well as anticipated. Clearly, the concept has a preference/bias for the understatement of the firm's net income (revenues-expenses) as well as for net assets in doubtful situations. In specific terms, if two estimates of some future amount are about equally likely, the preference should be for smaller amount/number while measuring assets or revenues and the larger for liabilities or expenses.

It is for this reason that inventories are valued at cost or market price, whichever is lower. Likewise, it is practice among the firms to provide for likely loss due to non-recovery from debtors by creating provision for bad and doubtful debts but not to create provision for likely discounts to be received/earned on payments to creditors. In sum, the conservative concept safeguards the business firm against over-estimating of profits and its consequences (say, higher bonus to employees, high compensation paid to senior executives, more dividends paid to shareholders and so on).

Realisation Concept

Realisation concept implies that revenue should be considered as earned/realised on the date of sale of goods/services to customers in consideration for cash/claims to cash and not on "pending" sales.

Realisation concept is closely related to the concept of conservatism in that it provides conservative basis for revenue recognition. According to the realisation concept, revenue should be considered as being earned/realised on the date when goods are sold or services are rendered to the customers in consideration for cash or claims to cash (i.e., debtors). In other words, revenue should not be reckoned/recognised for goods sold on approval till such time approval is received from the buyer by the firm; goods lying with customers are shown at cost price and not at the negotiated price of sale. Thus, the reaslisation concept prevents the firm from registering/posting profits on 'pending' sales. Viewed in this perspective, the spirit of realisation concept is in conformity with that of conservatism concept.

While cash sales as the basis of revenue recognition are self evident, a less obvious situation exists in the case of credit sales. When the firm sells goods on credit, it expects the customer/debtor to pay as credit sales are made, in general, to such customers who have a good credit record so that the receipt of payment is *reasonably certain* from them. However, in practice, it is true virtually for all the firms that all the credit customers/debtors may not pay their dues. Therefore, in measuring the revenues for the period, the realisation concept (as per the requirement of conservatism concept) requires the provision for likely loss in terms of bad debts to be created on credit sales/debtors outstanding. The past experience may serve as a useful guide to compute the *provision amount* for such a likely loss. It is normally expressed as percentage of debtors outstanding (say, 2% or 5%) on the closing date of financial year. Conceptually, it is desirable that the revenue should be shown net of the estimated amount of bad debts. In practice, however, the amount is often considered as an expense. This inflates gross profit but the net income remains unchanged.

It is important to note that though the spirit of conservatism and realisation concepts is the same, the conservatism concept is broader as it relates to income statement as well as balance sheet, whereas realisation concept is applicable only to income statement.

Accrual Concept

Accrual concept requires that expenses incurred/revenues earned should be considered as expenses/revenues of the same period whether paid/realised in cash or are in arrears/outstanding in that year.

The accounting period concept requires the preparation of income statement for a specific accounting period (say, a year w.e.f. 1st April 2016 to 31st March 2017). The accrual concept requires that expenses incurred for a particular accounting period should be considered as expenses of the same period whether they have been paid in cash or are in arrears (not paid/payable) in that year. Similarly, revenues earned in a specific accounting period should be considered as revenues of the same period, irrespective of whether realised in cash or not (for instance, realisation concept has shown that credit sales made in January, 2016 are considered revenues for accounting year 2015–16, though cash receipts may be realised in the next accounting year, 2016–17).

The accrual concept is of considerable significance to determine the true income of a business entity for each accounting period by considering accrued revenues and accrued expenses, and not cash revenues and cash expenses. For instance, assume a manufacturing firm has wages bill of ₹5 crore per month. On account of liquidity problems, it could not pay its workers for two months (say, February and March 2016). In other words, total wages paid in 2015–16 have been ₹50 crore (₹5 crore per month × 10 months). In accounting year (AY), 2016–17, the firm would be required to pay wages for 14 months (12 months for accounting year AY 2016–17 and for 2 months for AY 2015-16), that is, ₹5 crore × 14 months = ₹70 crore. Should the wages expenses be ₹50 crore and ₹70 crore in AY 2015–16 and AY 2016–17 respectively (based on cash basis) or ₹60 crore (on accrual basis) for both these years?

Obviously, ₹60 crore should be reckoned as wages expenses in both the accounting years. Otherwise, the total manufacturing costs of AY 2015–16, other things/costs being equal, would be lower by ₹20 crore compared to AY 2016–17, leading to more costs/lower profits of ₹20 crore of AY 2016-17 *vis-à-vis* AY 2015–16. These profit figures, in turn, have the risk of pseudo/distorted conclusions drawn about the better performance of AY 2015–16 compared to AY 2016–17.

Clearly, cash basis of expenses recognition suffers from serious limitation of distorting profit figures of accounting periods; it may indicate higher profits in one year (by postponing payment of expenses to subsequent year, as has been shown above) at the cost of profits of the subsequent year. Thus, cash basis of expense recognition misrepresents expenses figure (wages is one such example, the firm may defer payment of repairs and maintenance bill, payment of rent, property taxes, lease rent of equipment to show more profits). This, in turn, renders meaningless the management exercise of financial performance evaluation. The accrual concept of accounting overcomes these deficiencies.

Like expenses payable, accrual concept also calls for appropriate adjustment of expenses paid in advance. For instance, annual maintenance payment of ₹60 lakh (as on January 1, 2016) cannot be considered as expense of AY 2015–16; it needs to be pro-rated. Assuming April–March accounting period, annual maintenance payment for 3 months only (i.e., ₹15 lakh) would be considered as expense for AY 2015–16; the balance sum of ₹45 lakh would form expense of AY 2016–17.

The accounting treatment of revenues is akin to that of expenses. For instance, credit sales is the basis of revenue recognition and not receipts from debtors. Likewise, interest/dividends receivable (on 31st March 2016) on investments made by the firm are to be reckoned as its earnings for AY 2015–16, though the entity has not received them.

From the foregoing, it is apparent that 'accrual accounting' is superior to 'cash accounting'. Since accrual basis of accounting provides a sound conceptual framework of recognising revenues and expenses, it is adopted as the basis of income determination world-wide by the business firms.

Matching Concept

Matching concept requires that expenses recognised in an accounting period are matched with the revenue recognised in that period.

The matching concept—a logical extension of accrual concept—is regarded as the most comprehensive accounting principle as far as determination of net income/profit of a business firm (in a specified accounting period) is concerned. In operational terms, the matching concept involves two steps in computing net income: first, to determine the revenues earned in a given accounting period, and second, to determine the expenses/costs incurred to realise these revenues. The expenses recognised in an accounting period, then, are matched with the revenues recognised in that period. A firm is said to have earned profits when revenues exceeded expenses; losses result if expenses are more than revenues. The concept is logical, makes business sense and *per se* appears to be simple as far as drawing of income statement is concerned. The matching concept is illustrated by preparing a summarised income statement for the facts related to ATCPL contained in Example 2.1.

Income Statement of ATCPL for the period (1.1.2016 to 31.1.2016)

Particulars	*Amount*
Sales revenue (Cash sales, ₹1,25,000 + Credit sales, of ₹1,27,000)	₹2,52,000
Less cost of goods sold (Finished goods/toys purchased and sold)	2,00,000
Gross profit	52,000
Less other expenses* (salaries, rent, electricity, etc.)	32,000
Net profit	20,000

*In practice, amount incurred on each expense item is separately shown.

Observe that the net income figure (of ₹20,000) tallies with its earlier computation. The ATPCL example is very simple to understand the application of matching principle to determine net income of a business enterprise. In practice, the matching exercise is a difficult task. *Inter-se* estimation of revenues is relatively a simple exercise.

Revenues are equivalent to the amount of goods and services sold during the specific accounting period, irrespective of whether cash is realised against goods sold/services rendered.

Expenses are not so easy to compute. The reason is that there are many expenses which benefit more than one accounting year. Obviously, the entire amount of such expenses cannot be charged to income statement of single accounting year. Equity demands that the amount incurred on such expenses should be equitably spread over to all those accounting years which are likely to be benefited by such an expense. Though simple in theory, its application is difficult in practice in that the firm is required to ascertain the number of years the expense is likely to benefit as well as the quantum of benefit in each year. It is useful to classify expenses into two categories, namely, capital and revenue.

Capital expenditures (for instance, purchase of plant and machinery) are expenses whose benefit accrue beyond one accounting year. Usually, they involve large investments (having some salvage value at the end of their useful life) and are non-recurring in nature. The acquisition cost of plant and machinery (say, of ₹10 crore) in year 2016–17 cannot be considered as an expense of single accounting year (2016–17) as it would help in production for a number of years (say, 5 years). The machine might be more productive in the initial years compared to latter years. Further, the machine may become technologically obsolete before 5 year's estimated useful life or it may last longer than 5 years. Given these facts, it is obviously not easy to compute the share of ₹10 crore to be charged as an expense (technically referred to as depreciation) in each of these 5 years. Thus, for capital expense items, the matching concept is not easy to follow.

> **Capital expenditures** are expenses whose benefit accrue beyond one accounting year.

In contrast, **revenue expenses** (such as wages, insurance, property taxes, telephone bills, electricity and power, repairs etc.) occur in one accounting year and are expensed/written off against the revenues of the same year. They do not have re-sale value, are of relatively small amounts and occur annually or on a regular basis within a year. Clearly, the matching concept is easy to follow in respect of revenue expense items.

> **Revenue expenses** are expenses which benefit one accounting year.

However, it should be noted that there are a few notable revenue expense items (not having re-sale value) which benefit more than one accounting year, known as **deferred revenue expenses**. For example, substantial advertisement expenditure incurred at the time of launching a new product should not be considered as expense of the single accounting year in which it is incurred. Part of this expense should be shifted/charged to the subsequent accounting period(s) as they are likely to be benefited in terms of more sales revenue. Obviously, it is not easy to determine with precision the share of advertisement expense to be changed as expense of the future affected accounting period(s). Other notable expenses in this category are research and development expenses and flotation costs incurred by companies in raising funds through public offerings. Based on experience, the firms evolve some scientific criterion, in practice, to apportion such expenses over the years. In operational terms, there is subjectivity involved in apportioning both capital expenses and deferred revenue expenses (benefiting more than one accounting year) and to, that extent, there is *mismatch* in the net income determination process.

> **Deferred revenue expenses** are revenue expenses which benefit more than one accounting year, e.g. research and development expenditure.

In sum, therefore, net income figure determined as per income statement is not one hundred per cent accurate and precise; it is more an estimate/approximate figure rather than the actual/precise one. The more prefect is the matching, the more correct is the income determination and *vice versa*.

Consistency Concept/Principle

In the preparation of balance sheet and income statement, some accounting items can be treated in several ways. For example, a firm has various alternatives to value its inventory or charge depreciation on its assets, and so on. Which of these alternatives a firm would adopt is a matter of business policy. The consistency principle requires that once a firm has decided to adopt one of the alternatives, it will continue to adopt the same in future years also.

> **Consistency principle** requires consistency in accounting treatment of items such as depreciation and inventory valuation to ensure comparability over the years.

In other words, the consistency principle requires that there should be a consistency of accounting treatment of items (say, depreciation method, straight line or diminishing balance method—in respect of plan and machinery; method of valuation of inventory—LIFO, FIFO, weighted average and so on) in all the accounting periods. The amount of depreciation would be different under the two methods of depreciation. The change from one method of depreciation to another would affect the depreciation charged and, hence, the profits. Likewise, different methods of pricing inventory will lead to different costs of raw materials used in production. As a result of adoption of varying methods in different years, profit figures would not be comparable. The rational underlying this concept, therefore, is that if a firm does not follow a consistent policy, comparison of accounting figures would be vitiated.

Materiality Concept

Materiality concept requires full disclosure of all material information/events.

The materiality concept requires full disclosure of all important/material information/events. To put it differently, the insignificant events and information may not be reckoned in accounting records. The economic rationale underlying the concept is that some accounting items (say stationery, toiletries etc.) may be so trivial that the effort and cost involved in their estimation/record may not be justifiable. For instance, a brand new pad of papers, conceptually is an asset. Using a piece of paper implies that the part of the asses is used up. Theoretically, it is possible to count the number of pages remaining in the pad on closing day of the accounting period and show such an amount as an asset. The analogy can apply equally well to other stationery items such as pencils, rubber, fluid, carbon and so on. Given the insignificant amount involved, accountants more often prefer to show the entire amount spent on stationery items as expense of the same accounting year in which they have purchased instead of devoting energy to determine the amount of stationery unused and show it as an asset.

Further, many of the expense items at the best are either estimates or very close estimates. For instance, electricity and telephone bills (received normally each month) may not coincide with the time span of a month (in terms of specific dates) covered by the accounting period for which income statement is prepared. In such situations, there would not be a substantial advantage in terms of accuracy gained by estimating telephone/electricity bills for specific dates (say 1st January to 31st January, 2016) for which monthly income statement is prepared. Above all, since the amount of such bills are likely to be relatively stable month-wise, there is virtually no distortion in monthly income figures as computed by income statement (prepared on monthly basis). Thus, the materiality concept suggests that it is not worthwhile on the part of a firm to make an effort to refine estimates in situations as described above.

To conclude, the accounting principles, concepts and conventions (GAAPs) serve as a useful guide for accounting records and preparation of the balance sheet as well as income statement. Their worldwide following lends credence to the information contained in the financial statements of business firms.

Accounting Standards

Accounting standards provide guidelines relating to the accounting treatment as well as reporting of important accounting items with a view to standardise the diverse accounting policies/procedures.

LO 2.2 Explain significant accounting standards issued by the ICAI along with their usefulness in formulating accounting policies and practices

The accounting profession has developed accounting standards (ASs) to provide guidelines relating to the accounting treatment as well as reporting of important accounting items which have bearing, *inter-alia,* on income determination, asset valuation and presentation of financial statements (namely, income statement, balance sheet and cash flow statement). The primary objective of ASs is to standardise the diverse accounting policies and practices. The guidelines contained in ASs are mandatory in nature.

The mandatory status of an accounting standard implies that while discharging their audit functions, it will be the duty of the members of the Institute of Chartered Accountants of India (ICAI) to examine whether the accounting standard(s) is (are) complied with in the presentation of financial statements covered by their audit. In the event of any deviation from the accounting standard(s), it will be their duty to make adequate disclosures in their audit reports so that the users of financial statements are aware of such deviation.

Accounting standard compliance is mandatory for **(a)** enterprises whose equity or debt securities are listed on a recognised stock exchange in India or enterprises, whose securities are in the process of being issued and will be listed on a recognised stock exchange in India and **(b)** all other commercial enterprises whose turnover for the accounting year is more than ₹50 crore. The accounting standards issued by the ICAI are listed in Exhibit 2.2.

EXHIBIT 2.2 Indian Accounting Standards (Ind ASs) Issued by the ICAI

1. (Ind AS) 1:	Presentation of Financial Statements
2. (Ind AS) 2:	Inventories
3. (Ind AS) 7:	Statement of Cash Flows
4. (Ind AS) 8:	Accounting Policies, Changes in Accounting Estimates and Errors
5. (Ind AS) 10:	Events after the Reporting Period
6. (Ind AS) 11:	Construction Contracts
7. (Ind AS) 12:	Income Taxes
8. (Ind AS) 16:	Property, Plant and Equipment
9. (Ind AS) 17:	Leases
10. (Ind AS) 18:	Revenue
11. (Ind AS) 19:	Employee Benefits
12. (Ind AS) 20:	Accounting for Government Grants and Disclosure of Government Assistance
13. (Ind AS) 21:	The Effects of Changes in Foreign Exchange Rates
14. (Ind AS) 23:	Borrowing Costs
15. (Ind AS) 24:	Related Party Disclosures
16. (Ind AS) 27:	Consolidated and Seperate Financial Statements
17. (Ind AS) 28:	Investments in Associates
18. (Ind AS) 29:	Financial Reporting in Hyperinflationary Economies
19. (Ind AS) 31:	Interest in Joint Ventures
20. (Ind AS) 32:	Financial Instruments: Presentation
21. (Ind AS) 33:	Earnings Per Share
22. (Ind AS) 34:	Interim Financial Reporting
23. (Ind AS) 36:	Impairment of Assets
24. (Ind AS) 37:	Provisions, Contingent Liabilities and Contingent Assets
25. (Ind AS) 38:	Intangible Assets
26. (Ind AS) 39:	Financial Instruments: Recognition and Measurement
27. (Ind AS) 40:	Investment Property
28. (Ind AS) 101:	First-time Adoption of Indian Accounting Standards
29. (Ind AS) 102:	Share-based Payment
30. (Ind AS) 103:	Business Combinations
31. (Ind AS) 104:	Insurance Contracts
32. (Ind AS) 105:	Non-current Assets Held for Sale and Discontinued Operations
33. (Ind AS) 106:	Exploration for and Evaluation of Mineral Resources
34. (Ind AS) 107:	Financial Instruments: Disclosures
35. (Ind AS) 108:	Operating Segments

This part of the chapter gives a brief overview of the select accounting standards which have a bearing on income determination, preparation of financial statements and affect important notes and supplementary schedules annexed with financial statements.

Ind AS-1: Presentation of Financial Statements

Objective

The objective of this standard is to provide the basis for presentation of general purpose financial statements to ensure comparability both with the entity's financial statements of previous periods and with the financial statements of other entities. It sets out overall requirements for the presentation of financial statements, guidelines for their structure and minimum requirements for their contents.

Complete Set of Financial Statements

A complete set of financial statements comprises: (a) a balance sheet as at the end of the period (including statement of changes in equity which is presented as a part of the balance sheet); (b) a statement of profit and loss for the period; (c) a statement of cash flows for the period; (d) notes, comprising a summary of significant accounting policies and other explanatory information; and (e) a balance sheet as at the beginning of the earliest comparative period when an entity applies an accounting policy retrospectively or when it reclassifies items in its financial statements.

General Features

Presentation of True and Fair View and Compliance with Ind ASs Financial statements are required to present a true and fair view of the financial position, financial performance and cash flows of an entity. Presentation of true and fair view requires the faithful presentation of financial statements, representation of the effects of transactions, other events and conditions in accordance with the definitions and recognition criteria for assets, liabilities, income and expenses set out in the framework.

In the extremely rare circumstances in which management concludes that compliance with a requirement in an **Ind AS** would be so misleading that it would conflict with the objective of financial Indian Accounting Standards set out in the framework, the entity can depart from that requirement. In such a situation, it is expected to disclose (a) that it has complied with applicable Ind ASs, except that it has departed from a particular requirement to present a true and fair view; (b) the title of the **Ind AS** from which the entity has departed, the nature of the departure, including the treatment that the **Ind AS** would require, the reason why that treatment would be so misleading in the circumstances that it would conflict with the objective of financial statements set out in the framework, and the treatment adopted; and (c) for each period presented, the financial effect of the departure on each item in the financial statements that would have been reported in complying with the requirement.

Going Concern Financial statements are to be prepared on a going concern basis unless management either intends to liquidate the entity or to cease trading, or has no realistic alternative but to do so. When management is aware, in making its assessment, of material uncertainties related to events or conditions that may cast significant doubt upon the entity's ability to continue as a going concern, the entity is required to disclose those uncertainties. When an entity does not prepare financial statements on a going concern basis, it would disclose that fact, together with the basis on which it prepared the financial statements and the reason why the entity is not regarded as a going concern.

Accrual Basis of Accounting Financial statements, except for cash flow information, are to be prepared on the accrual basis of accounting. When the accrual basis of accounting is used, an entity recognises items as assets, liabilities, equity, income and expenses (the elements of financial statements) when they satisfy the definitions and recognition criteria for those elements in the framework.

Materiality and Aggregation An entity would present separately each material class of similar items.

Offsetting An entity would not offset assets and liabilities or income and expenses, unless required or permitted by an **Ind AS**.

Frequency of Reporting An entity would present a complete set of financial statements (including comparative information) at least annually. When an entity changes the end of its reporting period and presents financial statements for a period longer or shorter than one year, it is expected to disclose, in addition to the period covered by the financial statements, (a) the reason for using a longer or shorter period, and (b) the fact that amounts presented in the financial statements are not entirely comparable.

Comparative Information Except when **Ind ASs** permit or require otherwise, an entity should disclose comparative information in respect of the previous period for all amounts reported in the current period's financial statements. An entity should include comparative information for narrative and descriptive information when it is relevant to an understanding of the current period's financial statements.

Consistency of Presentation An entity is required to retain the presentation and classification of items in the financial statements from one period to the next unless it is apparent, following a significant change in the nature of the entity's operations, that another presentation or classification would be more appropriate.

Identification of the Financial Statements An entity should clearly identify the financial statements and distinguish them from other information in the same published document. **Ind ASs** apply only to financial statements, and not necessarily to other information presented in an annual report, a regulatory filing, or another document. Therefore, it is important that users can distinguish information that is prepared using **Ind ASs** from other information that is presented.

Balance Sheet

As a minimum, the balance sheet would include line items that present the following amounts:

(a) property, plant and equipment; (b) investment property; (c) intangible assets; (d) financial assets (excluding amounts shown under (e), (h) and (i)); (e) investments accounted for using the equity method; (f) biological assets; (g) inventories; (h) trade and other receivables; (i) cash and cash equivalents; (j) the total of assets classified as held for sale and assets included in disposal groups classified as held for sale in accordance with Ind AS-105: non-current assets held for sale and discontinued operations; (k) trade and other payables; (l) provisions; (m) financial liabilities (excluding amounts shown under (k) and (l)); (n) liabilities and assets for current tax, as defined in Ind AS-12: income taxes; (o) deferred tax liabilities and deferred tax assets, as defined in Ind AS-12; (p) liabilities included in disposal groups classified as held for sale in accordance with Ind AS-105; (q) non-controlling interests, presented within equity; and (r) issued capital and reserves attributable to owners of the parent.

An entity should present additional line items, headings and subtotals in the balance sheet when such presentation is relevant to an understanding of the entity's financial position.

When an entity presents current and non-current assets, and current and non-current liabilities, as separate classifications in its balance sheet, it is prohibited to classify deferred tax assets (liabilities) as current assets (liabilities). An entity would present current and non-current assets, and current and non-current liabilities, as separate classifications in its balance sheet.

Current Assets An entity would classify an asset as current when: (a) it expects to realise the asset, or intends to sell or consume it, in its normal operating cycle; (b) it holds the asset primarily for the purpose of trading; (c) it expects to realise the asset within twelve months after the reporting period; or (d) the asset is cash or a cash equivalent (as defined in **Ind AS 7**) unless the asset is restricted from being exchanged or used to settle a liability for at least twelve months after the reporting period. All other assets would be classified as non-current.

Current Liabilities An entity would classify a liability as current when: (a) it expects to settle the liability in its normal operating cycle; (b) it holds the liability primarily for the purpose of trading; (c) the liability is due to be settled within twelve months after the reporting period; or (d) it does not have an unconditional right to defer settlement of the liability for at least twelve months after the reporting period. All other liabilities would be classified as non-current.

An entity is required to disclose the following, either in the balance sheet or in the statement of changes in equity which is part of the balance sheet, or in the notes: (a) for each class of share capital: (i) the number of shares authorised; (ii) the number of shares issued and fully paid, and issued but not fully paid; (iii) par value per share, or that the shares have no par value; (iv) a reconciliation of the number of shares outstanding at the beginning and at the end of the period; (v) the rights, preferences and restrictions attaching to that class including restrictions on the distribution of dividends and the repayment of capital; (vi) shares in the entity held by the entity or by its subsidiaries or associates; and (vii) shares reserved for issue under options and contracts for the sale of shares, including terms and amounts; and (b) a description of the nature and purpose of each reserve.

Statement of Profit and Loss

An entity is required to present all items of income and expense including components of other comprehensive income recognised in a period in a single statement of profit and loss. As a minimum, the statement of profit and loss would include line items that present the following amounts for the period: (a) revenue; (b) finance costs; (c) share of the profit or loss of associates and joint ventures accounted for using the equity method; (d) tax expense; (e) a single amount comprising the total of: (i) the post-tax profit or loss of discontinued operations and (ii) the post-tax gain or loss recognised on the measurement to fair value less costs to sell or on the disposal of the assets or disposal group(s) constituting the discontinued operation; (f) profit or loss; (g) each component of other comprehensive income classified by nature (excluding amounts in (h)); (h) share of the other comprehensive income of associates and joint ventures accounted for using the equity method; and (i) total comprehensive income. An entity would disclose the following items in the statement of profit and loss as allocations for the period: (a) profit or loss for the period attributable to: (i) non-controlling interests, and (ii) owners of the parent. (b) total comprehensive income for the period attributable to: (i) non-controlling interests, and (ii) owners of the parent.

An entity would not present any items of income or expense as extraordinary items, in the statement of profit and loss or in the notes.

Profit or Loss for the Period An entity would recognise all items of income and expense in a period in profit or loss unless an **Ind AS** requires or permits otherwise.

Other Comprehensive Income for the Period An entity would disclose the amount of income tax relating to each component of other comprehensive income, including reclassification adjustments, either in the statement of profit and loss or in the notes. An entity would also disclose reclassification adjustments relating to components of other comprehensive income.

When items of income or expense are material, an entity is required to disclose their nature and amount separately. An entity would present an analysis of expenses recognised in profit or loss using a classification based on the nature of expense method.

An example of a classification using the nature of expense method is as follows:

Revenue,	X
Other income,	X
Changes in inventories of finished goods and work in progress,	X
Raw materials and consumables used,	X
Employee benefits expense,	X
Depreciation and amortisation expense,	X
Other expenses,	X
Total expenses,	(X)
Profit before tax,	X

Statement of Changes in Equity An entity would present a statement of changes in equity as a part of balance sheet and would include the following information: (a) total comprehensive income for the period, showing separately the total amounts attributable to owners of the parent and to non-controlling interests; (b) for each component of equity, the effects of retrospective application or retrospective restatement recognised in accordance with **Ind AS 8**; (c) for each component of equity, a reconciliation between the carrying amount at the beginning and the end of the period, separately disclosing each change resulting from: (i) profit or loss; (ii) each item of other comprehensive income; (iii) transactions with owners in their capacity as owners, showing separately contributions by and distributions to owners and changes in ownership interests in subsidiaries that do not result in a loss of control; and (iv) any item recognised directly in equity such as amount recognised directly in equity as capital reserve in accordance with **Ind AS 103**.

For each component of equity an entity would also present, either in the statement of changes in equity or in the notes, an analysis of other comprehensive income by item, the amount of dividends recognised as distributions to owners during the period, and the related amount of dividends per share.

Disclosure of Accounting Policies

An entity is required to disclose in the summary of significant accounting policies: (a) the measurement basis (or bases) used in preparing the financial statements, and (b) the other accounting policies used that are relevant to an understanding of the financial statements.

Sources of Estimation Uncertainty An entity would disclose information about the assumptions it makes about the future, and other major sources of estimation uncertainty at the end of the reporting period, that have a significant risk of resulting in a material adjustment to the carrying amounts of assets and liabilities within the next financial year. In respect of those assets and liabilities, the notes should include details of: (a) their nature, and (b) their carrying amount as at the end of the reporting period.

Capital An entity would disclose information that enables users of its financial statements to evaluate the entity's objectives, policies and processes for managing capital.

Other Disclosures An entity would disclose in the notes: (a) the amount of dividends proposed or declared before the financial statements were approved for issue but not recognised as a distribution to owners during the period, and the related amount per share; and (b) the amount of any cumulative preference dividends not recognised.

An entity would also disclose the following, if not disclosed elsewhere in information published with the financial statements: (a) the domicile and legal form of the entity, its country of incorporation and the address of its registered office (or principal place of business, if different from the registered office); (b) a description of the nature of the entity's operations and its principal activities; (c) the name of the parent and the ultimate parent of the group; and (d) if it is a limited life entity, information regarding the length of its life.

Ind AS–7: Statement of Cash Flows

This standard has been discussed in detail in Chapter 5.

Ind AS-8: Accounting Policies, Changes in Accounting Estimates and Errors

Objective

The objective of this standard is to prescribe the criteria for selecting and changing accounting policies, together with the accounting treatment and disclosure of changes in accounting policies, changes in accounting estimates and corrections of errors. The standard is intended to enhance the relevance and reliability of an entity's financial statements, and the comparability of those financial statements over time and with the financial statements of other entities.

Scope

This standard would be applied in selecting and applying accounting policies, and accounting for changes in accounting policies, changes in accounting estimates and corrections of prior period errors.

Definitions

Accounting policies are the specific principles, bases, conventions, rules and practices applied by an entity in preparing and presenting financial statements.

A change in accounting estimate is an adjustment of the carrying amount of an asset or a liability, or the amount of the periodic consumption of an asset, that results from the assessment of the present status of, and expected future benefits and obligations associated with assets and liabilities. Changes in accounting estimates result from new information or new developments and, accordingly, are not corrections of errors.

Prior period errors are omissions from, and mis-statements in, the entity's financial statements for one or more prior periods arising from a failure to use, or misuse of, reliable information that: (a) was available when financial statements for those periods were approved for issue; and (b) could reasonably be expected to have been obtained and taken into account in the preparation and presentation of those financial statements.

Such errors include the effects of mathematical mistakes, mistakes in applying accounting policies, oversights or misinterpretations of facts and fraud.

Retrospective application is applying a new accounting policy to transactions, other events and conditions as if that policy had always been applied. Retrospective restatement is correcting the recognition, measurement and disclosure of amounts of elements of financial statements as if a prior period error had never occurred.

Impracticable applying a requirement is impracticable when the entity cannot apply it after making every reasonable effort to do so. The possible situations are if: (a) the effects of the retrospective application or retrospective restatement are not determinable; (b) the retrospective application or retrospective restatement requires significant estimates of amounts and it is impossible to distinguish objectively information about those estimates.

Prospective application of a change in accounting policy and of recognising the effect of a change in an accounting estimate, respectively, are: (a) applying the new accounting policy to transactions, other events and conditions occurring after the date as at which the policy is changed; and (b) recognising the effect of the change in the accounting estimate in the current and future periods affected by the change.

Accounting Policies

Selection and Application of Accounting Policies When an **Ind AS** specifically applies to a transaction, other event or condition, the accounting policy or policies applied to that item should be determined by applying the Ind AS; in the absence of an **Ind AS**, management should use its judgement in developing and applying an accounting policy that results in information that is: (a) relevant to the economic decision-making needs of users; and (b) reliable so that the financial statements: (i) represent truly the financial position, financial performance and cash flows of the entity; (ii) are free from bias; (iii) are prudent; and (iv) are complete in all material respects.

In making the judgement, management would refer to, and consider the applicability of, the following sources in descending order: (a) the requirements in Ind ASs dealing with similar and related issues; and (b) the definitions, recognition criteria and measurement concepts for assets, liabilities, income and expenses in the framework. In making the judgement, management may also first consider the most recent pronouncements of International Accounting Standards Board and in absence thereof those of the other standard-setting bodies that use a similar conceptual framework to develop accounting standards, other accounting literature and accepted industry practices.

Consistency of Accounting Policies An entity is required to select and apply its accounting policies consistently for similar transactions, other events and conditions, unless an **Ind AS** specifically requires or permits categorisation of items for which different policies may be appropriate. If an **Ind AS** requires or permits such categorisation, an appropriate accounting policy should be selected and applied consistently to each category.

Changes in Accounting Policies An entity would change an accounting policy only if the change: (a) is required by an **Ind AS**; or (b) results in the financial statements providing reliable and more relevant information about the effects of transactions, other events or conditions on the entity's financial position, financial performance or cash flows.

The initial application of a policy to revalue assets in accordance with **Ind AS-16**: Property, Plant and Equipment or Ind AS-38: Intangible Assets is a change in an accounting policy to be dealt with as a revaluation in accordance with **Ind AS-16** or **Ind AS-38**, rather than in accordance with this standard.

Applying Changes in Accounting Policies (a) an entity would account for a change in accounting policy resulting from the initial application of an **Ind AS** in accordance with the specific transitional provisions, if any, in that Ind AS; and (b) when there are changes in an accounting policy voluntarily, it would apply the change retrospectively.

Disclosure When initial application of an **Ind AS** has an effect on the current period or any prior period, or might have an effect on future periods, an entity should disclose: (a) the title of the Ind AS; (b) when applicable; (c) the nature of the change in accounting policy; (d) the transitional provisions that might have an effect on future periods; (e) for the current period and each prior period presented, to the extent practicable, the amount of the adjustment: (i) for each financial statement line item affected; and (ii) if Ind AS-33: Earnings per Share applies to the entity, for basic and diluted earnings per share; and (f) the amount of the adjustment relating to periods before those presented, to the extent practicable.

Financial statements of subsequent periods need not repeat these disclosures.

Changes in Accounting Estimates and Errors

When an entity has not applied a new **Ind AS** that has been issued but is not yet effective, the entity would disclose: (a) this fact; and (b) known or reasonably estimable information relevant to assessing the possible impact that application of the new **Ind AS** will have on the entity's financial statements in the period of initial application.

The effect of change in an accounting estimate would be recognised prospectively by including it in profit or loss in: (a) the period of the change, if the change affects that period only; or (b) the period of the change and future periods, if the change affects both. On account of the uncertainties inherent in business activities, many items in financial statements cannot be measured with precision but can only be estimated. Estimation involves judgements based on the latest available, reliable information. For example, estimates may be required of: (i) bad debts; (ii) inventory obsolescence; (iii) the fair value of financial assets or financial liabilities.

To the extent that a change in an accounting estimate gives rise to changes in assets and liabilities, or relates to an item of equity, it should be recognised by adjusting the carrying amount of the related asset, liability or equity item in the period of the change.

An entity is required to correct material prior period errors retrospectively in the first set of financial statements approved for issue after their detection by: (a) restating the comparative amounts for the prior period(s) presented in which the error occurred; or (b) if the error occurred before the earliest prior period presented, restating the opening balances of assets, liabilities and equity for the earliest prior period presented.

Limitations on Retrospective Restatement A prior period error would be corrected by retrospective restatement except to the extent that it is impracticable to determine either the period-specific effects or the cumulative effect of the error. In such a situation, the entity would restate the opening balances of assets, liabilities and equity for the earliest period for which retrospective restatement is practicable.

Disclosure An entity would disclose the nature and amount of a change in an accounting estimate that has an effect in the current period or is expected to have an effect in future periods, except for the disclosure of the effect on future periods when it is impracticable to estimate that effect. If the amount of the effect in future periods is not disclosed because estimating it is impracticable, an entity should disclose that fact.

Disclosure of Prior Period Errors An entity would disclose the following: (a) the nature of the prior period error; (b) for each prior period presented, to the extent practicable, the amount of the correction: (i) for each financial statement line item affected; and (ii) if **Ind AS-33** applies to the entity, for basic and diluted earnings per share; (c) the amount of the correction at the beginning of the earliest prior period presented; and (d) if retrospective restatement is impracticable for a particular prior period, the circumstances that led to the existence of that condition and a description of how and from when the error has been corrected.

Financial statements of subsequent periods need not repeat these disclosures.

Ind AS-11: Construction Contracts

Definitions

A construction contract is a contract specifically negotiated for the construction of an asset or a combination of assets that are closely interrelated or interdependent in terms of their design, technology and function or their ultimate purpose or use. It also includes agreements of real estate development to provide services together with construction material in order to perform contractual obligation to deliver the real estate to the buyer.

A Fixed Price Contract is a construction contract in which the contractor agrees to a fixed contract price, or a fixed rate per unit of output, which in some cases is subject to cost escalation clauses.

A Cost Plus Contract is a construction contract in which the contractor is reimbursed for allowable or otherwise defined costs, plus a percentage of these costs or a fixed fee.

A construction contract may be negotiated for the construction of a single asset such as a bridge, building, dam, pipeline, road, ship or tunnel. A construction contract may also deal with the construction of a number of assets which are closely interrelated or interdependent in terms of their design, technology and function or their ultimate purpose or use; examples of such contracts include those for the construction of refineries and other complex pieces of plant or equipment.

For the purposes of this standard, construction contracts include: (a) contracts for the rendering of services which are directly related to the construction of the asset, for example, those for the services of project managers and architects; and (b) contracts for the destruction or restoration of assets, and the restoration of the environment following the demolition of assets.

Construction contracts are formulated in a number of ways which, for the purposes of this standard, are classified as fixed price contracts and cost plus contracts. Some construction contracts may contain characteristics of both a fixed price contract and a cost plus contract, for example in the case of a cost plus contract with an agreed maximum price. In such circumstances, a contractor needs to consider all the conditions carefully in order to determine when to recognise contract revenue and expenses.

Disclosure An entity is to disclose: (a) the amount of contract revenue recognised as revenue in the period; (b) the methods used to determine the contract revenue recognised in the period; and (c) the methods used to determine the stage of completion of contracts in progress.

Further, an entity should disclose each of the following for contracts in progress at the end of the reporting period: (a) the aggregate amount of costs incurred and recognised profits (less recognised losses) to date; (b) the amount of advances received; and (c) the amount of retentions.

Ind AS-12: Income Taxes

Objective

The objective of this standard is to prescribe the accounting treatment for income taxes. The principal issue in accounting for income taxes is how to account for the current and future tax consequences of: (a) the future recovery (settlement) of the carrying amount of assets (liabilities) that are recognised in an entity's balance sheet; and (b) transactions and other events of the current period that are recognised in an entity's financial statements.

Definitions

Accounting profit is profit or loss for a period before deducting tax expense. Taxable profit (tax loss) is the profit (loss) for a period, determined in accordance with the rules established by the taxation authorities, upon which income taxes are payable (recoverable).

Tax expense (tax income) is the aggregate amount included in the determination of profit or loss for the period in respect of current tax and deferred tax. Current tax is the amount of income taxes payable (recoverable) in respect of the taxable profit (tax loss) for a period. Tax expense comprises current tax expense and deferred tax expense.

Deferred tax liabilities are the amounts of income taxes payable in future periods in respect of taxable temporary differences.

Deferred tax assets are the amounts of income taxes recoverable in future periods in respect of: (a) deductible temporary differences; (b) the carry forward of unused tax losses; and (c) the carry forward of unused tax credits. Temporary differences are differences between the carrying amount of an asset or liability in the balance sheet and its tax base. The tax base of an asset or liability is the amount attributed to that asset or liability for tax purposes.

The tax base of an asset is the amount that will be deductible for tax purposes against any taxable economic benefits that will flow to an entity when it recovers the carrying amount of the asset.

Examples

1. A machine costs ₹100. For tax purposes, depreciation of ₹30 has already been deducted in the current and prior periods and the remaining cost will be deductible in future periods, either as depreciation or through a deduction on disposal. Revenue generated by using the machine is taxable, any gain on disposal of the machine will be taxable and any loss on disposal will be deductible for tax purposes. The tax base of the machine is ₹70.
2. A loan receivable has a carrying amount of ₹100. The repayment of the loan will have no tax consequences. The tax base of the loan is ₹100.
3. Current liabilities include accrued expenses with a carrying amount of ₹100. The related expense has already been deducted for tax purposes. The tax base of the accrued expenses is ₹100.
4. A loan payable has a carrying amount of ₹100. The repayment of the loan will have no tax consequences. Under this analysis, there is no deductible temporary difference.

Recognition of Current Tax Liabilities and Current Tax Assets

Current tax for current and prior periods, to the extent unpaid, is to be recognised as a liability. If the amount already paid in respect of current and prior periods exceeds the amount due for those periods, the excess amount paid is to be recognised as an asset.

Recognition of Deferred Tax Liabilities and Deferred Tax Assets

Deductible Temporary Differences Deferred tax asset is to be recognised for all deductible temporary differences to the extent that it is probable that taxable profit will be available against which the deductible temporary difference can be utilised.

Measurement Current tax liabilities (assets) for the current and prior periods are to be measured at the amount expected to be paid to (recovered from) the taxation authorities, using the tax rates (and tax laws) that have been enacted or substantively enacted by the end of the reporting period.

Deferred tax assets and liabilities are to be measured at the tax rates that are expected to apply to the period when the asset is realised or the liability is settled, based on tax rates (and tax laws) that have been enacted or substantively enacted by the end of the reporting period. The measurement of deferred tax liabilities and deferred tax assets would reflect the tax consequences that would follow from the manner in which the entity expects, at the end of the reporting period, to recover or settle the carrying amount of its assets and liabilities.

Recognition of Current and Deferred Tax

Items Recognised in Profit or Loss Current and deferred tax would be recognised as income or an expense and included in profit or loss for the period, except to the extent that the tax arises from: (a) a transaction or event which is recognised, in the same or a different period, outside profit or loss, either in other comprehensive income or directly in equity; or (b) a business combination.

Items Recognised Outside Profit or Loss Current tax and deferred tax would be recognised outside profit or loss if the tax relates to items that are recognised, in the same or a different period, outside profit or loss. Therefore, current tax and deferred tax that relates to items that are recognised, in the same or a different period: (a) in other comprehensive income, (b) directly in equity.

Offset An entity is entitled to offset current tax assets and current tax liabilities if, and only if, the entity: (a) has a legally enforceable right to set off the recognised amounts; and (b) intends either to settle on a net basis, or to realise the asset and settle the liability simultaneously. Moreover, an entity would offset deferred tax assets and deferred tax liabilities if, and only if: (a) the entity has a legally enforceable right to set off current tax assets against current tax liabilities; and (b) the deferred tax assets and the deferred tax liabilities relate to income taxes levied by the same taxation authority on either: (i) the same taxable entity; or (ii) different taxable entities which intend either to settle current tax liabilities and assets on a net basis, or to realise the assets and settle the liabilities simultaneously, in each future period in which significant amounts of deferred tax liabilities or assets are expected to be settled or recovered.

Disclosure

The major components of tax expense (income) are to be disclosed separately. These may include: (a) current tax expense (income); (b) any adjustments recognised in the period for current tax of prior periods; (c) the amount of deferred tax expense (income) relating to the origination and reversal of temporary differences; (d) the amount of deferred tax expense (income) relating to changes in tax rates or the imposition of new taxes; (e) the amount of the benefit arising from a previously unrecognised tax loss, tax credit or temporary difference of a prior period that is used to reduce current tax expense; (f) the amount of the benefit from a previously unrecognised tax loss, tax credit or temporary difference of a prior period that is used to reduce deferred tax expense; (g) deferred tax expense arising from the write-down, or reversal of a previous write-down, of a deferred tax asset; and (h) the amount of tax expense (income) relating to those changes in accounting policies and errors that are included in profit or loss in accordance with **Ind AS-8**, because they cannot be accounted for retrospectively.

The following are also to be disclosed separately: (a) the aggregate current and deferred tax relating to items that are charged or credited directly to equity; (b) the amount of income tax relating to each component of other comprehensive income; (c) an explanation of the relationship between tax expense (income) and accounting profit in either or both of the following forms: (i) a numerical reconciliation between tax expense (income) and the product of accounting profit multiplied by the applicable tax rate(s), disclosing also the basis on which the applicable tax rate(s) is (are) computed; or (ii) a numerical reconciliation between the average effective tax rate and the applicable tax rate, disclosing also the basis on which the applicable tax rate is computed; (d) an explanation of changes in the applicable tax rate(s) compared to the previous accounting period; (e) the amount (and expiry date, if any) of deductible temporary differences, unused tax losses, and unused tax credits for which no deferred tax asset is recognised in the balance sheet; (f) the aggregate amount of temporary differences associated with investments in subsidiaries, branches and associates and interests in joint ventures, for which deferred tax liabilities have not been recognised; (g) in respect of each type of temporary difference, and in respect of each type of unused tax losses and unused tax credits; (h) the amount of the deferred tax assets and liabilities recognised in the balance sheet for each period presented; (i) the amount of the deferred tax income or expense recognised in profit or loss, if this is not apparent from the changes in the amounts recognised in the balance sheet; the amount of income tax consequences of dividends to shareholders of the entity that were proposed or declared before the financial statements were approved for issue, but are not recognised as a liability in the financial statements; (j) if a business combination in which the entity is the acquirer causes a change in the amount recognised for its pre-acquisition deferred tax asset, the amount of that change; and (k) if the deferred tax benefits acquired in a business combination are not recognised at the acquisition date but are recognised after the acquisition date, a description of the event or change in circumstances that caused the deferred tax benefits to be recognised.

Yet another requirement in that an entity would disclose the amount of a deferred tax asset and the nature of the evidence supporting its recognition, when: (a) the utilisation of the deferred tax asset is dependent on future taxable profits in excess of the profits arising from the reversal of existing taxable temporary differences; and (b) the entity has suffered a loss in either the current or preceding period in the tax jurisdiction to which the deferred tax asset relates.

Finally, an entity would disclose the nature of the potential income tax consequences that would result from the payment of dividends to its shareholders. In addition, the entity would also disclose the amounts of the potential income tax consequences practicably determinable and whether there are any potential income tax consequences not practicably determinable.

Ind AS-16: Property, Plant and Equipment

Objective

The objective of this standard is to prescribe the accounting treatment for property, plant and equipment so that users of the financial statements can obtain information about an entity's investment in its property, plant and equipment and the changes in such investment. The principal issues in accounting for property, plant and equipment are the recognition of the assets, the determination of their carrying amounts and the depreciation charges and impairment losses to be recognised in relation to them.

Scope

This standard does not apply to: (a) property, plant and equipment classified as held for sale in accordance with **Ind AS-105**: Non-current Assets Held for Sale and Discontinued Operations; (b) biological assets related to agricultural activity; (c) the recognition and measurement of exploration and evaluation assets (**Ind AS-106**: Exploration for and Evaluation of Mineral Resources); or (d) mineral rights and mineral reserves such as oil, natural gas and similar non-regenerative resources. However, this standard applies to property, plant and equipment used to develop or maintain the assets described in (b)–(d).

Definitions

Carrying amount is the amount at which an asset is recognised after deducting any accumulated depreciation and accumulated impairment losses.

Cost is the amount of cash or cash equivalents paid or the fair value of the other consideration given to acquire an asset at the time of its acquisition or construction or, where applicable, the amount attributed to that asset when initially recognised in accordance with the specific requirements of other Indian Accounting Standards, e.g. **Ind AS-102** Share-based Payment.

Depreciable amount is the cost of an asset, or other amount substituted for cost, less its residual value.

Depreciation is the systematic allocation of the depreciable amount of an asset over its useful life. Entity-specific value is the present value of the cash flows an entity expects to obtain from the continuing use of an asset and from its disposal at the end of its useful life or expects to incur when settling a liability. Fair value is the amount for which an asset could be exchanged between knowledgeable, willing parties in an arm's length transaction.

An impairment loss is the amount by which the carrying amount of an asset exceeds its recoverable amount.

Property, plant and equipment are tangible items that: (a) are held for use in the production or supply of goods or services, for rental to others, or for administrative purposes; and (b) are expected to be used during more than one period.

Recoverable amount is the higher of an asset's fair value less costs to sell and its value in use.

Residual value of an asset is the estimated amount that an entity would currently obtain from disposal of the asset, after deducting the estimated costs of disposal, at the end of its useful life.

Useful life is: (a) the period over which an asset is expected to be available for use by an entity; or (b) the number of production or similar units expected to be obtained from the asset by an entity.

Recognition

The cost of an item of property, plant and equipment would be recognised as an asset only if: (a) it is probable that future economic benefits associated with the item will accrue to the entity; and (b) the cost of the item can be measured reliably.

Spare parts and servicing equipment are usually carried as inventory and recognised in profit or loss as consumed. However, major spare parts, stand-by equipment and servicing equipment qualify as property, plant and equipment when an entity expects to use them during more than one period.

Elements of Cost

The cost of an item of property, plant and equipment (by and large) comprises: (a) its purchase price, including import duties and nonrefundable purchase taxes, after deducting trade discounts and rebates; (b) any costs directly attributable to bringing the asset to the location and condition necessary for it to be capable of operating in the manner intended by management.

Directly attributable costs include: (a) costs of employee benefits (as defined in **Ind AS-19**: Employee Benefits) arising directly from the construction or acquisition of the item of property, plant and equipment; (b) costs of site preparation; (c) initial delivery and handling costs; (d) installation and assembly costs; (e) costs of testing whether the asset is functioning properly; and (f) professional fees.

Measurement of Cost An item of property, plant and equipment that qualifies for recognition as an asset would be measured at its cost. The cost of an item of property, plant and equipment is the cash price equivalent at the recognition date. If payment is deferred beyond normal credit terms, the difference between the cash price equivalent and the total payment is recognised as interest over the period of credit unless such interest is capitalised in accordance with **Ind AS-23**.

Cost Model: After recognition as an asset, an item of property, plant and equipment is to be carried at its cost less any accumulated depreciation and any accumulated impairment losses.

Revaluation Model: After recognition as an asset, an item of property, plant and equipment whose fair value can be measured reliably would be carried at a revalued amount, being its fair value at the date of the revaluation less any subsequent accumulated depreciation and subsequent accumulated impairment losses. Revaluations are required to be made with sufficient regularity to ensure that the carrying amount does not differ materially from that which would be determined using fair value at the end of the reporting period.

The fair value of land and buildings is usually determined from market-based evidence by appraisal that is normally undertaken by professionally qualified valuers. The fair value of items of plant and equipment is usually their market value determined by appraisal.

If there is no market-based evidence of fair value because of the specialised nature of the item of property, plant and equipment, and the item is rarely sold, except as part of a continuing business, an entity may need to estimate fair value using an income or a depreciated replacement cost approach.

A class of property, plant and equipment is a grouping of assets of a similar nature and use in an entity's operations. The following are examples of separate classes: (i) land; (ii) land and buildings; (iii) machinery; (iv) ships; (v) aircraft; (vi) motor vehicles; (vii) furniture and fixtures; and (viii) office equipment.

If an asset's carrying amount is increased as a result of a revaluation, the increase is required to be recognised in other comprehensive income and accumulated in equity under the heading of revaluation surplus. However, the increase would be recognised in profit or loss to the extent that it reverses a revaluation decrease of the same asset previously recognised in profit or loss.

If an asset's carrying amount is decreased as a result of a revaluation, the decrease is to be recognised in profit or loss. However, the decrease would be recognised in other comprehensive income to the extent of any credit balance existing in the revaluation surplus in respect of that asset. The decrease recognised in other comprehensive income reduces the amount accumulated in equity under the heading of revaluation surplus.

Each part of an item of property, plant and equipment with a cost that is significant is required to be depreciated separately. The depreciation charge for each period is to be recognised in profit or loss.

An entity would choose either the cost model or revaluation model (as its accounting policy); the chosen model is to be applied to an entire class of property, plant and equipment.

Depreciable Amount and Depreciation Period

The depreciable amount of an asset is to be allocated on a systematic basis over its useful life.

The residual value and the useful life of an asset are required to be reviewed at least at each financial year-end and, if expectations differ from previous estimates, the change(s) should be accounted for as a change in an accounting estimate in accordance with **Ind AS-8**: Accounting Policies, Changes in Accounting Estimates and Errors.

Depreciation is recognised even if the fair value of the asset exceeds its carrying amount, as long as the asset's residual value does not exceed its carrying amount. Repair and maintenance expenses incurred on an asset are to be additionally shown in profit and loss.

The depreciable amount of an asset is determined after deducting its residual value. The residual value of an asset may increase to an amount equal to or greater than the asset's carrying amount. If it does, the asset's depreciation charge is zero unless and until its residual value subsequently decreases to an amount below the asset's carrying amount. Depreciation of an asset begins when it is available for use, i.e. when it is in the location and condition necessary for it to be capable of operating in the manner intended by management. Further, depreciation does not cease when the asset becomes idle or is retired from active use unless the asset is fully depreciated. However, under usage methods of depreciation the depreciation charge can be zero while there is no production. The future economic benefits embodied in an asset are consumed by an entity principally through its use. However, other factors, such as technical or commercial obsolescence and wear and tear while an asset remains idle, often result in the diminution of the economic benefits that might have been obtained from the asset. Consequently, all the following factors are considered in determining the useful life of an asset: (a) expected usage of the asset in terms of expected capacity or physical output, (b) expected physical wear and tear, which depends on operational factors such as the number of shifts for which the asset is to be used and the repair and maintenance programme, and the care and maintenance of the asset while idle. (c) technical or commercial obsolescence arising from changes or improvements in production, or from a change in the market demand for the product or service output of the asset. (d) legal or similar limits on the use of the asset.

The useful life of an asset is defined in terms of the asset's expected utility to the entity. The asset management policy of the entity may involve the disposal of assets after a specified time or after consumption of a specified proportion of the future economic benefits embodied in the asset. Therefore, the useful (economic) life of an asset may be shorter than its physical useful life. The estimation of the useful life of the asset is a matter of judgement based on the experience of the entity with similar assets.

Land and buildings are separable assets and are accounted for separately, even when they are acquired together. With some exceptions, such as quarries and sites used for landfill, land has an unlimited useful life and therefore is not depreciated. Buildings have a limited useful life and therefore are depreciable assets. An increase in the value of the land on which a building stands does not affect the determination of the depreciable amount of the building.

Depreciation Method

The depreciation method used should reflect the pattern in which the asset's future economic benefits are expected to be consumed by the entity. The depreciation method applied to an asset should be reviewed at least at each financial year-end and, if there has been a significant change in the expected pattern of consumption of the future economic benefits embodied in the asset, the method should be changed to reflect the changed pattern. Such a change is to be accounted for as a change in an accounting estimate in accordance with **Ind AS-8**.

Derecognition

The carrying amount of an item of property, plant and equipment would be derecognised: (a) on disposal; or (b) when no future economic benefits are expected from its use or disposal.

The gain or loss arising from the derecognition of an item of property, plant and equipment is determined as the difference between the net disposal proceeds, and the carrying amount of the item.

Disclosure

The financial statements are required to disclose, for each class of property, plant and equipment: (a) the measurement bases used for determining the gross carrying amount; (b) the depreciation methods used; (c) the useful lives or the depreciation rates used; (d) the gross carrying amount and the accumulated depreciation (aggregated with accumulated impairment losses) at the beginning and end of the period; and (e) a reconciliation of the carrying amount at the beginning and end of the period showing: (i) additions; (ii) assets classified as held for sale or included in a disposal group classified as held for sale in accordance with **Ind AS-105** and other disposals; (iii) acquisitions through business combinations; (iv) increases or decreases resulting from revaluations and from impairment losses recognised or reversed in other comprehensive income in accordance with **Ind AS-36**; (v) impairment losses recognised in profit or loss in accordance with **Ind AS-36**; (vi) impairment losses reversed in profit or loss in accordance with **Ind AS-36**; (vii) depreciation; (viii) the net exchange differences arising on the translation of the financial statements from the functional currency into a different presentation currency, including the translation of a foreign operation into the presentation currency of the reporting entity; and (ix) other changes.

The financial statements are also to disclose: (a) the existence and amounts of restrictions on title, and property, plant and equipment pledged as security for liabilities; (b) the amount of expenditures recognised in the carrying amount of an item of property, plant and equipment in the course of its construction; and (c) the amount of contractual commitments for the acquisition of property, plant and equipment.

If items of property, plant and equipment are stated at revalued amounts, the entity is to disclose: (a) the effective date of the revaluation; (b) whether an independent valuer was involved; (c) the methods and significant assumptions applied in estimating the items' fair values; (d) the extent to which the items' fair values were determined directly by reference to observable prices in an active market or recent market transactions on arm's length terms or were estimated using other valuation techniques; (e) for each revalued class of property, plant and equipment, the carrying amount that would have been recognised had the assets been carried under the cost model; and (f) the revaluation surplus, indicating the change for the period and any restrictions on the distribution of the balance to shareholders.

Ind AS-18: Revenue

Objective

The primary issue in accounting for revenue is determining the stage of its recognition. Revenue is recognised when it is probable that future economic benefits will accrue to the entity and these benefits can be measured reliably. This standard identifies the circumstances in which these criteria will be met and, therefore, revenue will be recognised. It also provides practical guidance on the application of these criteria.

Scope

This standard would be applied in accounting for revenue arising from the following transactions and events: (a) the sale of goods; (b) the rendering of services; and (c) the use by others of entity assets yielding interest, royalties and dividends. Goods include goods produced by the entity for the purpose of sale and goods purchased for resale, such as merchandise purchased by a retailer or land and other property held for resale. The rendering of services typically involves the performance by the entity of a contractually agreed task over an agreed period of time. The services may be rendered within a single period or over more than one period. The use by others of entity assets gives rise to revenue in the form of: (a) interest—charges for the use of cash or cash equivalents or amounts due to the entity; (b) royalties—charges for the use of long-term assets of the entity, for example, patents, trademarks, copyrights and computer software; and (c) dividends—distributions of profits to holders of equity investments.

Definitions

Revenue is the gross inflow of economic benefits during the period arising in the course of the ordinary activities of an entity when those inflows result in increases in equity, (excluding contributions from equity participants).

Measurement of Revenue Revenue would be measured at the fair value of the consideration received or receivable.

Identification of the Transaction

The recognition criteria in this standard are usually applied separately to each transaction. However, in certain circumstances, it is necessary to apply the recognition criteria to the separately identifiable components of a single transaction in order to reflect the substance of the transaction. For example, when the selling price of a product includes an identifiable amount for subsequent servicing, that amount is deferred and recognised as revenue over the period during which the service is performed.

Sale of Goods Revenue from the sale of goods would be recognised when all the following conditions have been satisfied: (a) the entity has transferred to the buyer the significant risks and rewards of ownership of the goods; (b) the entity retains neither continuing managerial involvement to the degree usually associated with ownership nor effective control over the goods sold; (c) the amount of revenue can be measured reliably; (d) it is probable that the economic benefits associated with the transaction will accrue to the entity; and (e) the costs incurred or to be incurred in respect of the transaction can be measured reliably.

Rendering of Services When the outcome of a transaction involving the rendering of services can be estimated reliably, revenue associated with the transaction would be recognised by reference to the stage of completion of the transaction at the end of the reporting period. The outcome of a transaction can be estimated reliably when all the following conditions are satisfied: (a) the amount of revenue can be measured reliably; (b) it is probable that the economic benefits associated with the transaction will accrue to the entity; (c) the stage of completion of the transaction at the end of the reporting period can be measured reliably; and (d) the costs incurred for the transaction and the costs to complete the transaction can be measured reliably. When the outcome of the transaction involving the rendering of services cannot be estimated reliably, revenue should be recognised only to the extent of the expenses recognised that are recoverable.

Interest, Royalties and Dividends Revenue arising from the use by others of entity assets yielding interest, royalties and dividends would be recognised when: (a) it is probable that the economic benefits associated with the transaction will accrue to the entity; and (b) the amount of the revenue can be measured reliably.

Revenue would be recognised on the following bases: (a) interest is to be recognised using the effective interest method as set out in Ind AS 39; (b) royalties would be recognised on an accrual basis in accordance with the substance of the relevant agreement; and (c) dividends are to be recognised when the shareholder's right to receive payment is established.

Disclosure

An entity is required to disclose: (a) the accounting policies adopted for the recognition of revenue, including the methods adopted to determine the stage of completion of transactions involving the rendering of services; (b) the amount of each significant category of revenue recognised during the period, including revenue arising from: (i) the sale of goods; (ii) the rendering of services; (iii) interest; (iv) royalties; (v) dividends; and (c) the amount of revenue arising from exchanges of goods or services included in each significant category of revenue.

Ind AS-21: The Effects of Changes in Foreign Exchange Rates

Scope

This standard would be applied: (a) in accounting for transactions and balances in foreign currencies, except for those derivative transactions and balances that are within the scope of **Ind AS-39**: Financial Instruments: Recognition and Measurement; (b) in translating the results and financial position of foreign operations that are included in the financial statements of the entity by consolidation, proportionate consolidation or the equity method; and (c) in translating an entity's results and financial position into a presentation currency.

Definitions

Closing rate is the spot exchange rate at the end of the reporting period.

Exchange difference is the difference resulting from translating a given number of units of one currency into another currency at different exchange rates.

Exchange rate is the ratio of exchange for two currencies.

Fair value is the amount for which an asset could be exchanged, or a liability settled, between knowledgeable, willing parties in an arm's length transaction.

Foreign currency is a currency other than the functional currency of the entity.

Foreign operation is an entity that is a subsidiary, associate, joint venture or branch of a reporting entity, the activities of which are based or conducted in a country or currency other than those of the reporting entity.

Functional currency is the currency of the primary economic environment in which the entity operates.

A group is a parent and all its subsidiaries.

Monetary items are units of currency held and assets and liabilities to be received or paid in a fixed or determinable number of units of currency.

Net investment in a foreign operation is the amount of the reporting entity's interest in the net assets of that operation.

Presentation currency is the currency in which the financial statements are presented.

Spot exchange rate is the exchange rate for immediate delivery.

Reporting Foreign Currency Transactions in the Functional Currency

Initial Recognition Foreign currency transaction are to be recorded, on initial recognition in the functional currency, by applying to the foreign currency amount the spot exchange rate between the functional currency and the foreign currency at the date of the transaction.

Reporting at the End of Subsequent Reporting Periods At the end of each reporting period: (a) foreign currency monetary items would be translated using the closing rate; (b) non-monetary items that are measured in terms of historical cost in a foreign currency would be translated using the exchange rate at the date of the transaction; and (c) non-monetary items that are measured at fair value in a foreign currency would be translated using the exchange rates at the date when the fair value was determined.

Exchange differences arising on the settlement of monetary items or on translating monetary items at rates different from those at which they were translated on initial recognition during the period or in previous financial statements are to be shown in profit or loss in the period in which they arise, except: (i) exchange differences arising on a monetary item that forms part of a reporting entity's net investment in a foreign operation; (ii) where an entity exercises the option in respect of long-term monetary items.

When a gain or loss on a non-monetary item is recognised in other comprehensive income, any exchange component of that gain or loss is also required to be recognised in other comprehensive income. Likewise, when a gain or loss on a non-monetary item is recognised in profit or loss, any exchange component of that gain or loss is to be recognised in profit or loss.

Exchange differences arising on a monetary item that forms part of a reporting entity's net investment in a foreign operation would be recognised in profit or loss in the separate financial statements of the reporting entity or the individual financial statements of the foreign operations, as appropriate. In the financial statements that include the foreign operations and the reporting entity (e.g. consolidated financial statements when the foreign operation is a subsidiary), such exchange differences would be recognised initially in other comprehensive income and reclassified from equity to profit or loss on disposal of the net investment.

Change in Functional Currency When there is a change in an entity's functional currency, the entity is required to apply the translation procedures applicable to the new functional currency prospectively from the date of the change.

The results and financial position of an entity whose functional currency is not the currency of a hyperinflationary economy would be translated into a different presentation currency using the following procedures: (a) assets and liabilities for each balance sheet presented (i.e. including comparatives) would be translated at the closing rate at the date of that balance sheet; (b) income and expenses for each statement of profit and loss presented (i.e. including comparatives) would be translated at exchange rates at the dates of the transactions; and (c) all resulting exchange differences would be recognised in other comprehensive income.

The results and financial position of an entity whose functional currency is the currency of a hyperinflationary economy would be translated into a different presentation currency using the following procedures: (a) all amounts (i.e. assets, liabilities, equity items, income and expenses, including comparatives) would be translated at the closing rate at the date of the most recent balance sheet, except that (b) when amounts are translated into the currency of a non-hyperinflationary economy, comparative amounts would be those that were presented as current year amounts in the relevant prior year financial statements (i.e. not adjusted for subsequent changes in the price level or subsequent changes in exchange rates).

Ind AS-24: Related Party Disclosures

This standard has been discussed in detail in Chapter 4.

Ind AS-27: Consolidated and separate Financial Statements

This standard has been discussed in detail in Chapter 4.

Ind AS-28: Investments in Associates

This standard has been discussed in detail in Chapter 4.

Ind AS-29: Financial Reporting in Hyperinflationary Economies

Scope

This standard is to be applied to the financial statements, including the consolidated financial statements, of any entity whose functional currency is the currency of a hyperinflationary economy. In a hyperinflationary economy, reporting of operating results and financial position in the local currency (as they are) is not useful. Money loses purchasing power at such a rate that comparison of amounts from transactions and other events that have occurred at different times, even within the same accounting period, is misleading. The financial statements of an entity whose functional currency is the currency of a hyperinflationary economy, whether they are based on a historical cost approach or a current cost approach, would be stated in terms of the measuring unit current at the end of the reporting period. The corresponding figures for the previous period required by **Ind AS-1**: Presentation of Financial Statements and any information in respect of earlier periods would also be stated in terms of the measuring unit currency at the end of the reporting period. For the purpose of presenting comparative amounts in a different presentation currency, **Ind AS-21**: The Effects of Changes in Foreign Exchange Rates apply.

The gain or loss on the net monetary position should be included in profit or loss and separately disclosed.

Economies Ceasing to be Hyperinflationary

When an economy ceases to be hyperinflationary and an entity discontinues the preparation and presentation of financial statements prepared in accordance with this standard, it would treat the amounts expressed in the measuring unit currency at the end of the previous reporting period as the basis for the carrying amounts in its subsequent financial statements.

Disclosures

The following disclosures are to be made: (a) the fact that the financial statements and the corresponding figures for previous periods have been restated for the changes in the general purchasing power of the functional currency and, as a result, are stated in terms of the measuring unit currency at the end of the reporting period; (b) whether the financial statements are based on a historical cost approach or a current cost approach; and (c) the identity and level of the price index at the end of the reporting period and the movement in the index during the current and the previous reporting period; (d) the duration of the hyperinflationary situation existing in the economy.

Ind AS-32: Financial Instruments: Presentation

Objective

The objective of this standard is to establish principles for presenting financial instruments as liabilities or equity and for offsetting financial assets and financial liabilities. It applies to the classification of financial instruments, from the perspective of the issuer, into financial assets, financial liabilities and equity instruments; the classification of related interest, dividends, losses and gains; and the circumstances in which financial assets and financial liabilities should be offset.

The principles in this standard complement the principles for recognising and measuring financial assets and financial liabilities in **Ind AS-39** Financial Instruments: Recognition and Measurement, and for disclosing information about them in **Ind AS-107** Financial Instruments: Disclosures.

Scope

This standard would be applied to all entities and to all types of financial instruments except: (a) those interests in subsidiaries, associates or joint ventures that are accounted for in accordance with **Ind AS-27**, **Ind AS-28** or **Ind AS-31**. However, in some cases, **Ind AS-27**, **Ind AS-28** or **Ind AS-31** permits an entity to account for an interest in a subsidiary, associate or joint venture using **Ind AS-39**; in those cases, entities would apply the requirements of this standard. Entities would also apply this standard to all derivatives linked to interests in subsidiaries, associates or joint ventures; (b) employers' rights and obligations under employee benefit plans, to which **Ind AS-19** Employee Benefits applies; (c) insurance contracts as defined in **Ind AS-104** Insurance Contracts; (d) financial instruments that are within the scope of **Ind AS-104** because they contain a discretionary participation feature. The issuer of these instruments is exempt from applying to the specific features of this standard regarding the distinction between financial liabilities and equity instruments. However, these instruments are subject to all other requirements of this standard. Furthermore, this standard applies to derivatives that are embedded in these instruments; (e) financial instruments, contracts and obligations (by and large) under share-based payment transactions to which **Ind AS-102** Share-based Payment applies.

Definitions

A financial instrument is any contract that gives rise to a financial asset of one entity and a financial liability or equity instrument of another entity.

A financial asset is any asset that is: (a) cash; (b) an equity instrument of another entity; (c) a contractual right: (i) to receive cash or another financial asset from another entity; or (ii) to exchange financial assets or financial liabilities with another entity under conditions that are potentially favourable to the entity; or (d) a contract that will or may be settled in the entity's own equity instruments and is: (i) a non-derivative for which the entity is or may be obliged to receive a variable number of the entity's own equity instruments; or (ii) a derivative that will or may be settled other than by the exchange of a fixed amount of cash or another financial asset for a fixed number of the entity's own equity instruments.

A financial liability is any liability that is: (a) a contractual obligation: (i) to deliver cash or another financial asset to another entity; or (ii) to exchange financial assets or financial liabilities with another entity under conditions that are potentially unfavourable to the entity; or (b) a contract that will or may be settled in the entity's own equity instruments and is: (i) a non-derivative for which the entity is or may be obliged to deliver a variable number of the entity's own equity instruments; or (ii) a derivative that will or may be settled other than by the exchange of a fixed amount of cash or another financial asset for a fixed number of the entity's own equity instruments.

An equity instrument is any contract that evidences a residual interest in the assets of an entity after deducting all of its liabilities.

Fair value is the amount for which an asset could be exchanged, or a liability settled, between knowledgeable, willing parties in an arm's length transaction.

A puttable instrument is a financial instrument that gives the holder the right to put the instrument back to the issuer for cash or another financial asset or is automatically put back to the issuer on the occurrence of an uncertain future event or the death or retirement of the instrument holder.

Ind AS-33: Earnings per Share

Objective

The objective of this standard is to prescribe principles for the determination and presentation of earnings per share, so as to improve performance comparisons between different entities in the same reporting period and between different reporting periods for the same entity. Even though earnings per share data have limitations because of the different accounting policies that may be used for determining 'earnings', a consistently determined denominator enhances financial reporting. The focus of this standard is on the denominator of the earnings per share calculation.

Definitions

Antidilution is an increase in earnings per share or a reduction in loss per share resulting from the assumption that convertible instruments are converted, that options or warrants are exercised, or that ordinary shares are issued upon the satisfaction of specified conditions.

A contingent share agreement is an agreement to issue shares that is dependent on the satisfaction of specified conditions.

Contingently issuable ordinary shares are ordinary shares issuable for little or no cash or other consideration upon the satisfaction of specified conditions in a contingent share agreement.

Dilution is a reduction in earnings per share or an increase in loss per share resulting from the assumption that convertible instruments are converted, that options or warrants are exercised, or that ordinary shares are issued upon the satisfaction of specified conditions.

Options, warrants and their equivalents are financial instruments that give the holder the right to purchase ordinary shares.

A potential ordinary share is a financial instrument or other contract that may entitle its holder to ordinary shares.

Put options on ordinary shares are contracts that give the holder the right to sell ordinary shares at a specified price for a given period.

Measurement

Basic earnings per share should be calculated by dividing profit or loss attributable to ordinary equity holders of the parent entity (the numerator) by the weighted average number of ordinary shares outstanding (the denominator) during the period.

For the purpose of calculating basic earnings per share, the amounts attributable to ordinary equity holders of the parent entity in respect of: (a) profit or loss from continuing operations attributable to the parent entity; and (b) profit or loss attributable to the parent entity would be the amounts in (a) and (b) adjusted for the after-tax amounts of preference dividends and differences arising on the settlement of preference shares.

Where any item of income or expense which is otherwise required to be recognised in profit or loss in accordance with Indian Accounting Standards is debited or credited to securities premium account/other reserves, the amount in respect thereof would be deducted from profit or loss from continuing operations for the purpose of calculating basic earnings per share.

For the purpose of calculating basic earnings per share, **the number of ordinary shares** would be the weighted average number of ordinary shares outstanding during the period.

The weighted average number of ordinary shares outstanding during the period and for all periods presented would be adjusted for events, other than the conversion of potential ordinary shares, that have changed the number of ordinary shares outstanding without a corresponding change in resources.

Diluted Earnings Per Share

An entity would calculate diluted earnings per share amounts for profit or loss attributable to ordinary equity holders of the parent entity and, if presented, profit or loss from continuing operations attributable to those equity holders.

For the purpose of calculating diluted earnings per share, an entity would adjust profit or loss attributable to ordinary equity holders of the parent entity, and the weighted average number of shares outstanding, for the effects of all dilutive potential ordinary shares.

Additional adjustments required include: (a) any interest recognised in the period related to dilutive potential ordinary shares; and (b) any other changes in income or expense that would result from the conversion of the dilutive potential ordinary shares.

Dilutive Potential Ordinary Shares

Potential ordinary shares would be treated as dilutive when, and only when, their conversion to ordinary shares would decrease earnings per share or increase loss per share from continuing operations. For the purpose of calculating diluted earnings per share, an entity would assume the exercise of dilutive options and warrants of the entity. The assumed proceeds from these instruments would be regarded as having been received from the issue of ordinary shares at the average market price of ordinary shares during the period. The difference between the number of ordinary shares issued and the number of ordinary shares that would have been issued at the average market price of ordinary shares during the period would be treated as an issue of ordinary shares for no consideration. When an entity has issued a contract that may be settled in ordinary shares or cash at the entity's option, the entity should presume that the contract will be settled in ordinary shares, and the resulting potential ordinary shares would be included in diluted earnings per share if the effect is dilutive. For contracts that may be settled in ordinary shares or cash at the holder's option, the more dilutive of cash settlement and share settlement would be used in calculating diluted earnings per share.

Based on the above adjustments an entity would present in the statement of profit and loss basic and diluted earnings per share for profit or loss from continuing operations attributable to the ordinary equity holders of the parent entity and for profit or loss attributable to the ordinary equity holders of the parent entity for the period for each class of ordinary shares that has a different right to share in profit for the period. An entity would present basic and diluted earnings per share with equal prominence for all periods presented. An entity would present basic and diluted earnings per share, even if the amounts are negative (i.e. a loss per share).

Disclosure

An entity would disclose the following: (a) the amounts used as the numerators in calculating basic and diluted earnings per share, and a reconciliation of those amounts to profit or loss attributable to the parent entity for the period; (b) the weighted average number of ordinary shares used as the denominator in calculating basic and diluted earnings per share, and a reconciliation of these denominators to each other. The reconciliation should include the individual effect of each class of instruments that affects earnings per share; (c) instruments (including contingently issuable shares) that could potentially dilute basic earnings per share in the future, but were not included in the calculation of diluted earnings per share because they are antidilutive for the period(s) presented; (d) a description of ordinary share transactions or potential ordinary share transactions, that occur after the reporting period and that would have changed significantly the number of ordinary shares or potential ordinary shares outstanding at the end of the period if those transactions had occurred before the end of the reporting period.

If an entity discloses, in addition to basic and diluted earnings per share, amounts per share using a reported component of the statement of profit and loss other than one required by this standard, such amounts would be calculated using the weighted average number of ordinary shares determined in accordance with this standard. Basic and diluted amounts per share relating to such a component would be disclosed with equal prominence and presented in the notes. An entity would indicate the basis on which the numerator(s) is (are) determined, including whether amounts per share are before tax or after tax. If a component of the statement of profit and loss is used that is not reported as a line item in the statement of profit and loss, a reconciliation should be provided between the component used and a line item that is reported in the statement of profit and loss.

Ind AS-34: Interim Financial Reporting

This standard has been discussed in Chapter 4.

Ind AS-36: Impairment of Assets

Scope

This standard is to be applied in accounting for the impairment of all assets, other than: (a) inventories; (b) assets arising from construction contracts; (c) deferred tax assets; (d) assets arising from employee benefits; (e) financial assets; (f) biological assets related to agricultural activity that are measured at fair value less costs to sell; (g) deferred acquisition costs, and intangible assets, arising from an insurer's contractual rights under insurance contracts; and (h) non-current assets (or disposal groups) classified as held for sale in accordance with **Ind AS-105**: non-current assets held for sale and discontinued operations.

Definitions

An active market is a market in which all the following conditions exist: (a) the items traded within the market are homogeneous; (b) willing buyers and sellers can normally be found at any time; and (c) prices are available to the public.

Carrying amount is the amount at which an asset is recognised after deducting any accumulated depreciation (amortisation) and accumulated impairment losses thereon.

A cash-generating unit is the smallest identifiable group of assets that generates cash inflows that are largely independent of the cash inflows from other assets or groups of assets.

Corporate assets are assets other than goodwill that contribute to the future cash flows of both the cash-generating unit under review and other cash-generating units.

Costs of disposal are incremental costs directly attributable to the disposal of an asset or cash-generating unit, excluding finance costs and income tax expense.

Depreciable amount is the cost of an asset, or other amount substituted for cost in the financial statements, less its residual value.

Depreciation (Amortisation) is the systematic allocation of the depreciable amount of an asset over its useful life.

An impairment loss is the amount by which the carrying amount of an asset or a cash-generating unit exceeds its recoverable amount. The recoverable amount of an asset or a cash-generating unit is the higher of its fair value less costs to sell and its value in use.

Useful life is either: (a) the period of time over which an asset is expected to be used by the entity; or (b) the number of production or similar units expected to be obtained from the asset by the entity.

Value in use is the present value of the future cash flows expected to be derived from an asset or cash-generating unit.

Important Parameters Related to Impairment

Indicators An entity is required to assess at the end of each reporting period whether there is any indication that an asset may be impaired. If any such indication exists, the entity would estimate the recoverable amount of the asset.

Irrespective of whether there is any indication of impairment, an entity would also: (a) test an intangible asset with an indefinite useful life or an intangible asset not yet available for use for impairment annually by comparing its carrying amount with its recoverable amount. This impairment test may be performed at any time during an annual period; in subsequent years, it is to be performed at the same time. Different intangible assets may be tested for impairment at different times. However, if such an intangible asset was initially recognised during the current annual period, that intangible asset would be tested for impairment before the end of the current annual period. (b) test goodwill acquired in a business combination for impairment annually in accordance with rules laid down in this regard.

In assessing whether there is any indication that an asset may be impaired, an entity would consider, as a minimum, the following indications: (a) during the period, an asset's market value has declined significantly more than would be expected as a result of the passage of time or normal use; (b) significant changes with an adverse effect on the entity have taken place during the period, or will take place in the near future, in the technological, market, economic or legal environment in which the entity operates or in the market to which an asset is dedicated; (c) market interest rates or other market rates of return on investments have increased during the period, and those increases are likely to affect the discount rate used in calculating an asset's value in use and decrease the asset's recoverable amount materially; (d) the carrying amount of the net assets of the entity is more than its market capitalisation. Besides these external sources of information, there are internal sources of information. These include; (e) evidence is available of obsolescence or physical damage of an asset; (f) significant changes with an adverse effect on the entity have taken place during the period, or are expected to take place in the near future. These changes include the asset becoming idle, plans to discontinue or restructure the operation to which an asset belongs, plans to dispose of an asset; (g) evidence is available from internal reporting that indicates that the economic performance of an asset is, or will be, worse than expected.

Recognising and Measuring an Impairment Loss If, and only if, the recoverable amount of an asset is less than its carrying amount, the carrying amount of the asset would be reduced to its recoverable amount. That reduction is an impairment loss. An impairment loss would be recognised immediately in profit or loss, unless the asset is carried at revalued amount in accordance with another standard (for example, in accordance with the revaluation model in **Ind AS-16**). Any impairment loss of a revalued asset would be treated as a revaluation decrease in accordance with that other standard.

Identifying the cash-generating unit to which an asset belongs If there is any indication that an asset may be impaired, recoverable amount would be estimated for the individual asset. If it is not possible to estimate the recoverable amount of the individual asset, an entity would determine the recoverable amount of the cash generating unit (as per the procedure laid down in this regard) to which the asset belongs.

Impairment Loss for a Cash-Generating Unit An impairment loss would be recognised for a cash-generating unit (the smallest group of cash-generating units to which goodwill or a corporate asset has been allocated) if, and only if, the recoverable amount of the unit (group of units) is less than the carrying amount of the unit (group of units). The impairment loss would be allocated to reduce the carrying amount of the assets of the unit (group of units) in the following order: (a) first, to reduce the carrying amount of any goodwill allocated to the cash-generating unit (group of units); and (b) then, to the other assets of the unit (group of units) pro-rata on the basis of the carrying amount of each asset in the unit (group of units).

These reductions in carrying amounts would be treated as impairment losses on individual assets. In allocating an impairment loss, an entity would not reduce the carrying amount of an asset below the highest of: (a) its fair value less costs to sell (if determinable); (b) its value in use (if determinable); and (c) zero. The amount of the impairment loss that would otherwise have been allocated to the asset would be allocated pro-rata to the other assets of the unit (group of units).

Assets Value in Use

The following elements should be reflected in the calculation of an asset's value in use: (a) an estimate of the future cash flows the entity expects to derive from the asset; (b) expectations about possible variations in the amount or timing of those future cash flows; (c) the time value of money, represented by the current market risk-free rate of interest; (d) the price for bearing the uncertainty inherent in the asset; and (e) other factors, such as illiquidity, that market participants would reflect in pricing the future cash flows the entity expects to derive from the asset.

Basis for Estimates of Future Cash Flows In measuring value in use an entity would: (a) base cash flow projections on reasonable and supportable assumptions that represent management's best estimate of the range of economic conditions that will exist over the remaining useful life of the asset. Greater weight should be given to external evidence. (b) base cash flow projections on the most recent financial budgets/forecasts approved by management, but should exclude any estimated future cash inflows or outflows expected to arise from future restructurings or from improving or enhancing the asset's performance. Projections based on these budgets/forecasts would cover a maximum period of five years, unless a longer period can be justified. (c) the growth rate used in projections should not exceed the long-term average growth rate for the products, industries, or country or countries in which the entity operates, or for the market in which the asset is used, unless a higher rate can be justified.

Composition of Estimates of Future Cash Flows Estimates of future cash flows would include: (a) projections of cash inflows from the continuing use of the asset in its current condition; (b) projections of cash outflows that are necessarily incurred to generate the cash inflows from continuing use of the asset (including cash outflows to prepare the asset for use) and can be directly attributed, or allocated on a reasonable and consistent basis, to the asset; and (c) net cash flows, if any, to be received (or paid) for the disposal of the asset at the end of its useful life. The estimate of net cash flows to be received (or paid) for the disposal of an asset at the end of its useful life would be the amount that an entity expects to obtain from the disposal of the asset in an arm's length transaction between knowledgeable, willing parties, after deducting the estimated costs of disposal.

Estimates of future cash flows would not include: (a) cash inflows or outflows from financing activities; or (b) income tax receipts or payments.

Discount Rate The discount rate (rates) would be a pre-tax rate (rates) that reflect(s) current market assessments of: (a) the time value of money; and (b) the risks specific to the asset for which the future cash flow estimates have not been adjusted.

Disclosure

An entity is required to disclose the following for each class of assets: (a) the amount of impairment losses recognised in profit or loss during the period and the line item(s) of the statement of profit and loss in which those impairment losses are included; (b) the amount of reversals of impairment losses recognised in profit or loss during the period and the line item(s) of the statement of profit and loss in which those impairment losses are reversed; (c) the amount of impairment losses on revalued assets recognised in other comprehensive income during the period; (d) the amount of reversals of impairment losses on revalued assets recognised in other comprehensive income during the period.

An entity that reports segment information in accordance with **Ind AS-108** would disclose the following for each reportable segment: (a) the amount of impairment losses recognised in profit or loss and in other comprehensive income during the period. (b) the amount of reversals of impairment losses recognised in profit or loss and in other comprehensive income during the period.

An entity would also disclose the following for each material impairment loss recognised or reversed during the period for an individual asset, including goodwill, or a cash-generating unit: (a) the events and circumstances that led to the recognition or reversal of the impairment loss; (b) the amount of the impairment loss recognised or reversed; (c) for an individual asset: (i) the nature of the asset; and (ii) if the entity reports segment information in accordance with **Ind AS-108**, the reportable segment to which the asset belongs; (d) for a cash-generating unit: (i) a description of the cash-generating unit (such as whether it is a product line, a plant, a business operation, a geographical area, or a reportable segment as defined in **Ind AS-108**); (ii) the amount of the impairment loss recognised or reversed by class of assets and, if the entity reports segment information in accordance **Ind AS-108**, by reportable segment; and (iii) if the aggregation of assets for identifying the cash generating unit has changed since the previous estimate of the cash-generating unit's recoverable amount (if any), a description of the current and former way of aggregating assets and the reasons for changing the way the cash-generating unit is identified; (e) whether the recoverable amount of the asset (cash generating unit) is its fair value less costs to sell or its value in use; (f) if recoverable amount is fair value less costs to sell, the basis used to determine fair value less costs to sell (such as whether fair value was determined by reference to an active market); (g) if recoverable amount is value in use, the discount rate(s) used in the current estimate and previous estimate (if any) of value in use.

An entity would also disclose: (a) the aggregate impairment losses and the aggregate reversals of impairment losses recognised during the period; (b) the main classes of assets affected by impairment losses and the main classes of assets affected by reversals of impairment losses; (c) the main events and circumstances that led to the recognition of these impairment losses and reversals of impairment losses.

Ind AS-37: Provisions, Contingent Liabilities and Contingent Assets

Objective

The objective of this standard is to ensure that appropriate recognition criteria and measurement bases are applied to provisions, contingent liabilities and contingent assets and that sufficient information is disclosed in the notes to enable users to understand their nature, timing and amount.

Scope

This standard is to be applied by all entities in accounting for provisions, contingent liabilities and contingent assets, except: (a) those resulting from executory contracts, except where the contract is onerous; and (b) those covered by another standard.

Definitions

A provision is a liability of uncertain timing or amount.

A liability is a present obligation of the entity arising from past events, the settlement of which is expected to result in an outflow from the entity of resources embodying economic benefits.

An obligating event is an event that creates a legal or constructive obligation that results in an entity having no realistic alternative to settling that obligation. A legal obligation is an obligation that derives from: (a) a contract (through its explicit or implicit terms); (b) legislation; or (c) other operation of law.

A constructive obligation is an obligation that derives from an entity's actions where: (a) by an established pattern of past practice, published policies or a sufficiently specific current statement, the entity has indicated to other parties that it will accept certain responsibilities; and (b) as a result, the entity has created a valid expectation on the part of those other parties that it will discharge those responsibilities.

A contingent liability is: (a) a possible obligation that arises from past events and whose existence will be confirmed only by the occurrence or non-occurrence of one or more uncertain future events not wholly within the control of the entity; or (b) a present obligation that arises from past events but is not recognised because the amount of the obligation cannot be measured with sufficient reliability. A contingent liability is to be disclosed unless the possibility of an outflow of resources embodying economic benefits is remote.

A contingent asset is a possible asset that arises from past events and whose existence will be confirmed only by the occurrence or non-occurrence of one or more uncertain future events not wholly within the control of the entity.

An entity is not to recognise a contingent asset. Contingent assets usually arise from unplanned or other unexpected events that give rise to the possibility of an inflow of economic benefits to the entity. An example is a claim that an entity is pursuing through legal processes, where the outcome is uncertain.

An onerous contract is a contract in which the unavoidable costs of meeting the obligations under the contract exceed the economic benefits expected to be received under it.

Provisions A provision would be recognised when: (a) an entity has a present obligation (legal or constructive) as a result of a past event; (b) it is probable that an outflow of resources embodying economic benefits will be required to settle the obligation; and (c) a reliable estimate can be made of the amount of the obligation. If these conditions are not met, no provision would be recognised.

Best Estimate The amount recognised as a provision would be the best estimate of the expenditure required to settle the present obligation at the end of the reporting period. The risks and uncertainties that inevitably surround many events and circumstances should be taken into account in reaching the best estimate of a provision.

Present Value Where the effect of the time value of money is material, the amount of a provision would be the present value of the expenditures expected to be required to settle the obligation.

The discount rate would be a pre-tax rate that reflects current market assessments of the time value of money and the risks specific to the liability. The discount rate would not reflect risks for which future cash flow estimates have been adjusted.

Future events that may affect the amount required to settle an obligation would be reflected in the amount of a provision where there is sufficient objective evidence that they will occur.

Reimbursements Where some or all of the expenditure required to settle a provision is expected to be reimbursed by another party, the reimbursement is to be recognised when, and only when, it is virtually certain that reimbursement will be received if the entity settles the obligation. The reimbursement will be treated as a separate asset. The amount recognised for the reimbursement will not exceed the amount of the provision. In the statement of profit and loss, the expense relating to a provision may be presented net of the amount recognised for a reimbursement.

Disclosure

For each class of provision, an entity would disclose: (a) the carrying amount at the beginning and end of the period; (b) additional provisions made in the period, including increases to existing provisions; (c) amounts used (i.e. incurred and charged against the provision) during the period; (d) unused amounts reversed during the period; and (e) the increase during the period in the discounted amount arising from the passage of time and the effect of any change in the discount rate.

An entity would disclose the following for each class of provision: (a) a brief description of the nature of the obligation and the expected timing of any resulting outflows of economic benefits; (b) an indication of the uncertainties about the amount or timing of those outflows. Where necessary to provide adequate information, an entity would disclose the major assumptions made concerning future events; and (c) the amount of any expected reimbursement, stating the amount of any asset that has been recognised for that expected reimbursement.

Unless the possibility of any outflow in settlement is remote, an entity would also disclose for each class of contingent liability at the end of the reporting period a brief description of the nature of the contingent liability and, where practicable: (a) an estimate of its financial effect; (b) an indication of the uncertainties relating to the amount or timing of any outflow; and (c) the possibility of any reimbursement.

Where an inflow of economic benefits is probable, an entity would disclose a brief description of the nature of the contingent assets at the end of the reporting period, and, where practicable, an estimate of their financial effect, measured using the principles set out for provisions in this standard.

In extremely rare cases, when it is apprehended that the disclosure of some or all of the information required may prejudice seriously the position of the entity in a dispute with other parties on the subject matter of the provision, contingent liability or contingent asset. In such cases, an entity need not disclose the information, but is required disclose the general nature of the dispute, together with the fact that, and reason why, the information has not been disclosed.

Ind AS-38: Intangible Assets

Objective

The objective of this standard is to prescribe the accounting treatment for intangible assets that are not dealt with specifically in another standard. This standard requires an entity to recognise an intangible asset if, and only if, specified criteria are met. The standard also specifies how to measure the carrying amount of intangible assets and requires specified disclosures about intangible assets.

Definitions

An active market is a market in which all the following conditions exist: (a) the items traded in the market are homogeneous; (b) willing buyers and sellers can normally be found at any time; and (c) prices are available to the public.

Amortisation is the systematic allocation of the depreciable amount of an intangible asset over its useful life.

Carrying amount is the amount at which an asset is recognised in the balance sheet after deducting any accumulated amortisation and accumulated impairment losses thereon.

Depreciable amount is the cost of an asset, or other amount substituted for cost, less its residual value.

An intangible asset is an identifiable non-monetary asset without physical substance.

Research is original and planned investigation undertaken with the prospect of gaining new scientific or technical knowledge and understanding.

Useful life is: (a) the period over which an asset is expected to be available for use by an entity; (b) the number of production or similar units expected to be obtained from the asset by an entity.

An intangible asset would be recognised if, and only if: (a) it is probable that the expected future economic benefits that are attributable to the asset will accrue to the entity; and (b) the cost of the asset can be measured reliably. It would be measured initially at cost. Subsequent research and development incurred after the acquisition of that project are to be accounted for as per the procedure prescribed in this standard.

Development Phase

An intangible asset arising from development (or from the development phase of an internal project) would be recognised if, and only if, an entity can demonstrate all of the following: (a) the technical feasibility of completing the intangible asset so that it will be available for use or sale; (b) its intention to complete the intangible asset and use or sell it; (c) its ability to use or sell the intangible asset; (d) how the intangible asset will generate probable future economic benefits. Among other things, the entity can demonstrate the existence of a market for the output of the intangible asset or the intangible asset itself or, if it is to be used internally, the usefulness of the intangible asset; (e) the availability of adequate technical, financial and other resources to complete the development and to use or sell the intangible asset; (f) its ability to measure reliably the expenditure attributable to the intangible asset during its development.

Expenditure on an intangible item is to be recognised as an expense when it is incurred unless: (a) it forms part of the cost of an intangible asset that meets the recognition criteria; or (b) the item is acquired in a business combination and cannot be recognised as an intangible asset. If this is the case, it forms part of the amount recognised as goodwill at the acquisition date **(Ind AS-103)**.

However, expenditure on an intangible item that was initially recognised as an expense would not be recognised as part of the cost of an intangible asset at a later date.

Measurement After Recognition

An entity would choose either the cost model or the revaluation model as its accounting policy. If an intangible asset is accounted for using the revaluation model, all the other assets in its class are also be accounted for using the same model, unless there is no active market for those assets.

In the case of cost model, after initial recognition, an intangible asset would be carried at its cost less any accumulated amortisation and any accumulated impairment losses.

Revaluation Model After initial recognition, an intangible asset would be carried at a revalued amount, being its fair value at the date of the revaluation less any subsequent accumulated amortisation and any subsequent accumulated impairment losses. For the purpose of revaluations under this standard, fair value would be determined by reference to an active market. Revaluations are be made with such regularity that at the end of the reporting period the carrying amount of the asset does not differ materially from its fair value.

If the fair value of a revalued intangible asset can no longer be determined by reference to an active market, the carrying amount of the asset would be its revalued amount at the date of the last revaluation by reference to the active market less any subsequent accumulated amortisation and any subsequent accumulated impairment losses. If an intangible asset's carrying amount is increased as a result of a revaluation, the increase is to be recognised in other comprehensive income and accumulated in equity under the heading of revaluation surplus. However, the increase would be recognised in profit or loss to the extent that it reverses a revaluation decrease of the same asset previously recognised in profit or loss.

An entity would assess whether the useful life of an intangible asset is finite or indefinite and, if finite, the length of, or number of production or similar units would be considered to determine useful life. An intangible asset would be regarded to have an indefinite useful life when, based on an analysis of all of the relevant factors, there is no foreseeable limit to the period over which the asset is expected to generate net cash inflows for the entity. The useful life of an intangible asset that arises from contractual or other legal rights would not exceed the period of the contractual or other legal rights, but may be shorter depending on the period over which the entity expects to use the asset.

The depreciable amount of an intangible asset with a finite useful life would be allocated on a systematic basis over its useful life. Amortisation should begin when the asset is available for use, ie when it is in the location and condition necessary for it to be capable of operating in the manner intended by management. Amortisation would cease at the earlier of the date that the asset is classified as held for sale (or included in a disposal group that is classified as held for sale) in accordance with **Ind AS-105** and the date that the asset is derecognised. The amortisation method used should reflect the pattern in which the asset's future economic benefits are expected to be consumed by the entity. If that pattern cannot be determined reliably, the straight-line method has been recommended to be used. The amortisation charge for each period would be recognised in profit or loss unless this or another standard permits or requires it to be included in the carrying amount of another asset.

Residual Value The residual value of an intangible asset with a finite useful life would be assumed to be zero unless: (a) there is a commitment by a third party to purchase the asset at the end of its useful life; or (b) there is an active market for the asset and: (i) residual value can be determined by reference to that market; and (ii) it is probable that such a market will exist at the end of the asset's useful life.

The amortisation period and the amortisation method for an intangible asset with a finite useful life would be reviewed at least at each financial year-end. If the expected useful life of the asset is different from previous estimates, the amortisation period would be changed accordingly. If there has been a change in the expected pattern of consumption of the future economic benefits embodied in the asset, the amortisation method should also be changed to reflect the changed pattern. Such changes shall be accounted for as changes in accounting estimates in accordance with **Ind AS-8**.

Review of Useful Life Assessment The useful life of an intangible asset that is not being amortised would be reviewed each period to determine whether events and circumstances continue to support an indefinite useful life assessment for that asset. If they do not, the change in the useful life assessment from indefinite to finite should be accounted for as a change in an accounting estimate in accordance with **Ind AS-8**.

Retirements and Disposals An intangible asset would be derecognised: (a) on disposal; or (b) when no future economic benefits are expected from its use or disposal. The gain or loss arising from the derecognition of an intangible asset would be determined as the difference between the net disposal proceeds, if any, and the carrying amount of the asset.

Disclosure

An entity is required to disclose the following for each class of intangible assets, distinguishing between internally generated intangible assets and other intangible assets: (a) whether the useful lives are indefinite or finite and, if finite, the useful lives or the amortisation rates used; (b) the amortisation methods used for intangible assets with finite useful lives; (c) the gross carrying amount and any accumulated amortisation (aggregated with accumulated impairment losses) at the beginning and end of the period; (d) the line item(s) of the statement of profit and loss in which any amortisation of intangible assets is included; (e) a reconciliation of the carrying amount at the beginning and end of the period showing: (i) additions, indicating separately those from internal development, those acquired separately, and those acquired through business combinations; (ii) assets classified as held for sale or included in a disposal group classified as held for sale in accordance with **Ind AS-105** and other disposals; (iii) increases or decreases during the period resulting from revaluations and from impairment losses recognised or reversed in other comprehensive income in accordance with **Ind AS-36** (if any); (iv) impairment losses recognised in profit or loss during the period in accordance with **Ind AS-36** (if any); (v) impairment losses reversed in profit or loss during the period in accordance with **Ind AS-36** (if any); (vi) any amortisation recognised during the period; (vii) net exchange differences arising on the translation of the financial statements into the presentation currency, and on the translation of a foreign operation into the presentation currency of the entity; and (viii) other changes in the carrying amount during the period.

A class of intangible assets is a grouping of assets of a similar nature and use in an entity's operations. Examples of separate classes may include: (a) brand names; (b) publishing titles; (c) computer software; (d) licences and franchises; (e) copyrights, patents and other industrial property rights, service and operating rights; (f) recipes, formulae, models, designs and prototypes; and (g) intangible assets under development.

An entity would also disclose: (a) for an intangible asset assessed as having an indefinite useful life, the carrying amount of that asset and the reasons supporting the assessment of an indefinite useful life. In giving these reasons, the entity would describe the factor(s) that played a significant role in determining that the asset has an indefinite useful life; (b) a description, the carrying amount and remaining amortisation period of any individual intangible asset that is material to the entity's financial statements; (c) for intangible assets acquired by way of a government grant and initially recognised at fair value: (i) the fair value initially recognised for these assets; (ii) their carrying amount; and (iii) whether they are measured after recognition under the cost model or the revaluation model; (d) the existence and carrying amounts of intangible assets whose title is restricted and the carrying amounts of intangible assets pledged as security for liabilities; (e) the amount of contractual commitments for the acquisition of intangible assets.

If intangible assets are accounted for at revalued amounts, an entity would disclose the following: (a) by class of intangible assets: (i) the effective date of the revaluation; (ii) the carrying amount of revalued intangible assets; and (iii) the carrying amount that would have been recognised had the revalued class of intangible assets been measured after recognition using the cost model; (b) the amount of the revaluation surplus that relates to intangible assets at the beginning and end of the period, indicating the changes during the period and any restrictions on the distribution of the balance to shareholders; and (c) the methods and significant assumptions applied in estimating the assets' fair values.

Ind AS-40: Investment Property

Objective

The objective of this standard is to prescribe the accounting treatment for investment property and related disclosure requirements.

Scope

This standard would be applied in the recognition, measurement and disclosure of investment property.

Definitions

Carrying amount is the amount at which an asset is recognised in the balance sheet.

Cost is the amount of cash or cash equivalents paid or the fair value of other consideration given to acquire an asset at the time of its acquisition or construction or, where applicable, the amount attributed to that asset when initially recognised in accordance with the specific requirements of other Indian Accounting Standards, e.g. **Ind AS-102**.

Fair value is the amount for which an asset could be exchanged between knowledgeable, willing parties in an arm's length transaction.

Investment property is property (land or a building—or part of a building—or both) held (by the owner or by the lessee under a finance lease) to earn rentals or for capital appreciation or both.

Recognition and Measurement

Investment property would be recognised as an asset when, and only when: (a) it is probable that the future economic benefits that are associated with the investment property will accrue to the entity; and (b) the cost of the investment property can be measured reliably.

Under this recognition principle, an entity evaluates all its investment property costs at the time they are incurred. These costs include costs incurred initially to acquire an investment property and costs incurred subsequently to add to, replace part of, or service a property.

An investment property would be measured initially at its cost. Transaction costs would be included in the initial measurement.

Accounting Policy An entity would adopt as its accounting policy the cost model to all of its investment property.

Fair Value Determination The fair value of investment property would reflect market conditions at the end of the reporting period. There is a rebuttable presumption that an entity can reliably determine the fair value of an investment property on a continuing basis. However, in exceptional cases, there is clear evidence when an entity first acquires an investment property that the fair value of the investment property is not reliably determinable on a continuing basis. This arises when, and only when, comparable market transactions are infrequent and alternative reliable estimates of fair value (for example, based on discounted cash flow projections) are not available.

If an entity determines that the fair value of an investment property under construction is not reliably determinable but expects the fair value of the property to be reliably determinable when construction is complete, it would determine the fair value of that investment property either when its fair value becomes reliably determinable or construction is completed (whichever is earlier).

If an entity has previously determined the fair value of an investment property, it would continue to determine the fair value of that property until disposal (or until the property becomes owner-occupied property or the entity begins to develop the property for subsequent sale in the ordinary course of business) even if comparable market transactions become less frequent or market prices become less readily available.

Cost Model After initial recognition, an entity is required to measure all of its investment properties in accordance with **Ind AS-16's** requirements for cost model, other than those that meet the criteria to be classified as held for sale (or are included in a disposal group that is classified as held for sale) in accordance with **Ind AS-105** non-current assets held for sale and discontinued operations. Investment properties that meet the criteria to be classified as held for sale (or are included in a disposal group that is classified as held for sale) are required to be measured in accordance with **Ind AS-105**.

Disclosure

An entity, among others, would disclose: (a) its accounting policy for measurement of investment property; (b) the criteria it uses to distinguish investment property from owner-occupied property and from property held for sale in the ordinary course of business; (c) the methods and significant assumptions applied in determining the fair value of investment property, including a statement whether the determination of fair value was supported by market evidence or was more heavily based on other factors (which the entity would disclose) because of the nature of the property and lack of comparable market data; (d) the extent to which the fair value of investment property (as measured or disclosed in the financial statements) is based on a valuation by an independent valuer who holds a recognised and relevant professional qualification and has recent experience in the location and category of the investment property being valued. If there has been no such valuation, that fact is required be disclosed; (e) the amounts recognised in profit or loss for: (i) rental income from investment property; (ii) direct operating expenses (including repairs and maintenance) arising from investment property that generated rental income during the period; and (iii) direct operating expenses (including repairs and maintenance) arising from investment property that did not generate rental income during the period; (f) the existence and amounts of restrictions on the realisability of investment property or the remittance of income and proceeds of disposal; (g) contractual obligations to purchase, construct or develop investment property or for repairs, maintenance or enhancements.

In addition to the above disclosures, an entity would disclose: (a) the depreciation methods used; (b) the useful lives or the depreciation rates used; (c) the gross carrying amount and the accumulated depreciation (aggregated with accumulated impairment losses) at the beginning and end of the period; (d) a reconciliation of the carrying amount of investment property at the beginning and end of the period, showing the following: (i) additions, disclosing separately those additions resulting from acquisitions and those resulting from subsequent expenditure recognised as an asset; (ii) additions resulting from acquisitions through business combinations; (iii) assets classified as held for sale or included in a disposal group classified as held for sale in accordance with Ind AS-105 and other disposals; (iv) depreciation; (v) the amount of impairment losses recognised, and the amount of impairment losses reversed, during the period in accordance with **Ind AS-36**; (vi) the net exchange differences arising on the translation of the financial statements into a different presentation currency, and on translation of a foreign operation into the presentation currency of the reporting entity; (vii) transfers to and from inventories and owner-occupied property; and (viii) other changes; and (e) the fair value of investment property.

In the exceptional cases, when an entity cannot determine the fair value of the investment property reliably, it would disclose: (i) a description of the investment property (ii) an explanation of why fair value cannot be determined reliably; and (iii) if possible, the range of estimates within which fair value is highly likely to lie.

Ind AS-101: First-time Adoption of Indian Accounting Standards

This standard has been discussed in detail in Chapter 4.

Ind AS-105: Non-current Assets Held for Sale and Discontinued Operations

This standard has been discussed in detail in Chapter 4.

Ind AS-107: Financial Instruments: Disclosures

This standard has been discussed in detail in Chapter 4.

Ind AS-108: Operating Segments

This standard has been discussed in detail in Chapter 4.

SUMMARY

- Generally accepted accounting principles (GAAPs) and accounting standards provide sound conceptual framework for financial accounting records and preparation of credible and reliable financial statements, namely, statement of profit and loss, balance sheet and cash flow statement.
- Important GAAPs are: money measurement, separate entity, duality, going concern, cost, accounting period, conservatism, realisation, accrual, matching, consistency and materiality.
- As per money measurement concept, financial accounting should record only those business events/ transactions which are expressed in money terms; transactions which cannot be quantified in financial terms, irrespective of their importance, are outside the scope of accounting records. A further assumption of the money measurement concept is that the unit of measurement remains constant in terms of purchasing power over time. Financial accounting, thus, does not record all information about the operations of a firm.

- Business entity concept implies that the financial accounts should be prepared on the premise that a business firm has a separate entity from its owners. Accordingly, every item in financial accounts should be considered from the view point of the firm and not from the perspective of owners. Therefore, profits (since payable to owners) should be considered liabilities and losses (to be charged against owners) should be reckoned assets of the firm (and, hence, deducted from owner's equity).
- Duality concept implies that financial accounting records should be based on double entry system in that two accounting items are affected by each transaction. The total assets of a firm shown on one side of the balance sheet are always equal to the total liabilities shown on its other side. This equality, in turn, is the basis of fundamental accounting equation: Owners' equity + External liabilities = Assets.
- Apart from liabilities payable and assets owned basis of presenting balance sheet, another equally useful basis is that it is a statement which indicates sources of funds/finances and resources in which funds have been invested. Sources represent liabilities as they are payable and resources are assets as their ownership belongs to the firm. A balance sheet is always with reference to a particular point of time say, as on 31st March, 2017.
- Going concern concept implies that the business firm will continue to operate in future and will not cease doing business, sell its assets and make final payments to its creditors and owners. Therefore, current resale value of assets is not relevant. Their valuation is to be judged in terms of the likely value of goods product/services rendered by their use in future. Accordingly, assets should be valued at their acquisition cost (cost concept) less depreciation and not at their liquidation value. The operational implication of the going concern and cost concepts is that assets (in particular, long-term assets such as land and building and plant and machinery) do not reflect their current market value.
- The accounting period concept enables the management of the firm to assess its financial performance in terms of profit earned or loss suffered at periodic intervals (say, monthly, quarterly, or yearly). For taxation purposes, the required time-span is 12 months and for internal/managerial purposes, the time span is 1–3 months. Most of the domestic companies in India choose April 1–March 31 period (corresponding to fiscal year of the Government) and multi-national companies follow January 1 – December 31 period.
- The conservatism principle implies conservative/cautious approach in determining income by providing for all possible losses and ignoring profits till they are realised. In relation to the valuation of assets, the basis would be the cost or the current replacement value, whichever is lower.
- Realisation concept, closely related to conservatism concept, requires conservative basis to be followed in revenue recognition.
- Accrual concept requires that expenses related to a particular accounting period (say April 1, 2016 to March 31, 2017) should be considered as expenses of the same period, irrespective of whether they have been paid in cash or not (say, to be paid in May, 2017 or already paid in March 2017). Likewise, revenues earned in a specific accounting year are considered as revenues for the same period whether they are realised in cash or not. The expenses paid in advance and revenues/income received in advance should be adjusted.
- The matching concept involves two steps in computing net income: first, to determine revenues earned in a specific accounting year and, second, to determine expenses incurred to realise these revenues. The more perfect this matching is, the more correct is the determination of income (revenues – expenses). In estimating expenses, revenue expenses can be easily split between two or more accounting periods on the basis of time (as required by accrual concept). Capital expenditures and deferred revenue expenses (benefitting more than one accounting year) should be spread over in the form of depreciation/amortisation on the basis of some objective, equitable and scientific criterion.
- Consistency concept requires that there should be a consistency in accounting treatment of items (where there exists more than one basis of dealing them) year after year. The notable examples are depreciation methods used in the case of tangible long-term assets, amortisation period in respect of intangible assets and methods of inventory valuation.
- Materiality concept requires full disclosure of all material information and events.

- The primary objective of accounting standards (ASs) is to standardise accounting policies and practices. Unlike GAAPs, ASs are mandatory in nature. Though the International Accounting Standard Board (IASB) formulates international accounting standards, most of the individual countries have their own accounting standard boards.
- In India, ASs are formulated by the Accounting Standard Board (ASB) and are issued by the Council of the Institute of Chartered Accountants of India (ICAI). Being mandatory in nature, auditors are duly bound to examine whether the ASs are complied with in the preparation/presentation of financial statements or not. Their compliance is mandatory for **(a)** enterprises whose securities are listed or are in the process of being issued and will be listed on a recognised stock exchange in India and **(b)** all other commercial enterprises whose turnover for the accounting year is more than ₹50 crore.

LO 2.1

- The objective of AS-1 is to provide the basis for presentation of general purpose financial statements to ensure comparability both with the entity's financial statements of previous periods and with the financial statements of other entities. It sets out overall requirements for their presentation, guidelines and minimum requirements for their contents.

  Financial statements are required to present a true and fair view of the financial position/performance and cash flows. They should be prepared on a going concern and accrual bases of accounting at least annually. There should be consistency in presentation/classification of items and comparative information in respect of previous periods should be included. The balance sheet and the statement of profit loss should include all items specified in the AS-1. The entity should disclose the significant accounting policies.
- The AS-8 prescribes the criteria for selecting and changing accounting policies together with the accounting treatment and disclosures of changes in accounting policies/estimates and correction of errors. The accounting policies are the specific principles, bases, conventions, rules and practices applied by an entity in preparing/presenting financial statements. They are intended to enhance the relevance/reliability of financial statements and their comparability over time and with other entities.
- According to the AS-11, a construction contact is a contract specifically negotiated for construction of an asset or a combination of closely interrelated/ interdependent assets. It also includes agreements of real estate development. It prescribes disclosure requirements relating to contract revenue recognition.
- The objective of AS-12 is to provide the accounting treatment of income taxes, that is, how to account for the current and future tax consequences of future recovery of the carrying amount of assets/liabilities and transactions/other events of the current period recognised in the financial statements. The major components of tax expenses (income) should be disclosed separately. Other disclosures relating to taxes should be as prescribed by it.
- The AS-16 prescribes the accounting treatment for property, plant and equipment. The relevant issues in their accounting are the recognition of the assets, the determination of their carrying amounts and the depreciation charges/impairment losses in relation to them. Their cost should be recognised if the future benefits will accrue and they can be measured reliably. The cost should comprise the purchase price and any cost directly attributable to bringing it to the location and condition necessary for it to be capable of operating in the intended manner. The depreciable amount of an asset should be allocated on a systematic basis over its useful life. The depreciation method used should reflect the pattern in which the future economic benefits one expected to be consumed by the entity. The financial statements should disclose all the requirements provided by the AS-16.
- The primary issue in accounting for revenue is determining the stage of its recognition. Revenue is recognised when it is probable that future economic benefits will accrue and they can be measured reliably. The AS-18 identifies the circumstances in which these criteria will be met and, therefore, revenue will be recognised. It also prescribes practical guidance on the application of these criteria. The disclosure requirements in the financial statements are also prescribed.

- The AS-21 applies in accounting for transactions and balances in foreign currencies. It also applies in translating results and financial position of foreign operations included in the financial statements (a) by consolidation / proportionate consolidation or the equity methods, and (b) into a presentation currency.
- AS-29 is applicable to financial statements of an entity whose functional currency is the currency of a hyper inflationary economy. The financial statements of such an entity should be stated in terms of the measuring unit currency, at the end of the reporting period. The corresponding figures for the previous period(s) will also be similarly stated. The gain/loss on the net monetary position should be included in the profit/loss and separately disclosed. When the economy ceases to the hyper inflationary, the preparation/presentation of financial statements in accordance with AS-29 should be discontinued. The specified disclosures should be included in the financial statements.
- The objective of AS-32 is to establish principles for presenting financial instruments on liabilities or equity and for offsetting financial assets and financial liabilities. A financial instrument is a contract that gives rise to financial asset of one entity and a financial liability or equity of another entity. It applies to classification of financial instruments into financial assets, financial liabilities and equity instruments.
- AS-33 prescribes principles for the determination/presentation of earnings per share to enable performance comparison between/among different entities and over time. The basic earnings per share should be calculated by dividing profit attributable to the equityholders by the weighted average number of ordinary shares outstanding during the period. The entity should also calculate diluted earnings per share. The specified disclosures should be made by the entity in its financial statements.
- AS-36 is applicable in accounting for impairment of assets. Impairment loss is the amount by which the carrying amount of an asset/cash generating unit exceeds its recoverable amounts, the recoverable amount being the higher of its fair value less costs to sale and its value in use. It should be recognised in the statement of profit and loss. The specified disclosures should be made by the entity.
- The objective of AS-37 is to ensure that appropriate recognition criteria and measurement bases are applied to provisions, contingent liabilities/assets and that sufficient information is disclosed in the notes to the accounts to enable users to understand their nature, timing and amount. The specified disclosures should be made. When, however, it is apprehended that disclosure may prejudice seriously the position of the entity in a dispute with other entities, it may not disclose the information. It should disclose the general nature of the dispute together with the reason why it has not disclosed the information.
- An intangible asset is an identifiable non-monetary asset without physical substance. The AS-38 prescribes the accounting treatment for such assets; it requires an entity to recognise an intangible asset only if specified criteria are met. It also specifies how to measure its carrying cost. The specified disclosure about intangible assets should also be made.
- The objective of AS-40 is to prescribe the accounting treatment for investment property and the related disclosure requirements. it is applicable in the recognition, measurement and disclosure of investment property. It should be recognised only when the associated future economic benefits are likely to accrue and its cost can be measured reliably. An entity should adopt the cost model as its accounting policy. The specified disclosures should also be made. When an entity cannot determine the fair value of the property reliably, it should disclose a description of the property, an explanation why fair value cannot be determined reliably and the range of the estimates within which it is likely to lie.

LO 2.2

REFERENCES

1. Anthony, R.N., D.F. Hawkins and K.A. Merchant, *Accounting: Text and Cases*, (Tata McGraw-Hill, New Delhi, 2003), p.26.
2. Weygandt, Jerry, J., D.E. Kieso and P.D. Kimmel, *Financial Accounting* [John Wiley & Sons (Asia) Pvt. Ltd., Singapore, 2003], p.14.

3. *Op.cit.*, p.31.
4. *Ibid*, p.27.
5. *Ibid*, p.53.
6. *Ibid*, p.63.

REVIEW QUESTIONS

LOD: Easy

RQ.2.1 What is basic accounting equation? Can a business firm enter into a transaction in which only one side of the accounting equation is affected? If so, give concrete examples. LO 2.1

RQ.2.2 Name the two major claimants who have claim on the firm's assets. LO 2.1

RQ.2.3 In preparing balance sheet, would you use the historical cost or current market value while dealing with assets? Explain. LO 2.1

RQ.2.4 Name the accounting principle involved/violated/affected in the following: LO 2.1

- **(i)** The firm changes method of depreciation.
- **(ii)** The firm does not consider unused stationery as asset.
- **(iii)** The firm follows the policy of expensing all office equipments of less than ₹5,000.
- **(iv)** Capital is recorded on liabilities side.
- **(v)** Expenses are recognised as and when they are incurred and not when they are paid.
- **(vi)** Plant and machinery is valued at the current market price.
- **(vii)** Profit earned by owner in selling his personal house is not recorded in the firm's books.
- **(viii)** Anticipated profited are ignored.
- **(ix)** Massive advertisement expenditure incurred in launching a new product is not charged as an expense of one accounting year.
- **(x)** Accounting is not a record of all business events.

RQ.2.5 Ind AS-1 sets out overall requirements for the presentation of financial statements, guidelines for their structure and minimum requirements for their contents. Elaborate. LO 2.2

RQ.2.6 Explain the concepts of basic earnings per share and diluted earnings per share. How are they computed? LO 2.2

LOD: Medium

RQ.2.7 What is money measurement concept? State the impact of inflation on the monetary unit assumption. LO 2.1

RQ.2.8 Describe the accounting principle which explains losses are assets, and profits and capital are liabilities for a business firm. LO 2.1

RQ.2.9 "Accrual accounting is superior to cash accounting". Elaborate. LO 2.1

RQ.2.10 List the main elements of balance sheet and income statement. LO 2.1

RQ.2.11 What is the major revenue recognition criterion? LO 2.1

RQ.2.12 Using accounting equation, answer the following independent questions. LO 2.1

- **(i)** New company's assets are ₹250 lakh and its external liabilities are of ₹100 lakh, determine the amount of owners' equity.
- **(ii)** Royal Industries has total assets of ₹100 lakh and owners' equity of ₹70 lakh, compute the amount of external liabilities.

(iii) Small enterprise has following amounts appearing in balance sheet as at 31st December, 2007:

Capital, ₹50 lakh, Reserves and undistributed profits, ₹15 lakh and total external liabilities, ₹35 lakh, determine the amount of total assets.

(iv) At the beginning of the accounting year, Supreme Industries had total assets of ₹1,700 lakh and its total external liabilities of ₹1,000 lakh. During the year total assets increased by ₹300 lakh and total liabilities decreased by ₹160 lakh, compute the amount of owners' equity at the end of the year.

RQ.2.13 Ind AS-2 prescribes the criteria for selecting and applying accounting policies/estimates in correction of errors. Explain. LO 2.2

RQ.2.14 What is the criteria of revenue recognition? LO 2.2

RQ.2.15 Describe in brief disclosure requirements of accounting standards related to accounting for fixed assets and investments. LO 2.2

RQ.2.16 What is the basis of recognising intangible assets? How are they amortised? What are the major disclosure requirements of accounting standard for such assets? LO 2.2

RQ.2.17 Define provisions, contingent liabilities and contingent assets. State the major requirements of their accounting and disclosure of all the three to conform the needs of accounting standard. LO 2.2

RQ.2.18 What are the principal issues in accounting for property, plant and equipment according to the Ind AS-16?. LO 2.2

LOD: Difficult

RQ.2.19 "Profit and loss account provides only estimated figures of profit earned or loss suffered." Explain. LO 2.1

RQ.2.20 Explain the terms: **(i)** timing differences, **(ii)** permanent differences, **(iii)** deferred tax liability and **(iv)** deferred tax asset as per accounting standard related to taxes on income. LO 2.2

RQ.2.21 What is impairment of assets? Is reversal of impairment loss feasible? Explain your answer based on the requirements of accounting standard. LO 2.2

3

Accounting Cycle and Statements of Financial Information

Learning Objectives

After reading this chapter you will be able to:

LO 3.1 Identify the recording procedures of an accounting cycle and important accounting terms

LO 3.2 List various types of accounts

LO 3.3 Understand accounting books (Journals and ledgers) and the recordings of financial transactions

LO 3.4 Describe trial balance (Sheet of balances) and its limitations

LO 3.5 Illustrate special journals/ledgers

LO 3.6 Explain adjustments/closing/opening entries

LO 3.7 Discuss the contents of balance sheet

LO 3.8 Review profit and loss account and its content

LO 3.9 Show additional aspects related to profit and loss account

Introduction

In the preceding chapter, each accounting transaction was recorded in terms of its impact on balance sheet. Although this procedure is appropriate as an explanatory device to understand the reason why two sides of balance sheet always tally, it is not a *practical* way of handling the business transactions that occur in the actual operations of an organisation. The actual recording procedure should, obviously, provide all the details. For instance, cash balance (₹1.93 lakh) in Example 2.2 as on 31st January, *pre-se*, does not contain information of each cash inflow and outflow accounting transactions of ATCPL. This chapter describes the financial accounting system which provides complete information from the stage of its incurrence. Although most organisations use computer-based accounting system in practice, the manual system has been described in this chapter as the basic steps are the same in both the systems and it is easier to visualise these steps in a manual system. Accordingly, the procedural aspect of accounting records (technically referred to as accounting cycle) leading to the preparation of financial statements is the subject-matter of this chapter. The financial accounting framework to record transactions (i.e. accounting cycle) is outlined first. The contents of balance sheet and profit and loss account respectively have also been explained. The main points are summarised by way of recapitulation.

ACCOUNTING CYCLE

LO 3.1 Identify the recording procedures of an accounting cycle and important accounting terms

Accounting cycle refers to the procedural aspects of accounting records.

The accounting cycle has the following sequence of events: **(1)** Opening entry (in the case of existing firm) **(2)** Transaction analysis **(3)** Recording in special journal books **(4)** Posting in special ledger books **(5)** Preparation of trial balance **(6)** Adjustment entries **(7)** Closing entries in respect of nominal accounts (8) Preparation of financial statements, namely, profit and loss account, profit and loss appropriation account and balance sheet.

Important Accounting Terms

To understand the manual accounting system, it would be useful to know various important accounting terms, namely, account, debit and credit, normal balance (debit or credit) of assets, liabilities, revenues and expenses items, type of accounts and so on.

Account is a book-keeping device to record increases and decreases in each asset/liability item.

Account An account is a book-keeping device to record increases and decreases in each/specific asset or liability item. It facilitates in knowing the net change (along with all details of increases as well as decreases at one place) which has taken place in an item during a period for which the account has been prepared. In its simplest form, an account has two equal sides divided by a vertical line in between, given the look of the alphabet 'T' (hence, commonly called a 'T' account). **On its one side are recorded increases and on its other side are recorded decreases.** The procedure involved in its preparation is explained by drawing cash account (Format 3.1) of ATCPL (of Example 2.2). Being a new firm, ATCPL's opening balance at the beginning of the period is zero. By convention, left side (in cash account) records increases (cash inflows to the firm) and the right side records decreases (cash outflows) from the firm.

FORMAT 3.1 Cash Account of ATCPL

Cash Inflows (Receipts)	*Amount*	*Cash Outflows (Payments)*	*Amount*
Opening balance (January 1, 2016)	0	Bank deposit	₹7,00,000
Capital	₹10,00,000	Purchases (Toys)	2,00,000
Sales (Toys)	1,25,000	Expenses paid	32,000
			9,32,000
		Closing balance	1,93,000
	11,25,000		11,25,000
Opening balance (February 1, 2016)	1,93,000		

Observe that cash account has brought all cash transactions of ATCPL which have taken place during January 1–31, 2016 at one place. The reader has clear picture that the firm has total cash receipts of ₹11,25,000 and has total cash payments of ₹9,32,000 (along with description of each item). Since receipts are higher than payments, the firm has a closing cash balance of ₹1,93,000 (i.e., ₹11,25,000 – ₹9,32,000). In practice, all details as shown by cash account will obviously be required. The firm would like to know individual items affecting cash; more importantly, the details would be required for tax authorities.

Like the cash account, accounts are prepared for each asset and liability account providing full description of increases and decreases during the period for which these accounts are prepared.

However, preparation/understanding of other accounts is not as simple as that of cash account. Therefore, the widely used terms 'debit and credit' are required to be learnt.

Debit side is the left side of an account

Credit side is the right side of an account

Debit and Credit Conventionally, the left side of an account is designated as the debit side and the right side as the credit side. Amounts recorded on the left-hand side are called debits (abbreviated as Dr.) and amount recorded on the right-hand side are called credits (abbreviated as Cr.). This rule is applicable to all accounts. An account is said to have a debit balance if the total of debit side is greater than that of credit side. In case credit side total exceeds debit side total, an account has credit balance. In Format 3.1, cash account has a debit balance of ₹1,93,000 (as debit side total of ₹11,25,000 exceeds credit side total of ₹9,32,000)

Some accounts will have debit balance and some credit balance. Which account has Dr. balance and which has Cr. balance forms the basis of accounting records. In this context, it is reasonably safe to start with the premise that debtors have debit balance*. By recording an accounting transaction on debit side of a debtor's account, the balance of debtors account will increase and by recording on credit side, the balance will decrease. From this first step and given the accounting equation in Chapter 2 (Assets = Capital + External Liabilities), the following rules (pertaining to type of balance) can be inferred/deduced:

(1) Debtors have debit balance. Since amount is receivable from debtors, debtors are assets. Therefore, all assets (plant and machinery, land and buildings, furniture and office equipment, cash and bank balances and so on) will have debit balances.

(2) Since assets are equal to liabilities (duality concept), if assets have debit balance, all liabilities (creditors, loan, capital) will have credit balances.

(3) Profits are payable to owners (separate entity concept) and, hence, liabilities. Therefore, all revenue/income items (sales revenue, interest/dividends received and so on) contributing to profit will obviously have credit balances.

(4) Expenses are recoverable from owners/capital and, hence, in a way, are assets of the firm. Therefore, all expense items (wages, rent, insurance, telephone, electricity and power, repairs, depreciation and so on) will have debit balances. Viewed from another perspective, expenses are the opposite of revenues. As revenues have credit balances, expenses will have debit balances.

(5) Debiting accounts related to assets and expenses (having Dr. balances) will increase their balances and crediting such accounts will decrease them (Format 3.2). This inference is derived from points 1 and 4.

FORMAT 3.2 Meaning of Debit and Credit for Asset and Expense Accounts

Any Asset Account		*Any Expense Account*	
Debit for increase (+)	Credit for decrease (–) ↓	Debit for increase (+)	Credit for decrease (–) ↓

(6) Debiting accounts related to liabilities and revenues (having Cr. balances) will decrease their balances and crediting such accounts will increase them (based on points 1 and 3). (Format 3.3).

*Debit is derived from the Latin word **debitur** which means debtor and credit is derived from the Latin word credere which means creditor.

FORMAT 3.3 Meaning of Debit and Credit for Liability and Revenue Accounts

Any Liability Account		*Any Revenue Account*	
↓ Debit for decrease (–)	Credit for increase (+) ↑	↓ Debit for decrease (–)	Credit for increase (+) ↑

(7) From Formats 3.2 and 3.3, it is apparent that debit record results in increase in relation to assets and expense accounts whereas the debit transactions cause decrease in liabilities and revenue accounts. Evidently, debit does not imply increase and credit does not imply decrease.

What is debit? What is credit? In the context of the financial accounting, the *left side* of any account is *arbitrarily* called the *debit side* and amounts recorded on the left side are called *debits.* Entering an amount on the left side of an account is known as *debiting* the account. The reverse holds true for the *right-hand side* of an account; it is called the *credit side* and amounts recorded on the right side are called *credits.* Entering an amount on right side of an account is known as *crediting* the account. Thus, these terms serve as directional signals; they provide the basis of recording accounting transactions in books of accounts.

Each transaction has two-fold effect (as per duality concept). Therefore, for each transaction *debits must equal credits*. For this reason, financial accounting records are aptly referred to as *double-entry system* of *book-keeping.*

As stated above, for each transaction, the debit amount must equal the credit amount. Therefore, for all transactions (taken together) the total debit amount must equal the total credit amount. Any disagreement would imply an error. Clearly, double-entry system is a useful means of detecting errors. Equally important from this perspective is to know the *normal* balance (debit or credit) of an item. For instance, individual debtor account (to whom goods are sold on credit) is expected to have debit balance (being an asset). In case it indicates credit balance (Cr. side of an account exceeds Dr. side), it needs to be checked, being abnormal in nature. In concrete terms, it implies that the firm is to pay to the debtor. *Prima-facie,* it appears to be wrong. However, an occurrence of such a situation cannot be completely ruled out. Assume a firm has made credit sales of ₹20 lakh to Sohan, who has remitted cheque of ₹18 lakh. After a week, Sohan returns defective goods of ₹4 lakh. The firm owes ₹2 lakh (₹22 lakh – ₹20 lakh) and, accordingly, Sohan's account will show credit balance of ₹2 lakh (which is correct).

Unlike debtor account, cash account cannot have credit balance as it implies cash outflows of the firm exceeding the cash receipts. In the example of ATCPL (Format 3.1), the firm's cash outflows cannot be more than ₹11,25,000 (cash receipts). Assume for the sake of explanation only that the firm has cash outflows of ₹11,30,000. In operational terms, it implies that the firm has managed cash outflow transactions of the value of ₹11,30,000 while its cash receipts are ₹11,25,000. It is ridiculous to conceive of such a situation (in which cash account has credit balance) and, hence, the example reinforces the significance of knowing the normal balance of an item.

TYPE OF ACCOUNTS

LO 3.2 List various types of accounts

Accounting transactions of a firm can be classified into four major groups: assets, liabilities, revenues and expenses. While accounts maintained for assets and liabilities items (contained in balance sheet) are called *permanent accounts,* the accounts related to revenues and expenses items (summarised in income statement) are named as *temporary accounts/income statement accounts.*

Temporary accounts refer to revenue and expense accounts which are closed by transfer to profit and loss account.

Temporary Accounts It may be recalled that profit is determined by matching all expenses of an accounting year against the revenues earned in that year. All the expenses and revenue/income accounts are finally closed by transferring to income statement (with no balance of such items to be carried forward to the next accounting year). For this reason, these accounts are appropriately called *temporary accounts/nominal accounts* (which exist in name only). Thus, there are temporary accounts for sales revenue, commission received, interest/dividend received, cost of goods sold, administrative, selling and financial expenses, and so on. Revenue and expense transactions are recorded in their respective temporary accounts for the entire accounting period (say, from 1.4.2015 to 31.3.2016). On 31.3.2016, all the entries recorded, say, in sales revenue account can be added to determine the net sales for the period from 1.4.2015 to 31.3.2016. Likewise, entries recorded in various expenses accounts, say, wages power, insurance, rent, telephone and so on are added (in each account separately). The sum of each of these items (technically referred to balance) are then transferred to income statement. The summary of income statement in terms of net income (revenues > expenses) or the net loss (expenses > revenues) is finally transferred to profit and loss appropriation account/statement of retained earnings (explained later in the chapter). From the above description, it is apparent that all revenue and expense accounts are temporary in nature and are closed in the same accounting year.

Permanent Accounts In contrast, the balances of accounts pertaining to various assets and liabilities are taken to the balance sheet at the end of the accounting year (say, as at 31.3.2016). The balances of these items (namely, cash, plant and machinery, debtors, creditors, capital, etc.) are not closed in the same accounting year in that they would be carried/brought forward to the next accounting year (2016–17) as the year's opening balance. Permanent accounts can either be *personal* or *real* accounts.

Permanent accounts refer to assets and liability accounts which are carried forward.

Personal Accounts Personal accounts are the accounts of **(i)** *natural persons* (say Mohan, Sohan, Rohan) who deal with the firm in various capacities like buyers, sellers, lenders, investors and **(ii)** *legal/notional persons* like companies, financial institutions, banks, insurance companies, government organisations, and so on.

Personal accounts are accounts of natural and legal persons.

Real Accounts Real accounts stand for properties of a firm. These properties (or assets) can either be tangible or intangible. *Tangible* assets are those assets which can be felt, touched or seen. Plant and machinery, land and buildings, furniture, office equipment are notable examples of such assets. *Intangible* assets (not having physical existence) are valuable resources of a firm in that they have exchange value. Goodwill, patents, trademarks are the major examples of such assets.

Real accounts refer to assets which can be tangible or intangible.

Rules for Debit and Credit Corresponding to three types of accounts (nominal, personal and real), there are three sets of rules used for accounting records. These are now briefly explained.

Nominal Accounts Such account items relate to expenses and revenues. Recall that expense items have debit balances and revenues/income items have credit balances and, hence, the logical recording rule is: ***debit all expenses and losses and credit all revenues, incomes and gains***. In accounting terms, when expenses are incurred, say, rent paid, rent account is debited. On receipt of dividend, since dividend is income, dividend account is credited.

Nominal accounts relate to revenues and expenses.

Personal Accounts Such account items primarily relate to individuals and institutions. These are either debtors (sum receivable from them) or creditors (sum payable to them). Recall that debtors (being assets) have debit balances and creditors (being liabilities) have credit balances. Recall further that ATCPL has sold goods/toys on credit to Reliable Sound Buyers and Company. The company is receiver of goods and is to pay back to ATCPL in future and, therefore, its debtor. The ATCPL has purchased raw materials on credit from Supreme Plastics Limited. Obviously, ATCPL is to pay to Supreme Plastics which is supplier/giver of raw materials and, therefore, creditor. Therefore, the recording rule is: ***debit the receiver and credit the giver***. In the case of sale, Reliable Sound Buyers and Company's Account would be debited and in the case of purchase, Supreme Plastics Account would be credited in the books of ATCPL.

Real Account Such account deals with assets and assets have debit balances. Accordingly, balance of an asset account shows increase when it is debited and decrease when it is credited. Obviously, an asset account should show increase when it is purchased and revalued upwards and should show decrease when it is depreciated and sold. Hence, the rule is: ***debit what comes in and credit what goes out***. Recall, ATCPL has purchased machinery. According to this rule, machinery account is to be debited (as machinery has come-in). Debiting machinery account is relatively obvious. The less obvious is the amount of depreciation charged on machine. It causes decrease in the value of machine (and, hence, credited) but there is no 'going-out' of the machine. The notable point is that the literal application of the recording rule is not *always* possible; in such circumstances, the accounting transaction should be analysed with intent to ascertain its impact (increase/decrease) on the balance of an item. Depreciation of machine obviously would decrease the balance of machine account, and, hence, machine account should be credited with depreciation amount. Likewise, upward revaluation of building causes building balance to increase and, therefore, requires to be debited.

The above mentioned three rules are helpful to the accountant/book-keeper in recording virtually all the business transactions. In situations when straight application of these rules is not feasible (as observed in the case of depreciation and revaluation above), the understanding of the type of normal balance (debit or credit) an item carries is helpful guide in journalising the transactions.

Each transaction affects two items. One is debited and another item is credited. Both items involved in a transaction may not exclusively belong to one account (personal, real or nominal). One item may be personal and other item may relate to nominal or real or vice-versa. In fact, in most of the cases, it is important to note that the accounting transaction involves more than one type of account.

Account Books

LO 3.3 Understand accounting books (Journals and ledgers) and the recordings of financial transactions

There are two major books, namely, Journal and Ledger, used to record accounting transactions by a firm.

Journalising is the process of recording transactions in journal-the book of original entry.

Journal The *Journal* book provides a chronological record of transactions entered into by a firm. Since the accounting record of a transaction is *first* recorded in the journal book, it is called the book of the ***original or first entry***. **The entry (having one debit and one credit) is known as Journal entry.** Apart from debit and credit record, the entry also contains a brief narration/explanation about the transaction (for future reference). The process of recording transaction is called ***journalising***. The journal entry consists of the date of transaction, the specific accounts to be debited and credited along with the amount involved, brief narration of the transaction, ledger folio number (abbreviated L.F., showing ledger page number on which accounts are posted, explained later). All this is provided in Format 3.4.

Format 3.4 Journal Book

Date	Particulars	L.F.	Dr. Amount	Cr. Amount

The journal book contains date-wise record of all the business transactions of a firm. However, it fails to provide an *instant* answer to a lot of important information, for instance, the amount due from a debtor (at the quarter end June 30, 2016). Goods are sold at various points of time and so are the payments received. Occasionally, defective goods may also be returned by debtors. As a result, various credit sales transactions and bank-receipt transactions are likely to have been recorded at various dates in April to June 2016. Credit sale increases the amount receivable; both receipts of cash and returns of goods decrease the amount. Therefore, there is a need of a book where all information of credit sales, receipts, goods returned related to a specific debtor is available at one place. Likewise, the information may be required for a creditor from whom goods are purchased on credit and payments are frequently made. The firm may be interested in knowing the amount of expenses incurred and revenues earned during the quarter, so that income statement for the quarter period may be readily prepared. Ledger book, by providing details (increases as well as decreases) of each account serves this function; **it is known as the book of second entry**.

Ledger Refer to Format 3.1 which contains cash account of ATCPL. Observe that all cash receipts (January 1; 5–10) and all cash payments (January 2, 4, 28–31) of ATCPL have been shown at one place, thereby facilitating to know how much cash balance the firm should have on January 31. Like cash account, the firm will like to have individual accounts for the bank, capital, debtors, creditors, expense, revenue, machine and so on. The book in which these accounts are kept is known as a ledger. Thus, *ledger is a set of accounts*. In a manual system, it may be a bound book or a set of loose-leaf pages. Each account is placed on a separate page and is assigned the page number.

The process of transferring entry from the journal to the ledger is called ***posting***. Debit items/entries are posted on the debit side (with entry of credit side) and credit items/entries are posted on credit side (with entry of debit side). The ledger account (known as 'T' account) contains date, particulars (recording debit or credit item along with amount involved), Journal folio (J.F, the page number of Journal from where the item has been recorded). Its format is given in Format 3.5.

Posting
is the process of transferring entry from journal to ledger which is a set of accounts.

FORMAT 3.5 Ledger Account

Date	Particulars	J.F.	Dr. Amount	Date	Particulars	J.F.	Cr. Amount

The balance of an account is obtained by adding the items of both sides (debit and credit) separately. In case the total of debit side exceeds that of the credit side, the account is said to have ***debit balance***. Conversely, the account is said to have ***credit balance*** if the credit side total exceeds the debit side total. To equalise their totals, the balance amount is shown/inserted on the shorter side (by writing balance carried down, abbreviated as c/d). It is then shown on the higher side to show the opening balance as balance brought forward (abbreviated as b/f). Conventionally, one line is drawn above the total and two lines below the total. Where the totals of two sides equalise, the account is said to be in balance.

Debit balance
is the excess of debit side over credit side of an account.

Credit balance
is the excess of credit side over debit side of an account.

Recording Process in Journal and Ledger Before a transaction is recorded in a Journal, book it is necessary to determine its dual impact on the firm's accounts. This analysis facilitates to know which account is to be debited and which is to be credited. The journal entry should ensure that debits are equal to credits. It is often easy to record half of the journal entry (dealing with cash/bank account in particular) as its impact is obvious. The impact of the other half of the journal entry may not appear to be that obvious (for a beginner). It is suggested that whichever half of the entry (whether debit or credit part) is correctly understood, the same may first be recorded, and the remaining less obvious half entry then can be recorded, for instance, wages paid in cash. Cash is outflow; cash is real account; the rule is credit what goes out; cash is to be credited. The remaining half is wages account. Wages account is to be debited. Being a nominal account, expenses are to be debited. Likewise, capital brought in by the owner causes cash to increase. Accordingly cash account is to be debited and capital (the residual part) of the transaction is to be credited. Mathematically, it is correct. However, the reader should ascertain the accounting rule applicable (capital is personal account; giver is to be credited and, hence, capital account).

Once the accounts to be debited and credited are identified, the name of the account to be debited is written first, followed by the name of the account to be credited. The credit account is written in the following line *indented* (about half-an-inch) to the right with an objective to help the reader to demarcate the credit entry(ies) from the debit entry(ies). A simple journal entry involves one debit account and one credit account. A compound journal entry involves at least 3 accounts. After recording the journal entry, *narration*/supplementary information is provided below it (for instance, invoice number of the purchase or sale, cheque number of payment or receipt). A line is drawn after each journal entry.

Posting to the ledger book has already been explained. In brief, debit account items are posted on debit side (by inserting the name of credit account) and *vice-versa.*

◆ Example 3.1

In chapter 2, 10 accounting transactions of ATCPL were analysed and their impact was directly recorded in the balance sheet. The same set of transactions have now been used to explain accounting records made in Journal and Ledger Books.

Summary Sheet Showing Transaction Analysis

Transaction of January, 2013	*Type of accounts*					
	Real		*Personal*		*Nominal*	
	Debit	*Credit*	*Debit*	*Credit*	*Debit*	*Credit*
1	✓			✓		
2		✓	✓			
4	✓	✓				
5–10	✓					✓
15			✓	✓		
21	✓			✓		
22	✓			✓		
24			✓			✓
28 – 31		✓			✓	

Note: The transaction analysis facilitates the framing of journal entries.

Solution

Journal Book of ATCPL

Assume J.F. No. 1 (for transactions from 1-15 January) and J.F. No. 2 for transactions between 16-31 January)

Date	*Particulars*		*L.F.*	*Dr Amount (₹)*	*Cr Amount (₹)*
2016	Cash account	Dr.	10	10,00,000	
Jan. 1	To Capital account		15		10,00,000
	(Capital contributed by owners to start business)				

(Contd.)

(Contd.)

2	Bank account	Dr.	20	7,00,000	
	To Cash account		10		7,00,000
	(Amount deposited in Bank)				
4	Purchases account	Dr.	21	2,00,000	
	To Cash account		10		2,00,000
	(Toys bought for cash vide cash memo no... from...)				
5-10	Cash account	Dr.	10	1,25,000	
	To Sales account		31		1,25,000
	(Toys sold for cash vide cash memo nos. ...)				
15	Bank account	Dr.	20	8,00,000	
	To Loan account		35		8,00,000
	(Loan taken vide cheque No... at 12% rate of interest)				
21	Building shed account	Dr.	40	5,00,000	
	Machinery account	Dr.	42	7,00,000	
	To Bank account		20		12,00,000
	(Purchased Shed vide cheque No... and machinery vide cheque No...)				
22	Raw materials account	Dr.	45	1,00,000	
	To Supreme Plastics Limited		51		1,00,000
	(Purchased raw materials on credit vide invoice No...)				
24	Reliable Sound Buyers & Co.	Dr.	60	1,27,000	
	To sales account		30		1,27,000
	(Toys sold on credit vide invoice no.)				
28-31	Sundry Expenses	Dr.	70	32,000	
	To Cash account		10		32,000
	(Expenses paid in cash for month of January)				

Notes: (1) Refer to notes given at the end of ledger book to understand L.F. column.
(2) In practice, individual expense account (say, salary, telephone, rent, etc) would be debited.

LEDGER BOOK OF ATCPL

Date 2016	Particulars	J.F.	Dr. Amount (₹)	Date 2016	Particulars	J.F.	Cr. Amount (₹)
			Cash Account				(Folio No. 10 assumed)
Jan. 1	To Capital	1	10,00,000	Jan. 2	By Bank	1	7,00,000
5-10	To Sales	1	1,25,000	4	By Purchases	1	2,00,000
				28-31	By Sundry expenses	2	32,000
				31	By Balance c/d		1,93,000
			11,25,000				11,25,000
Feb. 1	To Balance b/f		1,93,000				

Date 2016	Particulars	J.F.	Dr. Amount (₹)	Date 2016	Particulars	J.F.	Cr. Amount (₹)
			Capital Account				(Folio No. 15 assumed)
Jan. 31	To Balance c/d		10,00,000	Jan. 1	By Cash	1	10,00,000
				Feb. 1	By Balance b/f		10,00,000

Date 2016	Particulars	J.F.	Dr. Amount (₹)	Date 2016	Particulars	J.F.	Cr. Amount (₹)
			Bank Account				(Folio No. 20 assumed)
Jan. 2	To Cash	1	7,00,000	Jan. 21	By Building shed	2	5,00,000
15	To 12% Loan	1	8,00,000		By Machinery	2	7,00,000
					By Balance c/d		3,00,000
			15,00,000				15,00,000
Feb. 1	To Balance b/f		3,00,000				

Date 2016	Particulars	J.F.	Dr. Amount (₹)	Date 2016	Particulars	J.F.	Cr. Amount (₹)
			Purchases Account				(Folio No. 21 assumed)
Jan. 4	To Cash	1	2,00,000	Jan. 31	By Balance c/d		2,00,000
Feb 1	To Balance b/f		2,00,000				

Date 2016	Particulars	J.F.	Dr. Amount (₹)	Date 2016	Particulars	J.F.	Cr. Amount (₹)
			Sales Account				(Folio No. 31 assumed)
Jan. 31	To Balance c/d		2,52,000	Jan.	By Cash	1	
				5-10	By Reliable Sound	2	
				24	Buyer & Company		1,27,000
			2,52,000				2,52,000
				Feb. 1	By Balance b/f		2,52,000

Date 2016	Particulars	J.F.	Dr. Amount (₹)	Date 2016	Particulars	J.F.	Cr. Amount (₹)
			Loan Account				(Folio No. 35 assumed)
Jan. 31	To Balance c/d		8,00,000	Jan. 15	By Bank	1	8,00,000
				Feb. 1	By Balance b/f		8,00,000

Date 2016	Particulars	J.F.	Dr. Amount (₹)	Date 2016	Particulars	J.F.	Cr. Amount (₹)
			Building Shed Account				(Folio No. 40 assumed)
Jan. 21	To Bank	2	5,00,000	Jan. 31	By Balance c/d		5,00,000
Feb. 1	To Balance b/f		5,00,000				

Date 2016	Particulars	J.F.	Dr. Amount (₹)	Date 2016	Particulars	J.F.	Cr. Amount (₹)
			Machinery Account				(Folio No. 42 assumed)
Jan. 21	To Bank	2	7,00,000	Jan. 31	By Balance c/d		7,00,000
Feb. 1	To Balance b/f		7,00,000				

Date 2016	Particulars	J.F.	Dr. Amount (₹)	Date 2016	Particulars	J.F.	Cr. Amount (₹)
			Raw Material Account				(Folio No. 45 assumed)
Jan. 22	To Supreme Plastics	2	1,00,000	Jan. 31	By Balance c/d		1,00,000
Feb. 1	To Balance b/f		1,00,000				

Date 2016	Particulars	J.F.	Dr. Amount (₹)	Date 2016	Particulars	J.F.	Cr. Amount (₹)
			Supreme Plastics Company Account				(Folio No. 51 assumed)
Jan. 31	To Balance c/d		1,00,000	Jan. 22	By Raw materials	2	1,00,000
				Feb. 1	By Balance b/f		1,00,000

Date 2016	Particulars	J.F.	Dr. Amount (₹)	Date 2016	Particulars	J.F.	Cr. Amount (₹)
			Reliable Sound Buyers & Company Account				(Folio No. 60 assumed)
Jan. 24	To Sales	2	1,27,000	Jan. 31	By Balance c/d		1,27,000
Feb.1	To Balance b/f		1,27,000				

Date 2016	Particulars	J.F.	Dr. Amount (₹)	Date 2016	Particulars	J.F.	Cr. Amount (₹)
			Sundry Expenses Account				(Folio No. 70 assumed)
Jan. 28-31	To Cash	2	32,000	Jan. 31	By Balance c/d		32,000
Feb. 1	To Balance b/f		32,000				

Notes: **(1)** It is a convention to write 'To' on debit side and 'By' on credit side while posting.

(2) As per GAAP, all expenses and revenue accounts are closed by transferring to profit and loss A/c. To help the reader to understand preparation of trial balance, the balance of these accounts have been shown/drawn.

(3) Each ledger account is assigned a page number, technically referred to as ledger folio (LF); accordingly, each ledger account is assigned LF number (mentioned along with account title).

(4) Likewise, each page of Journal book is also numbered (known as Journal Folio, JF).

(5) While the LF number indicates the ledger page number to which journal entry has been posted, the JF number shows the page number from which the journal entry has been brought to be recorded in ledger. In case of doubt/mistakes, these folio/page numbers help in retrieving/referring the accounting transaction and identifying/locating the error (if any) readily.

TRIAL BALANCE

LO 3.4 Describe trial balance (Sheet of balances) and its limitations

Under the double entry system, the sum of debit and credit balances of the ledger accounts must tally. For the purpose of such a verification, a sheet/statement of balances (known as *trial* balance) is prepared. Trial balance lists the account-names which have either debit or credit balances. In case, its two sides tally, it is *prima-facie,* a signal of arithmetic accuracy of books of accounts; if totals differ, there must be some error(s) which have occurred.

Trial balance is a statement of account balances and their totals.

The common errors in this regard are posting on the wrong side of a ledger account, posting wrong amount in a ledger account (say, ₹37,900 instead of ₹39,700), wrong totaling of either side of any ledger account, mistake in subtracting the lower side of a ledger account from the higher side and, hence, wrong balancing of account (referred to as *errors of commission).* Format 3.6 shows trial balance of ATCPL based on balances derived from Example 3.1.

FORMAT 3.6 Trial Balance of ATCPL as on 31.1.2016

Ledger account	*Dr. Balances*	*Cr. Balances*
Cash	₹1,93,000	
Capital		₹10,00,000
Bank	3,00,000	
Purchases	2,00,000	
Sales		2,52,000
12% Loan		8,00,000
Building shed	5,00,000	
Machinery	7,00,000	
Raw-materials	1,00,000	
Supreme Plastics Limited		1,00,000
Reliable Sound Buyers & Company	1,27,000	
Sundry expenses	32,000	
	21,52,000	21,52,000

However, it is important to note that the agreement of the two sides of trial balance is not a *conclusive proof* of accuracy of financial records. The reason is that trial balance fails to disclose/detect the following types of errors.

Error of omission arises from omission of a transaction from the journal.

Errors of Omission If a transaction has been *omitted* (entirely) to be recorded in the journal book, the trial balance agreement would not be disturbed as both debit and credit entries related to a transaction have been left out. Assume omission of credit sales transaction in a firm. In operational terms, it implies that the firm has neither debited debtor's account nor credited sales account in its journal book. Evidently, agreement of trial balance is not affected.

Error of principle arises from treatment of revanue expenditure as capital expenditure and *vice versa.*

Errors of Principle It may be recalled that capital expenditure items as well as revenue expense items have debit balances. Since both items have debit balances, a wrong transaction analysis, say, repairs of plant (which is an expense) charged to plant account (i.e., to an asset account) would not affect the agreement of the trial balance. However, it would cause over-estimation of profit.

Errors of compensation result from offsetting of one error by another error.

Errors of Compensation/Offsetting Errors These errors are of unique type in that the impact of one error which has occurred is nullified/neturalised by the unexpected incurrence of another error. For instance, a debit account has been posted an incorrect amount of ₹11,400 (instead of correct amount of ₹14,100); this mistake would be arithmetically offset if another error takes place which causes wrong debit of ₹14,100 instead of the correct debit of ₹11,400.

It is, thus, apparent that the agreement of trial balance is not a conclusive proof of accurate recording of accounting transactions. In spite of this deficiency of trial balances, it is a valuable statement which serves two principal purposes: **(1)** It shows whether there is an accurate recording of accounting transactions and **(2)** It provides a convenient summary of all ledger accounts at one place which, in turn, provides input to the preparation of income statement and balance sheet.

SPECIAL JOURNALS/LEDGERS

LO 3.5 Illustrate special journals and ledgers

The above procedure of recording accounting transactions in which only one general Journal and only one general ledger is maintained is one type of an accounting system. Its variant consists of a system in which there are more than one journal and more than one ledger book, each book specialising in one type of transaction. For instance, there can be one journal, recording exclusively credit sales transactions of goods (in which firm deals), known as *Sales Journal/Sales Book*. Likewise, there can be *Purchase Book* to record trade credit purchases; *Purchase Returns Book* and *Sales Return Book* to record returns of goods; *Cash Book* to record cash receipts and cash payments; *Bank Book* to record deposits and withdrawals and so on. In brief, there can be a separate journal book for each specific transaction which occurs frequently.

It is expected that the accounting record made in the above mentioned six *Special Journal* books (namely, sales, purchase, sales returns, purchase returns, cash and bank) is likely to cover the significant proportion of total business transactions of a business firm. *General Journal* can then serve the function of recording non-recurring transactions, say, bad debts, charging depreciation on plant and machinery, adjustment entries, closing and opening entries, and so on.

Obviously, maintaining accounting records based on special journals is more advantageous. Its three major advantages are: **(1)** There is less work load involved in journalising and posting. **(2)** It facilitates division of labour among employees working in accounts section of the firm. **(3)** It can relatively furnish more accurate information and that too more promptly. Firms would be well advised to adopt/prefer to maintain *special Journal instead of one General Journal.* Format 3.7 Provides the format of sales book.

FORMAT 3.7 Sales Book

Date	*Particulars*	*L.F.*	*Invoice Details*	*Amount*

While the format is the same for sales returns book, purchase book and purchase returns book, cash and bank transactions require different formats (Formats 3.8 and 3.9). Observe that cash and bank books have two sides whereas all other books have one side only.

FORMAT 3.8 Cash Book

Receipts				*Payments*			
Date	*Particulars*	*L.F.*	*Amount*	*Date*	*Particulars*	*L.F.*	*Amount*

Note: Discount column can also be inserted on both sides (before amount).

FORMAT 3.9 Bank Book

Deposits				*Withdrawals*			
Date	*Particulars*	*L.F.*	*Amount*	*Date*	*Particulars*	*L.F.*	*Amount*

Note: In case, the firm operates with more than one bank, it may maintain more than one bank book, or may operate with one bank book only. In the latter case, there will be additional amount columns (for each bank separately) on both sides.

Special Ledgers Like special journals, it would be equally advantageous to have more than one general ledger. The firm can have special ledgers, such as debtors ledger, creditors ledger, expense ledger, assets ledger and so on. These four ledgers are likely to cover the bulk of total posted items of a business firm. The firm can maintain one general ledger to take care of other accounts (say, accounts related to capital, loan etc.) as the the need for posting in these accounts is comparatively less frequent *vis-à-vis* the accounts related to debtors and creditors. The format is the same (already shown in Format 3.5) for all types of ledgers.

Posting Procedure from Special Journals The procedure is explained below.

(1) Sales Book (not pre-fixed with credit**)** Recall sales revenue has *credit* balance; therefore, total of sales book will obviously be posted to the *credit* side of sales revenue account in general ledger. To complete the double entry requirement, each credit sale transaction is to be posted to the *debit* side of the concerned debtor account in debtors ledger.

(2) Sales Returns Book It is opposite to sales revenue; it has *debit* balance; its total is posted to the *debit* side of sales returns account in general ledger. To conform to accounting equation, each sales return item is to be posted to the *credit* side of concerned debtor account in debtors ledger. (Hint: Recall that debtors have debit balance; sales return should reduce the debit balance and, hence, has to be credited).

(3) Purchase Book (not prefixed with credit) It has debit balance; accordingly, its total is to be posted to the *debit* side of purchase account in general ledger and to the *credit* side of individual creditors account in the creditors ledger. (Hint: Creditors have credit balance, credit purchases from them should increase this balance).

(4) Purchase Returns Book Being opposite to purchases account, it carries *credit* balance. Its total is therefore posted to the credit side of purchase returns account in general ledger. Since goods returned to suppliers reduce the sum payable to them, transactions of purchase returns are posted to the *debit* side of concerned creditor/supplier account in the creditors ledger.

(5) Cash Book Recall that a cash book has two sides. Accordingly, it serves the function of a cash account (as per ledger). *Debit* side of cash book is already conforming to the debit part of accounting equation; it is logical, therefore to post items appearing on debit side of cash book to the *credit* side of various relevant accounts of special ledgers and general ledgers. Likewise, items appearing on the *credit* side of cash book are to be posted to the *debit* side of relevant accounts.

(6) Bank Book Like cash book, bank book has also two sides and is akin to bank account (as per ledger). Its posting rules are the same as those of cash book.

Financial accounting system based on special journals and special ledgers is illustrated in comprehensive Example 3.2.

◆ Example 3.2

Record the following financial transactions in the appropriate books of accounts of M/s Growth firm. Also open various ledger accounts and draw trial balance as at March 31, 2016.

1. M/s Growth firm commenced business with a initial capital of ₹21 lakh in cash on January 1, 2016 contributed by the group of persons interested in the said business activity.
2. Deposited ₹20 lakh in bank.
3. Purchased following assets/raw material against cheque payments.
   (a) On January 5, land and building for ₹5 lakh
   (b) On January 10, plant and machinery for ₹10 lakh
   (c) On January 15, furniture and fixtures for ₹1 lakh
   (d) On January 20, raw material for ₹2 lakh
4. The firm processed raw material into finished goods and sold goods for ₹5 lakh as per following details:
   (a) On February 5 to Ramesh and Company for *₹1,00,000 on 30 days credit.* Ramesh and Company returned goods worth ₹25,000 on February 20 as they were not as per samples and paid ₹75,000 by cheque.

(b) On February 10 to Suresh and Company for ₹1,50,000 on 30 days credit. Payments from Suresh and Company were received on due date.
(c) On February 15 to Eximp and Company for ₹2,00,000 on cash basis.
(d) On February 15 to Solvent and Company for ₹50,000 on 30 days credit. Solvent and Company paid ₹.25,000 on due date and promised to pay balance ₹25,000 later on.

5. **(a)** The firm purchased goods for ₹2,50,000 from Creditnet and Company on March 1 (45 days credit) but returned ₹50,000 worth of goods due to different specifications/quality.
(b) The firm purchased goods for ₹1,00,000 from Chote Lal Company on March 3 and paid by cheque.

6. Other expenses for the period January to March are as under:

Particulars	*Total*	*January*	*February*	*March*
Wages and salaries	₹9,500	₹2,500	₹3,000	₹4,000
Rent	3,000	1,000	1,000	1,000
Electricity and fuel	2,500			2,500
Traveling	1,000			1,000
Repairs	3,000			3,000
Selling and administration	4,200			4,200
Postage	700			700
Telephone/fax etc	500			500
Stationery	1,500			1,500

Solution

Cash Book

Folio number 14 (assumed)

Receipts				*Payments*			
Date 2016	*Particulars*	*LF**	*Amount*	*Date 2016*	*Particulars*	*LF*	*Amount*
January 1	To Capital A/c	11	₹21,00,000	January 1	By Bank A/c	17	₹20,00,000
				31	By Wages/salary	114	2,500
				31	By Rent	115	1,000
				31	By Balance c/d		96,500
			21,00,000				21,00,000
February 1	To Balance b/f		96,500	February 28	By Wages/salary	114	3,000
15	To Sales A/c	33	2,00,000	28	By Rent	115	1,000
					By Balance c/d		2,92,500
			2,96,500				2,96,500
March 1	To Balance b/f		2,92,500	March 31	By Wages/salary	114	4,000
				31	By Rent	115	1,000
				31	By Electricity & fuel	116	2,500
				31	By Travelling	117	1,000
				31	By Repairs	118	3,000
					By Selling and administration	119	4,200
				31	By Postage	120	700
				31	By Tel/fax	121	500
				31	By Stationery	122	1,500
				31	By Balance c/d		2,74,100
			2,92,500				2,92,500
April 1	To Balance b/f		2,74,100				

*Ledger folio.

Bank Book

Folio number 17 (assumed)

Deposits				Withdrawals			
Date 2016	*Particulars*	*LF*	*Amount*	*Date 2016*	*Particulars*	*LF*	*Amount*
January 1	To Cash A/c	14	₹20,00,000	January 5	By Land and building	23	₹5,00,000
February 20	To Ramesh and Co.	34	75,000	10	By Plant and machinery	24	10,00,000
March 10	To Suresh and Co.	35	1,50,000	15	By Furniture	25	1,00,000
15	To Solvent and Co.	36	25,000	20	By Purchases	49	2,00,000
				March 3	By Purchases	49	1,00,000
				31	By Balance c/d		3,50,000
			22,50,000				22,50,000
April 1	To Balance b/f		3,50,000				

Sales Book

Folio number 02 (assumed)

Date 2016	*Particulars*	*LF*	*Invoice details (assumed)*	*Amount*
February 5	Ramesh and Company	34	Number 38 February 5	₹1,00,000
10	Suresh and Company	35	Number 142 February 10	1,50,000
15	Solvent and Company	36	Number 176 February 15	50,000
				3,00,000

Sales Return Book

Folio number 03 (assumed)

Date 2016	*Particulars*	*LF*	*Invoice details (assumed)*	*Amount*
February 20	Ramesh and Company	34	Number 53 February 20	₹25,000
				25,000

Purchase Book

Folio number 06

Date 2016	*Particulars*	*LF*	*Invoice details (assumed)*	*Amount*
March 1	Creditnet and Company	52	Number 45 March 1	₹2,50,000
				2,50,000

Purchase Returns Book

Folio number 04

Date 2016	*Particulars*	*LF*	*Invoice details (assumed)*	*Amount*
March 1	Creditnet and Company	52	Number 183 March 1	₹50,000
				50,000

DEBTOR'S LEDGER

Ramesh and Company's A/c

Ledger folio number 34 (assumed)

Debit				Credit			
Date 2016	*Particulars*	*JF@*	*Amount*	*Date 2016*	*Particulars*	*JF*	*Amount*
February 5	To Sales	2	₹1,00,000	February 20	By Sales return	3	₹25,000
				20	By Bank A/c	17	75,000
			1,00,000				1,00,000

Suresh and Company's A/c

Ledger folio number 35 (assumed)

Date 2016	*Particulars*	*JF*	*Amount*	*Date 2016*	*Particulars*	*JF*	*Amount*
February 2	To Sales	2	₹1,50,000	March 10	By Bank A/c	17	₹1,50,000

Solvent and Company's A/c

Ledger folio number 36 (assumed)

Date 2016	*Particulars*	*JF*	*Amount*	*Date 2016*	*Particulars*	*JF*	*Amount*
February 15	To Sales	2	₹50,000	March 15	By Bank A/c	17	₹25,000
				31	By Balance c/d		25,000
			50,000				50,000
April 1	To Balance b/f		25,000				

CREDITOR'S LEDGER

M/s Creditnet and Company

Ledger folio number 52 (assumed)

Debit				Credit			
Date 2016	*Particulars*	*JF*	*Amount*	*Date 2016*	*Particulars*	*JF*	*Amount*
March 1	To Purchase returns	4	₹50,000	March 1	By Purchases	06	₹2,50,000
March 31	To Balance c/d		2,00,000				
			2,50,000				2,50,000
				April 1	By Balance b/f		2,00,000

EXPENSES LEDGER

Wages and Salaries A/c

Folio number 114

Debit				Credit			
Date 2016	*Particulars*	*JF*	*Amount*	*Date 2016*	*Particulars*	*JF*	*Amount*
January 31	To Cash	14	₹2,500	March 31	By Balance c/d*		₹9,500
February 28	To Cash	14	3,000				
March 31	To Cash	14	4,000				
			9,500				
April 1	To Balance b/f		9,500				9,500

@Journal folio.

Rent A/c

Folio number 115

Debit				Credit			
Date 2016	*Particulars*	*JF*	*Amount*	*Date 2016*	*Particulars*	*JF*	*Amount*
January 31	To Cash	14	₹1,000	March 31	By Balance c/d*		₹3,000
February 28	To Cash	14	1,000				
March 31	To Cash	14	1,000				
			3,000				3,000
April 1	To Balance b/f		3,000				

Electricity and Fuel A/c

Folio number 116

Debit				Credit			
Date 2016	*Particulars*	*JF*	*Amount*	*Date 2016*	*Particulars*	*JF*	*Amount*
March 31	To Cash	14	₹2,500	March 31	By Balance c/d*		₹2,500
April 1	To Balance b/f		2,500				

Travelling A/c

Folio number 117

Debit				Credit			
Date 2016	*Particulars*	*JF*	*Amount*	*Date 2016*	*Particulars*	*JF*	*Amount*
March 31	To Cash	14	₹1,000	March 31	By Balance c/d*		1,000
April 1	To Balance b/f		1,000				

Repairs A/c

Folio number 118

Debit				Credit			
Date 2016	*Particulars*	*JF*	*Amount*	*Date 2016*	*Particulars*	*JF*	*Amount*
March 31	To Cash	14	₹3,000	March 31	By Balance c/d*		₹3,000
April 1	To Balance b/f		3,000				

Selling and Administration A/c

Folio number 119

Debit				Credit			
Date 2016	*Particulars*	*JF*	*Amount*	*Date 2016*	*Particulars*	*JF*	*Amount*
Marcsh 31	To Cash	14	₹4,200	March 31	By Balance c/d*		₹4,200
April 1	To Balance b/f		4,200				

Postage A/c

Folio number 120

Debit				Credit			
Date 2016	*Particulars*	*JF*	*Amount*	*Date 2016*	*Particulars*	*JF*	*Amount*
March 31	To Cash	14	₹700	March 31	By Balance c/d*		₹700
April 1	To Balance b/f		700				

Telephone/Fax A/c

Folio number 121

Debit				Credit			
Date 2016	Particulars	JF	Amount	Date 2016	Particulars	JF	Amount
March 31	To Cash	14	₹500	March 31	By Balance c/d*		₹500
April 1	To Balance b/f		500				

Stationery A/c

Debit				Credit			
Date 2016	Particulars	JF	Amount	Date 2016	Particulars	JF	Amount
March 31	To Cash	14	₹1,500	March 31	By Balance c/d*		₹1,500
April 1	To Balance b/f		1,500				

*In fact, as a matter of accounting principle, all expenses and revenue accounts are closed by transferring to Profit and Loss A/c; in order to help the reader to understand preparation of trial balance, balances of these accounts have been drawn/shown.

GENERAL LEDGER

Capital A/c

Folio number 11 (assumed)

Debit				Credit			
Date 2016	Particulars	JF	Amount	Date 2016	Particulars	JF	Amount
March 31	To Balance c/d		₹21,00,000	January 1	By Cash A/c	14	₹21,00,000
				April 1	By Balance b/f		21,00,000

Land and Building A/c

Folio number 23 (assumed)

Debit				Credit			
Date 2016	Particulars	JF	Amount	Date 2016	Particulars	JF	Amount
January 5	To Bank A/c	17	₹5,00,000	March 31	By Balance c/d		₹5,00,000
April 1	To Balance b/f		5,00,000				

Plant and Machinery A/c

Folio number 24 (assumed)

Debit				Credit			
Date 2016	Particulars	JF	Amount	Date 2016	Particulars	JF	Amount
January 10	To Bank A/c	17	₹10,00,000	March 31	By Balance c/d		₹10,00,000
April 1	To Balance b/f		10,00,000				

Furniture A/c

Folio number 25 (assumed)

Debit				Credit			
Date 2016	Particulars	JF	Amount	Date 2016	Particulars	JF	Amount
January 15	To Bank A/c	17	₹1,00,000	March 31	By Balance c/d		₹1,00,000
April 1	To Balance b/f		1,00,000				

Sales A/c

Folio number 33 (assumed)

Debit				Credit			
Date 2016	Particulars	JF	Amount	Date 2016	Particulars	JF	Amount
March 31	To Balance c/d		₹5,00,000	February 15	By Cash A/c	14	₹2,00,000
				March 31	By Sales book	02	3,00,000
			5,00,000				5,00,000
				April 1	By Balance b/f		5,00,000

Sales Return A/c

Folio number 93 (assumed)

Debit				Credit			
Date 2016	Particulars	JF	Amount	Date 2016	Particulars	JF	Amount
February 20	To Sales return book	03	₹25,000	February 28	By Balance c/d	21	₹25,000
March 28	To Balance b/f		25,000				

Purchase A/c

Folio number 49

Debit				Credit			
Date 2016	Particulars	JF	Amount	Date 2016	Particulars	JF	Amount
January 20	To Bank A/c	17	₹2,00,000	March 31	By Balance c/d		₹5,50,000
March 3	To Bank A/c	17	1,00,000				
March 31	To Purchase book	6	2,50,000				
			5,50,000				5,50,000
April 1	To Balance b/f		5,50,000				

Purchase Return A/c

Folio number 94

Debit				Credit			
Date 2016	Particulars	JF	Amount	Date 2016	Particulars	JF	Amount
March 31	To Balance c/d		₹50,000	March 31	By Purchase return book	04	₹50,000
				April 1	By Balance b/f		50,000

Trial Balance as at March 31, 2016

Particulars	Debit	Credit
Capital		₹21,00,000
Land and building	₹5,00,000	
Plant and machinery	10,00,000	
Furniture	1,00,000	
Sales		5,00,000
Sales return	25,000	
Cash	2,74,100	
Bank balance	3,50,000	
Wages and salary	9,500	

(Contd.)

(Contd.)

Rent	3,000	
Electricity and fuel	2,500	
Travelling	1,000	
Repairs	3,000	
Selling and administrative	4,200	
Postage	700	
Telephone/fax	500	
Stationery	1,500	
Sundry debtors	25,000	
Sundry creditors		2,00,000
Purchases	5,50,000	
Purchase return		50,000
Total	28,50,000	28,50,000

ADJUSTMENT/CLOSING/OPENING ENTRIES

LO 3.6 Explain adjustments/closing/opening entries

Trial balance indicates the debit and the credit balances of transactions that have been first recorded in journal books and subsequently posted to the ledger books. However, these balances are not adequate to prepare income statement and balance sheet. The reason is that all expenses pertaining to the accounting period (say w.e.f. 1.4.2015 to 31.3.2016) may not have been paid, by 31st March 2016. Likewise, there is need for adjustment for expenses paid in advance. Income/interest/dividend receivable also merits adjustment. Recall, these adjustments are required to conform to accrual accounting. This apart, entries are also required to conform to various other GAAPs. Charging depreciation on tangible assets, amortisation of intangible assets and creating provision for bad and doubtful debts are the notable items in this regard.

Obviously, these adjustments are required to determine true income and present true and fair financial position of a business firm. These adjustments are transmitted through ***adjustment entries***. The adjustment entries are akin to journal entries which have one debit item and another credit item. In most of the situations, one item relates to income statement and another to balance sheet. These entries are recorded on the last day of the accounting period (say, 31-3-2016). The entries are based on the debit and credit postulates.

Adjustment entries record outstanding expenses, expenses paid in advance and income in arrears, depreciation etc.

◆ **Example 3.3**

Adjustment Entries On 31.3.2016

Sr. No.	*Particulars*		*Dr Amount*	*Cr Amount*
(1)	Wages payable ₹50,000			
	Wages account	Dr.	₹50,000	
	To Wages payable account			₹50,000
	(Wages in arrears are recorded)			
(2)	Rent paid in advance ₹20,000			
	Rent paid in advance account	Dr.	20,000	
	To Rent account			20,000
	(Pre-paid rent has been adjusted)			
(3)	Depreciation on plant and machinery ₹1,00,000			
	Depreciation account	Dr.	1,00,000	
	To Plant and machinery account			1,00,000
	(Depreciation on plant and machinery charged)			

(Contd.)

(Contd.)

(4)	Interest receivable on investment ₹10,000			
	Interest receivable Account	Dr.	10,000	
	To Interest Account			10,000
	(Interest earned but not received)			

Explanation for Adjustment Entries:

(1) Unpaid wages ₹50,000 on 31st March, 2016 implies that actual wages expenses are more by ₹50,000 than shown in wages account. Since wages is a nominal account, it is debited and wages payable (being liability) is credited.

(2) Rent expense during Jan.–March, 2016 should be less to the extent of the amount of advance of ₹20,000. Since rent account has debit balance, the account is *credited* so that its balance decreases. The other half of the entry debited as rent paid in advance is an asset.

(3) Depreciation, being nominal account, has been debited. The balance of plant and equipment account (Dr. balance) is to be reduced on account of depreciation and, therefore, has been credited.

(4) Interest receivable account should augment income. Since income items have credit balance, interest account has been credited; interest amount is receivable in future and, therefore, represents assets (having debit balance).

Although it is common/convenient to have these adjustment entries carried out after the preparation of trial balance, conceptually, the adjustment entries can be recorded before the preparation of trial balance also. Irrespective of the fact whether adjustments have been made prior to, or after, the preparation of trial balance, the *modus-operandi* of incorporating their impact in financial statements is the same. In case these adjustments are carried out after the preparation of trial balance (in which debit balances are already = credit balances), the adjustment entry will affect one debit item and one credit item by identical amount so that the accounting equation (debit = credit) remains intact. If these adjustment entries are recorded prior to the preparation of the trial balance, their impact on both debit and credit items are reflected in the trial balance itself. In operational terms, adjustment item appearing in trial balance would be shown *one time only* either in income statement or balance sheet (as the case may be). For instance, wages payable in trial balance, having credit balance, will appear on liabilities side of the balance sheet as wages account appearing in trial balance has been adjusted for wages payable as a result of recording the adjustment entry. Depreciation on plant and machinery (Dr. balance), will be shown only on the debit side of profit and loss account as the depreciation amount has already been deducted from plant and machinery account.

Closing entries are entries that close all revenue and expense accounts by transfer to profit and loss account.

Closing Entries Recall that temporary/nominal accounts are closed by transferring to profit and loss account in the same accounting year so that profit and loss account of the next accounting year is not affected by the expenses and revenue accounts balances of the preceding year. Closing entries serve the purpose of closing all expenses and revenue accounts by transferring them to profit and loss account. The relevant closing entries are as follows:

(1) Closing Revenue Accounts Since revenue accounts (like sales, interest/dividend received and so on) have *credit* balances, they are closed by *debiting* them. The closing entry is:

Particulars		Dr Amount	Cr Amount
Sales revenue account	Dr.		
Interest received account	Dr.		
Commission received account	Dr.		
Discount received account	Dr.		
Any other income account (specify)	Dr.		
To Profit & Loss account			
(All revenue and other income accounts closed by transferring to P&L A/c)			

(2) Closing Expense Accounts Since expense accounts (say, wages, salaries, depreciation, repairs, power, telephone, freight, rent, insurance and so on) have debit balances, they are closed by crediting them. Accordingly, the closing entry is:

Particulars		Dr Amount	Cr Amount
Profit & Loss account	Dr.		
To Wages			
To Salaries			
To Depreciation			
To Repairs			
To Power			
To Telephone			
To Freight			
To Rent			
To Insurance			
To Any other expense (specify)			
(All expense accounts are closed by transferring to P&L A/c)			

(3) Closing Profit and Loss Account The balance of profit and loss account is transferred to profit and loss appropriation account (discussed later). Assuming profit and loss account has credit balance (implying firm has earned profits), the closing entry is

Particulars		Dr Amount	Cr Amount
Profit & Loss account	Dr.		
To Profit & Loss Appropriation account			

Note: In the case of loss, the last entry is to be reversed.

Opening entries are recorded to transfer all assets and liabilities from the previous year to the current year.

Opening Entries Recall that balances related to permanent accounts (real and personal) are carried/brought forward to next accounting year as the firm is to deal with these accounts in the coming year (unlike nominal accounts), for instance, receivables from debtors. Therefore, there is need to know the opening balance of debtors on day one of the next accounting year, say, 1.4.2016). Likewise, payables to creditors. There are closing balances in cash and bank accounts in the preceding year. These balances are to be used in the current year. Similarly, the assets like machines, building, office equipment, office furniture shown in the preceding year's balance sheet are used in the current year. To give effect to these permanent account balances, opening entries are to be recorded. In brief, opening entry (shown below) serves the purpose of transferring all assets (Dr. balances) and liabilities (Cr. balances) contained in balance sheet of the previous year to the current year.

Particulars		Dr Amount	Cr Amount
Cash account	Dr.		
Bank account	Dr.		
Machinery account	Dr.		
Building account	Dr.		
Furniture account	Dr.		
Office equipment account	Dr.		
Goodwill account	Dr.		
Patent account	Dr.		
Any other asset account (specify)	Dr.		
To Capital account			
To Profit & Loss Appropriation account (also known as retained earnings account)			
To Loan account			
To Creditors account			
To Expenses payable account			
To Any other liability account (specify)			

Example 3.4

From the trial balance (provided in Example 3.2) and following adjustments, (1) pass adjustment entries and closing entries on March 31, (2) prepare profit and loss account for the period 1st January to March 31, 2016 and balance sheet as at March 31st and (3) record opening entries on 1st April, 2016:

(a) Depreciation – ₹2,000 on furniture and ₹5,000 on plant and machinery.
(b) Wages payable are ₹500.
(c) Rent paid in advance, ₹1,200.
(d) Closing stock on 31st March, ₹2,00,000.
(e) Create provision for bad and doubtful debts at the rate of 5 per cent on debtors.
(f) Dividends (₹21,000) are to be paid. Assume the firm is not subject to taxes.

Solution

1(a). Adjustment Entries:

General Journal

Date 2016	Particulars		L.F.	Dr. Amount	Cr. Amount
March 31	Depreciation account	Dr.		₹7,000	
	To Furniture account				₹2,000
	To Plant and machinery account				5,000
	(Depreciation charged on furniture and plant and machinery)				
March 31	Wages account	Dr.		500	
	To Wages payable account				500
	(Outstanding wages of the current period recorded)				
March 31	Rent paid in advance account	Dr.		1,200	
	To Rent account				1,200
	(Excess rent paid in current year recorded)				
March 31	Closing stock account	Dr.		2,00,000	
	To Purchases account				2,00,000
	(Closing stock as on 31st March transferred to purchase account so that true cost of goods sold can be determined)				

(Contd.)

(Contd.)

March 31	Profit & Loss account	Dr.		1,250	
	To Provision for bad & doubtful Debts account				1,250
	(Provision for bad debts of ₹1,250 is created on sundry debtors)				
March 31	Profit & Loss Appropriation account		Dr.	21,000	
	To Dividend payable account				21,000
	(Dividends are payable to owners)				

1(b). Closing Entries:

Date 2016	*Particulars*		*L.F.*	*Dr. Amount*	*Cr. Amount*
March 31	Sales account	Dr.		₹5,00,000	
	Purchase return account	Dr.		50,000	
	To Profit & Loss account				₹5,50,000
	(Sales and purchase return accounts closed by transferring to P&L A/c)				
March 31	Profit & Loss account	Dr.		4,07,200	
	To Sales return account				25,000
	To Wages and salaries account*				10,000
	To Rent account*				1,800
	To Electricity and fuel account				2,500
	To Traveling account				1,000
	To Repairs account				3,000
	To Selling and administrative account				4,200
	To Postage account				700
	To Telephone/fax account				500
	To Stationery account				1,500
	To Purchases account*				3,50,000
	To Depreciation account*				7,000
	(All expense accounts closed by transferring to P&L A/c)				
March 31	Profit & Loss account	Dr.		1,41,550	
	To Profit & Loss Appropriation account				1,41,550
	(Profit transferred to P&L Appropriation Account)				

*Amounts are as per revised ledger account balances of these items (after incorporating the effect of adjustment entries)

2(a). Profit & Loss Account for the Period January to March 31, 2016

Particulars		*Dr. Amount*	*Particulars*		*Cr. Amount*
To Cost of goods sold			By Sales	₹5,00,000	
Purchases	₹5,50,000		Less sales returns	25,000	₹4,75,000
Less purchase returns	50,000				
Less closing stock	2,00,000	₹3,00,000*			
To Wages and salaries	9,500				
Add payable	500	10,000			
To Rent paid	3,000				
Less advance paid	1,200	1,800			
To Electricity and fuel		2,500			
To Travelling		1,000			
To Repairs		3,000			

(Contd.)

(Contd.)

To Selling and administration		4,200		
To Postage		700		
To Telephone/fax		500		
To Stationery		1,500		
To Depreciation:				
Plant & machinery	₹5,000			
Furniture	2,000	7,000		
To Provision for bad and doubtful debts		1,250		
To Profit (balance) transferred to P&L Appropriation Account		1,41,550		
		4,75,000		4,75,000

*represents cost of goods sold (Gross purchases, ₹5,50,000 Less returns, ₹50,000 Less closing stock unsold, ₹2,00,000). It is important to note that purchases is a real account. To the extent, goods purchased are sold, they acquire the form of nominal account. Goods left unsold (closing stock on 31st March), therefore, represents real account and is shown in balance sheet.

2(b). Profit & Loss Appropriation Account*

Particulars	*Dr. Amount*	*Particulars*	*Cr. Amount*
To Proposed dividends	₹21,000	By Profit transferred from P& L A/c	₹1,41,550
To Balance of profits retained taken to balance sheet	1,20,550		
	1,41,550		1,41,550

*indicates utilisation of profit by the firm.

2(c). Balance Sheet as at March 31, 2016

Liabilities	*Amount*	*Assets*		*Amount*
Capital	₹21,00,000	Land and building		₹5,00,000
Wages payable	500	Plant and machinery	₹10,00,000	
Sundry creditors	2,00,000	Less depreciation	5,000	9,95,000
Profit & Loss appropriation (retained earnings)	1,20,550	Furniture	₹1,00,000	
		Less depreciation	2,000	98,000
Dividends payable	21,000	Closing stock		2,00,000
		Cash		2,74,100
		Cash at bank		3,50,000
		Rent paid in advance		1,200
		Sundry debtors	₹25,000	
		Less provision for bad & doubtful debts	1,250	23,750
	24,42,050			24,42,050

3. Opening Entry (1st April, 2016)

Date 2013	*Particulars*		*Dr. Amount*	*Cr. Amount*
1st April	Land and building account	Dr.	₹5,00,000	
	Plant and machinery account	Dr.	9,95,000	
	Furniture account	Dr.	98,000	
	Closing stock account	Dr.	2,00,000	
	Cash account	Dr.	2,74,100	
	Bank account	Dr.	3,50,000	

(Contd.)

(*Contd.*)

Rent paid in advance account	Dr.	1,200	
Sundry debtors account	Dr.	25,000	
To Capital account			₹21,00,000
To Wages payable account			500
To Sundry creditors account			2,00,000
To P&L appropriation account			1,20,550
To Dividends Payable account			21,000
To Provision for bad and doubtful debts account			1,250
(Various assets and liabilities brought forward from the previous accounting year recorded)			

BALANCE SHEET

LO 3.7 Discuss the contents of balance sheet

The balance sheet is a significant financial statement of a firm. In fact, it is called the fundamental accounting report. Other terms to describe this financial statement are the *statement of financial position* or the *position statement.* As the name suggests, the balance sheet provides information about the financial standing/position of a firm at a particular point of time, say, as on March 31, 2016. It can be visualised as a snapshot of the financial status of a company. The financial position of the company is valid for only one day– the reference day. The position of the firm on the preceding or following day is most likely to be different.

Balance sheet provides information about financial position in terms of assets, liabilities and shareholders equity at a point of time.

The financial position of a firm as disclosed by the balance sheet refers to its resources and obligations, and the interests of its owners in the business. In operational terms, the balance sheet contains information regarding assets, liabilities and shareholders' equity.

Now, it is mandatory for balance sheet to be presented in vertical/report form. In this form a step-wise balance sheet is prepared (Format 3.10) listing assets first followed by liabilities and owner's equity.

FORMAT 3.10 Balance Sheet—Vertical Form

The Hypothetical Ltd. *Balance Sheet as on March 31, 2016*

Assets, liabilities and owner's equity	Amount
Fixed assets	
Land, building, plant, machinery, etc.	
Less: depreciation	
Investments (at cost)	
Current assets	
Inventory	
Debtors	
Cash and bank balance	
Advance deposits, etc.	
Less current liabilities and provisions	
Bills payable	
Creditors:	
For goods	
For expenses	

(*Contd.*)

(Contd.)

Customer's advances
Unclaimed dividend
Provision for dividend
Provision for taxation
Net current assets
Other assets
Total net assets
Financed by
Share capital
Reserves and surpluses
Shareholder's equity
Non-current liabilities
Debentures
Mortgages
Total obligations

The contents of the balance sheet, include assets of the firm and the means by which assets have been financed, that is, the liabilities and owner's equity. The mandatory format of balance sheet has been shown in Exhibit 4.1 (page 4.3) of Chapter 4. The main elements of these are described in what follows.

Assets

Asset is a valuable resource owned by a firm acquired at measurable money cost.

Assets may be described as valuable resources owned by a business which have been acquired at a measurable money cost. As an economic resource, they satisfy three requirements. In the first place, the resource must be valuable. A resource is valuable if **(i)** it is cash or convertible into cash or **(ii)** it can provide future benefits to the operations of the firm. Secondly, the resources must be owned. Mere possession or control of a resource would not constitute an asset; it must be owned in the legal sense of the term. Finally, the resource must be acquired at a measurable money cost. In case where an asset is not acquired with cash or a promise to pay cash, the criterion is, what the asset would have cost, had cash been paid for it.

The assets in the balance sheet are listed either in the order of liquidity–promptness with which they are expected to be converted into cash–or in reverse order, that is, fixity or listing of the least liquid asset (fixed) first, followed by others. All assets are grouped into categories, that is, assets with similar characteristics are put in one category. The assets included in one category are different from those in other categories. The standard classification of assets divides them into, **(i)** fixed assets, **(ii)** current assets, **(iii)** investments, and **(iv)** other assets.

Fixed assets are acquired to produce goods and services and not for sale.

Fixed/Long-term Assets As the name suggests, such assets are long-term in the sense that they are acquired to be retained in the business on a long-term basis to produce goods and services, and are not for resale. They are, in a sense, long-term resources in that they are held for longer than one accounting period. Such assets are obviously of crucial significance as the future earnings/revenue/ profits of firms are basically determined by them. They fall into two categories: tangible and intangible.

Tangible assets have a physical existance and are shown net of depreciation.

Tangible Fixed Assets Tangible Fixed Assets are those which have a physical existence and generate goods and services. Included in this category of fixed assets are land, buildings, plant, machinery, furniture, and so on. They are shown in the balance sheet, in accordance with the cost concept, at their cost to the firm at the time they were purchased. The cost of these assets is allocated to/charged against/spread over their useful life. The yearly charge is referred to as depreciation. As a result, the amount of tangible fixed assets shown in the balance sheet every year declines to the extent of the depreciation charged in that year and by the end of the useful life of the asset, it equals the salvage value, if any. Salvage value signifies the amount realised by the sale of the discarded asset at the end of its useful life.

Salvage value is the amount realised from sale of an asset after its useful life.

Intangible Fixed Assets Intangible Fixed Assets do not generate goods and services directly. In a way, they reflect the rights of the firm. This category of assets comprises patents, copyrights, trade marks and goodwill. These assets confer certain exclusive rights on their owners. Patents confer exclusive rights to use an invention; copyrights relate to production and sale of literary, musical and artistic works; trade marks represent exclusive rights to use certain names, symbols, labels, designs, and so on. Intangible fixed assets are also written off over a period of time.

Intangible assets reflect the rights of a firm and are amortised.

Current Assets The second category of assets included in the balance sheet are current assets. In contrast to long-term assets, current assets are short-term in nature. As short-term assets, they refer to assets/resources which are either held in the form of cash or are expected to be realised in cash within the accounting period or the normal operating cycle of the business whichever is more. The term "operating cycle" means the time span during which cash is converted into inventory, inventory into receivables/cash sales and receivables into cash. Conventionally, current assets designate assets which are held for a short period of time, usually not more than an year from the balance sheet date. These are also known as liquid assets. Current assets include cash, marketable securities, accounts receivable (debtors), notes/bills receivable and inventory.

Current assets are assets held for a period not exceeding one year. They generate liquirty.

Cash It is the most liquid current asset and includes cash in hand and cash at bank. It provides instant liquidity and can be used to meet obligations/acquire assets without any delay.

Marketable Securities These are short-term investments which are both readily marketable and which are expected to be converted into cash within a year. They provide an outlet to invest temporarily surplus/idle funds/cash. According to the Generally Accepted Accounting Principles, marketable securities are shown in the balance sheet at lower of the cost or the market price. When, however, shown at cost, the current market value is also shown in parenthesis.

Marketable securities are readily marketable and are shown at the lower of the cost or the market price.

Accounts Receivable They represent the amount the customers owe to the firm, arising from the sale of goods on credit. They are shown in the balance sheet as the amount owed less an allowance (bad debts) for the portion which may not be collected.

Accounts receivable is the amount the customers owe to the firm.

Bills Receivable These refer to amounts owed by outsiders for which written acknowledgements of the obligation are available.

Inventory It means the aggregate of those items which are held for sale in the ordinary course of business (finished goods), or are in the process of production for such sales (work-in-process), or are to be currently consumed in the production of goods and services (raw materials) to be available for sale.

Inventory is the aggregate of finished goods, work-in-process and raw materials.

It is the least liquid current asset. Included in inventory are raw materials, work-in-process (semi-finished) and finished goods. Each of these serves a useful purpose in the process of production and sale. Inventory is reported in the balance sheet at the cost or market value, whichever is lower.

Investments are assets outside the business of a firm.

Investments The third category of assets is investments. They represent investment of funds in the securities of another company. They are long-term assets outside the business of the firm. The purpose of such investments is either to earn a return or/and to control another company. It is customarily shown in the balance sheet with the market value shown in parenthesis.

Other Assets Included in this category of assets are what are called deferred charges, that is, advertisement expenditure, preliminary expenses, and so on. They are pre-payments for services/benefits for periods exceeding the accounting period.

Liabilities

Liabilities are the claims of outsiders against the firm.

The second major content of the balance sheet is liabilities of the firm. Liabilities may be defined as the claims of outsiders against the firm. Alternatively, they represent the amount that the firm owes to outsiders, that is, other than owners. The assets have to be financed by different sources. One source of funds is borrowing—long-term as well as short-term. The firms can borrow on a long-term basis from financial institutions/banks or through bonds/mortgages/debentures. The short-term borrowing may be in the form of purchase of goods and services on credit. These outside sources from which a firm can borrow are termed as liabilities. Since they finance the assets, they are, in a sense, claims against the assets.

Depending upon the periodicity of the funds, liabilities can be classified into **(i)** long-term liabilities, and **(ii)** current liabilities.

Long-term liabilities are obligations of a firm payable after one year.

Long-term Liabilities They are so called because the sources of funds included in them are available for periods exceeding one year. In other words, such liabilities represent obligations of a firm payable after the accounting period. The sources of long-term borrowings are **(i)** debentures, **(ii)** bonds, **(iii)**, mortgages, **(iv)** secured loans from financial institutions and commercial banks. They have to be repaid/redeemed either in lump sum at the maturity of the loan/debenture or in instalments over the life of the loan. Long-term liabilities are shown in the balance sheet net of redemption/repayment.

Current liabilities are obligations which mature within a year

Current Liabilities The second type of liability is current liabilities. In contrast, to the long-term liabilities, such liabilities are short-term maturing obligations to be met, as originally contemplated, within a year. It can be said to be the counterpart of the current assets. Conventionally, they are paid out of the current assets; in some cases, however, existing current liabilities can be liquidated through the creation of additional current liabilities. Included in this category of liabilities are **(i)** accounts payable, **(ii)** bills/notes payable, **(iii)** tax payable, **(iv)** accrued expenses, **(v)** deferred income, and **(vi)** short-term bank credit. The first two categories are also called trade credit.

Trade credit arise out of credit purchases and are also known as accounts payable.

Trade Credit represents the claims of such outsiders as have sold goods to the firm on credit for a short period depending upon trade practices. Usually, such credit is unsecured. One form of this type of short-term credit (current liability) is that the buyer–firm will pay the amount after a lapse of time but there is no formal written loan agreement. This type is known as *account payable.* When the claims of the supplier of the goods/services is evidenced by a note/bill—written acknowledgement of debt—it is called *bills/notes payable.* A bill/ note is a promise in writing to pay a certain sum of money at some specific date.

Short-term Bank Credit is another source of short-term funds (current liability) in the form of overdraft, cash credit, bill financing and loans and advances.

Tax Payable refers to the amount to be paid to the government as taxes.

Accrued Outstanding Expenses represent certain obligations which are claims against assets but there is no documentary evidence. Examples of this type of current liability are outstanding wages, salaries, rent and commission.

Deferred Income represents the liability that arises out of receipt of income in advance, for example, rent received in advance.

Owners' Equity

The third major content of a balance sheet is the owner's equity. Conceptually, it refers to the claims of the owners of the business against the assets of the firm. Alternatively, owners' equity may be viewed as that part of the resources of a firm which are supplied by its owners. The owners of a business are known as shareholders. There are two types of shareholders—ordinary and preference. The preference shareholders are entitled to a stated amount of dividend and return of principal at maturity. They are akin to creditors (liabilities) of the firm.

> **Owners equity** is the claim of the owners of business against its assets consisting of capital and retained earnings.

The ordinary shareholders, also called equityholders, are different from the preference shareholders as well as the creditors. They are entitled to the income/assets of the firm remaining after the claims of the creditors/preference shareholders are met in full. Their claim against the assets of the firm is, thus, *residual.* This is also known as the equity of the owners.

The owners' equity may be said to consist of two elements: **(i)** paid-up capital, that is, the initial amount of funds contributed by the shareholders; **(ii)** retained earnings/reserves and surplus, that is, that part of the profits belonging to the shareholders which is not paid out to them as dividends but instead is retained/ploughed back in the business.

Profit and Loss Account

LO 3.8 Review profit and loss account and its content

The second major statement of financial information is profit and loss account (P&L A/c). It is known by several other names such as income statement, statement of earnings and profit and loss statement.

> **Profit and loss account** portrays the operations of a firm during an accounting period.

While the balance sheet, as a stock statement, indicates the financial position/condition of a business firm at a particular point of time (say, 31st March, 2016), the P&L A/c as a flow statement, portrays the operations of a firm over/during a particular period of time (say, 1.4.2015 to 31.3.2016). The span of time covered is an accounting period (of one year). In practice, it is now usual for firms (in fact, mandatory for listed companies to prepare on quarterly basis) to prepare interim P&L A/c. Irrespective of the time span covered, it is useful to present P&L A/c in a number of sub-parts to assess the efficiency of operations it various levels.

Normally, the P&L A/c is divided into four parts: **(1)** Manufacturing account (with an objective to determine cost of goods manufactured); **(2)** Trading account (to know gross profit margin); **(3)** Profit & Loss A/c (to indicate earnings before interest and taxes (EBIT)/operating profit, net profits before taxes and after taxes); and **(4)** P&L Appropriation A/c (showing utilisation of profits earned).

The P&L A/c can be presented in the usual accounting form as well as in step-form. A summarised view of the accounting form of P&L A/c is presented in formats 3.11 to 3.14. While Formats 3.11 and 3.12 respectively deal with manufacturing account and trading account, the broad contents of P&L A/c and P&L Appropriation account are shown in Formats 3.13 and 3.14 respectively. The step-form of P&L A/c (known as income statement) is summarised in Format 3.15. The formats are followed by a comprehensive Example 3.5 related to the preparation of financial statements.

FORMAT 3.11 Manufacturing Account of Hypothetical Limited (for the period ...)

Particulars	*Dr. Amount*	*Particulars*	*Cr. Amount*
To Cost of direct raw materials used:		By Sale of scrap	- - -
Opening stock		By Closing stock of work-in-process	- - -
Add purchases (including freight)		By Cost of goods manufactured (balancing figure) transferred to Trading A/c	- - -
Less closing stock	- - -		
To Work-in-process (opening stock)	- - -		
To Direct labour cost	- - -		
To Other direct expenses	- - -		
To Manufacturing expenses:			
Factory rent			
Factory insurance			
Fuel and power			
Depreciation of plant and machinery			
Repairs/maintenance of machinery			
Consumable stores			
Indirect labour cost (salary of supervisors, foreman, factory manager)			
Other manufacturing expenses (specify)	- - -		

Note: In case the cost of goods manufactured (of finished output) is lower than purchase/buy cost from market, production department is efficient.

FORMAT 3.12 Trading Account of Hypothetical Limited (for the period ...)

Particulars	*Dr. Amount*	*Particulars*	*Cr. Amount*
To Cost of goods sold:		By Sales revenue (Gross)	
Opening stock of finished goods		Less Returns	- - -
Add production cost* (transferred from manufacturing A/c)			
Less closing stock of finished goods	- - -		
To Gross profit (balancing figure) transferred to P&L A/c	- - -		

*Purchase costs (including freight) are used in the case of trading/non-manufacturing firms; in such firms, goods purchased are sold without any further processing.

FORMAT 3.13 Profit & Loss A/c of Hypothetical Limited (for the period ...)

Particulars	*Dr. Amount*	*Particulars*	*Cr. Amount*
To Administrative expenses:		By Gross profit	- - -
Office salary		By Operating profit	
Office insurance		By Other incomes:	
Office rent		Interest received	
Depreciation on office equipments & furniture		Dividend received	
		Commission received	
Office electricity bills		Discount received	
Office stationary and postage		Other incomes (specify)	- - -
Office telephone, fax and internet			
Office traveling expenses			
Other office expenses (specify)	- - -		
To Selling expenses:			
Advertising			
Salesman salaries			
Salesman commission			
Bad debts			
Add provision for bad and doubtful debts created during current year			
Less provision created during last year			
Freight/Carriage on goods sold			
Depreciation of deliver vans (used to deliver goods at buyer place)			
Cost of free samples distributed			
Other selling expenses (specify)	- - -		
To Operating profit/EBIT (balancing figure)			
To Financial expenses:			
Interest on borrowings		By EBIT	- - -
Bank charges			
Amortisation cost of raising funds			
Other expenses (specify)	- - -		
To Profit before taxes	- - -		
To Provision for taxes	- - -	By Profit before taxes	- - -
To Net profit after taxes	- - -		

FORMAT 3.14 Profit & Loss Appropriation A/c of Hypothetical Limited (for the period ...)

Particulars	*Dr. Amount*	*Particulars*	*Cr. Amount*
To Statutory reserve	- - -	By Net profit after taxes	- - -
To General reserve	- - -		
To Long-term assets replacement reserve	- - -		
To Dividend (proposed)	- - -		
To Dividend equalisation reserve	- - -		
To Other reserves (specify)	- - -		
To Balance (representing retained earnings out of current year profits	- - -		

FORMAT 3.15 Income Statement of Hypothetical Limited (for the period ...)

Particulars	*Amount*
Revenues:	
Gross sales revenue	
Less returns	
Less operating expenses:	- - -
Cost of goods sold	
Administrative expenses (specify each)	
Selling expenses (specify each)	- - -
Operating profit/EBIT	- - -
Other incomes (specify each)	- - -
Less non-operating expenses:	
Financial expenses (specify each)	- - -
Profit before taxes	- - -
Less provision for taxes	- - -
Net profit after taxes	- - -
Less appropriations:	
Dividends (proposed)	- - -
General reserve	- - -
Others appropriations (specify each)	- - -
Retained earnings (out of current year profit)	- - -

Note: The required format of statement of profit and loss (as per Companies Act, 1956) is available in Exhibit 4.2 of Chapter 4.

◆ Example 3.5

From the following Trial Balance, prepare Manufacturing Account, Trading Account, Profit and Loss Account for the year ending March 31, 2016 and a Balance Sheet as on that date of Mr. Ajay:

Particulars	*Dr. Amount*	*Cr. Amount*
Cash in hand	₹12,500	
Cash at bank	2,00,000	
Sundry debtors	20,25,000	
Sundry creditors		₹22,80,000
Mr. Ajay's capital account		20,50,000
Mr. Ajay's drawing account	3,05,000	
Loan @ 10% per annum		3,00,000
Provision for bad debts (1.4.2015)		50,000
Patents	1,00,000	
Plant and machinery	10,00,000	
Land and building	13,00,000	
Purchase of raw materials	17,50,000	
Raw materials – April 1, 2015	1,75,000	
Finished stock – April 1, 2015	9,00,000	
Work-in-process – April 1, 2015	1,06,000	
Wages	13,50,000	

(Contd.)

(*Contd.*)

Salary of supervisors and foreman	2,80,000	
Factory expenses	1,70,000	
Factory rent and taxes	1,25,000	
Carriage on purchases	55,000	
Fuel and power	1,00,000	
Advertising	1,50,000	
Office rent and insurance	2,40,000	
Printing and stationery (office)	50,000	
Office expenses	2,90,000	
Carriage on sales	30,000	
Bad debts	37,500	
Office traveling expenses	70,000	
Commission received		55,000
Sales		61,70,000
Salesmen commission	60,000	
Interest on loan	30,000	
	1,09,05,000	1,09,05,000

Additional information

(i) Stock on 31st March, 2016 was as follows: ₹2,00,000 Raw materials, ₹14,00,000 Finished goods, ₹2,25,000 Work-in-process.

(ii) The outstanding expenses are: ₹12,500 Factory rent, ₹30,000 Wages and ₹1,50,000 Office salaries.

(iii) Provide 5 per cent for Doubtful debts.

(iv) Depreciate Building by 5 per cent, Plant by 10 per cent, and amortise Patents by 10 per cent.

(v) Office Rent and Insurance paid in advance is ₹40,000.

Solution

Manufacturing Account of Mr. Ajay for the Year Ending March 31, 2016

Particulars		*Dr. Amount*	*Particulars*	*Cr. Amount*
To Cost of direct raw materials used:			By Cost of finished goods transferred to	
Opening stock	₹1,75,000		Trading account,	₹38,97,500
Add purchases	17,50,000		By Closing work-in-process	
Less closing stock	(2,00,000)	₹17,25,000	(31st March, 2016)	2,25,000
To Work-in-process (opening stock)		1,00,000		
To Carriage on purchases		55,000		
To Fuels and power		1,00,000		
To Factory expenses		1,70,000		
To Salary of Supervisor and Foreman		2,80,000		
To Wages	₹13,50,000			
Add outstanding	30,000	13,80,000		
To Factory rent and taxes	₹1,25,000			
Add outstanding	12,500	1,37,500		
To Depreciation:				
Land and buildings	₹65,000			
Plant and machinery	1,00,000	1,65,000		
To Amortisation of patents		10,000		
		41,22,500		41,22,500

Trading Account *for the year ending March 31, 2016*

Particulars		Dr. Amount	Particulars	Cr. Amount
To Cost of goods sold:		₹61,70,000	By Sales	₹61,70,000
Opening stock	₹9,00,000			
Add production costs as per manufacturing account	38,97500			
Less closing stock	(14,00,000)	33,97,500		
To Gross profit		27,72,500		
		61,70,000		61,70,000

Profit and Loss Account *for the year ending March 31, 2016*

Particulars		Dr. Amount	Particulars	Cr. Amount
To Office traveling expenses		₹70,000	By Gross profit	₹27,72,500
To Salesmen commission		60,000	By Commission received	55,000
To Outstanding office salaries		1,50,000		
To Advertising		1,50,000		
To Printing and stationery		50,000		
To Office expenses		2,90,000		
To Carriage on sales		30,000		
To Office rent and Insurance	₹2,40,000			
Less paid in advance	40,000	2,00,000		
To Interest on loan		30,000		
To Provision for bad debts				
Required	₹1,01,250			
Add bad debts	37,500			
	1,38,750			
Less existing provision	50,000	88,750		
To Net profit carried to capital account		17,08,750		
		28,27,500		28,27,500

Balance Sheet of Mr Ajay *as on 31st March, 2016*

Liabilities		Amount	Assets		Amount
Capital account:			Current assets:		
Opening balance	₹20,50,000		Cash in hand		₹12,500
Add profit	17,08,750		Cast at bank		2,00,000
Less drawings	(3,05,000)	₹34,53,750	Sundry debtors	₹20,25,000	
Sundry creditors		22,80,000	Less provision for bad debts	1,01,250	19,23,750
Outstanding expenses			Closing stocks:		
(₹1,50,000 + 30,000 + 12,500)		1,92,500	Raw materials	₹2,00,000	
10% Loan		3,00,000	Work-in-process	2,25,000	
			Finished goods	14,00,000	18,25,000
			Prepaid office rent and insurance		40,000
			Long-term assets:		
			Patents	₹1,00,000	
			Less depreciation	10,000	90,000

(Contd.)

(Contd.)

	Plant and Machinery	₹10,00,000	
	Less depreciation	1,00,000	9,00,000
	Land and building	₹13,00,000	
	Less depreciation	65,000	12,35,000
62,26,250			62,26,250

Additional Aspects Related to Profit and Loss A/c

LO 3.9 Show additional aspects related to profit and loss account

Most of the items contained in formats 3.11 to 3.15 are self-explanatory and do not require additional explanation. However, certain important aspects related to income statement require more elaboration.

(1) Dealing With Estimated Expenses Recall that the income statement contains both actual and estimated expenses. The 'estimate category' requires determination of a fair share of capital expenditures (in terms of depreciation on tangible assets and amortisation on intangible assets) and deferred revenue expenditures to be charged as expenses of the accounting period. To avoid subjectivity, the Income-Tax Act has prescribed the method of depreciation to be used along with the schedule of depreciation rates at which various tangible long-term assets are to be depreciated. Likewise, there are provisions related to the time span during which intangible assets are to be amortised. Similarly, there are provisions relating to the treatment of other expense/provisions, and capital gains.

(2) Set of Income Statements Since the taxable income of a firm is to be computed in conformity with Income-Tax Act, the profit figure shown by the income statement to meet tax laws requirements would obviously differ from the profit figure computed to conform to the generally accepted accounting principles (enumerated in Chapter 2). Thus, there can be more than one set of income statement prepared by corporates to serve different needs: **(1)** for managerial purposes, **(2)** for tax purposes and **(3)** for reporting to the shareholders (to conform to provisions of Company Law, SEBI requirements and Accounting Standards).

(3) Extra-ordinary Transactions Extra-ordinary events in business firms cause abnormal losses and abnormal profits. They would portray a distorted picture of the performance of a firm, if abnormal events are reckoned in the year of occurrence only. For instance, a business firm may incur sizable abnormal loss due to fire, floods, riots and other natural calamities, beyond its control. With abnormal loss, the lower profits may erroneously be taken as indicator of inefficiency of management. Similarly, there can be abnormal profits on account of sale of a piece of land and a part of a building at prime location, upward revaluation of land and building and so on. As a result, the higher profits may be mistaken as an index of better performance of the management. Obviously, the reader of the income statement should exclude the impact of the extra-ordinary transactions to judge true efficiency of business operations of the entity as well as of its management. Moreover, their exclusion makes comparison of profit figures over the years more reliable.

Profit & Loss Appropriation Account Unlike non-corporate business firms, in which the total profit earned (or loss suffered) is taken directly to the capital account(s) of the owner(s), corporate enterprises, in practice, do not distribute the profits earned as dividends. In fact, the Indian Companies Act requires part of the profits to be transferred/appropriated to statutory reserve(s). Apart from the statutory requirement, the ***principle of financial prudence*** suggests that a part of the profits should

Profit and loss appropriation account deals with the use/ appropriation of profits.

be retained to strengthen the financial position of the company, in general, and in particular to cater to specific needs, such as payment of debentures, purchase of a new machine, extension/construction of building and so on. Thus, the use or appropriation of profits is dealt with in a separate account called profit and loss appropriation account (also known as the statement of retained earnings).

The P&L Appropriate Account of Hypothetical Limited is explained with imaginary figures in Format 3.16.

FORMAT 3.16 P&L Appropriation Account of Hypothetical Limited for the current year period ending on 31st March...

(Amount in ₹ lakh)

Particulars	*Dr. Amount*	*Particulars*	*Cr. Amount*
To Statutory reserve	28.0	By Net profit after taxes	280
To General reserve	35.0		
To Machine replacement reserve	30.0		
To Debenture redemption fund	20.0		
To Dividend proposed	84.0		
To Dividend equalisation reserve	16.0		
To Building construction fund	25.0		
To Balance c/d	42.0		
	280.0		280
		By Balance b/f	42.0

The Hypothetical Ltd has proposed a dividend of 30 per cent of net profit after taxes (₹84 lakh/₹280 lakh). The remaining amount has been retained in business to meet specific requirements, namely, payment of debentures, replacement of existing machine in use and construction of building. A dividend equalisation reserve has been created to be used in lean years of inadequate profits or losses (dividends can be paid out of the accumulated profits of the preceding years). While statutory reserve has been created to conform to the Companies Act, 1956 requirements, general reserve and balance of P&L appropriation account are meant to strengthen the financial position of the company.

An equally important aspect to note is that while payment of dividend causes cash outflows, the other appropriations (in terms of transfer to various funds/reserves) may not involve cash outflow (unless the company decides to invest them outside). The amount retained by the Hypothetical Ltd in business is ₹280 lakh – ₹84 lakh = ₹196 lakh (assuming no parking of funds outside the firm). Further, it is important to understand that ₹196 lakh has been used *internally* by the Hypothetical Ltd to finance its assets. Recall that retained profits are liabilities payable to the owners/shareholders. Liabilities are sources of financing assets. Viewed in this perspective, retained earnings (accumulated in the form of various reserves) constitute an important source of financing assets. In fact, all well established companies (e.g. Reliance Industries) have reserves which are significantly higher than the contribution of shareholders in the form of share capital. In brief, the reserves are important sources of financing the assets of a firm and are obviously not kept idle in the form of cash. However, more reserves, *prima-facie,* do not imply more liquidity.

In sum, net profit figure, due to estimated nature of some major expenses like depreciation, in particular for manufacturing companies, is not one-hundred per cent precise. Further, the net profit figure will vary depending on the purpose for which it is required, such as determination of income tax, preparation of annual report as per company law and managerial decision-making. Lastly, the term retained earnings is misnomer in that the amount retained in the business is more than the amount shown by retained earnings account.

SUMMARY

- The accounting cycle consists of seven sequential stages: **(1)** analysis of transaction, **(2)** recording accounting transactions in journal books, **(3)** posting them in ledger books, **(4)** preparing trial balance, **(5)** at the accounting period-end, recording adjustment entries in journal book, **(6)** passing closing entries to close account balances related to all expense and revenue/income items to prepare profit & loss account (P&L A/c), **(7)** prepare balance sheet (B/s) as on the last date of the accounting period. In the case of existing firms, the accounting cycle starts with opening entries of all liabilities and asset account balances of the preceding period (shown in the B/S) on the last day of the accounting period.
- An account is a book-keeping device to record increases and decreases in each specific asset or liability item. Accordingly, it facilitates to know the net change that has taken place in an item during the accounting period. It has two sides divided by a vertical line from the centre, giving it the appearance of alphabet 'T' and is, therefore, referred to as 'T'-account.
- Conventionally, the left side of an account is known as the debit (abbreviated Dr.) side and the right side as the credit (abbreviated Cr.) side. The account balance is always of the higher side.
- It is reasonably safe to assume that debtors have debit balance. Debtors are assets. Therefore, all assets have debit balances. Liabilities are opposite of assets and, therefore, have credit balances. Profits and revenue/income items are liabilities to and, hence, have credit balances. Conversely, expenses and loss items have debit balances.
- While debiting accounts related to assets and expenses increases their balances and crediting them decreases their balances, debiting liabilities and revenue items decrease their balances and crediting them increases their balances. By convention, the left side of an account is called debit side and the right side as the credit side.

LO 3.1

- All expenses and revenue/income accounts at the end of an accounting period are closed by transferring them to the P&L A/c with an objective to determine net profit earned or loss suffered during the period.
- There are three types of accounts, namely, nominal, personal and real. Corresponding to them, there are three sets of rules to record journal entry in journal book.
- Nominal account relates to expenses and revenues. The rule to record is: debit all expenses and losses and credit all revenues, incomes and gains. Personal accounts relate to individuals and institutions and the recording rule is: debit the receiver and credit the giver. Real accounts are concerned with assets. The recording rule is: debit what comes in and credit what goes out. It is important to observe that these rules are in conformity with the normal balances expected of accounts concerned.

LO 3.2

- There are two major books, namely, journal and ledger to record transaction of a business firm. Journal is a chronological record of transactions and is known as the book of original or first entry. Each business transaction has one journal entry. The simple journal entry has one debit item and one credit item (to conform to duality concept).
- While the journal book contains date-wise record of transaction of a firm, ledger book provides details (by listing increases as well as decreases) of each account and, thus, helps to know the balance in the case of assets and liabilities accounts and the total sum of each item pertaining to each expense revenue/ income account.
- The process of transferring entry from journal to ledger is called posting. The debit entries are posted on the debit side and the credit entries on the credit side. The balance of an account is obtained by adding debit and credit sides separately. The account is said to have debit balance if the total of the debit side is greater than that of the credit side; it has credit balance if the total of the credit side exceeds the total of the debit side.

- It is useful to analyse an accounting transaction to identify accounts to be debited and credited. Debit entry is recorded first, followed by credit entry in the following line indented (about half an inch) to the right. While the simple journal entry involves one debit account and one credit account, the compound entry's requirement is at least 3 accounts. Each journal entry contains brief narration about the transaction (considered useful for future reference purposes). From journal book, the items are posted to the ledger book.

LO 3.3

- Trial balance is a statement which contains the account names along with the balances in each account at a given point of time. It shows debit balances in one column and credit balances in another column. Tallying of the two sides of trial balance is a signal of arithmetic accuracy of records made in accounting books (journal and ledger). However, its agreement is not a conclusive proof that errors have not been made. A trial balance fails to detect certain types of errors, for instance, entries may have been omitted entirely; compensating/offsetting errors may have taken place; revenue transaction may have been incorrectly analysed as capital transaction or *vice-versa*. In spite of this deficiency, trial balance serves an important function of providing a convenient summary of all ledger account balances at one place which is helpful in the preparation of the financial statements.

LO 3.4

- There are two systems of keeping accounting records: **(1)** maintaining records in two books only, namely, one general journal and one general ledger, and **(2)** maintaining records in multiple books, namely, special journal books (separate book for sales, purchases, returns, cash, bank etc) and special ledger books (debtors ledger, creditors ledger, expense ledger etc). Maintaining accounting records in multiple books (each specialising in one type of transaction) is more advantageous. Most firms maintain records in this form.
- Accounting records from special journals are posted to special ledgers. For instance, the total of credit sales book is posted to the ***credit*** side of the sales account and to the ***debit*** side of the individual debtors account. The total of purchase book is posted to the ***debit*** side of the purchase account and to the ***credit*** side of the individual creditors account. Purchase returns book total is posted to the ***credit*** side of the purchase returns account and to the ***debit*** side of the account of the supplier. The sales returns book total is posted to the ***debit*** side of sales return account and ***credit*** side of debtor's account. Items from the ***debit*** side of cash and bank books are posted on the ***credit*** side and ***vice-versa.***

LO 3.5

- Adjustment entries (related to expenses/incomes in arrears or in advance, depreciation on long-term assets, creating provision for bad and doubtful debts) are required to determine true income and present correct picture of financial position of a firm. These adjustments are normally made on the last-day of the accounting period.
- Nominal accounts, known as temporary accounts, are closed at the end of the accounting period by transferring them to the profit and loss account. Closing entries serve this function. In contrast, real and personal accounts (related to assets and liabilities), referred to as permanent accounts, are brought forward to the following accounting year through an opening entry. This opening entry is recorded on the first day of the following accounting period.

LO 3.6

- The two financial statements, namely, the balance sheet and P&L A/c of a business firm contain useful information relating to its operations and financial health.
- A balance sheet (B/S) provides information about the financial position of a firm at a particular point of time, say, as on March 31, 2013. It is referred to as snapshot of the financial health of an enterprise. It is to be presented in the report form. Its contents consist of the assets owned by the firm and the sources/means by which the assets are financed, that is, external liabilities and owner's capital/equity.

- Assets are valuable resources owned by a business firm which have been acquired at a measurable money cost. Assets are broadly classified into 4 major groups, namely, fixed/long-term assets (categorised into tangible and intangible), current assets, investments and other assets.
- Long-term assets are acquired to be retained in the business on a long-term basis to produce goods and services, and are not meant for resale. Tangible assets have physical existence. Land, building, plant and machinery and furniture are notable examples. In contrast, intangible assets do not generate goods and services directly; they reflect the rights of the firm, indirectly contributing to revenues/incomes of the firm. Patents, copyrights, trade-marks and goodwill are the major examples in this group.
- Current assets refer to the assets/resources which are held either in the form of cash or are expected to be realised in cash within the accounting period or the normal operating cycle of the business, whichever is more. Current assets include cash, marketable securities, debtors, bills receivable and inventory.
- Long-term investments are made with intent to either earn interest/dividend income or/and to control another company. 'Other assets' category represents fictitious assets. They include deferred revenue expenses which have not been fully amortised till the date of the B/S such as advertisement expenditure, preliminary expenses, accumulated losses, issue of share/debenture expenses and so on.
- Liabilities can be broadly classified into external liabilities and owners' equity. External liabilities represent the amount the firm owes to outsiders other than owners. The owners' equity refers to the claims of the owners of the business against the assets of the firm. It consists of two elements, namely, capital contributed by the owners/shareholders and reserves and surplus (accumulated profits not distributed as dividends) ploughed back in the business.
- External liabilities can be classified into long-term liabilities and current liabilities. While long-term liabilities are intended to be paid in a time span of more than one year (such as long-term loans and debentures), current liabilities in contrast, are intended to be paid within one year from the date of their incurrence. Creditors, short-term bank credit, outstanding expenses and taxes payable are the major examples of current liabilities.

LO 3.7

- Profit and Loss Account (P&L A/c), known as income statement, summarises the revenue items and the expense items for an accounting period; the difference between the two is referred to as net income earned or net loss suffered. Thus, it represents the scoreboard of the performance of the firm in terms of the profitability of its operations and has three major contents: **(i)** Revenues, **(ii)** Expenses and, **(iii)** Net income/profit/loss; it can be presented either in the account form or step form.
- Revenue is defined as income that accrues to the firm by the sale of goods/services (known as sales revenue) and/or by the supply of the firm's resources to others and earning interest, dividend, royalty, commission, fee and so on. The cost of earning revenues is called expense. The major expense items are: **(i)** Cost of goods sold, **(ii)** Administrative expenses, **(iii)** Selling expenses, and **(iv)** Financial expenses.
- There are several variants of profit. The major variants are: **(i)** Gross profit: (Net sales – Cost of goods sold); **(ii)** Operating profit: (Gross profit – Administrative and selling expenses), **(iii)** Profit before taxes: (Operating profit + Other non-operating incomes – Financial expenses); and **(iv)** Profit after taxes : (Profit before taxes – Provision for taxes).
- Manufacturing account is prepared to determine the cost of goods manufactured so that decision may be taken whether own manufacturing is beneficial or buying from outside. Cost of goods manufactured = Cost of materials used + Direct labour cost + Factory expenses + Opening work-in-process – Closing work-in-process.
- While trading account facilitates determination of gross profit, operating profit, net profit before and after taxes are determined through the P&L A/c.
- Corporate enterprises prepare varied set of P&L A/c depending on the users and purpose, such as, determination of income-tax, preparation of annual report as per SEBI, accounting standards and Company Law, 2013 requirements and managerial decision-making.

LO 3.8

- Profit & Loss Appropriation A/c reports the use or appropriation of profits in terms of payment of dividends and creation/transfer to specific/general/statutory reserves. Appropriate in various reserves (unless invested outside to earn interest/dividend) are the significant sources of financing assets of a firm.
- Extra-ordinary items pertaining to abnormal losses and gains should be excluded to evaluate the true performance of a business enterprise.

LO 3.9

SOLVED PROBLEMS

P.3.1 Mr. Ashwin commenced business (in the name of M/s Ashwin Associates) from April 1, 2016 as a garment manufacturer. Following are the transactions for the six months ending September 30, 2016. LO 3.2,3,4,5 LOD: M

1. M/s Ashwin Associates commenced business activity with initial capital of ₹30,00,000 in cash on April 1.
2. Deposited ₹25,00,000 in bank on April 1.
3. Borrowed from GE Capital Company ₹10,00,000 against security (of personal house) on April 1.
4. Purchased following assets on April 1:
   (i) Installed furniture & fittings for ₹2,50,000.
   (ii) Machinery from Sewing Machinery Works for ₹15,00,000 (paid 50 per cent by cheque) and the balance is payable by October-end.
5. **(i)** On April 1 took a building (to be used as a factory for manufacturing garments) on rent of ₹10,000 per month.
   (ii) Deposited ₹20 lakh by cheque with HUDA for purchase of industrial plot.
6. On April 10, purchased raw-materials (cloth) valued ₹6,50,000 from Delicate Cloth House on credit and incurred freight expenses (for raw materials) of ₹20,000.
7. On May 3, purchased raw materials (cloth) from Vardhman Thread Company for ₹5,00,000 on credit but returned ₹1,50,000 worth of cloth due to different quality on May 4.
8. On June 15, sold goods (garments) on credit to Bombay Dying Men's Wear for ₹10,00,000.
9. On July 15, sold goods (garments) on credit to Fancy Ladies Showroom ₹15,00,000, but due to bad quality Fancy Ladies Showroom returned garments worth ₹1,50,000 on July 17.
10. On July 30, received cheque from Bombay Dying Men's Wear for ₹8,00,000.
11. On August 1, bought a car (to be used in office) for ₹5,00,000 and the payment was made by cheque.
12. On August 1, withdrew for personal use ₹50,000.
13. On August 17, cash sales made to Catmoss Fashion Wear for ₹8,00,000.
14. On August 30, received cheque from Fancy Ladies Showroom for ₹10,00,000.
15. On September 30, issued cheque to Delicate Cloth House for ₹5,00,000.
16. Other expenses for the period April to September (payable on the last date of the month) are as under:
   (i) Salary of supervisor, ₹10,000 per month.
   (ii) Wages of workers, ₹1,00,000 per month.
   (iii) Salary of accountant, ₹10,000 per month.
   (iv) Salary of salesmen, ₹15,000 per month.
   (v) Sundry expenses are incurred at the rate of ₹5,000 per month.
17. Advertisement expenses, ₹2,00,000 on September 30.
18. Packaging expenses, ₹50,000 on September 30.
19. Electricity bill of ₹20,000 payable by cheque on June 30 and ₹30,000 on September 30.
20. Telephone bill, ₹12,000 payable by cheque on June 30 and ₹8,000 on September 30.
21. On September 30, interest paid to GE Capital Company for 6 months, ₹50,000.

REQUIRED: **(i)** Journalise the above transactions into a general journal, **(ii)** Post them into a general ledger book and **(iii)** Prepare trial balance. (Assume 80 per cent of electricity bill is to be charged to factory).

Solution

(i) General Journal

Date 2016	Particulars		L.F.	Dr. Amount (₹)	Cr. Amount (₹)
April 1	Cash account	Dr.		30,00,000	
	To Capital account				30,00,000
	(Capital brought in by proprietor to start the business)				
April1	Bank account	Dr.		25,00,000	
	To Cash account				25,00,000
	(Amount deposited in the bank)				
April 1	Bank account	Dr.		10,00,000	
	To Loan account				10,00,000
	(Loan taken vide cheque no... at 10% rate of interest from GE Capital)				
April 1	Furniture and fittings account	Dr.		2,50,000	
	To Cash account				2,50,000
	(Furniture and fittings purchased in cash)				
April 1	Machinery account	Dr.		15,00,000	
	To Bank account				7,50,000
	To Sewing Machinery Works account				7,50,000
	(Purchased machinery vide invoice no. ... and 50 per cent payment is made by cheque No...)				
April 1	Advance for industrial plot account	Dr.		20,00,000	
	To Bank account				20,00,000
	(Advance deposited with HUDA vide cheque No...)				
April 10	Purchase account	Dr.		6,50,000	
	To Delicate Cloth House account				6,50,000
	(Cloth purchased on credit vide invoice no... from Delicate Cloth House)				
April 10	Freight expenses account	Dr.		20,000	
	To Cash account				20,000
	(Freight expenses paid in cash)				
April 30	Salary of supervisor account	Dr.		10,000	
	Wages account	Dr.		1,00,000	
	Salary account	Dr.		25,000	
	To Bank account				1,35,000
	(Salary expenses paid vide cheque No... for month of April)				
April 30	Sundry expenses account	Dr.		5,000	
	To Cash account				5,000
	(Expenses paid in cash for month of April)				
May 3	Purchases account	Dr.		5,00,000	
	To Vardhman Thread Company account				5,00,000
	(Cloth purchased on credit vide invoice no... from Vardhman Thread Company)				
May 4	Vardhman Thread Company account	Dr.		1,50,000	
	To Purchases return account				1,50,000
	(Returned goods on credit vide invoice No. to Vardhman Thread Co.)				
May 31	Salary of supervisor account	Dr.		10,000	
	Wages account	Dr.		1,00,000	

(Contd.)

(*Contd.*)

Date	Particulars		Debit	Credit
	Salary account	Dr.	25,000	
	To Bank account			1,35,000
	(Salary expenses paid through vide cheque No... for month of May)			
May 31	Sundry expenses account	Dr.	5,000	
	To Cash account			5,000
	(Expenses paid in cash for month of May)			
June 15	Bombay Dying Men's Wear Account	Dr.	10,00,000	
	To Sales account			10,00,000
	(Goods sold on credit vide invoice No. ...)			
June 30	Salary of supervisor account	Dr.	10,000	
	Wages account	Dr.	1,00,000	
	Salary account	Dr.	25,000	
	Electricity account	Dr.	20,000	
	Telephone account	Dr.	12,000	
	To Bank account			1,67,000
	(Salary expenses paid through vide cheque No... for month of June)			
June 30	Sundry expenses account	Dr.	5,000	
	To Cash account			5,000
	(Expenses paid in cash for month of June)			
July 15	Fancy Ladies Showroom account	Dr.	15,00,000	
	To Sales account			15,00,000
	(Goods sold on credit vide invoice No....)			
July 17	Sales returns account	Dr.	1,50,000	
	To Fancy Ladies Showroom account			1,50,000
	(Sold goods returned from Fancy Ladies Showroom)			
July 30	Bank account	Dr.	8,00,000	
	To Bombay Dying Men's Wear account			8,00,000
	(Receipt of payment vide cheque no...from Bombay Dying Mens Wear)			
July 31	Salary of supervisor account	Dr.	10,000	
	Wages account	Dr.	1,00,000	
	Salary account	Dr.	25,000	
	To Bank account			1,35,000
	(Salary expenses paid through vide cheque No... for month of July)			
July 31	Sundry expenses account	Dr.	5,000	
	To Cash account			5,000
	(Expenses paid in cash for month of July)			
Aug. 1	Car account	Dr.	5,00,000	
	To Bank account			5,00,000
	(Purchased Motor Lorry vide cheque no...)			
Aug. 1	Drawings account	Dr.	50,000	
	To Bank account			50,000
	(Amount withdrawn vide cheque No.... for personal use)			
Aug. 17	Cash account	Dr.	8,00,000	
	To Sales account			8,00,000
	(Garments sold for cash vide cash memo No... to Catmoss Fashion Wear)			
Aug. 30	Bank account	Dr.	10,00,000	
	To Fancy Ladies Showroom account			10,00,000

(*Contd.*)

(Contd.)

	(Receipt of payment vide cheque No... from Fancy Ladies Showroom)			
Aug. 31	Salary of supervisor account	Dr.	10,000	
	Wages account	Dr.	1,00,000	
	Salary account	Dr.	25,000	
	To Bank account			1,35,000
	(Salary expenses paid through vide cheque No... for month of August)			
Aug. 31	Sundry expenses account	Dr.	5,000	
	To Cash account			5,000
	(Expenses paid in cash for month of August)			
Sept. 30	Delicate Cloth House account	Dr.	5,00,000	
	To Bank account			5,00,000
	(Payment through vide cheque No... to Delicate Cloth House)			
	Factory rent account	Dr.	60,000	
	To Bank account			60,000
	(Factory rent paid for 6 months vide cheque No...)			
Sept 30	Salary of supervisor account	Dr.	10,000	
	Wages account	Dr.	1,00,000	
	Salary account	Dr.	25,000	
	To Bank account			1,35,000
	(Salary expenses paid vide cheque No... for month of September)			
Sept 30	Advertisement account	Dr.	2,00,000	
	Packaging account	Dr.	50,000	
	Electricity account	Dr.	30,000	
	Telephone account	Dr.	8,000	
	Interest on loan	Dr.	50,000	
	To Bank account			3,38,000
	(Expenses paid vide cheque No...)			
Sept. 30	Sundry expenses account	Dr.	5,000	
	To Cash account			5,000
	(Expenses paid in cash for month of September)			

(ii) General Ledger

Ashwin's Capital Account

Date 2016	*Particulars*	*JF*	*Amount*	*Date 2016*	*Particulars*	*JF*	*Amount*
Sept 30	To Balance c/d		₹30,00,000	April 1	By Cash		₹30,00,000
				Oct. 1	By Balance b/f		30,00,000

Loan (GE Capital Company) Account

Date 2016	*Particulars*	*JF*	*Amount*	*Date 2016*	*Particulars*	*JF*	*Amount*
Sept 30	To Balance c/d		10,00,000	April 1	By Bank		10,00,000
				Oct. 1	By Balance b/f		10,00,000

Furniture & Fittings Account

Date 2016	*Particulars*	*JF*	*Amount*	*Date 2016*	*Particulars*	*JF*	*Amount*
April 1	To Cash		2,50,000	Sept. 30	By Balance c/d		2,50,000
Oct. 1	To Balance b/f		2,50,000				

Date 2016	Particulars	JF	Amount	Date 2016	Particulars	JF	Amount
			Machinery Account				
April 1	To Bank		7,50,000	Sept 30	By Balance c/d		15,00,000
	To Sewing Machinery Works		7,50,000				
			15,00,000				15,00,000
Oct. 1	To Balance b/f		15,00,000				

Date 2016	Particulars	JF	Amount	Date 2016	Particulars	JF	Amount
			Advance For Industrial Plot Account				
April 1	To Bank		20,00,000	Sept 30	By Balance c/d		20,00,000
Oct. 1	To Balance b/f		20,00,000				

Date 2016	Particulars	JF	Amount	Date 2016	Particulars	JF	Amount
			Freight Expenses Account				
April 10	To Cash		20,000	Sept. 30	By Manufacturing A/c		20,000
			20,000				20,000

Date 2016	Particulars	JF	Amount	Date 2016	Particulars	JF	Amount
			Purchases Account				
April 10	To Delicate Cloth House		6,50,000	Sept. 30	By Manufacturing A/c		11,50,000
May 3	To Vardhman Thread Company		5,00,000				
			11,50,000				11,50,000

Date 2016	Particulars	JF	Amount	Date 2016	Particulars	JF	Amount
			Purchase Returns Account				
Sept 30	To Manufacturing A/c1,50,000			May 4	By Vardhman Thread Company		1,50,000
			1,50,000				1,50,000

Date 2016	Particulars	JF	Amount	Date 2016	Particulars	JF	Amount
			Vardhman Thread Company Account				
May 4	To Purchase Returns		1,50,000	May 3	By Purchases		5,00,000
Sept 30	To Balance c/d		3,50,000				
			5,00,000				5,00,000
				Oct. 1	By Balance b/f		3,50,000

Date 2016	Particulars	JF	Amount	Date 2016	Particulars	JF	Amount
			Bombay Dying Men's Wear Account				
June 15	To Sales		10,00,000	July 30	By Bank		8,00,000
				Sept. 30	By Balance c/d		2,00,000
			10,00,000				10,00,000
Oct. 1	To Balance b/f		2,00,000				

Date 2016	Particulars	JF	Amount	Date 2016	Particulars	JF	Amount
			Factory Rent Account				
For six Months	To Bank		60,000	Sept. 30	By Manufacturing A/c		60,000
			60,000				60,000

Date 2016	Particulars	JF	Amount	Date 2016	Particulars	JF	Amount
			Packaging Account				
Sept 30	To Bank		50,000	Sept 30	By P&L A/c		50,000
			50,000				50,000

Date 2016	Particulars	JF	Amount	Date 2016	Particulars	JF	Amount
			Sewing Machinery Works Account				
Sept 30	To Balance c/d		7,50,000	April 1	By Machinery		7,50,000
				Oct. 1	By Balance b/f		7,50,000

Date 2016	Particulars	JF	Amount	Date 2016	Particulars	JF	Amount
			Car Account				
Aug 1	To Bank		5,00,000	Sept 30	By Balance c/d		5,00,000
			5,00,000				5,00,000
Sept. 30	To Balance b/f		5,00,000				

Date 2016	Particulars	JF	Amount	Date 2016	Particulars	JF	Amount
			Delicate Cloth House Account				
Sept 30	To Bank		5,00,000	April 10	By Purchases		6,50,000
Sept 30	To Balance c/d		1,50,000				
			6,50,000				6,50,000
				Oct. 1	By Balance b/f		1,50,000

Date 2016	Particulars	JF	Amount	Date 2016	Particulars	JF	Amount
			Fancy Ladies Account				
July 15	To Sales		15,00,000	July 17	By Sales return		1,50,000
				Aug. 30	By Bank		10,00,000
				Sept. 30	By Balance c/d		3,50,000
			15,00,000				15,00,000
Oct. 1	To Balance b/f		3,50,000				

Date 2016	Particulars	JF	Amount	Date 2016	Particulars	JF	Amount
			Sales Account				
Sept 30	To Trading a/c		33,00,000	June 15	By Bombay Dying Men's Wear		10,00,000
				July 15	By Fancy Ladies Showroom		15,00,000
				Aug. 17	By Cash		8,00,000
			33,00,000				33,00,000

Date 2016	Particulars	JF	Amount	Date 2016	Particulars	JF	Amount
			Sales Return Account				
July 17	To Fancy Ladies Showroom		1,50,000	Sept. 30	By Trading a/c		1,50,000
			1,50,000				1,50,000

Date 2016	Particulars	JF	Amount	Date 2016	Particulars	JF	Amount
			Drawings Account				
Aug 1	To Bank		50,000	Sept. 30	By Balance c/d		50,000
			50,000				50,000
Oct 1	To Balance b/f		50,000				

Date 2016	Particulars	JF	Amount	Date 2016	Particulars	JF	Amount
			Electricity Account				
June 30	To Bank		20,000	Sept. 30	By Manufacturing A/c		40,000
Sept 30	To Bank		30,000	Sept. 30	By P&L A/c		10,000
			50,000				50,000

Date 2016	Particulars	JF	Amount	Date 2016	Particulars	JF	Amount
			Telephone Account				
June 30	To Bank		12,000	Sept. 30	By P&L A/c		20,000
Sept 30	To Bank		8,000				
			20,000				20,000

Date 2016	Particulars	JF	Amount	Date 2016	Particulars	JF	Amount
			Advertisement Account				
Sept 30	To Bank		2,00,000	Sept. 30	By P&L A/c		2,00,000
			2,00,000				2,00,000

Date 2016	Particulars	JF	Amount	Date 2016	Particulars	JF	Amount
			Interest on Loan Account				
Sept 30	To Bank		50,000	Sept. 30	By P&L A/c		50,000
			50,000				50,000

Date 2016	Particulars	JF	Amount	Date 2016	Particulars	JF	Amount
			Salary of Supervisor Account				
April 30	To Bank		10,000	Sept. 30	By Manufacturing A/c		60,000
May 31	To Bank		10,000				
June 30	To Bank		10,000				
July 31	To Bank		10,000				
Aug. 31	To Bank		10,000				
Sept 30	To Bank		10,000				
			60,000				60,000

Date 2016	Particulars	JF	Amount	Date 2016	Particulars	JF	Amount
			Wages Account				
April 30	To Bank		1,00,000	Sept. 30	By Manufacturing A/c		6,00,000
May 31	To Bank		1,00,000				

(Contd.)

(Contd.)

June 30	To Bank		1,00,000				
July 31	To Bank		1,00,000				
Aug 31	To Bank		1,00,000				
Sept 30	To Bank		1,00,000				
			6,00,000				6,00,000

Date 2016	*Particulars*	*JF*	*Amount*	*Date 2016*	*Particulars*	*JF*	*Amount*
			Salary Account				
April 30	To Bank		25,000	Sept. 30	By P&L A/c		1,50,000
May 31	To Bank		25,000				
June 30	To Bank		25,000				
July 31	To Bank		25,000				
Aug. 31	To Bank		25,000				
Sept. 30	To Bank		25,000				
			1,50,000				1,50,000

Date 2016	*Particulars*	*JF*	*Amount*	*Date 2016*	*Particulars*	*JF*	*Amount*
			Sundry Expenses Account				
April 30	To Cash		5,000	Sept. 30	By P&L A/c		30,000
May 31	To Cash		5,000				
June 30	To Cash		5,000				
July 31	To Cash		5,000				
Aug. 31	To Cash		5,000				
Sept. 30	To Cash		5,000				
			30,000				30,000

Cash Account

Receipts				*Payments*			
Date 2016	*Particulars*	*JF*	*Amount*	*Date 2016*	*Particulars*	*JF*	*Amount*
April 1	To Capital		₹30,00,000	April 1	By Bank		₹25,00,000
				April 1	By Furniture & fittings		2,50,000
				April 10	By Freight expenses		20,000
				April 10	By Sundry expenses		5,000
				April 30	By Balance c/d		2,25,000
			30,00,000				30,00,000
May 1	To Balance b/f		2,25,000	May 31	By Sundry expenses		5,000
				May 31	By Balance c/d		2,20,000
			2,25,000				2,25,000
June 1	To Balance b/f		2,20,000	June 30	By Sundry expenses		5,000
				June 30	By Balance c/d		2,15,000
			2,20,000				2,20,000
July 1	To Balance b/f		2,15,000	July 31	By Sundry expenses		5,000
				July 31	By Balance c/d		2,10,000
			2,15,000				2,15,000
Aug. 1	To Balance b/f		2,10,000	Aug. 31	By Sundry expenses		5,000
Aug. 17	To Sales		8,00,000	Aug. 31	By Balance c/d		10,05,000
			10,10,000				10,10,000

(Contd.)

(*Contd.*)

Sept. 1	To Balance b/f	10,05,000	Sept. 30	By Sundry expenses	5,000
			Sept. 30	By Balance c/d	10,00,000
		10,05,000			10,05,000
Oct. 1	To Balance b/f				10,00,000

Bank Account

Deposits				*Withdrawals*			
Date 2016	*Particulars*	*JF*	*Amount*	*Date 2016*	*Particulars*	*JF*	*Amount*
April 1	To Cash		₹25,00,000	April 1	By Machinery		₹7,50,000
April 1	To Loan (GE Capital Co.)		10,00,000	April 1	By Advance for plot		20,00,000
				April 30	By Salary of supervisor		10,000
					By Wages		1,00,000
					By Salary		25,000
				April 30	By Balance c/d		6,15,000
			35,00,000				35,00,000
May 1	To Balance b/f		6,15,000	May 31	By Salary of supervisor		10,000
					By Wages		1,00,000
					By Salary		25,000
				May 31	By Balance c/d		4,80,000
			6,15,000				6,15,000
June 1	To Balance b/f		4,80,000	June 30	By Salary of supervisor		10,000
					By Wages		1,00,000
					By Salary		25,000
					By Electricity		20,000
					By Telephone		12,000
				June 30	By Balance c/d		3,13,000
			4,80,000				4,80,000
July 1	To Balance b/f		3,13,000	July 31	By Salary of supervisor		10,000
July 30	To Bombay Dying Men's wear		8,00,000		By Wages		1,00,000
					By Salary		25,000
				July 31	By Balance c/d		9,78,000
			11,13,000				11,13,000
Aug. 1	To Balance b/f		9,78,000	Aug. 1	By Car		5,00,000
Aug. 30	To Fancy Ladies Showroom		10,00,000	Aug. 1	By Drawings		50,000
				Aug. 31	By Salary of supervisor		10,000
					By Wages		1,00,000
					By Salary		25,000
				Aug. 31	By Balance c/d		12,93,000
			19,78,000				19,78,000
Sept.1	To Balance b/f		12,93,000	Sept. 30	By Delicate Cloth House		5,00,000
				Sept. 30	By Factory rent		60,000
				Sept. 30	By Salary of supervisor		10,000
				Sept. 30	By Wages		1,00,000
				Sept. 30	By Salary		25,000
				Sept. 30	By Advertisement		2,00,000
				Sept. 30	By Packaging		50,000
					By Electricity		30,000
					By Telephone		8,000
					By Interest on loan from GE Capital		50,000
				Sept. 30	By Balance c/d		2,60,000
			12,93,000				12,93,000
Oct. 1	To Balance b/f		2,60,000				

(iii) Trial Balance* as at September 30, 2016

Particulars	*Dr. Amount*	*Cr. Amount*
Capital		₹30,00,000
Loan (GE Capital Company)		10,00,000
Machinery	₹15,00,000	
Furniture & fittings	2,50,000	
Car	5,00,000	
Advance for industrial plot	20,00,000	
Sales		33,00,000
Sales return	1,50,000	
Cash	10,00,000	
Bank balance	2,60,000	
Factory rent	60,000	
Electricity	50,000	
Telephone	20,000	
Purchases	11,50,000	
Purchase return		1,50,000
Sewing Machinery Works		7,50,000
Packaging	50,000	
Sundry expenses	30,000	
Delicate Cloth House		1,50,000
Freight expenses	20,000	
Vardhman Thread Company		3,50,000
Bombay Dying Men's Wear	2,00,000	
Drawings	50,000	
Fancy Ladies	3,50,000	
Advertisement	2,00,000	
Interest on GE Capital	50,000	
Salary of Supervisor	60,000	
Wages	6,00,000	
Salary	1,50,000	
	87,00,000	87,00,000

Note: Revenue and expense account balances have been included in trial balance with intent to check accuracy of financial records. Recall that such accounts in ledger have already been closed by transferring to trading account and P&L account.

P.3.2 From the trial balance drawn in **P.3.1** and from the following adjustment transactions **(a)** pass adjustment entries and prepare **(b) (i)** manufacturing account, **(ii)** trading account, **(iii)** P&L account for the period ending September 30, 2013 and **(iv)** balance sheet as at September 30, 2016. LO 3.6,7,8,9 LOD: D

(a) Closing stock of raw materials, ₹25,000.
Closing stock of finished goods, ₹75,000

(b) Depreciate machinery, Car and Furniture & fittings @ 10 per cent per annum.

(c) Provide 5 per cent per annum for doubtful debts.

(d) M/s Ashwin Associates decided to transfer, ₹2,50,000 to general reserve, ₹50,000 to insurance fund.

(e) Outstanding expenses: wages, ₹50,000, salaries, ₹25,000.

(f) Assume 80 per cent of electricity has been used in manufacturing activity.

Solution

(a) Adjustment Entries

Date 2016	Particulars		L.F.	Dr Amount	Cr Amount
Sept. 30	Closing stock of raw materials	Dr.		₹25,000	
	To Manufacturing account				₹25,000
	(Closing stock of raw materials transferred to manufacturing account)				
Sept. 30	Closing stock of finished goods	Dr.		75,000	
	To Trading account				75,000
	(Closing stock of finished goods transferred to trading account)				
Sept. 30	Depreciation account	Dr.		95,833	
	To Machinery account				75,000
	To Car account				8,333
	To Furniture & fittings account				12,500
	(Depreciation charged on various asset)				
Sept. 30	P&L account	Dr.		13,750	
	To Provision for doubtful debts				13,750
	(Provision for doubtful debts created)				
Sept. 30	Wages account	Dr.		50,000	
	To Outstanding wages				50,000
	(Outstanding wages transferred)				
Sept. 30	Salaries account	Dr.		25,000	
	To Outstanding salaries				25,000
	(Outstanding salaries transferred)				
Sept. 30	P&L Appropriation account	Dr.		3,00,000	
	To General reserve				2,50,000
	To Insurance fund				50,000
	(Part of profits transferred to general reserve and insurance fund)				

(b) (i) Manufacturing Account for the period from 1.4.2016 to 30.9.2016

Particulars		Amount	Particulars	Amount
To Cost of materials used:			By Cost of goods manufactured transferred to trading account	₹18,80,000
Purchases	₹11,50,000			
Less returns	1,50,000			
Less closing stock	25,000	₹9,75,000		
To Factory rent		60,000		
To Factory power (0.8 × ₹50,000)		40,000		
To Freight		20,000		
To Salary of supervisor		60,000		
To Wages	₹6,00,000			
Add payable	50,000	6,50,000		
To Depreciation on plant and machinery		75,000		
		18,80,000		18,80,000

(ii) Trading Account for the period from 1.4.2016 to 30.9.2016

Particulars		Amount	Particulars		Amount
To Cost of goods manufactured		₹18,80,000	By Sales	₹33,00,000	
To Gross profit		13,45,000	Less sales Return	1,50,000	₹31,50,000
			By Closing stock of finished goods		75,000
		32,25,000			32,25,000

(iii) Profit & Loss Account (from 1.4.2016 to 30.9.2016)

Particulars		Dr. Amount	Particulars	Cr. Amount
To Packaging		50,000	By Trading account (Gross profit)	₹13,45,000
To Electricity (0.2 × ₹50,000)		10,000		
To Telephone		20,000		
To Advertisement		2,00,000		
To Interest (GE Capital Company)		50,000		
To Sundry expenses		30,000		
To Salary	₹1,50,000			
Add salaries payable	25,000	1,75,000		
To Provision for doubtful debts		13,750		
To Depreciation on:				
Car		8,333		
Furniture & fittings		12,500		
To Profit & Loss Appropriation		7,75,417		
		13,45,000		13,45,000

(iv) Profit & Loss Appropriation Account as on 30.9.2016

Particulars	Dr. Amount	Particulars	Cr. Amount
To General reserve	₹2,50,000	By P&L A/c	₹7,75,417
To Insurance fund	50,000		
To Ashwin's capital	4,75,417		
	7,75,417		7,75,417

Balance Sheet of M/s Ashwin Associates For Six Months *as on September 30, 2016*

Liabilities		Amount	Assets		Amount
Ashwin Capital	₹30,00,000		Machinery	₹15,00,000	
Add profits	4,75,417		Less depreciation	75,000	₹14,25,000
Less drawings	50,000	₹34,25,417	Furniture & fittings	₹2,50,000	
General reserve		2,50,000	Less depreciation	12,500	2,37,500
Insurance fund		50,000	Car	₹5,00,000	
Loan (GE Capital Company)		10,00,000	Less depreciation	8,333	4,91,667
Sewing Machinery Works		7,50,000	Advance for Industrial Plot		20,00,000
Delicate Cloth House		1,50,000	Closing stock		
Vardhman Thread Company		3,50,000	Raw materials	₹25,000	
Outstanding wages		50,000	Finished stock	75,000	1,00,000
Outstanding salaries		25,000	Debtors		
			Bombay Dying		
			Men's Wear	₹2,00,000	
			Fancy Ladies Showroom	3,50,000	
			Less provision for		
			doubtful debts	13,750	5,36,250
			Bank		2,60,000
			Cash		10,00,000
		60,50,417			60,50,417

P.3.3 (a) Record closing entries for **P.3.2** and (b) opening entry as on October 1, 2016 in the books of Aswin Associates. LO 3.6 LOD: M

Solution

(b) Closing Entries
General Journal

Date 2016	Particulars		L.F.	Dr. Amount	Cr. Amount
Sept.30	Manufacturing account	Dr.		₹20,15,000	
	To Purchases account				₹11,50,000
	To Factory rent account				60,000
	To Freight account				20,000
	To Salary of supervisor account				60,000
	To Wages account				6,50,000
	To Depreciation on machinery account				75,000
	(Manufacturing cost accounts closed by transferring to manufacturing account)				
Sept. 30	Purchase returns account	Dr.		1,50,000	
	To Manufacturing account				1,50,000
	(Purchase returns account closed by transferring to manufacturing account)				
Sept 30	Trading account	Dr.		18,40,000	
	To Manufacturing account				18,40,000
	(Cost of goods manufactured transferred to transferred to trading account)				
Sept. 30	Sales account	Dr.		1,50,000	
	To Trading account				1,50,000
	(Sales account closed by transferring to trading account)				
Sept 30	Trading account	Dr.		13,85,000	
	To P&L account				13,85,000
	(Gross profit transferred to P&L A/c)				
Sept. 30	Profit & Loss account	Dr.		6,09,583	
	To Packaging account				50,000
	To Electricity account				50,000
	To Telephone account				20,000
	To Advertisement account				2,00,000
	To Interest (GE Capital account)				50,000
	To Sundry expenses account				30,000
	To Salary account				1,75,000
	To Provision for bad and doubtful debts account				13,750
	To Depreciation account				20,833
	(All expenses account closed by transferring to P&L A/c)				
Sept 30	Profit & Loss account	Dr.		7,75,417	
	To Profit & Loss Appropriation account				7,75,417
	(Profit transferred to P&L Appropriation A/c)				
Sept. 30	Profit and Loss Appropriation account	Dr.		7,75,417	
	To General Reserve				2,50,000
	To Insurance fund				50,000
	To Aswin's capital				4,75,417
	(Profit appropriated for creation of funds and balance transferred to capital account)				

(b) Opening Entry
General Journal

Date 2016	Particulars	L.F.	Dr Amount	Cr Amount
Oct. 1	Machinery	Dr.	₹14,25,000	
	Furniture & fittings	Dr.	2,37,500	
	Car	Dr.	4,91,667	
	Advance for industrial plot	Dr.	20,00,000	
	Closing stock (raw materials)	Dr.	25,000	
	Closing stock (finished goods)	Dr.	75,000	
	Sundry debtors	Dr.	5,50,000	
	Bank	Dr.	2,60,000	
	Cash	Dr.	10,00,000	
	To Aswin's capital			₹34,25,417
	To General reserve			2,50,000
	To Insurance fund			50,000
	To Loan (GE capital)			10,00,000
	To Sewing Machine Works			7,50,000
	To Sundry creditors			5,00,000
	To Outstanding wages			50,000
	To Outstanding salaries			25,000
	To Provision for bad & doubtful debts			13,750
	(Various assets and liabilities brought forward from the previous accounting period)			

P.3.4 Prepare special journal books from the transactions contained in **P.3.1.** LO 3.5 LOD: M

Solution

Special Journals

Cash Book

Receipts Date 2016	Particulars	LF	Amount	Payments Date 2016	Particulars	LF	Amount
April 1	To Capital		₹30,00,000	April 1	By Bank		₹25,00,000
				April 1	By Furniture & fittings		2,50,000
				April 10	By Freight expenses		20,000
				April 10	By Sundry expenses		5,000
				April 30	By Balance c/d		2,25,000
			30,00,000				30,00,000
May 1	To Balance b/f		2,25,000	May 31	By Sundry expenses		5,000
				May 31	By Balance c/d		2,20,000
			2,25,000				2,25,000
June 1	To Balance b/f		2,20,000	June 30	By Sundry expenses		5,000
				June 30	By Balance c/d		2,15,000
			2,20,000				2,20,000
July 1	To Balance b/f		2,15,000	July 31	By Sundry expenses		5,000
				July 31	By Balance c/d		2,10,000
			2,15,000				2,15,000
Aug. 1	To Balance b/f		2,10,000	Aug. 31	By Sundry expenses		5,000
Aug. 17	To Sales		8,00,000	Aug. 31	By Balance c/d		10,05,000
			10,10,000				10,10,000
Sept. 1	To Balance b/f		10,05,000	Sept. 30	By Sundry expenses		5,000
				Sept. 30	By Balance c/d		10,00,000
			10,05,000				10,05,000
Oct. 1	To Balance b/f		10,00,000				

Bank Book

Deposits				Withdrawals			
Date 2016	Particulars	LF	Amount	Date 2016	Particulars	LF	Amount
April 1	To Cash		₹25,00,000	April 1	By Machinery		₹7,50,000
April 1	To Loan (GE Capital Co.)		10,00,000	April 1	By Advance for plot		20,00,000
				April 30	By Salary of supervisor		10,000
					By Wages		1,00,000
					By Salary		25,000
				April 30	By Balance c/d		6,15,000
			35,00,000				35,00,000
May 1	To Balance b/f		6,15,000	May 31	By Salary of supervisor		10,000
					By Wages		1,00,000
					By Salary		25,000
				May 31	By Balance c/d		4,80,000
			6,15,000				6,15,000
June 1	To Balance b/f		4,80,000	June 30	By Salary of supervisor		10,000
					By Wages		1,00,000
					By Salary		25,000
					By Electricity		20,000
					By Telephone		12,000
				June 30	By Balance c/d		3,13,000
			4,80,000				4,80,000
July 1	To Balance b/f		3,13,000	July 31	By Salary of supervisor		10,000
July 30	To Bombay Dying Men's wear		8,00,000		By Wages		1,00,000
					By Salary		25,000
				July 31	By Balance c/d		9,78,000
			11,13,000				11,13,000
Aug. 1	To Balance b/f		9,78,000	Aug. 1	By Car		5,00,000
Aug. 30	To Fancy Ladies Showroom		10,00,000	Aug. 1	By Drawings		50,000
				Aug. 31	By Salary of supervisor		10,000
					By Wages		1,00,000
					By Salary		25,000
				Aug. 31	By Balance c/d		12,93,000
			19,78,000				19,78,000
Sept.1	To Balance b/f		12,93,000	Sept. 30	By Delicate Cloth House		5,00,000
				Sept. 30	By Factory rent		60,000
				Sept. 30	By Salary of supervisor		10,000
				Sept. 30	By Wages		1,00,000
				Sept. 30	By Salary		25,000
				Sept. 30	By Advertisement		2,00,000
				Sept. 30	By Packaging		50,000
					By Electricity		30,000
					By Telephone		8,000
					By Interest on loan from GE Capital		50,000
				Sept. 30	By Balance c/d		2,60,000
			12,93,000				12,93,000
Oct. 1	To Balance b/f		2,60,000				

Sales Book

Date 2016	Particulars	L.F.	Invoice details (assumed)	Amount
June 15	Bombay Dying Mens		1	₹10,00,000
July 15	Fancy Ladies Showroom		2	15,00,000
	Sales a/c			25,00,000

Sales Return Book

Date 2016	Particulars	L.F.	Invoice details (assumed)	Amount
July 17	Fancy Ladies Showroom		2	₹1,50,000
				1,50,000

Purchase Book

Date 2016	Particulars	L.F.	Invoice details (assumed)	Amount
April 10	Delicate Cloth House		1	₹6,50,000
May 3	Vardhman Thread Company		2	5,00,000
				11,50,000

Purchase Returns Book

Date 2016	Particulars	L.F.	Invoice details (assumed)	Amount
May 4	Vardhman Thread Company		2	₹1,50,000
				1,50,000

P.3.5 Small Toy Private Limited (STPC) has been manufacturing toys as well as buying from the market since 2001. The owners of the company are satisfied both with its profit margins its reputation in the market. They are planning for expansion of the business for which a high-tech machine costing ₹30 lakh is required to be purchased. The machine is expected to reduce cost of production as well as enhance productivity. Though the company has bank balance of ₹7 lakh, it is not adequate to meet the cost of machine and additional working capital requirements. The company is seeking a loan of ₹25 lakh from a bank. The bank is agreeable to considering the loan proposal and is asking for detailed financial statements (manufacturing account, trading account, P&L A/c and balance sheet). Unfortunately, the Senior Accountant who has already prepared the trial balance as at 31st March 2016 (duly adjusted for adjustment items except closing stock) is hospitalised for heart surgery and is likely to join in April-end. Since the owners do not want to delay the purchase of machine, they engage the services of Mr. Solution (chartered account) to prepare for them the required financial statements. The adjusted trial balance provided to him is as follows: **LO 3.6,7,8** **LOD: D**

Trial Balance (adjusted) of STPC *as on March 31, 2016*

Particulars	Dr. Amount	Cr. Amount
Opening stock of raw materials	₹3,00,000	
Opening stock of work-in-progress	3,90,000	

(Contd.)

(*Contd.*)

Opening stock of finished goods	10,95,000	
Purchases (raw materials)	10,00,000	
Custom duty (raw materials purchased)	60,000	
Wages (workers)	3,80,000	
Salary (works manager)	3,00,000	
Fuel and power	1,26,000	
Advertisement	3,60,000	
Bad debts	45,000	
Purchases (finished goods)	10,50,000	
Sales (less returns)		₹60,40,000
Depreciation on machinery	1,50,000	
Carriage on purchase of toys (finished goods)	46,500	
Expenses outstanding		75,000
Long-term loan		15,00,000
Capital		31,00,000
Reserves and surplus		6,53,000
Sundry creditors		2,00,000
Interest received		1,50,000
Discount allowed	30,000	
Insurance (office)	30,000	
Insurance (factory)	15,000	
Salaries (office)	2,40,000	
Rent (office)	60,000	
Printing and stationery	15,000	
Cash in hand	1,50,000	
Cash at bank	7,00,000	
Postage and telegram	6,000	
Legal expenses	30,000	
Heating and lighting (office)	30,000	
Audit fees	24,000	
Showroom expenses	33,000	
Sales commission	3,00,000	
Delivery van's expenses	27,000	
Interest on loan	66,000	
Commission earned		75,000
Income from investment		18,000
Short-term investment	3,00,000	
Sundry debtors	7,50,000	
Pre-paid expenses	60,000	
Land and building	15,00,000	
Plant and machinery	9,00,000	
Furniture and fittings	2,90,000	
Vehicles	1,50,000	
Goodwill	3,00,000	
Patents (purchased, March 2016)	1,80,000	
Licenses (purchased, March 2016)	1,50,000	
Depreciation (office furniture)	45,000	
Freight on goods sold	25,500	
Bank charges	12,000	
Drawings	90,000	
	1,18,11,000	1,18,11,000

The company is subject to tax at the rate of 35 per cent.

The closing stock on March 31, 2016: raw materials ₹2,40,000, work-in-process, ₹1,50,000, finished goods, ₹3,45,000.

(Hint: Items appearing in trial balance will appear at one place only)

Manufacturing Account of STPC *for the year ending March 31, 2016*

Particulars		*Dr. Amount*	*Particulars*	*Cr. Amount*
To Cost of raw materials used:			By Closing stock of work-in-process	₹1,50,000
Opening stock	₹3,00,000		By Cost of goods manufactured	
Add purchases	10,00,000		transferred to Trading A/c	23,31,000
Less closing stock	2,40,000	₹10,60,000		
To Custom duty (on raw materials)		60,000		
To Work-in-process (opening stock)		3,90,000		
To Wages (Workers)		3,80,000		
To Salary (Works-manager)		3,00,000		
To Fuel and power		1,26,000		
To Depreciation on machinery		1,50,000		
To Factory insurance		15,000		
		24,81,000		24,81,000

Trading Account of STPC *for the year-ending March 31, 2016*

Particulars		*Dr. Amount*	*Particulars*	*Cr. Amount*
To Cost of goods sold:			By Sales	₹60,40,000
Opening stock	₹10,95,000			
Add purchases	10,50,000			
Add production costs	23,31,000			
Less closing stock	3,45,000	₹41,31,000		
To Carriage on purchases (finished goods)		46,500		
To Gross profit transferred to P&L A/c		18,62,500		
		60,40,000		60,40,000

Profit & Loss A/c of STPC *for the year-ending March 31, 2016*

Particulars		*Dr. Amount*	*Particulars*	*Cr. Amount*
To Administrative expenses:			By Gross profit	₹18,62,500
Office insurance	₹30,000			
Salaries	2,40,000			
Rent	60,000			
Printing & stationery	15,000			
Postage & telegram	6,000			
Legal expenses	30,000			
Heating & lighting	30,000			
Audit fees	24,000			
Depreciation on office furniture	45,000	₹4,80,000		
To Selling expenses				
Advertisement	₹3,60,000			
Bad debts	45,000			
Discount allowed	30,000			
Showroom expenses	33,000			
Sales commission	3,00,000			
Delivery van's expenses	27,000			
Freight on goods sold	25,500	8,20,500		
To Operating profit		5,62,000		
		18,62,500		18,62,500

(*Contd.*)

To Financial expenses:			By Operating profit	5,62,000
Interest on loan	₹66,000		By Interest received	1,50,000
Bank charges	12,000	78,000	By Commission earned	75,000
To Profit before taxes		7,27,000	By Income from investment	18,000
		8,05,000		8,05,000
To Provision for taxes		2,54,450	By Profit before taxes	7,27,000
To Profit after taxes		4,72,550		
		7,27,000		7,27,000

Balance Sheet of STPC *as at March 31, 2016*

Particulars		*Dr. Amount*	*Particulars*	*Cr. Amount*
Capital		₹31,00,000	Current assets:	
Reserves & surplus		6,53,000	Cash in hand	₹1,50,000
Profit	₹4,72,550		Cash at bank	7,00,000
Less drawings	90,000	3,82,550	Short-term investment	3,00,000
Long-term loan		15,00,000	Sundry debtors	7,50,000
Current liabilities:			Prepaid expenses	60,000
Sundry creditors		2,00,000	Closing stock:	
Provision for taxes		2,54,450	Raw-materials	2,40,000
Outstanding expenses		75,000	Work-in-process	1,50,000
			Finished goods	3,45,000
			Long-term assets:	
			Land and building	15,00,000
			Plant and machinery	9,00,000
			Furniture and fittings	2,90,000
			Vehicles	1,50,000
			Goodwill	3,00,000
			Patents	1,80,000
			Licenses	1,50,000
		61,65,000		61,65,000

REVIEW QUESTIONS

LOD: Easy

RQ.3.1 Name the steps (in sequence form) involved in the accounting cycle. **LO 3.1**

RQ.3.2 Debit implies increase and credit implies decrease. Do you agree with the statement? Explain your answer. **LO 3.1**

RQ.3.3 What are nominal, real and personal accounts? Give four examples of each of them. **LO 3.2**

RQ.3.4 What is balancing of account? What are the two types of balances? Can a cash account have credit balance? **LO 3.3,4,5**

RQ.3.5 What is journal? State its two broad categories. Name the five special journal. **LO 3.5**

RQ.3.6 What is ledger? State its two broad types. Name three special ledger books. **LO 3.5**

RQ.3.7 What is a trial balance? Name the errors disclosed as well as not disclosed by trial balance. **LO 3.4**

RQ.3.8 Distinguish between the following:

(i) Long-term assets and Current assets **LO 3.7**

(ii) Tangible assets and Non-tangible assets **LO 3.7**

(iii) Long-term liabilities and Current liabilities **LO 3.7**

(iv) Gross profit and Operating profit **LO 3.8**

RQ.3.9 What is a manufacturing account? What is its objectives? Prepare a manufacturing account with appropriate imaginary figures. LO 3.8

RQ.3.10 What is a trading account? What are its major constituents? What is its major outcome? LO 3.8

RQ.3.11 What is a profit and loss account? Draw its format with as many items as possible. LO 3.8

RQ.3.12 Write short notes on the following:

(i) Account LO 3.1
(ii) Rules of debit and credit LO 3.1
(iii) Cost of goods sold LO 3.8
(iv) Errors of commission LO 3.4

RQ.3.13 Arrange the following information in the sequence of accounting cycle: LO 3.1

(a) Posting to the ledger,
(b) Trial balance is prepared,
(c) Business transaction takes place,
(d) Income statement is prepared,
(e) Closing entries are recorded, and
(f) Information is recorded in journal.

RQ.3.14 Indicate whether the following statements are true or false: LO 3.1,2,4,6,7,8,9

(a) All debit entries are posted on the left side of accounts and are indicative of decrease in the account balances.
(b) All credit entries are recorded on the right side of accounts and represent increase in the account balances.
(c) P&L account is prepared on cash basis.
(d) Reserves with companies are in cash form or are invested in marketable securities.
(e) Retained earnings are assets of a firm and therefore have debit balance.
(f) Purchase of plant on credit should be debited to purchase account and supplier's account should be credited.
(g) Trial balance agreement implies that books of accounts are correct.
(h) Opening entries are required for all types of accounts.
(i) Closing entries are needed to close nominal accounts.
(j) Adjustment entries can be recorded only after the preparation of trial balance.

[Answers: (a) False (b) False (c) False (d) False (e) False (f) False (g) False (h) False (i) True (j) False]

RQ.3.15 Refer to exercise 3.14. Correct the statements which are false. LO 3.2,4,6,7,8,9

RQ.3.16 Fill in the following blanks: LO 3.5,6,7,8,9

(i) Cost of goods sold = Opening stock of finished goods (+) ________ (–) Closing stock of finished goods in the case of trading firms.
(ii) Gross profit = Sales revenue (–) ________.
(iii) Operating profit = ________ (–) Operating expenses.
(iv) Cost of raw materials used = Opening stock of raw materials (+) Purchases (–) ________.
(v) Total of sales book is posted to *(Dr/Cr)* side of ________ account.
(vi) Total of purchase return book is posted to *(Dr/Cr)* side of ________ account.
(vii) Yearly charge on tangible long-term assets is called ________.
(viii) Bank overdraft is a ________ liability.
(ix) P&L A/c in the case of corporate enterprises is closed by transferring to ________.
(x) Debit entries from cash book are posted ________ side of concerned account.

[Answers: (i) Purchases, (ii) Cost of goods sold, (iii) Gross profit, (iv) Closing stock of raw materials, (v) Cr. side, sales account, (vi) Cr side, purchase returns account, (vii) Amortisation, (viii) Current liability, (ix) P&L appropriation A/c, (x) Cr. side]

RQ.3.17 Journalise the following transactions of a hypothetical firm during the period January 1 to January 31. **LO 3.3**

January 1	Ajit commenced business with cash, ₹10,00,000.
January 2	Deposited cash into bank, ₹7,50,000.
January 3	Purchased building for ₹2,00,000 and payment is made by cheque.
January 4	Purchased goods for cash, ₹50,000.
January 6	Purchased goods on credit, ₹1,00,000 from XYZ & Company.
January 6	Paid cartage on goods purchased, ₹5,000.
January 6	Cash purchase of furniture for office, ₹50,000.
January 10	Sold goods for cash, ₹1,75,000.
January 12	Sold goods on credit to Shyam, ₹60,000.
January 17	Withdrew from the bank, ₹30,000 for private use.
January 20	Paid sundry expenses, ₹10,000 in cash.
January 25	Paid salaries of office staff, ₹20,000 in cash.
January 31	Paid rent, ₹20,000 by cheque.

RQ.3.18 Enter the following transactions in cash book and bank book with discount columns. **LO 3.3**

2016

May 1	Balance of cash in hand ₹40,000, Overdraft at bank, ₹5,00,000.
May 4	Invested further capital of ₹20,00,000 out of which ₹6,00,000 deposited in the bank.
May 5	Sold goods for cash, ₹3,00,000.
May 6	Received cheques from debtors of last year, ₹8,00,000, discount allowed to them, ₹20,000.
May 10	Purchased goods for cash, ₹5,50,000.
May 11	Paid Raman Sharma (creditor), ₹2,50,000, discount allowed by him, ₹5,000.
May 13	Commission paid to sales agent, ₹60,000.
May 14	Office furniture purchased from Karan, ₹20,000 for cash.
May 14	Rent paid, ₹15,000.
May 14	Electricity charges paid, ₹1,000.
May 16	Draw cheque for personal use, ₹70,000.
May 17	Cash sales, ₹2,50,000.
May 18	Received cheque from Ajay, ₹4,00,000, deposited in the bank next day.
May 19	Draw from the bank for office use, ₹50,000.
May 22	Draw cheque for petty cash, ₹15,000.
May 24	Dividend received by cheque, ₹5,000, deposited in the bank on the same day.
May 25	Commission received by cheque, ₹25,000; deposited in the bank on 28th May.
May 29	Paid from the bank salary of the office staff, ₹1,50,000.
May 29	Paid salary of the manager by cheque, ₹50,000.
May 30	The cash amount in excess of ₹1,00,000 is required to deposited with bank as per the policy of the firm.

LOD: Medium

RQ.3.19 "Trial balance is not a conclusive proof as to the absolute accuracy of books of accounts. It may agree and yet there may be some errors in the books that remain undisclosed." Elaborate. Give concrete examples in support of your answer. **LO 3.4**

RQ.3.20 State the procedure of posting from 4 special journal books to ledger books. Explain the procedure with examples. What is the advantage of writing journal folio and ledger folio numbers? **LO 3.3,5**

RQ.3.21 What are adjustment entries? What is their rationale? Name 5 adjustment items and pass their adjustment entries. **LO 3.6**

RQ.3.22 What are closing entries? Why are they needed? Name the type of accounts (a) required to be closed and (b) not required to be closed. **LO 3.6**

RQ.3.23 What is an 'opening entry'? Why is it needed? Pass the opening entry with imaginary figures. **LO 3.6**

RQ.3.24 "Double entry implies that transaction is recorded in journal and ledger." Explain. **LO 3.3**

RQ.3.25 "While balance sheet is like a snapshot, profit and loss account is like a moving picture." Explain. **LO 3.7,8**

RQ.3.26 "While interest payment is an expense, dividend payment, in contrast, is not reckoned expense." Explain. **LO 3.8,9**

RQ.3.27 What is P&L Appropriation Account? What purpose does it serve? Do you require such an account in all type of firms? Draw such an account with imaginary figures. **LO 3.9**

RQ.3.28 "Capital expenditures and deferred revenue expenditures need to be apportioned to determine true income." Explain. Give 3 examples of each. **LO 3.7**

RQ.3.29 "Extraordinary items warrant exclusion to judge true operating performance of a business enterprise." Elaborate. Give 3 examples each of abnormal losses and of abnormal gains. **LO 3.9**

RQ.3.30 State the rules of debit and credit as applied to (a) expense accounts, (b) asset accounts (c) capital account. **LO 3.2**

RQ.3.31 Indicate whether the following accounts would normally possess a debit or credit balance: (a) Salaries, (b) Debtors, (c) Creditors, (d) Plant and machinery, (e) General reserve, (f) Patents, (g) Commission received, (h) Sales return, (i) Purchases, (u) Fuel and power, (k) Drawings, (l) Capital. **LO 3.2**

RQ.3.32 Journalise the following transactions. Post them into ledger and prepare trial balance. **LO 3.3,4,5**

2013

April 1	Mohan commenced business with cash, ₹20,00,000.
April 2	Deposited into bank, ₹17,00,000.
April 3	Bought goods for cash, ₹2,00,000.
April 4	Bought furniture for office for cash, ₹60,000.
April 10	Draw cash from bank for office, ₹50,000.
April 13	Goods sold to Gopal on credit, ₹1,00,000.
April 15	Bought goods from Ram on credit, ₹1,10,000.
April 18	Paid sundry expenses, ₹30,000.
April 19	Received cash from Gopal, ₹95,000. Allowed him discount, ₹5,000.
April 25	Paid salary, ₹20,000.
April 28	Paid Ram in full settlement, ₹1,06,000.
April 30	Paid rent, ₹20,000.
April 30	Purchased stationery in cash, ₹5,000.

RQ.3.33 Mittal & Co Pvt Ltd. ('MCPL'), registered on April 5, 2016 as a private limited company, is primarily engaged in fabrication and sale of steel products. For the transactions undertaken during the first quarter of its operation, you are required to pass journal entries. **LO 3.3**

Transactions

1. April 5. MCPL commenced its operations with the capital contribution of ₹50 lakh each by the two shareholders Jay Mittal and Ajay Mittal.
2. April 7. MCPL entered into a lease agreement with DLF Ltd for office building and factory space for a monthly rent of ₹1 lakh payable on 25th of each month. The lease agreement is for the period of 10 years and the value of building and factory provided on lease is estimated at ₹1 crore.

3. April 8. MCPL entered into contract with the Advanced Machine Suppliers ('AMS') for purchase and installation of machine. The machine along with installation costed ₹25 lakh, ₹10 lakh payable as down payment and balance is payable at installation. Quarterly Maintenance contract is also entered into with AMS for ₹10,000 per quarter payable at the end of each quarter.
4. April 10. The machinery was installed at the factory premises and 20 permanent labours and 15 casual labours were employed and trained by Ajay Mittal. Time spent by Ajay on training was 20 hours.
5. April 10-15. MCPL purchased raw material worth ₹1 crore from Mittal Steel. ₹25 lakh were paid as down payment and balance on delivery i.e., April 20.
6. April 25. MCPL bid for and secured a ₹2 crore export sales order for fabricated utensils to a Middle East Company; 50% of the contract value will be paid in advance and balance on delivery of goods. The delivery is due on June 15.
7. Per month salary of Jay and Ajay amounted to ₹50,000 each on 30th of each month. The wages paid to workers for every month amounted to ₹5 lakh.
8. Sales, general and administrative expenses for every month amounted to ₹1 lakh.
9. May 5. MCPL bagged another sales order of ₹50 lakh from Kali Limited on credit. The delivery of goods were made on May 25.
10. May 10–May 16. Jay Mittal became seriously ill and was not able to attend the business actively. Ajay was also not able to concentrate on business either. The business of MCPL of adversely affected and during the period lost a potential sales order of ₹1 crore to Khanna & sons.
11. May 20. Additional raw material was purchased on credit from Tata Steels for ₹50 lakh
12. May 25. MCPL obtained a loan of ₹2 crore from SIDBI at the annual interest rate of 8 percent. The interest is payable quarterly with the first payment due on June 30.
13. May 25–28. MCPL sold goods worth ₹50 lakh to local distributors for cash
14. May 28–30. usual expenses were paid off in cash
15. June 4. Kali Limited was declared insolvent and only 50 percent of the sales proceeds were recovered from Kali.
16. June 4. MCPL sold goods worth ₹1 crore to the local distributors on credit. MCPL expects that 2 per cent of the sales proceeds will not be recovered.
17. June 8. A small fire at factory damaged the machinery and stock. The damage caused by fire is estimated at ₹30 lakh. Machinery worth ₹5 lakh was scrapped and sold for ₹20,000 and additional ₹10,000 was incurred to restore the operations. The insurance claim of ₹20 lakh was paid on June 20.
18. June 25. MCPL was unable to fulfil order on time and, therefore, paid 1 percent of the contract value as damages to Middle-East Company.

RQ.3.34 From the following ledger balances of Mr. Dinesh, prepare a trading account, P&L account for the current year ended 31st March 2016 and a balance sheet as on that day, after making the necessary adjustments: **LO 3.7,8**

Dinesh's capital	₹8,00,000
Dinesh's drawings	60,000
Plant and machinery (1.4.2015)	2,00,000
Plant and machinery additions (1.7.2015)	50,000
Stock on 1.4.2015	1,50,000
Purchases during the year	8,20,000
Carriage on purchases	20,000
Furniture and fixtures	2,00,000

(Contd.)

(Contd.)

Carriage on sales	25,000
Sundry expenses	8,000
Printing, stationery and postage	12,000
Rent, rates and taxes	40,000
Bad debts	5,000
Sundry creditors	95,000
Sales	12,00,000
Purchase returns	10,000
Provision for bad and doubtful debts (1.4.2015)	8,000
Commission received	16,000
Sundry debtors	52,000
Insurance charges	10,000
Salaries	2,10,000
Cash in hand	62,000
Cash at bank	2,05,000

Adjustments are required for the following:

(1) Closing stock on 31.3.2016 was valued at ₹1,40,000.
(2) Create provision for bad and doubtful debts at the rate of 5 per cent on sundry debtors.
(3) Provide for depreciation on furniture & fixtures at 10 per cent per annum and on plant and machinery at 20 per cent per annum.
(4) Insurance paid in advance is ₹1,000.
(5) Commission receivable in arrears is ₹5,000.
(6) Salaries payable are ₹15,000.

LOD: Difficult

RQ.3.35 "Revenues are positive shareholders equity accounts while expenses are negative accounts in this regard." Explain. **LO 3.7.9**

RQ.3.36 From the following trial balance, prepare manufacturing account, trading account, P&L A/c for the year ending March 2016 and a balance sheet as on that date of small manufacturing firm owned by Sohan. **LO 3.7.8**

Particulars	*Dr. Amount*	*Cr. Amount*
Sohan's capital account		₹4,10,000
Sohan's drawing account	₹60,000	
Loan account		50,000
Cash in hand	10,000	
Cash at bank	30,000	
Sundry debtors	4,00,000	
Sundry creditors		4,40,000
Provision for bad and doubtful debts (1.4.2015)		10,000
Plant and machinery	4,70,000	
Purchases of raw materials	3,50,000	
Raw materials stock – 1.4.2015	35,000	
Work-in-process stock – 1.4.2015	20,000	
Finished stock – 1.4.2015	1,80,000	
Freight (on raw materials purchases)	10,000	
Wages (paid to workers)	2,70,000	
Wages of supervisor	60,000	
Factory expenses	30,000	

(Contd.)

(Contd.)

Factory insurance	16,000	
Fuel and power	22,000	
Factory rent	24,000	
Repairs and maintenance of machine	5,000	
Consumable stores	2,000	
Sales		13,00,000
Sales returns	40,000	
Advertising	30,000	
Patents	20,000	
Office insurance	6,000	
Office rent	36,000	
Office stationary, postage, and telephone	10,000	
Other office expenses	38,000	
Carriage on sales	26,000	
Bad debts during the year	7,000	
Discounts received		10,000
Discount allowed	13,000	
	22,20,000	22,20,000

Additional information:

(i) Stock on 31st March, 2016 was as follows: Raw materials, ₹35,000, Work-in-process, ₹60,000 and Finished goods stock, ₹3,00,000.

(ii) Create provision for bad and doubtful debts at 4 per cent.

(iii) Depreciate plant and machinery by 20 per cent.

(iv) Patents are to be amortised at 10 per cent.

(v) Outstanding wages are ₹5,000.

(vi) Factory insurance in advance is ₹4,000.

ANSWERS

RQ3.18 Cash book balance, ₹1,00,000; Bank book balance, ₹20,39,000.

RQ3.32 Total of trial balance, ₹21,04,000

RQ3.34 Gross profit, ₹3,60,000; Net loss, ₹5,100; Balance sheet total, ₹8,44,900.

RQ3.36 Cost of goods manufactured, ₹7,50,000; Gross profit, ₹6,30,000; Net profit, ₹3,72,000; Balance sheet total, ₹12,17,000

[Comprehensive solutions to all numerical review questions are available on the companion website: http://www.mhhe.com/khan_jain_ma7e]

Understanding Corporate Financial Statements and Reports

4

LEARNING OBJECTIVES

After reading this chapter you will be able to:

LO 4.1 Understand the provisions of the Indian Companies Act and the Indian Accounting Standards (IND AS) governing the preparation and presentation of corporate financial statements

LO 4.2 Explain Corporate Governance Report and other reports

LO 4.3 Analyse reporting under select accounting standards

INTRODUCTION

The preceding chapter has provided a bird's eye view of the financial accounting system leading to the preparation of the profit and loss account and the balance sheet of business firms. This chapter dwells on matters relating to the preparation and presentation of corporate financial statements and reports in conformity with the requirements of the Companies Act, the Ministry of Corporate Affairs, the Securities and Exchange Board of India (SEBI) and the accounting standards. It covers corporate financial statements as well as corporate reports. The main points are summarised by way of recapitulation.

CORPORATE FINANCIAL STATEMENTS

LO 4.1 Understand the provisions of the Indian Companies Act governing the preparation and presentation of corporate financial statements

Corporate financial statements, that is, financial statements/annual accounts of corporate enterprises, should conform to the Companies Act, 2013 requirements in their preparation and presentation. These are described below with reference to **(i)** books and accounts to be kept (Section 128), **(ii)** annual accounts and balance sheet

(Section 129), **(iii)** forms and contents of balance sheet and statement of profit and loss (Sections 129), **(iv)** authentication of balance sheet and statement of profit and loss (Section 134), **(v)** statement of profit and loss and auditors report annexed to the balance sheet (Section 134), **(vi)** forms and contents of balance sheet, **(vii)** requirements as to statement of profit and loss, and **(viii)** balance sheet abstract and company's general business profile.

Books of Accounts

Section 128 of the Companies Act, 2013 requires that every company should keep at its registered office **proper books of account** with respect to **(a)** all sums of money received and spent/receipts and expenditures by the company **(b)** all sales and purchases of goods by the company **(c)** the assets and liabilities of the company and **(d)** in the case of companies engaged in production, processing, manufacturing or mining activities, details relating to utilisation of material, or labour or other items of cost as may be prescribed, if is required by the Central Government to include such details in their books of accounts. **Proper books of accounts** would be deemed to have been kept if **(a)** the company keeps such books as are necessary to give a true and fair view of its own state of affairs or of its branch office to explain its transactions; and **(b)** such books are kept on accrual basis and according to the double entry-system of accounting.

In general, to satisfy the requirement of the Companies Act, companies maintain the following books: **(1)** Cash Book, **(2)** Bank Book, **(3)** Purchase Book, **(4)** Purchase Returns Book, **(5)** Sales Book, **(6)** Sales Returns Book, **(7)** Bills Receivable Book, **(8)** Bills Payable Book, **(9)** General Journal, **(10)** General Ledger, **(11)** Debtors Ledger and, **(12)** Creditors Ledger.

Financial Statements

Section 129 of the Companies Act 2013 stipulates that the financial statements should provide a true and fair view of the state of affairs of the company(ies), and comply with the prescribed accounting standards.

Annual Accounts and Balance Sheet

Section 129 of the Companies Act, 2013 stipulates that, at every annual general meeting of a company, the Board of Directors should lay **(a)** a balance sheet as at the end of the period and **(b)** statement of a profit and loss for the period (financial year). The financial year may be less or more than a calendar year but it should not exceed 15 months.

Form and Contents of Balance Sheet and Statement of Profit and Loss

Section 129 requires that every balance sheet of a company should not only provide a true and fair view of the state of affairs of a company as at the end of the financial year but also should be set out in the format prescribed in Part I of Schedule III of the Act, 2013. Likewise, statement of profit and loss of a company should provide a true and fair view of the profit or loss of the company for the financial year and comply with the requirements of Part II of Schedule III of the Act. Both these financial statements should also comply with the accounting standards (listed in Chapter 2), issued by the Institute of Chartered Accountants of India. In case of non-compliance, a company is under obligation to state **(a)** the reasons for such deviation and **(b)** the financial effect, if any, of such deviation.

Section 129 of the Act also requires, *inter-alia*, a holding company to annex with its balance sheet a copy each of the balance sheet, the statement of profit and loss, the report of Board of Directors, the report of auditors, of its subsidiaries and a statement of its interest in its subsidiary(ies).

Authentication of Balance Sheet and Statement of Profit and Loss

Section 134 of the Companies Act, 2013 requires that every balance sheet and statement of P&L duly approved by the Board of Directors should be signed on behalf of the Board of Directors of a company by its manager or secretary, if any, and at least two directors one of whom should be a managing director, if any. Only after such authentication, the financial statements can be submitted to the auditors for their report thereon.

Statement of Profit and Loss and Auditors' Report to be Annexed to Balance Sheet

Section 134 requires that the statement of profit and loss of a company is annexed to the balance sheet and the auditor's report including separate, special or supplementary report, if any.

Balance Sheet

The balance sheet should be prepared (in vertical form) in accordance with Companies (Indian Accounting Standards (IND AS)) Rules 2015*. The required contents of balance sheet are shown in Exhibit 4.1.

EXHIBIT 4.1 Form of Balance Sheet

Name of the company ....
Balance Sheet as at ....

(₹ in ....)

	Particulars	*Note No.*	*Figures as at the end of current reporting period*	*Figures as at the end of previous reporting period*
	1	*2*	*3*	*4*
I ASSETS				
(1)	**Non-current assets**			
	(a) Property, plant and equipment			
	(b) Capital work-in-progress			
	(c) Goodwill			
	(d) Intangible assets			
	(e) Intangible assets under development			

(Contd.)

* According to the Companies (Indian Accounting Standards (IND AS)) Rules 2015, it is mandatory for all companies having net worth greater than or equal to ₹250 crores. For companies having net worth of less than ₹250 crores, the adoption of the format is voluntary. The new format classifies assets only in two categories, namely, current assets and non-current assets (which are long-term assets). Likewise, sources of funds (hitherto referred to as Liabilities) have also been segregated in two groups, namely, Equity (representing shareholders' funds including preference share capital) and Liabilities (indicating external liabilities payable).

(*Contd.*)

	(f) Financial assets
	(i) Investments
	(ii) Loans
	(g) Other non-current assets
(2)	**Current assets**
	(a) Inventories
	(b) Financial assets
	(i) Investments
	(ii) Trade receivables
	(iii) Cash and cash equivalents
	(iv) Loans
	(v) Other financial assets
	(c) Other currents assets
TOTAL	
EQUITY AND LIABILITIES	
(1)	**Equity**
	(a) Equity share capital
	(b) Other equity
	(c) Non-controlling interest
(2)	**Liabilities**
	Non-current Liabilities
	(a) Financial liabilities
	(i) Borrowings
	(ii) Other financial liabilities
	(b) Deferred payment liabilities
	(c) Provisions
	(d) Deferred tax liabilities (Net)
	Current Liabilities
	(a) Financial liabilities
	(i) Borrowings
	(ii) Trade payables
	(iii) Other financial liabilities
	(b) Other current liabilities
	(c) Provisions
	Total Liabilities
	Total Equity and Liabilities

General Instructions for Preparation of Balance Sheet

1. An asset will be classified as current when it satisfies any of the following criteria:

(a) it is expected to be realised in, or is intended for sale or consumption in, the company's normal operating cycle;

(b) it is held primarily for the purpose of being traded;

(c) it is expected to be realised within 12 months after the reporting date; or

(d) it is in cash or cash equivalent unless it is restricted from being exchanged or used to settle a liability for at least twelve months after the reporting date.

All other assets will be classified as non-current.

2. An operating cycle is the time that elapses between the acquisition of assets for processing and their realisation in cash or cash equivalents. Where the normal operating cycle cannot be identified, it is assumed to have duration of 12 months.
3. A liability will be classified as current when it satisfies any of the following criteria:
   (a) it is expected to be settled in the company's normal operating cycle;
   (b) it is held primarily for the purpose of being traded; or
   (c) it is due to be settled within 12 months of the reporting date.
   All other liabilities will be classified as non-current.
4. A receivable will be classified as a 'trade receivable' if it is in respect of the amount due on account of goods sold or services rendered in the normal course of business.
5. A payable will be classified as a 'trade payable' if it is in respect of the amount due on account of goods purchased or services received in the normal course of business.
6. A company will disclose the following (in notes) to accounts.

A. Property, Plant and Equipment

(i) Property, plant and equipment will be classified as:
- **(a)** Land
- **(b)** Buildings
- **(c)** Plant and equipment
- **(d)** Bearer plants
- **(e)** Aircraft
- **(f)** Vehicles
- **(g)** Office equipment
- **(h)** Assets under lease

(ii) Land and building will be grouped as either one or two separate classes of property, plant and equipment. A class is defined as a group of assets of a similar nature and use in an entity's operations.

(iii) A reconciliation of the gross and net carrying amounts of each class of assets at the beginning and end of the reporting period – showing additions, disposals, acquisitions through business combinations and other adjustments and the related depreciation and impairment losses/reversals – will be disclosed separately.

B. Goodwill and other Intangible Assets

(i) Goodwill will be disclosed separately on the face of the balance sheet. Other intangible assets will be classified as follows:
- **(a)** Brands or trademarks
- **(b)** Computer software
- **(c)** Mastheads and publishing titles
- **(d)** Mining rights
- **(e)** Copyrights, patents and other intellectual property rights, services and operating rights
- **(f)** Recipes, formulae, models, designs and prototypes
- **(g)** Licenses and franchises

(ii) A reconciliation of the gross and net carrying amounts of each class of assets at the beginning and end of the reporting period showing additions, disposals, acquisitions through business combinations and other adjustments and the related amortisation and impairment losses/reversals will be disclosed separately.

(iii) Where sums have been written off on a reduction of capital or revaluation of assets or where sums have been added on revaluation of assets, every balance sheet subsequent to date of such write-off, or addition will show the reduced or increased figures as applicable and will by way of a note also show the amount of the reduction or increase as applicable together with the date thereof for the first five years subsequent to the date of such reduction or increase.

C. Investments

(i) Investments will be classified as:
- **(a)** Equity instruments;
- **(b)** Preference shares;
- **(c)** Government or trust securities;
- **(d)** Debentures or bonds;
- **(e)** Mutual funds;
- **(f)** Partnership firms; or
- **(g)** Other investments

(ii) Under each classification, details will be given of names of the bodies corporate (indicating separately whether such bodies are subsidiaries, associates, joint ventures and structured entities in which investments have been made and the nature and extent of the investment so made in each such body corporate (showing separately investments which are partly paid). The names of the body corporate (including nature and extent of the investment) is not required to be given where investments are made in instruments of parties other than subsidiaries, associates, joint ventures and structured entities.

(iii) Investments carried at an amount other than at cost should be separately stated specifying the basis for valuation thereof.

D. Non-current Loans

(i) Non-current loans will be classified as:
- **(a)** Capital advances
- **(b)** Security deposits
- **(c)** Loans and advances to related parties (giving details thereof)
- **(d)** Other loans and advances (specify nature)

(ii) The above will also be separately sub-classified as:
- **(a)** Secured, considered good
- **(b)** Unsecured, considered good
- **(c)** Doubtful

(iii) Allowance for bad and doubtful loans and advances will be disclosed under the relevant heads separately.

(iv) Loans and advances due by directors or other officers of the company or any of them either severally or jointly with any other persons or amounts due by firms or private companies respectively in which any director is a partner or a director or a member should be separately stated.

E. Other Non-current Assets

Other non-current assets will be classified as:

(i) Non-current trade receivables (including trade receivables on deferred credit terms)

(ii) Others (specify nature)

(iii) Non-current trade receivables will be sub-classified as:

(a) Secured, considered good;
(b) Unsecured considered good;
(c) Doubtful

- Allowance for bad and doubtful debts will be disclosed under the relevant heads separately.
- Debts which are due from directors or from other officers of the company or any of them either severally or jointly with any other person or from firms or private companies respectively in which any director is a partner or a director or a member should be separately stated.

F. Inventories

(i) Inventories will be classified as:

(a) Raw materials
(b) Work-in-progress
(c) Finished goods
(d) Stock-in-trade (in respect of goods acquired for trading)
(e) Stores and spares
(f) Loose tools
(g) Others (specify nature)

(ii) Goods-in-transit will be disclosed under the relevant sub-head of inventories. Mode of valuation will be stated.

G. Trade Receivables and Trade Payables

(i) A receivable will be classified as 'trade receivable' if it is in respect of the amount due on account of goods sold or services rendered in the normal course of business.

(ii) A payable will be classified as 'trade payable' if it is in respect of the amount due on account of goods purchased or services received in the normal course of business.

(iii) Schedule III requires disclosure of receivables due by directors or other officers of the company or any of them either severally or jointly with any other person or debts due by firms or private companies respectively in which any director is a partner or a director or a member.

H. Cash and Cash Equivalents

(i) Cash and bank balances will be classified as:

(a) Balances with banks
(b) Cheques, drafts on hand
(c) Cash on hand
(d) Others (specify nature)

(ii) Earmarked balances with banks (for example, for unpaid dividend) will be separately stated.

(iii) Balances with banks to the extent held as margin money or security against the borrowings, guarantees, other commitments will be disclosed separately.

(iv) Repatriation restrictions, if any, in respect of cash and bank balances will be separately stated.

(v) Bank deposits with more than 12 months maturity will be disclosed separately.

I. Current Loans

(i) Current loans will be classified as:

(a) Loans and advances to related parties (giving details thereof)
(b) Others (specify nature)

(ii) The above will also be sub-classified as:
 (a) Secured, considered good
 (b) Unsecured, considered good
 (c) Doubtful

(iii) Allowance for bad and doubtful loans and advances will be disclosed under the relevant heads separately.

(iv) Loans and advances due from directors or other officers of the company or any of them either individually or jointly with any other person or amounts due from firms or private companies respectively in which any director is a partner, or a director or a member, will be separately stated.

J. Biological Assets other than Bearer Plants

IND AS 41 defines bearer plant as a living plant that: (i)is used in the production or supply of agricultural produce, (ii) is expected to bear produce for more than one period, and (iii) has a remote likelihood of being sold as agricultural produce except for incidental scrap sales.

Schedule III requires reconciliation of the carrying amounts of each class of assets at the beginning and end of the reporting period showing additions, disposals, acquisitions through business combinations and other adjustments will be disclosed separately.

K. Deferred Tax and Liabilities shall be set off if, and only if:

(i) There is legally recognized right to set off current tax and liabilities, and

(ii) The deferred tax and liabilities relate to income taxes levied by the same taxation authority on either;
 (a) The same taxable entity, or
 (b) Different taxable entities which intend to settle current tax liabilities and assets on a net basis, or to realize the assets and settle the liabilities simultaneously, in each future period in which significant amounts of deferred tax liabilities or assets are expected to be settled or recovered.

(iii) The circumstances giving rise to a set off between entities in a consolidated entity are likely to be rare unless the entities are part of a tax consolidated group.

L. Asset Held for Sale

There is no requirement in either Ind AS 105 or Ind AS 1 to present assets of a disposal group separately from individual assets held for sale.

M. Other Current Assets (specify nature)

This is an all-inclusive heading, which incorporates current assets that do not fit into any other asset categories.

N. Equity

For each class of share capital (different classes of preference shares to be treated separately) following information need to be disclosed:

(i) The number and amount of shares authorised;

(ii) The number of shares issued, subscribed and fully paid, and subscribed but not fully paid;

(iii) Par value per share;

(iv) A reconciliation of the number of shares outstanding at the beginning and at the end of the reporting period;

(v) The rights, preferences and restrictions attached to each class of shares, including restrictions on the distribution of dividends and the repayment of capital;

(vi) Shares in respect of each class in the company held by its holding capacity or its ultimate holding company, including shares held by or by subsidiaries or associates of the holding company or the ultimate holding company in aggregate;

(vii) Shares in the company held by each shareholder holding more than 5 per cent shares, specifying the number of shares held;

(viii) Shares reserved for issue under options and contracts/commitments for the sale of shares/disinvestment, including the terms and amounts;

(ix) For the period of five years immediately preceding the date as at which the balance sheet is prepared:

- **(a)** Aggregate number and class of shares allotted as fully paid up pursuant to contract(s) without payment being received in cash
- **(b)** Aggregate number and class of shares allotted as fully paid up by way of bonus shares
- **(c)** Aggregate number and class of shares bought back

(x) Terms of any securities convertible into equity/preference shares issued along with the earliest date of conversion in descending order, starting from the farthest such date;

(xi) Calls unpaid (showing aggregate value of calls unpaid by directors and officers);

(xii) Forfeited shares (amount originally paid up).

Detailed notes on Equity are provided in Annexure 4-I given at the end of chapter.

O. Other Equity

(i) Other equity will be classified as follows:

- **(a)** Capital reserves
- **(b)** Capital redemption reserve
- **(c)** Securities premium reserve
- **(d)** Debenture redemption reserve
- **(e)** Revaluation reserve
- **(f)** Share options outstanding account
- **(g)** Other reserves (specify the nature and purpose of reserve and the amount in respect thereof)
- **(h)** Surplus, i.e. balance in Statement of Profit & Loss disclosing allocations and appropriations such as dividend, bonus shares and transfer to/from reserves, etc.

  (Additions and deductions since the last Balance Sheet to be shown under each of the specified head)

(ii) A reserve specifically represented by earmarked investments will be termed as a 'fund'.

(iii) Debit balance of statement of profit and loss will be shown as a negative figure under the head 'Surplus'. Similarly, the balance of 'Reserves and Surplus', after adjusting negative balance of surplus, if any, will be shown under the head 'Reserves and Surplus' even if the resulting figure is in the negative.

P. Borrowings

Schedule III requires the following disclosures:

(i) Borrowings will be sub-classified as secured and unsecured. Nature of security need to be specified.

(ii) Where loans have been guaranteed by directors or others, the aggregate amount of such loans under each head will be disclosed.

(iii) Bonds or debentures (along with rate of interest, and particulars of redemption or conversion, as the case may be) will be stated in descending order of maturity or conversion, starting from farthest redemption or conversion date, as the case may be. Where bonds/debentures are redeemable by installments, the date of maturity for this purpose must be reckoned as the date on which the first installment becomes due.

(iv) Particulars of any redeemed bonds or debentures which the company has power to reissue will be disclosed.

(v) Terms of repayment of term loans and other loans will be stated.

(vi) Period and amount of default as at the balance sheet date in repayment of borrowings and interest will be specified separately in each case.

Q. Other non-current Liabilities

Other non-current liabilities will be classified as:

(i) Trade payables

(ii) Others

R. Non-current Provisions

The amounts will be classified as:

(i) Provision for employee benefits, and

(ii) Others specifying the nature

S. Current Borrowings

(i) Current borrowings will be classified as:

- **(a)** Loans repayable on demand
  - from banks
  - from other parties
- **(b)** Loans and advances from related parties
- **(c)** Deposits
- **(d)** Other loans and advances (specify nature)

(ii) Borrowings will further be sub-classified as secured and unsecured. Nature of security will be specified separately in each case.

(iii) Where loans have been guaranteed by directors or others, the aggregate amount of such loans under each head will be disclosed.

(iv) Period and amount of default, as on the Balance Sheet date in repayment of loans and interest, will be specified separately in each case.

T. Other Current Liabilities

The amounts will be classified as:

(i) Current maturities of long-term debt

(ii) Current maturities of finance lease obligations

(iii) Interest accrued but not due on borrowings

(iv) Interest accrued and due on borrowings

(v) Income received in advance

(vi) Unpaid dividends

(vii) Application money received for allotment of securities and due for refund and interest accrued thereon

Share application money includes advances towards allotment of share capital. The terms and conditions including the number of shares proposed to be issued, the amount of premium, if any, and the period before which shares will be allotted will be disclosed. It will also be disclosed whether the company has sufficient authorised capital to cover the share capital amount resulting from allotment of shares out of such share application money. Further, the period for which the share application money has been pending beyond the period for allotment as mentioned in the document inviting application for shares along with the reason for such share application money being pending will be disclosed. Share application money not exceeding the issued capital and to the extent not refundable will be shown under the head 'Equity' and share application money to the extent refundable, i.e. the amount in excess of subscription or in case the requirements of minimum subscription are not met, will be separately shown under 'Other current liabilities'

(viii) Unpaid matured deposits and interest accrued thereon
(ix) Unpaid matured debentures and interest accrued thereon
(x) Other payables (specify nature)

U. Current Provisions

The amounts will be classified as:

(i) Provision for employee benefits
(ii) Others (specify nature)

V. Contingent Liabilities and Commitments (to the extent not provided for)

(i) Contingent liabilities will be classified as:
  (a) Claims against the company not acknowledged as debt
  (b) Guarantees
  (c) Other money for which the company is contingently liable
(ii) Commitments will be classified as:
  (a) Estimated amount of contracts remaining to be executed on capital account and not provided for
  (b) Uncalled liability on shares and other investments partly paid
  (c) Other commitments (specify nature)

W. The amount of dividends proposed to be distributed to equity and preference shareholders for the period and the related amount per share will be disclosed separately. Arrears of fixed cumulative dividends on preference shares will also be disclosed separately.

X. Where in case of an issue of securities made for a specific purpose, the whole or part of the amount has not been used for the specific purpose at the balance sheet date, the indication by way of a note as to how such unutilised amounts have been used or invested will be given.

Y. If, in the opinion of the Board, any of the assets other than fixed assets and non-current investments do not have a value on realisation in the ordinary course of business at least equal to the amount at which they are stated, the fact that the Board is of that opinion, will be stated.

Requirement as to Statement of Profit and Loss

The main requirements of Part II of Schedule III of the Companies Act, 2013 is that the statement of: Profit and loss should **(a)** be made in such a manner that it discloses clearly the result of the working of the company during the period covered by the account and **(b)** disclose every material feature, including credits or receipts and debits or expenses in respect of non-recurring transactions or transactions of an exceptional nature. Exhibit 4.2 shows the required contents/form of statement of profit and loss.

EXHIBIT 4.2 Form of Statement of Profit and Loss

Name of the company ....

Profit and loss statement for the year ended ....

(₹ in ....)

	Particulars	*Note No*	*Figures for the current reporting period*	*Figures for the previous reporting period*
I	**Revenue from operations (gross)**		xxx	xxx
II	**Other income**		xxx	xxx
III	**Total revenue (I + II)**		xxx	xxx
IV	**Expenses**			
	Cost of materials consumed		xxx	xxx
	Purchases of stock-in-trade		xxx	xxx
	Changes in inventories of finished goods, work-in-progress and stock-in-trade		xxx	xxx
	Employee benefits expense		xxx	xxx
	Finance costs		xxx	xxx
	Depreciation and amortisation expense		xxx	xxx
	Other expenses		xxx	xxx
	Total expenses		xxx	xxx
V	**Profit before exceptional and extraordinary items and tax (III – IV)**		xxx	xxx
VI	**Exceptional items**		xxx	xxx
VII	**Profit before extraordinary items and tax (V + VI)**		xxx	xxx
VIII	**Extraordinary items**		xxx	xxx
IX	**Profit before tax (VII + VIII)**		xxx	xxx
X	**Tax expense**			
	Current tax		xxx	xxx
	Deferred tax		xxx	xxx
XI	**Profit (Loss) for the period from continuing operations (VII – VIII)**		xxx	xxx
XII	**Profit (Loss) from discontinuing operations**		xxx	xxx
XIII	**Tax expense of discontinuing operations**		xxx	xxx
XIV	**Profit/(Loss) from discontinuing operations (after tax) (XII – XIII)**		xxx	xxx
XV	**Profit (Loss) for the period (XI + XIV)**		xxx	xxx
XVI	**Earnings per equity share:**		xxx	xxx
	(1) Basic		xxx	xxx
	(2) Diluted		xxx	xxx

See accompanying notes to the financial statements

General Instructions for Preparation of Statement of Profit and Loss

1. The provisions of this part will apply to the income and expenditure account referred to in Section 129 of the Act, in like manner as they apply to a statement of profit and loss.
2. **(A)** In respect of a company, other than a finance company, revenue from operations will disclose separately in the notes revenue from:
   (a) sale of products;
   (b) sale of services;
   (c) other operating revenues;
   Less:
   (d) excise duty.

   (B) In respect of a finance company, revenue from operations will include revenue from
   (a) Interest
   (b) Other financial services

   Revenue under each of the above heads will be disclosed separately by way of notes to accounts to the extent applicable.
3. **Finance Costs**
   Finance costs will be classified as:
   (a) Interest expense;
   (b) Other borrowing costs;
   (c) Applicable net gain/loss on foreign currency transactions and translation.
4. **Other income**
   Other income will be classified as:
   (a) Interest income (in case of a company other than a finance company);
   (b) Dividend income;
   (c) Net gain/loss on sale of investments
   (d) Other non-operating income (net of expenses directly attributable to such income).
5. **Additional Information**
   A Company will disclose by way of notes additional information regarding aggregate expenditure and income on the following items:
   (i) **(a)** Employee benefits expense [showing separately **(i)** salaries and wages, **(ii)** contribution to provident and other funds, **(iii)** expense on Employee Stock Option Scheme (ESOP) and Employee Stock Purchase Plan (ESPP), **(iv)** staff welfare expenses].
   (b) Depreciation and amortisation expense
   (c) Any item of income or expenditure which exceeds one per cent of the revenue from operations or ₹1,00,000 whichever is higher
   (d) Interest income
   (e) Interest expense
   (f) Dividend income
   (g) Net gain/loss on sale of investments
   (h) Adjustments to the carrying amount of investments
   (i) Net gain or loss on foreign currency transaction and translation (other than considered as finance cost)
   (j) Payments to the auditor as **(a)** auditor, **(b)** for taxation matters, **(c)** for company law matters, **(d)** for management services, **(e)** for other services, **(f)** for reimbursement of expenses

(k) Details of items of exceptional and extraordinary nature
(l) Prior period items

(ii) (a) In the case of manufacturing companies-
(1) Raw materials under broad heads
(2) Goods purchased under broad heads
(b) In the case of trading companies, purchases in respect of goods traded in by the company under broad heads
(c) In the case of companies rendering or supplying services, gross income derived from services rendered or supplied under broad heads
(d) In the case of a company, which falls under more than one of the categories mentioned in **(a)**, **(b)** and **(c)** above, it will be in sufficient compliance with the requirements herein if purchases, sales and consumption of raw material and the gross income from services rendered are shown under broad heads.
(e) In the case of other companies, gross income is derived under broad heads.

(iii) In the case of all concerns having works-in-progress under broad heads

(iv) (a) The aggregate, if material, of any amounts set aside or proposed to be set aside, to reserve, but not including provisions made to meet any specific liability, contingency or commitment known to exist at the date as to which the balance-sheet is made up
(b) The aggregate, if material, of any amounts withdrawn from such reserves

(v) (a) The aggregate, if material, of the amounts set aside to provisions made for meeting specific liabilities, contingencies or commitments
(b) The aggregate, if material, of the amounts withdrawn from such provisions, as no longer required

(vi) Expenditure incurred on each of the following items, separately for each item:
(a) Consumption of stores and spare parts
(b) Power and fuel
(c) Rent
(d) Repairs to buildings
(e) Repairs to machinery
(g) Insurance
(h) Rates and taxes, excluding, taxes on income
(i) Miscellaneous expenses

(vii) (a) Dividends from subsidiary companies
(b) Provisions for losses of subsidiary companies

(viii) The profit and loss account will also contain by way of a note the following information, namely:
(a) Value of imports calculated on C.I.F basis by the company during the financial year in respect of
- Raw materials
- Components and spare parts
- Capital goods

(b) Expenditure in foreign currency during the financial year on account of royalty, know-how, professional and consultation fees, interest, and other matters
(c) Total value of all imported raw materials, spare parts and components consumed during the financial year and the total value of all indigenous raw materials, spare parts and components similarly consumed and the percentage of each to the total consumption

(d) The amount remitted during the year in foreign currencies on account of dividends with a specific mention of the total number of non-resident shareholders, the total number of shares held by them on which the dividends were due and the year to which the dividends related

(e) Earnings in foreign exchange classified under the following heads:

- Export of goods calculated on F.O.B. basis
- Royalty, know-how, professional and consultation fees
- Interest and dividend
- Other income, indicating the nature thereof

Note: Broad heads will be decided taking into account the concept of materiality and presentation of true and fair view of financial statements.

2. This notification has come into force from 1-4-2011 (source: www.mca.gov.in)

The preparation of financial accounts as per the Companies (Indian Accounting Standards (IND AS)) Rules, 2015 is illustrated in Example 4.1. The major highlights of the financial statements of Reliance Industries Ltd for 2018 are given in Annexure 4-II given at the end of chapter.

◆ Example 4.1

From the following trial balance of Prakash Machineries Limited (which has decided to adopt Companies (Indian Accounting Standards (IND AS)) Rules 2015) and additional information, prepare final accounts of the company as per the Companies Act.

Particulars	*Amount*	*Particulars*	*Amount*
Opening stock		Sales	₹47,50,000
Raw materials	₹1,50,000	General reserve	25,000
Work-in-process	28,000	Provision for depreciation on	
Finished goods	1,90,000	plant and machinery	1,40,000
Purchases	15,50,000	Sundry creditors	1,35,000
Salaries and wages	2,30,000	Provision for depreciation on	
Plant & machinery (at cost)	12,10,000	furniture	30,000
Investment at cost		Purchases returns	25,000
(short-term)	3,29,000	Equity share capital	
Sundry debtors	1,58,000	(₹100 each)	30,00,000
Cash at bank	3,00,900	10% Preference shares capital	
Directors remuneration	80,000	(₹100 each)	5,00,000
Interim dividend	1,20,000	9% Debentures	6,00,000
Office furniture (at cost)	1,80,000	Debenture redemption	
Rates and taxes	17,000	reserve	3,00,000
Insurance	25,000	Bills payable	90,000
Audit fee	30,000	Securities premium	2,80,000
Sales return	70,000	Income from investments	30,000
Excise duty on finished goods	3,20,000	Excise duty payable	15,000
Rent	90,000	Profit and loss	20,000
Rent prepaid	20,000		
Bad debts	18,000		
Interest on debentures	27,000		
Freehold premises	47,30,000		
Other expenses	37,100		
Bills receivable	30,000		
	99,40,000		99,40,000

Additional information:

(1) Stock as at March 31, 2018
Raw materials and stores, ₹1,45,000; Work-in-process, ₹22,000; Finished goods, ₹1,98,000.

(2) Provide depreciation on written down value basis on plant and machinery @ 20 per cent per annum and on furniture @ 15 per cent per annum and on freehold premises @ 5 per cent per annum.

(3) In the middle of the year machine costing ₹3,00,000 was purchased and duly recorded.

(4) Sundry debtors include ₹18,000 due for more than six months. Provide for bad and doubtful debts @ 5 per cent on debtors.

(5) Market value of investments is ₹3,19,000.

(6) Make a provision for income-tax @ 35 per cent.

(7) Corporate dividend tax is 14.025 per cent including surcharge of 10 per cent and education cess of 2 per cent.

(8) The Board of Directors has recommended a final dividend @ 15 per cent on equity shares.

(9) Transfer ₹1,00,000 to debenture redemption reserve.

(10) Transfer minimum amount to statutory reserve as required by Company law.

(11) Provision for depreciation on freehold premises as on 31/3/2017 was ₹12,70,000.

(12) Interest on debentures becomes due on October 31 and March 31.

Solution

Name of the company: Prakash Machineries Limited

		Note No.	Figures as at March 31, 2018
I	**EQUITY AND LIABILITIES**		
(1)	**Shareholders' funds**		
	(a) Share capital	1	₹35,00,000
	(b) Reserves and surplus	2	10,81,545
	(c) Money received against share warrants		Nil
(2)	**Share application money pending allotment**		Nil
(3)	**Non-current liabilities**		
	(a) Long-term borrowings		6,00,000
	(b) Deferred tax liabilities (net)		Nil
	(c) Other long-term liabilities		Nil
	(d) Long-term provisions		Nil
(4)	**Current liabilities**		
	(a) Short-term borrowings		Nil
	(b) Trade payables	3	2,25,000
	(c) Other current liabilities	4	58,830
	(d) Short-term provisions	5	11,96,625
	Total		66,62,000
II	**ASSETS**		
	Non-current assets		

(Contd.)

(Contd.)

(1)	**(a)** Fixed assets		
	(i) Tangible assets	6	54,77,000
	(ii) Intangible assets		Nil
	(iii) Capital work-in-progress		Nil
	(iv) Intangible assets under development		Nil
	(b) Non-current investments		Nil
	(c) Deferred tax assets (net)		Nil
	(d) Long-term loans and advances		Nil
	(e) Other non-current assets		Nil
(2)	**Current assets**		
	(a) Current investments (at market value)		3,19,000
	(b) Inventories	7	3,65,000
	(c) Trade receivables	8	1,80,100
	(d) Cash and cash equivalents		3,00,900
	(e) Short-term loans and advances@		20,000
	(f) Other current assets		Nil
	Total		66,62,000

@ Includes prepaid rent.

STATEMENT OF PROFIT AND LOSS FOR THE YEAR ENDED MARCH 31, 2018

	Particulars	*Note No.*		*For the year ended March 31, 2018*
I	**Revenue from operations (gross)**			₹43,60,000
II	**Other income**			30,000
III	**Total revenue (I + II)**			43,90,000
IV	**Expenses**			
	Cost of materials consumed		₹15,30,000	
	Purchases of stock-in-trade		Nil	
	Changes in inventories of finished goods, work-in-progress and stock-in-trade			
	Finished goods		(8,000)	
	Work-in-progress		6,000	
	Stock-in-trade		Nil	
	Employee benefits expenses	9	3,10,000	
	Finance costs	10	54,000	
	Depreciation and amortisation expenses		4,73,000	
	Other expenses	11	2,35,000	
	Total expenses			26,00,000
V	**Profit before exceptional and extraordinary items and tax (III – IV)**			17,90,000

(Contd.)

(Contd.)

VI	**Exceptional items**	Nil
VII	**Profit before extraordinary items and tax (V + VI)**	17,90,000
VIII	**Extraordinary items**	Nil
IX	**Profit before tax (VII + VIII)**	17,90,000
X	**Tax expenses**	
	(1) Current tax	6,26,500
	(2) Deferred tax	Nil
XI	**Profit for the period from continuing operations (IX – X)**	11,63,500
XII	**Profit (Loss) from discontinuing operations**	Nil
XIII	**Tax expenses of discontinuing operations**	Nil
XIV	**Profit (Loss) from discontinuing operations (after tax) (XII – XIII)**	Nil
XV	**Profit (Loss) for the period (XI + XIV)**	11,63,500
XVI	**Earnings per equity share:**	
	(1) Basic*	36.88
	(2) Diluted	Nil

*(₹11,63,500 – ₹57,012.50 dividend on preference shares = ₹11,06,487.50/30,000 Equity shares)

NOTES

1. Equity

Authorised share capital	Nil
Issued and subscribed capital:	
30,000 equity shares of ₹100 each fully paid up	₹30,00,000
5000 preference shares of ₹100 each fully paid up	5,00,000
Total	35,00,000

2. Other Equity

Securities premium		₹2,80,000
Debenture redemption reserve		
As per last Balance Sheet	₹3,00,000	
Add: Transfer from profit and loss statement	1,00,000	4,00,000
General reserve		
As per last Balance Sheet	25,000	
Add: Statutory transfer from profit and loss statement	58,175	83,175
Surplus/(Deficit)		3,18,370
As per last Balance Sheet	20,000	
Add: Profit for the year	11,63,500	
Total	11,83,500	
Less: Interim dividend	1,20,000	

(Contd.)

(Contd.)

Proposed dividend:			
Equity	₹4,50,000		
Preference	50,000	5,00,000	
Corporate dividend tax payable (Interim dividend)		16,830	
Provision for dividend tax payable (Final dividend)		70,125	
Transferred to debenture redemption reserve		1,00,000	
Transferred to general reserve		58,175	
Total			10,81,545

3. Trade Payables

Bills payables	₹90,000
Sundry creditors	1,35,000
Total	2,25,000

4. Other Current Liabilities

Excise duty payable	₹15,000
Corporate dividend tax payable	16,830
Interest due on debentures	27,000
Total	58,830

5. Short Term Provisions

Provision for corporate dividend tax	₹70,125
Provision for proposed dividend (₹4,50,000 + ₹50,000)	5,00,000
Provision for tax	6,26,500
Total	11,96,625

6. Property, Plant and Equipment

Particulars of Assets	*Gross Block*			*Depreciation/ Amortisation*	*Net Block*
Tangible Assets	*Gross value*	*Purchases*	*Total*		
Freehold Premises	₹60,00,000	Nil	₹60,00,000	₹15,06,500	₹44,93,500
Plant and Machinery	9,10,000	₹3,00,000	12,10,000	3,54,000	8,56,000
Furniture	1,80,000	Nil	1,80,000	52,500	1,27,500
Total					54,77,000

7. Inventories

Raw Materials	₹1,45,000
Work-in-progress	22,000
Finished goods	1,98,000
Total	3,65,000

8. Trade Receivables

Debtors:			
Debts due for more than six months	₹18,000		
Other debts	1,40,000	₹1,58,000	
Less: Provision for bad debts		7,900	₹1,50,100
Bills Receivable			30,000
Total			1,80,100

9. Employee Benefits Expenses

Salaries and wages	₹2,30,000
Director's remuneration	80,000
Total	3,10,000

10. Finance Costs

Interest on Debentures	₹27,000
Add: Interest due	27,000
Total	54,000

11. Other Expenses

Rates and taxes	₹17,000
Insurance	25,000
Audit fees	30,000
Rent	90,000
Bad debts	18,000
Provision for bad debts	7,900
Loss on investment	10,000
Other expenses	37,100
Total	2,35,000

Corporate Reports

LO 4.2 Explain Corporate Governance Report and other reports

Corporates have to annex to their financial statements the corporate reports specified by the Companies Act. We discuss here the following reports: **(i)** Report of the Board of Directors, **(ii)** Management Discussion and Analysis, and **(iii)** Corporate Governance Report. **The major highlights of Corporate Reports of the Reliance Industries Ltd for 2018 are given in Annexure 4.III given at the end of chapter.**

Report of Board of Directors

The directors' report is an important constituent of corporate reports. It provides information relating to the past performance and future prospects of the company. The Companies Act requires the Board's report to provide information relating to **(a)** the state of the company's affairs; **(b)** the amount proposed to be carried to any reserves; **(c)** the amount recommended to be paid as dividends; **(d)** the material changes and commitments, if any, affecting the financial position of the company which have occurred between the end of the financial year of the company to which the balance sheet relates and the date of the report; **(e)** the conservation of energy, technology absorption, foreign exchange earnings and outgo in such manner as may be prescribed.

The Board report also should provide, so far as is material/important for the appreciation of the state of the company's affairs by its members and will not in the Board's opinion be harmful to the business of the company or any of its subsidiaries, about the changes which have occurred during the financial year **(a)** in the nature of the company's business; **(b)** in the nature of business carried on by its subsidiaries; and **(c)** generally in the class of businesses in which the company has an interest.

The Board report, *inter-alia,* should include a Directors' Responsibility Statement, indicating therein: **(a)** that the applicable accounting standards have been followed along with proper explanation to any material departure **(b)** that the Directors have selected such accounting policies and applied them consistently and made judgments and estimates that are reasonable and prudent so as to give a true and fair view of the state of affairs of the company at the end of the financial year and of its P&L A/c for the period **(c)** that the Directors have ensured maintenance of adequate accounting records in accordance with the provisions of Companies Act for safeguarding the assets of the company and for preventing and detecting frauds and other irregularities **(d)** that the directors had prepared the annual accounts on a going concern basis. The Board should also give the fullest information and explanations in its report on every reservation, qualification or adverse remark contained in the auditor's report.

Management Discussion and Analysis

Management's discussion and analysis is a discussion by management of the company's operating results, liquidity, solvency and other important developments having a bearing on the future performance of the company, such as uncertainties/risks faced by the company, opportunities and threats to the company's business, change in Government policy and its impact on the company's future prospects, impact of new accounting statement on the company's financial statements and so on.

Corporate Governance Report

Corporate governance refers to the distribution of rights and responsibilities among different participants in the company and spells out rules and procedures for making decision on corporate affairs.

Corporate governance refers to the distribution of rights and responsibilities among different participants in the company such as the Board of Directors, management, shareholders and other stakeholders (i.e., lenders and creditors) and spells out rules and procedures for making decisions on corporate affairs. The core principles of corporate governance practices are fairness, transparency, accountability and responsibility. In recognition of the importance of corporate governance as an integral part of corporate financial practices, the SEBI has mandated corporate governance in the listing requirement in Clause 49 of the Listing Agreement. There should be a separate section on corporate governance in the annual report of a company, with a detailed compliance report on corporate governance. The suggested list of mandatory items to be included in the report on corporate governance in the annual report of the companies are given in Exhibit 4.3. The non-mandatory requirements are listed in Exhibit 4.4.

EXHIBIT 4.3 Suggested List of Items to be Mandatorily Included in the Report on Corporate Governance in the Annual Report of Companies

1. A brief statement on company's philosophy on code of governance.
2. Board of Directors
   - **(i)** Composition and category of directors, for example, promoter, executive, non-executive, independent non-executive, nominee director, which institution represented as lender or a equity investor.
   - **(ii)** Attendance of each director at the Board of Directors (BOD) meetings and the last AGM.
   - **(iii)** Number of other BODs or Board committees in which he/she is a member or chairperson.
   - **(iv)** Number of BOD meetings held, dates on which held.
3. Audit Committee
   - **(i)** Brief description of terms of reference
   - **(ii)** Composition, name of members and chairperson
   - **(iii)** Meetings and attendance during the year
4. Remuneration Committee
   - **(i)** Brief description of terms of reference
   - **(ii)** Composition, name of members and chairperson
   - **(iii)** Attendance during the year
   - **(iv)** Remuneration policy
   - **(v)** Details of remuneration to all the directors, as per format in main report.
5. Shareholders Committee
   - **(i)** Name of non-executive director heading the committee
   - **(ii)** Name and designation of compliance officer
   - **(iii)** Number of shareholders' complaints received so far
   - **(iv)** Number not solved to the satisfaction of shareholders
   - **(v)** Number of pending complaints
6. General Body Meetings
   - **(i)** Location and time, where last three AGMs were held
   - **(ii)** Whether any special resolutions passed in the previous three AGMs
   - **(iii)** Whether any special resolution passed last year through postal ballot—details of voting pattern
   - **(iv)** Person who conducted the postal ballot exercise
   - **(v)** Whether any special resolution is proposed to be conducted through postal ballot
   - **(vi)** Procedure for postal ballot.
7. Disclosures
   - **(i)** Disclosures on materially significant related party transactions that may have potential conflict with the interests of the company at large
   - **(ii)** Disclosure of accounting treatment, if different, from that prescribed in Accounting Standards with explanation
   - **(iii)** Details of non-compliance by the company, penalties, strictures imposed on the company by stock exchange(s) or SEBI or any statutory authority, on any matter related to capital markets, during the last three years
   - **(iv)** Whistle blower policy and affirmation that no personnel has been denied access to the Audit Committee

8. Means of Communication

(i) Half-yearly report sent to each household of shareholders
(ii) Quarterly results
(iii) Newspapers wherein results normally published
(iv) Any web site, where displayed
(v) Whether it also displays official news releases
(vi) The presentations made to institutional investors or to the analysts
(vii) Whether management decision and analysis (MDA) is a part of annual report or not

9. General Shareholder Information

(i) AGM: Date, time and venue
(ii) Financial calendar
(iii) Date of book closure
(iv) Dividends payment date
(v) Listing on stock exchange(s)
(vi) Stock code
(vii) Market price data: high, low during each month in last financial year
(viii) Performance in comparison to broad-based indices such as BSE sensex, CRISIL index and so on.
(ix) Registrar and transfer agents
(x) Share transfer system
(xi) Distribution of shareholding
(xii) Dematerialisation of shares and liquidity
(xiii) Outstanding GDRs/ADRs/warrants or any convertible instruments, conversion date and likely impact on equity
(xiv) Plant locations
(xv) Address for correspondence

Exhibit 4.4 Non-Mandatory Requirements to be Included in Corporate Governance Report

---

(1) *The Board:* A non-executive Chairman may be entitled to maintain a Chairman's office at the company's expense and also allowed reimbursement of expenses incurred in performance of his duties. Independent Directors may have a tenure not exceeding, in the aggregate, a period of nine years, on the Board of a company.

(2) *Remuneration Committee*

(i) The Board may set up a remuneration committee to determine on their behalf and on behalf of the shareholders with agreed terms of reference, the company's policy on specific remuneration packages for executive directors including pension rights and any compensation payment.

(ii) To avoid conflicts of interest, remuneration committee, which would determine the remuneration packages of the executive directors may comprise of at least three directors, all of whom should be non-executive directors, the Chairman of committee being an independent director.

(iii) All the members of the remuneration committee could be present at the meeting.

(iv) The Chairman of the remuneration committee could be present at the Annual General Meeting, to answer the shareholder queries. However, it would be up to the Chairman to decide who should answer the queries.

(3) *Shareholder Rights:* A half-yearly declaration of financial performance including summary of the significant events in last six-months, may be sent to each household of shareholders.

(4) *Audit Qualifications:* The company may move towards a regime of unqualified financial statements.

(5) *Training of Board Members:* A company may train its Board members in the business model of the company as well as the risk profile of the business parameters of the company, their responsibilities as directors, and the best ways to discharge them.

(6) *Mechanism for Evaluating Non-executive Board Members*: The performance evaluation of non-executive directors could be done by a peer group comprising the entire Board of Directors, excluding the director being evaluated; and Peer Group evaluation could be the mechanism to determine whether to extend/continue the terms of appointment of non-executive directors.

(7) *Whistle Blower Policy:* The company may establish a mechanism for employees to report to the management concerns about unethical behaviour, actual or suspected fraud or violation of the company's code of conduct or ethics policy. This mechanism could also provide for adequate safeguards against victimisation of employees who avail of the mechanism and also provide for direct access to the Chairman and the Audit Committee in exceptional cases. Once established, the existence of the mechanism may be appropriately communicated within the organisation.

Compliance Report on Corporate Governance The company should obtain a certificate from either the auditor or practicing company secretary regarding compliance of conditions of corporate governance as stipulated in Clause 49. The compliance certificate should be annexed with the director's report which, in turn, is sent annually to all the shareholders of the company. The contents of quarterly compliance report on corporate governance is provided in Exhibit 4.5. Non-compliance of any mandatory requirement, that is, which is a part of the listing agreement with reasons thereof and the extent to which the non-mandatory requirements adopted should be specifically highlighted.

EXHIBIT 4.5 Quarterly Compliance Report on Corporate Governance

Name of the Company:
Quarter ending on:

Particulars	*Clause of Listing Agreement*	*Compliance Status Yes/No*	*Remarks*
I. Board of Directors	49 I		
(A) Composition of Board	49 (IA)		
(B) Non-executive Director's compensation and disclosures	49 (IB)		
(C) Other provisions as to Board and Committees	49 (IC)		
(D) Code of Conduct	49 (ID)		
II. Audit Committee	49 (II)		
(A) Qualified and Independent Audit Committee	49 (IIA)		
(B) Meeting of the Audit Committee	49 (IIB)		
(C) Powers of Audit Committee	49 (IIC)		

(Contd.)

(Contd.)

(D) Role of Audit Committee	49 (IID)
(E) Review of Information by Audit Committee	49 (IIE)
III. Subsidiary Companies	49 (III)
IV. Disclosures	49 (IV)
(A) Basis of Related Party Transactions	49 (IVA)
(B) Board Disclosures	49 (IVB)
(C) Proceeds From Public Issues, Rights Issues, Preferential Issues etc.	49 (IVC)
(D) Remuneration of Directors	49 (IVD)
(E) Management	49 (IVE)
(F) Shareholders	49 (IVF)
V. CEO/CFO Certification	49 (V)
VI. Report on Corporate Governance	49 (VI)
VII. Compliance	49 (VII)

Notes: (1) The details under each head shall be provided to incorporate all the information required as per the provisions of the Clause 49 of the Listing Agreement.

(2) In Column 3, compliance or non-compliance may be indicated by Yes/No/N.A. For example, if the Board has been composed in accordance with the Clause 49 (I) of the Listing Agreement, "Yes" may be indicated. Similarly, in case the company has no related party transactions, the words "N.A." may be indicated against 49 (IV-A).

(3) In the remarks column, reasons for non-compliance may be indicated, for example, in case of requirement related to circulation of information to the shareholders, which would be done only in the AGM/EGM, it might be indicated in the "Remarks" column as – "will be complied with at the AGM". Similarly, in respect of matters which can be complied with only where the situation arises, for example, "Report on Corporate Governance" is to be a part of Annual Report only, the words "will be complied in the next Annual Report" may be indicated.

Reporting Under Select Accounting Standards

LO 4.3 Analyse reporting under select accounting standards

The reporting requirement under select accounting standards are discussed below. The reporting standards are: **(i)** Ind AS-24: Related Party Disclosures, **(ii)** Ind AS-27: Consolidated and Separate Financial Statements, **(iii)** Ind AS-28: Investment in Associates, **(iv)** Ind AS-34: Interim Financial Reporting, **(v)** Ind AS-101: First time Adoption of Indian ASs, **(vi)** Ind AS-105: Non Current Assets Held for Sale, **(vii)** Ind AS-107: Financial Instruments Disclosures, and **(viii)** Ind AS-108: Operating Segments.

Ind AS-24: Related Party Disclosures

Objective

The objective of this standard is to ensure that an entity's financial statements contain the disclosures necessary to draw attention to the possibility that its financial position and profit or loss may have been affected by the existence of related parties and by transactions and outstanding balances, including commitments, with such parties.

Definitions

A related party is a person or entity that is related to the entity and preparing its financial statements. It implies (a) A person or a close member of that person's family related to a reporting entity if that person: (i) has control or joint control over the reporting entity; (ii) has significant influence over the reporting entity; or (iii) is a member of the key management personnel of the reporting entity or of a parent of the reporting entity. (b) An entity is related to a reporting entity if any of the following conditions applies: (i) The entity and the reporting entity are members of the same group (which means that each parent, subsidiary and fellow subsidiary is related to the others); (ii) One entity is an associate or joint venture of the other entity (or an associate or joint venture of a member of a group of which the other entity is a member); (iii) Both entities are joint ventures of the same third party; (iv) One entity is a joint venture of a third entity and the other entity is an associate of the third entity; (v) The entity is a post-employment benefit plan for the benefit of employees of either the reporting entity or an entity related to the reporting entity; (vi) The entity is controlled or jointly controlled by a person identified in (a); and (vii) A person identified in (a)(i) has significant influence over the entity or is a member of the key management personnel of the entity (or of a parent of the entity).

A related party transaction is a transfer of resources, services or obligations between a reporting entity and a related party, regardless of whether a price is charged.

Close members of the family of a person are the persons specified within meaning of 'relative' under the Companies Act 2013 and that person's domestic partner, children of that person's domestic partner and dependants of that person's domestic partner.

Control is the power to govern the financial and operating policies of an entity so as to obtain benefits from its activities.

Joint control is the contractually agreed sharing of control over an economic activity.

Key management personnel are those persons having authority and responsibility for planning, directing and controlling the activities of the entity, directly or indirectly, including any director (whether executive or otherwise) of that entity.

Significant influence is the power to participate in the financial and operating policy decisions of an entity, but is not control over those policies. Significant influence may be gained by share ownership, statute or agreement.

Government refers to government, government agencies and similar bodies whether local, national or international.

A government-related entity is an entity that is controlled, jointly controlled or significantly influenced by a government.

Disclosure

Relationships between a parent and its subsidiaries are required to be disclosed irrespective of whether there have been transactions between them or not.

An entity would disclose key management personnel compensation in total and for each of the following categories: (a) short-term employee benefits; (b) post-employment benefits; (c) other long-term benefits; (d) termination benefits; and (e) share-based payment.

If an entity has had related party transactions during the periods covered by the financial statements, it would disclose the nature of the related party relationship as well as information about those transactions and outstanding balances, including commitments, necessary for users to understand the potential effect of the relationship on the financial statements. At a minimum, disclosures should include: (a) the amount of the transactions; (b) the amount of outstanding balances, including commitments, and: (i) their terms and conditions, including whether they are secured, and the nature of the consideration to be provided in settlement; and (ii) details of any guarantees given or received; (c) provisions for doubtful debts related to the amount of outstanding balances; and (d) the expense recognised during the period in respect of bad or doubtful debts due from related parties.

The disclosures (stated above) would be made separately for each of the following categories: (a) the parent; (b) entities with joint control or significant influence over the entity; (c) subsidiaries; (d) associates; (e) joint ventures in which the entity is a venturer; (f) key management personnel of the entity or its parent; and (g) other related parties.

In the case of government-related entities, reporting entity is exempt from the above disclosure requirements in relation to related party transactions and outstanding balances, including commitments, with: (a) a government that has control, joint control or significant influence over the reporting entity; and (b) another entity that is a related party because the same government has control, joint control or significant influence over both the reporting entity and the other entity.

Ind AS-27: Consolidated and Separate Financial Statements

Scope

This standard is to be applied in the preparation and presentation of consolidated financial statements for a group of entities under the control of a parent. It would also be applicable in accounting for investments in subsidiaries, jointly controlled entities and associates when an entity elects, or is required by law, to present separate financial statements.

Definitions

Consolidated financial statements are the financial statements of a group presented as those of a single economic entity.

A group is a parent and all its subsidiaries. A parent is an entity that has one or more subsidiaries.

Separate financial statements are those presented by a parent, in a jointly controlled entity.

A subsidiary is an entity, including an unincorporated entity such as a partnership, that is controlled by another entity (known as the parent).

A parent is required to present consolidated financial statements in which it consolidates its investments in subsidiaries in accordance with this standard and in the desired format. Consolidated financial statements would include all subsidiaries of the parent.

Control is presumed to exist when the parent owns, directly or indirectly through subsidiaries, more than half of the voting power of an entity unless, in exceptional circumstances, it can be clearly demonstrated that such ownership does not constitute control. It also exists when the parent owns half or less of the voting power of an entity when there is: (a) power over more than half of the voting rights by virtue of an agreement with other investors; (b) power to govern the financial and operating policies of the entity under a statute or an agreement; (c) power to appoint or remove the majority of the members of the board of directors or equivalent governing body and control of the entity is by that board or body; or (d) power to cast the majority of votes at meetings of the board of directors or equivalent governing body and control of the entity is by that board or body.

Preparation of Financial Statements

The financial statements of the parent and its subsidiaries used in the preparation of the consolidated financial statements should be prepared as of the same date. When the end of the reporting period of the parent is different from that of a subsidiary, the subsidiary prepares, for consolidation purposes, additional financial statements as of the same date as the financial statements of the parent unless it is impracticable to do so.

When, the financial statements of a subsidiary used in the preparation of consolidated financial statements are prepared as of a date different from that of the parent's financial statements, adjustments should be made for the effects of significant transactions or events that occur between that date and the date of the parent's financial statements. Further, the difference between the end of the reporting period of the subsidiary and that of the parent should not be more than three months. The length of the reporting periods and any difference between the ends of the reporting periods should be the same from period to period.

Consolidated financial statements are required to be prepared using uniform accounting policies for like transactions and other events in similar circumstances.

For preparing separate financial statements, the entity would account for investments in subsidiaries, jointly controlled entities and associates either: (a) at cost, or (b) in accordance with **Ind AS-39**. The entity would apply the same accounting for each category of investments. Investments accounted for at cost would be accounted for in accordance with **Ind AS-105**. The measurement of investments accounted for in accordance with **Ind AS-39** is not changed in such circumstances. An entity is required to recognise a dividend from a subsidiary, jointly controlled entity or associate in profit or loss in its separate financial statements when its right to receive the dividend is established.

Disclosures

The following disclosures are to be made in **consolidated financial statements**: (a) the nature of the relationship between the parent and a subsidiary when the parent does not own, directly or indirectly through subsidiaries, more than half of the voting power; (b) the reasons why the ownership, directly or indirectly through subsidiaries, of more than half of the voting or potential voting power of an investee does not constitute control; (c) the end of the reporting period of the financial statements of a subsidiary when such financial statements are used to prepare consolidated financial statements and are as of a date or for a period that is different from that of the parent's consolidated and separate financial statements, and the reason for using a different date or period; (d) the nature and extent of any significant restrictions (e.g. resulting from borrowing arrangements or regulatory requirements) on the ability of subsidiaries to transfer funds to the parent in the form of cash dividends or to repay loans or advances; (e) a schedule that shows the effects of any changes in a parent's ownership interest in a subsidiary that do not result in a loss of control on the equity attributable to owners of the parent; and (f) if control of a subsidiary is lost, the parent is to disclose the gain or loss, if any.

Separate financial statements of a parent, venturer with an interest in a jointly controlled entity or an investor in an associate would disclose: (a) that the statements are separate financial statements; (b) a list of significant investments in subsidiaries, jointly controlled entities and associates, including the name, country of incorporation or residence, proportion of ownership interest and, if different, proportion of voting power held; and (c) a description of the method used to account for the investments listed under (b); and would identify that the financial statements have been prepared in accordance with this Standard or **Ind AS-28** and **Ind AS-31** to which they relate.

Ind AS-28: Investments in Associates

Scope

This standard is to be applied in accounting for investments in associates. However, it does not apply to investments in associates held by venture capital organisations; such investments are shown at fair value through profit or loss or are classified as held for trading and accounted for in accordance with **Ind AS-39**. Such investments are to be measured at fair value in accordance with **Ind AS-39**, with changes in fair value recognised in profit or loss in the period of the change.

Definitions

An associate is an entity, including an unincorporated entity such as a partnership, over which the investor has significant influence and that is neither a subsidiary nor an interest in a joint venture.

Consolidated financial statements are the financial statements of a group presented as those of a single economic entity. Control is the power to govern the financial and operating policies of an entity so as to obtain benefits from its activities. The equity method is a method of accounting whereby the investment is initially recognised at cost and adjusted thereafter for the post-acquisition change in the investor's share of net assets of the investee. The profit or loss of the investor includes the investor's share of the profit or loss of the investee.

Separate financial statements are those presented by a parent, an investor in an associate or a venturer in a jointly controlled entity, in which the investments are accounted for on the basis of the direct equity interest rather than on the basis of the reported results and net assets of the investees.

An investment in an associate would be accounted for in the investor's separate financial statements

A subsidiary is an entity, including an unincorporated entity such as a partnership, that is controlled by another entity (known as the parent).

Disclosure

The disclosures to be made include: (a) the fair value of investments in associates for which there are published price quotations; (b) summarised financial information of associates, including the aggregated amounts of assets, liabilities, revenues and profit or loss; (c) the reasons of the presumption that an investor significant influence even when it holds, directly or indirectly through subsidiaries, less than 20 per cent of the voting or potential voting power of the investee; (d) the reasons when an investor holds, directly or indirectly through subsidiaries, 20 per cent or more of the voting or potential voting power of the investee but concludes that it does not have significant influence; (e) the end of the reporting period of the financial statements of an associate, when such financial statements are used in applying the equity method and are as of a date or for a period that is different from that of the investor, and the reason for using a different date or different period; and (f) the nature and extent of any significant restrictions (for example, resulting from borrowing arrangements or regulatory requirements) on the ability of associates to transfer funds to the investor in the form of cash dividends, or repayment of loans or advances.

Further, investments in associates accounted for using the equity method are to be classified as non-current assets. The investor's share of the profit or loss of such associates, and the carrying amount of those investments, are to be separately disclosed. The investor's share of any discontinued operations of such associates would also be separately disclosed.

The investor's share of changes recognised in other comprehensive income by the associate would be recognised by the investor in other comprehensive income.

In accordance with **Ind AS-37** Provisions, Contingent Liabilities and Contingent Assets, the investor is required to disclose: (a) its share of the contingent liabilities of an associate incurred jointly with other investors; and (b) those contingent liabilities that arise because the investor is severally liable for all or part of the liabilities of the associate.

Ind AS-34: Interim Financial Reporting

Objective

Timely and reliable interim financial reporting improves the ability of investors, creditors, and others to understand an entity's capacity to generate earnings and cash flows and its financial condition and liquidity. Therefore, the objective of this standard is to prescribe the minimum content of an interim financial report (as per prescribed principles) in complete or condensed financial statements for an interim period.

Definitions

Interim period is a financial reporting period shorter than a full financial year.

Interim financial report means a financial report containing either a complete set of financial statements (as described in **Ind AS-1** Presentation of Financial Statements or a set of condensed financial statements as described in this standard) for an interim period.

In the interest of timeliness and cost considerations and to avoid repetition of information previously reported, an entity may be required to or may elect to provide less information at interim dates as compared with its annual financial statements. This standard defines the minimum content of an interim financial report as including condensed financial statements and selected explanatory notes. The interim financial report is intended to provide an update on the latest complete set of annual financial statements. Accordingly, it focuses on new activities, events, and circumstances and does not duplicate information previously reported.

Applying the Recognition and Measurement Principles

The measurement procedures to be followed in an interim financial report would be designed to ensure that the resulting information is reliable and that all material financial information that is relevant to an understanding of the financial position or performance of the entity is appropriately disclosed. While measurements in both annual and interim financial reports are often based on reasonable estimates, the preparation of interim financial reports generally will require a greater use of estimation methods than annual financial reports periods.

A change in accounting policy, other than one for which the transition is specified by a new Indian Accounting Standard, would be reflected by: (a) restating the financial statements of prior interim periods of the current financial year and the comparable interim periods of any prior financial years that will be restated in the annual financial statements in accordance with **Ind AS-8**; or (b) when it is impracticable to determine the cumulative effect at the beginning of the financial year of applying a new accounting policy to all prior periods, adjusting the financial statements of prior interim periods of the current financial year, and comparable interim periods of prior financial years to apply the new accounting policy prospectively from the earliest date practicable.

Minimum Components of an Interim Financial Report

An interim financial report shall include, at a minimum, the following components: (a) a condensed balance sheet (including condensed statement of changes in equity for the period which is presented as a part of the balance sheet); (b) a condensed statement of profit and loss; a condensed statement of cash flows; and (c) selected explanatory notes.

Form and Content of Interim Financial Statements If an entity publishes a complete set of financial statements in its interim financial report, the form and content of those statements should conform to the requirements of **Ind AS-1** for a complete set of financial statements.

If an entity publishes a set of condensed financial statements in its interim financial report, those condensed statements would include, at a minimum, each of the headings and subtotals that were included in its most recent annual financial statements and the selected explanatory notes as required by this standard. Additional line items or notes are to be included if their omission would make the condensed interim financial statements misleading.

In the statement that presents the components of profit or loss for an interim period, an entity would also present basic and diluted earnings per share for that period.

Disclosures

In addition to disclosing significant events and transactions, an entity should include the following information, in the notes to its interim financial statements, if not disclosed elsewhere in the interim financial report: (a) a statement that the same accounting policies and methods of computation are followed in the interim financial statements as followed in the most recent annual financial statements or, if those policies or methods have been changed, a description of the nature and effect of the change; (b) explanatory comments about the seasonality or cyclicality of interim operations; (c) the nature and amount of items affecting assets, liabilities, equity, net income or cash flows that are unusual because of their nature, size or incidence; (d) the nature and amount of changes in estimates of amounts reported in prior interim periods of the current financial year or changes in estimates of amounts reported in prior financial years; (e) issues, repurchases and repayments of debt and equity securities; (f) dividends paid (aggregate or per share) separately for ordinary shares and other shares; (g) the following segment information (disclosure of segment information is required in an entity's interim financial report only if Ind AS 108 Operating Segments requires that entity to disclose segment information in its annual financial statements): (i) revenues from external customers, if included in the measure of segment profit or loss reviewed by the chief operating decision maker or otherwise regularly provided to the chief operating decision maker; (ii) inter-segment revenues, if included in the measure of segment profit or loss reviewed by the chief operating decision maker or otherwise regularly provided to the chief operating decision maker; (iii) a measure of segment profit or loss; (iv) total assets for which there has been a material change from the amount disclosed in the last annual financial statements; (v) a description of differences from the last annual financial statements in the basis of segmentation or in the basis of measurement of segment profit or loss; (vi) a reconciliation of the total of the reportable segments' measures of profit or loss to the entity's profit or loss before tax expense (tax income) and discontinued operations. Material reconciling items would be separately identified and described in that reconciliation; (h) events after the interim period that have not been reflected in the financial statements for the interim period; (i) the effect of changes in the composition of the entity during the interim period, including business combinations, obtaining or losing control of subsidiaries and long-term investments, restructurings, and discontinued operations.

Disclosure of Compliance with Indian Accounting Standards If an entity's interim financial report is in compliance with this standard, that fact is to be disclosed. An interim financial report would not be considered as complying with Indian Accounting Standards unless it complies with all of the requirements of Indian Accounting Standards in preparation and presentation of interim financial statements.

Interim reports would include interim financial statements (condensed or complete) for periods as follows: (a) (i) balance sheet as at the end of the current interim period and a comparative balance sheet as at the end of the immediately preceding financial year and (ii) statement of changes in equity (which is presented as a part of the balance sheet) cumulatively for the current financial year to date, with a comparative statement for the comparable year-to-date period of the immediately preceding financial year; (b) statements of profit and loss for the current interim period and cumulatively for the current financial year to date, with comparative statements of profit and loss for the comparable interim periods (current and year-to-date) of the immediately preceding financial year; (c) statement of cash flows cumulatively for the current financial year to date, with a comparative statement for the comparable year-to-date period of the immediately preceding financial year.

In deciding how to recognise, measure, classify, or disclose an item for interim financial reporting purposes, materiality is to be assessed in relation to the interim period financial data. In making assessments of materiality, interim measurements may rely on estimates to a greater extent than measurements of annual financial data.

Disclosure in Annual Financial Statements If an estimate of an amount reported in an interim period is changed significantly during the final interim period of the financial year but a separate financial report is not published for that final interim period, the nature and amount of that change in estimate is required to be disclosed in a note to the annual financial statements for that financial year.

An entity would apply the same accounting policies in its interim financial statements as are applied in its annual financial statements, except for accounting policy changes made after the date of the most recent annual financial statements that are to be reflected in the next annual financial statements. However, the frequency of an entity's reporting (annual, half-yearly, or quarterly) should not affect the measurement of its annual results. For the purpose, measurements for interim reporting purposes would be made on a year-to-date basis. Revenues received seasonally, cyclically, or occasionally deferred as of an interim date if anticipation or deferral would not be appropriate at the end of the entity's financial year. Likewise, costs that are incurred unevenly during an entity's financial year should be anticipated or deferred for interim reporting purposes if, and only if, it is also appropriate to anticipate or defer that type of cost at the end of the financial year.

Ind AS-101: First-time Adoption of Indian Accounting Standards

Objective

The objective of this Indian Accounting Standard **(Ind-AS)** is to ensure that an entity's first Ind-AS financial statements, and its interim financial reports for part of the period covered by those financial statements, contain high quality information that: (a) is transparent for users and comparable over all periods presented; (b) provides a suitable starting point for accounting in accordance with **Ind-ASs**; and (c) can be generated at a cost that does not exceed the benefits.

Accounting policies

An entity would use the same accounting policies in its opening **Ind-AS** balance sheet and throughout all periods presented in its first **Ind-AS** financial statements. Those accounting policies are required to comply with each **Ind-AS** effective at the end of its first **Ind-AS** reporting period, with certain exceptions.

Estimates

An entity's estimates in accordance with **Ind-ASs** at the date of transition to **Ind-ASs** should be consistent with estimates made for the same date in accordance with previous GAAP (after adjustments to reflect any difference in accounting policies), unless there is objective evidence that those estimates were in error.

Comparative Information

To comply with **Ind AS-1**, an entity's first Ind-AS financial statements would include at least three balance sheets (including two statements of changes in equity), two statements of profit and loss, two statements of cash flows and related notes for those periods. However, in accordance with this **Ind-AS**, a first time adopter need not provide the corresponding previous period financial statements in accordance with Ind-AS when it reports its first **Ind-AS** financial statements. Irrespective of any of the following two options elected, in terms of this **Ind AS** the first time adopter is required to present latest corresponding previous periods' financial statements prepared as per the previous GAAP when presenting its first **Ind-AS** financial statements: (a) The first **Ind-AS** financial statements includes only two balance sheets (including one statement of changes in equity) and one statement of profit and loss, one statement of cash flows and related notes for the financial year prepared under **Ind-AS**. This first **Ind-AS** financial statements would include the previous years' comparative figures as per the previous GAAP. For example, a first time adopter for whom the first reporting period is financial statements for the year ending March 31, 2016 would only provide two Balance Sheets (including one statement of changes in equity) i.e. April 1, 2015 and March 31, 2016 and one statement of profit and loss, one statement of cash flows and related notes for the financial year ending March 31, 2016, accompanied by reclassified previous years financial statements for the year ending March 31, 2015 as per the previous GAAP to the extent practicable; or (b) In addition to (a) above, voluntarily provide the previous years' comparatives corresponding to the first **Ind-AS** financial statements also under Ind-AS on a memorandum basis. Only for compilation of previous years comparative financial statements under **Ind-ASs** on a memorandum basis the entity would assume that the deemed date of transition as at the beginning of the comparative period.

An entity's comparative financial statements under **Ind-ASs** should apply consistent accounting policies for the first **Ind- AS** financial statements and comparative period. However, it is entitled to the optional exemptions and exceptions prescribed in this standard consistently both as at the date of transition, i.e, beginning date of the financial year for which an entity presents financial information under Ind-ASs and deemed date of transition, i.e, beginning date of the comparative financial year for which an entity presents financial information under **Ind-ASs**. For example, the first time adopter for whom the first reporting period is financial statements for the year ending March 31, 2016 would apply the exemptions and exceptions as at April 1, 2014 and April 1, 2015; accordingly the Balance Sheet as at end of March 31, 2015 may not be equivalent to the opening Balance Sheet as at April 1, 2015.

Ind AS-105: Non-current Assets Held for Sale and Discontinued Operations

Objective

The objective of this standard is to specify the accounting for non-current assets held for sale, and the presentation and disclosure of discontinued operations. In particular, the standard requires: (a) assets that meet the criteria to be classified as held for sale should be measured at the lower of carrying amount and fair value less costs to sell, and depreciation on such assets cease to be charged; and (b) assets that meet the criteria to be classified as held for sale should be presented separately in the balance sheet; and (c) the results of discontinued operations should be presented separately in the statement of profit and loss.

Measurement of a Non-current Asset (or Disposal Group)

An entity would measure a non-current asset (or disposal group) classified as held for sale at the lower of its carrying amount and fair value less costs to sell.

An entity would measure a non-current asset (or disposal group) classified as held for distribution to owners at the lower of its carrying amount and fair value less costs to distribute.

An entity would present and disclose information that enables users of the financial statements to evaluate the financial effects of discontinued operations and disposals of non-current assets (or disposal groups). Any gain or loss on the remeasurement of a non-current asset (or disposal group) classified as held for sale that does not meet the definition of a discontinued operation shall be included in profit or loss from continuing operations.

Disclosure

An entity would disclose the following information in the notes in the period in which a non-current asset (or disposal group) has been either classified as held for sale or sold: (a) a description of the non-current asset; (b) a description of the facts and circumstances of the sale, or leading to the expected disposal, and the expected manner and timing of that disposal; (c) the gain or loss recognised (as per the prescription of this standard), and the caption in the statement of profit and loss that includes that gain or loss; (d) if applicable, the reportable segment in which the non-current asset (or disposal group) is presented in accordance with **Ind AS-108** Operating Segments.

Ind AS-107: Financial Instruments: Disclosures

An entity would disclose information that enables users of its financial statements to evaluate the significance of financial instruments for its financial position and performance; such a disclosure enables them to evaluate the nature and extent of risks arising from financial instruments to which the entity is exposed at the end of the reporting period and how they have been managed. These risks typically include, but are not limited to, credit risk, liquidity risk and market risk. Qualitative and quantitative disclosures contribute to disclosure of information in a way that better enables users to evaluate an entity's exposure to risks.

Disclosure

Qualitative Disclosures For each type of risk arising from financial instruments, an entity would disclose: (a) the exposures to risk and how they arise; (b) its objectives, policies and processes for managing the risk and the methods used to measure the risk; and (c) any changes in (a) or (b) from the previous period.

Quantitative Disclosures For each type of risk arising from financial instruments, an entity is required to disclose: summary quantitative data about its exposure to that risk at the end of the reporting period. This disclosure would be based on the information provided internally to key management personnel of the entity (as defined in **Ind AS-24** Related Party Disclosures), for example the entity's board of directors or chief executive officer.

In case, the quantitative data disclosed as at the end of the reporting period are unrepresentative of an entity's exposure to risk during the period, an entity is required to provide further information that is representative.

Credit Risk Disclosure (a) the amount that best represents its maximum exposure to credit risk at the end of the reporting period without taking account of any collateral held or other credit enhancements; this disclosure is not required for financial instruments whose carrying amount best represents the maximum exposure to credit risk; (b) a description of collateral held as security and other credit enhancements and their financial effect (e.g. a quantification of the extent to which collateral and other credit enhancements mitigate credit risk) in respect of the amount that best represents the maximum exposure to credit risk; (c) information about the credit quality of financial assets that are neither past due nor impaired; and financial assets that are either past due or impaired

An entity would disclose by class of financial asset: (a) an analysis of the age of financial assets that are past due as at the end of the reporting period but not impaired; and (b) an analysis of financial assets that are individually determined to be impaired as at the end of the reporting period, including the factors the entity considered in determining that they are impaired; and collateral and other credit enhancements obtained.

When an entity obtains financial or non-financial assets during the period by taking possession of collateral it holds as security or calling on other credit enhancements (e.g. guarantees), and such assets meet the recognition criteria in other Indian Accounting Standards, an entity would disclose for such assets held at the reporting date: (a) the nature and carrying amount of the assets; and (b) when the assets are not readily convertible into cash, its policies for disposing of such assets or for using them in its operations.

Liquidity Risk Disclosure An entity would disclose: (a) a maturity analysis for non-derivative financial liabilities (including issued financial guarantee contracts) that shows the remaining contractual maturities; (b) a maturity analysis for derivative financial liabilities. The maturity analysis would include the remaining contractual maturities for those derivative financial liabilities for which contractual maturities are essential for an understanding of the timing of the cash flows; (c) a description of how it manages the liquidity risk inherent in (a) and (b).

Market Risk Disclosure An entity would disclose: (a) a sensitivity analysis for each type of market risk to which the entity is exposed at the end of the reporting period, showing how profit or loss and equity would have been affected by changes in the relevant risk variable that were reasonably possible at that date; (b) the methods and assumptions used in preparing the sensitivity analysis; and (c) changes from the previous period in the methods and assumptions used, and the reasons for such changes.

If an entity prepares a sensitivity analysis, such as value-at-risk, that reflects interdependencies between risk variables (e.g. interest rates and exchange rates) and uses it to manage financial risks, it may use that sensitivity analysis in place of the analysis specified in this regard in this standard. The entity would also disclose: (a) an explanation of the method used in preparing such a sensitivity analysis, and of the main parameters and assumptions underlying the data provided; and (b) an explanation of the objective of the method used and of limitations that may result in the information not fully reflecting the fair value of the assets and liabilities involved.

Other Market Risk Disclosures When the sensitivity analyses disclosed in accordance with (preceding two paragraphs) are unrepresentative of a risk inherent in a financial instrument (for example because the year-end exposure does not reflect the exposure during the year), the entity is required disclose that fact and the reason it believes the sensitivity analyses are unrepresentative.

Ind AS-108: Operating Segments

An entity would disclose information to enable users of its financial statements to evaluate the nature and financial effects of the business activities in which it engages and the economic environments in which it operates.

Definition

An operating segment is a component of an entity: (a) that engages in business activities from which it may earn revenues and incur expenses (including revenues and expenses relating to transactions with other components of the same entity); (b) whose operating results are regularly reviewed by the entity's chief operating decision maker to make decisions about resources to be allocated to the segment and assess its performance; and (c) for which discrete financial information is available.

Not every part of an entity is necessarily an operating segment or part of an operating segment. For example, a corporate headquarters or some functional departments may not earn revenues or may earn revenues that are only incidental to the activities of the entity and would not be operating segments.

Aggregation Criteria

Operating segments often exhibit similar long-term financial performance if they have similar economic characteristics. For example, similar long-term average gross margins for two operating segments would be expected if their economic characteristics were similar. Two or more operating segments may be aggregated into a single operating segment if aggregation is consistent with the core principle of this Indian Accounting Standard, the segments have similar economic characteristics, and the segments are similar in each of the following respects: (a) the nature of the products and services; (b) the nature of the production processes; (c) the type or class of customer for their products and services; (d) the methods used to distribute their products or provide their services; and (e) if applicable, the nature of the regulatory environment, for example, banking, insurance or public utilities.

Quantitative Thresholds

An entity would report separately information about an operating segment that meets any of the following quantitative thresholds: (a) Its reported revenue, including both sales to external customers and inter-segment sales or transfers, is 10 per cent or more of the combined revenue, internal and external, of all operating segments. (b) The absolute amount of its reported profit or loss is 10 per cent or more of the greater, in absolute amount, of (i) the combined reported profit of all operating segments that did not report a loss and (ii) the combined reported loss of all operating segments that reported a loss. (c) Its assets are 10 per cent or more of the combined assets of all operating segments.

Operating segments that do not meet any of the quantitative thresholds may be considered reportable, and separately disclosed, if management believes that information about the segment would be useful to users of the financial statements.

Disclosure

An entity would disclose information to enable users of its financial statements to evaluate the nature and financial effects of the business activities in which it engages and the economic environments in which it operates.

To give effect to the principle, an entity should disclose the following for each period for which a statement of profit and loss is presented: (a) general information as per requirements of this standard; (b) information about reported segment profit or loss, including specified revenues and expenses included in reported segment profit or loss, segment assets, segment liabilities and the basis of measurement, per requirements of this standard; and (c) reconciliations of the totals of segment revenues, reported segment profit or loss, segment assets, segment liabilities and other material segment items to corresponding entity amounts.

An entity would report a measure of profit or loss for each reportable segment. An entity would report a measure of total assets and liabilities for each reportable segment if such amounts are regularly provided to the chief operating decision maker. An entity should also disclose the following about each reportable segment if the specified amounts are included in the measure of segment profit or loss reviewed by the chief operating decision maker, or are otherwise regularly provided to the chief operating decision maker, even if not included in that measure of segment profit or loss: (a) revenues from external customers; (b) revenues from transactions with other operating segments of the same entity; (c) interest revenue; (d) interest expense; (e) depreciation and amortisation; (f) material items of income and expense disclosed in accordance with the requirement of **Ind AS-1** Presentation of Financial Statements; (g) the entity's interest in the profit or loss of associates and joint ventures accounted for by the equity method; (h) income tax expense or income; and (i) material non-cash items other than depreciation and amortisation.

Entity-wide Disclosures

Some entities' business activities are not organised on the basis of differences in related products and services or differences in geographical areas of operations. Such an entity's reportable segments may report revenues from a broad range of essentially different products and services, or more than one of its reportable segments may provide essentially the same products and services. Similarly, an entity's reportable segments may hold assets in different geographical areas and report revenues from customers in different geographical areas, or more than one of its reportable segments may operate in the same geographical area.

Information about Products and Services An entity would report the revenues from external customers for each product and service, or each group of similar products and services, unless the necessary information is not available and the cost to develop it would be excessive, in which case that fact is required to be disclosed.

Information about Geographical Areas An entity would report the following geographical information, unless the necessary information is not available and the cost to develop it would be excessive: (a) revenues from external customers (i) attributed to the entity's country of domicile and (ii) attributed to all foreign countries in total from which the entity derives revenues. If revenues from external customers attributed to an individual foreign country are material, those revenues would be disclosed separately. An entity would disclose the basis for attributing revenues from external customers to individual countries; (b) non-current assets other than financial instruments, deferred tax assets, post-employment benefit assets, and rights arising under insurance contracts (i) located in the entity's country of domicile and (ii) located in all foreign countries in total in which the entity holds assets. If assets in an individual foreign country are material, those assets should be disclosed separately.

The amounts reported would be based on the financial information that is used to produce the entity's financial statements. If the necessary information is not available and the cost to develop it would be excessive, that fact needs to be disclosed. An entity may provide, in addition to the information required, subtotals of geographical information about groups of countries.

Information about Major Customers An entity would provide information about the extent of its reliance on its major customers. If revenues from transactions with a single external customer amount to 10 per cent or more of an entity's revenues, the entity should disclose that fact, the total amount of revenues from each such customer, and the identity of the segment or segments reporting the revenues.

The entity need not disclose the identity of a major customer or the amount of revenues that each segment reports from that customer. For the purposes of this Indian Accounting Standard, a group of entities known to a reporting entity to be under common control would be considered a single customer.

However, judgement is required to assess whether a government (including government agencies and similar bodies whether local, national or international) and entities known to the reporting entity to be under the control of that government are considered a single customer. In assessing this, the reporting entity would consider the extent of economic integration between those entities operating segment.

SUMMARY

- The preparation and presentation of corporate financial statements in India should conform to statutory requirements prescribed by the Companies Act, 2013 and the Indian Accounting Standards (IND AS).
- Section 128 of the Companies Act, 2013 requires every company to keep proper books of accounts with respect to **(a)** all receipts and all payments, **(b)** all expenditures and revenues, **(c)** all sales and purchases and **(d)** all assets and liabilities. In the case of manufacturing companies, details relating to utilisation of materials, labour other items of manufacturing costs are also required.
- Section 129 requires the Board of Directors to present balance sheet as at the end of the period and statement of profit and loss for the period in every annual general meeting.
- Section 129 requires the company's balance sheet and its statement of profit and loss to give a true and fair view of its state of affairs. While the balance sheet should be set out in the prescribed format in accordance with Schedule III of the Companies Act, the statement of profit and loss should include the prescribed contents. Both these financial statements should comply with accounting standards also, wherever applicable.
- Section 134 requires that balance sheet as well as statement of profit and loss should be signed by the manager or secretary (on behalf of the Board of Directors) and by at least two directors of the company, one of whom should be a managing director, if any. The financial statements so authenticated should be submitted to the auditors for their report.
- Section 134 requires the statement of profit and loss and the auditor's report to be annexed to the balance sheet.
- The balance sheet of a company should be presented (in vertical form) in accordance with Part I of Schedule III of the companies Act, 2013. The main heads representing assets are: (a) Non-current assets, and (b) Current assets. The major 'heads' representing equity and liabilities are: (a) Equity, (b) Liabilities, (i) Non-current liabilities, and (ii) Current liabilities.
- While there is no prescribed format for the statement of profit and loss, Part II of Schedule III lays down the requirements to be complied with in its preparation. The statement of profit and loss should be made out in such a manner that it discloses clearly and in a transparent manner the result of the working of the company during the period covered by the account. It requires disclosure of every material feature relating to credits, receipts, debits, expenses both of recurring and non-recurring/exceptional transactions. The major heads representing recurring expenses are: (a) Cost of materials consumed, (b) Purchases of stock, (c) Changes in all types of inventories, (d) Employee benefits expense, (e) Finance costs, (f) Depreciation and amortisation expenses, (g) Other expenses.

LO 4.1

- Corporate report primarily consists of financial statements, external auditor's report, Board of director's report, management discussion and analysis, corporate governance report, compliance report on corporate governance and select accounting standards (facilitating users of financial statements to make projections of an enterprise earnings – generating capacity and cash flows).
- The Board of Director's report provides information, among others, pertaining to the financial state of the company affairs, the dividend amount proposed, appropriations made for various reserves, major events and future plans, foreign exchange earnings and outflows, employee relations, and so on. It also includes a Directors' Responsibility statement stating the **(a)** adherence to the accounting standards, **(b)** selection of prudent accounting policies which are consistently followed and **(c)** response to every reservations, qualification or adverse remark contained in the auditor's report.
- Management discussion and analysis contains forward-looking statements relating to the operating results and company's financial performance, landmark events, likely opportunities and threats faced by the company's business, say, in the wake of change in Government policy.
- Corporate governance refers to the distribution of rights and responsibilities among different participants in the company, such as, the Board of Directors, management, shareholders and other stakeholders such as lenders/creditors and spells out rules and procedures for making decisions on corporate affairs.
- The SEBI has mandated corporate governance as a part of the requirements in Clause 49 of the listing agreement between the corporates and the stock exchange(s). The mandatory contents of the clause relate to **(a)** Board of Directors, **(b)** Audit committee, **(c)** Remuneration committee, **(d)** Shareholders committee, **(e)** General body meeting, **(f)** Disclosures, **(g)** Means of communication and **(h)** General shareholder information.
- Besides mandatory requirements, the company may make voluntary (non-mandatory) disclosures providing **(a)** additional information relating to Board and remuneration committee, **(b)** shareholder rights, **(c)** audit qualifications, **(d)** training of Board members, **(e)** mechanism for evaluating non-executive Board members and **(f)** whistle blower policy.
- A certificate relating to the compliance report on corporate governance should be obtained form either the auditor or practising company secretary. A compliance report should provide compliance status on items such as **(a)** Board of directors, **(b)** Audit committee, **(c)** Subsidiary companies, **(d)** Disclosures, **(e)** CEO/CFO certification and **(f)** Compliance. In the cases of non-compliance, reasons for non-compliance should be stated.

LO 4.2

- The objective of the AS-24 is to ensure that financial statements contain the disclosures necessary to draw attention to the possibility that financial position/profit or loss of an entity may have been affected by the related parties and by transactions/outstanding balances including commitments with them. A related party is a person/ entity related to the entity that is preparing the financial statements. The AS-24 has prescribed the disclosures to be made in the financial statements.
- AS-27 is applicable to the preparation /presentation of consolidated financial statements for a group of entities under common control. It is also applicable in accounting for investments in subsidiaries, jointly controlled entities and associates when an entity elects is required by law to present separate financial statements. The disclosure requirements for consolidate financial statements are specified by it.
- AS-28 is to be applied in accounting for investments in associates, that is, an entity over which the investor has significant influence and it is neither a subsidiary nor interest in joint venture. The financial statements of the investor should include the specified disclosures.
- Timely and reliable interim financial reporting improves the ability of investors, creditors and others to understand an entity's capacity to generate earnings and cash flows and its financial condition and liquidity. The AS-34 prescribes the minimum contents of an interim financial report in complete/condensed

financial statements for an interim period, that is, a reporting period shorter than a full financial year. The minimum components of an interim financial report are laid down by AS-34. The disclosures to be included in the notes to the interim financial statements are also prescribed by it.

- The objective of the AS-101 is to ensure that an entity's first set of financial statements (under Ind ASs) and its interim financial report contain high quality information that (i) is transparent for users and comparable over periods, (ii) provides a suitable starting point for accounting in accordance with the ASs and (iii) can be generated at a cost that does not exceed the benefits.
- The AS-105 specifies the accounting for non-current assets held for sale and the presentation and disclosure of discontinued operations. It requires that such assets should be (i) measured at the lower of carrying cost and fair value less cost to sell, (ii) presented separately in the balance sheet. The results of discontinued operations should be presented separately in the profit/loss statement. The entity should disclose the specified information in the notes to the account.
- The objective of AS-107 is to prescribe disclosures that enable users of financial statements to evaluate the significance of financial instruments for its financial position and performance. Such disclosures enable them to evaluate the nature and extent of risk associated with them to which the entity is exposed and how they have been managed. These risks typically include credit risk, liquidity risk and market risk. Qualitative and quantitative disclosures contribute to disclosure of information in a way that better enables the users to evaluate an entity's exposure to risk.
- An operating segment is a component of an entity (i) that engages in business activities from which it may earn revenues and income expenses, (ii) whose operating results are regularly reviewed to make decision about resources allocated to the segment and assess its performance, and (iii) for which discrete financial information is available. According to the AS-108, an entity should disclose information to enable users of its financial statements to evaluate the nature and financial effects of the business activities in which it engages and the economic environment in which it operates.

LO 4.3

SOLVED PROBLEMS

LO 4.1
LOD: E

P.4.1 From the following balances extracted from the books of Small Toy Limited as at March 31, 2016 (after preparation of the profit and loss account), prepare the balance sheet as at the above data.

Particulars	Dr. Amount	Particulars	Cr. Amount
Plant and machinery (at cost)	₹ 1,00,00,000	Share capital (10,00,000	
Debtors	30,00,000	shares of ₹ 10 each)	₹ 1,00,00,000
Stock at cost	28,00,000	12% Debentures	50,00,000
Cash in hand	7,00,000	Interest accrued on debentures	3,00,000
Bills receivable	5,00,000	General reserve	20,00,000
Investment at market value	37,00,000	Provision for taxation	5,00,000
Loose tools	7,00,000	Provision for depreciation	
Interest accrued on investments	95,000	on plant and machinery	11,50,000
		Provision for bad and doubtful debts	1,00,000
		Profit and loss A/c	10,00,000
		Creditors	9,20,000
		Bills payable	4,80,000
		Accrued expenses	45,000
	2,14,95,000		2,14,95,000

Additional Information:

(1) Debtors include debts of ₹10,00,000, which are outstanding for a period exceeding 6 months.
(2) Debentures are redeemable on or before March 31, 2019.
(3) Investments consist of 2,00,000 shares of ₹10 each of XYZ Ltd, acquired at a cost of ₹40,00,000.

Solution

Name of the Company: Small Toy Limited

Balance Sheet as at March 31, 2016

I	EQUITY AND LIABILITIES	Note No.	Amount as at March 31, 2016
(1)	**Shareholders' funds**		
	(a) Share capital	1	₹ 1,00,00,000
	(b) Reserves and surplus		30,00,000
(2)	**Share application money pending allotment**		Nil
(3)	Non-current liabilities		
	(a) Long-term borrowings		50,00,000
(4)	**Current liabilities**		
	(a) Trade payables	2	14,00,000
	(b) Other current liabilities	3	3,45,000
	(c) Short-term provisions(provision for taxation)		5,00,000
	Total		**2,02,45,000**
II	**ASSETS**		
	Non-current assets		
(1)	(a) Fixed assets		
	(i) Tangible assets	4	88,50,000
	(b) Non-current investments		37,00,000
(2)	**Current assets**		
	(a) Inventories	5	35,00,000
	(b) Trade receivables	6	34,00,000
	(c) Cash and cash equivalents		7,00,000
	(d) Other current assets@		95,000
	Total		**2,02,45,000**

@ Represents interest accrued on investments.

NOTES

1. Share Capital

Authorised share capital	
10,00,000 shares of ₹10 each	₹ 1,00,00,000
Issued and subscribed capital:	
10,00,000 equity shares of ₹10 each	1,00,00,000
Total	1,00,00,000

2. Trade Payables

Bills payables	₹ 4,80,000
Sundry creditors	9,20,000
Total	14,00,000

3. Other Current Liabilities

Interest accrued on debentures	₹ 3,00,000
Accrued expenses	45,000
Total	3,45,000

4. Tangible Assets

Particulars of Assets	Gross Block			Depreciation/ Amortisation	Net Block
Tangible Assets	Gross value	Purchases	Total		
Plant and Machinery	₹ 1,00,00,000	—	₹ 1,00,00,000	₹ 11,50,000	₹ 88,50,000

5. Inventories

Stock at cost	₹ 28,00,000
Loose tools	7,00,000
Total	35,00,000

6. Trade Receivables

Debtors due for more than six months	₹ 10,00,000
Other debtors	20,00,000
Less: Provision for bad debts	(1,00,000)
Bills Receivable	5,00,000
Total	34,00,000

P.4.2 Show the presentation of the following information under the appropriate heads of the balance sheet of a public limited company. **LO 4.1** **LOD: M**

(i) General reserve (beginning) stood at ₹ 30,00,000, profit and loss account (beginning) at ₹ 10,00,000. Profit made during the year was ₹ 60,00,000. Dividend proposed amounted to ₹ 28,00,000. Transfer made to the general reserve was ₹ 20,00,000. Profit and loss (year-end) stood at ₹ 22,00,000.

(ii) The cost of furniture (beginning) was ₹ 34,00,000. Furniture purchased during the year amounted to ₹ 12,00,000. Cost of furniture sold during the year was ₹ 8,00,000. Provision for depreciation (beginning) was ₹ 17,00,000, provision for depreciation (year-end) being ₹ 19,50,000.

(iii) Investments consists of: **(a)** 10,00,000 equity shares of A Ltd. of ₹ 10 each, ₹ 1,20,00,000, **(b)** 1,50,000, 13 per cent debentures of A Ltd of ₹ 100 each, ₹ 1,30,00,000, (c) 1,00,000 equity shares of Z Ltd of ₹ 100 each ₹ 60 called up, ₹ 80,00,000. Share capital of the company comprises 20,00,000 equity shares of ₹ 100 each, ₹ 90 called up and 5,00,000 14 per cent preference shares of ₹ 100 each fully paid up. Dividends on the preference shares are in arrears for the last 3 years.

Solution

(i) Balance Sheet (Equity and Liabilities Side)

Equity and Liabilities		Amount
Reserves and surplus:		
General reserve (beginning)	₹ 30,00,000	
Add transferred from profit and loss account	20,00,000	₹ 50,00,000
Profit and loss (beginning)	10,00,000	
Add profit during the year	60,00,000	
	70,00,000	
Less dividend proposed	28,00,000	
Less transferred to general reserve	20,00,000	22,00,000
Profit and loss (at year end)		
Current, Liabilities:		
(a) Short-term provisions:		
Dividends proposed		28,00,000

(ii) Balance Sheet (Assets Side)

Assets		*Amount*
Non current assets:		
(a) Fixed assets		
(i) Tangible assets		
Furniture at cost (beginning)	₹ 34,00,000	
Additions—purchased during the year	12,00,000	
	46,00,000	
Less cost of furniture sold	8,00,000	
	38,00,000	
Less provision for depreciation at the end	19,50,000	₹ 18,50,000

(iii) Balance Sheet

Equity and Liabilities		*Amount*	*Assets*		*Amount*
Share holders' funds			Non-current assets		
(a) share capital			(a) Non-current investments		
Authorised:			10,00,000 Equity shares of ₹ 10 each fully paid up, of A Ltd.		
Issued: 20,00,000 Equity shares of ₹ 100 each ₹ 20,00,00,000				₹ 1,00,00,000	
5,00,000 14% Preference share of ₹ 100 each	5,00,00,000	₹ 25,00,00,000	1,00,000 equity shares of ₹ 100 each ₹ 60 called up of Z Ltd		
Subscribed:				80,00,000	
20,00,000 Equity shares of ₹ 100 each, ₹ 90 called up ₹ 18,00,00,000			1,50,000 13% Debentures of A Ltd. (valued at cost)	1,30,00,000	₹ 3,10,00,000
5,00,000 14% Preference shares of ₹ 100 each fully paid up	5,00,00,000	₹ 23,00,00,000			

A footnote to the balance sheet: Contingent Liabilities:

1. Arrears of preference dividend for last 3 years, ₹ 2,10,00,000
2. Liability in respect of partly paid shares of Z ltd held by the company uncalled capital, ₹ 40,00,000.

P.4.3 The following is the Trial balance of Amit Ltd., as at March 31, 2016: **LO 4.1** **LOD: D**

(Amount in ₹ lakh)

Particulars	*Dr.*	*Cr.*	*Particulars*	*Dr.*	*Cr.*
Stock (April 1, 2009)	375	—	Purchases return	—	50.0
Purchases and sales	1,225	1,700	Wages	150	—
Discount	—	15	Carriage on purchases	2.75	—
Furniture and fittings	85	—	Salaries	37.5	—
Rent	20	—	Sundry expenses	45.25	—
Share capital 5 lakh shares @ ₹ 100 each)	—	500	Interim dividend	45	—
			Debtors and creditors	137.5	87.5
Plant and machinery	145		Cash at bank	251	—
General reserve	—	77.5	Patents and trade marks	24	—
Bills receivable	25	—	Development rebate reserve		28.0
Bills payable	—	35	Investments	2,250	
Profit and loss A/c (March 31, 2012)	—	75		5,068	5,068.0
10% Debentures	—	2,500			
Debenture interest	250				

Prepare statement of profit and loss for the year ended 31st March, 2016 and balance sheet as at that date after considering the following adjustments:

(i) Stock on 31st March 2016 was valued at ₹840 lakh.
(ii) Make a provision for income tax @ 35 per cent.
(iii) Transfer ₹10 lakh to the Development rebate reserve account on March 31, 2016.
(iv) Create debenture redemption reserve of ₹100 lakh.
(v) Depreciate plant and machinery @ 10 per cent, furniture & fittings @ 10 per cent and patents and trade marks @ 5 per cent.
(vi) On March 31, 2016, outstanding rent amounted to ₹4 lakh while outstanding salaries totaled ₹4.5 lakh.
(vii) Sundry debtors include outstanding ₹25 lakh for more than six months and make a provision for doubtful debts amounting to ₹15 lakh.
(viii) The directors proposed a dividend @ 15 per cent per annum for the year ended March 31, 2016 after transfer of 5 per cent to general reserve.
(ix) Provide for managerial remuneration of ₹45.18 lakh.

Solution

Name of the Company: Amit Limited

Balance Sheet as at March 31, 2016

(Amount in ₹ lakh)

			Note No.	Amount
I	**EQUITY AND LIABILITIES**			
(1)	**Shareholders' funds**			
	(a) Share capital (5 lakh shares @ ₹ 100 each)			₹ 500.00
	(b) Reserves and surplus		1	324.803
(2)	**Share application money pending allotment**			—
(3)	**Non-current liabilities**			
	(a) Long–term borrowings 10% Debentures			2,500.00
(4)	**Current liabilities**			
	(a) Short-term borrowings			
	(b) Trade payables		2	122.50
	(c) Other current liabilities		3	53.68
	(d) Short-term provisions		4	217.317
	Total			**3,718.30**
II	**ASSETS**			
	Non-current assets			
(1)	(a) Fixed assets			
	(i) Tangible assets		5	207.00
	(ii) Intangible assets			
	Patents and trade mark	₹ 24.00		
	Less amortisation	1.20		22.80
	(b) Non-current investments			2,250.00
(2)	**Current assets**			
	(a) Inventories			840.00
	(b) Trade receivables		6	147.50
	(c) Cash and cash equivalents			251.00
	Total			**3,718.30**

Statement of Profit and Loss

for the year ended March 31, 2016

(Amount in ₹ lakh)

	Particulars	Note No.		Amount
I	**Revenue from operations (gross)**			₹1,700.00
II	**Other income (discount received)**			15.00
III	**Total revenue (I+II)**			1,715.00
IV	**Expenses**			
	Purchases of stock-in-trade (₹ 1,225 lakh – ₹ 50 lakh returns)		1,175.00	
	Changes in inventories of finished goods		(465.00)	
	Employee benefits expenses	7	237.18	
	Finance costs (interest on debentures)		250.00	
	Depreciation and amortisation expenses	8	24.20	
	Other expenses	9	87.00	
	Total expenses			1,308.38
V	**Profit before exceptional and extraordinary items and tax (III – IV)**			406.62
VI	**Exceptional items**			-
VII	**Profit before extraordinary items and tax (V + VI)**			406.62
VIII	**Extraordinary items**			-
IX	**Profit before tax (VII + VIII)**			406.62
X	**Tax expenses (provision for taxation) (₹ 406.62 × 0.35)**			142.317
XI	**Profit for the period from continuing operations (IX – X)**			264.303
XII	**Earnings per equity share: Basic (₹264.303 lakh/5 lakh)**			52.86

NOTES

1. Reserves and Surplus

Debenture redemption reserve		₹ 100.00
General reserve:		
As per last balance sheet	₹ 77.50	
Add transfer from profit and loss statement	13.22	90.72
Development rebate reserve:		
As per last balance sheet	28.00	
Add transfer from profit and loss statement	10.00	38.00
Surplus (Deficit):		
As per last balance sheet	75.00	
Add profit for the year	264.303	
Total	339.303	
Less transfer to general reserve	13.22	
Less interim dividend	45.00	
Less proposed dividend	75.00	
Less transfer to debenture redemption reserve	100.00	
Less transfer to development rebate reserve	10.00	96.083
Total		324.803

2. Trade Payables

Sundry creditors	₹ 87.50
Bills payables	35.00
Total	122.50

3. Other Current Liabilities

Outstanding rent	₹ 4.00
Outstanding salaries	4.50
Managerial remuneration payable	45.18
Total	53.68

4. Short Term Provisions

Provision for taxation	₹ 142.317
Proposed dividend	75.00
Total	217.317

5. Tangible Assets

Particulars of Assets	*Gross Block*			*Depreciation/ Amortisation*	*Net Block*
Tangible Assets	*Gross value*	*Purchases*	*Total*		
Plant and Machinery	₹ 145.00	-	₹ 145.00	₹ 14.50	₹ 130.50
Furniture and fittings	85.00	-	85.00	8.50	76.50
Total					207.00

6. Trade Receivables

Debts outstanding for more than six months	₹ 25.00	
Add other debts	112.50	
Total	137.50	
Less: Provision for bad and doubtful debts	15.00	122.50
Bills Receivable		25.00
Total		147.50

7. Employee Benefits Expenses

Wages			₹ 150.00
Salaries	₹ 37.50		
Add payable		4.50	42.00
Managerial remuneration			45.18
Total			237.18

8. Depreciation and Amortisation Expenses

Depreciation on plant and machinery	₹ 14.50
Depreciation on furniture and fittings	8.50
Amortisation on patents and trade mark	1.20
Total	24.20

9. Other Expenses

Carriage on purchases		₹ 2.75
Rent	₹ 20.00	
Plus payable	4.00	24.00
Sundry expenses		45.25
Provision for doubtful debts		15.00
Total		87.00

REVIEW QUESTIONS

LOD: Easy

RQ.4.1 State whether the following statements are true or false. LO 4.1

(a) A company must prepare its profit and loss account in the format as prescribed by the Companies Act.

(b) It is statutory for the company to prepare its balance sheet in the format prescribed in Scheduled III of the Companies Act, 2013.

(c) A company must prepare its balance sheet as well as profit and loss account in the formats prescribed by the Companies Act, 2013.

(d) Schedule III of the Companies Act has prescribed the format for balance sheet and the requirements for the profit and loss account.

(e) Loose tools is an asset which is included under the head, current assets.

(f) Goodwill appears under the head, fixed assets.

(g) Provision for taxation as shown under the head of current liabilities and provisions.

(h) Proposed dividend is shown under the head reserves and surplus.

(i) A company can pay dividends only out of profits of the current year.

(j) Share premium account represents revenue reserves.

[Answer: (a) False, (b) True, (c) True, (d) True, (e) True, (f) True, (g) True, (h) False, (i) False, (j) False]

RQ.4.2 Fill in the blanks: LO 4.1 & 2

(a) SEBI has mandated corporate governance in the listing requirement in clause ____________ of the listing agreement.

(b) Apart from mandatory requirements listed in clause 49, the Board has also discretion to make ____________.

(c) Board of director's report should also include directors ____________ statement.

(d) It is ____________ for corporate enterprises whose equity or debt securities are listed on a recognised stock exchange in India to comply with accounting standards issued by the Institute of Chartered Accountants of India.

(e) Preliminary expenses to the extent not written-off will be shown under the head ____________ of ____________ side of balance sheet.

(f) The word 'fund', in relation to any reserve, should be used only where such a reserve is specifically represented by earmarked ____________.

[Answer: (a) 49, (b) Voluntary disclosures, (c) responsibility, (d) mandatory, (e) miscellaneous expenditures, assets, (f) investment]

RQ.4.3 State the particular items to be disclosed in a company's balance sheet as per Schedule III of the Companies Act 2013 in respect of (a) assets and (b) equity and liabilities. LO 4.1

RQ.4.4 Draw-up pro-forma balance sheet as per the requirements of Schedule III of the Companies Act 2013. LO 4.1

LOD: Medium

RQ.4.5 Name four contingent liabilities which may be shown as a footnote to balance sheet of a company. LO 4.1

RQ.4.6 Write short notes on the following: LO 4.3

(a) Operating segments

(b) Interim financial reporting

(c) Related party disclosures.

RQ.4.7 Enumerate, the mandatory and voluntary contents of Clause 49 of the listing agreement regarding corporate governance. LO 4.2

RQ.4.8 What is the objective of disclosing information about discontinued operations? Is abandonment of particular product in view of continuous decrease in market demand and diverting the resource to new substitute product is discontinuing operation? Explain your answer based on Ind AS-105. LO 4.3

RQ.4.9 The following balances have been extracted from the books of X Ltd as on March 31, 2016: LO 4.1

Particulars	*Amount*	*Particulars*	*Amount*
Profit and loss account [(Dr.) as on 1-4-2012]	₹ 20,00,000	Preliminary expenses	1,00,000
		Furniture and fixtures	2,00,000
Plant and machinery	10,00,000	Sales	2,00,00,000
Motor car	1,50,000	Opening stock of finished goods	30,00,000
Miscellaneous receipts	12,00,000	Closing stock of raw materials at cost	50,00,000
Consumption of raw materials	90,00,000	Share premium	36,00,000
Bank overdraft	10,50,000	Unsecured loan	30,00,000
Share capital	60,00,000	Salaries and wages	20,00,000
Sundry debtors (including ₹ 10,00,000 over six months)	70,00,000	Selling and distribution expenses	15,00,000
		Advance payment of income tax	30,00,000
Office administration expenses	40,00,000	Interim dividends	6,00,000
Sundry creditors	41,00,000		
Miscellaneous advances	4,00,000		

Additional Information:

(i) Closing stock of finished goods at cost is ₹60,00,000.

(ii) The original cost of fixed assets was: Plant and machinery ₹20,00,000; Furniture and fixtures ₹3,00,000; and Motor car ₹2,50,000.

Depreciation is to be charged on the written down value (a) 10 per cent on plant and machinery and furniture and fixtures; and 20 per cent on motor car. There were no additions or disposals during the year.

(iii) The entire authorised capital which consists of equity shares of ₹100 each has been issued and subscribed. The share capital is paid up to the extent of 30 per cent and there are no calls-in-arrears.

(iv) Provision for taxation ₹35,00,000.

(v) Preliminary expenses are to be written off.

(vi) Office administration expenses include auditors fee: ₹50,000 and director's fees ₹30,000.

(vii) The unsecured loan was taken on January 1, 2016 @ 18 per cent p.a. Interest is payable half yearly and necessary provisions are to be made in accounts.

(viii) The directors have proposed a final dividend of ₹6 on each equity share in addition to the interim dividend already declared.

You are required to prepare profit and loss account for the year ended March 31, 2016 and the balance sheet as on that date. You may ignore Company Law requirements in this regard.

LOD: Difficult

RQ.4.10 Explain the provisions relating to maintenance of books of account and presentation of financial statements of a company. LO 4.1

RQ.4.11 Explain the reporting and recognition requirement in the case of jointly controlled entities in (a) separate financial statement and (b) consolidated financial statements. Your answer is to be based on Ind AS-24. LO 4.3

RQ.4.12 Given below is the Trial Balance (rounded off to rupees thousands) of Supreme Chemical limited as at the end of their financial year 2015–16 and additional information to be considered while preparing the final accounts which you are required to do in details. You may ignore the required format of company law in this regard: LO 4.1

Trial Balance as on March 31, 2016

Particulars	*Dr. Amount*	*Cr. Amount*
Stock (1-4-2015)		
Raw materials	₹ 2,50,100	
Work-in-process	1,00,400	
Finished goods	4,99,500	
Fixed assets at cost	3,19,350	
Investments	950	
Loans and advances	2,900	
Cash at bank	1,600	
Sundry debtors	2,95,000	
Interest accrued	125	
Depreciation	17,750	
Other incomes		₹14,400
Other expenses	5,88,200	
Salaries and wages	1,48,550	
Purchases	22,42,000	
Sales		33,48,500
Share capital		1,00,000
General reserve		1,29,000
Development rebate reserve		11,700
Investment allowance reserve		21,250
Secured loans		67,400
Fixed deposits		80,000
Depreciation reserve		1,40,000
Provision for doubtful debts		300
Sundry creditors		5,53,875
	44,66,425	44,66,425

Additional Information:

(i) Stock at the end of March 31, 2016. Raw materials ₹1,50,050 thousand; Work-in-process ₹1,25,200 thousand; Finished goods ₹3,79,750 thousand;

(ii) Market value of investments ₹1,050 thousand.

(iii) Sundry debtors include ₹605 thousand due for more than six months out of which provision has been made for doubtful debts at ₹225 thousand during the year.

(iv) Income tax is to be provided at 35 per cent of taxable income.

(v) The authorised capital of the company is 100 lakh equity shares of ₹10 each.

(vi) ₹ 1,700 thousand are to be re-transferred from Development rebate reserve A/c.

(vii) Included in other expenses are:

(a) Fees to auditors ₹325 thousand out of which ₹75 thousand are in other capacities.

(b) Interest on fixed loans ₹3,100 thousand and other interest ₹5,000 thousand.

(viii) Provision is to be made for managing director's remuneration at 5 per cent of the net profits as provided under law, subject to the maximum of ₹600 thousand per annum.

(ix) Balance of profits is to transferred to general reserve after providing for dividend at 25 per cent on capital.

ANSWERS

RQ4.9 Net profit ₹ 38,15,000; Balance sheet total ₹2,26,00,000

RQ4.12 Net profit ₹ 1,11,020 (in thousands); Balance sheet total ₹11,34,625 (in thousands)

[Comprehensive solutions to all numerical review questions are available on the companion website: http://www.mhhe.com/khan_jain_ma7e]

ANNEXURE 4.I

Equity

Equity refers to the capital raised by a company by the issue of shares. A share in a company is one of the units into which the total capital of the company is divided. For example, if the capital of the company is ₹1,00,000 and is divided into 10,000 units of ₹10 each, each unit of ₹10 will be called a share of the company. It represents a fractional part of the share capital of the company. Share capital is of two types—preference or equity.

Preference share capital means that part of share capital of a company which carries preferential right in respect of both dividend payment and repayment of capital. Preference shares in India are cumulative in that arrears of dividends in any year due to inadequacy of profit would accumulate and become payable subsequently in an year of profits before any payment to shares of any other category. Preference shares in India are non-participating and are entitled to only a fixed dividend and do not participate in any surplus profit/asset remaining after payment to equity shareholders. All preference shares in India are redeemable within a period of ten years from the date of issue. Only non-convertible preference shares are issued by Indian companies.

Equity share capital All share capitals which are not preference share capital are equity share capital. In other words, holders of equity share capital can get dividend only after it is paid to preference shareholders. If no profits are left after the payment of dividend on the preference share capital, no dividend will be paid to equity shareholders. Similar is the treatment with regard to the return of capital on the winding up of the company.

Authorised share capital is the maximum amount of the equity share capital and preference share capital the company can raise in its life time. **Issued capital** is that part of the equity and preference share capital which has been actually issued by the company for cash and for considerations other than cash. **Subscribed capital** refers to that part of the equity and preference share capital which has been actually allotted by the company. **Called-up capital** refers to that part of the allotted capital which has been called-up by the company and the part which has not been called-up is the **uncalled capital**. **Paid-up capital** refers to the amount realised on the called-up capital and it is equal to the called-up capital minus unpaid calls.

The authorised capital of the company consists of 5,00,000 equity shares of ₹10 each and 10,000 14% preference shares of ₹100 each. The company issued 3,00,000 equity shares to the public, on which ₹8 per share had been called. On non-payment of the first call of ₹3 per share, 2,000 shares were forfeited of which 1,500 shares were reissued at ₹6 per share; 5,000 14% preference shares were issued to promoters for their services. The presentation of these facts in the balance sheet of a public limited company is shown below.

Balance Sheet (Equity and Liabilities Side)

Equity and Liabilities	Amount	Amount
Equity share capital		
Authorised Capital:		
5,00,000 Equity shares of ₹10 each	₹50,00,000	
10,000 14% Preference shares of ₹100 each	10,00,000	₹60,00,000
Issued Capital:		
3,00,000 Equity shares of ₹10 each	30,00,000	
5,000 14% Preference shares of ₹100 each	5,00,000	35,00,000
Subscribed Capital:		
2,99,500 Equity shares of ₹10 each, ₹8 called up	23,96,000	
5,000 14% Preference shares of ₹100 each	5,00,000	
	28,96,000	
Add shares forfeited account (500 x ₹5)	2,500	28,98,5000
(of the above shares, 5,000 14% preference shares of ₹100 each fully paid up were issued to promoters in recognition of their services)		
Other equity:		
Capital Reserves	4,500	

Note: Amount forfeited on 1,500 shares reissued [(1,500 × (₹8 – ₹3)] ₹7,500
Discount allowed on reissue [1,500 × (₹8 – ₹6)] ₹3,000
Capital profit on forfeiture and reissue [₹7,500 – ₹3,000] ₹4,500

ANNEXURE 4.II

Financial Statements of Reliance Industries Ltd. (Major Highlights)

Balance Sheet of Reliance Industries Limited
as at 31st March, 2018

(₹ in crore)

	Notes	As at 31st March, 2018	As at 31st March, 2017
ASSETS			
Non-current assets			
Property, plant and equipment	1	1,91,879	1,45,486
Capital work-in-progress	1	92,581	1,28,283
Intangible assets	1	9,085	9,092
Intangible assets under development	1	6,902	4,458

Financial assets			
Investments	2	1,71,945	1,40,544
Loans	3	17,699	10,418
Other non-current assets	4	3,522	2,184
Total non-current assets		4,93,613	4,40,465
Current Assets			
Inventories	5	39,568	34,018
Financial assets			
Investments	6	53,277	51,906
Trade receivables	7	10,460	5,472
Cash and cash equivalents	8	2,731	1,754
Loans	9	3,533	4,900
Other financial assets	10	3,856	3,372
Other current assets	12	10,487	4,859
Total current assets		1,23,912	1,06,281
Total assets		6,17,525	5,46,746
EQUITY AND LIABILITIES			
Equity			
Equity share capital	13	6,335	3,251
Other equity	14	3,08,312	2,85,062
Total equity		3,14,647	2,88,313
Liabilities			
Non-current liabilities			
Financial liabilities			
Borrowings	15	81,596	78,723
Provisions	16	2,205	2,118
Deferred tax liabilities (Net)	17	27,926	24,766
Other non-current liabilities	18	504	—
Total non-current liabilities		1,12,231	1,05,607
Current Liabilities			
Financial liabilities			
Borrowings	19	15,239	22,580
Trade payables	20	88,675	68,161
Other financial liabilities	21	48,250	43,920
Other current liabilities	22	37,565	16,897
Provisions	23	918	1,268
Total current liabilities		1,90,647	1,52,826
Total liabilities		3,02,878	2,58,433
Total equity and liabilities		6,17,525	5,46,746

Statement of Profit and Loss
for the year ended 31st March 2018

(₹ in crore)

	Notes	2017-18	2016-17
INCOME			
Value of sales	24	3,14,917	2,64,909
Income from services		440	132
Value of sales & services (Revenue)		3,15,357	2,65,041
Less: GST recovered		10,022	—
Revenue from operations		3,05,335	2,65,041
Other income	25	8,220	8,709
Total income		3,13,555	2,73,750
EXPENSES			
Cost of material consumed		1,98,029	1,64,250
Purchase of stock-in-trade		7,268	5,161
Changes in inventories of finished goods, Work-in-progress and stock-in-trade	26	(3,232)	(4,839)
Excise duty and service tax		15,293	23,016
Employee benefits expense	27	4,740	4,434
Finance costs	28	4,656	2,723
Depreciation / amortisation and depletion Expense	1	9,580	8,465
Other expenses	29	31,496	29,763
Total expenses		2,67,830	2,32,973
Profit before tax		45,725	40,777
Tax expenses			
Current tax	11	8,953	8,333
Deferred tax	17	3,160	1,019
Profit for the year		33,612	31,425
Other comprehensive income			
i. Items that will not be reclassified to profit or loss		(66)	35
ii. Income tax relating to items that will not be reclassified to Profit or Loss		14	(7)
iii. Items that will be reclassified to profit or loss	25.1	(4,388)	2,752
iv. Income tax relating to items that will be reclassified to profit or loss		937	(588)
Total other comprehensive income for the Year (Net of tax)		(3,503)	2,192
Total comprehensive income for the year		30,109	33,617
Earnings per equity share of face value of ₹10 each			
Basic (in ₹)	30	53.08	49.77*
Diluted (in ₹)	30	53.04	49.68 *

* After considering allotment of Bonus Equity Shares (Refer Note 30)

Notes on Financial Statements

for the year ended 31st March, 2018

1. PROPERTY, PLANT AND EQUIPMENT, CAPITAL WORK-IN-PROGRESS, INTANGIBLE ASSETS AND INTANGIBLE ASSETS UNDER DEVELOPMENT

Description	*GROSS BLOCK*				*DEPRECIATION / AMORTISATION AND DEPLETION*				*NET BLOCK*	
	As at 01-04-2017	*Additions / Adjustments*	*Deductions/ Adjustments*	*As at 31-03-2018*	*As at 01-04-2017*	*For the Year#*	*Deductions/ Adjustments*	*As at 31-03-2018*	*As at 31-03-2018*	*As at 31-03-2017*
Property, Plant and Equipment										
Own Assets :										
Leasehold Land	19,509	1	—	19,510	951	195	—	1,146	18,364	18,558
Freehold Land	36,780	181	7	36,954	—	—	—	—	36,954	36,780
Buildings	12,327	2,099	4	14,422	4,864	512	2	5,374	9,048	7,463
Plant and Machinery	1,71,706	48,235	332	2,19,609	92,165	6,520	294	98,391	1,21,218	79,541
Electrical Installations	4,774	1,700	152	6,322	3,066	365	144	3,287	3,035	1,708
Equipments $	3,510	2,235	4	5,741	2,528	395	4	2,919	2,822	982
Furniture and Fixtures	609	55	6	658	497	22	6	513	145	112
Vehicles	620	38	91	567	413	71	84	400	167	207
Ships	423	1	-	424	310	9	-	319	105	113
Aircrafts and Helicopters	46	—	—	46	36	1	—	37	9	10
Sub-Total	2,50,304	54,545	596	3,04,253	1,04,830	8,090	534	1,12,386	1,91,867	1,45,474
Leased Assets :										
Plant and Machinery	318	—	—	318	306	—	—	306	12	12
Ships	10	—	—	10	10	—	—	10	-	-
Sub-Total	328	—	—	328	316	—	—	316	12	12
Total (A)	**2,50,632**	**54,545**	**596**	**3,04,581**	**1,05,146**	**8,090**	**534**	**1,12,702**	**1,91,879**	**1,45,486**
Intangible Assets : *										
Technical Knowhow Fees	3,601	819	—	4,420	2,561	188	—	2,749	1,671	1,040
Software	1,003	30	—	1,033	915	42	—	957	76	88
Development Rights	41,304	859	—	42,163	33,363	1,462	—	34,825	7,338	7,941
Others	812	—	—	812	789	23	—	812	-	23
Total (B)	46,720	1,708	—	48,428	37,628	1,715	—	39,343	9,085	9,092
Total (A + B)	2,97,352	56,253	596	3,53,009	1,42,774	9,805	534	1,52,045	2,00,964	1,54,578
Previous Year	2,83,660	15,205	1,513	2,97,352	1,34,669	8,670	565	1,42,774	1,54,578	
Capital Work-in-Progress									92,581	1,28,283
Intangible Assets Under Development									6,902	4,458

$ Includes Office Equipments

* Other than internally generated

Depreciation / Amortisation and Depletion Expense for the year includes depreciation of ₹225 crore (Previous year ₹205 crore) capitalised during the year. Thus, the net amount ₹9,580 crore has been considered in Statement of Profit and Loss.

1.1 Buildings include

i) Cost of shares in Co-operative Societies ₹2,02,700 (Previous Year ₹2,00,200).

ii) ₹135 crore (Previous Year ₹135 crore) in shares of Companies / Societies with right to hold and use certain area of Buildings.

1.2 Additions in Property, Plant and Equipment, Capital Work-in-Progress, Intangible Assets and Intangible Assets under Development includes ₹823 crore (net loss) [Previous Year ₹2,166 crore (net loss)] on account of exchange difference during the year.

2. INVESTMENTS - NON-CURRENT

(₹ in crore)

Particulars	*As at 31st March, 2018*	*As at 31st March, 2017*
Category-wise Investment - Non-Current		
Financial Assets measured at Amortised Cost	3,542	3,324
Financial Assets measured at Cost	1,56,506	1,21,533
Financial Assets measured at Fair Value Through Other Comprehensive Income	3,039	7,765
Financial Assets measured at Fair Value Through Profit and Loss	8,858	7,922
Total Investment - Non-Current	1,71,945	1,40,544

3. LOANS - NON-CURRENT
(Unsecured and Considered Good)

(₹ in crore)

Particulars	*As at 31st March, 2018*	*As at 31st March, 2017*
LOANS - NON-CURRENT (Unsecured and Considered Good)		
Deposits with Related Parties (Refer Note 31(iv))	847	793
Loans and advances to Related parties (Refer Note 31(iv))	16,002	8,756
Other Loans and Advances*	850	869
Total	17,699	10,418

* Other Loans and Advances includes primarily fair value of interest free deposits.

4. OTHER NON-CURRENT ASSETS
(Unsecured and Considered Good)

(₹ in crore)

Particulars	*As at 31st March, 2018*	*As at 31st March, 2017*
OTHER NON-CURRENT ASSETS (Unsecured and Considered Good)		
Capital Advances	355	876
Advance Income Tax (Net of Provision)	1,605	992
Other Non-Current Assets with Related Parties (Refer Note 31(ii))	1,250	—
Others*	312	316
Total	3,522	2,184

* Include ₹295 crore (Previous Year ₹295 crore) deposited in Gas pool account (Refer Note 32.4 (b))

(₹ in crore)

	As at 31st March, 2018	As at 31st March, 2017
Advance Income Tax (Net of Provision)		
At start of year	992	360
Charge for the year - Current Tax	(8,953)	(8,333)
Others#	951	(595)
Tax paid (Net) during the year	8,615	9,560
At end of year	1,605	992

Pertain to Provision for tax on Other Comprehensive Income

5. INVENTORIES

(₹ in crore)

Particulars	*As at 31st March, 2018*	*As at 31st March, 2017*
INVENTORIES		
Raw Materials (Including Material in Transit)	19,164	16,225
Work-in-Progress	5,601	4,837
Finished Goods	10,864	9,208
Stock-in-Trade	68	55
Stores and spares	3,871	3,693
Total	39,568	34,018

6. INVESTMENTS - CURRENT

(₹ in crore)

Particulars	*As at 31st March, 2018*	*As at 31st March, 2017*
Category-wise Investment - Current		
Financial Assets measured at Amortised Cost	585	—
Financial Assets measured at Fair Value Through Other Comprehensive Income	21,547	22,918
Financial Assets measured at Fair Value Through Profit and Loss	31,145	28,988
Total Investment - Current	53,277	51,906

7. TRADE RECEIVABLES (Unsecured and Considered Good)

(₹ in crore)

Particulars	*As at 31st March, 2018*	*As at 31st March, 2017*
Trade Receivables	10,460	5,472
Total	10,460	5,472

8. CASH AND CASH EQUIVALENTS

(₹ in crore)

Particulars	*As at 31st March, 2018*	*As at 31st March, 2017*
Cash on Hand	8	5
Balances with Banks*	2,723	1,749
Cash and Cash Equivalents as per Balance Sheet	2,731	1,754
Cash and Cash Equivalents as per Standalone Cash Flow Statement	2,731	1,754

* Include Unclaimed Dividend of ₹259 crore (Previous Year ₹241 crore), Deposits of ₹158 crore (Previous Year ₹10,87,926) with maturity of more than 12 months and fixed deposits of ₹1,270 crore (Previous Year ₹1,335 crore) Pledged as collateral securities.

8.1 Cash and Cash Equivalents include deposits maintained by the Company with banks, which can be withdrawn by the Company at any point of time without prior notice or penalty on the principal.

9. LOANS - CURRENT (Unsecured and Considered Good)

(₹ in crore)

Particulars	*As at 31st March, 2018*	*As at 31st March, 2017*
Loans and Advances to Related Parties	2,883	4,250
Loans Others	650	650
Total	3,533	4,900

10. OTHER FINANCIAL ASSETS - CURRENT

(₹ in crore)

Particulars	*As at 31st March, 2018*	*As at 31st March, 2017*
Interest Accrued on Investment	118	176
Deposits	792	1,194
Others^	2,946	2,002
Total	3,856	3,372

^ Others include fair value of derivatives.

11. TAXATION

(₹ in crore)

Particulars	*Year ended 31st March, 2018*	*Year ended 31st March, 2017*
Income Tax recognised in Statement of Profit and Loss		
Current Tax	8,953	8,333
Deferred Tax	3,160	1,019
Total Income Tax expenses recognised in the current year	12,113	9,352

The income tax expenses for the year can be reconciled to the accounting profit as follows:

Particulars	Year ended 31st March, 2018	Year ended 31st March, 2017
Profit Before Tax	45,725	40,777
Applicable Tax Rate	34.608%	34.608%
Computed Tax Expense	15,825	14,112
Tax effect of :		
Exempted Income	(2,591)	(2,707)
Expenses Disallowed	3,530	3,044
Additional allowances net of MAT Credit	(7,811)	(6,116)
Current Tax Provision (A)	8,953	8,333
Incremental Deferred Tax Liability on account of Property, Plant and Equipment and Intangible Assets	2,788	1,229
Incremental Deferred Tax Liability / (Asset) on account of Financial Assets and Other Items	372	(210)
Deferred tax Provision (B)	3,160	1,019
Tax Expenses recognised in Statement of Profit and Loss (A+B)	12,113	9,352
Effective Tax Rate	26.49%	22.93%

12. OTHER CURRENT ASSETS (Unsecured and Considered Good)

(₹ in crore)

Particulars	As at 31st March, 2018	As at 31st March, 2017
Balance with Customs, Central Excise, GST and State Authorities	4,552	3,436
Other Current Assets to Related Parties (Refer Note 31 (ii))	75	—
Others*	5,860	1,423
Total	10,487	4,859

* Include primarily Intangible Assets Under Development held for sale amounting to ₹4,353 crore, prepaid expenses and claim receivables.

13. SHARE CAPITAL

(₹ in crore)

	Particulars	As at 31st March, 2018	As at 31st March, 2017
Authorised Share Capital			
14,00,00,00,000 (5,00,00,00,000)	Equity Shares of ₹10 each	14,000	5,000
1,00,00,00,000 (1,00,00,00,000)	Preference Shares of ₹10 each	1,000	1,000
		15,000	6,000
Issued, Subscribed and Paid up:			
6,33,46,51,022 (3,25,12,78,100)	Equity Shares of ₹10 each fully paid up	6,335	3,251
Less:	Calls in Arrears - by others [₹ Nil (Previous Year ₹2,303)]	—	—
Total		6,335	3,251

14. OTHER EQUITY

(₹ in crore)

Particulars	As at 31st March, 2018		As at 31st March, 2017	
Share Application Money Pending Allotment				
As per last Balance Sheet	4		8	
Add: Issue of Shares / Application money received	11		(4)	
		15		4
Capital Reserve				
As per last Balance Sheet		291		291
Capital Redemption Reserve				
As per last Balance Sheet	48		48	
Less: On issue of bonus shares	(48)		—	
		—		48
Securities Premium Reserve				
As per last Balance Sheet	49,080		48,387	
Add : On Employee Stock Options	126		693	
	49,206		49,080	
Less: On issue of Bonus shares	(3,032)		—	
Less: Calls in arrears - by others[₹Nil (Previous Year ₹1,03,189)]	—		—	
		46,174		49,080
Debentures Redemption Reserve				
As per last Balance Sheet	1,117		1,117	
Add: Transferred from Retained Earnings	4,134		—	
		5,251		1,117
Share Based Payments Reserve				
As per last Balance Sheet	16		18	
Less: On Employee Stock Options	(4)		(2)	
		12		16
General Reserve				
As per last Balance Sheet	2,00,000		1,75,210	
Add: Transferred from Retained Earnings	25,000		24,790	
		2,25,000		2,00,000
Retained Earnings				
As per last Balance Sheet	29,485		22,850	
Add: Profit for the year	33,612		31,425	
	63,097		54,275	

Add: Transferred from Share Based Payments Reserve	4		—	
Less: Appropriations				
Transferred to General Reserve	(25,000)		(24,790)	
Dividend on Equity Shares [Dividend per Share ₹11 (Previous year ₹ Nil)]	(3,255)		—	
Tax on Dividend	(661)		—	
Transferred to Debenture Redemption Reserve	(4,134)		—	
		30,051		29,485
Other Comprehensive Income (OCI)				
As per last Balance Sheet	5,021		2,829	
Add: Movement in OCI (Net) during the year	(3,503)		2,192	
		1,518		5,021
Total		3,08,312		2,85,062

15. BORROWINGS

(₹ in crore)

Particulars	As at 31st March, 2018		As at 31st March, 2017	
	Non-Current	Current	Non-Current	Current
Secured - At Amortised Cost				
Non-Convertible Debentures	500	503	1,003	133
	500	503	1,003	133
Unsecured - At Amortised Cost				
Non-Convertible Debentures	20,000	—	—	—
Bonds	22,177	1,884	23,979	536
Term Loans- from Banks	38,919	17,659	53,741	5,474
	81,096	19,543	77,720	6,010
Total	81,596	20,046	78,723	6,143

16. PROVISIONS - NON-CURRENT

(₹ in crore)

Particulars	As at 31st March, 2018	As at 31st March, 2017
Provision for decommissioning of Assets#	2,205	2,118
Total	2,205	2,118

The movement in the provision is towards (i) Utilisation for Tapti facilities, (ii) changes in the exchange rates and (iii) Unwinding of discount. Provision for Decommissioning of Assets is for Panna Mukta, Tapti, KGD6 and CBM Block. There exists uncertainty on the timing of abandonment of well and related facilities which would depend upon the ultimate life of the field and expected utilization of assets by other fields.

17. DEFERRED TAX LIABILITY (NET)

The movement on the deferred tax account is as follows:

(₹ in crore)

Particulars	*As at 31st March, 2018*	*As at 31st March, 2017*
At the start of the year	24,766	23,747
Charge/(credit) to Statement of Profit and Loss (Note 11)	3,160	1,019
At the end of year	27,926	24,766

Component of Deferred Tax Liabilities/(asset)

(₹ in crore)

Particulars	*As at 31st March, 2018*	*Charge/(credit) to Statement of Profit and Loss*	*As at 31st March, 2017*
Deferred tax liabilities / (asset) in relation to:			
Property, Plant and Equipment and Intangible Asset	25,088	2,788	27,876
Financial Assets	484	408	892
Loan and Advances	(21)	(6)	(27)
Provisions	(785)	(30)	(815)
Total	24,766	3,160	27,926

18. OTHER NON-CURRENT LIABILITIES

(₹ in crore)

Particulars	*As at 31st March, 2018*	*As at 31st March, 2017*
Advance from Related Parties (Refer Note 31 (ii))	504	—
Total	504	—

19. BORROWINGS – CURRENT

(₹ in crore)

Particulars	*As at 31st March, 2018*	*As at 31st March, 2017*
Secured - At Amortised Cost		
Working Capital Loans		
From Banks		
Foreign Currency Loans	—	5,837
Rupee Loans	1,653	3,621
	1,653	9,458

Unsecured - At Amortised Cost		
Other Loans and Advances		
From Banks		
Foreign Currency Loans	12	13,122
From Others		
Commercial Paper*	13,574	—
	13,586	13,122
Total	15,239	22,580

* Maximum amount outstanding at any time during the year was ₹21,876 crore.

19.1 Working Capital Loans from Banks of ₹1,653 crore (Previous Year ₹9,458 crore) are secured by hypothecation of present and future stock of raw materials, work-in-progress, finished goods, stores and spares (not relating to plant and machinery), book debts, outstanding monies, receivables, claims, bills, materials in transit, etc. save and except receivables of Oil and Gas Segment.

20. TRADE PAYABLES

(₹ in crore)

Particulars	*As at 31st March, 2018*	*As at 31st March, 2017*
Micro, Small and Medium Enterprises	210	242
Others	88,465	67,919
Total	88,675	68,161

20.1 There are no overdue amounts to Micro, Small and Medium Enterprises as at March 31, 2018 for which disclosure requirements under Micro, Small and Medium Enterprises Development Act, 2006 are applicable.

21. OTHER FINANCIAL LIABILITIES - CURRENT

(₹ in crore)

Particulars	*As at 31st March, 2018*	*As at 31st March, 2017*
Current maturities of Borrowings - Non-Current	20,046	6,143
Interest accrued but not due on Borrowings	1,138	370
Unclaimed Dividends#	259	241
Application money received and due for refund#	—	1
Unclaimed/ Unpaid matured Debentures and Interest accrued there-on#	—	1
Other Payables*	26,807	37,164
Total	48,250	43,920

These figures do not include any amounts due and outstanding, to be credited to Investor Education and Protection Fund except ₹19 crore (Previous Year ₹20 crore) which is held in abeyance due to legal cases pending.

* Includes Creditors for Capital Expenditure, Security Deposit and Financial liability at Fair Value.

22. OTHER CURRENT LIABILITIES

(₹ in crore)

Particulars	*As at 31st March, 2018*	*As at 31st March, 2017*
Other Payables^	37,565	16,897
Total	37,565	16,897

^ Includes advances from customers and statutory dues.

23. PROVISIONS - CURRENT

(₹ in crore)

Particulars	*As at 31st March, 2018*	*As at 31st March, 2017*
Provision for Employee Benefits (Refer Note 27.1)**	276	177
Other Provisions##	642	1,091
Total	918	1,268

** The provision for employee benefit includes annual leave and vested long service leave entitlement accrued and compensation claims made by employees.

The Company had recognised liability based on substantial degree of estimation for excise duty payable on clearance of goods lying in stock as on 31st March, 2017 of ₹596 crore as per the estimated pattern of dispatches. During the year, ₹596 crore was utilised for clearance of goods. Provision recognised under this class for the year is ₹274 crore which is outstanding as on 31st March, 2018. Actual outflow is expected in the next financial year. The Company had recognised customs duty liability on goods imported under various export incentive schemes of ₹419 crore as at 31st March, 2017. During the year, further provision of ₹805 crore was made and sum of ₹933 crore were reversed on fulfilment of export obligation. Closing balance on this account as at 31st March, 2018 is ₹291 crore.

24. VALUE OF SALES

(₹ in crore)

Particulars	*2017-18*	*2016-17*
Particulars of Sale of Products		
Petroleum Products	2,02,216	1,79,438
Petrochemical Products	1,09,614	82,095
Oil and Gas	2,468	2,787
Others	619	589
Total	3,14,917	2,64,909

25. OTHER INCOME

(₹ in crore)

Particulars	*2017-18*		*2016-17*	
Interest				
Bank deposits	85		356	
Debt instruments	3,231		2,933	
Other Financial Assets measured at Amortised Cost	270		246	
Others [₹11,56,621 (Previous Year ₹14,19,866)]	—		—	
		3,586		3,535

Dividend Income		**935**		**271**
Other Non-Operating Income		**253**		**787**
Gain on Financial Assets				
Realised Gain	3,483		2,948	
Unrealised Gain / (Loss)	(37)		1,168	
		3,446		4,116
Total		8,220		8,709

Above other income comprises of assets measured at Cost / Amortised Cost ₹1,725 crore (Previous Year ₹1,961 crore), Fair Value Through Profit and Loss ₹1,900 crore (Previous Year ₹2,847 crore) and Fair Value Through Other Comprehensive Income ₹4,342 crore (Previous year ₹3,114 crore) and Other Non-Operating Income ₹253 crore (Previous year ₹787 crore)

25.1 Other Comprehensive Income

(₹ in crore)

Particulars	*2017-18*	*2016-17*
Government Securities	—	(30)
Debentures or Bonds	(686)	220
Debt Income Fund	(1,769)	826
Commodity Hedge	(197)	—
Cash Flow Hedge	(1,736)	1,736
Total	(4,388)	2,752

26. CHANGES IN INVENTORIES OF FINISHED GOODS, WORK-IN-PROGRESS AND STOCK-IN-TRADE

(₹ in crore)

Particulars	*2017-18*	*2016-17*
Inventories (at close)		
Finished Goods / Stock-in-Trade	10,932	9,263
Work-in-Progress	5,601	4,837
	16,533	14,100
Inventories (at commencement)		
Finished Goods / Stock-in-Trade	9,263	7,663
Work-in-Progress	4,837	2,871
	14,100	10,534
Less: Capitalised during the year	799	1,273
	13,301	9,261
Total	(3,232)	(4,839

27. EMPLOYEE BENEFITS EXPENSE

(₹ in crore)

Particulars	*2017-18*	*2016-17*
Salaries and Wages	4,056	3,889
Contribution to Provident Fund and Other Funds	246	229
Staff Welfare Expenses	438	316
Total	4,740	4,434

28. FINANCE COSTS

(₹ in crore)

Particulars	*2017-18*	*2016-17*
Interest Expenses*	3,901	2,032
Applicable loss on foreign currency transactions and translation	755	691
Total	4,656	2,723

* Interest Expenses are net of Interest Capitalised of ₹3,302 crore (Previous Year ₹2,852 crore)

29. OTHER EXPENSES

(₹ in crore)

Particulars	*2017-18*	*2016-17*
Manufacturing Expenses		
Stores, Chemicals and Packing Materials	5,376	5,035
Electric Power, Fuel and Water	13,565	10,150
Labour Processing, Production Royalty and Machinery Hire Charges	1,495	1,638
Repairs to Building	97	84
Repairs to Machinery	1,145	1,064
Exchange Difference (Net)	52	40
Excise Duty#	(95)	234
Lease Rent	11	10
	21,646	18,255
Selling and Distribution Expenses		
Warehousing and Distribution Expenses	5,811	5,552
Sales Tax / VAT	854	1,428
Other Selling and Distribution Expenses	446	1,456
	7,111	8,436
Establishment Expenses		
Professional Fees	758	1,720
General Expenses	1,049	925
Rent	91	100
Insurance	902	862
Rates & Taxes	606	206

Other Repairs	427	310
Travelling Expenses	173	164
Payment to Auditors	18	23
Loss on Sale /Discard of Property, Plant and Equipments	17	69
Charity and Donations	790	654
	4,831	5,033
Less: Transferred to Project Development Expenditure	(2,092)	(1,961)
Total	31,496	29,763

Excise Duty shown under Manufacturing Expenses represents the aggregate of Excise Duty borne by the Company and difference between Excise Duty on opening and closing stock of finished goods.

29.1 Payment to Auditors as:

(₹ in crore)

Particulars	*2017-18*	*2016-17*
(a) Statutory Audit Fees	10	10
(b) Tax Audit Fees	1	1
(c) Certification and Consultation Fees	6	11
(d) Cost Audit Fees	1	1
Total	18	23

Certification and consultation fees primarily includes certification fees paid to auditors. Statute and regulation permit auditors to certify export / import documentation, quarterly filings, XBRL filings, transfer pricing and bond issuances among others.

29.2 Corporate Social Responsibility (CSR)

(a) CSR amount required to be spent as per Section 135 of the Companies Act, 2013 read with Schedule VII thereof by the Company during the year is ₹703 crore (Previous Year ₹620 crore)

(b) Expenditure related to Corporate Social Responsibility is ₹745 crore (Previous Year ₹659 crore).

Details of Amount spent towards CSR given below:

(₹ in crore)

Particulars	*2017-18*	*2016-17*
Rural Transformation	181	132
Health	148	267
Education	371	221
Sports for Development	43	24
Disaster Response	1	11
Urban Renewal (₹33,94,505)	—	3
Arts, Culture and Heritage	1	1
Total	745	659

30. EARNINGS PER SHARE (EPS)

(₹ in crore)

Particulars	*2017-18*	*2016-17*
Face value per Equity Share (₹)	10	10
Basic Earnings per Share (₹)	53.08	49.77*
Net Profit after Tax as per Statement of Profit and Loss attributable to Equity Shareholders (₹ in crore)	33,612	31,425
Weighted Average number of Equity Shares used as denominator for calculating Basic EPS	6,33,26,37,065	6,31,44,54,258
Diluted Earnings per Share (₹)	53.04	49.68*
Net Profit after Tax as per Statement of Profit and Loss attributable to Equity Shareholders (₹ in crore)	33,612	31,425
Weighted Average number of Equity Shares used as denominator for calculating Diluted EPS	6,33,76,93,539	6,32,56,40,411

* The Company has issued and allotted 308,03,34,238 equity shares to the eligible holders of equity shares on the book closure date (i.e., 9th September, 2017) as bonus equity shares by capitalizing reserves on 13th September, 2017. The Earnings Per Share figures for the year ended 31st March 2017 have been adjusted to give effect to the allotment of the bonus shares, as required by Ind AS-33.

27. NOTE

Significant Accounting Policies

- **Basis of Preparation and Presentation:** The Financial Statements have been prepared on the historical cost basis except for following assets and liabilities which have been measured at fair value amount:
  (i) Certain Financial Assets and Liabilities (including derivative instruments),
  (ii) Defined Benefit Plans - Plan Assets, and
  (iii) Equity settled Share Based Payments.

  The Financial Statements of the Company have been prepared to comply with the Indian Accounting standards ('Ind AS'), including the rules notified under the relevant provisions of the Companies Act, 2013.

  Company's Financial Statements are presented in Indian Rupees (₹), which is also its functional currency and all values are rounded to the nearest crore (₹00,00,000), except when otherwise indicated.

- **Property, Plant and Equipment:** Property, Plant and Equipment are stated at cost, net of recoverable taxes, trade discount and rebates less accumulated depreciation and impairment losses. In the case of land, the Company has availed fair value as deemed cost on the date of transition to Ind AS. Subsequent costs are included in the asset's carrying amount or recognised as a separate asset, as appropriate, only when it is probable that future economic benefits associated with the item will flow to the entity and the cost can be measured reliably.

  Depreciation on Property, Depreciation on Plant and Equipment is provided using written down value method on depreciable amount except in the case of certain assets from Refining segment and Petrochemical segment & SEZ units / developer which are depreciated using straight line method. Depreciation (by and large) is provided based on useful life of the assets as prescribed in Schedule II to the Companies Act, 2013.

- **Leases:** Leases are classified as finance leases whenever the terms of the lease, transfers substantially all the risks and rewards of ownership to the lessee. All other leases are classified as operating lease.
- **Intangible Assets:** Intangible Assets are stated at cost of acquisition net of recoverable taxes, trade discount and rebates less accumulated amortisation / depletion and impairment losses, if any. Such cost includes purchase price, borrowing costs, and any cost directly attributable to bringing the asset to its working condition for the intended use, net charges on foreign exchange contracts and adjustments arising from exchange rate variations attributable to the Intangible Assets.

  A summary of amortisation / depletion policies applied to the Company's Intangible Assets to the extent of depreciable amount is as follows:

Particular	Depreciation
Technical Know-How	Over the useful life of the underlying assets ranging from 5 years to 35 years.
Computer Software	Over a period of 5 years.
Development Rights	Depleted using the unit of production method. The cost of producing wells along with its related facilities including decommissioning costs are depleted in proportion of oil and gas production achieved vis-à-vis Proved Developed Reserves. The cost for common facilities including its decommissioning costs are depleted using Proved Reserves.
Others	In case of Jetty, the aggregate amount amortised to date is not less than the aggregate rebate availed by the Company.

  The amortisation period and the amortisation method for Intangible Assets with a finite useful life are reviewed at each reporting date.

- **Research and Development Expenditure:** Revenue expenditure pertaining to research is charged to the Statement of Profit and Loss. Development costs of products are charged to the Statement of Profit and Loss unless a product's technological and commercial feasibility has been established, in which case such expenditure is capitalised.
- **Finance Cost:** Borrowing costs include exchange differences arising from foreign currency borrowings to the extent they are regarded as an adjustment to the interest cost. Borrowing costs that are directly attributable to the acquisition or construction of qualifying assets are capitalised as part of the cost of such assets. A qualifying asset is one that necessarily takes substantial period of time to get ready for its intended use.

  Interest income earned on the temporary investment of specific borrowings pending their expenditure on qualifying assets is deducted from the borrowing costs eligible for capitalisation.

  All other borrowing costs are charged to the Statement of Profit and Loss for the period for which they are incurred.

- **Inventories:** Items of inventories are measured at lower of cost and net realisable value after providing for obsolescence, if any, except in the case of by-products which are valued at net realisable value. Cost of inventories comprises of cost of purchase, cost of conversion and other costs including manufacturing overheads net of recoverable taxes incurred in bringing them to their respective present location and condition.

Cost of raw materials, chemicals, stores and spares, packing materials, trading and other products are determined on weighted average basis.

- **Impairment of Non-Financial Assets - Property, Plant and Equipment and Intangible Assets:** The Company assesses at each reporting date as to whether there is any indication that any Property, Plant and Equipment and Intangible Assets or group of Assets, called Cash Generating Units (CGU) may be impaired. If any such indication exists, the recoverable amount of an asset or CGU is estimated to determine the extent of impairment, if any. When it is not possible to estimate the recoverable amount of an individual asset, the Company estimates the recoverable amount of the CGU to which the asset belongs.

  An impairment loss is recognised in the Statement of Profit and Loss to the extent, asset's carrying amount exceeds its recoverable amount.

  The impairment loss recognised in prior accounting period is reversed if there has been a change in the estimate of recoverable amount.
- **Provisions:** Provisions are recognised when the Company has a present obligation (legal or constructive) as a result of a past event, it is probable that an outflow of resources embodying economic benefits will be required to settle the obligation and a reliable estimate can be made of the amount of the obligation.
- **Employee Benefits Expense:** The undiscounted amount of **short term employee benefits** expected to be paid in exchange for the services rendered by employees are recognised as an expense during the period when the employees render the services.
- **Post-Employment Benefits:** The Company recognizes contribution payable to the provident fund scheme as an expense.

  The Company pays gratuity to the employees who have completed five years of service with the Company at the time of resignation/superannuation. The gratuity is paid @15 days salary for every completed year of service as per the Payment of Gratuity Act 1972.

  Compensation to employees who have opted for retirement under the voluntary retirement scheme of the Company is payable in the year of exercise of option by the employee. The Company recognises the employee separation cost when the scheme is announced and the Company is demonstrably committed to it.
- **Tax Expenses:** The tax expenses for the period comprise of current tax and deferred income tax. Tax is recognised in the Statement of Profit and Loss, except to the extent that it relates to items recognised in the Other Comprehensive Income or in equity. In which case, the tax is also recognised in Other Comprehensive Income or Equity.

  Current tax assets and liabilities are measured at the amount expected to be recovered from or paid to the Income Tax authorities, based on tax rates and laws that are enacted at the Balance sheet date.

  Deferred tax is recognised on temporary differences between the carrying amounts of assets and liabilities in the Financial Statements and the corresponding tax bases used in the computation of taxable profit.

Deferred tax liabilities and assets are measured at the tax rates that are expected to apply in the period in which the liability is settled or the asset realised, based on tax rates (and tax laws) that have been enacted or substantively enacted by the end of the reporting period. The carrying amount of Deferred tax liabilities and assets are reviewed at the end of each reporting period.

- **Foreign Currencies Transactions and Translation:** Transactions in foreign currencies are recorded at the exchange rate prevailing on the date of transaction. Monetary assets and liabilities denominated in foreign currencies are translated at the functional currency closing rates of exchange at the reporting date.
- **Revenue Recognition:** (i) Revenue from sale of goods is recognised when the significant risks and rewards of ownership have been transferred to the buyer, recovery of the consideration is probable, the associated cost can be estimated reliably, there is no continuing effective control or managerial involvement with the goods, and the amount of revenue can be measured reliably. (ii) Revenue from rendering of services is recognised when the performance of agreed contractual task has been completed. (iii) Revenue from operations is measured at the fair value of the consideration received or receivable, taking into account contractually defined terms of payment and excluding taxes or duties collected on behalf of the government.
- **Financial Assets (i) Initial Recognition and Measurement:** All Financial Assets are initially recognized at fair value. Transaction costs that are directly attributable to the acquisition or issue of Financial Assets, which are not at Fair Value through Profit or Loss, are adjusted to the fair value on initial recognition. Purchase and sale of Financial Assets are recognised using trade date accounting. (ii) Subsequent measurement: a) Financial Assets measured at Amortised Cost (AC): A Financial Asset is measured at Amortised Cost if it is held within a business model whose objective is to hold the asset in order to collect contractual cash flows and the contractual terms of the Financial Asset give rise on specified dates to cash flows that are solely payments of principal and interest on the principal amount outstanding. b) Financial Assets measured at Fair Value through Other Comprehensive Income (FVTOCI): A Financial Asset is measured at FVTOCI if it is held within a business model whose objective is achieved by both collecting contractual cash flows and selling Financial Assets and the contractual terms of the Financial Asset give rise on specified dates to cash flows that are solely payments of principal and interest on the principal amount outstanding. c) Financial Assets measured at Fair Value through Profit or Loss (FVTPL): A Financial Asset which is not classified in any of the above categories is measured at FVTPL.
- **Impairment of Financial Assets:** In accordance with Ind AS 109, the Company uses 'Expected Credit Loss' (ECL) model, for evaluating impairment of Financial Assets other than those measured at Fair Value Through Profit and Loss (FVTPL).

  Expected credit losses are measured through a loss allowance at an amount equal to:

  - o The 12-months expected credit losses (expected credit losses that result from those default events on the financial instrument that are possible within 12 months after the reporting date); or
  - o Full lifetime expected credit losses (expected credit losses that result from all possible default events over the life of the financial instrument).

For Trade Receivables the Company applies 'simplified approach' which requires expected lifetime losses to be recognised from initial recognition of the receivables. The Company uses historical default rates to determine impairment loss on the portfolio of trade receivables. At every reporting date these historical default rates are reviewed and changes in the forward looking estimates are analysed.

For other assets, the Company uses 12 month ECL to provide for impairment loss where there is no significant increase in credit risk. If there is significant increase in credit risk, full lifetime ECL is used.

- **Financial Liabilities:** (i) Initial Recognition and Measurement: All Financial Liabilities are recognized at fair value and in the case of borrowings, net of directly attributable cost. Fees of recurring nature are directly recognised in the Statement of Profit and Loss as finance cost. (ii) Subsequent Measurement: Financial Liabilities are carried at amortized cost using the effective interest method.

  For trade and other payables maturing within one year from the balance sheet date, the carrying amounts approximate fair value due to the short maturity of these instruments.
- **Derivative Financial Instruments and Hedge Accounting:** The Company uses various derivative financial instruments such as interest rate swaps, currency swaps, forwards & options and commodity contracts to mitigate the risk of changes in interest rates, exchange rates and commodity prices. Such derivative financial instruments are initially recognised at fair value on the date on which a derivative contract is entered into and are also subsequently measured at fair value. Derivatives are carried as Financial Assets when the fair value is positive and as Financial Liabilities when the fair value is negative.

  Any gains or losses arising from changes in the fair value of derivatives are (by and large) taken directly to the Statement of Profit and Loss.

  Hedges that meet the criteria for hedge accounting are accounted for as follows:
- **Cash Flow Hedge:** When a derivative is designated as a cash flow hedging instrument, the effective portion of changes in the fair value of the derivative is recognized in the cash flow hedging reserve being part of Other Comprehensive Income. Any ineffective portion of changes in the fair value of the derivative is recognized immediately in the Statement of Profit and Loss. If the hedging relationship no longer meets the criteria for hedge accounting, then hedge accounting is discontinued prospectively.
- **Fair Value Hedge:** The Company designates derivative contracts or non-derivative Financial Assets / Liabilities as hedging instruments to mitigate the risk of change in fair value of hedged item due to movement in interest rates, foreign exchange rates and commodity prices.

  Changes in the fair value of hedging instruments and hedged items that are designated and qualify as fair value hedges are recorded in the Statement of Profit and Loss. If the hedging relationship no longer meets the criteria for hedge accounting, the adjustment to the carrying amount of a hedged item for which the effective interest method is used is amortised to the Statement of Profit and Loss over the period of maturity.
- **De-recognition of Financial Instruments:** The Company derecognizes a Financial Asset when the contractual rights to the cash flows from the Financial Asset expire or it transfers the Financial Asset and the transfer qualifies for derecognition under Ind AS 109. A Finan-

cial liability (or a part of a financial liability) is derecognized from the Company's Balance Sheet when the obligation specified in the contract is discharged or cancelled or expires.

- **Offsetting:** Financial Assets and Financial Liabilities are offset and the net amount is presented in the balance sheet when, and only when, the Company has a legally enforceable right to set off the amount and it intends, either to settle them on a net basis or to realise the asset and settle the liability simultaneously.
- **Accounting for Oil and Gas Activity:** The Company has adopted Successful Efforts Method (SEM) of accounting for its Oil and Gas activities. The policy of recognition of exploration and evaluation expenditure is considered in line with the principle of SEM. Seismic costs, geological and geophysical studies, petroleum exploration license fees and general and administration costs directly attributable to exploration and evaluation activities are expensed off. The costs incurred on acquisition of interest in oil and gas blocks and on exploration and evaluation other than those which are expensed off are accounted for as Intangible Assets under Development. All development costs incurred in respect of proved reserves are also capitalized under Intangible Assets under Development. Once a well is ready to commence commercial production, the costs accumulated in Intangible Assets under Development are classified as Intangible Assets corresponding to prove developed oil and gas reserves. The exploration and evaluation expenditure which does not result in discovery of proved oil and gas reserves and all cost pertaining to production are charged to the Statement of Profit and Loss.

  The Company used technical estimation of reserves as per the Petroleum Resources Management System guidelines 2011 and standard geological and reservoir engineering methods. The reserve review and evaluation is carried out annually.
- **Critical Accounting Judgments and Key Sources of Estimation Uncertainty:** The preparation of the Company's Financial Statements requires management to make judgement, estimates and assumptions that affect the reported amount of revenue, expenses, assets and liabilities and the accompanying disclosures. Uncertainty about these assumptions and estimates could result in outcomes that require a material adjustment to the carrying amount of assets or liabilities affected in next financial years. (a) Estimation of Oil and Gas Reserves: The determination of the Company's estimated oil and natural gas reserves requires significant judgements and estimates to be applied and these are regularly reviewed and updated. Factors such as the availability of geological and engineering data, reservoir performance data, acquisition and divestment activity, drilling of new wells, and commodity prices all impact on the determination of the Company's estimates of its oil and natural gas reserves. The Company bases its proved reserves estimates on the requirement of reasonable certainty with rigorous technical and commercial assessments based on conventional industry practice and regulatory requirements.

  Estimates of oil and natural gas reserves are used to calculate depletion charges for the Company's oil and gas properties. The impact of changes in estimated proved reserves is dealt with prospectively by amortizing the remaining carrying value of the asset over the expected future production. Oil and natural gas reserves also have a direct impact on the assessment of the recoverability of asset carrying values reported in the Financial Statements. (b) Decommissioning Liabilities: The liability for decommissioning costs is recognized when the Company has an obligation to perform site restoration activity. The recognition and measurement of decommissioning provisions involves the use of estimates and assumptions. These include; the timing of abandonment of well and related facilities which would depend upon the ultimate life of the field, expected utilization of assets by other fields, the scope of abandonment activity and pre-tax rate applied for discounting. (c) Depreciation / Amortisation and useful lives of Property Plant and Equipment / Intangible Assets: Property, Plant and Equipment / Intangible Assets are depreciated / amortised over their estimated useful lives, after taking into account estimated residual value. Management reviews the estimated useful lives and residual values of the assets annually in order to determine the amount of depreciation / amortisation to be recorded during any reporting period. The useful lives and residual values are based on the Company's historical experience with similar assets and take into account anticipated technological changes. The depreciation / amortisation for future periods is revised if there are significant changes from previous estimates. (d) Recoverability of Trade Receivables: Judgements are required in assessing the recoverability of overdue trade receivables and determining whether a provision against those receivables is required. Factors considered include the credit rating of the counterparty, the amount and timing of anticipated future payments and any possible actions that can be taken to mitigate the risk of non-payment. (e) Provisions: Provisions and liabilities are recognized in the period when it becomes probable that there will be a future outflow of funds resulting from past operations or events and the amount of cash outflow can be reliably estimated. The timing of recognition and quantification of the liability requires the application of judgement to existing facts and circumstances, which can be subject to change. The carrying amounts of provisions and liabilities are reviewed regularly and revised to take account of changing facts and circumstances. (f) Impairment of Non-Financial Assets: The Company assesses at each reporting date whether there is an indication that an asset may be impaired. If any indication exists, the Company estimates the asset's recoverable amount. An asset's recoverable amount is the higher of an asset's or Cash Generating Units (CGU's) fair value less costs of disposal and its value in use. It is determined for an individual asset, unless the asset does not generate cash inflows that are largely independent of those from other assets or a groups of assets. Where the carrying amount of an asset or CGU exceeds its recoverable amount, the asset is considered impaired and is written down to its recoverable amount.

In assessing value in use, the estimated future cash flows are discounted to their present value using pre-tax discount rate that reflects current market assessments of the time value of money and the risks specific to the asset. In determining fair value less costs of disposal, recent market transactions are taken into account, if no such transactions can be identified, an appropriate valuation model is used. (g) Impairment of Financial Assets: The impairment provisions for Financial Assets are based on assumptions about risk of default and expected cash loss rates. The Company uses judgement in making these assumptions and selecting the inputs to the impairment calculation, based on Company's past history, existing market conditions as well as forward looking estimates at the end of each reporting period.

ANNEXURE 4.III

Corporate Reports of Reliance Industries Limited (Major Highlights)

The corporate reports of the Reliance Industries Limited (RIL) comprise of (i) Business Responsibility Report, (ii) Corporate Governance Report and (iii) Board's Report

Business Responsibility Report

At Reliance Industries Limited (RIL), sustainability is being viewed as being socially cognizant while remaining a technology driven organisation that delivers stakeholder expectations. This Business Responsibility Report (BRR) is one of the avenues to communicate the Company's obligations and performance to all its stakeholders for FY 2017-18.

RIL believes that the foundations of economic growth can be strengthened if the entire society is a part of the growth story. To achieve this vision, the Company strives to create value for India by elevating the quality of life across the entire socio-economic spectrum. Furthermore, the Company believes in the effectiveness of communication as the first step towards creating long-term stakeholder value.

This report conforms to the Business Responsibility Reporting (BRR) requirement of the SEBI (Listing Obligations and Disclosure Requirements) Regulations, 2015 and the National Voluntary guidelines (NVG) on Social, Environmental and Economic Responsibilities of Business released by the Ministry of Corporate Affairs, India. Furthermore, Reliance publishes its sustainability performance in a Sustainability Report which is prepared in accordance with Global Reporting Initiative (GRI) standards and is externally assured. All the Sustainability Reports published till date can be accessed at **www.ril.com**. This report is based on the following principles.

PRINCIPLE 1: Ethics, Transparency and Accountability Businesses should conduct and govern themselves with Ethics, Transparency and Accountability

PRINCIPLE 2: Product Life Cycle Sustainability Businesses should provide goods and services that are safe and contribute to sustainability throughout their life cycle

PRINCIPLE 3: Employees' Well-being Businesses should promote the well-being of all employees

PRINCIPLE 4: Stakeholder Engagement Businesses should respect the interests of, and be responsive towards all stakeholders, especially those who are disadvantaged, vulnerable and marginalised

PRINCIPLE 5: Human Rights Businesses should respect and promote human rights

PRINCIPLE 6: Environment Businesses should respect, protect and make efforts to restore the environment

PRINCIPLE 7: Policy Advocacy Businesses, when engaged in influencing public & regulatory policy, should do so in a responsible manner

PRINCIPLE 8: Inclusive Growth Businesses should support inclusive growth and equitable development

PRINCIPLE 9: Customer Value Businesses should engage with and provide value to their customers, and consumers in a responsible manner

Principle-Wise Performance Report is Listed Below:

Principle 1: Ethics, Transparency and Accountability Disclosures	Information/Reference Sections
Coverage of Code of Conduct policy and details of stakeholder complaints received and resolved in FY 2017-18.	Human Capital Page no. 120 Corporate Governance Report Page no. 208 For Investor grievances please refer to Corporate Governance Report Page no. 196
Principle 2: Products Life Cycle Sustainability Disclosures	**Information/Reference Sections**
Products and services incorporating environmental and social risks	**(a)** Zero / low antimony spun lace: Reliance has developed in-house technology which decreases the requirement of antimony (a known carcinogen) in continuous polymerisation for manufacturing zero/low antimony spun lace fibres, used mainly in hygiene products. **(b)** Bulk tankers to supply products: RIL has increased the PTA bag size from 1.1 MT to 1.2 MT at Hazira and Dahej to reduce the use of packing material and supplies via bulk tankers which results in reduced handling, decreased contamination and increased savings to customers. **(c)** Replacement of GPPS with PET: Polyethylene Terephthalate (PET) is now used in place of General Purpose Polystyrene (GPPS) on account of its techno-economic benefits, better recyclability and safer than GPPS. Manufactured capital Page no. 138-139
Recycled products and waste	Natural Capital Page no. 112-113
Procedures for sustainable sourcing and procuring goods and services from small and local vendors	Social and Relationship Capital Page no. 144
Principle 3: Employees' Well-being Disclosures	**Information/Reference Sections**
Total workforce by various indicators of diversity (e.g. gender, physical disability, contract type etc.) and efforts for their skill enhancement	From over 15 nationalities, RIL's total employee strength as on 31st March, 2018 is 29,533 which includes 1,521 female employees. The total number of permanent employees with disabilities at RIL as on 31st March, 2018 is 70. RIL takes the health and safety of its employees very seriously and regularly conducts related training programmes. RIL's contractual employees receive mandatory safety training before entering the Company's premises and also acquire on-the-job training through the contractor and the Company. At RIL, 71.92% of its permanent workforce received safety and skill up-gradation trainings and 70.22% of women employees received trainings through classroom and

	web-based training programmes. Out of 70 permanent employees with disabilities, 37.14% received safety and skill up gradation trainings. RIL ensures 100% employee participation in safety and mock fire drills. Human Capital Page no. 114
Workforce representation and grievance redressal	Human Capital Page no. 121
Principle 4: Stakeholder Engagement Disclosures	**Information/Reference Sections**
Identification and engagement with stakeholders including the vulnerable and marginalised groups	Report on Corporate Social Responsibility Page no. 164-179 Social and Relationship Capital Page no. 142-143
Principle 5: Human Rights Disclosures	**Information/Reference Sections**
Company's policy and practices for addressing human rights concerns	Human Capital Page no. 120
Principle 6: Environment Disclosures	**Information/Reference Sections**
Company's policies and practices for environmental protection including use of clean technologies, resource conservation and climate change adaptation and mitigation	Natural Capital Page no. 110-113 Board's Report Page no. 246-250
Ensuring compliance to environmental regulations	Natural Capital Page no. 110
Principle 7: Policy Advocacy Disclosures	**Information/Reference Sections**
Responsible policy advocacy in collaboration with policymakers	Social and Relationship Capital Page no. 144-145
Principle 8: Inclusive Growth Disclosures	**Information/Reference Sections**
Details of the Company's community development initiatives including financial contribution and ensuring long-term sustainability of projects	Report on Corporate Social Responsibility Page no. 164-179 Social and Relationship Capital Page no. 141-142 Board's Report Page no. 235-239 In FY 2017-18, RIL has spent ₹745 crore on community development initiatives.
Principle 9: Customer Value Disclosures	**Information/Reference Sections**
Ensuring customer satisfaction while conforming to regulatory requirements	Social and Relationship Capital Page no. 142 As on 31st March 2018, 2,183 customer complaints were received of which 2,080 have been successfully resolved. As a protocol followed at RIL, all the complaints received are resolved within 90 days. Subsequently, most of the remaining complaints have been resolved.

Independent Reasonable Assurance Statement to Reliance Industries Limited on their Sustainability Disclosures in the Integrated Annual Report for Financial Year 2017-18

To the Management of Reliance Industries Limited, 3rd Floor, Maker Chambers IV, 222, Nariman Point, Mumbai 400021, Maharashtra, India.

Introduction We ('KPMG in India', or 'KPMG') have been engaged for the purpose of providing assurance on the Sustainability disclosures presented in the Integrated Annual Report ('the Report') of Reliance Industries Limited ('RIL' or 'the Company') for FY 2017-18. Our responsibility was to provide reasonable assurance on the Report content as described in the boundary, scope and limitations, as part of the Company's sustainability reporting assurance process.

Reporting Criteria RIL has developed its report based on the applicable accounting standards and has incorporated the principles of the International Integrated Reporting Framework (<IR>) published by the International Integrated Reporting Council (IIRC) into the Management's Discussion and Analysis section of the Report.

Its sustainability performance reporting criteria has been derived from the GRI Standards of the Global Reporting Initiative, United Nation's Sustainable Development Goals (UN SDGs), American Petroleum Institute / The International Petroleum Industry Environmental Conservation Association (API/IPIECA) Sustainability Reporting Guidelines, and Business Responsibility Reporting Framework based on the principles of National Voluntary Guidelines on Social, Environmental and Economic Responsibilities of Business (NVG – SEE), World Business Council for Sustainable Development's focus areas and Accountability's AA1000APS 2008 (Principles of Inclusivity, Materiality and Responsiveness)

Other Frameworks/Initiatives RIL, has also referred to new and emerging frameworks such as Task Force on Climate-related Financial Disclosures (TCFD) recommendations, United Nations Guiding Principles on Business and Human Rights (UNGP), United Nations Global Compact (UNGC) Principles, Global Recycle Standard (GRS) Version 3.0, Natural Capital Protocol, Social return on investment (SROI) and the selected Government of India's initiatives supported by NITI Aayog.

Assurance Standards We conducted the assurance in accordance with

- Reasonable Assurance requirements of International Federation of Accountants' (IFAC) International Standard on Assurance Engagement (ISAE) 3000 (Revised) Assurance Engagements Other than Audits or Reviews of Historical Financial Information,
- Under this standard, we have reviewed the information presented in the report against the characteristics of relevance, completeness, reliability, neutrality and understand ability.

Scope, Boundary and Limitations

- The boundary of assurance covers the sustainability performance of RIL's manufacturing divisions, refineries, exploration and production in India; business divisions such as chemicals; fibre intermediates; petroleum; polyester; polymers; Reliance Foundation and corporate office at Reliance Corporate Park, for the period 1st April, 2017 to 31st March, 2018.
- The assurance process was limited to the selected sustainability disclosures in Business Responsibility Report, Management's Discussion and Analysis, Board's Report and Corporate Social Responsibility Report.

- The sustainability disclosures covered as part of the scope of the assurance process included water recycled and reused, reduction of energy consumption, total number of employees at RIL, total man-hours of training provided to RIL's workforce.
- The selected disclosures on the other reporting criteria and frameworks/initiatives were restricted to those that were shared by the company with KPMG and are mentioned in this report.

The assurance scope excludes;

- Aspects of the report other than those mentioned above;
- Data and information outside the defined reporting period;
- The Company's statements that describe expression of opinion, belief, aspiration, expectation, aim or future intention and assertions related to Intellectual Property Rights and other competitive issues.

Assurance Procedures Our assurance process involves performing procedures to obtain evidence about the reliability of specified disclosures. The nature, timing and extent of procedures selected depend on our judgment, including the assessment of the risks of material misstatement of the selected sustainability disclosures whether due to fraud or error. In making those risk assessments, we have considered internal controls relevant to the preparation of the Report in order to design assurance procedures that are appropriate in the circumstances.

Our assurance procedures also included:

- Assessment of RIL's reporting procedures regarding their consistency with the application of GRI Standards.
- Evaluating the appropriateness of the quantification methods used to arrive at the sustainability disclosures presented in the Report.
- Verification of systems and procedures used for quantification, collation, and analysis of sustainability disclosures included in the Report.
- Understanding the appropriateness of various assumptions, estimations and materiality thresholds used by RIL for data analysis.
- Discussions with the personnel responsible for the evaluation of competence required to ensure reliability of data and information presented in the Report.
- Discussion on sustainability aspects with senior executives at the different plant locations and at the corporate office to understand the risks and opportunities from sustainability context and the strategy RIL is following.
- Assessment of the stakeholder engagement process through personal interviews and review of relevant documentation.
- Assessment of data reliability and accuracy.
- For verifying the data and information related to RIL's financial performance we have relied on its audited Financial Statements for the FY 2017-18.
- Verification of disclosures through site visits to Manufacturing units at Barabanki, Dahej, Hazira, Hoshiarpur, Jamnagar DTA, Jamnagar SEZ, Nagothane, Naroda, Patalganga, Silvassa and Vadodara; On-shore and off-shore exploration and production facilities at Gadimoga; Corporate office at Reliance Corporate Park, Navi Mumbai and review of key performance data from Shahdol.

Appropriate documentary evidence was obtained to support our conclusions on the information and data verified.

Where such documentary evidence could not be collected due to sensitive nature of the information, our team verified the same at the company premises.

Conclusions Based on our assurance procedures and in line with the scope and limitations, we conclude that

- The selected sustainability parameters and disclosures presented in the Report by RIL are fairly represented.
- The sustainability disclosures as defined under scope of assurance are in alignment with the GRI standards.
- The company has initiated its alignment on sustainability disclosures with other reporting criteria and emerging frameworks as mentioned under reporting criteria.

We have provided our observations to the Company in a separate management letter. These, do not, however, affect our conclusions regarding the Report.

Independence The assurance was conducted by a multidisciplinary team including professionals with suitable skills and experience in auditing environmental, social and economic information in line with the requirements of ISAE 3000 (Revised) standard. Our work was performed in compliance with the requirements of the IFAC Code of Ethics for Professional Accountants, which requires, among other requirements, that the members of the assurance team (practitioners) as well as the assurance firm (assurance provider) be independent of the assurance client, in relation to the scope of this assurance engagement, including not being involved in writing the Report. The Code also includes detailed requirements for practitioners regarding integrity, objectivity, professional competence and due care, confidentiality and professional behaviour. KPMG has systems and processes in place to monitor compliance with the Code and to prevent conflicts regarding independence. The firm applies ISQC 1 and the practitioner complies with the applicable independence and other ethical requirements of the IESBA code.

Responsibilities RIL is responsible for developing the Report contents. RIL is also responsible for identification of material sustainability topics, establishing and maintaining appropriate performance management and internal control systems and derivation of performance data reported. This statement is made solely to the Management of RIL in accordance with the terms of our engagement and as per scope of assurance. Our work has been undertaken so that we might state to RIL those matters for which we have been engaged to state in this statement and for no other purpose. To the fullest extent permitted by law, we do not accept or assume responsibility to anyone other than RIL for our work, for this report, or for the conclusions expressed in this independent assurance statement. The assurance engagement is based on the assumption that the data and information provided to us is complete and true. We expressly disclaim any liability or co-responsibility for any decision a person or entity would make based on this assurance statement.

Corporate Governance Report

This report is prepared in accordance with the provisions of the Securities and Exchange Board of India (Listing Obligations and Disclosure Requirements) Regulations, 2015

('Listing Regulations'), and the report contains the details of Corporate Governance systems and processes at Reliance Industries Limited (RIL).

At RIL, Corporate Governance is all about maintaining a valuable relationship and trust with all stakeholders. We consider stakeholders as partners in our success, and we remain committed to maximising stakeholders' value, be it shareholders, employees, suppliers, customers, investors, communities or policy makers. This approach to value creation emanates from our belief that sound governance system, based on relationship and trust, is integral to creating enduring value for all. We have a defined policy framework for ethical conduct of businesses. We believe that any business conduct can be ethical only when it rests on the six core values, namely, customer value, ownership mindset, respect, integrity, one team and excellence.

Statement on Company's Philosophy on Code of Governance Corporate Governance encompasses a set of systems and practices to ensure that the Company's affairs are being managed in a manner which ensures accountability, transparency and fairness in all transactions in the widest sense. The objective is to meet stakeholders' aspirations and societal expectations. Good governance practices stem from the dynamic culture and positive mindset of the organisation. We are committed to meet the aspirations of all our stakeholders. This is demonstrated in shareholder returns, high credit ratings, awards & recognitions, governance processes and an entrepreneurial performance focused work environment. Additionally, our customers have benefited from high quality products delivered at extremely competitive prices.

The essence of Corporate Governance lies in promoting and maintaining integrity, transparency and accountability in the management's higher echelons. The demands of Corporate Governance require professionals to raise their competence and capability levels to meet the expectations in managing the enterprise and its resources effectively with the highest standards of ethics. It has thus become crucial to foster and sustain a culture that integrates all components of good governance by carefully balancing the complex inter-relationship among the Board of Directors, Board Committees, Finance, Compliance and Assurance teams, Auditors and the senior management. Our employee satisfaction is reflected in the stability of our senior management, low attrition across various levels and substantially higher productivity. Above all, we feel honoured to be integral to India's social development. Details of several such initiatives are available in the Report on Corporate Social Responsibility.

At RIL, we believe that as we move closer towards our aspirations of being a global corporation, our Corporate Governance standards must be globally benchmarked. Therefore, we have institutionalised the right building blocks for future growth. The building blocks will ensure that we achieve our ambition in a prudent and sustainable manner. RIL not only adheres to the prescribed Corporate Governance practices as per the Listing Regulations, but is also committed to sound Corporate Governance principles and practices. It constantly strives to adopt emerging best practices being followed worldwide. It is our endeavour to achieve higher standards and provide oversight and guidance to the management in strategy implementation, risk management and fulfilment of stated goals and objectives.

Over the years, we have strengthened governance practices. These practices define the way business is conducted and value is generated. Stakeholders' interests are taken into account, before making any business decision. RIL has the distinction of consistently rewarding its shareholders for four eventful decades from its first IPO. Since then, RIL has moved from one big idea to another and these milestones continue to fuel its relentless pursuit of ever-higher goals.

On standalone basis, we have grown by a Compounded Annual Growth Rate (CAGR) of Revenues 23.5%, Earnings before Interest Tax Depreciation and Amortisation (EBITDA) 25.4% and Net Profit 26.3%. The financial markets have endorsed our sterling performance and the market capitalisation has increased by CAGR of 31.4% during the same period. In terms of distributing wealth to our shareholders, apart from having a track record of uninterrupted dividend payout, we have also delivered consistent unmatched shareholder returns since listing. The result of our initiative is our ever widening reach and recall. Our shareholder base has grown from 52,000 after the IPO to a consolidated present base of around 2.3 million.

For decades, RIL is growing in step with India's industrial and economic development. The Company has helped transform the Indian economy with large projects and world-class execution. The quest to help elevate India's quality of life continues and is unabated. It emanates from a fundamental article of faith: 'What is good for India is good for Reliance'.

We believe, Corporate Governance is not just a destination, but a journey to constantly improve sustainable value creation. It is an upward-moving target that we collectively strive towards achieving. Our multiple initiatives towards maintaining the highest standards of governance are detailed in this report.

Appropriate Governance Structure with Defined Roles And Responsibilities The Company has put in place an internal governance structure with defined roles and responsibilities of every constituent of the system. The Company's shareholders appoint the Board of Directors, which in turn governs the Company. The Board has established seven Committees to discharge its responsibilities in an effective manner. The Chairman and Managing Director (CMD) provides overall direction and guidance to the Board. In the operations and functioning of the Company, the CMD is assisted by four Executive Directors and a core group of senior level executives. The CMD is responsible for corporate strategy, brand equity, planning, external contacts and all management matters.

The Chairman of the Board ('the Chairman') is the leader of the Board. The Chairman is responsible for fostering and promoting the integrity of the Board while nurturing a culture where the Board works harmoniously for the long-term benefit of the Company and all its stakeholders. The Chairman guides the Board for effective governance structure in the Company.

The Chairman takes a lead role in managing the Board and facilitating effective communication among Directors. The Chairman is responsible for matters pertaining to governance, including the organisation and composition of the Board, the organisation and conduct of Board meetings, effectiveness of the Board, committees and individual Directors in fulfilling their responsibilities. The Company Secretary assists the Chairman in management of the Board's administrative activities such as meetings, schedules, agendas, communication and documentation.

The Chairman actively works with the Human Resources, Nomination and Remuneration Committee to plan the Board and committees' composition, induction of directors to the Board, plan for directors' succession and provide constructive feedback and advice on performance evaluation to directors.

Board Leadership A majority of the Board, i.e. 8 out of 14 Directors, are Independent Directors. At RIL, it is our belief that an enlightened Board consciously creates a culture of leadership to provide a long-term vision and policy approach to improve the quality of governance. The Board's actions and decisions are aligned with the Company's best interests. It is committed to the goal of sustainably elevating the Company's value creation. The Company has defined guidelines and an established framework for the meetings of the Board and Committees. These guidelines seek to systematise the decision-making process at the meetings of the Board and Committees in an informed and efficient manner.

The Board critically evaluates the Company's strategic direction, management policies and their effectiveness. The agenda for the Board review inter alia include strategic review from each of the Committees, a detailed analysis and review of annual operating plans, capital allocation and budgets. Additionally, the Board reviews risks and risk mitigation measures, financial reports and business reports from each of the sector heads. Frequent and detailed interaction sets the agenda and provides the strategic roadmap for the Company's future growth.

Ethics / Governance Policies At RIL, we strive to conduct our business and strengthen our relationships in a manner that is dignified, distinctive and responsible. We adhere to ethical standards to ensure integrity, transparency, independence and accountability in dealing with all stakeholders. Therefore, we have adopted various codes and policies to carry out our duties in an ethical manner. Some of these codes and policies are:

- Code of Conduct
- Code of Conduct for Prohibition of Insider Trading
- Health, Safety and Environment (HSE) Policy
- Vigil Mechanism and Whistle-blower Policy
- Policy on Materiality of Related Party Transactions and on dealing with Related Party Transactions
- Corporate Social Responsibility Policy
- Policy for selection of Directors and determining Director's independence
- Remuneration Policy for Directors, Key Managerial Personnel and other employees
- Policy for determining Material Subsidiaries
- Code of Practices and Procedures for Fair Disclosure of Unpublished Price Sensitive Information
- Policy for Preservation of Documents
- Policy on Determination and Disclosure of Materiality of Events and Information and Web Archival Policy
- Dividend Distribution Policy

Audits and Internal Checks and Balances The Company has an Internal Audit Cell besides external firms acting as independent internal auditors that reviews internal controls and operating systems and procedures. A dedicated Legal Compliance Cell ensures that the Company conducts its businesses with high standards of legal, statutory and regulatory compliances. RIL has instituted a legal compliance programme in conformity with the best international standards, supported by a robust online system that covers all businesses of the Company and that of its subsidiaries. The purview of this system includes various statutes, such as industrial and labour laws, taxation laws, corporate and securities laws and health, safety and environmental laws.

At the heart of the processes is the extensive use of technology. This ensures robustness and integrity of financial reporting and internal controls, allows optimal use and protection of assets, facilitates accurate and timely compilation of financial statements and management reports and ensures compliance with statutory laws, regulations and company policies.

Management Initiatives for Controls and Compliance The Company has established the "Reliance Management System" (RMS) as part of its transformation agenda. RMS incorporates an integrated framework for managing risks and internal controls. The internal financial controls have been documented, embedded and digitised in the business processes. Internal controls are regularly tested for design, implementation and operating effectiveness.

Best Corporate Governance Practices RIL maintains the highest standards of Corporate Governance. It is the Company's constant endeavour to adopt the best Corporate Governance practices keeping in view the international codes of Corporate Governance and practices of well-known global companies. Some of the best implemented global governance norms include the following:

- The Company has a designated Lead Independent Director with a defined role.
- All securities related filings with Stock Exchanges are reviewed every quarter by the Stakeholders' Relationship Committee.
- The Company has independent Committees for matters related to Corporate Governance and stakeholders' interface and nomination of Board members.
- The Company's internal audit is also conducted by independent auditors.
- The Company undergoes quarterly secretarial compliance certification from an independent company secretary who is in whole-time practice.

Business Risk and Assurance Committees (BRACS) To have a better assessment of the business and functional risks and to monitor risk mitigation effectiveness based on risk evaluation, the concept of BRACs was introduced comprising senior management personnel in the said committee.

RIL'S Sustainability Reporting Journey RIL has been publishing Sustainability Reports annually since FY 2004-05 based on the Global Reporting Initiative's (GRI) reporting guidelines. For the last decade, the reports have been GRI checked with an 'A+' application level. Furthermore, the Company published its first sustainability report according to GRI Standards' (including Oil and Gas sector disclosures) 'In accordance – Comprehensive' option which was introduced in 2016-17. The report has been externally assured (Type II high level) indicating highest level of comprehensive disclosures for GRI Standards. RIL is also a member of World Business Council of Sustainable

Development (WBCSD) and Global Reporting Initiative (GRI). WBCSD's "Reporting matters" 2015 & 2017 has recognized RIL's sustainability report as leading example of the best practices. The reports are available at http://www.ril.com/Sustainability/CorporateSustainability.aspx

Integrated Reporting RIL has been at the forefront of adopting an integrated thinking in the Company's management approach. This approach reflects in the Company's business model which stands on the foundation of value creation for all stakeholder groups. While the model is designed to deliver superior financial performance, it also ensures that in the process, there is significant amount of value addition across the organisation's value chain and its related stakeholder groups.

RIL is a firm believer that the success of a business is not merely defined by the financial performance of the Company but also on how well it is able to meet its ambitions while maintaining the balance of the natural ecosystem and meeting the expectations of the people who are associated with it. Ensuring long-term societal value creation and propagating technological advancement are equally critical factors for the Company's long-term sustainability. For years, RIL has been living this philosophy and has based its business and investment decisions on this integrated approach.

Taking one step further in this direction, RIL published its maiden Integrated Annual Report in the FY 2016-17 aligned with the International Integrated Reporting Council's (IIRC) <IR> framework. The journey has been continued this year as well with renewed vigor and focus. The concept of the six capitals of business as suggested by the <IR> framework has been ingrained into the Company's management philosophy and has become an important enabler for RIL's value creation story. This integrated annual report builds on this story to showcase the Company's contribution towards each of the six capitals, namely, natural capital, human capital, intellectual capital, manufactured capital, financial capital and social and relationship capital.

Shareholders' Communications The Board recognises the importance of two-way communication with shareholders, giving a balanced report of results and progress and responding to questions and issues raised. RIL's corporate website (www.ril.com) has information for institutional and retail shareholders alike. Shareholders seeking information related to their shareholding may contact the Company directly or through the Company's Registrars and Transfer Agents, details of which are available on the Company's website. RIL ensures that complaints of its shareholders are responded to promptly. A comprehensive and informative shareholders' reference is available on the website of the Company.

Role of the Company Secretary in overall Governance Process The Company Secretary plays a key role in ensuring that the Board (including committees thereof) procedures are followed and regularly reviewed. The Company Secretary ensures that all relevant information, details and documents are made available to the Directors and senior management for effective decision-making at the meetings. The Company Secretary is primarily responsible to assist and advice the Board in the conduct of affairs of the Company, to ensure compliance with applicable statutory requirements, to provide guidance to directors and to facilitate convening of meetings. He interfaces between the management and regulatory authorities for governance matters.

Board of Directors

Board Composition and Category of Directors The Company's policy is to maintain optimum combination of Executive and Non-Executive Directors. The composition of the Board and category of Directors are as follows:

(i) Promoter Directors
(ii) Independent Directors
(iii) Executive Directors

Selection of Independent Directors Considering the requirement of skill sets on the Board, eminent people having an independent standing in their respective field / profession, and who can effectively contribute to the Company's business and policy decisions are considered by the Human Resources, Nomination and Remuneration Committee, for appointment, as Independent Director on the Board. The Committee, inter alia, considers qualification, positive attributes, area of expertise and number of Directorship(s) and Membership(s) held in various committees of other companies by such persons in accordance with the Company's Policy for Selection of Directors and determining Directors' independence. The Board considers the Committee's recommendation, and takes appropriate decision.

Every Independent Director, at the first meeting of the Board in which he participates as a Director and thereafter at the first meeting of the Board in every financial year, gives a declaration that he meets the criteria of independence as provided under the law.

Familiarisation Programmes for Board Members The Board members are provided with necessary documents / brochures, reports and internal policies to enable them to familiarise with the Company's procedures and practices.

Periodic presentations are made at the Board and Committee meetings on business and performance updates of the Company, global business environment, business strategy and risks involved. Detailed presentations on the Company's business segments are made at the separate meetings of the Independent Directors from time to time.

Quarterly updates on relevant statutory, regulatory changes and landmark judicial pronouncements encompassing important laws are regularly circulated to the Directors. Site visits to various plant locations are organised for the Independent Directors to enable them to understand and acquaint with the operations of the Company.

The details of such familiarisation programmes for Independent Directors are put up on the Company's website and can be accessed at http://www.ril.com/InvestorRelations/Downloads.aspx

Code of Conduct The Company has in place a comprehensive Code of Conduct ('the Code') applicable to the Directors and employees. The Code is applicable to Non-Executive Directors including Independent Directors to such an extent as may be applicable to them depending on their roles and responsibilities. The Code gives guidance and support needed for ethical conduct of business and compliance of law. The Code reflects the core values of the Company viz. Customer Value, Ownership Mindset, Respect, Integrity, One Team and Excellence.

A copy of the Code has been put up on the Company's website and can be accessed at http://www.ril.com/DownloadFiles/IRStatutory/Code-of-Conduct.pdf The Code has been circulated to Directors and Management Personnel, and its compliance is affirmed by them annually.

A declaration signed by the Company's Chairman and Managing Director is published in this Report.

Performance Evaluation Criteria for Directors The Human Resources, Nomination and Remuneration Committee has devised a criteria for evaluation of the performance of the Directors including Independent Directors. The said criteria provides certain parameters like attendance, acquaintance with business, communicate *inter se* board members, effective participation, domain knowledge, compliance with code of conduct, vision and strategy, benchmarks established by global peers etc., which is in compliance with applicable laws, regulations and guidelines.

Board Meetings, Committee Meetings and Procedures

Institutionalised Decision-making Process The Board of Directors is the apex body constituted by shareholders for overseeing the Company's overall functioning. The Board provides and evaluates the Company's strategic direction, management policies and their effectiveness, and ensures that shareholders' long-term interests are being served.

The Board has constituted seven Committees, viz. Audit Committee, Human Resources, Nomination and Remuneration Committee, Stakeholders' Relationship Committee, Corporate Social Responsibility and Governance Committee, Risk Management Committee, Health, Safety and Environment Committee and Finance Committee. The Board is authorised to constitute additional functional Committees, from time to time, depending on business needs.

The Company's internal guidelines for Board / Committee meetings facilitate decision-making process at its meetings in an informed and efficient manner. The following sub-sections deal with the practice of these guidelines at RIL.

Post Meeting follow-up Mechanism The guidelines for Board / Committee meetings facilitate an effective post meeting follow-up, review and reporting process for decisions taken by the Board and Committees thereof.

Important decisions taken at Board / Committee meetings are communicated promptly to the concerned departments / divisions. Action taken report on decisions / minutes of the previous meeting(s) is placed at the succeeding meeting of the Board / Committees for noting.

Compliance The Company Secretary, while preparing the agenda, notes on agenda and minutes of the meeting(s), is responsible for and is required to ensure adherence to all applicable laws and regulations, including the Companies Act, 2013 read with rules issued thereunder, Listing Regulations and Secretarial Standards issued by the Institute of Company Secretaries of India.

Terms of Reference and Other Details of Committees

Audit Committee The Committee's composition and terms of reference are in compliance with the provisions of Section 177 of the Companies Act, 2013 and Regulation 18 of the Listing Regulations. The composition of Committee is given in this Report.

Members of the Audit Committee possess requisite qualifications.

Terms of Reference of the Committee inter alia include the following

- Oversight of the Company's financial reporting process and the disclosure of its financial information to ensure that the financial statement is correct, sufficient and credible.
- Recommendation for appointment, remuneration and terms of appointment of auditors, including cost auditors, of the Company.
- Approval of payment to auditors, including cost auditors, for any other services rendered by them.
- Reviewing, with the management, the annual financial statements and auditors' report thereon before submission to the Board for its approval, with particular reference to:
  (a) matters required to be included in the Directors' Responsibility Statement to be included in the Board's Report;
  (b) changes, if any, in accounting policies and practices and reasons for the same;

(c) major accounting entries involving estimates based on the exercise of judgment by management;
(d) significant adjustments made in the financial statements arising out of audit findings;
(e) compliance with listing and other legal requirements relating to financial statements;
(f) disclosure of any related party transactions;
(g) modified opinion(s) in the draft audit report.

- Reviewing, with the management, the quarterly financial statements before submission to the Board for approval.
- Reviewing, with the management, the statement of uses / application of funds raised through an issue (public issue, rights issue, preferential issue, etc.), the statement of funds utilised for the purposes other than those stated in the offer document / prospectus / notice and the report submitted by the monitoring agency monitoring the utilisation of proceeds of a public or rights issue, and making appropriate recommendations to the Board to take up steps in this matter.
- Reviewing and monitoring the auditor's independence and performance and effectiveness of audit process.
- Approval or any subsequent modification of transactions with related parties of the Company.
- Scrutiny of inter-corporate loans and investments.
- Valuation of undertakings or assets of the Company, wherever it is necessary.
- Evaluation of internal financial controls and risk management systems.
- (a) Reviewing, with the management, performance of statutory and internal auditors;
  (b) Reviewing, with the management, adequacy of the internal control systems.
- Reviewing the adequacy of internal audit function, if any, including the structure of internal audit department, staffing and seniority of the official heading the department, reporting structure coverage and frequency of internal audit.
- Discussion with internal auditors of any significant findings and follow up there on.
- Reviewing the findings of any internal investigations by the internal auditors into matters where there is suspected fraud or irregularity or a failure of internal control systems of a material nature and reporting the matter to the Board.
- Discussion with statutory auditors before the audit commences, about the nature and scope of audit as well as post audit discussion to ascertain any area of concern.
- To look into the reasons for substantial defaults, in the payment to the depositors, debenture holders, shareholders (in case of non-payment of declared dividend) and creditors.
- (a) To review the functioning of the Whistle-blower mechanism;
  (b) To oversee the vigil mechanism
- Approval of appointment of Chief Financial Officer after assessing qualifications, experience and background etc. of the candidate.
- Mandatorily review the following:
  (a) Management Discussion and Analysis of financial condition and results of operations;
  (b) Statement of significant related party transactions (as defined by the Audit Committee), submitted by management;
  (c) Management letters/letters of internal control weaknesses issued by the statutory auditors;
  (d) Internal audit reports relating to internal control weaknesses;

(e) The appointment, removal and terms of remuneration of the chief internal auditor;

(f) Statement of deviations:

(i) quarterly statement of deviation(s) including report of monitoring agency, if applicable, submitted to stock exchanges(s) in terms of Regulation 32(1) of the Listing Regulations.

(ii) annual statement of funds utilised for purpose other than those stated in the offer document / prospectus in terms of Regulation 32(7) of the Listing Regulations.

- Reviewing financial statements, in particular the investments made by the Company's unlisted subsidiaries.
- Note report of compliance officer as per SEBI (Prohibition of Insider Trading) Regulation, 2015.
- Formulating the scope, functioning, periodicity of and methodology for conducting the internal audit.
- Annual performance evaluation of the Committee
- Review show cause, demand, prosecution notice(s) and penalty notice(s), which are materially important.
- Review any material default in financial obligations to and by the listed entity, or substantial non-payment for goods sold by the Company.
- Review any issue, which involves possible public or product liability claims of substantial nature, including any judgement or order which may have passed strictures on the conduct of the listed entity or taken an adverse view regarding another enterprise that may have negative implications on the Company.
- Review details of joint venture or collaboration agreement.
- Review sale of investments, subsidiaries, assets which are material in nature and not in normal course of business.
- Review quarterly details of foreign exchange exposures and the steps taken by management to limit the risks of adverse exchange rate movement, if material.
- To carry out any other function as is mandated by the Board from time to time and / or enforced by any statutory notification, amendment or modifications as may be applicable.

General The representatives of Statutory Auditors are permanent invitees to the Audit Committee meetings. The representatives of Statutory Auditors, Executives from Accounts department, Finance department, Corporate Secretarial department and Internal Audit department attend the Audit Committee meetings. The Cost Auditors attend the Audit Committee meeting where cost audit report is discussed. The due date for filing the cost audit report in XBRL mode for the financial year ended March 31, 2017 was August 19, 2017 and the cost audit report was filed by the Company on August 11, 2017. The cost audit report of the Company for financial year ended March 31, 2018 will be filed with Central Government on or before the due date as prescribed under Companies Act, 2013.

The Internal Auditor reports directly to the Audit Committee.

The Chairman of the Audit Committee was present at the last Annual General Meeting held on July 21, 2017.

Human Resources, Nomination and Remuneration Committee The Committee's composition and terms of reference are in compliance with the provisions of the Companies Act, 2013, Regulation 19 of the Listing Regulations and Securities and Exchange Board of India (Share Based Employee Benefits) Regulations, 2014, as amended from time to time. The composition of Committee is given in this Report.

Stakeholders' Relationship Committee The Committee's composition and terms of reference are in compliance with the provisions of the Companies Act, 2013 and Regulation 20 of the Listing Regulations. The composition of Committee is given in this Report.

The Stakeholders' Relationship Committee is primarily responsible to review all matters connected with the Company's transfer of securities and redressal of shareholders'/ investors'/ security holders' complaints.

Prohibition of Insider Trading With a view to regulate trading in securities by the directors and designated employees, the Company has adopted a Code of Conduct for Prohibition of Insider Trading.

Investor Grievance Redressal The number of complaints received and resolved to the satisfaction of investors during the year under review and their break-up are as under:

Type of Complaints	*Number of Complaints*
Non-Receipt of Annual Reports	131
Non-Receipt of Dividend	133
Non-Receipt of Interest/ Redemption Warrants	1
Transfer of securities	191
Total	456

As on March 31, 2018, no complaints were outstanding.

The response time for attending to investors' correspondence during financial year 2017-18 is as under:

Particulars	*Number*	*%*
Total number of correspondence received during 2017-18	2,37,389	100.00
Replied within 1 to 4 days of receipt	2,36,847	99.77
Replied within 5 to 7 days of receipt	542	0.23

Corporate Social Responsibility and Governance Committee The Committee's primary responsibility is to assist the Board in discharging its social responsibilities by way of formulating and monitoring implementation of the framework of corporate social responsibility policy, observe practices of Corporate Governance at all levels, and to suggest remedial measures wherever necessary. The Board has also empowered the Committee to look into the matters related to sustainability and overall governance.

The Committee's composition and terms of reference are in compliance with the provisions of the Companies Act, 2013. The composition of Committee is given in this Report.

Risk Management Committee The Committee's prime responsibility is to implement and monitor the risk management plan and policy of the Company. The Committee's composition is in compliance with the provisions of Regulation 21 of the Listing Regulations. The composition of Committee is given in this Report.

Terms of Reference of the Committee *'inter alia'* include the following:

- Framing of Risk Management Plan and Policy.
- Overseeing implementation / Monitoring of Risk Management Plan and Policy.
- Validating the process of Risk Management.
- Validating the procedure for Risk Minimisation.
- Periodically reviewing and evaluating the Risk Management Policy and practices with respect to risk assessment and risk management processes.
- Continually obtaining reasonable assurance from management that all known and emerging risks have been identified and mitigated or managed.
- Review of development and implementation of a risk management policy including identification therein of element of risk.
- Annual performance evaluation of the Committee.
- To carry out any other function as is mandated by the Board from time to time and / or enforced by any statutory notification, amendment or modification as may be applicable.

Health, Safety and Environment Committee The Committee is primarily responsible to monitor and ensure the highest standards of environmental, health and safety norms are maintained, and the Company's operations are in compliance with the applicable pollution and environmental laws across all locations. The Committee fulfils its responsibilities by reviewing with the management, health, safety, environmental and social impacts of the Company's various projects and operations.

Finance Committee The composition of Committee is given in this Report.

Terms of Reference of the Committee *'inter alia'* Include the following:

- Review the Company's financial policies, risk assessment and minimisation procedures, strategies and capital structure, working capital and cash flow management, and make such reports and recommendations to the Board with respect thereto, as it may deem advisable.
- Review banking arrangements and cash management
- Exercise all powers to borrow money (otherwise than by issue of debentures) within limits approved by the Board, and take necessary actions connected therewith, including refinancing for optimisation of borrowing costs.
- Give guarantees / issue letters of comfort / providing securities within the limits approved by the Board.
- Borrow money by way of loan and / or issue and allot bonds / notes denominated in one or more foreign currencies in international markets for the purpose of refinancing the existing debt, capital expenditure, general corporate purposes, including working capital requirements and possible strategic investments within limits approved by the Board.
- Provide corporate guarantee / performance guarantee within the limits approved by the Board.

- Approve opening and operation of Investment Management Accounts with foreign banks and appoint them as agents, establishment of representative / sales offices in or outside India.
- Other transactions or financial issues that the Board may desire to have them reviewed by the Finance Committee.
  (a) Forex derivative transactions
  (b) OTC trades
  (c) Note outstanding borrowings, inter-corporate investments, loans and guarantees
  (d) Note status report and hedging activities on commodity and forex products
- Delegate authorities from time to time to the executives / authorised persons to implement the Committee's decisions.
- Review regularly and make recommendations about changes to the charter of the Committee.
- Carry out any other function as is mandated by the Board from time to time.

Directors' Remuneration: Remuneration Policy The Company's Remuneration Policy for Directors, Key Managerial Personnel and other employees is annexed as 'Annexure IVB' to the Board's Report. Further, the Company has devised a Policy for performance evaluation of Independent Directors, Board, Committees and other individual Directors.

The Company's remuneration policy is directed towards rewarding performance based on review of achievements periodically. The remuneration policy is in consonance with the existing industry practice.

Subsidiary Companies' Monitoring Framework All subsidiary companies are Board managed with their Boards having the rights and obligations to manage such companies in the best interest of their stakeholders. The Company does not have any material unlisted subsidiary.

The Company monitors performance of subsidiary companies, inter alia, by the following means:

- Financial statements, in particular investments made by subsidiary companies, are reviewed quarterly by the Company's Audit Committee.
- Minutes of Board meetings of subsidiary companies are placed before the Company's Board regularly.
- A statement containing all significant transactions and arrangements entered into by subsidiary companies is placed before the Company's Board.
- Presentations are made by the senior management of major subsidiaries on business performance to the Board of Directors of the Company.

The Company's Policy for determining Material Subsidiaries is put up on the Company's website and can be accessed at http://www.ril.com/DownloadFiles/IRStatutory/Material-Subsidiaries.pdf

Disclosure on Materially Significant Related Party Transactions That May Have Potential Conflict with the Company's Interests at Large The Company's major related party transactions are generally with its subsidiaries and associates. The related party transactions are entered into based on considerations of various business exigencies, such as synergy in operations, sectoral specialisation and the Company's long-term strategy for sectoral investments, optimisation of market share, profitability, legal requirements, liquidity and capital resources of subsidiaries and associates.

All the contracts / arrangements / transactions entered by the Company during the financial year with related parties were in its ordinary course of business and on an arm's length basis. They were substantially on similar terms as in earlier years, as per the provisions of contract.

During the year, the Company had not entered into any contract / arrangement / transaction with related parties which could be considered material in accordance with the policy of the Company on materiality of related party transactions. Please refer Note 31 of Standalone Financial Statements, forming part of the Annual Report.

None of the transactions with any of related parties were in conflict with the Company's interest.

The Company's Policy on Materiality of Related Party Transactions and on dealing with Related Party Transactions is put up on the Company's website and can be accessed at http://www.ril.com/DownloadFiles/IRStatutory/Policy-on-Materiality-of-RPT.pdf

Whistle-Blower Policy The Company promotes ethical behaviour in all its business activities and has put in place a mechanism for reporting illegal or unethical behaviour. The Company has a Vigil Mechanism and Whistle-blower policy under which the employees are free to report violations of applicable laws and regulations and the Code of Conduct. The reportable matters may be disclosed to the Ethics and Compliance Task Force which operates under the supervision of the Audit Committee. Employees may also report to the Chairman of the Audit Committee. During the year under review, no employee was denied access to the Audit Committee.

Board's Report

In addition to the (i) financial results, (ii) results of operations and the state of affairs, (iii) financial performance review and analysis, (iv) dividends and (v) bonus shares. The highlights of the Board's report are as follows:

Management's Discussion and Analysis Report Management's Discussion and Analysis Report for the year under review, as stipulated under the Securities and Exchange Board of India (Listing Obligations and Disclosure Requirements) Regulations, 2015 ("Listing Regulations"), is presented in a separate section, forming part of the Annual Report. The developments in business operations / performance of the Company and its major subsidiaries consolidated with the Company are included in the report.

Credit Rating The Company's financial discipline and prudence is reflected in the strong credit ratings ascribed by rating agencies as given below:

Instrument	*Rating Agency*	*Rating*	*Outlook*	*Remarks*
International Debt	S&P	BBB+	Stable	Two notches above India's sovereign rating
International Debt	Moody's	Baa2	Stable	At par with India's sovereign rating
Long Term Debt	CRISIL	CRISIL AAA	Stable	Highest rating awarded by CRISIL
Long Term Debt	India Ratings	IND AAA	Stable	Highest rating awarded by India Ratings

Consolidated Financial Statement In accordance with the provisions of the Companies Act, 2013 ("the Act") and Ind AS 110 – Consolidated Financial Statement read with Ind AS - 28

Investments in Associates and Ind AS 31 – Interests in Joint Ventures, the audited consolidated financial statement is provided in the Annual Report.

Subsidiaries, Joint Ventures and Associate Companies A statement containing the salient features of the financial statement of subsidiary / associate / joint venture companies, as per Section 129(3) of the Act, is provided on consolidated financial statement.

The audited financial statement including the consolidated financial statement of the Company and all other documents required to be attached thereto is put on the Company's website. The financial statements of each of the subsidiaries is put on the Company's website. These documents will also be available for inspection on all working days, during business hours, at the Registered Office of the Company.

The Company has formulated a Policy for determining Material Subsidiaries.

Directors' Responsibility Statement Your Directors state that:

(a) in the preparation of the annual accounts for the year ended March 31, 2018, the applicable accounting standards read with requirements set out under Schedule III to the Act have been followed and there are no material departures from the same;

(b) the Directors have selected such accounting policies and applied them consistently and made judgments and estimates that are reasonable and prudent so as to give a true and fair view of the state of affairs of the Company as at March 31, 2018 and of the profit of the Company for the year ended on that date;

(c) the Directors have taken proper and sufficient care for the maintenance of adequate accounting records in accordance with the provisions of the Act for safeguarding the assets of the Company and for preventing and detecting fraud and other irregularities;

(d) the Directors have prepared the annual accounts on a going concern basis;

(e) the Directors have laid down internal financial controls to be followed by the Company and that such internal financial controls are adequate and are operating effectively; and

(f) the Directors have devised proper systems to ensure compliance with the provisions of all applicable laws and that such systems are adequate and operating effectively.

Corporate Governance The Company is committed to maintain the highest standards of Corporate Governance and adhere to the Corporate Governance requirements set out by the Securities and Exchange Board of India (SEBI). The Company has also implemented several best governance practices. The report on Corporate Governance as stipulated under the Listing Regulations forms an integral part of this Report. The requisite certificate from the Auditors of the Company confirming compliance with the conditions of Corporate Governance is attached to the report on Corporate Governance.

Business Responsibility Report As stipulated under the Listing Regulations, the Business Responsibility Report describing the initiatives taken by the Company from an environmental, social and governance perspective is attached as a part of the Annual Report.

Corporate Social Responsibility (CSR) During the year under review, the Company has won the Golden Peacock Award 2017 for the success of its Corporate Social Responsibility initiatives and in particular for the transformative work done by Reliance Foundation (RF), the CSR arm of the Company. Under the able leadership of its Founder and Chairperson, Smt. Nita M. Ambani,

RF has touched the lives of 20 million people across India covering more than 13,500 villages and 100 urban locations. The Company was recognized by the Awards Jury under the Chairmanship of Justice (Dr.) Arijit Pasayat, former Judge, the Supreme Court of India. Golden Peacock Award, is instituted by the Institute of Directors (IOD), India in 1991, and are regarded as a benchmark of Corporate Excellence worldwide.

The Corporate Social Responsibility and Governance Committee (CSR&G Committee) has formulated and recommended to the Board, a Corporate Social Responsibility Policy (CSR Policy) indicating the activities to be undertaken by the Company, which has been approved by the Board.

The key philosophy of CSR initiatives of the Company is guided by three core commitments of Scale, Impact and Sustainability.

The Company has identified following focus areas for CSR engagement:

- *Rural Transformation:* Creating sustainable livelihood solutions, addressing poverty, hunger and malnutrition.
- *Environment:* Environmental sustainability, ecological balance, conservation of natural resources and promoting bio-diversity.
- *Health:* Affordable solutions for healthcare through improved access, awareness and health seeking behaviour.
- *Education and Sports:* Access to quality education, training and skill enhancement, building sports & skills in young students.
- *Disaster Response:* Managing and responding to disaster.
- *Arts, Culture and Heritage:* Protection and promotion of India's art, culture and heritage.

The Company also undertakes other need based initiatives in compliance with Schedule VII to the Act.

Risk Management Your Company has an elaborate Group Risk Management Framework, which is designed to enable risks to be identified, assessed and mitigated appropriately. The Risk Management Committee of the Company has been entrusted with the responsibility to assist the Board in (a) Overseeing and approving the Company's enterprise wide risk management framework; and (b) Overseeing that all the risks that the organisation faces such as Strategic and Commercial, Safety and Operations, Compliance and Control and Financial risks have been identified and assessed and there is an adequate risk management infrastructure in place, capable of addressing those risks.

More details on Risk Management indicating development and implementation of Risk Management policy including identification of elements of risk and their mitigation are covered in Management Discussion and Analysis section, which forms part of this Report.

Internal Financial Controls Internal Financial Controls are an integrated part of the risk management process, addressing financial and financial reporting risks. The internal financial controls have been documented, digitised and embedded in the business processes.

Assurance on the effectiveness of internal financial controls is obtained through management reviews, control self-assessment, continuous monitoring by functional experts as well as testing of the internal financial control systems by the internal auditors during the course of their audits. We believe that these systems provide reasonable assurance that our internal financial controls are designed effectively and are operating as intended.

Performance Evaluation The Company has devised a Policy for performance evaluation of the Board, Committees and other individual Directors (including Independent Directors) which include criteria for performance evaluation of Non-executive Directors and Executive Directors. The evaluation process inter alia considers attendance of Directors at Board and committee meetings, acquaintance with business, communicating inter se board members, effective participation, domain knowledge, compliance with code of conduct, vision and strategy.

The Board carried out an annual performance evaluation of the Board, Committees, Individual Directors and the Chairperson. The Chairman of the respective Committees shared the report on evaluation with the respective Committee members. The performance of each Committee was evaluated by the Board, based on report on evaluation received from respective Committees.

The report on performance evaluation of the Individual Directors was reviewed by the Chairman of the Board and feedback was given to Directors.

Auditors and Auditors' Report The statutory auditors have confirmed that they are not disqualified from continuing as Auditors of the Company.

The Notes on financial statement referred to in the Auditors' Report are self-explanatory and do not call for any further comments. The Auditors' Report does not contain any qualification, reservation, adverse remark or disclaimer.

The Secretarial Audit Report does not contain any qualification, reservation, adverse remark or disclaimer.

Vigil Mechanism RIL has established a robust Vigil Mechanism and a Whistle-blower policy in accordance with provisions of the Act and Listing Regulations. The Vigil Mechanism is supervised by an 'Ethics & Compliance Task Force' comprising a member of the Board as the Chairperson and senior executives as members.

Protected disclosures can be made by a whistle-blower through an e-mail, or dedicated telephone line or a letter to the Task Force or to the Chairman of the Audit Committee. The Vigil Mechanism and whistle-blower policy is put on the Company's website.

Particulars of Loans Given, Investments Made, Guarantees Given and Securities Provided Particulars of loans given, Investments made, guarantees given and securities provided along with the purpose for which the loan or guarantee or security is proposed to be utilised by the recipient are provided in the standalone financial statement.

PART 3

FINANCIAL ANALYSIS

The focus of this part is on use of financial accounting by outside-users. While Chapter 5 deals with statement of cash flow, and financial statements analysis is described and illustrated in Chapter 6.

5 Statement of Cash Flows

LEARNING OBJECTIVES

After reading this chapter you will be able to:

- **LO 5.1** Explain the concept of statement of cash flows
- **LO 5.2** Determine cash inflows and cash outflows transactions
- **LO 5.3** Understand the usefulness of statement of cash flows
- **LO 5.4** Illustrate preparation of statement of cash flows
- **LO 5.5** Discuss cash flow statement as per AS-7

INTRODUCTION

The preceding two chapters have described the two major financial statements, namely, balance sheet and income statement of a business/corporate firm. A balance sheet shows the financial position of the a firm as at the last day of the accounting period. An income statement focuses on financial performance (profit or loss) due to the operating activities of a firm during the period. Revenues recorded in income statement do not reflect cash inflows as the debtors may pay later. Likewise, some of the expenses shown in income statement may be non-cash expenses (depreciation, amortisation etc.) and some may not be paid in full (goods purchased on credit, salaries payable etc). Thus, the period's profit or loss does not bear direct relationship to the cash flows associated with the period's operations. It does not evidently provide information about the investing and financing activities of the firm during the accounting period.

This chapter describes the third financial statement a company is required to prepare, namely, the statement of cash flows. The objective of the cash-flow statement is to provide information about the cash flows associated with operating, investing and financing activities of the firm during the accounting period. The information is significant to the stakeholders of a company. Dividends payable to the shareholders obviously are dependent on cash flows; interest payment and debt repayment to the lenders require the availability of cash; payment to the employees, suppliers and taxes in time is contingent upon the company's ability to generate adequate cash flows to meet these financial obligations.[1] For these reasons, statement of cash flows/cash flow statement (CFS) is the third major financial statement of a company. The meaning, sources and uses of cash, and usefulness of the CFS are outlined first. The preparation of CFS is also covered. Its preparation in conformity with Ind AS-7 is illustrated subsequently. Annexure I contains the actual cash flow statement of the Reliance Industries Ltd. The main points are summarised by way of recapitulation.

MEANING

LO 5.1 Explain the concept of statement of cash flows

Cash flow statement is a statement which indicates sources of cash inflows and transactions of cash outflows of a firm during an accounting period. The activities/transactions which generate cash inflows are known as sources of cash and activities which cause cash outflows are known as uses of cash. It is appropriately termed as "***Where Got Where Gone Statement***".

It may be emphasised that the information contained in the CFS are objective and, hence, more credible and reliable *vis-à-vis* the other financial statements. The reason is that ***cash is cash*** and the amounts of cash flows are not affected by the subjective judgments and estimates that are normally made in revenues, expenses and other accruals.[2] The CFS is a financial document as it leaves no scope for any maneuvering on the amounts of cash inflows and cash outflows.

SOURCES AND USES OF CASH

LO 5.2 Determine cash inflows and cash outflows transactions

Exhibit 5.1 shows major items of cash inflows and cash outflows.

EXHIBIT 5.1 Statement of Cash Flows of Hypothetical Limited

Particulars	*Amounts*
(I) Sources of Cash Inflows:	
(1) Business operations/operating activities	
(2) Non-business/operating activities (interest/dividend received)	
(3) Sale of long-term assets (plant, building and equipment)	
(4) Issue of additional long-term securities (equity, preference shares and debentures)	
(5) Additional long-term borrowings (banks and financial institutions)	
(6) Others sources (specify them)	
(II) Sources of Cash Outflows:	
(1) Purchase of long-term assets (plant and machinery, land and building, office equipments and furniture)	
(2) Redemption of preference shares and debentures	
(3) Repurchase of equity shares	
(4) Repayment of long-term borrowings	
(5) Cash dividends paid to shareholders (preference and equity)	
(6) Others items (specify)	
Net Increase (Decrease) in Cash **[I – II]**	

USEFULNESS OF STATEMENT OF CASH FLOWS

LO 5.3 Understand the usefulness of statement of cash flows

The cash flow statement helps to provide answers to users to some of the important questions related to the company such as the following:

- How much cash has been generated from normal business operating activities/operations of a company?
- What have been the other premier financing activities of the firm through which cash has been raised? What has happened to cash so obtained?

- How much cash has been spent on investment activities, say, on purchase of new plant and equipments?
- How was the redemption of preference shares and debentures accomplished?
- Have long-term sources of cash (internally generated plus raised externally) adequate to finance purchase of new long-term/fixed assets?
- What has been the proportion of debt and equity for cash raised from outside?
- Why are dividends not larger?
- Is the company borrowing to pay cash dividends?
- Has the liquidity position of the company improved?

Thus, the CFS enables the management to see whether the long-term funds are adequate to finance major fixed assets expansion. A situation in which short-term sources (bank overdraft, temporary loans, etc.) constitute the bulk of sources for long-term purposes may not be desirable. Such a pattern of financing is likely to cause problems for the firm to meet its current liabilities in future. Besides, the CFS also indicates the extent of reliance on external resources *vis-a-vis* the internal sources. Thus, the CFS clearly highlights the firm's financing and investment activities.

The CFS, when prepared on a projected basis, has immense potential/utility as a tool of financial planning. It shows the effect of various financing and investment decisions on future cashflows. If the implementation of the decision results in excessive or inadequate cash, steps may be taken to improve the situation or review the decisions. For instance, if the cash position is expected to deteriorate, funds may be raised by borrowing or issuing new equity shares. If the required amount is not feasible to be raised, plans for acquisition of assets may be postponed or alternative operative plans can be developed to ensure that the desired future level of business operations, expansion, and so on, are achieved. Thus, the CFS enables the management to revise/review its investments, operations and financing activities so as to conform to the desired financial inflow and outflow of resources. Above all, the long-term lenders can use the statement as a means of estimating the firm's ability to service their debts.

PREPARATION OF STATEMENT OF CASH FLOWS

LO 5.4 Illustrate preparation of statement of cash flows

You will remember that the balance sheet and income statement are prepared from the ledger account balances of a company. In contrast, the cash flow statement is derived from these two financial statements. The CFS explains factors which have caused changes in assets, liabilities and shareholders' funds between the opening and closing dates of the accounting period. Therefore, the CFS can be prepared by (i) finding the difference in amounts among the various items (say, changes in long-term liabilities, long-term assets) between the comparative balance sheets and then (ii) analysing the causes of difference. The analysis, in some cases, is facilitated by the use of 'T' accounts. The preparation of CFS is illustrated in Example 5.1.

Example 5.1

Given below are the balance sheets as on March 31, previous year and current year, and a statement of income and reconciliation of earnings for the current year of Electronics Ltd (EL). The only item in the plant and machinery account sold during the year was a specialised machine that originally cost ₹15,00,000. The accumulated depreciation on this machine at the time of sale was ₹8,00,000. The machine was sold for ₹6,00,000 and full payment was received in cash. Electronics Ltd. purchased patents for ₹16,00,000 during the year. Besides cash purchases of plant and equipment, the assets of another company were also purchased for ₹1,00,00,000 payable in fully paid-up shares, issued at par; the assets purchased being goodwill, ₹30,00,000 and plant, ₹70,00,000.

Comparative Balance Sheets

Particulars	*March 31 Previous Year (₹ lakh)*	*March 31 Current Year (₹ lakh)*
Cash	74	37
Sundry debtors	54	47
Inventories	312	277
Prepaid expenses	6	4
Land	60	60
Patents	55	65
Plant and machinery	420	550
Less: Accumulated depreciation	(105)	(120)
Goodwill	—	30
Total Assets	876	950
Sundry creditors	86	102
Provision for income tax	89	17
Debentures	220	60
Equity capital	250	560
Retained earnings	231	211
Total Liabilities	876	950

Statement of Income and Reconciliation of Earnings for Current Year

Particulars		*Amount (₹ lakh)*
Net sales		1,977
Less: Cost of goods sold		1,480
Gross profit		497
Less: Operating expenses (includes depreciation on plant and machinery and amortisation of patents)		486
Less: Interest on debentures		14
Net loss from operations		(3)
Add: Retained earnings (previous year)		231
		228
Less: Dividend paid	16	
Less: Loss on sale of assets	1	17
Retained earnings (March 31, current year)		211

From the foregoing information, prepare a statement of cash-flows for Electronics Ltd.

Solution

Statement of Cash Flows of Electronics Limited the current year

Particulars		*Amount (in ₹ lakh)*
(A) Sources of cash inflows		
Business operations		
Cash from customers/debtors (1)*	₹1,984	
Less payment to creditors (2)*	(1,429)	
Less operating expenses (5)*	(455)	
Less interest on debentures	14	
Less taxes paid (₹89-₹17)	72	14
Sale of machine		6
Issue of equity share capital (8)*		210
		230

(Contd.)

(Contd.)

(B) Cash outflows	
Purchase of long-term assets	
Plant and machinery (6)*	75
Patents	16
Redemption of debentures (7)*	160
Dividends paid to equity shareholders	16
	267
(C) Net decrease in cash (B-A)	37
Cash at beginning of year	37
Cash at year-end	74

Note: Figures in brackets refer to working note number.

Working Notes

(A) Determination of cash from business operation requires recasting of income statement from accrual basis to cash basis. Exclusion of non-cash items, namely, depreciation and amortisation is obvious. The less obvious is the computation of cash inflows from debtors/customers and cash payments to creditors for goods purchased and expenses. The following working notes provide these required inputs.

(1) Cash Receipts from Debtors:

Sundry Debtors Account

(Amount in ₹ lakh)

Particulars	*Amount*	*Particulars*	*Amount*
To Balance b/f (opening balance)	54	By Cash (receipts from debtors, balancing figure)	1,984
To Net sales (assumed credit sales)	1,977	By Balance c/d	47
	2,031		2,031

Alternatively

(in ₹ lakh)

Net sales	1,977
Add debtors due at the beginning of current year	54
Total amount receivable from debtors	2,031
Less debtors due at the end of current year	(47)
Cash receipts from debtors during current year	1,984

(2) Cash Payment to Creditors

Sundry Creditors Account

(Amount in ₹ lakh)

Particulars	*Amount*	*Particulars*	*Amount*
To Cash (payments to creditors, balancing figure)	1,429	By Balance b/f (opening balance)	86
To Balance c/d	102	By purchases* (assumed credit)	1,445
	1,531		1,531

*Cost of goods sold = Opening stock + Purchases – Closing stock
= ₹1,480 = ₹312 + Purchases – ₹277
= ₹1,480 – ₹312 + ₹277 = ₹1,445 (Purchases)

Alternatively

(in ₹ lakh)

Credit purchases	1,445
Add sundry creditors at the beginning of year	86
Total amount due/payable to creditors	1,531
Less sundry creditors at the year-end	(102)
Cash payment to creditors during the year	1,429

(3) Determination of Depreciation Charges

(a) T-Account Approach

Accumulated Depreciation Account

(Amount in ₹ lakh)

Particulars	*Amount*	*Particulars*	*Amount*
To Machine (accumulated depreciation written off on machine sold)	8	By Balance b/f	105
To Balance c/d	120	By P&L A/c (depreciation amount charged during the year, balancing figure)	23
	128		128

(b) Statement Approach

(Amount in ₹ lakh)

Opening balance at the beginning of year	105
Less depreciation written off on plant sold during current year	(8)
	97
Closing balance	120
Difference represents current year depreciation	23

(4) Determination of Amortisation Charges

Patent Account

(Amount in ₹ lakh)

Particulars	*Amount*	*Particulars*	*Amount*
To Balance b/f	55	By Amortisation (balancing figures)	6
To Cash (purchases)	16	By Balance c/d	65
	71		71

(5) Determination Cash Operating Expenses

(Amount in ₹ lakh)

Total operating expenses	486
Less depreciation (as it does not cause current cash outflow)	(23)
Less amortisation (non-cash expense)	(6)
Operating expenses (other than depreciation and amortisation)	457
Less prepaid expenses (already paid in previous year)	(6)
Add expenses paid in advance in current year	4
Operating expenses paid in cash	455

(B) Likewise, changes in *long term assets,* in particular, plant and machinery require a more careful analysis to ascertain cash obtained from their sales and cash used in their acquisition because the straight difference of the two years values do not indicate either purchase or sale. Such assets are subject to depreciation. Therefore, depreciation amount should be adjusted to ascertain the amount of such assets purchased/sold.

(6) Purchase of Plant and Machinery

(a) T-Account Approach

Plant and Machinery Account (Gross Basis)

(Amount in ₹ lakh)

Particulars	*Amount*	*Particulars*	*Amount*
To Balance b/f	420	By Cash (sale value)	6
To Equity share capital	70	By Loss (P&L A/c)	1
To Cash (purchases, balancing figure)	75	By Accumulated depreciation (on plant sold)	8
		By Balance c/d	550
	565		565

(b) Statement Approach

(Amount in ₹ lakh)

Opening balance of plant and machinery	420
Less original purchase price of plant sold (₹6 + 1 + 8)	15
	405
Closing balance	550
Difference represents purchases	145
Less purchases against issue of share capital	70
Cash purchases of plant	75

(c) Equation Approach

Opening balance of plant and machinery (PM) + Purchases of PM during the year – *Initial* acquisition cost of PM sold during the year = Closing balance of PM (5.1)

₹420 + Purchases – ₹15 = ₹550

Purchases = ₹550 – ₹420 + ₹15 = ₹145

Cash purchases = Total purchases ₹145 – Purchases through issue of equity share capital ₹75 = ₹70

OR

(a) T-Account Approach

Plant and Machinery (Net Basis)

(Amount in ₹ lakh)

Particulars	*Amount*	*Particulars*	*Amount*
To Balance b/f (₹420 – ₹105)	315	By Depreciation(charged during current year)	23
To Equtiy share capital	70	By Cash	6
To Cash (purchases, balancing figure	75	By P&L A/c (loss on sale of machine)	1
		By Balance c/d (₹550 – ₹120)	430
	460		460

(b) Statement Approach

(Amount in ₹ lakh)

Opening balance of plant and machinery	₹315
Less book value of plant sold	7
Less depreciation charged during the year	23
	285

(Contd.)

(Contd.)

Closing balance	430
Difference represents purchases	145
Less purchases against issue of share capital	70
Cash purchase of plant	75

(c) Equation Approach

Opening balance of PM + Purchases of PM during the year – Book value of PM sold during the year – Depreciation charges during the year = Closing balance of PM (5.2)

₹315 + Purchases – ₹7 – ₹23 = ₹430

Purchases = ₹430 – ₹315 + ₹7 + ₹23 = ₹145

Cash purchases = Total purchases ₹145 = Purchases through issue of equity share capital ₹75 = ₹70

(C) Treatment of changes in long-term liabilities are the easiest to deal. They relate to (i) fresh issue of shares and debentures or their redemption and (ii) additional long-term borrowings or their repayment. The increase is indicative of additional issue of securities or additional borrowings and, hence, is a source of cash.

The decrease represents repayment and, therefore, is use of cash, that is, cash outflow. However, if the increase in securities, say, in equity capital is caused due to issue of bonus shares, it is not a source of cash. Likewise, if increase in shares is an outcome of **(i)** payment for purchase of plant and machinery, land and building or any other asset and **(ii)** conversion of debentures into shares, such transactions do not affect cash inflow and are excluded.

(7) Redemption of Debentures *(Amount in ₹ lakh)*

Opening balance (at the year beginning)	220
Closing balance (at year-end)	60
Decrease in balance represents redemption of debentures	160

(8) Issue of Equity Share Capital for Cash *(Amount in ₹ lakh)*

Closing balance at current year-end	560
Less opening balance	250
Increase in balance represents additional issue	310
Less payment for goodwill (₹30) and for plant (₹70) by equity capital	100
Difference indicates additional cash raised through equity capital	210

It is emphasised that the amount of cash from business operations (in preparation of the CFS of Electronics Limited) has been determined using 'T' accounts extensively. Alternatively, cash from business operation can be computed by another approach. This approach uses less of 'T' account and involves two steps: **(i)** to determine working capital from business operations by excluding depreciation, amortisation, loss/gain on sale of long-term assets, non-operating incomes and **(ii)** to adjust the working capital from business operations by changes in current liabilities and current assets (except cash).

The rules for relating the changes in current assets and current liabilities to the profit and loss account in the computation of a flow of cash from operations are summarised below.

1. **All the increases in current assets excluding cash and decreases in current liabilities which increase working capital decrease cash**. The decrease in current liabilities takes place when they are paid in cash. For instance, decrease in creditors, bank overdrafts, bills payable and dividends payable will occur due to their payment. A word of explanation is necessary to show the negative impact of increase in current assets on cash. For instance, an

increase in sundry debtors takes place when credit sales are greater than cash collections from them; inventories increase when the cost of goods purchased is more than the cost of goods sold. Increase in prepaid expenses involves payment of more cash than is required for their current services. Evidently, increase in current assets decreases cash.

2. **From the first follows the second rule—all decreases in current assets other than cash and increases in current liabilities which cause a decrease in working capital increase cash.** Debtors would decrease when cash collections are more than current credit sales. Inventories would decrease because cost of goods sold is more than cost of goods purchased; decrease in prepaid expenses reflects that the firm has paid less for services than are currently used.

   Exhibits 5.2 and 5.3 show the procedure for determining cash from business operations.

EXHIBIT 5.2 Cash from Business Operations (Direct Method)

(A) Sales revenues
(B) *Less:* Expenses using working capital
- Cost of raw materials used (or cost of goods sold)
- Wages and salary expenses
- Others manufacturing expenses (excluding depreciation)
- Office expenses
- Selling and distribution expenses
- Interest
- Income tax

(C) Working capital from business operations
(D) Adjustment to convert to cash basis
- (i) *Add*: Decrease in WC (–CA or +CL)
  - Decrease in current assets other than cash (item-wise)
  - Increase in current liabilities (item-wise)
- (ii) *Less*: Increase in WC (+CA or –CL)
  - Increase in current assets other than cash (item-wise)
  - Decrease in current liabilities (item-wise)

(E) Cash flow from business operations

EXHIBIT 5.3 Cash from Business Operation (Indirect Method)

(A) Net income (or loss) as shown by profit and loss account
(B) *Add:* Depreciation expenses;
- Amortisation of goodwill, patents and other intangible assets;
- Amortisation of discount on debentures or share issue expenses;
- Amortisation of extraordinary losses occurred in previous years;
- Loss on sale of non-current assets;

(C) *Less:* Amortisation of premium received on debentures;
- Profit on sale of equipment (already included under sources)
- Profit on revaluation of non-current assets (does not contribute to working capital)
- Dividends and interest received on investments (reported separately).

(A + B – C) = Working capital from business operations.

(D) Adjustment to convert to cash basis:
- (i) *Add*: Decrease in WC (–CA or +CL)
  - Decrease in current assets other than cash (item wise)
  - Increase in current liabilities (item-wise)
- (ii) *Less*: Increase in WC (+CA or –CL)
  - Increase in current assets other than cash (item-wise)
  - Decrease in current liabilities (item-wise)

(E) Cash flow from business operations

Cash from business operations has been computed in Exhibits 5.4 and 5.5 for Electronics Limited using Exhibits 5.2 and 5.3 respectively.

Exhibit 5.4 Cash from Business Operation [Based on Exhibit 5.2] *(Amount in ₹ lakh)*

Net sales		1,977
Less cost of goods sold	1,480	
Less operating expenses (other than depreciation and amortisation)	457	
Less interest on debentures	14	1,951
Working capital from business operations		26
Add (Decrease in WC i.e. - CA or + CL):		
Debtors	7	
Inventories	35	
Prepaid expenses	2	
Creditors	16	60
Less (increase in WC i.e. - CA or – CL)		
Provision for income-taxes		(72)
Cash from business operation		14

Exhibit 5.5 Cash from Business Operations [Based on Exhibit 5.3]

Net loss as per income statement		(3)
Add depreciation on plant and machinery		23
Add amortisation on patents		6
Working capital from business operations		26
Add (Decrease in WC i.e. – CA or + CL)		
Debtors	7	
Inventories	35	
Prepaid expenses	2	
Creditors	16	60
Less (increase in WC i.e. – CA or – CL)		
Provision for income-taxes		(72)
Cash from business operations		14

◆ Example 5.2

From the following information furnished to you relating to plant and equipment account of Hypothetical Ltd., determine cash obtained from sale of old plant and equipment.

Particulars	*Previous year (₹ thousand)*	*Current year (₹ thousand)*
Plant and equipment (gross)	100	125
Accumulated depreciation	20	30
Additional information:		
(i) Loss on sale of plant and equipment		1
(ii) Depreciation charged during the year on plant and equipment		14
(iii) Purchase of new plant during the year		35

Solution

Equations 5.1 and 5.3 can be used to determine the required information to ascertain the sale proceeds from old plant and equipment (*PE*).

(i) Opening balance of *PE* (+) Purchases of *PE* during the year (–) Initial acquisition cost of *PE* sold during the year = Closing balance of *PE* (5.1)

= ₹1,00,000 + ₹35,000 – x = ₹1,25,000

= x = ₹1,35,000 – ₹1,25,000 = ₹10,000 (Purchase price of *PE* sold)

(ii) Opening balance of accumulated depreciation, *AD* + Depreciation charged during the year – *AD* written off on the *PE* sold during the year = Closing balance of *AD* (5.3)

= ₹20,000 + ₹14,000 – x = ₹30,000
= x = ₹34,000 – ₹30,000 = ₹4,000 (*AD* on *PE* sold)

The following information relating to the plant and equipment that has been sold is, thus, available:

Gross book value (purchase cost)	₹10,000
Accumulated depreciation	4,000
Net book value (₹10,000 – ₹4,000)	6,000
Therefore, sale proceeds of plant (₹6,000 – ₹1,000 loss)	5,000

The preceding information can also be obtained by preparing ledger accounts.

Plant and Equipment Account

Particulars	*Amount (₹ thousand)*	*Particulars*	*Amount (₹ thousand)*
Opening balance	100	Acquisition cost of sold plant (balancing figure)	10
Cash purchase of new plant	35	Closing balance	125
	135		135

Accumulated Depreciation Account

Total depreciation on sold plant (balancing figure)	4	Opening balance	20
Closing balance	30	Depreciation expenses charged during the year	14
	34		34

AS-7 - STATEMENT OF CASH FLOWS

LO 5.5 Discuss cash flow statement as per AS-7

The preparation and presentation of cash flow statement was prescribed by Accounting Standard-3 (AS3) issued by the Institute of Chartered Accountants of India (ICAI). As a part of the process of convergence of Indian Accounting Standards with International Financial Reporting Standards (IFRS), ICAI has issued a new accounting standard Ind AS-7 that deals with the statement of cash flows.

All listed and unlisted companies having net worth above ₹500 crore are to follow the new accounting standard from April 1, 2016. The deadline is also applicable for other entities having net worth of ₹500 crore or more. It would also apply to holding, subsidiary, joint venture or associate companies of these two classes of entities.

From April 1, 2017, Ind AS-7 has become mandatory for (i) Companies—whose equity and/or debt securities are listed or are in the process of being listed within India or outside — having a net worth of less than ₹500 crore. (ii) Other companies, that are unlisted having a net worth of ₹250 crore or more but less than ₹500 crore. Holding, subsidiary, joint venture or associate companies of these entities would have to comply with this deadline.

Companies whose securities are listed or in the process of listing on SME exchanges would not be required to apply Ind AS. Such companies would continue to comply with the existing accounting standard unless they choose otherwise.

We explain and illustrate below the CFS mandated by the Ind AS-7. **Annexure-5.I illustrates the CFS of the Reliance Industries Limited.**

Objectives

Information about the cash flows of an enterprise is useful in providing users of financial statements with a basis to assess the ability of the enterprise to generate cash and cash-equivalents and the needs of the enterprise to utilise those cash flows. The economic decisions that are taken by users require an evaluation of the ability of an enterprise to generate cash and cash-equivalents and the timing and certainty of their generation.

The CFS deals with the provision of information about the historical changes in cash and cash-equivalents of an enterprise by means of a cash flow statement which classifies cash flows during the period among **(i)** operating, **(ii)** investing and **(iii)** financing activities.

Benefits of Cash Flow Operation

Statement of Cash flows provides a summary of operating, investment and financing cashflows and reconciles them with changes in its cash and cash-equivalents (marketable securities) during the period.

A cash flow statement, when used in conjunction with the other financial statements, provides information that enables users to evaluate the changes in net assets of an enterprise, its financial structure (including its liquidity and solvency), and its ability to affect the amounts and timing of cash flows in order to adapt to changing circumstances and opportunities. Cash flow information is useful in assessing the ability of the enterprise to generate cash and cash-equivalents and enables users to develop models to assess and compare the present value of the future cash flows of different enterprises. It also enhances the comparability of the reporting of operating performance by different enterprises because it eliminates the effects of using different accounting treatments for the same transactions and events.

Definitions Associated with Cash Flow

Cash It consists of cash in hand and demand deposits with banks.

Cash Equivalents These are short-term highly liquid investments that are readily convertible into known amounts of changes in value. They have short maturity, say, of three months or less from the date of acquisition, for example, treasury bills.

Cash management includes the investment of excess cash in cash equivalents. Bank overdrafts (which are repayable on demand) are to be included as a component of cash and cash equivalents; the reason is that the bank balance often fluctuates from being positive to overdrawn.

Cash Flows These are inflows and outflows of cash and cash-equivalents.

Operating cashflows are directly related to production and sale of the firm's products/ services.

Operating Activities Cash inflows from operating activities primarily accrue from the major revenue producing activities (i.e., sale of goods and rendering of services) of the enterprise. Therefore, they generally result from the transactions and other events that enter into the determination of net profit or loss. Examples of cash flows from operating activities are as follows:

- Cash receipts from the sale of goods and the rendering of services
- Cash receipts from royalties, fees, commissions, and other revenues
- Cash payments to suppliers for goods and services
- Cash payments to and on behalf of employees
- Cash receipts and cash payments of an insurance enterprise for premiums and claims, annuities and other policy benefits
- Cash payments or refunds of income taxes unless they can be specifically identified with financing and investing activities
- Cash receipts and payments from contracts held for dealing or trading purposes.

Since the focus is on determining cash flows due to business/operating activities, non-operating expenses as well as non-operating incomes are excluded. In other words, both interest/dividend receipts and interest/dividend payments are excluded.

Investing Activities The investing activities relate to the acquisition and disposal of long-term assets and other investments not included in cash-equivalents. Their separate disclosure is important as they represent the extent to which expenditures have been made for resources intended to generate future income and cash flows. The principal items covered under this category of activities are as follows:

> **Investment flows** are cashflows associated with purchase/sale of both fixed assets and business interests.

- Cash payments to acquire property, plant and equipment, intangible and other long-term assets: fixed assets (including intangibles). These payments include those relating to capitalised research and development costs and self-constructed property, plant and equipment.
- Cash receipts from disposal of property, plant and equipment, intangible and other long-term assets.
- Cash payments to acquire shares, warrants or debt instruments of other enterprises and interests in joint ventures
- Cash receipts from disposal of shares, warrants, or debt instruments of other enterprises and interests in joint ventures
- Cash advances and loans made to third parties
- Cash receipts from the repayment of advances and loans made to third parties
- Cash payments for futures contracts, forward contracts, option contracts and swap contracts.
- Cash recently from futures contracts forward contracts, option contracts and swap contracts.

Financing Activities The financing activities report the changes in the size and composition of the share/owner's capital and debt of the enterprise. Their separate disclosure is useful in predicting claims on future cash flows by providers of funds (both capital and borrowings) to the enterprise. Examples of cash flows arising from financing activities are as follows:

> **Financing flows** are cash flows that result from debt/equity financing transactions and include incurrence and repayment of debt cashflows from the sale of shares and cash outflows to purchase shares or pay dividend.

- Cash proceeds from issue of shares or other equity instruments
- Cash proceeds from issue of debentures, loans, notes, bonds, mortgages and other short-term or long-term borrowings
- Cash repayments of amounts borrowed
- Dividend/interest paid
- Cash payments to owners to acquire or redeem the entity's shares i.e., buy back of shares and redemption of preference shares.
- Cash payments by a lessee for the reduction of the outstanding liability relating to a finance lease.

Reporting Cash Flows

From Operating Activities An enterprise is required to report cash flows from operating activities using either direct method or indirect method.

Direct Method Under this method, gross cash receipts and gross cash payments for the major items are disclosed, such as cash receipts from customers and cash paid to suppliers.

Indirect Method Under the indirect method, profit and loss account is adjusted for **(i)** the effects of transactions of non-cash nature such as depreciation, amortisation, deferred taxes, loss on sale of fixed assets and unrealised foreign exchange gains and losses, **(ii)** changes during the period in inventories and operating receivables and payables, and **(iii)** for all other items for which the cash effects are shown either in financing or investing activities.

From Investing and Financing Activities An enterprise is required to report separately major classes of gross cash receipts and gross cash payments arising from investing and financing activities. The cash flows from operating, financing and investing activities are to be reported on a *net* basis.

Treatment of Some Major Items

While most of the items (to be included in the CFS) are self-explanatory in nature, some transactions/items merit more explanation. These relate to **(i)** foreign currency, **(ii)** interest, **(iii)** dividends, **(iv)** taxes on income, **(v)** deferred taxes, **(vi)** investments in subsidiaries, associates and joint ventures, **(vii)** Changes in ownership interests in subsidiaries and other business units, **(viii)** non-cash transactions and **(ix)** other disclosures.

Foreign Currency Cash Flows Cash flows arising from transactions in a foreign currency should be recorded in an enterprise's functional currency by applying to the foreign currency amount the exchange rate between the functional currency and the foreign currency at the date of the cash flow. A rate that approximates the actual rate may be used if the result is substantially the same as would arise if the rates at the dates of the cash flows were used.

The effect of changes in exchange rates on cash and cash-equivalents held in a foreign currency are to be reported as a separate part of the reconciliation of the changes in cash and cash-equivalents during the period.

Evidently, unrealised gains and losses arising from changes in foreign exchange rates are not cash flows.

Interest In general, cash flows arising from interest paid should be classified as cash flows from financing activities, say interest on loans/debts; interest paid on working capital loan and any other loan taken to finance operating activities are to be shown as a part of operating activities. Unless stated otherwise, interest paid is to be reported with financing activities. The reason is that they are cost of obtaining financial resources.

Interest received from short-term investments (classified as cash equivalents) are to be reckoned as cash inflows from operating activities.

Cash flows arising from interest paid and interest received in the case of a financial enterprises should be classified as cash flows from operating activities. The reason that is borrowing and lending are the normal business activities for such enterprises.

Dividends While dividends paid are classified as financing activities as they are cost of obtaining financial resources, dividends received on investments constitute a part of investment activities. The reason is that they are the returns on investments.

For the financial enterprises, dividends received form a part of operating activities and dividends paid as a part of financing activities.

Taxes on Income Taxes paid on income as well as tax refunds are usually classified as cash flows from operating activities. In the event of their specific identification with investment or financing activities, the tax cash flow is classified as an investing or financing activity as appropriate.

Deferred Taxes There can be differences in the amount of taxes payable, determined on the basis of financial accounting *vis-à-vis* tax accounting. One such item which can cause this distortion relates to the treatment of depreciation. For instance, for income-tax reporting, the machine may be subject to higher rate of depreciation compared to financial accounting. This lowers the taxes payable in the early years of machine purchased and increases the taxes payable in the latter years. **Deferred taxes are to be treated just like other expenses on accrual basis.** Deferring tax liabilities to the future years is referred to as deferred taxes. As a result, increase in deferred tax liabilities are considered as cash inflows and decrease as cash outflows.

Investments in Subsidiaries, Associates and Joint Ventures Enterprises having investments in subsidiaries, associates and joint ventures are required to report in the CFS the cash flows between themselves and the investee/joint venture, for example, cash flows relating to dividends and advances.

Changes in Ownership Interests in Subsidiaries and Other Business Units The aggregate cash flows arising from obtaining or losing control of subsidiaries or other business units should be presented separately and classified as investing activities.

An enterprise should disclose, in aggregate, in respect of both obtaining and losing control of subsidiaries or other business units during the period, each of the following: **(i)** the total purchase or disposal consideration paid or received; and **(ii)** the portion of the purchase consideration discharged by means of cash and cash-equivalents.

Non-Cash Transactions Investing and financing transactions that do not require the use of cash or cash-equivalents should be excluded from a cash flow statement. Such transactions should be disclosed elsewhere in the financial statements in a way that provides all the relevant information about these investing and financing activities. Examples of non-cash transactions are: **(i)** the acquisition of assets/an enterprise by means of issue of shares and/or debentures, **(ii)** conversion of debt into equity and **(iii)** issue of bonus shares.

Other Disclosures An enterprise should disclose, together with a commentary by management, the amount of significant cash and cash-equivalent balances held by the enterprise that are not available for use by it. Examples include cash and cash-equivalent balances held by a branch of the enterprise that operates in a country where exchange controls or other legal restrictions apply as a result of which the balances are not available for use by the enterprise.

Exhibits 5.6 to 5.8 show the procedure of the preparation of the cash flow statement as per AS-3 (revised).

EXHIBIT 5.6 Direct Method Statement of Cash Flows

Cashflow From Operating Activities
Cash receipts from customers
Cash paid to suppliers and employees
Cash generated from operations
Income tax
Net cash from operating activities
Cashflow From Investing Activities
Purchase of fixed assets
Proceeds from sale of equipments
Interest received
Dividends received
Net cash from investing activities
Cashflow From Financing Activities
Proceeds from issuance of share capital
Proceeds from long-term borrowings
Repayments of long-term borrowings
Interest paid
Dividends paid
Net cash used in financing activities
Net Increase in Cash and Cash-equivalents*
Cash and cash-equivalents at the beginning of a period
Cash and cash-equivalents at the end of a period

*Consists of cash on hand and balance with banks, investment in money market (short-term) investments and effect of exchange rate changes.

EXHIBIT 5.7 Indirect Method Statement of Cash Flows

Cashflow From Operating Activities
- Net profit before taxation, and extraordinary items
- Adjustment for
  - Depreciation
  - Foreign exchange loss
  - Interest income
  - Dividend income
  - Interest expense
- Operating profit before working capital changes
- Decrease/(increase) in sundry debtors
- Decrease/(increase) in inventories
- Increase/(decrease) in sundry creditors
- Cash generated from operations
- Income tax paid

Net cash from operating activities

Cashflow From Investing Activities
- Purchase of fixed assets
- Proceeds from sale of equipment
- Interest received
- Dividends received

Net cash from investing activities

Cashflow From Financing Activities
- Proceeds from issuance of share capital
- Proceeds from long-term borrowings
- Repayment of long-term borrowings
- Interest paid
- Dividends paid

Net cash used in financing activities

Net Increases in Cash and Cash-equivalents
- Cash and cash-equivalents at the beginning of a period
- Cash and cash-equivalents at the end of a period

EXHIBIT 5.8 Statement of Cash Flows of a Financial Enterprise

Cashflows From Operating Activities
- Interest and commission receipts
- Interest payment
- Recoveries on loans previously written off
- Cash payments to employees and suppliers
- Operating profit before changes in operating assets
- Decrease (or increase) in operating assets:
  - Short-term funds
  - Deposit held for regulatory or monetary control purposes
  - Funds advanced to customers
  - Net increase in credit card receivables
  - Other short-term securities

Decrease (or increase) in operating liabilities
- Deposits from customers
- Certificates of deposit
- Net cash from operating activities before income tax
- Income taxes paid

(Contd.)

(*Contd.*)

Net cash from operating activities
Cashflows From Investing Activities
Dividends received
Interest received
Proceeds from sale of permanent investments
Purchase of permanent investments
Purchase of fixed assets
Net cash from investing activities
Cashflows From Financing Activities
Issue of shares
Repayment of long-term borrowings
Net decrease in other borrowings
Dividends paid
Net cash used in financing activities

For the Electronics Ltd. in Example 5.1, the cash flow statement as per AS-3 is shown in Exhibits 5.9 and 5.10.

EXHIBIT 5.9 Statement of Cash Flows of Electronics Limited for the Current Year (Direct Method)

(Amount in ₹ lakh)

Particulars		*Amount*
Cash Flows From Operating Activities		
Cash receipts from customers	1,984[1]	
Cash paid to suppliers and employees	1,884[2]	
Cash generated from operations	100	
Income taxes paid	(72)	
Net cash from operating activities		28*
Cash Flows From Investing Activities		
Purchase of plant and machinery	(75)	
Purchase of patents	(16)	
Proceeds from sale of plant	6	
Net cash used in investing activities		(85)
Cash Flows From Financing Activities		
Proceeds from issuance of equity share capital	210	
Repayment of debentures (₹220 – 60)	(160)	
Interest paid to debenture-holders	(14)	
Dividends paid	(16)	20
Net decrease in cash balance (₹85 – 48)		(37)
Less		
Cash and cash equivalents at beginning of the year		74
Cash and cash equivalents at end of the year		37

* It may be recalled that cash from operating activities (shown in Section II) was ₹14; the difference of ₹14 (₹28 as per AS3 and ₹14 as per CFS) is due to exclusion of interest payment on debentures (₹14); this interest payment is shown under financing activities.

WORKING NOTES

(Amount in ₹ lakh)

(1) Cash receipts from debtors and customers:	
Debtors at the beginning of the year	54

(*Contd.*)

(*Contd.*)

Add: Net sales during the year	1,977
Total sum receivable	2,031
Less: Debtors at the end of the year	47
Total	1,984
(2) Cash paid to suppliers and employees:	
Cost of goods sold	1,480
Add: Operating expenses excluding depreciation and amortisation (₹486 – 23 – 6)	457
Add: Current year prepaid expenses	4
Less Previous year prepaid expenses	(6)
	455
Add: Creditors at the beginning of the year	86
Add: Inventories at the end of the year	277
Less: Creditors at the end of the year	(102)
Less: Inventories at the beginning of the year	(312)
Total	1,884

EXHIBIT 5.10 Statement of Cash Flows of Electronics Limited for the Current Year (Indirect Method)

(Amount in ₹ lakh)

Particulars		*Amount*
Cash flows From Operating Activities		
Net loss before taxation and extra-ordinary items	(4)	
Adjustments for:		
Depreciation	23	
Amortisation of patent	6	
Interest expenses	14	
Loss on sale of assets	1	
Operating profit before working capital changes	40	
Add: Decrease in debtors	7	
Add: Decrease in inventories	35	
Add: Prepaid expenses	2	
Add: Increase in creditors	16	
Cash generated from operations	100	
Less: Income-tax paid	72	
Net cash from operating activities		28
Cash flows From Investing Activities		
Purchase of plant and machinery	(75)	
Purchase of patents	(16)	
Proceeds from sale of plant	6	
Net cash used in investing activities		(85)
Cash flows From Financing Activities		
Proceeds from issuance of equity share capital	210	
Repayment of debentures (220 – 60)	(160)	
Interest paid to debentureholders	(14)	
Dividends paid	(16)	20
Net decrease in cash balance (78 – 41)		(37)
Cash and cash equivalents at beginning of the year		74
Cash and cash equivalents at end of the year		37

The statement highlights that the firm does not have enough funds from its operating activities (₹28 lakh) and financing activities (₹20 lakh) to cater to investment requirement of ₹85 lakh, causing decline in cash (₹37 lakh).

ANNEXURE 5.1

Cash Flow Statement of Reliance Industries Limited for the Year 2015-16

(₹ in crore)

Particulars		*2015-16*		*2014-15*
A: CASH FLOW FROM OPERATING ACTIVITES				
Net Profit Before Tax as per Profit and Loss Statement		35,701		29,468
Adjusted for:				
Write off of Investment [₹ Nil (Previous Year ₹26,96,800)]	—		—	
Loss on Sale/Discard of Assets (Net)	20		31	
Depreciation/Amortisation and Depletion Expenses	9,566		8,488	
Effect of Exchange Rate Change	(2,911)		1,408	
Net Gain on Sale of Investments	(2,781)		(3,046)	
Dividend Income	(691)		(250)	
Interest Income	(3,936)		(5,414)	
Finance costs	2,454		2,367	
		1,721		3,584
Operating Profit before Working Capital Changes		**37,422**		**33,052**
Adjusted for:				
Trade and Other Receivables	146		5,462	
Inventories	8,517		6,381	
Trade and Other Payables	6,126		(3,528)	
		14,789		8,315
Cash Generated from Operations		**52,211**		**41,367**
Taxes Paid (Net)		(8,129)		(6,082)
Net Cash from Operating Activities		**44,082**		**35,285**
B: CASH FLOW FROM INVESTING ACTIVITIES				
Purchase of Fixed Assets		(21,322)		(42,720)
Sale of Fixed Assets		293		86
Purchase of Investments in Subsidiaries/ Trusts		(25,255)		(11,506)
Redemption of Investment in Subsidiaries		444		169
Purchase of other Investments		(668,990)		(655,591)
Sale/ Redemption of other Investments		6,68,877		6,43,525
Movement in Loans and Advances		(917)		(133)
Maturity of Fixed Assets		—		3,400
Interest Income		3,850		6,584
Dividend Income from Subsidiary and Associates		47		5
Dividend Income from Others		644		183
Net Cash (Used in) Investing Activities		**(42,329)**		**(55,998)**
C: CASH FLOW FROM FINANCING ACTIVITIES				
Proceeds from Issue of Share Capital		283		226
Share Application Money		8		17
Proceeds from Long Term Borrowings		7,552		20,310
Repayment of Long Term Borrowings		(4,591)		(4,555)
Short Term Borrowings (net)		1,843		(10,302)
Dividends Paid (Including Dividend Distribution Tax)		(7,259)		(3,268)
Interest Paid		(4,268)		(3,368)
Net Cash (used in)/From Financing Activities		**(6,432)**		**(940)**
Net (Decrease) in Cash and Cash Equivalents		(4,679)		(21,653)
Opening Balance of Cash and Cash Equivalents		11,571		33,224
Closing Balance of Cash and Cash Equivalents		**6,892**		**11,571**

SUMMARY

- Cash flow statement indicates sources of cash inflows and transactions of cash outflows of a firm during a period. It is also called "Where-Got Where-Gone" statement. The statement provides answers to many important questions related to financial position of an enterprise.

LO 5.1

- The major sources of cash inflows are cash from: **(i)** business operations, **(ii)** non-business operations (like interest, dividend etc), **(iii)** sale proceeds of long-term assets, **(iv)** raising additional share capital and **(v)** long-term borrowings. The principal uses of cash are: **(i)** purchase of long-term assets, **(ii)** redemption of preference shares/debentures, **(iii)** repayment of long-term borrowings and **(iv)** payment of dividends.

LO 5.2

- Cash flow statement (CFS) is an important tool of financial analysis. It clearly highlights the firm's operating, financing and investment activities. It enables the management to assess whether the firm has adequate long-term funds to finance major fixed assets expansion.

LO 5.3

- Preparation of cash flow statement is mandatory for all the listed companies as well as for all enterprises which have net worth of ₹500 crore or more.
- The CFS shows the sources and uses of cash and cash equivalents in terms of three components: **(i)** operating, **(ii)** financing and **(iii)** investing activities. The cash flows from each of these categories are to be reported on net basis.
- Cash flows from operating activities result from the major revenue producing activities of a firm. Accordingly, the income statement constitutes the main source of data. The major operating items are **(i)** cash receipts from customers, **(ii)** cash paid to suppliers and employees and **(iii)** income-tax.
- The items included in financing activities are: **(i)** proceeds from issue of share capital, **(ii)** proceeds from long-term borrowings, **(iii)** redemption of preference shares/debentures, **(iv)** repayment of long-term borrowings and **(v)** payment of interest and dividend to debenture-holders/lenders and shareholders respectively.
- Cash flows representing investment activities relate to capital expenditures incurred with intent to generate future earnings as cash flows and includes: **(i)** purchase of new fixed assets, **(ii)** proceeds from sale of existing fixed assets and **(iii)** interest and dividend received on investments made.

LO 5.4

REFERENCES

1. Anthony, R. N. et al., *Accounting: Text and Cases,* (Tata McGraw-Hill, New Delhi), 2003, p.339.
2. *Ibid.*, p. 339.

SOLVED PROBLEMS

P.5.1 Answer the following:

LO 5.4 LOD: E

(a) A company sold building for cash at ₹100 lakh. The profit and loss account has shown ₹40 lakh profit on sale of building. How will you report it in cash flow statement (based on Ind AS-7)?

(b) From the following information, determine cash received from debtors during current year: **LOD: E**

Debtors in the beginning of current year	₹100 lakh
Total sales	2,000
Cash sales	500
Debtors at the end of current year	300

(c) Determine cash paid to suppliers/creditors from the following data during current year: **LOD: E**

Cost of goods sold	₹480 lakh
Opening stock	30
Closing stock	50
Creditors at the beginning of year	60
Creditors at the end of the year	90
Cash purchases	40

(d) From the following **(i)** determine the gross amount of plant and machinery purchased and **(ii)** depreciation charged during the current year. **LOD: M**

- Plant assets (net of depreciation) at year-end ₹285 lakh and at the year-beginning ₹127 lakh.
- Gross plant assets increased by ₹186 lakh even through machine costing initially ₹58 lakh with book value of ₹38 lakh was sold at loss of ₹25 lakh.

(e) Account balances relating to equipment during 2015–16 are as follows: **LOD: M**

Particulars	*April 1, 2015*	*March 31, 2016*
Equipment	₹2,00,000	₹4,00,000
Less: Accumulated depreciation	50,000	70,000

Equipment with an original cost of ₹40,000, having an accumulated depreciation of ₹20,000, were sold at a gain of ₹5,000. Determine: **(i)** Cash provided by the sale of equipment; **(ii)** Cash used to acquire equipment; **(iii)** Depreciation expense on equipment during 2015–16.

(f) Would your answer for **(e) (i), (ii) and (iii)** be different if the equipment were sold at a loss of ₹5,000? **LOD: M**

Solution

(a) Cashflows from Investing Activities:
Proceeds from sale of building ₹100 lakh.

(b) Cash Receipts from Debtors:

Debtors at the beginning of current year	₹100 lakh
Plus credit sales (₹2,000 lakh – ₹500 lakh)	1,500
Total sum receivable from debtors	1,600
Less debtors at the end of current year	300
Cash received from debtors	1,300

(c) (i) Determination of Credit Purchases:

- Cost of goods sold = Opening stock + Purchases (x) – Closing stock
  ₹480 lakh = ₹30 lakh + x – ₹50 lakh
  x = ₹480 lakh – ₹30 lakh + ₹50 lakh = ₹500 lakh
- Credit purchases = ₹500 lakh – ₹40 lakh = ₹460 lakh

(ii) Determination of Payment to Creditors:

Creditors at the beginning of year	₹60 lakh
Plus credit purchases	460
Total sum payable	520
Less creditors at the year-end	90
Payment to creditors	430

(d) (i) Plant and Machinery Purchased:

Net increase in gross value	₹186 lakh
Add initial cost of plant sold	58
	244

(ii) Depreciation Charges:

Plant assets (net) at year beginning	₹127 lakh
Plus purchase cost of new plant	244
Less book value of plant sold	(38)
	333
Closing balance	285
Difference represents depreciation	48

(e) (i) Cash From the Sale of Equipment

Original cost of the sold equipment	₹40,000
Less: Accumulated depreciation on the sold equipment	(20,000)
Net book value	20,000
Plus: Gain on the sold equipment	5,000
Cash proceeds from sale of equipment	25,000

(ii) Cash Spent on Purchase of Equipment

Balance of equipment on April 1, 2015 (gross)	₹2,00,000
Less: Gross book value of the sold equipment	(40,000)
Balance of equipment on March 31, 2016 (without purchases)	1,60,000
Actual balance as on March 31, 2016 of equipment	4,00,000
Difference representing purchases made during 2015–16	2,40,000

(iii) Determination of Depreciation Amount Charged to the P&L A/c During 2015–16:

Balance of accumulated depreciation (1.4.2015)	₹50,000
Less: Depreciation written-off on sold equipment during 2015–16	(20,000)
Balance of accumulated depreciation without additional depreciation during 2015–16	30,000
Actual balance as on March 31, 2016 of accumulated depreciation	70,000
Difference representing depreciation amount charged during 2015–16	40,000

(f) Answers for parts **(e)(ii)** and **(e)(iii)** would remain unchanged. However, cash provided by the sale of equipment would be reduced by ₹10,000. The relevant calculations would be as follows:

Net book value	₹20,000
Less loss on sale of equipment	(5,000)
	15,000

P.5.2 Compute cash generated from operations during the year 2015-16, from the following data: **LO 5.4.5** **LOD: M**

Particulars	*April 1, 2015*	*March 31, 2016*
Sundry debtors	₹30,000	₹40,000
Sundry creditors	48,000	30,000
Outstanding expenses	3,000	6,000
Outstanding income	1,000	1,000
Stock in trade	55,000	60,000
Prepaid expenses	3,000	2,000

(Contd.)

(Contd.)

Accumulated depreciation (no retirements during the year)	50,000	60,000
Provision for doubtful accounts	1,500	2,000
Dividends payable	—	3,000
Bills receivable	10,000	12,000
Bills payable	8,000	6,000
Net income before taxes (as per profit and loss account)	—	80,000

Solution

Determination of Cash From Operations:

Net income as per P&L A/c		₹80,000
Add Depreciation		10,000
Working capital from business operations		90,000
Less: Transactions other than cash, increasing working capital:		
(i) Increase in current assets:		
Sundry debtors	₹10,000	
Outstanding income	500	
Stock-in-trade	5,000	
Bills receivable	2,000	(17,500)
(ii) Decrease in current liabilities:		
Sundry creditors	18,000	
Bills payable	2,000	(20,000)
Add: Transactions other than cash, decreasing working capital:		
(i) Decrease in current assets:	1,000	1,000
Prepaid expenses		
(ii) Increase in current liabilities:		
Outstanding expenses	3,000	
Provision for doubtful accounts	500	
Dividends payable	3,000	6,500
Cash from operations		60,000

P.5.3 From the following summary cash account of Y Ltd., prepare statement of cash flows for the current year ended March 31 in accordance with AS-7 using the direct method. The company does not have any cash equivalents. **LO 5.5** **LOD: M**

Summary Cash Account
for the Current Year Ended March 31

Cash inflows	₹ *('000)*	*Cash outflows*	₹ *('000)*
Opening balance	50	Payment to suppliers	2,000
Issue of equity shares	300	Purchase of fixed assets	200
Receipts from customers	2800	Overhead expenses	200
Sale of fixed assets	100	Wages and salaries	100
		Taxation	250
		Dividend	50
		Repayment of bank loan	300
		Closing balance	150
	3,250		3,250

Solution

Statement of Cash Flows Y Ltd.
as per AS-3 for the Current Year ended March 31

		Amount
Cash flows from operating activities:		
Cash receipts from customers	₹28,00,000	
Cash paid to suppliers	(20,00,000)	
Wages and salaries	(1,00,000)	
Overhead expenses	(2,00,000)	
Cash generated from operations	5,00,000	
Income tax paid	2,50,000	
Net cash from operating activities		₹2,50,000
Cash flows from investing activities:		
Purchase of fixed assets	(2,00,000)	
Sale of fixed assets	1,00,000	
Net cash used in investing activities		(1,00,000)
Cash flows from financing activities:		
Issue of equity shares	3,00,000	
Repayment of bank loan	(3,00,000)	
Dividend	(50,000)	
Net cash used in financing activities		(50,000)
Net increase in cash and cash-equivalent		1,00,000
Cash and cash equivalent at beginning of year		50,000
Cash and cash equivalent at the end of year		1,50,000

P.5.4 Charatlal, the president and majority shareholder, was a superb operating executive. He was an imaginative, aggressive marketing man and an ingenious, creative production man. But he had little patience with financial matters. After examining the most recent balance sheet and income statement, he muttered, "We have enjoyed ten years of steady growth, this year was our most profitable year. Despite this, we are in the worst cash position in our history. Just look those current liabilities in relation to our available cash! This whole picture of the more you make, the poorer you get, just does not make sense. These statements must be cockeyed." **LO 5.5** **LOD: M**

The balance sheets (in lakh of rupees) of Charat Engineering Ltd. are given below:

	March 31			March 31	
Assets	*Current Year*	*Previous year*	*Liabilities*	*Current year*	*Previous year*
Cash	2	10	Current liabilities	105	30
Receivables (net)	60	30	Long-term debt	150	—
Inventories	100	50	Stockholder's equity	207	160
Plan assets (net of accumulated depreciation)	300	100			
Total assets	462	190	Total equities	462	190

Net income before taxes, ₹81 lakh. Taxes paid are ₹27 lakh. Net income was ₹54 lakh. Cash dividend paid were ₹7 lakh. Depreciation was ₹20 lakh. Fixed assets were purchase for ₹220 lakh, ₹150 lakh of which was financed via the issuance of long-term debt outright for cash.

Using cash flow statement (based on AS-7), write a short memorandum to Mr Charatlal, explaining why there is such squeeze for cash. Show working.

Solution

Statement of Cash Flows of Charat Engineering Ltd. (Indirect Method)

Particulars		*Amount in ₹ lakh*
Cashflow from operating activities:		
Net profit before taxation	₹81	
Adjustment for		
Depreciation	20	
Operating profit before working capital changes	101	
Increase in receivables (net)	(30)	
Increase in inventories	(50)	
Increase in current liabilities	75	
Cash generated from operations	96	
Income tax paid	27	
Net cash from operating activities		69
Cashflow from investing activities:		
Purchase of fixed assets	(220)	(220)
Net cash used for investing activities		
Cashflow from financing activities:		
Issuance of long-term debt	150	
Dividends paid	(7)	
Net cash from financing activities		143
Net decrease in cash		(8)
Cash at the beginning of current year		10
Cash at the end of the year		2

Memorandum: The squeeze for cash has resulted from major fixed assets expansion programme. The cash flow statement highlights that the company does not have enough funds from operating activities (₹69 lakh) and financing activities (₹143 lakh) to cater to investment requirements of ₹220 lakh, causing decline in cash of ₹8 lakh.

P.5.5 Prepare a statement from the following financial information of ABC company, to explain the causes of increase in cash despite the firm incurring losses. **LO 5.5** **LOD: M**

Income statement		*(Amount in ₹ lakh)*
Sales		₹600.0
Dividends from investment in another company		3.6
		603.6
Expenses		
Cost of goods sold	₹400	
Depreciation	50	
Other operating expenditure	175	
Interest	1.6	
Loss on sale of plant (sale value, ₹7.2)	3.0	629.6
Net loss		(26)

Retained earnings	*(Amount in ₹ lakh)*
Beginning balance	₹50
Net loss	(26)
Dividends	(16)
Ending balance	8

Position statement		*(Amount in ₹ lakh)*
	Previous year	*Current year*
Cash	₹19.2	₹43.2
Sundry debtors	28.6	16.8
Inventory	33.0	22.0
Prepayments	2.2	1.8
Investments	18.0	18.0
Land	15.0	15.0
Plant and machinery	119.8	110.4
Accumulated depreciation	(75.2)	(78.4)
Total assets	160.6	148.8
Accounts payable	18.2	10.2
Accrued liabilities	1.2	2.4
Dividends payable	1.2	2.2
Debentures	12.0	16.0
Equity capital	50.0	60.0
Preference share capital	28.0	50.0
Retained earnings	50.0	8.0
Total liabilities	160.6	148.8

Solution

Cash Flow Statement of ABC Company (Indirect Method)

Particulars		*Amount (in ₹ lakh)*
Casflow from operating activities:		
Net loss before extraordinary items	(₹26)	
Adjustment for		
Depreciation	50	
Interest expenses	1.6	
Loss on sale of plant	3.0	
Dividend income	(3.6)	
Operating profit before working capital changes	25.0	
Decrease in sundry debtors	11.8	
Decrease in inventories	11.0	
Decrease in prepayments	0.4	
Decrease in accounts payable	(8.0)	
Increase in accrued liabilities	1.2	
Net cash from operating activities		41.4
Cash flow from investing activities:		
Purchase of plant and machinery	(47.6)	
Sale of plant	7.2	
Dividends received	3.6	
Net cash used in investing activities		(36.8)
Cash from financing activities:		
Proceeds from issuance of equity share capital	10	
Proceeds from issuance of preference share capital	22	
Proceeds from debentures	4	
Dividends paid to shareholders	(15)	
Interest paid on debentures	(1.6)	
Net cash from financing activities		19.4
Increase in cash		24.0
Cash at the beginning of current year		19.2
Cash at the end of current year		43.2

WORKING NOTES:

(i) Accumulated depreciation account

To Plant (accumulated deprecation on plant sold) (balancing figure)	₹46.8	By Balance b/d	₹75.2
To Balance c/d	78.4	By P&L A/c (depreciation of the current year)	50.0
	125.2		125.2

(ii) Gross value of plant sold

Cash A/c	Dr	₹7.2	
P&L A/c (Loss)	Dr	3.0	
Accumulated depreciation A/c	Dr	46.8	
To plant			₹57.0

(iii) Purchase of plant — *Plant account*

To Balance b/f	₹119.8	By Cash	₹7.2
To Plant purchased (balancing figure)	47.6	By P&L A/c	3.0
		By Accumulated depreciation A/c	46.8
		By Balance c/d	110.4
	167.4		167.4

(iv) *Dividends paid* = ₹1.2 payable of previous year + ₹16 of current year – ₹2.2 dividends payable at current year-end = ₹15

P.5.6 Nandini Ltd. provides the following data: **LO 5.5** **LOD: M**

Comparative trial balance *(Amount in ₹ lakh)*

Particulars	*March 31, year 2*	*March 31, year 1*	*Increase (decrease)*
Debit balance			
Cash	15	5	10
Working capital (other than cash)	₹185	₹95	₹90
Investments (long-term)	100	150	(50)
Building and equipment	500	400	100
Land	40	50	(10)
	840	700	140
Credit balance			
Accumulated depreciation	200	160	40
Bonds	100	50	50
Reserves	340	340	—
Equity shares	200	150	50
	840	700	140

Income Statement
for the period ending March 31, year 2 *(Amount in ₹ lakh)*

Sales		₹1000
Cost of goods sold		500
Selling expenses	₹50	
Administrative expenses	50	100
Operating income		400
Other charges and credits:		
Gain on sale of building and equipment	₹5	
Loss on sale of investments	(10)	
Interest	(6)	
Taxes	(189)	(200)
Net income after taxes		200

Notes: (a) The depreciation charged for the year was ₹60 lakh.

(b) The book value of the building and equipment disposed off was ₹10 lakh.

Prepare a cash flow statement (based on AS-7).

Solution

Statement of Cash Flows of Nandini Limited (Indirect Method)

Particulars		*Amount in ₹ lakh*
Cashflow from operating activities:		
Net profit before taxation	₹389	
Adjustment for		
Depreciation	60	
Gain on sale of building and equipment	(5)	
Interest expense	6	
Loss on sale of investments	10	
Operating profit before working capital changes	460	
Increase in working capital	(90)	
Cash generated from operations	370	
Income tax paid	189	
Net cash from operating activities		181
Cashflow from investing activities:		
Proceeds from sale of long-term investments (1)	40	
Proceeds from sale of land	10	
Proceeds from sale of building and equipment (₹10 lakh + ₹5 lakh gain)	15	
Purchase of building and equipment (2)	(130)	
Net cash used in investing activities		(65)
Cashflow from financing activities:		
Proceeds from issuance of bonds (₹100 – ₹50)	50	
Proceeds from issuance of equity shares (₹200 – ₹150)	50	
Interest on debentures	(6)	
Dividend to equity shareholders (3)	(200)	
Net cash used in financing activities		(106)
Net increase in cash		10
Cash at the beginning of year 2		5
Cash at the end of year 2		15

WORKING NOTES

(1) Proceeds from sale of long-term investments:

Investments at beginning of year -2	₹150 lakh
Less investment of year-end 2	100
Book value of investments sold	50
Less loss on sale of investments	(10)
Sale proceeds	40

(2) Purchase of building and equipment

Original cost of buildings and equipment at the beginning of year 2	₹400 lakh
Less original cost of building and equipment sold during year-2 (book value ₹10 lakh Plus accumulated depreciation ₹20 lakh*)	(30)
	370
Original cost of building and equipment at year-end 2	500
Difference represents purchases of building and equipment	130

*Accumulated Depreciation Account (in ₹ lakh)

Particular	Amount	Particular	Amount
To Building and equipment (accumulated depreciation on sale, balancing figure)	20	By Balance b/f	160
To Balance c/d	200	By P&L A/c (depreciation of current year)	60
	220		220

(3) Since there is no increase in reserves (₹340 lakh), the entire net income after taxes of ₹200 lakh represents payment of dividend to equity shareholders.

P.5.7 The manager of a small plastic manufacturing company has reviewed the annual financial statements for the current year and is unable to determine from a reading of the balance sheet the reasons for the changes in cash during the year. He asks you for assistance and presents the following balance sheets of the Hypothetical Ltd.

LO 5.5 **LOD: D**

Particulars	Previous year March 31	Current year March 31	Increase (Decreases)
Assets:			
Goodwill	₹1,00,000	(Nil)	₹(1,00,000)
Buildings	2,80,000	₹4,05,000	1,25,000
Land	75,000	70,000	(5,000)
Machinery	1,00,000	1,65,000	65,000
Tools	35,000	20,000	(15,000)
Trade investments	7,500	9,000	1,500
Inventories	1,09,000	1,05,000	(4,000)
Sundry debtors	46,000	90,000	44,000
Bills receivable	13,500	10,500	(3,000)
Cash in hand	4,500	1,000	(3,500)
Unexpired insurance	700	600	(100)
Unamortised discount on debentures	1,250	1,050	(200)
	7,72,450	8,77,150	1,04,700
Liabilities:			
Equity share capital	2,00,000	3,50,000	1,50,000
Debentures	50,000	75,000	25,000
Sundry creditors	26,000	29,000	3,000
Bank overdraft	—	4,000	4,000
Bills payable	5,000	4,500	(500)
Bank loans (short-term)	3,400	750	(2,650)
Accrued taxes	1,500	2,500	1,000
Accrued interest	3,000	5,000	2,000
Allowance for doubtful accounts	1,150	2,250	1,100
Accumulated depreciation	90,500	1,35,600	45,100
Retained earnings	3,91,900	2,68,550	(1,23,350)
	7,72,450	8,77,150	1,04,700

Additional Information:

(i) There were no purchases or sales of tools.

(ii) Equity shares were issued at a discount of 10 per cent.

(iii) Old machinery that cost ₹2,250 was scrapped and written off the books. Accumulated depreciation on such equipment was ₹1,650.

(iv) The income statement for the current year is:

Sales (net)	₹6,25,000
Less: Expenses:	
Operating charges:	
Materials and supplies	1,25,000
Direct labour	1,05,000
Manufacturing overhead	90,750
Depreciation	61,750
Selling expenses	1,22,500
General expenses	1,15,000
Interest expenses	3,750
Unusual items:	
Writing off of goodwill	1,00,000
Writing off of land	5,000
Loss on machinery	600
Discount on issue of equity shares 15,000	7,44,350
Net loss	(1,19,350)

You are required to prepare cash flow statement based on Ind AS-7.

Solution

Statement of Cash Flows of Plastic Manufacturing Company
for the Current Year (Indirect method)

Particulars		*Amount*
Cash flow from operating activities:		
Net loss	₹(1,19,350)	
Adjusted for		
Depreciation	61,750	
Interest expenses	3,750	
Writing off of goodwill	1,00,000	
Writing off of land	5,000	
Loss on machinery	600	
Discount on issue of shares	15,000	
Amortisation of discount on debentures	200	
Operating profit before working capital changes	66,950	
Adjusted for changes in working capital:		
Decrease in inventories	4,000	
Increase in sundry debtors	(44,000)	
Decrease in bills receivable	3,000	
Decrease in unexpired insurance	100	
Increase in creditors	3,000	
Increase in bank overdraft	4,000	
Decrease in bills payable	(500)	
Decrease in bank loans (short-term)	(2,650)	
Increase in accrued taxes	1,000	
Allowance for doubtful debts	1,100	
Net cash from operating activities		₹36,000
Cash flow from investing activities:		
Purchase of machine (1)	(67,250)	
Purchase of building	(1,25,000)	
Purchase of trade investments	1,500	
Net cash used in investing activities		1,93,750
Cash flow from financing activities:		
Proceeds from issue of equity shares	1,35,000	
Proceeds from issue of debentures	25,000	
Interest paid (2)	(1,750)	
Dividend paid (3)	(4,000)	
Net cash from financing activities		1,54,250
Net decrease in cash and cash-equivalents		(3,500)
Cash and cash equivalents at the beginning of current year		4,500
Cash and cash equivalents at the end of current year		1,000

WORKING NOTES

1. Purchase of Machine

Machinery at beginning of the year	₹1,00,000
Less scrap value of machine	2,250
	97,750
Closing balance of machine	1,65,000
Difference represents purchase of machine*	67,250

2. Interest paid

Accrued interest at the beginning of year	3,000
Interest due during the year	3,750*
	6,750
Less accrued interest at the end of the year	5,000
Interest paid	1,750

*Interest expenses are (₹1,750 paid + Payable, ₹2,000). In operating activities, ₹3,750 has been adjusted in determining figure of operating profit before working capital changes. Increase in accrued interest of ₹2,000 (₹5,000 – ₹3,000) is not adjusted subsequently as it would have added more to cash flow by ₹2,000. (to avoid double counting).

3. Determination of dividend amount:

Balance of retained earnings 31st March, previous year	₹3,91,900
Less*:* Net loss of current year	1,19,350
	2,72,550

However, the balance of retained earnings as on December 31, current year is ₹2,68,550, that is, ₹4,000 less. In the absence of any other information, this amount is assumed to have been paid as dividends to equityholders.

P.5.8 The following are the summarised balance sheets of Sound Ltd. as on March 31 for the two consecutive years 1 and 2: **LO 5.5** **LOD: D**

(₹ *in thousand*)

Particulars	*Year 2*	*Year 1*
Assets:		
Plant and machinery	1,980	1,010
Land and buildings	1,000	1,000
Long-term investments	550	550
Short-term investments	470	85
Sundry debtors	2,195	2,500
Inventories	1,400	1,300
Interest receivable	100	65
Cash in hand	300	500
Cash in bank	405	300
	8,400	7,310
Liabilities:		
Share capital	2,600	2,150
Reserve and surplus	1,460	900
15% debentures	2,000	1,800
Sundry creditors	440	650
Wages outstanding	40	20
Income-tax payable	400	450
Accumulated depreciation:		
Plant and machinery	910	840
Land and buildings	550	500
	8,400	7,310

Income Statement
for the period ending March 31, year 2 (₹ *in thousand)*

Sales revenue	45,300
Less: Cost of sales	39,000
(Contd.)	

(Contd.)

Gross profit	6,300
Less: Depreciation	(540)
Selling and administration expenses	(2,960)
Interest paid	(300)
Add: Interest income	65
Dividend income (gross)	95
Net profit before extraordinary items	2,660
Add: Insurance settlement received	10
	2,670
Less: Provision for income-taxes	550
Net profit after taxes	2,120

Additional information (₹ *in thousand*):

(1) 15% Debentures of ₹300 was redeemed during year 2.
(2) Tax deducted at source on dividends received (included in provision for taxes) amounts to ₹15.
(3) A plant costing ₹500, having accumulated depreciation of ₹420 was sold for ₹80.
(4) During year 2, interim dividend of ₹760 was paid; final dividend paid was ₹800.
(5) All sales and purchases are made on credit basis.

You are required to prepare a statement of cash flows as per Ind AS-7 (revised).

Solution

Direct Method Cash Flow Statement (₹ *in thousand)*

Cash flows from operating activities:		
Cash receipts from customers	45,605	
Cash paid to suppliers and employees	(42,250)	
Cash generated from operations	3,355	
Income tax paid	(585)	
Cash flow before extraordinary item	2,770	
Proceeds from insurance settlement	10	
Net cash from operating activities		2,780
Cash flows from investing activities:		
Purchases of plant and machinery	(1,470)	
Proceeds from sale of plant and machinery	80	
Interest received	30	
Dividends received (₹95 – 15)	80	
Net cash used in investing activities		(1,280)
Cash flows from financing activities:		
Proceeds from issuance of share capital	450	
Proceeds from issue of 15% debentures	500	
Redemption of 15% debentures	(300)	
Interest paid	(300)	
Dividends paid (interim + final)	(1,560)	
Net cash used in financing activities		(1,210)
Net increase in cash and cash-equivalent		290
Cash and cash-equivalent at beginning of year 2		885
Cash and cash-equivalents at the end of year 2		1,175

WORKING NOTES

(figures in ₹ '000)

1. Cash receipts from customers:

Sales	45,300
Add: Sundry debtors at the beginning of year 2	2,500
	47,800
Less: Sundry debtors at the end of year 2	(2,195)
	45,605

2. Cash paid to suppliers and employees:

Cost of sales	39,000
Add: Administrative and selling expenses	2,960
Sundry creditors at the beginning of year 2	650
Wages outstanding at the beginning of year 2	20
Inventories at the end of year 2	1,400
	44,030
Less: Sundry creditors at the end of year 2	(440)
Wages outstanding at the end of the year 2	(40)
Inventories at the end of year 1	(1,300)
	42,250

3. Income tax paid (including tax deducted at source from dividends received)

Income tax for year 2 (including tax deducted at source from dividends received)	550
Add: Income tax liability at the beginning of year 2	450
Less: Income tax liability at the end of year 2	(400)
	600

Out of ₹600, tax deducted at source on dividend received (amounting to ₹15) is included in cash flows from investing activities and the balance of ₹585 is included in cash flows from operating activities.

4. Interest received:

Interest income for year 2	65
Add: Interest receivable in the beginning of year 2	65
Less: Amount receivable at the end of year 2	(100)
	30

5. Machinery purchased:

Balance at the end of year 2	1,980
Add: Book value of machine sold	500
Less: Balance at the beginning of year 2	(1,010)
	1,470

Statement of Cash Flows Indirect Method *(Amount in '000 ₹)*

Cash flows from operating activities:	
Net profit before taxation	2,660
Adjustment for:	
Depreciation	540
Interest income	(65)
Dividend income	(95)
Interest expenses	300
Operating profit before working capital changes	3,740
Decrease in sundry debtors	305
Increase in wages outstanding	20

(Contd.)

(Contd.)

Increase in inventories	(100)	
Decrease in creditors	(210)	
Cash generated from operations	3,355	
Income taxes paid	(585)	
Cash flow before extraordinary item	2,770	
Add: Insurance settlement	10	
Net cash from operating activities		2,780
Cash flows from investing activities:		
Purchase of plant and machinery	(1,470)	
Proceeds from sale of plant and machinery	80	
Interest received	30	
Dividends received (95 – 15)	80	
Net cash used in investing activities		(1,280)
Cash flows from financial activities:		
Proceeds from issuance of share capital	450	
Proceeds from issue of 15% debentures	500	
Redemption of 15% debentures	(300)	
Interest paid	(300)	
Dividends paid (interim + final)	(1,560)	
Net cash used in financing activities		(1,210)
Net increase in cash and cash-equivalent		290
Cash and cash-equivalents at beginning of year 2		885
Cash and cash-equivalents at the end of year 2		1,175

Cash and Cash-equivalents *(Figures in '000 ₹)*

Particulars	*Year 2*	*Year 1*
Cash in hand	300	500
Cash at bank	405	300
Short-term investments	470	85
	1,175	885

P.5.9 The following are the summarised balance sheets of Hypothetical Ltd. as at March 31 for the two consecutive years 1 and 2. Prepare CFS as per Ind AS-7. **LO 5.5** **LOD: D**

(₹ in thousand)

Particulars		*Year 2*		*Year 1*
Assets				
Cash on hand and balances with banks		200		25
Short-term investments		670		135
Sundry debtors		1,700		1,200
Interest receivable		100		—
Inventories		900		1,950
Long-term investments		2,500		2,500
Fixed assets at cost	2,180		1,910	
Accumulated depreciation	(1,450)		(1,060)	
Fixed assets (net)		730		850
Total assets		6,800		6,660
Liabilities				
Sundry creditors		150		1,890
Interest payable		230		100
Income taxes payable		400		1,000
Long-term debt		1,110		1,040
Total liabilities		1,890		4,030

(Contd.)

(*Contd.*)

Shareholders' Funds		
Share capital	1,500	1,250
Reserves	3,410	1,380
Total shareholders' funds	4,910	2,630
Total liabilities and shareholders' funds	6,800	6,660

Statement of Profit and Loss
for the year 2 ended March 31

	(₹ '000)
Sales	30,650
Cost of sales	(26,000)
Gross profit	4,650
Depreciation	(450)
Administrative and selling expenses	(910)
Interest expense	(400)
Interest income	300
Dividend income	200
Foreign exchange loss	(40)
Net profit before taxation and extraordinary item	3,350
Extraordinary item-Insurance proceeds from earthquake disaster settlement	180
Net profit after extraordinary item	3,530
Income-tax	(300)
Net profit	3,230

Additional information (*₹ in thousand*)

(i) An amount of 250 was raised from the issue of share capital and a further 250 was raised from long-term borrowings.

(ii) Interest expense was 400 of which 170 was paid during the period. 100 relating to interest expense of the prior period was also paid during the period.

(iii) Dividends paid were 1,200.

(iv) Tax deducted at source on dividends received (included in the tax expense of 300 for the year) amounted to 40.

(v) During the period, the enterprise acquired fixed assets for 350. The payment was made in cash.

(vi) Plant with original cost of 80 and accumulated depreciation of 60 was sold for 20.

(vii) Foreign exchange loss of 40 represents the reduction in the carrying amount of a short-term investment in foreign-currency designated bonds arising out of a change in exchange rate between the date of acquisition of the investment and the balance sheet date.

(viii) Sundry debtors and sundry creditors include amounts relating to credit sales and credit purchases only.

Solution

Statement of Cash Flows Direct Method (*₹ '000*)

Cash flows from operating activities		
Cash receipts from customers	30,150	
Cash paid to suppliers and employees	(27,600)	
Cash generated from operations	2,550	
Income taxes paid	(860)	
Cash flow before extraordinary item	1,690	
Proceeds from earthquake disaster settlement	180	
Net cash from operating activities		1,870
Cash flows from investing activities		
Purchase of fixed assets	(350)	

(*Contd.*)

(*Contd.*)

Proceeds from sale of equipment	20	
Interest received	200	
Dividends received	160	
Net cash from investing activities		30
Cash flows from financing activities		
Proceeds from issuance of share capital	250	
Proceeds from long-term borrowings	250	
Repayment of long-term borrowings	(180)	
Interest paid	(270)	
Dividends paid	(1,200)	
Net cash used in financing activities		(1,150)
Net increase in cash and cash equivalents		750
Cash and cash equivalents at beginning of period (*see Note 1*)		160
Cash and cash equivalents at the end of period (*see Note 1*)		910

Statement of Cash Flows Indirect Method (*₹ '000*)

Cash flows from operating activities		
Net profit before taxation	3,350	
Adjustments for:		
Depreciation	450	
Foreign exchange loss	40	
Interest income	(300)	
Dividend income	(200)	
Interest expense	400	
Operating profit before working capital changes	3,740	
Increase in sundry debtors	(500)	
Decrease in inventories	1,050	
Decrease in sundry creditors	(1,740)	
Cash generated from operations	2,550	
Income taxes paid	(860)	
Cash flow before extraordinary item	1,690	
Proceeds from earthquake disaster settlement	180	
Net cash from operating activities		1,870
Cash flows from investing activities:		
Purchase of fixed assets	(350)	
Proceeds from sale of equipment	20	
Interest received	200	
Dividends received	160	
Net cash from investing activities		30
Cash flows from financing activities	250	
Proceeds from issuance of share capital	250	
Proceeds from long-term borrowings	(180)	
Repayment of long-term borrowings	(270)	
Interest paid	(1,200)	
Dividends paid		(1,150)
Net cash used in financing activities		750
Net increase in cash and cash equivalents		750
Cash and cash equivalents at beginning of period (*see Note 1*)		160
Cash and cash equivalents at end of period (*see Note 1*)		910

Notes to the cash flow statement (direct method and indirect method)

1. Cash and cash-equivalents

Cash and cash equivalents consist of cash on hand and balances with banks, and investments in money-market instruments. Cash and cash-equivalents included in the cash flow statement comprise the following balance sheet amounts.

	Year 2	Year 1
Cash on hand and balances with banks	₹200	₹25
Short-term investments	670	135
Cash and cash-equivalents	870	160
Effect of exchange rate changes	40	—
Cash and cash equivalents as restated	910	160

Cash and cash-equivalents at the end of the period include deposits with banks of 100 held by a branch which are not freely remissible to the company because of currency exchange restrictions. The company has undrawn borrowing facilities of 2,000 of which 700 may be used only for future expansion.

2. Total tax paid during the year (including tax deducted at source on dividends received) amounted to 900.

Alternative Presentation (indirect method):

As an alternative, in an indirect method cash flow statement, operating profit before working capital changes is sometimes presented as follows:

Revenues excluding investment income	₹30,650	
Operating expense excluding depreciation	(26,910)	
Operating profit before working capital changes		₹3,740

WORKING NOTES

(Figures in ₹ '000)

1. Cash receipts from customers		
Sales		30,650
Add: Sundry debtors at the end of the year		1,200
		31,850
Less: Sundry debtors at the end of the year		1,700
		30,150
2. Cash paid to suppliers and employees		
Cost of sales		26,000
Administrative and selling expenses		910
		26,910
Add: Sundry creditors at the beginning of the year	1,890	
Inventories at the end of the year	900	2,790
Less: Sundry creditors at the end of the year	150	29,700
Inventories at the beginning of the year	1,950	2,100
		27,600
3. Income taxes paid (including tax deducted at source from dividends received)		
Income tax expense for the year (including tax deducted at source from dividends received)		300
Add: Income tax liability at the beginning of the year		1,000
		1,300
Less: Income tax liability at the end of the year		400
		900

Out of 900, tax deducted at source on dividends received (amounting to 40) is included in cash flows from investing activities and the balance of 860 is included in cash flows from operating activities.

4. Repayment of long-term borrowings	
Long-term debt at the beginning of the year	1,040
Add: Long-term borrowing made during the year	250
	1,290
Less: Long-term borrowings at the end of the year	1,110
	180

5. Interest paid

Interest expense for the year	400
Add: Interest payable at the beginning of the year	100
	500
Less: Interest payable at the end of the year	230
	270

REVIEW QUESTIONS

LOD: Easy

RQ.5.1 Indicate whether the following statements are True or False. **LO 5.4.5**

(i) Cash from business operations can be determined from income statement.
(ii) Working capital from business operations can be determined from profit and loss account.
(iii) Sources of cash should always be more than uses of cash, in the context of cash flows statement.
(iv) Interest paid on debentures is a part of operating activities.
(v) Interest received on two-months deposits in bank is shown under investing activities.
(vi) Sources of cash and uses of cash are to be equal.
(vii) Cash flows are inflows and outflows of cash and cash-equivalents.
(viii) Revaluation of building affects cashflows.
(ix) Sale proceeds from machinery, being a source of finance, form part of financing activities.
(x) Cash flow statement is mandatory for all business firms.
(xi) In normal circumstances a firm has positive cash from operations and negative cash flow from investing activities.

[Answers: (i) False, (ii) True, (iii) False, (iv) False, (v) False, (vi) False, (vii) True, (viii) False, (ix) False, (x) False, and (xi) True]

RQ.5.2 Fill in the following blanks with right answer: **LO 5.4.5**

(i) Cash flow statement (based on AS-7) indicates change in __________ (cash/ bank/cash and cash-equivalents).
(ii) Decrease in creditors __________ (Decreases/Increases) cash.
(iii) Interest received on long-term investments is shown under __________ (Operating/ Financing/Investing activities).
(iv) Decrease in inventory __________ (Decreases/Increases) cash.
(v) Increase in pre-paid expenses __________ (Decreases/Increases) cash.
(vi) Cash payments to suppliers for goods and services are shown under __________ (Operating/Financing/Investing activities).
(vii) Cash-flow statement (based on AS-7) of listed companies should be presented as per the __________ (Indirect/Direct) method.
(viii) Cash payments to acquire long-term assets form part of __________ (Financing/Investing activities).
(ix) Buy back of shares is shown under (Financing/Investing activities).
(x) Dividends paid to shareholders are classified as __________ (Financing/Investing activities).

[Answers: (i) cash and cash-equivalents, (ii) decreases, (iii) investing activities, (iv) increases, (v) decreases, (vi) operating, (vii) indirect, (viii) investing, (ix) financing and (x) financing]

RQ.5.3 "The analysis of cash flow statement in any organisation can be very useful to the management." Elucidate the statement. LO 5.3

RQ.5.4 The cash flow statement is as useful to shareholders and lenders as to management. Explain. LO 5.3

RQ.5.5 Name three activities in which cash flows are classified as per Accounting Standard 7. Also give three examples of transactions covered in these activities. LO 5.5

RQ.5.6 Describe in brief the procedure of determining cash flow from operating activities as per indirect method of AS-7. Take an appropriate example to illustrate your answer. LO 5.5

RQ.5.7 The directors of Precision Tools Ltd. are worried at the deteriorating financial position of the company. The company has utilised full overdraft facility from the bank and is still not able to pay its creditors on due dates, although the profits earned are satisfactory. LO 5.5

The following are the balance sheets as on March 31 for the recent 2 years.

		Previous year		*Current year*
Share capital: shares of ₹10 each fully paid		₹10,00,000		₹10,00,000
P & L appropriation A/c		60,000		80,000
Overdraft from bank		1,60,000		6,00,000
Sundry creditors		2,00,000		6,00,000
		14,20,000		22,80,000
Land and buildings		3,00,000		5,00,000
Plant and machinery	₹5,00,000		₹6,00,000	
Less depreciation	1,20,000	3,80,000	1,80,000	4,20,000
Vehicles	1,16,000		1,24,000	
Less depreciation	56,000	60,000	84,000	40,000
Stock		2,20,000		7,20,000
Debtors		4,60,000		6,00,000
		14,20,000		22,80,000

During the year, a dividend of 10 per cent was distributed to the shareholders. On April 1 of the current year, a motor car, which originally costed ₹20,000, and showed a book value of ₹10,000, was sold for ₹16,000.

You are required to prepare a statement of cash flows based on Ind AS-7.

LOD: Medium

RQ.5.8 From the following financial information, select non-cash investing, financing and operating activities: LO 5.4,5

- Redemption of debentures by converting into equity shares
- Buy back of equity shares
- Purchase of fixed assets in exchange of preference shares
- Depreciation on fixed assets
- Increase in debtors
- Loss on sale of plant
- Decrease in inventories
- Amortisation of patents
- Issuance of equity share for cash
- Bonus shares

[Answer: (Non-cash activities)

Investing: Purchase of fixed assets in exchange of preference shares.

Financing: (i) Redemption of debentures by converting into equity shares,

(ii) Issue of preference shares for purchase of fixed assets, (iii) Bonus shares Operating: (i) Depreciation on fixed assets, (ii) Amortisation of patents, (iii) Loss on sale of plant]

RQ.5.9 Explain with example the two methods of determining cash provided by operating activities. **LO 5.5**

RQ.5.10 Explain why decrease in current liabilities decrease cash and decrease in current assets increase cash. **LO 5.4**

RQ.5.11 "Depreciation is a non-cash expense. Still it is an integral part of cash flows". Explain. **LO 5.4**

RQ.5.12 Write short notes on the following **LO 5.5**
 (i) Cash-equivalents
 (ii) Treatment of interest and dividends received in cash flow statement (based on AS-7).
 (iii) Major non-cash items.

RQ.5.13 Given the following data (₹ thousands), prepare a statement of cash flows based on Ind AS-7. **LO 5.5**

	Year 2	*Year 1*
Liabilities		
Equity share capital	₹3,600	₹3,600
Reserves	2,545	2,100
Total shareholder's equity	6,145	5,700
Debentures	16,000	16,000
Current liabilities		
Bills payable	3,900	2,800
Creditors	4,800	4,100
Provision for taxation	155	400
Total liabilities	31,000	29,000
Assets		
Fixed assets		
Land	300	300
Buildings, plant and machinery (net)	7,000	5,800
Total fixed assets	7,300	6,100
Current assets		
Bank	2,600	2,200
Inventories at cost	14,600	14,400
Investments	600	600
Debtors	5,300	5,100
Advances	600	600
Total current assets	23,700	22,900
Total assets	31,000	29,000

Statement of Income and Reconciliation of Retained Profits
for the year-end 2 *(₹ thousands)*

Sales		₹55,000
Cost of goods sold		40,000
Gross profit on sales		15,000
Other operating expenses		
Selling expenses	₹8,900	

(Contd.)

(*Contd.*)

Administrative	2,000	
Depreciation	1,000	11,900
Operating profit		3,100
Interest charged		800
Profit before tax		2,300
Provision for taxation (0.35)		805
Profit after taxation		1,495
Dividends		1,050
Net profit retained		445
Add reserves (beginning)		2,100
Reserves (closing)		2,545

RQ.5.14 From the information contained in income statement and balance sheet of 'A' Ltd., prepare cash flow statement (based on AS-7): **LO 5.5**

Income statement for the year ended March 31, 2016

Net sales	(A)	₹2,52,00,000
Less:		
Cash cost of sales		1,98,00,000
Depreciation		6,00,000
Salaries and wages		24,00,000
Operating expenses		8,00,000
Provision for taxation		8,80,000
	(B)	2,44,80,000
Net operating profit (*A* – *B*)		7,20,000
Non-recurring income – Profits on sale of equipment		1,20,000
		8,40,000
Retained earnings and profits brought forward		15,18,000
		23,58,000
Dividends declared and paid during the year		7,20,000
Profit and Loss Account balance as on March 31, 2016		16,38,000

Balance sheet as on

Assets	*March 31, 2015*	*March 31, 2016*
Fixed Assets:		
Land	₹4,80,000	₹9,60,000
Building and equipment	36,00,000	57,60,000
Current assets:		
Cash	6,00,000	7,20,000
Debtors	16,80,000	18,60,000
Stock	26,40,000	9,60,000
Advances	78,000	90,000
	90,78,000	1,03,50,000
Liabilities and Equity	March 31, 2015	March 31, 2016
Share capital	₹36,00,000	₹44,40,000
Surplus in profit and loss account	15,18,000	16,38,000
Sundry creditors	24,00,000	23,40,000
Outstanding expenses	2,40,000	4,80,000
Income-tax payable	1,20,000	1,32,000
Accumulated depreciation on buildings and equipments	12,00,000	13,20,000
	90,78,000	1,03,50,000

The original cost of equipment sold during the year 2015-16 was ₹7,20,000.

LOD: Difficult

RQ.5.15 The Balance Sheet of Royal Limited as on 31st March, 2015 and 31st March, 2016 are given below: **LO 5.5**

Balance Sheet as on *(Amount in ₹ thousands)*

Liabilities	*31.03.15*	*31.03.16*	*Assets*	*31.03.15*	*31.03.16*
Share capital	1,440	1,920	Fixed assets	3,840	4,560
Capital reserve	—	48	*Less:* Depreciation	1,104	1,392
General reserve	816	960		2,736	3,168
Profit and loss account	288	360	Investment	480	384
9% Debenture	960	672	Cash	210	312
Current liabilities	576	624	Other current assets (including stock)	1,134	1,272
Proposed dividend	144	174	Preliminary expenses	96	48
Provision for tax	432	408			
Unpaid dividend	—	18			
	4,656	5,184		4,656	5,184

Additional Informations:

(i) During the year 2015–2016, Fixed Assets costing ₹2,40,000 (accumulated depreciation ₹84,000) was sold for ₹1,20,000.

(ii) Provided ₹4,20,000 as depreciation.

(iii) Some investments are sold at a profit of ₹48,000 and Profit was credited to capital reserve.

(iv) It decided that stocks be valued at cost, whereas previously the practice was to value stock at cost less 10 per cent. The stock was ₹2,59,200 as on 31.03.15. The stock as on 31.03.16 was correctly valued at ₹3,60,000.

(v) It decided to write off fixed assets costing ₹60,000 on which depreciation amounting to ₹48,000 has been provided.

(vi) Debentures are redeemed at ₹105.

Required:

Prepare a Cash Flow Statement (based on Accounting Standard-7).

ANSWERS

RQ.5.7 Cash from operating activities, ₹4,12,000; Cash from investing activities, (₹3,12,000); Cash from financing activities, (₹1,00,000).

RQ.5.13 Cash from operating activities, ₹4,450; Cash from investing activities, (₹2,200); Cash from financing activities, (₹1,850).

RQ.5.14 Cash from operating activities, ₹30 lakh; Cash from investing activities, (₹30 lakh); Cash from financing activities, ₹1.2 lakh.

RQ.5.15 Cash from operating activities, ₹8,06,400; Cash from investing activities, (₹7,56,000); Cash from financing activities, ₹51,600.

[Comprehensive solutions to all numerical review questions are available on the companion website: http://www.mhhe.com/khan_jain_ma7e]

6 Financial Statements Analysis

LEARNING OBJECTIVES

After reading this chapter you will be able to:

- **LO 6.1** Know the meaning and rationale of ratio analysis
- **LO 6.2** Understand liquidity ratios
- **LO 6.3** Explain capital structure ratios
- **LO 6.4** Describe profitability ratios
- **LO 6.5** Interpret activity/efficiency ratios
- **LO 6.6** Discuss integrated analysis of ratios/Du Pont Chart
- **LO 6.7** Review the common size statements
- **LO 6.8** Illustrate the importance of ratio analysis
- **LO 6.9** Outline the limitations of ratio analysis

INTRODUCTION

As observed in the preceding Chapter, a basic limitation of the traditional financial statements comprising the balance sheet and the profit and loss account is that they do not give all the information related to the financial operations of a firm. Nevertheless, they provide some extremely useful information to the extent that the balance sheet mirrors the financial position on a particular date in terms of the structure of assets, liabilities and owners' equity, and so on and the profit and loss account shows the results of operations during a certain period of time in terms of the revenues obtained and the cost incurred during the year. Thus, the financial statements provide a summarised view of the financial position and operations of a firm. Therefore, much can be learnt about a firm from a careful examination of its financial statements as invaluable documents/performance reports. The analysis of financial statements is, thus, an important aid to financial analysis.

The focus of financial analysis is on key figures in the financial statements and the significant relationship that exists between them. The analysis of financial statements is a process of evaluating the relationship between component parts of financial statements to obtain a better understanding of the firm's position and performance.[1] The first task of the financial analyst is to select the information relevant to the decision under consideration from the total information contained in the financial statements. The second step is to arrange the information in a way to highlight significant relationships. The final step is interpretation and drawing of inferences and conclusions. *In brief, financial analysis is the process of selection, relation and evaluation.*[2]

The present chapter is devoted to an in-depth analysis of financial statements and its use for decision making by various external and internal parties interested in them. The focus of the Chapter is on ratio analysis as the most widely used technique of financial statement analysis. The Chapter also discusses common-size statements as method of analysis of financial statements. The importance of ratio analysis and its limitations are similarly briefly outlined. The major points are summarised by way of recapitulation.

RATIO ANALYSIS—MEANING

LO 6.1 Know the meaning and rationale of ratio analysis

Ratio Analysis is a widely-used tool of financial analysis. It can be used to compare the risk and return relationships of firms of different sizes. It is defined as the systematic use of ratio to interpret the financial statements so that the strengths and weaknesses of a firm as well as its historical performance and current financial condition can be determined. The term ratio refers to the numerical or quantitative relationship between two items/variables. This relationship can be expressed as **(i)** percentages, say, net profits are 25 per cent of sales (assuming net profits of ₹25 lakh and sales of ₹100 lakh, **(ii)** fraction (net profit is one-fourth of sales) and **(iii)** proportion of numbers (the relationship between net profits and sales is 1:4). These alternative methods of expressing items which are related to each other are, for purposes of financial analysis, referred to as ratio analysis. It should be noted that computing the ratios does not add any information not already inherent in the above figures of profits and sales. What the ratios do is that they reveal the relationship in a more meaningful way so as to enable equity investors, management and lenders make better investment and credit decisions.

Rationale

The rationale of ratio analysis lies in the fact that it makes related information comparable. A single figure by itself has no meaning but when expressed in terms of a related figure, it yields significant inferences. For instance, the fact that the net profits of a firm amount to, say, ₹10 lakh throws no light on its adequacy or otherwise. The figure of net profit has to be considered in relation to other variables. How does it stand in relation to sales? What does it represent by way of return on total assets used or total capital employed? If, therefore, net profits are shown in terms of their relationship with items such as sales, assets, capital employed, equity capital and so on, meaningful conclusions can be drawn regarding their adequacy. To carry the above example further, assuming the capital employed to be ₹50 lakh and ₹100 lakh, the net profits are 20 per cent and 10 per cent respectively. Ratio analysis, thus, as a quantitative tool, enables analysts to draw quantitative answers to questions such as: Are the net profits adequate? Are the assets being used efficiently? Is the firm solvent? Can the firm meet its current obligations and so on?

Basis of Comparison

Ratios, as shown above, are relative figures reflecting the relationship between variables. They enable analysts to draw conclusions regarding financial operations. The use of ratios, as a tool of financial analysis, involves their comparison, for a single ratio, like absolute figures, fails to reveal the true position. For example, if in the case of a firm, the return on capital employed is 15 per cent in a particular year, what does it indicate? Only if the figure is related to the fact that in the preceding year the relevant return was 12 per cent or 18 per cent, it can be inferred whether the profitability of the firm has declined or improved. Alternatively, if we know that the return for the industry as a whole is 10 per cent or 20 per cent, the profitability of the firm in question can be evaluated. Comparison with related facts is, therefore, the basis of ratio analysis. Four types of comparisons are involved: **(i)** trend ratios, **(ii)** interfirm comparison, **(iii)** comparison of items within a single year's financial statement of a firm, and **(iv)** comparison with standards or plans.

Trend ratios involve evaluation of financial performance over a period of time using finanical ratio analysis.

Trend ratios involve a comparison of the ratios of a firm over time, that is, present ratios are compared with past ratios for the same firm. The comparison of the profitability of a firm, say, year 1 through 5 is an illustration of a trend ratio. Trend ratios indicate the direction of change in the performance–improvement, deterioration or constancy–over the years.

Inter-firm comparison involves comparison of different firms' financial ratios at the same point of time; involves comparison of a firm's ratios to those of others in its industry or to industry average.

The **inter-firm comparison** involving comparison of the ratios of a firm with those of others in the same line of business or for the industry as a whole reflects its performance in relation to its competitors.

Other types of comparison may relate to comparison of items within a single year's financial statement of a firm and comparison with standards or plans.

Types of Ratios

Ratios can be classified into six broad groups: (i) Liquidity ratios, (ii) Capital structure/leverage ratios, (iii) Profitability ratios, (iv) Activity/Efficiency ratios and (v) Integrated analysis of ratios. **A checklist of financial ratios of Reliance Industries Limited (based on data for 2012 contained in Annexure 4.2 of chapter 4) is provided in Annexure 6.1.**

LIQUIDITY RATIOS

LO 6.2 Understand liquidity ratios

The importance of adequate liquidity in the sense of the ability of a firm to meet current/short-term obligations when they become due for payment can hardly be overstressed. In fact, liquidity is a prerequisite for the very survival of a firm. The short-term creditors of the firm are interested in the short-term solvency or liquidity of a firm. But liquidity implies, from the viewpoint of utilisation of the funds of the firm, that funds are idle or they earn very little. A proper balance between the two contradictory requirements, that is, liquidity and profitability, is required for efficient financial management. The liquidity ratios measure the ability of a firm to meet its short-term obligations and reflect the short-term financial strength/solvency of a firm. The ratios which indicate the liquidity of a firm are: **(i)** net working capital, **(ii)** current ratios, **(iii)** acid test/quick ratios, **(iv)** super quick ratios, **(v)** turnover ratios, **(vi)** defensive-interval ratios and **(vii)** cash flow from operations ratio.

Net Working Capital

Net working capital is a measure of liquidity calculated by subtracting current liabilities from current assets.

Net working capital (NWC) represents the excess of current assets over current liabilities. The term current assets refers to assets which in the normal course of business get converted into cash without dimunition in value over a short period, usually not exceeding one year or length of operating/cash cycle whichever is more. Current liabilities are those liabilities which at the inception are required to be paid in short period, normally a year. Although NWC is really not a ratio, it is frequently employed as a measure of a company's liquidity position. An enterprise should have sufficient NWC in order to be able to meet the claims of the creditors and the day-to-day needs of business. The greater is the amount of NWC, the greater is the liquidity of the firm. Accordingly, NWC is a measure of liquidity. Inadequate working capital is the first sign of financial problems for a firm.

There is, however, no predetermined criterion as to what constitutes adequate NWC. Moreover, the size of the NWC is not an appropriate measure of the liquidity position of a firm as shown in Table 6.1:

TABLE 6.1 Net Working Capital

Particulars	*Company A (₹ lakh)*	*Company B (₹ lakh)*
Total current assets	180	30
Total current liabilities	120	10
NWC	60	20

If the size of NWC is a measure of liquidity, Company A must be three times as liquid as Company B. However, a deeper probe would show that this is not so. A comparison of current liabilities and current assets of both the firms shows that for each rupee of current liability, B has ₹3 of current assets, while A has only ₹1.50. Thus, while A has three times the NWC of B, the current assets of the former are only 1.5 times its current liabilities as compared to 3 times in case of the latter. Obviously, from the viewpoint of the ability to meet its current obligations, firm B is in a better position than firm A. Another limitation of NWC, as a measure of liquidity, is that a change in NWC does not necessarily reflect a change in the liquidity position of a firm. Witness Table 6.2.

TABLE 6.2 Change in Net Working Capital

Particulars	*End-year 1 (₹ lakh)*	*End-year 2 (₹ lakh)*
Current assets	150	300
Current liabilities	75	200
NWC	75	100

Although the NWC has gone up for the firm in Table 6.2 from ₹75 lakh to ₹100 lakh, that is, by ₹25 lakh or 33.3 per cent between two points of time, there is, in reality, a deterioration in the liquidity position. In the first year, the firm had ₹2 of current assets for each rupee of current liabilities; but by the end of the second year the amount of current assets for each rupee of current liabilities declined to ₹1.5 only, that is, by 25 per cent. For these reasons, NWC is not a satisfactory measure of the liquidity of a firm for inter-firm comparison or for trend analysis.[3] A better indicator is the current ratio.

Current Ratio

Current ratio is a measure of liquidity calculated dividing the current assets by the current liabilities.

The **current ratio** is the ratio of total current assets to total current liabilities. It is calculated by dividing current assets by current liabilities:

$$\text{Current ratio} = \frac{\text{Current assets}}{\text{Current liabilities}} \tag{6.1}$$

The current assets of a firm, as already stated, represent those assets which can be, in the ordinary course of business, converted into cash within a short period of time, normally not exceeding one year and include cash and bank balances, marketable securities, inventory of raw materials, semi-finished (work-in-progress) and finished goods, debtors net of provision for bad and doubtful debts, bills receivable and prepaid expenses. The current liabilities defined as liabilities which are short-term maturing obligations to be met, as originally contemplated, within a year, consist of trade creditors, bills payable, bank credit, provision for taxation, dividends payable and outstanding expenses. The current ratio for firms A and B of Table 6.1 are shown in Table 6.3.

TABLE 6.3 Current Ratio

Particulars	Firm A (₹ lakh)	Firm B (₹ lakh)
$\frac{\text{Current assets}}{\text{Current liabilities}}$	$= \frac{180}{120}$	$= \frac{30}{10}$
	= 3 : 2 (1.5 : 1)	3 : 1

Rationale The current ratio of a firm measures its short-term solvency, that is, its ability to meet short-term obligations. As a measure of short-term/current financial liquidity, it indicates the rupees of current assets (cash balance and its potential source of cash) available for each rupee of current liability/obligation payable. *The higher the current ratio, the larger is the amount of rupees available per rupee of current liability, the more is the firm's ability to meet current obligations and the greater is the safety of funds of short-term creditors.* Thus, current ratio, in a way, is a measure of margin of safety to the creditors.

The need for safety margin arises from the inevitable unevenness in the flow of funds through the current assets and liabilities account. If the flows were absolutely smooth and uniform each day so that inflows exactly equalled absolutely maturing obligations, the requirement of a safety margin would be small. The fact that a firm can rarely count on such an even flow requires that the size of the current assets should be sufficiently larger than current liabilities so that the firm would be assured of being able to pay its current maturing debt as and when it becomes due. Moreover, the current liabilities can be settled only by making payment whereas the current assets available to liquidate them are subject to shrinkage for various reasons, such as bad debts, inventories becoming obsolete or unsaleable and occurrence of unexpected losses in marketable securities and so on. The current ratio measures the size of the short-term liquidity 'buffer'. A satisfactory current ratio would enable a firm to meet its obligations even when the value of the current assets declines.

Interpretation In the case of company A in the above example, the current ratio is 1.5 : 1. It implies that for every one rupee of current liabilities, current assets of one-and-half rupees are available to meet them. In other words, the current assets are one-and-half times the current liabilities. The current ratio of 3 : 1 for company B signifies that current assets are three-fold its short-term obligations. The liquidity position, as measured by the current ratio, is better in the case of B as compared to A. This is because the safety margin in the former (200 per cent) is substantially higher than in the latter (50 per cent). A slight decline in the value of current assets will adversely affect the ability of firm A to meet its obligations and, therefore, from the viewpoint of creditors, it is a more risky venture. In contrast, there is a sufficient cushion in firm B and even with two-thirds shrinkage in the value of its assets, it will be able to meet its obligations in full. For the creditors the firm is less risky. The interpretation is: *in interfirm comparison, the firm with the higher current ratio has better liquidity/short-term solvency.*

It is important to note that a very high ratio of current assets to current liabilities may be indicative of slack management practices, as it might signal excessive inventories for the current requirements and poor credit management in terms of overextended accounts receivable. At the same time, the firm may not be making full use of its current borrowing capacity.[5] Therefore, a firm should have a reasonable current ratio.

Although there is no hard and fast rule, conventionally, a current ratio of 2 : 1 (current assets twice current liabilities) is considered satisfactory. The logic underlying the conventional rule is that even with a drop-out of 50 per cent (half) in the value of current assets, a firm can meet its obligations, that is, a 50 per cent margin of safety is assumed to be sufficient to wardoff the worst of situations. The firm A of our example, having a current ratio of 1.5 : 1, can be interpreted, on the basis of the conventional rule, to be inadequately liquid from the point of view of its ability to always satisfy the claims of short-term creditors. The firm B, of course, is sufficiently liquid as its current ratio is 3 : 1. The rule of thumb (a current ratio of 2 : 1) cannot, however, be applied mechanically. What is a satisfactory ratio will differ depending on the development of the capital market and the availability of long-term funds to finance current assets, the nature of industry and so on.

In capital-rich countries, where long-term funds from the capital market are available in abundance, firms depend on current liabilities for financing a relatively small part of their current asset requirements and it is not unusual for a firm to finance two-thirds to three-quarters of its current assets by long-term sources.[6] This policy of relying to a limited extent on short-term credit (current liabilities) is probably to avoid the difficulty in which the firms may be put by the creditors in times of temporary adversity. In underdeveloped countries, there is no alternative to relying heavily on short-term financing. Yet, in view of the risk which such a practice entails, the firms would be well advised to keep the current liabilities within reasonable limits and finance a certain minimum part of the current assets by long-term sources.

Another factor which has a bearing on the current ratio is the nature of the industry. For in-stance, public utility companies generally have a very low current ratio, as normally such companies have very little need for current assets. The wholesale dealers, on the other hand, purchasing goods on cash basis or on credit basis for a very short period but selling to retailers on credit basis, require a higher current ratio. If, in our above example, firm A is a public utility, its liquidity position can be interpreted to be satisfactory even though its current ratio is less than the conventional norm. Thus, the standard norm of current ratio (2 : 1) may vary from industry to industry. However, a ratio of less than 1 : 1 would certainly be undesirable in any industry as at least some safety margin is required to protect the interest of the creditors and to provide cushion to the firm in adverse circumstances.

The current ratio, though superior to NWC in measuring short-term financial solvency, is a rather crude measure of the liquidity of a firm. The limitation of current ratio arises from the fact that it is a *quantitative* rather than a *qualitative* index of liquidity. The term quantitative refers to the fact that it takes into account the total current assets without making any distinction between various types of current assets such as cash, inventories and so on. A qualitative measure takes into account the proportion of various types of current assets to the total current assets. A satisfactory measure of liquidity should consider the liquidity of the various current assets *per se*. As already mentioned, while current liabilities are fixed in the sense that they have to be paid in full in all circumstances, the current assets are subject to shrinkage in value, for example, possibility of bad debts, unsaleability of inventory and so on. Moreover, some of the current assets are more liquid than others: cash is the most liquid of all; receivables are more liquid than inventories, the last being the least liquid as they have to be sold before they are converted into receivables and, then, into cash. A firm with a higher percentage of its current assets in the form of cash would be more liquid, in the sense of being able to meet obligations as and when they become due, than one with a higher percentage of slow moving and unsaleable inventory and/or slow paying receivables even though both have the same current ratio. In fact, the latter type of firm may encounter serious difficulties in paying its bills even though it may have a current ratio of 2 : 1, whereas the former may do well with a ratio lower than the conventional norm. Thus, the current ratio is not a conclusive index of the real liquidity of a firm. It fails to answer questions, such as, how liquid are the receivables and the inventory? What effect does the omission of inventory and prepaid expenses have on the liquidity of a firm? To answer these and related questions, an additional analysis of the quality of current assets is required. This is done in acid-test or quick ratio.

Acid-Test/Quick Ratio

As observed above, one weakness of the current ratio is that it fails to convey any information on the composition of the current assets of a firm. A rupee of cash is considered equivalent to a rupee of inventory or receivables. But it is not so. A rupee of cash is more readily available (i.e. more liquid) to meet current obligations than a rupee of, say, inventory. This impairs the usefulness of the current ratio. The acid-test ratio is a measure of liquidity designed to overcome this shortcoming of the current ratio. It is often referred to as quick ratio because it is a measurement of a firm's ability to convert its current assets quickly into cash in order to meet its current liabilities. Thus, it is a measure of quick or acid liquidity.

The **acid-test ratio** is the ratio between quick current assets and current liabilities and is calculated by dividing the quick assets by the current liabilities:

Acid-test ratio (quick ratio) is a measure of liquidity calculated dividing current assets minus inventory and prepaid expenses by current liabilities.

$$\text{Acid-test ratio} = \frac{\text{Quick assets}}{\text{Current liabilities}} \quad \textbf{(6.2)}$$

The term **quick assets** refers to current assets which can be converted into cash immediately or at a short notice without diminution of value. Included in this category of current assets are (i) cash and bank balances; (ii) short-term marketable securities and (iii) debtors/receivables. Thus, the current assets which are excluded are: prepaid expenses and inventory. The exclusion of inventory is based on the reasoning that it is not easily and readily convertible into cash. Prepaid expenses by their very nature are not available to pay off current debts. They merely reduce the amount of cash required in one period because of payment in a prior period.[8] The acid-test ratio is calculated in Table 6.4.

TABLE 6.4 Acid-Test Ratio

Cash	₹20 lakh
Debtors	20
Inventory	120
Total current assets	160
Total current liabilities	80
(i) Current ratio	2 : 1
(ii) Acid-test ratio	0.5 : 1

Interpretation The acid-test ratio is a rigorous measure of a firm's ability to service short-term liabilities. The usefulness of the ratio lies in the fact that it is widely accepted as the best available test of the liquidity position of a firm. That the acid-test ratio is superior to the current ratio is evident from Table 6.4. The current ratio of the hypothetical firm is 2 : 1 and can certainly be considered satisfactory. This interpretation of the liquidity position of the firm needs modification in the light of the quick ratio. Generally, an acid-test ratio of 1:1 is considered satisfactory as a firm can easily meet all current claims. In the case of the hypothetical firm the quick ratio (0.5 : 1) is less than the standard/norm, the satisfactory current ratio notwithstanding. The interpretation that can be placed on the current ratio (2 : 1) and acid-test (0.5 : 1) is that a large part of the current assets of the firm is tied up in slow moving and unsaleable inventories and slow paying debts. The firm would find it difficult to pay its current liabilities. The acid-test ratio provides, in a sense, a check on the liquidity position of a firm as shown by its current ratio. The quick ratio is a more rigorous and penetrating test of the liquidity position of a firm. Yet, it is not a conclusive test. Both the current and quick ratios should be considered in relation to the industry average to infer whether the firm's short-term financial position is satisfactory or not.

A variation of this ratio,[9] may be super-quick/cash ratio. This ratio is calculated by dividing the super-quick assets by the current liabilities of a firm. The super-quick current assets are cash and marketable securities. This ratio is the most rigorous and conservative test of a firm's liquidity position. Further, it is suggested that it would be useful, for the management, if the liquidity measure also takes into account 'reserve borrowing power' as the firm's real debt paying ability depends not only on cash resources available with it but also on its capacity to borrow from the market at short notice.

Turnover Ratio The liquidity ratios discussed so far relate to the liquidity of a firm as a whole. Another way of examining the liquidity is to determine how quickly certain current assets are converted into cash. The ratios to measure these are referred to as **turnover ratios.** These are, as activity ratios, covered in detail later in this chapter. In fact, liquidity ratios are not independent of activity ratios. Poor debtor or inventory turnover ratios limit the usefulness of the current and acid-test ratios. Both obsolete/unsaleable inventory and uncollectible debtors are unlikely to be sources of cash. Therefore, the liquidity ratios should be examined in conjunction with relevant turnover ratios affecting liquidity. The three relevant turnover ratios are **(i)** inventory turnover ratio; **(ii)** debtors turnover ratio; and **(iii)** creditors turnover ratio.

Inventory Turnover Ratio It is computed by dividing the cost of goods sold by the average inventory. Thus,

$$\text{Inventory turnover ratio} = \frac{\text{Cost of goods sold}}{\text{Average inventory}} \qquad \textbf{(6.3)}$$

The cost of goods sold means sales minus gross profit. The average inventory refers to the simple average of the opening and closing inventory. The ratio indicates how fast inventory is sold. A high ratio is good from the viewpoint of liquidity and *vice versa.* A low ratio would signify that inventory does not sell fast and stays on the shelf or in the warehouse for a long time. This is illustrated in Example 6.1.

◆ Example 6.1

A firm has sold goods worth ₹300 lakh with a gross profit margin of 20 per cent. The stock at the beginning and the end of the year was ₹35 lakh and ₹45 lakh respectively. What is the inventory turnover ratio?

Solution

$$\text{Inventory turnover ratio} = \frac{(₹300 \text{ lakh} - ₹60 \text{ lakh})}{(₹35 \text{ lakh} + ₹45 \text{ lakh}) \div 2} = 6 \text{ (times per year)}$$

$$\text{Inventory holding period} = \frac{12 \text{ months}}{\text{Inventory turnover ratio, (6)}} = 2 \text{ months}$$

Debtors Turnover Ratio It is determined by dividing the net credit sales by average debtors outstanding during the year. Thus,

$$\text{Debtors turnover ratio} = \frac{\text{Net credit sales}}{\text{Average debtors}} \qquad \textbf{(6.4)}$$

Net credit sales consist of gross credit sales minus returns, if any, from customers. Average debtors is the simple average of debtors (including bills receivable) at the beginning and at the end of year. The analysis of the debtors turnover ratio supplements the information regarding the liquidity of one item of current assets of the firm. The ratio measures how rapidly receivables are collected. A high ratio is indicative of shorter time-lag between credit sales and cash collection. A low ratio shows that debts are not being collected rapidly. This is shown in Example 6.2.

◆ Example 6.2

A firm has made credit sales of ₹240 lakh during the year. The outstanding amount of debtors at the beginning and at the end of the year respectively was ₹27.5 lakh and ₹32.5 lakh. Determine the debtors turnover ratio.

Solution

$$\text{Debtors turnover ratio} = \frac{₹240 \text{ lakh}}{(₹27.5 \text{ lakh} + ₹32.5 \text{ lakh}) \div 2} = 8 \text{ (times per year)}$$

$$\text{Debtors collection period} = \frac{12 \text{ months}}{\text{Debtors turnover ratio (8)}} = 1.5 \text{ month}$$

Creditors Turnover Ratio It is a ratio between net credit purchases and the average amount of creditors outstanding during the year. It is calculated as follows:

$$\text{Creditors turnover ratio} = \frac{\text{Net credit purchases}}{\text{Average creditors}} \quad \textbf{(6.5)}$$

Net credit purchases = Gross credit purchases *less* returns to suppliers

Average creditors = Average of creditors (including bills payable) outstanding at the beginning and at the end of the year

A low turnover ratio reflects liberal credit terms granted by suppliers, while a high ratio shows that accounts are to be settled rapidly. The creditors turnover ratio is an important tool of analysis as a firm can reduce its requirement of current assets by relying on supplier's credit. The extent to which trade creditors are willing to wait for payment can be approximated by the creditors turnover ratio. Consider Example 6.3.

◆ Example 6.3

The firm of Examples 6.1 and 6.2 has made credit purchases of ₹180 lakh. The amount payable to the creditors at the beginning and at the end of the year is ₹42.5 lakh and ₹47.5 lakh respectively. Find out the creditors turnover ratio.

Solution

$$\text{Creditors turnover ratio} = \frac{(₹180 \text{ lakh})}{(₹42.5 \text{ lakh} + ₹47.5 \text{ lakh}) \div 2} = 4 \text{ (times per year)}$$

$$\text{Creditor's payment period} = \frac{12 \text{ months}}{\text{Creditors turnover ratio (4)}} = 3 \text{ months}$$

The summing up of the three turnover ratios (known as a cash cycle) has a bearing on the liquidity of a firm. The cash cycle captures the interrelationship of sales, collections from debtors and payment to credi-tors. The combined effect of the three turnover ratios is summarised below:

Inventory holding period	2 months
Add: Debtor's collection period	+ 1.5 months
Less: Creditor's payment period	– 3 months
	0.5 months

As a rule, the shorter is the cash cycle, the better are the liquidity ratios as measured above and *vice versa*.

Defensive-Interval Ratio

Defensive interval ratio is the ratio between quick assets and projected daily cash requirement.

The liquidity ratios of a firm outlined in the preceding discussions throw light on the ability of a firm to pay its current liabilities. Apart from paying current liabilities, the liquidity position of a firm should also be examined in relation to its ability to meet projected daily expenditure from operations. The **defensive-interval ratio** provides such a measure of liquidity. It is a ratio between the quick/liquid assets and the projected daily cash requirements and is calculated according to Equation 6.6.

$$\text{Defensive-interval ratio} = \frac{\text{Liquid assets}}{\text{Projected daily cash requirement}} \qquad \textbf{(6.6)}$$

where

$$\text{Projected daily cash requirement} = \frac{\text{Projected cash operating expenditure}}{\text{Number of days in a year (365)}}$$

The projected cash operating expenditure is based on past expenditures and future plans. It is equivalent to the cost of goods sold excluding depreciation, plus selling and administrative expenditure and other ordinary cash expenses. Alternatively, a very rough estimate of cash oper-ating expenses can be obtained by subtracting the non-cash expenses like depreciation and amortisation from total expenses. Liquid assets, as already stated, include current assets excluding inventory and prepaid expenses.

The defensive-interval ratio measures the timespan a firm can operate on present liquid assets (comprising cash, marketable securities and debtors) without resorting to next year's income. Consider Example 6.4.

◆ Example 6.4

The projected cash operating expenditure of a firm from the next year is ₹182.5 lakh. It has liquid current assets amounting to ₹40 lakh. Determine the defensive-interval ratio.

Solution

$$\text{Projected daily cash requirement} = \frac{₹182.5 \text{ lakh}}{365} = ₹50{,}000$$

$$\text{Defensive-interval ratio} = \frac{₹40 \text{ lakh}}{₹50{,}000} = 80 \text{ days}$$

The figure of 80 days indicates that the firm has liquid assets which can meet the operating cash requirements of business for 80 days without resorting to future revenues. A higher ratio would be favourable as it would reflect the ability of a firm to meet cash requirements for a longer period of time. It provides a safety margin to the firm in determining its ability to meet basic operational costs. A higher ratio would provide the firm with a relatively higher degree of protection and tends to offset the weakness indicated by low current and acid-test ratios.[9] Sorter and Benston[10] have also suggested a ratio of liquid assets to daily cash operating expenditure as a measure of short-term solvency.

Cash-Flow From Operations Ratio

This ratio measures liquidity of a firm by comparing actual cash flows from operations (in lieu of current and potential cash inflows from CAs such as inventory and debtors) with current liability. It is calculated as per Equation 6.7

$$\text{Cash-flow from operations ratio} = \frac{\text{Cash flow from operations}}{\text{Current liabilities}} \tag{6.7}$$

Being a cash measure, the ratio does not encounter the problems of actual convertibility of current assets (such as debtors and inventory) and the need for maintaining minimum levels of these assets. In general, the higher the ratio, the better is a firm from the point of view of liquidity.

To conclude the discussion of liquidity ratios, the short-term solvency of a firm can be judged not merely in terms of the traditional liquidity ratios such as current and acid-tests, but the analysis should also be extended towards examining the quality of turnover of the items of current assets on which such ratios are based. These qualitative considerations (turnover ratios) coupled with the defensive-interval and cash flow from operation ratios would reveal the true liquidity position of the firm.

The liquidity ratios are, no doubt, primarily relevant from the viewpoint of the creditors of the firm. In theory, therefore, the higher the liquidity ratios, the better is the firm. But high ratios have serious implications from the firm's point of view. High current and acid-test ratios would imply that funds have unnecessarily accumulated and are not being profitably utilised. Similarly, an unusually high rate of inventory turnover may indicate that a firm is losing business by failing to maintain an adequate level of inventory to serve the customer's needs. A rapid turnover of debtors may reflect strict credit policies that hold revenue below levels that could be obtained by granting more liberal credit terms.

Finally, while interpreting the short-term position of the firm by the creditors, it should be recognised that the management may be tempted to indulge in 'window-dressing' just before the financial statements are prepared so as to make the current financial position appear better than what it actually is. For instance, by postponing purchases, allowing inventories to fall below the normal levels, using all available cash to pay off current liabilities and pressing collection on debtors, the current and acid-test ratios, and debtors turnover ratios may be artificially improved. Even when no deliberate attempt has been made to present a good picture, the current financial position shown by the year-end financial statements is probably more favourable than at any other time of the year. This is particularly true when a firm adopts a natural business year that ends during an ebb in the seasonal swing of business activity. At the time of peak activity, debtors, inventories and current liabilities tend to be at higher levels. In such cases, an analysis of current financial position based solely on year-end data will tend to over-state a firm's average liquidity position.[12]

LEVERAGE/CAPITAL STRUCTURE RATIOS

LO 6.3 Explain capital structure ratios

The second category of financial ratios is leverage or capital structure ratios. The long-term lenders/creditors would judge the soundness of a firm on the basis of the long-term financial strength measured in terms of its ability to pay the interest regularly as well as repay the instalment of the principal on due dates or in one lump sum at the time of maturity. The long-term solvency of a firm can be examined by using leverage or capital structure ratios. The leverage or capital structure ratios may be defined as financial ratios which throw light on the long-term solvency of a firm as reflected in its ability to assure the long-term lenders with regard to **(i)** periodic payment of interest during the period of the loan and **(ii)** repayment of principal on maturity or in predetermined instalments at due dates.

There are, thus, two aspects of the long-term solvency of a firm: **(i)** ability to repay the principal when due, and **(ii)** regular payment of the interest. Accordingly, there are two different, but mutually dependent and interrelated, types of leverage ratios. First, ratios which are based on the relationship between borrowed funds and owner's capital. These ratios are computed from the balance sheet and have many variations such as **(a)** debt-equity ratio, **(b)** debt-assets ratio, **(c)** equity-assets ratio, and so on. The second type of capital structure ratios, popularly called coverage ratios, are calculated from the profit and loss account. Included in this category are **(a)** interest coverage ratio, **(b)** dividend coverage ratio, **(c)** total fixed charges coverage ratio, **(d)** cash flow coverage ratio, and **(e)** debt services coverage ratio.

Debt-Equity Ratios

Debt-equity ratio measures the ratio of long-term or total debt to shareholders equity.

The relationship between borrowed funds and owner's capital is a popular measure of the long-term financial solvency of a firm. This relationship is shown by the debt-equity ratios. This ratio reflects the relative claims of creditors and shareholders against the assets of the firm. Alternatively, this ratio indicates the relative proportions of debt and equity in financing the assets of a firm. The relationship between outsiders' claims and owner's capital can be shown in different ways and, accordingly, there are many variants of the debt-equity (D/E) ratio.

One approach is to express the D/E ratios in terms of the relative proportion of long-term debt and shareholders' equity. Thus,

$$\text{D/E ratio} = \frac{\text{Long-term debt}}{\text{Shareholders' equity}} \tag{6.8}$$

The debt considered here is exclusive of current liabilities. The shareholders' equity includes **(i)** equity and preference share capital, **(ii)** past accumulated profits but excludes fictitious assets like past accumulated losses, **(iii)** discount on issue of shares and so on.

Another approach to the calculation of the debt-equity ratio is to relate the total debt (not merely long-term debt) to the shareholders' equity. That is,

$$\text{D/E ratio} = \frac{\text{Total debt}}{\text{Shareholders' equity}} \tag{6.9}$$

The D/E ratio is, thus, the ratio of total outside liabilities to owners' total funds. In other words, it is the ratio of the amount invested by outsiders to the amount invested by the owners of business.

The difference between this and the first approach is essentially in respect of the treatment of current liabilities. While the former excludes them, the latter includes them in the numerator (debt). Should current liabilities be included in the amount of debt to calculate the D/E ratio? While there is no doubt that current liabilities are short-term and the ability of a firm to meet such obligations is reflected in the liquidity ratios, their amount fluctuates widely during a year and interest payments on them are not large, they should form part of the total outside liabilities to determine the ability of a firm to meet its long-term obligations for a number of reasons. For one thing, individual items of current liabilities are certainly short-term and may fluctuate widely, but, as a whole, a fixed amount of them is always in use so that they are available more or less on a long-term footing. Moreover, some current liabilities like bank credit, which are ostensibly short-term, are renewed year after year and remain by and large permanently in the business. Also, current liabilities have, like the long-term creditors, a prior right on the assets of the business and are paid along with long-term lenders at the time of liquidation of the firm. Finally, the short-term creditors exercise as much, if not more, pressure on management. The omission of current liabilities in calculating the D/E ratio would lead to misleading results.

How should preference share capital be treated? Should it be included in the debt or equity? The exact treatment will depend upon the purpose for which the D/E ratio is being computed. If the object is to examine the financial solvency of a firm in terms of its ability to avoid financial risk, preference capital should be clubbed with equity capital. If, however, the D/E ratio is calculated to show the effect of the use of fixed-interest/dividend sources of funds on the earnings available to the ordinary shareholders, preference capital should be clubbed with debt.

Interpretation The D/E ratio is an important tool of financial analysis to appraise the financial structure of a firm. It has important implications from the view-point of the creditors, owners and the firm itself. The ratio reflects the relative contribution of creditors and owners of business in its financing. A high ratio shows a large share of financing by the creditors of the firm; a low ratio implies a smaller claim of creditors. The D/E ratio indicates the margin of safety to the creditors. If, for instance, the D/E ratio is 1 : 2, it implies that for every rupee of outside liability, the firm has two rupees of owner's capital or the stake of the creditors is one-half of the owners. There is, therefore, a safety margin of 66.67 per cent available to the creditors of the firm. The firm would be able to meet the creditors claims even if the value of the assets declines by 66.67 per cent. Conversely, if the D/E ratio is 2 : 1, it implies low safety margin (one-third) for the creditors.

If the D/E ratio is high, the owners are putting up relatively less money of their own. It is danger signal for the creditors. If the project should fail financially, the creditors would lose heavily. Moreover, with a small financial stake in the firm, the owners may behave irresponsibly and indulge in speculative activity. If they are heavily involved financially, they will strain every nerve to make the enterprise a success. In brief, the greater the D/E ratio, the greater is the risk to the creditors.

A high debt-equity ratio has equally serious implications from the firm's point of view also. A high proportion of debt in the capital structure would lead to inflexibility in the operations of the firm as creditors would exercise pressure and interfere in management. Secondly, such a firm would be able to borrow only under very restrictive terms and conditions. Further, it would have to face a heavy burden of interest payments, particularly in adverse circumstances when profits decline. Finally, the firm will have to encounter serious difficulties in raising funds in future.

The shareholders of the firm would, however, stand to gain in two ways: **(i)** with a limited stake, they would be able to retain control of the firm and **(ii)** the return to them would be magnified. With a larger proportion of debt in the financial structure, the earnings available to the owners would increase more than proportionately with an increase in the operating profits of the firm. This is because the debt carries a fixed rate of return and if the firm is able to earn on the borrowed funds a rate higher than the fixed-charge on loans, the benefit will go to the shareholders. This is illustrated in Table 6.5. Technically, this is referred to as **leverage** or **trading on equity**. The expression 'trading on equity' describes the practice of using borrowed funds carrying a fixed-charge in the expectation of obtaining a higher return to the equity-holders. The leverage can, of course, work in the opposite direction also, if the return on borrowed funds is less than the fixed charge.[13]

Trading on equity (leverage) is the use of borrowed funds in expectation of higher return to equity-holders.

A low D/E ratio has just the opposite implications. To the creditors, a relatively high stake of the owners implies sufficient safety margin and substantial protection against shrinkage in assets. For the company also, the servicing of debt is less burdensome and consequently its credit standing is not adversely affected, its operational flexibility is not jeopardised and it will be able to raise additional funds. The shareholders of the firm are deprived of the benefits of trading on equity or leverage.

TABLE 6.5 Trading on Equity *(Amount in ₹ thousand)*

Particular	*A*	*B*	*C*	*D*
(a) Total assets	1,000	1,000	1,000	1,000
Financing pattern:				
Equity capital	1,000	800	600	200
15% Debt		200	400	800
(b) Operating profit (EBIT)	300	300	300	300
Less: Interest	—	30	60	120
Earnings before taxes	300	270	240	180
Less: Taxes (0.35)	105	94.5	84	63
Earnings after taxes	195	175.5	156	117
Return on equity (per cent)	19.5	21.9	26	58.5

The preceding discussion should leave no doubt that both high and low D/E ratios are not de-sirable. What is needed is a ratio which strikes a proper balance between debt and equity. What is the reasonable relationship between debt and equity? There cannot be a rigid rule. It will de-pend upon the circumstances, prevailing practices and so on. The general proposition is: *other's money should be in reasonable proportion to the owner's capital and the owners should have sufficient stake in the fortunes of the enterprise.* For instance, in a capital-rich country, the practice is to use as little debt as possible. A D/E ratio of 1 : 3 is regarded as indicative of a fairly heavy debt; a ratio of 1 : 1 would indicate an extremely heavy and unsatisfactory debt situation.[14] In underdeveloped countries such standards cannot be expected. It was not unusual to find firms having a D/E ratio of 2 : 1 or even 3 : 1 in the case of joint stock enterprises in India. One reason for such heavy dose of debt was to be found in the fact that enterprises had to depend, by and large, on public financial institutions (PFIs) which provided most of the funds in the form of loans. This had made the financial structure of companies lopsided and, on canons of sound financing practices, highly imprudent. The borrowers were finding it extremely difficult to service the debt burden and the overdues of the financial institutions rose unabated.[15] With the shift in the post-1991 period of dependence of the corporates on the capital market, their dependence on loans/debt has significantly declined.

Secondly, the D/E ratio cannot be applied mechanically without regard to the circumstances of each case, such as type and size of business, the nature of the industry and the degree of risk involved. For example, firms having a stable income such as an electricity company, can afford to have a higher D/E ratio. Similarly, capital intensive industries and firms producing a basic product, like cement, tend to use a larger proportion of debt. The tolerable D/E ratio of a new company would be much lower than for an established one.

Finally, there is an important issue whether to use book or market values to compute leverage ratio. Valuation models in finance are generally based on the market value of debt and equity. Therefore, the use of market values can make the D/E ratio a more useful analytical tool. For instance, if the market value of equity is higher than its book value, the market value based D/E ratio will be lower than the one using book value. This would imply that the firm can raise funds at attractive financial costs. The financial costs would be higher if the market value of equity is lower than its book value as equity capital can be issued at a discount to book value.

Debt to Total Capital Ratio

The relationship between creditors' funds and owner's capital can also be expressed in terms of another leverage ratio. This is the debt to total capital ratio. Here, the outside liabilities are related to the total capitalisation of the firm and not merely to the shareholder's equity. Essentially, this type of capital structure ratio is a variant of the D/E ratio described above. It can be calculated in different ways.

One approach is to relate the long-term debt to the permanent capital of the firm. Included in the permanent capital are shareholders' equity as well as long-term debt. Thus,

$$\text{Debt to total capital ratio} = \frac{\text{Long-term debt}}{\text{Permanent capital}} \qquad \textbf{(6.10)}$$

Another approach to calculating the debt to capital ratio is to relate the total debt to the total assets of the firm. The total debt of the firm comprises long-term debt plus current liabilities. The total assets consist of permanent capital plus current liabilities. Thus,

$$\text{Debt to total assets/capital ratio} = \frac{\text{Total debt}}{\text{Total assets}} \qquad \textbf{(6.11)}$$

Proprietary ratio indicates the extent to which assets are financed by owners funds.

Still another variant of the D/E ratio is to relate the owner's/proprietor's funds with total assets. This is called the **proprietary ratio**. The ratio indicates the proportion of total assets financed by owners. Symbolically, it is equal to:

$$\frac{\text{Proprietor's funds}}{\text{Total assets}} \times 100 \qquad \textbf{(6.12)}$$

Finally, it may also be of some interest to know the relationship between equity funds (also referred to as net worth) and fixed-income bearing funds (preference shares, debentures and other borrowed funds). This ratio, called the **capital gearing ratio**, is useful when the objective is to show the effect of the use of fixed-interest/dividend source of funds on the earnings available to the equity shareholders.

Interpretation

As the ratio is like the D/E ratio, it gives results similar to the D/E ratio in respect of capital structure of a firm. The first of these (Equation 6.10), indicates what proportion of the permanent capital of a firm consists of long-term debt. If the ratio for a firm is 1 : 2, it implies that one-third of the total permanent capital of the firm is in the form of long-term debts. Although no hard and fast rules exist, conventionally a ratio of 1 : 2 is considered to be satisfactory.

The second ratio (Equation 6.11) measures the share of the total assets financed by outside funds. The third variant (Equation 6.12) shows what portion of the total assets are financed by the owner's capital. A low ratio of debt to total assets is desirable from the point of the creditors/ lenders as there is sufficient margin of safety available to them. But its implications for the shareholders are that debt is not being exploited to make available to them the benefit of trading on equity. A firm with a very high ratio would expose the creditors to higher risk. The implications of the ratio of equity capital of total assets are exactly opposite to that of the debt to total assets. A firm should have neither a very high ratio nor a very low ratio.

Coverage Ratios

Coverage ratios measure the firm's ability to pay certain fixed charges.

The second category of leverage ratios are **coverage ratios**. These ratios are computed from information available in the profit and loss account. For a normal firm, in the ordinary course of business, the claims of creditors are not met out of the sale proceeds of the permanent assets of the firm. The obligations of a firm are normally met out of the earnings or operating profits. These claims consist of **(i)** interest on loans, **(ii)** preference dividend, and **(iii)** amortisation of principal or repayment of the instalment of loans or redemption of preference capital on maturity. The soundness of a firm, from the view-point of long-term creditors, lies in its ability to service their claims. This ability is indicated by the coverage ratios. The coverage ratios measure the relationship between what is normally available from operations of the firms and the claims of the outsiders. The important coverage ratios are: **(i)** interest coverage, **(ii)** dividend coverage, **(iii)** total coverage, **(iv)** total cashflow coverage, and **(v)** debt service coverage ratio.

Interest coverage (time-interest-earned) ratio measures the firm's ability to make contractual interest payments.

Interest Coverage Ratio It is also known as **'time-interest-earned ratio'**. This ratio measures the debt servicing capacity of a firm insofar as fixed interest on long-term loan is concerned. It is determined by dividing the operating profits or earnings before interest and taxes (EBIT) by the fixed interest charges on loans. Thus,

$$\text{Interest coverage} = \frac{\text{EBIT}}{\text{Interest}} \tag{6.13}$$

It should be noted that this ratio uses the concept of net profits before taxes because interest is tax-deductible so that tax is calculated after paying interest on long-term loan. This ratio, as the name suggests, indicates the extent to which a fall in EBIT is tolerable in that the ability of the firm to service its interest payments would not be adversely affected. For instance, an interest coverage of 10 times would imply that even if the firm's EBIT were to decline to one-tenth of the present level, the operating profits available for servicing the interest on loan would still be equivalent to the claims of the lenders. On the other hand, a coverage of five times would indicate that a fall in operating earnings only to upto one-fifth level can be tolerated. From the point of view of the lenders, the larger the coverage, the greater is the ability of the firm to handle fixed-charge liabilities and the more assured is the payment of interest to them. However, too high a ratio may imply unused debt capacity. In contrast, a low ratio is a danger signal that the firm is using excessive debt and does not have the ability to offer assured payment of interest to the lenders.

Dividend Coverage Ratio It measures the ability of a firm to pay dividend on preference shares which carry a stated rate of return. This ratio is the ratio (expressed as x number of times) of net earnings after taxes (EAT) and the amount of preference dividend. Thus,

$$\text{Dividend coverage} = \frac{\text{EAT}}{\text{Preference dividend}} \tag{6.14}$$

It can be seen that although preference dividend is a fixed obligation, the earnings taken into account are after taxes. This is because, unlike debt on which interest is a charge on the profits of the firm, the preference dividend is treated as an appropriation of profit. The ratio, like the interest coverage ratio, reveals the safety margin available to the preference shareholders. As a rule, the higher the coverage, the better it is from their point of view.

Total fixed charge coverage ratios measure the firm's ability to meet all fixed payment obligations.

Total Fixed Charge Coverage Ratio While the interest coverage and preference dividend coverage ratios consider the fixed obligations of a firm to the respective suppliers of funds, that is, creditors and preference shareholders, the total coverage ratio has a wider scope and takes into account all the committed fixed obligations of a firm, that is, **(i)** interest on loan, **(ii)** preference dividend, **(iii)** lease payments, and **(iv)** repayment of principal. Symbolically,

$$\text{Total fixed charge coverage} = \frac{\text{EBIT + Lease payment}}{\text{Interest + Lease payments + (Preference dividend + Instalment of principal)/}(1-t)} \quad (6.15)$$

Total Cashflow Coverage Ratio However, coverage ratios mentioned above, suffer from one major limitation, that is, they relate the firm's ability to meet its various financial obligations to its earnings. In fact, these payments are met out of cash available with the firm. Accordingly, it would be more appropriate to relate cash resources of a firm to its various fixed financial obligations. The ratio, so determined, is referred to as ***total cash flow coverage ratio***. Symbolically,

$$\text{Total cash flow coverage} = \frac{\text{EBIT + Lease Payments + Depreciation + Non-cash expenses}}{\text{Lease payment + Interest} + \dfrac{\text{(Principal repayment)}}{(1-t)} + \dfrac{\text{(Preference dividend)}}{(1-t)}} \quad (6.16)$$

The overall ability of a firm to service outside liabilities is truly reflected in the total cash flow coverage ratio: the higher the coverage, the better is the ability.

Internally generated cash from operating activities (CFO) are required for investment as well as debt servicing. A typical firm requires funds both for growth, apart from replacement of existing fixed assets (in particular, plant and machinery) and servicing of debt. Accordingly, a firm's long-term solvency is a function of its ability **(i)** to finance the expansion and replacements needs of the business and **(ii)** to generate cash for servicing of debt.

Capital Expenditure Ratio measures the relationship between the firm's ability to generate CFO and its capital expenditure requirements. It is determined dividing CFO by capital expenditure. The higher the ratio, the better it is. The ratio greater than one indicates that the firm has cash to service debt as well as to make payment of dividends.

Debt-Service Coverage Ratio (DSCR) is considered a more comprehensive and apt measure to compute **debt service capacity** of a business firm. It provides the value in terms of the number of times the total debt service obligations consisting of interest and repayment of principal in instalments are covered by the total operating funds available after the payment of taxes: Earnings after taxes, EAT + Interest + Depreciation + Other non-cash expenditures like amortisation (OA). Symbolically,

> **Debt service capacity** is the ability of a firm to make the contractual payments required on a scheduled basis over the life of the debt.

$$\text{DSCR} = \frac{\sum_{t=1}^{n} \text{EAT}_t + \text{Interest}_t + \text{Depreciation}_t + OA_t}{\sum_{t=1}^{n} \text{Instalment}_t} \quad (6.17)$$

The higher the ratio, the better it is. A ratio of less than one may be taken as a sign of long-term solvency problem as it indicates that the firm does not generate enough cash internally to service debt. In general, lending financial institutions consider 2:1 as satisfactory ratio. Consider Example 6.5.

Example 6.5

Agro Industries Ltd has submitted the following projections. You are required to work out yearly debt service coverage ratio (DSCR) and the average DSCR: (Figures in ₹lakh)

Year	Net profit for the year	Interest on term loan during the year	Repayment of term loan in the year
1	21.67	19.14	10.70
2	34.77	17.64	18.00
3	36.01	15.12	18.00
4	19.20	12.60	18.00
5	18.61	10.08	18.00
6	18.40	7.56	18.00
7	18.33	5.04	18.00
8	16.41	Nil	18.00

The net profit has been arrived after charging depreciation of ₹17.68 lakh every year.

Solution

TABLE 6.6 Determination of Debt Service Coverage Ratio *(Amount in lakh of rupees)*

Year	*Net profit*	*Depre- ciation*	*Interest*	*Cash available (col. 2+3+4)*	*Principal instalment*	*Debt obligation (col.4+col.6)*	*DSCR [col. 5 ÷ col. 7 (No. of times)]*
1	*2*	*3*	*4*	*5*	*6*	*7*	*8*
1	21.67	17.68	19.14	58.49	10.70	29.84	1.96
2	34.77	17.68	17.64	70.09	18.00	35.64	1.97
3	36.01	17.68	15.12	68.81	18.00	33.12	2.08
4	19.20	17.68	12.60	49.48	18.00	30.60	1.62
5	18.61	17.68	10.08	46.37	18.00	28.08	1.65
6	18.40	17.68	7.56	43.64	18.00	25.56	1.71
7	18.33	17.68	5.04	41.05	18.00	23.04	1.78
8	16.41	17.68	Nil	34.09	18.00	18.00	1.89
Average DSCR (DSCR ÷ 8)							1.83

PROFITABILITY RATIOS

LO 6.4 Describe profitability ratios

Apart from the creditors, both short-term and long-term, also interested in the financial soundness of a firm are the owners and management or the company itself. The management of the firm is naturally eager to measure its operating efficiency. Similarly, the owners invest their funds in the expectation of reasonable returns. The operating efficiency of a firm and its ability to ensure adequate returns to its shareholders/owners depends ultimately on the profits earned by it. The profitability of a firm can be measured by its profitability ratios. In other words, the profitability ratios are designed to provide answers to questions such as **(i)** is the profit earned by the firm adequate? **(ii)** what rate of return does it represent? **(iii)** what is the rate of profit for various divisions and segments of the firm? **(iv)** what are the earnings per share? **(v)** what was the amount paid in dividends? **(vi)** what is the rate of return to equity-holders? and so on.

Profitability ratios can be determined on the basis of either sales or investments. The profitability ratios in relation to sales are **(a)** profit margin (gross and net) and **(b)** expenses ratio. Profitability in relation to investments is measured by **(a)** return on assets, **(b)** return on capital employed, and **(c)** return on shareholders' equity.

Profitability Ratios Related to Sales

These ratios are based on the premise that a firm should earn sufficient profit on each rupee of sales. If adequate profits are not earned on sales, there will be difficulty in meeting the operating expenses and no returns will be available to the owners. These ratios consist of **(i)** profit margin, and **(ii)** expenses ratios.

Profit Margin The profit margin measures the relationship between profit and sales. As the profits may be gross or net, there are two types of profit margins: Gross profit margin and Net profit margin.

Gross Profit Margin is also known as gross margin. It is calculated by dividing gross profit by sales. Thus,

Gross profit margin measures the percentage of each sales rupee remaining after the firm has paid for its goods.

$$\text{Gross profit margin} = \frac{\text{Gross profit}}{\text{Sales}} \times 100 \qquad \textbf{(6.18)}$$

If the sales of a firm amount to ₹40,00,000 and its gross profit is ₹10,00,000, the gross margin would be 25 per cent (₹10,00,000 ÷ ₹40,00,000). If the gross margin (25 per cent) is deducted from 100, the result (75 per cent) is the ratio of cost of goods sold to sales. The former measures profits in relation to sales, while the latter reveals the relationship between cost of production and sale price.

Gross profit is the result of the relationship between prices, sales volume and costs. A change in the gross margin can be brought about by changes in any of these factors. The gross margin represents the limit beyond which fall in sales prices are outside the tolerance limit. Further, the gross profit ratio/margin can also be used in determining the extent of loss caused by theft, spoilage, damage, and so on in the case of those firms which follow the policy of fixed gross profit margin in pricing their products.

A high ratio of gross profit to sales is a sign of good management as it implies that the cost of production of the firm is relatively low. It may also be indicative of a higher sales price without a corresponding increase in the cost of goods sold. It is also likely that cost of sales might have declined without a corresponding decline in sales price. Nevertheless, a very high and rising gross margin may also be the result of unsatisfactory basis of valuation of stock, that is, overvaluation of closing stock and/or undervaluation of opening stock.

A relatively low gross margin is definitely a danger signal, warranting a careful and detailed analysis of the factors responsible for it. The important contributory factors may be **(i)** a high cost of production reflecting acquisition of raw materials and other inputs on unfavourable terms, inefficient utilisation of current as well as fixed assets, and so on; and **(ii)** a low selling price resulting from severe competition, inferior quality of the product, lack of demand, and so on. A thorough investigation of the factors having a bearing on the low gross margin is called for.

A firm should have a reasonable gross margin to ensure adequate coverage for operating expenses of the firm and sufficient return to the owners of the business, which is reflected in the net profit margin.

Net Profit Margin is also known as net margin. This measures the relationship between net profits and sales of a firm. Depending on the concept of net profit employed, this ratio can be computed in three ways:

Net profit margin measures the percentage of each sales rupee remaining after all costs and expenses including interest and taxes have been deducted.

1. $$\text{Operating profit ratio} = \frac{\text{Earnings before interest and taxes (EBIT)}}{\text{Net sales}} \qquad \textbf{(6.19)}$$

2. $$\text{Pre-tax profit ratio} = \frac{\text{Earnings before taxes (EBT)}}{\text{Net sales}} \qquad \textbf{(6.20)}$$

3. Net profit ratio = $\dfrac{\text{Earnings after interest and taxes (EAT)}}{\text{Net sales}}$ **(6.21)**

The net profit margin is indicative of *management's ability to operate the business with sufficient success not only to recover from revenues of the period, the cost of merchandise or services, the expenses of operating the business (including depreciation) and the cost of the borrowed funds, but also to leave a margin of reasonable compensation to the owners for providing their capital at risk. The ratio of net profit (after interest and taxes) to sales essentially expresses the cost price effectiveness of the operation.*[16]

A high net profit margin would ensure adequate return to the owners as well as enable a firm to withstand adverse economic conditions when selling price is declining, cost of production is rising and demand for the product is falling.

A low net profit margin has the opposite implications. However, a firm with a low profit margin, can earn a high rate of return on investments if it has a higher inventory turnover. This aspect is covered in detail in the subsequent discussion. The profit margin should, therefore, be evaluated in relation to the turnover ratio. In other words, the overall rate of return is the product of the net profit margin and the investment turnover ratio. Similarly, the gross profit margin and the net profit margin should be jointly evaluated. The need for joint analysis arises because the two ratios may show different trends. For example, the gross margin may show a substantial increase over a period of time but the net profit margin may **(i)** have remained constant, or **(ii)** may not have increased as fast as the gross margin, or **(iii)** may actually have declined. It may be due to the fact that the increase in the operating expenses individually may behave abnormally. On the other hand, if either as a whole or individual items of operating expenses decline substantially, a decrease in gross margin may be associated with an improvement in the net profit margin.

Expenses Ratio Another profitability ratio related to sales is the **expenses ratio**. It is computed by dividing expenses by sales. The term 'expenses' includes **(i)** cost of goods sold, **(ii)** administrative expenses, **(iii)** selling and distribution expenses, **(iv)** financial expenses but excludes taxes, dividends and extraordinary losses due to theft of goods, good destroyed by fire and so on.

There are different variants of expenses ratios. That is,

1. Cost of goods sold ratio = $\dfrac{\text{Cost of goods sold}}{\text{Net sales}} \times 100$ **(6.22)**

2. Operating expenses ratio = $\dfrac{\text{Adminsitrative expenses + Selling expenses}}{\text{Net sales}} \times 100$ **(6.23)**

3. Administrative expenses ratio = $\dfrac{\text{Adminsitrative expenses}}{\text{Net sales}} \times 100$ **(6.24)**

4. Selling expenses ratio = $\dfrac{\text{Selling expenses}}{\text{Net sales}} \times 100$ **(6.25)**

5. Operating ratio = $\dfrac{\text{Cost of goods sold + Operating expenses}}{\text{Net sales}} \times 100$ **(6.26)**

6. Financial expenses ratio = $\dfrac{\text{Financial expenses}}{\text{Net sales}} \times 100$ **(6.27)**

Interpretation

The expenses ratio is closely related to the profit margin, gross as well as net. For instance, if the operating profit margin is deducted from 100 per cent, the resultant is the operating ratio. Alternatively, when the operating ratio is subtracted from 100 per cent, we get the operating profit margin. If the sales and total non-financial expenses of a firm are ₹40,00,000 and ₹32,00,000 respectively, the *operating ratio* would be 80 per cent. It implies that total operating expenses including cost of goods sold consume 80 per cent of the sales revenues of the firm and 20 per cent is left for meeting interest, tax and dividends obligations as also retaining profits for future expansion. *The cost of goods sold ratio* shows what percentage share of sales is consumed by cost of goods sold and, conversely, what proportion is available for meeting expenses such as selling and general distribution expenses as well as financial expenses consisting of taxes, interest and dividends, and so on.

The expenses ratio is, therefore, very important for analysing the profitability of a firm. It should be compared over a period of time with the industry average as well as firms of similar type. As a working proposition, a low ratio is favourable, while a high one is unfavourable. The implication of a high expenses ratio is that only a relatively small percentage share of sales is available for meeting financial liabilities like interest, tax and dividends, and so on. An analysis of the factors responsible for a low ratio may reveal changes in the selling price or the operating expenses. It is likely that individual items may behave differently. While some operating expenses may show a rising trend, others may record a fall. The specific expenses ratio for each of the items of operating cost may be calculated. These ratios would identify the specific cause. To illustrate, an increase in selling expenses, may be due to a number of reasons: **(i)** general rise in selling expenses, **(ii)** inefficiency of the marketing department leading to uncontrolled promotional and other expenses, **(iii)** growing competition, **(iv)** ineffective advertising, **(v)** inefficient utilisation of resources, and the like.

A low operating ratio is by and large a test of operational efficiency. In case of firms whose major source of income and expenses are non-operating, the operating ratio, however, cannot be used as a yardstick of profitability.

To conclude, the profitability ratios based on sales are an important indicator of the operational efficiency of a manufacturing enterprise. However, they suffer from a serious limitation in that they are not useful from the viewpoint of the owners of the firm. Consider Example 6.6.

◆ Example 6.6

From the following information of a firm, determine **(i)** gross profit margin and **(ii)** net profit margin.

1. Sales ₹200 lakh
2. Cost of goods sold 100 lakh
3. Other operating expenses 50 lakh

Solution

(i) Gross profit margin $= \dfrac{(₹200 \text{ lakh} - ₹100 \text{ lakh} = ₹100 \text{ lakh})}{₹200 \text{ lakh}} = 50$ per cent

(ii) Net profit margin (before taxes) $= \dfrac{(₹100 \text{ lakh} - ₹50 \text{ lakh} = ₹50 \text{ lakh})}{₹200 \text{ lakh}} = 25$ per cent

The operating efficiency of the firm is fairly good. Assume, however, that the investments are ₹1,000 lakh. The return on investments works out to be 5 per cent only. From the owner's point of view, rate of return on investments is a better measure of testing the profitability of a firm.

Profitability Ratios Related to Investments

Return on investments (ROI) measures the overall effectiveness of management in generating profits with its available assets.

As already observed, the profitability ratios can also be computed by relating the profits of a firm to its investments. Such ratios are popularly termed as return on investments (ROI). There are three different concepts of investments in vogue in financial literature: assets, capital employed and shareholders' equity. Based on each of them, there are three broad categories of ROIs. They are **(i)** return on assets, **(ii)** return on capital employed and **(iii)** return on shareholders' equity.

Return on Assets (ROA) Here, the profitability ratio is measured in terms of the relationship between net profits and assets. The ROA may also be called profit-to-asset ratio. There are various possible approaches to define net profits and assets, according to the purpose and intent of the calculation of the ratio. Depending upon how these two terms are defined, many variations of ROA are possible.

The concept of net profit may be **(i)** net profits after taxes, **(ii)** net profits after taxes plus interest, and **(iii)** net profits after taxes plus interest minus tax savings.[17] Assets may be defined as **(i)** total assets, **(ii)** fixed assets, and **(iii)** tangible assets. Accordingly, the different variants of the RAO are:

1. Return on assets (ROA) $= \dfrac{\text{Net profit after taxes}}{\text{Average total assets}} \times 100$ **(6.28)**

The ROA based on this ratio would be an underestimate as the interest paid to the lenders is excluded from the net profits. In point of fact, the real return on the total assets is the net earnings available to owners (EAT) and interest to lenders as assets are financed by owners as well as creditors. A more reliable indicator of the true return on assets, therefore, is the net profits inclusive of interest. It reports the total return accruing to all providers of capital (debt and equity).

2. ROA $= \dfrac{\text{Net profit after taxes + Interest}}{\text{Average total assets}} \times 100$ **(6.29)**

3. ROA $= \dfrac{\text{Net profit after taxes + Interest}}{\text{Average tangible assets}} \times 100$ **(6.30)**

4. ROA $= \dfrac{\text{Net profit after taxes + Interest}}{\text{Average fixed assets}} \times 100$ **(6.31)**

These measures, however, may not provide correct results for inter-firm comparisons particularly when these firms have markedly varying *capital structures* as interest payment on debt qualifies for tax deduction in determining net taxable income. Therefore the effective cash outflows is less than the actual payment of interest by the amount of tax shield on interest payment. As a measure of *operating performance*, therefore, Equations 6.29 to 6.31 should be substituted by the following.

$$\text{ROA} = \frac{\text{EAT + (Interest − Tax advantage on interest) or After tax interest cost}}{\text{Average total assets/Tangible assets/Fixed assets}} \quad \textbf{(6.32)}$$

This equation correctly reports the operating efficiency of firms as if they are all equity-financed.

The ROA measures the profitability of the total funds/ investments of a firm. It, however, throws no light on the profitability of the different sources of funds which finance the total assets. These aspects are covered by other ROIs.

Return on Capital Employed (ROCE) The ROCE is the second type of ROI. It is similar to the ROA except in one respect. Here the profits are related to the total capital employed. The term capital employed refers to long-term funds supplied by the lenders and owners of the firm. It can be computed in two ways. First, it is equal to non-current liabilities (long-term liabilities) plus owners' equity. Alternatively, it is equivalent to net working capital plus long-term assets. Second, it is equal to long-term funds minus investments made outside the firm. Thus, the capital employed basis provides a test of profitability related to the sources of long-term funds. A comparison of this ratio with similar firms, with the industry average and over time would provide sufficient insight into how efficiently the long-term funds of owners and lenders are being used. The higher the ratio, the more efficient is the use of capital employed.

The ROCE can be computed in different ways, using different concepts of profits and capital employed. Thus,

1. $$\text{ROCE} = \frac{\text{EBIT}}{\text{Average total capital employed}} \times 100 \qquad \textbf{(6.33)}$$

2. $$\text{ROCE} = \frac{\text{Net profit after taxes + Interest − Tax advantage on interest}}{\text{Average total capital employed}} \times 100 \qquad \textbf{(6.34)}$$

3. $$\text{ROCE} = \frac{\text{Net profit after taxes + Interest − Tax advantage on interest − (Interest and/or Dividends received − Taxes paid)}}{\text{Average total capital employed − Investments (long-term) made}} \times 100 \qquad \textbf{(6.35)}$$

Return on Shareholders' Equity This profitability ratio carries the relationship of return to the sources of funds yet another step further. While the ROCE expresses the profitability of a firm in relation to the funds supplied by the lenders and owners taken together, the return on shareholders' equity measures exclusively the return on the owners' funds.

> **Return on shareholders equity** measures the return on the owners (both preference and equity shareholders) investment in the firm.

The shareholders of a firm fall into two broad groups: preference shareholders and equity shareholders. The holders of preference shares enjoy a preference over equity shareholders in respect of receiving dividends. In other words, from the net profits available to the shareholders, the preference dividend is paid first and whatever remains belongs to the ordinary shareholders. The profitability ratios based on shareholders' equity are termed as *return on shareholders' equity*. There are several measures to calculate the return on shareholders equity: **(i)** Rate of return on **(a)** total shareholders' equity and **(b)** equity of ordinary shareholders; **(ii)** earnings per share; **(iii)** dividends per share; **(iv)** dividend–pay-out ratio; **(v)** dividend and earnings yield; and **(vi)** price-earnings ratio.

Return on Total Shareholders' Equity According to this ratio, profitability is measured by dividing the net profits after taxes (but before preference dividend) by the average total shareholders' equity. The term shareholders' equity includes **(i)** preference share capital; **(ii)** ordinary shareholders' equity consisting of **(a)** equity share capital, **(b)** share premium, and **(c)** reserves and surplus less accumulated losses. The ordinary shareholders' equity is also referred to as net worth. Thus,

$$\text{Return on total shareholders' equity} = \frac{\text{Net profit after taxes}}{\text{Average total shareholders' equity}} \times 100 \qquad \textbf{(6.36)}$$

The ratio reveals how profitably the owners' funds have been utilised by the firm. A comparison of this ratio with that of similar firms as also with the industry average will throw light on the relative performance and strength of the firm.

Return on Ordinary Shareholders' Equity (Net Worth) While there is no doubt that the preference shareholders are also owners of a firm, the real owners are the ordinary shareholders who bear all the risk, participate in management and are entitled to all the profits remaining after all outside claims including preference dividends are met in full. The profitability of a firm from the owners' point of view should, therefore, in the fitness of things be assessed in terms of the return to the ordinary shareholders. The ratio under reference serves this purpose.

Return on ordinary shareholders' equity measures the return on the total equity funds of ordinary shareholders.

It is calculated by dividing the profits after taxes and preference dividend by the average equity of the ordinary shareholders.

Thus,

$$\text{Return on equity funds} = \frac{\text{Net profit after taxes} - \text{Preference dividend}}{\text{Average ordinary shareholders' equity or net worth}} \times 100 \quad \textbf{(6.37)}$$

This is probably the single most important ratio to judge whether the firm has earned a satisfactory return for its equity-holders or not. Its adequacy can be judged by **(i)** comparing it with the past record of the same firm, **(ii)** inter-firm comparison, and **(iii)** comparisons with the overall industry average. The rate of return on ordinary shareholders' equity is of crucial significance in ratio analysis vis-a-vis from the point of the owners of the firm.

Earnings Per Share (EPS) measures the profit available to the equity shareholders on a per share basis, that is, the amount that they can get on every share held. It is calculated by dividing the profits available to the equity shareholders by the number of the outstanding shares. The profits available to the ordinary shareholders are represented by net profits after taxes and preference dividend. Thus,

$$\text{EPS} = \frac{\text{Net profit available to equity-holders}}{\text{Number of ordinary shares outstanding}} \quad \textbf{(6.38)}$$

Earnings Per Share (EPS) is a widely used ratio. Yet, EPS as a measure of profitability of a firm from the owner's point of view, should be used cautiously as it does not recognise the effect of increase in equity capital as a result of retention of earnings. In other words, if EPS has increased over the years, it does not necessarily follow that the firm's profitability has improved because the increased profits to the owners may be the effect of an enlarged equity capital as a result of profit retentions, though the number of ordinary shares outstanding still remains constant. Another limitation of EPS is that it does not reveal how much is paid to the owners as dividend, nor how much of the earnings are retained in the business. It only shows how much earnings *theoretically* belong to the ordinary shareholders (per share basis).

As a profitability ratio, the EPS can be used to draw inferences on the basis of **(i)** its trends over a period of time, **(ii)** comparison with the EPS of other firms, and **(iii)** comparison with the industry average.

Cash Earnings Per Share is computed using cash flows from business operations as the numerator. This value is determined by adding non-cash expenses, such as depreciation and amortisation to net profits available to equity owners. Thus,

$$\text{Cash EPS} = \frac{\text{Net profit available to equity–owners + Depreciation + Amortisation + Non-cash expenses}}{\text{Number of equity shares outstanding}} \quad \textbf{(6.39)}$$

The ratio indicates the cash generating ability (per equity share) of the firm. Like EPS, cash EPS should be used with caution. It is beset with all the limitations associated with EPS measure.

Book Value Per Share represents the equity/claim of the equity shareholder on a per share basis. It is computed dividing net worth (equity share capital + reserves and surplus – accumulated losses) by the number of equity shares outstanding (at balance sheet date), as shown in Equation 6.40)

$$\text{Book value per share} = \frac{\text{Net worth}}{\text{Number of equity shares outstanding}} \quad (6.40)$$

This ratio is sometimes used as a benchmark for comparisons with the market price per share. However, the book value per share has a serious limitation as a valuation tool as it is based on the historical costs of the assets of a firm. There may be a significant difference between the market value of assets from the book value of assets (as per balance sheet). Besides, there may be hidden assets or other intangible assets of uncertain value.

Price-to-Book Value Ratio Also known as price to book (P/B) ratio, measures the relationship between the market price of an equity share (MPS) with book value per share (BPS). Thus,

$$\text{P/B ratio} = \frac{\text{MPS}}{\text{BPS}} \quad (6.41)$$

The P/B ratio is significant in predicting future stock returns. For instance, Fama and French observed that the P/B ratio (along with size) was the best predictor of future stock returns[18]. Firms with low P/B ratios had consistently higher returns compared to the firms with high P/B ratios.

Dividend Per Share (DPS) is the dividends paid to the equity shareholders on a per share basis. In other words, DPS is the net distributed profit belonging to the ordinary shareholders divided by the number of ordinary shares outstanding. That is,

$$\text{DPS} = \frac{\text{Dividend paid to ordinary shareholders}}{\text{Number of ordinary shares outstanding}} \quad (6.42)$$

The DPS would be a better indicator than EPS as the former shows what exactly is received by the owners. Like the EPS, the DPS also should not be taken at its face value as the increased DPS may not be a reliable measure of profitability as the equity base may have increased due to increased retention without any change in the number of outstanding shares.

Dividend payout (D/P) ratio measures the proportion of dividends paid to earning available to shareholders.

Dividend Pay-out (D/P) Ratio is also known as pay-out ratio. It measures the relationship between the earnings belonging to the ordinary shareholders and the dividend paid to them. In other words, the D/P ratio shows what percentage share of the net profits after taxes and preference dividend is paid out as dividend to the equity-holders. It can be calculated by dividing the total dividend paid to the owners by the total profits/earnings available to them. Alternatively, it can be found out by dividing the DPS by the EPS. Thus,

1. $$\text{D/P ratio} = \frac{\text{Total dividend (cash dividend) to equityholders}}{\text{Total net profit belonging to equityholders}} \times 100 \quad (6.43)$$

2. $$\text{D/P} = \frac{\text{Dividend per ordinary share (DPS)}}{\text{Earnings per share (EPS)}} \times 100 \quad (6.44)$$

If the D/P ratio is subtracted from 100, retention ratio is obtained. The ratio indicates what percentage share of the net profits are retained in the business. To illustrate, if the net earnings after taxes and preference dividends are ₹50 lakh and the dividend paid to the ordinary shareholders amount to ₹30 lakh, the D/P = 60 per cent. This implies that 40 per cent of the profits of the firm are retained (retention ratio) and 60 per cent distributed as dividends. Similarly, if the DPS is ₹2 and EPS ₹5, the D/P is 60 per cent. While 60 per cent profits are used to pay dividends, 40 per cent are ploughed back.

The D/P ratio is an important and widely-used ratio. The pay-out ratio can be compared with the trend over the years or an inter-firm and intra-industry comparison would throw light on its adequacy.

Earnings and Dividend Yield is closely related to the EPS and DPS. While the EPS and DPS are based on the book value per share, the yield is expressed in terms of the market value per share. The earnings yield may be defined as the ratio of earnings per share to the market value per ordinary share. Similarly, the dividend yield is computed by dividing the cash dividends per share by the market value per share. That is,

1. Earnings yield $= \dfrac{\text{EPS}}{\text{Market value per share}} \times 100$ **(6.45)**

2. Dividend yield $= \dfrac{\text{DPS}}{\text{Market value per share}} \times 100$ **(6.46)**

The earnings yield is also called the earning-price ratio.

Price/Earnings (P/E) ratio measures the amount investors are willing to pay for each rupee of earnings; the higher the ratio, the larger the investors confidence in the firm's future.

Price Earnings (P/E) Ratio is closely related to the earnings yield/earnings price ratio. It is actually the reciprocal of the latter. This ratio is computed dividing the market price of the shares by the EPS. Thus,

$$P/E \text{ ratio} = \frac{\text{Market price of share}}{\text{EPS}} \quad \textbf{(6.47)}$$

The *P/E* ratio reflects the price currently being paid by the market for each rupee of currently reported EPS. In other words, the P/E ratio measures investors' expectations and the market appraisal of the performance of a firm. In estimating the earnings, therefore, only normally sustainable earnings associated with the assets are taken into account. That is, the earnings are adjusted for income from, say, discontinued operations and extraordinary items as well as many other items not expected to occur. This ratio is popularly used by security analysts to assess a firm's performance as expected by the investors.

ACTIVITY RATIOS

LO 6.5 Interpret activity/efficiency ratios

Activity ratios are concerned with measuring the efficiency in asset management. These ratios are also called **efficiency ratios** or **assets utilisation ratios.** The efficiency with which the assets are used would be reflected in the speed and rapidity with which assets are converted into sales. The greater is the rate of turnover or conversion, the more efficient is the utilisation of assets, other things being equal. For this reason, such ratios are also designated as turnover ratios. Turnover is the primary mode for measuring the extent of efficient employment of assets by relating the assets to sales. An activity ratio may, therefore, be defined as a test of the relationship between sales (more appropriately with cost of sales) and the various assets of a firm. Depending upon the various types of assets, there are various types of activity ratios.

Activity ratios measure the speed with which various accounts/assets are converted into sales or cash.

Inventory (or Stock) Turnover Ratio

Inventory (stock) turnover measures the activity/liquidity of inventory of a firm; the speed with which inventory is sold.

This ratio indicates the number of times inventory is replaced during the year. It measures the relationship between the cost of goods sold and the inventory level. The ratio can be computed in two ways.

First, it is calculated dividing the cost of goods sold by the average inventory. Symbolically,

$$\text{Inventory turnover} = \frac{\text{Cost of goods sold}}{\text{Average inventory}} \tag{6.48}$$

The average inventory figure may be of two types. In the first place, it may be the monthly inventory (stock) average. The monthly average can be found by adding the opening inventory of each month from, in case of the accounting year being a calendar year, January through January and dividing the total by thirteen. If the firm's accounting year is other than a calendar year, say a financial year, (April to March), the average level of inventory can be computed by adding the opening inventory of each month from April through April and dividing the total by thirteen.[19] This approach has the advantage of being free from bias as it smoothens out the fluctuations in inventory level at different periods. This is particularly true of firms in seasonal industries. However, a serious limitation of this approach is that detailed month-wise information may present practical problems of collection for the analyst. Therefore, average inventory may be obtained by using another basis, namely, the average of the opening inventory and the closing inventory.

Not only are there difficulties in getting detailed information regarding inventory level, but data may also not be readily available to an analyst in respect of the cost of goods sold. To solve the problem arising out of non-availability of the required data, the second approach to the computation of inventory turnover ratio is based on the relationship between sales and closing inventory. Thus, alternatively,

$$\text{Inventory turnover} = \frac{\text{Sales}}{\text{Closing inventory}} \tag{6.49}$$

In theory, this approach is not a satisfactory basis as it is not logical. For one thing, the numerator (sales) and the denominator (inventory) are not strictly comparable as the former is expressed in terms of market price, the latter is based on cost. Secondly, the closing inventory figures are likely to be underestimates as firms traditionally have lower inventory at the end of the year. The net effect will be that the ratio given by this approach will be higher than the one given by the first approach. Thus the ratio has built-in bias to show better utilisation of inventory.

In brief, of the two approaches to calculating the inventory turnover ratio, the first which relates the cost of goods sold to the average inventory is theoretically superior as it is logically consistent. The merit of the second approach is that it is free from practical problems of computation.

Interpretation The inventory/stock turnover ratio measures how quickly inventory is sold. It is a test of efficient inventory management. To judge whether the ratio of a firm is satisfactory or not, it should be compared over a period of time on the basis of trend analysis. It can also be compared with the level of other firms in that line of business as well as with industry average.

In general, a high inventory turnover ratio is better than a low ratio. A high ratio implies good inventory management. Yet,a very high ratio calls for a careful analysis. It may be indicative of underinvestment in, or very low level of, inventory. A very low level of inventory has serious implications. It will adversely affect the ability to meet customer demand as it may not cope with its requirements. That is, there is a danger of the firm being out of stock and incurring high 'stock out cost'. It is also likely that the firm may be following a policy of replenishing its stock in too many small sizes. Apart from being costly, this policy may retard the production process as sufficient stock of materials may not be available.

Similarly, a very low inventory turnover ratio is dangerous. It signifies excessive inventory or overinvestment in inventory. Carrying excessive inventory involves cost in terms of interest on funds locked up, rental of space, possible deterioration and so on. A low ratio may be the result of inferior quality goods, overvaluation of closing inventory, stock of unsaleable/obsolete goods and deliberate excessive purchases in anticipation of future increase in their prices and so on.

Thus, a firm should have neither too high nor too low inventory turnover. To avoid both 'stock out costs' associated with a high ratio and the costs of carrying excessive inventory with a low ratio, what is suggested is a reasonable level of this ratio. The firm would be well advised to maintain a close watch on the trend of the ratio and significant deviations on either side should be thoroughly investigated to locate the factors responsible for it. The computation of the turnover for the individual components of the inventory may be useful in this context. Such ratios can be computed in respect of raw materials and work-in-progress. Thus,

$$\text{Raw materials turnover} = \frac{\text{Cost of raw materials used}}{\text{Average raw material inventory}} \quad \textbf{(6.50)}$$

$$\text{Work-in-progress turnover} = \frac{\text{Cost of goods manufactured}}{\text{Average work-in-progress inventory}} \quad \textbf{(6.51)}$$

Receivables (Debtors) Turnover Ratio and Average Collection Period

Average collection period is the average amount of time needed to collect accounts receivable.

The second major activity ratio is the **receivables or debtors turnover ratio**. Allied and closely related to this is the average collection period. It shows how quickly receivables or debtors are converted into cash. In other words, the debtors turnover ratio is a test of the liquidity of the debtors of a firm.

The liquidity of a firm's receivables can be examined in two ways: **(i)** debtors/receivables turnover; **(ii)** average collection period.

The debtors turnover shows the relationship between credit sales and debtors of a firm. It can be calculated in two ways:

1. $$\text{Debtor turnover} = \frac{\text{Credit sales}}{\text{Average debtors} + \text{Average bills receivable (B/R)}} \quad \textbf{(6.52)}$$

This approach requires two types of data. First, credit sales, which may not be readily available to the analyst. Similarly, the computation of the figure of average debtors and bills receivable involves practical difficulties. In theory, these figures should be measured, as in the case of average inventory, on the basis of the monthly average. Since this type of information is not likely to be available to the analyst, the alternative is to use the average of the opening and closing balances of debtors and bills receivable.

To avoid the difficulty arising out of the non-availability of information in respect of credit sales and average debtors and bills receivable, the alternative method is to calculate the debtors turnover in terms of the relationship between total sales and closing balance of debtors. Thus,

2. $$\text{Debtors turnover}^{20} = \frac{\text{Total sales}}{\text{Debtors} + \text{Bills receivable}} \quad \textbf{(6.53)}$$

The first approach to the computation of the debtors turnover is superior in that the question of the speed of conversion of sales into cash arises only in the case of credit sales. The effect of adopting the second approach would be to inflate the receivables turnover ratio and deflate the collection period.

The second type of ratio for measuring the liquidity of a firm's debtors is the average collection period. This is, in fact, interrelated with, and dependent upon, the receivables turnover ratio. It is calculated dividing the days in a year by the debtors turnover. Thus,

$$\text{Average collection period} = \frac{\text{Months (days) in a year}}{\text{Debtors turnover}} \tag{6.54}$$

$$\text{Alternatively} = \frac{\text{Months (days) in a year } (\times) \text{ (Average Debtors + Average B/R)}}{\text{Total credit sales}} \tag{6.55}$$

◆ Example 6.7

The credit sales of a firm in a year amount to ₹120 lakh. The outstanding amount of debtors at the beginning and end of the year were ₹14 lakh and ₹16 lakh respectively. Determine the debtor turnover ratio and the average collection period.

Solution

1. Debtor turnover ratio $= \dfrac{₹120 \text{ lakh}}{(₹14 \text{ lakh} + ₹16 \text{ lakh})/2} = 8$ (times per year)

2. (i) Average debt collection period $= \dfrac{12 \text{ months}}{8} = 1.5$ months

(ii) (12 months × ₹15 lakh)/₹120 lakh = 1.5 months.

We can get the debtor turnover dividing the months (days) in the year by the average collection period (i.e. 12 ÷ 1.5 = 8). Likewise, if we divide the months (days) in the year by the debtor turnover ratio, we get the average collection period (12 ÷ 8 = 1.5).

Interpretation This ratio indicates the speed with which debtors/accounts receivable are being collected. A turnover ratio of 8 signifies that debtors get converted into cash 8 times in a year. The collection period of 1.5 months or 45 days implies that debtors on an average are collected in 45 days. Thus, it is indicative of the efficiency of trade credit management. The higher the turnover ratio and the shorter the average collection period, the better is the trade credit management and the better is the liquidity of debtors, as short collection period and high turnover ratio imply prompt payment on the part of debtors. On the other hand, low turnover ratio and long collection period reflect delayed payments by debtors. In general, therefore, short collection period (high turnover ratio) is preferable.

It is not, however, very prudent for a firm to have either a very short collection period or a very long one. A very long collection period would imply either poor credit selection or an inadequate collection effort. The delay in the collection of receivables would mean that, apart from the interest cost involved in maintaining a higher level of debtors, the liquidity position of the firm would be adversely affected. Moreover, there is the likelihood of a large number of accounts receivable becoming bad debts. Similarly, too short a period of average collection or too high a turnover ratio is not necessarily good. While it is true that it avoids the risk of receivables being bad debt as well as the burden of high interest on outstanding debtors, it may have an adverse effect on the volume of sales of the firm. Sales may be confined to only such customers as make prompt payments. The credit and collection policy of the firm may be very restrictive. Without reasonable credit, sales will be severely curtailed. Thus, a firm should have neither a very low nor a very high receivables turnover ratio; it should maintain it at a reasonable level. The reasonableness of the collection period can be judged in either of the following two ways.

First, the collection period of a firm can be compared with the industry practices of trade credit. Any notable deviation may result from **(i)** a more or less liberal policy of extending trade credit, or **(ii)** better/poor quality of receivables. A liberal trade credit policy may be aimed at augmenting sales.

Second, it may be more appropriately examined in relation to the credit terms and policy of the firm itself. In our example, the average collection period is 45 days or 1.5 months. This should be compared with the credit terms/period normally allowed by the firm. If the normal credit period, let us assume, as extended by the firm is 40-45 days, it means the firm is able to collect its receivables well within the due dates. If, however, the credit period normally allowed is 1 month or 30 days, it means that the debtors are outstanding for a period longer than warranted by the firm's credit policy. This may be a reflection on the efficiency of the credit collection department: it has made either poor credit selection or inadequate collection effort. The management should investigate the reasons for the difficulties in the collection of receivables.

Ageing schedule enables analysts to identify slow paying debtors.

A related aspect of the average collection period is the **ageing schedule.** While the former is concerned with the liquidity of debtors/receivables as a whole, the latter analyses them in a disaggregative manner by dividing the outstanding debtors on the basis of the duration during which they have been outstanding. The usefulness of the ageing schedule lies in the fact that it enables the analyst to identify the slow paying debtors in respect of whom the firm may have to encounter a serious collection problem. A hypothetical ageing schedule for the firm of our example, with an average collection period of 1.5 months is given in Table 6.7.

TABLE 6.7 Ageing Schedule

Outstanding period of debtors (1)	*Amount outstanding* (2)	*Percentage of total* (3)
Up to 30 days (1 month)	₹2,00,000	12.5
31-45 days (1.5 months)	4,00,000	25.0
46-60 days (2 months)	8,00,000	50.0
Above 60 days (more than two months)	2,00,000	12.5
	16,00,000	100

It can be seen from Table 6.7 that more than 60 per cent of the receivables are overdue as they remain outstanding beyond the average collection period of 45 days. Moreover, more than one-tenth of the outstanding debtors remain uncollected for more than 60 days. The ageing schedule, thus, supplements the collection period by showing how long the debtors are outstanding.

Assets turnover indicates the efficiency with which firm uses all its assets to generate sales.

Assets Turnover Ratio

This ratio is also known as the investment turnover ratio. It is based on the relationship between the cost of goods sold[21] and assets/investments of a firm. A reference to this was made while working out the overall profitability of a firm as reflected in its earning power. Depending upon the different concepts of assets employed, there are many variants of this ratio.

Thus,

1. Total assets turnover $= \dfrac{\text{Cost of goods sold}}{\text{Average total assets}}$ **(6.56)**

2. Fixed assets turnover $= \dfrac{\text{Cost of goods sold}}{\text{Average fixed assets}}$ **(6.57)**

3. Capital turnover $= \dfrac{\text{Cost of goods sold}}{\text{Average capital employed}}$ (6.58)

4. Current assets turnover $= \dfrac{\text{Cost of goods sold}}{\text{Average current assets}}$ (6.59)

5. Working capital turnover ratio $= \dfrac{\text{Cost of goods sold}}{\text{Net working capital}}$ (6.60)

Here, the total assets and fixed assets are net of depreciation and the assets are exclusive of fictitious assets like debit balance of profit and loss account and deferred expenditures and so on.

The assets turnover ratio, howsoever defined, measures the efficiency of a firm in managing and utilising its assets. The higher the turnover ratio, the more efficient is the management and utilisation of the assets while low turnover ratios are indicative of underutilisation of available resources and presence of idle capacity. In operational terms, it implies that the firm can expand its activity level (in terms of production and sales) without requiring additional capital investments. In the case of high ratios, the firm would normally be required, other things being equal, to make additional capital investments to operate at higher level of activity. To determine the efficiency of the ratio, it should be compared across time as well as with the industry average. In using the assets turnover ratios one point must be carefully kept in mind. The concept of assets/fixed assets is net of depreciation. As a result, the ratio is likely to be higher in the case of an old and established company as compared to a new one, other things being equal. The turnover ratio is in such cases likely to give a misleading impression regarding the relative efficiency with which assets are being used. It should, therefore, be cautiously used.

INTEGRATED ANALYSIS OF RATIOS

LO 6.6 Discuss integrated analysis of ratios/Du Pont Chart

The ratios discussed so far measure a firm's liquidity, solvency, efficiency of operations and profitability independent of one another. However, there exists interrelationship among these ratios. This aspect is brought out by integrated analysis of ratios. The disaggregation of ratios can reveal certain major economic and financial aspects, which otherwise would have been ignored. For instance, significant changes in profitability measured in terms of return on assets (ROA) and return on equity (ROE) are understood better through an analysis of its components.

The various profitability ratios discussed earlier throw light on the profitability of a firm from the viewpoint of **(i)** the owners of the firm, and **(ii)** the operating efficiency of the firm. The ratios covered under the rate of return to the equity-holders fall under the first category. The operating efficiency of a firm in terms of the efficient utilisation of the resources is reflected in net profit margin. It has been observed that although a high profit margin is a test of better performance, a low margin does not necessarily imply a lower rate of return on investments if a firm has higher investments/assets turnover. Therefore, the overall operating efficiency of a firm can be assessed on the basis of a combination of the two. The combined profitability is referred to as earning power/return on assets (ROA) ratio. The **earning power** of a firm may be defined as the overall profitability of an enterprise. This ratio has two elements: **(i)** profitability on sales as reflected in the net profit margin, and **(ii)** profitability of assets which is revealed by the assets/investment turnover. The earning power (ROA ratio) of a firm can be computed by multiplying the net profit margin and the assets turnover. Thus,

Earning power is the overall profitability of a firm; is computed by multiplying net profit margin and assets turnover.

$$\text{Earning power} = \text{Net profit margin} \times \text{Assets turnover} \tag{6.61}$$

where, Net profit margin = Earning after taxes/Sales

Asset turnover = Sales/Total assets

$$\text{Earning power} = \frac{\text{Earnings after taxes}}{\text{Sales}} \times \frac{\text{Sales}}{\text{Total assets}} = \frac{\text{EAT}}{\text{Total assets}} \tag{6.62}$$

The basic elements of the earning power of a firm are portrayed in Figure 6.1. This chart is known as the Du Pont Chart.

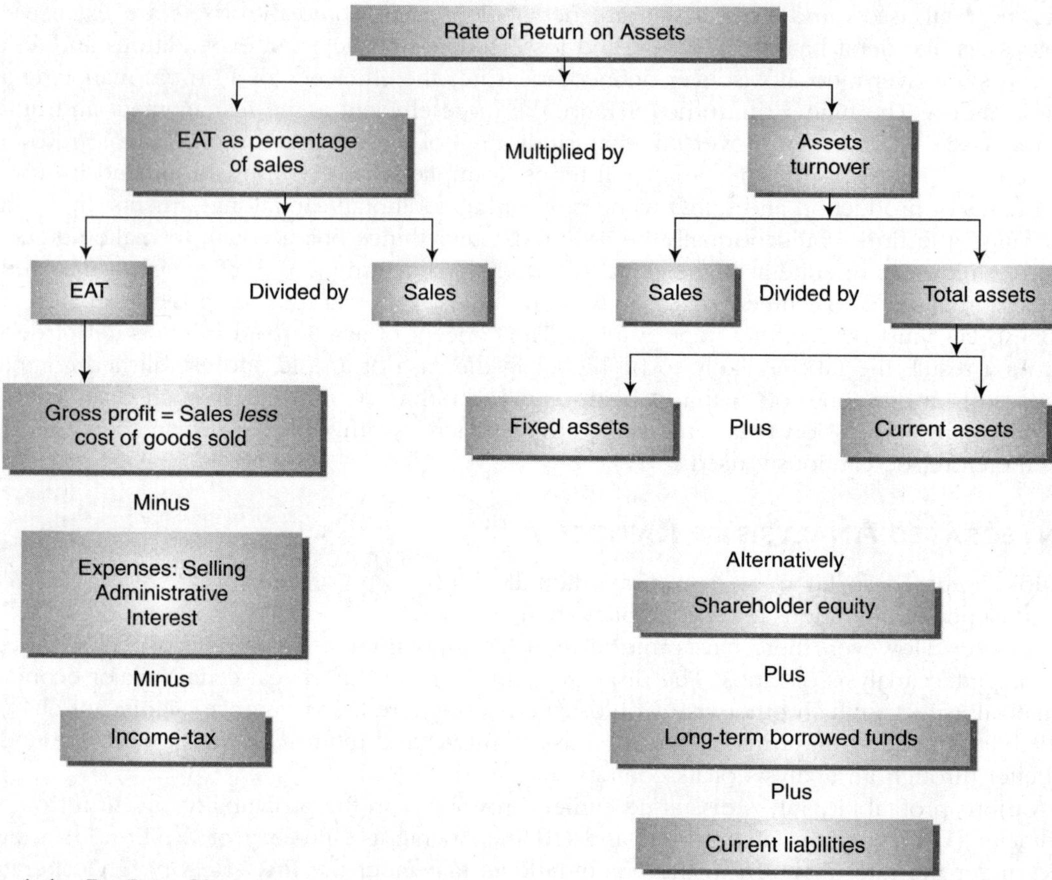

Fig. 6.1 *Du Pont Chart*

The ROA ratio is a central measure of the overall profitability and operational efficiency of a firm. It shows the interaction of profitability and activity ratios. It implies that the performance of a firm can be improved either by generating more sales volume per rupee of investment or by increasing the profit margin per rupee of sales. Consider Example 6.8.

Example 6.8

Assume that there are two firms, A and B, each having total assets amounting to ₹4,00,000, and average net profits after taxes of 10 per cent, that is, ₹40,000, each. Firm A has sales of ₹4,00,000, whereas the sales of firm B aggregate ₹40,00,000. Determine the ROA of firms A and B.

Table 6.8 shows the ROA based on two components.

Solution

TABLE 6.8 Return on Assets (ROA) of Firms A and B

Particulars	*Firm A*	*Firm B*
1. Net sales	₹4,00,000	₹40,00,000
2. Net profit	40,000	40,000
3. Total assets	4,00,000	4,00,000
4. Profit margin (2 ÷ 1) (per cent)	10	1
5. Assets turnover (1 ÷ 3) (times)	1	10
6. ROA ratio (4 × 5) (per cent)	10	10

Thus, the ROA of firms A and B is identical. While firm A has higher profit margin, B firm has higher assets turnover. Thus, the earning power is affected by two variables, namely, profit margin and assets turnover. Assets turnover ratio can further be segregated into inventory turnover, debtors turnover and fixed assets turnover ratios. Likewise, profit margin can be decomposed into gross profit, operating profit, profit before taxes and so on.

The usefulness of the integrated analysis lies in the fact that it presents the overall picture of the performance of a firm as also enables the management to identify the factors which have a bearing on profitability. In Example 6.8, if firm B could improve its profit margin even marginally, say, from 1 per cent to 2 per cent, its earning power (ROA) will be doubled, assuming sales are not affected. Similarly, firm A can double its earning power simply by a marginal increase in its investment turnover, as it indicates that the assets are used more efficiently, that is, more sales per rupee of investments. The two components of this ratio, namely, the profit margin and the investment turnover ratio, individually do not give an overall view as the former ignores the profitability of investments, while the latter fails to consider the profitability on sales.

The profitability analysis based on ROA can be extended further for a detailed examination of the return on equity (ROE). It is the most important measure of financial performance from the point of view of equityholders. The ROE can be decomposed into three following principal components:

$$\frac{\text{Earnings after taxes, EAT}}{\text{Sales}} \times \frac{\text{Sales}}{\text{Assets}} \times \frac{\text{Assets}}{\text{Equity}} \quad \textbf{(6.63)}$$

The three components in the ROE are indicative of net profit margin (profitability), assets turnover (efficiency in operations) and financial leverage (indicating the extent to which assets are financed by owners funds). Thus, the ROE is the product of the following three ratios:

Net profit ratio (×) Assets turnover (×) Financial leverage/Equity multiplier **(6.64)**

The equation indicates that the management of the firm has three levers through which it can control ROE: **(i)** the net profit margin per rupee of sales, **(ii)** the sales generated per rupee of assets employed and **(iii)** the amount of equity used to finance the assets. While profit margin summarises profit performance as reflected in the income statement of a firm, assets turnover and financial leverage measure its performance with respect to assets and liabilities side of its balance sheet respectively. Thus, these three levers capture the major elements of financial performance of a firm.[22]

Suppose in Example 6.7, Firm A uses equity capital of ₹2 lakh and B of ₹2.5 lakh in fin-ancing total assets of ₹4 lakh. The financial leverage of A is 2 (₹4 lakh assets/₹2 lakh equity) and of B is 1.6 (₹4 lakh/₹2.5 lakh). The ROE for A and B can be computed using Equation 6.65.

Net profit ratio × Assets turnover × Financial leverage **(6.65)**

$$10\% \times 1 \times 2 = 20\% \text{ (A)}$$

$$1\% \times 10 \times 1.6 = 16\% \text{ (B)}$$

Though the ROA for both firms is the same (10%), A has higher ROE (20%) than B (16%). The higher ROE of A primarily can be attributed to its higher financial leverage. The management of B can explore the possibility of increasing its financial leverage and thereby enhance the ROE of its equity owners. It will be profitable for B to employ more debt if the ROA is higher than the cost of debt. The relationship between ROA and ROE may be expressed as per Equation 6.66.

$$\text{ROE} = (\text{ROA} - \text{Interest cost} \div \text{Assets}) \times \text{Assets} \div \text{equity} \quad \textbf{(6.66)}$$

The three-component model of ROE (Equation 6.65) can be broadened further to consider the effect of interest and tax payments. The net profit ratio is to be disaggregated in the following three elements (the assets turnover and financial leverage ratios remaining unchanged).

$$\frac{\text{EAT}}{\text{Earnings before taxes (EBT)}} \times \frac{\text{EBT}}{\text{EBIT}} \times \frac{\text{EBIT}}{\text{Sales}} = \frac{\text{Net profit}}{\text{Sales}} \quad \textbf{(6.67)}$$

As a result of three sub-parts of net profit ratio, the ROE is composed of the following 5 components.

$$\frac{\text{EAT}}{\text{EBT}} \times \frac{\text{EBT}}{\text{EBIT}} \times \frac{\text{EBIT}}{\text{Sales}} \times \frac{\text{Sales}}{\text{Assets}} \times \frac{\text{Assets}}{\text{Equity}} \quad \textbf{(6.68)}$$

A 5-way break-up of ROE enables the management of a firm to analyse the effect of interest payments and tax payments separately from operating profitability.[23] To illustrate further assume 8 per cent interest rate, 35 per cent tax rate and other operating expense of ₹3,22,462 (Firm A) and ₹39,26,462 (Firm B) for the facts contained in Example 6.8. Table 6.9 shows the ROE (based on the 5 components) of Firms A and B.

Table 6.9 ROE (Five-way Basis) of Firms A and B

Particulars	*Firm A*	*Firm B*
Net sales	₹4,00,000	₹40,00,000
Less: Operating expenses	3,22,462	39,26,462
Earnings before interest and taxes (EBIT)	77,538	73,538
Less: Interest (8%)	16,000	12,000
Earnings before taxes (EBT)	61,538	61,538
Less: Taxes (35%)	21,538	21,538
Earnings after taxes (EAT)	40,000	40,000
Total assets	4,00,000	4,00,000
Debt	2,00,000	2,50,000
Equity	2,00,000	1,50,000
EAT/EBT (times)	0.65	0.65
EBT/EBIT (times)	0.79	0.84
EBIT/Sales (per cent)	19.4	1.84
Sales/Assets (times)	1	10
Assets/Equity (times)	2	1.6
ROE (per cent)	20	16

Table 6.9 shows that there is little impact of taxes and interest payment on the difference in the ROE of the two firms (as reflected in the EAT/EBT as well as EBT/EBIT ratios). The financial leverage ratio, as pointed out earlier, is a major explanatory factor for higher ROE of Firm A *vis-à-vis* Firm B.

ANNEXURE 6.I

Checklist of Financial Ratios of Reliance Industries Limited (For the Year 2012) (Amount is in ₹ Crore)

The ratios have been computed from the data in Annexure 4.II of Chapter 4:

1. Liquidity Ratios

$$\text{Current Ratio} = \frac{\text{Current assets}}{\text{Current liabilities}} = \frac{₹1,28,175}{₹68,888} = 1.86:1$$

Total current assets = Cash and bank + Inventories + Trade receivables + Other current assets + Loans and advances (Note 16) + Current investments
= ₹39,598 + ₹35,955 + ₹18,424 + ₹249 + (11,089 – 4,169@)
₹6920 + ₹27,029
= ₹1,28,175

@ Not usually available to pay current liabilities.

Total current liabilities = Short-term borrowings + Trade payables + Short-term provisions + Other current liabilities
= ₹10,593 + ₹40,324 + ₹13,713 + ₹4,258 = ₹68,888

2. $$\text{Acid-test ratio} = \frac{\text{Liquid assets}}{\text{Current liabilities}} = \frac{₹85,300}{₹68,888} = 1.24:1$$

Liquid assets = Total current assets – Inventories –Advances
= ₹1,28,175 – ₹35,955 – ₹6,920 = ₹85,300

3. (a) $$\text{Inventory turnover ratio (Finished goods)} = \frac{\text{Cost of goods sold}}{\text{Average finished goods inventory}} = \frac{₹2,97,023}{₹7,660} = 38.78 \text{ times}$$

Average finished goods inventory = (₹7,944 + ₹7,376)/2 = ₹7,660

(b) Inventory holding period = 365 Days/38.78 = 9.41 days

Cost of goods sold* = Opening stock of finished goods + Production cost – Closing stock of finished goods
= ₹7,376 + ₹2,97,591 – ₹7,944 = ₹2,97,023

Production cost = Opening stock in process + Raw materials consumed + Cash manufacturing expenses + Depreciation and amortisation (on net basis) + Other purchases (as per P/L Account) – Closing stock-in-process
= ₹4,909 + ₹2,74,814 + ₹10,307 + ₹11,394 + ₹1,441 – ₹5,274
= ₹2,97,591

*Source: Notes 13 and 25.

4. (a) Debtors turnover ratio (assuming all sales on credit basis)

$$= \frac{\text{Net credit sales}}{\text{Average debtors}} = \frac{₹3,39,792}{₹17,933} = 18.95 \text{ times}$$

(b) Debtors collection period = 365 Days/18.95 = 19.26 Days

Average debtors = (₹17,442 + ₹18,424)/2 = ₹17,933

(Ratio is based on gross turnover as the amount of taxes is also to be received)

5. (a) Creditors turnover ratio (assuming all purchases on credit basis)

$$= \frac{\text{Total credit purchases}^{@}}{\text{Average creditors}} = \frac{₹2,81,029}{₹37,584} = 7.47 \text{ times}$$

(b) Creditors payment period = 365 Days/7.47 = 48.86 Days

*Total credit purchases = Purchase of raw materials + Other purchases
= ₹2,79,588 + ₹1,441 = 2,81,029

Purchases of raw materials = Raw materials consumed + Closing stock of raw materials – Opening stock of raw materials
= ₹2,74,814 + ₹19,350 – ₹14,576 = ₹2,79,588

Average creditors = (₹34,844 + ₹40,324)/2 = 37,584

6. Cash flow from operations ratio* = $\frac{\text{Cash flow from operations}}{\text{Current liabilities}} = \frac{₹26,974}{₹68,888} = 0.39 : 1$

*(Source: Cash flow statement of Reliance Industries Ltd.)

II. Solvency Ratios

7. (a) Long-term debt to equity ratio = $\frac{\text{Long-term debt}}{\text{Shareholders' equity}} = \frac{₹60,156}{₹1,66,096} = 0.36 : 1$

Long-term debt = Long-term borrowings + Deferred tax liability (net)
= ₹48,034 + ₹12,122 = 60,156

(b) Total external obligations to equity ratio = $\frac{\text{Total external obligations}}{\text{Shareholders' equity}} = \frac{₹1,29,044}{₹1,66,096} = 0.78 : 1$

Total external obligations= Long-term borrowings + Short-term borrowings + Trade payables + Other current liabilities + Short-term provisions + Deferred tax liability (net)
= ₹48,034 + ₹10,593 + ₹40,324 + ₹13,713 + ₹4,258 + ₹12,122 = ₹1,29,044

(c) Total debt to equity Ratio = $\frac{\text{Total debt}}{\text{Shareholders' equity}} = \frac{₹70,749}{₹1,66,096} = 0.43 : 1$

(Gross D/E ratio)

Total debt= Long-term borrowings + Short-term borrowings + Deferred tax liability (net)
= ₹70,749

8. Total debt to assets ratio = $\frac{\text{Total debt}}{\text{Total assets}} = \frac{₹70,749}{₹2,95,140} = 0.24 : 1$

9. Long-term debt to assets ratio = $\frac{\text{Long-term debt}}{\text{Total assets}} = \frac{₹60,156}{₹2,95,140} = 0.20 : 1$

10. Total external obligations to assets ratio = $\frac{\text{Total external obligations}}{\text{Total assets}} = \frac{₹1,29.044}{₹2,95,140} = 0.44 : 1$

11. Proprietory ratio = $\frac{\text{Proprietor's funds/Shareholder's funds}}{\text{Total assets}} = \frac{₹1,66,096}{₹2,95,140} = 0.56 : 1$

12. Interest coverage ratio = $\frac{\text{EBIT}}{\text{Interest}} = \frac{₹27,716}{₹1,966} = 14.09 \text{ times}$

EBIT = EBT + Interest = ₹25,750 + ₹1,966 (see note 23) = ₹27,716

13. Total fixed charge coverage ratio = $\frac{\text{EBIT}}{\text{Finance Costs}} = \frac{₹27{,}716}{₹2{,}667} = 10.39$ times

14. Total cash flow coverage ratio = $\frac{\text{EBIT + Depreciation and amortisation}}{\text{Interest}}$

$$= \frac{₹27{,}716 + ₹11{,}394}{₹1{,}966} = 19.89 \text{ times}$$

III. Profitability Ratios

15. Gross profit margin = $\frac{\text{Gross profit} \times 100}{\text{Net sales}} = \frac{₹32{,}881}{₹3{,}29{,}904} \times 100 = 9.97\%$

Gross profit = Revenue from operations – Cost of goods sold
= ₹3,29,904 – ₹2,97,023 = ₹32,881

16. Operating profit ratio = $\frac{\text{EBIT} - \text{Other incomes}}{\text{Net sales}} \times 100 = \frac{₹27{,}716 - ₹6{,}192}{₹3{,}29{,}904} \times 100 = 6.52\%$

17. Pre-tax profit ratio = $\frac{\text{EBT}}{\text{Net sales}} \times 100 = \frac{₹25{,}750}{₹3{,}29{,}904} \times 100 = 7.8\%$

18. Net profit ratio = $\frac{\text{EAT}}{\text{Net sales}} \times 100 = \frac{₹20{,}040}{₹3{,}29{,}904} \times 100 = 6.07\%$

19. Cost of goods sold ratio = $\frac{\text{Cost of goods sold}}{\text{Net sales}} \times 100 = \frac{₹2{,}97{,}023}{₹3{,}29{,}904} \times 100 = 90.03\%$

20. Operating expenses ratio = $\frac{\text{Operating expenses}}{\text{Net sales}} \times 100 = \frac{₹10{,}595}{₹3{,}29{,}904} \times 100 = 3.21\%$

Operating expenses = Employee benefit expenses + Selling and distribution expenses + Establishment expenses
= ₹2,862 + ₹5,393 + ₹2,340 = ₹10,595

21. Administrative expenses ratio = $\frac{\text{Administrative expenses}}{\text{Net sales}} \times 100$

$$= \frac{₹5{,}202}{₹3{,}29{,}904} \times 100 = 1.58\%$$

Administrative expenses = Employees benefits expenses + Establishment expenses
= ₹2,862 + ₹2,340 = ₹5,202

22. Selling expenses ratio = $\frac{\text{Selling expenses}}{\text{Net sales}} \times 100 = \frac{₹5{,}393}{₹3{,}29{,}904} \times 100 = 1.63\%$

23. Operating ratio= $\frac{\text{Cost of goods sold + Operating expenses}}{\text{Net sales}} \times 100$

$$= \frac{₹2{,}97{,}023 + ₹10{,}595}{₹3{,}29{,}904} = 93.24\%$$

24. (a) Return on assets (ROA) = $\frac{\text{Net profit after taxes}}{\text{Average total assets}} \times 100 = \frac{₹20{,}040}{₹2{,}89{,}930} \times 100 = 6.9\%$

Average total assets = (2,95,140 + ₹2,84,719)/2 = ₹2,89,930

(b) ROA = $\dfrac{\text{Net profit after taxes + Interest}}{\text{Average total assets}} \times 100 = \dfrac{₹20{,}040 + ₹1{,}966}{₹2{,}89{,}930} \times 100 = 7.6\%$

(c) ROA = $\dfrac{\text{EAT + Interest – Tax advantage on interest}}{\text{Average total assets}} \times 100$

$= \dfrac{₹20{,}040 + ₹1{,}966 - (₹1{,}966 \times 0.339)}{₹2{,}89{,}930} \times 100$

$= \dfrac{₹21{,}353.29}{₹3{,}89{,}930} \times 100 = 7.36\%$

Corporate Tax Rate = 30% + 7.5% (Surcharge) + 3% (Education cess on taxes payable)
= 33.2%

25. (a) ROCE = $\dfrac{\text{EBIT – Other income}}{\text{Average long-term (fixed) assets used + Net working capital}}$

(Excluding capital work-in-progress as it does not contribute to operating income)

$= \dfrac{₹27{,}716 - ₹6{,}192}{₹1{,}28{,}219 + ₹59{,}287} \times 100 = 11.48\%$

Average long-term asset used = (₹1,13,723 + ₹1,42,707)/2 = ₹1,28,219
Net working capital = Current assets – Current liabilities
= ₹1,28,175 – ₹68,888 = ₹59,287

(b) ROCE = $\dfrac{\text{Net profit after tax + Interest – Tax advantage on interest – (other income attributed primarily from interest/dividends received from investments made outside-taxes paid)}}{\text{Average long-term assets used + Net working capital}} \times 100$

$= \dfrac{₹20{,}040 + ₹1{,}966 - ₹652.71 - (₹6{,}192 - ₹6{,}192 \times 0.332)}{₹1{,}87{,}506} \times 100 = 9.18\%$

26. Return on total shareholders' equity $= \dfrac{\text{Net profit after taxes}}{\text{Average shareholders' equity}} \times 100$

$= \dfrac{₹20{,}040}{₹1{,}58.818} \times 100 = 12.62\%$

Average shareholders' equity (₹1,66,096 + ₹1,51,540)/2 = ₹1,58.818

27. Return on equity funds = $\dfrac{\text{Net profit after taxes – Preference dividend*}}{\text{Average ordinary shareholders' equity}}$

*(Preference dividend is zero in this case)

$= \dfrac{₹20{,}040}{₹1{,}58{,}818} \times 100 = 12.62\%$

28. Earnings Per Share (EPS) = $\dfrac{\text{Net profit available to equity holders}}{\text{Number of ordinary shares outstanding}} = \dfrac{₹20{,}040}{327.10} = 61.27$ per share

29. Cash EPS = $\dfrac{₹20{,}040 + ₹11{,}394}{327.10} = ₹96.10$ per share

30. Book value per share = $\frac{\text{Net worth/Equity funds}}{\text{Number of equity shares outstanding}} = \frac{₹1,66,096}{327.10}$ = ₹507.78 per share

31. (a). Dividend per share = $\frac{\text{Dividend paid to ordinary shareholders*}}{\text{No. of ordinary shares outstanding}}$

$= \frac{₹2,531}{327.10}$ = ₹7.74 per share

*Excluding tax on dividend

(b) Dividend payout ratio = $\frac{\text{Total dividend paid to equity holders}}{\text{Total net profit}}$

$= \frac{₹2,941}{₹20,040} \times 100 = 14.68\%$

*Including tax on dividend

(c) Earnings yield = $\frac{\text{EPS}}{\text{Market price per share*}} \times 100 = \frac{₹61.27}{₹810.38} \times 100 = 7.56\%$

*Market price per share = ₹810.35 (as on March 31, 2012 at NSE)

(d) Dividend yield = $\frac{\text{DPS}}{\text{MPS}} = \frac{₹7.74}{₹810.35} \times 100 = 0.96\%$

(e) P/E ratio = $\frac{\text{MPS}}{\text{EPS}} = \frac{₹810.35}{₹61.27}$ = 13.22 times

IV. Efficiency Ratios

32. (a) Raw materials turnover = $\frac{\text{Cost of raw materials used}}{\text{Average raw materials inventory}} = \frac{₹2,74.814}{₹16,963}$ = 16.20 times

Average raw materials inventory = (₹14,576 + 19,350)/2 = ₹16,963

(b) Raw material holding period = 365 Days/16.20 = 22.53 Days

33. Stock-in-process turnover ratio = $\frac{\text{Cost of goods manufactured}}{\text{Average stock in process inventory}} = \frac{₹2,97,591}{₹5,089}$ = 58.48 times

Cost of goods manufactured = Cost of goods sold + Closing stock of finished goods – Opening stock of finished goods

= ₹2,97,023 + ₹7,944 – ₹7,376 = ₹2,97,591

Average stock-in-process = (₹4,904 + ₹5,274)/2 = ₹5,089

34. (a) Total assets turnover ratio = $\frac{\text{Cost of goods sold}}{\text{Average total assets}} = \frac{₹2,97,023}{₹2,89,930}$ = 1.02 times

(b) Total assets turnover ratio (Based on sales) = $\frac{\text{Net sales}}{\text{Average total assets}} = \frac{₹3,29,904}{₹2,89,930}$ = 1.14 times

35. (a) Fixed assets turnover ratio = $\frac{\text{Cost of goods sold}}{\text{Average fixed assets}} = \frac{₹2,97,023}{₹1,28,219}$ = 2.32 times

(b) Total assets turnover ratio (Based on sales) = $\frac{\text{Net sales}}{\text{Average fixed assets}} = \frac{₹3,29,904}{₹1,28,219}$ = 2.57 times

36. Capital turnover ratio = $\dfrac{\text{Cost of goods sold}}{\text{Average capital employed}} = \dfrac{₹2{,}97{,}023}{₹1{,}87{,}506} = 1.58$ times

37. Current assets turnover Ratio = $\dfrac{\text{Cost of goods sold}}{\text{Average current assets}} = \dfrac{₹2{,}97{,}023}{₹1{,}14.111} = 2.60$ times

(b) Total assets turnover ratio = $\dfrac{\text{Net sales}}{\text{Average current assets}} = \dfrac{₹3{,}29{,}904}{₹1{,}14{,}111} = 2.89$ times

Average current assets = (₹1,32,344 + ₹95,877)/2 = ₹1,14,111

38. Working capital turnover ratio = $\dfrac{\text{Net sales}}{\text{Net working capital}} = \dfrac{₹3{,}29{,}904}{₹59{,}287} = 5.56$ times

Net working capital = (₹1,28,175 – ₹68,888)

V. Integrated Ratios

39. (a) Earning power = Net profit margin × Assets turnover

Net profit margin = $\dfrac{\text{EAT}}{\text{Sales}} \times 100 = \dfrac{₹20{,}040}{₹3{,}29{,}904} \times 100 = 6.07\%$

Assets turnover = $\dfrac{\text{Sales}}{\text{Total assets}} = \dfrac{₹3{,}29{,}904}{₹2{,}95{,}140} = 1.12$ times

Earning power = 6.07% × 1.12 = 6.80%

(b) Return on Equity = $\dfrac{\text{EAT}}{\text{Sales}} \times \dfrac{\text{Sales}}{\text{Assets}} \times \dfrac{\text{Assets}}{\text{Equity}}$

$$= \frac{₹20{,}040}{₹3{,}29{,}904} \times \frac{₹3{,}29{,}904}{₹2{,}95{,}140} \times \frac{₹2{,}95{,}140}{₹1{,}66{,}096} = 11.96\%$$

or (c) ROE = $\dfrac{\text{EAT}}{\text{EBT}} \times \dfrac{\text{EBT}}{\text{EBIT}} \times \dfrac{\text{EBIT}}{\text{Sales}} \times \dfrac{\text{Sales}}{\text{Assets}} \times \dfrac{\text{Assets}}{\text{Equity}}$

$$= \left(\frac{₹20{,}040}{₹25{,}750} \times \frac{₹25{,}750}{₹27{,}716} \times \frac{₹27{,}716}{₹3{,}29{,}904} \times \frac{₹3{,}29{,}904}{₹2{,}95{,}140} \times \frac{₹2{,}95{,}140}{₹1{,}66{,}096}\right) \times 100 = 11.96\%$$

Common Size Statements

LO 6.7 Review the common size statements

Ratio analysis apart, another useful way of analysing financial statements is to convert them into common size statements by expressing absolute rupee amounts into percentages. When this method is pursued, the income statement exhibits each expense item or group of expense items as a percentage of net sales, and net sales are taken at 100 per cent. Similarly, each individual asset and liability classification is shown as a percentage of total assets and liabilities respectively. Statements prepared in this way are referred to as **common-size statements.**

Common-size comparative statements prepared for one firm over the years would highlight the relative changes in each group of expenses, assets and liabilities. These statements can be equally useful for inter-firm comparisons, given the fact that absolute figures of two firms of the same industry are not comparable. Financial statements and common-size statements of the Hypothetical Ltd are presented in Example 6.9.

Example 6.9

The accompanying balance sheet and profit and loss account relate to Hypothetical Ltd. Convert these into common-size statements.

Balance Sheet as at March 31 *(Amount in lakh of rupees)*

Particulars	*Previous Year*	*Current Year*
Liabilities		
Equity share capital (of ₹10 each)	240	240.0
General reserves	96	182.0
Long-term loans	182	169.5
Creditors	67	52.0
Outstanding expenses	6	—
Other current liabilities	9	6.5
	600	650.0
Assets		
Plant [net of accumulated depreciation]	402	390
Cash	54	78
Debtors	60	65
Inventories	84	117
	600	650

Income Statement for the Year Ended March 31 *(Amount in lakh of rupees)*

Particulars	*Previous year*	*Current year*
Gross sales	370	480
Less: Returns	20	30
Net sales	350	450
Less: Cost of goods sold	190	215
Gross profit	160	235
Less: Selling, general and administrative cost	50	72
Operating profit	110	163
Less: Interest expenses	20	17
Earning before taxes	90	146
Less: Taxes	31.5	51.5
Earning after taxes	58.5	94.9

Solution

Income Statement (Common-size) for the Years Ended March 31 *(Percentages)*

Particulars	*Previous year*	*Current year*
Net sales	100.0	100.0
Cost of goods sold	54.3	47.8
Gross profit	45.7	52.2
Selling, general and administrative expenses	14.3	16.0
Operating profit	31.4	36.2
Interest	5.7	3.8
Earnings before taxes	25.7	32.4
Taxes	9.0	11.4
Earnings after taxes (EAT)	16.7	21.0

Balance Sheets (Common-size as at March 31) *(Percentages)*

Particulars	*Previous year*	*Current year*
Owners' equity:		
Equity share capital	40.0	36.9
General reserves	16.0	28.0
	56.0	64.9
Long-term borrowings:		
Loan	30.3	26.1
Current liabilities:		
Creditors	11.2	8.0
Outstanding expenses	1.0	
Other liabilities	1.5	1.0
	13.7	9.0
Total liabilities	100.0	100.0
Fixed assets:		
Plant (net of accumulated depreciation)	67.0	60.0
Current assets:		
Cash	9.0	12.0
Debtors	10.0	10.0
Inventories	14.0	18.0
	33.0	40.0
Total assets	100.0	100.0

These percentage figures bring out clearly the relative significance of each group of items in the aggregative position of the firm. For instance, in the current year the EAT of Hypothetical Ltd has increased to 21 per cent from 16.7 per cent in the previous year. This improvement in profitability can mainly be traced to the decrease of 6.5 per cent in the cost of goods sold, reflecting im-provement in efficiency of manufacturing operations. The decrease in financial overheads (interest) by 1.9 per cent during the current year can be traced to the repayment of a part of long-term loans. Further analysis indicates that profitability would have been more but for an increase in operating expenses ratio by 1.7 per cent.

The common-size balance sheets show that current assets as a percentage of total assets have increased by 7 per cent over previous year. This increase was shared by inventories (4 per cent) and cash (3 per cent); the share of debtors remained unchanged at 10 per cent. The proportion of current liabilities (mainly due to creditors) was also lower at 9 per cent in the current year compared to 13.7 per cent in the previous year. These facts signal overall increase in the liquidity position of the firm. Further, the share of long-term debt has also declined and owners' equity has gone up from 56 per cent in the previous year to 64.9 per cent in the current year.

IMPORTANCE OF RATIO ANALYSIS

LO 6.8 Illustrate the importance of ratio analysis

As a tool of financial management, ratios are of crucial significance. The importance of ratio analysis lies in the fact that it presents facts on a comparative basis and enables the drawing of inferences regarding the performance of a firm. Ratio analysis is relevant in assessing the performance of a firm in respect of the following aspects: (i) liquidity position, (ii) long-term solvency, (iii) operating efficiency, (iv) overall profitability, (v) inter-firm comparison, and (vi) trend analysis.

Liquidity Position

With the help of ratio analysis conclusions can be drawn regarding the liquidity position of a firm. The liquidity position of a firm would be satisfactory if it is able to meet its current obligations when they become due. A firm can be said to have the ability to meet its short-term liabilities if it has sufficient liquid funds to pay the interest on its short-maturing debt usually within a year as well as to repay the principal. This ability is reflected in the liquidity ratios of a firm. The liquidity ratios are particularly useful in credit analysis by banks and other suppliers of short-term loans.

Long-term Solvency

Ratio analysis is equally useful for assessing the long-term financial viability of a firm. This aspect of the financial position of a borrower is of concern to the long-term creditors, security analysts and the present and potential owners of a business. The long-term solvency is measured by the leverage/capital structure and profitability ratios which focus on earning power and operating efficiency. Ratio analysis reveals the strengths and weaknesses of a firm in this respect. The leverage ratios, for instance, will indicate whether a firm has a reasonable proportion of various sources of finance or if it is heavily loaded with debt in which case its solvency is exposed to serious strain. Similarly, the various profitability ratios would reveal whether or not the firm is able to offer adequate return to its owners consistent with the risk involved.

Operating Efficiency

Yet another dimension of the usefulness of the ratio analysis, relevant from the viewpoint of management, is that it throws light on the degree of efficiency in the management and utilisation of its assets. The various activity ratios measure this kind of operational efficiency. In fact, the solvency of a firm is, in the ultimate analysis, dependent upon the sales revenues generated by the use of its assets–total as well as its components.

Overall Profitability

Unlike the outside parties which are interested in one aspect of the financial position of a firm, the management is constantly concerned about the overall profitability of the enterprise. That is, they are concerned about the ability of the firm to meet its short-term as well as long-term obligations to its creditors, to ensure a reasonable return to its owners and secure optimum utilisation of the assets of the firm. This is possible if an integrated view is taken and all the ratios are considered together.

Inter-firm Comparison

Ratio analysis not only throws light on the financial position of a firm but also serves as a stepping stone to remedial measures. This is made possible due to interfirm comparison and comparison with industry averages. A single figure of a particular ratio is meaningless unless it is related to some standard or norm. One of the popular techniques is to compare the ratios of a firm with the industry average. It should be reasonably expected that the performance of a firm should be in broad conformity with that of the industry to which it belongs. An interfirm comparison would demonstrate the firm's position *vis-a-vis* its competitors. If the results are at variance either with the industry average or with those of the competitors, the firm can seek to identify the probable reasons and, in that light, take remedial measures.

Trend Analysis

Finally, ratio analysis enables a firm to take the time dimension into account. In other words, whether the financial position of a firm is improving or deteriorating over the years. This is made possible by the use of trend analysis. The significance of a trend analysis of ratios lies in the fact that the analysts can know the direction of movement, that is, whether the movement is favourable or unfavourable. For example, the ratio may be low as compared to the norm but the trend may be upward. On the other hand, though the present level may be satisfactory but the trend may be a declining one.

LIMITATIONS OF RATIO ANALYSIS

LO 6.9 Outline the limitations of ratio analysis

Ratio analysis is a widely used tool of financial analysis. Yet, it suffers from various limitations. The operational implication of this is that while using ratios, the conclusions should not be taken on their face value. Some of the limitations which characterise ratio analysis are **(i)** difficulty in comparison, **(ii)** impact of inflation, and **(iii)** conceptual diversity.

Difficulty in Comparison

One serious limitation of ratio analysis arises out of the difficulty associated with their comparability. One technique that is employed is interfirm comparison. But such comparisons are vitiated by different procedures adopted by various firms. The differences may relate to:

- Differences in the basis of inventory valuation (e.g. last in first out, first in first out, average cost and cost);
- Different depreciation methods (i.e. straight line vs written down basis);
- Estimated working life of assets, particularly of plant and equipment;
- Amortisation of intangible assets like goodwill, patents and so on;
- Amortisation of deferred revenue expenditure such as preliminary expenditure and discount on issue of shares;
- Capitalisation of lease;
- Treatment of extraordinary items of income and expenditure; and so on.

Secondly, apart from different accounting procedures, companies may have different accounting periods, implying differences in the composition of the assets, particularly current assets. For these reasons, the ratios of two firms may not be strictly comparable.

Another basis of comparison is the industry average. This presupposes the availability, on a comprehensive scale, of various ratios for each industry group over a period of time. If, however, as is likely, such information is not compiled and available, the utility of ratio analysis would be limited.

Impact of Inflation

The second major limitation of the ratio analysis as a tool of financial analysis is associated with price level changes. This, in fact, is a weakness of the traditional financial statements which are based on historical costs. An implication of this feature of the financial statements as regards ratio analysis is that assets acquired at different periods are, in effect, shown at different prices in the balance sheet, as they are not adjusted for changes in the price level. As a result, ratio analysis will not yield strictly comparable and, therefore, dependable results. To illustrate, there are two firms which have identical rates of returns on investments, say 15 per cent. But one of these had acquired its fixed assets when prices were relatively low, while the other one had purchased them when prices were high. As a result, the book value of the fixed assets of the former type of firm would be lower, while that of the latter higher. From the point of view of profitability, the return on the investment of the firm with a lower book value would be overstated. Obviously, identical rates of returns on investment are not indicative of equal profitability of the two firms. This is a limitation of ratios.

Conceptual Diversity

Yet another factor which influences the usefulness of ratios is that there is difference of opinion regarding the various concepts used to compute the ratios. There is always room for diversity of opinion as to what constitutes shareholders' equity, debt, assets, profit and so on. Different firms may use these terms in different senses or the same firm may use them to mean different things at different times.

Reliance on a single ratio for a particular purpose may not be a conclusive indicator. For instance, the current ratio alone is not a adequate measure of short-term financial strength; it should be supplemented by the acid-test ratio, debtors turnover ratio and inventory turnover ratio to have a real insight into the liquidity aspect.

Finally, ratios are only a post-mortem analysis of what has happened between two balance sheet dates. For one thing, the position in the interim period is not revealed by ratio analysis. Moreover, they give no clue about the future.

In brief, ratio analysis suffers from some serious limitations. The analyst should not be carried away by its oversimplified nature, easy computation with a high degree of precision. The reliability and significance attached to ratios will largely depend upon the quality of data on which they are based. They are as good as the data itself. Nevertheless, they are an important tool of financial analysis.

SUMMARY

- Ratio analysis is a widely used tool of financial analysis. It is defined as the systematic use of ratio to interpret the financial statements so that the strengths and weaknesses of a firm, as well as its historical performance and current financial condition, can be determined.
- Ratios make the related information comparable. A single figure by itself has no meaning, but when expressed in terms of a related figure, it yields significant inferences. Thus, ratios are ***relative figures*** reflecting the relationship between related variables. Their use as tools of financial analysis involves their comparison as single ratios, like absolute figures, are not of much use. Three types of comparisons are generally involved: namely, **(i)** trend analysis, **(ii)** inter firm comparison, and **(iii)** comparison with standards or industry average.
- Trend analysis involves comparison of a firm over a period of time, that is, present ratios are compared with past ratios for the same firm. The comparison of the profitability ratios of a firm, say, year 1 to year 5, is an illustration of a trend analysis. It indicates the direction of change in the performance – improvement, deterioration or constancy – over the years.
- Interfirm comparison involves comparing the ratios of a firm with those of others in the same lines of business or for the industry as a whole. It reflects the firm's performance in relation to its competitors. Other types of comparisons may relate to the comparison of items within a single year's financial statement of firm and comparison with standards or plans.
- Ratios can broadly be classified into five groups: **(i)** liquidity, **(ii)** capital structure or leverage, **(iii)** profitability, **(iv)** activity and **(v)** integrated.

LO 6.1

- Liquidity ratios measure the ability of a firm to meet its short-term obligations and reflect its short-term financial strength or solvency. The important liquidity ratios are **(a)** current ratio, and **(b)** quick or acid test ratio.

  Current ratio is the ratio of total current assets (CAs) to total current liabilities (CLs). A satisfactory current ratio would enable a firm to meet its obligations, even if the value of its CAs decline. It is, however, a quantitative index of liquidity as it does not differentiate among the components of CAs, such as cash and inventory which are not equally liquid.

The quick or acid test ratio takes into consideration the differences in the liquidity of the components of CAs. It represents the ratio between quick CAs and the total CLs. It is a rigorous measure and superior to the current ratio. However, both these ratios should be used as complementary to each other to analyse the liquidity position of a firm.

The main liquidity ratios are computed as follows: **(i)** Current ratio = Current assets/Current liabilities. **(ii)** Acid test ratio = (Current assets – Stock – Pre-paid expenses)/Current liabilities. **(iii)** Super-quick ratio = (Cash + Marketable securities)/Current liabilities.

LO 6.2

- The capital structure or leverage ratios throw light on the long-term solvency of a firm. This is reflected in its ability to assure the long-term creditors with regard to periodic payment of interest and the repayment of loan on maturity, or in pre-determined instalments at due dates. There are two types of such ratios: **(a)** debt-equity or debt-assets, and **(b)** coverage.

The first type is computed from the balance sheet and reflects the relative contribution or stake of owners and creditors in financing the assets of the firm. In other words, such ratios reflect the safety margin to the long-term creditors.

The second category of such ratios is based on the income statement, which shows the number of times the fixed obligations are covered by earnings before interest and taxes or cash inflows. In other words, they indicate the extent to which a fall in operating profit or cash inflows is tolerable, in that the ability to repay would not be adversely affected.

The important leverage ratios are: **(i)** Debt/equity ratios = Total debt (long-term debt + current liabilities)/Shareholders' funds. **(ii)** Debt to total capital ratio = Total debt/Permanent capital (shareholder's funds + long-term debt). **(iii)** Debt to total assets ratio = Total debt/Total assets. **(iv)** Proprietary ratio = Owner's funds/Total assets. **(v)** Capital gearing ratio = (Preference share capital + Debentures + Other borrowed funds)/Equity funds (net worth). **(vi)** Interest coverage ratio (times-interest earned) = Earnings before interest and taxes (EBIT/Interest. **(vii)** Dividend coverage ratio = Earnings after taxes (EAT)/ Preference dividend (D_p).

(viii) Total coverage ratio = $$\frac{\text{EBIT + Lease payment}}{\text{Interest lease payment} + \left(\frac{D_p}{1-t}\right) + \frac{\text{Instalment of principal}}{(1-t)}}$$

(ix) Cash flow coverage ratio = $$\frac{\text{EBIT + Lease payment + Depreciation}}{\text{Interest Lease payment} + \left(\frac{D_p}{1-t}\right) + \frac{\text{Instalment of principal}}{(1-t)}}$$

(x) Debt service coverage ratio = $$\frac{\sum_{t=1}^{n} \text{EAT}_t + \text{Depreciation}_t + \text{Interest}_t + \text{Other non – cash expenses}_t}{\sum_{t=1}^{n} \text{Principal}_t + \text{Interest}_t}$$

LO 6.3

- The profitability of a firm can be measured by the profitability ratios. Such ratios can be computed either from sales or investment.

The profitability ratios based on sales are **(a)** profit margin (gross and net), and **(b)** expenses or operating ratios. They indicate the proportion of sales consumed by operating costs and the proportion available to other expenses.

The profitability ratios related to investments include **(i)** return on assets, **(ii)** return on capital employed, and **(iii)** return on shareholders' equity, including earnings per share, dividend per share, dividend-payout ratio, earning and dividend yield.

The procedure of calculating profitability ratios based on sales are: **(i)** Gross profit ratio/margin = Gross profit (sales – cost of goods sold)/Net sales. **(ii)** Operating profit ratio/margin = EBIT/Net sales. **(iii)** Net profit ratio/margin = Earnings after taxes (EAT)/Net sales. **(iv)** Cost of goods sold ratio = Cost of goods sold/Net sales. **(v)** Operating expenses ratio = (Administrative expenses + Selling expenses)/Net sales. **(vi)** Administrative expenses ratio = Administrative expenses/Net sales. **(vii)** Selling expenses ratio = Selling expenses/Net sales. **(viii)** Operating ratio = (Cost of goods sold + Operating expenses)/Net sales.

Ratios related to total investment are calculated as follows: **(i)** Return on total assets = (*EAT* + Interest – Tax advantage on interest)/Average total assets. **(ii)** Return on capital employed = (EAT + Interest – Tax advantage on interest)/Average total capital employed. **(iii)** Return on shareholders' equity = EAT/Average total shareholders' equity. **(iv)** Return on equity funds = (EAT – Preference dividend)/Average ordinary shareholders' equity (net worth). **(v)** Earnings per share (EPS) = Net profit available to equity shareholders' (EAT – D_p)/Number of equity shares outstanding (*N*) **(vi)** Dividends per share (DPS) = Dividend paid to ordinary shareholders/Number of ordinary shares outstanding (*N*). **(vii)** Earnings yield = EPS/Market price per share. **(viii)** DPS/Market price per share. **(ix)** Dividend payment/payout (D/P) ratio = DPS/EPS. **(x)** Price-earnings (P/E) ratio = Market price of a share/EPS. **(xi)** Book value per share = Ordinary shareholders' equity/Number of equity shares outstanding.

LO 6.4

- The activity ratios (also known as efficiency or turnover ratios) are concerned with measuring the efficiency in asset management. The efficiency with which assets are managed/used is reflected in the speed and rapidity with which they are converted into sales. Thus, the activity ratios are a test of relationship between sales/cost of goods sold and assets. Depending upon the type of assets, activity ratios may be **(a)** inventory/stock turnover, **(b)** receivables/debtors turnover, and **(c)** total assets turnover.

  The first of these indicates the number of times inventory is replaced during the year or how quickly the goods are sold. It is a test of efficient inventory management.

  The second category of turnover ratios indicates the efficiency of receivables management and shows how quickly trade credit is collected.

  The total assets turnover represents the ratio of total assets to sales/cost of goods sold. It reveals the efficiency in managing and utilizing the total assets.

  The computation procedure of these ratios is as follows: **(i)** Raw material turnover = Cost of raw materials used/Average raw materials inventory. **(ii)** Work-in-process turnover = Cost of goods manufactured/Average work-in-process inventory. **(iii)** Finished goods inventory turnover = Cost of goods sold/Average finished goods inventory. **(iv)** Debtors turnover ratio = Total credit sales/(Average debtors + Averages bills receivable). **(v)** Average collection period = Months (days) in year/Debtors turnover ratio. **(vi)** Total assets turnover = Cost of goods sold/Average total assets. **(vii)** Fixed assets turnover = Cost of goods sold/Average fixed assets. **(viii)** Current assets turnover = Cost of goods sold/Average current assets. **(ix)** Working capital turnover ratio = Cost of goods sold/Average net working capital. If data about cost of goods sold are not available, sales figures are used in the numerator.

LO 6.5

- Integrated ratios provide better insight about financial and economic analysis of a firm. For instance of the rate of return on assets (ROA) can be decomposed in to net profit margin (EAT/Sales) and assets turnover (Sales/Total assets). Likewise, the ROE can be decomposed in the following two ways: **(i)** (EAT/Sales) × (Sales/Assets) × (Assets/Equity) and **(ii)** (EAT/EBT) × (EBT/EBIT) × (EBIT/Sales) × (Sales/Assets) × (Assets/Equity).

LO 6.6

- Preparation of common-size financial statements is an extension of ratio analysis. These statements convert absolute sums into more easily understood percentages of some base amount. It is sales in the case of income statement and totals of assets and liabilities in the case of the balance sheet.

LO 6.7

- Ratio analysis in view of its several limitations should be considered only as a tool for analysis rather than as an end in itself. The reliability and significance attached to ratios will largely hinge upon the quality of data on which they are based. They are as good or as bad as the data itself. Nevertheless, they are an important tool of financial analysis.

LO 6.9

REFERENCES

1. Metcalf, R W and P L Titard, *Principles of Accounting*, W B Saunders, (Philadelphia) 1976, p 157.
2. Meigs, W B and others, *Intermediate Accounting*, McGraw-Hill, New York, 1978, p 1049.
3. It is, of course, useful in certain situations. In brief, NWC, as a measure of liquidity, is useful for purposes of internal control.
4. White, Gerald I, et. al. The Analysis and use of Financial Statements (John Wiley & Sons, New York), 1998, p 160.
5. Spiller, E A, *Financial Accounting*, Richard D Irwin, Homewood, Ill. 1977, p 644.
6. Bryce, M D, *Industrial Development*, McGraw-Hill, New York, 1960, p 256.
7. Metcalf, R W and P L Titard, *op. cit.*, p 170.
8. Davidson, S, and R L, Weil, *Handbook of Modern Accounting*, McGraw-Hill, (New York), 1977, pp 4-8.
9. Kieso, D E and J J Weygandt, *Intermediate Accounting*, John Wiley, (New York), 1969, pp 1023-1024.
10. Quoted in Davidson and Weil, *op. cit.*, pp 4-9.
11. White Gerald I, et. al, *op. cit.*, p 160.
12. Meig, W B and Others, *op. cit.*, p 1069.
13. This aspect has been discussed in great detail in Chapter 15.
14. Bryce, M D, *op. cit.*, p 254.
15. For a detailed account please refer to Khan, M Y, *Indian Financial System*, TMH, New Delhi, 2003.
16. Helfert, E A, *Techniques of Financial Analysis*, Richard D Irwin, Homewood Ill. 1972, p 53, Used with the permission of Richard D Irwin, USA.
17. Suggested by Spiller, E A, *op. cit.*, pp 653-54. This figure of profit represents what might have been earned if all assets had been financed by equity capital.
18. Fama, E and K R French, "The Cros-section of Expected Stock Returns, *Journal of Finance* (June, 1992), pp 427-66.
19. Metcalf and Titard, *op. cit.*, p 174.
20. Deduction should not be made in respect of provision for bad and doubtful depts.
21. If the information regarding the cost of goods sold is not available, the figure of sales can be used.
22. Higgins, R.C., *Analysis for Financial Managment,* Irwin McGraw-Hill, Boston, 2001, pp 34-5.
23. White, G. I et al, *The Analysis and Use of Financial Statments* (John Wiley & Sons, New York), 1998, p 186.
24. There are varying practices regarding its treatment. Assuming going concern concept and RIL to be profitable in future, it is treated as liability.

SOLVED PROBLEMS

P.6.1 B Raj Ltd sells goods on cash as well as credit. The following particulars are extracted from their books of accounts for the current year-end. LO 6.2 LOD: E

Particulars	*Amount (in lakh of rupees)*
Total gross sales	100
Cash sales (included in above)	20
Sales returns	7
Total debtors at the end	9
Bills receivable	2
Provision for doubtful debts at the end of the year	1
Total creditors at the end	10

Calculate the average collection period.

Solution

Total net credit sales = Gross sales – Cash sales – Sales returns = ₹100 lakh – ₹20 lakh – ₹7 lakh = ₹73 lakh

$$\text{Debtors turnover} = \frac{\text{Credit sales}}{\text{Debtors + Bills receivable}} = \frac{₹73 \text{ lakh}}{₹11 \text{ lakh}} = \frac{73}{11}$$

$$\text{Average collection period} = \frac{365 \text{ days}}{\text{Debtors turnover (73/11)}} = 55 \text{ days}$$

P.6.2 The following are the ratios relating to the activities of National Traders Ltd: LO 6.3 LOD: D

Debtors velocity (months)	3
Stock velocity (months)	8
Creditors velocity (months)	2
Gross profit ratio (%)	25

Gross profit for the current year ended December 31 amounts to ₹4,00,000. Closing stock of the year is ₹10,000 above the opening stock. Bills receivable amount to ₹25,000 and bills payable to ₹10,000. Find out: **(a)** Sales, **(b)** Sundry debtors, **(c)** Closing stock, and **(d)** Sundry creditors.

Solution

(a) Determination of sales: $\text{Sales} = \frac{₹4,00,000}{25} \times 100 = ₹16,00,000$

(b) Determination of sundry debtors: Debtors velocity is 3 months. In other words, debtors' collection period is 3 months, or debtors' turnover ratio is 4. Assuming all sales to be credit sales and debtors turnover ratio being calculated on the basis of year-end figures,

$$\text{Debtors turnover ratio} = \frac{\text{Credit sales}}{\text{Closing debtors + Bills receivable}}$$

or

$$\text{Closing debtors + Bills receivable} = \frac{\text{Credit sales}}{\text{Debtors turnover ratio}} = \frac{₹16,00,000}{4} = ₹4,00,000$$

$$\text{Closing debtors} = ₹4,00,000 - ₹25,000 = ₹3,75,000$$

(c) Determination of closing stock: Stock velocity of 8 months signifies that the inventory holding period is 8 months, stock turnover ratio is 1.5 = (12 months ÷ 8).

$$\text{Stock turnover} = \frac{\text{Cost of goods sold (Sales – Gross profit)}}{\text{Average stock}}$$

$$1.5 = \frac{₹12{,}00{,}000}{\text{Average stock}}$$

$$\text{Average stock} = \frac{₹12{,}00{,}000}{1.5} = ₹8{,}00{,}000$$

$$\text{Closing stock} - \text{Opening stock} = ₹10{,}000 \quad (1)$$

$$\frac{\text{Closing stock} + \text{Opening stock}}{2} = ₹8{,}00{,}000 \quad (2)$$

$$\text{Closing stock} + \text{Opening stock} = ₹16{,}00{,}000 \quad (3)$$

or

Subtracting (1) from (3) we have,

$$2 \text{ Opening stock} = ₹15{,}90{,}000$$

$$\text{Opening stock} = ₹7{,}95{,}000$$

Therefore, Closing stock = ₹8,05,000

(d) Determination of sundry creditors: Creditors velocity of 2 months signifies that the credit payment period is 2 months. In other words, creditors' turnover ratio is 6 (12 months ÷ 2). Assuming all purchases to be credit purchases and creditors turnover is based on year-end figures,

$$\text{Creditors turnover ratio} = \frac{\text{Credit purchases}}{\text{Creditors + Bills payable}}$$

$$6 = \frac{₹12{,}10{,}000}{\text{Creditors} + ₹10{,}000}$$

$$\text{Creditors} + ₹10{,}000 = \frac{₹12{,}10{,}000}{6} = ₹2{,}01{,}667$$

$$\text{Creditors} = ₹2{,}01{,}667 - ₹10{,}000 = ₹1{,}91{,}667$$

Credit purchases are calculated as follows:

Cost of goods sold = Opening stock + Purchases – Closing stock
₹12,00,000 = ₹7,95,000 + Purchases – ₹8,05,000
₹12,00,000 + ₹10,000 = Purchases
₹12,10,000 = Purchases (credit).

P.6.3 The Avon Ltd has a capital of ₹10,00,000; its turnover is 3 times the capital and the net profit margin on sales is 6 per cent. What is the return on investment? LO 6.4 LOD: E

Solution

Rate of return on investment = Margin of profit × Capital/Investment turnover

$$= \frac{\text{Net profit}}{\text{Sales}} \times \frac{\text{Sales}}{\text{Capital}} = 0.06 \times 3 = 18 \text{ per cent}$$

P.6.4 The capital of E. Ltd. is as follows: LO 6.4 LOD: M

9% Preference shares, ₹10 each	₹3,00,000
Equity shares of ₹10 each	8,00,000
	11,00,000

Additional information: Profit (after tax at 35 per cent), ₹2,70,000; Depreciation, ₹60,000; Equity dividend paid, 20 per cent; Market price of equity shares, ₹40.

You are required to compute the following, showing the necessary workings:

(a) Dividend yield on the equity shares.

(b) Cover for the preference and equity dividends.

(c) Earnings per shares.
(d) Price-earnings ratio.

Solution

(a) Dividend yield on the equity shares: $= \dfrac{\text{Dividend per share}}{\text{Market price per share}} \times 100$

$$= \frac{₹2\ (0.20 \times ₹10)}{₹40} \times 100 = 5 \text{ per cent}$$

(b) Dividend coverage ratio:

(i) Preference

$$= \frac{\text{Profit after taxes}}{\text{Dividend payable to preference shareholders}} = \frac{₹2,70,000}{₹27,000\ (0.09 \times ₹3,00,000)} = 10 \text{ times}$$

(ii) Equity $= \dfrac{\text{Profit after taxes} - \text{Preference share dividend}}{\text{Dividend payable to equity shareholders at current rate of ₹2 per share}}$

$$= \frac{₹2,70,000 - ₹27,000}{₹1,60,000\ (80,000 \text{ shares} \times ₹2)} = 1.52 \text{ times}$$

(c) Earnings per equity share $= \dfrac{\text{Earnings available to equity shareholders}}{\text{Number of equity shares outstanding}} = \dfrac{₹2,43,00}{80,000} = ₹3.04$ per share

(d) Price-earning (P/E) ratio $= \dfrac{\text{Market price per share}}{\text{Earnings pe share}} = \dfrac{₹40}{₹3.04} = 13.2$ time

P.6.5 Z Ltd purchased a retail store and commenced business on April 1. From the following information, you are required to prepare in as much details as possible, a trading and profit and loss account for the current year ended March 31 and a balance sheet as at the date. LO 6.1,4,5 LOD: D

Capital introduced on April 1	₹47,000
Drawings during the year	5,000
Working capital (current assets less current liabilities) at March 31	23,000
Depreciation of fixed assets during the year, based on a rate of 20 per cent per annum on cost	3,000
Ratio of annual sales to year-end values of fixed assets plus working capital	2:1
Ratio of current assets to current liabilities at the year-end	2:1
Ratio of liquid assets (cash plus debtors) to current liabilities on March 31	5:4
Debtors at the year-end as per cent of annual sales	12
General expenses (excluding depreciation) as per cent of annual sales	20

The current assets consist of stocks (which are unchanged throughout the year), debtors and cash. Stocks are turned over four times during the year. The current liabilities consist only of creditors.

Solution

Trading A/c of Z Ltd for the Current Year ended March 31

To Cost of sales	₹69,000	By Sales	₹1,00,000
To Gross profit c/f to P&L A/c	31,000		
	1,00,000		1,00,000

Profit and Loss A/c for the Current Year ended March 31

To General Expenses	₹20,000	By Gross profit b/f from trading A/c	₹31,000
To Depreciation	3,000		
To Net profit c/f to capital A/c	8,000		
	31,000		31,000

Balance Sheet as at March 31, Current Year

Liabilities		*Amount*	*Assets*		*Amount*
Capital	₹47,000		Fixed assets	₹30,000	
Add: Net profit	8,000		*Less:* Depreciation	3,000	₹27,000
	55,000				
Less: Drawings	5,000	₹50,000	Current assets		
			Cash	16,750	
Creditors		23,000	Debtors	12,000	
			Stock	17,250	46,000
		73,000			73,000

WORKING NOTES

1. Determination of current assets and current liabilities:

$$CA - CL = ₹23,000 \quad (1)$$

$$0.5\ CA - CL = 0 \quad (2)$$

Subtracting equation (2) from equation (1)

$$0.5\ CA = ₹23,000$$

$$CA = ₹46,000$$

CL = ₹23,000 = Creditors as there are no other current liabilities.

2. Determination of fixed assets: Depreciation rate, 10 per cent = ₹3,000

$$\text{Cost of fixed assets} = ₹3,000 \times \frac{100}{10} = ₹30,000$$

3. Determination of sales $= \dfrac{\text{Sales}}{\text{Fixed assets + Working capital}} = 2$

$$\frac{\text{Sales}}{₹27,000 + ₹23,000} = 2$$

$$\text{Sales} = ₹1,00,000$$

4. Determination of liquid assets: liquid ratio $= \dfrac{\text{Liquid assets}}{\text{Current liabilities}}, 1.25 = \dfrac{\text{Liquid assets}}{₹23,000}$

$$₹28,750 = \text{Liquid assets (cash + debtors)}$$

(a) Debtors are 12 per cent of annual sales = ₹12,000 (0.12 × ₹1,00,000)

(b) Cash = ₹28,750 – ₹12,000 = ₹16,750

5. Determination of stock: Current assets – Liquid assets

₹46,000 – ₹28,750 = ₹17,250

6. Determination of cost of sales: Stock turnover ratio $= \dfrac{\text{Cost of sales}}{\text{Average stock}}$

$$4 = \frac{\text{Cost of sales}}{₹17,250}$$

$$₹69,000 = \text{Cost of sales.}$$

P.6.6 Using the following information, complete the balance sheet given below: **LO 6.2,3,4,5** **LOD: D**

Total debt to net worth: 0.5 to 1.
Turnover of total assets (based on year-end sales figures): 2.
Gross profit: 30 per cent
Average collection period (based on 360-day-year): 40 days
Inventory turnover (based on cost of goods sold and year-end inventory): 3 times.
Acid test ratio: 0.75:1.

Balance sheet

Cash		Notes and accounts payable	
Accounts receivable		Common stock	₹2,00,000
Inventory		Retained earnings	3,00,000
Plant and equipment			
Total		Total	

Solution

Balance sheet

Cash	₹20,833	Notes and accounts payable	₹2,50,000
Accounts receivable	1,66,667	Common stock	2,00,000
Inventory	3,50,000	Retained earnings	3,00,000
Plant and equipment	2,12,500		
Total	7,50,000	Total	7,50,000

Working Notes

1. $$\text{Debt to net worth ratio} = \frac{\text{Total debt}}{\text{Net worth (Common stock + Retained earnings)}}$$

$$0.5 = \frac{\text{Total debt}}{₹5,00,000}$$

$$₹2,50,000 = \text{Total debt (notes and accounts payable)}$$

2. Substituting the value of 'notes and accounts payable' on the liabilities side, we have ₹7,50,000 as the total sum of liabilities and so the total assets will be ₹7,50,000.

$$\text{Total assets turnover} = \frac{\text{Sales}}{\text{Total assets}}$$

$$2 = \frac{\text{Sales}}{₹7,50,000}$$

$$\text{or} \quad ₹15,00,000 = \text{Sales}$$

3. $$\text{Gross profit ratio} = \frac{\text{Gross profit}}{\text{Sales}} \times 100$$

$$30 = \frac{\text{Gross profit}}{₹15,00,000} \times 100$$

$$₹4,50,000 = \text{Gross profit}$$

Cost of goods sold = Sales – Gross profit = ₹15,00,000 – ₹4,50,000 = ₹10,50,000

4. Assuming all sales to be credit sales, the figure of accounts receivable would be determined as follows:

$$\text{Accounts receivable turnover ratio} = \frac{\text{360 days}}{\text{Average collection period}} = \frac{\text{360 days}}{\text{40 days}} = 9$$

$$\text{Accounts receivable turnover ratio} = \frac{\text{Credit sales}}{\text{Average debtors}}$$

$$9 = \frac{₹15,00,000}{\text{Average debtors}}$$

$$\text{Average debtors} = \frac{₹15,00,000}{9} = ₹1,66,667$$

In the absence of any figure of the opening debtors and closing debtors, it is assumed that accounts receivable ratio is calculated on the basis of year-end figures. Accordingly, the amount of ₹1,66,667 represents the balance of accounts receivable at the end of the year.

5. Inventory turnover ratio $= \frac{\text{Cost of goods sold}}{\text{Closing inventory}}$

$$3 = \frac{₹10,50,000}{\text{Closing inventory}}$$

or ₹3,50,000 = Closing inventory

6. Acid test ratio $= \frac{\text{Liquid assets}}{\text{Current liabilities}}$

$$0.75 = \frac{\text{Liquid assets}}{₹2,50,000}$$

₹1,87,500 = Liquid assets

₹1,87,500 = Cash + Accounts receivable

₹1,87,500 – ₹1,66,667 = ₹20,833 = Cash

P.6.7 As the manager of a financial services company, you have received a proposal seeking a term loan of ₹300 lakh, from a firm planning an investment in fixed assets of ₹500 lakh in a new project. The loan is indicated to be repayable in three annual instalments commencing from the end of the second year. The following information concerning the project is available: (₹ in lakhs) LO 6.3 LOD: M

Particulars	*Year* 1	2	3	4
Gross profit (before depreciation)	75	100	150	150
Depreciation	50	45	40	35
Interest on term loan	25	45	30	15
Working capital borrowing (interest)	10	15	20	20
Provision for tax	—	—	10	30

Assuming other *techno-economic* criteria to be satisfactory, you are required to:

(a) compute appropriate financial ratio which, in your opinion, would guide the financing decision, and

(b) interpret briefly the ratio so computed and give your views on the proposal.

Solution

(a) Debt service coverage ratio is the most appropriate ratio for the lending company as it indicates relationship between the total cash funds available with the borrowing firm to service debt/instalment (consisting of principal repayment and interest).

Debt-Service Coverage Ratio (DSCR): (Amount in lakhs of rupees)

Particulars	Year			
	1	2	3	4
Gross profit (before depreciation)	75	100	150	150
Less interest on working capital borrowing	10	15	20	20
Less provision for tax	—	—	10	30
(i) Cash available to service term loan	65	85	120	100
Debt service obligations:				
Interest on term loan	25	45	30	15
Instalment payment	—	100	100	100
(ii) Total debt service obligations	25	145	130	115
(iii) DSCR (i ÷ ii) (Number of times)	2.6	0.59	0.92	0.87

(b) COMMENT: The DSCR is very unsatisfactory as it is less than one for all the three years in which instalmetns are to be paid. The firm will not have enough cash to service instalment and is likely to commit default. The proposal is not financially viable and term loan should not be sanctioned by the financial services company.

P.6.8 The information below is taken from the records of two companies in the same industry. The companies are X Ltd and Y Ltd; and the data is as follows: LO 6.2,3,4 LOD: M

Particulars	X Ltd	Y Ltd
Cash	₹2,10,000	₹3,20,000
Debtors (net)	3,30,000	6,30,000
Stock	12,30,000	9,50,000
Plant and equipment	16,95,000	24,00,000
Total assets	34,65,000	43,00,000
Sundry creditors	9,00,000	10,50,000
8% Debentures	5,00,000	10,00,000
Equity share capital	11,00,000	17,50,000
Retained earnings	9,65,000	5,00,000
Total liabilities	34,65,000	43,00,000
Sales	56,00,000	82,00,000
Cost of goods sold	40,00,000	64,80,000
Other operating expenses	8,00,000	8,60,000
Interest expenses	40,000	80,000
Income taxes	2,66,000	2,73,000
Dividends	1,00,000	1,80,000

Answer each of the following questions by making a comparison of one, or more, relevant ratios.

(i) Which company is using the equity shareholders' money more profitably?
(ii) Which company is better able to meet its current debts?
(iii) If you were to purchase the debentures of one company, which company's debentures would you buy?
(iv) Which company collects its receivables faster, assuming all sales to be credit sales?
(v) Which company is extended credit for a longer period by the creditors, assuming all purchases (equivalent to cost of goods sold) to be credit purchases?
(vi) How long does it take each company to convert an investment in stock to cash?
(vii) Which company retains the larger proportion of income in the business?

Solution

(i) *Rate of return (ROR) on shareholders' funds*

= (₹4,94,000*/₹20,65,000**) × 100 = 23.9 per cent (X Ltd)

= (₹5,07,000**/₹22,50,000) × 100 = 22.5 per cent (Y Ltd)

X Ltd is using the shareholders' money more profitably.

(ii) (a) *Current ratio* = ₹17,70,000/₹9,00,000 = 1.97 (X), ₹19,00,000/ ₹10,50,000 = 1.81 (Y)

(b) *Acid test ratio* = ₹5,40,000/₹9,00,000 = 0.6 (X), ₹9,50,000/ ₹10,50,000 = 0.9 (Y)

Y Ltd is better able to meet its current debts.

(iii) (a) *Debt-equity ratio* = ₹14,00,000/₹20,65,000 = 0.68 (X), ₹20,50,000/ ₹22,50,000 = 0.91 (Y)

(b) *Interest coverage ratio* = ₹8,00,000/₹40,000 = 20 times (X), ₹8,60,000/ ₹80,000 = 10.75 times (Y)

The debentures of X Ltd should be bought.

(iv) *Debtors collection period* = (360 × ₹3,30,000)/₹56,00,000 = 21 days (X Ltd), (360 × ₹6,30,000)/₹82,00,000 = 28 days (Y Ltd)

X Ltd collects its receivables faster.

(v) *Creditors payment period* = (360 × ₹9,00,000)/₹40,00,000 = 81 days (X Ltd), (360 × ₹10,50,000)/₹64,80,000 = 58 days (Y Ltd)

X Ltd is extended credit for a longer period by the creditors.

(vi) *Stock turnover ratio* = ₹40,00,000/₹12,30,000 = 3.25 times (X), ₹64,80,000/₹9,50,000 = 6.82 times (Y)

= 360 days/3.25 = 111 days (X), 360 days/6.82 = 53 days (Y)

Length of time required for conversion of investment in stock to cash:

111 days + 21 days = 132 days (X)

53 days + 28 days = 81 days (Y)

(vii) *Dividend payout ratio* = ₹1,00,000/₹4,94,000 = 20.2 per cent (X), ₹1,80,000/₹5,07,000 = 35.5 per cent (Y)

Retention ratio = 100 – 20.2 = 79.8 per cent (X), 100 – 35.5 = 64.5 per cent (Y)

X Ltd retains the larger proportion of its income in the business

* ₹56,00,000 – ₹51,06,000

** ₹82,00,000 – ₹76,93,000

P.6.9 The following information was taken from the financial statements of XYZ Ltd *(amount in thousand of rupees)* **LO 6.5** **LOD: M**

Particulars	Year 1	Year 2	Year 3
Total assets	750	850	860
Credit sales	420	520	550
Cost of goods sold	450	595	645
Cash	50	60	55
Debtors	150	165	180
Inventory	130	160	170
Net fixed assets	120	260	250
Creditors	75	85	100
Short-term debt	125	175	170
Long-term debt	125	185	175
Equity	125	200	210

Calculate those ratios which indicate the efficient use of assets and discuss potential sources of trouble.

Solution

The efficient use of assets is indicated by the following key ratios: **(a)** Current assets turnover, **(b)** Debtors' turnover, **(c)** Inventory turnover, **(d)** Fixed assets turnover, and **(e)** Total assets turnover.

Computation or ratios

Particulars	Year 1	Year 2	Year 3
(a) Current assets turnover ratio (cost of goods sold ÷ total current assets)	1.36	1.55	1.59
(b) Debtors' turnover (credit sales ÷ average debtors)	2.8*	3.30	3.19
(c) Inventory turnover (cost of goods sold ÷ average inventory)	3.46*	4.10	3.91
(d) Fixed assets turnover (cost of goods sold ÷ fixed assets)	3.75	2.29	2.58
(e) Total assets turnover (cost of goods sold ÷ total assets)	1.00	0.92	0.98

*Based on debtors and inventory at the end, as their opening balances are not available.

COMMENTS: The first three ratios indicate the efficiency of current assets usage, and the latter two, namely, fixed assets turnover and total assets turnover ratio, show the efficacy of utilisation of these. Current assets utilisation appears to be very satisfactory as reflected in the first three types of ratios. No major change is noticeable in their values over a period of time, which is presumably indicative of consistency in debtors collection period and inventory turnover. There does not seem to be any significant problem regarding utilisation of current assets.

However, it appears that fixed assets are not being fully utilised. Investments in fixed assets have more than doubled during years 2 and 3. The fixed assets turnover ratio has sharply fallen to 2.58 in year 3 from 3.75 in year 1. Thus, investments in fixed assets are either excessive, or the capacity of the additional plant is under-utilised. This is corroborated by the fact that sales in the latter 2 years have increased by around 15 per cent. Therefore, the remedy lies in utilising the plant capacity by increasing production and sales.

P.6.10 From the ratios and other data set forth below for the Auto Accessories Ltd, indicate your interpretation of the company's financial condition: LO 6.2,4,5 LOD: M

Particulars	Year 3	Year 2	Year 1
Current ratio (per cent)	302	278	265
Acid-test ratio	99	110	155
Working capital turnover (times)	3.25	3.00	2.75
Receivable turnover (times)	7.2	8.41	9.83
Collection period (days)	50	43	37
Inventory to working capital (per cent)	110	100	95
Inventory turnover (times)	5.41	6.01	6.11
Income per equity share (₹)	2.5	4.05	5.10
Net income to net worth (per cent)	7	8.5	11.07
Operating expenses to net sales (per cent)	25	23	22
Sales increase during the year (per cent)	23	16	10
Cost of goods sold to net sales (per cent)	73	71	70
Dividend per share (₹)	3	3	3
Fixed assets to net worth (per cent)	22.7	18.0	16.4
Net profit on net sales (per cent)	2.0	5.09	7.03

Solution

The interpretation of the financial condition of Auto Accessories Ltd, as revealed by the ratios and other data, yields the following inferences:

(i) Declining profitability is evident from the following:

(a) Decrease in gross profit ratio from 30 in year 1 to 27 per cent in year 3, **(b)** decrease in net profit ratio from 7 in year 1 to 2 in year 3 and **(c)** decrease in rate of return on net worth from 11.1 per cent in year 1 to 7 per cent in year 3. This is in spite of increase in sales from 10 per cent in year 1 to 23 per cent in year 3.

In interpreting the profitability of the company, another relevant factor is the expenses ratios. The ratio of cost of goods sold to net sales has gone up from 70 to 73 per cent during the period. Likewise, there has been an increase in operating expenses ratio from 22 to 25 per cent. The high inventories as reflected in lower inventory turnover ratio of 5.41 in year 3 as compared to 6.11 in year 1 have also adversely affected the profit margin.

As a consequence, the EPS has declined by more than 50 per cent during year 1-3 from ₹5.1 in year 1 to ₹2.5 in year 3.

(ii) The emerging liquidity position of the company appears to be highly satisfactory. The current ratio has increased from 2.65 in year 1 to 3.02 in year 3. Though, the acid-test ratio has declined from 1.55 1 to 0.99, it meets the standard. The company is unlikely to encounter any serious difficulty in paying the short-term obligations as and when they become due for payment.

However, the management should realise that the policy relating to collection of debt is not sound as reflected in the declining trend of receivables turnover from 9.83 in year 1 to 7.2 in year 3. In other words, the average debt collection period has increased from 37 days to 50 days. There is carelessness either (i) in collecting the payments from debtors, or (ii) in extending credit sales to customers leading to an increase in bad debts and thereby an increase in the expenses ratio. Further, the inventory holding period requires investigation as the consistent increase in the current ratio and the consistent decrease in the acid-test ratio result from large accumulation of inventories. The excessive investment in current assets seem to be affecting the rate of return.

The investment in fixed assets appears excessive as shown by a consistent increase in the ratio of fixed assets to net worth. However, the overinvestment in fixed assets is not as clear as the overinvestment in working capital.

The stable dividend policy of the company is commendable and is likely to have a salutary effect on the market price of its shares.

In conclusion, the firm's financial position has not become so bad that it cannot be cured. What is required is a thorough probe into overinvestment in working capital, particularly inventories and fixed assets.

P.6.11 Below is given the balance sheet of Best Ltd, as on March 31, of the current year: **LO 6.2,3,4,5** **LOD: D**

Equity and Liabilities	Amount	Assets	Amount
Equity share capital	₹20,00,000	Fixed assets (cost)	₹50,00,000
7.5% Preference share capital	10,00,000	Depreciation written-off	16,00,000
General reserve	4,00,000		34,00,000
6% Debentures	6,00,000	Stock	6,00,000
Sundry creditors	10,00,000	Sundry debtors	8,00,000
		Cash	2,00,000
	50,00,000		50,00,000

The following additional information is available:

(1) Fixed assets costing ₹10,00,000 to be installed on April 1, and would become operative on that date, payment to be made on March 31 of next year.
(2) The fixed assets turnover ratio (on the cost of the fixed assets) would be 1.5.
(3) The stock turnover ratio would be 14.4 (calculated on the basis of the average of the opening and closing stocks).
(4) The break-up of cost and profit would be as follows (percentages):

Materials	40
Labour	25
Manufacturing expenses	10
Office and selling expenses	10
Depreciation	5
Profit	10
Sales	100

The profit is subject to debenture interest and taxation @ 35 per cent.
(5) Debtors would be 1/9 of turnover.
(6) Creditors would be 1/5 of materials consumed.
(7) In March next year a dividend of 10 per cent on equity capital would be paid.
(8) ₹5,00,000, 6% debentures would be issued on April 1, next year.

You are required to prepare the forecast balance sheet as on March 31, next year and calculate the resultant:
(a) Current ratio;
(b) Fixed Assets/Net worth ratio; and
(c) Debt-equity ratio
(The turnover above refers to the value of sales).

Solution

Forecast Balance Sheet of Best Ltd as on March 31, Next Year

Equity and Liabilities	*Amount*	*Assets*		*Amount*
Equity share capital	₹20,00,000	Fixed assets:		
13.5% Preference share capital	10,00,000	Cost	₹60,00,000	
General reserves	6,67,100	*Less:* Depreciation	20,50,000	₹39,50,000
15% Debentures	11,00,000	Sundry debtors		10,00,000
Sundry creditors	7,20,000	Stock		6,50,000
Provision for taxation	2,91,900	Cash		1,79,000
	57,79,000			57,79,000

Resultant ratio:

	Ratio		*Formula*	*Computation*
(i)	Current ratio		Current assets / Current liabilities	₹18,29,00 / ₹11,37,000 = 1.61
(ii)	Fixed assets to net worth		Fixed assets / Net worth	₹39,50,000 / ₹35,42 000 = 1.12
(iii)	Debt-equity ratio	(a)	External dept / Internal equity	₹22,37,00 / ₹35,42,000 = 0.63
		(b)	Long term debt / Internal equity	₹11,00,000 / ₹35,42,000 = 0.31

WORKING NOTES

1. Determination of sales:

$$\text{Fixed assets turnover ratio} = \frac{\text{Sales}}{\text{Fixed assets}}$$

Or $$1.5 = \frac{\text{Sales}}{₹60,00,000}$$

Or $$₹90,00,000 = \text{Sales}$$

2. Determination of actual expenses

Particulars	*Percentage of sales*	*Amount*
Materials	40	₹36,00,000
Manufacturing expenses	10	9,00,000
Labour	25	22,50,000
Office & selling expenses	10	9,00,000
Depreciation	5	4,50,000
Profit	10	9,00,000
	100	90,00,000

3. Determination of net fixed assets:

Opening balance		₹50,00,000
Add: Purchases		10,00,000
		60,00,000
Less: Depreciation:		
Accumulated	₹16,00,000	
Additional	4,50,000	20,50,000
Closing balance		39,50,000

4. Determination of closing stock:

$$\text{Average stock} = \frac{\text{Sales}}{\text{Stock turnover ratio}}$$

$$= \frac{₹90,00,000}{14.4} = ₹6,25,000$$

$$\text{Average stock} = \frac{\text{Opening stock + closing stock}}{2}$$

$$₹12,50,000 = ₹6,00,000 + \text{Closing stock}$$

$$₹\ 6,50,000 = \text{Closing stock}$$

5. Determination of debtors:

$$\text{Debtors} = \frac{\text{Sales}}{9} = \frac{₹90,00,000}{9} = ₹10,00,000$$

6. Determination of creditors:

$$\text{Creditors} = \frac{\text{Materials consumed}}{5} = \frac{₹36,00,000}{5} = ₹7,20,000$$

7. Determination of interest and provision for taxation:

Net profit	₹9,00,000
Less: Interest (0.06 × ₹11,00,000)	66,000
	8,34,000
Less: Taxes (0.35 × ₹8,34,000)	2,91,900
Net-profit after taxes	5,42,100

8. Determination of amount to be transferred to general reserves:

Opening balance of general reserve		₹4,00,000
Transfer from the current year:		
Net profit	₹5,42,100	
Less: Preference dividend	(75,000)	
Less: Equity dividend	(2,00,000)	2,67,100
Closing balance		6,67,100

9. Determination of cash:

Cash flow statement

Sources of cash:			
Cash from operations:			
Profit after tax		₹5,42,100	
Add: Depreciation		4,50,000	
		9,52,100	
Add: Increase in current liabilities (provision for taxation):		2,91,900	
Less: Increase in current assets and decrease in current liabilities:			
Stock	₹50,000		
Debtors	2,00,000		
Creditors	2,80,000	(5,30,000)	₹ 7,54,000
Issue of debentures			5,00,000
Total cash (sources) (A)			12,54,000
Uses of cash:			
Purchase of fixed assets			10,00,000
Payment of dividend:			
Preference		75,000	
Equity		2,00,000	2,75,000
Total cash (uses) (B)			12,75,000
Net decrease in cash (B – A)		(21,000)	
Opening balance of cash		2,00,000	
Less: Decrease in cash		21,000	1,79,000
Closing balance of cash			

P.6.12 You have been supplied data for the Supreme Plastic Company Ltd, and its industry averages: LO 6.2,3,4,5 LOD: M

1. Determine the indicated ratios for the Supreme Plastic Company.

2. Indicate the company's strengths and weaknesses as shown by your analysis.

Balance sheet as at March 31

Equity and Liabilities	*Amount*	*Assets*	*Amount*
Equity share capital	₹12,00,000	Net fixed assets	₹6,05,000
10% Debentures	2,30,000	Cash	2,20,000
Sundry creditors	1,65,000	Sundry debtors	2,75,000
Bills payable	2,20,000	Stock	8,25,000
Other current liabilities	1,10,000		
	19,25,000		19,25,000

Statement of profit for the year ending March 31, current year

Sales		₹27,50,000
Less: Cost of goods sold:		
Materials	₹10,45,000	
Wages	6,60,000	
Factory overheads	3,24,500	20,29,500
Gross profit		7,20,500
Less: Selling and distribution expenses		2,75,000
Less: Administrative and general expenses		3,07,000
Earnings before interest and taxes		1,38,500
Less: Interest		23,000
Earnings before taxes		1,15,500
Less: Income taxes (0.35)		40,425
Net profit		75,075

Ratios

Ratios	*Industry*	*Supreme Plastic*
Current assets/current liabilities	2.4	
Sales/debtors	8.0	
Sales/stock	9.8	
Sales/total assets	2.0	
Net profit/sales (per cent)	3.3	
Net profit/total assets (per cent)	6.6	
Net profit/net worth (per cent)	12.7	
Total debt/total assets (per cent)	63.5	

Solution

(1) Determination of Ratios

Ratios	*Computation*	*Indicated result*	*Industry*
Current assets / Current liabilities	₹12,20,000 / ₹4,95,000	2.7	2.4
Sales / Debtors	27,50,000 / 2,75,000	10.0	8.0
Sales / Stock	27,50,000 / 8,25,000	3.3	9.8
Sales / Total assets	27,50,000 / 19,25,000	1.4	2.0
Net profit / Sales (per cent)	75,075 / 27,50,000	2.7	3.3
Net profit / Total assets (per cent)	75,075 / 19,25,000	3.9	6.6
Net profit / Equity share capital	75,075 / 12,00,000	6.3	12.7
Total debt / Total assets	7,25,000 / 19,25,000	37.7	63.5

2. The level of stock maintained by Supreme Plastics is alarmingly high in that it is almost three times the industry average. The other turnover ratios are in conformity with that of the industry. In fact, current ratios and debtors turnover reflecting debt collection period of the company are better than those of the industry.

The greatest weakness of the company is the high level of inventories. It has caused a steep decline in the total assets turnover. The cost of carrying stocks is likely to adversely affect the profit margin. As a result of its low turnover and profit margin, the company's rate of return on net worth is less than one-half of the industry. The rate of return on equity capital of the company is also low because the company is using relatively less debt, i.e. 37.7 per cent as against the industry average of 63.5 per cent.

P.6.13 From the following particulars, prepare the balance sheet of Shri Mohan Ram and Co. Ltd as at March 31, current year. LO 6.2,3,4,5 LOD: D

Current ratio, 2
Working capital, ₹4,00,000
Capital block to current asset, 3:2
Fixed asset to turnover, 1:3
Sales cash/credit, 1:2
Debentures/share capital, 1:2
Stock velocity, 2 months
Creditors velocity, 2 months
Debtors velocity, 2 months
Gross profit ratio, 25 per cent (to sales)
Capital block:
    Net profit, 10 per cent of turnover
    Reserve, 2.5 per cent of turnover

Solution

Balance Sheet as at March 31

Liabilities	*Amount*	*Assets*	*Amount*
Share capital	₹6,00,000	Fixed assets (net)	₹8,00,000
Reserves	60,000	Current assets:	
Profit and loss A/c	2,40,000	Stock	3,00,000
Debentures	3,00,000	Debtors	2,66,667
Creditors	3,50,000	Other current assets	2,33,333
Other current liabilities	50,000		
	16,00,000		16,00,000

WORKING NOTES

1. Current ratio of 2 implies that CA_s = twice CL, i.e., CA – 2CL = 0
   Further, CA - CL = ₹4,00,000 or, CL = ₹4,00,000 and CA = ₹8,00,000.
2. Capital block to current assets ratio of 3:2 implies that long-term capital funds (equity funds + debentures) are 1.5 times current assets, i.e., ₹8,00,000 × 1.5 = ₹12,00,000.
3. Total assets = Total liabilities = ₹16,00,000 (₹12,00,000 long-term funds + ₹4,00,000 CL).
4. Fixed assets = ₹16,00,000, Total assets – ₹8,00,000, CA = ₹8,00,000.
5. FA/Turnover (sales) = 1/3 or Sales = ₹8,00,000 × 3 = ₹24,00,000.
6. Proportion of cash sales to credit sales is 1:2 or cash sales are one-third of total sales, i.e. 1/3 × ₹24,00,000 = ₹8,00,000; credit sales = ₹16,00,000.
7. Gross profit = 0.25 × ₹24,00,000 = ₹6,00,000; cost of goods sold = ₹18,00,000.
8. Debtors = ₹16,00,000/6 (Debtors turnover ratio, 12 ÷ 2) = ₹2,66,667.
9. Stock = ₹18,00,000/6 (Stock turnover ratio, 12 ÷ 2) = ₹3,00,000.
10. Other CAs = ₹8,00,000 – (₹2,66,667 + ₹3,00,00) = ₹2,33,333.
11. Reserves = 0.025 × ₹24,00,000 = ₹60,000.

12. Credit purchases = Cost of goods sold + Closing stock = ₹18,00,000 + ₹3,00,000 = ₹21,00,000.
13. Creditors = ₹21,00,000 ÷ 6 (creditors turnover ratio, 12 ÷ 2) = ₹3,50,000.
14. Other CLs = Total CL – Creditors, i.e. ₹4,00,000 – ₹3,50,000 = ₹50,000.
15. Debentures to share capital ratio of 1:2 implies that debentures in value are equal to one-half of share capital (2 Debentures = Share capital). Further, capital block (as per working note 3) is ₹12,00,000.
₹12,00,000 = Debentures + Share capital + Net profit + Reserves
₹12,00,000 = 3 Debentures + ₹2,40,000 (10 per cent of sales) + ₹60,000
₹3,00,000 = Debentures; Share capital = ₹6,00,000

P.6.14 The following items appear in the accounts of XYZ Ltd as at March 31, current year: LO 6.4 LOD: M

Cash	₹4,860	Bank overdraft	₹5,200
Land and building	80,000	Equity shares (₹10 each)	1,00,000
Deposits and payments in advance	6,200	Profit and loss A/c (Cr.)	21,700
Stock	37,280	Proposed equity dividend for current year	8,625
Trade creditors	40,575	Trade investments	2,000
General reserve	10,000	Provision for taxation	12,400
Debtors	52,300	Dividend reserve	14,000
Bills receivable	2,260	Bills payable	1,800
Plant and machinery	54,400	Net sales for current year	2,18,240
12% Debentures (secured)	25,000	Net profit for current year before taxation and dividend	32,783

Note:
The values of all fixed assets reflect current price levels after provision of depreciation.

You are required to arrange the above items in the form of financial statement and find out the rate of return on capital employed (by using different ways).

Solution

Financial Statement of XYZ Ltd as at March 31

Particulars			*Amount*
Shareholders' funds:			
Equity share capital			₹1,00,000
General reserve			10,000
Profit and loss account (credit)			21,700
Dividend reserve			14,000
			1,45,700
Add: 12% Debentures (secured)			25,000
Long-term funds (capital employed)			1,70,700
Investment of funds in:			
Fixed assets:			
Land and building		₹80,000	
Trade investments		2,000	
Plant and machinery		54,400	1,36,400
Working capital (net)			
Current assets:			
Cash	₹4,860		
Deposit and payments in advance	6,200		
Stock	37,280		
Debtors	52,300		
Bills receivable	2,260	1,02,900	

(Contd.)

(*Contd.*)

Less: Current liabilities:			
Trade creditors	40,575		
Bank overdraft	5,200		
Provision for taxation	12,400		
Bills payable	1,800		
Proposed equity dividends	8,625	(68,600)	34,300
			1,70,700

Rate of return on capital employed (ROCE)

(i) $\frac{\text{EBIT}}{\text{Capital employed}} \times 100 = \frac{₹32{,}783 + ₹3{,}00^{@}}{₹1{,}70{,}700} \times 100 = 21\%$ per cent

@Interest on 12% Debentures is ₹25,000 × 0.12 = ₹3,000

(ii) $\frac{\text{EAT + Interest}}{\text{Capital emploted}} \times 100 = \frac{₹32{,}783 - ₹12{,}400 + ₹3{,}000}{₹1{,}70{,}700} \times 100 = 13.7\%$ per cent

(iii) $\frac{\text{EAT + Interest – tax advantage on interest}^{@@}}{\text{Capital employed}} \times 100 = \frac{₹20{,}383 + \text{Rs}\,3{,}000 - ₹1{,}134}{₹1{,}70{,}700} \times 100 = 13\%$ per cent

@@(Effective tax rate = ₹12,400/₹32,783 = 37.8 per cent)

P.6.15 Towards the end of previous year, the directors of *A* Ltd decided to expand the business. The annual accounts of the company for the previous year and current year are summarised as given: LO 6.4,5 LOD: M

Particulars	*Previous year*		*Current year*	
Sales: Cash	₹30,000		₹32,000	
Credit	2,70,000	₹3,00,000	3,42,000	₹3,74,000
Cost of goods sold		2,36,000		2,98,000
Gross margin		64,000		76,000
Expenses:				
Warehousing		13,000		14,000
Transport		6,000		10,000
Administration		19,000		19,000
Selling		11,000		14,000
Debenture interest		—		2,000
		49,000		59,000
Net profit		15,000		17,000
Fixed assets (*less* depreciation)		30,000		40,000
Current assets:				
Stock	60,000		94,000	
Debtors	50,000		82,000	
Cash	10,000	1,20,000	7,000	1,83,000
Less: Current liabilities (trade creditors)		50,000		76,000
Net current assets		70,000		1,07,000
		1,00,000		1,47,000
Share capital		75,000		75,000
Reserves and undistributed profit		25,000		42,000
Debentures		—		30,000
		1,00,000		1,47,000

You are informed that, **(a)** all sales were from stocks in the company's warehouse, **(b)** the range of merchandise was not changed and buying prices remained steady throughout the 2 years, **(c)** the stocks as on April 1 previous year was ₹40,000 and **(d)** the debenture loan was received on April 1 current year and fixed assets were purchased on that date.

You are required to work out the following accounting ratios for both the years.

(i) Gross profit ratio
(ii) Operating expenses to sales
(iii) Operating profit ratio
(iv) Capital turnover ratio
(v) Stock turnover ratio
(vi) Net profit to capital employed ratio and
(vii) Debtors collection period (in days).

Your answer should give the figures calculated to one decimal place, together with possible reasons for changes in the ratios for 2 years. Ratios relating to capital employed should be based on the capital at the end of the year. Ignore taxation.

Solution

(i) Gross profit ratio (gross profit/sales) × 100

Previous year (₹64,000/₹3,00,000) × 100 = 21.3 per cent
Current year (₹76,000/₹3,74,000) × 100 = 20.3 per cent

The gross profit ratio has declined by 1 per cent. The possible reasons may be **(i)** decrease in unit selling price, **(ii)** increase in direct expenses other than purchases and value of stock and/or **(iii)** any combination of **(i)** and **(ii)**.

(ii) Operating expenses to sales (OES) ratio

Previous year (₹49,000/₹3,00,000) × 100 = 16.3 per cent
Current year (₹57,000/₹3,74,000) × 100 = 15.2 per cent

Operating expenses may not change *pari passu* with sales as such expenses are partly fixed in nature. As a result, the OES ratio has fallen in current year in spite of increase in sales. For instance, administration expenses remained unchanged (at ₹19,000) resulting in a decline in administration expenses ratio from 6.3 to 5.1 per cent. The warehousing expenses have similarly fallen from 4.3 to 3.7 per cent. These cost savings have been partly offset by increase in transport expenses ratio (from 2 per cent to 2.7 per cent and selling expenses ratio from 3.7 to 3.8 per cent) presumably caused by additional transport expenses and selling expenses due to market expansion and tapping of more distant customers.

(iii) Operating profit ratio (EBIT/sales) × 100

Previous year (₹15,000/₹3,00,000) × 100 = 5 per cent
Current year (₹19,000/₹3,74,000) × 100 = 5.1 per cent

The increase in operating profit ratio by 0.1 per cent is the result of (i) decrease in operating expenses ratio by 1.1 per cent (increase in profits) and (ii) decrease in gross profit ratio by 1 per cent. It implies that there is virtually no gain to the company from increased sales.

(iv) Capital turnover ratio (sales/capital employed)

Previous year (₹3,00,000/₹1,00,000) = 3 times
Current year (₹3,74,000/₹1,47,000) = 2.5 times

The reduction in capital turnover ratio signifies that the company is unable to employ the additional funds as profitably as the existing funds. The expected increase in sales does not seem to have materialised.

(v) Stock turnover ratio (cost of goods sold/average stock)

Previous year (₹2,36,000/₹50,000) = 4.7 times

Current year (₹2,98,000/₹77,000) = 3.9 times

The increase in sales was less than proportionate increase in stock.

(vi) Net profit to capital employed ratio [(net profit + interest)/capital employed] × 100

Previous year (₹15,000/₹1,00,000) × 100 = 15 per cent

Current year (₹19,000/₹1,47,000) × 100 = 12.9 per cent

The company seems to have failed to maintain the earning rate on the funds employed.

(vii) Debtors' collection period (debtors/average credit sales per day)

Previous year (₹50,000/₹739.7) = 68 days

Current year (₹82,000/₹937) = 88 days

The increase in debtors' collection period implies relaxation in credit terms to promote sales, in particular, to penetrate new market/customers.

To sum up, the expansion of the business does not seem to have yielded the anticipated benefits.

P.6.16 Hypothetical Industries Ltd (HIL) has submitted the following projections. (₹lakh) You are required to determine yearly debt service coverage ratio (DSCR) and the average DSCR and comment. LO 6.3 LOD: M

Year	EAT	Interest on loan	Repayment of term loan
1	20	19	11
2	35	17	18
3	40	15	18
4	20	12	18
5	18	10	18
6	18	7	8
7	16	5	8
8	16	2	8

The net profit (EAT) has been arrived at after charging depreciation of ₹20 lakh every year.

Solution

Determination of Debt Service Coverage Ratio (amount in lakh of rupees)

Year	EAT	Depreciation	Interest	Cash available (Col. 2 + 3 + 4)	Principal instalment	Debt obligations	DSCR (Col. 5 ÷ Col. 7)
1	2	3	4	5	6	7	8
1	20	20	19	59	11	30	1.97
2	35	20	17	72	18	35	2.06
3	40	20	15	75	18	33	2.27
4	20	20	12	52	18	30	1.73
5	18	20	10	48	18	28	1.71
6	18	20	7	45	8	15	3.00
7	16	20	5	41	8	13	3.15
8	16	20	2	38	8	10	3.80
Average DSCR (ΣDSCR/8) = 19.69/8 =							2.46

COMMENT: The DSCR of HIL is very satisfactory.

P.6.17 The financial statement of Excel AMP Graphics Limited are as under:

LO 6.6 LOD: D

Balance sheet as at 31st March, 2013 (₹ in crore)

Sources of funds:		2013	2012
Shareholders' funds			
Share capital	₹1,121		₹931
Reserves and surplus	8,950	₹10,071	7,999
			8,930
Loan funds:			
Secured loans	—		259
Finance lease obligations	74		—
Unsecured loans	171	245	115
			374
		10,316	9,304
Application of funds:			
Fixed assets			
Gross block	6,667		5,747
Less: Depreciation	3,150		2,561
Net block	3,517		3,186
Capital work-in-progress	27	3,544	28
			3,214
Investments		288	222
Current assets, loans and advances:			
Inventories	2,709		2,540
Sundry debtors	9,468		9,428
Cash and bank balances	3,206		662
Loans and advances	2,043		1,712
	17,426		14,342
Less: Current liabilities and provisions:			
Current liabilities	10,109		7,902
Provisions	513		572
	10,622		8,474
Net current assets		6,804	5,868
Net deferred tax liability		(320)	—
		10,316	9,304

Profit and loss account for the year ended 31 March, 2013 (₹ in crore)

Particulars		2013		2012
Income:				
Sales and services		23,436		17,849
Other income		320		306
		23,756		18,155
Expenditure:				
Cost of materials		15,179		10,996
Personnel expenses		2,543		2,293
Other expenses		3,546		2,815
Depreciation	419		383	
Less: Transfer from revaluation reserve	7	412	6	377
Interest		164		88
			21,844	16,569
Profit before tax			1,912	1,586
Provision for tax:				
Current tax			450	371
Deferred tax			(6)	—
Profit after tax			1,468	1,215

REQUIRED:

(i) Compute and analyse the return on capital employed (ROCE) in a Du-Pont control chart framework.
(ii) Compute and analyse the average inventory holding period and average collection period.
(iii) Compute and analyse the return on equity (ROE) by bringing out clearly the impact of financial leverage.

Solution

(i) *Determination of Return on Capital Employed (ROCE) as per Du-Pont chart* *(Amount in ₹ crore)*

Particulars	*2013*	*2012*
(a) Determination of EBIT:		
Profit before tax	₹1,912	₹1,586
Add back interest	164	88
Less other incomes	(320)	(306)
Earnings before interest and taxes (EBIT)	1,756	1,368
(b) Determination of capital employed		
Shareholders funds	10,071	8,930
Add loan funds	245	374
Less capital work-in-progress	(27)	(28)
Less investments	(288)	(222)
Less loans and advances	(2,043)	(1,712)
Capital employed in business	7,958	7,342
(c) Sales and services (operating revenues)	23,436	17,849
(d) EBIT/sales (%)	7.49	7.66
(e) Sales/capital employed (times)	2.945	2.431
(f) ROC/= (d × e) (%)	22.06	18.62

(ii) *Computation of average inventory holding period and average collection period*

(Amount in ₹ crore)

Particulars	*2013*	*2012*
Cost of materials used during the year	₹15,179	₹10,996
Inventories at year-end	2,709	2,540
Average inventory holding period (365 days × Closing inventory)/ Cost of materials used (days)	65	84
Sales and services (assumed to be on credit)	23,436	17,849
Debtors at year-end	9,468	9,428
Average collection period (365 days × Closing debtors)/ Credit sales (days)	147	193

ANALYSIS: It is a matter of satisfaction for the firm that there has been a decrease in inventory holding period as well as debtors collection period in year 2001 *vis-à-vis* year 2000. There seems to be potentials of further reduction in debtors collection period. Debtors collection period of nearly 5 months (in 2001) *per-se* is high still.

(iii) *Return on Equity and Impact of Financial Leverage* *(Amount in ₹ crore)*

Particulars	*2013*	*2012*
(a) Return on equity:		
Profit after tax (EAT)	₹1,468	₹1,215
Shareholders funds (SHF)	10,071	8,930
ROR on equity (EAT/SHF) × 100 (%)	14.58	13.61

(Contd.)

(Contd.)

(b) Return on capital employed (post-tax basis) (%)		
ROCE (before tax)	22.06	18.62
Tax rate	35	35
ROCE	14.34	12.1
(c) Debt funds to total funds:		
Loan funds	245	374
Total funds	10,316	9,304
Share of loan funds to total funds (%)	2.37	4.02

ANALYSIS: The return on equity is marginally higher than the return on total assets/capital employed. The reason is loan funds constitute a meager portion of total funds. In other words, the impact of financial leverage (use of debt to magnify the ROE) is negligible.

P.6.18 The financial statistics pertaining to profitability of Asian Paints (India) Limited for years 1–6 are tabulated below: LO 6.6 LOD: D

(Amount is in ₹ crore)

Particulars	*Year, March 31*					
	1	*2*	*3*	*4*	*5*	*6*
EBIT	107.06	120.77	125.82	163.47	177.20	194.99
Interest	21.68	19.58	22.33	20.29	22.12	14.59
EBT	85.38	100.19	103.49	143.18	155.08	180.40
Tax provisions	30.00	33.00	24.00	45.75	49.50	66.09
EAT	55.38	67.19	79.49	97.43	105.58	114.31
Sales	938.11	1,046.80	1,158.38	1,383.55	1,526.01	1,659.72
Total assets	534.49	647.66	685.84	771.09	882.20	893.52
Average total assets (ATA)	—	591.07	666.75	728.46	826.64	887.86
Equity funds	226.41	260.50	304.51	357.41	411.20	410.56
Average equity funds (AEF)	—	243.45	282.50	330.96	384.30	410.88
Net fixed assets	194.28	256.68	306.87	333.29	382.95	375.76
Inventory (Finished goods)	72.66	81.60	86.58	106.50	114.50	88.26
Sundry debtors	66.92	80.74	79.95	86.67	121.65	118.96
Average fixed assets	—	225.48	281.77	320.08	358.12	379.35
Average inventory	—	77.13	84.09	96.54	110.50	101.38
Average debtors	—	73.83	80.34	83.31	104.16	120.30

From the above financial information, you are required to prepare a disaggregative analysis related to ROA and ROE (both on pre-tax and post-tax basis) and intrepret the results.

Solution

Disaggregation of Pretax ROA and ROE of Asian Paints (India) Ltd

	(I) Return on Assets (TA)				*(II) Return on Equity (EF)*		
	Operating profit margin	× *Assets turnover*	= *Pre-interest and tax ROA*	– *Interest on Assets*	*Post-interest ROA*	× *Leverage*	= *Pretax ROE*
Year	*EBIT/sales (%)*	× *Sales/ATA* (times)*	= *EBIT/ATA (%)*	– *I/ATA (%)*	*EBT/ATA (%)*	× *ATA/AEF (times)*	*EBT/AEF (%)*
2	11.54	1.77	20.43	3.31	17.12	2.43	41.6
3	10.86	1.74	18.90	3.35	15.55	2.36	36.70
4	11.82	1.90	22.46	2.79	19.67	2.20	43.27
5	11.61	1.85	21.48	2.68	18.80	2.15	40.42
6	11.75	1.87	21.97	1.64	20.33	2.16	43.91
Average	11.521.83	21.08	2.75	18.33	2.26	41.18	

*Average total assets.

Component Disaggregation of Return on Equity (After-tax) of Asian Paints

Year	Profitability (×) (EAT/Sales) (×) (%)	Assets turnover Sales/ATA = (times)	EAT/ATA (×) (%)	(×) Solvency = ATA/AEF = (times)	ROE EAT/AEF (%)
2	6.42	1.77	11.36	2.43	27.60
3	6.86	1.74	11.94	2.36	28.18
4	7.04	1.90	13.38	2.20	29.44
5	6.92	1.85	12.80	2.15	27.52
6	6.89	1.87	12.88	2.16	27.82
Average	6.83	1.83	12.50	2.26	28.11

Five-component Disaggregation of ROE (After-tax) of Asian Paints

Effects of: Year	Profitability (×) Taxes EAT/EBT (×) (times)	Turnover Financing EBT/EBIT (×) (times)	Operations EBIT/Sales (=) (%)	EAT/Sales (×) (%)	Sales/ATA = (times)	EAT/ATA (%)	(×) Solvency = ATA/AEF (times)	ROE EAT/AEF (%)
2	0.67	0.83	11.54	6.42	1.77	11.36	2.43	27.60
3	0.77	0.82	10.86	6.86	1.74	11.94	2.36	28.18
4	0.68	0.88	11.82	7.04	1.90	13.38	2.20	29.44
5	0.68	0.88	11.61	6.92	1.85	12.80	2.15	27.52
6	0.63	0.93	11.75	6.89	1.87	12.88	2.16	27.82
Average	0.69	0.87	11.52	6.83	1.83	12.50	2.26	28.11

INTERPRETATION: There has been no significant change in ROA (based on EBIT) of Asian Paints during year 2–6 (and in particular 4–6). The two components of ROA, namely, operating profit margin and assets turnover also do not show any noticeable change during the period. Except during year 3, the EBIT/sales ratio varied in a narrow range of 11.54 per cent and 11.82 per cent. Minor change is also observed in respect of assets turnover, the range being 1.74 – 1.90. Between the two components, the change in the operating profit margin largely accounted for the change in ROA.

REVIEW QUESTIONS

LOD: Easy

RQ.6.1 Indicate whether the following statements are true or false: LO 6.2,3,4,5

(i) Current ratio and acid-test ratio of a business firm are virtually the same; this implies that the firm has low investment in inventory.

(ii) A company's current ratio is 2.0. If it uses cash to pay creditors, this transaction would cause a decrease in current ratio.

(iii) Solvency ratios measure the firm's ability to cater to the obligations arising out of long-term debt.

(iv) Equity funds are greater than equity capital in a loss-incurring firm.

(v) In general, low turnover ratios are desirable.

(vi) Earnings yield is determined dividing EPS by acquisition price per equity share.

(vii) Return on equity funds is determined by dividing EAT by average net worth.

(viii) Internal growth rate is the maximum rate at which the firm can grow without external financing of any kind.

(ix) It is conceptually correct to determine stock turnover ratio (finished goods) by dividing cost of goods sold by average stock.

[Answers: (i) True, (ii) False, (iii) True, (iv) False, (v) False, (vi) False, (vii) False, (viii) True, (ix) True.]

RQ.6.2 Fill in the blanks with the correct answer (out of the choices provided). LO 6.2,3,4,5,6

(i) An analyst applied the DuPont System to the following data of a company: (a) equity turnover 4.2, (b) net profit margin 5.5%, (c) total assets turnover 2.0 and (d) dividend payout ratio 30%; the company's rate of return on equity is ________ (11%/23.1%).

(ii) Four-times stock turnover ratio implies ________ months inventory holding period (3/4).

(iii) The following information is given about a company: (a) current assets ₹900 lakh and current liabilities ₹450 lakh in current year and (b) current assets ₹1,100 lakh and current liabilities ₹530 in previous year. The approximate percentage decrease in current ratio is ________ (0.04%/4.0%).

(iv) Presently, current assets and current liabilities of a company are ₹16 lakh and ₹8 lakh respectively. The current ratio will ________ (increase/decrease) on purchase of new machinery of ₹6 lakh.

(v) Purchase of treasury bills will (weaken/not affect) acid-test ratio.

(vi) Assume that the company's existing debt-equity ratio is 2:1, the ploughing back of profits by a company will ________ (increase/decrease) it.

(vii) A two-months debtor collection period implies that debtors turnover ratio is ________ (6 times/2 times).

(viii) ________ is a more rigorous test of the solvency position of a business firm. (Interest coverage ratio/Debt service coverage ratio).

(ix) ROR on shareholders' equity is computed dividing EAT by ________ (share capital/ shareholders' funds).

(x) Issue of 12% preference shares will ________ debt-equity ratio of a corporate enterprise. (decrease/increase)

[Answers: (i) 23.1%, (ii) 3, (iii) 4.0%, (iv) decrease, (v) not affect, (vi) decrease, (vii) 6 times, (viii) debt service coverage ratio, (ix) shareholders' funds, (x) decrease.]

RQ.6.3 What is the importance of ratio analysis? Briefly discuss the importance of the following accounting ratios: LO 6.2,3,4,5
(a) Liquidity ratio, **(b)** Debt-equity ratio, **(c)** Stock-turnover rate, and **(d)** Ratio of debtors to turnover.

RQ.6.4 What procedure would you adopt to study the liquidity of a business firm? LO 6.2,3,4

RQ.6.5 What is indicated when the average age of accounts receivable for a firm is 45 days, but credit terms require customers to pay accounts within 30 days? LO 6.5

RQ.6.6 What are the limitations of financial ratios as a technique for appraising the financial position of a company? LO 6.9

LOD: Medium

RQ.6.7 How would you analyse the financial position of a company from the point of view of **(a)** an investor, **(b)** a creditor, and **(c)** a long-term lender? LO 6.8

RQ.6.8 Discuss the importance of ratio analysis for interfirm and intrafirm comparisons, including circumstances responsible for its limitations. If any.

RQ.6.9 Distinguish between percentage analysis and ratio analysis relating to the interpretation of financial statements. What is the value of these two types of analysis? LO 6.1,7,8

RQ.6.10 How does the acid-test ratio differ from the current ratio? How are they similar? What is the usefulness of the defensive interval ratio? LO 6.2

RQ.6.11 What is the relationship of the assets turnover rate to the rate of return on total assets? LO 6.6

RQ.6.12 Discuss some inherent limitations of single-year financial statements for purposes of analysis and interpretation. To what extent are these limitations overcome by the use of the common size statements? LO 6.1,7

RQ.6.13 You have been furnished with the financial information of Aditya Mills Ltd. for the current year.

Balance sheet, March 31, current year

Liabilities	*Amount (₹ thousand)*	*Assets*		*Amount (₹ thousand)*
Equity share capital (₹100 each)	1,000	Plant and equipment		640
Retained earnings	368	Land and buildings		80
Sundry creditors	104	Cash		160
Bills payable	200	Sundry debtors	360	
Other current liabilities	20	*Less:* Allowances	40	320
		Stock		480
		Prepaid insurance		12
	1,692			1,692

Statement of profit, year ended March 31, current year

Particulars	*(₹ thousand)*
Sales	4,000
Less: Cost of goods sold	3,080
Gross profit on sales	920
Less: Operating expenses	680
Net profit	240
Less: Taxes (0.35)	84
Net profit after taxes	156

Sundry debtors and stock at the beginning of the year were ₹3,00,000 and ₹4,00,000 respectively.

(a) Determine the following ratios of the Aditya Mills Ltd: **(i)** Current ratio, **(ii)** Acid-test ratio, **(iii)** Stock turnover, **(iv)** Debtors turnover, **(v)** Gross profit ratio, **(vi)** Net profit ratio, **(vii)** Operating ratio, **(viii)** Earnings per share, **(ix)** Rate of return on equity capital, and **(x)** Market value of the shares if P/E ratio is 10 times, LO 6.2,3,4,5

(b) Indicate for each of the following transactions whether the transaction would improve, weaken or have an effect on the current ratio of the Aditya Mills Ltd: **(i)** Sell additional equity shares, **(ii)** Sell 10% debentures, **(iii)** Pay bills payable, **(iv)** Collect sundry debtors, **(v)** Purchase additional plant, **(vi)** Issuing bills payable to creditors, **(vii)** Collecting bills receivable from debtors, **(viii)** Purchase of treasury bills, and **(ix)** Writing off bad debt. LO 6.2

RQ.6.14 The XYZ Ltd's financial statement contains the following information: **LO 6.2,3,4,5**

Balance sheet as at March 31, current year

Particulars	*Previous year (₹ thousand)*	*Current year (₹ thousand)*
Cash	200	160
Sundry debtors	320	400
Temporary investments	200	320
Stock	1,840	2,160
Prepaid expenses	28	12
Total current assets	2,588	3,052
Total assets	5,600	6,400
Current liabilities	640	800
15% Debentures	1,600	1,600
Equity share capital	2,000	2,000
Retained earnings	468	904

Statement of profits year ended March 31, current year

Particulars	*(₹ thousand)*
Sales	4,000
Less: Cost of goods sold	2,800
Less: Interest	160
Net profit for current year	1,040
Less: Taxes	364
Earnings after taxes	676
Dividend declared on equity shares	220

From the above, appraise the financial position of the company from the points of view of **(a)** liquidity, **(b)** solvency, **(c)** profitability, and **(d)** activity.

RQ.6.15 You have been supplied data for Royal Plastic Ltd. and its industry averages. **LO 6.2,3,4,5**

(a) Determine the indicated ratios for the Royal Plastic Ltd.

(b) Indicate the company's strengths and weaknesses in terms of liquidity, solvency and profitability, as revealed by your analysis.

Balance sheet, March 31, current year

Liabilities		*Assets*	
Equity share capital	₹1,00,000	Plant and equipment	₹1,51,000
10% Preference share capital	40,000	Cash	12,300
Retained earnings	27,400	Debtors	36,000
Long-term debt	34,000	Stock	60,800
Sundry creditors	31,500		
Outstanding expenses	1,200		
Other current liabilities	26,000		
	2,60,100		2,60,100

Statement of profit, year ended March 31, current year

Sales—net		₹2,25,000
Less: Cost of goods sold	₹1,52,500	
Selling expenses	29,500	
Administrative expenses	14,800	
Research and development expenses	6,500	
Interest	2,900	2,06,200
Earnings before taxes		18,800
Less: Income taxes (0.35)		6,580
Net income		12,220
Dividends paid to equity holders		5,000

Financial ratios of industry

1. Current ratio	2.2 : 1
2. Stock turnover (times)	2.8
3. Collection period (days)	56
4. Total debt/shareholders' equity (percentage)	45
5. Interest coverage ratio (times)	10
6. Turnover of assets (times)	1.35
7. Income before tax/sales (percentage)	11.9
8. Rate of return on shareholders' equity (percentage)	10.9

RQ.6.16 Below are selected ratios for two companies in the same industry, along with industry average: LO 6.2,3,4,5

Ratios	*A*	*B*	*Industry*
Current ratio	221	561	241
Acid-test ratio	121	301	131
Debt-asset ratio	36	5	35
Operating expenses ratio	18	17.5	20
Number of times interest earned	6	12	5
Stock turnover	8.5	6.5	7.0
Debtors turnover	11.0	15.0	11.4
Rate of return on total assets	17	10	13.5

Can we say on the basis of above ratios and information that company B is better than company A because its ratios are better in six out of eight areas (all except stock turnover and rate of return on total assets)? The company B is better than the industry average in the same six categories.

RQ.6.17 The following data are extracted from the published accounts of two companies, ABC Ltd. and XYZ Ltd., in an industry. LO 6.2,3,4,5

Particulars	*ABC Ltd.*	*XYZ Ltd.*
Sales	₹32,00,000	₹30,00,000
Net profit after tax	1,23,000	1,58,000
Equity capital (₹10 per share fully paid)	10,00,000	8,00,000
General reserves	2,32,000	6,42,000
Long-term debt	8,00,000	5,60,000
Creditors	3,82,000	5,49,000
Bank credit (short-term)	60,000	2,00,000
Fixed assets	15,99,000	15,90,000
Inventories	3,31,000	8,09,000
Other current assets	5,44,000	4,52,000

Prepare a statement of comparative ratios showing liquidity, profitability, activity and financial position of the two companies.

RQ.6.18 Hypothetical Industries Ltd. (HIL) has submitted the following projections (₹ lakh). You are required to determine yearly debt service coverage ratio (DSCR) and the average DSCR and comment. LO 6.3

Year	EAT	Interest on loan	Repayment of term loan
1	20	19	11
2	35	17	18
3	40	15	18
4	20	12	18
5	18	10	18
6	18	7	8
7	16	5	8
8	16	2	8

The net profit (EAT) has been arrived at after charging depreciation of ₹20 lakh every year.

LOD: Difficult

RQ.6.19 There are four groups of financial ratios; liquidity, leverage, activity, and profitability. Financial analysis is conducted by four types of analysts: management, equity investors, long-term creditors and short-term creditors. You are required to **(a)** explain each type of ratio, **(b)** explain the emphasis of each type of analyst, **(c)** state if the same basic approach to financial analysis should be taken by each group of analysts. LO 6.2,3,4,5

RQ.6.20 Two companies have the same amount of working capital. The paying ability of short-term maturing obligations one company is much weaker than that of the other. Explain how this could occur. LO 6.2

RQ.6.21 'A uniform system of accounts, including identical forms for balance sheets and income statements is a prerequisite of inter firm comparisons.' Elucidate. LO 6.1,7

RQ.6.22 A partial list of trend and common-size percentage for ABC Ltd. for years 1 and 2 is given below: LO 6.7

Particulars	Year 2	Year 1
Trend percentages:		
Sales (net)	120	100
Cost of goods sold	?	100
Gross profit on sales	?	100
Operating expenses and income taxes	?	100
Net income	?	100
Common size percentages:		
Sales (net)	100	100
Cost of goods sold	?	?
Gross profit on sales	40	?
Operating expenses and income taxes	20	25
Net income	20	10
		= (₹20,000)

(a) Determine the missing trend and common-size percentages.
(b) Compute the net income for year 2.

RQ.6.23 Presented below is the financial information of two companies—A and B, belonging to the same industry: LO 6.3

Particulars	*A*	*B*
Current ratio	3.2:1	2.0:1
Acid-test ratio	1.7:1	1.1:1
Debt-equity ratio (percentage)	30	40
Number of times interest earned	6	5

Assume you are loan officer of a bank and both the companies have requested a loan of equal amount to be repaid over the next two years. Based on the information above,
(a) If you could grant a loan to only one company, which would it be? Explain.
(b) If you could grant a loan to both the companies, would you be willing to do so? Explain.

RQ.6.24 Below are selected ratios for three years ending March 31 for the Worst Company Ltd: LO 6.2,3,4,5

Ratios	*Year 1*	*Year 2*	*Year 3*
Current ratio	200	500	150
Acid-test ratio	110	320	80
Debt-asset ratio	15	40	55
Operating expenses ratio	24	25	32
Number of times interest earned	6	6	(–1)
Stock turnover	5	4	3
Debtors turnover	12	10	6
Rate of return on total assets	15	10	5

Outline possible explanations for the drastic changes in some of the ratios during these years.

RQ.6.25 From the following details, prepare a statement of proprietary funds with as many details as possible: LO 6.2,4,5

(a) Stock velocity = 6
(b) Capital turnover = 2
(c) Fixed assets turnover ratio = 4
(d) Gross profit turnover ratio = 20
(e) Debtors velocity = 2 months
(f) Creditors velocity = 73 days

The gross profit was ₹60,000; Reserves and surplus amounted to ₹20,000; Closing stock was ₹5,000 in excess of opening stock.

RQ.6.26 From the following information of a textile company complete the proforma balance sheet if its sales are ₹32,00,000. **LO 6.2,3,4,5**

Sales to net worth (times)	2.3
Current debt to net worth (ratio)	42
Total debt to net worth (ratio)	75
Current ratio (times)	2.9
Net sales to inventory (times)	4.7
Average collection period (days)	64
Fixed assets to net worth (ratio)	53.2

RQ.6.27 From the following selected financials of Jet Airways for the period 2006-2011, appraise its financial health from the point of view of liquidity, solvency, and profitability.

(Amount in ₹ crore)

SELECTED FINANCIAL DATA AND RATIOS

Description	*2006*	*2007*	*2008*	*2009*	*2010*	*2011*
Share capital	86.33	86.33	86.33	86.33	86.33	86.33
Reserves and surplus	2,219.55	2,150.92	4,465.32	3,332.06	3,284.73	3,237.40
Total shareholder's fund	2,305.88	2,237.25	4,551.65	3,418.39	3,371.06	3,323.73
Long term borrowings	4,300.82	3,174.71	9,547.67	13,746.52	11,362.15	11,027.65
Short term borrowings	594.78	2,881.59	2,054.87	2,302.01	2,365.31	2,452.74
Deferred payment liability	-	-	412.50	275.00	137.50	-
Deferred tax liability	320.66	331.06	160.23	-	-	33.63
Sundry creditors	251.52	749.77	1,739.77	1,423.26	1,725.55	1,835.54
Other current liabilities	814.10	1,102.87	2,049.31	1,858.24	1,848.00	2,546.59
Provisions	262.98	248.16	189.24	178.83	144.21	186.89
Total Current Liabilities	1,923.38	4,982.39	6,033.19	5,762.34	6,083.07	7,021.76
Inventory	405.25	438.99	545.03	595.67	584.79	711.18
Sundry debtors	433.15	603.90	1,313.73	732.25	810.77	965.77
Advances	932.71	1,224.94	1,208.54	1,628.28	1,613.81	2,732.91
Cash	2,104.25	1,096.64	855.14	1,394.50	772.83	587.71
Current investments	187.23	68.93	10.35	100.00	100.00	80.00
Total Current Assets	4,062.59	3,433.40	3,932.79	4,450.70	3,882.20	5,077.57
Total fixed assets	2,122.48	3,297.49	14,084.17	16,261.94	14,429.92	13,615.81
Profit & Loss account (debit balance)/Loss	-	-	-	261.44	729.08	719.39
Liquid assets	2,724.63	1,769.47	2,179.22	2,226.75	1,683.60	1,633.48
Interest	241.60	240.15	492.75	738.03	993.01	1,028.36
Total equity	2,305.88	2,237.25	4,551.65	3,418.39	3,371.06	3,323.73
Total debt	5,216.26	6,387.36	12,175.27	16,323.53	13,864.96	13,514.02
Long term debt	4,621.48	3,505.77	10,120.40	14,021.52	11,499.65	11,061.28
Total external obligations	6,544.86	8,488.16	16,153.59	19,783.86	17,582.72	18,083.04
Total assets	8,850.74	10,725.41	20,705.24	23,202.25	20,953.78	21,406.77
Operating revenue	5,645.83	7,057.78	8,811.10	11,476.98	10,469.64	12,776.83
Non operating revenue	441.74	343.53	739.86	309.90	153.28	174.21
Total revenue	6,087.57	7,401.31	9,550.96	11,786.88	10,622.92	12,951.04
Aircraft fuel expenses	1,678.93	2,427.64	3,293.03	4,915.01	3,151.65	4,366.70
Selling and distribution expenses	726.12	800.85	982.86	1,098.17	984.91	1,261.72
Other operating expenses	2,718.66	3,881.31	5,125.46	6,670.36	6,031.35	6,418.05
Interest	241.60	240.15	492.75	738.03	993.01	1,028.36
EBT	722.26	51.36	–343.14	–1,634.69	–538.00	–123.79

EBIT	963.86	291.51	149.61	–896.66	455.01	904.57
EAT	452.04	27.94	–253.06	–402.34	–467.64	9.69
Average debtors	342.73	518.53	958.82	1,022.99	771.51	888.27
Average inventory	368.89	422.12	492.01	570.35	590.23	647.99
Average current assets	3,851.36	3,748.00	3,683.10	4,191.75	4,166.45	4,479.89
Average fixed assets	2,365.56	2,709.99	8,690.83	15,173.06	15,345.93	14,022.87
Average total assets	7,565.76	9,788.08	15,715.33	21,953.75	22,078.02	21,180.28
Average equity funds	2,158.02	2,271.57	3,394.45	3,985.02	3,394.73	3,347.40
Average capital employed	6606.7	5411.96	14099.32	17164.91	14733.21	14351.38

Financial Ratios

Particulars	*2006*	*2007*	*2008*	*2009*	*2010*	*2011*
Liquidity Ratios:						
Net working capital (₹ crore)	2,139.21	–1,548.99	–2,100.4	–1,311.64	–2,200.87	–1,944.19
Current ratio	2.11	0.69	0.65	0.77	0.64	0.72
Acid test ratio	1.42	0.36	0.36	0.39	0.28	0.23
Debtors turnover ratio	17.76	14.27	9.96	11.52	13.77	14.58
Debtors collection period (Days)	20.55	25.57	36.64	31.68	26.51	25.03
Solvency Ratios:						
Total debt to equity ratio	2.26	2.86	2.67	4.78	4.11	4.07
Long term debt to equity ratio	2.00	1.57	2.22	4.10	3.41	3.33
Total debt to assets ratio	0.59	0.60	0.59	0.70	0.66	0.63
Total external obligations to assets ratio	0.74	0.79	0.78	0.85	0.84	0.84
Interest Coverage Ratio	3.99	1.21	0.30	Negative	0.46	0.88
Profitability Ratios:						
Net profit ratio %	7.43	0.38	–2.65	–3.41	–4.40	0.07
ROR on capital employed %	12.33	4.46	2.46	2.15	3.29	7.14
ROR (Total assets) %	9.17	2.74	1.53	1.53	2.38	4.90
ROR (Equity funds) %	20.95	1.23	–7.46	–10.10	–13.78	0.29
Efficiency Ratios:						
Total assets turnover ratio	0.80	0.76	0.61	0.54	0.48	0.61
Fixed assets turnover ratio	2.57	2.73	1.10	0.78	0.69	0.92
Current assets turnover ratio	1.58	1.97	2.59	2.81	2.55	2.89

RQ.6.28 From the following selected financials of Dabur India Ltd for the period 2006-2011, appraise its financial health from the point of view of liquidity, solvency, profitability and efficiency.

Selected Financial Data of Dabur India Ltd.

1. Related to liquidity Analysis

(In ₹ crore)

Particulars	*2006*	*2007*	*2008*	*2009*	*2010*	*2011*
CURRENT ASSETS	295.23	466.04	753.62	862.83	1,163.91	1,702.86
Inventory	115.61	157.37	201.15	261.72	298.44	460.58
Debtors	26.94	60.98	100.46	112.36	130.48	202.46
Advances	73.77	117.82	181.11	227.28	321.22	430.03
Cash and bank balance	38.04	50.25	68.26	143.69	163.91	192.41
Current investments	40.87	79.62	202.64	117.78	249.86	417.38
CURRENT LIABILITIES	320.33	372.36	594.51	803.28	966.94	1,278.14

Sundry creditors	85.45	124.01	140.07	153.03	159.74	252.56
Short-term borrowings	13.02	16.28	11.88	136.79	94.78	246.50
Provisions	113.89	77.49	265.41	315.10	440.10	535.36
Other current liabilities	107.97	154.58	177.15	198.36	272.32	243.72
Net working capital	-25.10	93.68	159.11	59.55	196.97	424.72
Liquid assets	105.85	190.85	371.36	373.83	544.25	812.25
Credit sales	1,369.68	1,778.02	2,117.79	2,423.68	2,879.54	3,295.36
Cost of goods sold	462.26	640.67	829.77	951.42	1,079.75	1,322.38
Cost of raw materials used	401.52	595.63	737.20	892.13	988.10	1,274.10
Credit purchases	394.69	601.24	748.24	913.72	1,004.30	1,357.70
Average debtors	38.11	43.96	80.72	106.41	121.42	166.47
Average creditors	107.70	104.73	132.04	146.55	156.39	206.15
Average inventory	121.82	136.49	179.26	231.44	280.08	379.51
Current ratio	0.92	1.25	1.27	1.07	1.2	1.33
Acid test ratio	0.33	0.51	0.62	0.47	0.56	0.64
Debtors turnover Ratio	35.94	40.45	26.24	22.78	23.72	19.8
Creditors turnover ratio	3.66	5.74	5.67	6.23	6.42	6.59
Inventory turnover ratio	11.24	13.03	11.81	10.47	10.28	8.68
Inventory holding period (days)	32.46	28.02	30.9	34.85	35.5	42.04
Debtors cycle (days)	10.16	9.02	13.91	16.03	15.39	18.44
Creditors cycle (days)	99.59	63.58	64.41	58.54	56.84	55.42

2. Related to Solvency Analysis

	2006	*2007*	*2008*	*2009*	*2010*	*2011*
Equity capital	57.33	86.29	86.40	86.51	86.90	174.07
Reserves and surplus	390.54	316.90	441.92	651.70	662.50	927.09
Equity fund	447.87	403.19	528.32	738.20	749.38	1,101.16
Long-term borrowings	7.55	3.80	5.46	2.19	15.19	10.94
Deferred tax liabilities (net)	16.72	22.64	27.28	30.49	11.95	17.40
Short-term borrowings	13.02	16.28	11.88	136.79	94.78	246.50
Current liabilities & provisions	320.33	320.33	320.33	320.33	320.33	320.33
Long-term debt	24.27	26.44	32.74	32.68	27.14	28.34
Total debt	37.29	42.72	44.62	169.47	121.92	274.84
Total external obligations	344.60	346.77	353.07	353.01	347.47	348.67
EBT	214.36	284.22	365.18	425.00	527.03	596.26
Interest	5.66	4.43	8.55	13.34	13.49	12.93
EBIT	220.02	288.65	373.73	438.34	540.52	609.19
Total assets	792.47	749.96	881.39	1,091.21	1,096.85	1,449.83
Total debt to equity ratio	0.08	0.11	0.08	0.23	0.16	0.25
Long-term debt to equity ratio	0.05	0.07	0.06	0.04	0.04	0.03
Total debt to assets ratio	0.05	0.06	0.05	0.16	0.11	0.19
Interest coverage ratio	38.87	65.16	43.71	32.86	40.07	47.11
Long-term debt to total assets ratio	0.03	0.04	0.04	0.03	0.02	0.02

3. Related to profitability analysis

	2006	*2007*	*2008*	*2009*	*2010*	*2011*
Sales (Net)	1,375.03	1,794.54	2,083.40	2,396.16	2,855.96	3,264.37
Cost of goods sold	462.26	640.67	829.77	951.42	1,079.75	1,322.38

Gross profit	912.77	1,153.87	1,253.63	1,444.74	1,776.21	1,941.99
EBIT	220.02	288.65	373.73	438.34	540.52	609.19
EBT	214.36	284.22	365.18	425.00	527.03	596.26
EAT	188.57	252.08	316.77	373.55	433.33	471.41
Interest	5.66	4.43	8.55	13.34	13.49	12.93
Average fixed assets	195.22	218.93	266.74	327.23	405.49	474.25
Average total capital employed	401.79	431.21	470.39	637.09	752.48	938.34
Average total assets	757.09	771.22	815.68	986.30	1,094.03	1,273.34
Average equity funds	392.97	425.53	465.76	633.26	743.79	925.27
Gross profit %	66.38	64.3	60.17	60.29	62.19	59.49
Net profit ratio %	13.71	14.05	15.2	15.59	15.17	14.44
Cost of goods sold ratio %	33.62	35.7	39.83	39.71	37.81	40.51
ROR on capital employed (ROCE) %	48.34	59.49	69.16	60.73	59.38	51.62
ROR (Total assets) %	25.65	33.26	39.88	39.23	40.84	38.04
ROR (Equity funds) %	48	59	68	59	58	51

4. Related to efficiency analysis

	2006	*2007*	*2008*	*2009*	*2010*	*2011*
Sales (Net)	1,375.03	1,794.54	2,083.40	2,396.16	2,855.96	3,264.37
Average total assets	757.09	771.22	815.68	986.30	1,094.03	1,273.34
Average fixed assets	195.22	218.93	266.74	327.23	405.49	474.25
Average current assets	295.49	380.64	609.83	808.23	1,013.37	1,433.39
Debtors turnover ratio	35.94	40.45	26.24	22.78	23.72	19.8
Creditors turnover ratio	3.66	5.74	5.67	6.23	6.42	6.59
Inventory turnover ratio	11.24	13.03	11.81	10.47	10.28	8.68
Inventory holding period (days)	32.46	28.02	30.9	34.85	35.5	42.04
Debtors cycle (days)	10.16	9.02	13.91	16.03	15.39	18.44
Creditors cycle (days)	99.59	63.58	64.41	58.54	56.84	55.42
Current assets turnover ratio	4.65	4.71	3.42	2.96	2.82	2.28
Fixed assets turnover ratio	7.04	8.2	7.81	7.32	7.04	6.88
Total assets turnover ratio	1.82	2.33	2.55	2.43	2.61	2.56

ANSWERS

RQ.6.13 **(a)** **(i)** 3:1, **(ii)** 1.48:1, **(iii)** 7 times, **(iv)** 12.12 times, **(v)** 23 per cent, **(vi)** 3.9 per cent, **(vii)** 94 per cent, **(viii)** ₹15.6 **(ix)** 11.4 per cent, **(x)** ₹156,

(b) **(i)** Improve, **(ii)** Improve, **(iii)** Improve, **(iv)** No effect, **(v)** Weaken, **(vi)** No effect, **(vii)** No effect, **(viii)** No effect, **(ix)** Weaken.

RQ.6.14 The company's position is sound from the points of view of **(a)** liquidity, **(b)** profitability but its activity ratios do not seem to be adequate.

RQ.6.15 **(a)** **(1)** 1.86, **(2)** 2.51 times, **(3)** 58 days, **(4)** 55 per cent, **(5)** 7.48 times, **(6)** 0.58 times, **(7)** 8.36 per cent, **(8)** 5.45 per cent. **(b)** Company's position both in terms of profitability and solvency is weaker than that of industry.

RQ.6.16 Not necessarily.

RQ.6.17 ABC Limited is better placed than XYZ Ltd. in respect of liquidity, activity and solvency ratios; XYZ Limited has an edge over ABC Limited in respect of profitability ratio.

RQ.6.18 Average DSCR is 2.46; it is very satisfactory.

RQ.6.22 **(a)** Trend percentages: Cost of goods sold 110.8 per cent, Gross profit on sales 137.14 per cent, Operating expenses and income taxes 96.00 per cent, Net income 240 per cnet; Common-size percentages: Cost of goods sold 60 per cent year 2 and 65 per cent year 1, Gross profit on sales 35 per cent year 1 **(b)** Net income ₹48,000.

RQ.6.23 **(a)** Loan would be granted to company A on account of its lower debt-equity ratio and higher interest coverage ratio. **(b)** Yes. Company B's debt-equity ratio of 40 per cent and interest coverage ratio of 5 times are fairly satisfactory solvency ratios.

RQ.6.24 The reasons for the drastic changes may be conceived in terms of the **(a)** high operating expenses ratio not matched by increase in sales price, **(b)** excessive interest cost due to large amount of borrowings, **(c)** higher inventory cost, and **(d)** liberal grant of credit causing bad debts.

RQ.6.25 Proprietary funds, ₹1,20,000, Fixed assets, ₹60,000, Stock, ₹42,500, Debtors, ₹50,000, Cash, ₹16,500 and Creditors, ₹49,000.

RQ.6.26 Net worth ₹13,91,304, Long term debt ₹4,59,130, Current debt ₹5,84,348, Fixed assets ₹7,40,173, Cash ₹4,44,869, Stock ₹6,80,851 and S. debtors ₹5,68,889. Total of balance sheet ₹24,34,782.

[Comprehensive solutions to all numerical review questions are available on the companion website: http://www.mhhe.com/khan_jain_ma7e]

CASES

C.6.1 From the following selected financials of RIL for the period 2004-5 to 2015-16, appraise its financial health from the point of view of liquidity, solvency, profitability and efficiency.

Selected financial data and ratios (Amount in ₹ crore)

Description	2005	2006	2007	2008	2009	2010	2011	2012	2013	2014	2015	2016
(I) Related to Liquidity Analysis												
CURRENT ASSETS	24,258.04	22,062.33	25,908.92	40,133.24	53,051.10	67,870.64	93,814	1,28,175.00	1,40,302.00	130,967	109,389.00	85,591.00
Inventory	7,412.88	10,119.82	12,136.51	14,247.54	14,836.72	26,981.62	29,825	35,955	42,729	42,932	36,551.00	28,034.00
Debtors	3,927.81	4,163.62	3,732.42	6,227.58	4,571.38	11,660.21	17,442	18,424	11,880	10,664	4,661.00	3,495.00
Loans & Advances	3,711.64	3,609.84	6,024.56	12,019.68	8,545.04	7,247.20	9,851	6,920	7,300	6,911	5,544.00	6,965.00
Current Investments	3,509.26	1,997.83	2,177.01	3,285.85	2,873.57	8,427.56	9,361	27,029	28,366	33,370	50,515.00	39,429.00
Cash and bank balance	3,608.79	2,146.16	1,835.35	4,280.05	22,176.53	13,462.65	27,135	39,598	49,547	36,624	11,571.00	6,892.00
Other current assets	2,087.66	25.06	3.07	72.54	47.86	91.4	199	249	480	466	547.00	776.00
CURRENT LIABILITIES	20,572.23	21,804.33	26,741.53	32,560.59	41,928.87	45,650.70	66,525	68,888	83,286	95,566	91,301.00	125,022.00
Short-term bank borrowings	3,440.71	5,349.85	8,163.13	8,522.50	6,226.97	5,950.29	12,304	10,593	11,511	22,770	12,914.00	14,490.00
Trade Payables	13,209.76	12,166.87	16,467.24	20,590.45	31,579.09	36,055.60	48,846	40,324	45,787	57,862	54,470.00	54,521.00
Other current liabilities	449.96	396.63	398.29	455.02	1,111.91	79.38	811	13,713	21,640	10,767	19,063.00	54,841.00
Short-term provisions	3,471.80	3,890.98	1,712.87	2,992.62	3,010.90	3,565.43	4,563	4,258	4,348	4,167	4,854.00	1,170.00
Net working capital	3,685.81	258	–832.61	7,572.65	11,122.23	22,219.94	27,289	59,287	57,016	35,401	18,088.00	–39,431.00
Credit sales	73,164.10	89,124.16	1,18,353.71	1,39,269.46	1,46,328.07	2,00,399.79	2,58,651.20	3,39,721	3,71,021	4,01,200	340,727.00	251,100.00
Cost of goods sold	52,939.81	63,325.00	87,830.79	1,07,100.52	1,19,021.00	1,64,818.70	2,13,307.60	2,97,023	3,25,405	3,55,773	293,312.00	188,056.00
Cost of raw material used	43,575.32	55,826.18	76,871.66	90,303.85	1,04,805.05	1,47,919.20	1,93,233.90	2,74,814	3,06,127	3,29,313	255,998.00	152,769.00
Credit purchases	45,771.35	58,763.24	78,988.52	1,00,240.39	1,04,729.50	1,59,825.60	1,94,251.30	2,81,029	3,08,981	3,31,589	258,652.00	152,321.00
Average debtors	3,558.87	4,045.71	3,948.02	4,980.00	5,399.48	8,115.80	14,551	17,933	15,152	11,272	7,662.00	5,106.00
Average creditors	11,515.68	12,688.32	14,317.06	18,528.85	26,084.77	33,817.35	42,451	44,585	43,056	51,825	56,166.00	54,495.00
Current ratio	1.18	1.01	0.97	1.23	1.27	1.49	1.41	1.86	1.68	1.37	1.20	0.68

Acid test ratio	0.64	0.38	0.29	0.43	0.71	0.74	0.81	1.24	1.08	0.85	0.74	0.40
Debtors turnover	20.56	22.03	29.98	27.97	27.1	24.69	17.78	18.94	24.49	35.59	44.47	49.18
Creditors turnover	3.97	4.63	5.52	5.41	4.01	4.73	4.58	6.3	7.18	6.4	4.61	2.80
Debtors cycle (days)	17.8	16.61	12.21	13.09	13.51	14.82	20.59	19.32	14.91	10.25	8.20	7.42
Creditors cycle (days)	92.08	79.03	66.34	67.65	91.16	77.44	79.98	58.07	50.86	57.05	79.34	130.59
(II) Related to Solvency Analysis												
Share Capital	1,393.09	1,393.17	1,393.21	1,453.39	1,573.53	3,270.37	3,273.37	3,271.00	3,229.00	3,232	3,236.00	3,240.00
Equity Share Suspense	0	0	60.14	0	69.25	0	0	0	0	0	0.00	0.00
Equity Share Warrants	0	0	0	1,682.40	0	0	0	0	0	0	0.00	0.00
Reserves and surplus	39,010.23	48,411.09	62,513.78	78,312.81	1,24,730.19	1,33,900.24	1,48,266.95	1,62,825.00	1,76,766.00	1,93,842.00	212,923.00	236,936.00
Shareholders' fund	**40,403.32**	**49,804.26**	**63,967.13**	**81,448.60**	**1,26,372.97**	**1,37,170.61**	**1,51,540.32**	**1,66,096.00**	**1,79,995.00**	**1,97,074.00**	**216,159.00**	**240,176.00**
Long-term borrowings	15,343.88	16,515.76	19,662.60	27,957.18	67,677.51	56,544.40	55,092.34	48,034.00	43,012.00	62,711	76,227.00	77,866.00
Short-term bank borrowings	3,440.71	5,349.85	8,163.13	8,522.50	6,226.97	5,950.29	12,304.34	10,593.00	11,511.00	22,770	12,914.00	14,490.00
Deferred Tax Liability	4,266.82	4,970.82	6,982.02	7,872.54	9,726.30	10,926.30	11,561.80	12,122.00	12,193.00	12,215	12,677.00	13,159.00
Total debt	**23,051.41**	**26,836.43**	**34,807.75**	**44,352.22**	**83,630.78**	**73,420.99**	**78,958.48**	**70,749.00**	**66,716.00**	**97,696**	**101,818.00**	**105,515.00**
Long term debt	19,610.70	21,486.58	26,644.62	35,829.72	77,403.81	67,470.70	66,654.14	60,156.00	55,205.00	74,926	90,308.00	92,514.00
Total External obligations	40,182.93	43,290.91	53,386.15	68,390.31	1,19,332.68	1,13,121.40	1,33,179.08	1,29,044.00	1,38,491.00	1,70,492.00	180,205.00	216,047.00
EBT	9,068.68	10,704.06	14,520.47	23,010.14	18,433.23	20,547.44	25,242.24	25,750.00	26,284.00	27,818	29,468.00	35,701.00
Interest	1,468.66	877.04	1,188.89	1,077.36	1,745.23	1,997.21	2,327.62	1,966.00	2,574.00	1,867	1,540.00	1,527.00
EBIT	10,537.34	11,581.10	15,709.36	24,087.50	20,178.46	22,544.65	27,569.86	27,716.00	28,858.00	29,685	31,008.00	37,228.00
Total Assets	**80,586.25**	**93,095.17**	**1,17,353.28**	**1,49,838.91**	**2,45,705.65**	**2,50,292.01**	**2,84,719.40**	**2,95,140.00**	**3,18,486.00**	**3,67,566.00**	**397,785.00**	**457,720.00**
Total debt-equity ratio	0.57	0.54	0.54	0.54	0.66	0.54	0.52	0.43	0.37	0.5	0.47	0.44

Long-term debt-equity ratio	0.49	0.43	0.42	0.44	0.61	0.49	0.44	0.36	0.31	0.38	0.42	0.39
Interest coverage ratio	7.17	13.2	13.21	22.36	11.56	11.29	11.84	14.1	11.21	15.9	20.14	24.38
total debt asset ratio	0.29	0.29	0.3	0.3	0.34	0.29	0.28	0.24	0.21	0.27	0.26	0.23
Long term debt asset ratio	0.24	0.23	0.23	0.24	0.32	0.27	0.23	0.2	0.17	0.2	0.23	0.20
Total External obligations to asset ratio	0.5	0.47	0.45	0.46	0.49	0.45	0.47	0.44	0.43	0.46	0.45	0.47
(III) Related to Profitability Analysis												
Revenue from operations	66,051.30	81,211.33	1,11,692.72	1,33,443.00	1,41,847.47	1,92,461.02	2,48,170.00	3,29,904.00	3,97,062.00	3,90,117.00	329,076.00	233,158.00
Cost of goods sold	53,345.03	65,535.84	83,015.64	1,02,253.38	1,19,021.00	1,64,818.70	2,13,307.60	2,97,023.00	3,25,405.00	3,55,773.00	293,312.00	188,056.00
Gross Profit	12,706.27	15,675.49	28,677.08	31,189.62	22,826.47	27,642.32	34,862.40	32,881.00	71,657.00	34,344.00	35,764.00	45,102.00
EBIT	10,537.34	11,581.10	15,709.36	24,087.50	20,178.46	22,544.65	27,569.86	27,716.00	28,858.00	29,685.00	31,008.00	37,228.00
Other Incomes	1,449.81	682.92	478.28	5,628.79	2,059.88	2,460.47	3,051.71	6,192.00	7,867.00	8,936.00	8,721.00	7,582.00
Operating profit	9,087.53	10,898.18	15,231.08	18,458.71	18,118.58	20,084.18	24,518.15	21,524.00	20,991.00	20,749.00	22,287.00	29,646.00
EAT	7,571.68	9,069.34	11,943.40	19,458.29	15,309.32	16,235.67	20,286.30	20,040.00	21,003.00	21,984.00	22,719.00	27,417.00
Average total capital employed	52,978.70	61,033.61	74,974.88	96,517.76	1,51,728.13	1,93,882.75	2,00,173.84	2,10,381.33	2,18,568.50	2,41,396.00	276,084.00	305,214.00
Average total assets	76,206.70	86,840.71	1,05,224.23	1,33,596.10	1,97,772.28	2,47,998.83	2,67,505.71	2,89,929.70	3,06,813.00	3,43,026.00	382,684.00	427,753.00
Average equity funds	37,427.89	45,103.79	56,885.70	72,707.87	1,03,910.79	1,31,771.79	1,44,355.47	1,58,818.16	1,73,045.50	1,88,535.00	206,616.00	228,168.00
Gross profit %	19.24	19.3	25.67	23.37	16.09	14.36	14.05	9.97	18.05	8.8	10.87	19.34
Operating profit ratio %	13.76	13.42	13.64	13.83	12.77	10.44	9.88	6.52	5.29	5.32	6.77	12.71
Net profit ratio %	11.46	11.17	10.69	14.58	10.79	8.44	8.17	6.07	5.29	5.64	6.90	11.76
Cost of goods sold ratio%	80.76	80.7	74.33	76.63	83.91	85.64	85.95	90.03	81.95	91.2	89.13	80.66
ROR (Equity funds)	20.23	20.11	21	26.76	14.73	12.32	14.05	12.62	13.62	12.65	11.00	12.02

ROR on capital employed (ROCE)1	17.06	16.3	17.52	21.28	11.24	9.4	11.3	10.46	10.79	9.88	8.23	8.98
ROR (Total assets)2	11.86	11.45	12.48	15.37	8.62	7.35	8.45	7.59	7.68	6.95	5.94	6.41
(IV) Related to Efficiency Analysis												
Cost of raw materials used	43,575.32	55,826.18	76,871.66	90,303.85	1,04,805.05	1,47,919.20	1,93,233.90	2,74,814.00	3,06,127.00	3,29,313.00	255,998.00	152,769.00
Average raw materials inventory	3,315.10	3,958.83	4,317.08	6,429.29	7,253.28	10,568.13	14,800.00	16,963.00	20,526.00	22,578.00	21,214.00	16,629.00
Cost of goods manufactured	52,196.39	64,688.04	89,214.01	1,05,598.14	1,18,778.63	1,68,081.63	2,14,520.40	2,97,591.00	3,28,230.00	3,55,025.00	292,650.00	186,242.00
Average stock in process	861.92	1,355.53	1,814.17	1,706.35	1,858.93	2,536.37	3,893.98	5,089.00	5,817.50	6,453.50	5,877.00	4,040.00
Cost of goods sold	52,939.81	63,325.00	87,830.79	1,07,100.52	1,19,021.00	1,64,818.70	2,13,307.60	2,97,023.00	3,25,405.00	3,55,773.00	293,312.00	188,056.00
Average total assets	76,206.70	86,840.71	1,05,224.23	1,33,596.10	1,97,772.28	2,47,998.83	2,67,505.71	2,89,929.70	3,06,813.00	3,43,026.00	382,684.00	427,753.00
Average fixed assets	31,021.08	42,984.87	59,688.61	62,772.05	81,113.35	1,26,801.47	1,47,983.18	1,28,215.00	1,11,735.50	1,09,577.00	111,985.00	122,986.00
Average capital employed	52,978.70	61,033.61	74,974.88	96,517.76	1,51,728.13	1,93,882.75	2,00,173.84	2,10,381.33	2,18,568.50	2,41,396.00	276,084.00	305,214.00
Average current assets	20,055.98	23,160.19	23,985.63	33,021.08	46,592.17	60,460.87	80,842.20	1,14,111.00	1,34,238.50	1,35,634.50	120,178.00	97,490.00
Net working capital	3,685.81	258	–832.61	7,572.65	11,122.23	22,219.94	27,288.81	59,287.00	57,016.00	35,401.00	18,088.00	(39,431.00)
Net sales	66,051.30	81,211.33	1,11,692.72	1,33,443.00	1,41,847.47	1,92,461.02	2,48,170.00	3,29,904.00	3,97,062.00	3,90,117.00	329,076.00	233,158.00
Raw materials turnover ratio	13.14	14.1	17.81	14.05	14.45	14	13.06	16.2	14.91	14.59	12.07	9.19
Raw materials holding period (in days)	27.77	25.88	20.5	25.99	25.26	26.08	27.96	22.53	24.47	25.02	30.27	39.76
Stock in process turnover ratio	60.56	47.72	49.18	61.89	63.9	66.27	55.09	58.48	56.42	55.01	49.80	46.10
Stock in process cycle (in days)	6.03	7.65	7.42	5.9	5.71	5.51	6.63	6.24	6.47	6.63	7.33	7.92
Total assets turnover ratio (Based on COGS)	0.69	0.73	0.83	0.8	0.6	0.66	0.8	1.02	1.06	1.04	0.77	0.44

Total assets turnover ratio (Based on sales)	0.87	0.94	1.06	1	0.72	0.78	0.93	1.14	1.29	1.14	0.86	0.55
Fixed assets turnover ratio(Based on COGS)	1.71	1.47	1.47	1.71	1.47	1.3	1.44	2.32	2.91	3.25	2.62	1.53
Fixed assets turnover ratio (Based on sales)	2.13	1.89	1.87	2.13	1.75	1.52	1.68	2.57	3.55	3.56	2.94	1.90
Capital turnover ratio	1.25	1.33	1.49	1.38	0.93	0.99	1.24	1.57	1.82	1.62	1.06	0.62
Current assets turnover ratio (Based on COGS)	2.64	2.73	3.66	3.24	2.55	2.73	2.64	2.6	2.42	2.62	2.44	1.93
Current assets turnover ratio (Based on sales)	3.29	3.51	4.66	4.04	3.04	3.18	3.07	2.89	2.96	2.88	2.74	2.39
Working capital turnover ratio	17.92	314.77	–134.15	17.62	12.75	8.66	9.09	5.56	6.96	11.02	18.19	–5.91

Notes:

1. Liquid assets = Total current assets – Inventories – Advances
2. Cost of goods sold = Opening stock of finished goods + Production cost* – Closing stock of finished goods
3. Production cost* = Opening stock in process + Raw material consumed + Cash manufacturing expenses + Depreciation + Other purchases (as per profit and loss account) – Closing stock in process
4. Total credit purchases = Purchases of raw materials* + Other purchases
5. Purchases of raw material* = Raw material consumed + Closing stock of raw materials – Opening stock of raw materials
6. Total assets = Shareholders' funds + Long term borrowings + Deferred tax liability + Current liability & provisions
7. Total external obligations = Long term borrowings + Current liabilities & provisions + Deferred tax liability
8. Average total capital employed = Average long term assets used (excluding capital work-in-progress as it does not contribute to operating income) + Net working capital
9. EBIT = EBT + Interest
10. ROCE = (EAT + Interest) / Average capital employed
11. ROR (Total assets) = (EAT + Interest) / Average assets
12. Cost of goods manufactured = Cost of goods sold + Closing stock of finished goods – Opening stock of finished goods

Solution

The appraisal of financial health of RIL is presented below.

I. Liquidity Analysis: The liquidity position of RIL during the period of 2005-16 has shown both upward and downward trends. For instance, in the initial years, the current ratio was alarmingly low (1.01 in 2006 and less than one, i.e., 0.97 in 2007). Then, it steadily improved through the years 2008 to 2013 and increased from 1.23 to 1.68. However, in the subsequent years, from 2014, the current ratio witnessed a downward trend again. It decreased to 1.37 in 2014 to 1.20 in 2015 and finally was at alarmingly low level of less than one, in 2016. This sharp decrease in current ratio is a matter of concern. The closer analysis indicates that from 2015 to 2016, there has been a reduction in inventory, debtors, cash and bank balances and current investment; further, there has been a significant increase in 'other current liabilities', which has been the main driver for pulling the current ratio below 1.

We observe a similar pattern for the acid test ratio. A very low ratio in the initial years (0.38 in 2006 and 0.27 in 2007), has steadily improved from 2008 to 2012. In fact, in 2012 and 2013, the ratio was very satisfactory at 1.24 and 1.08 respectively (Conventionally, the ratio of 1:1 is considered satisfactory). However, from 2014 onwards acid test ratio started declining. It reached an alarmingly low level of 0.40 in 2016. Following the trend of current ratio, we find that significant increase in 'other current liabilities' along with decrease in debtors, cash and bank balances and current investment have contributed to such low/ unsatisfactory levels of acid test ratio.

The other notable observation is that RIL seems to be banking on bank borrowings (may be in the form of cash credit, enabling it to operate at lower liquidity ratios) to finance its working capital requirements as reflected in a substantial increase in such borrowing over the years. From ₹3,440.71 crore (in 2005), the amount steadily increased to ₹8,522.50 crore (by 2008) and to ₹10,593 crore by 2012 and finally touching ₹14,490 crore by 2016 (registering more than 4 times increase in 2016 compared to 2005).

The net working capital position has shown both an upward and downward trend during the period 2005-16. During the period 2008-2013, the net working capital position showed commendable improvement. From the negative sum of ₹832.61 crore in 2007, the amount has consistently increased over the years, the relevant figures being ₹27,288.81 crore and 59,287 crore in 2011 and 2012 respectively. From 2014, the net working capital has started to decline from ₹35,401 crore in 2014 to ₹18,088 crore in 2015 and has become negative ₹39,431 crore in 2016.

The other notable observation is that RIL has the advantage of much higher creditors payment period compared to debtors collection period. The debtors collection period (varying from 17 days in 2005 to around 20 days in 2012) has shown a further improvement in that the collection period has decreased to 10 days in 2014 and 7 days in 2016. Evidently, the debtors collection period is at a very satisfactory level.

In marked contrast, the creditors payment period is very high. It varied in the range of 66 days to 92 days till 2015. However; in 2016, it saw a sharp rise to 130 days. In 2016, the creditors payment period is 18 times the debtors collection period. This favourable gap provides some leverage to RIL to operate at relatively low liquidity ratios. However, a point of caution must not be ignored here. RIL has witnessed decreasing revenues from 2014 to 2016. A very low debtors turnover ratio could be responsible for the same and requires thorough investigation.

To conclude, the liquidity position of RIL at present does not appear to be satisfactory; it needs improvement.

II. Solvency Ratios: The solvency position of RIL is sound for two reasons: First, it has a satisfactory level of interest coverage ratio during all these years, being in the impressive range of 7.17 and 24.38. It is not likely to commit default in payment of interest to its lenders as its operating profits (EBIT) have incredible margins to meet its interest obligations.

Secondly, its various capital structure ratios have shown a substantial decrease (improvement) over the years. For instance, its total debt to equity ratio has shown a notable decrease from 0.57 in 2005 to 0.44 by 2016. Likewise, long-term debt to equity ratio has registered a substantial decrease from 0.49 in 2005 to 0.39 by 2016. Similarly, total external obligations to assets ratio has recorded a decrease (albeit small) over the years. In view of this commendable financial statistics, it can be concluded that solvency position of RIL is sound. As a result, it enjoys a very high credit rating among international credit rating agencies as well as domestic ones.

III. Profitability Ratios: The profit margins (gross, operating and net) of the RIL over the years had increased in the initial years (2005-08). After that (from 2009-12), the gross, operating and net profit margins have declined significantly. For instance, gross profit margins have declined to 9.97%, operating profit margins declined to 6.52% and net profit margins to 6.07% in the year 2012. Then, in the year 2013, gross profit margin hit a high of 18%, but subsequently dropped to 8% and 10% in 2014 and 2015 respectively. It has again shown a sharp rise in 2016, by jumping straight up to 19%.

The operating profit ratio and net margin ratio remained relatively stable at around 6% from 2012 to 2015. But, in 2016, they also jumped to 12% and 11% respectively.

This trend in operating profit margins has had an impact on the ROR on capital employed which has come down from 21.28% in 2008 to 10.46% in 2012 and is now at 8.98% in 2016.

It is also significant to note that there has been a significant decline in other rates of return too. For instance, the ROR on total assets has come down to 7.35% in 2010 from 15.37% in 2008. It has been consistently decreasing since 2009 and touched 5.94% in 2015. However, it showed improvement in 2016 by increasing to 6.41%.

Likewise, a notable decrease has been observed in ROR on equity funds. From 26.76 percent in 2008, it has decreased to 12.62% in 2012. Since then, it has been relatively stable in the range of 11 percent to 12% till 2016.

All this decline is primarily (perhaps) attributable to increase in the cost of goods sold ratio which touched a peak level of 90% in 2012 from 76 percent in 2008. Even when the cost of goods sold ratio declined considerably from 90% in 2012 to 80% in 2016, considerable improvement in ROR has not been noticed.

In conclusion, the profitability position of Reliance is less satisfactory and declining profits is a matter of concern and requires investigation.

IV. Efficiency: In terms of inventory turnover, raw materials holding period has varied in the range of 20 to 30 days during the period 2005-11. This period, *prima-facie*, appears to be satisfactory. However, it showed a sharp increase to 39 days in 2016. Such high inventory holding period merits a close examination.

In terms of debtors, debtors collection period of 20 to 28 days till 2012 appears to be satisfactory. However, its subsequent decrease to 7 days in 2016 compared to 13 days in 2013 though *prima-facie*, is a sign of notable improvement in the efficiency of debtors collection department, it needs to be carefully evaluated as the lower credit period offered to debtors may or could be the cause of lower sales (and hence of unsatisfactory profits) of RIL.

The Current assets turnover ratio during the period under study has been in the range of 2.89 to 4.66.

The fixed assets turnover ratio varied from 1.30 in 2010 to 2.62 in 2015. However, it has shown a sharp decrease in 2016 to 1.53.

RIL, being a capital intensive industry, the ratio of more than 2 (in most of the year, 2010-2016) seems to be indicative of the fact that long-term assets, by and large, operate at their higher levels of capacity.

To summarise its financial position, RIL has a sound solvency position. However, its liquidity position at present (2016) does not appear to be satisfactory. It needs improvement. Although its business operations are profitable, its margins of profits (on sales) as well as rates of return (on total assets, on capital employed and equity funds) have witnessed decline during 2012-16. Finally, it goes to the credit of RIL that it manages its assets/resources (by and large) well (as indicated by efficiency ratios).

C.6.2 From the following selected financials of ITC for the period 2011-12 to 2015-16, appraise its financial health from the point of view of liquidity, solvency, profitability and efficiency.

(Figures in ₹ crore)

Particulars	*2011-12*	*2012-13*	*2013-14*	*2014-15*	*2015-16*
(I) Related to Liquidity Analysis					
CURRENT ASSETS	14443.57	17591.47	20928.73	23955.03	24134.74
Current Investment	4363.31	5059.43	6311.26	5963.82	6461.34
Inventory	5637.83	6600.20	7359.54	7836.76	8519.82
Trade receivables	986.02	1163.34	2165.36	1722.40	1686.35
Cash and bank balances	2818.93	3615.00	3289.37	7588.61	6563.95
Short-term loans and advances	500.59	512.14	783.51	549.89	501.84
Other current assets	136.89	641.36	1019.69	293.55	401.44
CURRENT LIABILITIES	9101.83	10330.73	11504.32	11681.91	14587.86
Short-term bank borrowings	1.77	0.00	0.14	0.02	3.60
Trade payables	1424.84	1668.98	1987.59	1904.62	2265.59
Other current liabilities	3371.27	3528.62	3631.88	3671.18	4000.08
Short-term provisions	4303.95	5133.13	5884.71	6106.09	8318.59
Credit sales	34871.86	41809.82	46712.62	49964.82	51582.45
Cost of goods sold	12631.09	14747.90	17213.41	18219.98	17380.36
Cost of raw materials used	7660.91	8936.21	10263.28	10987.83	11054.75
Credit purchases	9698.12	12312.13	13284.75	14886.49	13644.83
Average debtors	935.56	1072.86	1664.35	1943.88	1704.38
Average creditors	1410.08	1559.10	1828.29	1946.11	2085.11
Current ratio	1.59	1.70	1.82	2.05	1.65
Acid test ratio	0.97	1.06	1.18	1.38	1.07
Net working capital	5341.74	7260.74	9424.41	12273.12	9546.88
Debtors turnover ratio	37.27	38.97	28.07	25.70	30.26
Creditors turnover ratio	6.88	7.90	7.27	7.65	6.54
Debtors cycle(days)	9.79	9.37	13.00	14.20	12.06
Creditors cycle(days)	53.07	46.22	50.23	47.72	55.78
(II) Related to Solvency Analysis					
Share Capital	781.84	790.18	795.32	801.55	804.72
Reserves and Surplus	18010.05	21497.67	25466.70	29934.14	32124.28
Shareholder's Funds	**18791.89**	**22287.85**	**26262.02**	**30735.69**	**32929.00**
Long Term Borrowings	77.32	66.40	51.00	38.69	25.83
Short Term Borrowings	1.70	0.00	0.14	0.02	3.60

Deferred Tax liabilities	872.72	1203.72	1296.96	1631.60	1848.42
Total Debt	**951.74**	**1270.12**	**1348.10**	**1670.31**	**1877.85**
Long Term Debt	950.04	1270.12	1347.96	1670.29	1874.25
Total External Borrowings	10174.51	11729.58	12967.37	13459.97	16589.43
EBT	8897.53	10684.18	12659.11	13997.52	14958.39
Interest	66.98	65.97	2.95	35.41	49.13
EBIT	8964.51	10750.15	12662.06	14032.93	15007.52
Total Assets	**28966.40**	**34017.43**	**39299.39**	**44195.66**	**49518.43**
Total debt-equity ratio	0.05	0.06	0.05	0.05	0.06
Long term debt-equity ratio	0.05	0.06	0.05	0.05	0.06
Interest coverage Ratio	133.84	162.96	4292.22	396.30	305.47
Total debt to asset Ratio	0.03	0.04	0.03	0.04	0.04
Long term debt to assets Ratio	0.03	0.04	0.03	0.04	0.04
Total external obligations to assets Ratio	0.35	0.34	0.33	0.30	0.34
(III) Related to Profitability					
Revenue from operations	25173.82	29901.27	33238.6	36507.4	36837.39
Cost of goods sold	12631.09	14747.90	17213.41	18219.98	17380.36
Gross profit	12542.73	15153.37	16025.19	18287.42	19457.03
EBIT	8964.51	10750.15	12662.06	14032.93	15007.52
Other income	825.34	938.7	1107.14	1543.13	1803.74
Operating profit	8139.17	9811.45	11554.92	12489.80	13203.78
EAT	6162.37	7418.39	8785.21	9607.73	9844.71
Average net block	8722.15	10154.27	11611.04	13095.62	14191.51
Average total capital employed	17587.82	22198.91	25429.34	30399.61	32429.74
Average total assets	27200.11	31502.82	36623.41	41712.53	46857.05
Average equity funds	17372.58	20539.87	24274.94	28498.86	31832.35
Gross profit ratio	50%	51%	48%	50%	53%
Operating profit ratio	32%	33%	35%	34%	36%
Net profit ratio	24%	25%	26%	26%	27%
Cost of goods sold ratio	50%	49%	52%	50%	47%
ROR on capital employed	51%	48%	50%	46%	46%
ROR on total assets	33%	34%	35%	34%	32%
ROR on equity funds	35%	36%	36%	34%	31%
(IV) Related to Efficiency Analysis					
Cost of materials used	7660.91	8936.21	10263.28	10987.83	11054.75
Cost of goods sold	12631.09	14747.90	17213.41	18219.98	17380.36

Average total assets	27200.11	31502.82	36623.41	41712.53	46857.05
Average fixed assets	8722.15	10154.27	11611.04	13095.62	14191.51
Average capital employed	17587.82	22198.91	25429.34	30399.61	32429.74
Average current assets	13744.56	16027.26	19260.10	22441.88	24044.89
Net working capital	5341.74	7260.74	9424.41	12273.12	9546.88
Net sales	25173.82	29901.27	33238.60	36507.40	36837.39
Total assets turnover ratio (based on COGS)	0.46	0.47	0.47	0.44	0.37
Total assets turnover ratio (based on Sales)	0.93	0.95	0.91	0.88	0.79
Fixed assets turnover ratio (based on COGS)	1.45	1.45	1.48	1.39	1.22
Fixed assets turnover ratio (based on Sales)	2.89	2.94	2.86	2.79	2.60
Capital turnover ratio	0.72	0.66	0.68	0.60	0.54
Current assets turnover ratio (based on COGS)	0.92	0.92	0.89	0.81	0.72
Current assets turnover ratio (based on Sales)	1.83	1.87	1.73	1.63	1.53
Working Capital Turnover ratio	2.36	2.03	1.83	1.48	1.82

Solution

The appraisal of the financial health of ITC is presented below:

I. Liquidity Analysis: The liquidity ratios of ITC appears to be satisfactory. In 2011, the current ratio was around 1.59 and it increased to 2.05 in 2014-15. Conventionally, a ratio of 2:1 is considered satisfactory. However, in 2015-16, the current ratio took a sharp decrease to 1.65. Closer analysis shows that there has been a substantial increase in current liabilities, contributing to the decrease in current ratio.

Similar trends are observed for the acid test ratio. A ratio of 0.97 in 2011-12, got stronger over the years and touched a high of 1.38 in 2014-15. However, it decreased in 2015-16 and reached 1.07 by the end of the 2016. A quick ratio of 1:1 is considered ideal, which ITC has maintained throughout.

Another observation is that net working capital of ITC has consistently increased during the period under reference. But, it has improved from ₹5,341 crores in 2011-12 to ₹12,273 crores in 2014-15. There has been a decline in net working capital in 2016 to ₹9,546 crores; in spite of this decrease, the liquidity position of ITC can be considered as satisfactory.

We also observe that ITC is enjoying a much higher creditors payment period as compared to the debtors collection period. The debtors collection period varied in the range of 9-12 days during 2012-16. In contrast, the creditors payment period was in the range of 53-55 days during the same period. This favourable gap provides leverage for the company and ensures better liquidity position of ITC to meet its short-term maturing obligations in time.

II. Solvency Analysis: The solvency position of ITC appears robust. Firstly, the interest coverage ratio is exorbitantly high. It was already very high i.e. 133 in 2011, and this further increased to become 305 in 2016. With such high ratio, the company is not likely to face any problem paying in interest to its lenders.

The various leverage ratios have been relatively stable and shows ITC does not heavily depend on debt for its financing. The total debt to assets ratio has been around 0.03 to 0.04 during the period under study. Similarly, the long-term debt to assets ratio has also been in the same range. Total debt to equity and long term debt to equity ratio has been stable around 0.05 to 0.06.

Evidently, the solvency position of the company is very sound.

III. Profitability Analysis: The profitability analysis is equally impressive. Over the years, there has been stability in its profitability ratios. For instance, the gross profit ratio has been in the range of 48% to 53%. Its net profit ratio also is stable in the range of 24% to 27%.

The rates of return on capital employed as well as total assets are also notable. For instance, ROR on capital employed has been as high as 51% and ROR on total assets touched a high of 35% in 2013-14. The ROR on equity funds is also lucrative at 31% to 35% during the five year period of the study.

IV. Efficiency Ratios: Analysing the performance with respect to utilisation of assets, we find it is unsatisfactory. The fixed assets turnover ratio has substantially declined from 2.89 in 2011-12 to 2.60 in 2015-16. The Current assets turnover ratio has also declined from 1.83 in 2011-12 to 1.53 in 2015-16. Better utilisation of assets can further augment its profitability.

To conclude, the financial health of ITC is sound given its liquidity, solvency and profitability ratios. However, the efficiency ratios have potential for further improvement.

C.6.3 From the following selected financials of Tata Motors for the period 2011-12 to 2015-16, appraise its financial health from the point of view of liquidity, solvency, profitability and efficiency.

(Amount in ₹ crore)

Particulars	*2011-12*	*2012-13*	*2013-14*	*2014-15*	*2015-16*
(I) Related to Liquidity Analysis					
CURRENT ASSETS	13633.39	10027.16	6700.55	8506.83	10616.45
Current Investment	2590.26	1762.68	100.85	20.22	1736.00
Inventory	4588.23	4455.03	3862.53	4802.08	4902.20
Trade receivables	2708.32	1818.04	1216.70	1114.48	1568.46
Cash and bank balances	1840.96	462.86	226.15	944.75	452.08
Short-term loans and advances	1792.21	1424.29	1185.26	1508.27	1704.86
Other current assets	113.41	104.26	109.06	117.03	252.85
CURRENT LIABILITIES	22138.17	21104.61	18797.53	20370.63	17751.06
Short-term bank borrowings	3007.13	6216.91	4769.08	7762.01	3351.74
Trade payables	8705.53	8455.02	9672.36	8852.65	8916.60
Other current liabilities	7470.95	4923.10	2463.18	3142.88	4267.23
Short term provisions	2954.56	1509.58	1892.91	613.09	1215.49
Credit sales	58650.42	48665.28	37101.74	38829.49	45879.45
Cost of goods sold	44303.71	36932.75	29152.13	33236.85	35816.47
Cost of raw materials used	33894.82	27244.28	20492.87	22155.23	24313.08
Credit purchases	40328.77	33108.73	25542.69	27920.47	29572.35
Average debtors	2655.56	2263.18	1517.37	1165.59	1341.47
Average creditors	8781.05	8580.28	9063.69	9262.51	8884.63
Current ratio	0.62	0.48	0.36	0.42	0.60

Acid test ratio	0.41	0.26	0.15	0.18	0.32
Net working capital	–8504.78	–11077.45	–12096.98	–11863.80	–7134.61
Debtors turnover ratio	22.09	21.50	24.45	33.31	34.20
Creditors turnover ratio	4.59	3.86	2.82	3.01	3.33
Debtors cycle (days)	16.53	16.97	14.93	10.96	10.67
Creditors cycle (days)	79.47	94.59	129.52	121.09	109.66
(II) Related to Solvency Analysis					
Share Capital	634.75	638.07	643.78	643.78	679.18
Reserves and Surplus	18732.91	18496.77	18532.87	14218.81	21688.90
Shareholder's Funds	**19367.66**	**19134.84**	**19176.65**	**14862.59**	**22368.08**
Long-term Borrowings	8004.50	8051.78	9746.45	12318.96	10687.94
Short-term Borrowings	3007.13	6216.91	4769.08	7762.01	3351.74
Deferred Tax liabilities	98.80	–126.88	–1360.32	764.23	–83.84
Total Debt	**11110.43**	**14141.81**	**13155.21**	**20845.20**	**13955.84**
Long Term Debt	8103.30	7924.90	8386.13	13083.19	10604.10
Total External Borrowings	34893.27	33049.93	30557.77	35080.58	30058.17
EBT	1926.27	600.80	–485.94	–3570.97	513.60
Interest	849.44	1051.45	1008.62	1151.07	1108.24
EBIT	2775.71	1652.25	522.68	–2419.90	1621.84
Total Assets	**13712.92**	**10134.96**	**6739.06**	**8572.97**	**10705.91**
Total debt-equity ratio	0.57	0.74	0.69	1.40	0.62
Long term debt-equity ratio	0.42	0.41	0.44	0.88	0.47
Interest coverage ratio	3.27	1.57	0.52	–2.10	1.46
Total debt to asset Ratio	0.81	1.40	1.95	2.43	1.30
Long term debt to assets Ratio	0.59	0.78	1.24	1.53	0.99
Total external obligations to assets Ratio	2.54	3.26	4.53	4.09	2.81
(III) Related to Profitability					
Revenue from operations	54306.56	44765.72	34288.11	36294.74	42369.82
Cost of goods sold	44303.71	36932.75	29152.13	33236.85	35816.47
Gross profit	10002.85	7832.97	5135.98	3057.89	6553.35
EBIT	2775.71	1652.25	522.68	–2419.90	1621.84
Other Income	574.08	2088.20	3833.03	1881.41	2132.92
Operating profit	2201.63	–435.95	–3310.35	–4301.31	–511.08
EAT	1242.23	301.81	334.52	–4738.95	234.23
Average net block	14218.30	15237.63	15348.16	15511.90	15773.60
Average total capital employed	28006.56	26219.56	24543.31	23465.61	28104.84

Average total assets	54354.87	53222.85	50959.59	49838.80	51184.71
Average equity funds	19819.65	19251.25	19155.75	17019.62	18615.34
Gross profit ratio	18%	17%	15%	8%	15%
Operating profit ratio	4%	–1%	–10%	–12%	–1%
Net profit ratio	2%	1%	1%	–13%	1%
Cost of goods sold ratio	82%	83%	85%	92%	85%
ROR on capital employed	10%	6%	2%	–10%	6%
ROR on total assets	5%	3%	1%	–5%	3%
ROR on equity funds	6%	2%	2%	–28%	1%
(IV) Related to Efficiency Analysis					
Cost of materials used	33894.82	27244.28	20492.87	22155.23	24313.08
Cost of goods sold	44303.71	36932.75	29152.13	33236.85	35816.47
Average total assets	54354.87	53222.85	50959.59	49838.80	51184.71
Average fixed assets	14218.30	15237.63	15348.16	15511.90	15773.60
Average capital employed	28006.56	26219.56	24543.31	23465.61	28104.84
Average current assets	12342.29	11923.94	8437.01	7656.02	9639.44
Net working capital	–8504.78	–11077.45	–12096.98	–11863.80	–7134.61
Net sales	54306.56	44765.72	34288.11	36294.74	42369.82
Total assets turnover ratio (based on COGS)	0.82	0.69	0.57	0.67	0.70
Total assets turnover ratio (based on Sales)	1.00	0.84	0.67	0.73	0.83
Fixed assets turnover ratio (based on COGS)	3.12	2.42	1.90	2.14	2.27
Fixed assets turnover ratio (based on Sales)	3.82	2.94	2.23	2.34	2.69
Capital turnover ratio	1.58	1.41	1.19	1.42	1.27
Current assets turnover ratio (based on COGS)	3.59	3.10	3.46	4.34	3.72
Current assets turnover ratio (based on sales)	4.40	3.75	4.06	4.74	4.40
Working capital turnover ratio	–5.21	–3.33	–2.41	–2.80	–5.02

Solution

The appraisal of the financial health of Tata Motors is presented below:

I. Liquidity Analysis: The liquidity ratios of Tata Motors do not portray its satisfactory position. In 2011, the current ratio was around 0.62 and it substantially reduced to an alarmingly low level of 0.36 in 2013-14. Although, since then the ratio improved to 0.60 (close to what it was in 2011), still it is at an unsatisfactory level. Conventionally, a ratio of 2:1 is considered satisfactory and Tata Motors is way below that level. Similar trends are observed for the acid test ratio. A weak ratio of 0.42 in 2011, got weaker over the years and touched a low of 0.15 in 2013. In spite of the fact that it has shown improvement and reached 0.32 by the end of the 2016, it remains at unsatisfactory level. There has been a substantial decrease in cash and bank balances since 2012-13, and this appears to be a significant contributor to the decreased levels of current ratio and acid test ratio.

Another observation is that the net working capital of Tata Motors has consistently been negative during the period. But, it has improved from ₹8,500 crores in 2011-12 to ₹7,100 crores in 2015-16. The decline in the sales revenue during the years could also be a factor for the reduced working capital needs.

We also observe that Tata Motors is enjoying a much higher creditors payment period as compared to the debtors collection period. The debtors collection period was about 17 days in 2011 and further dipped to 10 days in 2015. In contrast, the creditors payment period was 80 days in 2011 and increased to 109 days by the end of the period under study. This favourable gap provides some leverage/solace for the company to operate at such low liquidity ratios. However, a point of caution is the decreasing debtors collection period. A low credit period of 10 days could be the reason of declining sales and requires thorough investigation.

II. Solvency Analysis: The solvency position of Tata Motors also appears to be unsatisfactory. Firstly, the interest coverage ratio is inadequate. It was somewhat at a satisfactory level of 3.27 in 2011, it decreased to become -2 in 2014 (when the company suffered losses and had a negative EBIT). However, since then this ratio improved to 1.46. Even though the ratio is positive now, it is not satisfactory and may pose problems for the company to service its interest payments to lenders.

The total debt to assets ratio has increased from 0.81 in 2011-12 to 2.43 in 2014-15 and then decreased to 1.30 in 2015-16. Similarly, the long-term debt to assets ratio has increased from 0.59 in 2011-12 to 1.53 in 2014-15 and then decreased to 0.99 in 2015-16. Although there has been a decrease in total external obligations/debt to assets ratio as well as long term debt to assets ratio in 2016, given its very low interest coverage ratio, the level of debt of the firm seems to be on the higher side and needs to be reduced.

III. Profitability Analysis: The profitability analysis looks disturbing. Over the years, there has been a dip in its profitability ratios. For instance, the gross profit ratio decreased from 18% in 2011-12 to 15% in 2015-16. Its net profit ratio also decreased from 2% in 2011-12 to become negative in 2015 and finally to 1% in 2015-16. Consequently, the rates of return on capital employed as well as total assets declined during the period. ROR on capital employed declined from 10% to 6% and ROR on total assets declined from 5% to 3%. The ROR on equity funds presents a dismal picture as it turns negative in 2014-15. However, this ratio did improve in the subsequent year.
Overall, the profitability of Tata Motors is a matter of serious concern.

IV. Efficiency Ratios: Analysing the performance with respect to utilisation of assets, we find it is unsatisfactory. The total assets turnover ratio has declined from 0.82 in 2011-12 to 0.07 in 2015-16.

Also, the fixed assets turnover ratio has substantially declined from 3.12 in 2011-12 to 2.27 in 2015-16. For an automobile manufacturer, fixed assets form an important part in the total assets, and a decline in this ratio implies unutilised capacity.

The current assets turnover ratio has been stable varying from 3.59 in 2011-12 to 3.72 in 2015-16. This could be due to the inadequate amount of current assets with the company.

Conclusion: We can thus conclude, that the financial health of Tata Motors is not sound given its unsatisfactory liquidity, solvency, profitability and efficiency ratios.

PART 4

COST ACCUMULATION

Full cost-based data is one of the three basic types of information used in management accounting. Part 4 is devoted to a discussion of cost accumulation procedures based on full cost. Chapter 7 treats the cost concepts in relation to different managerial needs. Chapters 8-11 describe cost elements of material, labour and overheads. While Chapters 8 and 9 deal with cost of material and labour respectively, the factory overheads and administrative and selling overheads are dealt in Chapters 10 and 11 respectively. The activity-based costing is illustrated in Chapter 12. Chapters 13-15 discuss the cost accumulation procedure in different situations. Chapter 13 deals with job costing. Cost accumulation in process costing and joint costing is examined in Chapter 14. The variable and absorbing costing methods for income determination are described in Chapter 15.

7

Cost Concepts and Management Needs

Learning Objectives

After reading this chapter you will be able to:

LO 7.1 Explain cost concepts relating management needs to income measurement
LO 7.2 Illustrate cost concepts relating to profit planning
LO 7.3 Discuss cost concepts relating to control
LO 7.4 Analyse cost concepts relating to decision-making

Introduction

One of the important inputs in managerial decision-making is cost data. There is, however, no single concept of cost, which can cater to all management needs. The "needs concept" of cost depends on the conditions under which the costs are required to be measured and the purpose for which measurement is required. In other words, cost data which are relevant and useful in one situation may be quite irrelevant and useless in another. Developing the data on the required lines can be designated as "the concept of cost relevancy."1 The concept implies the need of different sets of cost data for different objectives, purposes and situations. The object of the present chapter is to describe the various concepts of cost related to managerial needs. Management needs can be classified into four broad groups:

1. Income measurement
2. Profit planning
3. Costs control
4. Special situations requiring special decisions.

Cost Concepts Relating to Income Measurement

There are four cost concepts which pertain to income measurement. These are: **(i)** Product costs and Period costs; **(ii)** Absorbed costs and Unabsorbed costs; **(iii)** Expired costs and Unexpired costs; and **(iv)** Joint product costs and Separable costs.

LO 7.1 Explain cost concepts relating management needs to income measurement

Product Costs and Periods Costs

Product costs are costs which can be identified with goods produced for resale.

Product Costs The distinction between product costs and period costs assumes significance in the income determination process. In a variable costing system, only variable costs are recognised as product costs. The rationale is that it is only these costs which are affected by the production volume. If there is no production, there will be no material and direct labour cost (elements of variable costs) and, hence, no production cost. Therefore, variable costs are often called product costs. Thus, production costs can be defined as *those costs, which can be identified with goods produced or purchased for resale.* They vary with production. Raw material and direct labour are the examples of product costs.

Period costs are costs which are matched against the revenue of the current period.

Period Costs In contrast, period costs are costs which vary with the passage of time and not with volume of production. Rent, insurance, salary of a works manager and general manager, and so on. will vary *pari passu* with the time period. For instance, factory rent may be paid per month. Every month, this sum is to be paid irrespective of the volume of production. Likewise, insurance instalment of a quarter is to be paid whether there is production or no production. Logically, therefore, they should be considered expenses of the year in which they have been incurred and not be carried forward to the next year as part of the inventory costs. In brief, period cost may be defined as *costs which are matched against the revenue of the current period,* that is, the sum of period costs is deducted as expenses from the revenue of the current period only.

Absorbed Costs and Unabsorbed Cost

Absorbed costs are costs absorbed by the revenues of the period in which product has been sold.

The importance of this classification in the income determination process emanates from the fact that variable production costs are not the only true costs. Product costs should include some proportion of fixed costs. This can best be understood by an example. Let us assume that the management decides that product manufactured on an operator-controlled machine be henceforth manufactured on an automated process involving high cost machinery. Assume further, that as a result of the change in the production process, there will be no variation in material costs or variable manufacturing costs per unit. There will be a change only in direct labour cost which henceforth will become part of the fixed cost associated with the machine. According to the definition of product costs (as per variable costing), the cost of production will be reduced by the direct labour cost, simply because of a change in the method of manufacture. Certainly, this is not a logical viewpoint. Therefore, the argument that the benefits of fixed costs lapse with the passage of time and, hence, must be absorbed by the revenues of that period only to which they relate ignores the point that facilities represented by those costs are value-creating[2].

From the above it follows that fixed costs add value to the product and this value is well taken account of in determining the selling price. Therefore, such costs must be absorbed by the revenues of the period in which the products have been sold and not necessarily in the year in which they have been incurred. The fact that goods are held as inventories so that they can be sold in future further reinforces the above contention. Therefore, fixed costs are relevant and inventoriable. This argument is in line with another cost concept, namely, expired and unexpired cost.

Expired cost is a cost which cannot contribute to the production of future revenues.

Unexpired cost has the capacity to contribute to the production of revenue in the future.

Expired and Unexpired Cost

An expired cost is one which cannot contribute to the production of future revenues. In contrast, an unexpired cost is one which has the capacity of contributing to the production of revenue in the future. Inventory constitutes a good example of unexpired cost, as it can be sold in subsequent years and will influence total future revenues. These arguments, then, constitute the rationale of the concept of the absorbed and unabsorbed costs, the problem of allocating fixed costs notwithstanding. Fixed factory or production costs are related to capacity to produce. They are necessary to be spent to create infrastructure facilities so that the manufacturing process can set in. Therefore, they are as necessary costs of production as the variable costs. Accordingly, production should absorb fixed costs at a certain pre-fixed standard rate, which normally is determined with reference to the budgeted fixed cost and the normal capacity to produce. Suppose that fixed costs are ₹30,000 and the normal production is 15,000 units. The standard fixed overhead rate (SFOR) of recovery is ₹2 per unit (₹30,000 ÷ 15,000 units). In other words, every unit of production absorbs ₹2 of fixed costs. If the company produces 10,000 units, the total absorbed costs will be ₹20,000 (10,000 units × ₹2, SFOR). Obviously, ₹10,000 constitutes unabsorbed costs (₹30,000, actual cost – ₹20,000, absorbed costs). Thus, absorbed costs may be defined as those costs, which have been charged to production. Costs, which remain uncharged to production are referred to as unabsorbed costs. In contrast, overabsorbed costs represent the positive difference of fixed costs charged to production and actual fixed costs. Such a situation will arise if actual production is more than the normal production. In the above example, if the company produces 16,250 units, the costs charged to production will be ₹32,500 (16,250 units × ₹2, SFOR). The overabsorbed cost will be ₹2,500 [₹30,000, actual fixed costs (AFC) – ₹32,500 charged to production]. Figure 7.1 portrays these relationships.

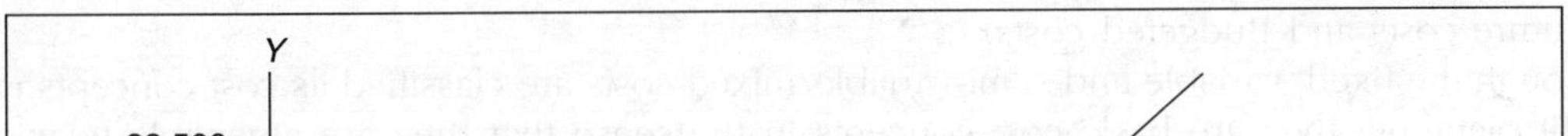

FIG. 7.1 *Absorbed and Unabsorbed Costs*

Symbolically,

$$\text{Absorbed costs} = \text{Units produced} \times \text{SFOR} \quad (7.1)$$

$$\text{Unabsorbed costs} = [\text{AFC} - (\text{Units produced} \times \text{SFOR})] \quad (7.2)$$

$$\text{Overabsorbed costs} = [\text{Units produced} \times \text{SFOR}) - \text{AFC}] \quad (7.3)$$

Joint Product Costs and Separable Costs

Joint product costs are the costs of a single process, or a series of processes that simultaneously produce two or more products of significant sales value. Such costs are not attributable to different individual products until after a certain stage of production known as the split-off point.[3]

Separable cost, in contrast, refers to any cost that can be attributed exclusively and wholly to a particular product, process, division or department.

The above cost concepts are helpful in the determination of the true costs of a particular segment of the business and, hence, the correct income.

COST CONCEPTS RELATING TO PROFIT PLANNING

LO 7.2 Illustrate cost concepts relating to profit planning

Profit planning is concerned with taking a series of decisions where alternatives are available. Planning deals with the future. Therefore, future costs are relevant costs in the profit planning function. Cost volume profit relationship is an integral part of profit planning, that is, how the costs and profits vary with sales volume. The relevant cost concept are:

1. Fixed, Variable and Semi-variable/Mixed costs,
2. Future costs and Budgeted costs.

Although the fixed, variable and semi-variable/mixed costs are classified as cost concepts relevant to profit planning, they are basic cost concepts in the sense that they are amenable to wider application.

Fixed costs are costs which do not change with changes in volume of output/activity within a specified (relevant) range for a given budget period.

Fixed Costs

Fixed costs are costs associated with those inputs, which do not vary with changes in volume of output or activity within a specified range of activity or output (relevant range) for a given budget period. Fixed costs, thus, remain constant whether activity increases or decreases within a relevant range. For example, the rent of factory or office premises, property insurance, senior executives' salaries, lease payments, depreciation, and so on remain the same whether there is an increase or decrease in the volume of activity. However, fixed costs are not fixed for all times to come. Fixed cost, like any other cost, is subject to change over a period of time. For instance, rent may increase, property insurance rates may go up, executives' salaries may increase, and so on in the next period but these increases are not the result of an increase in the firm's output. In a way, therefore, the terminology "fixed cost" is not very appropriate; "non-variable" is a more appropriate name for these costs.

Since fixed costs are unaffected by volume changes, any increase in volume implies that the costs will be allocated to a greater number of units and as a result fixed cost per unit will become progressively smaller as volume increases. Conversely, when a smaller number of units is produced, the fixed costs per unit will become larger. Such a variation in unit fixed cost creates problems in product costing, the cost being dependent on the number of units produced. This aspect has been referred to as "troublesome fixed costs."[4]

Table 7.1 illustrates the nature of fixed costs.

TABLE 7.1 Production Volume and Fixed Costs

Production (in units)	*Total fixed cost (TFC)*	*Average fixed cost per unit*
1,000	₹10,000	₹10
2,000	10,000	5
5,000	10,000	2
10,000	10,000	1

Figure 7.2 portrays the relationship between volume and total fixed costs. The relationship between volume and fixed costs per unit is exhibited by Figure 7.3. While fixed cost remain constant at ₹10,000 in total, cost per unit starts decreasing as the volume increases. Thus, there is an inverse relationship between production volume and average fixed cost (AFC) per unit (Figure 7.3). Hence, fixed costs are constant on an aggregative basis but are variable on a unit basis.

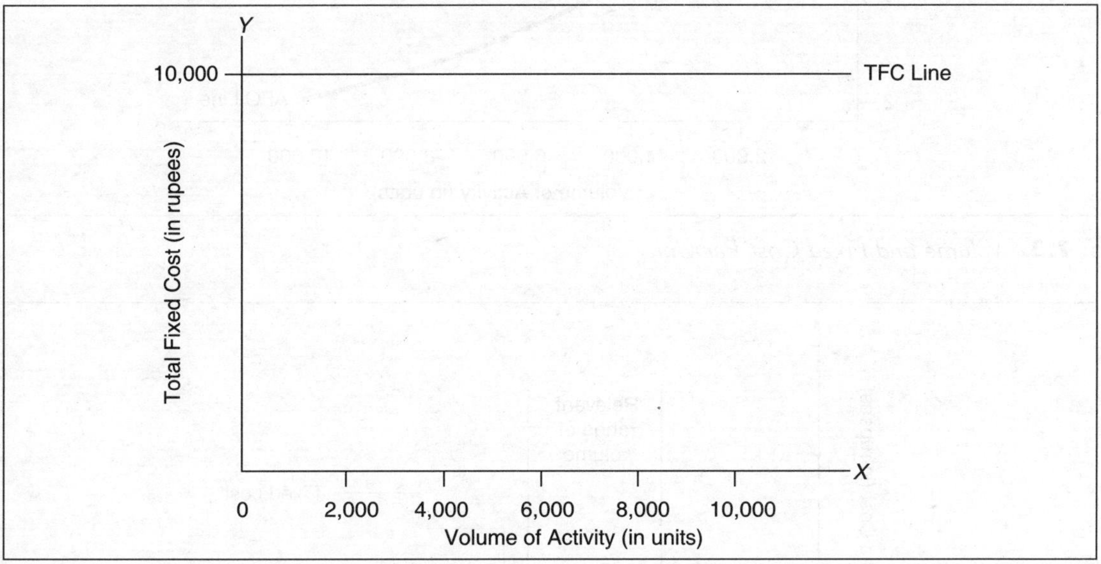

FIG. 7.2 *Volume and Total Fixed Costs*

As stated earlier, fixed costs will not change over a wide range of volume (the relevant range). They will fluctuate before and beyond that range. For example, prolonged strike or lockout may cause fixed costs to be reduced if executives or employees are laid off. Likewise, an expansion of activity beyond the present capacity will require purchase of new plant and equipment, engaging additional foremen and supervisors and, hence, additional fixed costs will result from these new inputs.[5] Such costs behaviour is shown in Figure 7.4. It is for this reason that fixed costs are sometimes called "capacity costs" as they measure the capacity for manufacturing, sales, administration and research. They reflect the capability for sustaining a planned volume of activity.[6]

It is useful to sub-divide fixed costs into "committed" fixed costs and "discretionary" fixed costs from the point of view of profit planning and control.

Committed fixed costs are costs caused by the acquisition of capacity-producing assets.

Committed Fixed Costs Fixed costs caused by the purchase of capacity producing assets such as plant and equipment are called committed costs. These costs are on an increase in a growing firm as usually such a firm

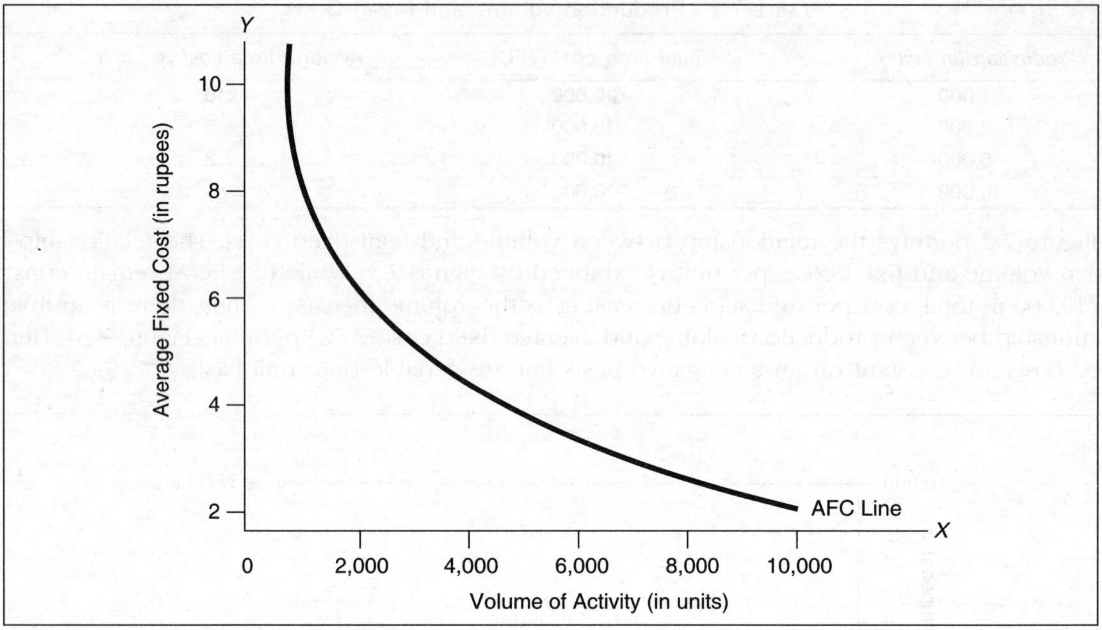

FIG. 7.3 *Volume and Fixed Cost Per Unit*

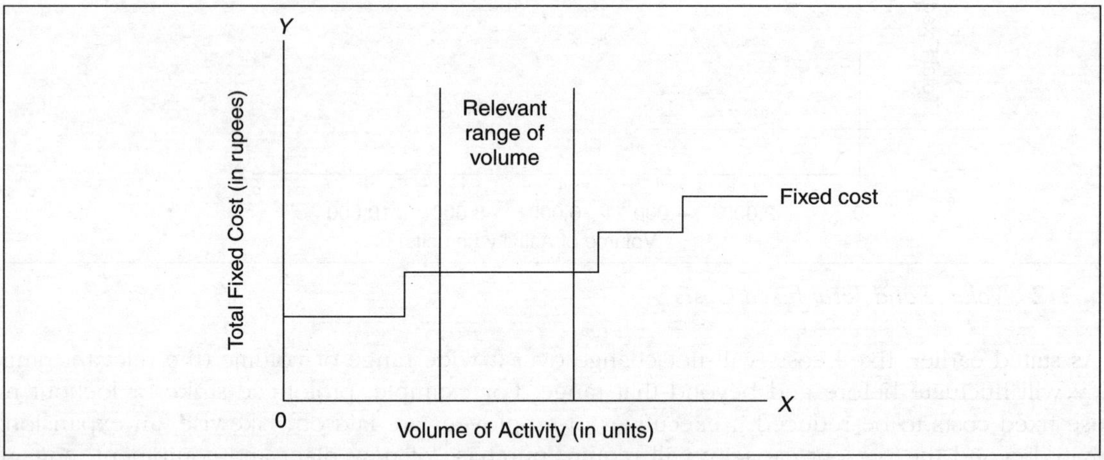

FIG. 7.4 *Behaviour of Fixed Costs*

switches over to automatic plant operation from a manual one, resulting in higher expenditure on plant and equipment. Depreciation, rent, property taxes, salaries of key personnel, insurance, and so on are examples of committed fixed costs. These costs are known as committed fixed costs because the company has committed itself to incur such costs by making long range decisions which will extend several years into the future. Such costs cannot be reduced substantially without impairing the organisation's competence to meet long range goals. The committed fixed costs are the least responsive of the fixed costs, because they tend to be less affected by month-to-month and year-to-year decisions. For instance, once buildings are constructed and machinery is installed, little can be done in day-do-day operations to affect the total level of committed costs. From the point of view of the management, therefore, the stress should be to increase current utilisation of these facilities so as to augment income. It is for this reason that fixed costs are ignored for short-term decisions, that is, the management decides to sell a product at a price below the total cost but higher than variable cost. In such situations, the concept of the contribution margin as a decision-criterion becomes important. Contribution margin per unit is the difference between the selling price and the variable cost per unit.

Discretionary fixed costs are costs caused by management policy decisions.

Discretionary Fixed Costs These costs are also known as *programmed costs or managed costs.* The costs caused by management policy decisions to undertake activities such as research and development, training programmes for its employees, advertising and sales promotion, charitable and/or political donations, management consulting services, and so on, are called discretionary fixed costs. Such costs can be reduced substantially (and in extreme cases almost entirely) for a given year in difficult times at the discretion of management. For instance, the management may decide not go give any donations, may stop making advertisements in newspapers or other media and, thus, eliminate these costs.

The amount/size of discretionary fixed costs is decided by the top management at the beginning of the budget period, specifying the allocation for each of the expenditure items listed above. For example, the management may decide to allocate ₹2 lakh for market research and development, ₹1 lakh for sales promotion and advertising, and so on. These expenditures are allocated in the light of the long-term goals of the company. The advantages accruing from such expenditures cannot be expected in the same budget period in which they have been incurred. For example, even a technological break-through that could shorten production time appreciably would have no effect until it was properly tested, installed and checked—a process that would most likely extend into some future budgeted period.[7] Therefore, discretionary fixed costs are not subject to ordinary engineering input-output analysis which holds true for most other costs.[8]

Variable Costs

Variable costs are costs that tend to vary in direct proportion to change in production in relevant range.

Costs that tend to vary in direct proportion or in a one-to-one relationship to changes in production activity, sales activity or some other measure of volume within relevant range for a given budget period are referred to as variable costs.[9] Material costs, direct labour costs and supplies are examples of variable cost. The cost of these inputs increases/ decreases in proportion to increase/decrease in volume. It is so because these inputs are used in the exact quantities needed. Table 7.2 portrays relationship between direct material, direct labour and total variable costs and production volume.

TABLE 7.2 Production Volume and Variable Costs

Production (units)	*Direct Material costs (@ ₹8 per unit)*	*Direct Labour costs (@ ₹2 per unit)*	*Total variable costs (@ ₹10 per unit)*
8,000	64,000	16,000	80,000
8,100	64,800	16,200	81,000
8,300	66,400	16,600	83,000
8,500	68,000	17,000	85,000

Table 7.2 shows that each change of one unit of product causes a change of ₹10 of variable cost (₹8 materials and ₹2 labour). As output increases, so do the variable costs increase in the same proportion. For instance, at 8,000 units production level, variable costs are ₹80,000; at 8,500 units,

such costs become ₹85,000. Expressed mathematically, there is a linear relationship between volume and variable costs. Thus, total variable costs vary in direct proportion to volume and, consequently, are constant per unit of volume. Figures 7.5 and 7.6 illustrate this relationship. In view of their behaviour, variable costs are sometimes called "engineered costs". An engineered costs is any cost that has an explicit, specified, physical relationship with a selected measure of activity. Most variable costs are of this type. An "engineered" variable cost is said to exist when work measurement techniques (material standards with the help of production engineers, labour standards through time and motion study) have carefully established an optimum relationship between input and output.[10] Direct material and direct labour are a prime example of engineered costs. Like fixed costs, some of the variable costs are discretionary in nature, that is, they are dependent upon management policy. As an illustration, let us suppose that the management has pre-determined that *X* per cent of the sales revenue will be spent for items such as market research and advertising. These costs will, obviously, vary in direct proportion to the sales revenue but the reasons for variability are not the same as in case of direct materials or direct labour.

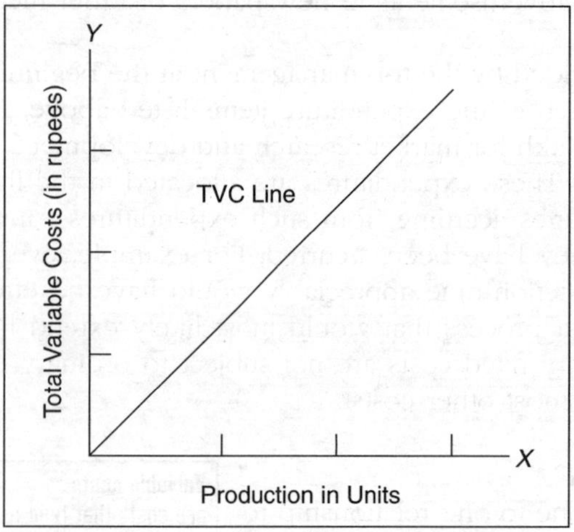

FIG. 7.5 *Total Variable Cost*

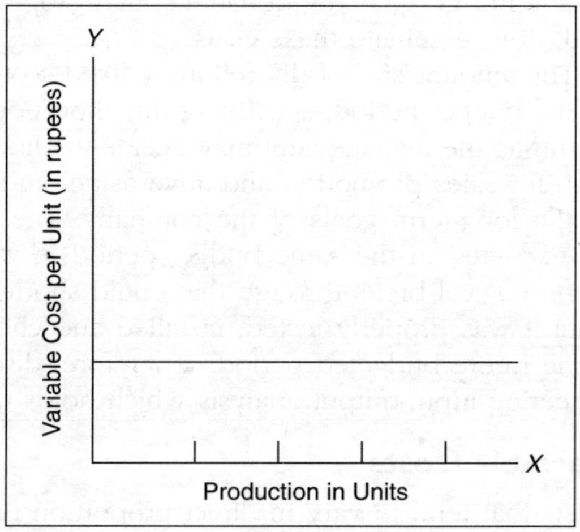

FIG. 7.6 *Variable Cost per Unit*

Semi-Variable Costs (Mixed Costs)

Mixed costs are costs which consist of partly fixed costs and partly variable costs.

All costs which are neither perfectly variable nor absolutely fixed in relation to volume changes are called semi-variable costs. Semi-variable costs are also known as mixed costs as they consist both of fixed costs and variable costs. The fixed component of mixed costs represents the cost of providing capacity, whereas the variable component is caused by using the capacity. The first part is not affected by the changes in activity (and is thus like the fixed cost), while the latter part is influenced by the changes in activity (and is, thus, like the variable cost). Thus, semi-variable costs change in the same direction as volume but not in direct proportion thereto. Figure 7.7 exhibits such a relationship.

Telephone, power, repairs and maintenance costs are some of the examples of mixed costs. For example, a telephone bill involves the twin elements of cost: fixed charge consisting of basic cost for telephone service (telephone rent) irrespective of the calls made; and variable charge consisting of actual number of telephone calls made. In the case of power expenses, meter rent is a fixed charge and power usage is a variable charge.

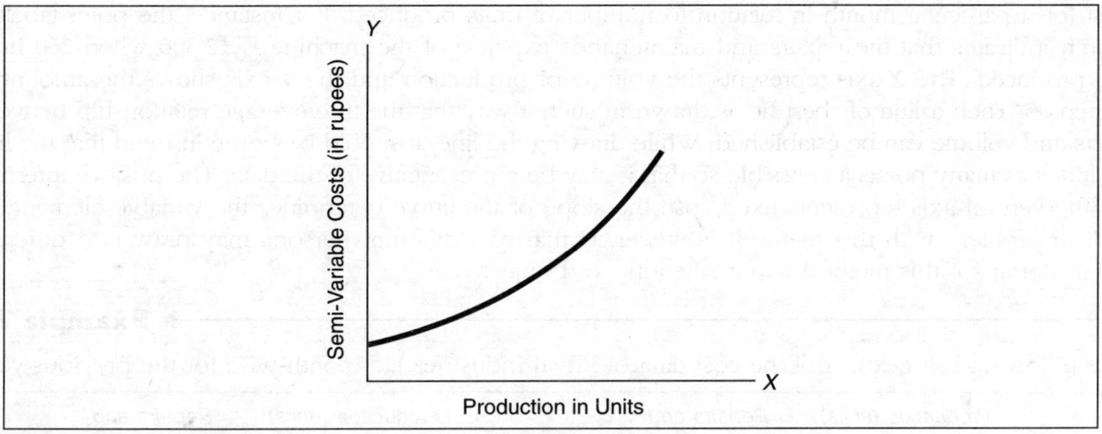

FIG. 7.7 *Semi-Variable Costs*

Ideally, semi-variable costs should be bifurcated into fixed and variable elements as the functions of profit planning, cost control and decision-making assume that costs are either variable or fixed.

Methods of Mixed Cost Segregation There are four methods to bifurcate mixed costs:

1. Graphic Method (Scatter Diagram)
2. Two Point Method (High-Low Method)
3. Analytical Approach
4. Method of Least Squares.

Graphic Method The graphic method of dividing mixed costs into their fixed and variable components makes use of all relevant past data pertaining to cost-volume relationships. The data are plotted on a scatter graph, as shown in Figure 7.8, on the basis of Example 7.1. Each point on a chart represents

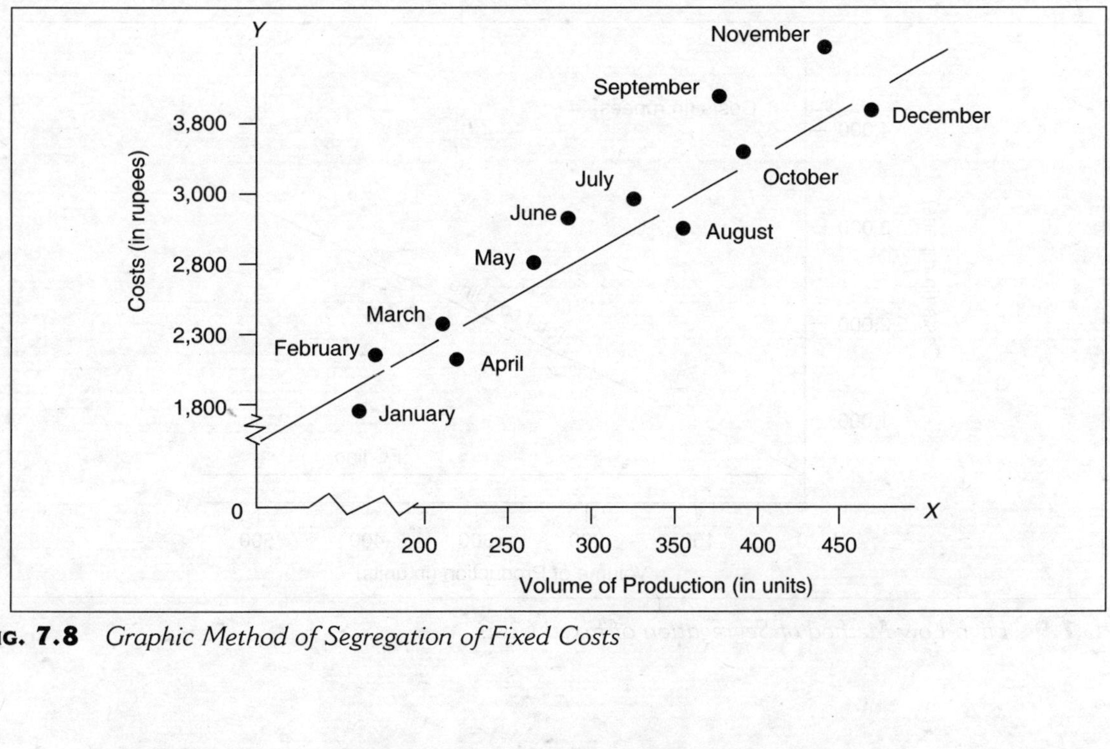

FIG. 7.8 *Graphic Method of Segregation of Fixed Costs*

cost for a particular month in relation to number of units produced. For instance, the point labelled March indicates that the repairs and maintenance expense of the machine is ₹2,300 when 250 units are produced. The *X* axis represents the volume of production and the *Y* axis shows the amount of expenses. Then a line of "best fit" is drawn in such a way that the true average relationship between costs and volume can be established. While drawing the line, it should be borne in mind that the line includes as many points as possible so that it may be representative of the data. The positive intercept on the vertical axis represents fixed cost: the slope of the curve determines the variable element.

The problem with this method, however, is that two different persons may draw two different lines. Being so, this method is not scientific and objective.

◆ Example 7.1

The following is an extract of the cost data of Royal Industries Ltd month-wise for the previous year:

Month	*Production (units)*	*Repairs and maintenance costs*	*Month*	*Production (units)*	*Repairs and maintenance costs*
January	200	₹1,800	July	350	₹3,000
February	200	1,900	August	350	2,950
March	250	2,300	September	400	3,350
April	250	2,250	October	400	3,300
May	300	2,650	November	450	3,750
June	300	2,750	December	450	3,650

High-Low Method As the name suggests, this method makes use of two observations rather than all the observations for drawing the cost line. The two points chosen are: (i) The high cost point; and (ii) The low cost point corresponding g to some specific volume (may be number of units produced as in Example 7.1 or any other measure of volume such as, labour-hours, machine-hours, telephone calls made, power consumed, and so on). Figure 7.9 shows the relationship on the basis of data contained in Example 7.1. The relevant data are plotted as follows.

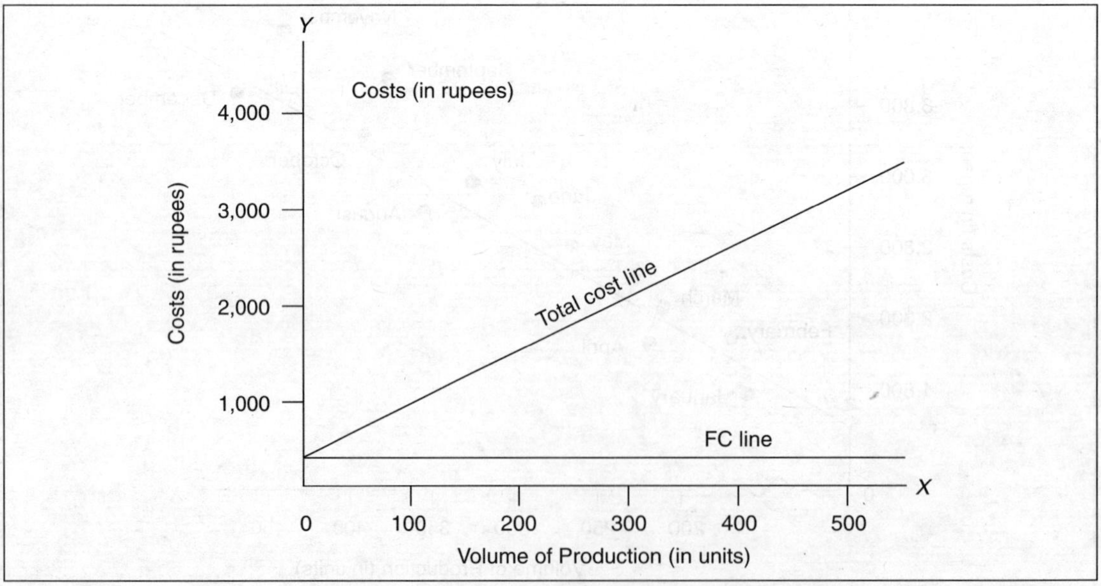

FIG. 7.9 *High Low Method of Segregation of Fixed Costs*

The intercept on the vertical axis represents fixed cost and the slope of the cost line represents the variable element of the cost.

Month	Production (in units)	Costs
January	200 (P_l) (lower production)	₹ 1,800 (Low cost point, C_L)
November	450 (P_H) (higher production)	3,750 (High cost point, C_H)

The algebraic method will yield identical results as shown below:
Variable rate = Difference in cost ($C_H - C_L$) ÷ Difference in production ($P_H - P_L$) = ₹1,950 ÷ 250 units = ₹7.8 per unit
Fixed overhead component at P_L = ₹1,800 – (₹7.8 × 200) = ₹240
P_H = ₹3,750 – (₹7.8 × 450) = ₹240
Thus, mixed cost = ₹240 + ₹7.8X

In statistical terms, total cost (Y) is a function of (i) fixed element, a, and (ii) variable element, b, multiplied by number of units produced, X:

$$Y = a + bX$$

In Example, 7.1, the cost equation (flexible budget cost line)

$$Y = ₹240 + ₹7.8\ X$$

The high-low method is statistically not desirable as its results are based only on two extreme observations. Because of the danger of relying on extreme points, which may not be representative of normal situations, the high-low method is not recommended.[11] From the point of view of obtaining reliable and representative results, all data points should be used and not just two, as a basis of cost estimation. Therefore, the method is unscientific and inaccurate.

Analytical Method This method is also called the "degree of variability" technique because the genesis of this method lies in measuring the extent of variability of costs with volume. In other words, the technique is based on a careful analysis of each item to determine how far the cost varies with volume.[12] Some of the mixed cost may have a 40 per cent degree of variability while others may have only 20 per cent. The virtue of this method, apart from easy understanding, is that it closely examines each constituent of the mixed costs, and therefore, is likely to give most accurate figures of fixed and variable elements. But it may be emphasised again that this method also suffers from subjectivity in that the degree of variability associated with each part of semi-variable costs is to be determined by the accountant/some other person entrusted with the job. Obviously, two different persons will assign two different percentages to the degree of variability attached with an element of semi-variable cost. But then there is no accurate method of apportioning the mixed cost into fixed and variable components. One can only approximate. Such an analysis is of particular significance in making flexible budgets.

◆ Example 7.2

The analysis of factory overheads of Hypothetical Ltd reveals that on an average there is a 40 per cent degree of variability at 100 per cent level of activity. Budgeted mixed overheads are ₹10,000. What would they be at 50, 70 and 90 per cent levels of activity?

Solution

Variable overheads = (Budgeted mixed overheads × Degree of variability) = ₹10,000 × 0.40 = ₹4,000
Fixed overheads at 100 per cent capacity = (₹10,000 – ₹4,000) = ₹6,000
Variable overheads at 1 per cent capacity = Total variable overheads ÷ 100 = ₹4,000 ÷ 100 = ₹40
Flexible Budget (Overheads Costs)

Particulars	Level of capacity (per cent)		
	50	70	90
Fixed overheads	₹6,000	₹6,000	₹6,000
Variable overheads (level of capacity × ₹40)	2,000	2,800	3,600
Total	8,000	8,800	9,600

Method of Least Squares This method is perhaps the most accurate and scientific to apportion mixed costs. The line is not plotted arbitrarily like the scatter diagram method. It is located by means of solving the two linear equations based on the formula for drawing a straight line regression equation. The basic equation is:

$$Y = a + bX \tag{7.4}$$

Where Y = Total cost

a = Fixed element of mixed cost

b = Variable cost to volume ratio

X = Any measure of volume (production, hours, and so on)

From Equation 7.4 follows the two simultaneous linear equations:

$$\Sigma Y = na + b\,\Sigma X \tag{7.5}$$

$$\Sigma XY = a\,\Sigma X + b\,\Sigma X^2 \tag{7.6}$$

◆ **Example 7.3**

ABC Ltd furnishes the following overhead cost behaviour of mixed cost for the first 6 months of the current year. You are required to segregate these costs into fixed and variable.

Month	Units produced	Cost		
	(X)	(Y)	XY	X^2
January	20	₹900	₹18,000	₹400
February	10	700	7,000	100
March	30	1,100	33,000	900
April	20	900	18,000	400
May	00	500	00	00
June	30	1,300	39,000	900
	110	5,400	1,15,000	2,700

Solution

Substituting the values in Equations 7.5 and 7.6

$$5{,}400 = 6a + 110b \tag{1}$$

$$1{,}15{,}000 = 110a + 2{,}700b \tag{2}$$

Multiplying Equation 1 by 110 and 2 by 6, we have

$$5{,}94{,}000 = 660a + 12{,}100b$$

$$6{,}90{,}000 = 660a + 16{,}200b$$

Subtracting Equation 1 from Equation 2,

$$96{,}000 = 4{,}100b$$

$$\therefore \quad b = 23.41$$

Substituting b in Equation 1 we have $6a = 2{,}824.39$ or $a = 470.73$.

Thus, the least squares equation is

$$Y = 470.73 + 23.41\ X$$

The equation indicates that fixed costs are ₹470.73, when volume X is zero and for each unit of production beyond zero costs will increase by ₹23.41 (variable costs). The results of this equation can be used to estimate total costs for any volume within the relevant range. Figure 7.10 exhibits this relationship.

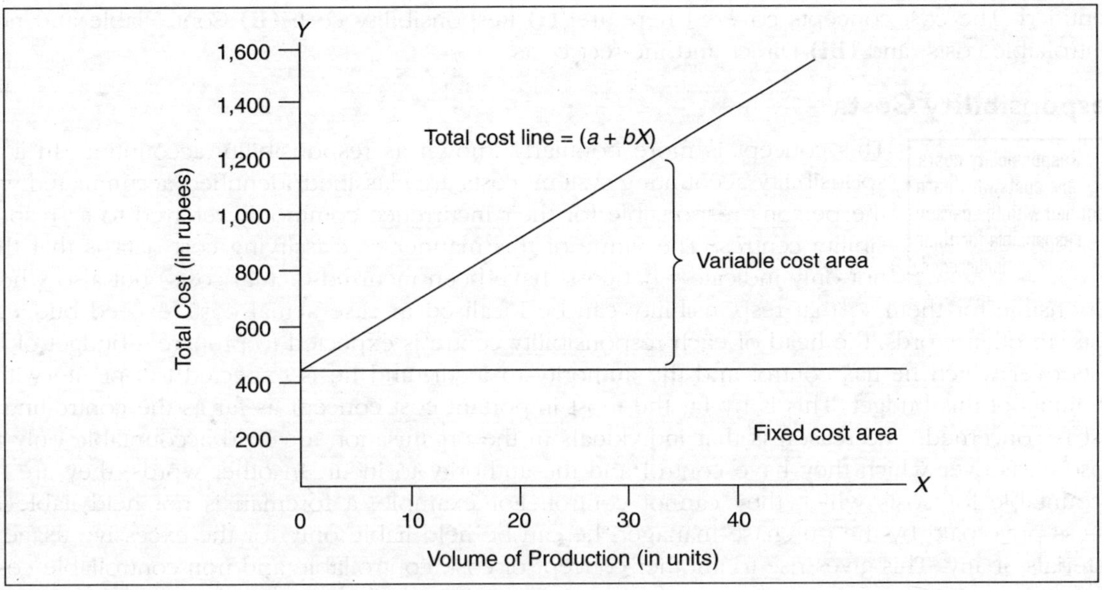

FIG. 7.10 *Total Cost at Various Levels of Production*

This method is by far the best among the four methods of segregating mixed costs.

Future Costs

> **Future costs** are costs reasonably expected to be incurred at some future date as a result of a current decision.

Future costs are relevant costs in the profit planning function of management. Those costs which are reasonably expected to be incurred at some future date as a result of a current decision are called future costs. Since they deal with a future period, they are estimated costs based on expectations, Such costs are of paramount importance to the management as they are the only costs over which it can exercise any control. In the case of historical costs, there can only be retrospection and nothing much can be done about them if they are more than the budgeted cost, for the simple reason that they have already been incurred. However, future costs can be planned for and planned to be reduced. If they are too high, resources can be planned to meet the high costs and efforts can be made, if possible, to reduce them. Thus, the measurement of future costs is critically associated with the active management functions of planning and control.[13]

Budgeted Costs

> **Budgeted costs** are costs which are incorporated formally in the budget of a specific period.

When an operating plan involving future costs is accepted, and incorporated formally in the budget for a specific period, such costs get converted to what may be referred to as budgeted costs. Budgeted costs are important elements in that they provide the basis for measuring the actual performance of different cost centres and, therefore, constitute an important input of responsibility accounting.

Cost Concepts for Control

LO 7.3 Discuss cost concepts relating to control

Once costs have been planned, the next step is to see that actual costs are in conformity with planned costs. It is in this context that management needs cost data so that responsibility for incurrence of cost can be identified. The cost concepts covered here are: **(i)** Responsibility cost; **(ii)** Controllable and non-controllable costs; and **(iii)** Direct and indirect costs.

Responsibility Costs

Responsibility costs are costs which are identified with the person responsible for their incurrence.

This concept is more popularly known as responsibility accounting. In a responsibility accounting system, costs are classified/identified/accumulated with the persons responsible for their incurrence commonly referred to as responsibility centres. The virtue of this manner of classifying cost data is that they not only indicate what costs have been incurred (actual costs) but also who is responsible for them so that responsibility can be localised in case actual costs exceed budgeted costs. In other words, the head of each responsibility centre is expected to prepare a budget of the costs over which he has control and the authority to incur, and he is expected to operate within the limits of this budget. This is by far the most important cost concept as far as the controlling of cost is concerned. The reason is that individuals in the organisation are held accountable only for those costs over which they have control and the authority to incur. In other words, they are not accountable for costs which they cannot control. For example, a foreman is not held liable for excess price paid by the purchase manager; he can be held liable only for the excessive usage of materials, if any. This gives rise to another concept of cost: controllable and non-controllable costs.

Controllable costs are costs the amount of which is significantly influenced by the action of the manager of the responsibility centre.

Controllable and Non-controllable Costs "An item of cost is controllable if the amount of cost incurred in (or assigned to) a responsibility centre is significantly influenced by the actions of the manager of the responsibility centre. Otherwise, it is non-controllable."[14]

The important characteristics of controllable costs are: **(i)** They are in relation to a particular responsibility centre (or the managerial area of responsibility involved); **(ii)** The head of the responsibility centre has *significant* influence but *not complete* influence on its controllability; **(iii)** They are relevant for the time period under review. For instance, the purchase manager has entered into a price contract, say for three months, with a supplier of raw materials used in production. Then price is not controllable by him for the relevant period of contract (three months) but is possibly controllable after the expiry of the contract period. Likewise, the sales manager may have entered into a contract for making advertisements for a certain period at an agreed amount.

The first characteristic indicates that the concept of controllable costs is a relative concept in the sense that when a company is viewed as a single entity, all costs are controllable at one level or another level of management. For instance, the top management may decide to close down one of the departments/divisions/segments of the business and, thus, reduce its cost to zero. The management may also decide to purchase a component from an outside supplier, hitherto manufactured by the company itself. These examples indicate that costs are uncontrollable only at intermediate and lower levels of management. For instance, a departmental supervisor has no control over the fixed costs allocated to his department, a sales manager has no control over the price/cost at which goods have been transferred to his department by the production manager. Thus, allocated costs are not controllable by the responsibility centre to which the allocation is made.

Since all costs are controllable at the higher echelons of management, the management control system should focus on those costs which are controllable at lower/intermediate levels of management. It is important to stress here that cost controllability does not involve eliminating costs, but its endeavour is to keep them as close as possible to some desirable and reasonably attainable levels or standards.[15]

Direct costs are costs which can be identified logically and practically in their entirety to a particular department/product.

Direct and Indirect Costs The various items of cost in a responsibility centre may be classified as either direct or indirect. Those costs which can be identified logically and practically in their entirety to a particular department or a product are called direct costs. Those costs which are not practically identifiable exclusively and wholly to a particular product, division or segment are called indirect cost. Indirect costs are frequently called "common costs" as they are allocated between two or more products/departments/divisions of a business. The salary of the chief executive who looks after the entire business, is an example of indirect cost. A divisional manager's salary is a direct cost if that division happens to be one specific responsibility centre. However, within divisions, if there are a number of products to be manufactured, then for each product unit (which is a separate responsibility centre), the divisional manager's salary will be the indirect cost. Thus, the distinction between a direct cost and an indirect cost depends upon the unit under consideration. If a cost can be directly and wholly traced to a particular responsibility centre under consideration, it is direct cost and if it is allocated to it from somewhere else in the organisation, it is an indirect cost.

This distinction is important as only direct costs are controllable costs for various responsibility centres. Indirect costs are not controllable.

COST CONCEPTS FOR DECISION-MAKING

LO 7.4 Analyse cost concepts relating to decision-making.

Management is concerned with two types of decisions: (i) Long-range (capacity decisions) which cover a long time span and take into account the time value of money, (ii) Short-range or operating decisions cover a short span of time and, therefore, time value of money is not considered to be significant. Decisions involving production, output, pricing of special orders, addition or dropping of a product line, make or buy, processing further or sell, temporary shutdown and so on are examples of short-range decisions. To have correct decision, management requires estimates of all future benefits and costs concerning a particular decision. The relevant cost concepts affecting the latter type of decisions are: **(i)** Relevant and irrelevant costs; **(ii)** Incremental cost/differential cost; **(iii)** Out of pocket costs and sunk costs; **(iv)** Opportunity costs and imputed costs.

Relevant and Irrelevant Costs

Relevant costs are costs which are influenced by a decision.

Cost which is influenced by a decision is a relevant cost and, hence, is important for decision-makers. Cost which is not affected by a decision is irrelevant cost, that is, it will be the same regardless of the choice that is made. As a result, such a cost is of no relevance to decision-makers. Therefore, it should be ignored while taking decisions. Committed fixed costs are irrelevant costs. However, it should not be taken to mean that relevant costs are equivalent to variable costs. In situations where additional fixed costs are to be incurred as a result of a decision, fixed costs are as much the relevant costs as the variable costs are. As an illustration, if the company wants to make a component hitherto purchased from the outside suppliers, the relevant costs will be: **(i)** Cost of material and direct labour (variable cost) and **(ii)** Fixed costs (required for creating new facilities so that the manufacturing process of making a component can start). Thus, relevant costs, truly speaking, are incremental costs, fixed and variable classification notwithstanding.

Incremental Cost/Differential Cost

Incremental costs are additional costs caused by a particular decision.

Differential cost is the difference in cost between any two acceptable alternatives.

This is by far the most important concept of cost in the decision-making process. Incremental costs are the additional costs which will be incurred if management chooses one course of action as opposed to another. They are the extra, or incremental costs, caused by a particular decision.

A differential cost is the difference in cost between any two available, acceptable alternatives. This approach compares the two alternatives directly by looking at the differences between them.[16] The difference in cost between buying a component from outside and making it in the company is a differential cost, relevant for decision-making. Furthermore, differential costs always relate to a specific time period. What it implies is that with the passage of time and change of situation, the amount of differential costs will vary. It is a broader concept than variable cost as it also takes into account additional fixed costs caused by a management decision.

Out of Pocket Costs and Sunk Costs

Sunk costs are costs which have already been incurred and would not require current cash expenditure.

A cost which requires current or future cash expenditures as a result of a decision is labelled as an out of pocket cost. In situations where funds/cash resources available are limited, such costs become very decisive in the decision-making process. In contrast, those costs which have already been incurred in the past and will not require current cash expenditure are called sunk costs.

Thus, the two cost concepts are the opposites of each other. In the case of the sunk cost a prior investment of cash resources has been made, while cash will be required currently or in the near future period in the cash of out of pocket costs.

Depreciation, depletion and amortisation of intangible assets (like preliminary expenses, cost of issue of shares and debentures) are some of the examples of sunk costs. Since sunk costs are the results of past commitments, they should be ignored/disregarded for purposes of decision-making. "*Do not cry over spilt milk*" should be the management's attitude towards such costs.

From the above it will be erroneous to infer that all variable costs are out of pocket costs and that all fixed costs are sunk costs. The chief executive's salary may be fixed but is very much an out of pocket cost as it requires current cash outlay. Similarly, in certain situations, variable costs may not be affected by the decision and, therefore, will be sunk costs. For example, assume that a company is considering a change in the manufacturing process with no change in production volume; the variable costs will remain unchanged and, therefore, will be labelled as sunk costs with respect to the decision. Consider the facts in Table 7.3.

TABLE 7.3 Differential Cost

Particulars	*Present manufacturing process*	*Proposed manufacturing process*
Direct material	₹2,00,000	₹2,00,000
Direct labour	3,00,000	3,00,000
Factory overheads	3,50,000	2,50,000
Total costs	8,50,000	7,50,000

The materials and labour costs are estimated at ₹5,00,000 under both the manufacturing processes. They are sunk costs in this situation. The decrease of factory overheads in the proposed manufacturing process is the differential cost relevant for decision-making, though it is largely in the nature of a fixed cost.

The above illustration highlights the fact that variable costs are not always relevant costs and fixed costs are not always irrelevant costs from the points of view of decision-making. Included in the category of relevant costs for decision-making are all those costs which differ among the alternatives at hand. It is not significant whether the cost belongs to the fixed or variable category. Therefore, differential costs (incremental costs) are the only "material" costs for effective and efficient decision-making. It is this concept of differential costing, also known as incremental analysis, which is used for short-term non-recurring decision-making.

Opportunity Costs and Imputed Costs

Opportunity costs represent benefits foregone by not choosing the second best alternative in favour of the best one.

Opportunity costs represent the benefits foregone by not choosing the second best alternative in favour of the best one. When we decide to follow one alternative, we are also deciding not to follow another. As a result, all the benefits that would have accrued are given up. To the extent they can be quantified/measured, they are opportunity costs of the decision and relevant costs for a decision. Assume that a company owns a building; it could be either used for business purposes or be rented to others. If a decision is taken to use the building, the amount of rent foregone constitutes the opportunity cost. Opportunity costs are associated only with feasible alternatives. The lost rent is an opportunity cost only if there are potential tenants willing to hire the building. Since they are hypothetical/theoretical costs, they are not entered in the accounting records. But the cost of the second best alternative must be taken into account before taking a decision.

Imputed costs are similar to the opportunity costs in that they are not recorded in the accounting books. However, they are hypothetical costs that must be taken into account if a correct decision is to be arrived at. Interest is the principal example of imputed costs.

SUMMARY

- From the viewpoint of managerial needs, cost concepts fall into four broad categories—income measurement, profit planning, cost control, and special situations.
- There are four cost concepts pertaining to income measurement. These are Product and period costs; Absorbed and unabsorbed costs; Expired and unexpired costs; and Joint and separable costs.
- Production costs are costs which can be identified with goods produced/purchased for resale. Period costs are costs which are matched against the revenue of the current period.
- Absorbed costs are costs which must be absorbed by the revenue of the period in which the products have been sold and not necessarily in the year in which they have been incurred.
- An expired cost is one which can not contribute to the production of future revenues. An unexpired cost has the capacity to contribute to the production of revenue in future, for example, inventory.
- Joint product costs are the costs of a single process/series of processes that simultaneously produce two or more products of significant sale value. Separable costs refer to any cost that can be attributed exclusively and wholly to a particular product/process/division/department.

LO 7.1

- The cost concepts relevant to profit planning are: **(i)** Fixed, variable and semi-variable/mixed costs, and **(ii)** Future and budgeted costs.
- Fixed (non-variable) costs do not change with changes in volume of output or activity within a specified range of activity/output (relevant range) for a given budget period. Fixed costs caused by the purchase of capacity producing assets such as plants are called committed fixed costs. The discretionary fixed (managed) costs are caused by management policy decision to undertake activities such as research and development, training programme for employees, advertising and sales promotion and so on.
- Costs that tend to vary in total in direct proportion or in one-to-one relationship to changes in production/sales/some other measure of volume are variable costs.
- All costs which are neither perfectly variable nor absolutely fixed in relation to volume changes are called semi-variable (mixed) costs. They consist of both fixed costs and variable costs.
- The methods of segregating of mixed costs are the graphic method, the high-low method, the analytical method and the method of least squares.

LO 7.2

- The concepts relating to cost control are Responsibility costs, Controllable and non-controllable costs, and Direct and indirect costs.
- Responsibility costs are costs which are classified/identified/accumulated with the person(s) responsible for their incurrence.
- An item of cost is controllable if the amount of cost incurred in (assigned to) a responsibility centre is significantly influenced by the actions of the manager of the responsibility centre. Otherwise, it is non-controllable.
- Those costs which can be identified logically and practically in their entirety to a particular department/product are called direct costs. Those costs which are not practically identifiable exclusively and wholly to a particular product/division/segment are called indirect (common) costs.

LO 7.3

- The cost concepts affecting decision-making are Relevant and irrelevant costs, Differential costs, out-of-pocket costs and sunk costs, and Opportunity costs and imputed costs.
- Costs which are influenced by a decision are a relevant cost and cost which is not affected by a decision is irrelevant cost.
- Differential/incremental costs are the differential/additional costs which would be incurred if the management chooses one course of action as opposed to another. They are incremental costs caused by a particular decision.
- A cost which requires a current/future cash expenditure as a result of a decision is an out of pocket cost. Costs which have already been incurred in the past are sunk costs.
- Opportunity cost represents the benefits foregone by not choosing the second best alternative in favour of the best one. Imputed costs are hypothetical costs that must be considered for correct decision, for example, interest cost.

LO 7.4

REFERENCES

1. P.F. Bourke in D.L. Anderson and Donald L. Raun, *Information Analysis in Management Accounting*, (Santa Barbara, New York, 1978), p. 6.
2. *Ibid.*, p 9.

3. C.T. Horngren, *Introduction to Management Accounting*, (Prentice-Hall, New Jersey, 1978), p. 118.
4. C.L. Moore and R.K. Jaedicke, *Managerial Accounting*, (South Western Publishing Company, Chicago, 1972), pp. 263-64.
5. R.M. Copeland and P.E. Dascher, *Managerial Accounting*, (John Wiley, New York, 1978), p. 75
6. Horngren, C.T., and G.L. Sundlem, *Introduction to Management Accounting*, (Prentice Hall, New Delhi, 1990), p. 206.
7. Copeland and Dascher, *op.cit.*, p. 76.
8. Horngren, *op.cit.*, p. 208.
9. The phrase 'relevant range' is important. It can be explained with reference to direct material cost (the most important constituent of variable costs). Assume purchase cost of 1 kg of materials is ₹10; for 10 kgs it would be ₹100; if purchases are of 100 kgs, the material cost per kg may be less than ₹10 (say, it is ₹9.5 per kg); extending the purchase size to 1,000 kg, the cost per kg may further decrease (say to ₹8.5 per kg), as the quantity purchased is substantially higher at 1,000 kgs compared to 100 kgs earlier). Given the fact of having trade discounts on bulk purchases, the per unit cost of material would depend on quantity of materials to be purchased. In real situation, the firm (based on its budgeted production) would have its budgeted requirement of direct materials. Based on the likely quantity of direct materials to be purchased (say 10,000 kg for ₹80,000) per kg material cost would be ₹8; the direct material cost at the rate of ₹8 per kg would be valid only if the quantity purchased are in the vicinity of 8,000 kg; in case, there is substantial decrease/increase in the purchased quantity, per unit cost may increase/decrease. This then constitutes the rationale of having relevant range as a part of definition of VC.
10. *Ibid.*, p. 208.
11. *Ibid.*, p. 224.
12. J.L. Brown and L.R. Howard, *Principles and Practice of Management Accounting*, (Macdonald and Evans Ltd, London, 1969), p. 249
13. Fremgen, *Accounting for Managerial Analysis*, (Illinois, Irwin, 1976), p. 17.
14. R.N. Anthony and G.A. Welsh, *Fundamentals of Management Accounting*, (Richard D. Irwin, Homewood, Illinois, 1977, p. 451).
15. Fremgen, *op.cit.*, p. 28.
16. D.T. Decoster, *Management Accounting: A Decision Emphasis*, (John Wiley and Sons, New York, 1979), p. 10.

REVIEW QUESTIONS

LOD: Easy

RQ.7.1 In the following multiple choice questions, select the correct answers. LO 7.2,3,4

(i) A company undertakes job-works. Which one of the following is likely to be a variable cost? (a) the wages of workers paid on monthly basis, (b) the salary of the factory manager, (c) the wages of shop floor workers paid by piece rate, (d) the rent of the factory.

(ii) A company makes plastic windows and doors. Which one of the following is likely to be a fixed cost?
(a) the cost of heating the factory, (b) the cost of the plastic, (c) sales commission, (d) none of these.

(iii) When units produced increase, total variable costs ____________
(a) increase in proportion to the units produced, (b) increase at a greater rate than units produced, (c) increase at a lesser rate than units produced, (d) do not change.

(iv) As production increases (within relevant range), total fixed costs __________
(a) increase in proportion to the units produced, (b) increase at a greater rate than units produced, (c) increase at a lesser rate than units produced, (d) do not change.

(v) When units produced increase (within relevant range), variable cost per unit __________
(a) increase in proportion to the units produced, (b) increase at a greater rate than units produced, (c) increase at a lesser rate than units produced, (d) do not change.

(vi) As production increases, fixed cost per unit __________
(a) decreases, (b) increases, (c) we can't tell, (d) do not change.

(vii) The line equation expressing the total costs (y) might be expressed (based on the following information: total fixed costs = ₹10,000; and variable cost per unit = ₹5) as follows:
(a) $x = 5y - 10,000$, (b) $x = 10,000y - 5$, (c) $y = 5x + 10,000$, (d) $y = 10,000x + 5$

(viii) The Scattergraph method __________
(a) is a more accurate method of analysing mixed costs than the high-low method, (b) is a less accurate method of analysing mixed costs than the high-low method, (c) is as accurate method of analyzing mixed costs as the high-low method, (d) is more accurate than method of least squares.

(ix) All opportunity costs are
(a) relevant costs, (b) irrelevant costs, (c) increment costs, (d) none of these

(x) Most of the historical costs are
(a) relevant costs, (b) irrelevant costs, (c) increment costs, (d) none of these

[Answers: (i) c (ii) a (iii) a (iv) d (v) d (vi) a (vii) c (viii) a (ix) a (x) b]

RQ.7.2 Fill in the following blanks. LO 7.1,2,3,4

(i) The volume range over which cost relationships are valid is termed as __________.

(ii) Future costs that differ under proposed alternatives are __________.

(iii) Costs that are important to decision-makers, but are not recorded in financial accounting records are __________.

(iv) Costs which increase with increase in production volume are __________.

(v) The vertical axis intercept of total cost function represents __________.

(vi) Fixed costs like rent, insurance, salaries etc. are also known as __________.

(vii) Incremental and opportunity costs are __________ for decision-making.

(viii) The synonymous term for existing fixed costs is __________ from the perspective of decision-making.

(ix) __________ the most scientific method of segregating mixed costs into fixed and variable components.

(x) Indirect costs are __________ from the perspective of cost control.

[Answers: (i) relevant range, (ii) relevant costs, (iii) opportunity costs, (iv) incremental costs, (v) fixed costs, (vi) period costs, (vii) relevant costs, (viii) sunk costs, (ix) method of least squares, (x) non-controllable costs.]

RQ.7.3 Why are sunk costs not relevant in decision-making? LO 7.4

RQ.7.4 "All future costs are relevant." Do you agree? Why? LO 7.4

RQ.7.5 "Fixed costs are really variable. The more you produce the less they become." Do you agree? Explain. LO 7.2

LOD: Medium

RQ.7.6 (a) Are all fixed costs sunk costs? Explain. LO 7.2

(b) What are opportunity costs? Are opportunity costs relevant in decision-making? Give examples in support of your answer. LO 7.4

RQ.7.7 (a) "Certain costs are controllable and certain other costs are non-controllable." This is a meaningless statement unless we define what portion of the organisation is being discussed. Explain. **LO 7.3**

(b) Write short notes on controllable and uncontrollable costs. **LO 7.3**

RQ.7.8 (a) "All controllable costs are direct costs. Not all direct costs are controllable." Explain with the help of suitable examples. **LO 7.3**

(b) Distinguish between (i) engineered, (ii) discretionary, and (iii) committed costs. Give suitable examples. Are all these costs controllable? **LO 7.2**

LOD: Difficult

RQ.7.9 Direct costs and controllable costs are not necessarily the same. Comment. **LO 7.3**

RQ.7.10 What are the various methods by which you would split mixed costs in its fixed and variable elements? **LO 7.2**

RQ.7.11(a) The classification of costs as controllable and non-controllable depends upon a point of reference. Explain. **LO 7.3**

(b) Direct costs and controllable costs are not necessarily the same. Comment.

CASES

7.C.1 (Cost Concepts) Sycon Technology Inc (STI) is a NRI-owned company headquartered in Silicon Valley, California, U.S.A. The STI provides software services and software products in the area of telecom and networking technologies. The main line of work is in turnkey software projects in those areas. It has been growing phenomenally in the past two years. Yet, it has to refuse projects since it is unable to handle more business. Anupam Singh, the CEO, STI, is concerned about the state of affairs since refusing business is not in the long-term interest of the company. Due to non-availability of experienced persons, he is seriously constrained in expanding his business.

The Chief Operating Officer (COO) of STI, N.K. Singh, has suggested to the CEO that a possible solution could be to set up a development centre in India. Since a lot of talented software engineers are available there and the cost of operating the centre would be much lower than expanding the company in the USA itself. To carry a feasibility study of setting up the new development centre, Anupam Singh hires the services of Delhi-based consultant - ABC Consultants.

ABC Consultants identified three locations for setting up the development centre: Delhi, Noida and Gurgaon. The major cost elements associated with these three locations identified by ABC after wide-ranging consultations/survey are summarised below:

- Rental of office space: Delhi office, ₹3,000 per square feet per annum; Noida office, ₹700; and Gurgaon office, ₹900. The development centre would require the office for 50 engineers. On an average, 100 square feet per engineer would be required after taking into account all service areas also.
- Setup costs including architect's fee: Delhi office, ₹12,00,000; Noida office, ₹35,00,000; and Gurgaon office, ₹17,00,000

- Cost of 64 kpbs STP Internet link shared with other companies through Software Technology Park (STP): Delhi site, ₹10,00,000; Noida site, ₹8,00,000; and Gurgaon site ₹12,00,000. However, the running costs for all the three sites would be ₹3,00,000 per annum.
- Average price of personal computers, ₹60,000 and workstation cost to buy additional equipment to set up the office such as UPS, LAN hubs, routers and ethernet switch and so on, ₹85,000 per work station at all the sites.
- Employee compensation:
  - (i) Annual salary, ₹2,00,000
  - (ii) Housing facility/Monthly rent of a two-bed room apartment: Delhi, ₹9,500; Noida, ₹5,000; and Gurgaon, ₹4,500.
  - (iii) Transport facility/hiring of buses (monthly charges): Delhi, ₹17,000; Noida and Gurgaon ₹22,000 each.
- Cost of running offices:
  - (i) Electricity charges (annual): Delhi, ₹6,00,000; Noida, ₹7,00,000; and Gurgaon, ₹5,50,000
  - (ii) Annual water charges: Delhi, ₹25,000; Noida, ₹28,000 and Gurgaon, ₹38,000.
  - (iii) Telephone charges, ₹20,000 monthly irrespective of the location.
- Consultants fee/charges: ₹3,00,000.

Based on the above facts, ABC Consultants prepared a report (cost schedule) for consideration of the CEO, as given in Exhibit 1:

EXHIBIT 1 Cost Schedule/Report (Annual Costs) Relating to Development Centres

Cost Elements	*Location*		
	Delhi	*Gurgaon*	*Noida*
Fixed Costs*: (A)			
Space rental	₹1,50,00,000@	₹45,00,000@@	₹35,00,000@@
Setup costs	12,00,000	17,00,000	35,00,000
STP link costs	10,00,000	12,00,000	8,00,000
Equipment costs	42,50,000	42,50,000	42,50,000
Consultant's fee	3,00,000	3,00,000	3,00,000
	2,17,50,000	1,19,50,000	1,23,50,000
Variable Costs**(B)			
Salary	1,00,00,000	1,00,00,000	1,00,00,000
Employee housing	57,00,000[1]	27,00,000[2]	30,00,000[3]
Employee transport	6,12,000[4]	7,92,000[5]	7,92,000[6]
Electricity charges	6,00,000	4,50,000	7,00,000
Water charges	25,000	38,000	28,000
Telephone charges	2,40,000[7]	2,40,000	2,40,000
STP link usage charges	3,00,000	3,00,000	3,00,000
	1,74,77,000	1,46,20,000	1,50,60,000
Total (A + B)	3,92,27,000	2,65,70,000	2,74,10,000

@(50 × 100 × ₹3,000) @@(50 × 100 × ₹900) @@@(50 × 100 × ₹700)

[1](₹9,500 × 12 × 50) [2](₹4,500 × 12 × 50) [3](₹5,000 × 12 × 50)

[4](3 × ₹17,000 × 12) [5](3 × ₹22,000 × 12) [6](3 × ₹22,000 × 12)

[7](₹20,000 × 12)

*Costs which do not vary with a change in number of employees

**Costs which change directly with the change in number of employees.

On the basis of the above cost analysis, ABC consultants has recommended that the STI's development centre in India should be located in Gurgaon.

REQUIRED: Should the Consultant's recommendation be accepted?

Before taking a final decision, the CEO referred the Consultants' report to the CFO, Nipon Shah for review. His findings/comments on the report are summarised below:

- Fixed costs are non-time cost and should be recovered over the life of the asset. The setup costs and STP link costs are fixed costs, having 4-year lives. They should be assumed to have been incurred throughout the 4-year period.
- The Consultant fee is sunk cost.
- Equipment costs, salary and telephone charges are the same for all the locations and, therefore, irrelevant cost with respect to the decision to locate the development centre.

In the light of these, the CFO prepared the following cost report.

Cost Elements	*Delhi*	*Noida*	*Gurgaon*
(A) Fixed Costs			
Space rental	₹1,50,00,000	₹45,00,000	₹35,00,000
Setup costs (total ÷ 4)	3,00,000	42,50,000	8,75,000
STP link costs (total ÷ 4)	10,00,000	12,00,000	8,00,000
	1,55,00,000	52,25,000	45,75,000
(B) Variable Costs			
Employee housing	57,00,000	27,00,000	30,00,000
Employee transport	6,12,000	7,92,000	7,92,000
Electricity charges	6,00,000	4,50,000	7,00,000
Water charges	25,000	38,000	28,000
	69,37,000	40,80,000	45,20,000
Total (A + B)	2,24,87,000	93,05,000	90,95,000

RECOMMENDATION: The CFO has recommended the setting of the development centre at Gurgaon.

ANNEXURE 7.1

COST ASCERTAINMENT/PRODUCT COSTING

An important objective of cost accounting is product costing. Cost ascertainment is the process of determining costs on the basis of actual data. The cost ascertainment involves: (i) Collection and classification of cost/expenditure according to cost elements; (ii) Its allocation /apportionment to cost centres/units; (iii) Choice of an appropriate method of costing; and (iv) Selection of an appropriate costing technique.

Elements of Cost

There are three broad elements of cost: direct material, direct labour, and overheads.

Direct Material The substance from which the product is made is known as material. All materials which become an integral part of the finished product and which can be conveniently assigned to specific physical units are direct material.

Direct Labour Human efforts, both physical and mental, used for conversion of materials into finished products is labour. Labour cost which can be wholly, conveniently identified with a specific physical unit of product is direct labour cost. Such costs are specifically and conveniently traceable to a specific product.

Overheads These include (i) Indirect material cost (ii) Indirect labour cost, and (iii) Indirect expenses.

Indirect Material Cost It is the cost of materials which cannot be conveniently assigned to a specific physical units of production. The examples of such a cost are consumable stores, oil and waste, and so on.

Indirect Labour Cost It cannot be conveniently traced to a specific unit of product/output. It includes, wages of storekeepers, foremen, time-keepers, directors fee, salary of salesmen, and so on.

Indirect Expenses The expenses which cannot be directly, conveniently and wholly allocated to specific cost units/centres are treated as indirect expenses. They consist of: (i) Factory/manufacturing/workers/production expenses, (ii) Office and administrative expenses, and (iii) Selling and distribution expenses.

Indirect Manufacturing Expenses These are incurred in the factory. Included in these are expenses relating to production management, such as rent, rates and insurance of factory premises, power used in factory, depreciation of plant and machinery, and so on.

Office and Administrative Expenses These pertain to management of business and include office rent, lighting and heating, postage, telephone, fax and other charges, depreciation of office furnitures and equipments, legal charges, audit fee, and so on.

Selling and Distribution Charges These are incurred for marketing of products, dispatching goods sold, and so on and include (i) advertisement expenses, cost of preparing tenders, travelling expenses, bad debts, collection charges, (ii) warehouse charges, packing and loading charges and carriage outwards, and so on.

The various elements of cost are depicted in Figures 7A.1 and 7A.2.

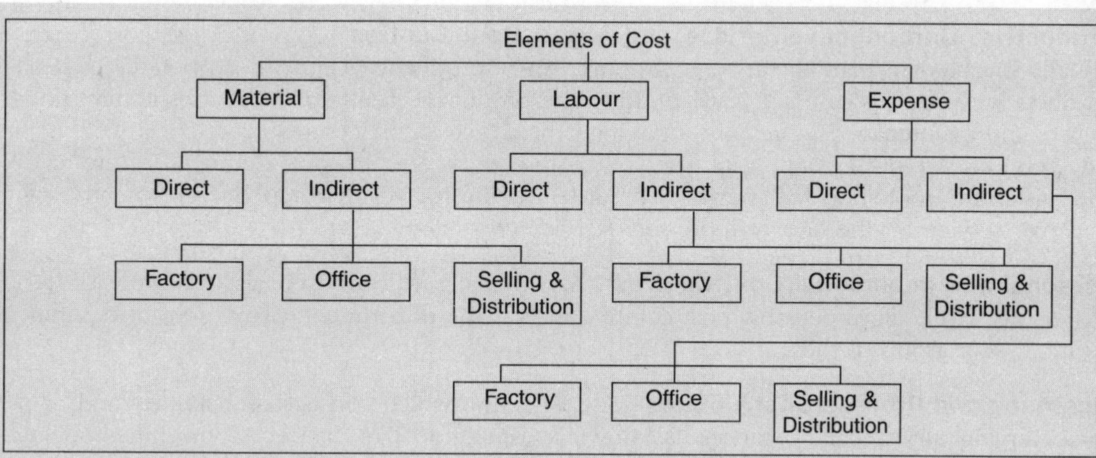

FIG. 7A.1 *Elements of Cost*

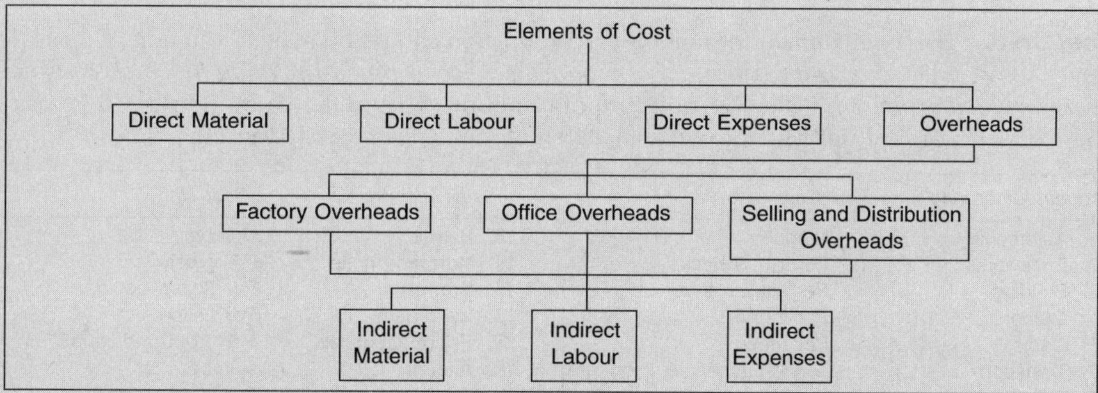

FIG. 7A.2 *Elements of Cost*

Cost Centres and Cost Units

The second element in cost ascertainment is allocation/apportionment of cost/expenses to cost centres/units.

Cost Centres While ascertaining cost, various cost elements are accumulated cost centre-wise. A cost centre means "*a location, person, or item of equipment (or a group of these) for which costs may be ascertained and used for the purpose of cost control*". It is an organisational segment/area of activity to accumulate costs. In other words, a cost centre refers to a convenient segment into which the organisation is appropriately divided for product costing. For instance, in a laundry, various activities such as collecting, sorting, marking and washing are performed. For purposes of cost accumulation, each of these activities may be treated as cost centre. All costs relating to particular activity (cost centre) would be separately accumulated to compute the cost of production of that cost centre. Cost centres can be classified into:(i) Productive, unproductive/service and mixed, (ii) Personal and impersonal, and (iii) Operation and process.

Productive, Unproductive/Service and Mixed Cost Centres A productive cost centre is actually engaged in manufacturing a product. An unproductive centre does not directly make products but provides essential service/aid to the productive centre and includes administration, repairs and maintenance, stores and drawing office. Mixed cost centres produce as well as provide services. A typical example of a mixed cost centre is a tool shop. The manufacture of dyes and jigs in the tool shop for specific jobs/orders is illustrative of productive cost centre, while its repair service for the factory represents service cost centre.

Personal and Impersonal Cost Centres A personal cost centre consists of a person/group of persons, while an impersonal cost centre consists of a department, plant, item of equipment, location, or a group of these.

Operation and Process Cost Centres A cost centre which consists of machines and/or persons carrying out similar operations is known as operation cost centre. All machines/operators performing the same operation are combined into one cost centre to ascertain the cost of each operation irrespective of location in the factory. Process cost centre consists of a specific process/ a continuous sequence of operations. An example of such cost centres is chemical industry.

Cost Units The ascertainment of unit cost of production should be related to a unit of measurement. A cost unit is "*a unit of quantity of product, service or time in relation to which costs may be ascertained/expressed.*" The cost units are not uniform. They differ from industry to industry. The examples of cost units for products in different industries are listed in Fig. 7A.3.

Industry/Enterprise	*Cost Unit*	*Industry/Enterprise*	*Cost Unit*
1. Automobile	Number	13. Bicycle	Number
2. Brickworks	Per 1,000 bricks	14. Nuts and bolts	Per gross
3. Building	Per square foot	15. Brewery	Per dozen bottle
4. Cement	Per tonne	16. Ice cream	Per gallon
5. Cable	Per meter	17. Pharmaceuticals	Per 1,000 tablets
6. Transport	Tonne/passenger kilometre	18. Aircraft	Number
7. Gas	Cubic foot/meter	19. Confectionery	Per kilogramme
8. Power	Kilowatt hour	20. Timber	Per cubic foot
9. Paper	Ream	21. Steel	Per tonne
10. Textiles	Metres	22. Soft drinks	Per case of 24 bottles
11. Hospital	Per/bed/outpatient visit	23. Sugar	Tonnes/kilogramme
12. Road contractors	Per mile/kilometer	24. Oil	Tonnes/Kilogramme Gallon/litre

Fig. 7A.3 *Cost Units*

Costing Methods

As observed earlier, costing is the process and technique of ascertaining costs. Different methods can be applied to ascertain costs. The method to be used differs from industry to industry and according to nature of business. It primarily depends on the manufacturing process and the method of measuring the departmental and finished products. Basically, there are two methods of costing, namely, specific order costing or job/ terminal costing and operations/process/ period costing.

Specific Order/Job/Terminal Costing This category of basic costing methods is applicable where the work consists of separate jobs/batches/contracts as per specific orders and customer specifications and includes: (i) Job costing, (ii) Batch costing, and (iii) Contract costing.

Job Costing According to this method, costs are collected for each job/work/project separately. Where production is not repetitive, and consists of distinct jobs/ lots with which costs can be identified, job costing method is used. It is applicable to enterprises engaged in printing, machine tool manufacturing, foundaries and forging shops, general engineering workshops, house-building, and ship building. The cost unit is the specific job.

Batch Costing It is an extension of job costing. A batch consists of a number of similar products. The cost of a group of products constituting the batch and not the single item within the batch is ascertained. It is applicable for the production of nuts and bolts, medicines, biscuits, garments, and spare parts and components and so on. Each batch constitutes the cost unit.

Contract Costing A contract is a big job and is spread over a period of time. Contract costing is applicable to builders, civil engineering contractors, construction and mechanical engineering firms. The contract is the cost unit.

Operations/Process/Period Costing This basic method of costing is applicable where standardised products result from a sequence of repetitive and, more or less, continuous operations/processes to which costs are charged. The costs cannot be traced to specific units and are averaged for the number of units manufactured. This method includes: (i) Process costing, (ii) Unit/output costing, and (iii) Service/ operating costing.

Process Costing Where (i) production is continuous, (ii) manufacturing is carried on by distinct and well defined processes, (iii) the finished product of one process (stage) becomes the raw material of the subsequent process, (iv) different products with/without byproducts are produced simultaneously of the same process, and (v) products are exactly identical, the costing method is called process costing. Cost has to be computed (a) for each process and (b) for each unit at each process by averaging the total process cost. The industries in which this method is applicable are textiles, chemicals, paper, tanneries, paints, food, explosives, soaps, and so on.

Unit/Output/Single Costing Where a single item is produced and the final product is homogeneous, the costing method is known as unit/output/single costing. The per unit cost is computed, dividing the total cost by the number of units manufactured. Industries in which this method is applicable are brick making, collieries, flour mills, paper mills, cement manufacturing, oil drilling, and so on.

Operating (Service) Costing This method is suitable for enterprises/industries which provide services and do not manufacture any physical goods. Examples are transport undertakings, electricity companies, hospitals, hotels, railways, and so on. The cost units differ among these service organisations depending on the nature of service being provided. There is usually a composite cost unit such as tonne-passenger kilometer (transport undertakings), kilowatt-hour (power companies), patient-day (hospitals), and so on.

Costing Techniques/Types

The various costing methods outlined above can be used under different costing techniques. These techniques/types refer to the manner of ascertaining cost for cost control and decision-making purposes and include uniform costing, variable costing, absorption costing, historical costing, and standard costing.

Uniform Costing It is the use of standarised principles, practices and methods of cost accounting by several undertakings for a common control or comparison of costs. It includes methods of costing, accounting classification, methods of defining costs and charging depreciation, allocation/apportionment of overheads to cost centres/cost units, and so on.

Variable Costing It is a technique of cost ascertainment in which all variable costs only which arise due to a change in volume of production, are charged to products/operations/processes. The fixed costs are accounted for in the profits of the period in which they arise. This technique is employed to ascertain the effect of change in volume/product mix and so on profit.

Absorption Costing This technique charges all costs, that is, all variable as well as all fixed, to operations/products/processes.

Historical Costing It is a system of costing in which costs are determined after they have been incurred. It ascertains actual cost incurred in the past.

Standard Costing Standard costs are predetermined in conformity with the most efficient operation and use of resources. The standard costing technique compares actual cost with standard cost. The variances between them, if any, are analysed and, in the light of the analysis of the probable causes, remedial actions are initiated by the management.

8

Costing and Control of Materials

LEARNING OBJECTIVES

After reading this chapter you will be able to:

LO 8.1 Identify the prerequisites to an effective control system for materials

LO 8.2 Explain the purchase and issue procedures for materials, system of accounting for materials issued and inventory control techniques

LO 8.3 Understand the cost of inventory

LO 8.4 Illustrate methods of pricing of materials issued/inventory costing

LO 8.5 Describe an appropriate inventory valuation method

LO 8.6 Discuss just-in time inventory/production

INTRODUCTION

Raw materials constitute an essential element of production. After raw materials are purchased and temporarily placed in store, they are processed/transformed into finished goods. This chapter explores the costing and control of materials. The control of materials is analysed first. The costing of materials is examined subsequently. The chapter also describes the just-in time inventory/production. The main points are summarised by way of recapitulation.

CONTROL OF MATERIALS

LO 8.1 Identify the prerequisites to an effective control system for materials

Rigid control over materials are necessary not only to guard against theft, but also to minimise waste and misuse from causes such as excessive inventories, overissue, deterioration, spoilage, and obsolescence. There are certain prerequisites to an effective control system for materials:[1]

- Materials of the desired quantity will be available when needed;
- Materials will be purchased only when a need exists and in economical qualities;

- Purchases of materials will be made at most favourable prices;
- Vouchers for the payments of materials purchased will be approved only if the materials have been received in good condition;
- Materials will be protected against loss by proper physical control;
- Issue of materials will be properly authorised and accounted for; and
- All materials, at all times, will be charged, as the responsibility of some individual.

The control of materials, as an element of cost of production, is illustrated with reference to the purchase and issues procedures, inventory systems, and inventory control techniques.

ORGANISATION FOR CONTROL: PURCHASE AND ISSUES PROCEDURES

LO 8.2 Explain the purchase and issue procedures for materials, system of accounting for materials issued and inventory control techniques

Control is achieved in part through an organisational structure that allows specialisation, and at the same time it defines authority, fixes responsibility and provides a system of checks and balances. To secure the advantage of specialisation, the function related to material acquisition (purchase) and handling, are usually subdivided. A centralised purchasing department is charged with the responsibility of planning orders for materials with reliable vendors at the right time and at the right price. A receiving department inspects incoming shipments/purchased goods and verifies the quantities received on orders. A stores department is held responsible for protecting materials against physical deterioration and ensuring that it is properly issued. Record-keeping is centralised in the accounting department where transactions are entered in the accounts only after documentary evidence has been supplied by other departments. Invoices are paid in the finance/credit department after approval by the accounting department. Checks and balances (that is, effective internal controls) are provided by making each department independent of the others.

Accounting for materials usually involves two activities: **(i)** Purchase of materials and **(ii)** Issue of materials.

Purchase of Materials Generally, there is a purchasing department whose function is to order/purchase materials and supplies for production. The purchase manager is responsible for ensuring that the items ordered: **(a)** Meet the quality standards, **(b)** Are acquired at the lowest price and **(c)** Are delivered on a timely basis. A typical purchase procedure involves three steps: **(1)** Purchase requisition, **(2)** Purchase order, and **(3)** Receipt of materials.

Purchase Requisition Purchase is initiated through a purchase requisition. It is a written request, sent to inform the purchasing department of a need for materials and supplies. The purchase requisition serves two purposes:

1. It notifies the purchasing department that a need exists for materials to start the purchase process in motion;
2. It fixes responsibility for the purchase request.

Although a purchase requisition is usually preprinted according to the specifications of a particular company, most forms include the requisition (serially numbered); name of the department/individual making the request; quantity of the items requested; identifying the catalogue number; description of the item; unit price; total price; shipping, handling, insurance and related costs; total cost of entire requisition; order date; required delivery date, and authorised signature. Figure 8.1 shows a purchase requisition.

Avon Company Ltd — Number

Purchase Requisition

Department/Individual making request...............................

Order date..............................Delivery date requested..............................

Quantity	Catalogue number	Description	Unit price	Total

Approved by.. Total cost

FIG. 8.1 *Purchase Requisition*

Two copies of purchase requisition are customarily made, the original going to the purchasing department (to place the order), and the copy remaining with the stores clerk who requested the purchase order (to keep track of orders placed).

Purchase Order After the requisition has been approved, the purchasing department places order. For routine purchases, the order is usually sent through established sources of supply; in other cases, the purchasing department may ask for bids or send out requests for quotations before placing the order. A purchase order is a written request to a supplier for specified goods at an agreed price. The request also stipulates terms of delivery and terms of payment. The purchase order authorises the supplier to deliver goods and submit a bill. To provide control over issuance of purchase orders, they are serially numbered. The items commonly included in a purchase ordered are: preprinted name and address of the company placing the order; purchase order number; name and address of supplier; order date; date delivery requested, delivery and payment terms; quantity of items ordered; catalogue number; description, unit and total price; shipping, handling, insurance and related costs; total cost of entire order; and authorised signature. Figure 8.2 shows a purchase order.

Avon Company Ltd — Number

(full address)

Purchase Order

Supplier................................. Order date.................................

Address................................. Date delivery requested by ....

Delivery terms......................... Payment terms.................................

Quantity	Catalogue number	Description	Unit price	Total

Approved by.. Total cost

FIG. 8.2 *Purchase Order*

The original order is sent to the supplier (to place the order). Copies of the purchase order usually go to the: **(i)** Accounting department (to be used in checking the supplier's invoice when a voucher is being prepared for payment, and for future recording in the purchase journal and the general and subsidiary ledgers); **(ii)** Receiving department (to alert them to expect a delivery), and **(iii)** Credit/finance department (for eventual payment within the discount period). A copy is retained by the purchasing department to maintain a file of all purchase orders issued.

Receiving Materials When the goods that were ordered are delivered, the receiving department unpacks and counts them. In order to ensure that the goods delivered are actually counted, the copy of the purchase order sent to the receiving department does not show/deliberately omit the quantity ordered. The supplier sends a packing slip giving details of the goods supplied/shipped. To ensure that the goods are not damaged and that they meet the specifications of the purchase order and the packing list, they are checked by the receiving department. Quantities and condition on receipt of goods are noted by the receiving department on a Receiving Report as shown in Figure 8.3. The report includes the suppliers' name, purchase order number; date, delivery was received; quantity received; description of goods, discrepancies, if any, from the purchase order (or mention of damaged goods), and authorised signature. While the original report is kept with the receiving department, copies are sent to:

- Purchasing department, to indicate that the material was received, as well as to supply information about the goods received that might be useful in evaluating the suppliers'/vendors' performance in sending the materials on schedule;
- Credit/finance department, to be matched against the purchase order and the suppliers' bill. If the receiving report, purchase order and suppliers' bill tally, payment is authorised;
- Accounting department, to record in journal and ledger together with the related liability; and
- Stores, to infom that the goods have arrived.

Avon Company Ltd — Number

Receiving Report

Supplier..................................

Purchase order number..

Date received...

Quantity	Catalogue number	Description	Unit price	Total
Authorised signature...................................				

Fig. 8.3 *Receiving Report*

In brief, for purposes of internal control over materials, the purchase order, receiving report, and the suppliers'/vendors' invoice should be matched/approved by an independent party. The accounting department should be responsible for checking and approving payment since they would not have a conflict of interest. Figure 8.4 illustrates the use of the three forms, namely purchase requisition, purchase order, and receiving reports together with the vendors' invoice.

Storing and Issuance of Materials Materials are transferred from the receiving department to the stores. The person in charge of the stores is responsible for proper storage, protection and issue of all materials. Efficient storing is another important step in materials control system. The basic accounting records of any inventory system are the documents required to authorise and record materials movements in/out of the store, namely, stocks/stores/materials ledger cards, bin cards and materials requisition note.

Stock/Stores/Materials Ledger Cards They show quantities on order, expected delivery dates and quantities reserved/required for work to be processed. They show the account number; descrip-

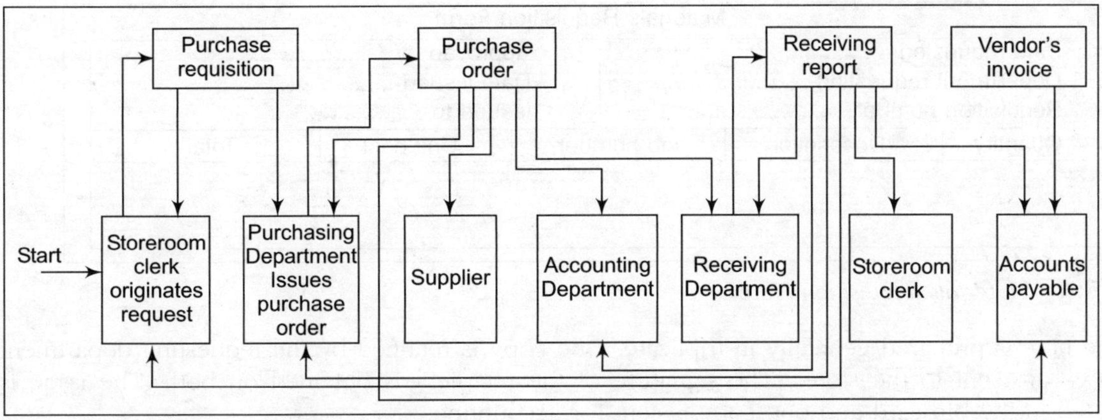

FIG. 8.4 *Purchase Requisition, Purchase Order, Receiving Report and Vendors' Invoice*

tion/type of material; location; unit measurement; minimum and maximum quantities to carry; details about the materials received; issued and balance. This is the basis of stock control as it is used to determine when additional stock needs to be acquired.

Bin card shows quantities of each type of material received, issued and on hand.

Bin Card This usually shows quantities of each type of material received, issued and on hand. It is placed in the bin/shelf or is hung over the almirah/rack otherwise known as bin. Separate bin cards are prepared for each item of stores. A bin card is shown in Figure 8.5.

Avon Company Ltd
Bin Card

Description.......................... Bin card.......................
Stores ledger number.......................... Code number.......................
Minimum level.......................... Unit number.......................

Date	Received		Issue		Balance quantity	Check
	Reference	Quantity	Reference	Quantity		

FIG. 8.5 *Bin Card*

Materials Requisition Note/Form As an element of material control system, no materials can be issued from the store without proper authorisation by competent authority. The insurance of materials is authorised by means of a materials requisition form prepared by the production manager/departmental supervisor. It shows the job number/department requesting the goods; their quantity and description and the unit cost and total cost of the materials issued. Figure 8.6 shows a material requisition note/form.

Materials Requisition Form				
Date requested .... Department requesting .... Requisition number		Approved by .... Date issued .... Issued to		
Quantity	Description	Job number	Unit cost	Total

FIG. 8.6 *Materials Requisition Note*

The note is prepared generally in triplicate. One copy is retained by the requesting department and two are sent to the stores. The signature of the recipient is obtained on both. The issue is recorded in the bin card and one copy is sent for accounting.

Materials Returned to Stores Materials requisitioned from store, and not needed, or found to be defective are returned to the stores. A returned material report is prepared, either by the person returning the material or by the incharge of the store upon receipt of the material. The original is used as a basis for crediting the accounts charged, while the duplicate copy is filed in the department returning the materials.

When summary of materials is prepared, the quantity and value of goods returned to the stores are deducted from the total materials issued. Similarly, the amount is deducted from the total amount charged to each department. Alternatively, returned materials may be recorded in the receipts section while putting a symbol/notation in red ink to indicate that it is not a receipt of new materials. The entry in red is helpful in insolating department consistently over requisitioning materials.

Some of the departments may prefer to use the excess materials on the next job instead of returning them to the store. A materials transfer note is prepared to transfer costs from one original job to the new job and also, the transfer is noted in the stock records.

System of Accounting for Materials Issued/Inventory Systems

Either the periodic inventory system or the perpetual inventory system may be used to account for materials issued to production and ending materials inventory.

> **Periodical inventory system** involves physical count of materials on hand at periodical intervals to arrive at the ending inventory.

Periodic Inventory System Under the periodic inventory system, the purchase of materials is recorded in Purchase of Raw Materials Account. The opening/beginning inventory, if any, is recorded in a separate Materials Inventory-Opening Account. The materials available for use during a period equal purchases plus opening inventory. A physical count is made of the materials on hand at the end of the period to arrive at the closing/ending materials inventory. The cost of materials for the period is determined as shown in Exhibit 8.1.

EXHIBIT 8.1 **Cost of Materials Issued**

Materials inventory-opening
+ Purchases
= Materials available for use
– Materials inventory-closing (based on physical count)
= Cost of materials issued

The entire book inventory is verified at a given date by an actual count of materials on hand. This physical inventory is usually taken near the end of the accounting year/period. This method provides for the recording of the purchases on a daily basis but does not provide for a continuous inventory-taking. Neither does it provide for a daily/continuous computation of cost of goods sold. At the end of each accounting year, a physical count is made of the quantity of goods on hand, and the value of the inventory is determined by using an appropriate pricing method and attaching costs to units counted. It is assumed that goods not on hand at the end of the period have been sold. There is no system and accounting for shrinkage, losses, theft and wastage throughout the accounting period, and they can be discovered only at the end.

Perpetual Inventory System The purchase of materials is recorded under the perpetual inventory system in Materials Inventory Account rather than in a Purchase of Raw Materials Account. The opening/beginning materials inventory, if any, is also shown on the debit side of the Materials Inventory Account. The Materials Inventory Account is credited for the cost of materials issued, with a corresponding debit to Work-in-Process Inventory Account. The effect is that the cost of materials issued is charged to production at the time when the materials are issued and the balance in the Material Inventory Account shows the cost of materials still available for use/issue. Therefore, both the cost of materials issued and the ending materials inventory can be directly ascertained after each transaction.

Perpetual inventory system shows both cost of materials issued and ending materials inventory directly.

The perpetual inventory system is superior to the periodic inventory system. It provides better inventory/materials control and more information than the periodic inventory system. The recording and accounting of material cost is, therefore, illustrated below, using perpetual inventory system.

Recording/Accounting for Material Cost When a perpetual inventory system is used to account for materials inventory, a subsidiary ledger records card is maintained. Its total must equal the amount/balance in the Materials Inventory Control Account in the general ledger. The materials subsidiary ledger has a separate inventory record card for each item of inventory. Figure 8.7 shows an inventory record card. It shows the date, quantity and amount of materials received (debit) and issued (credit), and the resulting balance (debit).

Inventory Record Card

Item........................... Description.................................

Received			Issued			Balance		
Date	Quantity	Amount	Date	Quantity	Amount	Date	Quantity	Amount

FIG. 8.7 *Inventory Record Card*

The use of perpetual inventory system also involves physical count of materials on hand, at least once a year, in order to check for possible loss or shrinkage due to theft or spoilage. If the physical count does not match with the balance in the inventory record cards, the book figures are adjusted upward/downward to reflected the actual count.

Journal Entries The purchase and issue of materials (direct as well indirect) are journalised as follows:

(i) When materials are purchased:
Direct Materials Inventory A/c Dr
To Cash/Accounts Payable (credit purchases)
Indirect Material Inventory A/c Dr
To Cash/Accounts Payable A/c (credit purchase)

(ii) Issue of direct materials for production:
Work-in-process Inventory A/c Dr
To Materials Inventory A/c

(iii) Issue of indirect materials for production:
Factory Overhead Control A/c Dr
To Materials Inventory A/c

Direct materials are debited to work-in-process inventory because they represent a major element of production cost and, therefore, require separate recognition to provide better control. On the other hand, indirect materials represent insignificant amounts and/or are not directly traceable to a product and are, therefore, charged to factory overhead control account. The factory overhead control account accumulates all indirect cost of production such as indirect materials, indirect labour, factory depreciation, and so on. Factory overheads are discussed in detail in Chapter 10.

◆ Example 8.1

The following data relate to wood pulp inventory of Premier Supply Company Ltd for the month of April.

April	1	Opening inventory, 10,000 kilos of wood pulp costing ₹50 per kilo
	10	Purchases: 3,000 kilos @ ₹55/kilo
	16	Issued: 3,000 kilos
	26	Issued: 7,500 kilos
	28	Purchases: 4,000 kilos @ ₹60/kilo
	30	Issued: 3,500 kilos

All purchases are cash purchases. Journalise the above transactions under a perpetual inventory system. Also, compute the cost of materials issued and ending materials inventory. The company uses FIFO (first-in-first-out) method to value ending inventory.

Solution

Journal Entries:

April	10	Materials inventory (3,000 × ₹55)	Dr	₹1,65,000	
		To Cash			₹1,65,000
	16	Works-in-process inventory	Dr	1,50,000	
		To Materials inventory (3,000 × ₹50)			1,50,000
	26	Work-in-process inventory	Dr	3,77,500	
		To Materials inventory [(7,000 × ₹50) + (500 × ₹55)]		3,77,500	
	28	Materials inventory (4,000 × ₹60)	Dr	2,40,000	
		To Cash			2,40,000
	30	Work-in-process inventory	Dr	1,97,500	
		To Materials inventory [(2,500 × ₹55) + (1,000 × ₹60)]		1,97,500	

Computation of Cost:

Materials Inventory A/c

April 1	To opening stock	₹5,00,000	April 16	By work-in process	₹1,50,000
10	To cash	1,65,000	26	By work-in process	3,77,500
28	To cash	2,40,000	30	By work-in process	1,97,500
			30	By balance c/d	1,80,000
		9,05,000			9,05,000

Work-in-Process A/c

April 16	To materials inventory	₹1,50,000
26	To materials inventory	3,77,500
30	To materials inventory	1,97,500
		7,25,000

Summary:

Cost of materials issued	₹7,25,000
Ending materials inventory	1,80,000

Adjustment for Discrepancies As observed earlier, physical count of materials under the perpetual inventory system may not tally with the inventory record cards (stores ledger). The discrepancy may result from: (a) Unavoidable reasons such as evaporation; absorption/moisture; temperature changes affecting the volume of stock; shrinkage; deterioration in quality, for example, through rust; and loss due to breaking bulk or cutting up and (b) Avoidable reasons such as pilferage, unsuitable storage, careless handling, under and over issues, and materials unused but not returned to stores. The stores ledger records should be corrected to tally with the physical units in inventory irrespective of the reasons for inventory shortage. The following adjusting entries are made in different situations.

(a) When book inventory is more than the physical inventory and the shortage is normal:

Factory Overheads Control A/c Dr
  To Stores Ledger Control A/c

(b) When the shortage in physical inventory is due to non-recording of inventory shortage:

Work-in-process Control A/c Dr
  To Stores Ledger Control A/c

In both the above situations, in the stores ledger, an entry for both quantity and value is recorded in the Issue Column and a reduction is made in the Balance Column.

(c) In case of inventory gain, that is, when the stores ledger balance is less than the physical inventory (inventory overages), reverse adjusting entries of (a) and (b) above are passed. In the stores ledger, an entry for quantity and value both is recorded in the Received Column and addition is made in the Balance Column.

(d) The above adjustments are made when the inventory shortage/overage is normal and is expected in the normal course of business operations. If the loss is abnormal/due to unusual circumstances such as fire, theft, sabotage, the proper treatment is to transfer it to costing profit and loss account:

Costing Profit and Loss A/c Dr
  To Stores Ledger Control A/c

Abnormal loss is considered a non-manufacturing loss, and is taken as a period charge against income of the current accounting period.

(e) If the discrepancies are slight, the balance of the stores ledger may be accepted for inventory verification and accounting purposes. No adjustment is required in such a situation.

Inventory Control Techniques

The important techniques covered here are: **(i)** ABC analysis, **(ii)** Economic order quantity (EOQ), **(iii)** Reorder-point and **(iv)** Safety stock.

ABC system assumes different degrees of control on different items of inventory.

ABC System: Classification Problem The first step in the inventory control process is classification of different types of inventories to determine the type and degree of control required for each. The ABC System is a widely-used classification technique to identify various items of inventory for purposes of inventory control. This technique is based on the assumption that a firm should not exercise the *same* degree of control on *all* items of inventory. It should rather keep more rigorous control on items that are: **(1)** Most costly, and/or **(2)** Slowest-turning, while items that are less expensive should be given less control effort.

On the basis of the cost involved, the various inventory items are, according to this system, categorised into three classes: A, B and C. The items included in group A involve the largest investment. Therefore, inventory control should be the most rigorous and intensive, and the most sophisticated inventory control techniques should be applied to these items. The C group consists of items of inventory which involve relatively small investments, although the number of items is fairly large. These items warrant the minimum attention. The B group stands midway. It deserves less attention than A but more than C. It can be controlled by employing less sophisticated techniques.

The task of inventory planning is to properly classify all the inventory items into one of these three categories. The typical breakdown of inventory items looks approximately as shown in Table 8.1.[2]

TABLE 8.1 Inventory Breakdown Between Number of Items and Inventory Value

Group	Number of items (per cent)	Inventory value (per cent)
A	15	70
B	30	20
C	55	10
Total	100	100

Some points emerge from Table 8.1. While group A is the least important in terms of the number of items, it is by far the most important in terms of the investments involved. With only 15 per cent of the number, it accounts for as much as 70 per cent of the total value of inventory. The firm should direct most of its inventory control efforts to the items included in this group. The items comprising the B group account for 20 per cent of the investments in the inventory. They deserve less attention than A but more than C which involves only 10 per cent of the total value although, number-wise its share is as high as 55 per cent. The A B C analysis is illustrated in Example 8.2.

◆ Example 8.2

A firm has seven different items in its inventory. The average number of each of these items held, along with their unit costs, is listed below.

Items number	Average number of units in inventory	Average cost per unit
1	20,000	₹60.80
2	10,000	102.40
3	32,000	11.00
4	28,000	10.28
5	60,000	3.40
6	30,000	3.00
7	20,000	1.30

The firm wishes to introduce an A B C inventory system. Suggest a breakdown of the items into A, B and C classifications.

Solution

The ABC analysis is presented in Table 8.2.

TABLE 8.2 ABC Analysis

Item (1)	Units (2)	Per cent of Total (3)		Unit Cost (4)	Total Cost (5)	Per cent of Total (6)	
1	20,000	10	15	₹ 60.80	₹ 12,16,000	₹ 38.00	70
2	10,000	5		102.40	10,24,000	32.00	
3	32,000	16	30	11.00	3,52,000	11.00	20
4	28,000	14		10.28	2,88,000	9.00	
5	60,000	30	55	3.40	2,04,000	6.38	10
6	30,000	15		3.00	90,000	2.80	
7	20,000	10		1.30	26,000	0.82	
Total	2,00,000	100	100		32,00,000	100.00	100

The A B C system of classification of various items of inventory for determining degree of inventory control effort is a very useful technique. It should, however, be used with caution. For example, an item of inventory may be very inexpensive. Under the A B C system, it would be classified into C category. But it may be very critical to the production process and may not be easily available. It, therefore, deserves the special attention of management. But in terms of the A B C framework, it would be included in the category which requires the least attention. This is a limitation of the A B C analysis.

Economic Order Quantity Model (EOQ): Order Quantity Problem After various inventory items are classified on the basis of the A B C analysis, the management becomes aware of the type of control that would be appropriate for each of the three categories of the inventory items. The A group of items warrant the maximum attention and the most rigorous control. A key inventory problem particularly in respect of group A items relate to the determination of the size or quantity in which inventory should be acquired. In other words, while purchasing raw materials or finished goods, the questions to be answered are: *How much inventory should be bought in one lot under one order on each replenishment? Should the quantity to be purchased be large or small? Or should the requirements of material during a given period (say six months or one year) be acquired in one lot or should it be acquired in instalments or in several small lots?* Such inventory problems are called order quantity problems.

The determination of the appropriate quantity to be purchased in each lot to replenish stock as a solution to the order quantity problem necessitates a resolution of conflicting goals. Buying in large quantities implies higher average inventory level, which will assure: (i) Smooth production/

sale operations, and (ii) Lower ordering or set-up costs. But it will involve higher carrying costs. On the other hand, small orders would reduce the carrying costs of inventory by reducing the average inventory level but the ordering costs would increase, as also there is a likely interruption in operations due to stock-outs. A firm should place neither too large nor too small orders. On the basis of a trade-off between benefits derived from the availability of inventory and the cost of carrying that level of inventory, the appropriate or optimum level of the order to be placed should be determined. The optimum level of inventory is popularly referred to as the Economic Order Quantity (EOQ). It is also known as the Economic Lot Size. *The economic order quantity may be defined as that level of inventory order that minimises the total cost associated with inventory management.* Stated with reference to the cost perspectives, EOQ refers to the level of inventory at which the total cost of inventory comprising acquisition/ordering/set-up costs and carrying costs is the minimum.

EOQ is the level of inventory order that minimises the total cost associated with inventory management.

For analysing the EOQ as an inventory management technique, several sophisticated and mathematical models are available.[3] These are, however, outside the scope of this book. We illustrate here the analysis of EOQ on the basis of a simple non-mathematical approach. Nevertheless, the main elements of the order quantity problem are covered by the analytical method followed here.

Assumptions The EOQ model, as a technique to determine the economic order quantity, illustrated by us, is based on three restrictive assumptions, namely:

(i) The firms knows with certainty the annual usage (consumption) of a particular item of inventory.

(ii) The rate at which the firm uses inventory is steady over time,

(iii) The orders placed to replenish inventory stocks are received at exactly the point in time when inventories reach zero.

In addition, it may also be assumed that ordering and carrying costs are constant over the range of possible inventory levels being considered.

Approaches The EOQ model can be illustrated: **(i)** By long/analytical approach or trial and error approach, and **(ii)** By the shortcut or simple mathematical approach.

Trial and Error Approach Given the total requirements of inventory during a given period of time depending upon the inventory planning horizon, a firm has different alternatives to purchase its inventories. For instance, it can buy its entire requirements in one single lot at the beginning of the inventory planning period. Alternatively, the inventories may be procured in small lots periodically, say, weekly, monthly, quarterly, six-monthly, and so on. If the purchases are made in one big lot, the firm's average inventory holdings would be relatively large, whereas, it would be relatively small in case of acquisition of inventory in small lots. The smaller the lot, the lower the average inventory and *vice-versa.* The high average inventory would involve high carrying costs. On the other hand, low inventory holdings are associated with high ordering cost. The trial and error or long analytical approach to determine EOQ uses different permutations and combinations of lots of inventory

Carrying costs are cost associated with the maintenance/ holding of inventory.

Ordering costs are costs associated with acquisition of/ placing order for inventory.

purchases so as to find out the least ordering and carrying cost combination. In other words, according to this approach, the carrying and acquisition costs for different sizes of orders to purchase inventories are computed, and the order-size with the lowest total cost (ordering plus carrying) of inventory is the economic order quantity. The mechanics of the computation of EOQ with the trial and error approach is illustrated in Example 8.3.

◆ Example 8.3

A firm's inventory planning period is one year. Its inventory requirement for this period is 1,600 units. Assume that its acquisition costs are ₹50 per order. The carrying costs are expected to be ₹1 per unit per year for an item. The firm can procure inventories in various lots as follows: **(i)** 1,600 units, **(ii)** 800 units, **(iii)** 400 units, **(iv)** 200 units, and **(v)** 100 units. Which of these order quantities is the economic order quantity?

Solution

The calculations of the inventory costs for the data in Example 8.3 for different order quantities are shown in Table 8.3.

TABLE 8.3 Inventory Cost for Different Order Quantities

1.	Size of order (units)	1,600	800	400	200	100
2.	Number of orders	1	2	4	8	16
3.	Cost per order	₹50	₹50	₹50	₹50	₹50
4.	Total ordering cost (2 × 3)	50	100	200	400	800
5.	Carrying cost per unit	1	1	1	1	1
6.	Average inventory (units)	800	400	200	100	50
7.	Total carrying cost (5 × 6)	₹800	₹400	₹200	₹100	₹50
8.	Total cost (4 + 7)	₹850	₹500	₹400	₹500	₹850

WORKING NOTES

(i) Number of orders = Total inventory requirement/ Order size

(ii) Average inventory = Order size/2

It can be seen from Table 8.3 that the carrying and ordering costs taken together are the lowest for the order size of 400 units. This, therefore, is the economic order quantity.

The calculation of EOQ is further developed in Example 8.4.

◆ Example 8.4

The following details are available in respect of a firm:

1. Inventory requirement per year, 6,000 units
2. Cost per unit (other than carrying and ordering costs), ₹5
3. Carrying costs per item for one year, ₹1
4. Cost of placing each order, ₹60
5. Alternative order size (units): 6,000, 3,000, 2,000, 1,200, 1,000, 600 and 200.

Determine the EOQ.

Solution

The EOQ is determined in Table 8.4.

TABLE 8.4 Determination of Economic Order Quantity

1. Cost of items purchased each year	₹30,000	₹30,000	₹30,000	₹30,000	₹30,000	₹30,000	₹30,000
2. Order size (units)	6,000	3,000	2,000	1,200	1,000	600	200
3. Number of orders	1	2	3	5	6	10	30
4. Average inventory (units)	3,000	1,500	1,000	600	500	300	100
5. Total carrying cost	₹3,000	₹1,500	₹1,000	₹600	₹500	₹300	₹100
6. Total ordering costs	60	120	180	300	360	600	1,800
7. Total cost (carrying plus ordering cost)	3,060	1,620	1,180	900	860	900	1,900

Clearly, the EOQ is 1,000 units.

WORKING NOTES

(i) Total carrying costs = Average inventory × Carrying cost per unit

(ii) Total ordering costs = Number of orders × Cost per order

Mathematical (Short-cut) Approach The economic order quantity can, using a short-cut method, be calculated by the following equation:

$$EOQ = \sqrt{2\ AB/C} \tag{8.1}$$

Where A = Usage unit for the inventory planning period (total inventory requirement in units)
B = Ordering cost per buying order*
C = Carrying cost per unit

◆ Example 8.5

Using the facts in Example 8.3, find out the EOQ by applying the short-cut mathematical approach.

Solution

$$EOQ = \sqrt{\frac{2 \times 1{,}600 \times 50}{1}} = 400 \text{ units}$$

Limitations While using the EOQ model, it should be noted that it suffers from shortcomings which arise mainly due to the restrictive nature of the assumptions on which it is based. The important limitations are:

1. The assumption of a constant consumption/usage and the instantaneous replenishment of inventory are of doubtful validity. As discussed subsequently, deliveries from suppliers may be slower than expected for reasons beyond control. It is also possible that there may be unusual and unexpected demand for the stocks. To meet such contingencies, firms have to make provision by keeping additional inventories which are known as safety stocks.
2. Another weakness of the EOQ model is that the assumption of a known annual demand for inventories is open to question. There is the likelihood of a discrepancy between the actual and the expected demand leading to a wrong estimate of the economic order quantity.
3. In addition to the above, there are some computational problems involved. For instance, Equation 8.1 may give the EOQ in fractional figures, say, 232.5 units. A more difficult situation

may occur with the use of the model in that the number of orders to be may turn out to be a fraction.

Reorder Point: Order Point Problem The EOQ technique determines the size of an order to acquire inventory so as to minimise the carrying as well as the ordering` costs. In other words, the EOQ provides an answer to the question: How much inventory should be ordered in one lot? Another important question pertaining to efficient inventory management is: When should the order to procure inventory be placed? This aspect of inventory management is covered under the order point problem.

Reorder point is that level of inventory which is equal to the consumption during the lead time.

The reorder point is stated in terms of the level of inventory at which an order should be placed for replenishing the current stock of inventory. In other words, reorder point may be defined as that level of inventory when a fresh order should be placed with the suppliers for procuring additional inventory equal to the economic order quantity. Although some sophisticated reorder point formulae are available, they are outside the scope of this book We have, therefore, used a simple formula to calculate the reorder point. It is based on the following assumptions: (i) Constant daily usage of inventory and (ii) Fixed lead time. In other words, the formula assumes a condition of certainty.

$$\text{The reorder point} = \text{Lead time in days} \times \text{Average daily usage of inventory} \quad (8.2)$$

The term, "lead time" refers to the time normally taken in receiving the delivery of inventory after placing orders with the suppliers. It covers the time span from the point when a decision to place an order for the procurement of inventory is made to the actual receipt of the inventory by the firm. In other words, the lead time consists of the number of days required by the suppliers to receive and process the order as well as the number of days during which the goods will be in transit from the supplier. The lead time may also be called the procurement time of inventory.

The average usage means the quantity of inventory consumed daily. We can, therefore, define reorder point *as that inventory level which should be equal to the consumption during the lead time.*

◆ Example 8.6

Suppose the average consumption (daily usage) of inventory of a firm is 5,000 units. The number of days required to receive the delivery of inventory after placing the order (lead, that is, processing and transit time) is 15 days. The reorder point = 5,000 units × 15 days = 75,000 units. The implication is that the firm should place an order for replenishing the stock of inventory as soon as the level reaches 75,000 units. The size of the order would obviously be equal to the EOQ.

Safety Stock The economic order quantity and the reorder point, as inventory management techniques, have been explained so as to keep the discussion simple, on the assumption of certainty conditions. That is, we had assumed: **(i)** Constant/fixed usage/requirement of inventory and **(ii)** Instantaneous replenishment of inventory. The assumptions are, however, of questionable validity in real world situations, that is, under conditions of uncertainty. For instance, the demand for inventory is likely to fluctuate from time to time. In particular, at certain points of time the demand may exceed the anticipated level. In other words, a discrepancy between the assumed (anticipated/expected) and the actual usage rate of inventory is likely to occur in practice. Similarly, the receipt of the inventory from the suppliers may be delayed beyond the expected lead time. The delay may result from factors beyond control such as strikes, floods, transportation, and other bottlenecks. Thus, a firm would come across situations in which the actual usage of inventory is higher than the anticipated level, and/or the delivery of the inventory from

Safety stock is the minimum additional inventory to serve as a safety margin to meet unanticipated increase in usage.

the suppliers is delayed. Another way of saying the same thing is that the demand for inventory cannot be anticipated with certainty, that is, the likely demand for inventory is uncertain.

The effect of increased usage and/or slower delivery would be shortage of inventory. That is, the firm would disrupt production schedule and alienate the customers. The firm would, therefore, be well advised to keep a sufficient safety margin by having additional inventory to guard against stock-out situations. Such stocks are called safety stocks. This would act as a buffer/cushion against a possible shortage of inventory caused by either increased usage or delayed delivery of inventory. The safety stock may, thus, be defined as *minimum additional inventory to serve as safety margin/buffer/cushion to meet unanticipated increase in usage resulting from unusually high demand and/or uncontrollable late receipt of incoming inventory.*

Figure 8.8 has been drawn to show clearly the interrelationship that exists among various concepts of inventory discussed so far. It serves the useful purpose of presenting an integrated picture at one place. In the figure, inventory of 400 units is delivered on Day 0. The company has the policy of maintaining a safety stock of 200 units. With the receipt of 400 units inventory on Day 0, the inventory level reaches 600 units (the maximum level). With the withdrawal of raw material inventory from the store at the rate of 40 units per day, the balance of inventory stock declines to 360 units after 6 days [600 units — (40 units × 6 days)]. This level is the reorder point. If delivery is on time, the next replenishment point is reached at Day 10. On the 10th day the company has a maximum level of stock of 600 units. If, however, inventory is not received in time, the company has a safety stock of five days to fall back upon.

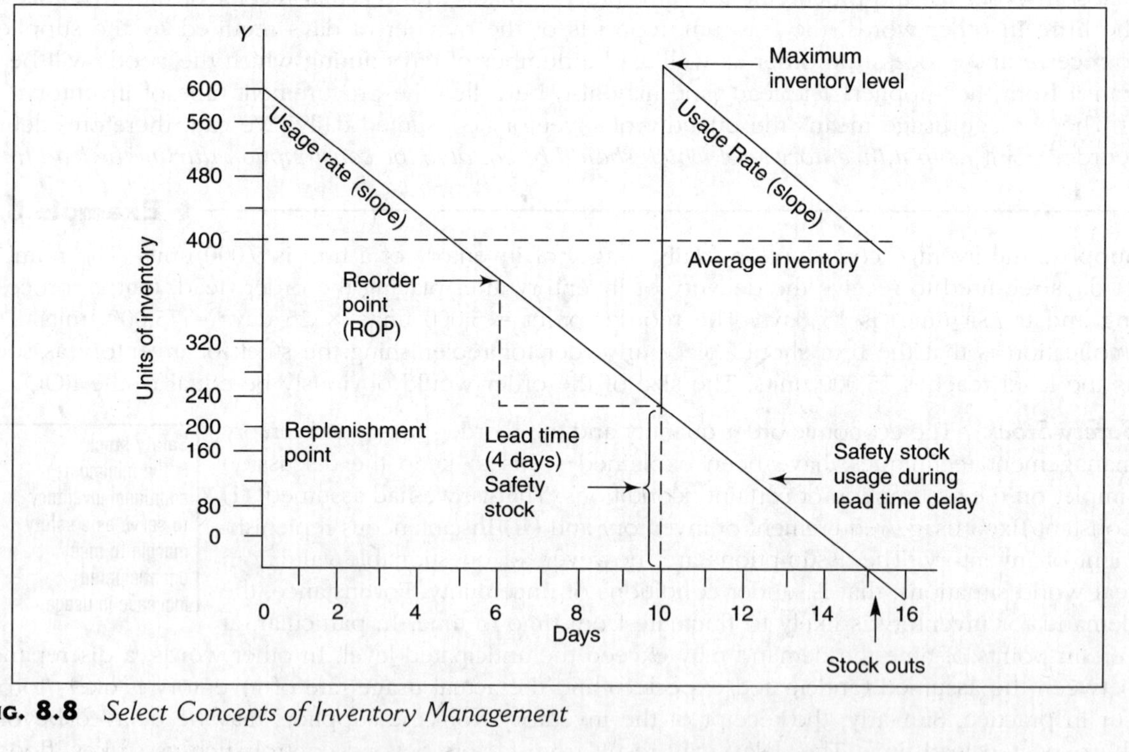

Fig. 8.8 *Select Concepts of Inventory Management*

How can the decision-maker determine the safety stock? What is his responsibility? The safety stock involves two types of costs: **(i)** Stockout and **(ii)** Carrying costs. The job of the financial manager is to determine the appropriate level of safety stock on the basis of a trade-off between these two types of conflicting costs.

Stock-out costs are costs associated with the shortage (stock-out) of inventory.

The term, 'stock-out-costs' refers to the cost associated with the shortage (stock-out) of inventory. It is, in fact, an opportunity cost in the sense that due to shortage of inventory the firm would be deprived of certain benefits. The denial of the benefits which would otherwise be available to the firm are the stock-out costs. The first, and the most obvious, of these costs is the loss of profits which the firm could have earned from increased sales if there was no shortage of inventory. Another category of stock-out costs is in terms of damage to relations with customers.[4] Since, due to shortage of inventory the firm would not be able to meet customer's requirements, the latter may turn to the firm's competitors. Of course, this type of cost cannot be easily and precisely quantified. The shortage of inventory may also disrupt the production schedule of the firm. The production process would grind to a halt, involving idle time.

The carrying costs are the costs associated with the maintenance of inventory. Since the firm is required to maintain additional inventory, in excess of the normal usage, additional carrying costs are involved.

The stock-out and the carrying costs are counterbalancing. The larger the safety stock, the larger the carrying costs and *vice versa.* Conversely, the larger the safety stock, the smaller the stock-out costs. In other words, if the firm minimises the carrying costs, the stock-out costs are likely to rise; on the other hand, attempt to minimise the stock-out costs imply increased carrying costs. The object of the financial managers should be to have the lowest total cost (carrying cost plus stock-out cost). The safety stock with the minimum carrying and stock-out costs is the economic (appropriate) level which financial managers should aim at. In brief, the appropriate level of the safety stock is determined by the trade-off between the stock-out and the carrying costs. We illustrate below, using a simple method,[5] the determination of the optimum (least cost) safety stock. Consider Example 8.7.

Example 8.7

The experience of a firm of being out of stock is summarised below:

(A) *Stock-out (number of units)*	*Number of times*	
500	1	(1)
400	2	(2)
250	3	(3)
100	4	(4)
50	10	(10)
0	80	(80)
Total	100	(100)

Figures in brackets represent percentage of time the firm has been out of stock.

(B) Assume that the stock-out cost are ₹40 per unit.

(C) The carrying cost of inventory per unit is ₹20.

Determine the optimal level of stock-out inventory.

Solution

TABLE 8.5 Computation of Expected Stock-out Costs

Safety stock level (units)	*Stock-out (units)*	*Stock-out costs (₹40 per unit)*	*Probability of stock-out*	*Expected stock-out cost [(3) × (4)]*	*Total expected stock-out cost*
(1)	*(2)*	*(3)*	*(4)*	*(5)*	*(6)*
500	0	0	0	0	0
400	100	₹4,000	0.01	₹40	₹40
250	250	10,000	0.01	100	
	150	6,000	0.02	120	220
100	400	16,000	0.01	160	
	300	12,000	0.02	240	
	150	6,000	0.03	180	580
50	450	18,000	0.01	180	
	350	14,000	0.02	280	
	200	8,000	0.03	240	
	50	2,000	0.04	80	780
0	500	20,000	0.01	200	
	400	16,000	0.02	320	
	250	10,000	0.03	300	
	100	4,000	0.04	160	
	50	2,000	0.10	200	1,180

WORKING NOTES

(i) The determination of the optimum safety stock involves dealing with uncertain demand. The first step, therefore, is to estimate the size of stock-out in terms of the shortage of inventory at different levels of safety stock as well as the probability of being out of stock.

Size of stock-out (units): The shortage of inventory at different levels of safety stock can be computed as follows:

(a) Assuming the firm's experience has been that it has been short of inventory by 500 units only once in 100 times. If, therefore, the level of safety stock is 500 units, it will never be short of inventory. It means that with 500 units of safety stock, the size of stock-out would be zero.

(b) When the firm has a safety stock of 400 units, it could be short by 100 units.

(c) Further, with 250 units of safety stock, the firm could be short by 250 units if the actual demand turns out to be 500 units greater than expected; 150 units short, if the demand turns out to be 400 units greater than the expected. Thus, the size of stock-out could be 250 units or 150 units depending upon the level of actual demand.

(d) It should be obvious that the size of stock-out increases with a decrease in the level of safety stock. The size of the stock-out for safety stock levels of 100 units, 50 units and 0 units can be computed on the lines of step (c) above.

The stock-out size at a different safety stock levels is computed in column (2) of Table 8.5.

Probability of stock-out: The probability of stock-out at different levels of safety stock can be computed as follows:

(a) If the safety stock of the firm is 500 units, there is no chance of the firm being out of stock. The probability of stock-out is, therefore, zero.

(b) When the safety stock is 400 units, there is 1 per cent chance that the firm will be short of inventory. The probability of stock-out is, therefore, 0.01.
(c) The probability of stock-out for other levels of safety stock is similarly computed in column 4 of Table 8.5.

(ii) After the determination of the size and probability of stock-out, the next step is the calculation of the stock-out cost. The stock-out cost can be found out by multiplying the stock-out by the stock-out cost per unit and the probability of stock-out cost.

When the stock-out is expected to be 100 units (safety stock being 400 units), the stock-out cost would be 100 × ₹40 = ₹4,000. But the probability of stock-out of this size is only 0.01. Therefore, the expected stock out cost would be ₹4,000 × 0.01 = ₹40. For other levels of safety stock, the stock-out cost can be similarly computed (column 5 of Table 8.5).

(iii) The next step is to compute the total expected stock-out costs (column 6 of Table 8.5).

(iv) Then, the carrying costs should be calculated. The carrying costs are equal to the safety stock multiplied by the carrying costs per unit (column 3 of Table 8.5).

(v) Finally, the carrying costs and the expected stock-out costs at each safety stock level should be added (column 4 of Table 8.5). The optimum safety stock would be that level of inventory at which the total of these two costs is the lowest. This is shown in Table 8.6.

TABLE 8.6 Computation of Total Safety Stock Costs

Safety stock level (units) (1)	*Expected stock-out costs* (2)*	*Carrying costs (₹20 per unit) (3)*	*Total safety stock cost (2+3) (4)*
0	₹1,180	₹0	₹1,180
50	780	1,000	1,780
100	580	2,000	2,580
250	220	5,000	5,220
400	40	8,000	8,040
500	0	10,000	10,000

*From Table 8.5 column 6.

Thus, the optimum safety stock is zero unit.

COST OF INVENTORY AND COSTING METHODS

This section presents and evaluates the alternative practices and policies to measure the cost of inventory. We first discuss what is included in the cost of inventory. This is followed by a discussion of the inventory costing methods. In the light of the requirements of management, an evaluation of these methods is also presented.

Cost of Inventory

LO 8.3 Understand the cost of inventory

The cost of inventory may be said to be composed of two elements: **(i)** Inventory quantities determined on the basis of either physical count or perpetual inventory records and **(ii)** Unit cost. In other words, inventory value/cost can be found out by multiplying physical quantity of inventory by unit cost/cost per unit. The physical quantity can be determined from the cost accounting records. The term *unit* cost merits some elaboration.

In general, the basis of inventory valuation is the "lower of cost or market" or more appropriately "the lower of actual cost or replacement cost." Although replacement costs can be estimated for interim periods, and adjustments made later on to reflect the conditions at the close of the year, the market value can be known with certainty only at the close of the accounting period.

As regards the actual cost, there are several elements associated with it. They are: **(i)** Invoice cost, **(ii)** Freight charges and costs of buying, receiving and storing, and **(iii)** Discounts-trade/quantity as well as cash. In valuing inventory, management has to decide which of these should be included to determine the actual cost.

In theory, all the costs which are necessary to acquire the materials and to put them in a position where they are ready to be used should be considered in valuing inventory. It can, therefore, be argued on theoretical grounds that in addition to the invoice cost, the other two components are also relevant. In other words, the value of inventory should consist of invoice cost net of all discounts plus appropriate portions of the cost of freight, buying, receiving, and storing.

However, there are practical difficulties in computing unit cost on the basis of the theoretical ideal. For instance, appropriate portions of the cost of buying, receiving, and storing are exceedingly difficult to determine. Similar difficulties may sometimes be countered with identifying the relevant freight costs. On the contrary, the inclusion of discounts also does not seem to be very appropriate. The trade and quantity discounts exist for the purpose of defining the true invoice cost of the material. Cash discounts are considered as a reward for early payment (absence of such discounts may signify as penalty for late payment). The reward can be interpreted as income while the penalty can be interpreted as a loss rather than a part of unit cost.

Thus, items like freight, cost of storing, and discount are amenable to different treatments depending on facts and circumstances. However, whichever way they are treated, the firm should consistently follow the practice.

METHODS OF INVENTORY COSTING/PRICING OF MATERIALS ISSUED

LO 8.4 Illustrate methods of pricing of materials issued/inventory costing

There are a number of generally accepted methods of determining the cost of inventories at the close of the accounting period. As already observed, our interest in discussing these methods is to identify a suitable method as a basis of inventory valuation. The selection of a suitable method assumes significance in view of the fact that it has a direct bearing on the cost of goods sold and consequently on profit. Therefore, the method should be selected in the light of the probable effects on profits over a period of years.[6] The discussion here of the methods to value inventory should, therefore, be viewed in this perspective.

First In First Out (FIFO) Method The calculation of inventory according to the FIFO method is illustrated in Table 8.7.

TABLE 8.7 Inventory Valuation (FIFO Method)

Date	Receipts			Issues			Inventory		
	Quantity (1)	*Cost (2)*	*Value (3)*	*Quantity (4)*	*Cost (5)*	*Value (6)*	*Quantity (7)*	*Cost (8)*	*Value (9)*
January 1							10,000	₹21	₹2,10,000

(Contd.)

(Contd.)

9	1,000	₹22.1	₹22,100				11,000	—	2,32,100
12				2,000	₹21	₹42,000	9,000	—	1,90,100
27	1,000	23.10	23,100				10,000	—	2,13,200
February									
10				4,000	21	84,000	6,000	—	1,29,200
16	2,000	24.10	48,200				8,000	—	1,77,400
March									
3	2,000	24.10	48,200				10,000	—	2,25,600
17				4,000	21	84,000	6,000	—	1,41,600
29	4,000	22.90	91,600				10,000	—	2,33,200
April									
4	2,000	21.40	42,800				12,000	—	2,76,000
18				4,000	@	93,400	8,000	—	1,82,600
23	2,000	20.40	40,800				10,000	—	2,23,400
May									
12				1,000	24.10	24,100	9,000	—	1,99,300
24	3,000	20.00	60,000				12,000	—	2,59,300
June									
10				1,000	24.10	24,100	11,000	—	2,35,200
30	2,000	20.20	40,400				13,000	—	2,75,600
Total	19,000		4,17,200	16,000		3,51,600			

@ 1,000	₹22.10	₹22,100
1,000	23.10	23,100
2,000	24.10	48,200
4,000	—	93,400

FIFO method assumes that the inventory is consumed in chronological order, that is, those received first are issued/consumed first and value fixed accordingly.

The FIFO method of valuation of inventory is based on the assumption that the inventory is consumed in chronological order, that is, those received first are deemed to have been issued/consumed first and priced accordingly.[7] It can be seen from Table 8.7 that with an opening inventory of 10,000 units at ₹21, the first 10,000 units issued/consumed are charged to the cost of goods sold at this opening inventory rate (₹21). The April 18 issue or consignment of 4,000 units is costed on the basis of the first receipts of the year: January 9, 1,000 units at ₹22.10, January 27, 1,000 units at ₹23.10, and February 16, 2,000 units at ₹24.10. The 1,000 each issued on May 12 and June 10 are costed on the basis of the 2,000 received on March 3. Therefore, the cost of the 13,000 inventory on June 30 is composed of the receipts of March 29, April 4 and 23, May 24 and June 30 and the value is the sum of the costs of these receipts.

Average Cost Method According to the average cost method, each purchase is added to inventory and an average cost determined. Materials are charged into cost of sales at this average until another lot is received, when a new average unit inventory cost is calculated. Using the basic data contained in Table 8.7, the average cost of inventory is calculated in Table 8.8.

TABLE 8.8 Inventory Valuation (Average Cost Method)

Date	Receipts			Issues			Inventory		
	Quantity (1)	Cost* (2)	Value (3)	Quantity (4)	Cost** (5)	Value (6)	Quantity (7)	Cost** (8)	Value (9)
January									
1							10,000	₹21.00	₹2,10,000
9	1,000	₹22.10	₹22,100				11,000	21.10	2,32,100
12				2,000	₹21.10	₹42,200	9,000	21.10	1,89,900
27	1,000	23.10	23,100				10,000	21.30	2,13,000
February									
10				4,000	21.30	85,200	6,000	21.30	1,27,800
16	2,000	24.10	48,200				8,000	22.00	1,76,000
March									
3	2,000	24.10	48,200				10,000	22.42	2,24,200
17				4,000	22.42	89,680	6,000	22.42	1,34,520
29	4,000	22.90	91,600				10,000	22.612	2,26,120
April									
4	2,000	21.40	42,800				12,000	22.41	2,68,920
18				4,000	22.41	89,640	8,000	22.41	1,79,280
23	2,000	20.40	40,800				10,000	22.008	2,20,080
May									
12				1,000	22.008	22,008	9,000	22.008	1,98,072
24	3,000	20.00	60,000				12,000	21.506	2,58,072
June									
10				1,000	21.506	21,506	11,000	21.506	2,36,566
30	2,000	20.20	40,400				13,000	21.30	2,76,966
Total	19,000		4,17,200	16,000		3,50,234			

* Actual
** Average

LIFO method assumes valuation of inventory on the basis of inverse sequence of receipts.

Last In First Out (LIFO) Method As discussed above, under the FIFO as well as the average cost methods, it is possible to calculate the cost of sales each month, and at the same time determine a known inventory cost rate for the succeeding period(s). Under the LIFO method, on the other hand, the cost of goods sold and the value of closing inventory can be determined only after the final lot of the year has been received. This is because of the assumption underlying the valuation of inventory, according to this method. As the name LIFO suggests, the use of inventory is valued on the basis of the inverse sequence of receipts. Materials received last are deemed to have been issued first and priced accordingly; physical movement of materials need not be in that order. The calculations of the value of inventory on the basis of this method are illustrated in Table 8.9.

TABLE 8.9 Inventory Valuation (LIFO Method)

	Quantity	Cost		Value
PART A				
Straight LIFO:				
Inventory (January 1)	10,000	₹21.0	—	₹2,10,000
Receipts	19,000	—	—	4,17,200
Total	29,000	—	—	6,27,200

(Contd.)

(Contd.)

Inventory (June 30)		13,000			
Inventory (January 1)	10,000	—	21.0	2,10,000	
Receipts (January 9)	1,000	—	22.10	22,100	
(January 27)	1,000	—	23.10	23,100	
(February 16)	1,000	—	24.10	24,100	
	13,000				2,79,300
Cost of inventory issued		16,000			3,47,900
PART B					
Additions at average cost:					
Inventory (January 1)		10,000	21.0		2,10,000
Receipts		19,000	21.958 app.		4,17,200
Total		29,000			6,27,200
Inventory (June 30)		13,000			
Inventory (January 1)	10,000	—	21.00	2,10,000	
Added Inventory	3,000	—	22.322	66,966	
	13,000	—			2,76,966
Cost of inventory issued		16,000			3,50,234
PART C					
Additional at FIFO cost:					
Inventory (January 1)	—	10,000	21.0		2,10,000
Receipts	—	19,000	—		4,17,200
Total	—	29,000	—		6,27,200
Inventory (June 30)	—	13,000			
March 29	4,000	—	22.90	91,600	
April 4		2,000	—	21.40	42,800
April 23	2,000	—	20.40	40,800	
May 24	3,000	—	20.00	60,000	
June 30	2,000	—	20.20	40,400	
	13,000	—	—		2,75,600
Cost of inventory issued		16,000			3,51,600

As can be seen from Table 8.9, LIFO method has three variations which are shown in parts A, B, and C respectively of the table. Under the first of these, namely, the straight LIFO method (Part A), the costs to addition to inventory in any year are the cost of the first equivalent quantity of purchases of the year. Under the second (Part B), the costs of the additions in taken at the average cost of the year. Under the third variations (Part C), the costs of the additions in any year are the costs of the last equivalent quantity or purchases in the year. In other words, additions to a LIFO inventory can be valued at FIFO cost, average cost, or LIFO cost.

However, regardless of the variation of the LIFO method used for costing additions to inventory in any one year, the years are on a straight LIFO basis regarding additions and reductions. Thus, the cost used for valuation in the first year in the LIFO method is the cost used for that quantity in every year so long as the quantity at the close of any year is not less than the original quantity. Cost of additions in a year as determined by the method selected (FIFO, Average, or LIFO for the year), is also used year after year so long as that quantity plus the original quantity remain on inventory. Reductions in inventory result in the elimination of the additions of the most recent year, and from there on back into the original quantity, if the inventory drops that far. Table 8.10 shows closing inventories for six years. As the quantities on hand at the close of the year increased in the first and second years, they were costed at the applicable rate for the respective year. In the third year, the reduction in quantities removed the additions of the second year and 1,000 those of the first year. In the fourth year, quantities increased, and the increase was costed on the basis of the cost of that year. In the fifth year, a substantial reduction in quantities took out the fourth and the first year's additions and 1,000 of the original quantity. LIFO costs of these passed out of the picture with this reduction, and in the sixth year the increase over the fifth year was costed on the basis of acquisitions in the sixth year.

TABLE 8.10 Inventory Valuation (LIFO Method—6 Years)

Particulars	*Quantity*	*Rate*	*Value*
Opening inventory at cost—first year'	10,000	₹21.00	₹2,10,000
Closing inventory:			
First year—opening inventory	10,000	21.00	2,10,000
First year's additions	3,000	23.10	69,300
Total	13,000	—	2,79,300
Second year—first year's opening	10,000	21.00	2,10,000
First year's additions	3,000	23.10	69,300
Second year's additions	2,000	22.00	44,000
Total	15,000	—	3,23,300
Third year—first year's opening	10,000	21.00	2,10,000
First year's additions	2,000	23.10	46,200
Total	12,000	—	2,56,200
Fourth year—first year's opening	10,000	21.00	2,10,000
First year's additions	2,000	23.10	46,200
Fourth year's additions	1,000	25.00	25,000
Total	13,000	—	2,81,200
Fifth year—remainder of first year's opening	9,000	21.00	1,89,000
Sixth year—remainder of first year's opening	9,000	21.00	1,89,000
Sixth year's additions	1,000	26.00	26,000
Total	10,000	—	2,15,000

Specific Identification/Actual Cost Method Under this method, the materials issued are priced at their actual cost which involves identification of each lot purchased. It is the simplest but also the most time-consuming method of determining cost of materials used and cost of the ending inventory. It entails keeping a record of the purchase price of each specific unit and the quantity of specific units used. Cost of material used is computed by multiplying the quantity used by the specific price of each material. In many cases, when materials are purchased, a tag showing the price is attached in order to identify them. This method may be usefully applied if purchase prices are fairly stable and material is readily identifiable.

Base stock is the minimum quantity of stock of materials that a firm has to maintain all times.

Base Stock Prices Method The base stock refers to the minimum quantity of stock of materials that a firm has to maintain at all times. Under this method, it is assumed that the minimum stock which must always be carried is in the nature of fixed assets, and is never realised while the business continues. The minimum stock is carried at original cost of acquisition. The quantity of materials in excess of the base stock is available for production, while the base stock is used only in case of emergency. The excess is priced in conjunction with one of the other methods such as FIFO or LIFO. Thus, this method cannot be used independently. Moreover, estimation of base stock may be difficult. It can be used in industries having relatively long processing period, and where the cost of finished product is largely made up of basic raw materials such as crude oil, hides and so on.

Standard Price Method This method of pricing issues is based on a standard price for a specified period. A standard price is fixed for each class of materials in advance after proper investigation. The method is suitable where standard costing is relevant. The difference between actual price and standard price is transferred to purchase price variance which reveals to what extent actual costs are different from standard material cost. This method is simple to operate and provides stability in costing system. However, standard price/cost does not often reflect actual/expected cost but only a notional cost/generalised target. The stock value does not show actual cost incurrence and, therefore, does not necessarily conform to acceptable principles of stock valuation.

Replacement/Market Price Method Under this method, materials are issued at the price at which they can be replaced, that is, at the market price prevailing on the date of issue. This method could be applied principally to materials purchased in advance for use in large quantities, in anticipation of economic/profitable use, or in such items of stores which are either obsolete or are lying unused for a long time in store. It reflects current cost of production and may be useful in such cases where quotations based on competitive market prices of materials are sent. However, it may be difficult to ascertain current price of each item of material at the time of issue. It is also not based on actual cost incurred and, therefore, may add confusion and complications in cost accounting.

Replacement price is the market price prevailing on the date of issue of materials.

CHOICE OF A METHOD

LO 8.5 Describe an appropriate inventory valuation method

We now attempt to select an appropriate method. First, the implications of the different methods from the viewpoint of cost, and consequently their impact on profits, are analysed. The factors which are responsible for the differences among the methods in so far as their impact on cost flows and profits is concerned, are then identified. Finally, the suitability of the different methods to value inventory is examined. The Institute of Chartered Accountants of India issued in 1999 fresh accounting standard for inventory valuation. Our focus here is, therefore, on the relative suitability of FIFO, LIFO, and Average methods.

Implications of Different Inventory Valuation Methods As stated earlier, inventory is, from the accounting point of view, included in the profit and loss account/income statement as cost of goods sold, and in the balance sheet as inventory on the assets side. The different methods of valuing inventory will have their impact on the flow of cost through the balance sheet into the profit and loss account. If, therefore, different methods to value inventory produce differing inventory values, they will also show differing amounts of cost of goods sold which will inevitably affect the profits. The implications of different methods of valuing inventory, in other words, is that depending upon the method selected, the amount of profit as shown by the profit and loss account will be different. From the viewpoint of income determination, thus, the choice of an appropriate method assumes significance. The impact of the various methods on profits through their impact on the flow of cost for the data contained in Tables 8.7 through 8.10 is illustrated in Table 8.11.

TABLE 8.11 Impact of Inventory Valuation on Cost Flows/Profits

	FIFO	*Average cost*	*LIFO*
Beginning inventory	₹2,10,000	₹2,10,000	₹2,10,000
Add: Receipts	4,17,200	4,17,200	4,17,200
Total	6,27,200	6,27,200	6,27,200
Deduct: Ending inventory	2,75,600	2,76,966	2,75,600
Materials put into process	3,51,600	3,50,234	3,51,600

It is clear from the table that each method produces a different figure for the transfer of raw materials to work-in-process. Ultimately, when the goods are sold, the varying methods of inventory valuation will have their impact on cost of goods sold and, thus, on profits.

Causes of Differences The exclusive reason for the difference in cost and profit according to the different inventory valuation methods is the changing purchase price or unit cost. If the purchase prices do not change at all or remain stable, all the inventory valuation methods will produce identical cost and profit figures. To elaborate, let us assume the following facts about the purchase of materials by a hypothetical firm.

Date of purchase (1)	*Units acquired* (2)	*Unit cost (stable price)* (3)	*Unit cost (rising price)* (4)	*Unit cost (falling price)* (5)
January 1	2	₹10	₹10.00	₹10.00
15	4	10	10.20	9.70
31	3	10	10.50	9.40

If the inventory on January 31 consists of two units, the inventory values and cost flows for each-inventory method, assuming no beginning inventory, are presented in Table 8.12.

TABLE 8.12 Cost Flows Under Different Assumptions of Price Levels

	FIFO	*Average*	*LIFO*
(A) *Stable price level*			
Ending inventory (2 units)	₹20.00	₹20.00	₹20.00
Materials put in process (7 units)	70.00	70.00	70.00
(B) *Rising price level*:			
Ending inventory (2 units)	21.00	20.50	20.00
Materials in process (7 units)	71.30	71.80	72.30
(C) *Falling price level*			
Ending inventory (2 units)	18.80	19.40	20.00
Materials in process (7 units)	68.20	67.60	67.00

The conclusions emerging from Table 8.12 are:

1. When prices are stable, all inventory valuation methods give the same figure of cost.
2. When prices are rising, the LIFO produces the highest cost flow and the lowest inventory. The FIFO has exactly the opposite effect.
3. When prices are falling, the LIFO method produces the lowest cost and the highest inventory. The impact of FIFO is exactly opposite.
4. Thus, the LIFO and the FIFO methods are extremes and the average methods falls in between.

Evaluation There is no one best method of inventory valuation. The three methods–FIFO, Average and LIFO–are suitable under different circumstances. As already observed, different methods affect the income determination (profit and loss account) and asset measurement (balance sheet). The discussion of the choice of a suitable method here is accordingly divided into two parts: The implications **(i)** On income determination and **(ii)** On asset measurement.

***Income Determination:* FIFO Method** The FIFO method is based on an assumption regarding the physical flow of materials. As observed earlier, the implicit physical flow is the chronological order, that is, materials which are purchased/received first are consumed/issued/sold first. This assumption of the pattern of flow of materials closely approximates a theoretically sound method of inventory valuation, namely, *specific identification.* The term, "specific identification," means that the units in inventory should be identified with the specific unit costs to which they apply. The merit of the FIFO method is that the physical flow of materials match the flow of cost.[8]

LIFO Method The LIFO method cannot be justified on the basis of the physical flow of materials. The justification of this method is based on *cost flow.* Under conditions of changing prices, the LIFO method matches costs and revenues. Since the LIFO method assumes that the latest item in, is the first item out, the current cost of materials are matched with the current selling price/current revenues. *This matching of current costs with current revenues is the essence of the argument for the LIFO method.*

Average Method The average method is mid-way between FIFO and LIFO. The justification for the average method has two aspects. First, it differs from the FIFO and LIFO methods in respect of the physical flow of the materials. While the FIFO fits a first-in-first-out system and the LIFO fits a last-in-first-out (current cost) system, the average method fits a system, which has no specific pattern of physical flow. Therefore, where the units in inventory are identical, interchangeable and do not follow any specific pattern of physical flow, the average cost system would be appropriate. But such a situation is more imaginary than real. It provides no justification for the appropriateness of the average cost method. The second aspect is that it is a statistical technique. As an averaging technique, it can balance the effect of changes in purchase price on inventories and cost of materials put into prices, and ultimately in the cost of goods sold.

In brief, there is not one best method to value inventories. The method chosen should fit a particular situation. In case of a physical flow pattern, the FIFO method may be appropriate. The lack of a clearly identifiable physical flow pattern may justify the use of the Average method. The relevance of cost flows, as distinct from physical flows, particularly in periods of changing prices, would warrant the use of the LIFO method.

Asset Measurement We now highlight the effect of these methods on the inventory value to be shown in the balance sheet.

FIFO Method Under this method, as noted earlier, inventory is valued on the assumption of chronological cost flow. This implies that the unused/unsold inventory consists of the most recent purchases and, therefore, can be assumed to be valued at current cost. The value of inventory as shown in the balance sheet would reflect the *current cost,* if the FIFO method is used.

LIFO Method According to this method, obviously, the inventory figure would *not* appear in the balance sheet at the *current cost.* It will reflect rather the cost of raw materials purchased in the past year. Assuming rising prices, the inventory value based on the LIFO method would tend to be *undervalued* (Table 8.10). It can be seen from the table that inventory (not in physical terms but for purposes of costing) may consist of inventory purchased as early as six years or more. In that situation, the inventory figure included in the balance sheet would be actually the price paid on the purchase of inventory six years ago. In a period of rising prices, this value would naturally be grossly out of line with the currently prevailing price. This would imply that the balance sheet will not reflect the current worth of the inventory. That the inventory value will not be correct is another way of saying that the balance sheet will present a distorted picture of the affairs of the firms.

A possible solution to correct the above distortion in the balance sheet implicit in the *undervaluation* of inventory with the LIFO method is a modified/adjusted LIFO method. According to the latter, inventory should be shown in the balance sheet in two parts: **(i)** As usual and **(ii)** The current cost should be shown in the *inner* column. To illustrate, the inventory data contained in Table 8.10 would appear in the balance sheet (sixth year) as follows:

	Balance Sheet	
	Inventory(Current cost, ₹2,60,000)	₹2,15,000

The modified LIFO method will, thus, serve the needs of correct income determination as well as correct asset measurement. However, this is subject to a qualification, namely, the current year's purchases (units) should exceed the current year's consumption (units). If for reasons such as strike/lockouts, transportation problems, and so on, the current consumption exceeds the current purchases, profits will rise. The increase will depend upon the extent of liquidation of the previous years' inventory. This increase in profit is termed as *liquidation profit*,[9] which is equal to the difference between the current cost of the inventory and the cost of the inventory purchased in the past. Assume 2 lakh units of the previous years' inventory has been used in the current year (2013), the difference in the current cost of the inventory and the cost of the inventory purchased is ₹25 per unit. The liquidation profit is ₹50 lakh (2 lakh units × ₹25).

The reporting of the liquidation profit separately from the operating profit would be found useful by management for a comparison of profits over a period of time. An additional advantage of such a policy would be that tax payment would be deferred by the firm, which will ultimately result in lower tax incidence due to time value of money.

JUST-IN TIME INVENTORY/PRODUCTION

Just-in-time refers to acquiring materials and manufacturing goods only as needed to fill customer orders.

LO 8.6 Discuss just-in time inventory/ production

The level of inventories by retailers are influenced by the demand patterns of their customers and supply relationship with their distributors and manufacturers, the suppliers to their manufacturers and so on. Supply chain describes the flow of goods/services/information from the initial source of materials and services to the delivery of products to consumers regardless of whether those activities occur in the same organisation or in other organisations. There are significant gains to companies in the supply chain from coordinating their activities and sharing information. There would be (a) fewer stock outs at the retail level, (b) reduced manufacture of goods not immediately needed by retailers, (c) fewer manufacturing orders that have to be "rushed" or "expedited" and (d) lower inventories held by each company in the supply chain. Of the numerous systems developed by manufacturing companies to plan and implement production and inventory activities within their plants, just-in-time (JIT) production/inventory is a widely used system.

Concept

The JIT is an innovative manufacturing system. It refers to acquiring materials and manufacturing goods only as needed to fill customer orders. The JIT production, also called *lean production,* is a **demand-pull**[10] manufacturing system because each component in a production line is produced as soon as and only when needed by the next step in the production line. Demand triggers each step of the production process, starting with customer demand for a finished product at the end of the process and working all the way back to the demand for direct materials at the beginning of the process. In this way, demand pulls an order through the production line. The JIT production systems aim to simultaneously (i) meet customer demand in a timely way, (ii) with high quality products and (iii) at the lowest possible total cost.[11]

As a demand-pull manufacturing system, JIT contrasts with more traditional *supply push* system in which manufacturers simply produce as many goods as possible. The JIT system is characterised by extremely small/non-existent inventories of material, work-in-process, and finished goods. Materials are scheduled to arrive only as needed, and products flow quickly from one production process to the next without having to move into temporary storage facilities. Finished goods in excess of existing customer orders are not produced.

Non-value added activities refers to those functions that do not directly increase the worth of a product to a customer.

The JIT is, however, more than an approach to inventory management. It is a philosophy of eliminating *non-value-added activities* and increasing product quality throughout the manufacturing process. Non-value-added activities refer to those functions that do not directly increase the worth of a product to a customer. Examples of such activities are: storing direct materials, setting up machinery and time during which machinery/employees stand idle. Cost savings through the reduction/elimination of such activities usually do not influence customer satisfaction. In contrast, value-added-activities do increase the value of the product to the customers. Included in such activities are product design, all manufacturing processes, manufacturing to customer specifications and convenient channels of distribution.

Value added activities do increase the value of a product to the customers.

Financial Benefits of JIT and Relevant Costs

In computing the relevant benefits and costs of reducing inventories in JIT production systems, account should be taken of all benefits. In addition to lower carrying costs of inventory, other benefits of lower inventory are[12]: **(i)** greater transparency of the production process, **(ii)** heightened emphasis on eliminating the specific causes of rework, scrap and waste, and **(iii)** lower manufacturing to lead times.

Illustration To illustrate, Hindustan Tools Corporation (HTC), manufacturer of brass fittings, is considering implementing a JIT production system. The HTC would have to incur ₹10,00,000 in annual tooling costs to reduce setup times. It is expected that JIT will reduce average inventory by ₹50,00,000. The relevant costs of insurance, storage, materials handling and setup are likely to decline by ₹3,00,000. The HTC's required rate of return on inventory investment is 10 per cent.

The other benefits associated with low inventories in JIT production system of HTC are: (i) improved quality and reduced rework on 500 units each year would result in a saving of ₹500 per unit; and (ii) better quality and faster delivery will enable HTC to charge ₹20 more per unit on the 20,000 units that it sells every year.

Based on the cost savings in carrying costs of inventory only, HTC would not find the implementation of JIT system feasible as the additional tooling cost (₹10,00,000) exceeds the annual cost savings in carrying costs of ₹8,00,000 [(0.10 × ₹50,00,000) + ₹3,00,000]. However, on the basis of the total benefits in terms of cost savings in carrying costs plus the annual relevant quality and delivery benefits, HTC would be well advised to implement the JIT systems as the total benefits exceed the annual implementation costs of ₹10,00,000 as shown below.

1. Cost savings in carrying cost of inventory		₹8,00,000
2. Plus quality and delivery benefits:		
• Rework savings (₹500 × 500 units)	₹2,50,000	
• Additional contribution margin (₹20 × 20,000)	4,00,000	6,50,000
		14,50,000

Performance Measure

The measures that managers can use to evaluate and control JIT production are discussed below.

Personal Observation The production layout in a JIT plant is streamlined and operations are not obscured by piles of inventory/rework. For this reason, personal observation is more effective in JIT plants compared to traditional plants.

Financial Performance Measure The financial measure that is widely used is inventory turnover ratio, that is, cost of goods sold ÷ inventory. This ratio would increase in a JIT system.

Non-financial Performance Measures Included in this category of measures are:

- Decrease in manufacturing lead time
- Increase in units produced per hour
- Decrease in number of days inventory on hand
- Decrease in total setup time for machines ÷ total manufacturing time
- Decrease in number of units requiring rework or scrap ÷ total number of units started and completed.

Effect on Costing System

The JIT system has effect on the costing systems. In the first place, by reducing material handling, warehousing and inspection, it reduces overhead costs. Second, it facilitates direct tracing of some costs usually classified as indirect, for example, material handling, and machine operating costs. Finally, the use of multi-skilled workers allows the costs of setup, maintenance and quality inspection to be traced as direct costs.

SUMMARY

- Materials are the basic input that are transformed into finished goods in the production process. Materials costs based on relationship with finished goods, can be broken down into direct and indirect costs.
- Accounting for materials in a manufacturing company usually involves two activities: purchase of materials (requiring a purchase requisition, purchase order, and receiving report) and the issue of materials requiring a materials requisition form.
- Materials may be entered into accounting records under either the periodic or the perpetual system. The periodic system is relatively simple and does not maintain a continuous record of the large volume of materials issued. In contrast, under the perpetual system, the cost of materials is determined as the material are placed in production.

LO 8.2

- The first step in the inventory planning/control process is the classification of different types of inventory to determine the type and degree of control required for each. The ABC system is a widely-used classification technique for the purpose. On the basis of the cost involved, the various items are classified into three categories: **(i) A**, consisting of items with the largest investment, **(ii) C**, with relatively small investments, but fairly large number of items, and **(iii) B**, which stands mid-way between category A and C. Category A needs the most rigorous control, C requires minimum attention, and B deserves less attention than A but more than C.
- The second key inventory problem relates to determination of the size/quantity of inventory which would be acquired. This is the order quantity problem. The economic order quantity, or economic lot size (EOQ) is that level of inventory order which minimises the total cost associated with inventory management. Stated with reference to cost perspective, EOQ refers to the level of inventory at which the total cost of inventory comprising (i) order/setup cost, and (ii) carrying costs is the minimum.
Symbolically,

$$EOQ = \sqrt{2\,AB/C}$$

where A = Annual usage of inventory in units, B = Buying cost per order, C = Carrying cost per unit per year
- Yet another important question relating to inventory planning and control is: When should the order to procure inventory be placed? It is what is called the order point problem. The re-order point is that level of inventory when a fresh order should be placed with suppliers to procure additional inventory equal to the EOQ. It is that inventory level which is equal to the consumption during the lead time or procurement time.
  Re-order level = (Daily usage × Lead time) + Safety stock
  Minimum level = Re-order level – (Normal usage × Average delivery time)
  Maximum level = Reorder level – (Minimum usage × Maximum delivery time) + Re-order quantity
  Average stock level = Minimum level + (Re-order quantity)/2
  Danger level = (Average consumption per day × Lead time in days for emergency purchases)
- The safety stocks are the minimum additional inventory which serve as a safety margin to meet an unanticipated increase in usage. This increase may be due to an usually high demand or because of uncontrollable late receipt of incoming inventory. The following steps are involved in determining the level of safety stocks:
  (i) The first step is to estimate the probability of being out of stock, as well as the size of stock-out in terms of the shortage of inventory at different levels of safety stock.
  (ii) After the determination of the size and probability of stock-out, the next step is the calculation of the stock-out cost. The stock-out cost can be found out by multiplying the stock-out by the cost per unit, and the probability of stock-out.
  (iii) Then, the carrying cost should be calculated. The carrying cost are equal to the safety stock multiplied by the carrying costs per unit.
  (iv) Finally, the carrying costs and the expected stock-out costs at each safety level should be added. The optimum safety stock would be that level of inventory at which the total of these two costs is the lowest.

LO 8.2

- The proper costing of inventory is important from the point of view of the income determination and asset measurement. The important inventory costing methods are: FIFO, Weighted Average, LIFO and Inflated Cost Method. The FIFO method ***assumes*** that the inventory is consumed in chronological order, that is, items received first are deemed to have been issued/consumed first and priced accordingly. The LIFO method is based on the ***assumption*** that the cost of inventory is computed on the basis of the inverse sequence of receipts. According to the Weighted Average Method, the weighted average price of purchases and inventory is taken as the basis for determining the cost of the inventory. The Inflated Cost Method takes into account normal material losses caused due to transportation, material handling and storage losses.

LO 8.4

- The implication of different inventory costing method is: **(i)** When prices are stable, all inventory valuation methods give the same figure of cost, **(ii)** when prices are rising, the LIFO produces the highest cost flow and the lowest inventory, **(iii)** When prices are falling, the LIFO method produces the lowest cost and the highest inventory. The impact of FIFO is exactly opposite, and **(iv)** the LIFO and the FIFO methods are extremes and the weighted average method falls in between.

LO 8.5

- JIT, as an innovative manufacturing system, refers to acquiring materials and manufacturing goods only as needed to fill customer orders. Also called lean production system, it is a demand-pull manufacturing system because each component in a production line is produced as soon as and only when needed by the next step in the production line.
- However, it is more than an approach to inventory management. It is a philosophy of eliminating non-value-added activities.
- The benefits of JIT are in addition to lower carrying cost of inventory, improved quality, reduced rework, faster delivery and so on.
- The measures of performance that managers use to evaluate and control JIT are personal observations, financial, and non-financial measures.
- The effects of JIT on costing system are reduced overheads and direct tracing of some indirect costs.

LO 8.6

REFERENCES

1. Polimeni, R.S., Fabozzi, F.J., Adelberg, A.H., Kole, M.A., *Cost Accounting*, (McGraw-Hill, 1991, New York), p. 90.
2. Based on studies By A. Synder, "*Principles of Inventory Management*", Financial Executive, April, 1964, pp 13-21.
3. For instance, for a detailed development and discussion of such models refer to R.I. Levin and C.A. Kirkpatrick, *Quantitative Approaches to Management*, (McGraw-Hill), New York, 1975).
4. S.E. Bolten, *Managerial Financial*, (Houghton Mifflin Co., Boston, 1976), p. 392.
5. For a more comprehensive and sophisticated treatment refer to M.C. Findlay, and E.E. Williams, *An Integrated Analysis for Managerial Finance*, (Prentice-Hall. Englewood Cliffs, 1970), p. 87.
6. It may not be out of place to mention that once a method is selected, it must be used consistently and cannot be changed from year to year.
7. In practice, the physical movement of materials may not follow the chronological order; in fact, in many situations, materials received last may be issued first as the strict adherence to the chronological order needs the removal of materials received in the 'last' so that the materials received 'first'/'earlier' can be issued. This obviously adds to the logistic inconvenience (which is avoidable). The chronological movement is desired when materials are perishable in nature.

8. I.W. Keller and W.L. Ferrara, *Management Accounting for Control,* (Tata McGraw-Hill Publishing Company Ltd., New Delhi, 1979), p. 81.
9. M.J. Gordon and G. Shillinglow, *Accounting: A Management Approach,* (Richard D. Irwin, Homewood, Illinois, 1974), p. 286.
10. Williams, J. R., *Financial and Management Accounting,* TMH, 2004, p. 788.
11. Horngren, C.T., *Cost Accounting,* Pearson, 2004, p. 697.
12. *Ibid,* pp. 697-698.

SOLVED PROBLEMS

P.8.1 If the price of the material is ₹15 per unit and the annual consumption is 4,000 units, the interest and store-keeping charges are 20 per cent of the value and the cost of placing of an order and receiving the goods is ₹60, how much material should be ordered at one time? LO 8.2 LOD: E

Solution

$$EOQ = \sqrt{\frac{2\ AB}{C}}$$

Where A = Annual usage of inventory (in units)
B = Ordering cost per buying order
C = Carrying cost per unit

$$EOQ = \sqrt{\frac{2 \times 4{,}000 \times 60}{3}} = 400 \text{ units.}$$

400 units should be ordered at one time.

WORKING NOTES

$$\text{Total carrying cost} = \frac{4{,}000 \times ₹15 \times 20}{100} = ₹12{,}000$$

$$\text{Carrying cost per unit} = \frac{₹12{,}000}{4{,}000 \text{ units}} = ₹3$$

P.8.2 Two components, A and B are used as follows: LO 8.2 LOD: M

Normal usage	:	50 units each per week
Minimum usage	:	25 units each per week
Maximum usage	:	75 units each per week
Re-order quantity	:	A: 300 units; B: 500 units
Re-order period	:	A: 4 to 6 weeks; B: 2 to 4 weeks

Calculate for each component: **(a)** Re-order level, **(b)** Minimum level, **(c)** Maximum level, and **(d)** Average stock level.

Solution

(a) *Re-order level* = (Maximum usage × Maximum delivery time)
A = 75 × 6 weeks = 450 units
B = 75 × 4 weeks = 300 units

(b) *Minimum level* = Re-order level — (Normal usage × Average delivery time in weeks)
A = 450 units — (50 units × 5 weeks) = 200 units
B = 300 units — (50 units × 3 weeks) = 150 units

(c) *Maximum level* = Re-order level — (Minimum usage × Minimum delivery time) + Re-order quantity

A = 450 units — (25 × 4) + 300 units = 650 units

B = 300 units — (25 × 2) + 500 units = 750 units

(d) (i) Average stock level = Minimum level + (Re-order quantity)/2

A = 200 + (300)/2 = 350 units

B = 150 + (500/2) = 400 units

(ii) (Minimum level + Maximum level)/2

A = (200 + 650)/2 = 425 units

B = (150 + 500)/2 = 325 units

P.8.3 The following information pertaining to a firm are available: LO 8.2 LOD: M

Annual consumption	12,000 units (360 days)
Cost per unit	₹1
Cost per order	12
Inventory carrying cost (%)	20
Lead time (maximum, normal and minimum) (days)	30-15-5
Daily consumption: (maximum, normal and minimum) (units)	45-33-15

Calculate inventory levels.

Solution

(a) *Economic-order quantity* $= \sqrt{\dfrac{2AB}{C}} = \sqrt{\dfrac{2 \times 12{,}000 \times ₹12}{0.20}}$ = 1,200 units

Carrying cost per unit= $\left(\dfrac{₹12{,}000 \times 0.2}{12000 \text{ units}}\right)$ = ₹0.20

(b) Re-order level = (Maximum usage × Maximum delivery time) = 45 units × 30 days = 1,350 units

(c) Minimum level = Re-order level — (Normal usage × Average delivery time in days)

= 1,350 units — (33 units × 15 days) = 855 units

(d) Maximum Level = Re-order level — (Minimum usage × Minimum delivery time) + Re-order quantity

= 1,350 units — (15 units × 5 days) + 1,200 units

= 1,350 units — 75 units + 1,200 units = 2,475 units

(e) (i) Average stock level = Minimum level + (Re-order quantity)/2 = 855 units + 600 = 1,455 units

(ii) (Minimum level + Maximum level)/2 = (855 units + 2,475 units)/2 = 1,665 units

P.8.4 Peekay Company Ltd has been buying a given item in lots of 1,200 units which is a six months' supply, the cost per unit is ₹12, order cost is ₹8 per order, and carrying cost is 25 per cent. You are required to calculate the savings per year by buying in economical lot quantities. LO 8.2 LOD: D

Solution

EQQ = $\sqrt{2\,AB/C}\ \sqrt{(2 \times 2{,}400 \times 8)/3}$ = 114 units

Total carrying cost = 2,400 × ₹12 × 25/100 = ₹7,200

Carrying cost per unit (C)= 7,200 ÷ 2,400 units = ₹3

Savings due to EOQ:

Particulars	*Present*	*With EOQ*
1. Size of order (units)	1,200	114
2. Number of order	2	22
3. Cost per order	₹8	₹8

(Contd.)

(Contd.)

4. Total ordering cost (2 × 3)	16	176
5. Carrying cost per unit	3	3
6. Average inventory (units)	600 (1,200 ÷ 2)	57 (114 ÷ 2)
7. Total carrying cost (5 × 6)	1,800	171
8. Total cost (4 + 7)	1,816	347
Differential costs (savings)	₹1,469	

P.8.5 Ganges Pump Company Ltd. uses about 75,000 valves per year and the usage is fairly constant at 6,250 per month. The valve cost of ₹1.50 per unit when bought in large quantities, and the carrying cost is estimated to be 20 per cent of average inventory investment on an annual basis. The cost to place an order and process the delivery is ₹18. LO 8.2 LOD: M

It takes 45 days to receive delivery from the date of an order and a safety stock of 3,250 valves is desired.

You are required to determine: **(i)** The most economical order quantity and frequency of orders, **(ii)** The order point, and **(iii)** The most economical order quantity if the valves cost ₹4.50 each instead of ₹1.50 each.

Solution

EOQ = $\sqrt{2\text{ AB/C}} = \sqrt{(2 \times 75{,}000 \times 18)/0.30}$ = 3,000 units

WORKING NOTES

(i) *Total carrying cost* = (75,000 × ₹1.50 × 20) ÷ 100 = ₹22,500
Carrying cost per unit = ₹22,500/75,000 = ₹0.30 per unit

(ii) Order point (Lead time × normal usage during lead time) + safety stock
(1.5 months × 6,250 units per month) + 3,250 units = 12,625 units.

(iii) *EOQ when cost per valve is ₹4.50:* = $\sqrt{2\text{ AB/C}} = \sqrt{(2 \times 75{,}000 \times ₹18)/₹0.90}$ =1,733 units
Total carrying cost = (75,000 × ₹4.50 × 20) ÷ 100 = ₹67,500
Carrying cost per unit = ₹67,500/75,000 = ₹0.90

P.8.6 Precision Engineering Factory Ltd consumes 50,000 units of a component per year. The ordering, receiving and handling cost are ₹3 per order while the trucking costs are ₹12 per order. Further details are as follows: deterioration and obsolescence cost, ₹0.004 per unit per year; storage cost, ₹1,000 per year for 50,000 units. Interest cost is ₹0.06 per unit per year. Calculate the economic order quantity. LO 8.2 LOD: M

Solution

EOQ = $\sqrt{2\text{ AB/C}} = \sqrt{2 \times 50{,}000 \times 15/0.084}$ = 4,226 units

Carrying cost per unit: Interest cost, ₹0.060 + Deterioration and obsolescence cost, ₹0.004 + Storage, ₹0.020 (₹1,000/50,000) = ₹0.084.

P.8.7 A customer has been ordering 5,000 special design metal columns at the rate of 1,000 per order during the past year. The production cost is ₹12 a unit–₹8 for materials and labour and ₹4 for overheads (fixed) cost. It costs ₹1,500 to set up for one run of 1,000 columns, and inventory carrying cost is 20 per cent. Since this customers may buy at least 5,000 columns this year, the company would like to avoid making five different production runs. Find the most economic production run. LO 8.2 LOD: M

Solution

Economic production run is given by the formula of EOQ in which B is setting up costs for one production run in place of buying cost per order. Accordingly economic production run = $\sqrt{(2 \times 50{,}000 \times 1{,}500)/₹2.40}$ = 2,500 units

P.8.8 Royal Industries Ltd manufacturers plastic lunch boxes in a moulding process. On an annual basis, the industry manufacturers 1,000 plastic lunch boxes at a cost of ₹4 per unit. The industry's differential costs of carrying the item in the finished goods inventory are 20 per cent LO 8.2 LOD: M of the inventory value per year, and the set-up costs per production run is ₹200. What is the optimum production-run?

Solution

Optimum production = $\sqrt{2\ AB/C} = \sqrt{2 \times 1{,}000 \times ₹200/0.080}$ = 707 units

P.8.9 M/s Tubes Ltd are the manufacturers of picture tubes for T.V. The following are the details of the operation during the current year: LO 8.2 LOD: M

Average monthly market demand (tubes)	2,000
Ordering cost (per order)	₹100
Inventory carrying cost (per cent per annum)	20
Cost of tubes (per tube)	500
Normal usage (tubes per week)	100
Minimum usage (tubes per week)	50
Maximum usage (tubes per week)	200
Lead time to supply (weeks)	6-8

Compute from the above:

1. Economic order quantity. If the supplier is willing to supply quarterly 1,500 units at a discount of 5 per cent, is it worth accepting?
2. Maximum level of stock
3. Minimum level of stock
4. Reorder level.

Solution

1. *Economic order quantity*

Annual demand (A) = Normal usage per week × 52 weeks = 100 tubes × 52 = 5,200 tubes. Ordering cost per order (B) = ₹100 per order

Inventory carrying cost per unit per annum(C) = ₹500 × 0.20 = ₹100 per unit per annum

EOQ = $\sqrt{2\ AB/C} = \sqrt{(2 \times 5{,}200 \text{ units} \times ₹100) \div ₹100}$ = 102 tubes

If supplier is willing to supply 1,500 units at a discount of 5 per cent:

Total cost (When order size is 1,500 units) = Cost of 5,200 units + Ordering cost + Carrying cost

= [5,200 × (500 × 0.95)) + [(5,200/1,500) × ₹100) + ($\frac{1}{2}$ × 1,500 × 0.20 × 475)]

= ₹24, 70,000 + ₹346.67 + ₹71, 250 = ₹25, 41,596.67

Total cost (when order size is 102 units) = (5,200 × 500) + (5,200/102 × ₹100)
+ (1/2 × 102 × 0.20 × 500)
= ₹26,00,000 + ₹5,098.03 + ₹5,100 = ₹26, 10,198.03

Since the total cost under quarterly supply of 1,500 units with 5 per cent discount is lower than when order size is 102 units, the offer should be accepted. While accepting this offer, consideration of capital blocked on order size of 1,500 units per quarter has been ignored.

2. Maximum level of stock = Reorder level+Reorder quantity—(Minimum usage × Minimum reorder period)
= 1,600 units + 102 units — (50 units × 6 weeks) = 1,402 units

3. Maximum level of stock = Reorder level—(Normal usage × Average reorder period)
= 1,600 units—(100 units × 7 weeks) = 900 units

4. Reorder level = Maximum consumption × Maximum reorder period = 200 units × 8 weeks = 1,600 units.

P.8.10 IPL Limited uses a small casting in one of its finished products. The castings are purchased from a foundry. IPL Limited purchases 54,000 castings per year at a cost of ₹800 per casting. LO 8.2 LOD: D

The castings are used evenly throughout the year in the production process on a 360-day-per-year basis. The company estimates that it costs ₹9,000 to place a single purchase order and about

₹300 to carry one casting in inventory for a year. The high carrying costs result from the need to keep the castings in carefully controlled temperature and humidity conditions, and from the high cost of insurance.

Delivery from the foundry generally takes 6 days, but it can take as much as 10 days. The days of delivery time and percentage of their occurrence are shown in the following tabulation:

Delivery time (days)	6	7	8	9	10
Percentage of occurrence	75	10	5	5	5

REQUIRED: **(i)** Compute the economic order quantity (EOQ). **(ii)** Assume the company is willing to assume a 15 per cent risk of being out of stock. What would be the safety stock? The re-order point? **(iii)** Assume the company is willing to assume a 5 per cent risk of being out of stock. What would be the safety stock? The re-order point? **(iv)** Assume 5 per cent stock-out risk. What would be the total cost of ordering and carrying inventory for one year? **(v)** Refer to the original data. Assume that using process re-engineering the company reduces its cost of placing a purchase order to only ₹600. In addition, the company estimates that when the waste and inefficiency caused by inventories are considered, the true cost of carrying a unit in stock is ₹720 per year.

(a) Compute the new EOQ.

(b) How frequently would the company be placing an order, as compared to the old purchasing policy?

Solution

(i) *Computation of economic order quantity (EOQ):*

$$\text{EOQ} = \sqrt{\frac{2AB}{C}} = \sqrt{\frac{2 \times 54{,}000 \times ₹9{,}000}{₹300}} = 1.800 \text{ castings}$$

(ii) *Safety stock:* (Assuming a 15 per cent risk of being out of stock)
Safety stock for one day = 54,000/360 days = 150 castings
Reorder point = Minimum stock level + Average consumption
= 150 + (6 × 150) = 1,050 castings

(iii) *Safety stocks:* (Assuming a 5 per cent risk of being out of stock)
Safety stock for three days = 150 × 3 days = 450 castings
Reorder point = 450 castings + 900 castings = 1,350 castings.

(iv) Total cost of ordering = (54,000/1,800) × ₹9,000 = ₹2,70,000
Total cost of carrying = (450 +1/2 × 1,800) × ₹300 = ₹4,05,000

(v) (a) Computation of new EOQ:

$$\text{EOQ} = \sqrt{\frac{2 \times 54{,}000 \times 600}{720}} = 300 \text{ castings}$$

(b) Under the new purchasing policy, the order will be placed more frequently. In fact, each order is to be placed after 2 days (1 year = 360 days). Under old purchasing policy each order was placed after 12 days.

LO 8.2 LOD: D

P.8.11 RST Limited has received an offer of quantity discount on its order of materials as under:

Price per tonne	*Tonnes number*
₹9,600	Less than 50
9,360	50 and less than 100
9,120	100 and less than 200
8,880	200 and less than 300
8,640	300 and above

The annual requirement for the material is 500 tonnes. The ordering cost per order is ₹12,500 and the stock holding cost is estimated at 25 per cent of the material cost per annum.
Required: (i) Compute the most economical purchase level. (ii) Compute EOQ if there are no quantity discounts and the price per tonne is ₹10,500.

Solution

(1) *Calculation of Most Economical Purchase Level:*

(1) Order size (Q) (Units)	40	50	100	200	300
(2) No. of orders (Units) [A/Q]	12.5	10	5	2.5	1.67
(3) Cost of purchase (A) × Per unit cost	₹48,00,000 (500 × 9,600)	₹46,80,000 (500 × 9,360)	₹45,60,000 (500 × 9,120)	₹44,40,000 (500 × 8,880)	₹43,20,000 (500 × 8,640)
(4) Ordering cost [(A/Q) × ₹12,500]	1,56,250	1,25,000	62,500	31,250	20,875
(5) Carrying cost [(Q/2) × c × 25%]	48,000 [(40/2) × 9,600 × 0.25)	58,000 [(50/2) × 9,360 × 0.25)	1,14,000 [(100/2) × 9,120 × 0.25)	2,22,000 [(200/2) × 8,880 × 0.25]	3,24,000 [(300/2) × 8,640 × 0.25)]
Total cost (3 + 4 + 5)	₹50,04,250	₹48,63,500	₹47,36,500	₹46,93,250	₹46,64,875

Total cost is minimum (₹46,64,875) when the order size is 300 units. Hence, the most economical purchase level is 300 units.

(2) $\text{EOQ} = \sqrt{\frac{2AB}{C}} = \sqrt{\frac{2 \times 500 \times ₹12{,}500}{10{,}500 \times 0.25}} = 69 \text{ tonnes}$

P.8.12 SK Enterprise manufactures a special product "ZE". The following particulars were collected for the year 2004: LO 8.2 LOD: M

Annual consumption	12,000 units (360 days)
Cost per unit	₹1
Ordering cost	₹12 per order
Inventory carrying cost	24%
Normal lead time	15 days
Safety stock	30 days consumption

REQUIRED: (i) Re-order quantity (ii) Re-order level (iii) What should be the inventory level (ideally) immediately before the material order is received?

Solution

(i) Re-order quantity/EOQ = $\sqrt{2AB/C} = \sqrt{(2 \times 12{,}000 \times ₹12) \div ₹0.24}$ = 1,095 units

Carrying cost per unit (c) = (12,000 units × 0.24)/12,000 units = ₹0.24 per unit

(ii) Re-order level = (Normal lead time × Daily consumption) + Safety stock
= (15 days × 33.33 units) + (30 days × 33.33 units) = 1,500 units

(iii) Minimum ideal level = Re-order level — (Normal usage per day × Average delivery time in days)
= 1,500 units — (33.33 units × 15 days) = 1,000 units

P.8.13 G. Ltd. produces a product which has a monthly demand of 4,000 units. The product requires a component X which is purchased at ₹20. For every finished product, one unit of component is required. The ordering cost is ₹120 per order and the holding cost is 10 per cent per annum. LO 8.2 LOD: D

You are required to calculate:

(i) Economic order quantity.

(ii) If the minimum lot size to be supplied is 4,000 units, what is the extra cost, the company has to incur?

(iii) What is the minimum carrying cost, the company has to incur?

Solution

(i) *Determination of EOQ*

$$EOQ = \sqrt{\frac{2AB}{C}} = \sqrt{\frac{2 \times 48{,}000 \text{ units} \times ₹120}{₹2}} = 2{,}400 \text{ units}$$

A = 4,000 units per month × 12 months = 48,000 units

C = ₹20 cost per unit × 0.10 = ₹2 per unit per annum

(ii) *Determination of Extra Cost when Lot Size is 4,000 Units*

Particulars	Cost when lot size is	
	4,000 units	2,400 units
1. Annual usage (units)	48,000	48,000
2. Size of order	4,000	2,400
3. Number of orders (1 ÷ 2)	12	20
4. Cost per order	₹120	₹120
5. Total ordering costs (3 × 4)	1,440	2,400
6. Carrying cost per unit per annum	2	2
7. Average inventory (size of order/2)	2,000	1,200
8. Total carrying cost (6 × 7)	₹4,000	₹2,400
9. Total costs (5 + 8)	₹5,400	₹4,800

Extra costs to be incurred is ₹640 (₹5,440 — ₹4,800), when the order size is 4,000 units.

(iii) *There is a positive relationship between the total carrying cost the firm incurs and the size of the average inventory it carries; this average size of inventory, in turn, is positively related to the size of order. In view of these facts, the minimum carrying costs, the firm is to incur is ₹2,400 (corresponding to EOQ of 2,400 units and the average inventory level of 1,200 units)*

P.8.14 A company manufactures a product from a raw material, which is purchased at ₹60 per kg. The company incurs a handling cost of ₹360 plus freight of ₹390 per order. The incremental carrying cost of inventory of raw material is ₹0.50 per kg. per month. In addition, the cost of working capital finance on the investment in inventory of raw material is ₹9 per kg per annum. The annual production of the product is 1,00,000 units and 2.5 units are obtained from one kg of raw material. LO 8.2 LOD: D

REQUIRED:

(i) Calculate the economic order quantity of raw materials.

(ii) Advise, how frequently should orders for procurement be placed.

(iii) If the company proposes to rationalise placement of orders on quarterly basis, what percentage of discount in the price of raw materials should be negotiated?

Solution

(i) $EOQ = \sqrt{\frac{2AB}{C}} = \sqrt{\frac{2 \times 40{,}000 \text{ kgs} \times ₹750}{₹15}} = 2{,}000 \text{ kgs}$

Annual usage in kgs (A) = 1,00,000 units/2.5 units = 40,000 kgs

Ordering cost per order (B) = ₹360 + ₹390 = ₹750

Carrying cost per kg per annum (C) = (₹0.50 per kg per month ×12 months) + ₹9 per kg cost of working capital finance per annum = ₹15

(ii) *Frequency of placing an order in a year*

Annual usage (in kgs)	40,000
EOQ (in kgs)	2,000
Number of orders placed in a year (40,000 kgs/2,000 kgs)	20*

* Frequency of placing an order is 18 days (360 days/20)

(iii) (a) *Incremental Total Cost to be Incurred when Orders are Placed on quarterly basis i.e., 10,000 kgs (40,000 Annual usage/4 Quarters)*

Particulars	On EOQ Basis	On Quarterly Basis
1. Annual usage (kgs)	40,000	40,000
2. Size of orders	2,000	10,000
3. Number of orders (1 ÷ 2)	20	4
4. Cost per order	₹750	₹750
5. Total orderings costs (3 × 4)	15,000	3,000
6. Carrying cost per unit	15	15
7. Average inventory (size of order/2) (kgs)	1,000	5,000
8. Total carrying cost (6 × 7)	₹15,000	₹75,000
9. Total cost (5 + 8)	30,000	78,000
Incremental costs (₹78,000 – ₹30,000) per year = ₹48,000		

(b) The firm should be able to earn discount of ₹48,000 on its total annual purchases of 40,000 kgs (40,000 kgs × ₹60 per kg = ₹24,00,000). The negotiated discount sum will be: (₹48,000/₹24,00,000) × 100 = 2 per cent.

P.8.15 The Complete Gardener is deciding on the economic order quantity for two brands of lawn fertilizer: Super Grow and Nature's Own. The following information is collected: **LO 8.2** **LOD: M**

Particulars	Fertilizer	
	Super Grow	Nature's Own
Annual demand	2,000 Bags	1,280 Bags
Relevant ordering cost per purchase order	₹1,200	₹1,400
Annual relevant carrying cost per bag	480	560

Required:

(i) Compute EOQ for Super Grow and Nature's Own.

(ii) For the EOQ, what is the sum of the total annual relevant ordering costs and total annual relevant carrying costs for Super Grow and Nature's Own?

(iii) For the EOQ, compute the number of deliveries per year for Super Grow and Nature's Own.

Solution

(i) $\text{EOQ} = \sqrt{\frac{2AB}{C}} = \sqrt{\frac{2 \times 2,000 \times 1,200}{480}}$ = 100 bags (Super Grow)

$= \sqrt{\frac{2 \times 1,280 \times 1,400}{560}}$ = 80 bags (Nature's Own)

(ii) and **(iii)** Statement showing Total Relevant Costs for Super Grow and Nature's Own Fertilizer

Particulars	Super Grow	Nature's Own
Annual demand (bags)	2,000	1,280
EOQ (bags)	100	80
Number of orders/deliveries	20	16
Multiplied by ordering cost per order	₹1,200	₹1,400
(a) Total ordering cost	24,000	22,400
Average inventory (1/2 × EOQ) of bags	50	40
Multiplied by carrying cost per bag	480	560
(b) Total carrying cost	24,000	22,400
(c) Total cost (a) + (b)	48,000	44,800

P.8.16 A Company has the option to procure a particular material from two sources: Source I assures that defectives will not be more than 2 per cent of supplied quantity. Source II does not give any assurance, but on the basis of past experience of supplies received from it, it is observed that defective percentage is 2.8 per cent. LO 8.3 LOD: M

The material is supplied in lots of 1,000 units. Source II supplies the lot at a price, which is lower by ₹100 as compared to source 1. The defective units of material can be rectified for use at a cost of ₹5 per unit.

You are required to find out which of the two sources is more economical.

Solution

Statement showing Comparative Costs Associated with two Sources of Material Supplies

Particulars	*Material source I*	*Material source II*
1. Material supplied (in units)	1,000	1,000
2. Defective units (in percentage)	2	2.8
3. Total defective units (I × 2)	20	28
4. Rectification cost per unit	₹5	₹5
5. Total rectification (3 × 4)	100	140
6. Additional price paid in Source I	100	—
7. Total additional costs (5 + 6)	200	140

Material Source II is more economical as it entails lower costs. The company is advised to buy materials from Source II.

P.8.17 A factory uses 4,000 varieties of inventory. In terms of inventory holding and inventory usage, the following information is compiled. LO 8.2 LOD: M

Number of varieties of inventory	*Percentage*	*% value of inventory holding (average)*	*% of inventory usage (in end-product)*
3,875	96.875	20	5
110	2.750	30	10
15	0.375	50	85
4,000	100.00	100	100

Classify the items of inventory as per ABC analysis with reasons.

Solution

(i) 15 number of varieties of inventory items should be classified as 'A' category (as per ABC analysis) as, while they constitute less than one per cent (0.375 per cent) of total number of inventory items handled by the store, their value is 50 per cent. Besides, these varieties (15) account for 85 per cent of total inventory usage (in end-product). Thus, this group is the most important.

(ii) 3,875 number of inventory items should be classified as 'C' category as they constitute 96.875 per cent of total varieties of inventory items handled by the store; such inventories account for only for 20 per cent of total value and 5 per cent of total inventory usage (in-end product). Thus, this group is the least important.

(iii) 110 number of inventory items should be classified as 'B' category as they occupy intermediate position between A category (15 items) and C category (3,875 items). These items (110) require more attention than C category items but less attention than A category items as per ABC analysis. In financial terms also, these items require 30 per cent investment (less than A category but more than C category) with 2.75 per cent of total number of varieties of inventory handled by store; such number is much higher for C category (96.875 per cent) and lower for A category (0.375 per cent).

LO 8.4
LOD: E

P.8.18 From the following informations prepare a stores ledger account under FIFO method:

1-1-X6	Opening stock, 1,000 units at ₹5 each
5-1-X6	Purchased, 900 units at ₹6 each
10-1-X6	Issued, 1,200 units
12-1-X6	Purchased, 800 units at ₹6.20 each
15-1-X6	Purchased, 300 units at ₹6.40 each
19-1-X6	Issued, 400 units
22-1-X6	Issued, 600 units
27-1-X6	Purchased, 200 units at ₹6.50 each
31-1-X6	Issued, 600 units

Solution

Stores Ledger (FIFO Method)

Date		Receipts			Issues			Balance		
		Quantity	Rate	Amount	Quantity	Rate	Amount	Quantity	Rate	Amount
January	1							1,000	₹5	5,000
	5	900	₹6	₹5,400				1,900	—	10,400
	10				1,000	₹5	₹5,000			
					200	6	1,200	700	—	4,200
	12	800	6.20	4,960				1,500		9,160
	15	300	6.40	1,920				1,800		11,080
	19				400	6	2,400	1,400		8,680
	22				300	6	1,800			
					300	6.20	1,860	800		5,020
	27	200	6.50	1,300				1,000		6,320
	31				500	6.20	3,100			
					100	6.40	640	400		2,580

LO 8.4
LOD: M

P.8.19 The following is a summary of receipts and issues of materials in a factory during January, current year:

January	1	Opening balance, 500 units @ ₹25 per unit
	3	Issue, 70 units
	4	Issue, 100 units
	8	Issue, 80 units
	13	Received from supplier, 200 units @ ₹24.50 per unit
	14	Returned to store, 15 units @ ₹24 per unit
	16	Issue, 180 units
	20	Received from supplier, 240 units @ ₹24.75 per unit
	24	Issue, 304 units
	25	Received from supplier, 320 units @ ₹24.50 per unit
	26	Issue, 112 units
	27	Returned to store, 12 units @ ₹24.50 per unit
	31	Received from supplier, 100 units @ ₹25 per unit.

Work out on the basis of First-in-First-Out price at which materials are to be issued and the value of stock as on January, 31. The physical verification revealed that on January, 15 there was a shortage of 5 units and another of 8 units on January 28.

Solution

Cost of Inventory Used and its Valuation (FIFO Method)

Date		Receipts			Issues			Balance		
		Quantity	Rate	Amount	Quantity	Rate	Amount	Quantity	Rate	Amount
January	1							500	₹25	₹12,500
	3				70	25	1,750	430	—	10,750
	4				100	25	2,500	330	—	8,250
	8				80	25	2,000	250	—	6,250
	13	200	₹24.5	₹4,900				450	—	11,150
	14	15[1]	24.0	360				465	—	11,510
	15				5[2]	25	125	460	—	11,385
	16				180	25	4,500	280	—	6,885
	20	240	24.75	5,940				520	—	12,825
	24									
					65	25	1,625			
					200	24.5	4,900			
					15	24.0	360			
					24	24.75	594	216	—	5,346
	25	320	24.50	7,840			2,772	536	—	13,186
	26				112	24.75	424	—	10,414	
	27	12[1]	24.50	294				436	—	10,708
	28				8[2]	24.75	198	428	—	10,510
	31	100	25.0	2,500				528	—	13,010

1. Returned to stores; 2. Shortage (deemed to be an issue and priced accordingly)
Value of material on January 31, ₹13,010.

P.8.20 Assume everything to be the same as provided in **P. 8.19**, work out on the basis of LIFO, the price at which materials are to be issued and the value of stock as on January 31. LO 8.4 LOD: M

Solution

Cost of Inventory Used and its Valuation (LIFO Method)

Date		Receipts			Issues			Balance		
		Quantity	Rate	Amount	Quantity	Rate	Amount	Quantity	Rate	Amount
January	1							500	₹25	₹12,500
	3				70	25	₹1,750	430	—	10,750
	4				100	25	2,500	330	—	8,250
	8				80	25	2,000	250	—	6,250
	13	200	₹24.5	₹4,900				450	—	11,150
	14	15[1]	24.0	360				465	—	11,510
	15				5[2]	24	120	460	—	11,390
	16				10	24	240		—	
					170	24.5	4,165	280		6,985
	20	240	24.75	5,940				520	—	12,925
	24				240	24.75	5,940			
					30	24.50	735			
					34	25.00	850	216		5,400
	25	320	24.50	7,840				536	—	13,240
	26				112	24.50	2,744	424	—	10,496
	27	12[1]	24.50	294				436	—	10,790
	28				8[2]	24.50	196	428	—	10,594
	31	100	25.00	2,500				528	—	13,094

1. Returned to stores; 2. shortage
Value of materials on January 31, ₹13,094

P.8.21 The following are the transactions in respect of purchase and issue of components forming a part of an assembly of a product manufactured by a firm which required to update its cost of production, very often for bidding tenders and finalising cost plus contracts: **LO 8.5 LOD: M**

January	5	1,000 units purchased @ ₹12 each
	11	Issued 2,000 units to production
February	1	1,500 units purchased @ ₹13 each
	18	Issued 2,400 units to production
	26	Issued 1,000 units to production
March	8	1,000 units purchased @ ₹14 each
	17	1,500 units purchased @ ₹15 each
	28	2,000 units issued to production

Stock on January, 1 was 5,000 units valued at ₹11 each. State the method you would adopt in pricing the issue of components, giving reasons. What value would you place on stocks as on March 31, which happens to be financial year-end?

Solution

The LIFO method is ideal under conditions of rising prices (as is in the present question), as it matches current costs (higher costs) with current revenues, leading to correct income determination. Stores ledger, based on LIFO is given below.

Stores Ledger (LIFO Method)

Date		*Receipts*			*Issues*			*Balance*		
		Quantity	*Rate*	*Amount*	*Quantity*	*Rate*	*Amount*	*Quantity*	*Rate*	*Amount*
January	1							5,000	₹11	₹55,000
	5	1,000	12	₹12,000				6,000	—	67,000
	11				1,000	12	₹12,000			
					1,000	11	11,000	4,000	—	44,000
								5,500		63,500
February	1	1,500	13	19,500						
	18				1,500	13	19,500	3,100		34,100
					900	11	9,900	2,100		23,100
	26				1,000	11	11,000			
March	8	1,000	14	14,000				3,100		37,100
	17	1,500	15	22,500				4,600		59,600
	28				1,500	15		22,500		
					500	14		7,000		30,100

Stock on March, 31 = ₹30,100.

P.8.22 From the following details of store receipts and issues of material "Exe" in a manufacturing unit, prepare the store ledger using weighted average method of valuing the issues. **LO 8.4 LOD: M**

November	1	Opening stock, 2,000 units @ ₹5 each
	3	Issued, 1,500 units to production
	4	Received, 4,500 units @ ₹6 each
	8	Issued, 1,600 units to production
	9	Returned to stores, 100 units by production department (from the issues of November 3)
	16	Received, 2,400 units @ ₹6.50 each
	19	Returned to supplier, 200 units out of the quantity received on November 4
	20	Received, 1,000 units @ ₹7.00 each
	24	Issued to production, 2,100 units
	27	Received, 1,200 units @ ₹7.50 each
	29	Issued to production, 2,800 units.

Note: Use rates up to two decimal places.

Solution

Stores Ledger (Weighted Average Method)

Date		Receipts			Issues			Balance		
		Quantity	Rate	Amount	Quantity	Rate	Amount	Quantity	Rate	Amount
November	1							2,000	₹5	₹10,000
	3				1,500	₹5	₹7,500	500	5	2,500
	4	4,500	₹6	₹27,000	1,600	5.9	9,440	5,000	5.9	29,500
	8							3,400	5.9	20,060
	9	100[1]	5	500				3,500	5.87	20,560
	16	2,400	6.50	15,600				5,900	6.13	36,160
	19				200[2]	6.0	1,200	5,700	6.13	34,960
	20	1,000	7.00	7,000				6,700	6.26	41,960
	24				2,100	6.26	13,146	4,600	6.26	28,814
	27	1,200		9,000				5,800	6.52	37,814
	29		7.50		2,800	6.52	18,256	3,000	6.52	19,558

1. Returned to stores; 2. Returned to supplier.

P.8.23 The following information is provided by Sunrise Industries Ltd for the fortnight of April, current year in respect of material Exe: LO 8.4 LOD: M

Stock on April	1	100 units @ ₹5 per unit
Purchases:		
	5	300 units @ ₹6 per unit
	8	500 units @ ₹7 per unit
	12	600 units @ ₹8 per unit
Issues:		
	6	250 units
	10	400 units
	14	500 units

REQUIRED: (a) Calculate using FIFO and LIFO methods of pricing issues (i) the value of materials consumed during the period and (ii) the value of stock materials on April 15, current year; (b) Explain why the figures in (i) and (ii) in part (a) of this question are different under the two methods of pricing of materials issued/used. You need not draw up the stores ledgers.

Solution

(a) *(i) Value of Materials Exe Consumed during April (FIFO Basis)*

Date		Receipts			Issues			Balance		
		Quantity	Rate	Amount	Quantity	Rate	Amount	Quantity	Rate	Amount
April	1							100	₹5	₹500
	5	300	₹6	₹1,800				400	—	2,300
	6				100	₹5	₹500			
					150	6	900	150	—	900
	8	500	7	3,500				650	—	4,400
	10				150	6	900			
					250	7	1,750	250		1,750
								850		6,550
	12	600	8	4,800	250	7	1,750			
	14				250	8	2,000	350		2,800

(ii) *Value of Materials Exe Consumed during April (LIFO Basis)*

Date		Receipts			Issues			Balance		
		Quantity	Rate	Amount	Quantity	Rate	Amount	Quantity	Rate	Amount
April	1							100	₹5	₹500
	5	300	₹6	₹1,800				400	—	2,300
	6				250	₹6	₹1,500	150	—	800
	8	500	7	3,500				650		4,300
	10				400	7	2,800	250		1,500
	12	600	8	4,800				850		6,300
	14				500	8	4,000	350		2,300

Cost of materials consumed	*FIFO*	*LIFO*
April 6	₹1,400	₹1,500
10	2,650	2,800
14	3,750	4,000
Total cost of materials used	7,800	8,300
Value of stock		
Balance, opening	₹500	₹500
Add purchases	10,100	10,100
Less value of materials consumed	(7,800)	(8,300)
Closing stock	2,800	2,300

(b) Cost of materials issued under LIFO method is higher by ₹500 (₹8,300, LIFO-₹7,800, FIFO), therefore, value of stock in LIFO method is lower by ₹500 (₹2,800—₹2,300).

LO 8.4 LOD: M

P.8.24 The following transactions occur in the purchase and issue of a material.

January	2	Purchased, 4,000 units at ₹4 per unit.
	20	Purchased, 500 units at ₹5 per unit
February	5	Issued, 2,000 units
	10	Purchased, 6,000 units at ₹6 per unit
	12	Issued, 4,000 units
March	2	Issued, 1,000 units
	5	Issued, 2,000 units
	15	Purchased, 4500 units at ₹5.50 per unit
	20	Issued, 3,000 units

Prepare stores ledger account using (a) Simple Average Method, (b) Weighted Average Method.

Solution

(a) *Stores Ledger (Simple Average Method)*

Date		Receipts			Issues			Balance		
		Quantity	Rate	Amount	Quantity	Rate	Amount	Quantity	Rate	Amount
January	2	4,000	₹4	₹16,000				4,000	₹4	₹16,000
	20	500	5	2,500				4,500	—	18,500
February	5				2,000	4.5[1]	9,000	2,500	—	9,500
	10	6,000	6	36,000				8,500	—	45,500
	12				4,000	5.0[2]	20,000	4,500	—	25,500
March	2				1,000	6.0[3]	6,000	3,500	—	19,500
	5				2,000	6.0	12,000	1,500	—	7,500
	15	4,500	5.50	24,750				6,000	—	32,250
	20				3,000	5.75[4]	17,250	3,000	—	15,000

Note: (1) (₹4 + ₹5)/2 = ₹4.50; (2) (₹4 + ₹5 + ₹6)/3 = ₹5; (3) ₹6; (4) (₹6 + ₹5.50)/2 = ₹5.75

(b) *Stores ledger (weighted average method)*

Date		Receipts			Issues			Balance		
		Quantity	Rate	Amount	Quantity	Rate	Amount	Quantity	Rate	Amount
January	2	4000	₹4	₹16,000				4,000	₹4	₹16,000
	20	500	5	2,500				4,500	4.11	18,500
February	5				2,000	₹4.11	₹8,220	2,500	4.11	10,280
	10	6,000	6	36,000				8,500	5.44	46,280
	12				4,000	5.44	21,760	4,500	5.45	24,520
March	2				1,000	5.45	5,450	3,500	5.45	19,070
	5				2,000	5.45	10,900	1,500	5.45	8,170
	15	4,500	5.50	24,750				6,000	5.49	32,920
	20				3,000	5.49	16,470	3,000	5.49	16,470

P.8.25 The following information is extracted from the stores ledger: LO 8.4 LOD: M

Material X

Opening Stock		Nil
Purchases:		
January	1	100 @ ₹1 per unit
	20	100 @ ₹2 per unit
Issues:		
	22	60 for job W-16
	23	60 for job W-17

Complete the receipts and issues valuation by adopting the First-in-first-out, Last-in-last-out and the Weighted Average Method.

Solution

Stores Ledger Account (FIFO, LIFO, Weighted Average Cost Method)

Date		Receipts			Issues			Balance		
		Quantity	Rate	Amount	Quantity	Rate	Amount	Quantity	Rate	Amount
(a) FIFO										
January	1	100	₹1	₹100				100	₹1	₹100
	20	100	2	200				200	—	300
	22				60	₹1	₹60	140	—	240
	23				40 20	1 2	40 40	80	—	160
(b) LIFO										
January	1	100	1	100				100	1	100
	20	100	2	200				200	—	300
	22				60	2	120	140	—	180
	23				40 20	2 1	80 20	80		80
(c) Weighted Average Cost Method										
January	1	100	1	100				100	1	100
	20	100	2	200				200	1.5	300
	22				60	1.5	90	140	1.5	210
	23				60	1.5	90	80	1.5	120

P.8.26 A manufacturer of Surat purchased three chemicals, A, B and C from Bombay. The invoice gave the following information: LO 8.3 LOD: D

Chemical A:	3,000 kgs @ ₹42 per kg	₹1,26,000
Chemical B:	5,000 kgs @ ₹38 per kg	1,90,000
Chemical C:	2,000 kgs @ ₹47.50 per kg	95,000
Sales tax		20,550
Railway freight		10,000
Total cost		4,41,550

A shortage of 200 kgs in chemical A, of 280 kgs in chemical B and of 100 kgs in chemical C was noticed due to breakages. At Surat, the manufacturer paid octroi duty @ ₹1 per kg. He also paid cartage, ₹2,000 for chemical A, ₹6,000 for chemical B and ₹3,000 for chemical C. Calculate the stock rate that you would suggest for pricing issue of chemicals assuming a provision of 5 per cent towards further deterioration.

Solution

Statement showing Determination of Issue Price of Materials

Particulars	*Chemical A*	*Chemical B*	*Chemical C*
Purchase price	₹1,26,000	₹1,90,000	₹95,000
Add sales tax (0.05[1] × purchase price)	6,300	9,500	4,750
Add railway freight (apportioned in the ratio of quantity, 3:5:2)	3,000	5,000	2,000
Add octroi @ ₹1 per kg of material received	2,800	4,720	1,900
Add cartage charges	2,000	6,000	3,000
Total cost	1,40,100	2,15,220	1,06,650
Divided by expected quantity available for issue (kgs)	2,660	4,484	1,805
Issue price per kg	52.67	48.00	59.09

Working Notes

1. Sales tax = (Total sales tax/Total purchase price) × 100 = (₹20,550/₹4,11,000) × 100 = 5 per cent

2. Statement showing the quantity (kgs) of chemicals available for issue

Particulars	*Chemical A*	*Chemical B*	*Chemical C*
Quantity purchased	3,000	5,000	2,000
Less shortage*	200	280	100
Quantity received at store	2,800	4,720	1,900
Less provision for further loss (5 per cent)*	140	236	95
Quantity available for issue	2,660	4,484	1,805

*It is assumed that both shortages due to breakage and deterioration in quantity of materials are normal losses.

LO 8.4 LOD: D

P.8.27 A Ltd furnishes the following stores transactions for September of current year:

September 1	Opening balance, 25 units; value, ₹162.50
4	Issues (Requisition 85), 8 units
6	Receipts from B and Co. (GNR 26), 50 units @ ₹5.75 per unit
7	Issues (Requisition 97), 12 units
10	Returns to B and Co., 10 units
12	Issues (Requisition 10), 15 units
13	Issues (Requisition 110), 20 units
15	Receipts from M and Co. (GNR 33), 25 units @ ₹6.10 per unit
17	Issues (Requisition 121). 10 units
19	Received replacement from B and Co. (GRN 38), 10 units
20	Returned from department material of B and Co. (MRR 4), 5 units
22	Transfer from Job 182 to Job 187 in department (MTR 6), 5 units

(Contd.)

(Contd.)

26	Issue (Requisition 146), 10 units
29	Transfer from Department A to Department B (MTR 10), 5 units
30	Shortage in stock-taking, 2 units

Write up the stores ledger under FIFO method and LIFO method.

Solution

Stores Ledger (FIFO Method)

Date	Receipts			Issues			Balance		
	Quantity	Rate	Amount	Quantity	Rate	Amount	Quantity	Rate	Amount
September 1						25	₹6.5	₹162.5	
4				8	₹6.50	₹52	17	—	110.5
6	50	₹5.75	₹287.50				67		398.0
7				12	6.50	78	55	—	320.0
10				10[1]	5.75	57.5	45	—	262.5
12				5	6.50	32.5			
				10	5.75	57.5	30	—	172.5
13				20	5.75	115.0	10	—	57.5
15	25	6.10	152.50				35	—	210.0
17				10	5.75	57.5	25	—	152.50
19	10	5.75[2]	57.50				35	—	210.00
20	5	5.75[3]	28.75				40		238.75
26				5[4]	5.75	28.75			
				5	6.10	30.50	30		179.50
30				2[5]	6.10	12.20	28		167.30

Note: (1) Returned to supplier; (2) Replacement from supplier (obviously at initial sale price of ₹5.75 per unit; (3) Returned to stores; (4) The material received as replacement from vendor has been treated as a fresh supply and hence will be used after supplies purchased on September 15 are exhausted. Since, materials returned (5 units) on September 20 (from within) relate to purchases of September 6, these units have been priced at ₹5.75 per unit; (5) Shortage (deemed to be am issue and priced accordingly); (6) The transfer from one job to another (September, 22) and from one department to another (September, 29) are book entries for adjusting the cost of respective jobs and, therefore, have not been taken into account in stores ledger account.

Stores Ledger (LIFO Method)

Date	Receipts			Issues			Balance		
	Quantity	Rate	Amount	Quantity	Rate	Amount	Quantity	Rate	Amount
September 1						25	₹6.5	₹162.5	
4				8	₹6.50	₹52	17	—	110.5
6	50	₹5.75	₹287.50				67	—	398
7				12	5.75	69	55		329
10				10	5.75	57.50	45		271.5
12				15	5.75	86.25	30		185.25
13				13	5.75	74.75			
				7	6.50	45.50	10		65
15	25	6.10	152.50				35		217.50
17				10	6.10	61.00	25		156.50

(Contd.)

(Contd.)

19	10	5.75	57.50				35	214
20	5	5.75	28.75				40	242.75
26				10	5.75	57.50	30	185.25
30				2	6.10	12.20	28@	173.05

@ Closing stock consists of

10 units @ ₹6.50	=	₹65
5 units @ ₹5.75	=	28.75
13 units @ ₹6.10	=	79.30
		173.05

P.8.28 With help of the following information, prepare the store ledger based on the weighted average method of pricing issues. **LO 8.4** **LOD: M**

September 1	Opening balance	24,000 kgs @ ₹7.5 per kg
1	Purchased	44,000 kgs @ ₹7.6 per kg
2	Issued	10,000 kgs
5	Issued	16,000 kgs
12	Issued	24,000 kgs
13	Purchased	10,000 kgs @ ₹8 per kg
18	Issued	24,000 kgs
22	Purchased	50,000 kgs @ ₹8 per kg
28	Issued	30,000 kgs
30	Issued	22,000 kgs

Note: Use rates up to two decimals.

Solution

Store Ledger (Weighted Average Method)

Date	Receipts			Issues			Balance		
	Quantity	Rate	Amount	Quantity	Rate	Amount	Quantity	Rate	Amount
September 1							24,000	₹7.5	₹1,80,000
1	44,000	₹7.6	₹3,34,400				68,000	7.56	5,14,400
2				10,000	₹7.56	₹75,600	58,000	7.56	4,38,800
5				16,000	7.56	1,20,960	42,000	7.56	3,17,840
12				24,000	7.56	1,81,440	18,000	7.56	1,36,400
13	10,000	8.0	80,000				28,000	7.73	2,16,400
18				24,000	7.73	1,85,520	4,000	7.73	30,880
22	50,000	8.0	4,00,000				54,000	7.98	4,30,880
28				30,000	7.98	2,39,378	24,000	7.98	1,91,502
30				22,000	7.98	1,75,560	2,000	7.97	15,942

REVIEW QUESTIONS

LOD: Easy

RQ.8.1 Indicate whether the following statements are 'true' or 'false'. **LO 8.2,4**

(i) It is desired that the company should exercise same degree of control on all items of inventory.
(ii) ABC analysis classifies all the material in the organisation into three categories, namely, X, Y and Z.
(iii) In ABC analysis, A category of materials warrants maximum attention followed by B and C category of materials.

(iv) Economic order quantity (EOQ) helps in determining the order size that should be placed in order to minimise the total costs associated with inventory management.
(v) EOQ assumes that the rate of consumption of inventory is constant over a period of time.
(vi) The higher is the EOQ, the higher are the ordering costs.
(vii) The lower is the EOQ, the lower are the carrying costs.
(viii) Re-order point signifies that level of inventory which is expected to be consumed during the lead time period.
(ix) Safety stock is the amount of inventory that needs to be maintained to meet the unforeseenable condition, say, increase in daily usage, increase in lead time, etc.
(x) The FIFO method assumes that materials received first are issued first.
(xi) Liquidation profits occur at the time of winding-up of a business firm

[Answers: (i) False, (ii) False, (iii) True, (iv) True, (v) True, (vi) False, (vii) True, (viii) True, (ix) True, (x) False, (xi) False]

RQ.8.2 Fill in the blanks: LO 8.2,4
(i) ________ appropriate costing method when prices of raw materials are increasing.
(ii) ________ costing method serves the needs of correct income determination as well as correct asset measurement.
(iii) ________ is the formula used to determine EOQ.
(iv) In EOQ, average inventory is determined dividing ________
(v) Minimum level = ________.
(vi) ________ form is the basis of issuing materials from the store.
(vii) Purchase of materials is initiated through ________.
(viii) ________ card is hung over the rack or shelf where material is stored.

[Answers: (i) LIFO, (ii) Modified LIFO method, (iii) ($\sqrt{2AB/C}$), (iv) Order size/2, (v) Reorder level — (Normal usage per day × Average delivery time in days), (vi) Material requisition, (vii) Purchase requisition form, (viii) Bin.]

RQ.8.3 Describe the functions and responsibilities of the purchasing department. LO 8.2

RQ.8.4 What is meant by the ABC inventory control system? On what key premise is this system based? What are its limitations? LO 8.2

RQ.8.5 Define economic order quantity (EOQ). How can it be computed? What are the limitations of the EOQ model? LO 8.2

RQ.8.6 In connection with inventory ordering and control, certain terms are basic. Explain the meaning of each of the following: LO 8.2
1. Economic order quantity
2. Re-order point
3. Lead time
4. Safety stock

RQ.8.7 Define JIT. Explain its features. LO 8.6

LOD: Medium

RQ.8.8 Identify the three forms commonly used to purchase goods. What items are usually included in them? LO 8.2

RQ.8.9 How is the cost of materials issued determined? LO 8.3

RQ.8.10 Write notes on: LO 8.2
(i) Periodic inventory system
(ii) Perpetual inventory system.

RQ.8.11 Compare LIFO with FIFO methods of inventory valuation **LO 8.4**

RQ.8.12 Explain with the help of a suitable example how current costs can be shown on both the income statement and the balance sheet under the LIFO inventory method. **LO 8.5**

RQ.8.13 Explain and contrast the use of FIFO and LIFO methods of inventory pricing on income determination and asset valuation in a period of inflation. Illustrate your answer with respect to the following data: **LO 8.4**

January	1	Inventory	1,000 units at ₹3 each
	31	Purchases	1,200 units at ₹4 each
February	28	Purchases	1,100 units at ₹5 each
March	28	Purchases	1,400 units at ₹6 each
	31	Sales	4,000 units at ₹8 each

RQ.8.14 Purchases of a certain product during March are set out below: **LO 8.4**

March	1	100 units @ ₹10.00
	12	100 units @ ₹9.80
	15	50 units @ ₹9.60
	20	100 units @ ₹9.40

Units sold during the month were as follows: March 10, 80 units; March 14, 100 units; March 30, 90 units. There were no opening inventories.

You are required to determine the cost of goods sold for March under three different valuation methods: FIFO, LIFO, and Weighted average cost.

RQ.8.15 In what manner do the various methods of inventory valuation affect reporting profits? Which method of inventory valuation would you recommend in an inflationary situation? **LO 8.4,5**

RQ.8.16 What are the methods of pricing materials issues? When do you advocate pricing the issues at cost price based on Last-In-First-Out method? **LO 8.4,5**

RQ.8.17 What are the benefits of JIT? What measures can managers take to control and evaluate JIT? **LO 8.6**

RQ.8.18 After the annual stock-taking you come to know of some significant discrepancies between book stock and physical stock. You gather the following information: **LO 8.2**

Items	*Stock card (units)*	*Store ledger (units)*	*Physical check (units)*	*Cost/unit*
A	600	600	560	₹60
B	380	380	385	40
C	750	780	720	10

What action should be taken to record the information shown above, assuming discrepancies are to be treated as abnormal?

RQ.8.19 From the following data, determine the EOQ. **LO 8.2**

(a) List price of product X is ₹800 per gross.
(b) 40 per cent trade discount is allowed on list price on purchases in gross lots.
(c) Freight cost is ₹20 per gross from the transport company to the factory premises.
(d) Annual usage or product X: 36 gross per year.
(e) Cost of placing an order is ₹10, the cost of receiving an order is ₹20.
(f) Carrying cost is 20 per cent of the effective purchase price of goods per year.
(g) Insurance and taxes are approximately 12 per cent of the net delivered cost of inventory.

(i) Determine the total annual cost of inventory based on uniform order lot sizes of 1, 2, 3, 4, 5 and 6 gross of product X.

(ii) Determine the minimum stock re-order point of product X, given the following: (a) working days: 240; (b) normal delivery time to receive an order: 20 working days from the date of purchase request is initiated; (c) safety stock: 1 gross.

RQ.8.20 JP Limited manufacturers of a special product, follows the policy of EOQ for one of its components. The component's details are as follows: LO 8.2

Purchase price per component, ₹200
Cost of an order, ₹100
Annual cost of carrying one unit in inventory, 10 per cent of purchase price
Annual usage of components, 4,000

The company has been offered a discount of 2 per cent on the price of the component provided the lot size is 2,000 components at a time. You are required to (i) compute the EOQ, (ii) advise whether the quantity discount offer can be accepted (assume that the inventory carrying cost does not vary according to discount policy) and (iii) would your advise differ if the company is offered 5 per cent discount on a single order?

LOD: Difficult

RQ.8.21 "Management makes policy decision, at one time or another, regarding methods of inventory valuation. These decisions are important because they directly affect the way income will be computed." Discuss. LO 8.5

RQ.8.22 "LIFO is acceptable, because it makes use of historical cost; replacement cost is not acceptable because it adjusts cost figures to a value that is not related to the amount paid for them." Examine this point of view for dealing with the problem of changes in the purchasing power of money. How would you match the cost of non-current assets with current revenue? LO 8.4,5

RQ.8.23 ABC Ltd. has several items of inventory. The average number of each of these as well as their unit costs is listed below: LO 8.2

Item	*Average inventory (units)*	*Average cost per unit*	*Item*	*Average inventory (units)*	*Average cost per unit*
1	4,000	₹19.6	11	1,800	₹250
2	200	100	12	130	27
3	440	24	13	4,400	95
4	2,000	168	14	3,200	26
5	20	1,650	15	1,920	20
6	300	60	16	800	12
7	160	760	17	3,400	22
8	3,000	30	18	2,400	100
9	1,200	19	19	120	210
10	6,000	5	20	320	40

The company wishes to adopt an ABC inventory system. How should the items be classified into A, B and C?

RQ.8.24 The following information is available relating to the stockout of a firm: LO 8.2

Stockout (units)	*Number of times*
800	2
600	3
400	5
200	10
0	30
	50

The selling price of each unit is ₹200. The carrying costs are ₹19 per unit. The stockout costs are ₹50 per unit.

(i) If the firm wishes to never miss a sale, what should be its safety stock? What is the total cost associated with this level of safety stock? What are the associated costs with safety stock of 600, 400 and 200 units, respectively?

(ii) What is the optimal safety stock level?

RQ.8.25 The store ledger account for Material X in a manufacturing concern reveals the following data for the quarter ended September 30: LO 8.4,5

Date		Receipts Quantity	Receipts Price	Issues Quantity	Issues Price
July 1	Balance b/d	1,600	₹20	—	—
9		3,000	22	—	—
13		—	—	1,200	₹25,560
August 5		—	—	900	19,170
17		3,600	24	—	—
24		—	—	1,800	41,220
September 11		2,500	25	—	—
27		—	—	2,100	49,710
29		—	—	700	16,560

Physical verification on September 30 revealed an actual stock of 3,800 units. You are required to:

(a) Indicate the method of pricing employed in the above.

(b) Complete the above account by making entries you would consider necessary including adjustments, if any, and giving explanations for such adjustments.

ANSWERS

RQ.8.18 For items A and C, there is shortage of ₹3,000. For item B, there is abnormal gain of ₹200. These amounts will be transferred to costing profit and loss account.

RQ.8.19 **(i)** EOQ 4 gross (as purchases are allowed in gross lots) Annual cost of inventory ₹1,136 (1 gross), ₹652 (2 gross), ₹528 (3 gross), ₹494 (4 gross), ₹496 (5 gross), ₹516 (6 gross)
(ii) 4 gross

RQ.8.20 **(i)** 200 units
(ii) Quantity discount offer of 2 per cent should be accepted
(iii) Advised to avail 5 per cent trade discount.

RQ.8.23 Items 11, 13, 4, 18 are to be classified as A category (% value 68.24). Items 7, 8, 14, 1 are to be classified as B category (% value 21.17). The remaining items are to be classified as C category (% value 10.56).

RQ.8.24 **(i)** 800 units safety stock (costs are ₹15,200); 600 units (₹11,800), 400 units (₹9,000), 200 units (₹7,200) **(ii)** 200 units

RQ.8.25 **(a)** weighted average cost method **(b)** closing stock: 3,800 units @ ₹23.7 = ₹90,060; shortage of 200 units to be charged at ₹23.7 per unit.

[Comprehensive solutions to all numerical review questions are available on the companion website: http://www.mhhe.com/khan_jain_ma7e]

Costing and Control of Labour

9

LEARNING OBJECTIVES

After reading this chapter you will be able to:

LO 9.1 Illustrate accounting for labour in terms of three key activities
LO 9.2 Discuss special problems relating to accounting for labour
LO 9.3 Explain labour turnover in terms of its measurement, causes, costs and treatment
LO 9.4 Review two interrelated efficiency rating procedures: job evaluation and merit rating

INTRODUCTION

Manufacturing is a process by which raw materials are converted into finished products. The two elements of conversion costs are direct labour, and factory overheads. If the manufacturing process is labour-intensive, labour costs constitute a significant component in the conversion process. This chapter explores the costing and control of labour. The costing and control of factory overheads follow in Chapter 10.

The compensation paid to the employees engaged in production related activities represents factory labour cost. The principal labour cost is *wages* paid to production workers made on hourly, daily, monthly, or price work basis. Included in labour costs are not only the regular earnings of the workers but also supplementary costs such as pensions, vocation and holiday pays, insurance benefits and other fringe benefit costs. Labour costs are direct or indirect.

Direct labour cost consists of the wages paid to labourers who work on a product directly, either manually or using a machine. It comprises wages which can be identified with, and allocated to, cost units. Direct labour, in other words, is the labour that: **(i)** Is directly involved in the production of a finished product, **(ii)** Can be easily traced to a product, and **(iii)** Represents a major labour cost of manufacturing that product.[1] Examples are assembly-line workers, machine operators, moulders, samplers, and finishers.

Indirect labour is a factory labour which is not engaged in production. It is not directly traceable to a product. It cannot be allocated but can be apportioned to/absorbed by cost centres/units. Examples of indirect labour who are indirectly related to production are product designers, job supervisors, product inspectors, and so on. Indirect labour is included in factory overhead cost.

We first illustrate accounting for labour. Some problems relating to accounting for labour and labour turnover are also discussed. The efficiency rating procedures, namely, job evaluation and merit rating are briefly examined subsequently. The main points are summarised by way of recapitulation.

ACCOUNTING FOR LABOUR

LO 9.1 Illustrate accounting for labour in terms of three key activities

Accounting for labour by a manufacturing organisation usually involves three activities: **(i)** Time-keeping, **(ii)** Computation of total payroll (wages), and **(iii)** Allocation of total payroll costs.

Timekeeping

The timekeeping function involves two major activities in labour costing and control: **(i)** It accumulates the total number of hours worked by each worker so as to calculate his earnings and **(ii)** It determines how the labour - hours were spent so that proper distribution can be made in the cost records.

Timekeeping is usually centred in a separate time-keeping section of the personnel department. In small plants, however, timekeeping is mostly taken care of by each department head or, in some cases, by the workers themselves. The two source-documents commonly used in time keeping are: **(a)** Time or clock card and **(b)** Labour job ticket.

Time/Clock Card It is inserted in a time clock by the workers several times each day, that is: **(i)** Upon arrival, **(ii)** Going for lunch, **(iii)** Taking a break, and **(iv)** Leaving for the day. This provides a reliable source for computing and recording total payroll costs. Figure 9.1 shows a time card.

Time Card

Employee name.................... Department...........................

Employee/clock number.......................... Week..........................

Shift..........................

Day	Regular (time)				Overtime		Hours	
	In	Out	In	Out	In	Out	Regular	Overtime
						Total		

FIG. 9.1 *Time Card*

Labour Job Tickets They are prepared daily by workers for each job worked on. They indicate the number of hours worked, a description of the work performed and the workers' wage rate (inserted by the payroll department). The total of the labour cost and hours for different jobs as shown on labour job tickets should equal the total labour cost and labour-hours for the period as shown on time cards. Figure 9.2 shows a labour job ticket.

Labour Job Ticket

Employee............................. Nature of work......................
Shift................................ Units completed......................
Job number........................... Department.......................
Date...............................

Time started	Time stopped	Hours worked	Rate	Amount

Approved by............

FIG. 9.2 *Labour Job Payroll*

Computation of Total Payroll

The payroll department computes the total payroll including the gross amount earned and the net amount payable to employees after deduction of taxes and so on. It distributes the payroll and maintains records of employees' earnings, wage rate and job classification. The procedure is that the time cards are entered on the payroll sheet/summary. Figure 9.3 shows a payroll sheet. It forms the basis for the preparation of payroll vouchers authorising disbursements for the net amount payable to workers.

Payroll Sheet

Week.......

Employee	Hours worked	Rate	Gross pay	Deduction	Net pay

FIG. 9.3 *Payroll Summary*

Allocation of Payroll Costs

On the basis of the time cards and job tickets, the cost accounting departments allocate the total payroll costs to individual jobs/departments/products. Alternatively, the payroll department itself prepares the allocation and sends it to cost accounting department for accounting in the form of appropriate journal entries. The total payroll cost must equal the sum of labour costs allocated to the individual jobs/departments/products.

Journal Entries to Record Labour Costs Payrolls are generally prepared weekly, fortnightly or monthly. Gross wages for an individual worker are determined by multiplying the hours shown on time cards by the hourly rate, plus any bonus or overtime. The payroll and related liabilities for deductions are journalised for each payroll period. The employee payroll expenses and payroll cost distribution are usually journalised at the end of the month. The basic journal entries to record factory labour costs are as follows:

(A) To record the payroll:

Work-in-process Inventory (direct labour)	Dr
Factory Overhead Control (indirect labour)	Dr
To Payroll Payable	

(B) To record deductions and payment of payroll (wages):

Payroll Payable	Dr
To Employee Deductions Payable	
To Cash (to employees)	

(C) To record fringe benefits costs (pension, insurance, and so on):

Factory Overhead Control	Dr
To Employee Benefits Payable	

Special Problems Relating to Accounting for Labour

LO 9.2 Discuss special problems relating to accounting for labour

The accounting for labour involves special problems that are not encountered in the accounting for materials. The problem areas discussed in this section are:

- Workers/employees taxes
- Employer taxes and fringe benefits
- Shifts premiums
- Overtime
- Idle time
- Minimum guaranteed wages and incentive plans.

Workers Taxes

Employers are required to deduct income taxes as well as social security payments, such as provident fund/pension contributions, which are remitted to government/social security organisations on a monthly/quarterly basis.

Fringe Benefit Costs

Employers are required to pay a matching contribution towards provident/pension funds of workers. They also bear the cost of workman's compensation insurance to provide funds to employees who are injured on the job.

Example 9.1

Journalise the following payroll cost for the week ending April 15:

Factory payroll:		
Direct labour-Job 10	₹1,80,000	
Indirect labour	1,44,000	₹3,24,000
Other payroll:		
Salesmen's salaries	1,45,800	
Administrative salaries	70,200	2,16,000
Gross payroll		5,40,000
Social security contribution payable (employees contribution)		37,800
Social security contributions payable (employers contribution)		37,800
Income-tax deducted at source		1,35,000
Employees pension fund (paid by employer)		39,960

Solution

Assuming all employers contribution and fringe benefits are recorded on a weekly basis, the following journal entries would be made on April 15:

(a) To record the payroll:			
Work-in-process Inventory—Job 10	Dr	₹1,80,000	
Factory Overhead Control (indirect labour)	Dr	1,44,000	
Selling Expenses Control	Dr	1,45,800	
Administrative Expenses Control	Dr	70,020	
To Payroll Payable			₹5,40,000
(b) To record employee taxes and pay the payroll:			
Payroll Payable	Dr	₹5,40,000	
To Employee Income Taxes Payable			₹1,35,000
To Employee Social Security Contribution Payable			37,800
To Cash (to employees – residual balance)			3,67,200
(c) To record employer contribution and fringe benefit costs:			
Factory Overhead Control (₹3,24,000 × 14.4 %*)	Dr	₹46,656	
Selling Expenses Control (₹1,45,800 × 14.4%)	Dr	20,995	
Administrative Expenses Control (₹70,200 × 14.4%)	Dr	10,109	
To Employer Social Security Contribution payable			₹37,800
To Employers Pension Fund			39,960
(d) To pay on a periodic basis all taxes/contribution and fringe benefit liabilities:			
Employee Income Taxes Payable	Dr	₹1,35,000	
Employee Social Security Contribution Payable	Dr	37,800	
Employer Social Security Contribution Payable	Dr	37,800	
Employer Pension Fund Contribution Payable	Dr	39,960	
To Cash/Bank			₹2,50,560

* (₹37,800 + ₹39,960)/₹5,40,000 = 14.4%

Shift Premiums

Shift premium is the payment of higher hourly rates for working in less desirable (night) shifts.

The shift premium/differential refers to the payment of higher hourly rates for working in less desirable evening/night shift(s). It is charged to factory overhead control rather than work-in-process, and spread over all units produced because they are not caused by specific units. If day shift rate is ₹65 per hour and the night shift rate for the same job is ₹70, for a worker working 50-hours week in the night shift, the entry would be:

Work-in-process Inventory (50 hours × ₹65)	Dr	₹3,250	
Factory Overhead Control-Shift Premium (50 hours × ₹5/hour)	Dr	250	
To Payroll Payable (50 hours × ₹70/hour)			₹3,500

Overtime Premium

Regular earnings represent the total hours worked, including overtime hours multiplied by the regular pay rate. But a higher rate may be paid for overtime work. This is called overtime premium and represents the overtime hours multiplied by the premium rate. The premium rate is usually a fraction of the regular rate.

Accounting Treatment Depending on the underlying cause of overtime, overtime premium is treated in three ways when overtime results from: **(i)** Random scheduling of jobs, **(ii)** Requirements of a specific job, and **(iii)** Negligence or poor workmanship.

Random Scheduling of Jobs Overtime premium should be treated like shift premium and charged to factory overhead control. The entry to record overtime premium is:

Work-in-process Inventory—Job No. (Total hours worked × Normal hourly rate) Dr
Factory Overhead Control-Overtime Premium (Overtime hours × Overtime premium rate) Dr
To Payroll Payable

Requirements of a Specific Job The overtime premium should be charged to the specific job that caused the overtime. If a rush order caused overtime for which the customer agrees to pay as a special service, the entry would be:

Work-in-process—Job No. Dr
To Payroll Payable

Negligence/Poor Workmanship The overtime premium should be charged to as a loss and the entry would be:

Work-in-process Inventory—Job No. Dr
Loss from Overtime Premium Dr
To Payroll Payable

The treatment accorded to overtime premium would determine action to be taken by management in planning and control of labour costs. The recording of loss, for example, would call for closer supervision/better on-the-job training.

Idle Time

Idle time results from payment when workers have no work.

When workers have no work to perform but are still paid for their time, idle time results. The accounting treatment from the point of view of labour cost control depends upon the reason for idle time. It could be normal or due to negligence/inefficiency.

If idle time is normal for the production process and is unavoidable, the cost of idle time is charged to factory overhead control and the entry is:

Work-in-process Inventory—Job No. (Hours worked × Rate per hour) Dr
Factory Overhead Control-Idle Time (Hours × Hourly rate) Dr
To Payroll Payable

If idle time is caused by negligence/inefficiency, it is charged to a loss account and the entry would be:

Work-in-process Inventory Dr
Loss from Idle Time Dr
To Payroll Payable

Minimum Guaranteed Wage and Incentive Plans

Under the piecework rate system of wage payment, employees earnings is equal to the number of units produced multiplied by the piecework rate. Several manufacturing organisations have a system of wage payment under which employees are paid a minimum guaranteed wage with a stipulation that they can earn more if they produce more. If the output multiplied by the piece rate results in an amount less than the guaranteed wage, the difference is charged to the factory overhead control; if the former exceeds the latter, it should be charged to the work-in-process inventory. Thus, under this system of wage payment, an average employee is expected to earn not only the minimum wage but a bonus as well. Employees who produce more than a specified number of units (piecework) receive a bonus.

The incentive (bonus) plans vary in format and application. They fall into two categories: **(1)** Differential piece rates schemes and **(2)** Premium bonus plans.

Differential Piece Rates Schemes Included in this category are **(i)** Taylor Differential Piece Rate System, **(ii)** Merrick Differential Piece Rate System, and **(iii)** Gantt Task and Bonus Plan.

Taylors Differential Piece Rate System Under this system, there are two price wage rates: a low rate for output below standard performance, and a higher rate applicable to workers whose production is above standard. The efficiency of a worker may be determined as a percentage of: **(i)** Time allowed for a job to the actual time taken or **(ii)** Actual output to standard output within a specified time. For example, if standard time allowed for a job is 15 hours, while the actual time taken is 20 hours, workers efficiency/performance is (15 × 100) ÷ 20 = 75 per cent. Similarly, if standard output is 5 units per hour, and the actual output is 6 units per hour, efficiency = (6 × 100) ÷ 5 = 120 per cent. The merit of this system is that it provides a strong incentive to the efficient workers. The slow worker is penalised while the efficient worker is duly rewarded.

◆ Example 9.2

The standard production in Hypothetical Ltd is 20 units per hour. For the first week of April, a workers' record (working 8 hours per day) is as follows:

Monday	140 units	Wednesday	175 units
Tuesday	160 units	Thursday	180 units
Friday	200 units		

Compute the workers daily earnings. The effective hourly rate and the labour cost per unit under the Taylor Differential Piece Rate System with piece rates are as specified below: ₹2 per unit below standard; ₹2.40 at standard and upto 20 per cent above standard; and ₹3 per unit when daily output exceeds 20 per cent above standard.

Solution

Taylor Differential Piece Rate System

Days	*Standard output*	*Actual output*	*Efficiency (%)*	*Piece rate* ₹2	₹2.40	₹3	*Effective hourly rate*	*Cost per unit*
Monday	160	140	87.5	280	—	—	₹35.0	₹2
Tuesday	160	160	100.0	—	384	—	48.0	2.4
Wednesday	160	175	109.4	—	420		52.5	2.4
Thursday	160	180	112.5	—	432		54.0	2.4
Friday	160	200	125.0	—	—	600	75.0	3.0

◆ Example 9.3

Assuming the following facts, calculate the earnings of workers under Taylor Differential Piece Rate System:

- Standard time per piece; 20 minutes
- Normal rate per hour, ₹27
- In a 9-hour day, A produces 25 units and B produces 30 units.
- Differential to be applied: 80 per cent of piece rate below standard and 120 per cent above standard.

Solution

Efficiency of A = 92.6 per cent = (25/27) × 100
B = 111 per cent = (30/27) × 100

Piece rate of A = 0.80 × ₹9 = ₹7.2
B = 1.2 × ₹9 = ₹10.8

Earnings of A = 25 × ₹7.2 = ₹180
B = 30 × ₹10.8 = ₹324

Merrick Differential Piece Rate System This is a modification of/improvement over the Taylor Differential Piece Rate System. It uses three piece rates. Normal piece rates are paid when output is upto 83 per cent of the standard output; 110 per cent of normal piece rates are paid for output between 83 - 100 per cent; and 120 per cent is paid if the output exceeds 100 per cent. While it rewards efficient workers, it does not penalise less efficient workers as minimum upto 83 per cent could possibly be achievable by all workers.

Example 9.4

From the under-mentioned facts, calculate the earnings of A, B and C under the Merrick Differential Piece Rate System:

- Normal piece rate (upto 83 per cent of high task output), ₹30 per unit;
- High task, 40 units per week
- Output for the week: A, 32 units; B, 37 units; C, 42 units.

Solution

Efficiency of A = (32 × 100) ÷ 40 = 80 per cent
B = (37 × 100) ÷ 40 = 92.5 per cent
C = (42 × 100) ÷ 40 = 105 per cent

Wages of A = (32 × ₹30) = ₹960
B = (37 × ₹30 × 110) ÷ 100 = ₹1,221
C = (42 × ₹30 × 120) ÷ 100 = ₹1,512

Gantt Task and Bonus Plan This system is a mixture of a guaranteed time rate with a bonus and piece rate plan using the differential principle. When output is below standard/high task (efficiency below 100 per cent), time rate is guaranteed. In case of output at standard level (100 per centefficiency), bonus @ 20 per cent on time rate is payable, while higher price rate on whole output is paid if output exceeds standards. At the same time, it provides security/encouragement to less efficient workers.

Example 9.5

Calculate the wages of workers A, B and C under the Gantt Task and Bonus Plan from the facts given below:

- Time rate, ₹30 per hour for 40-hours week
- Standard production, 40 units per week
- Piece rate above standard output, ₹36
- Weekly output: A, 32 units; B, 37 units; C, 42 units

Solution

Wages: A = ₹1,200 (40 × ₹30): output below standard (32 units)
B = ₹1,200 (40 × ₹30): output below standard (37 units)
C = ₹1,512 (42 × ₹36): output above standard (42 units)

Premium Bonus Plans Under the time rate basis of wage payment, additional production beyond normal level benefits the employers, whereas, with piece rate system the benefit goes to the employees. Bonus plans are a mid-way in the sense that savings are shared between them. The plans included in premium bonus plans are Halsey Premium Plan, Halsey-Weir Plan, Rowan Plan, and Bedaux Point Plan.

Halsey Premium Plan Under this system, time rate is guaranteed and if a worker completes his jobs within/in more than standard time, he is paid the standard rate. But if the job is completed in less than the standard time, he is given wages for actual hours taken plus bonus equal to normally 50 per cent of the wages of the time saved; the remaining portion represents the share of the employer. The earning of a worker is computed according to Equation 9.1.

Workers earnings = (Time taken × Rate) + [0.50 × (Standard time – Time taken) × Rate] (9.1)

Halsey-Weir Premium Plan This plan is similar to the Halsey Plan with the only difference that the bonus/premium is usually applied on 33.33: 66.67 basis.

◆ Example 9.6

The standard time to complete the work is 10 hours. The wage rate is ₹40 per hour. If the job is completed in 8 hours, compute the earnings per hour using Halsey Premium and Halsey-Weir Premium plans.

Solution

Computation of Wages and Earnings per Hour

	Halsey premium		*Halsey-Weir plan*	
Total wages	(8 × ₹40) + 0.50 × (2 × ₹40) =	₹360	(8 × ₹40) + 0.333 × (2 × ₹40) =	₹346.67
Earnings per hour	(₹360 ÷ 8) =	45	(₹346.67 ÷ 8) =	43.33

Rowan Plan This scheme is similar to the Halsey Plan in that a standard time is fixed for the completion of a job and bonus is paid in respect of the time saved. But a ceiling is applied to the size of the bonus. The bonus hours are computed as a proportion of the time taken, while time saved bears to the time allowed and is paid for at time rate.

The bonus = (Time taken ÷ Time allowed) × Time saved × Time rate (9.2)

The earnings are calculated according to Equation 9.3.

Earnings (Time taken × Rate per hour) + [(Standard time – Time taken) ÷ Standard time] × Time taken × Rate per hour (9.3)

◆ Example 9.7

From the undermentioned facts, calculate bonus, total earnings, and rate of earnings per hour under the Rowan plan:

- Time allowed, 6 hours
- Time taken, 4 hours
- Hourly rate, ₹30

Solution

Bonus = [(4/6) × 2] × ₹30 = ₹40*

Earnings = (4 × ₹30) + ₹40* or 40* [(6 – 4) ÷ 6] × 4 × ₹30

Earnings per hour = ₹160 ÷ 4 = ₹40

Bedaux Point Plan Under this plan, a guaranteed hourly rate is paid until standard production is achieved, and a premium or additional wage is paid for units in excess of standard. Instead of being paid as piece rate, an hour's production is converted into points by dividing a standard hour's production in units into 60 minutes. A minute of standard time is termed as Bedaux Point (B), 60 units making one hour's work and the number of B points determined accordingly for each job. For instance, if 10 units are standard, each unit is 6 points (B). At standard performance, a worker produces a point per minute and for the first 60 points produced in an hour, he gets the hourly rate. For additional production, a bonus of 75 per cent of the rate is given to the workers; the remaining 25 per cent is paid to the supervisory staff and other indirect labour. Thus, under the Bedaux Point Plan, the guaranteed daily wage would apply for production upto standard. In excess of 60 points in an hour, bonus is paid equal to 75 per cent.

◆ Example 9.8

From the information given below, compute bonus and total earnings according to Bedaux Point Plan:
Standard production for 8 hours daily = 100 (number)
Actual production for hours daily = 120 (number)
Hourly wage rate = ₹30

Solution

Standard points = 8 × 60 = 480 (B)
Actual points = (120 × 480) ÷ 100 = 576 (B)
Points saved = 576 – 480 = 96 × 0.75 = 72
Bonus earned = (72 × ₹30) ÷ 60 = ₹36
Total earnings = (8 × ₹30) + ₹36 (bonus) = ₹276

While incentive plans of wage payments are intended to improve labour performance/efficiency, their possible negative effects must be examined by management. They involve increased clerical cost due to additional record keeping. Moreover, quantity may become the main consideration to the detriment of quality of production. Therefore, incentive plans should be introduced only if increase in total payroll costs is offset by increase in production/sales, as well as reduction in labour cost per unit and/or labour-related costs per unit.

LABOUR TURNOVER

LO 9.3 Explain labour turnover in terms of its measurement, causes, costs and treatment

Labour turnover is the rate at which employees leave employment at a factory.

Labour turnover may be defined as the rate of change in the composition of the labour force in an organisation. It is the rate at which employees leave employment at a factory. Labour turnover has important implications for labour cost, efficiency and productivity. The objective should be to keep labour turnover at minimal.

Measurement of Labour Turnover

There are three methods to measure labour turnover: (i) Separation method, (ii) Flux/Separation-cum-replacement method, and (iii) Replacement/Net labour turnover method.

Separation Method Labour turnover is measured according to Equation 9.4.

Labour turnover = [(Employees leaving (number of separations) in a period ÷ Average number of workers employed)] × 100 (9.4)

Flux or Separation-cum-Replacement Method Labour turnover is measured according to Equation 9.5.

Labour turnover = [(Number of separations (employees leaving) + Number of replacements (new employees, excluding those recruited for expansion)] ÷ (Average number employed) × 100 (9.5)

Replacement/Net Labour Turnover Method Labour turnover is computed according to Equation 9.6.

Labour turnover = (Number of workers replaced in a period ÷ Average number employed) × 100 (9.6)

◆ Example 9.9

The information relating to the workforce of Premier Industries Ltd during the latest month is listed below:

- Number of workers in the beginning and end of the month 19,000 and 21,000 respectively;
- During the month workers discharged, 600 and left on their own, 200;
- During the month workers engaged, 2,000 out of which workers appointed against vacancies caused by separation, 400 and on account of expansion, the remaining 1,600.

Compute the monthly labour turnover rate and the equivalent annual rates under the three methods of labour turnover measurement.

Solution

1. Separation Method:
Labour turnover rate = (800 × 100) ÷ 20,000* = 4 per cent *(19,000 + 21,000) ÷ 2
Equivalent annual turnover = (4 × 365 days) ÷ 30 days = 48.67 per cent

2. Flux Method:
Labour turnover rate = (800 + 400) ÷ 20,000* = 6 per cent
Equivalent annual rate = (6 × 365) ÷ 30 = 73 per cent

3. Replacement Method:
Labour turnover rate = (400 × 100) ÷ 20,000* = 2 per cent
Equivalent annual rate = (2 × 365) ÷ 30 = 24.33 per cent

Of the three, separation method is a better indicator of the labour turnover in a factory organisation.

Causes of Labour Turnover

The causes of labour turnover may be avoidable and unavoidable.

Avoidable Causes Such causes are avoidable in the sense that with suitable measures they can be eliminated. They include:

- Low wage rates and earnings
- Dissatisfaction with job/Unsatisfactory working conditions
- Unsatisfactory relationship with supervisors/fellow workers
- Lack of conveyance, accommodations, medical, educational, recreational and housing facilities
- Unfair methods of promotion/lack of promotional avenues
- Seasonal nature of job.

Unavoidable Causes They include

- Change for better jobs
- Retirement and death
- Domestic/family responsibilities/constraints
- Dismissal/discharge due to insubordination, negligence, inefficiency and
- Retrenchment/lay off.

Costs of Labour Turnover

The cost of labour turnover consists of two elements; preventive and replacements.

Preventive Costs This include all those costs which are incurred to keep the labour turnover rate as low as possible to prevent workers from leaving the organisation and keeping them satisfied. High preventive costs would result in low labour turnover. The preventive costs, *inter alia,* include costs of providing to workers/families:

- Medical, housing and recreational facilities
- Benefits like pension, gratuity and bonus
- Educational facilities to children of employees
- Good working conditions
- Other welfare facilities.

Replacement Costs These costs arise on account of labour turnover and consequent replacement of employees. They include costs which are incurred for recruitment/training of new workers as well as those which result from wastages, losses, lower production due to less competent and inexperienced new employees:

Personnel Department Expenses This is for recruitment/training new employees and loss of production time during training period.

Inefficiency of New Workers This has an adverse effect on production.

Delay in Recruitment of New Workers Recruitment of new workers is time-consuming, necessitating overtime payment to existing employees and the consequent burden on the organisation.

Cost of Abnormal Breakages This pertains to tools, equipments by new/inexperienced workers as well as machine break-down and the consequent interruption of production.

Cost of Spoilage and Defectives More spoilage/defectives are likely to occur due to mishandling/carelessness of new workers. The greater the spoilage/defectives, the larger is the production costs.

The replacement cost of labour turnover can be computed in two ways: **(i)** By separation and replacement method and **(ii)** By profit forgone method.

Separation and Replacement Method Under this method, the specific costs associated with separation (turnover) and replacements (recruitment/training) are accumulated. The separation costs include terminal pay, gratuity and other benefits. The replacement costs include costs associated with selection/training of new employees. Another relevant cost is the lost contribution in terms of sales less additional variable cost due to labour cost of lost hours due to replacement, and increase in material and variable overhead due to increase in potential sales.

◆ Example 9.10

From the information given below, calculate the cost of labour turnover, using separation and replacement method:

Income Statement for the Year Ended March 31, Current Year

Sales		₹40,00,000
Variable costs:		
Materials	₹10,00,000	
Direct labour	8,00,000	
Variable overheads	8,00,000	26,00,000
Contribution		14,00,000
Less fixed overheads		9,00,000
Profit before tax		5,00,000

The direct labour-hours worked during the period were 20,300 of which 500 hours pertained to new workers on training. Only 40 per cent of trainee's time was productive. As replacement of workers left was delayed for some time, 600 productive hours were lost.

The company incurred direct costs as a consequence of separation/replacements detailed below: Separation, ₹40,000; Selection, ₹60,000, and Training, ₹1,00,000.

Solution

Cost of Labour Turnover

Direct labour-hours worked		20,300
Less unproductive time of new workers (0.60 × 500)		300
Productive hours		20,000
Loss labour hours:		
Replacement	600	
Training	300	900
Unit sales per productive labour hour (₹40,00,000 ÷ 20,000)		₹200
(i) Loss of potential sales (900 hours × ₹200)		1,80,000
Direct labour cost per hour worked (₹8,00,000 ÷ 20,300)		39.41
(ii) Increase in direct labour cost of lost hours due to replacement (600* hours × ₹39.41)		23,646
* (300 hours already included while calculating hourly rate)		
(iii) Increase in material and variable overheads due to increase in potential sales (₹18,00,000 ÷ ₹40,00,000) × ₹1,80,000		81,000
(iv) Total increase in cost [(ii) + (iii)]		1,04,646
Contribution foregone [(i) – (iv)]		75,354
Add separation, selection and training costs (₹40,000 + ₹60,000 + ₹1,00,000)		2,00,000
Cost of labour turnover		2,75,354

Profit Forgone Method According to this method, the cost of labour turnover equals the profit foregone in terms of the difference between the actual profit for the period and the estimated profit that would have been earned had no labour turnover occurred. Alternatively, contribution lost due to labour turnover and costs incurred consequent on labour turnover equal profit foregone.

◆ Example 9.11

The sales of Premier Industries Ltd in the previous year aggregated ₹1,66,06,600 and the P/V (profit – volume) ratio was 20 per cent. The actual hours worked was 4.45 lakh. The actual direct hours included 30,000 hours attributable to training of new recruits of which 50 per cent represented unproductive hours. As a result of delays in filling vacancies caused by labour turnover, 1,00,000 potentially productive hours were lost.

The cost associated with labour turnover were: **(i)** Settlement cost due to leaving, ₹87,640; **(ii)** Recruitments cost, ₹53,480; **(iii)** Selection costs, ₹25,500, and **(iv)** Training costs, ₹60,980.

Assuming the potential production loss consequent upon labour turnover could have been sold at the prevailing price, find the profit foregone in the previous year on account of labour turnover.

Solution

Determination of Profit Foregone

Contribution foregone (working note)	₹7,72,400
Settlement cost	87,640
Recruitment cost	53,480
Selection cost	25,500
Training cost	60,980
Total	10,00,000

WORKING NOTE

Determination of contribution foregone:

Actual hours worked	4,45,000
Less unproductive hours (0.50 × 30,000)	15,000
Actual productive hours	4,30,000
Sales lost (₹1,66,06,600 ÷ 4,30,000 hours) × 1,00,000 hours	₹38,62,000
Contribution lost (₹38,62,000 × 0.20, P/V ratio)	7,72,400

Treatment of Labour Turnover Costs Labour turnover costs are usually treated as factory overhead. The preventive costs are distributed among different departments on the basis of workers in each department. The replacement costs are shared by the departments affected by the labour turnover on the basis of number of workers replaced.

Control of Labour Turnover Costs: Labour Turnover Report This report is prepared by the personnel department periodically with a view to minimising labour turnover costs by taking appropriate measures. It contains turnover statistics, turnover rate and reasons for turnover divided into avoidable and unavoidable. It shows whether workers are leaving through dissatisfaction or are being dismissed because of unsuitability/bad relations. A specimen of labour turnover report is given in Figure 9.4.

Labour Turnover Report Date..............

	Month	Cumulative since beginning of year	Last year
Number of employees			
Employees leaving			
Labour turnover (%)			
Reasons for leaving:			
Avoidable:			
....			
....			
....			
Total			
Percentage			
Unavoidable:			
....			
....			
....			
Total			
Percentage			
Number of replacements			
Percentages			

FIG. 9.4 *Labour Turnover Report*

EFFICIENCY RATING PROCEDURES

LO 9.4 Review two interrelated efficiency rating procedures: job evaluation and merit rating

This Section examines the two interrelated efficiency rating procedures, namely, job evaluation and merit rating.

Job Evaluation

Job evaluation is the systematic technique of analysis and assessment of jobs to ascertain their comparative worth.

Meaning Job evaluation is the systematic technique of analysis and assessment of jobs to ascertain their comparative labour/job worth. Every job has its own characteristics. Depending upon these, jobs demand varying degrees of qualifications, skill, experience and soon on the part of the operators performing them. For instance, some jobs may require physical ability, others may need a high degree of mental ability, yet others may need skill, experience and high educational qualification. Thus, job evaluation is the process of review, analysis and systematic classification of a job in accordance with its characteristics in terms of the varying factors it demands from the employees/workers. In other words, it grades all jobs with reference to their main characteristics so that the relative merit of each job in terms of work value/worth may be ascertained. Its focus is on the job and it has nothing to do with the rating of the employees.

Objectives/Importance/Uses The uses to which job evaluation may be put to, and the advantages acccruing from it, are specified below:

Fixation of Wage Structure The main aim/utility of job evaluation relates to fixation of a systematic, rational and equitable basis for differential wages/salaries in an organisation. Fixation of wages on an impersonal basis, solely based on the job requirements, eliminates personal biases and errors. This results in simplified and balanced wage structure which are fair both for the employees as well as the employers. A related dimension is that anomalies in the wages of employees can be identified by comparing the actual wages *vis-a-vis* the job evaluation.

Help in Recruitment of New Workers The job evaluation technique generates useful information for recruitment of new workers. Since the exact requirement of each job is known, the personnel department can select only those workers who satisfy the requirements of the specific job. Likewise, promotions, transfers and so on can be made on a rational basis for different employees in the organisation.

Improvement of Labour Relations Job evaluation improves labour relations as it obviates scope for unfairness, favouritism, nepotism and so on.

Methods of Evaluation The job evaluation methods may be **(i)** qualitative or **(ii)** quantitative. The qualitative/non-qualitative methods include **(1)** job ranking method, and **(2)** job grading/grade description method. The quantitative method is primarily a point rating method.

Job ranking is the evaluation and ranking of jobs on the basis of relative difficulty in performance and responsibilities

Job Ranking Method According to this method, different jobs are evaluated and ranked on the basis of relative difficulty in performance and responsibilities. As a first step, all jobs are properly studied in terms of job requirements, qualification, responsibilities, hazards, working conditions and so on. On the basis of comparison of the job with the same components of another job, jobs are ranked in ascending/descending order. It is a method of informal arrangement of a hierarchy of jobs from the lowest to the highest or *vice versa*. After ranking, each job is put in ranked scale of jobs.

The ranking method of job evaluation is simple to use, easy to understand and less costly to operate. But it is less accurate. It could be usefully employed by small organisations only where jobs are few and well defined. Where jobs are complex in large organisations, the usefulness of this method would be rather limited.

Job grading is ranking of jobs on the basis of predetermined standard/scale.

Job Grading/Grade Description Method This method is a variant of the job ranking method. It is also an improvement over the ranking method. Under the job grading method, a predetermined/hypothetical scale/standard of job values is determined on the basis of education, experience, skill, responsibilities and so on and each job is placed in suitable grades/classes. The jobs within each grade are approximately of similar nature. The method is simple, less costly and administratively feasible. It attempts applying a rational basis for grading jobs. But like the ranking method, it is less accurate and is not suitable for large/complex organisations.

Factor ranking is the analysis of job factors such as skills, efforts, responsibilities and working conditions.

Point/Factor Ranking Method According to this method, each job is analysed in terms of job factors consisting of elements like basic skills and knowledge, mental and physical efforts, responsibilities, working conditions and so on. As a first step, depending upon its nature and the extent to which it requires the various factors for its performance, each job is assigned points/weightage. A job requiring a large number of these factors would rank high in the process of job evaluation compared to those requiring smaller number of these factors. Moreover, two dissimilar jobs may have the same gradation if each has the same number of points. An illustrative/list of characteristic which may be taken into account for job evaluation and hypothetical points allotted against each is summarised in Figure 9.5.

The second step is to review the specification of a job, analyse it into various factors/characteristics and evaluate each job in terms of assigning points. This is illustrated below:

Job Factors

Job	*Background skill and knowledge*	*Skill and efforts required for job performance*	*Responsibility*	*Working conditions*	*Total point*
A	40	80	100	80	300
B	120	20	70	140	350
C	50	160	200	20	430
D	300	40	60	100	500
E	400	200	10	180	790

Finally, jobs are ranked in the order of points and are placed in a number of arbitrary grades for each of which wages scales/ranges of pay are fixed. The gradation/fixation of wages for the various grades are shown below:

Wages Scales/Grades

Points Value	*Grade*	*Pay Scale (per month)*
100-198	I	₹6,000-7,000
200-398	II	7,000-8,000
400-498	III	8,000-10,000
500-598	IV	10,000-12,000
600-898	V	12,000-13,800
900-1.098	VI	13,800-16,000
1,100-1,198	VII	16,000-20,000
1,200-1,300	VIII	20,000-24,000

Basic Factors	Points	Main Factors	Points	Sub-factors	Points
Basic Factors; Background skill and knowledge	400	Main Factors:			
		Education	100		
		Training	150		
		Experience	150	Sub-factors:	
				Education:	100
			400	Non-matriculate	10
				High School	20
				Intermediate	30
				Degree	40
					100
Skill and efforts	400	Mental:			
		Reasoning	100		
		Observation	60		
		Initiation	20		
		Physical:			
		Mascular	100		
		Stamina	100		
		Dexterity	20	Training:	75
			400		
Responsibilities	300	Degree of supervision	100		
		Responsibility for material	100		
		Safety for others	50		
		Confidential information	50		
			300		
Working condition	200	Hazard	60	Physical:	
		Risk and safety	80	Mascular:	
		Disagreeableness	60	High	50
			200	Medium	30
				Ordinary	20
		Total	1,300		100

Fig. 9.5 *Job Characteristics/Factors*

This method is theoretically sound and objective but it is difficult to operate. The relative points/weights of different job factors need to be developed very carefully and in an objective manner.

Merit Rating

> **Merit rating** is the comparative appraisal of the individual merit of an employee through some performance standards.

Meaning As a systematic method of determining the relative worth of employees, merit rating is the comparative appraisal of the individual merits of an employee. It is a technique to rate an employees' performance through some norms/standards. The factors/characteristics that are considered in merit appraisal of the employees are:

- Quantity of work done
- Quality of work done
- Sense of responsibility
- Initiative
- Reliability and integrity
- Knowledge, skill, experience and aptitude for work
- Cooperation and discipline
- Sense of judgement
- Attendance and punctuality and so on.

Each of these factors is assigned a point rating/value and each employee is rated according to the extent of the point value he possesses. The employees may be ranked individually in order of the points they score. Alternatively, they may be arranged in groups according to their common ratings. The individual/group rating may also be expressed as a ratio of the normal/standard rating.

Comparison With Job Evaluation While job evaluation is the process of analysis and classification of jobs according to their characteristics, merit rating refers to the evaluation of the merits of employees and their classification into groups on that basis. Merit rating differs from job evaluation in several respects. In the first place, job evaluation is the assessment of the relative worth of jobs in an organisations; merit rating in the assessment of the relative worth of an employee with respect to a job. In other words, while job evaluation rates jobs, merit rating rates employees on their jobs. Secondly, job evaluation helps in establishing a rational wage/salary structure. In contrast, merit rating provides a scientific basis for determining fair wages for each employee based on his ability/competence and performance. Finally, job evaluation simplifies wage/salaries administration by rationalising and bringing uniformity in the wage/salary rates. But merit rating helps in determining a fair rate of pay for different employees on the basis of their relative performance.

Objectives The main objectives of merit rating are the following:

- To find out the suitability of an employee for a particular job
- To assess an employee's merit for promotion, grant of increment, payment of reward for good work and so on.
- To serve as a basis for incentive payment and for simplification of wage structure and
- To analyse the employee's defects/bring out their strength and special abilities.

Shortcomings/Limitations Merit rating improves labour relations, reduces labour turnover and stimulates competition among employees and, thus, contributes to increased production, improved productivity and so on. Nevertheless, it suffers from certain limitations/shortcomings. Being a matter of mostly opinion/subjective, the rating may be erroneous and may result in unrest/dissatisfaction among the employees. Moreover, raters may be influenced by past ratings of an employee. This may vitiate their judgement. The employee(s) may have improved in course of time. Further, irrelevant factors may be given prominence by the raters. For example, raters may be highly influenced by one specific/strong good/adverse factor. If merit rating is inaccurate/unreliable/subjective, it may not serve the intended purpose.

SUMMARY

- Labour is the physical/mental effort expended in the production of a product. Labour costs can be broken down into direct and indirect, based on the employees' relationship with the finished product. Total labour costs are based on elements other than just gross wages. The additional costs include bonus payments, vacation pay, pension costs and other fringe benefits including employees contribution to health, life and other insurance.
- The accounting for labour in a manufacturing organisation generally involves three activities: timekeeping, computation of total payroll and allocation of payroll costs. Journal entries to record the payroll (wages) payments and associated liabilities for amounts withheld are made for each period.

LO 9.1

- The accounting for labour involves special problems that are not encountered in the accounting for materials. They are: taxes and fringe benefit costs, shift premiums, overtime, idle time, and minimum guaranteed wage and incentive plans. The incentive/bonus plans vary in format and applications. They fall into two categories: differential price rate schemes and premium bonus plans. Included in the first category are **(1)** Taylor Differential Piece Rate **(2)** Merrick Differential Piece Rate, and **(3)** Gantt Task and Bonus Plan.
- Under the Taylor Differential Piece Rate System, there are two piece wage rates: a low rate for output below standard performance and a higher rate applicable to workers where production is above standard. The efficiency of a worker may be determined as a percentage of **(i)** time allowed for a job to the actual time taken or **(ii)** actual output to standard output within a specified time.
- Merrick Differential Piece Rate System is a modification of/improvement over the Taylor Differential Piece Rate System. It uses three piece rates. Normal piece rates are paid when output is upto 83 per cent of the standard output; 110 per cent of normal piece rates are paid for output between 83–100 per cent; 120 per cent is paid if the output exceeds 100 per cent.
- Gantt Task and Bonus Plan is a mixture of a guaranteed time rate with a bonus and piece rate plan using the differential plan when output is below standard (efficiency below 100 per cent), time rate is guaranteed. In case of output at standard level (100 per cent efficiency) bonus at the rate of 20 per cent on time rate is payable while a higher piece rate on the whole output is paid if output exceeds standard.
- Under the time rate basis of wage payment, additional production beyond normal level benefits the employer(s); with piece rate system, the benefit goes to the employee(s). Bonus plans are a mid-way in the sense that the savings are shared between them. These plans include **(i)** Halsey/Halsey-Weir Plan and **(ii)** Rowan Plan.
- Under the Halsey Premium Plan the earnings and bonus of a worker is computed as below:
  Earnings = (Time taken × rate) + [0.50 × (Standard time – Time taken) × Rate]
  Bonus = [0.50 × (Standard time – Time taken) × Rate]
- Halsey-Weir Premium Plan is similar to Halsey Plan with the difference that the bonus/premium is usually applied on 33.33:66.67 basis.
- According to the Rowan Plan earnings and bonus are computed as below:]
  Workers earnings = (Time taken × Rate per hour) + [(Standard time – Time taken) ÷ Standard time] × Time taken × Rate Per hour
  Bonus = (Time taken ÷ Time allowed) × Time saved × Time rate

LO 9.2

- Labour turnover is the rate at which employees leave employment. It has implications for labour cost. The objective should be to keep the labour turnover at minimal. Labour turnover can be measured in three ways: by Separation method, Flux method and Replacement method.
- According to the separation method, labour turnover = [Employees leaving (number of separations) in a period ÷ Average number of workers employed] × 100
- According to flux/separation-cum-replacement method, labour turnover = [(Number of employees leaving) + Number of employees joining/replacements against vacancies of those leaving (new employees) ÷ Average number employed)] × 100
- According to replacement/net labour turnover method, labour turnover = (Number of workers replaced in a period ÷ Average number employed) × 100
- The causes of labour turnover may be avoidable in the sense that with suitable measures they can be eliminated or unavoidable. The labour turnover cost consists of two elements, that is, preventive cost and replacement. The replacement can be computed in either of two ways: **(i)** Separation and replacement method and **(ii)** Profit forgone method.
- Under separation and replacement method, the specific costs associated with separation (turnover) and replacements (recruitment/training) are accumulated. The separation costs include terminal pay, gratuity and other benefits. The replacement costs include costs associated with selection/training of new

employees. Another relevant cost is the lost contribution in terms of sales less additional variable cost due to labour cost of lost hours due to replacement, and increase in material and variable overhead costs due to increase in potential sales.

- According to profit foregone method, the cost of labour turnover equals the profit foregone in terms of the difference between the actual profit for the period and the estimated profit that would have been earned had no labour turnover occurred. Alternatively, contribution lost due to labour turnover and costs incurred consequent on labour turnover equal profit foregone.
- Labour turnover costs are usually treated as factory overhead. While the preventive costs are distributed among different departments, the replacements costs are shared by the department(s) affected by the labour turnover. The personnel department prepares a labour turnover report periodically to minimise turnover by taking appropriate measures.

LO 9.3

- Job evaluation is the systematic technique of analysis and assessment of jobs to ascertain their comparative labour/job worth. It grades all jobs with reference to their main characteristics so that the relative merit of each job in terms of work value may be ascertained. Its focus is on jobs and it has nothing to do with the rating of the employees. The job evaluation methods are: **(i)** job ranking method, **(ii)** job grading/grade description method and **(iii)** point rating method.
- According to the job ranking method, different jobs are evaluated and ranked on the basis of relative difficulty in performance and responsibilities.
- Under the job grading method, a predetermined/hypothetical scale/standard of job value is determined on the basis of education, experience, skill, responsibilities and so on and each job is placed in suitable grade(s)/class(es).
- According to the point/factor ranking method, each job is analysed in terms of job factors consisting of elements like basic skills and knowledge, mental and physical efforts, responsibilities, working conditions and so on. Each job is assigned points/weightage.
- As a systematic method of determining the relative worth of employees, merit rating is the comparative appraisal of the individual merits of an employee. It rates an employees' performance through some norms/standards.

LO 9.4

REFERENCE

1. Polimeni, Fabbozi and Adelberg, *op. cit.*, p. 100.

SOLVED PROBLEMS

P. 9.1 Calculate the earnings of a worker under **(1)** Halsey Plan and **(2)** Rowan Plan from the following particulars: **(i)** Hourly rate of wages guaranteed, ₹50 per hour; **(ii)** Standard time for producing one dozen articles—3 hours; **(iii)** Actual time taken by the worker to produce 20 dozen articles—48 hours. LO 9.2 LOD: E

Solution

Determination of Earnings of a Worker

(i) Halsey plan: (Hours worked × Rate per hour) + [(50% Time saved (Hours) × Rate per hour)]
= (48 × ₹50) + (0.5 × 12 × ₹50) = ₹2,700

(ii) Rowan plan: (Hours worked × Rate per hour) + (Time saved/Time allowed) × Time taken × Rate per hour) = (48 × ₹50) + [(12/60) × 48 × ₹50] = ₹2,880.

P. 9.2 During a week a worker produced 300 units, working for 48 hours. The hourly rate is ₹40. The estimated time to produce a unit is 10 minutes. Under incentive scheme, 20 per cent additional time is allowed. Calculate his gross earnings under Halsey and Rowan Plans.

LO 9.2
LOD: E

Solution

Determination of Earnings of a Worker

(i) *Halsey Plan* : (Hours worked × Rate per hour) + (50% Time saved × Rate per hour)
: (48 hours × ₹40) + [0.5 (60 hours[1] – 48 hours) × ₹40]
: ₹1,920 + (6 × ₹40) = ₹2,160

(1) Normal time allowed (10 minutes × 300 units) =	3,000 minutes
Plus 20 per cent additional time (0.2 × 3,000) =	600
Standard time allowed (60 hours)	3,600 minutes

(ii) *Rowan Plan* : (Hours worked × Rate per hour) + (Time saved/Time allowed) × Time taken × Rate per hour
: (48 hours × ₹40) + (12 hours/60 hours) × 48 hours × ₹40
: ₹1,920 + (1/5 × 48 × ₹40) = ₹2,304

P. 9.3 A workman's wages for a guaranteed 44 hours week is ₹75 per hour. The estimated time to produce one article is 30 minutes and under an incentive plan, the time allowed is increased by 20 per cent.

During a week, a worker produced 100 articles. Calculate the wages under: (a) Time rate, (b) Rowan system and (c) Halsey system.

LO 9.2
LOD: M

Solution

Determination of Earnings of a Worker

(i) Time Rate : (44 hours × ₹75) = ₹3,300
(ii) Rowan System : (44 hours × ₹75) + (16 hours/60 hours)[1] × 44 hours × ₹75
: ₹3,300 + ₹880 = ₹4,180
(iii) Halsey Plan : (44 hours × ₹75) + (8 hours × ₹75) = ₹3,300 + ₹600 = ₹3,900

1	Normal time per article (minutes)	30
	Plus 20 per cent extra time allowed	6
	Standard time per article (minutes)	36
	Standard time for 100 articles (60 hours)	
	Time saved (60 hours – 44 hours worked) (hours)	16

P. 9.4 An employee working under a bonus scheme saves 10 hours in a job for which the standard time is 60 hours. Calculate the rate per hour worked and wages payable to him if incentive bonus of 10 per cen on the hourly rate is payable when standard time (namely, 100 per cent efficiency) is achieved, and a further incentive bonus of 1 per cent on hourly rate for each 1 per cent excess of that 100 per cent efficiency is payable. Assume that the normal rate of payment is ₹50 per hour.

LO 9.2
LOD: M

Solution

Determination of Total Wages and Effective Rate per Hour

Wages (50 hours × ₹50)	₹2,500
Plus bonus (0.10 × ₹2,500)	250
Plus incentive (1% for efficiency in excess of 100%)	
Efficiency (60 actual hours/50 standard hours) = 120%	
Plus incentive (120% – 100%) × 2,500	500
Total wages	3,250
Effective rate per hour (₹3,250/50 hours)	65

P. 9.5 Calculate the earnings of workers A, B and C under Straight Piece Rate System and Merrick's Multiple Piece Rate System from the following particulars:

LO 9.2
LOD: M

Normal rate per hour	₹54
Standard time per unit	1 minute

Output per day is as follows:

Worker A—390 units

Worker B—450 units

Worker C—600 units

Working hours per day are 8.

Solution

Earnings of Workers Under Straight Piece Rate System

Worker A = (390 units × ₹0.90@) =	₹351
Worker B = (450 units × ₹0.90@) =	405
Worker C = (600 units × ₹0.90@) =	540

@ ₹54/60 units = ₹0.90

Earnings of Workers under Merrick's Multiple Piece Rate System

Particulars/Workers	A	B	C
1. Actual output per day	390	450	600
2. Standard output per day (8 hours)	480	480	480
3. Efficiency level (1 ÷ 2) × 100 (%)	81.25	93.75	125
4. Revised wage rate per unit	₹0.90*	₹0.99**	₹1.08***
5. Earnings (1 × 4)	351	445.50	648

* Normal rate; ** 10 per cent above normal rate; *** 20 per cent above normal rate.

P. 9.6 A job can be executed either through workman A or B. A takes 32 hours to complete the job while B finishes it in 30 hours. The standard time to finish the job is 40 hours. LO 9.2 LOD: D

The hourly wage rate is same for both the workers. In addition, workman A is entitled to receive bonus according to Halsey Plan (50 per cent sharing) while B is paid bonus as per Rowan Plan. The works overheads are absorbed on the job at ₹7.50 per labour-hour worked. The factory cost of the job comes to ₹2,600 irrespective of the workman engaged. Find out the hourly wage rate and cost of raw materials input. Also, show cost against each element of cost included in factory cost.

Solution

Statement of Factory Cost of Jobs A and B

Particulars/Workman	Job A	Job B
Material cost	₹X	₹X
Wages (workmen)	36 Y	37.5 Y
Work overheads @ ₹7.50 per hour worked	240	225
Factory cost	2,600	2,600
Standard time (hours)	40	40
Actual time taken (hours)	32	30
Time saved (hours)	8	10
Bonus	4 Y(1)	7.5Y(2)
Wages paid	32 Y	30 Y
Total wages paid	36 Y	37.5Y

1. Bonus for A under Halsey Plan: Time saved × 0.50 × Hourly rate = 8 × 0.50 × ₹Y = 4 Y
2. Bonus for B under Rowan Plan: (Time saved ÷ Standard time) × Time taken × Hourly rate) = (10 × 40) ÷ 30 × ₹Y = 7.5 Y

Now, from the above we can deduce that:

₹X + ₹36 Y + ₹240 = ₹2,600

₹X + ₹37.5 Y + ₹225 = ₹2,600

Solving above equations, we get:

X = ₹2,000

Y = ₹10 per hour.

Therefore, material cost (X) is ₹2,000, and hourly wage rate (Y) is ₹10 per hour.

P. 9.7 Supreme Industries Ltd recently adopted an incentive plan. Factory workers are paid at ₹3.75 per unit with a guaranteed minimum wages of ₹1,000 per week. Following is a report on employees' productivity for the week ending March, current year. All employees had worked the full 40-hour week. Weekly summary is as follows: LO 9.2 LOD: D

Workers' name	*Units produced*
A	240
B	275
C	250
D	280
E	220
F	300

Required (a) Compute each employee's gross wages per week, (b) What amount should be charged to work-in-process charged to factory overheads?

Solution

(a) ***Statement showing Determination of Gross Wages***

Name	*Units produced*	*Piece rate*	*Piecework earnings*	*Below minimum*	*Total earnings*
A	240	₹3.75	₹900.00	₹100	₹1,000.00
B	275	3.75	1,031.25	—	1,031.25
C	250	3.75	937.50	62.50	1,000.00
D	280	3.75	1,050.00	—	1,050.00
E	220	3.75	825.00	175.00	1,000.00
F	300	3.75	1,125.00	—	1,125.00
			5,868.75	337.50	6,206.25

(b) Amount to be charged to work-in-process (WIP) inventory is ₹5,868.75

(c) Amount to be charged to factory overheads is ₹337.50.

P. 9.8 In an engineering concern, the employees are paid incentive bonus in addition to their normal wages at hourly rates. Incentive bonus is calculated in proportion of time taken to time allowed, of the time saved. The following details are made available in respect of employees X, Y and Z for a particular week: LO 9.2 LOD: M

	X	*Y*	*Z*
Normal wages (per hour)	₹40	₹50	₹60
Completed units of production	6,000	3,000	4,800
Time allowed per 100 units (hour)	0.8	1.5	1.0
Actual time taken (hours)	42	40	48

You are required to work out for each employee: **(i)** The amount of bonus earned, **(ii)** The total amount of wags received, and **(iii)** The total wages cost per 100 units of output.

Solution

Statement showing the amount of Bonus Earned, Wages Received, and Wages Cost per 100 units of Output

	X	Y	Z
Completed units of production	6,000	3,000	4,800
Time allowed for units produced	48	45	48
Actual time taken (hours)	42	40	48
Time saved (hours)	6	5	—
Normal wages (per hour)	₹40	₹50	₹60
Basic wages (Actual hours × Normal rate)	1,680	2,000	2,880
(i) Bonus earned (Time taken/Time allowed) × Time saved × Wage rate	210	222.20	—
(ii) Total wages cost	1,890	2,222.20	2,880
(iii) Wages cost per 100 units	31.50	74.10	60

P. 9.9 The time allowed for a job is 8 hours. The hourly rate is ₹8. Prepare a statement showing: bonus earned, **(ii)** The total earnings of labour, and **(iii)** Hourly earnings under the Halsey System with 50 per cent bonus for time saved, and Rowan System for each hour saved respectively. LO 9.2 LOD: D

Solution

Determination of Bonus, Total Earnings of Labour and Hourly Earnings as per Halsey and Rowan Systems

				Bonus		Total earnings		Hourly earnings	
Time allowed (hours)	*Time taken (hours)*	*Time saved (hours)*	*Basic wages at ₹8 per hour*	*Halsey System@*	*Rowan System@@*	*Halsey System (Col. 4 + Col. 5)*	*Rowan System (Col. 4 + Col. 6)*	*Halsey System (Col. 7 ÷ Col. 2)*	*Rowan System (Col. 8 ÷ Col. 2)*
1	2	3	4	5	6	7	8	9	10
8	8	Nil	₹64	—	—	₹64	₹64	₹8	₹8.0
8	7	1	56	₹4	₹7	60	63	8.57	9.0
8	6	2	48	8	12	56	60	9.33	10.0
8	5	3	40	12	15	52	55	10.40	11.0
8	4	4	32	16	16	48	48	12.00	12.0
8	3	5	24	20	15	44	39	14.67	13.0
8	2	6	16	24	12	40	28	20.0	14.0
8	1	7	8	28	7	36	15	36.0	15.0

@ Standard wage rate × 0.5 × Time saved

@@ Standard wage rate × (Time saved/Time allowed) × Time taken

P.9.10 A skilled worker in XYZ Ltd is paid a guaranteed wage rate of ₹30 per hour. The standard time per unit for a particular product is 4 hours. P, a machineman, has been paid wages under the Rowan Incentive Plan and he had earned an effective hourly rate of ₹37.50 on the manufacture of that particular product. LO 9.2 LOD: D

What could have been his total earnings and effective hourly rate, had he been put on Halsey Incentive Scheme (50 per cent)?

Solution

(i) Total Earnings of Machineman, P as per Haley Incentive Scheme (50 per cent)
= (Time taken × Rate per hour) + [0.50 × (Standard time – Time taken) × Rate per hour
= (3 hours × ₹30) + [0.5(4 Hours – 3 Hours) × ₹30]
= ₹90 + ₹15 = ₹105

(ii) *Effective Hourly Rate = Total earnings/Number of hours = ₹105/3 = ₹35*

WORKING NOTES

Determination of Time Taken by a Machineman

Earnings as per Rowan Incentive Plan are = (Time taken × Rate per hour) + [(Standard time – Time taken) ÷ Standard time] × Time taken × Rate per hour

Let time taken by x

$$₹37.50 = ₹30x + [(4 - x) \div 4] \times x ₹30$$

Let both sides be divided be $1/x$

$$= ₹37.50 = ₹30 + \left[\frac{4 - x}{4}\right] \times ₹30 = ₹37.50 = ₹30 + \left[\frac{₹120 - 30x}{4}\right]$$

$$₹7.5 = ₹30 - 7.5\,x$$

$$7.5x = ₹225 \quad \text{or} \quad x = ₹22.5/7.5 = 3 \text{ hours}$$

P.9.11. Calculate the earnings of workers A, B and C under Straight Piece Rate System and Merrick's Multiple Piece Rate System from the following particulars: LO 9.2 LOD: M

Normal rate per hour	₹54
Standard time per unit (minutes)	1

Output (units) per day is as follows:

Worker A	390
Worker B	450
Worker C	600

Working hours per day are 8.

Solution

Determination of Wages under Straight Piece Rate System

Worker	*(Output per day × Rate per unit)*	*Amount*
A	(390 Units × ₹0.90)[1]	₹351
B	(450 Units × ₹0.90)	405
C	(600 Units × ₹0.90)	540

1. Normal rate per hour ₹54 ÷ Standard output per hour 60 = ₹0.90

(i) *Determination of Wages under Merrick's Multiple Piece Rate System*

Worker	*Efficiency ratio (Actual production/ Standard production i.e., 60 × 8 = 480 units) (%)*	*Rate per unit**	*Actual units produced*	*Wages payable*
A	(390/480) = 81.25	₹0.90	390	₹351
B	(450/480) = 93.75	0.99	450	445.50
C	(600/480) = 125.00	1.08	600	648

*Normal piece rate is paid when output is upto 83 per cent of the standard output (and hence ₹0.90 per unit for worker A); 110 per cent of normal piece rate when output is between 83- 100 per cent (and hence ₹0.99 per unit for worker B); and 120 per cent is paid when output exceeds 100 per cent (and hence ₹1.08 per unit for worker C).

P.9.12 From the following information, calculate labour turnover rate and labour flux rate: LO 9.3 LOD: M

Number of workers as on January 1 = 7,600

Number of workers on December 31 = 8,400

During the year, 80 workers left while 320 workers were discharged. 1,500 workers recruited during the year; of these 300 workers were recruited because of exits and the rest were recruited in accordance with expansion plans.

Solution

(i) *Separation Method* = [(Number of workers leaving i.e., (left + discharged in a period) ÷ Average number of workers employed] × 100
= [(80 + 320)/ (7,600 + 8,400) ÷ 2] = 5 per cent

(ii) *Replacement Method* = (Number of workers replaced in a period) ÷ (Average number of workers employed) × 100
= (300/8,000) × 100 = 3.75 per cent

(iii) *Labour Flux Rate* = [(Number of workers leaving + Number of workers replaced excluding those who were recruited for expansion) ÷ (Average number of workers employed)] × 100
= [(400 + 300)/8000] × 100 = 8.75 per cent

P. 9.13 The cost accountant of Y Ltd has computed labour turnover rates for the quarter ended March 31, current year as 10 per cent, 5 per cent, and 3 per cent respectively under Flux Method. Replacement Method and Separation Method. If the number of workers replaced during that quarter is 30, find out the number of **(1)** workers recruited and joined and **(2)** workers left and discharged. LO 9.3 LOD: D

Solution

Average number of workers on roll: Labour turnover rate (replacement method) = [Number of replacement ÷ Average number of workers on roll]
(N) × 100
0.05 = 30/N
Therefore, average number of workers on roll (N) is 600.

1. Labour turnover rate (Separation Method) = (Number of separation (s) ÷ Average number of workers on roll) × 100
0.03 = S/600
S = 18
Therefore, number of workers left and discharged is 18.

2. Number of workers recruited and joined
Labour turnover rate (Flux Method) = [Number of separation (S) + Number of replacement (R)] ÷ Average number of workers (N) × 100
0.10 = (18 + R)/600
R = 42

Therefore, workers recruited and joined are 42.

P. 9.14 The management of In and Out Limited are worried about their increasing labour turnover in the factory, and before analysing the causes and taking remedial steps, they want to have an idea of the profit forgone as a result of labor turnover in the last year. LO 9.3 LOD: M

Last year, sales amounted to ₹8,30,33,000 and the profit-volume ratio was 20 per cent. The total number of actual hours worked by the direct labour force was 4.45 lakh. As a result of the delays by the Personnel Department in filling vacancies due to labour turnover, 1,00,000 potentially productive hours were lost. The actual direct labour-hours included 30,000 hours attributable to training new recruits, out of which half of the hours were unproductive.

The cost incurred consequent to labour turnover revealed on analysis the following:

Settlement costs due to leaving	₹4,38,200
Recruitment costs	2,67,400
Selection costs	1,27,500
Training costs	3,04,900

Assuming the potential production lost as a consequence of labour turnover could have been sold at prevailing prices, find the profit forgone last year on account of labour turnover.

Solution

Statement showing Profit Foregone due to Labour Turnover Last year

Settlement costs due to leaving	₹4,38,200
Recruitment costs	2,67,400
Selection costs	1,27,500
Training costs	3,04,900
Contribution lost due to lost sales	38,62,000
Total loss	50,00,000

WORKING NOTES

Direct labour-hours paid for	4,45,000
Less unproductive direct labour-hours	15,000
Actual direct labour-hours (productive)	4,30,000
Sales lost for 1,00,000 hours (₹8,30,33,000/4,30,000) × 1,00,000 hours	₹1,93,10,000
Contribution lost (₹1,93,10,000 × 0.20)	38,62,000

P. 9.15 The Managing Director of AII Found Limited is very much perturbed to see that labour turnover is increasing every year. Before taking an appropriate action, he desires to know the profit forgone on account of labour turnover. You are required to calculate the profit forgone on account of labour turnover from the following: LO 9.3 LOD: M

Income statement for the current year ended March, 31

Sales		₹20,00,000
Variable costs:		
Material	₹5,00,000	
Direct labour	4,00,000	
Variable overheads	4,00,000	13,00,000
Contribution		7,00,000
Less fixed overheads		2,00,000
Profit before taxes		5,00,000

The direct labour-hours worked in the concern during the period were 20,300, of which 500 hours pertained to the new workers on training. Only 40 per cent of the trainees time was productive. As replacement for the worker left was delayed for some time, 600 productive hours were lost.

The direct costs incurred by the company as a consequence of labour separation and replacement were as follows:

Separation costs	₹20,000
Selection costs	30,000
Training costs	50,000

Solution

Statement showing Determination of Profit Forgone due to Labour Turnover

Separation costs	₹20,000
Selection costs	30,000
Training costs	50,000
Contribution forgone	37,680
	1,37,680

WORKING NOTES

(i) Direct labour hours paid for	20,300
Less unproductive time of new workers (0.6 × 500)	300
Productive hours	20,000
Total labour hours lost including 600 for replacement	900
Unit sales per productive labour-hour (₹20,00,000/20,000)	₹100
Loss of potential sales (900 hours × ₹100)	90,000

Less variable costs:

Material costs (₹5,00,000/₹20,00,000) × ₹90,000	22,500
Variable overheads (₹4,00,000/₹20,00,000) × ₹90,000	18,000
Increase in direct labour cost (600 hours) (₹4,00,000/20,300 hours)	11,820
Contribution foregone	37,680

P. 9.16 A company is undecided as to what kind of wage scheme should be introduced. The following particulars have been compiled in respect of three systems, which are under consideration of the management:

LO 9.2 LOD: D

Particulars	*Workers*		
	A	*B*	*C*
Actual hours worked in a week	38	40	34
Hourly rate of wages	₹60	₹50	₹72
Production in units:			
Product P	21	—	60
Product Q	36	—	135
Product R	46	25	—
Standard time allowed per unit of each product is:			
	P	**Q**	**R**
Minutes	12	18	30

For the purpose of piece rate, each minute is valued at ₹1.

You are required to calculate the wages of each worker under:

(i) Guaranteed hourly rates basis

(ii) Piece work earnings basis, but guaranteed 75 per cent of basic pay (guaranteed hourly rate) if his earnings are less than 50 per cent of basic pay.

(iii) Premium bonus where the worker receives bonus based on Rowan scheme.

Solution

(i) *Computation of Wages of Workers under Guaranteed Hourly Rate Basis*

Particulars	*Workers*		
	A	*B*	*C*
1. Actual hours worked in a week	38	40	34
2. Multiply by hourly rate of wages	₹60	₹50	₹72
3. Guaranteed wages per week	₹2,280	₹2,000	₹2,448

(ii) *Computation of Wages of Workers under Piece Work Earnings Basis*

Product	*Piece rate per unit*	*Units produced by workers*			*Wages of workers*		
		A	*B*	*C*	*A*	*B*	*C*
1	2		3			4 (2 × 3)	
P	(12 minutes × ₹1) = ₹12	21	—	60	₹252	—	₹720
Q	(18 minutes × ₹1) = 18	36	—	135	648	—	2,430
R	(30 minutes × ₹1) = 30	46	25	—	1,380	750	—
					2,280	150[@]	3,150

@ Since ₹750 is less than 50% of basic pay (of ₹2,000), he would be paid 75 per cent × ₹2,000 = ₹1,500.

(iii) *Rowan scheme provides the following basis of computing bonus.*

Bonus = (Time taken/Time allowed) × Time saved × Time rate

(a) *Determination of Time Allowed to Workers*

Product	Standard time allowed per unit (in minutes)	Units produced by workers			Total standard time allowed to workers (in hours)		
		A	B	C	A	B	C
P	12	21	—	60	252	—	720
Q	18	36	—	135	648	—	2,430
R	30	46	25	—	1,380	750	—
					2,280	750	3,150

(b) Determination of Bonus Payable under Rowan Scheme

Workers	Time (in hours)			Wage rate per hour	Earnings	Bonus	Total earnings + bonus
	Taken	Allowed	Saved				
A	38	38	—	₹60	₹2,280	—	₹2,280
B	40	12.5	NA	50	2,000	—	2,000
C	34	52.5	18.5	72	2,448	862.6[1]	3,310.60

1 = (34/52.5) × 18.5 × ₹72 = ₹862.60

P. 9.17 ZED Ltd is working by employing 50 skilled workers. It is considering the introduction of incentive scheme-either Halsey scheme (with 50 per cent bonus) or Rowan scheme of wage payment for increasing the labour productivity to cope up the increasing demand for the product by 40 per cent. It is believed that proposed incentive scheme could bring about an average 20 per cent increase over the present earnings of the workers; it could act as sufficient incentive for them to produce more. **LO 9.2** **LOD: D**

Because of assurance, the increase in productivity has been observed as revealed by the figures for the month of April.

Hourly rate of wages (guaranteed)	₹30
Average time for producing one unit by one worker at the previous performance (This may be taken as time allowed)	1.975 hours
Number of working days in the month	24
Number of working hours per day of each worker	8
Actual production during the month	6,120 units

REQUIRED: **(i)** Calculate the effective rate of earnings under the Halsey scheme and the Rowan scheme. **(ii)** Calculate the savings to the ZED Ltd in terms of direct labour cost per piece. **(iii)** Advise ZED Ltd about the selection of the scheme to fulfill their assurance.

Solution

(i) *Determination of Effective Rate of Earnings*

Halsey Scheme: (Hours worked in a month × Rate per hour) + (0.50 of time saved × Rate per hour)
= (24 days × 8 hours per day × 50 workers = 9,600 hours × ₹30 per hour) + [0.50 × (Time allowed 6,120 units × 1.975 hours = 12,087 hours – 9,600 hours) × ₹30)]
= ₹2,88,000 + 37,305 = ₹3,25,305
Effective earnings per hour = (₹3,25,305/9,600 hours) = ₹33.89
Rowan Scheme: (Hours worked in a month × Rate per hour) + [(Time saved/Time allowed) × Time taken × Rate per hour]
= (9,600 hours × ₹30) + [(2,487/12,087) × 9,600 × ₹30]
= ₹2,88,000 + ₹59,258 = ₹3,47,258
Effective earnings per hour (₹3,47,258/9,600) = ₹36.17

(ii) *Computation of Savings in Direct Labour Cost per Unit/Piece*

Halsey Scheme:	
Current production cost per unit (1.975 hours x ₹30 per hour)	₹59.25
Less production cost under Halsey scheme (₹3,25,305/6,120 units)	53.15
Savings per unit	6.10
Rowan Scheme:	
Current production cost	₹59.25
Less production cost under Rowan Scheme (₹3,47,258/6,120 units)	56.74
Savings per unit	2.51

(iii) Zed Ltd. has assured workers the increase in wages by 20 per cent (i.e. from present level of ₹2,88,000 to 3,45,600); this assurance can be fulfilled only under Rowan scheme as only under this scheme, the wage payable is ₹3,47,258. The total wage amount under Halsey scheme is ₹3,25,305 only (increase of 13 per cent only). Therefore, Zed Ltd is advised to adopt Rowan scheme.

REVIEW QUESTIONS

LOD: Easy

RQ.9.1(a) Indicate whether the following statements are true or false. LO 9.2,3

(i) Piece work system of wage payment is good for quality-conscious organisations producing aesthetic products or decorative items.

(ii) Taylor piece rate system has differential piece rates.

(iii) Merrick differential piece rate system has two wage rates: a lower rate for output below standard performance and higher rate for output above standard performance.

(iv) Gantt task and bonus plan is a mixture of guaranteed time rate with bonus and piece rate plan using the differential principle.

(v) Cost of labour turnover includes preventive and replacements costs.

(b) In the following multiple choice questions select the correct answers. LO 9.2

(vi) Which of the following are earnings of workers A and B under Taylor differential piece rate system, given the following data?

— Standard time per piece; 20 minutes

— Normal rate per hour, ₹9

— In a 9-hour day, A produces 25 units and B produces 30 units.

— Differential to be applied: 80 per cent of piece rate below standard and 120 per cent above standard.

(a) ₹50, ₹90, (b) ₹60, ₹108, (c) ₹75, ₹90, (d) ₹50, ₹188.

(vii) Which of the following are the earnings of A, B and C under Merrick differential piece rate system, given the following data?

— Normal piece rate (upto 83% of high task output), ₹10 per unit

— High task, 40 units per week

— Weekly output: A, 32 units; B, 37 units; C, 42 units

(a) ₹320, ₹407, ₹504, (b) ₹352, ₹407, ₹504, (c) ₹320, ₹444, ₹504, (d) ₹300, ₹407, ₹504.

(viii) Which of the following are the earning of A, B and C under Gantt task and bonus plan given the following data?

— Time rate ₹10 per hour for 48 hours week.

— Standard production, 48 units per week.
— Piece rate above standard output, ₹12.
— Weekly output A, 38 units; B, 45 units; C, 50 units.
(a) ₹480, ₹480, ₹600, (b) ₹480, ₹480, ₹500, (c) ₹380, ₹450, ₹500, (d) ₹480, ₹450, ₹600.

(ix) Which is the earning (per hour) payable to A under Halsey premium plan given the following data?
— Time given to complete the work- 8 hours
— Wage rate ₹4 per hour
— Job completed in 6 hours
(a) ₹4.67 per hour., (b) ₹4 per hour, (c) ₹3.5 per hour, (d) ₹4.5 per hour.

(x) Which of the following is the earning of A (as per data given in Question No ix), under Halsey-Weir premium plan?
(a) ₹26.67, (b) ₹24, (c) ₹28, (d) ₹29.33.

(xi) Which of the following is the earning (per hour) of A (as per data given in Question No ix), under Rowan plan?
(a) ₹30 or ₹5/hour, (b) ₹30 or ₹3.75/hour, (c) ₹30 or ₹4/hour, (d) ₹30 or ₹3/hour.

(xii) Under the Bedaux point plan which is the amount of bonus and earnings given the information below?
— Standard production – 8 hours daily = 100 (units).
— Actual production for hours daily = 125 (units).
— Hourly wage rate = ₹3.
(a) ₹4.5 and ₹28.5, (b) ₹4 and ₹28, (c) Nil and ₹24, (d) ₹4.8 and ₹28.8.

[Answers: (i) False, (ii) True, (iii) False, (iv) True, (v) True, (vi) b (vii) a (viii) a (ix) a (x) a (xi) a (xii) a.]

RQ.9.2 What are the costs included in total labour cost besides gross wages? LO 9.1

RQ.9.3 Explain timekeeping and book keeping and state the detailed records normally maintained under them. LO 9.1

RQ.9.4 What is idle time? How is it treated in costing of labour? LO 9.2

RQ.9.5 What is labour turnover? How is it measured? What are its costs? How can they be reduced? LO 9.3

RQ.9.6 The time taken for a particular operation for operator X in the Process Division of a manufacturing concern on three different counts was 24, 22 and 27 minutes while that of operator Y was 20, 23 and 26 minutes. It has been ascertained that the rating of 'X' is 70/60 and that of 'Y' is 55/60. Allowance for fatigue, personal needs are assumed at 15 per cent. Calculate, using the above information as a base, for that particular operation, (i) the standard time, and (ii) the time allowed under an incentive allowance of 30 per cent of standard time. LO 9.2

LOD: Medium

RQ.9.7 What is overtime premium? Discuss its treatment in cost accounting and suggest a procedure for its control. LO 9.2

RQ.9.8 What are incentive plans? Describe the main types of incentives plans. LO 9.2

RQ.9.9 Explain and illustrate the differential price rate schemes type of incentive/bonus plans. LO 9.2

RQ.9.10 Write notes on the different types of premium bonus plans. Illustrate your answer with examples. LO 9.2

RQ.9.11 A skilled worker is allowed to take 9 hours to complete a job on daily wages and 6 hours on a scheme of payment by results. His daily rate is ₹75 per hour. The material cost is ₹400 and the overheads are recovered at 150 per cent of the total direct wages. Calculate the factory cost of the product under (i) piece-work plan, (ii) Halsey Plan and (iii) Rowan Plan, assuming work is completed in 6 hours. LO 9.2

RQ.9.12 Mr. A is working by employing 10 skilled workers. He is considering the introduction of some incentive scheme — either Halsey Scheme (with 50 per cent bonus) or Rowan Scheme — of wage payment for increasing the labour productivity to cope with the increased demand for the product. He feels that if the proposed incentive scheme could bring about an average 20 per cent increase over the present earnings of the workers, it could act as sufficient incentive for them to produce more and he has accordingly given this assurance to the workers. As a result of the assurance, the increase in productivity observed as revealed by the following figures for the current month: LO 9.2

Hourly rate of wages (guaranteed)	₹20
Average time for producing 1 piece by one worker at the previous performance (This may be taken as time allowed) (hours)	2
Number of working days in the month	25
Number of working hours per day for each worker	8
Actual production during the month (units)	1,250

REQUIRED:

(a) Calculate effective rate of earnings per hour under Halsey Scheme and Rowan Scheme.

(b) Calculate the savings to Mr. A in terms of direct labour cost per piece under the schemes.

(c) Advise Mr. A about the selection of the scheme to fulfill assurance.

RQ.9.13 From the following data provided to you, find out the labour turnover rate by applying (a) Flux method, (b) Replacement method, and (c) Separation method. LO 9.3

Number of workers on the payroll: At the beginning of the month, 500; At the end of the month, 600.

During the month, 5 workers left, 20 persons were discharged and 75 workers were recruited. Of these, 10 workers were recruited in the vacancies of those leaving, while the rest were engaged for an expansion scheme.

LOD: Difficult

RQ.9.14 Your organisation is experiencing a high labour turnover in recent years and management would like you to submit a report on the loss suffered by the Company due to such labour turnover. Following figures are available for your consideration: LO 9.3

Sales (₹lakhs)	₹600
Direct materials	150
Direct labour (4,80,000 man-hours)	48
Other variable expenses	60
Fixed overheads	80

The direct man-hours include 9,000 man-hours spent on trainees and replacement, only 50 per cent of which were productive. Further, during the year, 12,000 man-hours of potential work could not be availed of because of delayed replacement. The cost incurred due to separations and replacements amounted to ₹1 lakh.

On the basis of above data, prepare comparative statement showing actual profit *vis-à-vis* the profit which would have been realised had there been no labour turnover.

ANSWERS

RQ.9.6 **(i)** 28.45 minutes **(ii)** 37 minutes

RQ.9.11 **(a)** **(i)** ₹450, **(ii)** ₹562.50, **(iii)** ₹675 wages; **(b)** Factory cost **(i)** ₹1,525, **(ii)** ₹1,806.25, **(iii)** ₹2,087.50

RQ.9.12 **(a)** Halsey Scheme, ₹22.50; Rowan Scheme ₹24, **(b)** Halsey Scheme, ₹4.0; Rowan Scheme ₹1.60; **(c)** The Rowan plans is advised to be adopted.

RQ.9.13 **(a)** Flux method (6.36 per cent), **(b)** Replacement method (1.82 per cent), **(c)** Separation method (4.55 per cent)

RQ.9.14 Loss of profit due to labour turnover ₹13,33,312

[Comprehensive solutions to all numerical review questions are available on the companion website: http://www.mhhe.com/khan_jain_ma7e]

Costing and Control of Factory (Manufacturing) Overheads

10

LEARNING OBJECTIVES

After reading this chapter you will be able to:

LO 10.1 Explain the concept of factory overhead costs
LO 10.2 Discuss and illustrate the factory overheads application/absorption rate
LO 10.3 Show the methods/procedures of allocating costs of service departments to production departments
LO 10.4 Describe the methods of absorption of factory overheads
LO 10.5 Illustrate the treatment of under/over-absorption of factory overheads

INTRODUCTION

The previous two chapters discussed costing and control of direct material costs (Chapter 8) and direct labour costs (Chapter 9) that are incurred in manufacturing of products. The third element of production costs, namely, factory overheads is the subject matter of this chapter. The chapter deals with determination of factory overheads. It also deals with determination of factory overheads application/absorption rate. The methods/procedure of allocating costs of service departments to production departments are discussed subsequently. We also explain the methods of absorption of factory overheads. The treatment of the difference between actual factory overheads incurred and factory overheads absorbed, that is, under-absorption/over-absorption of factory overheads has also been explained. The main points are summarised by way of recapitulation.

FACTORY OVERHEAD COSTS

LO 10.1 Explain the concept of factory overhead costs

Factory overhead costs refer to all indirect manufacturing costs which cannot be identified with particular orders or units of product. These costs include the following:

Factory overhead costs refer to all indirect manufacturing costs which cannot be identified with a particular order/unit/product.

- Indirect materials and indirect labour.
- Factory rent, rates, lighting, power, and fuel.

- Depreciation on factory plant and equipments and factory building.
- Insurance, repairs and maintenance of factory plant and equipments and building.
- Storekeeping, toolroom costs.

FACTORY OVERHEAD APPLICATION/ABSORPTION RATE

LO 10.2 Discuss and illustrate the factory overheads application/absorption rate

Cost allocation is the allotmant of whole items of costs to cost centres/units.

Direct costs normally can be conveniently identified/allocated to specific jobs. Material requisitions and workers' time sheets provide sufficient indication where these costs are to be charged. The same is, however, not true for the indirect manufacturing costs as they are incurred for the factory as a whole. Being *common costs,* they are divided/shared/charged among various *cost centres* and/or *cost units.*

Cost apportioniment is the allotment of common costs to cost centres on the basis of benefits received

The procedure for allotting factory overheads to cost centres/objects/units cover cost allocation, cost apportionment, and overhead absorption. While the allotment of whole items of cost to cost centres or cost units is referred to as *cost allocation,* the allotment of common costs to two or more cost centres on the estimated basis of benefits received is known as cost *apportionment.* The allotment of factory overheads to cost units/objects by means of predetermined factory overhead application rate is called *overhead absorption.*

Overhead absorption is the allotmant of factory overheads to cost units objects by means of overhead application rate.

The factory overhead absorption rate can either be *actual* overhead rate or a *predetermined* overhead rate. Normally, a predetermined overhead rate is preferred, the reason being: **(a)** It is useful in 'bidding' cases to determine quotation prices; **(b)** It enables individual jobs to be costed immediately on their completion; and **(c)** Such a rate levels out the fluctuations which may be caused by variations in actual factory overhead costs and/or actual level of activity.

The two key factors to determine the factory overhead application rate for a period are: **(a)** To select a volume/level of production (more commonly referred to as capacity) to be used as a base for applying factory overheads to production (denominators) and **(b)** To budget factory overheads at the capacity selected (numerator).

Concepts of Capacity Choice of the capacity to be used as a base in applying factory overheads often raises a difficult question. The reason is that there are more than one basis of determining capacity. For instance, capacity can be based on the physical facilities that have been installed, or productive capacity that can be utilised (giving due allowance for unavoidable lost hours both in respect of machines and workers), or actual capacity used in relation to the expected sales volume. While one capacity level relates to the level of production (determined by engineers, with no regard to the expected sales volume) the other is the expected product sales. The choice (by and large *subjective* in nature) is to be made from one of the following four possibilities: **(i)** Maximum/Theoretical idle capacity, **(ii)** Practical capacity **(iii)** Normal/Long-term production capacity, and **(iv)** Expected/Short-term actual capacity.

Maximum or Theoretical Idle Capacity It refers to the volume of production that a particular production department or factory is capable of producing if the plant were in continuous operation at *peak efficiency at all times.* In other words, such a capacity base does not have any provision for either a lack of sales orders or interruptions in production (due to machine break-down, machine downtime for repairs and maintenance, set-up time, holidays, weekends, and so on). At this capacity level, the plant is assumed to function 24 hours a day, 7 days a week, 52 weeks a year without any interruptions, in order to yield the highest physical output possible, that is, 100 per cent of plant capacity.[1]

Practical Capacity Unlike theoretical capacity measure, practical capacity does notexpect full utilisation of the plant; it makes due allowances for unavoidable idleness of workers and machinery caused by repairs and maintenance, machine set-up, fatigue, and time lost through vacations and holidays. However, this measure does not take into consideration plant and personnel made idle due to the lack of sales orders. In *operational* terms, it is the maximum capacity expected when the plant operates at *a planned level of efficiency.*

> **Practical capacity** is the maximum capacity expected when the plant operates at a planned level of efficiency

Normal or Long-run Productive Capacity Unlike practical capacity, normal capacity allows for idleness both of plant and personnel caused due to a lack of sales orders. Normally, capacity is equal to, or less than, practical production capacity depending upon the volume of expected sales. More often, normal capacity is less than practical capacity. Further, normal capacity is not based just on one year's sales; it is the average annual volume of production needed to meet ordinary and usual sales demand over a cycle of years long enough (say 5 years) to even out seasonal, cyclical, and other variations in customer demand.

> **Normal capacity** is equal to, or less than, practical capacity depending on the volume of expected sales.

Expected or Short-run Actual Capacity It is the volume of production required to meet the estimated/projected demand for the next period/year (that is in a single year only). Thus, expected actual capacity differs from normal capacity in the length of time to determine capacity base; this measure does not smoothen out cyclical variations in sales that are likely to occur over a period of time as it is guided by one year projections only. Such a measure may appeal to those firms which are interested more in short-term planning and control.
Example 10.1 illustrates these 4 concepts of capacity.

◆ Example 10.1

The Hypothetical Manufacturing Company Ltd wishes to determine various capacity levels both in terms of production units and machine-hours. One machine-hour produces 10 units of finished product. The production department in which the machine is located normally operates 6 days a week (except Sunday) on a single, eight-hour shift. The plant is closed for 10 working days each year for holidays.

Plant is closed for 200 hours each year for its repairs and maintenance. Normal sales demand averages 20,000 units a year over a 5-year period (extensive product changes are made every five years). The expected sales volume for the next year is 19,000 units. Show the machine-hours and production capacity at the four levels.

Solution

Machine-hours and production capacity at 4 levels of capacity are shown in Table 10.1.

TABLE 10.1 Capacity at Various Levels

Details of computation		*Capacity*	
		Machine-hours	*Production units @ 10 units per hour*
1. Maximum capacity (365 days × 8 hours per day)		2,920	29,200
2. Practical capacity			
Maximum capacity (in hours)	2,920		
Less idle capacity:			
Sundays (52 days × 8 hours)	416		
Holidays (10 days × 8 hours)	80		
Plant maintenance	200	2,224	22,240
3. Normal capacity		2,000	20,000
4. Expected capacity		1,900	19,000

Table 10.1 shows that factory overhead applied rate will markedly vary among 4 capacity measures and thereby affect production costs, inventory costs, and profits. Therefore, it is important to select an appropriate capacity level to determine reliable and correct factory overhead application rate.

The first measure based on theoretical ideal/maximum capacity is more of academic significance rather than of practical relevance, as it is practically infeasible for plant to operate at such a capacity (for instance, in Example 10.1, it is not always possible for the firm to produce 29,200 units).

Likewise, practical capacity level suffers from lack of realism in that it focuses more on production than sales it can achieve. In practice, it is not a tenable assumption that the firm will produce without taking into account its sales level. However, this measure can be fruitfully applied if a manufacturing firm has captive market, that is, it can sell *all* it produces. But, in practice, this is rarely the case for the majority of the firms; most firms are expected to produce only as much as they can sell.

From the foregoing, it follows that sales projections are a vital factor in the planning process and must be considered while estimating production levels. For most manufacturing firms, either normal productive capacity or expected productive capacity is used to determine factory overhead application rate as both these bases explicitly recognise expected product sales.

Between the two, the normal long-run productive capacity base should be preferred. Such a measure, assuming all other factors remain constant, **(i)** Yields uniform product costs per unit across different time periods; **(ii)** Eliminates the possibility of manipulation of unit product cost by varying production levels intentionally. The latter situation is likely to arise in firms selling products which exhibit pronounced variations in their demand pattern across different time periods (over a cycle of years, say 5 years).

In sum, therefore, normal capacity level is conceptually correct measure to determine factory overhead application rate.

Budgeted Factory Overhead Costs Once the estimated level of production (capacity) has been decided, a manufacturing firm prepares a budget of expected production/factory overheads likely to be incurred in the next year. For estimating budgeted factory overheads, past historical cost data are normally taken as the base and adjustments are made for likely changes in prices/rates of various cost constituents of factory overheads. These overhead costs are classified based on their behaviour in relation to production into three categories: fixed, variable, and mixed costs; mixed costs, in turn, are segregated into fixed and variable.[3] Budgeted factory overheads are computed as shown in Format 10.1.

FORMAT 10.1 Determination of Budgeted Factory Overhead Costs

Total budgeted fixed factory overheads	______
Add variable factory overheads (Budgeted capacity level × Budgeted variable overhead rate)	______
Total	______

◆ Example 10.2

For Hypothetical Ltd in Example 10.1, assume further that the budgeted fixed overhead costs are estimated at ₹6 lakh and variable overhead costs at ₹100 per unit as the basis of determining factory overhead application rate. Compute the factory overhead application rate.

Solution

TABLE 10.2 Determination of Factory Overhead Application Rate

(a)	*Total budgeted fixed overheads*	
	Fixed overhead costs	₹6,00,000
	Variable overhead costs (2,000 hours × ₹100)	2,00,000
		8,00,000
(b)	Normal capacity (machine-hours)	2,000
(c)	(i) Factory overhead application rate (₹8,00,000/2,000) per hour	400
	(ii) Factory overhead application rate (₹8,00,000/20,000 units) per unit	40

COST ALLOCATION

LO 10.3 Show the methods/procedures of allocating costs of service departments to production departments

When a company produces more than one product, it is important that the factory overhead costs (as determined above) are allocated to various production departments or cost centres. These departments, in turn, assign these costs to product(s) on some equitable basis. Thus, when multiple products are produced, a single factorywide factory overhead application rate is not appropriate for allocating factory overheads. On grounds of equity, the production departments receiving greater benefits should be charged a higher share of these overheads and *vice-versa*. This process of assigning direct and indirect manufacturing costs to various cost centres is referred to as *cost allocation*. Proper cost allocation is of crucial significance as wrong cost allocation can distort income determination, asset valuation, performance evaluation, and decision-making in a firm.

The cost allocation process is comprised of three basic activities.[4]

1. Accumulating the costs on the basis of department or division or product.
2. Identifying the cost objects or recipients of the allocated costs, say, a unit of product or a department.
3. Selecting a method for relating the costs so accumulated to the cost objects.

The third aspect is the most difficult as common costs cannot be directly associated with a single unit, or production department, or division. Some meaningful base needs to be developed to relate costs and cost objects.

While no allocation base can be hundred per cent foolproof (in terms of precision and accuracy), following bases are commonly used for allotting fixed overheads:

Labour-related Factory Overheads

(Say supervisor's salaries, canteen expenses) are usually allocated on the basis of number of employees, direct labour-hours, wages paid or similar other labour related criteria.

Machine-related Factory Overheads

(Say insurance, maintenance, depreciation) are normally allocated on the basis of machine-hours, current book value of machinery, number of machines, or similar other machine-related criteria.

Space-related Factory Overheads

(Say factory building rent and insurance, lighting, maintenance of building) are usually allocated on the basis of space occupied or similar other space-related criteria.

Service-related Costs

(Say materials handling, utility) are normally allocated on the basis of value, quantity, time and similar other service related criteria.

While the principle of cost allocation, in theory, appears to be easy, it is not so simple when it is put to practice. Methods used in practice are often somewhat arbitrary. As far as possible, each factory overhead cost item should be analysed on its own merit to arrive at the most suitable/ equitable base.

Departmental Rates

It is common for manufacturing firms to have several departments that are involved either directly or indirectly in production. The discussion that follows dwells on determination of departmental rates related to factory overheads.

Direct Departmental Costs These are the costs which can be easily traced to specific departments. For instance, indirect materials used in production department (say X) can be traced through requisitions on store and can wholly be allocated to department X; likewise, indirect labour (foreman's and supervisor's salaries) wholly engaged in department X can be traced through payroll records; the same applies for depreciation on machines and plants exclusively used in the department X and annual maintenance contact payment for these machines.

Indirect Departmental Costs These are the costs which are common to more than one department and, hence, need to be shared/apportioned among the departments receiving benefits. Building occupancy costs (such as rent, maintenance and light); factory insurance premium, power charges for machine operations (where there are no separate metres for departments) are the major costs included in this category.

Charging Cost of Service Departments

It is a important to take into account costs incurred on service departments to compute factory overheads application rate of production departments.

A service department is a department which provides benefits to producing departments and/ or service departments. For instance, maintenance department (responsible for the upkeep of the machinery and building), utility department (responsible for providing power and electricity for a factory), personnel department (responsible for keeping records of personnel employed), are the examples of service departments. Since the output of such service departments is not sold to outside customers, their costs must be covered by production departments, receiving their services.

Accordingly, apportioned service department costs to production departments (in which material conversion or production takes place) can be construed similar to indirect manufacturing costs. The following methods are used to apportion total budgeted costs of service department to production departments (also known as secondary distribution of factory overheads; allocation of indirect manufacturing costs like indirect labour and indirect materials to production departments is referred as primary distribution): **(i)** Direct method, **(ii)** Step method, **(iii)** Repeated distribution method, and **(iv)** Algebraic method.

Direct Method Total budgeted costs of service departments are apportioned between/among production departments only, ignoring any services provided by service departments to each other. This method is the most appropriate when there is virtually no provision of rendering services on reciprocal basis among the service departments. This method has the virtue of simplicity as far as its use in assigning costs to production departments is concerned.

Example 10.3 illustrates how total budgeted costs of five service departments in a manufacturing company are apportioned between its two production departments. It also shows the *modus operandi* of determining factory overhead application/absorption rate for each of the two production departments (after taking into account the share of service departments).

Example 10.3

A manufacturing company has 5 service departments and 2 production departments. The total budgeted costs for the period for each department were as follows:

Service Departments:	
Building and grounds	₹1,00,000
Personnel	10,000
General factory and administration	2,60,900
Cafeteria	16,400
Storeroom	26,700
Production Departments:	
Machinery	3,47,000
Assembly	4,89,000

The following schedule was prepared to assist in allocating service department costs:

Department	*Direct labour-hours*	*Number of employees*	*Square feet*	*Total labour-hours*	*Number of requisitions*
Building and grounds	—	—	—	—	—
Personnel	—	—	2,000	—	—
General factory administration	—	35	7,000	—	—
Cafeteria	—	10	4,000	1,000	—
Storeroom	—	5	7,000	1,000	—
Machinery	5,000	50	30,000	8,000	2,000
Assembly	15,000	100	50,000	17,000	1,000
	20,000	200	1,00,000	27,000	3,000

The company management decided that the appropriate bases used by each service department would be the following:

Building and grounds	Square feet
Personnel department	Employees
General factory administration	Total labour-hours
Cafeteria	Employees
Storeroom	Requisitions

Direct labour-hours are used as the basis for computing the production dapartment's factory overhead application rates.

You are required to allocate the total budgeted costs of the service departments by using direct method. Also, determine the factory overhead absorption rates for the production departments.

Solution

TABLE 10.3 Determination of Factory Overhead Absorption Rates for Production Departments (Machinery and Assembly)

Items	*Basis of charge*	*Service Departments*					*Production Departments*	
		Building and grounds	*Personnel*	*General factory administration*	*Cafeteria*	*Storeroom*	*Machinery*	*Assembly*
Budgeted costs	Allocation	₹1,00,000	₹10,000	₹2,60,900	₹16,400	₹26,700	₹3,47,000	₹4,89,000
Cost of service departments apportioned to production departments:								
Building and grounds	Square feet ratio (3:5)	(1,00,000)					37,500	62,500
Personnel	Employees (1:2)		(10,000)				3,333	6,667
General factory administration	Total labour-hours (8:17)			(2,60,900)			83,488	1,77,412
Cafeteria	Employees (1:2)				(16,400)		5,467	10,933
Storeroom	Requisitions (2:1)					(26,700)	17,800	8,900
Total cost		—	—	—	—	—	4,94,588	7,55,412
Direct labour-hours							5,000	15,000
Factory overhead absorption rate (Total cost/Direct labour-hours)							98.92	50.36

Step Method In situations, when one service department renders services to another (that is reciprocity exists), the step method is more appropriate than the direct method. This method takes into consideration the *total/true* cost of each service department (and not partial) in assigning them to production departments.

The following is a list of steps used for the purpose of apportioning budgeted costs of service departments:[5]

(i) It is usual to apportion first the cost of that service department which renders services to the largest number of other service departments.

(ii) The budgeted costs of the service department that renders services to the next largest number of service departments are then apportioned. Obviously, any apportioned costs added to this service department from step 1 are included. The sum of budgeted service cost, so arrived at, is then apportioned among the remaining service departments (whose costs are yet to be assigned). The service department whose budgeted costs were apportioned as per the step 1 will not receive any cost share from the second department.

(iii) This sequence is continued, step-by-step, until all the budgeted service department costs have been apportioned to production departments.

Using the facts given in Example 10.3, cost apportionment of service departments as per Step method is shown in Table 10.4.

TABLE 10.4 Determination of Factory Overhead Absorption Rates for Production Departments (Machinery and Assembly)

Items	*Basis of charge*	*Service Departments*					*Production Departments*	
		Building and grounds	*Personnel*	*General factory administration*	*Cafeteria*	*Storeroom*	*Machinery*	*Assembly*
Budgeted costs	Allocation	₹1,00,000	₹10,000	₹2,60,900	₹16,400	₹26,700	₹3,47,000	₹4,89,000
Distribution of factory overheads of:								
Building and grounds	Square feet ratio	(1,00,000)	2,000	7,000	4,000	7,000	30,000	50,000
Personnel	Employees		(12,000)	2,100	600	300	3,000	6,000
General factory administration	Total labour-hours			(2,70,000)	10,000	10,000	80,000	1,70,000
Cafeteria	Employees				(31,000)	1,000	10,000	20,000
Storeroom	Requisition					(45,000)	30,000	15,000
Total cost		—	—	—	—	—	5,00,000	7,50,000
Direct labour-hours (DLH)							5,000	15,000
Factory overhead absorption rate (Total cost/DLH)							100	50

The allocation of 5 service departments (SD) is made in the following order: **(a)** Building and grounds (shared with 4 SD), **(b)** Personnel department (shared with 3 SD), **(c)** General factory administration (shared with 2 SD), **(d)** Cafeteria (with one SD), and **(e)** Service departments costs of storeroom is apportioned only with 2 production departments and not with any service department.

It may be noted that under direct method, budgeted costs of each of the five service departments were apportioned between 2 production departments only; service departments had not been apportioned any costs, at any stage.

Repeated Distribution Method The process of apportioning service departments overhead is continued until the figures of unapportioned sum(s) of service department(s) become negligible: The following steps are involved in its application:

(i) The first service department's (to be identified on the basis of the order in which their names are stated) budgeted costs are to be apportioned. As a result, the balance of the first service department becomes nil; its costs are apportioned among other departments (on the basis of their percentage share or some other base stated).

(ii) The budgeted costs of the second service department (consisting of original amount plus the apportioned sum from the first service department) is to be apportioned among other departments including the first service department.

(iii) This process continues for all the remaining/other service departments. The steps shown as per (i) to (iii) refer to the first phase.

(iv) The second phase of cycle starts once again with the first service department; it will consist only of apportioned amounts from other service departments. As a result, the total costs of service departments become less and less with each phase of apportionment.

(v) The process comes to an end when it is found that the residual sum (to be apportioned) has been either exhausted or has become virtually insignificant.

Consider Example 10.4.

Example 10.4

A small company has three production departments and two service departments. Distribution summary of overheads (per week) is as follows:

Production departments:	
A	₹13,600
B	14,700
C	12,800
Service departments:	
X	9,000
Y	3,000

The expenses of service departments are charged on a percentage basis, which is as follows:

Department	*A*	*B*	*C*	*X*	*Y*
X	40	30	20	—	10
Y	30	30	20	20	—

Apportion the cost of service departments by using the repeated distribution method.

Solution

TABLE 10.5 Apportionment of Cost of Service Departments to Production Departments

Particulars	*Production departments*			*Service departments*	
	A	*B*	*C*	*X*	*Y*
Primary apportionment	₹13,600	₹14,700	₹12,800	₹9,000	₹3,000
Department X overheads apportioned in ratio of (4:3:2:1)	3,600	2,700	1,800	(9,000)	900
Department Y overheads (₹3,900) apportioned in the ratio of (3:3:2:2)	1,170	1,170	780	780	(3,900)
Department X overheads (₹780) apportioned in the ratio of 4:3:2:1	312	234	156	(780)	78
Department Y overheads (₹78) apportioned in the ratio of 3:3:2:2	23	23	16	16	(78)
Department X overheads (₹16) apportioned in the ratio of 4:3:2:1	6	5	3	(16)	2
Department Y overheads (₹2) apportioned in the ratio of 3:3:2:2	1	1	—	—	(2)
Total	18,712	18,833	15,555	—	—

Algebraic Method This method is the most appropriate of all the four methods when reciprocal services exist between service departments. It is also called the reciprocal services method as it takes into account cost flows in both directions between service departments that render services to each other. Typically, the service departments provide services to each other in most of the manufacturing firms in practice. This method provides conceptually the most correct budget cost estimates of service departments and their subsequent apportionment.

Example 10.5 illustrates its application.

◆ Example 10.5

Tiny Industries Ltd has 2 service (SD) and 2 production departments (PD). It employs the algebraic method to allocate budgeted service department costs. The following information is available:

Department	*Budgeted costs*	*Services provided by*	
		Department A	*Department B*
Total costs:			
SD A	₹1,00,000	—	20 %
SD B	2,00,000	35 %	—
Factory overhead costs:			
PD_1	1,40,000	15	45
PD_2	60,000	50	35
	5,00,000	100 %	100 %
Direct labour-hours (DLH):			
PD_1	20,000		
PD_2	10,000		

From the above information, you are required to: **(a)** Allocate the service departments costs to production departments. Use algebraic equation method, **(b)** Compute factory overhead absorption rate, based on direct labour-hours.

Solution

(a) Let X be the total overhead costs of SD A and Y be of SD B

X = ₹1,00,000 + 0.20Y

Y = ₹2,00,000 + 0.35X

Substituting,

X = ₹1,00,000 + 0.20 × (₹2,00,000 + 0.35X) = ₹1,00,000 + ₹40,000 + 0.07X

= ₹1,40,000/0.93 = ₹1,50,538

Y = ₹2,00,000 + 0.35 × (₹1,50,538) = ₹2,52,688

Allocation of Overheads Among Production Departments

Items	*Production Departments*		*Total*
	P_1	P_2	
Direct overheads	₹1,40,000	₹60,000	₹2,00,000
SD A (15:50)	22,581	75,269	97,850
SD B (45:35)	1,13,709	88,441	2,02,150
Total	2,76,290	2,23,710	5,00,000

WORKING NOTES

1. Total expenses of SD A	₹1,50,538
Less share of SD B (0.35 × ₹1,50,538)	52,688
Amount to be divided between production departments	97,850
2. Total expenses of SD B	2,52,688
Less share of SD A (0.20 × ₹2,52,688)	50,538
Amount to be divided between production departments	2,02,150

(b) *Factory Overhead Absorption Rate (based on DLH) for Production Departments*

For P_1 (₹2,76,290/20,000, DLH)	₹13.8145
For P_2 (₹2,23,710/10,000, DLH)	22.3710

ABSORPTION OF FACTORY OVERHEADS

LO 10.4 Describe the methods of absorption of factory overheads

Absorption rate is the equitable allotment of factory overheads to cost units/objects.

If in production cost centre/department, all units produced are identical, the total factory overheads of production department could be shared equally among the units produced. For instance, if the total budgeted production department costs (inclusive of apportioned share from service departments) are ₹1,50,000 per month, budgeted production units are 15,000; factory overhead (predetermined) rate would be ₹10 per unit.

However, when the units are not normally identical and different facilities are used in their production, if a unit rate were used, some units would be over-charged and others under-charged. This will cause wrong cost estimation of various products and, hence, incorrect income reporting of these products to the management. On the basis of income reporting, the management may like to encourage more profitable products (in terms of expansion) in future; it may be possible that these products, in effect, may not be more profitable as they have been charged lower share of factory overheads than their due. Further, the management may like to discontinue products (which appear to be less profitable or loss-incurring) due to overcharge of factory overheads.

Thus, it is imperative to have an equitable allotment of factory overheads to cost units. This allotment of factory overheads to cost units/cost objects is referred to as *absorption*. The absorption rate is usually expressed in terms of rupee(s) per unit of estimated activity base (called denominator activity).

There are no definitive rules for determining which base to use as the denominator activity. However, a close nexus between the denominator activity base and factory overhead costs should be ensured. This will facilitate determination of equitable and fair absorption rate. Besides, the method used should be simple and economical; as far as possible, denominator activity base "must be a factor that is common to all jobs, has a high correlation with the incurrence of overhead costs, and is easy to measure."[6]

Some common bases for absorption of factory overhead are: **(i)** Units of production **(ii)** Direct materials cost, **(iii)** Direct labour cost **(iv)** Prime cost method **(v)** Direct labour-hours and **(vi)** Machine-hours.

Units of Production Method

Under this method, factory overheads are absorbed at a uniform rate for each unit produced. This method is suitable when a production department manufacturers only one type of product. The factory overhead absorption rate is computed using Equation 10.1.

Estimated factory overhead costs ÷ Estimated units of production **(10.1)**

Direct Material Cost Method

Direct material cost method the overhead recovery rate is given by dividing estimated overhead costs by the estimated direct material cost.

This method is an appropriate basis of charging fixed overheads to production when overhead costs are closely related to direct materials cost. In an assembly area, where many of the costs correspond to the quantity of materials used, it may be equitable to assign factory overhead costs on the basis of direct materials costs. The overhead recovery rate (in terms of percentage of direct materials cost) is computed, using Equation 10.2.

(Estimated factory overhead costs ÷ Estimated direct materials cost) × 100 **(10.2)**

However, in practice, this method should not be normally followed (except in situation when factory overhead costs are significantly correlated to direct material costs) for the following reasons:

(a) While cost of materials is often subject to considerable fluctuations, factory overhead costs are not normally accompanied by similar fluctuations.

(b) For firms using job costing, this method may give very distorted results. The mere fact that a job uses materials of a very expensive nature is no justification for the assumption that the factory overhead appropriate to that job will be proportionately heavier.[7]

(c) Overheads attributable to jobs tend to vary more in tune with time spent on them rather than on the value of materials used by them as most factory overheads, say, rent, rates insurance and salaries accrue on time basis. For this reason, time should be reckoned the key factor in charging factory overhead costs to production.

Direct Labour Costs Basis/Method

This method is suggested for the following reasons:

(a) There is built-in mechanism to consider time factor; it is reasonable to assume that the greater the direct labour costs attributed to a job, the longer is likely to be the time spent on that job.

(b) Labour rates are usually more stable than material prices.

(c) Variable factory overhead costs are likely to vary, to some extent, with the number of employees and, thus, with direct labour costs.

Direct labour cost basis computes the factory overhead rate as a percentage of direct labour cost.

However, this method may not provide correct results in situations when different types of labour personnel (obviously subject to different wage rates) are used in different jobs. For instance, assume in Job A, skilled labour is used (which is paid at ₹20 per hour); unskilled labour is used in Job B, paid @ ₹10 per hour. As per this method, factory overheads will be charged twice in Job A compared to Job B, assuming both jobs use the same hours. Thus, the wages incurred on different jobs may not be necessarily in the same ratio as the hours spent and, hence, distortion in absorption of overheads. The question of overtime further compounds the problem.

(d) This method will also be inappropriate if the major share of factory overhead costs consists of depreciation, repairs and maintenance, and other machine-related costs. In such a situation, there is likely to be a little relationship between factory overhead costs and direct labour costs.

The factory overhead rate in terms of percentage of direct labour cost is computed, using Equation 10.3.

(Estimated factory overhead costs ÷ Estimated direct labour costs) × 100 **(10.3)**

Prime Cost Method

Since both direct materials and direct labour give rise to factory overheads, both these costs (prime cost) should be the basis to arrive at factory overhead absorption rate. Equation 10.4 provides the computation basis (in terms of percentage of prime cost).

(Estimated factory overhead costs ÷ Estimated prime costs) × 100 **(10.4)**

This method is an ideal in the most unlikely situation (or rare situation) when the same material and the same type of labour (drawing uniform wages) is engaged in production/jobs carried out by the manufacturing firms. Conversely, this method has the drawback of giving very distorted results if different types of materials as well as different types of labour is used in production/jobs.

Direct Labour-hours

This method is an appropriate absorption base when there is a direct relationship between factory overhead costs and direct labour-hours. It is likely to be so for businesses where most of the work is accomplished by labour. The results under this method are not distorted even when there is a marked difference among hourly wage rates as this method takes into account *hours* used on the job and not *the labour cost.* As stated earlier, factory overheads are likely to vary more in tune with time and not with labour cost; therefore this method is more logical than direct labour cost method. The factory overhead absorption rate per direct labour-hour is computed using Equation 10.5.

Estimated factory overhead costs ÷ Estimated direct labour-hours **(10.5)**

This method, however, will be inappropriate if factory overhead costs are primarily based on machine-related activity.

Machine-hour Rate

Machine-hour rate is calculated by dividing the etimated factory overhead costs by the estimated machine- hours.

This method is the most ideal method of absorbing factory overheads of those production departments in which machinery represents the predominant factor of production, that is, where most of the work is done through machines. This generally occurs in those production departments which are largely automated; as a result, the major share of factory overhead costs consist of depreciation on plant and machinery installed/used in that department. Firms, providing computer services, normally charge their costs based on computer time used. The factory overhead absorption rate per machine-hour (MHR) is computed according to Equation 10.6.

Estimated factory overhead costs ÷ Estimated machine-hours **(10.6)**

Since most of the work is done through machines, machine-hour rate is normally adopted to absorb factory overheads.

In cases where production department has several machines (serving different needs), the factory overheads among different machines (each machine/block of machine constitutes a cost centre) should be apportioned on equitable basis. For instance, **(i)** rent and rates, lighting and heating costs can be apportioned on the basis of *effective* floor space occupied (that is, allowing for reasonable space to operate the machine; **(ii)** insurance may be apportioned on the basis of book value of machines; **(iii)** depreciation may be computed on the basis of effective cost of the machine and its effective useful life in hours; **(iv)** power costs should be charged on the basis of actual units consumed; **(v)** supervision costs are to be apportioned on the basis of the degree of supervision required by each machine. Similarly, other production department costs are to be apportioned on the most equitable basis. The estimated productive machine-hours should be based on effective hours for which the machine works. It should exclude time lost due to setting-up of the machine and its maintenance.

Further, total overheads related to machine should be segregated in two categories, normally: fixed costs (commonly called standing charges), and variable costs (referred to as machine expenses) for cost control purposes, as also for decision-making purposes. Included in machine expenses are depreciation, power, repairs and maintenance; standing charges include rent and rates, general lighting, insurance, and supervisor's salary.

Where the work performed by direct labour personnel is identifiable with a particular machine group, their direct wages should be included as part of the machine group cost. Thus production/job will be charged with a machine-hour rate which is inclusive of direct wages.[8] Such a rate is known as *comprehensive* machine-hour rate.

Examples 10.6 and 10.7 illustrate the computation of machine-hour rate and comprehensive machine-hour rate respectively.

Example 10.6

Compute the machine-hour rate from the following data:

Cost of machine	₹30,00,000
Estimated scrap value after the expiry of its useful life (5 years)	5,00,000
Rent and rates for the shop per month	10,000
General lighting for the shop per month	6,000
Insurance premium for the machine per annum	48,000
Repairs and maintenance expenses per annum	50,000
Power consumption — 10 units per hour @ ₹6 per unit	60
Estimated working hours per annum 2,200 (including setting-up time of 200 hours; no power is required during setting-up time)	
Shop supervisor's salary per month	30,000

The machine occupies one-fourth of the total area of the shop. The supervisor is expected to devote one-fifth of his time for supervising the machine.

Determine machine-hour rate.

Solution

Determination of Machine-hour Rate

Particulars		*Rate per hour*
Standing charges:		
Rent and rates (₹10,000 per month × 12)/4	₹30,000	
General lighting (₹6,000 per month × 12)/4	18,000	
Insurance premium per annum	48,000	
Shop supervisor's salary (₹30,000 per month × 12)/5	72,000	
Total standing charges	1,68,000	
Productive working machine-hours (2,200 – 200, setting-up time)	2,000	
Standing charges per hour (₹1,68,000/2,000)		₹84.00
*Machine expenses**:		
Repairs and maintenance expenses (₹50,000/2,000 hours)	25.0	
Depreciation [(₹30 lakh – ₹5 lakh)/5 years] ÷ 2,000 hours	250.0	
Power consumption per hour	60.0	335.00
Machine-hour rate per hour		419.00

*are in the nature of mixed and variable costs.

Example 10.7

A machine costs ₹9 lakh and is deemed to have a scrap value of 10 per cent at the end of its effective life (9 years). Ordinarily, the machine is expected to run for 2,400 hours per annum but it is estimated that 150 hours will be lost for normal repairs and maintenance and further 750 hours will be lost due to staggering. The other details in respect of machine shop are:

Wages, bonus and provident fund contribution of each of two operators (each operator is in charge of two machines) (per year)	₹1,80,000
Rent of the shop (per year)	1,20,000
General lighting of the shop (per month)	10,000
Insurance premium for one machine (per year)	32,000
Cost of repairs and maintenance per machine (per month)	10,000
Shop supervisor's salary (per month)	20,000
Power consumption of machine per hour 20 units @ ₹6 per unit	
Other factory overheads attributable to the shop (per annum)	1,60,000

There are four identical machines in the shop. The supervisor is expected to devote one-fifth of time for supervising the machine. Compute a comprehensive machine-hour rate from the above details.

Solution

Determination of Comprehensive Machine-hour Rate per Hour (per machine)

Particulars		*Amount per hour*
Standing charges per annum		
Rent and rates (₹1,20,000/4 machines)	₹30,000	
General lighting (₹10,000 × 12)/4 machines	30,000	
Insurance premium	32,000	
Supervisor's salary (₹20,000 × 12)/5	48,000	
Other factory overheads (₹1,60,000/4 machines)	40,000	
Total standing charges	1,80,000	
Standing charges per hour (₹1,80,000/1,500[1] machine-hours)		₹120
Machine charges per hour		
Wages, bonus and provident fund (₹1,80,000/2 machines) = ₹90,000/1,500 machine-hours	60	
Repairs and maintenance (₹10,000 × 12)/1,500	80	
Power (20 units × ₹6 per unit)	120	
Depreciation [(₹9 lakh – ₹0.90 lakh)/9 years] ÷ 1,500	60	320
Machine-hour rate		440

Note: Productive machine–hours (2,400 – 150 – 750) = 1,500

There is no absorption method which is the best to charge factory overheads in all situations. Selection of the method that best serves a firm's needs can be made only after the factory overheads have been carefully analysed and their incurrence has been observed to exhibit direct/close association with the method (say machine-hours, labour-hours, direct wage cost, direct material cost) chosen for absorption of factory overheads.

Underabsorption and Overabsorption of Factory Overheads

LO 10.5 Illustrate the treatment of under/over-absorption of factory overheads

Once the factory overhead absorption/application rate has been determined, it is used as the basis to charge factory overhead costs to actual production. The rate is applied to production on an ongoing basis as goods are manufactured according to the method used (say, direct labour-hours, machine-hours, units produced). For instance, assume that factory overhead absorption rate is ₹50 per machine-hour, using machine-hour as a base and that, 10,000 machine-hours were used, ₹5,00,000 (10,000 machine-hours × ₹50) of factory overheads will be charged to production. If the actual factory overheads are ₹6,00,000, it implies they are underabsorbed/underapplied by ₹1,00,000 (₹6,00,000 – ₹5,00,000). Alternatively, if the actual factory overheads are ₹4,50,000, it is the case of overabsorption/overapplied factory overheads by ₹50,000 (₹5,00,000 – ₹4,50,000).

Overhead variance is the difference between the actual factory overhead costs and the absorbed factory overheads.

The under-absorption and overabsorption of factory overheads are computed as per Equations 10.7 and 10.8.

Under-absorption of factory overheads = Actual factory overheads – Overheads charged to production **(10.7)**

Overabsorption of factory overheads = Overheads charged to production – Production overheads **(10.8)**

The difference between the actual factory overhead costs and absorbed factory overheads is referred to as overhead variance.[9] Overhead variances may be disposed of by following either of the two methods:

First, they may be treated as a period costs and, therefore, assigned to the income statement of current period. The adjustment is made through cost of goods sold account. Journal entries will be as follows:

Cost of Goods Sold A/c . . . . Dr
    To Factory Overhead Control A/c
(For charging under-absorbed factory overheads)

Factory Overhead Control A/c . . . . Dr
    To Cost of Goods Sold A/c
(For adjusting over-absorbed factory overheads)

This method is normally used when variance is insignificant in amount.

In the second method, it may be considered as the cost of production of the current period and the amount is pro-rated to work-in-process inventory, finished goods inventory, and cost of goods sold in proportion to the unadjusted factory overhead balance in each account. This method is normally used when the variance is significant in amount. The objective is to allocate the under-or overabsorbed factory overhead costs to those accounts which were distorted by using incorrect absorption rate and to bring their ending balances close to what they would have been if the correct application rate had been used. Journal entries would be as follows:

Work-in-process Inventory A/c . . . . Dr
Finished Goods Inventory A/c . . . . Dr
Cost of Goods Sold A/c . . . . Dr
    To Factory Overhead Control A/c
(For charging under-applied factory overheads)

Factory Overhead Control A/c . . . . Dr
    To Work-in-process Inventory A/c
    To Cost of Goods Sold A/c
(For adjusting over-applied factory overheads)

Apart from the magnitude of variance, the treatment would also depend on the nature of such variances. If the variance has been an outcome of abnormal factors/unusual events (say, defective planning), it should be considered as period costs and taken to current year's cost of goods sold account. On the contrary, if such a variance has been caused by errors in estimation (either of budgeted factory overhead or activity base), it should be pro-rated to work-in-process inventory, finished goods inventory and cost of goods sold.

◆ Example 10.8

In a manufacturing unit, factory overhead was recovered at a predetermined rate of ₹25 per manday. The total factory overhead expenses incurred and the mandays actually worked were ₹41.50 lakh and 1.5 lakh, respectively. Out of the 40,000 units produced during a period, 30,000 were sold.

On analysing the reasons, it was found that 60 per cent of the unabsorbed overheads were due to defective planning and the rest were attributable to increase in overhead costs.

How would unabsorbed overheads be treated in cost accounts?

Solution

Determination of Unabsorbed Factory Overheads

Factory overhead expenses incurred	₹41,50,000
Less factory overheads absorbed (1,50,000 mandays × ₹25 per manday)	37,50,000
Unabsorbed factory overheads	4,00,000

Treatment of Unabsorbed Factory Overheads:

(1) 60 per cent of unabsorbed overheads are attributed to defective planning. Being abnormal in nature, ₹2,40,000 (0.60 × ₹4 lakh) is charged to costing profit and loss account		₹2,40,000
(2) ₹1,60,000 is to be pro-rated between cost of goods sold (30,000 units) and finished goods inventory (10,000 units):		
— Cost of goods sold (₹1,60,000 × 3/4)	₹1,20,000	
— Finished goods inventory (₹1,60,000 × 1/4)	40,000	1,60,000
		4,00,000

◆ Example 10.9

The XYZ Ltd has the following information relating to applied and actual factory overheads for the current month:

Factory overheads, incurred	₹1,52,500
Applied factory overheads	1,98,500

Applied factory overhead costs are in the following accounts:

Cost of goods sold	1,60,000
Ending work-in-process inventory	17,500
Ending finished goods inventory	21,000

You are required to allocate the under or overapplied factory overheads to relevant accounts and pass necessary journal entries at the month-end.

Solution

Overapplied/Overabsorbed Factory Overheads:

Applied factory overheads	₹1,98,500
Less factory overheads incurred	1,52,500
	46,000
Over-absorbed factory overheads will be pro-rated in the following accounts:	
Cost of goods sold (₹1,60,000/₹1,98,500) × ₹46,000	37,078
Ending work-in-process inventory (₹17,500/₹1,98,500) × ₹46,000	4,055
Ending finished goods inventory (₹21,000/₹1,98,500) × ₹46,000	4,867
	46,000

Journal Entries:

Factory Overhead Applied A/c. . . . . . .Dr	₹1,98,500	
To Over-applied Factory Overhead A/c		₹46,000
To Factory Overhead Control A/c		1,52,500
Overapplied Factory Overhead A/c. . . . . . .Dr	46,000	
To Cost of Goods Sold A/c		37,078
To Ending Work-in-process Inventory A/c		4,055
To Ending Finished Goods Inventory A/c		4,867

SUMMARY

- Factory overheads represent all indirect manufacturing costs. Unlike direct costs, these costs cannot be conveniently and wholly charged to product cost centres. All of the factory overhead costs find their way into production costs through a somewhat difficult method of allocations and apportionments and reallocations and reapportionments. Allotment of common costs/factory overheads to cost centres/cost objects/cost units is often made on a somewhat arbitrary basis. Cost allocation procedures are costly as they use the time of cost accountants and decision-makers. Therefore, cost allocation should be justified on the basis of cost-benefit considerations. Yet, cost allocation is necessary to determine the true cost of products, particularly in the case of multi-product firms.
- Costing and control of factory overheads involves **(i)** Determination of factory overheads application role, **(ii)** Allocation of overheads, **(iii)** Absorption of overheads and **(iv)** Under/over absorption of overheads.

LO 10.1

- Factory overheads costs are normally allocated at a predetermined factory overhead application rate. It is determined dividing budgeted factory overhead costs (consisting of fixed costs, variable costs and mixed costs) for the coming period/year by capacity level. Among four capacity measures, normal capacity and expected capacity levels (theoretical capacity, practical capacity), normal capacity (based on long-run productive capacity) is considered as the best denominator measure.

LO 10.2

- Cost common to more than one department are to be allocated among the production departments receiving benefits, and service department costs are to be distributed among producing departments. Cost incurred in service departments are apportioned by **(i)** Direct method, **(ii)** Step method, **(iii)** Repeated distribution method, and **(iv)** Algebraic method, among production departments as part of factory overhead costs.
- According to direct method, total budgeted costs of service departments are apportioned between/among production departments, ignoring any services provided by service departments to each other.
- In situations when one service department renders services to another (that is reciprocity exits), the step method is more appropriate than the direct method. This method takes into consideration the ***total/true*** cost of each service department (and not partial) in assigning them to production departments.

  The following is a list of steps used for the purpose of apportioning budgeted costs of service departments.

  (i) It is usual to apportion first the cost of that service department which renders services to the largest number of other service departments.

  (ii) The budgeted costs of the service department that renders services to the next largest number of service departments are then apportioned. Obviously, any apportioned costs added to this service department from step 1 are included. The sum of budgeted service cost, so arrived at, is then apportioned to note that the service department (whose costs are yet to be assigned). It is important to note that the service department whose budgeted costs were apportioned as per the step 1 will not receive any cost share from the second department.

  (iii) This sequence is continued, step-by-step, until all the budgeted service department costs have been apportioned departments.
- The process of apportioning service departments overhead according to repeated distribution method is continued until the figures of unapportioned sum(s) of service department(s) become negligible: The following steps are involved in its application:

- **(i)** The first service department's (to be identified on the basis of the order in which their names are stated) budgeted costs are to be apportioned. As a result, the balance of the first service department becomes nil; its costs are apportioned among other departments (on the basis of their percentage share or some other stated base).
- **(ii)** The budgeted costs of the second service department (consisting of original amount plus the apportioned sum from the first service department) is to be apportioned among other departments including the first service department.
- **(iii)** This process continues for all the remaining/other service departments. The steps shown as per (i) to (iii) refer to the first phase.
- **(iv)** The second phase of cycle starts once again with the first service department; it will consist only of apportioned amounts from other service departments. As a result, the total costs of service departments becomes less and less with each phase of apportionment.
- **(v)** The process comes to an end when it is found that the residual sum (to be apportioned) has been either exhausted or has become virtually insignificant.

- The algebraic method is the most appropriate of all the four methods when reciprocal services exist between service departments. This method is also called the reciprocal services method as it takes into account cost flows in both directions between service departments that render services to each other. This is typical for the service departments to provide services to each other in most of the manufacturing firms in practice. This method provides conceptually the most correct budget cost estimates of service departments and their subsequent apportionment.

LO 10.3

- Factory overheads of production departments (inclusive of appropriate apportioned share from other services departments) are to be applied to production/jobs. Some common bases of absorption of factory overheads are: **(i)** Units of production, **(ii)** Direct materials cost, **(iii)** Direct labour cost, **(iv)** Prime cost method, **(v)** Direct labour-hours, and **(vi)** Machine-hours.
- According to units of production method, the factory overhead absorption rate = Estimated/budgeted factory overhead costs ÷ Estimated/budgeted units of production
- According to the direct material cost method, the overhead recovery rate in terms of percentage of direct material cost = (Estimated/budgeted factory overhead cost/Estimated direct material cost) × 100
- The factory overhead rate according to direct labour cost method = (Estimated factory overhead cost/Estimated direct labour cost) × 100
- According to prime cost method the factory overhead rate = (Estimated factory overhead cost/Estimated prime cost) × 100
- The factory overhead absorption rate per direct labour hour = Estimated factory overhead costs ÷ Estimated direct labour-hours
- According to the machine-hour rate, the factory overhead absorption rate per machine-hour (MHR) = Estimated factory overhead costs ÷ Estimated machine-hours
- Since most of the work is done through machines, machine-hour rate is normally adopted to absorb factory overheads.
- In cases where production department has several machine (serving different needs), the factory overheads among different machines (each machine/block of machine constitutes a cost centre) should be apportioned on equitable basis. For instance, **(i)** rent and rates, lighting and heating costs can be apportioned on the basis of ***effective*** floor space occupied (that is, allowing for reasonable space to operate the machine); **(ii)** insurance may be apportioned on the basis of book value of machines; **(iii)** depreciation may be computed on the basis of effective cost of the machine and its effective useful life in hours; **(iv)** power costs should be charged on the basis of actual units consumed; **(v)** supervision costs are to be apportioned on the basis of the degree of supervision required by each machine. Similarly, other production departments costs are to be apportioned on the most equitable basis. The estimated

productive machine-hours should be based on effective hours for which the machine works. It should exclude time lost due to setting-up of the machine and its maintenance.

- Further, total overheads related to machine should be normally segregated in two categories: fixed costs (commonly called standing charges), and variable costs (referred to as machine expenses) for cost control purposes, as also for decision-making purposes. Included in machine expenses are depreciation, power, repairs and maintenance; standing charges include rent and rates, general lighting, insurance, and supervisor's salary.
- Where the work performed by direct labour personnel is identifiable with a particular machine group, their direct wages should be included as part of the machine group cost. Thus production/job will be charged with a machine-hour rate which is inclusive of direct wages. Such a rate is known as ***comprehensive*** machine-hour rate.
- Direct labour-hour rate (where factory overhead costs consist primarily of labour activity) and machine-hour rate (where indirect manufacturing costs predominantly comprise of machine-related activity) are the two suitable methods. Further, for cost control and decision-making purposes, factory overhead absorption rate should be computed separately both for fixed costs and variable costs.

LO 10.4

- When predetermined factory overhead applied rate is used as the basis of absorption of indirect manufacturing costs, it is seldom that the total factory overhead costs applied to production (or jobs) in a given period are equal to the total factory overhead costs incurred in that period. When the absorbed factory overheads exceed the actual, it is a situation of overabsorption; under-absorption results when the actual factory overhead costs exceed the factory overheads charged to production. At the end of accounting period, if the over/under-applied overhead balance is insignificant, it is normally closed by transferring to cost of goods sold; if it is being sizeable, it is pro-rated to work-in-process inventory, finished goods inventory and cost of goods sold.

LO 10.5

REFERENCES

1. Polimeni, R.S., *et. al.*, *Cost Accounting: Concepts and Application for Managerial Decision Making* (New York, McGraw-Hill), 1991, p. 143.
2. *Ibid.*, 143-44.
3. For methods of segregating mixed costs, please refer to Chapter 7.
4. Deakin, E.B. and M.W. Maher, *Cost Accounting*, (Illinois, Irwin), 1984, p. 89.
5. Polimeni, R.S., *et. al.*, *op. cit.*, p. 160.
6. Morse, W.J., *Cost Accounting*, (Massachusetts, Addison-Wesley Publishing Co.), 1978, p. 66
7. Wald, J., *Bigg's Cost Accounts*, (London, Macdonald & Grans Limited), 1978, p. 118
8. *Ibid.*, p. 124
9. For details of overhead variances, please refer to Chapter 16 of this book.

SOLVED PROBLEMS

P.10.1 Atlas Engineering Limited accepts a variety of jobs which require both manual and machine operations. The budgeted profit and loss account for the current period is as follows: (₹in lakh) LO 10.4 LOD: E

Sales		75
Cost:		
Direct materials	10	
Direct labour	5	
Prime cost	15	
Production overheads	30	
Production cost	45	
Administrative, selling and distribution overheads	15	60
Profit		15

Other budgeted data:

Labour-hours for the period	25,000
Machine-hours for the period	15,000
Number of jobs for the period	300

An enquiry has been received recently from a customer and the production department has prepared the following estimate of the prime cost required for the job.

Direct material	₹2,500
Direct labour	2,000
Prime cost	4,500
Labour-hours required	80
Machine-hours required	50

You are required to:

(a) Calculate by different methods, six overhead absorption rates for absorption of production overhead and comment on the suitability of each.

(b) Calculate the production overhead cost of the order based on each of the above rates.

(c) Give your recommendation to the company.

Solution

(a) *Statement showing Determination of Production Overhead Rate under various Methods of Absorption.*

Method of absorption	*Production overhead absorption rate*
1. Percentage of direct material cost (₹30 lakh/₹10 lakh) × 100	300 per cent (3 times) of direct material cost
2. Percentage of direct labour cost (₹30 lakh/₹5 lakh) × 100	600 per cent (6 times) of direct labour cost
3. Percentage of prime cost (₹30 lakh/₹15 lakh) × 100	200 per cent (twice) of prime cost
4. Machine-hour rate (₹30 lakh/15,000 hours)	₹200 per machine-hour
5. Direct labour-hour rate (₹30 lakh/25,000 hours)	₹120 per labour-hour
6. Production unit method (₹30 lakh/300 Jobs)	₹10,000 per job

(b) *Statement showing Determination of Production Overhead Cost of a Job under various Methods of Absorption.*

Method	*Production overhead cost*
1. Percentage of direct material cost	₹2500 × 3 = ₹7,500
2. Percentage of direct labour cost	₹2,000 × 6 = ₹12,000
3. Percentage of prime cost	₹4,500 × 2 = ₹9,000
4. Machine-hour rate	50 hours × ₹200 = ₹10,000
5. Direct labour-hour rate	80 hours × ₹120 = ₹9,600
6. Production unit method	1 × ₹10,000 = ₹10,000

(c) RECOMMENDATION The company is advised to apply machine-hour rate to compute production overhead cost as mechanisation is high.

P.10.2 A company's production costs for the current ending March 31 are given below: LO 10.3 LOD: M

Item	*Production departments*			*Service departments*			*Total*
	P_1	P_2	P_3	Office	Stores	Workshop	
Direct wages	₹2,00,000	₹2,50,000	₹3,00,000	—	—	—	₹7,50,000
Direct materials	3,00,000	3,50,000	4,50,000	—	—	—	11,00,000
Indirect materials	20,000	30,000	30,000	₹10,000	₹20,000	₹20,000	1,30,000
Indirect wages	30,000	30,000	40,000	1,00,000	1,00,000	50,000	3,50,000
Area (sq. metres)	200	250	300	150	100	250	1,250
Book value of machinery	3,00,000	3,50,000	2,50,000	—	—	1,50,000	10,50,000
Total horse power (H.P.) of machines	15	20	25	—	—	5	65
Machine-hours worked	10,000	20,000	15,000	—	—	5,000	50,000

The other expenses are as follows:

Rent	₹1,25,000
Insurance	10,500
Depreciation (per cent of value of machinery)	15
Power	38,000
Light	12,500

You are required to prepare an overhead analysis sheet for the departments showing clearly the basis of apportionment where necessary.

Solution

Overhead Analysis Sheet

Item	*Basis*	*Production departments*			*Service departments*			*Total*
		P_1	P_2	P_3	Office	Stores	Workshop	
Indirect materials	Allocation	₹20,000	₹30,000	₹30,000	₹10,000	₹20,000	₹20,000	₹1,30,000
Indirect wages	Allocation	30,000	30,000	40,000	1,00,000	1,00,000	50,000	3,50,000
Rent	Area	20,000	25,000	30,000	15,000	10,000	25,000	1,25,000
Insurance	Value of machine	3,000	3,500	2,500	—	—	1,500	10,500
Depreciation	Value of machine	45,000	52,500	37,500	—	—	22,500	1,57,500
Power	Horse power	8,770	11,690	14,620	—	—	2,920	38,000
Light	Area	2,000	2,500	3,000	1,500	1,000	2,500	12,500
Total		1,28,770	1,55,190	1,57,620	1,26,500	1,31,000	1,24,420	8,23,500
office overheads	Direct wages	33,730	42,170	50,600	(1,26,500)	—	—	—
Stores overheads	Direct materials	35,730	41,680	53,590	—	(1,31,000)	—	—
Workshop overheads	Machine-hours	27,650	55,300	41,470	—		(1,24,420)	—
Total overheads		2,25,880	2,94,340	3,03,280	—	—	—	8,23,500

P.10.3 Deccan Manufacturing Limited has three departments which are regarded as production departments. Service department's costs are distributed to these production departments using the "Step Ladder Method" of distribution. Estimates of factory overhead costs to be incurred by each department in the forthcoming quarter are as follows. Data required for distribution is also shown against each department. LO 10.2 LOD: M

Department	*Factory overheads*	*Direct labour-hours*	*Number of employees*	*Area in square metres*
Production				
X	₹1,93,000	4,000	100	3,000
Y	64,000	3,000	125	1,500
Z	83,000	4,000	85	1,500
Service				
P	45,000	1,000	10	500
Q	75,000	5,000	50	1,500
R	1,05,000	6,000	40	1,000
S	30,000	3,000	50	1,000

The overhead costs of the 4 service departments are distributed in the same order, namely, P,Q,R and S respectively on the following basis:

Departments	*Basis*
P	Number of employees
Q	Direct labour-hours
R	Area in square metres
S	Direct labour-hours

You are required to: **(a)** Prepare a schedule showing the distribution of overhead costs of the four service departments to the three production departments; and **(b)** Calculate the overhead recovery rate per direct labour-hour for each of the three production departments.

Solution

(a) *Statement showing Distribution of Factory Overhead Costs of Service Department among Production Departments as per Step Ladder Method*

Particulars	*Service departments*				*Production departments*		
	P	Q	R	S	X	Y	Z
Factory overhead costs	₹45,000	₹75,000	₹1,05,000	₹30,000	₹1,93,000	₹64,000	₹83,000
Distribution of factory overhead of Department P (in the ratio of number of employees)	(45,000)	5,000	4,000	5,000	10,000	12,500	8,500
Distribution of factory overhead of Department Q, ₹80,000 (in the ratio of direct labour-hours)	—	(80,000)	24,000	12,000	16,000	12,000	16,000
Distribution of factory overheads of Department R, ₹1,33,000 (in the ratio of area used)	—	—	(1,33,000)	19,000	57,000	28,500	28,500
Distribution of factory overheads of Department S,	—	—	—	(66,000)	24,000	18,000	24,000

(*Contd.*)

(Contd.)

₹66,000 (in the ratio of direct labour-hours)			
Total cost	3,00,000	1,35,000	1,60,000
(b) Divided by direct labour-hours	4,000	3,000	4,000
Overhead recovery rate per hour (Total cost/DLH)	75	45	40

P.10.4 Modern Machines Limited has three production departments (A, B and C) and two service departments (D and E). From the following figures extracted from the records of the company, calculate the overhead rate per labour-hour of production departments. Total direct labour hours of departments A, B and C are 5,000, 5,000 and 2,000 respectively. LO 10.3 LOD: M

Indirect materials	₹1,50,000
Indirect wages	1,00,000
Depreciation on machinery	2,50,000
Depreciation on buildings	50,000
Rent, rates and taxes	1,00,000
Electric power for machinery	1,50,000
Electric power for lighting	5,000
General expenses	1,50,000

Items	*Total*	*A*	*B*	*C*	*D*	*E*
Drect materials (₹)	6,00,000	2,00,000	1,00,000	1,90,000	60,000	50,000
Direct wages (₹)	4,00,000	1,50,000	1,50,000	40,000	20,000	40,000
Value of machinery (₹)	25,00,000	6,00,000	10,00,000	4,00,000	2,50,000	2,50,000
Floor area (sq. feet)	50,000	15,000	10,000	10,000	5,000	10,000
Horse power of machines	150	50	60	30	5	5
Number of light points	50	15	10	10	5	10
General expenses	1,50,000	50,000	50,000	20,000	10,000	20,000

The expenses of service departments D and E are to be apportioned as follows:

	A	B	C	D	E
Department D (%)	40	20	30	—	10
Department E (%)	30	30	40	—	—

Solution

Determination of Departmental Overhead Rates of Production

Item	*Basis of charge*	*Total*	*Production departments*			*Service departments*	
			A	*B*	*C*	*D*	*E*
Direct materials	Allocation	₹1,10,000	—	—	—	₹60,000	₹50,000
Direct wages	Allocation	60,000	—	—	—	20,000	40,000
Indirect materials	Direct materials usage ratio	1,50,000	₹50,000	₹25,000	47,500	15,000	12,500
Indirect wages	Direct wages usage ratio[1]	1,00,000	37,500	37,500	10,000	5,000	10,000
Depreciation (machinery)	Value of machinery	2,50,000	60,000	1,00,000	40,000	25,000	25,000

(Contd.)

(Contd.)

Depreciation (building)	Floor area	50,000	15,000	10,000	10,000	5,000	10,000
Rent, rates and taxes	Floor area	1,00,000	30,000	20,000	20,000	10,000	20,000
Electric power (machinery)	Horse power	1,50,000	50,000	60,000	30,000	5,000	5,000
Electric power (lighting)	Light points	5,000	1,500	1,000	1,000	500	1,000
General expenses	Labour-hours	1,50,000	50,000	50,000	20,000	10,000	20,000
Total		11,25,000	2,94,000	3,03,500	1,78,500	1,55,500	1,93,500
Cost of service Department D apportioned			62,200	31,100	46,650	(1,55,500)	15,550
Cost of service Department E apportioned		—	62,720	62,710	83,620	—	(2,09,050)
Total overheads		11,25,000	4,18,920	3,97,310	3,08,770	—	—
Labour-hours		—	5,000	5,000	2,000	—	—
Overhead rate per direct labour-hour			83.78	79.46	154.39	—	

1. May also be based on the basis of direct labour-hours.

P.10.5 A factory is having three production departments: A, B and C, and two service departments, namely, Boiler House (BH) and Pump Room (PR). The Boiler House is to depend upon the Pump Room for supply of water and Pump Room, in turn, is dependent on the Boiler House for supply of power for driving the pump. The expenses incurred by the production departments during a period are: A, ₹8,00,000; B, ₹7,00,000; and C, ₹5,00,000. The expenses for Boiler House are ₹2,34,000 and the Pump Room are ₹3,00,000. **LO 10.3** **LOD: D**

The expenses of the Boiler House and Pump Room are apportioned to the production departments on the following basis:

	A	B	C	B.H.	P.R.
Expenses of Boiler House (%)	20	40	30	—	10
Expenses of Pump Room (%)	40	20	20	20	—

Show clearly as to how the expenses of Boiler House and Pump Room would be apportioned to A, B and C departments. Use algebraic equation method.

Solution

Let X be total overhead costs of Boiler House, and

Y be total overhead costs of Pump Room

X = ₹2,34,000 + 0.2Y

Y = ₹3,00,000 + 0.1X

Or, X = ₹2,34,000 + 0.2 × (₹3,00,000 + 0.1X) = ₹2,34,000 + ₹60,000 + 0.02X = ₹2,94,000/0.98

= ₹3,00,000

Y = ₹3,00,000 + 0.1 × (₹3,00,000) = ₹3,30,000

Allocation of Overheads among Production Departments

Particulars	Production departments			Total
	A	B	C	
Direct overheads	₹8,00,000	₹7,00,000	₹5,00,000	₹20,00,000
Boiler House (2:4:3)	60,000	1,20,000	90,000	2,70,000 [1]
Pump Room (4:2:2)	1,32,000	66,000	66,000	2,64,000 [2]
Total	9,92,000	8,86,000	6,56,000	25,34,000

WORKING NOTES

1. Total expenses of Boiler House	₹3,00,000
Less share of Pump Room (0.10 × ₹3,00,000)	30,000
Amount to be apportioned among production departments	2,70,000
2. Total expenses of Pump Room	3,30,000
Less share of Boiler House (0.20 × ₹3,30,000)	66,000
Amount to be apportioned among production departments	2,64,000

P.10.6 A factory has three production departments (P_1, P_2 and P_3) and two service departments (S_1 and S_2). Budgeted overheads for the next year have been allocated/apportioned by the cost department among the five departments. The secondary distribution of service department overheads is pending and the following details are given to you: LO 10.3 LOD: D

Department	*Overheads apportioned/allocated*	*Estimated level of activity*
P_1	₹48,000	500 labour-hours
P_2	1,12,000	1,200 machine-hours
P_3	52,000	600 labour-hours
Apportionment of service department costs		
S_1	16,000	P_1 (20 per cent), P_2, (40 per cent), P_3 (20 per cent), S_2 (20 per cent)
S_2	24,000	P_1 (10 per cent), P_2 (60 per cent), P_3 (20 per cent), S_1 (10 per cent)

Calculate the overhead rate of each production department after completing the distribution of service department costs.

Solution

Let, X be total overhead costs of S_1

Y be total overhead costs of S_2

We get simultaneous equations,

X = ₹16,000 + 0.1Y

Y = ₹24,000 + 0.2X

Or, X = ₹16,000 + 0.10 × (₹24,000 + 0.2X) or 0.98X = ₹18,400

X = ₹18,775

Y = ₹24,000 + 0.20 (₹18,775) = ₹27,755

Allocation of Overheads among Production Departments

Particulars	*Production departments*		
	P_1	P_2	P_3
Direct overheads	₹48,000	₹1,12,000	52,000
Allocation of overheads			
Department S_1 (₹18,775)	3,755 (0.20)	7,510 (0.40)	3,755 (0.20)
Department S_2 (₹27,755)	2,776 (0.10)	16,653 (0.60)	5,551 (0.20)
Total cost	54,531	1,36,163	61,306
Estimated capacity	500 (labour-hours)	1,200 (machine-hours)	600 (labour-hours)
Overhead cost per hour	₹109.10	₹113.50	₹102.20

P. 10.7 E-books is an online book retailer. The company has four departments. The two sales departments are corporate sales and consumer sales. The two support-departments are Administrative (Human resources, Accounting), and Information systems. Each of the sales departments conducts merchandising and marketing operations independently. LO 10.3 LOD: D

The following data are available for October, 2013:

Departments	*Revenues*	*Number of employees*	*Processing time used (in minutes)*
Corporate sales	₹16,67,750	42	2,400
Consumer sales	8,33,875	28	2,000
Administrative	—	14	400
Information systems	—	21	1,400

Cost incurred in each of four departments for October, 2013 are as follows:

Corporate sales	₹12,97,751
Consumer sales	6,36,818
Administrative	94,510
(Information systems)	3,04,720

The company uses number of employees as a basis to allocate administrative costs and processing time as a basis to allocate information systems costs.

REQUIRED:

(i) Allocate the support department costs to the sales departments using the direct method. **(ii)** Rank the support departments based on percentage of their services rendered to other support departments. Use this ranking to allocate support costs based on the step-down allocation method. **(iii)** How could you have ranked the support departments differently? **(iv)** Allocate the support department costs to two sales departments using the reciprocal allocation method.

Solution

(i) *Statement showing the Allocation of Support Department Costs to the Sales Departments (using Direct Method)*

Particulars	*Basis of allocation*	*Sales department*		*Support department*	
		Corporate sales	*Consumer sales*	*Administrative*	*Information systems*
Cost incurred	No. of employees	₹12,97,751	₹6,36,818	₹94,510	₹3,04,720
Administrative cost	(6:4)	56,706	37,804	(94,510)	—
Information systems cost	Processing time (6:5)	1,66,211	1,38,509	—	(3,04,720)
		15,20,668	**8,13,131**	—	—

(ii) *Ranking of Support Departments based on Percentage of their Services Rendered to other Support Departments*

(a) Administrative support department provides 23.077 per cent [21/(42 + 28 + 21) × 100] of its services to information systems support department. Thus, 23.077 per cent of ₹94,510 = ₹21,810.

(b) Information system support department provides [400/(2,400 + 2,000 + 400) × 100] 8.33 per cent of its services to administration support department. Thus 8.33 per cent of ₹3,04,720 = ₹25,383.

Statement showing Allocation of Support Costs (using Step-down Allocation Method)

Particulars	Basis of allocation	Support department		Sales department	
		Administrative	Information systems	Corporate sales	Consumer sales
Cost		₹94,510	₹3,04,720	₹12,97,751	₹6,36,818
Reallocation of administrative department cost	No. of employees (6:4:3)	(94,510)	21,810	43,620	29,080
			3,26,530		
Reallocation of information system department cost	Processing time (6:5)	—	(3,26,530)	1,78,107	1,48,423
				15,19,478	8,14,321

(iii) *An alternative ranking is based on the rupee amount (figures obtained under requirement (ii) of services rendered to other service departments. This approach would use the following sequence of ranking:*

— Allocation of information systems overheads as first (₹25,383 provided to administrative department)

— Allocated administrative overheads as second (₹21,810 provided to information systems).

(iv) *Statement showing Allocation of Support Department Costs to the Sales Departments (using Reciprocal Allocation Method)*

Particulars	Sales department	
	Corporate sales	Consumer sales
Costs	₹12,97,751	₹6,36,818
Reallocation of cost of administrative department (46.16% and 30.77% of ₹1,22,243)	56,427	37,614
Reallocation of cost of information systems department (50% and 41.67% of ₹3,32,922)	1,66,461	1,38,729
	15,20,639	8,13,161

WORKING NOTES

(i) *Percentage of Services Provided by Service Department between themselves and Sales Departments.*

Particulars	Service departments		Sales departments	
	Administrative	Information system	Corporate sales	Consumer sales
Administrative	—	23.07%	46.16%	30.77%
Information systems	8.33%	—	50%	41.67%

(ii) *Determination of Total Cost of Support Department: (using Simultaneous Equation Method)*

Let X and Y be the total costs of support departments Administrative overheads and Information systems respectively.

X = ₹94,510 + $0.0833Y$

Y = ₹3,04,720 + $0.2307X$

Or X = ₹94,510 + 0.0833 (₹3,04,720 + $0.2307X$)

Or X = ₹94,510 + ₹25,383 + $0.01922X$

Or $X - 0.01922X$ = ₹1,19,893

Or $0.98078X$ = ₹1,19,893

X = ₹1,19,893/0.98078 = ₹1,22,243

Y = ₹3,04,720 + 0.2307 (₹1,22,243)

Y = ₹3,04,720 + 28,202 = ₹3,32,922

P.10.8 A machine was purchased on January 1, in the current year. The following information relate to the machine: LO 10.4 LOD: E

Cost of machine	₹4,20,000
Estimated life	10 years of 2,000 hours per year
Estimated scrap value	₹20,000
Estimated repairs for whole life	₹1,05,000
Power consumed per hour	5 units @ ₹5 per unit
Insurance (on original cost)	0.75% per month
Consumable stores	₹300 per month

The machine is installed in a department whose monthly rent is ₹5,000 and this machine occupies 1/5 of the area. Total monthly lighting expenses is ₹4,000 for 10 light points, of which 3 relate to the machine. A supervisor with monthly salary of ₹16,000, devotes 1/4 of his time to this machine. Calculate machine hour rate.

Solution

Determination of Machine-hour Rate

	Per year	Per hour
Standing charges:		
Insurance (0.75% per month × 12 × ₹4,20,000)	₹37,800	
Rent (₹5,000 per month × 12 months × 1/5)	12,000	
Lighting charges (₹400 per point per month × 12 months × 3 points)	14,400	
Supervisor's salary (₹16,000 per month × 12 months × 1/4)	48,000	
Total standing charges	1,12,200	
Standing charges per hour (₹1,12,200/2,000 hours)		₹56.10
Machine expenses:		
Depreciation per hour (₹4,20,000 – ₹20,000)/10 years = ₹40,000/2,000		20.00
Consumable stores (₹300 per month × 12 months)/2,000		1.80
Power consumed (5 units × ₹5)		25.00
Repairs (₹1,05,000/10 years) = ₹10,500/2,000		5.25
Machine-hour rate per hour		108.15

P.10.9 A machine was purchased on April 1 in the current year for ₹5 lakh. The total cost of all machinery inclusive of the new machine was ₹75 lakh. The following particulars are further available: LO 10.4 LOD: M

Expected life of machine, 10 years
Scrap value at the end of 10 years, ₹5,000
Repairs and maintenance for the machine during the year, ₹20,000
Expected number of working hours of machine per year, 4,000
Insurance premium annually for all the machines, ₹45,000
Electricity consumption for the machine per hour (@ ₹5 per unit), 10 units
Area occupied by the machine, 100 sq. feet
Area occupied by other machines, 1,500 sq. feet
Rent per month of the department, ₹8,000
Lighting charges for 20 points for the whole department, out of which 3 points are for the machine, ₹1,200 per month.

Compute the machine-hour rate for the new machine on the basis of the data given above.

Solution

Computation of Machine-hour Rate of New Machine

	Per annum	Per hour
Standing charges:		
Insurance premium (₹45,000 × ₹5 lakh)/₹75 lakh	₹ 3,000	
Rent (₹96,000 per year × 100 sq. feet)/1,600 sq. feet	6,000	
Lighting charges (₹14,400 per year × 3 points)/20 points	2,160	
Total standing charges	11,160	
Standing charges per hour (₹11,160 ÷ 4,000 hours)		₹2.790
Machines expenses:		
Depreciation per hour (₹5 lakh – ₹5,000)/40,000 hours		12.375
Power charges (10 units × ₹5)		50.000
Repairs and maintenance (₹20,000/4,000 hours)		5.000
Machine-hour rate		70.165

P.10.10 X Ltd, having fifteen different types of automatic machines furnishes information as under for current year. **LO 10.4** **LOD: M**

(i) Overhead expenses: Factory rent, ₹9,60,000 (floor area 80,000 sq. ft.); Heat and gas, ₹4,50,000, and Supervision, ₹12,00,000.

(ii) Wages of the operator are ₹480 per day of 8 hours. He attends to one machine when it is under set-up and two machines while they are under operation.

(iii) Cost of machine ₹4,50,000; Life of machine, 10 years, and scrap value at the end of its life, ₹50,000.

(iv) Annual expenses on special equipment attached to the machine are estimated at ₹30,000.

(v) Estimated operation time of the machine is 3,600 hours while set-up time is 400 hours per annum.

(vi) The machine occupies 5,000 sq. ft. floor area.

(vii) Power costs ₹25 per hour while machine is in operation.

Find out the comprehensive machine-hour rate of machine B. Also find out machine costs to be absorbed in respect of use of machine B on the following two work orders:

	Work order 31	Work order 32
Machine set-up time (hours)	10	20
Machine operation time (hours)	90	180

Solution

Statement showing Comprehensive Machine-hour Rate of Machine B of X Ltd

Particulars		Amount
Standing charges:		
Factory rent (₹9,60,000/80,000 sq. ft.) × 5,000 sq. ft.		₹60,000
Heat and gas (₹4,50,000/15 machines)		30,000
Supervision (₹12,00,000/15 machines)		80,000
Depreciation [(₹4,50,000 – ₹50,000)/10 years]		40,000
Annual expenses on special equipment		30,000
Total		2,40,000
Machine-hours		4,000
Fixed cost per hour		60
	Set up rate per hour	Operation rate per hour
Fixed cost	₹60	₹60
Power	—	25
Wages	60	30
Comprehensive machine-hour rate	120	115

Statement of Machines B Costs to be Absorbed on the Two Work Orders

Particulars	Work order 31			Work order 32		
	Hours	Rate	Amount	Hours	Rate	Amount
Set up time cost	10	₹120	₹1,200	20	₹120	₹2,400
Operation time cost	90	115	10,350	180	115	20,700
Total cost			11,550			23,100

P.10.11 A machine shop cost centre contains 6 machines of equivalent capacities. Three operators are employed on each machine: one at ₹50 per hour and two at ₹25 per hour each. The factory works a 40-hour week which includes 4 hours for setup time. The work is jointly done by the operators. The operators are paid fully for the 40 hours. In addition, they are paid a bonus of 10 per cent on productive time. Costs are reported for this company on the basis of 13 four-week periods. **LO 10.4** **LOD: D**

The company for the purposes of computing machine-hour rate includes direct wages of the operators and also recoups the factory overheads allocated to the machines. The following details of factory overheads applicable to the cost centre are available:

1. Setup time as described above.
2. Depreciation, 10 per cent per annum on original cost on each machine (original cost of each machine is ₹1,30,000)
3. Maintenance and repairs per week per machine is ₹2,500
4. Consumable stores per week per machine is ₹3,600
5. Power, 20 units per hour per machine at ₹5 per unit
6. Apportionment to the cost centre:

Rent per annum	₹1,44,000
Heat and light per annum	5,40,000
Foreman's salary (2 in number)	7,20,000
Total expenses for 6 machines	14,04,000

From the above, you are required to compute: (a) The cost of running one machine for a 4-week period and (b) The machine-hour rate.

Solution

(a) *Determination of Cost of Running one Machine for a 4-week period.*

Standing charges:		
Rent per annum (₹1,44,000/6 machines)	₹24,000	
Heat and light per annum (₹5,40,000/6)	90,000	
Foreman's salary per annum (₹7,20,000/6)	1,20,000	
Total expenses for one machine per annum	2,34,000	
Expenses for a 4-week period (₹2,34,000/13)		₹18,000
Wages for a 4-week period		17,440[1]
Total standing charges		35,440
Machine expenses		
Depreciation (₹1,30,000 × 0.10 × 1/13)		1,000
Repairs an maintenance (₹2,500 × 4 weeks)		10,000
Consumable stores (₹3,600 × 4 weeks)		14,400
Power (144 Hours × 20 units × ₹5 per unit)		14,400[2]
Total machine expenses		39,800
Total cost (₹35,440 + ₹39,800)		75,240

(b) *Machine-hour rate* = ₹75,240/144 (36 hours × 4) productive hours = ₹522.50.

WORKING NOTES

(1) Determination of wages:

Hours for 4 weeks	160
Rate per hour [(1 operator × ₹50) + (2 operators × ₹25)]	₹100
Wages for 4 weeks (160 × ₹100)	16,000
Add bonus for productive time (36 hours per week × 4 weeks × ₹100 per hour) × 0.1	1,440
	₹17,440

(2) It is assumed that no power is used during setup time of the machine.

P.10.12 A machine shop has 8 identical drilling machines manned by 6 operators. The original cost of all these 8 machines, works out to ₹80 lakh. These particulars are furnished for a 6-month period: LO 10.4 LOD: M

Normal available hours per month	208
Absenteeism with pay (hours)	18
Leave with pay (hours)	20
Normal idle time unavoidable (hours)	10
Average rate of wages per day of 8 hours	₹200
Production bonus estimated (per cent on wages)	15
Value of power consumed	80,500
Supervision and indirect labour	33,000
Lighting and electricity	12,000

These particulars are for a year:

Repairs and maintenance including consumables, 3 per cent on value of machines. Insurance, ₹4,00,000

Depreciation, 10 per cent on original cost

Other sundry works expenses, ₹1,20,000

General management expenses allocated, ₹5,45,300

You are required to work out a comprehensive machine-hour rate.

Solution

Determination of Comprehensive Machine-hour Rate of Machine Shop

		Amount (6 months)
Standing charges:		
Supervision and indirect labour	₹33,000	
Lighting and electricity	12,000	
Insurance (₹4,00,000 × 6/12)	2,00,000	
Other sundry works expenses (₹20,000 × 6/12)	60,000	
General management expenses (₹5,45,300 × 6/12)	2,72,650	₹5,77,650
Machine charges:		
Power	80,500	
Repairs and maintenance including consumables (0.03 × ₹80 lakh × 0.5 year)	1,20,000	
Depreciation (.10 × ₹80 lakh × 0.5 year)	4,00,000	
Operators wages	1,71,000[1]	
Production bonus (0.15 × ₹1,71,000)	25,650	7,97,150
Total		13,74,800
Machine-hour rate (₹13,74,800/5,760 hours[2])		238.70

WORKING NOTES

1. Determination of wages payable to operators:

Normal available hours per month	208
Less absenteeism hours per month (without pay)	18

Number of hours for which wages are to be paid	190
Wages paid for 6 operators for 6 months @ ₹25 per hour (₹200/8 hours) = 190 hours × ₹25 × 6 months × 6 operators)	₹1,71,000

2. Determination of machine-hours available for work (for 6 months):

Normal available hours per operator (per month)	208
Less absenteeism hours	18
Less leave hours	20
Less normal idle time hours	10
Effective hours available per operator per month	160
Total effective hours for 6 operators for 6 months (160 × 6 × 6)	5,760

P.10.13 Gemini Enterprise Ltd undertakes three different jobs: A, B, and C. All of them require the use of a special machine and also the use of computer. The computer is hired and the hire charges work out to be ₹4,20,000 per annum. The expenses regarding the machine are estimated as follows: **LO 10.4** **LOD: M**

Rent for the quarter	₹ 17,500
Depreciation per annum	2,00,000
Indirect charges per annum	1,50,000

During the first month of operation, the following details were taken from the job register:

Job	*A*	*B*	*C*
Number of hours the machine was used			
(a) Without the use of the computer	600	900	—
(b) With the use of computer	400	600	1,000

You are required to compute the machine-hour rate (a) for the firm as a whole for the month when the computer was used and when the computer was not used, (b) for the individual jobs: A,B and C.

Solution

(a) *Determination of Machine-hour rate when the Computer was not used:*

Total overheads of machine per month:	
Rent (₹17,500/3 months) per month	₹5,833
Depreciation (₹2,00,000/12 months) per month	16,667
Indirect charges (₹1,50,000/12 months) per month	12,500
	35,000
Total machine-hours in a month:	
Without the use of computer	1,500
With the use of computer	2,000
	3,500
Machine-hour rate (without use of computer) ₹35,000/3,500 hours)	10
When computer is used:	
Machine-hour rate per hour (determined above)	10
Add computer charges per hour(₹4,20,000/12 months) = ₹35,000 per month/2,000 hours	17.50
	27.50

(b) *Determination of Machine-hour Rate (MHR) for Jobs A, B and C*

Particulars	*Jobs*					
	A		*B*		*C*	
	Hours	*Amount*	*Hours*	*Amount*	*Hours*	*Amount*
MHR, without computer @ ₹10 per hour	600	₹6,000	900	₹9,000	—	—

(Contd.)

(Contd.)

MHR with use of computer @ ₹27.50 per hour	400	11,000	600	16,500	1,000	₹27,500
Total	1,000	17,000	1,500	25,500	1,000	27,500
MHR		17		17		27.50

P.10.14 In a machine shop, the machine-hour rate is worked out at the beginning of a year on the basis of a 13-week period which is equal to three calendar months. The following estimates for operating a machine are relevant. LO 10.4 LOD: M

Total working hours available per week	48
Maintenance time included in the above	2
Setting up time included in the above	2
Cost details:	
Operator's wages per month	₹13,000
Supervisor's salary per month	20,000
Written down value of machine (depreciation at 12 per cent)	18,00,000
Repairs and maintenance per annum	1,60,000
Consumable stores per annum	3,00,000
Rent, rates and taxes (for the quarter apportioned)	48,108

Power consumed is 10 units per hour @ ₹5 per unit. Power is required for productive hours only. Setting-up time is part of productive time but no power is required for setting-up jobs.

The operator and supervisor are permanent. Repairs and maintenance and consumable stores are variable.

You are required to:

(a) Work out the machine-hour rate

(b) Work out the rate for quoting to the outside party for utilising the idle capacity in the machine shop assuming a profit of 20 per cent above variable cost.

Solution

(a) *Determination of Machine-hour Rate*

Standing charges:			
Operator's wages (₹13,000 × 3 months)		₹39,000	
Supervisors' salary (₹20,000 × 3 months)		60,000	
Rent, rates and taxes		48,108	
Total standing fixed charges		1,47,108	
Standing charges per hour (₹1,47,108/598 productive hours, that is, 46 hours × 13 weeks)			₹246.00
Variable cost per hour:			
Power (10 units × ₹5 per unit × 44/46 hours)	₹47.83		
Repairs and maintenance (₹40,000/598)	66.89		
Consumable stores (₹75,000/598)	125.42		
Depreciation [(₹18 lakh × 0.12)/4] ÷ 598 hours	90.30		330.44
Machine-hour rate			576.44

(b) *Determination of Quotation Price:*

Variable cost per machine-hour	₹330.44
Add 20 per cent profit	66.09
Quotation price per hour	396.53

ASSUMPTION Depreciation is treated as machine charges and, hence, is more close to variable cost category.

P.10.15 The budgeted working conditions for a cost centre are as follows: LO 10.4, 5 LOD: M

Normal working week, 40 hours
Number of machines, 10
Normal weekly loss of hours on maintenance, and so on, 5 hours per machine
Estimated annual factory overheads, ₹50,40,000
Estimated direct wages rate, ₹30 per hour
Number of weeks worked per year, 48

Actual results in respect of a 4 week period are:

Factory overheads incurred, ₹5,80,000
Wages incurred, ₹49,200
Machine-hours produced, 2,000

You are required to calculate: **(a)** The overhead rate per machine-hour and **(b)** The amount of under or over-absorption of both factory overheads and wages.

Solution

(a) Machine-hour rate = ₹50,40,000/16,800[1] hours = ₹300

(b) *Determination of Overheads Under-or Overabsorbed:*

Factory overheads incurred	₹5,80,000
Overheads absorbed (2,000 hours × ₹300)	6,00,000
Overheads overabsorbed (₹6,00,000 – ₹5,80,000)	20,000

Determination of Wages Under or Overabsorbed:

Wages incurred	₹49,200
Wages absorbed (10 machines × 40 hours per week × 4 weeks × ₹30 per hour)	48,000
Wages underabsorbed (₹49,200 – ₹48,000)	1,200

WORKING NOTES

(1) Normal working hours per year for 10 machines (40 hours × 10 machines × 48 weeks)	19,200
Less hours lost due to maintenance in a year (5 hours × 10 machines × 48 weeks)	2,400
	16,800

P.10.16 In a small factory, overheads of a particular department are recovered on the basis of ₹50 per machine-hour. The total expenses incurred and the actual machine-hours for the department for the month of August were ₹8,00,000 and 10,000 respectively. Of the amount of ₹8,00,000, ₹1,50,000 became payable due to an award of the Labour Court and ₹50,000 was in respect of expenses of the previous year booked in the current month (August). Actual production was 40,000 units, of which 30,000 units were sold. On analysing the reasons, it was found that 60 per cent of the under-absorbed overhead was due to defective planning and the rest was attributed to normal cost increase. How would you treat the under-absorbed overhead in the cost accounts? LO 10.5 LOD: M

Solution

Determination of Underabsorbed Overhead Expenses

Total expenses incurred in August	₹8,00,000
Less amount paid as per Labour Court award (assumed to be abnormal expense)	1,50,000
Less expenses paid related to previous year	50,000
Overhead expenses relating to current month	6,00,000
Less overheads recovered (10,000 machine-hours × ₹50)	5,00,000
Underabsorbed factory overheads	1,00,000

Treatment of underabsorbed overheads in cost accounts

1. 60 per cent of underabsorbed factory overheads (₹1,00,000) is attributed to defective planning. Being abnormal in nature, the amount of ₹60,000 is to be charged to costing profit and loss account

2. Balance 40 per cent of underabsorbed factory overheads is prorated between cost of sales (30,000 units) and finished goods inventory (10,000 units).
Accordingly, ₹40,000 distribution between the two is as follows:

Cost of sales	₹30,000	
Finished goods	10,000	₹40,000
Total unabsorbed overheads (₹60,000 + ₹40,000)		1,00,000

P.10.17 ABC Ltd manufactures a single product and absorbs the production overheads at a predetermined rate of ₹100 per machine-hour. LO 10.5 LOD: M

At the end of current financial year, it has been found that actual production overheads incurred were ₹6,00,000. It included ₹45,000 on account of 'written off' obsolete stores and ₹30,000 being the wages paid for the strike period under an award.

The production and sales data for the current year is as under:

Production:	
Finished goods (units)	20,000
Work-in-progress (50% complete in all respects) (units)	8,000
Sales:	
Finished goods (units)	18,000

The actual machine-hours worked during the period were 4,800. It has been found that one-third of the under-absorption of production overheads was due to lack of production planning and the rest was attributable to normal increase in costs.

You are required to:

(i) Calculate the amount of under-absorption of production overheads during the current year; and

(ii) Show the accounting treatment of under-absorption of production overheads.

Solution

(i) *Determination of Unabsorbed Production Overheads*

Production overhead expenses incurred (gross)		₹6,00,000
Less "written off" obsolete stores	₹45,000	
Less wages paid for the strike period	30,000	75,000
Net relevant production overheads expenses		5,25,000
Less production overheads absorbed (4,800 machine-hours × ₹100 per machine-hour)		4,80,000
Unabsorbed production overheads		45,000

(ii) *Treatment of Unabsorbed Production Overheads:*

(1) One-third of unabsorbed overheads are attributed to lack of production planning. Being abnormal in nature ₹15,000 (₹45,000 × 1/3) is charged to costing profit and loss account		₹15,000
(2) The balance sum of ₹30,000 is to be pro-rated among Cost of goods sold (18,000 units), work-in-progress(4,000 units i.e., 8,000 units × 50 per cent completion) and finished goods inventory 2,000 units) as follows:		
Cost of goods sold (₹30,000 × 18/24)	₹22,500	
Work-in-progress (₹30,000 × 4/24)	5,000	
Finished goods inventory (₹30,000 × 2/24)	2,500	30,000
		45,000

Journal entry will be as follows:

Cost of goods sold A/c	.... Dr	₹22,500	
Work-in-progress A/c	.... Dr	5,000	
Finished goods inventory A/c	.... Dr	2,500	
To Factory overhead control A/c			₹30,000

REVIEW QUESTIONS

LOD: Easy

RQ.10.1 **(a)** Indicate whether the following statements are 'True' or 'False'. **LO 10.1,2**

(i) Factory overheads are direct manufacturing costs.
(ii) Indirect labour and indirect materials form part of factory overheads.
(iii) Factory overheads are common costs and are shared among various cost centres.
(iv) Allotment of whole items of cost to cost centres is referred to as cost apportionment.
(v) Allotment of factory overheads to cost units by means of predetermined factory overhead application rate is called overhead absorption.
(vi) Normal capacity is less than theoretical capacity.

(b) In the following multiple choice questions, select the correct answers: **LO 10.2,4,5**

(vii) Which of the following is correct factory overheads application rate given:
Budgeted fixed overhead costs – ₹6 lakh; Variable overhead cost ₹100 per unit; Theoretical capacity – 3,000 units; and Normal capacity – 2,000 units.
(a) ₹400 per unit, (b) ₹300 per unit, (c) ₹350 per unit, (d) None of these.

(viii) Compute the machine hour rate from the data below:
Cost of machine ₹3,00,000; Estimated scrap value after expiry of its useful life (5 years) ₹50,000. Assume machine is subject to straight line method of depreciation; Rent and rates per month ₹2,000; Insurance premium/annum ₹6,000; and Estimated working hours/annum 2,000.
(a) ₹40 per machine hour, (b) ₹30 per machine hour,
(c) ₹35 per machine hour, (d) None of these.

(ix) Following data is available: Factory overhead absorption rate is 50 per machine-hour; 10,000 machine-hours were used; If actual factory overheads are ₹6,00,000. This implies that firm has
(a) Under-absorption, (b) Over-absorption, (c) Under-allocation, (d) Over-allocation.

[Answers: (i) False, (ii) True, (iii) True, (iv) False, (v) True, (vi) True, (vii) a, (viii) a, (ix) a.]

RQ.10.2 What do you understand by fixed overheads? Why are they called 'burdens'? **LO 10.1,2**

RQ.10.3 What two key factors determine the factory overhead application rate for a period? Why are these factors important? **LO 10.2**

RQ.10.4 What are the six bases commonly used to compute the factory overhead absorption rate and when is each one appropriate to use? **LO 10.4**

RQ.10.5 A manufacturing unit has added a new machine to its fleet of five existing machines. **LO 10.4** The total cost of purchase and installation of the machine is ₹7,50,000. The machine has an estimated life of 5 years and is expected to realise ₹30,000 as scrap at the end of its working-life.

Other relevant data are as follows:

(i) Budgeted working-hours is 2,400 based on 8 hours per day for 300 days. This includes 400 hours for plant maintenance.
(ii) Power used by the machine is 5 units per hour at a cost of ₹6 per unit. No current is drawn during maintenance.
(iii) The machine requires special oil for heating which is replaced once in every month at a cost of ₹2,500 on each occasion.
(iv) Estimated cost of maintenance of the machine is ₹1,000 per week of 6 working days.
(v) 3 operators control the operations of the entire battery of six machines and the average wages per person amounts to ₹4,500 per week *plus* 40 per cent fringe benefits.

(vi) Departmental and general works overheads allocated to the operation during the last year was ₹6,00,000. During the current year, it is estimated that there will be an increase of 12.5 per cent of this amount. No incremental overhead is envisaged for the installation of the new machine.

You are required to compute the machine-hour rate for recovery of the running cost of the machine.

RQ.10.6 From the following particulars calculate labour cost per hour: LO 10.4

(a) Basic salary, ₹200 per working day
(b) Dearness allowance per month, ₹5 per/ every point over 100 cost of living index (current cost of living index is 700 points)
(c) Leave salary, 10 per cent of [(a) + (b)]
(d) Employer's contribution to provident fund, 8 per cent of [(a) + (b) + (c)]
(e) Employer's contribution to state insurance, 2.5 per cent of [(a) + (b) + (c)]
(f) Expenditure on amenities to labour, ₹1,000 per head per month
(g) Number of working days in a month, 25 days of 8 hours each.

LOD: Medium

RQ.10.7 What do you understand by classification, allocation, apportionment, and absorption in relation to overhead expenses? Explain with examples. LO 10.3,4,5

RQ.10.8 (a) Distinguish between cost allocation, cost apportionment and cost absorption, LO 10.3
(b) Explain in brief various methods for apportionment of service department's cost over production departments.

RQ.10.9 Describe how costs are allocated under the direct method, the step method, and the algebraic method. LO 10.3

RQ.10.10 What are the requisites of a good method of absorption of factory overheads? LO 10.4

RQ.10.11 What information is necessary to calculate machine-hour rate for overhead absorption? State the conditions in which this method is most effective. LO 10.4

RQ.10.12 What is meant by absorbed overhead? Under what circumstances will a difference arise between absorbed and actual overheads? How would you dispose of the balance? LO 10.5

RQ.10.13 What is meant by under/overabsorption of factory overheads? How will you account for them in cost accounts? Does it bear any impact while submitting quotations? LO 10.5

RQ.10.14 A company has three production cost centres A, B, and C and two service cost centres X and Y. Costs allocated to service centres are required to be apportioned to the production centres to find out cost of production of different products. LO 10.3

It is found that benefit of service cost centres is also received by each other along with the production cost centres. Overhead costs as allocated to the five cost centres and estimates of benefit of service cost centres received by each of them are as under:

Cost centres	*Overhead costs as allocated*	*Estimates of benefits received from service centres (%)*	
		X	*Y*
A	₹80,000	20	20
B	40,000	30	25
C	20,000	40	50
X	20,000	—	5
Y	10,000	10	—

Required: Work out final overhead costs of each of the production departments including reapportioned cost of service centres using (a) continuous distribution method and (b) simultaneous equation method.

RQ.10.15 XYZ Ltd. has three production departments (P, Q, and R) and two service departments (X and Y). The following data relate to these departments: **LO 10.3**

Particulars	*P*	*Q*	*R*	*X*	*Y*
Direct wages	₹30,000	₹20,000	₹30,000	₹15,000	₹1,950
Worked hours	3,070	4,475	2,419	—	—
Value of machine	6,00,000	8,00,000	10,00,000	50,000	50,000
HP of machines	60	30	50	10	—
Light points	10	15	20	10	5
Floor space (square feet)	2,000	2,500	3,000	2,000	500

Additional information

Rent	₹50,000
Lighting	6,000
Power	15,000
Indirect wages	19,390
Depreciation on machines	1,00,000
Sundries	96,950

Determine overhead recovery rate per hour for production departments, if X's expenses are distributed to P, Q, R, and Y in the ratio of 2 : 3 : 4 : 1 and Y's expenses are distributed in the ratio of 4 : 2 : 3 : 1 to P, Q, R, and X respectively.

RQ.10.16 The following data pertains to the machine shop of an engineering company, relating to the current year. The machine shop has 3 cost centres A, B, and C, each having 3 distinct set of machines. **LO 10.4**

Particulars	*A*	*B*	*C*	*Total*
Number of workers	400	400	800	1,600
Number of machine-hours	50,000	50,000	60,000	1,60,000
Percentage of HP	40	25	35	100
Value of assets	₹20,00,000	₹35,00,000	₹30,00,000	₹85,00,000
Direct wages	16,00,000	20,00,000	24,00,000	60,00,000
Indirect wages				18,00,000
Supervisory salaries				7,00,000
Depreciation				8,50,000
Insurance				4,25,000
Electricity charges				12,00,000
Welfare expenses				9,00,000
Office and other expenses				16,00,000

Work out a composite machine-hour rate for each of the cost centres, showing the basis of apportionment of expenses amongst the cost centres.

LOD: Difficult

RQ.10.17 What do you understand by the terms production department and service department? Explain the rationale for allocating the service department costs to production departments. Using your own figures, illustrate how the expenses are absorbed over the production department? Consider at least three service departments that are to be absorbed by production departments. **LO 10.3**

RQ.10.18 A company has two production departments and two service departments. The data relating to a period are as under: LO 10.3

	Production Departments		Service Departments	
	PD_1	PD_2	SD_1	SD_2
Direct Materials	₹8,00,000	₹4,00,000	₹1,00,000	₹2,00,000
Direct Wages	9,50,000	5,00,000	2,00,000	1,00,000
Overheads	8,00,000	5,00,000	3,00,000	2,00,000
Power requirement at normal capacity operations (Kwh)	20,000	35,000	12,500	17,500
Actual Power consumption during the period (Kwh)	13,000	23,000	10,250	10,000

The power requirement of these departments are met by a power generation plant. The said plant incurred an expenditure, which is not included above, of ₹12,18,750 out of which a sum of ₹8,43,750 was variable and the rest fixed.

After apportionment of power generation plant costs to the four departments, the service department overheads are to be redistributed on the following bases:

	PD_1	PD_2	SD_1	SD_2
SD_1	50 per cent	40 per cent	—	10 per cent
SD_2	60 per cent	20 per cent	20 per cent	—

You are required to:

(i) Apportion the power generation plant costs to the four departments.

(ii) Re-apportion service department cost to production departments.

(iii) Calculate the overhead rates per direct labour hour of production departments, given that the direct wage rates of PD_1 and PD_2 are ₹50 and ₹40 per hour respectively.

ANSWERS

RQ.10.5 Machine hour rate ₹377

RQ.10.6 Labour hour rate, ₹53.60.

RQ.10.14 **(a)** Final overhead costs ₹86,523 **(A)**, ₹49,196 **(B)**, ₹34,271 **(C)**
(b) ₹86,533 **(A)**, ₹49,196 **(B)**, ₹34,271 **(C)**

RQ.10.15 Overhead recovery rate ₹30.10 **(P)**, ₹20.20 **(Q)**, ₹50.30 **(R)**

RQ.10.16 Machine hour rate ₹75.20 **(A)**, ₹86.50 **(B)**, ₹89.83 **(C)**.

RQ.10.18 **(i)** ₹10,83,240 **(PD_1)**, ₹9,99,410 **(PD_2)**, ₹2,08,900 **(SD_1)**, ₹2,27,200 **(SD_2)**
(ii) ₹20,64,898 **(PD_1)**, ₹15,53,852 **(PD_2)** **(iii)** ₹108.70 **(PD_1)**, ₹124.30 **(PD_2)**

[Comprehensive solutions to all numerical review questions are available on the companion website: http://www.mhhe.com/khan_jain_ma7e]

Costing and Control of Administrative, Selling and Distribution Overheads

11

Learning Objectives

After reading this chapter you will be able to:

LO 11.1 Discuss the nature, accounting and control of administrative overheads

LO 11.2 Explain the nature of selling and distribution overheads, their accounting treatment and control and the related aspect of analysis of sales

Introduction

The previous chapter has illustrated the costing and control of factory (manufacturing) overheads. Though the control techniques used in manufacturing costs/overheads are by and large applicable to non-manufacturing costs/overheads, due to difficulty in cost-benefit analysis as the benefits are not easily measurable, such overheads require accounting and control treatment different from that of the factory overheads. The non-manufacturing overheads fall into two groups: **(i)** Administrative costs and **(ii)** Selling and distribution costs. The costing and control of these two categories of non-manufacturing costs are discussed in the chapter. The main points are summarised by way of recapitulation.

Administrative Overheads/Costs

This section discusses the meaning/nature, accounting, and control of administration overheads.

LO 11.1 Discuss the nature, accounting and control of administrative overheads

Meaning and Nature

The administrative overheads are those costs which are incurred for formulating policy to be followed, directing the organisation in a manner that these policies are effectively carried out, and controlling its operations. They are, in other words, incurred for planning, general management and control of organisation. They have, therefore, some special features which distinguish them from other

Administrative overheads are incurred for planning, general management and control of an organisation.

overheads, namely, factory/manufacturing and selling and distribution. In most cases, the amount of such costs is relatively small. Moreover, due to the nature of most of the items of expenses, it is difficult to fix suitable norms/standards for comparison with the actual costs. Such overheads are, therefore, not susceptible to the same degree of control as are other overheads. The methods of absorption of administrative overheads in product costing are, in addition, mostly arbitrary as a result of which it is not possible to have an accurate/equitable cost ascertainment. They, however, do not show wide fluctuations as they are not related to output/sales.

Depending on the organisational structure, two types of administrative costs are typically incurred in a large manufacturing organisation: **(i)** Those incurred within the plant/factory in terms of provision of staff and other administrative support to the factory. The associated costs are controllable at the factory level; **(ii)** Those incurred centrally in the head office and allocated to various plants on an equitable basis. The associated costs are controllable at the head office level.

The administrative overheads include, *inter alia,* the following costs items:

- **Indirect material: (i)** Printing and stationery used in office and **(ii)** Other office supplies.
- **Indirect labour: (i)** Salary and allowances/fee of office and administrative staff including Board of Directors, Managing Director, Chairman, accounting and secretarial staff; **(ii)** Salary/allowances/fee of legal advisor/public relations officer and staff, and internal and statutory auditors.
- **Indirect expenses: (i)** Office rent, rates, and insurance; **(ii)** Office lighting, heating, and cleaning; **(iii)** Depreciation and repairs of office building, furniture and fittings; **(iv)** Legal charges; **(v)** Bank charges; **(vi)** Trade subscriptions and donations and **(vii)** Miscellaneous office expenses.

Accounting for Administrative Overheads

The procedures for the primary accounting and analysis of administrative overheads, namely, classification, allocation and departmentalisation follow the same patterns as in the case of factory overheads described in the preceding chapter. In brief, as a first step, they are classified according to the nature and purpose of cost. Each type of cost is allotted a separate Control Account Number for this purpose. A control account, namely, Administrative Overhead Control Account, is opened in the cost books to record the total administrative overheads incurred in an accounting period. The next step, similar to the procedure adopted for factory overhead, is to departmentalise the cost. These administrative departments serve as cost centres for the purpose of collection and control of these overheads. A typical list of such departments is given in Exhibit 11.1.

EXHIBIT 11.1 Departmentalisation of Administrative Overheads

1. Accounts Department	4. Legal Department
2. Factory Estate Department	5. Personnel Departmen
3. General Office	6. Secretarial Department

The expenses that can be identified with specific departments are allocated directly. Those that cannot be so identified are apportioned to the various departments on a suitable basis in a manner similar to that for manufacturing overheads.

Accounting Methods There are three methods of accounting of administrative overheads: **(i)** Transfer to costing profit and loss account; **(ii)** Apportionment to manufacturing, selling and distribution divisions/functions, and **(iii)** Addition as a separate item of cost.

Transfer to Costing Profit and Loss Account According to this method, administrative overheads are treated as period costs to be excluded from product costs for two reasons: **(i)** They are mainly fixed costs which do not vary with production/sales and **(ii)** There is no equitable basis to charge them to other products/divisions/functions/departments. The accounting treatment is simple. At the end of the accounting period, as a step in closing the books, Profit and Loss Account is debited and the Administrative Overhead Control Accounts credited. However, non-inclusion of administrative overheads results in understatement of product costs.

Apportionment to Manufacturing and Selling, and Distribution Divisions This method recognises only two basic functions of a manufacturing organisation, namely, **(i)** manufacturing and **(ii)** selling and distribution. As administrative overheads are incurred for manufacturing as well as selling and distribution, these suitably are apportioned between production and selling and distribution expenses. As a result, they lose their identity and are merged with manufacturing and selling and distribution costs.

The expenses apportioned to manufacturing and selling and distribution overheads respectively are treated in the same way as other items of such overheads. Each item is first allocated to service cost and production centres. The cost of the service centre is then apportioned to the production cost centres and ultimately absorbed in cost units. These overheads incurred are debited to Administrative Overhead Control Account. On apportionment, the amount pertaining to manufacturing is transferred to Works/Manufacturing/Factory Overhead Control Account/Work-in-Process Account, and those pertaining to selling and distribution are debited to Selling and Distribution Control Account.

The main problem with this method of accounting of administrative overheads is the selection of a suitable/equitable basis for their apportionment. As the nature of the various items of these overheads is different from each other, each item is analysed separately for the purpose. Some of the items can be allocated directly on the basis of the amount spent. In the case of most items, however, equitable bases have to be adopted for apportionment of each item of expenditure. The bases adopted for apportionment of factory overheads would be useful here also. An illustrative list of items and the basis of their apportionment is given in Exhibit 11.2.

EXHIBIT 11.2 Apportionment of Administrative Overheads

Item/Expense	*Basis of Apportionment*
1. Office rent and rates	Floor area
2. Depreciation of office building	Floor area or capital value
3. Legal expenses	Number of employees
4. Personnel department expenses	Number of employee
5. Filing	Number of items handled
6. Typing	Number of letters typed
7. Invoicing	Number of invoices
8. Correspondence	Number of letters drafted

Addition as a Separate Item of Cost Under this method, administrative overhead is added as a separate cost element to the cost units sold. It is apportioned to the cost of product/goods sold on the basis of an equitable administrative overhead rate much in the same way as is done for the determination of factory overhead rate. Depending upon the suitability and equitability under the given circumstances, the administrative overhead rate can be computed using one of the following bases: **(i)** Sales value/quantity; **(ii)** Cost of sales/selling cost; **(iii)** Works/manufacturing cost; **(iv)** Conversion costs; **(v)** Production units, and **(vi)** Gross profit.

Control of Administrative Overheads

As administrative overheads typically relate to the general and financial management of an organisation, their major portion represents policy costs that are mostly fixed in nature and, therefore, largely non-controllable. Moreover, fixation of norm/standard to measure the effectiveness of such costs is beset with serious difficulties, coupled with the fact that the amount involved is rather small. The introduction and operation of a control system is difficult as well as not very worthwhile. Nonetheless, the normal methods of controlling costs may, with suitable adjustments, be applied to such costs as well, as explained below.

Comparison with Past Performance The administrative overheads allocated to various administrative/service departments/cost centres may be compared periodically with the corresponding expenditure in a previous period. The effectiveness of this method would depend upon the level of activity during the period of comparison. Alternatively, the cost of a department may be compared with the cost of similar services from outside. Similarly, the administrative overhead absorption rate my also be compared over a period of time and the relative efficiency of a department would be reflected in the extent of under/over absorption.

Budgetary Control The technique of budgetary control can be used and periodic comparison with actuals would reveal relative efficiency.

Standard Costing Although standards cannot be set with the same degree of precision as in case of manufacturing costs, standards for certain types of administrative work with standard units of measurement can be established. The examples of such types of work are clerical, typing, posting, filing and billing, and so on. The standard costing techniques, however, cannot be applied to fixed administrative costs such as depreciation of office buildings/machines/equipments, and so on. They may be included in a separate fixed cost budget for the information of the top management.

SELLING AND DISTRIBUTION OVERHEADS

LO 11.2 Explain the nature of selling and distribution overheads, their accounting treatment and control and the related aspect of analysis of sales

This section discusses the nature of selling and distribution overheads, their accounting treatment, and control, and the related aspect of analysis of sales.

Nature

Although the selling and distribution functions are separate but as *after-production costs*, there is overlapping between the two. They are, therefore, dealt with together for accounting and control purposes. As most of the items of such costs are not identifiable with specific products, they are in the nature of indirect costs/overheads.

Selling overheads are costs incurred in selling to existing customers, retaining customers and in promoting sales to potential customes.

Selling Overheads Selling overheads/costs include the costs incurred in selling to existing customers, retaining customers and in promoting sales to potential customers. They consist of the following items.

Direct Selling Costs Such costs are incurred for soliciting/obtaining orders, market research, and supply of goods to customers. They are paid to sales executives/staff/office.

Advertising and Sales Promotion Costs The major items of expenditure are:

- Advertising;

- Sales promotion: exhibitions, displays, posters, films, distribution of samples and free gifts/ diaries/calendars

Credit and Collection Costs These include expenses relating to collection of receivables and bad debts.

Financial and General Administration Costs Included in this category are **(i)** royalty on sales, **(ii)** discounts and allowances, **(iii)** sales invoicing, and **(iv)** accounts.

Distribution Overheads Distribution overheads begin when a order has been obtained, and generally end when goods are to be despatched. They include the following.

Transportation Costs Such costs consist of expenditure on different modes of transport, comprising salary of staff, maintenance/depreciation/insurance of vehicles, demurrage and wharfage and dispatch of goods, and so on.

Warehousing and Storage Costs The main items of such costs are the cost of storage such as warehouse rent, salary of warehouse staff, warehouse office expenses, depreciation, and insurance.

Financial and General Administration The distribution expenses covered under this head are **(i)** cost of carrying stock and **(ii)** financial/cost accounting costs, and so on.

Accounting of Selling and Distribution Overheads

The accounting of selling and distribution overheads involves three-stage analysis: **(i)** By nature/object, **(ii)** By function/cost centre, and **(iii)** By product/cost units.

Analysis by Nature/Object The selling and distribution costs are analysed according to the nature/ object of different items of such costs. An illustrative list of such cost items nature-wise includes: **(i)** advertising, **(ii)** commission/remuneration, **(iii)** customs excise/duty, **(iv)** depreciation, **(v)** discounts and allowances, **(vi)** fees, **(vii)** freight, **(viii)** heating, **(ix)** insurance, **(x)** lighting/ power **(xi)** materials and consumable stores/supplies, **(xii)** packing, **(xiii)** postage, **(xiv)** rent, **(xv)** repairs, **(xvi)** services, and so on. Like the manufacturing costs, selling and distribution overheads may be fixed, variable, and semi-variable.

Functional Analysis The functional analysis of selling and distribution costs is similar to departmentalisation and apportionment of manufacturing overheads to cost centres. The main operational functions with reference to such costs my be further classified into **(i)** direct selling, **(ii)** advertising and sales promotion, **(iii)** transportation, **(iv)** warehousing and storage, **(v)** credit and collection, **(vi)** financial, **(vii)** general administration, **(viii)** warranty claims, and **(ix)** miscellaneous. The functional analysis can be extended to locations, namely, territories/sales offices/customers/salesmen. Each function and location constitutes a cost centre for accounting and control of selling and distribution costs. Such costs are allocated to functions/locations to which they relate, for example, freight charges, packing materials, remuneration of salesmen, postage and stationery, and so on. The items/expenses which cannot be allocated may be apportioned on some suitable basis. An illustrative list of bases for such apportionment is given in Exhibit 11.3.

EXHIBIT 11.3 Apportionment of Selling and Distribution Overheads

Expense item	Basis
1. Advertising	Sales vale/physical units
2. Credit control	Number of orders
3. Depreciation	Value of assets
4. Insurance	Property value
5. Rent	Floor space
6. Warehousing	Sales volume
7. Transport	Weight/number of packages/distance carried

Analysis by Products/Groups of Products Selling and distribution costs can also be analysed by products/groups of products, for example, products A and B and location-wise, that is, Territory/Zone 1 (East), 2 (South), 3 (West), and 4 (North). This type of analysis is somewhat similar to absorption of manufacturing overheads to cost units. Such an analysis can also be made for a group of products based on some common factors such as prices, sales order, and salesmen. There are two other related methods of analysis of such overheads, namely, by channels of distribution/methods of sale and by customers.

Apportionment of Functional Costs The direct functional costs are allocated to cost units. The indirect functional costs which cannot be allocated directly are apportioned to cost units on the basis of following methods: **(i)** Rate per article based on number/other physical unit of the product (i.e. advertisement, transportation and warehousing expenses); **(ii)** Percentage of turnover (i.e. direct selling costs, general administration/finance cost); **(iii)** Percentage of cash collected (bad debts and credit collection expenses); **(iv)** Percentage of works cost (e.g. fixed selling and distribution costs); **(v)** Percentage of stock of finished goods; **(vi)** Number of orders; **(vii)** Number of invoices, and **(viii)** Percentage of value added (i.e. total sales less cost of materials). Each item of such expenses should be analysed and allocated to different products (cost centres) on the basis of services rendered.

◆ Example 11.1

Following data is available relating to ABC Ltd. for a certain month:

	Territory I	*Territory II*	*Territory III*
Selling expenses	₹76,000	₹42,000	₹62,400
Distribution costs	40,000	18,000	20,000
Number of units sold	16,000	6,000	10,000
Sales	7,60,000	2,80,000	5,20,000

The company adopts sales basis and quantity basis for application of selling and distribution costs respectively. Compute **(a)** the territory-wise overhead recovery rates separately for selling and distribution costs and **(b)** the amount of selling and distribution costs chargeable to a consignment of 2,000 units of a product, sold in each territory at ₹45 per unit.

Solution

(a) *Statement Showing Determination of Overhead Recovery Rates for Selling and Distribution Costs*

(i) *Selling cost recovery rate:* (Selling expenses/Sales) × 100
Territory I (₹76,000/₹7,60,000) × 100 = 10 per cent of sales
Territory II (₹42,000/₹2,80,000) × 100 = 15 per cent of sales
Territory III (₹62,400/₹5,20,000) × 100 = 12 per cent of sales

(ii) *Distribution cost recovery rate per unit sold:* (Distribution costs/Number of units sold)
Territory I (₹40,000/16,000 units) = ₹2.50 per unit sold
Territory II (₹18,000/6,000 units) = ₹3
Territory III (₹20,000/10,000 units) = ₹2

(b) ***Statement Showing Determination of Selling and Distribution Costs Charged to Consignment of 2,000 units***

Particulars	Territory I	Territory II	Territory III
Number of units sold	2,000	2,000	2,000
Sales revenue	₹90,000	₹90,000	₹90,000
Selling cost	9,000	13,500	10,800
Distribution cost	5,000	6,000	4,000
Total cost	14,000	19,500	14,800

◆ Example 11.2

The Hypothetical Ltd. is making a study of the relative profitability of two products—A and B. In addition to direct costs, indirect selling and distribution costs to be allocated between the two products are as under:

Insurance charge for inventory (finished)	₹78,000
Storage costs	1,40,000
Packing and forwarding charges	7,20,000
Salesman salaries	8,50,000
Invoicing costs	4,50,000

Other details are:

	Product A	Product B
Selling price per unit	₹500	₹1,000
Cost per unit (exclusive of indirect selling and distribution cost)	300	600
Annuals sales (in units)	10,000	8,000
Average inventory (in units)	1,000	800
Number of invoices	2,500	2,000

One unit of product A requires a storage space twice as much as product B. The cost to pack and forward is the same for both the products. The salesmen are paid salary plus commission @ 5 per cent on sales and equal amount of efforts are put forth on the sales of each of the products.

REQUIRED: **(i)** Set up a schedule sharing the apportionment of the indirect selling and distribution costs between the two products, **(ii)** Prepare a statement sharing the relative profitability of two products.

Solution

(i) ***Schedule Showing Apportionment of Indirect Selling and Distribution Costs Between Products A and B***

Particulars	Basis of apportionment	Products A	B	Total
Insurance charges	Value of average inventory (₹500 × 1,000): (₹1,000 × 800) = 5:8	₹30,000	₹48,000	₹78,000
Storage costs	Storage space occupied by inventory (1000 × 2): (800 × 1) = 20:8	1,00,000	40,000	1,40,000

(Contd.)

(Contd.)

Packing and forwarding	Annual sales (units) = 10:8	4,00,000	3,20,000	7,20,000
Salesmen's salaries	Efforts of salesmen (1:1)	4,25,000	4,25,000	8,50,000
Salesmen's commission	Sales value (₹500 × 1,000) : (₹1,000 × 800)	2,50,000	4,00,000	6,50,000
Invoicing costs	Number of invoices (2500:2000) = 5:4	2,50,000	2,00,000	4,50,000
Total cost		14,55,000	14,33,000	28,88,000

(ii) *Statement Showing Relative Profitability of Two Products—A and B*

Particulars	Product A	Product B
Annual sales revenue	₹50,00,000	₹80,00,000
Loss cost of goods sold	30,00,000	48,00,000
Gross profit	20,00,000	32,00,000
Less indirect selling and distribution costs	14,55,000	14,33,000
Profit	5,45,000	17,67,000
Profit as përcentage of sales	10.9	22.09

Control of Selling and Distribution Overheads

The control of selling and distribution costs is comparatively difficult due to the special nature of such costs. The incidence of such costs is dependent upon various external factors such as distance of market, sales terms and extent of competition, and so on. The problems associated with their control are: **(i)** Absence of control over customers/competitors; **(ii)** Lack of proper definition of capacity of a sales organisation; **(iii)** Absence of control/direct supervision over staff/representatives employed outside, necessitating the use of incentive plans of remuneration for them; **(iv)** Fixation of market prices without reference to cost of production; **(v)** Difficulty in obtaining data regarding market operations; and **(vi)** Difficulty in accurately determining the market capacity. Most of the items of selling and distribution overheads are in the nature of policy/discretionary costs which are largely uncontrollable at lower levels of management. Nevertheless, control of such costs may be effected by comparison with past performance (actual) or with the help of budgets and standards like the administrative and factory overheads.

A contributory factor to effective planning and control is the analysis of sales.

Sales Analysis Sales may be analysed in a number of ways according to market segments. The methods of analysis, according to different market segments and the purpose served by each are discussed below.

Salesmen-wise The turnover by each salesman is ascertained for comparison of **(a)** actual sales with past/budgeted sales/sales quota or inter-salesmen comparison for corrective action, and **(b)** sales volume *vis-à-vis* selling costs for control of cost and fixing up commission/bonus payable to salesmen.

Performance Evaluation of Salesmen As much of the success of marketing strategy of a company depends on the efficiency of its salesmen including selling agents/offices, their performance evaluation is an important element in sales analysis. Such evaluation is made on the basis of performance in relation to one/more standards/targets specified below:

- Sales turnover
- Gross profit/contribution on sales
- Percentage of sales quota achieved

- Number/volume of new business obtained/lost
- Number of calls made.

Sales Territory The analysis of sales by territory enables **(i)** comparison with budgets/potential sales, **(ii)** determination of each territory's contribution to net profits, **(iii)** control of selling and distribution costs through correlation with sales volume, **(iv)** assessment of the extent of penetration of competitors, and so on.

Product/Product Lines-wise The usefulness of such analysis is based on **(i)** ascertainment of profit of each product/product line and comparison with past data for control purposes, **(ii)** product planning in terms of choice of product mix based on profitability, **(iii)** ascertainment of sales trends for each product, and **(iv)** control of selling and distribution costs in relation to sales volume of each product.

Customer-wise This analysis of sales is useful to:

- Ascertain profit by each type of customer,
- Maintain a reasonable balance between the types of customers and the extent of discount allowed to each
- Ascertain by type of customers the potential for future sales
- Determine their preferences in respect of quality/type of products.

Distribution Channel-wise Sales Such analysis is useful to ascertain profits of various channels of distribution and to assess their relative viability. The distribution channels refer to the series of middlemen/intermediary agencies through whom the products of a manufacturer reach the consumers. They include wholesalers, retailers, selling agents, commission agents, distributors, and so on. The choice of a channel of distribution is related to improvement in sales and provision of more effective customer service. Each distribution system produces different level of sales/profits and incurs different distribution costs. The main objective of evaluation of distribution alternatives is to determine/select the one which would bring in the highest sales/profits through the least cost. The evaluation process is based on a consideration of the relationship between sales value and the related costs for each alternative.

By Size of Order The analysis of sales on the basis of size of orders would enable comparison of cost of handling and transportation with the sales volume of various sizes as well as decision regarding trade discount for sales of various sizes.

Unit Price-wise This analysis of sales provides information relating to price trends which may be useful in the formulation of a price policy for products.

Period-wise A comparison of sales over a period of time would reveal trends, periodic/cyclical movements, seasonal/fluctuating characteristics of the product and assist in formulating sales policy on long-term basis.

SUMMARY

- The non-manufacturing overheads consist of administrative and selling and distribution costs. The administrative costs are incurred for policy formulation, direction, organisation and control of operations of an organisation.

- Their special features are that their amount is relatively small, fixation of standards for them is difficult and their absorption in product costing is arbitrary. There are three methods of accounting of administrative overheads: **(i)** transfer to costing profit and loss account, **(ii)** apportionment to manufacturing, selling and distribution functions, and **(iii)** addition as a separate item of cost.
- Though the introduction and operation of a control system is both difficult as well as not very useful, the normal methods of controlling cost, namely, comparison with past record, budgeting control and standard costing, may with suitable adjustments, be applied to such cost as well.

LO 11.1

- Although the selling and distribution functions are separate but as after-production costs, there is overlapping between the two. These are, therefore, dealt with together for costing and control purposes. The selling overheads are incurred for selling to existing customers/retaining customers and for promoting sales to potential customers.
- The distribution overheads begin when an order is obtained and generally ends when goods are despatched. The accounting of selling and distribution overheads involves three-stage analysis: **(i)** by nature, **(ii)** by function, and **(iii)** by product. The control of such costs is comparatively difficult due to their special nature.
- important factor in their control is sales analysis. Sales may be analysed in a number of ways and according to market segments. The methods of analysis are:
  - — By salesmen
  - — By territories
  - — By product
  - — By customer
  - — By distribution channel
  - — By size of order
  - — By period.

LO 11.2

SOLVED PROBLEMS

P.11.1 A company is producing three types of products A, B and C. The sales territory of the company is divided into three areas X, Y and Z. The estimated sales for the year are as under: LO 11.2 LOD: E

	Territories		
Product	*X*	*Y*	*Z*
A	₹5,00,000	₹2,00,000	—
B	3,00,000	—	₹8,00,000
C	—	7,00,000	4,00,000

Budgeted advertising cost is as under:

	Territories			
Product	*X*	*Y*	*Z*	*Total*
Local cost	₹32,000	₹45,000	₹42,000	₹1,19,000
Common cost				58,000

You are required to prepare the statement showing cost (per cent on sales) for each product and territory.

Solution

Statement showing Determination of Product-wise Advertising Cost

Particulars of Cost	Products			Total
	Product A	Product B	Product C	
Local cost:				
Territory X[1]	₹20,000	₹12,000	—	₹32,000
Territory Y[2]	10,000	—	35,000	45,000
Territory Z[3]	—	28,000	14,000	42,000
Common cost: (apportioned as % of sales)[4]	14,000	22,000	22,000	58,000
Total apportioned cost	44,000	62,000	71,000	1,77,000
Sales	7,00,000	11,00,000	11,00,000	29,00,000
Per cent on sales	6.29	5.64	6.45	6.10

Statement showing Determination of Territory-wise Advertising Cost

Particulars	Territory X	Territory Y	Territory Z	Total
Local cost (direct allocation)	₹32,000	₹45,000	₹42,000	₹1,19,000
Common cost (apportionment as % of sales, territory-wise)[5]	16,000	18,000	24,000	58,000
Total apportioned costs	48,000	63,000	66,000	1,77,000
Total sales	8,00,000	9,00,000	12,00,000	29,00,000
Per cent on sales	6.00	7.00	5.50	6.10

WORKING NOTES

Local/territory costs are apportioned to products on the basis of their sales value.

1. Local cost of territory X (₹32,000) has been apportioned in the ratio of 5:3, i.e.
   Product A (₹32,000 × 5/8) = ₹20,000
   Product B (₹32,000 × 3/8) = 12,000
2. Local cost of territory Y (₹45,000) is apportioned in the ratio of 2:7:
   Product A (₹45,000 × 2/9) = ₹10,000 Product C (₹45,000 (7/9) = 35,000
3. Costs of Territory Z (₹42,000) are apportioned in the ratio of 8:4:
   Product B (₹42,000 × 8/12) = ₹28,000
   Product C (₹42,000 × 4/12) = 14,000
4. (₹58,000/₹29,00,000) × ₹7,00,000 = ₹14,000 (Product A)
   (₹58,000/₹29,00,000) × ₹11,00,000 = 22,000 (Product B)
   (₹58,000/₹29,00,000) × ₹11,00,000 = 22,000 (Product C)
5. ₹5,800 common costs are apportioned in territories X, Y, Z in proportion of sales made in each of these territories, i.e. (8:9:12)
   (₹58,000/₹29,00,000) × ₹8,00,000 = ₹16,000 (Territory X)
   (₹58,000/₹29,00,000) × ₹9,00,000 = ₹18,000 (Territory Y)
   (₹58,000/₹29,00,000) × ₹12,00,000 = ₹24,000 (Territory Z)

P.11.2 XYZ Ltd., having an extensive marketing network throughout the country, sells its products throughout four zonal sales offices, namely, A, B, C and D. The budgeted expenditure for the year are given below: **LO 11.2** **LOD: M**

Sales manager's salary	₹12,00,000
Expenses relating to sales manager's office	8,00,000
Travelling salesmen's salaries	32,00,000
Travelling expenses	3,60,000
Advertisements	3,00,000

(Contd.)

(Contd.)

Godown rent: Zone	A	₹1,50,000	
	B	2,52,000	
	C	98,000	
	D	1,80,000	6,80,000
Insurance on inventories			2,00,000
Commision on sales @ 5% on sales			60,00,000

The following further particulars are also available:

Zone	*Sales (₹lakh)*	*Number of salesmen*	*Total mileage covered*	*Allocation of advertisement (%)*	*Average stock in ₹lakh*
A	360	5	6,000	30	60
B	480	6	14,000	30	80
C	160	2	4,500	20	40
D	200	3	5,500	20	20

Based on the above details, compute zone-wise selling overheads, as a percentage to sales.

Solution

Statement showing Determination of Zone-wise Selling Overhead Rates

Particulars	*Basis of apportionment*	*Zones* A	B	C	D	*Total*
Sales manager salary	Sales ratio	₹3,60,000	₹4,80,000	₹1,60,000	₹2,00,000	₹12,00,000
Office expenses of sales	Sales ratio	2,40,000	3,20,000	1,00,667	1,33,330	8,00,000
Travelling salesman's salaries	No. of salesmen	10,00,000	12,00,000	4,00,000	6,00,000	32,00,000
Travelling expenses	Mileage covered	72,000	1,68,000	54,000	66,000	3,60,000
Advertisement	(3:3:2:2)	90,000	90,000	60,000	60,000	3,00,000
Godown rent	Actual	1,50,000	2,52,000	98,000	1,80,000	6,80,000
Insurance (stock)	(6:8:4:2)	60,000	80,000	40,000	20,000	2,00,000
Commission	(5% of sales)	18,00,000	24,00,000	8,00,000	10,00,000	60,00,000
Total overheads		37,72,000	49,90,000	17,18,670	22,59,330	1,27,40,000
Sales revenue		3,60,00,000	4,80,00,000	1,60,00,000	2,00,00,000	12,00,00,000
Selling overheads as % of sales		10.48	10.40	10.74	11.30	10.62

P.11.3 A manufacturing concern sells its sale product in three sizes of packages—small, medium, and large—each package containing one, two and three dozen units of the product respectively. Sales for the year were: **LO 11.2** **LOD: M**

	Number of packages sold	*Sales rate*
Small size	20,000	₹10
Medium size	5,00,000	15
Large size	5,00,000	20

The factory cost was 30 paise per unit of product and the administration overhead was added at 2% of sales. The following selling and distribution expenses were incurred:

Advertising:	
Small	₹30,000
Medium	6,00,000
Large	15,00,000
Packages:	
Small	5,000
Medium	5,00,000
Large	5,00,000
General advertising (as % of sales)	1
Commission (as % of sales)	10
Sales office expenses (as % of sales)	2
Travelling expenses:	
Small	1,000
Medium	80,000
Large	30,000

Prepare a comparative income statement for each size of package.

Solution

Income Statement, Package-wise

Particulars	Packages		
	Small	*Medium*	*Large*
Number of units	₹2,40,000	₹120,00,000	₹18,00,00,000
Sales revenue	2,00,000	75,00,000	1,00,00,000
Factory cost (₹0.3 per unit)	72,000	36,00,000	54,00,000
Administration overheads	4,000	1,50,000	2,00,000
Advertising	30,000	6,00,000	15,00,000
Packaging expenses	5,000	5,00,000	5,00,000
General advertising	2,000	75,000	1,00,000
Commission	20,000	7,50,000	10,00,000
Sales office expenses	4,000	1,50,000	2,00,000
Traveling expenses	1,000	80,000	30,000
Total cost of sales	1,38,000	59,05,000	89,30,000
Profit (Sales-Cost of sales)	62,000	15,95,000	10,70,000

P.11.4 Alpha limited has decided to analyse the profitability of its five new customers. It buys bottled water at ₹90 per case and sells to retail customers at a list price of ₹108 per case. The data pertaining to five customers are: LO 11.2 LOD: M

	Customers				
	A	*B*	*C*	*D*	*E*
Cases sold	4,680	19,688	1,36,90	71,550	8,775
List selling price	₹108	108	108	108	108
Actual selling price	108	106.20	99	104.40	97.20
Number of purchase orders	15	25	30	25	30
Number of customer visits	2	3	6	2	3
Number of deliveries	10	30	60	40	20
Kilometers travelled per delivery	20	6	5	10	30
Number of expedited deliveries	0	0	0	0	1

Its five activities and their cost drivers are:

Activity	Cost driver rate
Order taking	₹750 per purchase order
Customer visits	₹600 per customer visit
Deliveries	₹5.75 per delivery km travelled
Product handling	₹3.75 per case sold
Expedited deliveries	₹2,250 per expedited delivery

REQUIRED:

(i) Compute the customer-level operating income of each of five retail customers now being examined (A,B,C,D and E). Comment on the results. **(ii)** What insights are gained by reporting both the list selling price and the actual selling price for each customer? **(iii)** What factors should Alpha Limited consider in deciding whether to drop one or more of five customers?

Solution

(i) *Statement showing Operating Income of Customers A to E*

Particulars	Customers				
	A	B	C	D	E
Cases sold	4,680	19,688	1,36,800	71,550	8,775
Revenues (at listed price)	₹5,05,440	₹21,26,304	₹1,47,74,400	₹77,27,400	₹9,47,700
Less costs:					
Cost of goods sold (cases sold x ₹90)	4,21,200	17,71,920	1,23,12,000	64,39,500	7,89,750
Discount	—	35,438	12,31,200	2,57,580	94,770
		(19,688 × ₹1.80)	(1,36,800 × ₹9)	(71,550 × ₹3.60)	(8,775 × ₹10.80)
Order taking costs (No. of purchase orders × ₹750)	11,250	18,750	22,500	18,750	22,500
Customer visits costs: (No. of customer visits × ₹600)	1,200	1,800	3,600	1,200	1,800
Delivery vehicles travel costs (₹5.75 per km)	1,150	1,035	1,725	2,300	3,450
Product handling costs (cases sold × ₹3.75)	17,550	73,830	5,13,000	2,68,313	32,906
Cost of expediting deliveries	—	—	—	—	2,250
Operating income	53,090	2,23,531	6,90,375	7,39,757	274

COMMENT: Although the number of cases sold is maximum in the case of customer C, the most profitable customer is D. The primary reason is that customer C gets 2.5 times discount *vis-à-vis* customer D, the respective discount rates being ₹9 per case and ₹3.60. Further, customer E is the least profitable as he gets the maximum discount of ₹10.80 per case, places orders more frequently, requires more customer visits as well as more traveling costs compared to other customers.

(ii) *Insights gained by reporting the two sets of prices, i.e., the listed selling price (LSP) and the actual selling price (ASP) for each customer*

The difference between the LSP and the ASP represents discount. The discount amount offered to customers enables Alpha Limited to examine whether the discount offered to various customers has bearing on the sales made to them. In general, the expectation is the higher is the amount of discount, the higher is the likely sales volume. The relevant data showing the relationship between the two is contained in the following table:

Discount per case	*Sales volume in cases (customer)*
₹0.00	4,680 (Customer A)
1.80	19,688 (Customer B)
3.60	71,550 (Customer D)
9.00	1,36,800 (Customer C)
10.80	8,775 (Customer E)

There is direct relationship between discount amount and sales, except in the case of customer E. There is need to examine (a) the reason for higher discount (of ₹10.80) in the case of customer E and (b) whether it will be profitable to offer discount to customer A also.

(iii) *Factors to be considered in dropping one or more customers*

Since there is profit from each customer, the decision of dropping the customers should be the last option/resort. The major factors to be considered are: (a) To determine the projected profitability in respect of each customer. In particular, the company should examine profitability in respect of customers E (the least profitable) and A (low profitable). (b) There is need to segregate cost data into avoidable costs and unavoidable costs. Based on such data, profitability for each customer should be determined. (c) The company should explore to ascertain whether it is possible to have more profits by offering different discount rate structure to different customers (in particular between customers C and D).

REVIEW QUESTIONS

LOD: Easy

RQ.11.1 Indicate whether the following statements are 'true' or 'false'. **LO 11.1,2**

(i) Apportionment of office rent and rates is done on the basis of floor area.
(ii) Selling and distribution expenses form part of selling and administrative overheads.
(iii) Selling and distribution expenses are exclusively indirect costs.
(iv) Warehousing and storage costs are part of selling overheads.
(v) Selling overheads generally include indirect selling cost, advertising and sales promotion costs and credit and collection costs.
(vi) Distribution expenses primarily include transportation cost, warehousing and storage costs.
(vii) Huge advertisement cost, which would yield benefits over a period of time in future, should still be charged to profit and loss account in which it is incurred.
(viii) Sales analysis has only on two bases, namely, product and territory.
(ix) Warehousing costs are apportioned on the basis of sales volume.

[Answers: (i) True, (ii) False, (iii) False, (iv) False, (v) True, (vi) True, (vii) False, (viii) False, (ix) True.]

RQ.11.2 Explain the term administrative overheads and briefly discuss three methods of treatment thereof in cost accounts. **LO 11.1**

RQ.11.3 What are non-manufacturing costs? Give a few examples of such costs. **LO 11.1,2**

RQ.11.4 A company is making a study of the relative profitability of the two products A and B. In addition to direct costs, indirect selling and distribution costs to be allocated between the two products are as under: **LO 11.2**

Insurance charges for inventory (finished)	₹78,000
Storage costs	1,40,000
Packing and forwarding charges	7,20,000
Salesmen salaries	8,50,000
Invoicing costs	4,50,000

Other details are:

	Product A	*Product B*
Selling price per unit	₹500	₹1,000
Cost per unit (exclusive of indirect selling and distribution costs)	300	600
Annual sales in units	10,000	8,000
Average inventory (units)	1,000	800
Number of invoices	2,500	2,000

One unit of product A requires a storage space twice as much as product B. The cost to pack and forward one unit is the same for both the products. Sales men are paid salary *plus* commission @ 5 per cent on sales and equal amount of efforts are put forth on the sales of each of the products.

Required:

(i) Set up a schedule showing the apportionment of the indirect selling and distribution costs between the two products.

(ii) Prepare a statement showing the relative profitability of the two products.

LOD: Medium

RQ.11.5 What, according to you, are the steps to be followed in controlling administrative overheads? **LO 11.1**

RQ.11.6 What problems are encountered in applying administrative costs partly to the manufacturing and partly to the selling department of a business firm? **LO 11.1,2**

RQ.11.7 What are selling and distribution overheads? Give four examples of such costs. How can such costs be controlled? **LO 11.2**

RQ.11.8 Distinguish between selling costs and distribution costs. What is the relevance of such a distinction? **LO 11.2**

RQ.11.9 For purposes of product costing, explain how would you allocate or apportion each of the following items of overhead: **LO 11.2**

(a) Traveler's salaries, commissions and expenses

(b) After-sales services costs

(c) Warehousing costs

(d) Market research costs

RQ.11.10 How would you deal with the following items in the cost accounts of a manufacturing concern? **LO 11.1,2**

(a) Packing expenses

(b) Sales promotion expenses

(c) Director's fees and salaries

(d) Bad debts

RQ.11.11 Marketing Division of company wishes to discontinue the sale of one of the products in view of unprofitable operations. Following details are available with regard to turnover, costs, and activity for the current year ending 31st March. **LO 11.2**

	Products			
	P	Q	R	S
Sales turnover	₹6,00,000	₹10,00,000	₹5,00,000	₹9,00,000
Cost of sales	3,50,000	8,00,000	3,70,000	4,80,000
Storage area (square metres)	40,000	60,000	70,000	30,000
Number of cartons sold	2,00,000	3,00,000	1,50,000	3,50,000
Number of bills raised	1,00,000	1,20,000	80,000	1,00,000

Overhead costs and basis of apportionment are:

Fixed expenses

		Basis of apportionment
Administrative wages and salaries	₹1,00,000	Number of bills raised
Salesmen's salaries and expenses	1,20,000	Sales turnover
Rent and insurance	60,000	Storage area
Depreciation	20,000	Number of cartons

Variable costs

Commission	4 per cent of sales
Packing materials and wages	₹0.50 per carton
Stationery	₹0.20 per bill

Based on the above data, you are required to:

(i) prepare a statement showing summary of Selling and Distribution Costs to the products, and

(ii) prepare a Profit and Loss Statement showing contribution and profit or loss on sale of each of the products to enable the marketing department and take an appropriate decision on discontinuance of the sale of a product.

ANSWERS

RQ.11.4 **(i)** Product A, ₹14,55,000; Product B, ₹14,33,000
(ii) Net profit Product A, ₹5,45,000; Product B, ₹17,67,000

RQ. 11.11 **(i)** Product A, ₹10,00,000; B, ₹2,09,000; C, ₹3,08,000; D, ₹1,75,000; Product E, ₹3,06,000
(ii) Product Q may be discontinued as it has maximum loss of ₹1,08,000

[Comprehensive solutions to all numerical review questions are available on the companion website: http://www.mhhe.com/khan_jain_ma7e]

12

Activity Based Costing System

LEARNING OBJECTIVES

After reading this chapter you will be able to:

LO 12.1 Understand how traditional cost systems, distort product and customer costs
LO 12.2 Illustrate the measurement of the cost of resource capacity
LO 12.3 Show activity-based costing for marketing, selling, distribution and administration jobs
LO 12.4 Discuss the role of activity-based cost systems for service companies
LO 12.5 Explain the pros and cons of activity-based costing system

INTRODUCTION

The focus of traditional cost accounting is on product costing by tracing costs to the product and allocating indirect costs through cost centres. While the direct costs are in proportion to the volume of production, the indirect costs (i.e. the production/administration/selling/distribution overheads) are apportioned to the individual products on the basis of volume-related methods such as machine-hour rate, labour-hour rate, percentage of direct cost/labour, and so on. These (normal) methods of apportionment/allocation are inadequate to prorate common costs of different functions/activities to the product costs. The activity-based costing system provides a solution to the inadequacies of the traditional method of overhead absorption/allocation. The focus of the chapter is on **(i)** traditional (manufacturing) costing system, its limitations and activity-based cost (ABC) management **(ii)** measuring the cost of resource capacity **(iii)** marketing, selling and distribution expenses and managing customer profitability **(iv)** service companies and **(v)** pros and cons of ABC system. The main points are summarised by way of recapitulation.

Traditional Manufacturing Costing System

LO 12.1 Understand how traditional cost systems, distort product and customer costs

The traditional costing system (TCS), as discussed in Chapter 10, assigns direct (material and labour) costs to products. The indirect costs/overheads [e.g. machine expenses, scheduling, quality control, purchasing, maintenance, supervision and general factory expenses (for building depreciation, insurance, utilities and housekeeping)] are accumulated as support department expenses. These expenses, in turn, are allocated, first, to production departments (cost centres). Second, the accumulated indirect costs in production departments are assigned to individual jobs/products on the basis of pre-determined overhead allocation rates. These are based on/in proportion to some measure of volume such as direct labour cost, directly labour-hour rate, machine-hour rate and so on. An illustrative cost allocation process for Montex Pen Manufacturing Company Ltd. is shown in Exhibit 12.1.

Exhibit 12.1 Montex Pen Total and Product Profitability

	Blue Pens (1)	*Black Pens* (2)	*Red Pens* (3)	*Purple Pens* (4)	*Total* (5)
Production/Sales volume	25,000	20,000	4,500	500	50,000
Unit sale price	₹45	₹45	₹46.5	₹49.5	
Sales (a)	11,25,000	9,00,000	2,09,250	24,750	₹22,59,000
Material costs	3,75,000	3,00,000	70,200	8,250	7,53,450
Direct labour costs	1,50,000	1,20,000	27,000	3,000	3,00,000
Overheads (300% of direct labour)	4,50,000	3,60,000	81,000	9,000	9,00,000*
Total costs (b)	9,75,000	7,80,000	1,78,200	20,250	19,53,450
Total operating income [(a) – (b)]	1,50,000	1,20,000	31,050	4,500	3,05,550
Return on sales (%)	13.3	13.3	14.8	18.2	13.5

Limitations/Inadequacies of Traditional Costing System

The TCS, using only the measure of production as allocation base, has the merit of being simple, easy to use and understand, and applied consistently from year to year. It is adequate for financial reporting of inventory valuation. The problem with the TCS is that it assumes that all overheads costs are proportionate to production volume, for example, when volume increase by 20 per cent, overheads increase by 20 per cent, when volume increases by 50 per cent, overheads increase by 50 per cent, and so on. However, many overhead costs (such as the cost of setting up equipment for a production run, the cost of inspecting raw materials, and the cost of handling materials) are not proportionate to volume. In fact, many overhead costs are affected by product complexity rather than volume. The result is that simple high volume products would be overcosted whereas complex low-volume products would be undercosted. To illustrate, consider the overhead costs associated with starting a production line. Both a high-volume product (which is associated with a large number of labour and machine-time) and a low-volume product (which is associated with a small amount of labour and machine-time) many require the same amount of set up time/cost. However, since setup costs (along with all other overheads) are allocated only on the basis of production volume, the high-volume product would receive a larger **allocation** of set up cost. Thus, it would be overcosted. The low-volume product would obviously receive a smaller **allocation** of setup cost, and, thus, would be undercosted.

Cost distortion results from overcosting of high-volume products and undercosting of low-volume products.

The use of volume-related allocation base for allocating overheads/production cost centre expenses to products/jobs would, thus, lead to product **cost distortion** in an environment of complex and high product variety. **Cost distortion results from overcosting of high-volume products and undercosting of low-volume products**. To illustrate the nature of the distortion, consider the case of two pen manufacturers: **(i)** Montex Pen Manufacturing Company Ltd. and **(ii)** Luxor Pen Manufacturing Company Ltd.

Assume Luxor makes one-model one-colour (black) 5,00,000 pens. Montex also makes 5,00,000 pens, but of different colours, sizes, varieties ranging between specialty pens with annual production as low as 50 pens per year to high volume standard (blue and black) pens whose annual production volume are each about 50,000 per year. Even though both Luxor and Montex make the same product and physical output, Montex has a highly varied mix. It would have about the same cost of materials, require the same number of labour/machine-hours for actual production but it would also require much higher indirect and support costs because of its more varied product mix and complex production task as compared to Luxor. The requirement of much larger production support staff of Montex would be to **(i)** schedule machine and production runs, **(ii)** perform setups, **(iii)** inspect produced items after setup, **(iv)** move materials, **(v)** ship orders, **(vi)** expedite orders, **(vii)** rework defective items, **(viii)** design new products, **(ix)** improve existing products, **(x)** negotiate with vendors, **(xi)** schedule material receipts, **(xii)** order, receive and inspecting materials and parts, and **(xii)** update and maintain the much larger computer-based information system. It would also operate with considerably higher levels of idle time, setup time, overtime, inventory, rework and scrap.[1] Montex would naturally require many more resources to support its highly varied mix.

Based on the TCS, the overhead costs would be allocated/applied on the basis of their respective production volumes. The black and blue pens (50,000 each) represent about 10 per cent of Montex's output (5,00,000 units). About 10 per cent of its overhead would be applied to each of them. A low volume specialty product (50 pens per year) represents only 0.1 per cent of its output. Obviously, 0.1 per cent of its overhead would be allocated to the low-volume product. The TCS would, therefore, report essentially identical product costs for **all** products (standard/high-volume as well as specialty/low-volume) irrespective of their relative production volumes. However, considerably more of Montex's per unit indirect and support costs are required for the low-volume specialty pens than for the high-volume black and blue pens. Thus, the TCS would systematically and grossly underestimate the cost of resources for low-volume pens and would overestimate the cost of high-volume/standard black and blue pens (products). **The activity-based costing (ABC) system eliminates this major source of cost distortion**. The next section illustrates how the ABC system provides a solution to the inadequacies of the TCS in terms of these cost distortions.

Activity Based Costing/Management (ABC/ABM) System

The traditional costing system uses actual departments or cost centres for accumulating and redistributing/allocating costs. The ABC system, instead of using **cost centres**, uses **activities** for accumulating costs. The focus shifts from what the money was being spent on (e.g. labour, equipment, supplies and so on) to what the resources required by the spending were actually doing. The resource expenses are assigned to activities based on how much of the resource expenses are required or used to perform the activities. **The ABC system is a system based on activities linking spending on resources to the products/services produced/delivered to customers.**

The ABC system first accumulates indirect resource costs for each of the activities of a particular plant, department, value-chain function or organisation and then assigns the costs of activities to the products, services or other costs o the activity. One of the most important difference between the TCS and the ABC system is the extent of allocation across the value chain. The TCS generally allocates only indirect production costs to the products. These are the only costs that can be added to the inventory value of a product for financial reporting purpose and the TCS often focuses on simply measuring such inventory values. It normally does not allocate the costs of other value chain functions because these are not appropriate costs to include in inventory. The ABC system, in contrast, focuses on the costs that are important to decision-makers. It often expands allocation of costs beyond production to processes such as design, marketing, order processing and customer services. As a result, though more complex, ABC generates more accurate and useful costs to aid decision-making.

ABC System is a system based on activities linking spending on resources to the products/services produced/delivered to customers.

The basic idea of ABC is that costs are grouped accordingly to what drives (causes) them to be incurred. These cost drivers are used as the absorption base. **Cost drivers** are defined as those activities/transactions that are significant determinants of cost. In other words, the cost driver is an activity that generates cost. It is a structural determinant of cost-related activity. Since activities are presumed to cause costs, a link should be made between activities and products by assigning costs of activities to products based on an individual products demand for each activity. Costs are grouped into pools according to the activities which derive them. For example, a cost pool may be procurement of goods. All the costs associated with procurement, namely, ordering, inspection, storing and so on would be included in this cost pool and cost driver identified. The procurement cost per acquisition is then calculated. This provides a means to trace the cost of procurement to individual products. Thus, ABC focuses on different costs for different purposes and the identification of only those costs that are relevant to a particular decision.

Cost Allocation

The ABC system uses a two-stage approach, similar to but more general than traditional cost system: **(i)** tracing costs to activities and **(ii)** tracing costs from activities to products.

Tracing Costs to Activities The first step in cost allocation under the ABC system is to identify major activities that cause overhead costs to be incurred. Some of the activities are related to production volume but others are not. The costs of resources consumed performing these activities are grouped into costs pools. Some common activities and associated costs are listed in Exhibit 12.2 (Columns 1 and 2).

EXHIBIT 12.2 Common Activities and Associated Costs/Cost Drivers

Major Activities (1)	*Associated Costs* (2)	*Cost Driver* (3)
Processing purchase orders for materials and parts	Labour costs for workers determining order quantities, contacting vendors, and preparing purchase orders	Number of purchase orders processed
Handling material and parts	Labour costs for workers handling material and parts, depreciation of equipment used to move material and parts	Number of material requisitions
Inspecting incoming material and parts	Labour costs for workers performing inspections, depreciation of equipment used to test strength of materials, tolerances, etc.	Number of receipts

(*Contd.*)

(*Contd.*)

Setting up equipment	Labour costs for workers involved in setups, depreciation of equipment used to adjust equipment	Number of setups
Producing goods using manufacturing equipment	Depreciation on manufacturing equipment	Number of machine-hours
Supervising assembly workers	Salary of assembly supervisors	Number of assembly labour-hours
Inspecting finished goods	Labour cost for finished goods inspections, depreciation of equipment used to test whether finished goods meet customer specifications, etc.	Number of inspections
Packing customer orders	Labour cost for packing workers, cost of packing materials, etc.	Number of boxes packed

Tracing Costs from Activities to Products The next step is to assign costs to products using cost driver as a measure of activity. Activity cost drivers represent the quantity of activities used to produce individual products. ***Activity cost drivers are measures that identify the linkage between activities and cost objects; they serve as quantitative measures of the output of activities***. Cost drivers associated with some activities are listed in Exhibit 12.3 (Column 3).

Activity cost drivers are measures that identify the linkage between activities and cost objects; they serve as quantitative measures of the output of activities.

It may be noted that some of the cost drivers are volume-related, for example, machine-hours and assembly labour-hours. One example of costs not related to production volume is number of inspections. Some low-volume products that involve complex/fragile parts may need a large number of inspections, whereas some high-volume products that involve simple/rugged parts may need relatively few inspections. Similarly, number of setups is another cost driver that may not be related to volume. Both low-volume and high-volume products may require the same number of setups.

Selecting Activity Cost Drivers Activity cost drivers are the central innovation of ABC system. They are also the most difficult to measure, particularly the quantity of each activity cost driver used by each product. Each firm must decide how many separate activities and related cost pools and cost drivers to identify. If too many activities are identified, the system will be unnecessarily costly and confusing. For example, if a company produces 200 products and identifies 100 key activities, it must account for 20,000 (200 × 100) product-activity relations. On the other hand, if too few activities are used, ABC system is not likely to produce accurate data. The selection of an activity cost driver reflects a subjective trade-off between accuracy and cost of measurement.

A firm can choose from three types of activity cost drivers: **(i)** Transaction, **(ii)** Duration, and **(iii)** Intensity (direct charging).

Transaction Drivers **Transaction drivers are used to count the frequency of an activity/the number of times an activity is performed**. They assume that the same quantity of resources is required every time an activity is performed. An example of transaction driver is the number of setups. If the variation in the quantity of resources used by each activity is small, that is, all setup times are between, say, 40 and 50 minutes, a transaction driver would be fine for assigning activity expenses to the cost object. If, however, the amount of resources required to perform the activity varies considerably, that is, the setup times range from 40 minutes to 7 hours, transaction driver would be the least expensive as well as the least accurate. The use

Transaction drivers are used to count the frequency of an activity/number of times an activity is performed.

of a transaction driver will overcost simple products and undercost complex products. Duration drivers avoid this distortion.

Duration drivers represent the amount of time required to perform an activity.

Duration Drivers **Duration drivers represents the amount of time required to perform an activity**. Example of duration drivers are setup-hours, inspection-hours, direct labour-hours. They are more accurate than transaction drivers but more expensive to implement.

Intensity drivers are used to charge directly for the resources used each time an activity is performed.

Intensity Drivers **Intensity drivers are used to charge directly for the resources used each time an activity is performed**. In cases where a particularly complex product may require special setup and quality control personnel, as well as special gauging and test equipment each time the machine is setup to produce the product, activity costs should be charged directly to the output based on work orders or other records that accumulate the activity expenses incurred for that output. Intensity drivers are the most accurate but the most expensive to implement.

The choice of an appropriate cost driver involves balancing the benefits of increased accuracy against the cost of increased measurement. The goal of the ABC system should be to have the best cost system—not the most accurate.

Activity cost driver rate is the amount determined by dividing the activity expenses by the total quantity of the activity cost driver.

Activity Cost Driver Rate The next step is to compute the Activity Cost Driver Rate (ACDR). **The ACDR is the amount determined by dividing the activity expenses by the total quantity of the activity cost driver.** This rate is used to assign activity costs to individual products.

Activity-Based Costing Products Profitability Report Finally, ABC Products Profitability Report is prepared. It combines activity expenses assigned to each product with their direct (labour and material) costs. The activity expenses assigned to a product is arrived at by multiplying the ACDR by the quantity of each activity cost driver used by each product.

Illustration We will now illustrate the step-wise cost allocation of overhead costs and the preparation of the ABC Products Profitability Report for the Montex Pen Manufacturing Company in Exhibit 12.1.

(A) The total overheads (aggregating ₹9,00,000) were comprised of the following:

Expense category	*Expenses*
Indirect labour	₹3,00,000
Fringe benefits	2,40,000
Computer system expenses	1,50,000
Machinery	1,20,000
Maintenance	60,000
Energy	30,000
Total	9,00,000

(B) The activities and activity expenses of the Montex Pen Manufacturing Company are summarised below:

Overhead Cost Items	*Cost Driver*				*Total Expenses*
	Handle Production Runs	*Set up*	*Support Machines*	*Run Machine Products*	
1 Indirect labour and 1/2 fringe benefits	50%	40%	10%	—	₹4,20,000

(Contd.)

(Contd.)

2 Computer expenses	80%	—	20%	—	1,50,000
3 Machine depreciation	—	—	—	100%	1,20,000
4 Maintenance	—	—	—	100%	60,000
5 Energy	—	—	—	100%	30,000
Activity Expenses	₹3,30,000*	₹1,68,000†	₹72,000□	₹2,10,000△	7,80,000

*(₹4,20,000 × 0.50) + (₹1,50,000 × 0.80) = ₹2,10,000 + ₹1,20,000 = ₹3,30,000

†(₹4,20,000 × 0.40) = ₹1,68,000

□(₹4,20,000 × 0.10) + (₹1,50,000 × 0.20) = ₹42,000 + ₹30,000 = ₹72,000

△(₹1,20,000 + ₹60,000 + ₹30,000) × 1.00 = ₹2,10,000

Activity Cost Driver	*Products*				
	Blue Pens	*Black Pens*	*Red Pens*	*Purple Pens*	*Total@*
Direct labour-hour/unit	0.02	0.02	0.02	0.02	2,000
Machine-hour/unit	0.10	0.10	0.10	0.10	10,000
Production runs	70.00	65.00	50.00	15.00	200
Setup time/run	4.00	2.40	5.60	5.60	—
Total setup time (hour)	280.00	156.00	280.00	84.00	800
Number of products	1.00	1.00	1.00	1.00	4

@Total labour and machine-hours are obtained by multiplying the unit amounts by the quantity of each type of pen sold (from Exhibit 12.1), that is, 25,000 blue, 20,000 black, 4,500 red and 500 purple pens.

(C) The activity cost driver rates and the activity expenses assigned to products are shown below:

Activity	*Activity Expense*	*Activity Cost Driver*	*Activity Cost Driver Quantity*	*Activity Cost Driver Rate*	
Handle production runs	₹3,30,000	Number of production runs	200	₹1,650	per run
Set up machines	1,68,000	Number of setup hours	800	210	per setup hour
Support products	72,000	Number of products	4	18,000	per product
Run machines	2,10,000	Number of machine-hours	10,000	2.10	per machine-hour
Total	7,80,000				

Activity Expenses Assigned to Products

Activity	*ACDR*	*ACDQ for Blue*	*Activity Expenses: Blue*	*ACDQ for Black*	*Activity Expenses: Black*	*ACDQ For Red*	*Activity Expenses: Red*	*ACDQ for Purple*	*Activity Expenses: Purple*
(1)	*(2)*	*(3)*	*(4)*	*(5)*	*(6)*	*(7)*	*(8)*	*(9)*	*(10)*
Handle Production Run	₹1,650	70	₹1,15,500	65	₹1,07,250	50	₹82,500	15	₹24,750
Setup Machines	210	280	58,800	156	32,760	280	58,800	84	17,640
Support Products	18,000	1	18,000	1	18,000	1	18,000	1	18,000
Run Machines	2.10	5,000	1,05,000	4,000	84,000	900	18,900	100	210

Note: ACDR = Activity Cost Driver Rate; ACDQ = Activity Cost Driver Quantity

(D) The ABC product profitability report for the Montex Pen Manufacturing Company is shown in Exhibit 12.3.

EXHIBIT 12.3 Activity-Based Costing Products Profitability Report

	Blue Pens	Black Pens	Red Pens	Purple Pens	Total
Sales revenues	₹11,25,000	₹9,00,000	₹2,09,250	₹24,750	₹22,59,000
Material cost	3,75,000	3,00,000	70,200	8,250	7,53,450
Direct labour cost	1,50,000	1,20,000	27,000	3,000	3,00,000
Gross Margin	6,00,000	4,80,000	1,12,050	13,500	12,05,550
Overheads:					
— 50% fringe benefit on direct labour	60,000	48,000	10,800	1,200	1,20,000
— Handle production runs	1,15,500	1,07,250	82,500	24,250	3,30,000
— Setup machines	58,800	32,760	58,800	17,640	1,68,000
— Support products	18,000	18,000	18,000	18,000	72,000
— Run machines	1,05,000	84,000	18,900	2,100	2,10,000
Total	3,57,300	2,90,010	1,89,000	63,690	9,00,000
Operating income	**2,42,700**	**1,89,990**	**(76,950)**	**(50,190)**	**3,05,550**
Return on sales (%)	21.7	21.1	(36.8)	(202.8)	13.5

COMMENT: First, the return on sale (as a measure of profitability) according to the ABC system (Exhibit 12.3) is quite different from the return on sale according to the TCS (Exhibit 12.1). The two specialty pens (red and purple) are the most profitable according to the TCS. In sharp contrast, the blue and black pens are the only profitable pens according to the ABC systems and the red and purple pens are the most unprofitable. The reason for these differences is that incremental revenues from sale of red and purple pens are not able to cover the additional expenses caused by increase in overhead resources cost to support a large computer system and more indirect and support employees. The TCS, allocating overhead costs proportional to direct labour cost has assigned too much costs to the high-volume, simple products (black and blue pens) and too little cost to the low-volume and more complex products (red and purple pens). The production of complex, low-volume products creates disproportionate demands for resources that perform setups, handle production runs and support products. Secondly, the ABC profitability report contains far more information than the highly aggregated TCS-based report. In a single item (overheads), it aggregates a complex set of activities performed by the indirect and support resources for the four types of pens. The ABC-based report shows the cost of all the activities performed for each type of pen.

Activity-Based Management (ABM)

The ABM is a management tool that involves analysing and costing activities with the goal of improving efficiency and effectiveness. It is closely related to the ABC but it differs from the **ABC** in its primary goal. While ABC focuses on activities with the object of measuring costs of products/activities produced by them, the focus of ABM is on activities with a view to managing the activities themselves. In other words, resources are traced in ABC to activities to facilitate costing of products/services; resources are traced in ABM to activities to facilitate evaluation of activities. To clarify the difference, consider activity involved in setting up equipment for a production run. The ABC seeks to measure the cost of setup and then assign a cost to product based on how many setups each product requires. The ABM would focus on ways to improve the setup process and ways to eliminate the demand for setup activity (thus reducing setup costs).

Activity-based management refers to a set of actions that management can take, based on information from an ABC study to increase/improve profitability.

The ABM refers to a set of actions that management can take, based on information from an ABC study/system, to increase/improve profitability. The information contained in Exhibit 12.3 provides numerous insights about how to increase the profitability of Montex pens. To be able to compete in both the high-volume (blue and black pens) and the low-volume, specialty (red and purple pens), the profitability of the Montex pens can be significantly increased by a combination of a set of actions, namely, **(i)** repricing, **(ii)** increase in sales volume, **(iii)** process improvement and **(iv)** engineering and design improvements.

Repricing of Unprofitable Products One set of actions to improve profitability of Montex pens involves repricing of the two unprofitable pens—red and purple so as to cover their production costs. The red and purple pens can also be made profitable by **(i)** modifying distribution arrangements, **(ii)** changing their product design so that they can be built with simpler and fewer parts and **(iii)** imposing minimum order sizes to eliminate short, unprofitable production runs.

Increase in Sales Volume A simultaneous set of actions to improve profitability of Montex pens is to increase the sales volume of the highly profitable pens, namely, blue and black to generate incremental revenues in excess of their incremental costs.

Process Improvement Yet another ABC-based management action to improve profitability of Montex pens may relate to improving processes. For example, the Montex Pen Manufacturing Company may focus on how to reduce setup times so that the low-volume red and purple pens would require less resources and, therefore, less cost to produce, rather than try to run their production equipment faster.

Engineering and Design Improvements This set of actions would focus on seeking ways to design products that would be easier to produce and would require fewer modifications once introduced. This would reduce the resource demands by a product-sustaining activity.

The combined effect of the above set of actions would be that Montex Pen Company would produce the same volume and mix of products with fewer resources.

Cost of Resource Capacity[2]

LO 12.2 Illustrate the measurement of the cost of resource capacity

For the computation of the activity cost driver rates (ACDRs) in the preceding section, the expenses of each activity were divided by the output form that activity (such as number of production runs, number of setup-hours, number of products and number of machine-hours) to obtain the average cost. It is, however, possible that resources supplied exceeded the used resources. For example, in the Montex Pen case in the preceding section, although only 200 production runs were scheduled during the quarter, the indirect labour supplied could have performed 240 production runs. The unit cost per production was (₹3,30,000 ÷ 200 runs) ₹1,650. The ₹3,30,000 of resources could actually have handled 240 productions runs. There was, in other words, overestimation of the cost of handling each production run. A better estimate for the cost of resources to handle each production can, therefore, be obtained by dividing the capacity expenses by the practical capacity of work the resources could perform.

Practical capacity is the maximum amount of work that can be performed by resources supplied for production/services.

Practical Capacity

Practical capacity is the maximum amount of work that can be performed by resources supplied for production/services. It is expressed as a predetermined percentage of theoretical capacity. **Theoretical capacity means the normal working hours of a machine/worker (employee).** If the theoretical capacity is 50 hours per week and the practical capacity is 80 per cent of the theoretical capacity, the practical capacity would be 40 hours (50 × 0.80) per week per employee. The practical capacity of 80 per cent

Theoretical capacity means the normal working hours of a machine/worker/employee.

(40 hours per week) is based on the assumption that 20 per cent time of employees is utilised for breaks, arrival and departure and so on, which are not related to actual work performance. Similarly, 20 per cent represents allowance for downtime of machines due to maintenance, repair and rescheduling fluctuations and so on. The unit cost per production run = cost of capacity supplied ÷ practical cost of resources supplied, that is, ₹3,30,000 ÷ 240 runs = ₹1,375. Compared to the cost per production run based on actual work performed (₹1,650), the unit cost based on practical capacity is considerably lower (₹1,375).

Unused Capacity

Cost of unused capacity is the amount/expense of resources unused during production.

The cost per production run based on the actual work performed (i.e. 200 production runs) of ₹1,650, thus, includes, in effect, two types of costs: **(i)** the cost of resources used for actual production runs handled and **(ii)** cost of unused capacity. **The cost of unused capacity is the amount/expense of resources unused during production** (240 – 200 = 40 production runs).

The unused capacity should not be treated as general cost to be shared across all production lines. Such a cost should not be assigned to products produced/customers served during a period. It should also not be ignored. In order to ensure that the activity cost driver rate reflects the efficiency of allocation of cost to each production run, the cost of supply resources capacity to do work (₹3,30,000) should be related to the quantity of work the resources **can** perform rather than that actually performed (i.e. 240 production runs and not 200 production runs).

The cost of unused capacity should be assigned to the person/department/customer/market segment concerned with/responsible for it. For example, if the unused capacity was intended to meet anticipated demands from a particular customer/market segment, such cost caused by lower-than-expected demand can be assigned to the person/organisational unit responsible for that customer/segment on a lump-sum basis. Similarly, the cost of unused capacity related to a particular product line should be assigned to the product line concerned due to non-materialistion of demand. In brief, in assigning costs of unused capacity, the costs should be traced at the level where decisions affecting supply of capacity resources and the demand for these resources are made in the organisation/company.

ABC for Marketing, Selling and Distribution Expenses

LO 12.3 Show activity-based costing for marketing, selling, distribution and administration jobs

In the preceding section, we have illustrated the ABC system for allocation of manufacturing overheads. With focus on customer satisfaction and market-oriented strategies, expenses related to marketing, selling and distribution have become significant components of the overheads costs of companies. Many of these expenses do not relate to individual products/product lines but are associated with individual customers, market segments and distribution channels. This section illustrates activity-based costing for marketing, selling, distribution and administration costs.

Tracing Costs to Customers

The focus of ABC system is on tracing marketing, selling and distribution costs to customer segments. To illustrate, consider two customers, Simple and Complex, of Avon Industries Ltd. Avon Ltd. currently uses the traditional/conventional cost accounting system and distributes the marketing, selling and distribution to customers based on sales revenue, that is, approximately one-third of total sales. The traditional costing-based profitability of Simple and Complex (customers) is summarised in Exhibit 12.4:

EXHIBIT 12.4 Traditional Costing Based Customer Profitability Analysis

Particulars	*Simple*	*Complex*
Sales revenue	₹12,80,000	₹12,60,000
Costs of goods sold	6,16,000	6,24,000
Gross margin	6,64,000	6,36,000
Marketing, selling, distribution and administrative expenses (0.33 × sales)	4,22,000	4,15,800
Operating profit	2,41,600	2,20,200
Profit (as percentage of sale)	18.8	17.5

Identification of Activities and Cost Drivers The first step in the ABC system for marketing, selling and distribution overheads is identifying the activities performed by the resources and selecting activity cost drivers linking each activity to individual customers. The activity, activity cost description and activity cost driver are listed below:[3]

Activity	*Activity Cost Driver*
1 Marketing and technical support	1 Estimated proportion of time spent on each customer
2 Travel to customers	2 Actual expenditure
3 Distribution of sales catalogue	3 Number of mailings
4 Servicing of customers	4 Estimated proportion of time spent on each customer and supplies used by them
5 Handle customer orders	5 Number or orders
6 Warehouse inventory for customers	6 Quality of inventory and space required by customer
7 Shipping/despatch to customers	7 Actual records

Identify Resource Spending The next step is to identify the resource spending in the various accounts. The customer profile of Simple and Complex is as follows. Simple orders only a few products in large quantities, places order predictably and with long lead times, and requires little sales and technical support. But Complex requires a great deal of handholding and continuously inquires whether products could be modified to meet his specific needs. In addition to marketing resources, many technical resources are required to service Complex. Complex also places many small orders for special products, requires expeditious delivery and pays slowly, increasing the demands on order processing, invoicing and accounts receivable process of Avon Ltd. Suppose the following marketing, selling, distribution and administrative costs are identified for the two customers.

Activity	*Simple*	*Complex*
1 Marketing and technical support	₹28,000	₹2,16,000
2 Travel to customers	4,800	28,800
3 Distribution of sales catalogue	400	400
4 Servicing of customers	16,000	1,68,000
5 Handling customer orders	2,000	72,000
6 Warehouse inventory	3,200	35,200
7 Ship/despatch to customers	50,400	168,000
Total activity expenses	1,04,800	6,88,400

Customer Profitability Analysis Report The next step is to prepare a customer profitability analysis as shown in Exhibit 12.5.

EXHIBIT 12.5 Activity-Based Costing Customer Profitability Analysis

Particulars	*Simple*	*Complex*
Sales revenue	₹12,80,000	₹12,60,000
Cost of goods sold	6,16,000	6,24,000
Gross margin	6,64,000	6,36,000
Marketing, selling and distribution expenses:		
Marketing and technical support	28,000	2,16,000
Travel to customers	4,800	28,000
Distribution of sales catalogue	400	400
Servicing of customers	16,000	1,68,000
Handling customer orders	2,000	72,000
Warehouse inventory	3,200	35,000
Ship/despatch to customers	50,400	1,68,000
Total activity expenses	1,04,800	6,88,400
Operating profit	5,59,200	(–52,400)
Profits as percentage of sales (operating margin)	43.7	(–4.2)

COMMENT: Both customers—Simple and Complex—are profitable according to the traditional customer profitability analysis (Exhibit 12.4). But according to the ABC customer profitability analysis (Exhibit 12.5), Simple is a highly profitable customer while Complex is a very unprofitable customer. The reason is that ordering and support activities of Simple places few demands on the Avon's marketing, selling, distribution and administrative resource as a result of which its operating margin is much higher.

Managing Customer Profitability[4]

Managing customer profitability is the use of ABC customer profitability analysis to manage profitable and unprofitable customers.

The ABC customer profitability analysis of Avon Ltd. can be used to manage its profitable and unprofitable customers.

Profitable Customers Such customers are low-cost ones to serve and also offer high margin. Avon Ltd should, if necessary, offer discounts, incentives and special services to retain such valuable customers to protect them from competitors.

Unprofitable Customers These customers drag down the profitability of companies due to low margin and high cost of servicing which can be caused by **(i)** unpredictable order patterns, **(ii)** small order size, **(iii)** large demand on technical and sales personnel and so on. The unprofitable customers can be transformed into profitable ones through a whole range of actions, such as, process improvement, activity-based pricing and managing customer relationships.

Process Improvement One set of actions to make unprofitable customers profitable is to improve the internal operations to reduce/lower the costs of servicing customers. For example, the problem associated with smaller order sizes could be resolved by reducing the batch-related costs, namely, setups and order handling. This would enable accommodation of customer preferences without increasing overall prices. Electronic systems greatly reduce the cost of processing larger quantities of small orders. Similarly, companies can customise their products at the latest possible stage to meet customer preferences for large variety of products. They can also use information technology to increase the linkages from design to manufacturing so as to be able to offer greater variety and customisation without additional costs.

Activity-Based Pricing Activity-based pricing prices orders and not products. When prices are based on valid cost information, customers would shift their ordering, shipping/despatching and distribution patterns in a way so as to lower total supply-chain costs for the benefit of customers as well as suppliers.

Pricing is the most powerful tool to transform unprofitable customers into profitable customers. Activity-based pricing sets a base price for a standard quantity for each standard product. For any special services, the company may provide several options with associated prices. The prices for special services may recover the activity-based cost-to-serve and allow the customer to choose from the features of services it wishes at a price to cover the cost of providing those features/services for the customers.

Another option for the Avon Ltd. may be to earn a margin on special services by pricing them above the cost of services. Price surcharges could be imposed after designing and producing special variants for a customer's particular needs. Discounts could be offered when the ordering pattern lowers the cost of supplying it.

Managing Relationships Finally, companies can convert unpredictable customers into profitable customers by persuading them to increase the scope of the purchases of their other products/services. The margin from increased purchases of other products/services would contribute to cover customer-sustaining costs.

ABC FOR SERVICE COMPANIES

LO 12.4 Discuss the role of activity-based cost systems for service companies

The ABC system is as much applicable and useful to a service company as it is to a manufacturing company. Service organisations include companies in **(a)** financial services (i.e. banks, insurance organisations, money managers), **(b)** transportation (i.e. airlines, roads and railways), **(c)** telecommunications, **(d)** wholesale and retail, **(e)** healthcare and so on. This section illustrates the ABC model for a service company with particular reference to a telecommunication company.

Cost Structure of Service Companies

As shown in an earlier section, the ABC system in a manufacturing company focuses on the service component and not on the direct (material and labour) costs of manufacturing operations. It addresses the support resources for the manufacturing process, such as, purchasing, scheduling, inspecting, designing, supporting products and processes and handling customers and orders. The direct costs are traced to individual products.

Service companies have a unique cost structure. Virtually all the costs of a service company are indirect/fixed. A service company has little or no direct material—its personnel provide indirect support to products/customers—and, hence the company does not have direct/traceable costs to serve as allocation base. The variable cost (i.e. the increase in spending due to an incremental transaction/customer) is practically zero. For example, for a telecommunication company, handling one more phone call from a customer/one more data transfer involves no incremental spending. Therefore, the cost to provide a service based on variable costs by a service company may be close to zero.

Customer Costs

Customer costs Basic operating costs of service companies are determined by customer behaviour.

In contrast to manufacturing companies, customer behaviour determines the basic operating costs of products/services of service companies. For example, customers of a telecommunications company can order a basic service in several ways, namely, through a phone call, a letter, or a visit to a local unit.

A customer may order two/one phone line(s). An engineer may have to go there to install a new line or may make a change at the local switching centre. A customer may make only one request or several and can pay either by direct debit over the Internet, a telephone banking transfer, a mailed cheque or in person. The cost of each option is obviously quite different. Therefore, far more relevant and useful information would be available to the telecom company by measuring revenues/costs at the customer level rather than at the product level. Service companies should, therefore, identify the differential profitability of individual customers as they determine the quantity of demands for the operating activities.

In addition, a customer may have more than one relationship with a service company. For example, a customer of a telecom company may have, in addition to the basic phone line, a high speed data line, a long distance account, a service contract, equipment rentals and so on. The service company should act on total relationship profitability of a customer and not on the profitability of just a single service.

ABC Model Illustrated

The structure/construction of the ABC system in a service company is almost identical to that of a manufacturing company, that is, **(i)** identify activities, **(ii)** assign resources expenses to activities, **(iii)** determine activity cost drivers, **(iv)** calculate activity cost driver rate and **(v)** compute product/customer cost. We illustrate below the ABC model for a service company with reference to IBM-Daksh.

The billing department of IBM-Daksh customer care centre requires accurate and useful information about the cost of providing account inquiry and bill printing services for its 1,20,000 residential and 20,000 commercial customer accounts. A local service centre has offered to provide all the functions currently performed by IBM-Daksh's billing department at ₹21.5 per residential account and ₹40 per commercial account.

All costs in the billing department are indirect. There are no direct or unallocated costs. The resources used to support the billing department of IBM-Daksh in the previous month are summarised below:

Expense	*Expense amount*
Telecommunications	₹2,92,600
Computer expenses	8,90,000
Supervisors	1,68,000
Paper	36,000
Occupancy	2,35,000
Account inquiry labour	8,67,300
Printing machines	2,75,000
Billing labour	2,81,750
Verification labour	56,250
Other resources	3,35,000
	34,37,500

The billing department of IBM-Daksh uses a traditional costing system that allocates all indirect costs based on (i) the number of account inquiries, namely, 20,000 (80 per cent) for residential customers and 5,000 (20 per cent) for commercial customers.

Suppose IBM-Daksh wants to introduce ABC system for its billing department. They have identified the following activities and the related cost drivers:

Activity	*Cost driver*
Account billing	Number of printed pages
Bill verification	Number of accounts verified
Account inquiry	Number of inquiries
Correspondence	Number of letters
Other activities	Number of printed pages

The resources used to perform the activities and the activities performed are shown here:

Resources Used to Perform Activity	*Activity Performed (%)*					
	Account Inquiry	*Correspondence*	*Billing*	*Verification*	*Others*	*Total*
Supervisor	40	10	30	—	20	100
Account inquiry labour	90	10	—			100
Billing labour	—	—	30	70	—	100
Verification labour	—	—	—	100	—	100
Paper	—	—	100	—	—	100
Computer	45	5	35	10	5	100
Telecommunications	90	—	—	—	10	100
Occupancy	65	—	15	—	20	100
Printing machines	—	5	90	—	5	100
All other resources	—	—	—	—	100	100

The number of cost driver units for the billing department of IBM-Daksh is shown below:

Activity	*Cost driver units*	*Number of cost driver units*		
		Residential	*Commercial*	*Total*
1 Account inquiry	Number of inquiries	20,000	5,000	25,000
2 Correspondence	Number of letters	1,800	1,000	2,800
3 Bill printing	Number of printed pages	1,20,000	40,000	1,60,000
4 Verification	Number of accounts verified	—	20,000	20,000
5 Other activities	Number of printed pages	1,20,000	40,000	1,60,000

REQUIRED:

(a) Using the traditional costing system, should the IBM-Daksh accept the offer of the local service centre to perform all the functions?

(b) Would the decision be different with ABC system?

Solution

(a) Cost Computation for Billing Department (Traditional Costing System)

Particulars	*Residential*		*Commercial*
1 Cost	₹27,50,000@		₹6,87,500@@
2 Number of inquiries	20,000	(0.80)	5,000 (0.20)
3 Number of accounts	1,20,000		20,000
4 Cost per account (1 ÷ 3)	22.9		34.4

@₹34,37,500 × (0.80)   @@₹34,37,500 × (0.20)

Decision: The billing department should accept the offer of the local service centre to service residential accounts as there is a saving of ₹1.4 per account (₹22.9 – ₹21.5). But it should continue to service the commercial accounts because of lower cost of ₹5.6 (₹40 – ₹34.4).

(b) The computation of activity-based cost per account for each customer class (residential and commercial is illustrated below).

(b) (i) Total Traceable Costs

Resource	*Cost*	*Activity Cost Pool*				
		Account Inquiry	*Corres-pondence*	*Billing*	*Verification*	*Others*
1 Supervisors	₹1,68,000	₹67,200[a]	₹16,800[b]	₹50,400[c]	—	₹33,600[d]
2 Account inquiry labour	8,67,300	7,80,570	86,730	—	—	—
3 Billing labour	2,81,250	—	—	84,375	₹1,96,875	—
4 Verification labour	56,250	—	—	—	56,250	—
5 Paper	36,600	—	—	36,600	—	—
6 Computer	8,90,000	4,00,500	44,500	3,11,500	89,000	44,500
7 Telecommunications	2,92,600	2,63,340	—	—	—	29,260
8 Occupancy	2,35,000	1,52,750	—	35,250	—	47,000
9 Printing machines	2,75,000	—	13,750	2,47,500	—	13,750
10 Others	3,35,000	—	—	—	—	3,35,500
Total traceable cost	34,37,500	16,64,360	1,61,780	7,65,625	3,42,125	5,03,610

[a](₹16,8,000 × 0.40) [b](₹16,8,000 × 0.10) [c](₹1,68,000 × 0.30) [d](₹16,8,000 × 0.20)

(b) (ii) Costs Driver

Activity	*Traceable costs (1)*	*Number of Driver Units (2)*	*Cost per Driver Units [(1) ÷ (2)]*
Account inquiry	₹16,64,360	25,000 inquiries	₹66.5744
Correspondence	1,61,780	2,800 letters	57.7786
Account billing	7,65,625	1,60,000 printed pages	4.7852
Bill verification	3,42,125	20,000 accounts verified	17.1062
Other activities	5,03,610	1,60,000 printed pages	3.1476

(b) (iii) Cost per Customer Class

Activity	*Cost Per Driver Unit*	*Residential Customer Accounts*		*Commercial Customer Accounts*	
		Number of Driver Units	*Cost*	*Number of Driver Units*	*Cost*
(1)	*(2)*	*(3)*	*(4)*	*(5)*	*(6)*
Account inquiry	₹66.5744	20,000 inquiries	₹13,31,490	5,000 inquiries	₹3,32,870
Correspondence	57.7786	2,800 letters	1,04,001	1,000 letters	57,779
Account billing	4.7852	1,20,000 pages	5,74,224	40,000 pages	1,91,408
Billing verification	17.1062	—		— 20,000	accounts
3,42,124					
Other activities	3.1476	1,20,000 pages	3,77,712	40,000 pages	1,25,904
Total Costs			23,87,415		10,50,085
Number of accounts			1,20,000		20,000
Cost per account			₹19.90		₹52.50
Cost per account (traditional system)			22.90		34.40

COMMENTS: The traditional costing system overcosts the high-volume residential accounts (₹22.9) and substantially undercosts the low-volume complex commercial accounts (₹34.40). The cost per account for residential accounts using ABC system (₹19.9) is 13 per cent less than the cost generated by the traditional system [₹22.9 – ₹19.9 = (₹3 ÷ ₹22.9) × 100]. The cost per account of commercial accounts, using ABC system, is similarly more than the cost from the traditional system [₹52.50 – ₹34.10 = (₹16.42 ÷ ₹24.10) × 100 = 53%].

Decision: The ABC system gives a diametrically opposite decision. The billing department of IBM-Daksh should accept the offer of the local service centre to service commercial accounts as there is a saving of ₹12.10 (₹52.50 – ₹40). But it should continue to service the residential accounts because of lower cost of ₹1.6 (₹21.5 – ₹19.9).

PROs AND CONs

LO 12.5 Explain the pros and cons of activity-based costing system

The ABC system offers some real advantages but it also suffers from some major limitations. This section briefly describes the pros and cons of ABC system.

Advantages

A major benefit of ABC system is that, in contrast to the traditional costing system, it is not likely to undercost complex low-volume products and overcost high-volume simple products. This is so because the cost drivers used by the ABC system to assign costs are unrelated to volume and many more cost drivers are used.

The second benefit of the ABC system is that it may result in improved cost control. This is so because costs are broken into a number of activities rather than into a few cost pools. The managers know the costs of setups, inspections, order taking, stocking, moving inventory, and other key activities so that they see a need to improve efficiency and reduce costs.

Disadvantages

A major disadvantage of ABC system is that it is more expensive/costly to develop and maintain compared to a traditional costing system. For example, consider an ABC system with 25 cost pools applied to 100 different products. Assigning cost to 25 pools will be costly and 2,500 (25 pools × 100 products) allocations will have to be made to assign costs to products.

The most serious limitation of ABC system is that, in practice, it is used to develop the **full cost** of products. Since full costs include allocation of costs that are fixed (e.g. depreciation and supervisory salaries), the cost per unit generated by the ABC system does not measure the incremental costs needed to produce an item. An incremental information is required for decision-making. The fixed costs are sunk costs and sunk costs are not relevant for decisions since they are not incremental.

To conclude, for companies which do not use the information generated by the ABC system in an overly simplistic way (i.e. treat the full cost information as if it were full cost information), an ABC is likely to be, on the whole, quite beneficial.

SUMMARY

- The traditional costing system (TCS) assigns indirect costs/overheads to job/products in two stages: first, the accumulated cost are allocated to production departments (cost centers), second, the accumulated costs in cost centres are assigned to individual job/products on the basis of an overhead allocation rate based on/in proportion to some measure of volume of production such as direct labour cost, direct labour-hour rate, machine-hour rate and so on. It has the merit of being simple, easy to use and understand, and applied consistently from year to year. It is adequate for financial reporting of inventory valuation.

- It has, however, serious limitations/inadequacies due to its assumption that all overheads are proportionate to volume of production. Many overheads costs are, actually, not proportionate to volume. Examples of such costs are setup costs of machines/equipment, cost of inspection/handling of materials and so on. They are affected by complexity rather than volume. As a result, simple high-volume products would be overcosted (i.e. receive a larger allocation of overheads) and low-volume complex products would be undercosted (i.e. receive a smaller allocation of overheads). The use of volume-related allocation base of TCS for allocating overheads would result in product cost distortion in an environment of complex and high product variety. The ABC system eliminates this source of cost distortion.

LO 12.1

- The ABC system also uses a two-stage overhead allocation: **(i)** tracing costs to activities and **(ii)** tracing costs from activities to products/jobs.
- The first step is to identify major activities that cause/drive overhead costs to be incurred. Some of the activities are related to production volume (such as production runs, salary of supervisors and so on) but others are not (such as inspection/handling of materials, setting up equipment and so on). The cost of resources consumed in performing these activities are grouped into cost pools.
- The next step is to assign costs to products/jobs using cost drivers as a measure of activity. Cost drivers represent the quantity of activities used to produce individual products. They identify the linkage between activities and cost objects and serve as quantitative measures of the output of activities. In fact, they are the central innovation of ABC system. A firm can choose from three types of cost drivers: **(i)** transaction, **(ii)** duration and **(iii)** intensity (direct charging).
- Transaction cost drivers are used to count the frequency of an activity/number of times an activity is performed. It is the least expensive as well as the least accurate. Duration drivers represent the amount of time required to perform an activity (e.g. inspection-hours). They are more accurate than transaction drivers, but more expensive to implement. Intensity drivers are used to charge directly for the resources used each time an activity is performed. They are the most accurate but the most expensive to implement. The choice of an appropriate activity cost driver involves balancing the benefits of increased accuracy against the cost of increased measurement.
- The activity costs are assigned to individual jobs/products on the basis of activity cost driver rate (ACDR). The ACDR = activity expenses ÷ total quantity of the activity cost driver. The activity expenses assigned to a product = ACDR × quantity of each activity cost driver used by the product concerned.
- The activity-based management (ABM) refers to a set of actions that management can take, based on information from an ABC study, to increase/improve profitability. These include a combination of **(i)** repricing of unprofitable products, **(ii)** increasing sales volume of highly profitable products, **(iii)** process improvement (e.g. how to reduce setup times in contrast to faster run of production, equipment and **(iv)** engineering and design improvements. Their combined effect would be production of the same volume and mix of products with fewer resources.
- Practical capacity is a better measure of cost of resources to handle each production (i.e. capacity expenses ÷ practical capacity). It is the maximum amount of work that can be performed by resources supplied for production/services and is expressed as a percentage of theoretical capacity. Theoretical capacity means the normal working hours of a machine/working employee. The difference between theoretical capacity and practical capacity is the time utilised by the employees for breaks, arrivals, departures and so on, which are not related to actual work performance. It may also represent allowances for downtimes of machines due to maintenance, repair and rescheduling fluctuations and so on. The expenses of resources unused during the production (difference between theoretical capacity and practical capacity) is the cost of unused capacity. Such a cost should be assigned to the person/customer/department/market segment concerned with/responsible for it.

LO 12.2

- Marketing, selling and distribution expenses are significant components of overhead costs of companies. Most of these costs are associated with customers, market segments and distribution channels rather than to individual products. The ABC is applicable to such costs also. Its focus is on tracing these costs to customer segments. The activities performed by these services are first identified together with activity cost drivers linking each activity to individual customers. The resource spending in the various customer accounts are then identified. The final stage is preparation of customer profitability analysis.
- The ABC customer profitability analysis can be used to manage its profitable and unprofitable customers. To protect them from competitive inroads profitable customers may be offered discounts/incentives and special services to retain them. The unprofitable customers can be transformed into profitable customers through a number of actions: **(i)** process improvement, **(ii)** activity-based pricing and **(iii)** managing customer relationships.

LO 12.3

- The ABC system is as much applicable to service companies as it is to a manufacturing company. Service companies have a unique cost structure. Virtually all their costs are indirect/fixed. In contrast to manufacturing companies, customer behaviour determines the basic operating costs of products/services of service companies. They should, therefore, identify the differential profitability of individual customers as they determine the quantity of demands for their operating activities. Moreover, service companies should act on total relationship profitability of a customer and not on the profitability of just a single customer. The structure/construction of the ABC system of a service company is identical to that of a manufacturing company.

LO 12.4

- The ABC system has advantages as well as limitations. Its major benefits are: **(i)** it does not undercost complex low-volume products and overcost high-volume simple products, **(ii)** it may result in improved cost control. The limitations of ABC system are two-fold: **(a)** it is costly to develop and maintain and **(b)** it is used to develop full costs and does not measure the incremental costs needed to produce an item.

LO 12.5

REFERENCES

1. Anthony A.A., Kaplan, R.S. and Young, S.M., *Management Accounting*, Pearson (London, 2004), p. 126.
2. Ibid, p. 137.
3. Ibid, p. 144.
4. Ibid, p. 145.

SOLVED PROBLEMS

LO 12.2
LOD: E

P.12.1 Image Furnishing Ltd. manufacturers a variety of premium board room chairs. Its job-costing system is designed using an activity-based approach. There are two direct cost categories consisting of direct materials and direct manufacturing labour and three indirect costs pools representing three activity areas at the plant:

Manufacturing activity area	*Budgeted costs*	*Cost driver used as allocation base*	*Cost allocation rate*
Material handling	₹2,00,000	Parts	₹0.25
Cutting	21,60,000	Parts	2.50
Assembly	20,00,000	Direct manufacturing labour-hours	25.00

Two styles of chairs were produced in March: executive chair and chairman chair. Their quantities, direct material costs and other data for March are as follows:

Type of chair	Units produced	Direct material costs	Number of parts	Direct manufacturing labour-hours
Executive	5,000	₹6,00,000	1,00,000	7,500
Chairman	100	25,000	3,500	500

The direct manufacturing labour rate is ₹20 per hour. Assuming no beginning/ending inventory, compute the total manufacturing costs and units costs of the two types of chairs.

Solution

(a) Manufacturing Costs with Activity-based Costing

Particulars	Executive chair	Chairman chair
Direct manufacturing costs:		
Direct material costs	₹6,00,000	₹25,000
Direct manufacturing labour [(executive chair 7,500 labour-hours, chairman chair, 500 labour-hours) × ₹20]	1,50,000	10,000
	7,50,000	35,000
Indirect manufacturing costs:		
Material handling [(Executive chair, 1,00,000 parts; Chairman chair, 3,500 parts) × ₹0.25]	25,000	875
Cutting [(Executive chair, 1,00,000 parts; Chairman chair, 3,500 parts) × ₹2.50]	2,50,000	8,750
Assembly [(Executive chair, direct manufacturing labour-hours, 7,500; Chairman chair, direct manufacturing labour-hours, 500) × ₹25]	1,87,500	12,500
	4,62,500	22,125
Total manufacturing costs	12,12,500	57,125

P.12.2 The Aeronautical Ltd. has production facility specialising in jobs for the aircraft components market. The traditional costing system has two direct-cost categories, namely, direct materials and direct manufacturing labour and a single direct cost pool, that is, manufacturing overhead allocated on the basis of direct labour-hours. The indirect cost allocation rate would have been ₹115 direct manufacturing labour-hour. **LO 12.1, 2** **LOD: M**

The company has now decided to replace the single indirect cost pool with five indirect cost pools, representing five activity areas each with its own supervising and budget responsibility. The relevant data are as follows:

Activity area	Cost driver used as an allocation base	Cost allocation rate
Material handling	Parts	₹0.40
Lathe work	Turns	0.20
Milling	Machine-hours	20.00
Grinding	Parts	0.80
Testing	Units tested	15.00

Two representative jobs processed under the new system of the facility at the most recent period had the following features:

Particulars	Job 101	Job 102
Direct material costs per job	₹9,700	₹59,900
Direct manufacturing labour cost per job	750	11,250
Direct manufacturing labour-hours per job	25	375
Parts per job	500	2,000
Turns per job	20,000	60,000
Machine-hours per job	150	1,050
Units per job	10	200

REQUIRED:

(a) Compute the per unit manufacturing costs of each job under the traditional job-cutting system.
(b) Compute the per unit manufacturing costs of each job under the activity-based costing system.

Solution

(a) Manufacturing Costs with Traditional Job Costing System

Particulars	*Job 101*	*Job 102*
Direct manufacturing costs per job:		
Direct materials per job	₹9,700	₹59,900
Direct manufacturing labour per job	750	11,250
	10,450	71,150
Indirect manufacturing costs per job: (Job 101, 25 labour-hours; job 102, 375 labour-hours) × ₹115	2,875	43,125
Total manufacturing costs per job	13,325	1,14,275

(b) Manufacturing Costs with Activity-based Costing System

Particulars	*Job 101*	*Job 102*
Direct manufacturing costs per job:		
Direct materials per job	₹9,700	₹59,900
Direct manufacturing labour per job	750	11,250
	10,450	71,150
Indirect manufacturing costs:		
Material handling [(Job 101, 500 parts; Job 102, 2,000 parts) × ₹0.40]	200	800
Lathe work [(Job 101, 20,000 turns; Job 102, 60,000 turns) × ₹0.20]	4,000	12,000
Milling [(Job 101,150 machine-hours; Job 102, 1050 machine-hours) × ₹20]	3,000	21,000
Grinding [(Job 101, 500 parts; Job 102, 2,000 parts) × ₹0.80]	400	1,600
Testing [(Job 101, 10 units; Job 102, 200 units) × ₹15]	150	3,000
	7,750	38,400
Total manufacturing costs	18,200	1,09,550

P.12.3 A company, manufacturing two products, furnishes the following data for a year: **LO 12.1, 2** **LOD: E**

Product	*Annual output (Units)*	*Total machine-hours*	*Total number of purchase orders*	*Total number of set-ups*
A	5,000	20,000	160	20
B	60,000	1,20,000	384	44

The annual overheads are as under:

Volume-related activity costs	₹5,50,000
Setup-related costs	8,20,000
Purchase-related costs	6,18,000

You are required to calculate the cost per unit of each product A and B based on:

(i) Traditional method of charging overheads
(ii) Activity based costing method.

Solution

(i) Statement showing Cost per unit of Products: (A and B based on Traditional Method of Charging Overheads)

Total annual overheads (₹5,50,000 + 8,20,000 + 6,18,000)	₹19,88,000
Total machine hours	1,40,000
Machine-hour rate (₹19,88,000/1,40,000 hours)	14.2

Particulars	*Products*	
	A	*B*
Annual output (units)	5,000	60,000
Total machine-hours	20,000	1,20,000
Overhead cost	₹2,84,000*	₹17,04,000**
Overhead cost per unit	₹56.80@	₹28.40@@

*(20,000 × ₹14.20) **(1,20,000 × ₹14.20)

@(₹2,84,000/5,000 units) @@(₹17,04,000/60,000 units)

(ii) Statement showing Cost per unit Products (A and B based on Activity based Costing Method)

Machine-hour rate (₹5,50,000/1,40,000 hours)	₹3.93
Cost of one setup (₹8,20,000/64 setups)	12,812.50
Cost of purchase order (₹6,18,000/544 orders)	1,136.03

Particulars	*Products*	
	Product A	*Product B*
Total machine-hours	20,000.00	1,20,000.00
Cost related to volume activities	₹78,600.00@	4,71,600.00@@
Cost related to purchases	₹1,81,764.80*	₹4,36,235.52**
Cost related to setups	2,56,250.00$	₹5,63,750.00$$
Total costs	5,16,614.80	14,71,585.52
Annual output (units)	(÷) 5,000.00	(÷) 60,000.00
Cost per unit	₹103.32	₹24.53

@(20,000 hours × ₹3.93) @@(1,20,000 hours × ₹3.93)

*(160 orders × ₹1,136.03) **(384 orders × ₹1,136.03)

$(20 setups × ₹12,812.50) $$(44 set-ups × ₹12,812.50)

P.12.4 Family Store wants information about the profitability of individual product lines: soft drinks, fresh produce and packaged food. The store provides the following data for the current year for each product line: **LO 12.2** **LOD: M**

	Soft drinks	*Fresh produce*	*Packaged food*
Revenues	₹7,93,500	₹21,00,600	₹12,09,000
Cost of goods sold	6,00,000	15,00,000	9,00,000
Cost of bottles returned	12,000	0	0
Number of purchase orders placed	360	840	360
Number of deliveries received	300	2,190	660
Hours of shelf-stocking time	540	5,400	2,700
Items sold	1,26,000	11,04,000	3,06,000

Family Store also provides the following information for the current year:

Activity	Description of activity	Total cost	Cost-allocation base
Bottle returns	Returning of empty bottles	₹12,000	Direct tracing of soft drink line
Ordering	Placing of orders for purchases	1,56,000	1,560 purchase orders
Delivery	Physical delivery and receipt of goods	2,52,000	3,150 deliveries
Shelf-stocking	Stocking of goods on store shelves and on-going restocking	1,72,800	8,640 hours of shelf-stocking time
Customer support	Assistance provided to customers including checkout	3,07,200	15,36,000 items sold

REQUIRED:

(i) Family Store currently allocates support cost (all costs other than cost of goods sold) to product lines on the basis of cost of goods sold of each product line. Calculate the operating income and operating income as a % of revenues for each product line. **(ii)** If Family Store allocates support costs (other than cost of goods sold) to product lines using an activity-based costing system, calculate the operating income and operating income as a % of revenues for each product line. **(iii)** Comment on your answers in requirements **(i)** and **(ii)**.

Solution

(i) Statement showing Operating Income and Operating Income as a Percentage of Revenues for 3 Products of Family Store

Particulars	Soft drinks	Fresh produce	Packaged food	Total
Revenues	₹7,93,000	₹21,00,600	₹12,09,000	₹41,04,000
Cost of goods sold (COGS)	6,00,000	15,00,000	9,00,000	30,00,000
Support cost (30% of COGS)	1,80,000	4,50,000	2,70,000	9,00,000
Total cost	7,80,000	19,50,000	11,70,000	39,00,000
Operating income	13,500	1,50,600	39,900	2,04,000
Operating income as a % of revenue	1.70	7.17	3.30	4.97

WORKING NOTES

1. Total Support Cost:

Bottle returns	₹12,000
Ordering	1,56,000
Delivery	2,52,000
Shelf-stocking	1,72,800
Customer support	3,07,200
Total support cost	9,00,000

2. Percentage of Support Cost of Goods Sold (COGS)
= (₹9,00,000/30,00,000) × 100 = 30%

(ii) Statement showing Operating Income and Operating Income as a Percentage of Revenues for 3 Products of Family Store

Particulars	Soft drinks	Fresh produce	Packaged foods	Total
Revenues	₹7,93,500	₹21,06,000	₹12,09,900	₹41,04,000
Cost of goods sold	6,00,000	15,00,000	9,00,000	30,00,000
Cost of bottles returned	12,000	—	—	12,000
Ordering cost [360:840:360]	36,000	84,000	36,000	1,56,000
Delivery cost [300:2,190:660]	24,000	1,75,200	52,800	2,52,000

(Contd.)

(Contd.)

Shelf-stocking cost [540:5,400:2,700]	10,800	1,08,000	54,000	1,72,800
Customer support cost [1,26,000:11,04,000:3,06,000]	25,200	2,20,800	61,200	3,07,200
Total cost	7,08,000	20,88,000	11,04,000	39,00,000
Operating income	85,500	12,600	1,05,900	2,04,000
Operating income as % of revenues	10.78	0.60	8.75	4.97

WORKING NOTE

Computation of Cost for each Cost Activity:

Activity	*Total cost*	*Cost allocation base*	*Cost activity rate*
Ordering	₹1,56,000	1,560 purchase orders	₹100 per purchase order
Delivery	2,52,000	3,150 deliveries	80 per delivery
Shelf-stocking	1,72,800	8,640 hours	20 per stocking hours
Customer support	3,07,200	15,36,000 items sold	0.20 per items sold

(iii) COMMENT: The operating income margins are more credible and authentic under the ABC costing system *vis-à-vis* the traditional costing system. The reason is that the ABC method provides more equitable basis of allocation of costs among user units.

P.12.5 RST Limited specialises in the distribution of pharmaceutical products. It buys from the pharmaceutical companies and resells to each of the three different markets: **LO 12.2, 3** **LOD: D**

(i) General supermarket chains
(ii) Drugstore chains
(iii) Chemist shops

The following data for the month of April current year in respect of RST Limited has been reported:

	General supermarket chains	*Drugstore chains*	*Chemist shops*
Average revenue per delivery	₹84,975	₹28,875	₹5,445
Average cost of goods sold per delivery	82,500	27,500	4,950
Number of deliveries	300	825	2,750

In the past, RST Limited has used gross margin percentage to evaluate the relative profitability of its distribution channel.

The company plans to use activity-based costing for analysing the profitability of its distribution channels. The activity analysis of RST Limited is as under:

Activity area	*Cost driver*
Customer purchase order processing	Purchase orders by customers
Line-item ordering	Line-items per purchase order
Store delivery	Store deliveries
Cartons dispatched to stores	Cartons despatched to a store per delivery
Shelf-stocking at customer store	Hours of shelf-stocking

The April, current year operating costs (other than cost of goods sold) of RST Limited are ₹8,27,970. These operating costs are assigned to five activity areas. The cost in each area and the quantity of the cost allocation basis used in that area for April, current year, are as follows:

Activity area	Total cost in April, current year	Total unit of cost allocation base used in April, current year
Customer purchase order processing	₹2,20,000	5,500 orders
Line-item ordering	1,75,560	58,520 line items
Store delivery	1,95,250	3,905 store deliveries
Cartons despatched to store	2,09,000	2,09,000 cartons
Shelf-stocking at customer store	28,160	1,760 hours

Other data for April, current year include the following:

	General supermarket chains	Drugstore chains	Chemist shops
Total number of orders	385	990	4,125
Average number of line items per order	14	12	10
Total number of store deliveries	330	825	2,750
Average number of cartons shipped per store delivery	300	80	16
Average number of hours of shelf-stocking per store delivery	3	0.6	0.1

REQUIRED:

(i) Compute for April, current year, gross-margin percentage for each of its three distribution channels and compute RST Limited's operating income.

(ii) Compute the April, current year rate per unit of the cost-allocation base for each of the five activity areas.

(iii) Compute the operating income of each distribution channel in April, current year using the activity-based costing information. Comment on the results. What new insights are available with activity-based cost information?

(iv) Describe four challenges one would face in assigning the total April, current year operating costs of ₹8,27,970 to five activity areas.

Solution

(i) Statement showing Operating Income and Gross Margin Percentage of three Distribution Channels of RST Limited

Particulars	General super market chains	Drugstore chains	Chemist shops	Total
Revenues	₹2,80,41,750	₹2,38,21,875	₹1,49,73,750	₹6,68,37,375
	(330 × ₹84,975)	(825 × ₹28,875)	(2,750 × ₹5,445)	
Less cost of goods sold	2,72,25,000	2,26,87,500	1,36,12,500	6,35,25,000
	(330 × ₹82,500)	(825 × ₹27,500)	(2,750 × ₹4,950)	
Gross margin	8,16,750	11,34,375	13,61,250	33,12,375
Less operating costs				8,27,970
Operating income				24,84,405
Gross margin (%)	2.91	4.76	9.09	4.96
Operating income (%)				3.72

(ii) Computation of rate per unit of cost allocation for five activity areas for April current year

1 Customer purchase order processing (₹2,20,000/5,500 orders)	₹40 per order
2 Line-item ordering (₹1,75,560/58,520 line items)	3 per line item hours
3 Store delivery (₹1,95,250/3,905 store deliveries)	50 per delivery
4 Cartons despatched (₹2,09,000/2,09,000 deliveries)	1 per despatch
5 Shelf-stocking at customer store (₹28,160/1,760 hours)	16 per hour

(iii) Statement showing Operating Income Statement of Distribution Channels in April, current year (using Activity Based Costing Information)

Particulars	*General supermarket chains*	*Drugstore chains*	*Chemist shops*
Gross margin	₹8,16,750	₹11,34,375	₹13,61,250
Less operating costs:			
Customer purchase	15,400	39,600	1,65,000
Order processing	(₹40 × 385 orders)	(₹40 × 990 orders)	(₹40 × 4,125 orders)
Line-item ordering	16,170 (₹3 × 14 × 385 orders)	35,640 (₹3 × 12 × 990 orders)	1,23,750 (₹3 × 10 × 4,125 orders)
Store delivery	16,500 (₹50 × 330 deliveries)	41,250 (₹50 × 825 deliveries)	1,37,500 (₹50 × 2,750 deliveries)
Cartons dispatched	99,000 (₹1 × 300 cartons × 330 deliveries)	66,000 (₹1 × 80 cartons × 825 deliveries)	44,000 (₹1 × 16 cartons × 2,750 deliveries)
Shelf-stocking	15,840 (₹16 × 330 deliveries × 3 Activity hours)	7,920 (₹16 × 825 deliveries × 0.6 Activity hours)	4,400 (₹16 × 2,750 deliveries × 0.1 Activity hours)
Operating income	6,53,840	9,43,965	8,86,600
Operating income (%)	2.33	3.96	5.92

COMMENT: The activity based costing technique focuses on different costs for different purposes and identifies only those costs which are relevant to a particular decision.

It highlights the distribution channel, namely, chemist shops which use larger amount RST Limited's resources per rupee of revenue earned *vis-à-vis* the other two distribution channels. Ratio of operating costs of revenues for 3 channels is as follows:

General supermarket chains	0.58%
Drugstore chains	0.80%
Chemist shops	3.17%

(iv) Challenges faced in assigning total operating cost of ₹8,27,970:
- Selection of an appropriate cost-allocation base
- Development of a reliable data base for the chosen cost base
- Developing the rate per unit of each cost allocation base
- Behavioural factors

P.12.6 MST Limited has collected the following data for its two activities. It calculates activity cost rates based on cost driver capacity. **LO 12.2** **LOD: E**

Activity	*Cost driver*	*Capacity*	*Cost*
Power	Kilowatt-hours	50,000 hours	₹2,00,000
Quality inspections	Number of inspections	10,000 inspections	₹3,00,000

The company makes three products, M, S and T. For the year ended March 31, current year, the following consumption of cost drivers was reported:

Product	*Kilowatt-hours*	*Quality inspections*
M	10,000	3,500
S	20,000	2,500
T	15,000	3,000

REQUIRED:

(i) Compute the costs allocated to each product from each activity, (ii) Calculate the cost of unused capacity for each activity.

Solution

(i) Statement showing Cost Allocation to each Product from each Activity:

Product	*Power*		*Quality inspections*	
M	(10,000 hours × ₹4)	₹40,000	(3,500 inspections × ₹30)	₹1,05,000
S	(20,000 hours × ₹4)	80,000	(2,500 inspections × ₹30)	75,000
T	(15,000 hours × ₹4)	60,000	(3,000 inspections × ₹30)	90,000
		1,80,000		2,70,000

WORKING NOTE

(i) Computation of rate per unit of cost driver:
Power (₹2,00,000/50,000 hours) = ₹4 per hour
Quality inspection (₹3,00,000/10,000 inspections) = ₹30 per inspection

(ii) Cost computation of unused capacity for each activity

Power (₹2,00,000 – ₹1,80,000)	₹20,000
Quality inspections (₹3,00,000 – ₹2,70,000)	30,000
Total cost of unused capacity	50,000

P.12.7 MNP Suits is a ready-to-wear suit manufacturer. It has four customers: two wholesale-channel customers and two retail-channel customers. MNP Suits has developed the following activity-based costing system: LO 12.3 LOD: M

Activity	*Cost driver*	*Rate in next year*
Order processing	Number of purchase orders	₹1,225 per order
Sales visits	Number of customer visits	7,150 per visit
Delivery-regular	Number of regular deliveries	1,500 per delivery
Delivery-rushed	Number of rushed deliveries	4,250 per delivery

List selling price per suit is ₹1,000 and average cost per suit is ₹550. The CEO of MNP Suits wants to revaluate the profitability of each of the four customers in the current year to explore opportunities for increasing the profitability of his company in next year. The following data are available for the current year:

Item	*Wholesale customers*		*Retail customers*	
	W	*H*	*R*	*T*
Total number of orders	44	62	212	250
Total number of sales visits	8	12	22	20
Regular deliveries	41	48	166	190
Rush deliveries	3	14	46	60
Average number of suits per order	400	200	30	25
Average selling price per suit	₹700	₹800	₹850	₹900

REQUIRED:

(i) Calculate the customer-level operating income, current year. (ii) What do you recommend to the CEO of MNP Suits to do to increase the company's operating income next year? (iii) Assume MNP Suits' distribution channel cost are ₹17,50,000 for its wholesale customers and ₹10,50,000 for the retail customers. Also, assume that its corporate sustaining costs are ₹12,50,000. Prepare the income statement of MNP Suits for the current year.

Solution

(i) Statement showing Computation of Customer-level Operating Income in the Current Year.

Particulars	*Wholesale customers*		*Retail customers*	
	W	*H*	*R*	*T*
Revenue at list price	₹1,76,00,000 (44 × 400 × 1,000)	₹1,24,00,000 (62 × 200 × 1,000)	₹63,60,000 (212 × 30 × 1,000)	₹62,50,000 (250 × 25 × 1,000)
Less discount	52,80,000 (44 × 400 × 300)	24,80,000 (62,200 × 200)	9,54,000 (212 × 30 × 150)	6,25,000 (250 × 25 × 100)
Revenue at actual prices	1,23,20,000	99,20,000	54,06,000	56,25,000
Less cost of goods sold	96,80,000 (44 × 400 × 550)	68,20,000 (62,200 × 550)	34,98,000 (212 × 30 × 550)	34,37,500 (250 × 25,550)
Gross margin	26,40,000	31,00,000	19,08,000	21,87,500
Customer level operating costs:				
Order processing (44,62,212,250) ÷ (₹1,225)	53,900	75,950	2,59,700	3,06,250
Sales visits (8,12,22,20) ÷ (₹7,150)	57,200	85,800	1,57,300	1,43,000
Delivery regular (41,48,166,190) ÷ (₹1,500)	61,500	72,000	2,49,000	2,85,000
Delivery rushed (3,14,46,60) ÷ (₹4,250)	12,750	59,500	1,95,500	2,55,000
Customer-level operating income	24,54,650	28,06,750	10,46,500	11,98,250
Customer level operating income as percentage on revenues at actual prices	19.92	28.29	19.35	21.30

(ii) The activity based costing (ABC) system is a far more refined costing system and reports costs that better measure the way jobs/products/customers use the resources of the company.

The ABC cost system reveals areas where R and T (retail customers) cause more costs to the company. The identified areas are high number of orders, high number of customer visits and high number of rushed deliveries.

The CEO needs to explore if this high level of activity can be reduced without reducing customer revenues.

(iii) Income Statement of MNP Suits for the Current Year

Particulars	*Wholesale customers*	*Retail customers*	*Total*
Operating income	₹52,61,400	₹22,44,750	₹75,06,150
Less distribution channel cost	17,50,000	10,50,000	28,00,000
Distribution channel level operating income	35,11,400	11,94,750	47,06,150
Less corporate sustaining costs			12,50,000
Operating income			34,56,150

P.12.8 Garden Tools Manufactures Ltd. (GTML) produces garden tools and lawn maintenance products that are sold through an All-India chain of stores. The GTML manufactures more than 50 products and approximately 20 per cent of its revenue comes from selling small home garden tools such as rakes, pruners and spades. It also manufacturers high-quality lawn movers, edgers and blowers for professional lawn service companies. Sales of these products, however, have not been a major source of revenue. **LO 12.1, 2** **LOD: D**

The CFO of GTML, Harsha Desai, is concerned about the apparent profitability of two of its products, namely, **(i)** a high-volume product Model-300 spade and **(ii)** a low-volume product, Model-800 mowers.

At the beginning of current year, the total estimated manufacturing overhead was ₹20,00,00,000 and the estimated total labour cost was ₹4,00,00,000. For the current year, the expected sales revenues from sale of Model-300 spade and Model-800 mowers are summarised below:

Particulars	Model-300 Spade	Model-800 Mower
1 Number of units sold	42,500	400
2 Sales revenue	₹38,25,000	₹12,00,000
3 Direct labour cost	4,59,000	60,000
4 Direct material cost	7,65,000	2,40,000

The GTML allocates manufacturing overheads to products based on direct labour cost. The product process for spades is fairly simple. The GTML uses one supplier for the metal handle and blade. It produces shafts on an automatic lathe and the handles, blades and shafts are assembled by hand at single workstation.

The production process for mowers is much more complicated. Twenty suppliers are used to supply the 50 components involved in producing the Model-800. Moreover, assembly of mowers makes uses of 15 separate assembly workstations.

The estimated total manufacturing overhead (₹20,00,00,000) is related to four cost drivers as shown below:

Overhead cost item/pool	Annual cost	Cost driver	Estimated annual value	Cost per driver unit
(1)	(2)	(3)	(4)	(5)
1 Set up costs	₹2,00,00,000	Number of setups	1,000	₹20,000
2 Material handling cost	1,00,00,000	Number of material requisitions	2,000	5,000 per requisition
3 Depreciation of equipment	5,00,00,000	Number of requisition	20,000	2,500 per machine-hour
4 Others 12,00,000		Number of work-stations used in production of product	3,000 work-stations across all products	40,000 per workstation

The production information for 42,500 spades (Model-300) and 400 Mowers (Model-800) is summarised below:

Particulars	Model-300 spade	Model-800 mower
1 Number of setups	2	5
2 Number of material requisitions	3	50
3 Number of machine-hours	40	100
4 Number of workstations	1	15

REQUIRED:

From the above information, compute the profitability of the two products: M-300 spade and M-800 mowers, using **(a)** traditional costing approach/system and **(b)** ABC system/approach to allocate manufacturing overheads. Comment on the differences in **(a)** and **(b)**.

Solution

(a) Profitability of Models 300 and 800 (Traditional/Production Volume based Approach)

Particulars	Model-300 spade (42,500 units)		Model-800 mower (400 units)
1 Sales revenue (42,500 × ₹90)	₹38,25,000	(400 × ₹3,000)	₹12,00,000
2 Direct labour cost	4,59,000		60,000
3 Direct material cost	7,65,000		2,40,000
4 Overheads	22,95,000[@]		3,00,000[@@]
5 Total cost (2 + 3 + 4)	35,19,000		6,00,000
6 Gross profit (1 – 5)	3,06,000		6,00,000
7 Cost per unit [(5) ÷ 42,500]	82.8	[(5) ÷ 400]	–1,500
8 Gross profit per unit [(6) ÷ 42,500]	7.2	[(6) ÷ 400]	1,500
9 Gross profit as % of sales (%) (6 ÷ 1)	8.0		50

[@]Direct labour cost, ₹4,59,000 × 5 (manufacturing cost, ₹20,00,00,000 ÷ ₹4,00,00,000, labour cost) = ₹22,95,000

[@@]₹60,000 × 5 = ₹3,00,000

(b) Profitability of Model-300 and Model-800 (ABC Approach)

Particulars		*Model-300 spade (42,500 units)*	*Model-800 mower (400 units)*
1 Direct labour cost		₹4,59,000	₹60,000
2 Direct material cost		7,65,000	2,40,000
3 Overheads:			
(i) Setup costs	(₹20,000 × 2)	40,000	
	(₹20,000 × 5)		1,00,000
(ii) Material handling cost			
	(₹5,000 × 3)	15,000	
	(₹5,000 × 50)		2,50,00
(iii) Depreciation of equipment			
	(₹2,500 × 40)	1,00,000	
	(₹2,500 × 100)		2,50,000
(iv) Others			
	(₹40,000 × 1)	40,000	
	(₹40,000 × 15)		6,00,000
Total overheads		1,95,000	12,00,000
4 Total cost		14,19,000	15,00,000
5 Cost per unit		33.4	3,750
6 Selling price per unit		90.0	3,000
7 Gross profit per unit		56.6	(–750)
8 Gross profit as % of sales (%)		63.0	(25)

(c) Comparison of Profitability of Model-300 and Model-800

Particulars	*Traditional approach*		*ABC approach*	
	Model-300	*Model-800*	*Model-300*	*Model-800*
1 Cost per unit	₹82.8	₹1,500	₹33.4	₹3,750
2 Gross profit as % of sales	8.0	50	63.0	(25)

COMMENT: The cost of Model 300-drops from ₹82 in the traditional approach to ₹33.4 per unit in the ABC approach and the cost of Model-800 increases from ₹1,500 to ₹3,750. The ABC approach reveals that the high-volume product (Model-300 spades) is very profitable as reflected in the gross profit margin (63%) while the selling price (₹3,000) does not cover even the full cost (₹3,750) of the low-volume product (Model-800) with a negative (–25%) gross margin.

P.12.9 Bajaj Electric Company (BEC) produces electric motors used by manufacturing companies such as those of home appliances. Each motor is made to customer specifications. The BEC has an activity-based costing system with the following overhead costs and cost drivers: **LO 12.1, 2** **LOD: M**

Cost pool	*Annual amount*	*Annual cost driver*
Direct labour-related	₹20,00,000	₹50,00,000 direct labour cost
Material ordering	5,00,000	25,000 purchase orders
Material inspection	30,00,000	20,000 receiving reports
Equipment setup	10,00,000	5,000 setups
Quality control	20,00,000	10,000 inspection of motors
Machine-related	40,00,000	20,000 machine-hours
Miscellaneous	20,00,000	₹2,00,00,000 of product costs other than miscellaneous overheads
Total overheads	1,45,00,000	

The BEC has received an order from Prakash Electronics Store (PES) for 5 identical motors. The BEC estimated the following costs (total) and activities related to the order:

- Material cost, ₹5,000
- Labour cost, ₹2,000
- Purchase order, 2
- Receiving reports, 2
- Setups, 1
- Inspections, 1
- Machine-hours 10

REQUIRED:

(a) Calculate the cost of PES job, assuming the BEC uses a traditional costing system with labour cost as the allocation base.

(b) Calculate the cost using the ABC system.

(c) Comment on the differences in (a) and (b).

Solution

(a) Calculation of Cost of PES Job (Traditional Costing)

Material		₹5,000
Labour		2,000
Overheads (₹2.9[@] × ₹2,000)		5,800
		12,800
[@]Total overheads	₹1,45,00,000	
Total labour cost	₹50,00,000	
Overhead rate per rupee of labour cost (₹1,45,00,000 ÷ ₹50,00,000)	2.9	

(b) Calculation of Cost of PES job (ABC Approach)

Material cost		₹5,000
Labour cost		2,000
Overheads:		
• Labour-related (0.40 × ₹2,000)	₹800	
• Material ordering (₹200 × 2)	400	
• Material inspection (₹1,500 × 2)	3,000	
• Setups (₹2,000 × 1)	2,000	
• Quality control (₹2,000 × 2)	4,000	
• Machine-related (₹200 × 10)	2,000	
• Miscellaneous (0.10 × cost other than Miscellaneous, ₹17,200)	1,720	
Total		13,920
Total cost		20,920

WORKING NOTES

Cost pool	Overhead rate (annual amount ÷ annual driver)
1 Direct labour-related (₹20,00,000 ÷ ₹50,00,000 direct labour cost)	₹0.40 per direct labour cost
2 Material ordering (₹5,00,000 ÷ 25,000 purchase orders)	200 per purchase order
3 Material inspection (₹30,00,000 ÷ 20,000 receiving reports)	1,500 per receiving report
4 Equipment setup (₹10,00,000 ÷ 5,000 setups)	2,000 per setup
5 Quality control (₹20,00,000 ÷ 10,000 inspections)	2,000 per inspection
6 Machine-related (₹40,00,000 ÷ 20,000 machine-hours)	200 per machine-hour
7 Miscellaneous (₹20,00,000 ÷ 2,00,00,000 product costs other than miscellaneous overheads)	0.10 per rupee of product other than miscellaneous overheads

COMMENT: Costs are higher in the ABC system as the PES job is relatively small and makes use of a number of activities whose costs are not proportionate to volume.

P.12.10 The management of Reliance Telecom Gurgaon area customer care centre is contemplating the implementation of the ABC system. The centre has 1,96,000 residential customers and 50,000 commercial customers. The relevant data are summarised below:

LO 12.3
LOD: M

Resource	*Monthly cost*	*Percentage of resource used in activity (%)*				
		Billing	*Account inquiry*	*Correspondence*	*Verification*	*Others*
1 Supervisors	₹1,22,000	40	35	8	—	17
2 Account inquiry labour	4,08,000	—	85	15	—	—
3 Billing labour	1,80,000	70	—	—	30	—
4 Paper	23,200	100	—	—	—	—
5 Computers	5,72,000	30	48	7	10	5
6 Telecommunications	1,98,400	—	85	—	—	15
7 Occupancy	2,24,000	15	70	—	—	15
8 Printers	3,00,000	80	—	5	—	15
9 Others	2,36,000	—	—	—	—	100
	22,63,680					

Activity	*Cost driver*	*Monthly number of cost driver units*		
		Residential	*Commercial*	*Total*
1 Printing	Lines	23,52,000	25,00,000	48,52,000
2 Account inquiry	Inquiries	19,600	15,000	34,600
3 Correspondence	Letters	3,920	5,000	8,920
4 Verification	Accounts	98,000	25,000	1,23,000

The management of Reliance Telecom has decided not to allocate the other resource costs.

REQUIRED:

(a) Prepare schedules to determine the cost per driver unit for each activity and the activity-based cost per account for each customer type.

(b) Consider the verification activity. Suppose the cost per account verified is ₹0.90. The centre verifies 50 per cent of residential and accommodation bills. Given that there are, on an average, 50 lines on each commercial bill and only 12 lines on each residential bill, comment on the use of accounts verified as a cost driver. What could be a more plausible and reliable cost driver?

Solution

(a) (i) Traceable Cost of Activities of Billing Department of Reliance Telecom

Resource	*Cost*	*Activity*				
		Billing inquiry	*Account*	*Correspondence*	*Verification*	*Others*
(1)	(2)	(3)	(4)	(5)	(6)	(7)
1 Supervisors	₹1,22,000	₹48,800[a]	₹42,700[b]	₹9,760[c]	—	₹20,740[d]
2 Account inquiry labour	4,08,000	—	3,46,800	61,200	—	—
3 Billing labour	1,80,000	1,26,000	—	—	₹54,000	—
4 Paper	23,200	23,200	—	—	—	—
5 Computers	5,72,000	1,71,600	3,43,200	50,050	57,200	28,600
6 Telecommunications	1,98,400	—	1,68,708	—	—	29,772
7 Occupancy	2,24,000	33,600	1,56,800	—	—	33,600

(Contd.)

(Contd.)

8 Printers	3,00,000	2,40,000	—	15,000	—	45,000
9 Others resources	2,36,000	—	—		—	2,36,000
Total traceable cost	22,63,680	6,43,200	9,89,568	1,26,000	1,11,200	3,93,712

[a](₹1,22,000 × 0.40) [b](₹1,22,000 × 0.35) [c](₹1,22,000 × 0.08) [d](₹1,22,000 × 0.17)

(ii) Cost per Driver Unit

Activity (driver units)	*Driver costs*		
	Traceable costs	*Total number of driver units*	*Cost per driver unit*
	(1)	*(2)*	*(3) [(1) ÷ (2)]*
Account inquiry (inquiries)	₹9,89,568	34,600 inquiries	₹28.600231
Correspondence (letters)	1,26,000	8,920 letters	14.12556
Account billing (lines)	6,43,200	48,52,000 lines	0.13256
Bill verification (accounts verified)	1,11,200	1,23,000 accounts verified	0.90406

(iii) Cost per Customer Class

Activity	*Cost per Driver Unit*	*Customer Class*			
		Residential		*Commercial*	
		Number of Driver Units	*Cost*	*Number of Driver Units*	*Cost*
Account inquiry	₹28.600231	19,600 inquiries	₹5,60,564	15,000 inquiries	₹4,29,004
Correspondence	14.12556	3,920 letters	55,372	5,000 letters	70,628
Account billing	0.13256	23,52,000 lines	3,11,788	25,00,000 lines	3,31,412
Bill verification	0.90406	98,000 accounts	88,596	25,000 accounts	22,600
Total cost			10,16,324		8,53,644
Number of accounts			1,96,000		50,000
Cost per account			5.18		17.08

(b) The ABC system allocates 79.7 per cent [98,000 ÷ 1,23,000 (98,000 + 25,000)] of verification costs to residential accounts based on the number of accounts verified. However, the work performed to verify a bill is rather closely related to the number of lines on the bill. The amount of effort of employees would depend on the number of lines in each account rather than on the number of accounts. The lines verified is, therefore, a more reliable cost driver.

The number of lines verified for residential accounts are: 12 lines per account × 98,000 accounts = 11,76,000 lines. The number of lines verified for commercial accounts are: 50 lines per account × 25,000 accounts verified = 12,50,000 lines. Therefore, 48.5 per cent [11,76,000 ÷ 24,26,000 (11,76,000 + 12,50,000)] of verification costs should be allocated to residential accounts based on lines verified.

P.12.11 The new Controller of Bharti Telecom (BT) has discovered that BT's customers differ greatly in their ordering pattern and interaction with BT's sales force. He feels that BT's costing system does not accurately assign marketing, distribution and selling expenses to customer. He has developed an ABC system to assign these expenses to customers. He has identified the following marketing, selling and distribution costs for two customers, Alpha and Beta. **LO 12.3** **LOD: D**

	Alpha	*Beta*
1 Travelling by sales representatives	₹36,000	₹1,68,000
2 Servicing customers	60,000	4,40,000
3 Handling customer orders	4,000	48,000
4 Shipping to customers	96,000	2,88,000
	196,00	9,44,000

(Contd.)

(Contd.)

The following additional information is available:		
1 Sales	17,20,000	14,00,000
2 Cost of goods sold	8,80,000	6,20,000

REQUIRED:

(a) Using the current costing approach of assigning marketing, selling and distribution expenses to customers using 33 per cent of sales revenue, determine the operating profit of the two customers.

(b) Using the ABC information provided, determine their operating profits.

(c) Which of the two methods produces more accurate assignment of marketing, selling and distribution expenses to customers? Explain.

Solution

(a) Customer Profitability Analysis (Current Costing Approach)

Particulars	*Alpha*	*Beta*
Sales revenue	₹17,20,000	₹14,00,000
Cost of goods sold	8,80,000	6,20,000
Gross margin	8,40,000	7,80,000
Marketing, selling and distribution expenses (0.33 × sales revenue)	5,67,600	4,62,000
Operating profit	2,72,400	3,18,000
Profit (as percentage of sales)	15.8	22.7

(b) Customer Profitability Analysis (ABC Approach)

Particulars	*Alpha*	*Beta*
Sales revenue	₹17,20,000	₹14,00,000
Cost of goods sold	8,80,000	6,20,000
Gross margin	8,40,000	7,80,000
Marketing, selling and distribution expenses:		
— Travelling by sales representatives	36,000	1,68,000
— Servicing customer	60,000	4,40,000
— Handling customer orders	4,000	48,000
— Shipping to customers	96,000	2,88,000
Total activity expenses	1,96,000	9,44,000
Operating profit	6,44,000	(–1,64,000)
Profit (as percentage of sales)	37.4	(–11.7)

(c) Beta customer is more profitable than Alpha customer according to the current costing system. Moreover, both the customers are profitable. But customer Alpha emerges as highly profitable and Beta emerges as the most unfavourable customer according to the ABC approach. The ABC obviously produces more accurate assignment of marketing, selling and distribution expenses. As can be seen from the computations, travel, customer services and shipping to customers, have huge demands on Beta's marketing, selling and distribution resource in contrast to Alpha's. But the current costing system fails to make this distinction between them.

P.12.12 Hinduja Health Centre (HHC) runs three programmes: **(1)** alcoholic rehabilitation, **(2)** drug addict rehabilitation, and **(3)** aftercare (counseling and support of patients after release from a mental hospital). LO 12.4 LOD: D

The HHC's budget for current year follows:

Professional salaries:		
4 physicians × ₹3,00,000	₹12,00,000	
18 psychologists × ₹1,50,000	27,00,000	
20 nurses × ₹60,000	12,00,000	₹51,00,000
Medical supplies		3,00,000
General overhead (administrative salaries, rent, utilities, etc.)		8,80,000
		62,80,000

Dr. Anupam Verma, the Director of the HHC, is keen on determining the cost of each programme. He has compiled the following data describing employees allocations to individual programmes:

	Alcohol	*Drug*	*Aftercare*	*Total employees*
Physicians		4		4
Psychologists	6	4	8	18
Nurses	4	6	10	20

Eight patients are in residence in the alcohol programme, each staying for about six months. Thus, the clinic provides 40 patient-years of service in the alcohol programme. Similarly, 100 patients are involved in the drug programme for about six months each. Thus, the clinic provides 50 patient-years of service in the drug programme.

Dr Verma has recently become aware of activity-based costing as a method to refine costing systems. He asks his accountant, Kulkarni, how he should apply this new technique. Kulkarni obtains the following information:

(a) Consumption of medical supplies depends on the number of patient-years.

(b) General Overhead Costs consist of

Rent and clinic maintenance	₹1,80,000
Administrative costs to manage patient charts, food, laundry	6,00,000
Laboratory services	1,00,000
Total	8,80,000

(c) Other Information about Individual Departments:

	Alcohol	*Drug*	*Aftercare*	*Total employee*
Square feet of space occupied by each programme	9,000	9,000	12,000	30,000
Patient-years of service	40	50	60	150
Number of laboratory tests	400	1,400	70	2,500

REQUIRED:

1. Using an activity-based costing approach to cost analysis, calculate the cost of each programme and the cost per patient-year of the alcohol and drug programmes. What benefits can HHC obtain by implementing the ABC system?
2. What factors, other than cost, do you think HHC should consider in allocating resources to its programmes?

Solution

1. Activity-based Costs for each Programme and Cost per Patient-year of the Alcohol and Drug programmes:

	Alcohol	Drug	Aftercare
Direct labour:			
Physicians [₹3,00,000 × (0;4;0)]	—	₹12,00,000	—
Psychologists [₹1,50,000 (× 6;4;8)]	₹9,00,000	6,00,000	₹12,00,000
Nurses labour costs	2,40,000	3,60,000	6,00,000
Direct labour costs	11,40,000	21,60,000	18,00,000
Medical supplies[1] [₹2,000 × (40; 50; 60)]	80,000	1,00,000	1,20,000
Rent and clinic maintenance[2] [₹6 × (9,000; 9,000; 12,000)]	54,000	54,000	72,000
Administrative costs to manage patient charts, food, and laundry[3] [₹4,000 × (40; 50; 60)]	1,60,000	2,00,000	2,40,000
Laboratory services[4] [₹40 × (400; 1,400; 7,000]	16,000	56,000	28,000
Total costs	14,50,000	25,70,000	22,60,000

Cost per patient = ₹14,50,000/40 = ₹ 36,250 (alcohol)
= 25,70,000 ÷ 50 = 56,400 (drug).

[1]Allocated using patient-years
[2]Allocated using square feet of space
[3]Allocated using patient-years
[4]Allocated using number of laboratory tests

The ABC system allocates costs more accurately because it identifies better cost drivers. It chooses cost driers for overhead costs that have a cause-and-effect relationship between the cost drivers and the costs.

By implementing the ABC system, Dr Verma can gain a more detailed understanding of costs and cost drivers. This is valuable information from a cost management perspective. The system can yield insight into the efficiencies with which various activities are performed. Dr Verma can then examine if redundant activities are performed. He can study trends and work toward improving the efficiency of the activities.

In addition, the ABC system will help Dr Verma determine which programmes are the most costly to operate. This will be useful in making long-run decisions as to which programme to offer or emphasise on. The ABC system will also assist Dr Verma in setting up those prices for the programmes that reflect their costs more accurately.

2. The concern with using costs per patient-year as the rule to allocate resources among its programmes is that it emphasises "input" to the exclusion of "outputs" or effectiveness of the programmes. Afterall, the goal is to cure patients while controlling costs, not to minimise costs per-patient year. The problem, of course, is measuring outputs.

Unlike many manufacturing companies, where the outputs are obvious because they are tangible and measurable, the outputs of service organisations are more difficult to measure. Examples are "cured" patients as distinguished from "processed" or "discharged" patients, "educated" as distinguished from "partially educated" students, and so on.

REVIEW QUESTIONS

LOD: Easy

RQ.12.1 Indicate whether the followings statements are 'True' or 'False'. **LO 12.1,2,5**

(i) Activity based costing (ABC) system is applicable only for allocation of manufacturing overheads.

(ii) ABC system has the potential of eliminating cost distortion.
(iii) Higher-volume products would have higher share of indirect costs in ABC system.
(iv) ABC system uses cost centres for accumulating costs.
(v) Cost drivers are significant determinants of costs in ABC system.
(vi) Duration drivers represent the number of times an activity is performed.
(vii) Transaction drivers represent the amount of time required to perform an activity.
(viii) Intensity drivers are used to charge directly for the resources used each time an activity is performed.
(ix) Practical capacity is higher than theoretical capacity.
(x) Activity based costing prices products.
(xi) ABC system is appropriate only for manufacturing firms.
(xii) ABC based costing systems are more costly than traditional costing systems.

[Answers: (i) False, (ii) True, (iii) False, (iv) False, (v) True, (vi) False, (vii) False, (viii) True, (ix) False, (x) False, (xi) False, (xii) True.]

RQ.12.2 Fill in the following blanks: LO 12.1,2

(i) In traditional costing system, the accumulated costs, first, are allocated to ____________ and then such costs are assigned to ____________.
(ii) ABC system first traces costs to ____________ and then to ____________.
(iii) Costs are assigned to products/jobs using ____________ as a measure of activity.
(iv) In ABC system, a firm can choose from three types of cost drivers, namely, ____________
(v) Among three types of cost drivers, ____________ is the least accurate in ABC system.
(vi) ____________ are the most accurate cost drivers.
(vii) Activity costs are assigned to individual jobs/products on the basis of ____________
(viii) Activity cost driver rate = ____________ divided by total quantity of activity cost driver.
(ix) Activity expenses assigned to a product = ____________ (×) Quantity of each activity cost driver used by the product/job.
(x) Cost incurred in performing activities are grouped into ____________

[Answers: (i) Production/cost centres; (iv) Transaction, duration and intensity, (v) Transaction cost drivers, (vi) Intensity drivers, (vii) Activity cost driver rate, (viii) Activity expenses, (ix) Activity cost driver rate, (x) Cost pools.]

RQ.12.3 Briefly explain how traditional methods of allocation of overheads to products may underallocate costs to low-production-volume products and overallocate costs to high-volume products. LO 12.1

RQ.12.4 How does ABC differ from the traditional costing approach? LO 12.1,2

RQ.12.5 When would ABC give more accurate costs than traditional costing system? LO 12.1,2

RQ.12.6 What are the benefits and limitations of ABC? LO 12.5

RQ.12.7 What do the terms 'activity cost driver' and 'activity cost driver rates' mean? LO 12.2

RQ.12.8 How do activity-based costing systems avoid distortions in tracing costs to products? LO 12.2

RQ.12.9 Aptech Computers manufactures mouse devices for computers. They make 12 different models of mouse devices as well as several other types of computer components. They use activity-based costing to assign manufacturing overheads to products. The data relating to one of their products–wireless remote mouse–and the ABC cost pools are given below. LO 12.2

(a) Wireless Remote Mouse: Annual production, 20,000 units; Direct materials per unit, ₹310; Direct labour per unit, ₹60.

(b) Manufacturing overhead cost pools

Cost pool	Cost	Cost driver
1 Materials ordering	₹80,00,000	Number of purchase orders
2 Materials inspection	40,00,000	Number of receiving reports
3 Equipment setup	2,00,00,000	Number of setups
4 Quality control	90,00,000	Number of inspections
5 Others	15,00,00,000	Direct labour cost
Total manufacturing overheads	19,10,00,000	

(c) Activity information related to cost drivers

Cost pool	Annual activity	
	All products	Remote Mouse
1 Materials ordering	10,00,000 orders	10,000 orders
2 Materials inspection	20,000 receiving reports	3,000 reports
3 Equipment setup	1,000 setups	10 setups
4 Quality control	40,000 inspections	4,000 inspections
5 Others	10,00,000 direct labour hours	1,20,000 direct labour hours

REQUIRED:

(a) Calculate the overhead rate per unit of activity for each of the 5 cost pools.
(b) Calculate the total overhead assigned to the production of the remote mouse.
(c) Calculate the overhead cost per unit for the remote mouse.
(d) Calculate the total unit cost for the remote mouse.

RQ.12.10 The HDFC Bank Ltd. is contemplating to implement an ABC system for its teller department. The activities identified and the associated cost drivers for its New Friends Colony Branch are summarised below: **LO 12.4**

Support activity	Estimated cost	Activity cost driver	Quantity
1 Process deposits	₹1,48,150	Number of deposits processed	1,66,250
2 Process withdrawals	1,30,400	Number of withdrawals processed	1,13,750
3 Answer inquiries	1,24,000	Number of customer inquiries	2,25,000
4 Negotiable instruments' selling	24,300	Number of negotiable instruments sold	5,500
5 Balance drawers	21,450	Number of drawers balanced	6,500

REQUIRED:

(a) Compute the activity cost driver rates for each of the support facilities.
(b) Estimate in total monthly support costs for a typical amount from the information given below:

Support activity	Average monthly volume
1 Process deposits	11,500
2 Process withdrawals	30,000
3 Answer customer inquiries	10,500
4 Sell negotiable instruments	2,500

RQ.12.11 The Delhi Manufacturers Ltd. (DML) manufactures two products. Their estimated unit cost and production data are summarised below: **LO 12.4**

Item	Product	
	D1	D2
Direct material cost	₹120	₹180
Direct labour cost (₹48 per hour)	96	240
Estimated production (units)	4,00,000	1,50,000

The manufacturing support costs are estimated to be ₹2,61,40,000 for the current year. The activity cost pools and cost drivers are as given below:

Activity	Costs	Activity cost driver	Practical capacity	Cost driver units required by	
				D1	D2
1 Machine setups	₹17,00,000	Setup hours	13,000	4,000	8,400
2 Purchase ordering	40,000	Number of orders	200	50	100
3 Machining	2,40,00,000	Number of machine-hours	1,50,000	80,000	30,000
4 Inspection	1,44,000	Number of batches	2,400	800	1,200
5 Packing and despatch	2,56,000	Number of despatches	3,200	160	3,000
Total	2,61,40,000				

REQUIRED:

(a) Estimate the manufacturing cost per unit of each product if support costs are assigned to products using activity-based cost driver rates based on practical capacity.

(b) Compute the variance/difference between the estimated manufacturing support costs and the support costs assigned to DML's products in (a).

LOD: Medium

RQ.12.12 How does ABC differ from activity-based management? LO 12.2

RQ.12.13 Explain the two-stage allocation of overheads in activity-based costing. LO 12.2

RQ.12.14 "Conventional product costing systems are likely to overcost high-volume products". Do you agree with this statement? Explain. LO 12.1

RQ.12.15 How are cost driver rates selected in activity-based costing system? LO 12.2

RQ.12.16 In ABC, what are the trade-offs made in choosing among transaction, duration and intensity activity cost drivers. LO 12.2

RQ.12.17 How can the information from an ABC systems guide improvement in operations and decisions about products/customers? LO 12.2,5

RQ.12.18 Why should practical capacity be used in calculating activity cost drivers? LO 12.2

RQ.12.19 The Sports Manufacturers Ltd. produces two products: (i) a recreational whitewater play boat and (ii) a high performance competition boat. The recreation boat is uniform in style and dimensions. The competition boat is customer designed to fit the individual requirement. The data related to the two products for the most recent year are summarised below: LO 12.1,2

	Recreation boat	Competition boat
1 Sales and production (number)	900	100
2 Sales price (per boat)	₹3,000	₹3,300

(Contd.)

(Contd.)

3 Unit costs:				
Direct material	₹750		₹1,000	
Direct labour	500		500	
Overheads@	675	1,925	675	2,175
Gross profit (2 – 3)		1,075		1,125

@Overheads (total):

• Depreciation of building	₹1,25,000
• Depreciation of equipment	1,25,000
• Materials ordering	75,000
• Quality control	50,000
• Maintenance and security	50,000
• Setup and drafting	1,00,000
• Supervision	1,50,000
	6,75,000

Overhead rate based on direct labour cost:

Total overhead	6,75,000	
Total labour (₹500 × 900) + (₹500 × 100)	5,00,000	
Rate (overhead labour) per direct labour cost		1.35

REQUIRED:

(a) The traditional costing system that Sports Manufacturers is using, assigns the total overheads on the basis of direct labour cost. Discuss why this is not an accurate way to assign overheads to the two products.

(b) Assume that a consultant to create an ABC system for Sports Manufactures develops the following data:

Cost pool	*Amount*	*Driver*	*Driver activity*	
			Recreation boat	*Competition boat*
Building	₹1,25,000	Square footage	6,000	1,000
Equipment	1,25,000	Machine-hours	3,400	600
Material ordering	75,000	Number of orders	200	150
Quality control	50,000	Number of inspections	300	150
Maintenance and security	50,000	Square footage	6,000	1,000
Setup and drafting	1,00,000	Number of setups	20	40
Supervision	1,50,000	Direct labour cost	₹4,50,000	₹50,000

Determine the overhead allocation to each line of boats using an ABC approach and compute the total unit cost for each model.

(c) Discuss why activity-based allocations are different from those generated by the traditional method?

LOD: Difficult

RQ.12.20 Discuss some of the special considerations in designing a cost accounting system for service organisations. **LO 12.4**

RQ.12.21 Reliable Automative Manufacturers Ltd. (RAML) is an automatic components/parts supplier. The Hyundai Motors has approached the RAML to expand its production part P-808 to a total annual quantity of 4,000 units. P-808 is a low-volume, complex product with a high gross margin that is based on a proposed/quoted unit sale price of ₹15. The RAML uses the traditional costing system, allocating indirect manufacturing costs currently at 400 per cent of direct labour cost (i.e. ₹1,32,00,000 annual factory overhead ÷ ₹33,00,000 annual direct labour cost). Producing 4,000 units of part P-808 requires ₹20,000 of direct materials and ₹4,000 of direct labour. The unit cost and gross margin percentage of P-808 according to the traditional costing system are computed below: **LO 12.2**

Particulars	Total cost (1)	Per unit cost (2) [(1) ÷ 4,000]
Direct materials	₹20,000	₹5.00
Direct labour	4,000	1.00
Indirect manufacturing (400 × direct labour)	16,000	4.00
Total cost	40,000	10.00
Sales price quoted		15.00
Gross margin		5.00
Gross margin percentage		33.00

The management of RAML has decided to examine the effectiveness of their traditional costing system versus an activity-based costing system. The following data have been collected by a team of accounting and engineering analysts:

Activity	Traceable factory overhead costs (annual)	Cost drivers	Annual cost-driver quantity	Cost-driver consumption (4,000 units of P-808)
1 Quality	₹32,00,000	Number of pieces scrapped	20,000	240
2 Production scheduling and setups	26,00,000	Number of setups	1,000	8
3 Shipping	12,00,000	Number of containers shipped	1,20,000	20
4 Shipping administration	2,00,000	Number of shipments	2,000	10
5 Production	60,00,000	Number of machine-hours	20,000	30

REQUIRED:

(a) Calculate the unit cost and gross margin of part P-808 using the ABC approach.

(b) Based on (a) which course of action would you recommend regarding the Hyundai's proposal?

ANSWERS

RQ.12.9 **(a)** Material ordering ₹80 per order, Material inspection ₹200 per report, Equipment set up ₹20,000 per set up, Quality control ₹225 per inspection, Others ₹150 per direct labour hour

(b) ₹1,97,80,000

(c) ₹989

(d) ₹1,359

RQ.12.10 **(a)** Process deposits ₹0.891 per deposit processed, ₹1.146 per withdrawal processed, ₹0.55 per customer enquiry, ₹4.41 per negotiable instrument sold ₹3.3 per drawer balanced.

(b) ₹61,426.50

RQ.12.11 **(a)** D_1 ₹249.48, D_2 ₹461.54

(b) Costs under the ABC system ₹1,96,24,336, Costs under traditional costing system ₹2,61,40,000; difference is ₹65,15,664.

RQ.12.19 **(a)** Major share of factory overhead costs consists of depreciation, supervision, maintenance and other related costs. In such a situation, there is likely to be a little relationship between factory overhead costs and direct labour costs.

(b) (i) Recreation boat ₹1,806.41, (ii) ₹3,242.27

(c) The ABC system allocates more accurately as it identifies better cost drivers. It chooses cost drivers that have a cause and effect relationship between the cost drivers and overhead costs. In contrast, all overhead costs are allocated on the basis of direct labour costs.

RQ.12.21 **(a)** Unit cost ₹23.35, Gross margin (₹8.35) per unit.
(b) Since there is negative gross margin, proposal should not be accepted.

[Comprehensive solutions to all numerical review questions are available on the companion website: http://www.mhhe.com/khan_jain_ma7e]

CASES

12.C.1 ABC and Customer Profitability

To increase its share of deposits accounts, the UTI Bank Ltd (UBL) took two actions recently: first, to respond to depositor-customers inquiries about account balances, clearance of cheques and fee charged, it set up a call centre; second, it paid year-end bonuses to branch managers who met the target in terms of additional customers. Inspite of the fact that 75 per cent of the branch managers met the target increase in the number of customers, the profits of the UTI Bank Ltd (UBL) continued to decline. It was not clear to the CEO, Pulin Naik, why inspite of serving more customers, profits of the UBL were declining. The branch manager of Cannaught Circle Branch, Dinesh Parekh, noticed that retail customers were increasing but there was a decline in the number of business customers.

The costing system of the UBL was developed in 1996 when it was setup. It is still in operation. According to current practice, no costs are traced directly to customers. The total indirect costs are assigned simply to customer lines (i.e. retail customers and business customers) in terms of the total number of cheques processed.

Dinesh suspected that the current costing system of UBL was responsible for the state of affairs. He wondered if an ABC system, with customer-line as the primary cost object, could be introduced in UBL.

The top management of UBL was initially skeptical about any such move in view of the decline in its profit. Dinesh Parekh finally succeeded in pursuading the CEO, Pulin Naik, to allow a pilot ABC study for the five branches of UBL located in Delhi. An implementation team including Dinesh and the managers of the other four branches of UBL was constituted for the purpose.

As a first step, the implementation team identified three activities: **(i)** cheque payments, **(ii)** tellers withdrawals and deposits and **(iii)** customer service call centre.

The second step was to scrutinise the total indirect costs of all the New Delhi branches. The implementation team of the pilot study classified the components of the indirect cost into appropriate activity pools as summarised below:

Cost	*Activity cost pool to which cost is assigned*	*Estimated total cost for New Delhi Branches*
1 Salary of cheque-processing personnel	Cheque payments	₹22,00,000
2 Depreciation on cheque-processing equipment	Cheque payments	35,00,000
3 Teller salary	Teller withdrawals/deposits	60,00,000
4 Salary at call centre	Customer service call centre	22,50,000
5 Toll free phone lines at call centre	Customer service call centre	3,00,000
Total indirect costs		1,42,50,000

The implementation team also identified the following cost drivers:

Activity cost pool	*Activity cost driver*
1 Cheque payments	Number of cheques processed
2 Teller withdrawals/deposits	Number of teller transactions
3 Customer service call centre	Number of calls

The ABC team then identified the retail customer lines and business customer lines listed below:

Activity cost driver	*Number of units of activity cost driver by retail customers*	*Number of units of activity cost driver used by business customers*	*Total*
(1)	*(2)*	*(3)*	*(4)*
1 Cheques processed	57,00,000	2,28,00,000	2,85,00,000
2 Teller transactions	16,00,000	4,00,000	20,00,000
3 Customer call centres	4,75,000	25,000	5,00,000
4 Deposit accounts	7,50,000	2,50,000	10,00,000

The average revenues (from interest earned on account balances) from each type of account earned by the UBL is: **(i)** per retail customer account, ₹50 and **(ii)** per business customer account, ₹200.

REQUIRED:

(A) Using the current cost accounting practices of UBL:
1. compute the indirect cost allocation rate,
2. determine the total indirect cost assigned to the retail customer lines and business customer lines,
3. compute the proportion of the total indirect cost assigned to the retail customer line and business customer line,
4. determine the indirect cost per retail and business account,
5. assuming that there are no direct costs, compute the average profit per account for retail and business customers.

(B) Using the proposed ABC System:
1. compute the indirect cost allocation rate for each of the three activities: cheque payments, teller withdrawal/ deposits and customer call centre,
2. calculate the activity-wise total indirect costs allocated to each retail and business customer lines,
3. compute the proportion of each activity's resources used by the retail and business customer lines,
4. compute the indirect cost per retail and business customer account,
5. compute the average profit per account of both retail and business customers.

(C) Was UBL's bonus-based incentive plan to increase the number of deposit accounts a sound strategy? In the light of the ABC analysis, what changes would you suggest in the strategy? What benefits can UBL get from the ABC analysis?

Solution

(A) (1) Computation of indirect cost allocation rate

Total indirect cost	₹1,42,50,000
Total number of cheques processed	2,85,00,000
Indirect cost per cheque processed (₹1,42,50,000/2,85,00,000)	Re. 0.50

(2) Computation of total indirect cost assigned to retail and business customer lines

Particulars	*Retail customer lines*	*Business customer lines*
Number of cheques processed	57,00,000	2,28,00,000
Indirect cost allocated @ Re.0.50 per cheque processed	₹28,50,000	₹1,14,00,000

(3) Computation of the proportion of the total indirect cost assigned to retail and business customer lines

Total indirect cost allocated	₹1,42,50,000
Proportion of indirect cost allocated to retail customer lines (28,50,000/1,42,50,000)	0.20
Proportion of indirect cost allocated to business customer lines (1,14,00,000/1,42,50,000)	0.80

(4) Computation of indirect cost per retail and business account

Particulars	*Retail account*	*Business account*
Total indirect cost allocated	₹28,50,000	₹1,14,00,000
Number of deposit accounts	7,50,000	2,50,000
Indirect cost per account	₹3.8	₹45.6

(5) Statement showing average profit per retail and business account

Particulars	*Retail account*	*Business account*
Average revenue per account	₹50	₹200
Indirect cost per account	3.8	45.6
Average profit per account	46.2	154.4

(B) (1) Computation of indirect cost allocation rate under ABC system

Activity	*Total cost*	*Activity cost driver*	*Number of units of activity cost*	*Cost allocation rate driver*
Cheque payments	₹57,00,000	Cheques Processed	2,85,00,000	Re. 0.20 per cheque processed
Teller withdrawal/deposits	60,00,000	Teller transactions	20,00,000	₹3.00 per teller transaction
Customer call centre	25,50,000	Customer calls	5,00,000	₹5.10 per customer call

(2) Computation of activity-wise total indirect cost assigned to retail and business customer lines under ABC system

Particulars	*Retail customer lines*	*Business customer lines*
Cheque payments	₹11,40,000	₹45,60,000
Teller withdrawal/deposits	48,00,000	12,00,000
Customer call centre	24,22,500	1,27,500
Total	83,62,500	58,87,500

(3) Computation of the proportion of activity resources used by retail and business customer lines under ABC system

Activity	*Proportion used by retail customer lines*	*Proportion used by business customer lines*
Cheque payments	0.20	0.80
Teller withdrawal/deposits	0.80	0.20
Customer call centre	0.95	0.05

(4) Computation of indirect cost per retail and business account under ABC system

Particulars	*Retail account*	*Business account*
Total indirect cost allocated	₹83,62,500	₹58,87,500
Number of deposit accounts	7,50,000	2,50,000
Indirect cost per account	₹11.15	₹23.55

(5) Statement showing average profit per retail and business account under ABC system

Particulars	*Retail account*	*Business account*
Average revenue per account	₹50	₹200
Indirect cost per account	11.15	23.55
Average profit per account	38.85	176.45

(C) UBL's bonus-based incentive plan to increase the number of deposit accounts was not a sound strategy as it resulted in increase in the number of retail customers and decrease in the number of business customers.

The ABC analysis reveals that retail customers place greater demands on UBL's resources. Retail customers account for 80 per cent of teller withdrawals/deposit transactions and 95 per cent of customer calls while the revenue per retails customer is only 25 percent of that of a business customer. As a result, the indirect cost per retail customer account is approximately 22 per cent of revenue compared to 12 per cent for a business customer account. As business coustomers are more profitable, UBL should adopt a strategy that will increase the number of business customers.

Based on the ABC analysis, UBL can work towards making its retail customer accounts more profitable by either imposing restrictions on number of withdrawals/deposits and customer calls for retail customers or by increasing the revenue per retail customer.

12.C.2 ABC and Distribution Channel Profitability In January, current year, the top management of Color Plus Ltd. was debating the relative profitability of its three distribution channels: (a) catalogue sales, (b) corporate sales and (c) retail sales. They asked Deepak Parekh, a financial analyst, to conduct a channel profitability analysis. The results of his analysis would have a significant bearing on the company's distribution strategy.

Color Plus Ltd. sells garments. It contracts out the manufacturing of all products to outside supplies. Its employees maintain a large catalogue mailing list. The catalogue buyers, mostly individuals, place generally small quantity orders by phone or over the Internet.

The corporate sales orders are generally large-quantity orders and are brought in through the field sales force of Colur Plus. About three-quarters of corporate orders involve time-consuming order specification and/or price negotiation by the salesman and usually some design experts.

Most of the retail orders are also procured by the field sales force through personal visits to retail outlets. The buyers generally purchase medium quantities of goods at wholesale prices. Some of the retailers require special product labelling and packaging.

Currently all the three distribution channels look profitable as shown in Exhibit 1.

Exhibit 1 Gross Margin Levels of Distribution Channels

	Distribution Channels (Amount ₹thousands)			
	Catalogue	*Corporate*	*Retail*	*Total*
Sales	₹1,50,000	₹50,000	₹1,00,000	₹3,00,000
Cost of sales	75,000	32,500	70,000	1,77,500
Gross margin	75,000	17,500	30,000	1,22,500

The CFO of Color Plus believes that the gross margin-level measure may be a misleading performance indicator. He noted that the selling, general and administrative (SGA) expenses were "below" the gross margin line. His institution was that if the SGA costs were allocated to distribution channels, quite a different performance picture may result. To address his concern, Deepak Parekh was assigned the responsibility of looking into the SGA costs.

During the course of the study to identify the relevant SGA expenses, Deepak noticed that direct sales force was paid a 10 per cent commission on the sales brought in by them. The other SGA expenses for current year were found by Deepak as given below:

Item	*Amount (₹thousand)*
1 Marketing and sales support	₹30,000
2 Design	4,500
3 Information system	10,000
4 General administration	15,000
	59,500

After identifying the relevant SGA expenses, Deepak proceeded to identify the major activities that were the cause of SGA expenses. Exhibit 2 shows Deepak Parkeh's estimate of the proportion of each of the SGA expense items caused by each of the activities identified by him.

EXHIBIT 2 Activity-wise SGA Expenses

SGA Items	*Activities*						
	Customer mailing	*Take phone or internet order*	*Take field order*	*Special negotiation field order*	*Process customer invoice*	*Others*	*Total*
1 Marketing and sales support	10%	10%	30%	50%	—	—	100%
2 Design	—	—	—	90%	—	10%	100%
3 Information system	—	10%	—	—	10%	80%	100%
4 General administration	—	—	—	10%	10%	80%	

Deepak Parekh's next task was to assign the costs of each of the activities to the distribution channels. The information collected by him is given in Exhibit 3.

EXHIBIT 3 Channel-wise Cost of Activities

Activity	*Channels*			
	Catalogue	*Corporate*	*Retail*	*Total*
1 Customer mailings	1,96,000	2,000	2,000	2,00,000
2 Number of phone orders	6,000	60	120	6,180
3 Number of field orders	—	800	800	1,600
5 Number of field orders requiring special negotiation	—	600	200	800
5 Total number of orders (2 + 3)	6,000	860	920	7,780

REQUIRED:

(a) Calculate the profitability of each of the three distribution channels both in terms of total amount and return on sales.

(b) What are the implications of these for the distribution strategy of Color Plus?

Solution

(a) Statement showing Profitability of Distribution Channels

Particulars	*Catalogue*	*Corporate*	*Retail*	*Total*
Sales	₹1,50,000	₹50,000	₹1,00,000	₹3,00,000
Cost of sales	75,000	32,500	70,000	1,77,500
Gross margin	75,000	17,500	30,000	1,22,500
SGA expenses				
Sales commission		5,000	10,000	15,000
Customer mailing	2,940	30	30	3,000
Take phone/internet orders	3,882	39	79	4,000
Take field orders		4,500	4,500	9,000
Special negotiation field order		15,412	5,138	20,550
Process customer invoices	1,927	277	296	2,500
Others	15,771	2,261	2,418	20,450
Net margin/(loss)	50,480	(10,019)	7,539	48,000
Return on sales (%)	67.3	(57.3)	25.1	39.2

WORKING NOTE

1. Computation of Activity costs

	Expense Head				
	Marketing and sales support	*Design*	*Information system*	*General administration*	*Total*
Activity					
Customer mailing	₹3,000	—	—	—	₹3,000
Take phone/Internet orders	3,000	—	₹1,000	—	4,000
Take field orders	9,000	—	—	—	9,000
Special Negotiation	15,000	₹4,050	—	₹1,500	20,550
Processing Invoices	—	—	1,000	1,500	2,500
Others	—	450	8,000	12,000	20,450
Total	30,000	4,500	10,000	15,000	59,500

2. Computation of activity cost driver rates

Activity	*Total activity cost*	*Activity cost driver*	*Number of units of activity cost driver*	*Activity cost driver rate*
Customer mailing	₹3,000	Customer Mailings	2,00,000	Re. 0.015 per customer mailing
Take phone/internet orders	4,000	Number of phone/ internet orders	6,180	Re. 0.647 per phone/ internet/order
Take field orders	9,000	Number of field Orders	1,600	₹5.625 per field order
Special negotiations	20,550	Number of special negotiation orders	800	₹25.688 per special negotiation order
Processing invoices	2,500	Total number of orders	7,780	Re. 0.3213 per order
Others	20,450	Total number of	7,780	₹2.6285 per order

(b) The analysis carried out in part (a) shows that the corporate distribution channel is incurring a loss. This channel incurs an expense of nearly 40% of its sales revenue on taking field orders and negotiating special orders. Almost the entire design costs are incurred on special negotiation corporate orders. The order size is small and is not sufficient to absorb the design and sales support costs. To make the channel profitable, the company may fix the minimum size of a special order and also exhort its sales force to increase sales from the corporate channel.

12.C.3 ABC and Product Pricing Jay Engineering manufacturers electronic testing and measurement instruments. Many products are customer designed with recent orders for function generators, harmonic analysers, logic analysers, temperature measurement instruments and data logging instruments. Jay prices its instruments at 33 per cent over estimated cost (excluding administrative and selling costs).

It has come to the notice of the CEO of Jay that its sales-mix has changed. It is receiving fewer larger orders for simple instruments and more small orders for complex instruments. The CEO intuitively feels that the reason for Jay not being price competitive for simple products may the current cost accounting system. On the suggestion of Director (operations), he hires Jain Consultants to conduct a study to switch to ABC system.

Jain Consultants have selected two recent orders for study: (i) a 1,600 unit order for a temperature monitoring instrument and (ii) an order for 2 harmonic analysers. The costs and price data relating to them are given in Exhibit 1.

Exhibit 1 Cost and Price Data

	Temperature Monitor	*Harmonic Analyser*
1 Component cost per unit	₹800	₹8,000
2 Direct labor per unit	80	1,600
3 Overhead per unit	400	8,000
4 Cost per unit	1,280	17,600
5 Markup (30%)	384	5,280
6 Price per unit	1,664	22,880
7 Number of units	1,600	2
8 Value or order	26,62,400	45,760

Currently, the overhead (₹16,00,00,000 annually) is applied based on direct labour cost (₹3,20,00,000). Jain Consultants have broken down the annual overheads into six cost pools and identified the related cost driver as given in Exhibit 2.

Exhibit 2 Cost Pools and Cost Drivers

Cost Pools	*Annual Cost*	*Annual Cost Driver*
1 Production design	₹2,40,00,000	2,40,000 design-hours
2 Material ordering and handling	3,20,00,000	2,00,000 unique part numbers
3 Inspection	1,00,00,000	8,00,000 inspections
4 Setup	60,00,000	1,00,000 setups
5 Labour-related overheads	2,40,00,000	₹3,20,00,000 direct labour cost
5 Depreciation of plant and equipment	6,40,00,000	4,00,00,000 machine-hours
Total	16,00,00,000	

Jain Consultants have also estimated that the temperature monitoring instrument and the harmonic analyser make use of the cost drivers as shown in Exhibit 3.

EXHIBIT 3 Use of Cost Drivers by the Monitor and Analyser

	For 1,600 Monitors	For 2 Analysers
Number of design-hours	84	200
Number of unique parts	30	40
Number of inspections	400	30
Number of setups	1	1
Machine-hours	200	10

REQUIRED:

(a) Based on Jain Consultants data, compute the cost per unit of each product using the ABC approach.

(b) Based on Jain Consultants work, Jay Engineering has introduced an ABC system (as per Exhibit 2). Recently, Jay has received order from Amity International for a unique data logging device, requiring ₹32,000 of components and ₹8,000 of direct labour together with the following requirements:

- Number of design-hours 50
- Number of unique parts 30
- Number of inspections 20
- Number of setups 1
- Machine-hours 16

Amity International has indicated that they already have a quote from another supplier for ₹38,000. Calculate the cost of data logging device, using the ABC approach. How does it stand in relation to the competitors quote?

Solution

(a) Statement showing cost per unit using the ABC approach

	Temperature Monitor	Harmonic Analyser
Component cost per unit	₹800	₹8,000
Direct labour per unit	80	1,600
Overhead per unit	72	14,626
Cost per unit	952	24,226

WORKING NOTES

1. Computation of cost driver rate using the ABC approach

Activity	Annual cost	Cost driver	Number of units of cost driver per annum	Cost driver rate
Production design	₹2,40,00,000	design hours	2,40,000	₹100 per design hour
Material ordering and handling	3,20,00,000	unique part numbers	2,00,000	₹160 per unique part
Inspection	1,00,00,000	inspections	8,00,000	₹12.5 per Inspection
Setup	60,00,000	setups	1,00,000	₹60 per setup
Labour-related overheads	2,40,00,000	direct-labour cost	₹3,20,00,000	75% of direct labour cost
Depreciation of plant and equipment	6,40,00,000	machine-hours	4,00,00,000	₹1.60 per machine hour

2. Computation of overhead cost per unit using the ABC approach

Activity	*Cost driver rate*	*For 1,600 Monitors*		*For 2 Analysers*	
		Units of cost driver	*Cost*	*Units of cost driver*	*Cost*
Production design	₹100	84	₹8,400	200	₹20,000
Material ordering and handling	160	30	4,800	40	6,400
Inspection	12.5	400	5,000	30	375
Setup	60	1	60	1	60
Labour related overhead	75% of direct labour cost	₹1,28,000	96,000	₹3,200	2,400
Depreciation of plant	1.6	200	320	10	16
Total overhead cost			1,14,580		29,251
Overhead cost per unit (rounded off)			72		14,626

(b) Statement showing the cost of data logging device using the ABC approach

Component cost	₹32,000
Direct labour cost	8,000
Overhead cost	16,136
	56,136
Mark-up (30%)	16,841
Price per unit	72,977

WORKING NOTE

Computation of overhead cost per unit using the ABC approach

Activity	Cost driver rate	Units of cost driver	Cost
Production design	₹100	50	₹5,000
Material ordering and handling	160	30	4,800
Inspection	12.5	20	250
Setup	60	1	60
Labour related overhead labour cost	75% of direct	₹8,000	6,000
Depreciation of plant	1.6	16	26
Total overhead cost per unit			16,136

The cost of the company for a unit of the data logging device is nearly 48% higher than the quoted price of the other supplier.

13

Job-order, Batch and Service Costing

Learning Objectives

After reading this chapter you will be able to:

LO 13.1 Understand job/order costing
LO 13.2 Explain batch costing
LO 13.3 Describe service costing

Introduction

This chapter describes and illustrates the systems of job/order, batch costing and service costing. The main points are also summarised by way of recapitulation.

Job/Order Costing

LO 13.1 Understand job/order costing

This Section illustrates job costing as a method of cost accumulation. As the system of costing depends upon the operating environment/production procedure, we first outline the nature of job costing in terms of the situations/manufacturing processes in which such a costing method is appropriate. This is followed by the cost accounting cycle for jobs. The cost recording procedure under job costing is dependent on whether the firm maintains both the general and factory ledgers or only the general ledger. The cost accumulation in job costing is illustrated here in both situations.

Job order costing is the procedure to accumulate cost when work is performed pursuant to an order to meet individual customer's specifications.

Nature and Suitability

As the name implies, job-order costing refers to a costing system that determines the production cost of individual orders/jobs. Under this system, costs are assigned to, and accumulated for, each job. Such a system of cost accumulation is related to the flow of production in which a firm has to work on a job in pursuance of an order received from a customer. The order may be for a single item or a number of identical items manufactured as a group, that is, a batch. For instance, a book publishing company prints performed pursuant to an order, and when products are manufactured or services rendered to meet individual customers' specifications.

The essence of job costing is that as all jobs/orders are not necessarily alike, they do not pass through the same manufacturing process. In other words, since each job requires varying amounts of materials and labour and different levels of skills or attention, the cost of one job would differ from another. Thus, the cost should be recorded separately for each job. Therefore, the job-order costing system traces costs with individual production orders/jobs. In other words, in the case of certain manufacturing processes/situations, whether dealing with a product or service, is the relative uniqueness of the work (specific identity) performed for each job/client/order. Therefore, in this system of costing, each job or batch is regarded as a cost unit from the viewpoint of cost accumulation. Thus, the distinguishing feature of job-order costing is the ability to identify costs with a specific project/job/order or group of units.[1]

It follows from the above that job-order costing is, in general, appropriate in situations when each job (work) is unique, easily identifiable, and can serve as a cost objective[2] Such a system can be appropriately applied to accumulate costs in the following situations:

1. Auto-repair shops, where each repair job requires varying amounts of material and labour. The mechanic will charge the cost of any replaced parts and the number of labour-hours spent in repairing.
2. Automobile assembly, where each car includes a variety of different options.
3. Printing shops, where each print order requires a different type of paper, ink, design and so on.
4. Foundries, where special parts are to be manufactured as per order.
5. Hospitals, where the costs of services provided to each patient are billed separately.
6. Contractors, shipbuilders and motion picture companies.
7. Machine shops, tool shops and design engineers.
8. Public accounting firms and other similar professions, where each audit, tax return, or management services engagement needs varying amounts of professional time and attention.
9. Furniture making firms, where they may produce a batch of similar chairs, tables, sofas, and so on. Each batch may be treated as a job.

Cost Accounting Cycle/Job Cost Sheet

This section discusses the work flow and cost recording procedure in job costing. The backbone of the job costing system is the *job cost sheet.*

On receipt of an order by a firm employing job costing, a job cost sheet is prepared. Every job order is given a specific number. For identification, a job cost sheet bearing the allotted number is maintained for each job put into production. General information in respect of the job order is recorded at the top of the job sheet. As regards specific information, the job cost sheet enumerates the appropriate inputs required in three basic categories: direct material, direct labour and overhead to carry out the order. Depending on data requirements for planning, controlling costs and evaluating performance, additional information such as labour-hours, machine-hours, quantity and quality of the materials to be used may also be recorded in the job sheet. Besides, it also contains information regarding the quantum and quality of the final output and the date by which the supply is to be made; it may also provide reference of the customer. In some job cost situations, the job sheet follows the job physically through the production process, serving not only to accumulate costs, but also providing the appropriate routing for the job.[3] The labour and materials used by each production department on the job are recorded on the job sheet. A reference of the overhead criterion such as, direct material, direct labour, machine-hour rate or labour-hour rate used is also recorded on the job sheet. On completion of the work in one department, the goods are transferred to the next relevant department along with the job sheet. This process is repeated till the job is completed. At the final stage, the job sheet contains all the materials, labour and overhead costs that were incurred on each job, as the work on an order progresses through various stages of production. As a result, profit earned or loss suffered on the job can be easily determined. The job sheet also provides room for comparing the actual total costs with estimated costs. The reasons for variance in these costs are determined so as to prevent their future occurrence. All this information is vital to the management for evaluating employee performance and controlling the costs. Thus, the job cost sheet constitutes the backbone of the job-order system. In fact, it is a vital document for subsequent accounting records. The format of the cost sheet varies from firm to firm depending on their individual requirements. Exhibit 13.1 is the commonly used cost-sheet format. Columns may be added or deleted as circumstances warrant.

EXHIBIT 13.1 Job Cost Sheet

		Job No.	
Customer name		Date started	
and address		Date promised	
Description		Date finished	
Quantity		Special remarks, if any	

	Materials			*Labour*			*Overheads*		
	Quantity	Rate	Amount	Hours	Rate	Amount	Hours	Rate	Amount
Department 1									
Department 2									
Department 3									

Cost Summary

	Materials	*Labour*	*Overheads*	*Total*	
				Actual	*Estimate*
Department 1					
Department 2					
Department 3					
Job order price					
Profit (Loss)					

Discrepancies between actual and estimated costs are explained below:

1.
2.
3.

Recording Job Costs in Accounts

The accounting system of recording job costs will depend on whether the general ledger records all cost transactions or a special ledger called factory ledger is *separately* maintained for the purpose. It is ideal/preferable if the cost accountant is concerned with recording the costs in respect of the use of material and labour closer to the scene of production operations in the factory ledger, and the financial accountant is concerned with paying the bills and the records are maintained in the general ledger. Such a system of record keeping also rules out duplication of clerical effort.

The *modus operandi* is that a factory ledger account is opened in the general ledger to substitute for the accounts, which have been recorded in the factory ledger. Likewise, a general ledger account is provided in the factory ledger. Such cost recording can be said to be on a *self-balancing basis* as the general ledger and the factory ledger are independent of each other. The balances in these accounts are kept equal at all times. When an entry is made in the factory ledger accounts at the general office, it is offsetted by an entry made in the general ledger account at the factory office. In view of the usefulness of keeping a separate cost record in the factory ledger, it is commended for adoption. The accounting procedure to be adopted if both the factory and general ledgers are maintained is explained first. The accounting procedure when no separate ledger is kept and all transactions are recorded in a general ledger is illustrated subsequently. We have first explained the procedure relating to the: **(i)** Accounting for materials, **(ii)** Accounting for labour, **(iii)** Accounting for overheads, and **(iv)** Accounting for completed jobs. A comprehensive illustration follows the theoretical discussion.

Accounting for Materials Certain raw materials may be purchased to cater to the specifications of particular jobs. Typically, more basic materials of common use on a number of jobs are acquired and held in the materials inventory. For each type of raw material held by the manufacturing firm, a separate materials ledger card is prepared which indicates the quantity and cost of materials held for future use. When the materials are needed for a job, the job supervisor or any other authorised person, requisitions them through a *materials requisition slip/form* which forms the basis for the entry transferring materials from materials inventory (materials and supplies) account to the concerned job account. This form identifies the job order number and lists the type and quantity of materials drawn from the inventory. Any material not used in the job for which it was requisitioned would be returned. The relevant accounting entries in the factory and general ledgers to record the **(i)** purchase, **(ii)** issue, and **(iii)** return of materials would be as follows:

Factory ledger:

1. Debit materials inventory/materials and supplies A/c, and Credit general ledger.
2. Debit work-in-process A/c, and Credit materials inventory/materials and supplies A/c.
3. Reversal of entry (2)

General ledger:

1. Debit factory ledger, and Credit accounts payable/cash or bank.
2. No entry
3. No entry

Materials inventory is also used for indirect materials and supplies. Often, it is not worthwhile to assign the costs of these materials directly to the jobs in which they are used, as their value is insignificant compared to the total cost of the job. Hence, they are charged to the indirect manufacturing overhead account *(indirect manufacturing costs control account).* The journal entry for the acquisition of indirect materials is the same as that for the purchase of direct materials in both sets of ledgers. However, the issue of such materials to production is considered as an addition to indirect manufacturing cost and is charged to the manufacturing overhead cost control account. Subsequently, indirect material costs are allocated to jobs on the basis of some predetermined rate of absorption of indirect overheads.

Accounting for Labour In job-order costing, direct labour costs are payments for the services of employees directly engaged in manufacturing activities on jobs in progress—for example, wages paid to machinists, drill press operators, welders, and assemblers.

It is usual for manufacturing firms to pay wages to production workers on the basis of time; moreover, they are also usually provided with *a job time card* on which they record the number of hours spent on each job on a working day. The direct labour cost of any job is ascertained by the product of the number of hours spent on that job and the worker's hourly wage rate. In determining true hourly wage rate, calculations should not be limited to only the wage amount paid to him, but should also include the employer's contribution to the provident fund, pension and insurance plans, and other fringe benefits that are paid to him by the firm.

It is important to recognise here the element of indirect labour cost in the aggregate payments made to production workers. Indirect labour includes the costs of supervisors, foremen, maintenance, security and time keeping personnel; it also includes the costs of idle time, machine setup time, rework time and overtime wages paid to direct labourers. The justification in including overtime premium in indirect overhead is the fact that overtime is the result of overall activity. If the overall level of activity were lower, the job worked on during overtime hours would be worked on during regular hours. Accordingly, overtime premiums are allocated to all jobs through the overhead account.[4] However, if overtime premium accrues on account of a "*rush*" job where the customer is willing to pay for shorter than normal delivery time, the premium amount can be charged directly to a specific job.

The following journal entries would be recorded in respect of the labour cost:

> *Factory ledger:*
> Debit work-in-process A/c (for direct labour) and Debit factory overhead control (A/c (for indirect labour) and *Credit general ledger.*
> *General ledger:*
> Debit factory ledger A/c, and Credit wages payable A/c /cash or bank.

Accounting for Manufacturing Overheads Unlike direct material and labour costs which can wholly and exclusively be identified with specific jobs, costs relating to manufacturing overheads cannot be conveniently traced to a particular job as overhead costs are indirect in nature and pertain to the factory or organisation as a whole. In other words, they are not caused by a specific job. Nevertheless, each job requires the services of indirect overheads. This gives rise to the need for charging each job with its fair share of indirect overheads to determine its true cost.

> **Predetermined overhead rate** is budgeted manufacturing overheads divided by budgeted activity

Manufacturing overheads can be charged to various jobs either at the actual overhead rate or a *predetermined* overhead rate. The merits of a predetermined overhead rate are: **(a)** It is useful in 'bidding' cases to determine the tender/quotation price; **(b)** It enables individual jobs to be costed as soon as they are completed and, thus, helps in providing more rapid product cost information to the management; and **(c)** Such a rate levels out the fluctuations which may be caused by variations in actual overhead costs and actual activity. For these reasons, manufacturing overheads are often applied to jobs at a predetermined overhead rate:

Predetermined overhead rate = Budgeted manufacturing overheads/Budgeted activity **(13.1)**

For estimating budgeted manufacturing overheads, past historical cost data are taken as the base and adjustments are made for likely changes in prices/rates of various elements of overheads. The overheads are segregated into two categories: variable (for example, power and heating, indirect materials, repairs and maintenance) and fixed (for example, insurance, rent, property taxes, work manager's salary). Thus,

Budgeted manufacturing overheads =
[Total budgeted fixed overheads + Budgeted variable overhead rate] × Budgeted activity **(13.2)**

The budgeted activity measure "must be a factor that is common to all jobs, has a high correlation with the incurrence of overhead costs, and is easy to measure.[5] Where most of the work is done by machines, the machine-hour rate is often used to charge indirect overheads to jobs. The labour-hour rate or direct labour cost is useful in situations where most of the work is accomplished by labour.

Like manufacturing overheads, one reasonable way of estimating budgeted activity can be to make adjustments in the previous year's activity level on the basis of the management's expectation for the coming year.

Consider Example 13.1.

◆ Example 13.1

(Determining Predetermined Overheads Rate)

Hypothetical Ltd employs job-order costing. It uses an annual predetermined rate for applying manufacturing overheads to jobs. The company furnishes you with the following information regarding its overheads for the coming year at normal activity: Fixed overheads, ₹20,00,000; and Variable overheads, ₹15,00,000.

The estimates of the direct labour cost, direct labour hours and machine-hours at normal activity along with a set of correlation coefficients between overheads and various measures of activity, as compiled from past records, are also given:

	Normal level of activity	*Correlation coefficient with overheads*
Direct labour cost	₹10,00,000	0.7
Direct labour hours	20,000	0.8
Machine hours	10,000	0.6

Determine the predetermined (i) fixed, (ii) variable, and (iii) total overhead rates.

Solution

Predetermined overhead rates should be based on direct labour-hours (DLH):

(i) Predetermined fixed overhead rate = ₹20,00,000 ÷ 20,000 = ₹100
(ii) Predetermined variable overhead rate = ₹15,00,000 ÷ 20,000 = ₹75
(iii) Total predetermined overhead rate = ₹35,00,000 ÷ 20,000 = ₹175

Further assume that Hypothetical Ltd during the first quarter received an invitation from a regular customer to bid on a job. The job was estimated to require ₹1,00,000 of direct materials and the following: Direct labour cost, ₹50,000; Direct labour-hours, 1,500; and Machine-hours, 500

Determine the bid price the company should quote assuming its normal practice of charging 20 per cent on factory cost to cover other administrative overheads and profit. Assume further that the company uses a predetermined factory overhead rate to assign factory overheads to jobs.

Solution

Job Cost Sheet to Determine the Bid Price

Particulars	Amount
Direct materials	₹1,00,000
Direct labour cost	50,000
Prime cost	1,50,000
Add factory overheads (1,500 direct labour-hours @ ₹175 per hour)	2,62,500
Factory cost	4,12,500
Add 20 per cent for administrative overheads and profit	82,500
Bid price	4,95,000

Over-applied or Under-applied Manufacturing Overheads When predetermined overhead rate is used as the basis of absorption of overheads, it is seldom that the total overhead costs applied to jobs in a given period are equal to the total overhead costs of that period. When the applied overhead exceeds the actual, it is referred to as over-applied/absorbed overhead. It is known as under-applied/absorbed in case the applied is less than the actual. The difference between the actual and applied manufacturing overhead costs is designated as the *variance.*

Suppose in Example 13.1, the company's actual overheads were ₹9,00,000 and total direct labour-hours used were 4,500 in the first quarter. The applied overheads would amount to ₹7,87,500 [4,500 DLH × ₹175 (Total predetermined overhead rate per hour)]; overhead is under-applied by ₹1,12,500 (₹9,00,000 – ₹7,87,500).

Disposition of Variance Overhead variances may be disposed of by following either of the two methods: **(i)** They may be assigned to the income statement of the current period by charging the entire amount to the cost of goods sold account; or **(ii)** They may be considered as the cost of production of the current period and accordingly may be pro-rated to work-in-process, finished goods and cost of goods sold. The treatment would depend on the nature of such variance.

If the variance has been an outcome of unusual events of the current period, it should be charged to the cost of goods sold. But if such a variance has been caused by errors in estimation or fundamental changes in cost structure, it should be pro-rated over work-in-process, finished goods and cost of goods sold. For the firm in Example 13.1, consider the following additional information:

Job No.	Direct costs	Overheads charged in quarter	Status of job at the end of the quarter
50	₹11,00,000	₹3,60,000	Cost of goods sold
51	9,00,000	2,25,000	Finished goods inventory
52	6,50,000	2,02,500	Work-in-process inventory
	26,50,000	7,87,500	

Show the process of adjusting under-applied overheads.

Solution

Manufacturing/Factory Overhead Adjustment

Account	Overhead-charged in quarter	Percentage of overhead applied in quarter	Under-applied overheads (₹1,12,500) × (percentage)	Total costs assigned to jobs after adjustment
Cost of goods sold	₹3,60,000	45.7	₹51,412.50	₹4,11,412.50
Finished goods inventory	2,25,000	28.6	32,175.00	2,57,175.00
Work-in-process inventory	2,02,500	25.7	28,912.50	2,31,412.50
	7,87,500	100.00	1,12,500.00	9,00,000.00

The following journal entries would be required to give effect to manufacturing overheads.

Factory ledger

1. Debit Factory Overhead Control A/c, and Credit General Ledger
   (For indirect manufacturing costs incurred).
2. Debit Work-in-Process/Individual Jobs A/c, and Credit Factory Overhead Control A/c
   (For charging indirect overheads to jobs).
3. Debit Cost of Goods Sold A/c, and Credit Factory Overhead Control A/c
   (For charging under-applied overheads to cost of goods sold account under first method).
   Entry number (3) would be reversed in the case of over-applied overheads.
4. Debit Work-in-Process/Individual Jobs
   Debit Finished Goods inventory
   Debit Cost of Goods Sold, and
   Credit Factory Overhead Control A/c
   (For charging under-applied overheads under pro-rating method).
   Entries (3) and (4) would be reversed in the case of over-applied overheads.

General ledger

1. Debit Factory Ledger A/c, and Credit Various Credits (Accounts Payable), Credit Accumulated Depreciation, and so on.
   (For indirect manufacturing costs incurred).

For subsequent transactions no entry is required in the general ledger as these transactions do not affect the general ledger accounts.

Accounting for Completed Jobs Normally, in a job costing system when work on a job is completed, it would be available for delivery to a customer. At the time of completion, all work-in-process account balances pertaining to that job are transferred directly to cost of goods sold account. In case, production is made in anticipation of future sale, relevant costs from work-in-process will be transferred to the finished goods inventory account. The journal entries in the factory ledger would be as follows:

1. *Production is as per order*
   Debit Cost of Goods Sold A/c, and
   Credit Work-in-process A/c
   (Transfer of cost on completion of the job).
2. *Production is for future sale*
   (a) Debit Finished Goods Inventory A/c, and
   Credit Work-in-process A/c
   (b) *At the time of sale*
   Debit Costs of Goods Sold A/c, and
   Credit finished goods inventory.

Accounting for Non-Manufacturing Costs Costs such as sales commissions, freight and delivery charges, can sometimes be related directly to particular jobs. Since these costs are incurred subsequent to the completion of the job, they cannot be classified as the cost of production. They should be separately shown as the direct costs of selling, distributing, and servicing particular jobs in job cost sheets which can be modified to add non-manufacturing costs. This information is useful in estimating future job costs and in bidding on prices.

We now illustrate the cost recording procedure in job costing with a comprehensive example.

◆ **Example 13.2**

(Job Costing System: Factory Ledger and General Ledger Method)

Jay Engineering Company Ltd uses a job-order cost system. The following is a summary of its operations during January:

1. Purchases of raw materials and supplies, ₹37,500.
2. Materials and supplies were requisitioned and issued as follows:
   Direct materials:

Job No.	101	₹6,000	
	102	9,000	
	103	1,400	₹16,400
Indirect materials			400

3. Factory payroll sent to the general office for payment was distributed as follows:
   Direct labour:

Job No.	101	₹5,400	
	102	6,000	
	103	600	
			₹12,000
Indirect labour			4,000

4. Indirect miscellaneous manufacturing costs incurred, ₹5,200.
5. Indirect manufacturing costs were applied using a rate of 70 per cent of direct labour cost.
6. Job No. 101 (100 units) and Job No. 102 (50 units) were completed and transferred to finished goods.
7. Goods despatched to customers were as follows: From Job No. 101, 50 units; From Job No. 102, 100 units.

Prepare the required ledger accounts to record the above transactions in the factory ledger.

Solution

Job Ledger

Particulars	Job No. 101	Job No. 102	Job No. 103
Raw materials and supplies	₹6,000	₹9,000	₹1,400
Direct labour	5,400	6,000	600
Indirect manufacturing costs applied	3,780	4,200	420
	15,180	19,200	2,420

Factory Ledger Accounts

Raw Materials and Supplies A/c

To general ledger (purchase of inventory)	₹37,500	By work-in-process	₹16,400
		By factory overhead control A/c	400

Work-in-Process A/c

To raw materials and supplies	₹16,400	By finished goods (cost of Job Nos. 101 and 102	₹34,380
To general ledger (direct labour payment)	12,000		
To factory overhead control (applied A/c)	8,400		

Finished Goods Inventory A/c

To work-in-process	₹34,380	By cost of goods sold (₹7,590 + ₹12,800)	₹20,390

Cost of Goods Sold A/c

To finished goods inventory	₹20,390		

Factory Overhead Control A/c

To raw materials and supplies	₹400		
To general ledger (indirect labour payment)	4,000		
To general ledger (miscellaneous expenses)	5,200		

Factory Overhead Control Applied A/c

		By work-in-process	₹8,400

General Ledger Accounts

		By raw materials and supplies	₹37,500
		By work-in-process	12,000
		By factory overhead control A/c	4,000
		By factory overhead control A/c	5,200

Note: Ledger accounts are not balanced as the transactions pertain to only a month's period.

General Ledger Accounts

Factory Ledger (A/c)

To accounts payable	₹37,500		
To wages payable	16,000		
To miscellaneous credits	5,200		

Accounts Payable A/c*

		By factory ledger A/c	₹37,500

Wages Payable A/c*

		By factory ledger A/c	₹16,000

Miscellaneous Credits A/c*

		By factory ledger A/c	₹5,200

*Debits in these accounts would be made when payments are made.

The above cost recording procedure is valid when a *separate* factory ledger is maintained. We now enumerate the accounting system when the general ledger records *all* transactions and no separate factory ledger is maintained. A comprehensive illustration (Example 13.3) demonstrates the actual recording procedure.

◆ Example 13.3

(Job Order Costing: General Ledger Method)

The following transactions occurred at the Small Machine Manufacturing Company Ltd:

1. Issued ₹1,000 in supplies from the materials inventory.
2. Purchased materials worth ₹20,000.
3. Purchased materials costing ₹15,800 on cash basis.
4. Paid for the materials purchased.

5. Issued materials worth ₹17,000 to the production department.
6. Incurred wages of ₹42,000 which were debited to a temporary account called the wages payable account. Of this amount, ₹8,000 was withheld for taxes; the balance was paid in cash to the employees.
7. Analysis of the wage accounts reveals that 60 per cent was direct labour, 30 per cent indirect manufacturing labour and 10 per cent administrative and selling costs.
8. Paid cash for utilities, power, equipment maintenance, and other miscellaneous items for the manufacturing plant. The total amount was ₹21,600.
9. Applied overhead on the basis of 175 per cent of direct labour costs.
10. Depreciation on plant and equipment is to be charged at ₹10,500.
11. The following balances appeared in the accounts of company:

	Opening	*Closing*
Materials inventory	₹37,050	—
Work-in-process inventory	8,250	—
Finished goods inventory	41,500	₹33,200
Cost of goods sold		65,850

You are required to prepare T accounts to show the costs during the period.

Solution

Ledger Accounts

Materials Inventory A/c

To balance b/d	₹37,050	By factory overhead control A/c	₹1,000
To accounts payable	20,000	By work-in-process inventory	17,000
To cash (purchases)	15,800	By balance c/d	54,850
	72,850		72,850
To balance b/d	54,850		

Work-in-Process Inventory A/c

To balance b/d	₹8,250	By finished goods inventory A/c	₹57,550
To raw materials inventory	17,000	By balance c/d	37,000
To factory overhead control A/c	44,100		
To wages control A/c (₹42,000 × 0.60)	25,200		
	94,550		94,550
To balance b/d	37,000		

Finished Goods Inventory A/c

To balance b/d	₹41,500	By cost of goods sold	₹65,850
To work-in-process inventory (balancing figure)	57,550	By balance c/d	33,200
To balance b/d	33,200		
	99,050		99,050

Factory Overhead Control A/c

To raw materials inventory	₹1,000	By work-in-process A/c (₹25,200 × 1.75)	₹44,100
To wages control A/c (₹42,000 × 0.30)	12,600	By factory-overhead control applied A/c (under-absorbed)	1,600
To cash (for various overheads)	21,600		
To accumulated depreciation on plant	10,500		
	45,700		45,700

Apart from the manufacturing firms, service organisations such as engineering, consulting and accounting, firms can also usefully apply the job-order costing system. The job-order costing procedure is basically the same in both service and manufacturing organisations, except that the former do not make use of any direct materials. Instead of having an indirect manufacturing overhead account, service firms can have the title of service overhead account, to represent and accumulate costs in respect of indirect materials, indirect labour and other overheads.

Evaluation

Job order costing is useful in the following ways:

1. Job costing data can be utilised for estimating the production costs of specific jobs or lots of production. If, for example, a customer places an order with the firm to manufacture a specific type of product that has unique characteristics different from the other products manufactured by the company, a job-order cost system should be utilised to accumulate the production costs associated with this product. In other words, job costing system provides the basis for determining the 'bidding' price for similar jobs that will be considered in the future.
2. Estimates of future job costs serve not only as a basis for bidding and price setting but also as a standard for measuring efficiency and evaluating the performance through comparisons with the actual costs incurred. Since under this system, all costs such as direct materials, direct labour and other expenses which can be traced directly to particular or specific jobs must be forecast as separate identifiable amounts, subsequent comparisons between actual job costs incurred and estimated job costs can be made on an item-by-item basis. This process helps the management in assigning responsibilities for variance in costs to different responsibility centres that worked on the job. Thus, this process assists the management in discharging its control function.
3. From the point of view of accounting also, the system is easy to operate as the costs are recorded order or job-wise.
4. Finally, job cost sheets which are the focal point of job order system can be utilised by the management to segregate jobs on the basis of contributions/profits made by them. This information, in turn, will help the management in deciding which types of jobs should be accorded priority.

The only drawback visualised in the system is that it requires detailed record-keeping for each of the jobs, and, therefore, may prove to be more expensive to use.

Batch Costing

LO 13.2 Explain batch costing

This Section illustrates batch costing, as a system of cost accumulation. As mentioned earlier, batch costing is a variant of job costing. It is a natural type of system to be utilised in situations when a firm manufactures products in readily identifiable batches or definite lots.

The I.C.M.A. London has defined batch costing as "that form of specific order costing which applies where similar articles are manufactured in batches either for sale or for use within the company". In most cases, this costing is similar to job-costing. "A batch is a cost unit which consists of a group of similar articles, which maintain its identity throughout one or more stages of production:" In such a system, each batch can serve as a cost objective for identification of costs as each job is a cost objective in the job-order costing system. Hence, the cost recording procedure in the batch costing system is similar to that of the job costing system.

For identification purposes, each batch is required to be numbered in batch costing as each job is numbered in the job costing system. Similarly, direct material, direct labour and any other direct costs which can be traced directly to a specific batch are charged to it and indirect manufacturing overheads are applied at the predetermined rate. Thus, the normal principles of job-order costing system apply to batch costing also. However, there are some points of distinction between the two.

The unique feature which distinguishes job costing from batch costing is that, while in the former production is tailored to meet the customers' specifications, in the latter, in general, goods are produced to inventory them for future sale to customers. The situations in which batch costing might gainfully be applied include, furniture making, small tool making, manufacture of fabric, clothing and toys, as well as certain food processing undertakings.

The determination of batch/quantity to be produced in each job is another salient feature which distinguishes it from job costing. The determination of the appropriate size of the batch produced necessitates a resolution of conflicting goals. Production in large quantities implies lower *setting-up* costs as such costs are normally fixed per batch. Thus, the unit cost falls with an increase in size of the batch. But an increase in size of the batch produced would involve higher carrying costs of holding inventory in stock. These costs include the cost of storage, risk of pilferage, spoilage and obsolescence and loss interest on the investment blocked in inventories. Therefore, the size of batch produced should neither be too small nor too large. On the basis of a trade-off between benefits derived from setting-up costs and the costs of carrying the inventory, an appropriate production level of the batch should be determined. Stated with reference to the cost perspective, the economic batch quantity (EBQ), can be determined by Equation 13.3. This is similar to the method of determining the economic order quantity (EOQ):

$$EBQ = \sqrt{2\,AS/C} \qquad \textbf{(13.3)}$$

Where A = annual requirements of the product
S = setting-up costs per batch
C = carrying cost per unit of inventory per annum

◆ Example 13.4

The following details are available in respect of a small tool manufacturing firm:

Annual estimated demand per year (units)	1,600
Cost of production per unit	₹5
Carrying costs per unit for one year	1
Setting up cost per batch	50

Determine EBQ.

Solution

Using Equation 13.3,

$$EBQ = \sqrt{\frac{2 \times 1{,}600 \times ₹50}{₹1}} = 400 \text{ units}$$

SERVICE COSTING

LO 13.3 Describe service costing

The term service costing is applied to unit costing of services as opposed to that of products. It is applicable where standardised services are provided, either by an undertaking or by a service cost centre within an undertaking. Thus, service (also known as operating) costing is suitable for public utility undertakings providing services to the community at large, such as road and rail transport companies, electricity undertakings, hospitals and theatres. It is also suitable for cost ascertainment by ancillary services departments of manufacturing units such as power house, boiler house, hospital, internal transport and canteen for the benefit of employees.

The cost per unit in service costing is based on average cost. Example of units to express average cost are as follows:

Organisation	*Cost unit*
Transport undertakings	Passenger– km (passenger traffic) or Tonne– km (goods transport)
Electricity boards/Organisation	Kilowatt– hours
Hospitals	Patient– days, outpatients treated, cost per major or minor surgical operation
Boiler houses	Quantity (kg or lb) of steam generated
Canteens	Meals served; cups of tea sold.

The unit costs in service organisations are ascertained in the form of operating cost sheet. It is a statement of operating costs (and sometimes profit also) in operating costing. Corresponding to the fixed costs, variable costs and semi-variable costs in manufacturing organsiations, the operating costs in service organisations are generally categorised into three groups, namely, standing charges, running costs and repairs and maintenance. The repairs and maintenance is often clubbed with running costs. The main elements of these categories of costs in the case of a transport undertaking are detailed as follows.

Standing Charges

Standing charges are those, which are incurred irrespective of the mileage run. They are like fixed costs. Included in this category are the following expenses:

1. License fees
2. Insurance premium
3. Road tax
4. Garage costs and administration
5. Drivers' wages (gross) including provident fund contribution of employers
6. Attendant-cum-cleaner's wages
7. Interest on capital (if considered as a part of cost).

Running Costs

Running costs are those which vary more or less in direct proportion to the mileage run. The following is a list of such expenses:

1. Cost of fuel (diesel, petrol etc.)
2. Lubricants, grease and oil
3. Repairs and maintenance (strictly semi–variable)
4. Cost of tyres, tubes and other spare parts
5. Depreciation.

In costing transport undertakings, the cost unit is normally passenger– km (in the case of passenger traffic) and tonne– km (in the case of goods transport). However, passenger– km/tonne– km unit may not be applicable in all situations. For instance, where the material is bulky but of small weight, say, empty containers (drums and tins), a certain maximum volume is often considered as equivalent to one tonne. For example, in sea freight, a maximum volume of 40 cubic feet is considered equivalent to one tonne for freight purposes. Likewise, some other standard freight measure is adopted for items such as cars, televisions, refrigerators, and so on.

In transport, the total operating cost should be determined with reference to each vehicle under suitable cost headings, namely, standing charges, running charges and maintenance charges. The passenger–km or tonne–km can be conceived as a function of the following variables:

1. The number of vehicles (fleet)
2. The carrying capacity of the vehicle in terms of number of passengers/freight
3. Distance travelled
4. Number of days on an average for which the vehicle is likely to be in operation
5. Number of trips in a day; going and coming should be considered as two trips
6. Passenger/weight actually carried on an average.

◆ Example 13.5

DHT Ltd. is running 4 buses between two towns which are 100 kms apart: the seating capacity of each bus is 50 passengers and 80 per cent of this capacity is actually used. Each vehicle makes 2 round trips daily and the vehicles are working on an average of 25 days a month. Determine the passenger–kms. Also, determine cost per passenger–km, if the total operating costs for 4 buses are ₹160,00,000.

Solution

Passenger– km = Number of buses × Distance × Capacity × Trips × 2 × Days × Percentage of the capacity used = (4 × 100 × 50 × 2 × 2 × 25) × 0.80 = 16,00,000

Cost per passenger–km = Total costs/Total passenger–kms = ₹160,00,000/16,00,000 = ₹10

When the transport undertaking owns vehicles having different capacities, cost unit should be determined with reference to varying capacities.

◆ Example 13.6

(Determination of Cost Unit When Vehicle Have Different Rated Capacities)

A transport company operates the following fleet: 20 trucks of 10 tonne capacity, 10 trucks of 5 tonne capacity, 5 mini-trucks of 2 tonne capacity.

The first two types of trucks are used for long distances and the mini-truck is utilised for local transport only. In a week, the following distances were covered by each of the trucks: 10 tonne capacity truck 600 kms, 5 tonne capacity truck; 500 kms; 2 tonne capacity truck, 300 kms.

If the total cost is ₹14,80,000, determine the cost per tonne–km, assuming that all vehicles worked to their full capacity during the period.

Solution

Determination of Total Tonne – Kilometres (Kms)

Number of vehicle	*Capacity in tonnes*	*Distance in kms*	*Tonne– kms*
20	10	600	1,20,000
10	5	500	25,000
5	2	100	3,000
			1,48,000

Cost per tonne – kilometre = ₹17,76,000/ 1,48,000 = ₹10

Each vehicle, in a way, is a *cost centre* in operating costing. Therefore, a separate cost sheet is maintained for each vehicle in the cost accounting department. Detailed information to be incorporated in the cost sheet is available from the *daily log sheet* maintained by the bus operators. The daily log sheet provides complete information in respect of each journey. For instance, it records kilometers travelled, weight or passengers carried, the time when the journey commenced and when it was completed. Apart from the journey, the log sheet also records the supplies of petrol, diesel or other materials made to the vehicle. Cost in respect of road tax, insurance, tyres and spares are entered directly in the records already maintained. Wages of the drivers and assistants are recorded from the payroll register.

When a transport company maintains its own repairs and maintenance department, the vehicle can be charged for the cost and the time mechanics spend on its repairs and maintenance. For this purpose, they maintain *time sheets* to record time spent by them on each vehicle. Subsequently, these time sheets are the guiding reference to apportion cost of this department among various vehicles. Likewise, the materials issued (tyres, tubes, and other spares) from the central store are classified and the relevant costs of such materials transferred to the concerned cost sheet of each vehicle.

At suitable periodical intervals, the costs are transferred from the vehicle cost sheets to the summary statement of the operating cost of the fleet as a whole. Costs are recorded under suitable headings of running costs and standing costs. The cost classification enables a comparison of each vehicle's performance. The total costs so determined are averaged out to determine cost per km or cost per tonne–km or cost per passenger–km as applicable. Comparison can be made with operating cost of other transport companies/ undertakings operating in that region to judge the operating efficiency of the firm.

Apart from inter-firm comparisons, certain ratios can also be determined and used for the purpose. One such ratio can be the *capacity utilisation ratio.* This ratio would measure the relationship between the capacity used (tonne–km/passenger–km) and the capacity available. The higher the ratio, the better it is. This ratio can be compared with the corresponding ratio of earlier years also. Another important ratio in this regard can be the *cost revenue ratio.* This ratio would establish the relationship between cost per tonne–km incurred and revenue per tonne–km realised; the lower the ratio, the better it is. The ratio of more than 1 (or 100 per cent) signals unprofitability and very high ratios point to deteriorating profitability.

Finally, for control purposes, the following data may be compiled for each vehicle at periodical intervals: **(i)** the mileage run, **(ii)** fuel consumed and the km per litre, **(iii)** lubricants consumed, and **(iv)** working days analysis in respect of **(a)** running under load, **(b)** under repair, **(c)** loses through abnormal causes such as driver's absence or breakdown of vehicle. This exercise also helps in assessing whether it is profitable to operate a particular vehicle on a certain route or not.

SUMMARY

- A job defined as the work done in pursuance of an order from a customer for the supply of a specific type of product to suit his needs. The job costing system is applicable in the case of a single item or batch. It is also applicable both to manufacturing and service activities.
- In this system of costing, each job is regarded as a cost unit as each job is different from the other. Such a system of cost accumulation is applicable to firms such as auto repair shops, printing shops, foundaries, hospitals, machine/tool shops, design engineers, accounting firms, furniture-making firms and so on.
- The procedure of determining cost according to this method is to trace/attach costs of the specific job by means of a cost sheet set up for each job. Direct materials and direct labour costs are traced directly to the specific jobs; indirect manufacturing costs are applied to jobs by means of a predetermined overhead application rate. The pre-determined rate = Budgeted overheads/Budgeted/normal activity.

- At the end of the accounting period, there will be an over or under-applied overhead balance. If this balance is insignificant in nature, it is usually closed to the cost of goods sold, but significant amounts may need to be ***pro-rated*** to appropriate accounts, that is, work-in-process, finished goods and cost of goods sold. The procedure of recording cost depends on whether a firm maintains only a general ledger or whether it records transactions in a general as well as a factory ledger.

LO 13.1

- Batch costing is a variant of job costing. The distinguishing feature between the two is that production is tailored to meet the customers' specifications in job costing; in contrast, goods are produced to inventory them for future sale to customers.

LO 13.2

- Service costing is applied to service organisations as well as to service departments of manufacturing organsiations. The cost per unit in service costing is based on average cost such as passenger–km, tonne–km and kilowatt– hours. Another distinguishing feature of this type of costing is the basis of cost classification. The major elements of cost are standing charges (fixed costs) and running cost (variable costs).

LO 13.3

REFERENCES

1. Morse, W.J., *Cost Accounting*, (Addison-Wesley Publishing Co., Massachusetts), 1978, p. 55.
2. Chatfield, M. and Weilson, D., *Cost Accounting*, (Harcourt Brance Joyanvich, New York), 1983, p. 115.
3. Moriarity, S. and Allen, C.P. *Cost Accounting*, (Harper and Row Publishers, New York), p. 516.
4. Morse, W.J., *op. cit.*, p. 58.
5. *Ibid.*, p. 66.

SOLVED PROBLEMS

P. 13.1 The normal expenses attributable to machine No. III and the normal hours for which the machine is expected to be utilised in the current year are indicated below: LO 13.1 LOD: E

Fixed		₹20,000
Variable:		
Power	₹15,000	
Repairs	9,000	
Lubricants	6,000	30,000
		50,000

Predetermined normal hours of working:	
To make ready	200
Running on jobs	800
Total	1,000

From the data furnished below, compute the cost of job No. 8237:

Materials consumed (10 units of ₹50 per unit)	₹500
Direct labour cost:	
To make ready: 2 machine-hours at ₹10	20
Running on job: 8 machine-hours at ₹10	80
	600

Note: Whenever a job is to be put on the machine, the machine is cleaned, any tools or jigs already on the machine are removed, and new tools and so on. suitable for the particular job are fitted before commissioning the machine for the job and the time involved is to be charged to the job as 'Make ready' time.

Solution

Job Cost Sheet

Customer name .... Job No. 8237 ....
Description and quantity .... Date started ....
Special remarks .... Date promised ....
(Machine III is used on job) .... Date finished ....

Particulars	*Rate*	*Hours/units*	*Amount*
Materials (Requisition No....)	₹50	10	₹500
Wages: (To make ready)	10	2	20
(Running on job)	10	8	80
Prime cost			600
Factory overheads:			
To make ready	20	2	40
Running on job (see working note)	57.50	8	460
Cost of production			1,100

WORKING NOTES

Determination of factory overheads: Total normal machine-hours are 1,000; of which setting-up time (to make ready) is 200 hours. Fixed expenses will be pro-rated on the basis of 1,000 hours and variable expenses on the basis of 800 hours the machine worked. The rates, so determined would be:

Fixed overhead rate to make ready (₹20,000, total expenses ÷ 1,000)	₹20.00
Variable (₹30,000, total expenses ÷ 800)	37.50
Overhead rate to make ready	20.00
Overhead rate for running time would be the sum of the two rates, (₹20 + ₹37.50)	57.50

P. 13.2 A shop-floor supervisor of a small factory presents the following per unit cost for Job No. 421 to determine the selling price: **LO 13.1** **LOD: E**

Materials	₹70
Direct wages (1.8 hours @ ₹25) (Department X, 0.8 hour; Department Y, 0.6 hour; Department Z, 0.4 hour)	45
Chargeable expenses (special stores items)	5
Prime cost	120
Add 33.33 per cent for expenses	40
Total	160

Analysis of the profit and loss A/c for the current quarter shows the following:

Materials used		₹1,50,000	Sales less returns	₹2,50,000
Direct wages:				
Department X	₹10,000			
Department Y	12,000			
Department Z	8,000	30,000		
Special stores items		4,000		
Overheads:				
Department X	5,000			
Department Y	9,000			
Department Z	2,000	16,000		
Gross profit c/d		50,000		
		2,50,000		2,50,000
Selling expenses		20,000	Gross profits b/d	50,000
Net profit		30,000		
		50,000		50,000

It is also noted that average hourly wage rates for the 3 departments, X, Y, and Z are similar. Direct labour-hour method is followed to absorb overheads.

You are required to: **(i)** Draw up a job cost sheet; **(ii)** Calculate revised cost for the current year, using actual figures as basis; and **(iii)** Add 20 per cent to total costs to determine selling price.

Solution

Job Cost Sheet

Customer name .... Job No. 421

Description and quantity .... Date started..

Special remarks .... Date promised

Date finished ....

Particulars	*Rate*	*Hours/quantity*	*Amount*
Materials used			₹70.00
Direct wages:			
Department X	₹25	0.8	20.00
Department Y	25	0.6	15.00
Department Z	25	0.4	10.00
Direct expenses			5.00
Prime cost			120.00
Indirect overheads: (see working note)			
Department X	12.50	0.8	10.00
Department Y	18.75	0.6	11.25
Department Z	6.25	0.4	2.50
Cost of production (total cost)			143.75
Add 20 per cent profit margin on cost			28.75
Selling price			172.50

Working Notes

Determination of Overhead Rate

Department	*Overheads*	*Direct labour-hours (Total wages ÷ hourly rates)*	*Rate per hour*
X	₹5,000	400	₹12.50
Y	9,000	480	18.75
Z	2,000	320	6.25

P. 13.3 The Rathi Engineering Company Ltd manufactures special-purpose small machines to order. In the beginning of the year, there were two jobs in process, namely, Job No. 100 and Job No. 101. The following costs were applied to these jobs in the previous year: **LO 13.1** **LOD: M**

	Job 100	*Job 101*
Direct materials	₹25,000	₹40,000
Direct labour	20,000	15,000
Overheads	22,200	16,650
	67,200	71,650

During January of the current year, the following transactions took place:

1. Raw materials costing ₹2,00,000 were purchased on account.
2. Supplies costing ₹40,000 were purchased for cash.
3. Jobs 102, 103 and 104 were started and the following costs applied to them:

	Job 102	Job 103	Job 104
Direct materials	₹15,000	₹50,000	₹35,000
Direct labour	25,000	30,000	20,000

4. Jobs 100 and 101 were completed; additional direct labour costs incurred on them were ₹10,000 and ₹20,000 respectively.
5. Wages paid to production employees during January totalled ₹1,25,000, of which accrued wages of the previous year were ₹25,000; wages payable at the end of the current month were ₹20,000.
6. Depreciation for the month totalled ₹50,000.
7. Utilities bills totalling ₹60,000 were received for the January operations.
8. Supplies costing ₹10,000 were used.
9. Miscellaneous overhead expenses totalled ₹12,000 for January.

Actual overhead is applied for individual jobs at the end of each month using a rate based on actual direct-labour costs. You are required to

(a) Determine the overhead rate for the month of January.
(b) Pass the necessary journal entries for each of the transactions that book place during January.
(c) Specify all subsidiary records affected by each transaction.
(d) Determine the amount of profit earned on Jobs 100 and 101, assuming job prices of ₹1,10,000 and ₹1,70,000 respectively.
(e) Prepare a statement of cost of goods manufactured.

Solution

(a) *Determination of Overhead Rate (January)*

Indirect labour:			
Wages paid		₹1,25,000	
Less wages outstanding of previous year(25,000)			
Add wages outstanding of current month		20,000	
		1,20,000	
Less direct labour			
Job 100	₹10,000		
101	20,000		
102	25,000		
103	30,000		
104	20,000	(1,05,000)	₹15,000
Depreciation			50,000
Utilities			60,000
Supplies			10,000
Miscellaneous overhead			12,000
Total overheads			1,47,000
Actual direct labour cost			1,05,000
Overhead rate (₹1,47,000 ÷ ₹1,05,000) × 100 (per cent)			140

(b) and **(c)** *Subsidiary Records Affected by the Transactions are shown along with Journal Entry.*

Particulars		Dr Amount	Cr Amount
Stores control A/c	Dr	₹2,00,000	
To accounts payable			₹2,00,000
(Inventory ledger cards, payable ledger)			
Supplies inventory A/c	Dr	40,000	
To bank			40,000

(Contd.)

(Contd.)

(Supplies inventory may have separate records and accordingly subsidiary ledgers would be affected)			
Work-in-process A/c	Dr	1,00,000	
To stores control			1,00,000
(Job cost sheets and inventory ledger cards)			
Factory overhead control A/c	Dr	15,000	
(individual labour)			
Work-in-process	Dr	1,05,000	
To wages payable			1,20,000
(Overhead ledger cards, job cost sheets and payable ledger)			
Wages payable A/c	Dr	1,25,000	
To bank/cash			
(Payables ledger)			1,25,000
Factory overhead control A/c	Dr	1,32,000	
To accumulated depreciation			50,000
To accounts payable (utilities)			60,000
To supplies inventory			10,000
To sundry accounts			12,000
(overheads ledger *cards payables ledger and fixed assets ledger)*			
Accounts payable (utilities)	Dr	50,000	
To bank/cash			50,000
(Accounts payable ledger)			
Work-in-process A/c	Dr	1,47,000	
To factory overhead control			1,47,000
(Job cost sheets and overhead ledger cards)			
Finished stock inventory	Dr	2,10,850	
To work-in-process			2,10,850

(d) *Job Cost Sheet (for jobs 100 and 101)*

Particulars	*Job 100*	*Job 101*
Opening work-in-process		
Direct materials	₹25,000	₹40,000
Direct labour	20,000	15,000
Overhead	22,200	16,650
	67,200	71,650
Add current month cost		
Direct labour	10,000	20,000
Overhead (140 per cent)	14,000	28,000
Total cost	91,200	1,19,650
Profit (balancing figure)	18,800	50,350
Job prices	1,10,000	1,70,000

(e) *Statement of Cost of Goods Manufactured for the month of January*

Particulars	*Amount*
Direct materials	₹1,00,000
Direct labour	1,05,000
Prime cost	2,05,000

(Contd.)

(Contd.)

Add factory overheads		
Indirect labour	₹15,000	
Depreciation	50,000	
Utilities	60,000	
Supplies	10,000	
Miscellaneous overheads	12,000	1,47,000
Gross factory cost		3,52,000
Add work-in-process (opening)		
Job 100	67,200	
Job 101	71,650	1,38,850
Less closing work-in-process		
Job 102 (₹15,000 + ₹25,000 + ₹35,000)	75,000	
Job 103 (₹50,000 + ₹30,000 + ₹42,000)	1,22,000	
Job 104 (₹35,000 + ₹20,000 + ₹28,000)	83,000	(2,80,000)
Cost of goods manufactured		2,10,850

P.13.4 The Philips Company Ltd produces gramophone records and has several different recording companies as clients. Since each order is separately identifiable, a job order accounting system is in use. Two departments are utilised, and the following overhead budget data at normal activity are available for the whole current year as well as the actual overhead cost for the first month (January): **LO 13.1** **LOD: D**

Particulars	*Overhead budget for the current year at normal level of activity*	*Actual overheads(January)*
Department X		
Fixed	₹7,20,000	₹66,000
Variable	6,00,000	63,000
Department Y		
Fixed	10,80,000	87,000
Variable	9,00,000	51,000

During January, 2 jobs were in production (209 and 210). The following is a summary of some of the data from their respective job cost sheets.

	Job 209		*Job 210*	
	Departments		*Departments*	
Items	X	Y	X	Y
Direct labour	₹1,08,000	₹15,000	₹36,000	₹42,000
Direct labour-hours	24,000	3,000	6,000	9,000
Machine-hours	4,800	24,000	3,000	12,000

The estimates of the departments' direct-labour cost, direct labour-hours, and machine-hours at normal activity are also provided in the following table, along with a set of correlation coefficients between overheads and the various measure of activity that have been compiled from past production and cost data.

	Department X		*Department Y*	
	Normal level of activity	*Correlation co-efficient with overheads*	*Normal level of activity*	*Correlation co-efficient with overheads*
Direct labour cost	₹15,00,000	0.8	₹7,20,000	0.6
Direct labour-hours	30,000	0.9	15,000	0.8
Machine-hours	9,000	0.5	6,000	0.9

During January, the company received an invitation from a regular customer to bid on a job which, if won, would be executed in February. The job was estimated to require ₹1,50,000 of materials and to involve:

	Department X	Department Y
Direct labour cost	₹75,000	₹33,000
Direct labour-hours	1,500	600
Machine-hours	300	210

How much overhead would you include in the bid? Estimate the bid price, the company should quote, assuming the company's normal practice of charging 20 per cent on cost price as profit.

Solution

Job Cost Sheet to Determine the Tender Price

Particulars	*Amount*		*Amount*
Direct materials			₹1,50,000
Direct labour cost:			
Department X	₹75,000		
Department Y	33,000		1,08,000
Prime cost			2,58,000
Add overhead costs			
Department X:			
Fixed (1,500 × ₹24)	36,000		
Variable (1,500 × ₹20)	30,000	₹66,000	
Department Y:			
Fixed (210 × ₹180)	37,800		
Variable (210 × ₹150)	31,500	69,300	1,35,300
Factory cost			3,93,300
Add estimated profit @ 20 per cent on cost			78,660
Bid price			4,71,960

WORKING NOTES

Determination of overhead rates:

Department X [Direct labour hours (DLH) has been taken as basis. The reason is there is the highest correlation between DLH and overhead incurred]

Fixed = ₹7,20,000 ÷ 30,000 DLH = ₹24

Variable = ₹6,00,000 ÷ 30,000 DLH = ₹20

Department Y [Machine-hour rate (MHR) has been taken as the basis. The reason there exists the highest correlation between MHR and overhead]:

Fixed = ₹10,80,000 ÷ 6,000 = ₹180

Variable = ₹9,00,000 ÷ 6,000 = ₹150

P.13.5 A jobbing factory has undertaken to supply 200 pieces of a component per month for the ensuing 6 months. Every month a batch order is opened against which materials and labour-hours are booked at actuals; overheads are levied at a per/labour hour rate. The selling price contracted for is ₹8 per piece. From the following data, present the cost and profit per piece of each batch order and overall position of the order for 1,200 pieces: LO 13.2 LOD: M

Months	*Batch output*	*Material cost*	*Direct wages*	*Direct labour-hours*
January	210	₹650	₹120	24
February	200	640	140	28
March	220	680	150	28
April	180	630	140	27
May	200	700	150	30
June	220	720	160	32

The other details are:

Month	Chargeable expenses	Direct labour-hours
January	₹12,000	480
February	10,560	440
March	12,000	500
April	10,580	460
May	13,000	500
June	12,000	480

Solution

Batch Cost Sheet for six months (January to June)

Month	Material	Cost of production			Batch output (units)	Cost per unit (5 × 6)	Selling price per unit	Profit (loss) per unit
		Direct wages	Overheads*	Total				
(1)	(2)	(3)	(4)	(5)	(6)	(7)	(8)	(9)
January	₹650	₹120	₹600	₹1,370	₹210	₹6.52	₹8	₹1.48
February	640	140	672	1,452	200	7.26	8	0.74
March	680	150	672	1,502	220	6.83	8	1.17
April	630	140	621	1,391	180	7.73	8	0.27
May	700	150	780	1,630	200	8.15	8	(0.15)
June	720	160	800	1,680	220	7.64	8	0.36
	4,020	860	4,145	9,025	1,230			

*Overheads = (Direct labour-hours × Labour-hour rate)

Labour-hour rate = (Chargeable expenses ÷ Direct labour-hours)

Overall position of the order of 1,200 units

Sale revenue (1,200 × ₹8)	₹9,600
Less cost of production (₹9,025/1,230) × 1,200	8,805
Profit	795

P.13.6 You are required to prepare a cost-sheet of an engineering work showing the actual and estimated cost of a batch of 100 units from the following information: **LO 13.2** **LOD: M**

The batch passes through 3 departments, A, B and C. Materials used for the batch:

Department A—600 units @ ₹10 per unit

Department B—50 units @ ₹20 per unit

Direct labour

Department A—10 hours @ ₹20 per hour

Department B—2 hours @ ₹25 per hour

Department C—10 hours @ ₹15 per hour

Factory overhead

Department A—150 per cent on direct wages

Department B—₹10 per labour hour

Department C—66.67 per cent on direct wages.

After the batch is complete, 100 units of raw materials issued to department A are found to be surplus and are returned to stores.

A comparison of the actual costs with the estimated costs of the direct materials and the factory overhead has shown that the actual costs exceed the respective estimated costs by 20 per cent, whereas the actual labour costs is 25 per cent lower than the estimated costs.

You are required to show in the cost sheet, the costs of the batch and the difference between the estimated costs and the actual costs. Show detailed workings separately.

Solution

Batch Cost Sheet (100 units)

Special remarks .... Batch no. ....

Date started. .... Date finished..

Particulars			Cost Actual	Cost Estimated	Adverse (A) Favourable (F)
Materials: (Requisition no....)					
Department A (600 units × ₹10)		₹6,000			
Less returns (100 units × ₹10)		1,000	₹5,000	₹4,167	₹833A
Department B (50 units × ₹20)			1,000	833	167A
Direct labour:					
Department	A (10 hours × ₹20)		200	250	50F
	B (2 hours × ₹25)		50	62	12F
	C (10 hours × ₹15)		150	188	38F
Factory overhead:					
Department	A (200 × ₹150%)		300	250	50A
	B (20 × ₹10)		200	167	33A
	C (150 × ₹66.67%)		100	83	17A
Total			7,000	6,000	1,000A

Summary of Variances: Department-wise

Particulars		Actual	Estimated	Variance
Department A:	Materials	₹5,000	₹4,167	₹833A
	Labour	200	250	50F
	Overheads	300	250	50A
Total		5,500	4,667	833A
Department B:	Materials	1,000	833	167A
	Labour	50	62	12F
	Overheads	200	167	33A
Total		1,250	1,062	188A
Department C:	Materials	150	188	38F
	Labour	100	83	17A
Total		250	271	21F

P. 13.7 From the following data calculate the cost per km of a vehicle. LO 13.3 LOD: E

Value of vehicle	₹15,000,00
Road license for the year	36,000
Insurance charges per year	24,000
Garage rent per year	30,000
Driver's and conductor wages per month	10,000
Cost of diesel per litre	40
Proportional charge for tyre and maintenance per km	2
Estimated life (kms)	1,50,000
Estimated annual mileage (kms)	30,000
Petrol consumption (kms/litre)	8

Solution

Operating Cost Statement to Determine Cost per km

Particulars	*Total annual cost of 6,000 kms*	*Cost per km*
(A) Standing charges:		
Road licence fee for the year	₹36,000	₹1.20
Insurance charges for the year	24,000	0.80
Garage rent per year	30,000	1.00
Driver's wages per year (₹10,000 × 12)	1,20,000	4.00
Total	2,10,000	7.00
(B) Running charges:		
Depreciation of vehicle		
(₹15,00,000 × 30,000) ÷ 1,50,000	3,00,000	10.00
Cost of diesel		
(₹40 × 30,000) ÷ 8	1,50,000	5.00
Tyre and maintenance	60,000	2.00
Total	5,10,000	17.00
(C) Total running cost per km (A+B)	7,20,000	24.00

P. 13.8 The Delhi Bus Company Ltd. operates a number of buses in Delhi city. The firm's buses make 200 trips per week with an average distance of 50 kms. Fares are ₹1.0 per km per passenger and each bus can carry 40 passengers. The firm has the following cost structure. **LO 13.3** **LOD: E**

Driver's pay, ₹2,000 per week per driver	₹40,000
Conductors' pay, ₹1,500 per week per conductor	30,000
Other salaries and wages per week	30,000
Depreciation and maintenance of buses	50,000
Petrol, diesel and variable costs (per bus per km)	10

Determine the firm's weekly income if it operates with its buses on an average 75 per cent utilisation.

Solution

Statement of Operating Cost and Profit for a week (3,00,000 passenger– kms)

Particulars		*Amount*
(A) Revenue (3,00,000 × ₹1)		₹3,00,000
(B) Operating costs		
(a) Standing charges:		
Driver's pay	₹40,000	
Conductor's pay	30,000	
Other salaries and wages	30,000	
Total	1,00,000	
(b) Running costs:		
Depreciation and maintenance	50,000	
Petrol, diesel and other variable costs		
(₹10 × 10,000 kms)[@]	1,00,000	
Total	1,50,000	
(c) Total costs (a + b)		2,50,000
(C) Profit (A – B)		50,000

[@](200 Trips × 50 kms)

Determination of passenger– kms= (Trips × kms × passengers capacity) × 0.75 = (200 × 50 × 40) × 0.75 = 3,00,000 kms

P. 13.9 Iron ore is transported from two mines, A and B and unloaded at plots in a railway station. A is at a distance of 10 kms and B is at a distance of 15 kms from the railway plots. A fleet of lorries of 5-tonne carrying capacity is used for transport of ore from mines. Records reveal that lorries average a speed of 30 kms per hour when running and regularly take 10 minutes to unload at the railhead. At mine A, loading time averages 30 minutes per load while at mine B, loading time averages 20 minutes per load. LO 13.3 LOD: M

Drivers wages, depreciation, insurance, and taxes are found to cost ₹90 per hour of operating. Fuel, oil, tyres, repairs and maintenance cost ₹12 per km. Draw up a statement showing the per tonne–km cost of carrying iron ore from each mine.

Solution

Operating Cost Statement determining Cost per tonne– km of carrying iron ore from two mines, A and B

Particulars	Mine A	Mine B
1 Distance from railway station (one way) (kms)	10	15
2 Distance from railway station (kms) (both ways or length of journey per trip)	20	30
3 Speed of lorries (kms per hour)	30	30
4 Time taken per trip (2) ÷ (3) (minutes)	40	60
5 Loading time at mines (minutes)	30	20
6 Unloading time at railway station (minutes)	10	10
7 Total time taken per trip (4 + 5 + 6)	80	90
8 Driver's wages, depreciation, insurance and taxes (per hour ₹)	90	90
9 Driver's wages, depreciation insurance etc. per trip	120*	135**
10 Fuel, oil, tyres, repairs and maintenance cost (₹ per km)	12	12
11 Fuel oil, tyres, repairs, etc. per trip (2) × (10)	240	360
12 Total cost (9 + 11)	360	495
13 Total tonne– kms (kms × capacity)	50	75
14 Cost per tonne– km (12 ÷13) (₹)	7.2	6.6

* = (80 × ₹90) ÷ 60 = ₹120

** = (90 × ₹90) ÷ 60 = ₹135

P. 13.10 A practising chartered accountant now spends ₹10 per km on taxi fare for his client's work. He is considering two other alternatives: the purchase of a new small car or an old big car. The estimated costs figure are: LO 13.3 LOD: E

Particulars	New small car	Big old car
Purchase price	₹3,50,000	₹2,00,000
Sale price of car after 5 years	1,90,000	1,20,000
Repairs and servicing per year	10,000	12,000
Taxes and insurance per year	17,000	7,000
Diesel price per litre	40	40
Diesel consumption (kms/litre)	10	7

He estimates that he covers 10,000 kms annually. Which of these alternatives will be cheaper? If his practice expands and he has to cover 19,000 kms per annum, what should be his decision?

Solution

Comparative Operating Cost Statement

Particulars	Total cost			
	10,000 kms per year		19,000 kms per year	
	New small car	Big old car	New small car	Big old car
(A) Standing charges:				
Taxes and insurance per year	₹17,000	₹7,000	₹17,000	₹7,000
(B) Running charges:				
Repair and servicing per year	10,000	12,000	10,000	12,000
Depreciation per year (purchase price – salvage value) ÷ 5	32,000	16,000	32,000	16,000
Cost of Diesel	40,000	57,143	76,000	1,08,571
Total	82,000	85,143	1,18,000	1,36,571
(C) Total operating cost (A + B)	99,000	92,143	1,35,000	1,43,571

Conclusions: **(i)** Buying the big old car would be cheaper at 10,000 kms. **(ii)** Buying the new small car would be cheaper at 19,000 kms. However, it is important to recognise the interest cost. The new small car requires a cash outlay of ₹1,50,000 over and above the big old car. Assuming 10 per cent interest, the total cost of the new small car would be ₹1,35,000 + ₹15,000 (₹1,50,000 × 0.10) = ₹1,50,000 and the decision then would be different.

P.13.11 A transport company supplies the following details in respect of a truck of 5 tonne capacity. **LO 13.3** **LOD: M**

Cost of truck	₹18,00,000
Diesel, oil, grease (per trip each way)	1,200
Repairs and maintenance (per month)	30,000
Driver's (monthly) wages	12,000
Cleaner–cum–attendant's wages (monthly)	6,000
Insurance (per year)	1,80,000
Road licence (per year)	72,000
General supervision charges (per year)	1,44,000
Estimated life (years)	10

The truck carries goods to and from the city covering a distance of 50 kms each way. While going to the city, freight is available for a full load of the truck and on its return journey it can fetch freight only up to 20 per cent of its capacity. Truck has no salvage value at year-end 10.

On the assumption that the truck runs on an average 25 days a month, you are required to determine the following: **(i)** operating cost per tonne–km, **(ii)** rate per tonne per trip that the company should charge if profit of 100 per cent on cost is to be earned, and **(iii)** what price would you charge if one wants to engage the truck for one day for a trip to the city and back?

Solution

Operating Cost Statement to determine Cost per km

Particulars	Total cost per month of 7,500 tonne–kms	Cost per tonne–km
(A) Standing charges		
Driver's wages	₹12,000	₹1.6
Cleaner–cum–attendant's wages	6,000	0.8

(Contd.)

(*Contd.*)

	Insurance (₹1,80,000 ÷ 12)	15,000	2.0
	Road licence (₹72,000 ÷ 12)	6,000	0.8
	General supervision (₹1,44,000 ÷ 12)	12,000	1.6
	Total	51,000	6.8
(B)	Running charges		
	Depreciation (₹18,00,000 ÷ (12 × 10)	15,000	2.0
	Diesel, oil, grease (₹1,200 × 50 trips that is, 2 trips daily for 25 days)	60,000	8.0
	Repairs and maintenance	30,000	4.0
	Total	1,05,000	14.0
(C)	Total cost per tonne–km (A + B)	1,56,000	20.8

WORKING NOTES

(i)	*Determination of tonne–km per month:*	
	Trip to city: 50 kms × 5 tonnes capacity × 25 days	6,250
	Return back from city: 50 kms × 25 days × 1 tonne	1,250
		7,500
(ii)	Determination of freight rate:	
	Cost per tonne	₹20.8
	Add desired profit 100 per cent of cost	20.8
	Freight rate per tonne km	41.6
(iii)	*Quotation price:*	
	Freight tonne– km in both trips (250 + 50)	300
	Multiplied by freight rate per tonne– km	₹41.6
		12,480

P.13.12 A cement manufacturing company is facing the problem of transportation of limestone from its quarry. The quarry is situated 25 kms away and the only means of transport available is the roadways. The company has received quotations from some of the local transporters at ₹325, ₹340 and ₹350 per tonne of limestone transported, with an escalation clause in respect of diesel/oil costs. The quantity of limestone to be transported per month is 24,000 tonnes. While examining the feasibility of departmental transport the following facts come to be recgonised. **LO 13.3** **LOD: D**

1. Two types of trucks are available in the market, namely, 10–tonners and 8–tonners.
2. Details of operating costs for the trucks are:

	10–tonners	*8–tonners*
Purchase price	₹25,00,000	₹20,00,000
Estimated useful life (years)	5	5
Residual value	4,00,000	2,00,000
Km per litre of diesel (kms)	3	4
Estimated repairs and maintenance cost per truck per month	20,000	16,000
Vehicle and road tax per quarter	6,000	6,000

3. Cost of diesel per litre, ₹45.
4. Cost of finance for purchase of trucks, 12 per cent per annum.
5. Each vehicle can run 5 trips (up and down) each day and can run on an average 24 days each month.

6. Drivers will have to be recruited according to the number of trucks to be purchased. In addition, one extra driver for every 5 vehicles will be required for the entire fleet. Each driver will cost ₹8,000 per month.
7. An additional transport supervisor would be required at a cost of ₹15,000 per month.
8. Yet another possibility is to hire sufficient number of trucks (10–tonners only) from a transport company at the rate of ₹50,000 per month per truck. The transport company bears repair and maintenance costs as well as the vehicle and road tax. The cement company has to bear the cost of drivers, supervisor and other operational costs.

You are required to advise the company on an appropriate choice among the above alternatives, considering also the option of entrusting the job to the transport operators.

Solution

Statement of Operating Costs under Alternative Means of Transporting Limestone

Details of costs	*Purchase of trucks*		*Hiring of 10–tonners*
	10–tonners	*8–tonners*	
1 Repairs and maintenance per month	₹20,000	₹16,000	—
2 Vehicle and road tax per month	2,000	2,000	—
3 Cost of diesel per month (see working note 1)	90,000	67,500	₹90,000
4 Depreciation cost per month (see working note 2)	35,000	30,000	—
5 Finance cost per month(see working note 3)	25,000	20,000	—
6 Hiring charges per month	—	—	50,000
7 Supervisor's salary	15,000	15,000	15,000
8 Salary of drivers (see working note 5)	1,92,000	2,40,000	1,92,000
9 Total cost per truck per month[total (1) to (6)]	3,79,000	3,90,500	3,47,000
10 Number of trucks needed (see working note 4)	20	25	20
11 Total cost of entire fleet [(9) × (10) + (8) + (7)]	75,80,000	97,62,500	69,40,000
12 Cost per tonne limestone transported (11 ÷ 24,000)	315.83	406.77	289.16

The company is advised to hire 20 (10–tonner) trucks as it would involve the lowest cost per tonne of limestone transported. There is no question of entrusting the job to local transporters as their charges are higher, that is, ₹325, ₹340 and ₹350.

WORKING NOTES

Particulars	*10–tonners*	*8–tonners*
1 Cost of diesel per month		
Distance to be covered per trip (kms)	50	50
(×) Number of trips	5	5
Total distance per day (kms)	250	250
(×) Number of days	24	24
Total distance per month (kms)	6,000	6,000
÷ Km covered per litre of diesel	3	4
Total diesel consumption (litres)	2,000	1,500
× Rate per litre	₹45	₹45
	90,000	67,500

(*Contd.*)

(Contd.)

2 *Depreciation cost per month*		
Purchase price	₹25,00,000	₹20,00,000
Less residual value	4,00,000	2,00,000
Depreciation cost	21,00,000	18,00,000
÷ Life (in months)	60	60
Depreciation per month	35,000	30,000
3 *Finance cost per year*	3,00,000*	2,40,000**
Finance cost per month [(3) ÷ 12]	25,000	20,000
4 *Number of trucks required*		
(a) Limestone to be transported (tonnes)	24,000	24,000
(b) Limestone transported in 24 days (tonnes)	1,200@	960@@
Number of trucks required (a ÷ b)	20	25
5 Number of drivers (regular)	20	25
Number of drivers (extra)	4	5
Total number of drivers	24	30
× Salary per driver per month	₹8,000	₹8,000
Total salary bill	1,92,000	2,40,000

* (₹25,00,000 × 0.12), ** (₹20,00,000 × 0.12)
@(5 × 10 × 24), @@ (5 × 8 × 24)

P. 13.13 Shankar has been promised a contract to run a tourist car on a 20-kms long route for the chief executive of a multinational firm. He buys a car costing ₹3,00,000. The annual cost of insurance and taxes are ₹9,000 and ₹2,400 respectively. He has to pay ₹500 per month for a garage where he keeps the car when it is not in use. The annual repair costs are estimated at ₹8,000. The car is estimated to have a life of 10 years, at the end of which the scrap value is likely to be ₹50,000. LO 13.3 LOD: D

He hires a driver who is to be paid ₹6,000 per month and 10 per cent of the takings as commission. Other incidental expenses are estimated at ₹2,000 per month.

Diesel and oil cost ₹500 per 100 kms. The car will make 4 round trips every day. Assuming that a profit of 15 per cent on takings is desired and that the car will be on the road for 25 days on an average per month, what should Shankar charge per round trip?

Solution

Operating Cost Statement Showing Determination of Charges per Round Trip

Particulars	*Total amount*
(i) Standing charges per month	
Insurance (₹9,000 ÷ 12)	₹750
Taxes (₹2,400 ÷ 12)	200
Garage Charges	500
Driver's salary	6,000
Incidental expenses	1,300
	8,750
(ii) Running charges per month	
Repairs cost (₹8,000 ÷ 12)	666.67
Diesel and oil (20 kms × 2 × 4 round trips × 25 days × ₹5 per km)	20,000.00
Depreciation (₹3,00,000 – ₹50,000) ÷ 120 months	2,083.33
	22,750

(Contd.)

(Contd.)

(iii) Total operating cost (i + ii) excluding commission	31,500
(iv) Driver's commission (*see working notes*)	4,200
(v) Desired profit (*see working notes*)	6,300
(vi) Total charges per 100 trips (25 days × 4 round trips)	42,000
(vii) Charges per round trip (₹42,000 ÷ 100)	420

Working Notes

1. *Determination of takings per month*
   Let 'X' be the sum of total takings per month.
   Driver's commission is 10% of X = 0.10X
   Desired profit 15% of X = 0.15X
   Total takings per month = Total cost + Driver's commission + Desired profit
   X = ₹31,500 + 0.10X + 0.15X
   X – 0.10X – 0.15X = ₹31,500, or, 0.75X = ₹31,500
   X = ₹42,000 i.e. (₹31,500/0.75)
2. *Driver's commission* = 0.10 × ₹42,000 = ₹4,200
3. *Desired profit* = 0.15 × ₹42,000 = ₹6,300

P 13.14 From the following data relating to two different vehicles A and B, compute the cost running kilometer: **LO 13.3** **LOD: M**

Particulars	*A*	*B*
Kilometers run (annual)	15,000	6,000
Cost of vehicles	₹5,00,000	₹3,00,000
Road license (annual)	9,250	8,000
Insurance (annual)	7,000	4,000
Garage rent (annual)	6,000	5,000
Driver wages per hour	20	20
Cost of diesel per litre	40	40
Kilometers run per litre	20	15
Repair charges per kilometer	1.65	2.00
Tyre cost per kilometer	2.00	2.00
Estimated life of the vehicle (kilometers)	1,00,000	75,000
Vehicle run per hour (kilometers)	20	20

Solution

Operating Cost Statement showing Cost per Running km of Vehicles A and B

Particulars	*Total Cost*	
	Vehicle A	*Vehicle B*
(i) Standing charges per year:		
Road license	9,250	8,000
Insurance	7,000	4,000
Garage rent	6,000	5,000
	22,250	17,000
(ii) Running charges per year:		
Depreciation (₹5,00,000 ÷ 1,00,000 kms) ÷ 15,000	75,000	—
(₹3,00,000 ÷ 75,000 kms) × 6,000	—	24,000
Driver wages (15,000 km ÷ 20 kms) × ₹20 per hour	15,000	—
(6,000km ÷ 20 kms) ₹20 per hour	—	6,000

(Contd.)

(Contd.)

Diesel cost (15,000 km ÷ 20 kms) × ₹40 per litre	30,000	—
(6,000 km ÷ 15 kms) × ₹40 per litre		16,000
Repair Charges (15,000 kms × ₹1.65)	24,750	
(6000 kms × ₹2.00)	12,000	
Tyre cost (15,000 kms × ₹2.00)	30,000	
(6,000 kms × ₹2.00)		12,000
	1,74,750	70,000
(iii) Total charges (i + ii)	1,97,000	87,000
(iv) Total kilometers run	15,000	6,000
(v) Cost per running km (iii ÷ iv)	13.13	14.50

P.13.15 A lorry starts with a load of 20 tonnes of goods from station A. It unloads 8 tonnes at station B and rest of goods at station C. It reaches back directly to station A after getting reloaded with 16 tonnes of goods at station C. The distance between A to B, B to C and then from C to A are 80 kms, 120 kms and 160 kms respective. Compute 'Absolute tones-kms' and 'Commercial tones-kms'. **LO 13.3** **LOD: D**

Solution

(a) *Determination of Absolute Tonne-kms*

(Number of tonnes added × Distance in kms):		
From Station A to B	(20 tonnes × 80 kms)	1,600
From Station B to C	(12 tonnes × 120 kms)	1,440
From Station C to A	(16 tonnes × 160 kms)	2,560
Total tonnes-kms		5,600

(b) *Determination of Commercial Tonne-kms*

Average load × Total kms travelled

[(20 + 12 + 16)/3] × 30 kms = 5,760 tonnes-km

REVIEW QUESTIONS

LOD: Easy

RQ.13.1 Indicate whether the followings statements are 'True' or 'False'. **LO 13.1**

(i) In job order system of costing, each order is regarded as cost unit from the point of view of cost accumulation.

(ii) Process costing is appropriate when each job (work) is unique and easily identifiable.

(iii) A job cost-sheet is the backbone of job costing.

(iv) A job-cost sheet does not enumerate the appropriate inputs required, say, direct materials, direct labour and overheads.

(v) A job cost sheet does not contain date of starting the work and the delivery date.

(vi) A job-cost sheet does not help out in comparing the actual cost of job with the standard cost already set.

(vii) Under-absorption of overheads implies that overheads charged to various jobs are higher than actual overheads.

(viii) When an organisation deals in such products that all the time it gets orders which are totally different from last served ones, the job order costing should not be applied as it may result into biased bidding rates.

(ix) Job costing data may be used for estimating the production cost of specific jobs or job of production.

(x) Manufacturing overheads can be identified with specific jobs.

(xi) Direct materials and direct labour cost are traced to jobs by means of materials requisition forms and job time card.

(xii) In an oil refinery, job costing is more appropriate.

[Answer: (i) True, (ii) False, (iii) True, (iv) False, (v) False, (vi) False, (vii) False, (viii) False, (ix) True, (x) False, (xi) True, (xii) False.]

RQ.13.2 What are the characteristics of companies that are likely to be using job order cost system? Specify five concrete situations when use of job order cost system is most appropriate. **LO 13.1**

RQ.13.3 What is a job-cost sheet? Prepare a comprehensive job-cost sheet of a firm having two departments. **LO 13.1**

RQ.13.4 Explain the meaning of batch costing. How does such a costing differ from job costing? **LO 13.1,2**

RQ.13.5 What is service costing? Describe the type of industries in which such a system would be suitable. **LO 13.3**

RQ.13.6 Describe in brief the cost accumulating procedure (with suitable illustration) under service costing. **LO 13.3**

RQ.13.7 A Ltd. employs a job-order costing system. The factory expenses incurred in the month of March of the current year (as shown by the factory overhead control account) are as follows: **LO 13.1**

Cutting shop	₹3,62,500
Assembly shop	47,550
Spraying shop	6,700
Finishing shop	79,000

Overheads have been debited to jobs as follows:

Cutting–₹130 per machine-hour for 2,200 hours.

Assembly–140 per cent of direct labour cost. Direct labour cost is ₹33,000.

Spraying–₹6 per piece for 925 pieces.

Finishing–₹75 per direct labour-hour for 1,100 hours.

All expenses are charged to a factory overhead control account and are transferred from this account at the end of each month to the departmental overhead account.

You are required to (a) record the necessary journal entries for factory overheads incurred and absorbed, and (b) state the amount of over- or under-absorption of overheads in each department. Assume that the company maintains both factory ledger and general ledger.

RQ.13.8 A job shop commenced its operations on January 1 of the current year. During the first quarter, the following transactions took place: **LO 13.1**

(i) Materials costing ₹4,00,000 were purchased on account.

(ii) Materials purchased were placed in process.

(iii) A total of 2,000 direct labour-hours were charged to individual jobs at the rate of ₹50 per hour.

(iv) The fixed manufacturing overhead totalled ₹1,60,000.

(v) The variable manufacturing overhead totalled ₹40,000.

(vi) Only job 10, with material charges of 40,000, direct labour charges of ₹20,000, and applied overhead rate, was in process at the end of the period.

Additional information:

(i) The firm uses an actual job-order cost system.

(ii) The variable manufacturing overhead is a function of direct labour-hours.

(iii) All overheads are allocated to individual jobs on the basis of a single rate based on direct labour-hours.

You are required to record journal entries for the current quarter assuming only general ledger is maintained.

RQ.13.9 Mumbai Transport Ltd operates a fleet of lorries. The following information relates to lorry 10 for the month of June: **LO 13.3**

Days available	26
Days operated	22
Total kms covered	1,600
Total trips made	28
Total tonnage carried	3,000

Operating costs (June): Petrol, oil, and grease, ₹9,600; Wages - driver, ₹10,000, attendant, ₹6,000 and mechanic, ₹6,000. *Maintenance costs* (estimated for the year): ₹9,600. *Fixed costs* (estimated for the year): Insurance, ₹9,600, Road tax, ₹3,600 and miscellaneous, ₹2,400. *Capital cost,* ₹7,26,000; Residual value estimated to be ₹1,20,000 with an effective life of 5 years. *Administration and other overheads* for the year, ₹1,20,000.

Prepare operating cost statement determining cost per km operated.

LOD: Medium

RQ.13.10 Enumerate, in brief, the cost recording procedure in a job-order cost system. Illustrate your answer with examples. **LO 13.1**

RQ.13.11 Why is it difficult to identify manufacturing overheads with products manufactured? Also, state the difference between the manufacturing overheads control account and manufacturing overhead applied account. **LO 13.1**

RQ.13.12 How is job costing in service organisations different from job costing in manufacturing organisations? **LO 13.1,3**

RQ.13.13 A firm is engaged in manufacturing jobs of long duration. Examine the detailed procedure suitable for costing purposes. **LO 13.1**

RQ.13.14 A small factory can produce 60,000 units per annum at its optimum capacity. The estimated unit costs of production are as under: **LO 13.1**

Direct material	₹3
Direct labour	2
Indirect expenses	
Fixed (per annum)	1,57,000
Variable (per unit)	5
Semi-variable per annum up to 50 per cent capacity and an extra ₹10,000 for every 25 per cent increase in capacity or part thereof.	50,000

The factory produces only against orders (and not for stock). The production programme of the factory is as indicated below. The management desires to ensure a profit of ₹1,00,000 for the year. Work out the average selling price at which each unit should be quoted.

First 3 months of the year	:	50 per cent of the capacity
Remaining 9 months	:	80 per cent of the capacity

Ignore selling and administration overheads.

RQ.13.15 An entrepreneur own a bus which runs from Delhi to Agra and back for 25 days in a month. The distance from Delhi to Agra is 170 kms. The bus completes the trip from Delhi to Agra and back on the same day. Calculate the fare the entrepreneur should charge a passenger if he wants to earn a profit of 33.33 per cent on cost. The following information is further available: **LO 13.3**

Cost of bus	₹30,00,000
Salary of driver per month	10,500
Salary of conductor per month	7,000
Salary of part-time accountant per month	8,500
Insurance per annum	33,600
Diesel consumption 4 kms. per litre costing	30
Local taxes per annum	12,000
Lubricant oil per 100 kms	40
Repairs and maintenance per annum	20,000
Licence fee per annum	36,925
Normal capacity (person)	50
Depreciation rate per annum	20

The bus usually runs full up to 90 per cent of its capacity (50 passengers) both ways. Interest is payable on the cost of bus at 10 per cent per annum.

RQ.13.16 A factory which uses a large amount of coal is situated between two collieries, X and Y, with both being at a distance of 5 and 10 kms, respectively, from the factory. A fleet or lorries of 5 tonnes carrying capacity is used for collecting coal from the pitheads. The lorries average a speed of 20 kilometres per hour when running and generally take 10 minutes to unload in the factory premises. At colliery X, loading time averages 30 minutes per load, while at colliery Y it is 20 minutes per load. **LO 13.3**

Driver's wages, licences, insurance, depreciation, garage, and similar charges cost ₹60 per hour operated. Fuel, oil, tyres repairs and similar charges cost ₹6 per km run.

Draw up a statement showing the cost per-tonne-kilometre of carrying coal from each colliery. If the coal is of same quality and price at pithead, which of the collieries should the company prefer to make purchases?

RQ 13.17 Mr Ahuja runs a tempo service in the town and has two vehicles. He furnishes you the following data from which you are to compute the cost per running mile. **LO 13.3**

Particulars	*Vehicle A*	*Vehicle B*
Cost of vehicle	₹5,00,000	₹3,00,000
Road licence per year	7,000	7,500
Supervision and salary (yearly)	66,000	48,000
Driver's wages per hour	40	40
Cost of fuel per litre	42	42
Repairs and maintenance per mile	3.0	4.0
Tyre cost per mile	2.00	2.00
Garage rent per year	18,000	10,000
Insurance premium yearly	9,000	7,000
Km run per litre	6	5
Km run during the year	15,000	6,000
Estimated life of vehicles (kms)	1,00,000	75,000

Charge interest at 10 per cent per annum on the cost of vehicle. The vehicles run 20 kms. per hour on an average.

RQ.13.18 From the following particulars, calculate the cost per running kilometer of a vehicle: LO 13.3

Cost of vehicle	₹25,00,000
Road licence fee for the year	75,000
Driver's and conductor wages per hour	100
Cost fuel per litre	40
Repairs per kilometer	1.50
Tyre cost per kilometer	2.00
Garage rent per year	1,32,500
Insurance per year	85,000
Kilometers run per litre	6
Kilometers run during the year	15,000
Estimated life of vehicles (kms)	1,00,000
Charge interest at 10 per cent on the cost of vehicle.	
The vehicle runs 20 kms per hour on an average.	

LOD: Difficult

RQ.13.19 Union Transport Company Ltd supplies the following details in respect of a truck of a 5-tonne capacity: LO 13.3

Cost of truck	₹18,00,000
Estimated life (years)	10
Diesel, oil grease, etc. per trip each way	450
Repairs and maintenance per month	10,000
Driver's wages per month	10,000
Cleaner's wages per month	5,000
Insurance per year	24,000
Tax per year	12,000
General supervision charges per year	84,000

The truck carries goods to and from the city covering a distance of 50 kms each way.

On outward trip, freight is available up to the full capacity and on return trip, 20 per cent of capacity. Assume that the truck runs on an average of 25 days a month. Work out:

(a) Operating cost per tonne-km, and

(b) Rate per tonne per trip that the company should charge if a profit of 50 per cent on freight is to be earned.

RQ.13.20 A transport company is running 4 buses between two towns which are 50 kms apart. Seating capacity of each bus is 40 passengers. The following particulars were obtained from their books for April month of the current year: LO 13.3

Wages of drivers and conductors	₹1,20,000
Salaries to office staff	50,000
Diesel and other oil	2,00,000
Repairs and maintenance	40,000
Taxes and insurance	80,000
Depreciation	1,30,000
Interest and other charges	1,00,000
	7,20,000

Actual passengers carried were 75 per cent of the seating capacity. All the four buses run on all days of the month. Each bus made one round trip per day. Find out the cost per passenger km.

ANSWERS

RQ.13.7 **(a)** Under absorption ₹76,500 (Cutting shop), ₹1,350 (Assembly shop), ₹1,150 (Spraying shop)
(b) Over-absorption ₹3,500 (Finishing shop).
RQ.13.8 Cost of goods completed and transferred ₹6,00,000; Overhead rate per hour ₹100
RQ.13.9 ₹33.625
RQ.13.14 Average selling price ₹22
RQ.13.15 ₹104.72 or ₹105
RQ.13.16 Colliery X should be preferred. Carrying cost per tonne ₹26 (X) and ₹42 (Y)
RQ.13.17 ₹29.0 (Vehicle A) and ₹37.4 (Vehicle B)
RQ.13.18 ₹75.83
RQ.13.19 **(a)** ₹9.67
(b) ₹19.34
RQ.13.20 ₹2.0

[Comprehensive solutions to all numerical review questions are available on the companion website: http://www.mhhe.com/khan_jain_ma7e]

14

Process, Joint and By-product Costing

Learning Objectives

After reading this chapter you will be able to:

- **LO 14.1** Understand the nature of process costing, its comparison with job costing and its suitability
- **LO 14.2** Illustrate the accounting procedure involved in process costing
- **LO 14.3** Discuss accounting procedure for joint products
- **LO 14.4** Describe the costing treatment of by-products
- **LO 14.5** Explain the costing for selling at split-off point or processing further

Introduction

The purpose of this chapter is to discuss and illustrate process costing–a system of costing applicable to organisations whose products pass through different processes. The nature of process costing in terms of its comparison with job costing and the types of organisations for which it is suitable is examined first. The accounting procedure involved in computing the cost under this system of costing is also illustrated with reference to: **(a)** Completed units, **(b)** Partially completed/incomplete units, **(c)** Spoilage, and **(d)** Inter-process profits. The related aspects of joint products and by-products are dealt with subsequently. The costing for selling at split-off point or processing further is also discussed in this chapter. The major points are summarised by way of recapitulation.

Process costing is used when identical units are produced through an on-going series of production steps (processes).

Nature and Suitability

LO 14.1 Understand the nature of process costing, its comparison with job costing and its suitability

The process costing system refers to the procedure of determining the average unit cost in situations in which the product passes through more than one stage of the manufacturing process. In other words, it is used when identical units are produced through an on-going series of uniform production steps. The process costing system, as a cost accumulation procedure, can be applied when: **(i)** The output is homogeneous, that is, the units produced are alike in all respects, **(ii)** Production is continuous, **(iii)** Production precedes sales, and **(iv)** There is feasibility of segmentation of the manufacturing operations into clearly identifiable processes or departments. In view of these features, process costing is appropriate for industries such as chemicals, food processing, breweries, petroleum refining, glass, metal manufacturing, steel making, paper, and so on.

The process costing system can be distinguished from the job costing system in several respects. In the first place, in job costing, jobs receive varying degrees of skill and attention from each production department or operation; in process costing, units of output produced receive identical attention from each production department or operation. Secondly, the job-order cost system identifies costs essentially with a specific job, while the process cost system identifies costs with units of work performed during a period of time. Thirdly, in job costing, unit costs are determined continuously as each job is completed, whereas in process costing, unit costs are determined periodically. Fourthly, in job costing, production is for a specific order to meet an individual customer's specifications; therefore, sales normally precede production. In process costing, production is for building up inventories for future sales and, therefore, production precedes sales. Further, the materials needed for jobs would depend on the receipt of specific job-order, and therefore, the materials inventory/stock held is small/minimum in job costing. In process costing, the materials needed for output are known and, hence, the materials inventory kept on hand tends to be higher *vis-à-vis* job costing. In addition, in job costing most of the costs are directly traceable to the jobs and, therefore, a major part of the total costs normally consists of direct costs; overheads form a relatively low proportion of these costs. In process costing, automation/mechanisation is feasible to a greater extent entailing higher overhead costs, but in job costing production runs are relatively short since the number of units produced each time depends on specific orders received. In marked contrast, in process costing, production being on a mass scale, production runs are long and often continuous. Finally, job cost sheets for each job are the backbone of the job/order costing system. Cost-of-production reports for each production process, department or operation constitute the focal points of the process costing system.

The foregoing differences notwithstanding, job and process costing systems are not mutually exclusive, that is, a firm need not limit itself to the adoption of either of the two systems. For, the same firm can use both the methods to serve cost information needs. For instance, automobile manufacturing firms may employ job costing in their engineering departments and process costing in their main assembly lines. Similarly, heavy equipment manufacturing firms often use job costing to determine the total cost of a large machine but the costs of mass produced machine components like switches, valves, and so on, are first determined by the process cost method.

Cost Accumulation/Accounting Procedure in Process Costing

LO 14.2 Illustrate the accounting procedure involved in process costing

The process cost system accumulates production costs according to departments or processes. Each department/process constitutes a *responsibility centre* from the point of view of cost control and performance evaluation through techniques such as standard costing, responsibility accounting, budgeting, and so on, It provides unit cost measures that are helpful in establishing selling price particularly when the firm employs 'cost plus' or some other type of cost-based product pricing.

Process costing assumes a sequential flow of costs from one process to another as units of output pass through a number of specified production processes. That is, the units leave the first process and take their costs with them to the second process, the units leave the second process and take their costs with them to the third process, and this process continues till the last process, when output is finally completed. Each process performs part of the total operation and transfers its 'finished' output to the next process, in which it is the input/raw material for further processing. The finished product of the last process is transferred to the finished goods inventory. Thus, the cost becomes cumulative as production moves along, the final process determining the total cost.

In process costing, a work-in-process account (process account) is set up for each production process, and the material, labour and indirect manufacturing overhead costs are recorded as the work progresses. Direct materials and direct labour costs are assigned to the respective process accounts using materials requisition forms and payroll records. Likewise, indirect manufacturing overhead costs are often allocated to the units of each process on the basis of a predetermined departmental overhead application rate.

Process costing assumes a sequential flow of cost from one process to another as units of output pass through a number of specified production processes.

The procedure to determine the cost under process costing will depend on the stage of completion of the product in each process. From the point of view of the level of completion, a product may be fully or partially complete. During the production process, some units may be wasted. Moreover, the output of one process may be transferred at cost price or market/inflated price. We, therefore, elaborate the computation of unit costs in each of these situations in the discussions that follow.

Completed Units

Example 14.1 shows the calculation of costs when units are fully complete.

◆ Example 14.1

A product passes through two processes, A and B. During the month ended June 30, 1,500 units were produced. The detailed cost break-up is as follows:

	Process A	*Process B*
Direct materials	₹90,000	₹75,000
Direct labour	75,000	1,50,000
Direct expenses	15,000	18,000

Indirect overhead costs during the period were ₹60,000 apportioned to the processes on the basis of direct labour cost. No work-in-progress existed at the beginning and end of the period.

Prepare relevant process accounts.

Solution

Process A Account

To direct materials	₹90,000	By cost of output transferred	
To direct labour	75,000	to process B	₹2,00,000
To direct expenses	15,000		
To indirect overheads (₹60,000 × 1/3)	20,000		
	2,00,000		2,00,000

Process B Account

To process A (cost transferred)	₹2,00,000	By cost of output transferred	
To direct material	75,000	to finished goods inventory	₹4,83,000

(Contd.)

(Contd.)

To direct labour	1,50,000	
To direct expenses	18,000	
To indirect overheads (₹60,000 × 2/3)	40,000	
	4,83,000	4,83,000

Finished Goods Inventory

To process B (cost of output)	₹4,83,000

Incomplete Units

Given the nature of the production process, some units may remain incomplete at the time of accounting for the total cost of production. In such a situation, some units are complete while others are incomplete/partially complete. For the purpose of cost accumulation, the units of production are to be converted into comparable units. They are referred to as *equivalent units.* For instance, 100 units of inventory estimated to be 40 per cent complete are considered equivalent to 40 completed units. Therefore, for cost determination purposes, 100 partially completed units will be considered equal to 40 units of equivalent production. Symbolically:

Equivalent units = Actual number of partially completed units × Stage of completion **(14.1)**

The computation of equivalent units is illustrated in Examples 14.2 and 14.3, assuming that the stage of completion is uniform in respect of all items of cost and it is different in respect of raw materials and conversion costs (labour and overheads) respectively.

◆ Example 14.2

From the following information of ABC Manufacturers Limited, prepare a statement of equivalent units.

Opening inventory: Partially completed units (40 per cent complete)	600
Units introduced during the period	10,000
Closing inventory (partially completed units: 70 per cent complete)	2,000

Solution

Statement of Equivalent Units

1. Work necessary to complete opening inventory (600 × 0.60)	360
2. Work necessary to start and finish units introduced during the current year (10,000 – 2,000 partially completed units)	8,000
3. Work performed on closing inventory (2,000 × 0.70)	1,400
Total number of equivalent units	9,760

◆ Example 14.3

From the following production record of XYZ Manufacturing Company Ltd, prepare a statement of equivalent units:

Units in process-opening	2,000
Stage of completion (%): material	100
labour	60
overheads	50

(Contd.)

(Contd.)

New units introduced	20,000
Units completed	18,000
Units in process-closing	4,000
Stage of completion (%): material	100
labour	50
overheads	40

Solution

Table 14.1 Statement of Equivalent Units

Input	*Particulars*	*Number of units (completed or otherwise)*	*Work performed during the current period [stage of completion (per cent)]*			*Equivalent produced units: input units × stage completion in respect of*		
			Material	*Labour*	*Overheads*	*Material*	*Labour*	*Overheads*
Opening inventory 2,000 units	Work expended on opening inventories (100 per cent stage of completion)	2,000	Nil	40	50	—	800	1,000
+ 20,000 units introduced during the current period	Units started and completed during the current period (18,000 total units completed inventory)	16,000	100	100	100	16,000	16,000	16,000
	Closing inventory (work-in-process)	4,000	100	50	40	4,000	2,000	1,600
22,000		22,000				20,000	18,800	18,600

Process Accounts/Production Cost Report

Under the process costing system, the cost of production can be shown in form of production cost reports and/or process cost accounts.

Production Cost Report The cost of production report forms the backbone of the process cost records. It provides the summary of the production activity and costs of each process or department. On the basis of information regarding production activity in the report, it is possible to determine the number of equivalent units processed, unit costs per equivalent unit, and the quantity and cost of ending work-in-process inventories and of units completed and transferred to subsequent processing departments/finished goods inventory account. Cost of production report provides production and cost information, generally, in the following sequence of steps for a given period:

Equivalent units are incomplete units expressed in terms of completed units.

1. It accounts for physical flow of *all* units irrespective of their stage of completion during the period under reference.
2. It shows the computation of *equivalent* units of materials, labour and overheads; often the last two items are clubbed together and shown under the head of conversion costs.
3. It provides information for the total costs to be accounted for, consisting of the cost of opening work-in-process plus the costs of material, labour and factory overhead that were assigned to these units during the current period.

4. It shows very explicitly the procedure of determining the cost per equivalent unit of output processed.
5. Finally, it indicates the manner of allocating the cost of processing to ending work-in-process and to units completed and transferred.

The total cost of production of each process is split into: **(i)** Cost of output and **(ii)** Closing inventory. The distribution between these two elements would depend on the method of valuation of work-in-process (closing inventory), namely, weighted average method and first-in-first-out (FIFO) method.

Weighted Average Cost Method Under this method, total costs in process are divided by *equivalent* units produced by the process to ascertain the cost per equivalent unit. Total cost in process is the sum of the current production costs and the costs of opening work-in-process. Total equivalent units produced by the process are determined by adding units completed during the current period and equivalent units of work performed on opening and closing inventories.

FIFO Method Unlike the weighted average cost method, this method is based on the assumption that units in process at the beginning of the period are the first to be completed and accordingly the first costs incurred in the current period should be attached to the units of the opening work-in-process inventory. Therefore, under this method, the cost of the units that are completed from the opening inventory is separated from the cost of the units that have been introduced and completed during the current period. As a result, under the FIFO method, closing work-in-process inventory is based on the cost pertaining to the current period only *vis-à-vis* average cost under the weighted average cost method.

Exhibits 14.1 and 14.2 show the process accounts prepared as per the weighted average cost and FIFO methods respectively.

EXHIBIT 14.1 Process Account (Weighted Average Cost Method)

To work-in-process (opening inventory)	By cost of completed units transferred to next process/finished goods inventory A/c
To current costs	By closing work-in-process
Material	
Labour	
Overheads	
To closing work-in-process inventory to be carried to the next period	

EXHIBIT 14.2 Process Account (FIFO Method)

To work-in-process opening inventory during the current period (units partially completed in earlier period)	By units completed
To current costs	1. Units started in earlier period and completed during the current period
1. To complete opening inventory units	2. Units started and completed during the current period
2. To work initiated on new units in the current period in this process:	3. Units started but not completed during the current period
(a) Some of which are completed and transferred	
(b) Some of which are not yet completed and carried as opening inventory for next period	
To closing work-in-process inventory to be carried forward to the next period	

The effect of the two methods of valuation is that a larger share of the total cost will be allocated to the closing inventory according to the FIFO method, whereas with the weighted average cost method the current output will be charged at a relatively higher amount. Example 14.4 illustrates the process costs using both these methods.

◆ Example 14.4

For the firm in Example 14.3, assume the following:

Cost of 2,000 units in process (opening):	
Materials	₹6,000
Labour	3,600
Overheads	2,400
Processing costs during the current period	
Materials	69,900
Labour	56,560
Overheads	58,360

Prepare a cost of production report for the current period using **(a)** weighted average and **(b)** FIFO costing methods.

Solution

Cost of Production Report of Process A (Weighted average cost method)

Flow of completed or partially completed units:				
Opening	2,000			
Introduced	20,000			
Total in process	22,000			
Less completed	18,000			
In process	4,000			
Equivalent units in process:				
		Conversion costs		
	Material	*Labour*	*Overhead*	
Units completed	18,000	18,000	18,000	
Equivalent units in ending inventory	4,000	2,000	1,600	
	22,000	20,000	19,600	
Total cost to be accounted for:				
	Material	*Labour*	*Overheads*	*Total*
Work-in-process (opening)	₹6,000	₹3,600	₹2,400	₹12,000
Current costs	69,900	56,560	58,360	1,84,820
Total cost in process	75,900	60,160	60,760	1,96,820
Equivalent units (EU) in process	22,000	20,000	19,600	—
Cost per equivalent unit in process (Total cost ÷ EU)	3.45	3.008	3.1	9.558
Costs accounted for:				
Transferred to finished goods inventory (18,000 × ₹9.558)				1,72,044
Work-in-process (closing inventory)				
Materials (4,000 × 100 per cent × ₹3.45)		₹13,800		
Labour (4,000 × 0.50 × ₹3.008)		6,016		
Overheads (4,000 × 0.40 × ₹3.1)		4,960		24,776
Total costs accounted for				1,96,820

Cost of Production Report of Process A (FIFO method)

Flow of completed or partially completed units:			
Opening	2,000		
Introduced	20,000		
Total in process	22,000		
Less completed	18,000		
In process	4,000		
Equivalent units manufactured:			

		Conversion costs		
	Material	*Labour*	*Overheads*	
Units completed	18,000	18,000	18,000	
Equivalent units in ending inventory	4,000	2,000	1,600	
Equivalent units in process	22,000	20,000	19,600	
Less equivalent units in opening inventory	2,000	1,200	1,000	
Equivalent units manufactured	20,000	18,800	18,600	
Total costs to account for:				
	Material	*Labour*	*Overheads*	*Total*
Opening work-in-process		—	—	₹12,000
Current costs	₹69,900	₹56,560	₹58,360	1,84,820
Total costs in process				1,96,820
Equivalent units manufactured	20,000	18,800	18,600	—
Cost per equivalent unit manufactured	3.495	3.0085	3.1376	9.6411
Costs accounted for:				
Transferred to finished goods inventory				
First batch:				
Work-in-process opening inventory		₹12,000		
Add conversion costs:				
Labour (2,000 × 0.40 × ₹3.0085)		2,406.8		
Overheads (2,000 × 0.50 × ₹3.1376)		3,137.6		₹17,544.4
Second batch:				
Started and completed (16,000 × ₹9.6411)				1,54,257.6
Work-in-process (closing):				
Materials (4,000 × 100 per cent × ₹3.495)		13,980		
Labour (4,000 × 0.50 × ₹3.0085)		6,017		
Overheads (4,000 × 0.40 × ₹3.1376)		5,020.16		25,017.16
				1,96,819.16

Comparison For comparison of the two costing methods, summary results of important items are listed below:

	FIFO		*Weighted average cost*
(A) Cost of output transferred from			
(i) Opening inventory	₹17,544.40		₹1,72,044
(ii) Current production	1,54,257.60	₹1,71,802	
(B) Closing work-in-process		25,017.16	24,776
		1,96,819.16	1,96,820

Spoilage

In the case of firms whose output passes through several stages, some wastage/spoilage of units takes place for a variety of reasons, such as breakdown of machines, use of substandard material, poor workmanship, evaporation, shrinkage, and so on. The effect of wastage is that the actual units produced are less than the units introduced initially.

The treatment of spoiled units depends on the nature of the spoilage/wastage/loss. The wastage may be normal or abnormal. *Normal loss* may be defined as the loss of units which is an inherent part of the production process caused by natural or unavoidable causes such as milling, drying, breaking, weighing, evaporating, processing, loading, unloading, and so on. Any loss in excess of the normal spoilage is called *abnormal loss.* It is a controllable loss. It involves consumption of resources without accruing corresponding benefits to the firm. On the other hand, if the number of units actually lost are less than the number of units normally expected to get lost, the difference would represent an abnormal gain/effectiveness.

Spoilage is wastage of units due to breakdown of machines, use of sub-standard material, poor workmanship, evaporation, shrinkage and so on.

Normal spoilage forms part of the product cost. Since it is inherent in the production process, it occurs even under efficient operating conditions. Therefore, the cost of production of spoiled units is recovered from the good units. Abnormal loss is treated as a period cost and is written off as a loss of the period in which it occurs. It is relevant for determining the process cost. Likewise, abnormal gain is transferred to the profit and loss account of the period.

Normal spoilage is the loss of units which is an inherent part of the production process caused by natural/ unavoidable causes.

It is likely that the wasted units (normal as well as abnormal) may have salvage value. The sale proceeds of the units in normal waste would reduce the cost of production. The loss on abnormal wastage charged against the costing profit and loss account will be lower to the extent of the revenue received from their sale.

The unit cost with normal spoilage and with salvage value is computed as per Equation 14.2 and the amount of loss on account of abnormal spoilage to be transferred to profit and loss account is determined as in Equation 14.3.

$$\text{Cost per unit} = (\text{Total process cost} - \text{Salvage value of normal spoilage}) \div (\text{Total units introduced} - \text{Normal loss in units}) \quad \textbf{(14.2)}$$

$$\text{Abnormal loss} = [\text{Abnormal loss in units} \times \text{Unit production cost}] - \text{Salvage value of abnormal spoilage} \quad \textbf{(14.3)}$$

The treatment of spoilage is illustrated in Example 14.5.

◆ Example 14.5

Six hundred kgs of material was charged to process I at the rate of ₹40 per kg. The direct labour accounted for ₹2,000 and the other departmental expenses amounted to ₹7,600. The normal loss is 10 per cent of input. During the period, the actual production was 500 kgs and 100 kgs was scrap. Assuming that the scrap is saleable at ₹20 per kg, prepare a ledger account of process I, showing the values of normal and abnormal losses.

Solution

Process I Account

Particulars	Units (kgs)	Amount	Particulars	Units (kgs)	Amount
To materials	600	₹24,000	By normal loss (600 × 0.10)	60	₹1,200
To wages		2,000	By abnormal loss	40	2,400
To departmental expenses		7,600	By process II (500 units transferred at ₹60 each)	500	30,000
	600	33,600		600	33,600

WORKING NOTES

Cost per unit = (₹33,600 - ₹1,200)/540 units = ₹60

Amount of abnormal loss

Units introduced	600
Less normal loss (10 per cent)	60
Normal output expected	540
Less actual output achieved	500
Abnormal loss (units)	40
(×) Cost per unit	₹60
Total loss	₹2,400
Less sale value of scrap (40 × ₹20)	800
Effective loss	1,600

We now take comprehensive examples (14.6 to 14.10) to illustrate the preparation of process accounts under different situations.

◆ Example 14.6

(Closing Work-in-Process with Process Loss or Gain)

AB Ltd is engaged in the process engineering industry. During the month of April, 2,000 units were introduced in process X, the normal loss was estimated at 5 per cent of input. At the end of the month, 1,400 units had been produced and transferred to process Y; 460 units were incomplete and 140 units had to be scrapped during the process. The incomplete units had reached the following stages of completion: Material, 75 per cent; Labour, 50 per cent; Overhead, 50 per cent. Further information on process X:

Cost of the 2,000 units	₹58,000
Additional direct material	14,400
Direct labour	33,400
Direct overhead	16,700

Scrapped units realised ₹10 each.

Prepare a statement of equivalent production, statement of cost, statement of apportionment of cost and process X account.

Solution

Statement of Equivalent Production

Input	*Particulars*	*Number of units (completed or otherwise)*	*Stage completion (per cent)*			*Equivalent units (units × stage of completion)*		
			Material	*Labour*	*Over-heads*	*Material*	*Labour*	*Over-heads*
2,000	Units introduced		100	100	100	1,400	1,400	1,400
	Units produced	1,400						
	Normal loss (0.5 × 2,000)	100	—	—	—	—	—	—
	Abnormal loss (140 units – 100, normal)	40	100	100	100	40	40	40
	Closing inventory	460	75	50	50	345	230	230
		2,000				1,785	1,670	1,670

Statement of Cost

Particulars	Total cost	Equivalent production (units)	Cost per unit
Materials			
Cost of units introduced	₹58,000		
Additional direct material	14,400		
	72,400		
Less sale proceeds of scrap material (100 units × ₹10)	1,000		
	71,400	1,785	₹40
Direct labour	33,400	1,670	20
Direct overheads	16,700	1,670	10
	1,21,500		70

Statement of Apportionment of Cost

Particulars	Element of cost	Equivalent production	Cost per unit	Cost	Total cost
Finished production	Material	1,400	₹40	₹56,000	
	Labour	1,400	20	28,000	
	Overhead	1,400	10	14,000	₹98,000
Abnormal loss	Material	40	40	1,600	
	Labour	40	20	800	
	Overhead	40	10	400	2,800
Work-in-process	Material	345	40	13,800	
	Labour	230	20	4,600	
	Overhead	230	10	2,300	20,700
					1,21,500

Process X Account

Particulars	Units	Amount	Particulars	Units	Amount
To raw material	2,000	₹58,000	By normal loss	100	₹1,000
To other direct materials		14,400	By abnormal loss	40	2,800
To direct labour		33,400	By process Y (transferred @ ₹70)	1,400	98,000
To direct overheads		16,700	By work-in-process	460	20,700
	2,000	1,22,500		2,000	1,22,500

◆ Example 14.7

(Opening and Closing Work-in-Process with Process Loss/Gains)

The finished output of a factory passes through two processes, the entire material being introduced at the beginning of the first process. From the following production and cost data relating to the first process, work out the value of closing inventory and the value of materials transferred to the second process. Also prepare process I account.

Process I: Opening stock, 10,000 units at ₹50,000

Stage of completion of opening inventory: Materials, 100 per cent; Labour, 60 per cent; Overheads; 50 per cent.

Units introduced during the process: 50,000 units at ₹1,44,000; Direct labour, ₹81,000; Overheads, ₹80,000.

Units transferred to next process, 38,000

Spoilage during the process (units), 7,000

Stage of completion of closing inventory, 15,000 units: Material, 100 per cent; Labour, 50 per cent; Overheads, 40 per cent.
Normal loss, 10 per cent of input.
Sale value of spoilage, ₹2 per unit.

Solution

Statement of Cost

Particulars	Total cost	Equivalent production (units)	Cost per unit
Materials	₹1,44,000		
Less sale value of normal scrap (6,000 × ₹2)	12,000		
	1,32,000	44,000	₹3
Direct labour	81,000	40,500	2
Overheads	80,000	40,000	2
	2,93,000		7

Statement of Equivalent Production

Input units	Particulars	Number of units (completed or otherwise)	Stage completion (per cent)			Equivalent units (units × stage of completion)		
			Material	Labour	Overheads	Material	Labour	Overheads
10,000	Opening stock (100 per cent stage of completion)	10,000	Nil	40	50	—	4,000	5,000
50,000	Units started and completed (38,000 – 10,000, opening inventory)	28,000	100	100	100	28,000	28,000	28,000
	Normal loss (0.10 × 60,000)	6,000	—	—	—	—	—	—
	Abnormal loss (7,000 – 6,000)	1,000	100	100	100	1,000	1,000	1,000
	Closing work-in-process	15,000	100	50	40	15,000	7,500	6,000
60,000		60,000				44,000	40,500	40,000

Note: FIFO method of cost flow has been assumed.

Statement of Apportionment of Cost

Particulars	Element of cost	Equivalent production	Cost per unit	Total cost	
Opening inventory (combined)	—	—	—	₹50,000	—
	Material	—	—	—	—
	Labour	4,000	₹2	8,000	
	Overheads	5,000	2	10,000	₹68,000
Units introduced and completed	Material	28,000	3	84,000	
	Labour	28,000	2	56,000	
	Overheads	28,000	2	56,000	1,96,000
Abnormal loss	Material	1,000	3	3,000	
	Labour	1,000	2	2,000	
	Overheads	1,000	2	2,000	7,000

(Contd.)

(Contd.)

Closing work-in-process	Material	15,000	3	45,000	
	Labour	7,500	2	15,000	
	Overheads	6,000	2	12,000	72,000

Process I Account

Particulars	Units	Amount	Particulars	Units	Amount
To opening work-in-process	10,000	₹50,000	By normal loss	6,000	12,000
			By abnormal loss	1,000	7,000
To direct material costs	50,000	1,44,000	By process II (₹68,000 + ₹1,96,000)	38,000	2,64,000
To direct labour		81,000			
To overheads		80,000	By work-in-process	15,000	72,000
	60,000	3,55,000		60,000	3,55,000

◆ Example 14.8

(Determination of Abnormal Loss When Units are Scrapped and Spoiled Units are at Different Stages of Completion)

In **Example 14.7**, assume the stages of completion in respect of 7,000 spoiled units are as follows: Material, 100 per cent; Labour, 50 per cent; Overheads, 60 per cent.

Determine the abnormal loss.

Solution

Determination of Abnormal Loss

Cost element	Number of units	Stage of completion (per cent)	Equivalent units	Cost per unit	Total cost
Material	1,000	100	1,000	₹3.000	₹3,000.00
Labour	1,000	50	500	2.025	1,012.50
Overheads	1,000	60	600	2.020	1,212.00
					5,224.50

Material cost	(₹1,32,000 ÷ 44,000)	=	₹ 3.00 per unit
Labour cost	(₹81,000 ÷ 40,000)	=	2.025 per unit
Overhead costs	(₹80,000 ÷ 39,600)	=	2.02 per unit

◆ Example 14.9

(Abnormal Loss and Abnormal Gain with no Work-in-process Inventory)

XYZ Chemical Ltd processes a range of products including a detergent, 'Washo', which passes through 3 processes before completion and transfer to the finished goods warehouse. During April, data relating to this product were as follows:

Particulars	Process I	Process II	Process III	Total
Basic raw material (1,000 units)	₹6,000	—	—	₹6,000
Direct raw material added in process	8,500	9,500	5,500	23,500
Direct wages	4,000	6,000	12,000	22,000
Direct expenses	1,200	930	1,340	3,470
Production overhead				16,500
Output (units)	920	870	790	
Normal loss in process of input (per cent)	10	5	10	
Scrap value per unit	2	5	10	

The production overhead is absorbed as a percentage of direct wages. There was no stock at the start or at the end of any process.

You are required to prepare the following accounts: **(i)** Process I; **(ii)** Process II; **(iii)** Process III; **(iv)** Abnormal loss; and **(v)** Abnormal gain.

Solution

Process I Account

Particulars	Units	Amount	Particulars	Units	Amount
To raw materials	1,000	₹6,000	By normal loss (0.10 × 1,000)	100	₹200
To other direct raw materials		8,500	By process II (transferred @ ₹25 per unit: ₹22,500 ÷ 900)	920	23,000
To direct wages		4,000			
To direct expenses		1,200			
To manufacturing overheads [0.75 × (₹16,500 ÷ ₹22,000) of wages]		3,000			
To abnormal gain (920 – 900, normal output)	20	500			
	1,020	23,200		1,020	23,200

Process II Account

Particulars	Units	Amount	Particulars	Units	Amount
To output transferred from process I	920	₹23,000	By normal loss (0.05 × 920)	46	₹230
To direct raw materials		9,500	By process III (transferred @ ₹50: ₹43,700 ÷ 874)	870	43,500
To direct wages		6,000	By abnormal loss (8,74 normal output – 8,70)	4	200
To direct expenses		930			
To manufacturing overheads (0.75 × ₹6,000)		4,500			
	920	43,930		920	43,930

Process III Account

Particulars	Units	Amount	Particulars	Units	Amount
To output transferred from process II	870	₹43,500	By normal loss (870 × 0.10)	87	₹870
To direct material		5,500	By finished stock A/c (final output transferred @ ₹90 per unit)	790	71,100
To direct wages		12,000			
To direct expenses		1,340			
To manufactured overhead (0.75 × ₹12,000)		9,000			
To abnormal gain (790 – 783, normal output)	7	630			
	877	71,970		877	71,970

Abnormal Loss Account

Particulars	Units	Amount	Particulars	Units	Amount
To process II	4	200	By sale proceeds of scrap @ ₹5 per unit	4	20
			By profit @ loss A/c (loss transferred)		180
	4	200		4	200

Abnormal Gain Account

To normal loss			By process I A/c	20	500
Process I	20	40	By process III A/c	7	630
Process II	7	70			
To profit and loss account (profit transferred)		1,020			
	27	1,130		27	1,130

◆ Example 14.10

(Intermediate Process Output is Partially Sold and Partially Transferred)

A chemical company processes a patent material used in buildings. The material is produced in three consecutive grades: soft, medium and hard. The details of its operations are as follows:

	Process I	Process II	Process III
Raw material used (kgs.)	1,000		
Cost per kg.	₹200		
Total manufacturing expenses	87,500	₹39,500	₹10,710
Weight lost (per cent of input of the process)	5	10	20
Scrap (Sale price ₹50 per kg.) (kgs.)	50	30	51
Sale price per kg.	350	500	800

Management expenses were ₹7,500 and selling expenses, ₹5,000. Two-thirds of the output of process I and one-half of the output of process II is passed on to the next process and the balance is sold. The entire output of process III is sold.

Prepare relevant process accounts.

Solution

Process I Account

Particulars	kgs.	Amount	Particulars	kgs.	Amount
To direct raw materials	1,000	₹2,00,000	By weight lost	50	—
To manufacturing expenses		87,500	By scrap sales	50	₹2,500
To profit		10,000	By sales (900 × 1/3)	300	1,05,000
			By Process II	600	
			(₹2,85,000 × 2/3)	—	1,90,000
	1,000	2,97,500		1,000	2,97,500

Process II Account

Particulars	kgs.	Amount	Particulars	kgs.	Amount
To process I			By weight lost	60	—
(transferred from)	600	₹1,90,000	By scrap sales	30	₹1,500
To manufacturing expenses		39,500	By sales (510 × 1/2)	255	1,27,500
To profit		13,500	By process III (transferred)		
			(₹2,28,000 × 1/2)	255	1,14,000
	600	2,43,000		600	2,43,000

Process III Account

Particulars	kgs.	Amount	Particulars	kgs.	Amount
To process II			By weight loss	51	—
(transferred from)	255	₹1,14,000	By scrap sales	51	₹2,550
To manufacturing expenses		10,710	By sales	153	1,22,400
To profit		240			
	255	1,24,950		255	1,24,950

Statement of Profit

Profit from		
Process I	₹10,000	
II	13,500	
III	240	
Total		₹23,740
Less: management expenses	7,500	
selling expenses	5,000	12,500
Net profit		11,240

Note: Weight lost as well as scrap material is assumed to be normal loss.

Inter-Process Profits

Inter-process profit is the profit arising out of transfer of the product of one process to the other on the basis of market/inflated price.

The transfer of the output of one process to another can either be at the cost or at the market/inflated price. The cost basis of inter-process transfer of output has a serious limitation in that the efficiency or inefficiency of one process is passed on to the next. The market price basis overcomes this weakness.

The efficiency of process operations can be judged by comparing the value of output of a process with the price which would be paid for purchasing material from the market. If the market price is lower, the process operations are clearly not efficient. Conversely, if the market price is higher, efficiency of the process operations should be recognised in terms of profits contributed by the process equal to the excess of market price over its cost. Naturally, for true comparison of efficiency of, say, process II, the output of process I should be transferred at market price and not at the cost price. '*Market/inflated price transfer formula*' has an additional advantage in that the final process account is not artificially distorted by inclusion of a figure of profit which has, in fact, accrued throughout the sequence of prior processes. Each process is, thus, made to stand by itself. The determination of the true cost of each process independent of others is of utmost significance particularly for those process industries where there are clear-cut possibilities of getting the intermediate supplies form the market. Therefore, the '*economy cost*' of performing such operations should be determined. For these reasons, inter-process transfer should be at the current market value or by the addition of an arbitrary percentage to cost. Such transfers would involve inter-process profits.

One important consequence of inflated transfer price (for inter-processes output) would be on valuation of closing stock. The inter-processes profit should be deducted from the closing inventory to show the inventory at cost price. This is illustrated in Examples 14.11 and 14.12.

◆ Example 14.11

(Inter-Process Profits)

A product passes through three processes, A, B, and C. The output of process A and B is charged to the next process at a price calculated to give a profit of 16.67 per cent on transfer price while the output of process C is charged to the finished stock account at a profit of 13.33 per cent on the transfer price. From the following particulars, prepare the process cost accounts and calculate the amount of reserve that should be made in respect of the stock in hand.

	Process A	*Process B*	*Process C*
Materials and labour	₹7,000	₹2,800	₹4,800
Closing stock	2,000	2,800	2,000

There was no stock in hand at the beginning of the period. The closing stocks are valued at prime cost in each process.

Solution

Process A Account

Particulars	*Amount*	*Particulars*	*Amount*
To materials and labour	₹7,000	By closing stock	₹2,000
To profit (₹6,000 × 0.1667)	1,000	By process B (₹5,000 × 120/100)	6,000
	8,000		8,000

Process B Account

Particulars	*Amount*	*Particulars*	*Amount*
To process A	₹6,000	By closing stock	₹2,800
To material and labour	2,800	By process C (₹6,000 × 120/100)	7,200
To profit (₹7,200 × 0.1667)	1,200		
	10,000		10,000

Process C Account

Particulars	*Amount*	*Particulars*	*Amount*
To process B	₹7,200	By closing stock	₹2,000
To materials and labour	4,800	By finished goods (10,000 × 115.38/100)	11,538
To profit (₹11,538 × 0.1333)	1,538		
	13,538		13,538

WORKING NOTES

1. Profit of 16.67 per cent on transfer means 20 per cent on cost price.
2. Likewise, profit of 13.33 per cent on transfer price means 15.38 per cent on cost.
3. Provision for unrealised profit:
   Process A: Nil
   Process B: (₹1,000 × 2,800)/8,800 = ₹318
   Process C: Closing stock of process C of ₹2,000 is made up of respective cost proportions of C: B, that is, 2:3 (₹4,800: ₹7,200).
   Process C's share is = ₹2,000 × 2/5 = ₹800
   Process B's share is = ₹2,000 × 3/5 = ₹1,200
   Profit included in ₹1,200 (process B's cost) is = ₹1200 × 20/120 = ₹200 (i)
   Profit included in ₹1,000. This includes part of process A's costs: ₹1,000 × 60/88= ₹682.
   ₹682 includes profit element of = ₹682 × 20/120 = ₹113 (ii)
   Total profit included in process C = ₹313 (200 + 113) (i + ii)

Statement of Profit

Process A		₹1,000
Process B	₹1,200	
Less provision for unrealised profit	318	882
Process C	1,538	
Less provision for unrealised profit	313	1,225
Profit realised		3,107

Alternatively

Process A Account

Particulars	Total	Cost	Profit	Particulars	Total	Cost	Profit
To materials and labour	₹7,000	₹7,000	—	By closing stock	₹2,000	₹2,000	—
To profit (₹5,000 × 50/3 × 3/250)	1,000	—	₹1,000	By process B (transferred)	6,000	5,000	₹1,000
	8,000	7,000	1,000		8,000	7,000	1,000

Process B Account

	Total	Cost	Profit		Total	Cost	Profit
To process A	₹6,000	₹5,000	₹1,000	By Closing stock (2,800 × 1,000) ÷ 8,800	₹2,800	₹2,482	₹318
To materials and labour	2,800	2,800	—	By process C (transferred)	7,200	5,318	1,882
To profit and loss A/c (₹6,000 × (50 × 3) ÷ (3 × 250))	1,200	—	1,200				
	10,000	7,800	2,200		10,000	7,800	2,200

Process C Account

	Total	Cost	Profit		Total	Cost	Profit
To process B	₹7,200	₹5,318	₹1,882	By closing stock	₹2,000	₹1,687	₹313
To materials and labour	4,800	4,800	—	By finished goods A/c (at 115.38 per cent of cost)	11,538	8,431	3,107
To profit and loss A/c (0.1333 × ₹11,538)	1,538	—	1,538				
	13,538	10,118	3,420		13,538	10,118	3,420

◆ Example 14.12

(Inter-Process Profit When Opening Inventory of Processes is Given)

A Ltd makes a product which passes through two processes before it is completed and transferred to finished stock. The following data related to the month of December:

Particulars	Process I	Process II	Finished stock
Opening stock	₹7,500	₹9,000	₹22,500
Direct materials	15,000	15,750	
Direct wages	11,200	11,250	

(Contd.)

(*Contd.*)

Factory overheads	10,500	4,500	
Closing stock	3,700	4,500	11,250
Inter-process profit included in opening stock		1,500	8,250

Output of process I is transferred to process II at 25 per cent profit on the transfer price. Output of process II is transferred to finished stock at 20 per cent profit on the transfer price. Stocks in process are valued at prime cost. Finished stock is valued at the price at which it is received from process II. Sales during the period were ₹1,40,000.

Prepare process cost account and finished goods account showing the profit element at each stage.

Solution

Process I Account

Particulars	Total	Cost	Profit	Particulars	Total	Cost	Profit
To opening stock	₹7,500	₹7,500	—	By process II (₹40,500 × 133.33/100)	₹54,000	₹40,500	₹13,500
To direct materials	15,000	15,000	—				
To direct wages	11,200	11,200	—				
Less closing stock	(3,700)	(3,700)					
Prime cost	30,000	30,000					
To factory overheads/ process cost	10,500	10,500					
Process cost	40,500	40,500					
To profit & loss A/c(0.25 × ₹54,000)	13,500		₹13,500				
	54,000	40,500	13,500		54,000	40,500	13,500

Process II Account

Particulars	Total	Cost	Profit	Particulars	Total	Cost	Profit
To opening stock	₹9,000	₹7,500	₹1,500	By finished stock (₹90,000 × 125/100)	₹1,12,500	₹75,750	₹36,750
To process I (transferred from)	54,000	40,500	13,500				
To direct materials	15,750	15,750	—				
To direct wages	11,250	11,250	—				
Less closing stock	(4,500)	(3,750)	(750)				
Prime cost	85,500	71,250	14,250				
To factory overheads	4,500	4,500					
Process cost	90,000	75,750	—				
To profit & loss A/c	22,500	—	22,500				
	1,12,500	75,750	36,750		1,12,500	75,750	36,750

Finished Stock Account

To opening stock	₹22,500	₹14,250	₹8,250	By closing stock	₹11,250	₹7,500	₹3,750
To Process II (transferred from)	1,12,500	75,750	36,750	By sales	1,40,000	82,500	57,500
To profit & loss A/c (profit transferred)	16,250	—	16,250				
	1,51,250	90,000	61,250		1,51,250	90,000	61,250

WORKING NOTES

1. If ₹90,000 prime cost includes ₹15,000 profit, then ₹4,500 closing stock would include: ₹15,000 × ₹4,500)/₹90,000 = ₹750
2. *Statement of Profit*

Particulars		*Amount*
Process I:		₹13,500
Process II:	₹22,500	
Adjustment: provision for unrealised profit		
Add for opening stock	1,500	
Less for closing stock	750	23,250
Finished stock account	16,250	
Adjustment of provision for unrealised profit		
Add for opening stock	8,250	
Less for closing stock	3,750	20,750
		57,500

3. If ₹1,35,000 includes ₹45,000 profit, then ₹11,250 closing stock would include: (₹45,000 × ₹11,250) ÷ ₹1,35,000 = ₹3,750

The process accounts prepared in columnar form are more informative and useful as they provide classified information regarding cost and profit. This information shows inter-process profits included in the value of output (stock) transferred from one process to another, while such profits are to be computed separately in non-columnar form of process accounts.

JOINT PRODUCTS

LO 14.3 Discuss accounting procedure for joint products

Joint products are a feature of industries which process natural raw materials such as petroleum, chemicals, dairy products, wood products, mining and extractive industries. Two or more products produced simultaneously from a common set of inputs through a single manufacturing process (joint process), are called joint products.

Since joint products are the result of the use of some common items of cost, these items of cost are known as common/joint costs. The joint/multiple products resulting from common costs can be either sold at this stage of production or they can be processed further. Therefore, this stage of the joint production process is known as the *split-off point*. *Split-off point* is that stage in the manufacturing process where the joint products are separately identifiable. Prior to the point of split-off/ separation, products are not subject to identification nor are the costs. Therefore, production costs incurred prior to the split-off point are called *joint costs*, and those incurred after the split-off point are called *separable costs*. Being so, separable costs can be directly traced to specific products and, therefore, do not entail any problem of cost allocation while the same is not true of joint costs.

Split-off point is that stage in the manufacturing process where the joint products are separately identifiable.

Allocation of Joint Costs

The critical problem in accounting for joint products is that of allocating common process costs among the separate/multiple outputs that emerge from the joint process. The allocation method used will determine the amount of common processing cost allocated to each of the joint outputs. The commonly-used methods for allocating joint processing costs include:

Joint cost are the costs incurred prior to the split-off point.

1. Physical quantities method/Unit method.
2. Relative sales value method/Net realisable value method.
3. Net realisable value less normal profit method.
4. Weighted averages cost method.

Physical Quantities Method/Unit Method Under this method, the total costs (material, labour and overhead) incurred in the joint production process are allocated to various products in proportion to the physical measurement of the output. The physical measure might be volume, weight, surface area or any other common measure of the physical characteristics. Thus, under this method, the common attribute is aggregated and the joint costs are allocated on the basis of each product's relative share of it. This is illustrated in Example 14.13.

Physical quantity method allocates joint costs in proportion to the physical measurement of the output, e.g., volume, weight, surface area.

◆ Example 14.13

(Allocation of Joint Costs Under Unit Method)

Royal Industries Ltd manufactures products X, Y and Z by processing a specific raw material in Department 1. The production process is such that every 1,100 kgs of raw materials that is put into Department 1 yields 400 kgs of X, 250 kgs of Y and 350 kgs of Z. The total cost of processing a batch of 1,100 kgs of raw materials through Department 1 is ₹22,000. Allocate the joint costs to the three products using the physical quantity method.

Solution

Joint Cost Allocation Using Unit Method

Product	*Output (kgs)*	*Rates (per cent)*	*Allocated joint cost*	*Cost per unit*
X	400	40	₹8,800	₹22
Y	250	25	5,500	22
Z	350	35	7,700	22
	1,000	100	22,000	22

This method results in identical unit costs for each product. Identical benefits exist only if the products are homogeneous. It will, therefore, provide a satisfactory basis of allocating joint cost if the different products are homogeneous and their sale prices are relatively close to each other. Otherwise, it may lead to misleading results in that there will be wide divergence in the gross margin of the different products as shown in Table 14.2.

TABLE 14.2 Gross Margin of Different Products

	Product X	*Product Y*	*Product Z*
Sales price	₹33	₹44	₹66
Less cost of production	22	22	22
Cross margin	11	22	44
Gross margin percentage	33.33	50	66.67

Relative Sales Value/Net Realisable Value (NRV) Method As per this method, joint costs are *prorated* among multiple products on the basis of the market value of the products manufactured. This method is based on the premise that if a product has a higher sale price, it costs more to produce and, hence, the market value basis to allocate join costs.

Net realisable value is the sale value after further processing less further processing cost.

If the joint products can be sold at the split-off point, sales price measure can *directly and conveniently* be applied for joint costs allocation. In case the products are not readily marketable at the split-off point, but require further processing, it is necessary to estimate the sales value at the split-off-point. This is usually estimated by taking the sale value after further processing and deducting the additional processing costs.

Net realisable value = Sales value after further process — Further processing cost (14.4)

From the facts in **Example 14.13 and Table 14.2** and assuming all products are sold at the split-off point, joint cost allocation under the relative sale value method would be, as shown in Table 14.3.

TABLE 14.3 Joint Cost Allocation Using Sales Value Method

Product	*Output (kgs)*	*Market price*	*Market value*	*Rates*	*Allocated joint cost*	*Cost per unit*
X	400	₹33	₹13,200	132/473	₹6,140	₹15.35
Y	250	44	11,000	110/473	5,116	20.46
Z	350	66	23,100	231/473	10,744	30.70
	1,000		47,300		22,000	22.00

Thus, the costs per unit are in proportion to the sale prices. The relative sale price method generates the same margin percentage (53.48 per cent) for all products. Thus, this approach implies a matching of input costs with revenues generated by each output.

In practice, however, it may so happen that the joint products may not be in a condition to be sold at the split-off point; they may need further processing to become marketable. In such cases, a hypothetical sales value needs to be estimated at the split-off point to allocate joint costs. The resulting hypothetical sales value/net realisable value is used for joint cost allocation in the same way as actual market value at the split-off point. Assuming that for the firm in Example 14.13, the additional processing for products X, Y and Z is done in departments 2, 3 and 4 respectively. Following are the costs incurred in these departments to process the batch of 1,100 kgs of materials:

Product	*Output (kgs)*	*Department*	*Further processing/ separable cost*	*Unit cost*
X	400	2	₹6,000	₹15
Y	250	3	4,500	18
Z	350	4	7,000	20

Assuming no change in market price, joint costs of Royal Industries Ltd would be allocated as shown in Table 14.4.

TABLE 14.4 Allocation of Joint Costs [Net Realisable Value (NRV) Method]

Product	*Output (kgs)*	*Market price*	*Market value*	*Separable cost*	*Net realisable value*	*Rates*	*Allocated joint costs*	*Joint cost per unit*
X	400	₹33	₹13,200	₹6,000	₹7,200	72/298	₹5,315	₹13.28
Y	250	44	11,000	4,500	6,500	65/298	4,799	19.19
Z	350	66	23,100	7,000	16,100	161/298	11,886	33.96
	1,000		47,300	17,500	29,800		22,000	22.00

The gross margin rates for each product according to this method are shown in Table 14.5.

TABLE 14.5 Gross Margin Rates

	Product X	*Product Y*	*Product Z*
Sales price	₹33.00	₹44.00	₹66.00
Less cost of production:			
Joint cost	13.28	19.19	33.96
Separable cost	15.00	18.00	20.00
	28.28	37.19	53.96
Gross margin	4.72	6.81	12.04
Gross margin rate (percentage)	14.3	15.5	18.21

The NRV method is based on the assumption that the processing costs incurred subsequent to the split-off point contribute nothing to profit; the increase in the product's sales value is equal to the separable costs. This supposition is fundamentally wrong as it implies that the firm would be willing to process its products further even if they do not contribute to profits. This is not likely to be true in practice for manufacturing firms. Therefore, it may be more logical to argue that profit is earned over the entire span of production rather than just during the joint span. Thus, this method of allocating joint costs ignores the profits from further processing of the product beyond the split-off point.

Net Realisable Value Less Normal Profit Method This method is based on the fundamental axiom that profits are earned on total cost incurred, and not on joint costs only. The following are the steps required to apply this method:

(i) Determine the ratio of the total production cost (joint and separable) to total final market value. This ratio is an average cost ratio per rupee of sales.
(ii) Subtract the average cost ratio form 100 per cent to find an average/normal profit ratio.
(iii) Finally, subtract the sum of the separable costs and normal profit from the market value. The amount so arrived at would be allocated joint costs corresponding to each product. Table 14.6 shows the cost allocation.

TABLE 14.6 Joint Cost Allocation Using NRV Less Normal Profit Method

Product	*Output (kgs)*	*Market value*	*Normal profit*	*Separable costs*	*Joint cost allocation*	*Joint cost per unit*
X	400	₹13,200	₹2,177	₹6,000	₹5,023	₹12.557
Y	250	11,000	1,814	4,500	4,686	22.744
Z	350	23,100	3,809	7,000	12,291	35.117
	1,000	47,300	7,800	17,500	22,000	

WORKING NOTES

Normal profit ratio = 100 per cent — [Total costs — (Joint + Separable) × 100] ÷ Total market value = 100 per cent — [(₹22,000 + ₹17,500) × 100 ÷ ₹47,300, 83.5 per cent = 16.5 per cent]

It may be noted that gross profit margin is uniform (16.5 per cent) for all the products as per this method which may not be a desirable characteristic. Therefore, this method should again not be taken as a perfect measure of allocating joint costs but, certainly, it is one, which is logically superior to others discussed so far.

Weighted Average Method Where the products are heterogeneous, the weighted average method can provide a reasonable basis for allocating joint costs. This method is theoretically superior to the physical quantity method as this method, by assigning different weights to different products, recognises some significant characteristics of the output. As the weight factors can reflect the varying amounts of time required to process the units, the difficulty of the processing procedure, the amount of material and labour used and other significant factors, there would be a positive correlation between these factors and the assigned value of weights. The sale price is one of the widely-used weight factors in practice.

According to this method, the volume of output for each product is multiplied by a weight that reflects the collective differences among the products. In order to have reliable results from the method, weights should be assigned after giving due and careful consideration to all the relevant characteristics of the product.

Continuing with the example of Royal Industries Ltd, assume that the following are the weights assigned to products X, Y and Z after taking into consideration a variety of factors: X, 1; Y, 2; Z, 4. Using the weighted average method, the joint costs are allocated in Table 14.7.

TABLE 14.7 Joint Cost Allocation Using Weighted Average Method

Product	*Output (kgs)*	*Weight*	*Weighted output*	*Ratio*	*Allocated joint cost*	*Cost per unit*
X	400	1	400	4/23	₹3,826	₹9.56
Y	250	2	500	5/23	4,783	19.13
Z	350	4	1,400	14/23	13,391	38.26
	1,000		2,300		22,000	

Thus, according to this method, joint cost per unit is in direct proportion to the weights assigned to various products. The major limitation of the method is the problem of establishment of the weights. These weights are frequently the result of individual judgement and, therefore, may not be objective. In all fairness, this method would be an ideal one if weights could be objectively determined.

BY-PRODUCTS

LO 14.4 Describe the costing treatment of by-products

A by-product is incidental to the process of manufacturing the main/joint products. It is an output whose value does not contribute materially to the revenues of the firm. Its amount, relative to the value of the main product, is small. Chemical residues, sawdust and shavings, and slag are typical by-products of the chemicals, timber and steel processing industries respectively. By-products differ from scrap. For instance, scrap is sold as it is while by-products may have to undergo additional processing before sale. Moreover, it may so happen that the disposal of scrap may involve some expenses instead of yielding any revenue, whereas a by-product always generates some revenue.

By-products is incidental to the process of manufacturing the main/joint products.

The accounting treatment of by-products will depend on whether the by-product is sold at the split-off point or processed further. The former is discussed here while the latter is covered in the next section. The two most commonly used methods of accounting for by-products are: **(1)** Miscellaneous income method, and **(2)** Net realisable value method (NRV).

Miscellaneous Income Method

Under this method, sales revenue contributed by the by-products is considered as miscellaneous income of the firm. All costs are assigned to only the main products and not to the by-products. This method is considered as the most appropriate when the value of the by-product is uncertain or so trivial that it is not likely to have any significant/noticeable effect on inventory or profit.

Net Realisable Value Method

In case the value of a by-product is large enough to have a significant effect on inventory or profits, the by-product should be valued at its net realisable value/sale value. This treatment would cause *reduction in the cost of production of the main products.* The cost of the joint process is assigned to the joint products as well as to by-products. Therefore, the cost of production of the main output would be lower by the proportionate charge to the by-product. There are two variants of this method: **(i)** Recognition of no profit on the sale of by-products **(ii)** Recognition of some normal profit.

Recognition of No Profit on the Sale of By-products As per this variant, the sale price of the by-product would be considered to consist of two elements, namely, **(i)** Production cost assigned to it out of joint costs, and **(ii)** Selling and distribution cost. Accordingly, the share of joint costs allocated to by-products would be:

Sale price of by-products – Selling and distribution cost of by-products = Joint process cost allocated to by-products **(14.5)**

Recognition of Some Normal Profit on the Sale of By-products A second variant is to recognise some normal profit from the sales of by-products. Accordingly, the sale price of by-product would be considered consisting of three elements, namely, **(i)** Production cost (share of joint costs) allocated to it; **(ii)** Selling and distribution cost; and **(iii)** Normal profit. The share of joint costs allocated to by-products would be determined as follows (Equation 14.6).

Sale price of by-products – Normal profit – Selling and distribution cost of by-products **(14.6)**

◆ Example 14.14

For the facts contained in **Example 14.13**, let as assume further that joint production process also yields by-product (70 kgs) in addition to three main products X, Y, Z. Its selling price is ₹2 per kg and selling costs are ₹0.50 per kg. Determine the share of joint costs **(i)** if firm does not recognise profit on the sale of its by-product; and **(ii)** if it recognises 10 per cent profit on such sales.

Solution

Share of Joint Costs

(i) When no profits are recognised:	
Sales revenue (70 kgs × ₹2)	₹140
Less selling costs (70 kgs × ₹0.50)	35
Share of joint costs (70 kgs × ₹1.50)	105
(ii) When 10 per cent profits are recognised:	
Sales revenue (70 kgs × ₹2)	140
Less normal profit (₹140 × 0.10)	14
Less selling costs (70 kgs × ₹0.50)	35
Share of joint costs (70 kgs × ₹1.30)	91

SELL NOW (AT SPLIT-OFF POINT) OR PROCESS FURTHER

LO 14.5 Explain the costing for selling at split-off point or processing further

As mentioned in the preceding section, a joint product can be sold at the split-off point or processed further and sold later as a completed production unit. This section explains the accounting for the sale or further processing of the main products as well as the by-products. This exercise will be helpful to the management in arriving at a decision, whether the product should be sold at the split-off point or processed further. From the point of view of managerial decision-making, incremental costs of further processing should be compared with the incremental revenue. This aspect is comprehensively elaborated in a subsequent chapter dealing with short-term decisions.

Main Products Requiring Further Processing

Examples 14.15 and 14.16 illustrate the application of process costing to the main products.

◆ Example 14.15

(Sell Now or Process Further: Single Product)

A B C Ltd manufactures a single product which it sells to firms which process it further before sale. The normal quarterly operating volume for the company is 50,000 units produced and sold. The relevant cost data are as follows:

Selling price		₹10.00
Less standard costs:		
Direct materials	₹3.00	
Direct labour	1.50	
Variable manufacturing overheads	1.00	
Fixed manufacturing overheads (₹25,000 per quarter)	0.50	
Variable selling overheads	1.00	
Fixed selling expenses (₹12,500 per quarter)	0.25	7.25
Standard (budgeted) profit per unit		2.75

The company's management is considering the possibility of further processing the product and selling it directly to the customers. The management estimates that the product can be sold @ ₹14 per unit after further processing. The following are the estimates of the *additional* (*per unit/ quarter*) costs of processing 50,000 units:

Direct labour	₹1.00
Variable manufacturing overheads	0.50
Variable selling costs	0.20
Additional fixed manufacturing overheads (per quarter)	10,000
Additional sales expenses (per quarter)	5,000

You are required to compute the cost (i) without, and (ii) with further processing. Is further processing advisable?

Solution

Cost Comparison: Incremental Analysis

Particulars	*Without further processing*		*With further processing*		*Difference from further processing*	
	Per unit	*Total*	*Per unit*	*Total*	*Per unit*	*Total*
Sales	₹10.00	₹5,00,000	₹14.00	₹7,00,000	₹4.00	₹2,00,000
Less variables costs:						
Direct material	3.00	1,50,000	3.00	1,50,000	0.00	—
Direct labour	1.50	75,000	2.50	1,25,000	1.00	50,000
Manufacturing						

(Contd.)

(*Contd.*)

overheads	1.00	50,000	1.50	75,000	0.50	25,000
Selling overheads	1.00	50,000	1.20	60,000	0.20	10,000
Total	6.50	3,25,000	8.20	4,10,000	1.70	85,000
Contribution	3.50	1,75,000	5.80	2,90,000	2.30	1,15,000
Less separable identifiable fixed costs:						
Manufacturing		—		10,000		10,000
Sales		—		5,000		5,000
Product margin		1,75,000		2,75,000		1,00,000
Less common fixed costs:						
Manufacturing		25,000		25,000		—
Sales		12,500		12,500		—
Net income		1,37,500		2,37,500		1,00,000

Since further processing would result in a greater product margin and net income, the new proposal is acceptable.

◆ Example 14.16

(Sell Now or Process Further: Multiple Products)

XYZ Ltd produces three products, A, B and C. One type of a raw material is used for all these products. Raw material enters the process in department 1 of the factory. Department 1 separates material for products A, B and C. During the last quarter, ₹4,00,000 of material was issued to Department 1. Other direct costs of operating Department 1 were ₹2,00,000. The output of products A, B and C from Department 1 was: A, 10,000 units; B, 5,000 units; C, 2,000 units.

Products A, B and C can be sold after being processed from Department 1 (split-off point) at prices of ₹60, ₹30 and ₹20 respectively. After the split off, product A could be processed further in Department 2. With additional processing, product A can be sold at ₹70 per unit. After the split-off, product B could be processed further in Department 3 for ₹30,000 additional cost, and will fetch ₹35 per unit after processing. Product C is not suitable for further processing and has to be sold at the point of split-off. What action should be management take?

Solution

Sell or Process Further: Decision Analysis

Particulars	*Product A*			*Product B*		
	Sell now	*Process further*	*Difference from further processing*	*Sell now*	*Process further*	*Differences from further processing*
Sales	₹6,00,000	₹7,00,000	₹1,00,000	₹1,50,000	₹1,75,000	₹25,000
Less separable costs	—	50,000	50,000	—	30,000	30,000
Joint cost of ₹6,00,000 from Department 1	Irrelevant as costs not affected by the decision					
Contribution (decrease)	₹6,00,000	6,50,000	50,000	1,50,000	1,45,000	(5,000)

Thus, it is profitable to process product A further because it yields an incremental profit of ₹50,000, (additional revenue being ₹1,00,000 and additional cost, ₹50,000). The decision is based on the assumption that there is no other opportunity cost for using the facilities of Departments 2 and 3.

By-Products Processed Further

There are several methods of accounting for costs of further processing: **(i)** Recognition of no profit on sale of by-products; **(ii)** Recognition of normal profit on by-products; and **(iii)** Separate cost records for by-products.

Recognition of No Profit on Sale of By-products Method Under this method, share of joint costs allocated to by-products would be determined by subtracting both selling and further processing costs from the sale price of by-products.

Sale price of by-products — Further processing cost beyond split-off point — Selling cost = Joint costs **(14.7)**

Recognition of Normal Profit on Sale of By-Products/Reversal Cost Method The share of joint costs assigned to by-products is given by Equation 14.8.

Sale-price-Further processing cost beyond shift off point-Selling cost-Estimated normal profit. **(14.8)**

This method is also known as the reversal cost/replacement/opportunity cost method and is most appropriate when by-products are used/utilised in the firm itself as material for manufacturing/processing some other products. Under this method, by-products are valued at the price which would have been paid by the firm in making outside purchases for these products.

Separate Cost Record for By-products This method is most appropriate in situations when the joint manufacturing process yields by-products which are relatively of high value and/or of large quantity; they also require further processing after separation from the joint manufacturing process. In such situations, the by-products cease to be by-products; they become as significant as the main products. Accordingly, they must normally be treated as main products and the cost allocated on some equitable and rational basis.

◆ **Example 14.17**

(Reversal Cost Method)

In manufacturing the main product, Hypothetical Ltd processes the incidental waste into two products, A and B. From the following data relating to the products, you are required to prepare a comparative profit and loss statement showing the individual costs and other details. The total costs upto separation point were ₹3,10,400.

	Main product	*By-product A*	*By-product B*
Sales	₹8,00,000	₹64,000	₹96,000
Costs after separation	80,000	12,800	14,400
Estimated net profit			
(per cent to sales value)		20	30
Estimated selling expenses			
(as per cent to sales value)	20	10	15

Solution

Statement Showing Allocation of Joint Costs

Particulars	*By-product A*	*By-product B*
Sales	₹64,000	₹96,000
Less: estimated net profit on sale		
(20 per cent, A; and 30 per cent, B)	12,800	28,800
estimated selling expenses		

(Contd.)

(*Contd.*)

(10 per cent, A, and 15 per cent, B)	6,400	14,400
separable costs	12,800	14,400
Share of joint costs allocated	32,000	38,400

Share of main products in joint costs, therefore, would be: ₹3,10,400 — (₹32,000 + ₹38,400) = ₹2,40,000.

Comparative Profit and Loss Account

Particulars	*Main product*	*By-product A*	*By-product B*
Sales revenue	₹8,00,000	₹64,000	₹96,000
Less cost of production:			
Joints costs	2,40,000	32,000	38,400
Separable costs	80,000	12,800	14,400
Gross profit	4,80,000	19,200	43,200
Less selling expenses	1,60,000	6,400	14,400
Net profit	3,20,000	12,800	28,800

SUMMARY

- The process costing system measures the cost of products under conditions of continuous production, sequential processing and homogeneous output. The procedure under such a system of costing essentially involves averaging the total costs of a process or a department. It is used in industries such as chemicals, food processing, breweries, petroleum refining, paper, glass, metal manufacturing and so on.

LO 14.1

- The procedure to determine the cost will depend on, firstly, the stage of completion of the product, in each process, secondly, the extent of wastage, spoilage of units in the process and, thirdly, the inter-process profits.
- In cases where some units are complete, while others are incomplete or partially complete, for the purpose of cost accumulation, the partially completed units are to be converted into comparable equivalent units. Equivalent units = [Actual number of partially completed units × Stage ofcompletion]
- The cost of production is shown in the form of a production cost report and/or process cost account. The total cost of production of each process is split into the cost of output and the closing inventory/work-in-process. The distribution between these two elements depends on the method of valuation of work-in-process, namely, weighted average method and first-in-first-out (FIFO) method.
- The spoilage of units under process costing may take place due to a variety of reasons, like use of sub-standard material, poor workmanship, evaporation, shrinkage, break-down of machines, and so on. The effect of spoilage is that the number of actual units produced is less than the units introduced initially. The spoilage or wastage may be normal or abnormal. The unit cost with normal spoilage

$$= \left(\frac{\text{Total process costs} - \text{Salvage value of normal spoilage}}{\text{Total units introduced} - \text{Normal loss in units}}\right)$$

- Abnormal loss = [(Abnormal loss in units × Unit production cost) – Salvage value of abnormal spoilage]
- The transfer of output of one process to the other can either be at cost or the inflated/market price. Transfers at the latter price involve inter-process profits. These profits should be deducted from closing inventory to determine true profits.

LO 14.2

- Two or more products produced simultaneously from a common set of inputs through a single manufacturing (joint) process are called joint products. The joint products can be sold either at the stage of production (split-off point) itself or they can be processed further. The costs incurred before the split-off point are called joint/common/inseparable costs and the costs incurred beyond that point are known as separable costs. The crucial factor in accounting for joint products is the allocation of joint costs among the joint/multiple products from the joint process.

- The commonly used methods of allocating joint process costs are: **(i)** Physical quantities method/unit method, **(ii)** Relative sales value method/net realisable value method, **(iii)** Net realisable value less normal profit method, and **(iv)** Weighted average cost method.
- Under the physical quantities method, the total joint costs are allocated to the joint products in proportion to the physical measurement of output.
- In the net realisable value method, joint costs are pro-rated on the basis of the market value of the joint products.
- The net realisable value less normal profit method differs from the net realisable value method to the extent the joint costs less normal profits are pro-rated.
- Where the joint products are heterogeneous, the weighted average cost method provides a reasonable basis for allocating the joint costs.

LO 14.3

- A by-product is incidental to the process of manufacturing the main/joint product. The accounting treatment depends on whether the by-product is sold at the split-off point or is processed further. The two most commonly-used methods of accounting for by-products are: **(i)** Miscellaneous income method, and **(ii)** Net realisable value method, ***(NRV).***
- Under the miscellaneous income method, the income generated by the by-products is treated as a miscellaneous income and all the associated costs are charged to the main product.
- According to the NRV method, the by-product is valued at its net realisable value and the joint costs are pro-rated between the main product and the by-product. Joint process cost allocated to by-product = (Sale price of by-products – Selling and distribution costs of by-products)
- A variation of this is to recognise some normal profit from the sale of by-products.
- Joint cost allocated to by-products = (Sale price of by-products – Normal profit – Selling and distribution costs of by-product)

LO 14.4

SOLVED PROBLEMS

P.14.1 The product of ABC Ltd passes through three distinct processes for completion. From past experience, it is ascertained that normal wastage in each process is as under: LO 14.2 LOD: E

Process	Wastage (%)	Sale value of wastage per unit
A	2	₹0.25
B	4	0.50
C	2.5	0.60

The expenses were as follows:

	Process A	Process B	Process C
Materials	₹12,000	₹10,000	₹9,000
Direct labour	16,000	5,000	4,900
Manufacturing expenses	2,000	3,400	3,590
Other factory expenses	3,500	2,005	2,004

4,000 units were initially introduced in process at a cost of ₹13,560. The output of each process was as under: A, 3,850 units; B, 3,600 units; and C, 3,500 units.

Prepare process accounts and also work out the sale price per unit of finished stock so as to realise 20 per cent profit on selling price.

Solution

Process A Account

Particulars	Units	Amount	Particulars	Units	Amount
To units introduced	4,000	₹13,560	By normal wastage	80	₹20
To materials		12,000	By abnormal wastage@ ₹12 per unit	70	840
To direct labour		16,000	By process B (output transferred @ ₹12 per unit, ₹47,040 ÷ 3,920, normal output)	3,850	46,200
To manufacturing expenses		2,000			
To other factory expenses		3,500			
	4,000	47,060		4,000	47,060

Process B Account

Particulars	Units	Amount	Particulars	Units	Amount
To process A (transferred from)	3,850	₹46,200	By normal wastage	154	₹77
To materials		10,000	By abnormal loss @ ₹18 per unit	96	1,728
To direct labour		5,000	By process C (output transferred @ ₹18 per unit, ₹66,528÷ 3,696, normal output)	3,600	64,800
To manufacturing expenses		3,400			
To other factory expenses		2,005			
	3,850	66,605		3,850	66,605

Process C Account

Particulars	Units	Amount	Particulars	Units	Amount
To process B (transferred from)	3,600	₹64,800	By normal wastage	90	₹54
To materials		9,000	By abnormal loss @ ₹24 per unit	10	240
To direct labour		4,900	By finished stock (output transferred @ ₹24 per unit, ₹84,240 ÷ 3,510 units)	3,500	84,000
To manufacturing expenses		3,590			
To other factory expenses		2,004			
	3,600	84,294		3,600	84,294

Selling price per unit = ₹30 (₹24 + ₹6, profit)

P.14.2 A product passes through two consecutive processes having relative standard output of 80 per cent and 90 per cent of inputs. In addition, standard yield is obtained by giving scrap allowances of 10 per cent and 5 per cent of outputs of process I and II respectively. Scraps of each process are sold at ₹1,000 per tonne. LO 14.2 LOD: M

There was no work-in-process at any stage, all materials were issued in process I as follows and all scraps arising from the processes were sold, except closing stock of 10 tonnes (opening stock was nil).

Material issued: 'A'; 100 tonnes @ ₹2,000 per tonne; 'B'; 400 tonnes @ ₹1,500 per tonne; and 'C'; 500 tonnes @ ₹1,200 per tonne.

The actual outputs and scraps were 85-per cent and 8 per cent in process I and 80 per cent and 10 per cent in process II. Assume that there was no price variance.

You are required to find out the standard cost and actual cost per tonne of a product.

Solution

(a) *Value of Materials Used*

Type of materials	*Quantity (tonnes)*	*Rate*	*Amount*
A	100	₹2,000	₹2,00,000
B	400	1,500	6,00,000
C	500	1,200	6,00,000
	1,000		14,00,000

(b) *Statement of Production–Standard and Actual*

Particulars	*Standard*		*Actual*	
	Percentage	*Quantity (tonnes)*	*Percentage*	*Quantity (tonnes)*
(i) Process I				
Input in process I	100	1,000	100	1,000
Output of process I	80	800	85	850
Less scrap	10	80	8	68
Finished output of process transferred to process II		720		782
(ii) Process II				
Inputs to process II	100	720	100	782
Output of process II	90	648	80	625.60
Less scrap	5	32.40	10	62.56
Finished output (yield) of process II		615.60		563.04

(c) *Cost of Finished Product per Tonne*

	Standard	Actual
Value of materials used	₹14,00,000	₹14,00,000
Less scrap sale value		
Standard: (102.4 tonnes @ ₹1,000)		
Less closing stock of 10 tonnes @ ₹1,000	10,000	
102.4 tonnes sold @ ₹1,000 per tonne	1,02,400**	
Actual: (120.56 tonnes@ ₹1,000)		
Less closing stock of 10 tonnes @ ₹1,000		10,000
120.56 tonnes sold @ 1,000 per tonne		1,20,560***
Net cost	12,87,600	12,69,440
Finished output in tonnes	615.60	563.04
Cost of finished output per tonne	2,092	2,255

** (Process I 80 tonnes + Process II 32.4 tonnes-closing stock 10 tonnes) = 1,02,400

*** (Process I 68 tonnes + Process II 62.56 tonnes-closing stock 10 tonnes) = 1,20,560

P.14.3 A product passes through two processes. The output of Process 1 becomes the input of Process II and the output of Process II is transferred to warehouse. The quantity of raw materials introduced into Process I is 20,000 kgs at ₹10 per kg. The cost and output data for the month under review are as under: LO 14.2 LOD:M

Particulars	*Process I*	*Process II*
Direct materials	₹60,000	₹40,000
Direct labour	40,000	30,000
Production overheads	39,000	40,250
Normal loss	8%	5%
Output	18,000	17,400
Loss realisation of ₹/Units	2.00	3.00

The company's policy is to fix the selling price of the end product in such a way as to yield a profit of 20 per cent on selling price.

REQUIRED:

(i) Prepare the process accounts **(ii)** Determine the selling price per unit of the end product.

Solution

(i)

Process I Account

Particulars	*Kgs*	*Amount*	*Particulars*	*Kgs*	*Amount*
To raw materials	20,000	₹2,00,000	By normal loss	1,600	₹3,200
To direct materials			By abnormal loss		
To direct labour		60,000	@ ₹18.25 per kg	400[1]	7,300[2]
To production		40,000	By process II		
overheads			(output transferred		
		39,000	@ ₹18.25 per kg)	18,000	3,28,500
	20,000	3,39,000		20,000	3,39,000

Process II Account

Particulars	*Kgs*	*Amount*	*Particulars*	*Kgs*	*Amount*
To process I account	18,000	₹3,28,500	By normal loss	900	₹2,700
To direct materials		40,000	By finished stock		
To direct labour		30,000	(output transferred		
To production			@ ₹25.50 per kg)		
overheads	40,250			17,400	4,43,700
To abnormal gain @					
₹25.50 per kg.	300	7,650[3]			
	18,300	4,46,400		18,300	4,46,400

WORKING NOTES

1. *Abnormal Loss in Process I Account*

Normal output expected (20,000 kgs. – 8% Normal loss)	18,400 kgs
Less actual output	18,000
Abnormal loss	400

2. *Value of Abnormal Loss in Process I*

Total cost of process I	₹3,39,000
Less sales value of normal loss (1,600 kgs × ₹2)	3,200
Normal cost of normal output (20,000 kgs – 1,600 kgs)	3,35,800
Normal cost per kg (₹3,35,800/18,400 kgs)	18.25
Value of abnormal loss (400 kgs × ₹18.25)	7,300

3. *Abnormal Gain in Process II Account*

Normal output expected (18,000 kgs – 5% normal loss)	17,100 kgs
Actual output	17,400
Abnormal gain	300

4. *Value of Abnormal Gain in Process II Account*

Normal cost of normal output (17,100 kgs) (i.e., ₹4,38,750 – ₹2,700)	₹4,36,050
Normal cost per kg (₹4,36,050/17,100 kgs)	25.50
Value of abnormal gain (300 kgs × ₹25.50)	7,650

(ii) *Determination of Selling Price per Kg*

Cost per kg	₹25.50
Add desired profit @ 20% of selling price [₹20 on selling price of ₹100 or 20 on cost of ₹80 cost i.e., 25% on cost price (₹25.50 × 0.25)]	6.375
Selling price per kg	31.875

P.14.4 S.M. Limited furnishes you the following information relating to process B for the month of October: **LO 14.2** **LOD: M**

1. Opening work-in-process, Nil
2. Units introduced, 10,000 units @ ₹3 per unit
3. *Expenses debited to the process*
   Direct materials, ₹14,650
   Labour, ₹21,148
   Overheads, ₹42,000
4. Normal loss in process, 1 per cent of input
5. Closing work-in-process, 350 units
   Degree of completion
   Material, 100 per cent
   Labour and overheads, 50 per cent
6. Finished output, 9,500 units
7. Degree of completion of abnormal loss:
   Material, 100 per cent
   Labour and overheads, 80 per cent
8. Units scrapped as normal loss were sold at ₹1 per unit.
9. All the units of abnormal loss were sold at ₹2.50 per unit.

Prepare: **(a)** Statement of equivalent production, **(b)** Statement of cost, **(c)** Process B account, and **(d)** Abnormal loss account.

Solution

(a) *Statement of Equivalent Production in Process B*

Input	*Particulars*	*Units completed or otherwise*	*Stage of completion (per cent)*		*Equivalent units*	
			Material	*Conversion cost*	*Material*	*Conversion cost*
10,000	Units introduced					
	Units produced	9,500	100	100	9,500	9,500
	Normal loss (10,000 × 0.01)	100	—	—	—	—
	Abnormal loss (150 units – 100 normal)	50	100	80	50	40
	Work-in-process	350	100	50	350	175
10,000		10,000			9,900	9,715

(b) *Statement of Cost*

Particulars	Total cost	Equivalent production in units	Cost per unit
Cost of units introduced	₹30,000		
Additional direct materials	14,650		
	44,650		
Less sale proceeds of normal loss units (100 units × ₹1)	100		
Total material cost	44,550	9,900	₹4.5
Conversion costs			
Direct labour	21,148		
Overheads	42,000		
Total conversion costs	63,148	9,715	6.5
Total cost	1,07,698		11.00
Value of work-in-process			
Material (350 units × ₹4.50)		₹1,575.00	
Conversion costs (175 units × ₹6.50)		1,137.50	
		2,712.50	
Value of abnormal loss			
Materials (50 units × ₹4.50)		225	
Conversion costs (40 units × ₹6.50)		260	
		485	

(c) *Process B Account*

Particulars	Units	Amount	Particulars	Units	Amount
To materials	10,000	₹30,000	By normal loss	100	₹100
To direct materials		14,650	By abnormal loss	50	485
To labour		21,148	By finished stock		
To overheads		42,000	@ ₹11 per unit	9,500	1,04,500
			By work-in-process inventory	350	2,713
	10,000	1,07,798		10,000	1,07,798

(d) *Abnormal Loss Account*

Particulars	Units	Amount	Particulars	Units	Amount
To process B	50	₹485	By sales	50	₹125
			By costing profit and loss A/c	—	360
	50	485		50	485

P.14.5 A company within the food industry mixes ingredients in two different processes to produce one product. The output of process I becomes the input of process II and the output of process II is transferred to the packing department. From the information given below, you are required to open accounts for process I, process II, abnormal loss and packing department and to record the transactions for the week ended May. **LO 14.2** **LOD: M**

Process I		
Input:		
	Material A	600 kgs at ₹5 per kg
	Material B	400 kgs at ₹10 per kg
	Mixing labour	43 hours at ₹20 per kg
	Normal loss	5 per cent of weight input, disposed of at ₹1.60 per kg
Output		920 kgs

Process II

Input:

Material C	660 kgs at ₹12.50 per kg
Material D	420 kgs at ₹7.50 per kg
Flavouring essence	₹330
Mixing labour	37 hours at ₹20 per hour
Normal waste	5 per cent of weight input with no disposal value
Output	1,800 kgs

No work-in-process at the beginning of the week but 100 kgs in process at the end of the week and estimated to be only 50 per cent complete so far as labour and overheads were concerned.

Overhead of ₹3,200 incurred by the two processes to be absorbed on the basis of mixing labour-hours.

Solution

Process I Account

Particulars	*Quantity*	*Amount*	*Particulars*	*Quantity*	*Amount*
To material A	600	₹3,000	By normal loss	50	₹80
To material B	400	4,000	By abnormal loss	30	300
To mixing labour (43 hours @ ₹20 per hour)		860	By transfer to process II @ ₹10 per kg	920	9,200
To overhead (@ ₹40 per hour)		1,720			
	1,000	9,580		1,000	9,580

Process II Account

To Process I	920	₹9,200	By normal waste	100	
To material C	660	8,250	By work-in-process	100	₹1,160
To material D	420	3,150	By packing department	1,800	21,960
To flavouring essence		300	(1,800 kgs × ₹12.20)		
To mixing labour		740			
To overhead		1,480			
	2,000	23,120		2,000	23,120

Abnormal Loss Account

To process A/c	30	₹300	By sale	30	₹48
			By balance to P/L A/c		252
	30	300		30	300

Packing Department Account

To Process II	1,800	₹21,960	By balance c/d		₹21,960
		21,960			21,960

WORKING NOTES

(i) *Statement of Equivalent Production (Process II)*

Input	*Particulars*	*Units completed or otherwise*	*Stage of completion*		*Equivalent units produced*	
			Material	*Conversion cost*	*Material*	*Conversion cost*
920 kgs (output from process I) + 1,080 kgs introduced during process II	Kgs output completed	1,800	100	100	1,800	1,800
	Normal loss (0.05 × 2,000 kgs)	100	—	—	—	—
	Work-in-process	100	100	50	100	50
2,000		2,000			1,900	1,850

(ii) *Statement of Cost*

Particulars	*Total cost*	*Equivalent production (kg)*	*Cost per unit/kg*
Materials transferred from Process I	₹9,200		
Add current process costs:			
Material C	8,250		
Material D	3,150		
Flavouring essence	300		
Total material cost	20,900	1,900	₹11
Conversion cost			
Mixing labour	740		
Overhead	1,480		
	2,220	1,850	1.2

(iii) *Statement of Apportionment of Cost*

Particulars	*Element of cost*	*Equivalent production*	*Cost per kg*	*Cost*	*Total*
Finished input	Material	1,800	₹11	₹19,800	
	Conversion costs	1,800	1.2	2,160	₹21,960
Work-in-process	Material	100	11.0	1,100	
	Conversion costs	50	1.2	60	1,160
					23,120

(iv) *Determination of overhead absorption rate* = ₹3,200 (Total labour-hours (43 + 37) = ₹40 per labour-hour

(v) *Cost per kg of output* = (₹9,580 — ₹80) ÷ 950 = ₹10

P.14.6 Product B passes through two processes before it is completed and transferred to finished stock. The following data are available for the month of March of the current year: **LO 14.2** **LOD: D**

Particulars	*Process I*	*Process II*
Opening stock (at prime cost)	₹5,000	₹8,000
Direct materials	40,000	12,000
Direct labour	35,000	40,000
Production overheads	20,000	24,000
Closing stock (at prime cost)	10,000	4,000

Output of processes are transferred to the next ones at the following transfer prices:

Process I–@ 25 per cent on the transfer price to Process I

Process II–@ 25 per cent on the transfer price to finished stock.

Finished stocks are valued at the price at which they are received from Process II, and are as follows: Opening stock, ₹20,000; Closing stock, ₹30,000. Sales for the month amounted to ₹3,00,000. Provision for internal process profits as on March 1 were as follows:

Included in work-in-process of Process II, ₹1,500; Included in finished stock, ₹6,500

Calculate: **(a)** Process costs, **(b)** Gross profit, and **(c)** Write up the provision for inter-process profit account.

Solution

(a) *Process I Account*

Particulars	*Total*	*Cost*	*Profit*	*Particulars*	*Total*	*Cost*	*Profit*
To opening stock	₹5,000	₹5,000	—	By Process III			
To direct materials	40,000	40,000	—	(output transferred			
To direct labour	35,000	35,000	—	at $133\frac{1}{3}$% of cost			

(*Contd.*)

(*Contd.*)

Less closing stock	(10,000)	(10,000)	—	(₹90,000 ×			
Prime cost	70,000	70,000	—	$133\frac{1}{3}$ %)	₹1,20,000	₹90,000	₹30,000
To factory overheads	20,000	20,000					
Process costs	90,000	90,000					
To profit and loss A/c (profit at 25% on transfer price or $33\frac{1}{3}$ % on cost)	30,000	—	30,000				
	1,20,000	90,000	30,000		1,20,000	90,000	30,000

Process II Account

To opening stock	₹8,000	₹6,500	₹1,500	By finished stock A/c (output transferred)	₹2,50,000	₹1,69,200	₹80,800
To Process I (transferred from)	1,20,000	90,000	30,000				
To direct materials	12,000	12,000	—				
To direct labour	40,000	40,000	—				
Less closing stock@	(4,000)	(3,300)	(700)				
Prime cost	1,76,000	1,45,200	30,800				
To factory overheads	24,000	24,000	—				
Process cost	2,00,000	1,69,200	30,800				
To profit and loss A/c (profit at 20% on transfer price or 25% on cost)	50,000	—	50,000				
	2,50,000	1,69,200	80,800		2,50,000	1,69,200	80,800

@Cost of closing stock is worked out proportionately: (₹1,48,500 × ₹4,000) ÷ ₹1,80,000 = ₹3,300
Profit = ₹4,000 — ₹3,300, cost = ₹700

Finished Stock Account

Particulars	*Total*	*Cost*	*Profit*	*Particulars*	*Total*	*Cost*	*Profit*
To balance b/d	₹20,000	₹13,500	₹6,500	By closing stock	₹30,000	₹20,300@	₹9,700
To Process I (transferred from)	2,50,000	1,69,200	80,800	By sales	3,00,000	1,62,400	1,37,600
To profit and loss A/c (profit transferred)	60,000	—	60,000				
	3,30,000	1,82,700	1,47,300		3,30,000	1,82,700	1,47,300

@Cost of closing stock = (₹1,82,700 × ₹30,000) ÷ ₹2,70,000 = ₹20,300

(b) *and* **(c)** *Statement of profit*

Process I		₹30,000
Process II	₹50,000	
Adjustment of provision for unrealised profit		
Add on opening stock	1,500	
Less on closing stock	(700)	50,800
Finished stock account	60,000	
Adjustment of provision for unrealised profit		
Add on opening stock	6,500	
Less on closing stock	(9,700)	56,800
		1,37,600

P.14.7 The Food Specialists Ltd has two cost centres: **(i)** Cooking and **(ii)** Mix-pack. Material is added at the beginning of production in each cost centre, and labour is added equally during production in each cost centre. The FIFO method is used in the Cooking department and the weighted average method in the Mix-pack department. LO 14.2 LOD: D

The following information is available for the month of January:

Particulars	*Cooking*	*Mix-Pack*
Work-in-process opening, January 1		
Materials	₹4,980	₹570
Labour	500	300
Overhead	400	240
Prior department cost	—	2,130
Current month's cost		
Materials	1,98,000	76,380
Labour	50,250	80,000
Overhead	40,200	64,000

Inventory and production records show that Cooking had 500 litres, 40 per cent processed in the beginning of the month and 400 litres, 50 per cent processed at the end of the month; Mix-pack had 300 litres, 50 per cent processed in the beginning of the month and 400 litres, 30 per cent processed at the end of the month.

Production reports for the month show that 'Cooking' started 20,000 litres into production and completed and transferred 20,100 litres to Mix-pack; Mix-pack completed and transferred 20,000 one-litre containers of the finished product to the warehouse.

You are required to prepare a process cost report for the Cooking department as well as for Mix-pack department. Also prepare relevant process accounts.

Solution

Production Cost Report of Cooking Centre for the month of January (FIFO basis)

1. *Units schedule*		
Opening inventory (40 per cent)		500
Add introduced during the month		20,000
Total		20,500
Less closing work-in-process inventory (50 per cent)		400
Units completed and transferred		20,100
2. *Cost to be accounted for*		
Opening inventory (₹4,980 + ₹500 + ₹400)		₹5,880
Materials		1,98,000
Conversion costs:		
Labour	₹50,250	
Overhead	40,200	90,450
		2,94,330

3. *Equivalent units and unit cost*	*Material*	*Conversion cost*
Opening inventory	Nil	300
Units introduced and completed (20,000 – 400)	19,600	19,600
Closing inventory	400	200
Equivalent units produced	20,000	20,100
Costs	₹1,98,000	₹90,450
Cost per unit	9.90	4.50

(Contd.)

(*Contd.*)

4. *Accounting for total costs transferred to Mix-pack*		
Opening inventory	₹5,880	
Costs to complete (300 × ₹4.50)	1,350	₹7,230
Started and completed 19,600 × (₹9.90 + ₹4.50)		2,82,240
Closing work-in-process inventory		
Materials (400 × ₹9.90)	3,960	
Conversion costs (200 × ₹4.50)	900	4,860
Total costs accounted for		2,94,330

Cooking Process Account

Particulars	*Unit (litres)*	*Amount*	*Particulars*	*Unit (litres)*	*Amount*
To opening inventory	500	₹5,880	By Mix-pack	20,100	₹2,89,470
To material	20,000	1,98,000	By closing work-in-process	400	4,860
To labour		50,250			
To overheads		40,200			
	20,500	2,94,330		20,500	2,94,330

Cost of Production Report of Mix-pack Department for the month of January (Weighted Average Cost basis)

1. *Units schedule*

Opening inventory (50 per cent)	300
Add units transferred from Cooking centre	20,100
Total	20,400
Less closing work-in-process inventory	400
Units completed and transferred	20,000

2. *Cost to be accounted for*

	Cooking centre	*Mix-pack Material*	*Mix-pack Conversion costs*	*Total costs*
Opening inventory	₹2,130	₹570	₹540	₹3,240
Current period costs	2,89,470	76,380	1,44,000	5,09,850
	2,91,600	76,950	1,44,540	5,13,090

3. *Equivalent units and unit cost*

	Cooking centre	*Mix-pack Material*	*Mix-pack Conversion costs*
Units completed	20,000	20,000	20,000
Plus closing work-in-process	400	400	120
	20,400	20,400	20,120
Cost per equivalent unit	₹14.2941	₹3.772	₹7.184

4. *Accounting for total costs*

Transferred to finished goods inventory [20,000 × ₹25.2501 (₹14.2941 + ₹3.772 + ₹7.184)]		₹5,05,002
Work-in-process (closing)		
Cooking centre (400 × ₹14.294)	₹5,717.60	
Material (400 × ₹3.772)	1,508.80	
Conversion costs (120 × ₹7.184)	862.08	8,088.48
Total costs accounted for		5,13,090.48

Mix-pack Process Account

Particulars	*Unit (litres)*	*Amount*	*Particulars*	*Unit (litres)*	*Amount*
To opening work-in -process inventory	300	₹3,240	By finished goods inventory account (transferred to)	20,000	₹5,05,002

(*Contd.*)

(Contd.)

To cooking process A/c (transferred from)	20,100	2,89,470	By work-in-process	400	8,088
To materials		76,380			
To labour		80,000			
To overheads		64,000			
	20,400	5,13,090		20,400	5,13,090

P.14.8 RST Ltd. manufactures plastic moulded chairs (for kids). Three models of moulded chairs, all variation of the same design are standard, deluxe and executive. The company uses an operation costing system. LO 14.2 LOD: D

RST Ltd. has extrusion, form, trim and finish operations. Plastic sheets are produced by the extrusion operation. During the forming operation, the plastic sheets are moulded into chair seats and the legs are added. The standard model is sold after this operation. During the trim operation, the arms are added to the deluxe and executive models and the chair edges are smoothed. Only the executive model enters the finish operation, in which padding is added. All of the units produced received the same steps within each operation. In April, units of production direct material cost incurred are as follows:

	Units produced	*Extrusion materials*	*Form materials*	*Trim materials*	*Finish materials*
Standard model	10,500	₹1,26,000	₹42,000	₹0	₹0
Deluxe model	5,250	63,000	21,000	15,750	0
Executive model	3,500	42,000	14,000	10,500	21,000
	19,250	2,31,000	77,000	26,250	21,000

The total conversion costs for the month of April, are:

	Extrusion operation	*Form operation*	*Trim operation*	*Finish operations*
Total conversion costs	₹6,06,375	₹2,97,000	₹1,55,250	₹94,500

REQUIRED:

(i) For each product produced by RST Ltd. during April, determine the unit cost and the total cost.

(ii) Now consider the following information for May. All unit costs in May are identical to the April unit costs calculated as above in (i). At the end of May, 1,500 units of the Deluxe model remain in work-in-progress. These units are 100 per cent complete as to materials and 65 per cent complete in the trim operation. Determine the cost of the Deluxe model work-in-process inventory at the end of May.

Solution

Statement showing Unit Cost and Total Cost of three models of Chairs

Particulars	*Standard model cost*	*Deluxe model cost*	*Executive model cost*
Extrusion material	₹12	₹12	₹12
Form material	4	4	4
Trim material	—	3	3
Finish material	—	—	6
Extrusion operation	31.50	31.50	31.50
Form operation	15.43	15.43	15.43
Trim operation	—	17.74	17.74
Finish operation	—	—	27.00
Total unit cost	62.93	83.67	116.67
Units produced	10,500	5,250	3,500
Total cost	6,60,765	4,39,267.5	4,08,345

WORKING NOTES

(i) *Statement of Material and Conversion Cost per Equivalent Unit:*

Particulars	*Extrusion*	*Form*	*Trim*	*Finish*
Equivalent units (1)	19,250*	19,250*	8,750**	3,500
Material cost (2)	₹2,31,000	₹77,000	₹26,250	₹21,000
Conversion cost (3)	6,06,375	2,97,000	1,55,250	94,500
Material cost per equivalent unit (2/1)	12	4	3	6
Conversion cost per equivalent unit (3/1)	31.50	15.43	17.74	27

*(10,500 + 5,250 + 3,500)
**(5,250 + 3,500)

(ii) *Statement showing Cost of 1,500 units of Deluxe Model of Chairs (Work-in-process inventory) at the end of May*

Particulars	*Equivalent (1)*	*Unit cost (2)*	*Total cost (3) = (1) × (2)*
Extrusion materials	1,500	₹12	₹18,000
Form materials	1,500	4	6,000
Trim materials	1,500	3	4,500
Extrusion operation	1,500	31.50	47,250
Form operation	1,500	15.43	23,145
Trim operation (1,500 x 65%)	975	17.74	17,296.50
Total cost			1,16,191.5

P.14.9 Following information is available regarding process A for the month of February, related to the current year. **LO 14.2** **LOD: M**

Production record:	
Units in process as on February 1	
(All materials used, 25 per cent complete for labour and overheads)	4,000
New units introduced	16,000
Units completed	14,000
Units in process as on February 28	
(All materials used, 33-1/3 per cent complete for labour and overheads)	6,000
Cost records:	
Work-in-process as on February 1	
Materials	₹6,000
Labour	1,000
Overheads	1,000
	8,000
Cost during the month	
Materials	25,600
Labour	15,000
Overheads	15,000
	55,600

Presuming that average method of inventory is used, prepare:

(i) Statement of equivalent production.
(ii) Statement showing cost for each element
(iii) Statement of apportionment of cost.
(iv) Process cost account for process A.

Solution

(i) *Statement of Equivalent Production (Average Cost Method)*

Flow of completed or partially completed units:	
Opening (at the beginning of month)	4,000
Introduced during the month	16,000
Total in process	20,000
Less units completed	14,000
Units in process	6,000

Particulars	*Number of units completed or otherwise*	*Stage of completion (per cent)*			*Equivalent units*		
		Materials	*Labour*	*Overheads*	*Materials*	*Labour*	*Overheads*
Units completed	14,000	100	100	100	14,000	14,000	14,000
Units in process	6,000	100	$33\frac{1}{3}$	$33\frac{1}{3}$	6,000	2,000	2,000
					20,000	16,000	16,000

(ii) *Statement showing Cost for each Element*

Particulars	*Materials*	*Labour*	*Overheads*	*Total*
Opening work-in-process	₹6,000	₹1,000	₹1,000	₹8,000
Cost incurred during February	25,600	15,000	15,000	55,600
Total cost	31,600	16,000	16,000	63,600
Equivalent units	20,000	16,000	16,000	—
Cost per equivalent unit	₹1.58	₹1	₹1	₹3.58

(iii) *Statement of Apportionment of Cost*

Particulars	*Element of cost*	*Equivalent production (in units)*	*Cost per unit*	*Total cost*	
Finished production	Materials	14,000	₹1.58	₹22,120	
	Labour	14,000	1.00	14,000	
	Overheads	14,000	1.00	14,000	₹50,120
Work-in-process	Materials	6,000	1.58	₹9,480	
	Labour	2,000	1.00	2,000	
	Overheads	2,000	1.00	2,000	13,480
					63,600

(iv) *Process A Account*

Particulars	*Units*	*Amount*	*Particulars*	*Units*	*Amount*
To Opening Work-in-process	4,000	₹8,000	By Completed units	14,000	₹50,120
To Materials	16,000	25,600	By Closing work-in-process	6,000	13,480
To Labour		15,000			
To Overheads		15,000			
	20,000	63,600		20,000	63,600

P.14.10 The following information is given in respect of Process 3 for the month of January, current year. LO 14.2 LOD: M

Opening stock – 2,000 units made-up of:	
Direct materials-I	₹12,350
Direct materials-II	13,200
Direct labour	17,500
Overheads	11,000

(Contd.)

(*Contd.*)

Transferred from Process 2: 20,000 units @ ₹6 per unit.	
Transferred to Process 4: 17,000 units	
Expenditure incurred in Process 3:	
Direct materials	30,000
Direct labour	60,000
Overheads	60,000
Scrap: 1,000 units – Direct materials, 100 per cent; Direct labour, 60 per cent; Overheads, 40 per cent	
Normal loss: 10 per cent of production.	
Scrapped units realised: ₹4 per unit	
Closing Stock: 4,000 units – Degree of completion: Direct materials, 80 per cent, Direct labour, 60 per cent and Overheads, 40 per cent	

Prepare Process 3 Account using average price method, alongwith necessary supporting statements.

Solution

Statement of Equivalent Production (Average Cost Method)

Particulars	Total units to be accounted for	Stage of completion(%)				Equivalent units			
		Materials I	Materials II	Labour	Over -heads	Materials I	Materials II	Labour	Over -heads
Units completed	17,000	100	100	100	100	17,000	17,000	17,000	17,000
Normal loss (10%) (2,000 units + 20,000 units – 4,000 units)	1,800	—	—	—	—	—	—	—	—
Closing stock (work-in-process)	4,000	100	80	60	40	4,000	3,200	2,400	1,600
Abnormal gain (balancing figure)	(800)*	100	100	100	100	(800)	(800)	(800)	(800)
Total	22,000	—	—	—	—	20,200	19,400	18,600	17,800

* 22,800 — 22,000 (total units to be accounted for i.e., 2,000 opening stock units + 20,000 transferred from Process No. 2).

It may be noted that units completed include units due to abnormal gain also.

Statement of Cost

Particulars	Total cost	Equivalent units	Equivalent per unit cost
Direct materials-I:			
Opening stock	₹12,350		
Add cost of 20,000 units transferred form process 2@ ₹6 per unit	1,20,000		
	1,32,350		
Less scrap value of normal loss units (1,800 x ₹4)	7,200		
	1,25,150	20,200	₹6.2
Direct materials-II:			
Opening stock	₹13,200		
Introduced in process 3	30,000		
	43,200	19,400	2.2268
Direct labour:			
Included in opening stock	17,500		
Costs incurred as per process 3	60,000		
	77,500	18,600	4.1667
Overheads:			
Included in opening stock	11,000		
Costs incurred as per process 3	60,000		
	71,000	17,800	3.9888
Total cost per unit			16.5778

Statement showing Apportionment of Costs

Cost of completed units	(17,000 units × ₹16.5778)		₹2,81,822.60
Valuation of abnormal gain	(800 units × ₹16.5778)		13,262.24
Valuation of closing stock (Work-in-process):			
Direct materials I	(4000 Units × ₹6.1955)	₹24,782	
Direct Materials II	(3,200 Units × 2.2268)	7,125.76	
Direct Labour	(2,400 Units × 4.1667)	10,000.08	
Overheads	(1,600 Units × 3.9888)	6,382.08	48,289.92

Process 3 Account

Particulars	Units	Amount	Particulars	Units	Amount
To opening work-in-process	2,000	₹54,050	By Normal loss	1,800	₹7,200
To Process 2	20,000	1,20,000	By Finished goods	17,000	2,81,822
To Direct materials II		30,000	By Closing work-in-process	4,000	48,290
To Direct labour		60,000			
To Overheads		60,000			
To Abnormal gain	800	13,262			
	22,800	3,37,312		22,800	3,37,312

P.14.11 A factory producing P also produces a by-product Q which is further processed into a finished product. The joint cost of manufacture is given below: Material, ₹5,000; Labour, ₹3,000; and Overheads, ₹2,000. LO 14.3 LOD: M

Subsequent costs are as under:

	P	Q
Material	₹3,000	₹1,500
Labour	1,400	1,000
Overheads	600	500
	5,000	3,000

Selling prices are: P, ₹16,000; Q, ₹8,000.

Estimated profits on selling prices are 25 per cent for P and 20 per cent for Q.

Assume that selling and distribution expenses are in proportion of sales price.

Show how you would apportion joint costs of manufacture, and prepare a statement showing cost of production of P and Q.

Solution

Apportionment of Joint Costs

Particulars	P	Q
Selling price	₹16,000	₹8,000
Less profits @ 25 per cent (P) and 20 per cent (Q) on selling price	4,000	1,600
Less selling and distribution expenses (2:1)	267	133
Cost of production	11,733	6,267
Less separable costs subsequent to split-off point	5,000	3,000
Share of joint costs (6,733: 3,267 for P and Q)	6,733	3,267

Statement showing Cost of Production of P and Q

Elements	Joint costs		Separable costs		Total cost	
of cost	P	Q	P	Q	P	Q
Materials	₹3,367	₹1,633	₹3,000	₹1,500	₹6,367	₹3,133
Labour	2,020	980	1,400	1,000	3,420	1,980
Overheads	1,346	654	600	500	1,946	1,154
	6,733	3,267	5,000	3,000	11,733	6,267

WORKING NOTES

Determination of Selling and Distribution Expenses

Sales revenue (P and Q)		₹24,000
Less profit (P and Q)		5,600
Cost of sales		18,400
Less cost of production		
Joint costs	₹10,000	
Separable costs [₹5,000 (P) + ₹3,000 (Q)]	8,000	18,000
Selling and distribution expenses		400

P.14.12 X Ltd manufactures product A which yields two by-products, B and C. In a period the amount spent upto the point of separation was ₹20,600. Subsequent expenses were: LO 14.4 LOD: E

	A	B	C
Materials	₹300	₹200	₹250
Direct wages	400	300	200
Overhead	300	270	180
	1,000	770	630

Gross sales value of products A, B and C was ₹15,000, ₹10,000, and ₹5,000 respectively. It was estimated that the net profit as a percentage of sales in case of products B and C would be 25 per cent and 20 per cent respectively. Ascertain the profit earned on A.

Solution

Statement showing the Allocation of Joint Costs between Products B and C (NRV less Normal Profit Method)

Products	*Sales value*	*Profit*	*Separable costs*	*NRV/Joint costs*
B	₹10,000	₹2,500	₹770	₹6,730
C	5,000	1,000	630	3,370

Joint cost to be allocated to A would be: ₹20,600 — (₹6,730 + ₹3,370) = ₹10,500

Statement showing Profit Earned by Product A

Sales revenue			₹15,000
Less cost of production			
Joint cost		₹10,500	
Separable costs:			
Material	₹300		
Direct wages	400		
Overheads	300	1,000	11,500
Profit			3,500

P.14.13 From the following information, find the profit made by each product apportioning joint costs on sales-value basis: LO 14.3 LOD: E

Joint costs		
Direct material		₹1,26,000
Power		25,000
Petrol, oil, lubricants		5,000
Labour		7,500
Other charges		4,100
		1,67,600
	Product X	*Product Y*
Selling costs	₹20,000	₹80,000
Sales	1,52,000	1,68,000

Solution

Statement showing Profit after Apportionment of Joint Costs

Particulars	Product X	Product Y	Total
Sales	₹1,52,000	₹1,68,000	₹3,20,000
Less cost of production			
(In the ratio of sales: 19:21)			
Direct material	59,850	66,150	1,26,000
Power	11,875	13,125	25,000
Petrol, oil, lubricants	2,375	2,625	5,000
Labour	3,562.50	3,937.50	7,500
Other charges	1,947.50	2,152.50	4,100
Gross profit	72,390	80,010	1,52,400
Less selling costs	20,000	80,000	1,00,000
Profit	52,390	10	52,400

P.14.14 XYZ Chemicals Manufacturing Company Ltd buys a particular raw material at ₹4 per litre. At the end of the processing in department 1, this raw material splits-off into products, X, Y and Z. Product X is sold at the split-off point, with no further processing. Products Y and Z require further processing before they can be sold. Product Y is processed in department 2, and product Z is processed in department 3. Following is a summary of costs and other related data for the end of the current year. LO 14.5 LOD: M

	Department		
	1	2	3
Cost of raw material	₹2,40,000	—	—
Direct labour	35,000	₹2,25,000	₹3,25,000
Manufacturing overhead	24,000	1,05,000	2,25,000
	Products		
	X	Y	Z
Litres sold	10,000	15,000	22,500
Closing inventory	5,000	—	7,500
Sales	₹1,50,000	₹4,80,000	₹7,50,000
Sale price per litre	15	32	25

There were no opening and closing inventories of basic raw materials at the beginning as well as at the end of the year. All finished goods inventory of litres was complete as to processing. The company uses the relative sales value method of allocating joint costs.

You are required to prepare: **(i)** Schedule showing the allocation of joint cost; **(ii)** Cost of sales of each product, the cost of each ending inventory; and **(iii)** A comparative statement of profit.

Solution

(i) *Schedule showing Allocation of Joint Cost*

Product	Output (litres)	Market price	Total market price	Separable costs	Net realisable value	Joint cost	Total cost	Cost per unit
X	15,000	₹15	₹2,25,000	—	₹2,25,000	₹1,17,000	₹1,17,000	₹7.8
Y	15,000	32	4,80,000	₹3,30,000	1,50,000	78,000	4,08,000	27.2
Z	30,000	25	7,50,000	5,50,000	2,00,000	1,04,000	6,54,000	21.8
				8,80,000		2,99,000	11,79,000	

Joint cost = [₹2,40,000 + ₹35,000 + ₹24,000] = ₹2,99,000 of Department 1 allocated in the ratio of 9:6:8 among products X, Y, and Z respectively.

(ii) *Schedule showing Cost of Sales and Ending Inventory of each Product*

Product	Cost per unit	Units sold (litres)	Cost of sales	Inventory units (litres)	Inventory cost
X	₹7.8	₹10,000	₹78,000	5,000	₹39,000
Y	27.2	15,000	4,08,000	—	—
Z	21.8	22,500	4,90,500	7,500	1,63,500

(iii) *Comparative Statement of Profit*

Particulars	Product X	Product Y	Product Z
(a) Sales revenue	₹1,50,000	₹4,80,000	₹5,62,500
Less cost of sales			
Production cost			
(i) Joint cost	1,17,000	78,000	1,04,000
(ii) Separable cost	—	3,30,000	5,50,000
Total cost	1,17,000	4,08,000	6,54,000
Less closing inventory	39,000	—	1,63,500
(b) Cost of goods sold	78,000	4,08,000	4,90,500
(c) Gross profit [(a) – (b)]	72,000	72,000	72,000

P.14.15 The ABC Ltd makes three products from one common input. Process I is the joint process and every 100 kgs of input yields: 60 kgs of product A; 30 kgs of product B; and 5 kgs of product C and the remaining 5 kgs is a waste product with no market value. LO 14.5 LOD: M

Product A requires further processing in process II at an average cost of ₹10 per kg. It is then sold at ₹100 per kg. Product B is sold at split-off point at ₹50 per kg. Product C after further processing in process III (at ₹2.5 per kg), is sold at ₹5 per kg. The selling expenses associated with C are negligible, and the company desires the cost of product C to be such as to earn a profit of 10 per cent on sales.

During the current period, 1,00,000 kgs of input was processed through process I (assume no inventories), and the total operating costs in Process I were ₹51,85,000.

You are required: **(i)** To determine the amount of Process I cost assigned to by-product C; **(ii)** To determine the amount of joint costs to be assigned to A and B using the relative sales value approach; **(iii)** To determine the amount of joint costs to be assigned to A and B, using the net realisable value less normal profit approach.

Solution

(i) *Determination of Cost of By-product C*

Sales revenue (₹5 × 5,000 kgs, that is, 1,00,000 kgs × 0.5)	₹25,000
Less separable costs in Process III (₹2.5 × 5,000 kgs)	12,500
Less profit [10 per cent of selling price (0.10 × ₹25,000)]	2,500
Cost of Process I (joint costs) assigned to product C	10,000

(ii) *Statement showing Allocation of Joint Cost between Products A and B (Relative Sales Value Approach)*

Product	Output (kgs)	Sales price	Total market value	Separable costs	NRV	Joint cost
A	60,000	₹100	₹60,00,000	₹6,00,000	₹54,00,000	₹40,50,000
B	30,000	50	15,00,000	—	15,00,000	11,25,000
			75,00,000		69,00,000	51,75,000

(iii) *Statement showing the Allocation of Joint Cost between Products A and B (NRV Less Normal Profit Approach)*

Product	*Market value*	*Normal profit*	*Separable cost*	*NRV*	*Joint cost*
A	₹60,00,000	₹13,80,000	₹6,00,000	₹40,20,000	₹40,20,000
B	15,00,000	3,45,000	—	11,55,000	11,55,000

Normal profit ratio = 100 per cent — (₹51,75,000+₹6,00,000) ÷ ₹75,00,000 = 100 —77 = 23 per cent

P.14.16 The XYZ Chemical Company Ltd produces chemicals X and Y from material Z. 10 litres of raw material Z yield 8 litres of X and 2 litres of Y as a result of processing it in department I. Product X requires furhter processing in department II and then is sold at ₹150 per litre. Product Y is sold at the split-off point for ₹112.50 per litre. The following additional data are available for the current period.

LO 14.5 **LOD: E**

Department I	
Inventory (in litres)	100
Percentage completion of conversion costs	50
Cost of material Z added in current period (1,100 litres)	₹22,000
Conversion costs in current period	31,500
Department II	
Inventory (in litres)	200
Percentage completion of conversion costs	25
Conversion costs in current period	₹52,000
Finished goods inventories	
Product X	100
Product Y	50

Prepare a statement apportioning the joint costs of Department I between Products X and Y using the net realisable value less normal profit method.

Solution

Department I

Total cost (₹22,000 + ₹31,500)		₹53,500
Less cost of closing inventory (work-in-process):		
Material cost (100 litres × ₹20)	₹2,000	
Conversion cost [100 × 0.50 × ₹31.500 ÷ 1,050)]	1,500	3,500
Cost to be allocated between products X and Y		50,000

WORKING NOTES

(i) 1,050 are equivalent units: (1,000, completed units + 100 units, work in process × 0.50 complete).

(ii) Litres produced, 1,000
Product X (0.80 × 1,000) = 800 litres
Product Y (0.20 × 1,000) = 200 litres

Department II (Product X)

Equivalent units started and finished (800 litres from Department I - 200 litres, closing inventory)	600
Add closing equivalent units inventory (200 × 0.25)	50
Equivalent units produced	650
Conversion costs	₹52,000
Cost per equivalent unit (₹52,000 ÷ 650)	80

Statement Apportioning Joint Cost of Department I between Products X and Y (NRV Less Normal Profit Method)

Product	Output (litres)	Selling price	Total market value	Normal profit	Separable costs	Joint costs
X	800	₹150	₹1,20,000	₹24,000	₹64,000	₹32,000
Y	200	112.50	22,500	4,500	—	18,000

Normal profit rate = 100 – [₹50,000 + (₹80 × 800)] ÷ ₹1,42,500 = 100 – 80 = 20 per cent
Separable costs for completed 800 units @ ₹80 per equivalent unit = (₹80 × 800) = ₹64,000.

P.14.17 X Ltd is in the food processing industry. In one of its processes, three joint products are manufactured. Traditionally, the company apportions costs incurred upto the joint products' pre-separation point on the basis of weight of output of the product. LO 14.3 LOD: M

You are required to prepare statements for the management to express:

(a) The profit or loss of each product as ascertained, using weight basis of apportioning pre-separation joint cost.

(b) The optimal contribution which could be obtained from the manufacture of these products.

The following process data for December are given. Costs incurred upto separation point are ₹96,000.

	Product A	Product B	Product C
Cost incurred after separation point	₹20,000	₹12,000	₹8,000
Selling price per tonne:			
Completed product	500	800	600
Estimated, if sold at separation point	250	700	450
Output (tonnes)	100	60	80

The cost of any unused capacity after the separation point should be ignored.

Solution

Comparative Profit and Loss Account for Products, A, B and C

Particulars	Products A	B	C	Total
Sales revenue	₹50,000	₹48,000	₹48,000	₹1,46,000
Less cost of production:				
Joint costs (allocated in of proportion output 10:6:8)	40,000	24,000	32,000	96,000
Separable costs	20,000	12,000	8,000	40,000
Profit/(loss)	(10,000)	12,000	8,000	10,000

(b) In order to ascertain whether the firm is following a sound policy regarding processing all products beyond the split-off point, we should adopt the incremental analysis which compares incremental revenue from further processing with incremental costs (separable costs) incurred by the firm.

Particulars	Product A	Product B	Product C
(i) Number of units (tonnes)	100	60	80
(ii) Incremental revenue from further processing per unit	₹250	₹100	₹150
(iii) Total incremental revenue (i) × (ii)	25,000	6,000	12,000
(iv) Incremental cost from further processing	20,000	12,000	8,000
(v) Incremental profit/loss [(iii) – (iv)]	5,000	(6,000)	4,000

The incremental analysis suggests that products A and C should be processed further beyond the split-off point as they yield positive contributions. Product B should be sold at split-off point because further processing cost is more than the incremental revenue it fetches. Accordingly, contributions would be maximum and optimal when products A and C are processed further and product B is sold at the split-off point. This is shown in the following statement:

Statement Showing Optimal Contribution

Particulars	Product A	Product B	Product C	Total
Sales revenue	₹50,000	₹42,000	₹48,000	₹1,40,000
Less variable costs for further processing	20,000	—	8,000	28,000
Contribution	30,000	42,000	40,000	1,12,000
Less joint costs		Not required		96,000
Profit				16,000

P.14.18 Two products P and Q are obtained in a crude form and require processing at a cost of ₹5 for P and ₹4 for Q per unit before sale. Assuming a net margin of 25 per cent on cost, their sale prices are fixed at ₹13.75 and ₹8.75 per unit respectively. During the period, the joint cost was ₹88,000 and the outputs were: P, 8,000 units; Q, 6,000 units. Ascertain the joint cost per unit

LO 14.3
LOD: M

Solution

Statement for Ascertaining Joint Cost per Unit

Product	P	Q
Output (units)	8,000	6,000
Selling price per unit	₹13.75	8.75
Less, profit margin @ 25 per cent on cost or 20 per cent on sales	(2.75)	(1.75)
	11	7
Less post split off cost	(5)	(4)
Pre-split off net joint cost per unit	6	3
Share in joint cost of units of P and Q can be obtained by apportioning in ratio of 8:3[1]	64,000	24,000
Joint cost per unit	8@	4@@

@(₹64,000/8000 units) @@(₹24,000/6,000 units)

WORKING NOTES

1. *Calculation of Ratio of Apportionment of Joint Cost*

Products	P	Q
Units	8,000	6,000
Pre-split off net joint cost per unit	₹6	₹3
Total output cost	48,000	18,000
Ratio	8 :	3

P.14.19 A company purchases raw materials worth ₹11.04 lakh and processes them into four products P, Q, R and S, which have a unit sale price of ₹3, ₹9, ₹16, and ₹60, respectively at split-off point, as they could be sold as such to other processors. However, during year, the company decided to further process and sell products P, Q and S, while product R would be sold at split-off point to other processes. The processing of raw materials into the four products cost ₹28 lakh to the company. The other data for the year were as under (amount in ₹lakh):

LO 14.3
LOD: M

Product	Output (units)	Sales	Additional processing (variable) cost after split-off
P	10,00,000	46.00	12.00
Q	20,000	4.00	2.40
R	10,000	1.60	
S	18,000	12.00	0.40

You are required to work out the company's annual income If the joint costs are allocated amongst the four products on the basis of 'net realisable value' at split-off point, what would be the compan's annual income?

Solution

Statement showing Annual Income for four Products (₹in lakh):

Products	Sales	Joint cost (working note 1)	Additional processing cost after split-off	Total cost (3+4)	Net income (2–5)
(1)	(2)	(3)	(4)	(5)	(6)
P	46.00	27.20	12.00	39.20	6.80
Q	4.00	1.28	2.40	3.68	0.32
R	1.60	1.28	—	1.28	0.32
S	12.00	9.28	0.40	9.68	2.32
Total	63.60	39.04	14.80	53.84	9.76

WORKING NOTES

1. Statement showing Allocation of Joint Cost amongst the Products P, Q, R and S (under Net Realisable Values at Split-off Point Method) (₹in lakh)

Products	Sales value	Less additional processing cost	Net realisation value beyond split-off point	Computation	Joint costs
(1)	(2)	(3)	(4)	(5)	(6)
P	46.00	12.00	34.00	$\frac{39.04 \times 34.00}{48.80}$	27.20
Q	4.00	2.40	1.60	$\frac{39.04 \times 1.60}{48.80}$	1.28
R	1.60	—	1.60	$\frac{39.04 \times 1.60}{48.80}$	1.28
S	12.00	0.40	11.60	$\frac{39.04 \times 11.60}{48.80}$	9.28
Total:	63.60	14.80	48.80		39.04

P.14.20 JKL Ltd produces two products — J and K together with a by-product L from a single main process (process I). Product J is sold at the point of separation for ₹55 per kg, whereas product K is sold for ₹77 per kg after further processing into product k2. By-product L is sold without further processing for ₹19.25 per kg. **LO 14.3,5** **LOD: D**

Process I is closely monitored by a team of chemists, who planned the output per 1,000 kg of input materials to be as follows:

Product J	500 kgs
Product K	350 kgs
Product L	100 kgs
Toxic waste	50 kgs

The toxic waste is disposed at a cost of ₹16.50 per kg, and arises at the end of processing. Process II which is used for further processing of product K into product K2, has the following cost structure:

Fixed costs	₹2,64,000 per week
Variable cost	16.50 per kg processed

The following actual data relate to the first week of the month:

Process I	
Opening work-in-progress	Nil
Material input	40,000 kgs costing ₹6,60,000
Direct labour	4,40,00
Variable overheads	1,76,000
Fixed overheads	2,64,000
Outputs:	
Product J	19,200 kgs
Product K	14,400 kgs
Product L	4,000 kgs
Toxic waste	2,400 kgs
Closing work-in-progress	Nil
Process II	
Opening work-in-progress	Nil
Input of product K	14,400 kgs
Output of product K2	13,200 kgs
Closing work-in-progress (50% converted and conversion costs were incurred in accordance with the planned cost structure)	1,200 kgs

REQUIRED:

(i) Prepare process I account for the first week of the month using the final sales value method of attribute the pre-separation costs to join products. **(ii)** Prepare the toxic waste account and process I account for the first week of the month. **(iii)** Comment on the method used by the JKL limited to attribute the pre-separation costs to joint products. **(iv)** Advise the management of JKL limited whether or not, on purely financial grounds, it should continue to process product K into product K2:

(a) If product k could be sold at the point of separation for ₹47.30 per kg; and

(b) If the 60 per cent of the weekly fixed costs of process II were avoided by not processing product K further.

Solution

(i) *Process I Account*

Particular	*Units in Kg*	*Rate per kg*	*Amount*	*Particulars*	*Units in kg*	*Rate per kg*	*Amount*
To material				By sales	4,000	₹19.25	₹77,000
To direct labour	40,000	₹16.50	₹6,60,000	(product L)			
To variable				By normal loss	2,000	(16.50)	(33,000)*
overheads			4,40,000	By abnormal loss	400	44	17,600
To fixed				By product J	19,200		7,21,171
overheads			1,76,000	By product K	14,400		7,57,229
			2,64,000				
	40,000		15,40,000		40,000		15,40,000

*Disposal costs and, therefore, deducted.

WORKING NOTES

1. *Valuation of Abnormal Loss per kg:*
   = (₹15,40,000 – ₹77,000 + ₹33,000)/(40,000 kgs × 0.85 excluding product L and waste)
   = ₹14,96,000/34,000 kgs = ₹44 per kg

2. *Calculation of Joint Cost of the Output (J and K):*
= ₹15,40,000 + Disposal cost, [₹33,000 – ₹77,000 – ₹17,600] = ₹14,78,400

3. *Allocation of Joint Cost between Joint Products J and K (using Final Sales Value Method)*

Products	*Quantity (kgs)*	*Sales value*	*Joint cost*
J	19,200	₹10,56,000 (19,200 kgs × ₹55)	₹7,21,171
K	14,400	11,08,800 (14,400 kgs × ₹77)	7,57,229
		21,64,800	14,78,400

(ii) *Toxic Waste Account*

Particulars	*Units in kg*	*Rate per kg*	*Amount*	*Particulars*	*Units in kg*	*Rate per kg*	*Amount*
To process I A/c	2,000	16.50	(₹33,000)	By balance c/d		16.50	(₹33,000)

Process II Account

Particulars	*Units in kg*	*Rate per kg*	*Amount*	*Particulars*	*Units in kg*	*Rate per kg*	*Amount*
To process I A/c (product K)	14,400	₹52.585	₹7,57,229	By product K2	13,200	—	₹11,73,917
To variable overheads			2,37,600	By closing work-in-process	1,200	—	84,912
To fixed overheads		16.50	2,64,000				
			12,58,829				12,58,829

WORKING NOTES

1. *Valuation of 1,200 kgs of Closing Work-in-process*

Material 100% complete (1,200 kgs × ₹52.585)	₹63,103
Fixed and variable overheads [(₹2,37,600 + ₹2,64,000)/(13,800 units [14,200 – 600])] × 600 units	21,809
	84,912

(iii) *Comment on the Method used by JKL Ltd:*

JKL Ltd has used the commonly used method of final sales value for allocating joint costs between products J and K. Other methods used are: (a) Physical measure method, (b) Constant gross margin percentage method and (c) Net realisable value method.

(iv) *Whether Further Processing of Product K to K_2 should be undertaken or not:*

Incremental sales revenue per kg from further processing (₹77 – ₹47.30)	₹29.70
Less incremental variable cost per kg of further processing	16.50
Incremental contribution per kg from further processing	13.20
Total incremental contribution (14,400 kgs × ₹13.20)	1,90,080
Less avoidable fixed cost (60% × ₹2,64,000)	1,58,400
Incremental profit	31,680.00

Break-even point = Avoidable fixed costs/Incremental contribution per kg = ₹1,58,400/13.20 = 12,000 kgs
The company should opt for further processing in case the output is expected to exceed 12,000 kgs per week.

P.14.21 Pokemon Chocolates manufactures and distributes chocolate products. It purchases Cocoa beans and processes them into two intermediate products: **LO 14.3,5** **LOD: D**
Chocolate powder liquor base
Milk-chocolate liquor base.

These two intermediate products become separately identifiable at a single split off point. Every 500 pounds of cocoa beans yields 20 gallons of chocolate — powder liquor base and 30 gallons of milk-chocolate liquor base.

The chocolate power liquor base is further processed into chocolate powder. The milk-chocolate liquor base is further processed into milk-chocolate. Every 30 gallons of milk-chocolate liquor based yields 340 pounds of milk chocolate.

Production and sales data for October, current year are:

Cocoa beans processed 7,500 pounds

Costs of processing Cocoa beans to split off point (including purchase of beans) = ₹7,12,500

	Production	*Sales*	*Selling price*
Chocolate powder	3,000 pounds	3,000 pounds	₹190 per pound
Milk chocolate	5,100	5,100	₹237.50 per pound

The October, separable costs of processing chocolate-powder liquor into chocolate powder are ₹3,02,812.50. The October, 2004 separable costs of processing milk-chocolate liquor base into milk-chocolate are ₹6,23,437.50.

Pokemon could have sold the chocolate powder liquor based for ₹997.50 a gallon and the milk-chocolate liquor base for ₹1,235 a gallon.

REQUIRED:

(i) Calculate how the joint cost of ₹7,12,500 would be allocated between the chocolate powder and milk-chocolate liquor bases under the following methods:

(a) Sales value at split off point **(b)** Physical measure (gallons) **(c)** Estimated net realisable value, (NRV) and **(d)** Constant gross-margin percentage NRV.

(ii) What is the gross-margin percentage of the chocolate powder and milk-chocolate liquor bases under each of the methods in requirements (i)? **(iii)** Could Pokemon have increased its operating income by a change in its decision to fully process both of its intermediate products? Show your computation.

Solution

(i) *Allocation of Joint Cost under Various Methods*

Particulars	*Chocolate powder liquor base*	*Milk chocolate liquor base*	*Total*
(a) Sales value at split of point method:			
Sales value of products at split off	₹2,99,250 (300 × ₹997.50)	₹5,55,750 (450 gallons × ₹1,235)	₹8,55,000
Weights (in proportion of sale value)	0.35	0.65	1.00
Joint cost allocated	(₹7,12,500 × 0.35) ₹2,49,375	(₹7,12,500 × 0.65) ₹4,63,125	7,12,500
(b) Physical measure method:			
Output	300 gallons	450 gallons	750 gallons
Weights (300:450)	(300/750) = 0.40	(450/750) = 0.60	
Joint cost allocated (in proportion of output)	(₹7,12,500 × 0.40) = ₹2,85,000	(₹7,12,500 × 0.60) = ₹4,27,500	1.00 ₹7,12,500
(c) Net realisable value (NRV) method:			
Final sales value of production	(3,000 pounds × ₹190) = ₹5,70,000	(5,100 pounds × ₹237.50) = ₹12,11,250	₹17,81,250
Less separable costs	3,02,812.50	6,23,437.50	9,26,250
Net realisable value at split off point	2,67,187.50	5,87,812.50	8,55,000
Weights (in proportion of NRV)	0.3125	0.6875	1.00

(*Contd.*)

(Contd.)

Joint cost allocated	(₹7,12,500 × 0.3125) = ₹2,22,656.25	(₹7,12,500 × 0.6875) = ₹4,89,843.75	₹7,12,500
(d) Constant gross margin percentage NRV method:			
Final sales value of production	₹5,70,000	₹12,11,250	₹17,81,250
Less gross margin (8%)	45,600	96,900	1,42,500
Cost of goods available for sale	5,24,400	11,14,350	16,38,750
Less separable costs	3,02,812,50	623,437.50	9,26,250
Joint cost allocated	2,21,587.50	4,90,912.50	7,12,500

WORKING NOTES

Computation of Gross Margin

Final sales value of total production	₹17,81,250
Less joint and separable cost	16,38,750
Gross margin	1,42,500
Gross margin (%) (₹1,42,500/₹17,81,250)/ × 100	8

(ii) *Computation of Gross Margin of Chocolate Powder and Milk Chocolate Liquor Bases under various Methods*

Particulars	*Sales value at split off*	*Physical measure*	*Net realisable value*	*Constant gross margin NRV*
Chocolate powder liquor base:				
Final sales value	₹5,70,000	₹5,70,000	₹5,70,000	₹5,70,000
Less separable costs	3,02,812.50	3,02,812.50	3,02,812.50	3,02,812.50
Less joint costs	2,49,375.00	2,85,000.00	2,22,656.25	2,21,587.50
Gross margin	17,812.50	(17,812.50)	44.531.25	45,600.00
Gross margin (%)	3.125	(3.125)	7.8125	8
Milk chocolate liquor base:				
Final sales value	₹12,11,250	₹12,11,250	₹12,11,250	₹12,11,250
Less separable costs	6,23,437.50	6,23,437.50	6,23,437.50	6,23,437.50
Less joint costs	4,63,125	4,27,500	4,89,843.75	4,90,912
Gross margin	1,24,687.50	1,60,312,50	97,968.75	96,900.50
Gross margin (%)	10.29	13.23	8.08	8

(iii) *Further Processing of Chocolate Powder Liquor Base into Chocolate Powder*

Particulars	*Amount*
Incremental revenue [₹5,70,000 – (₹997.50 × 300)]	₹2,70,750
Less incremental costs	3,02,812,50
Incremental operating income	(32,062.50)

Further Processing of Milk Chocolate Liquor Base into Milk Chocolate

Particulars	*Amount*
Incremental revenue [₹12,11,250 – (450 × ₹1,235)]	₹6,55,500
Less incremental cost	6,23,437,50
Incremental operating income	32,062.50

From the above, it is clear that Pokemon Chocolates could increase operating income (by ₹32,062.50) by processing further milk chocolate liquor base into milk chocolate and selling chocolate liquor base at split off point itself.

P.14.22 The Sunshine Oil Company purchases crude vegetable oil. It does refining of the same. The refining process results in four products at the split-off point: M,N,O and P. LO 14.3,5 LOD: M

Product O is fully processed at the split-off point. Product M,N and P can be individually further refined into 'Super M', 'Super N' and 'Super p'. In the most recent month (October), related to current year the output (in gallons) at split-off point was:

Product M	3,00,000
Product N	1,00,000
Product O	50,000
Product P	50,000

The joint cost of purchasing the crude vegetable oil and processing it were ₹40,00,000.

Sunshine had no beginning or ending inventories. Sales of Product O in October were ₹20,00,000. Total output of products M, N and P was further refined and then sold. Data related to October are as follows:

Particulars	Further processing costs to make Super Products	Sales
'Super M'	₹80,00,000	₹1,20,00,000
'Super N'	32,00,000	40,00,000
'Super P'	36,00,000	48,00,000

Sunshine had the option of selling products M, N and P at the split-off point. This alternative would have yielded the following sales for October:

Product M	₹20,00,000
Product N	12,00,000
Product P	28,00,000

You are required to answer:

(i) How would the joint cost of ₹40,00,000 be allocated between each product under each of the following methods (a) sales value at split-off: (b) physical output (gallons): and (c) estimated net realizable value?

(ii) Could Sunshine have increased its October operating profits by making different decisions about the further refining of product M, N or P? Show the effect of any change you recommend on operating profits.

Solution

(i) *(a) Joint Cost Allocation using Sales Value at Split-off Method*

Products (1)	Sales value at split-off point (2)	Basis of joint cost allocation (3)	Joint cost allocated (Col 3 × ₹40 lakh) (4)
M	₹20,00,000	20/80	₹10,00,000
N	12,00,000	12/80	6,00,000
O	20,00,000	20/80	10,00,000
P	28,00,000	28/80	14,00,000
	80,00,000		40,00,000

* assumed sales value at split-off point.

(b) Joint Cost Allocation using Physical Output Method

Products (1)	Output (gallons) (2)	Basis of joint cost allocation (3)	Joint cost allocated (Col 3 × ₹40 lakh) (4)
M	₹3,00,000	3/5	₹24,00,000
N	1,00,000	1/5	8,00,000
O	50,000	1/10	4,00,000
P	50,000	1/10	4,00,000
	5,00,000		40,00,000

(c) Joint Cost Allocation using Estimated Net Realisable Value Method

Products (1)	Sales value after further processing (2)	Further processing costs (3)	Net realisable value (Col.2 - Col. 3) (4)	Basis of joint cost allocation (5)	Joint cost allocated (Col. 5 x 40 lakh) (6)
M	₹1,20,00,000	₹80,00,000	₹40,00,000	40/80	₹20,00,000
N	40,00,000	32,00,000	8,00,000	8/80	4,00,000
O	—	—	20,00,000	20/80	10,00,000
P	48,00,000	36,00,000	12,00,000	12/80	6,00,000
			80,00,000		40,00,000

(ii) *Sell or Process Further: Decision Analysis*

Particulars	Products M	N	P
Sales value after further processing	₹1,20,00,000	₹40,00,000	₹48,00,000
Less sales value before further processing	20,00,000	12,00,000	28,00,000
Incremental sales revenue	1,00,00,000	28,00,000	20,00,000
Less further processing costs	80,00,000	32,00,000	36,00,000
Incremental profit (loss) from further processing	20,00,000	(4,00,000)	(16,00,000)

Sunshine would have increased profits by ₹20 lakh if it had processed Product M further; further processing of products N and P would have caused losses.

P.14.23 Two products P and Q are obtained in a crude form and require further processing at a cost of ₹5 for P and ₹4 for Q per unit before sale. Assuming a net margin of 25 per cent on cost, their sale prices are fixed at ₹13.75 and ₹8.75 per unit respectively. During the period, the joint cost was ₹88,000 and the outputs were: P, 8,000 units; Q, 6,000 units Ascertain the joint cost per unit. **LO 14.3.5** **LOD: M**

Solution

Statement showing Allocation of Joint Costs

Particulars	Products P	Q
Selling price per unit	₹13.75	₹8.75
Less estimated net profit (25 per cent on cost or 20 per cent on sales)	2.75	1.75
Less separable post split-off cost	5.00	4.00
Pre-split/joint cost per unit	6.00	3.00
Multiplied by output (in units)	8,000	6,000
Joint costs are to be shared between products P and Q in the ratio of 48000: 18,000 i.e., 8:3 respectively	48,000	18,000
Share of joint costs (P: ₹88,000 × 8/11 and Q: ₹88,000 × 3/11	64,000	24,000

P.14.24 ABC Ltd operates a simple chemical process to convert a single material into three separate items, referred to here as X, Y an Z. All three end products are separated simultaneously at a single split-off point. **LO 14.3.5** **LOD: M**

Product X and Y are ready for sale immediately upon split-off without further processing or any other additional costs. Product Z, however, is processed further before being sold. There is no available market price for Z at the split-off point.

The selling prices quoted here are expected to remain the same in the coming year. During 2002-03, the selling prices of the items and the total amounts sold were:

X—186 tons sold for ₹1,500 per ton
Y—527 tons sold for ₹1,125 per ton
Z—736 tons sold for ₹750 per ton

The total joint manufacturing costs for the year were ₹6,25,000. An additional ₹3,10,000 was spent to finished product Z.

There were no opening inventories of X, Y or Z. At the end of the year, the following inventories of complete units are on hand:

X—180 tons
Y—60 tons
Z—25 tons

There was no opening or closing work-in-progress.

Required:

(i) Compute the cost of inventories of X, Y and Z for balance sheet purposes and cost of goods sold for income statement purposes as of March 31, 2016, using:

(a) Net realisable value (NRV) method of joint cost allocation.

(b) Constant gross-margin percentage NRV method of joint-cost allocation.

(ii) Compare the gross-margin percentages for X, Y and Z using two methods given in requirement (i).

Solution (i) (a)

Statement showing Joint Cost Allocation among Products X, Y and Z (Net Realisable Value Method)

Particulars	Products			
	X	Y	Z	Total
Final sales value of total production	₹5,49,000[@]	₹6,60,375[£]	₹5,70,750*	₹17,80,125
Less further processing costs	—	—	3,10,000	3,10,000
Net realisable value	5,49,000	6,60,375	2,60,750	14,70,125
Joint cost allocated[1]	2,33,398	2,80,748	1,10,854	6,25,000

[@](366 tons × ₹1,500) [£](587 tons × ₹1,125) *(761 tons × ₹750)

WORKING NOTES

1. *Apportionment of joint cost:*

X = (₹6,25,000/₹14,70,125) × ₹5,49,000 = ₹2,33,398

Y = (₹6,25,000/14,70,125) × ₹6,60,375 = ₹2,80,748

Z = (₹6,25,000/14,70,125) × ₹2,60,750 = ₹1,10,854

(i) (a) *Cost of Goods Sold for the year and Cost of Closing Inventory as of March 31, 2016 (NRV Method)*

Products	Allocated joint cost	Further processing cost	Cost of goods available for sale	Cost of ending inventory[2]	Cost of goods sold
(1)	(2)	(3)	(4) = (2) + (3)	(5)	(6) = (4) – (5)
X	₹2,33,378	—	₹2,33,398	₹1,14,785	₹1,18,613
Y	2,80,748	—	2,80,748	28,692	2,52,056
Z	1,10,854	3,10,000	4,20,854	13,846	4,07,008
Total	6,25,000	3,10,000	9,35,000	(1,57,323)	7,77,677

2. *Computation of Total Production:*

Products	Quantity sold in tons	Quantity of ending inventory in tons	Total production	Ending inventory percentage
(1)	(2)	(3)	(4) (2) + (3)	(5) = (3)/(4)
X	186	180	366	49.18%
Y	527	60	587	10.22
Z	736	25	761	3.29

Income Statement (based on Net Realisable Value Method)

Products	Sales revenue	Cost of goods sold	Gross margin	Gross margin %
X	₹2,79,000[@]	₹1,18,613	₹1,60,387	57.49%
Y	5,92,875*	2,52,056	3,40,819	57.49
Z	5,52,000[£]	4,07,008	1,44,992	26.26
Total	14,23,875	7,77,677	6,46,198	

[@](186 tons × ₹1,500)
[£](527 tons × ₹1,125)
*(736 tons × ₹750)

(i) (b) *Statement showing Joint Cost Allocation among Products X, Y and Z (Gross Margin Percentage Net Realisable Value Method)*

Particulars	Products X	Y	Z	Total
Final sales value of total production	₹5,49,000	₹6,60,375	₹5,70,750	₹17,80,125
Less gross margin[3] (refer to working note)	2,60,641	3,13,517	2,70,967	8,45,125
	2,88,359	3,46,858	2,99,783	9,35,000
Less additional cost			3,10,000	3,10,000
Joint cost allocated	2,88,359	3,46,858	(10,217)	6,25,000

3. *Gross Margin Percentage*

Final sales value of production	₹17,80,125
Less joint costs and additional costs	9,35,000
Gross margin	8,45,125
Gross margin %(₹8,45,125/17,80,125) × 100	47.4756%

Cost of Goods Sold for the year and Cost of Closing Inventory as of March 31, 2016 (using Constant Gross Margin percentage NRV method)

Particulars	Products X	Y	Z	Total
Allocated joint cost	₹2,88,359	₹3,46,858	(₹10,217)	₹6,25,000
Add additional cost			3,10,000	3,10,000
Cost of goods available for sale (CGAS)	2,88,359	3,46,858	2,99,783	9,35,000
Less cost of ending inventory	1,41,815*	35,449[@]	9,863[£]	1,87,127
Cost of goods sold	1,46,544	3,11,409	2,89,920	7,47,873

*(49.18% × 2,88,359)
[@](10.22% × 3,46,858)
[£](3.29% × 2,99,783)

Income statement (based on constant gross margin percentage NRV method)

Particulars	X	Y	Z	Total
	Products			
Sales revenue	₹2,79,000	₹5,92,875	₹5,52,000	₹14,23,875
Less cost of goods sold	1,46,544	3,11,409	2,89,920	7,47,873
Gross margin	1,32,456	2,81,466	2,62,080	6,76,002
Gross margin (%)	47.48	47.48	47.48	47.48

Comparative statement of gross margin percentage for X, Y and Z (using net realisable value and constant gross margin percentage NRV methods)

Method	Product gross margin percentage		
	X	Y	Z
Net realisable value	57.49	57.49	26.26
Constant gross margin percentage NRV	47.48	47.48	47.48

REVIEW QUESTIONS

LOD: Easy

RQ.14.1 (a) Indicate whether the followings statements are 'True' or 'False'. **LO 14.1,2,3**

(i) Process costing is appropriate when the output is heterogeneous and/or the production process is generally intermittent.

(ii) In process costing, unit cost is determined periodically.

(iii) Less amount of inventory needs to be maintained in process costing as compared to job costing.

(iv) Job costing and process costing are mutually exclusive systems of costing.

(v) Process costing usually does not include a work-in-process account.

(vi) In process costing, the units of production in process need to be converted into equivalent units.

(vii) 100 units of inventory estimated to be 40 per cent complete are considered equivalent to 60 per cent completed units.

(viii) The split of production cost into (a) cost of output, and (b) closing inventory would remain same in FIFO as well as weighted average method of valuing work-in-process closing inventory.

(ix) In process costing, both normal and abnormal losses are controllable losses.

(x) Normal spoilage and abnormal spoilage are treated as product cost in process costing.

(xi) Abnormal spoilage cost is treated as a period cost and is written off as a loss in the period in which it occurs.

(xii) Transfer of output from one process to another can be either at cost or at market/inflated prices.

(xiii) The cost basis of inter-process transfer of output is better than market price basis.

(xiv) In process costing, production normally precedes sales.

(xv) Normal spoilage forms part of product costs.

(xvi) Normal loss is a controllable loss.

(xvii) Production costs incurred after the split-off point are joint costs.

(xviii) Physical quantities method results in identical unit costs for each product.

(b) In the following multiple choice questions, select the correct answers.

The following data of ABC Ltd. is given below.

Process I

— Raw material charged — 600 kg @ ₹4/kg.

— Direct labour ₹200.

— Departmental expenses ₹760.

— Normal loss is 10 per cent of input.

— During the period actual production was 500 kg and 100 kg was scrap. The scrap is sellable at ₹2/kg.

(xix) Calculate cost per unit which is cost per unit for ABC Ltd.

(a) ₹6 per unit, **(b)** ₹5.6 per unit, **(c)** ₹5 per unit, **(d)** None of these.

(xx) What is the amount of effective abnormal loss for ABC Ltd.?

(a) ₹240, **(b)** ₹160, **(c)** ₹200, **(d)** None of these.

[Answers: (i) False, (ii) True, (iii) False, (iv) False, (v) False, (vi) True, (vii) False, (viii) False, (ix) False, (x) False, (xi) True, (xii) True, (xiii) False, (xiv) True, (xv) True, (xvi) False, (xvii) True, (xviii) True, (xix) a (xx) b.]

RQ.14.2 Fill in the following blanks

(i) _______________ report forms the backbone of the process cost records (Cost of production/Job cost sheet). LO 14.1,2,3

(ii) Loss in excess of the normal spoilage is _______________ (abnormal loss/normal waste).

(iii) Production costs incurred prior to split-off point are called _______________ (joint costs/seperable costs).

(iv) Another name of unit method used for allocating joint costs is _______________ (physical quantities method/relative sales value).

(v) Where the joint products are heterogeneous, it is appropriate to use _______________ method (weighted average cost/net reliable value).

[Answers: (i) cost of production, (ii) abnormal loss, (iii) joint costs, (iv) physical quantities method, (v) weighted average cost.]

RQ.14.3 Specify the production situations that are more suitable to the process costing system. LO 14.1

RQ.14.4 Distinguish between process costing and job costing. Why is cost accumulation easier under the process costing system than under the job costing system? LO 14.1

RQ.14.5 Specify the important elements of a production report. LO 14.2

RQ.14.6 Compare the weighted average method with the FIFO method in calculating unit costs. LO 14.2

RQ.14.7 A product passes through two processes, A and B. The output of A passes on to B and that of B becomes the finished product. From the following information, prepare the process accounts: LO 14.2

	Process A	*Process B*
Materials consumed	₹24,000	₹12,000
Direct labour	28,000	16,000
Manufacturing expenses	8,010	8,000
Input in process A (units)	20,000	
Input in process A	20,000	
Output (units)	18,000	16,600
Normal wastage of input (%)	5	10
Value of normal wastage per 100 units	16	20

RQ.14.8 In manufacturing the main product A, a company processes the resulting waste material into two by-products, M_1 and M_2. Using the method of working backwards from the sales value to an estimated cost, prepare a comparative profit and loss statement of the three products from the following data: LO 14.3

(i) Total costs upto separation point was ₹1,36,000.

	A	M_1	M_2
(ii) Sale (all production)	₹3,28,000	₹32,000	₹48,000
(iii) Cost after separation	—	9,600	14,400
(iv) Estimated net profit percentage to sales values	—	20	30
(v) Estimated selling expenses as percentage of sales values	20	20	20

LOD: Medium

RQ.14.9 Explain clearly the difference between scrap, by-products, and joint products. Give the cost accounting treatment for each. LO 14.3,4

RQ.14.10 What is meant by 'equivalent units?' Discuss its importance in valuing work-in-process. LO 14.2

RQ.14.11 Explain normal and abnormal wastage and state how they should be dealt with in process cost accounts. LO 14.2

RQ.14.12 Under what circumstances are identical results obtained under weighted average and FIFO process costing? LO 14.2

RQ.14.13 Define joint products and by-products. Explain the various methods available for apportionment of joint costs to joint products. LO 14.3,4

RQ.14.14 What is meant by the split-off point? What is its significance in product costing? LO 14.5

RQ.14.15 A manufacturer can sell part of the output of process 1 as it is or process it further in process 2. What cost are relevant in a decision to sell it as it is or to process it further? What costs are irrelevant? LO 14.5

RQ.14.16 What are inter-process profits? How are such profits taken into account while valuing closing stock from the point of view of the balance sheet? Do you subscribe to the view that the output of one process should be transferred to another at a profit? LO 14.2

RQ.14.17 From the following data, prepare process accounts for a single product: LO 14.2

	Process I	*Process II*
(i) Period: December of the current year		
(ii) Work-in-process at the beginning	Nil	Nil
(iii) *Cost incurred in the period*		
Direct materials	₹60,000	—
Labour	12,000	₹16,000
Factory overheads	24,000	20,000
(iv) *Units of production*		
Received in process	40,000	36,000
Completed and transferred	36,000	32,000
Remaining in process at the end of the period	2,000	2,500
Loss-in-process (normal loss)	2,000	1,500
(v) *Production remaining in process should be valued at:*		
Material, 100 per cent		
Labour and overheads, 50 per cent.		

RQ.14.18 The following information is available from the records of a company engaged in manufacturing a single product. LO 14.2

Opening work-in-process	Quantity (units)	16,000
	Material	₹1,48,000
	Wages	33,000
	Overhead	29,000
Added during the year	Quantity (units)	69,000
	Material	5,62,000
	Labour	1,67,000
	Overhead	1,51,000
Finished during the year	Quantity (units)	56,000
Closing work-in-progress	Quantity (units)	24,000
	Material: 100% complete	
	Labour and overhead: 1/3 complete	

Tabulate the production and cost figures to give quantities, units values and total value for completed output and value of each element of cost for closing work-in-progress. Weighted average method of valuation may be used.

RQ.14.19 A manufacturing company makes a product using two processes. For the month of June, the information recorded for the second process is: A work-in-progress balance of 400 units brought forward from May was valued at ₹5,760. During June, 17,040 units were transferred from the first to the second process at a cost of ₹1,32,320. Costs incurred by the second process were: LO 14.2

Direct material issued	₹64,288
Direct wages	31,696
Overheads	15,848

The transfer of finished goods to the stock was 15,120 units. Number of units scrapped during the period was 880; 1,440 units were in work-in-progress at the end of the month.

There was a normal loss of 5 per cent of production. Units scrapped were sold at ₹3 each. The particulars relating to degree of completion are as follows:

	Degree of completion (%)		
	Opening stock	*Closing stock*	*Scrap*
Direct material	70	80	100
Direct wages	50	60	80
Overheads	50	60	80

Prepare the necessary accounts.

RQ.14.20 G.H. & Company Ltd. manufactures a product in the process costing and its work-in-progress stock at the end of each month is valued at FIFO basis. LO 14.2

At the beginning of the month of June, the inventory of work-in-progress showed 400 units, 40 per cent complete, valued as follows:

Material	₹3,600
Labour	3,400
Overheads	1,000
	8,000

In the month of June, materials were purchased for ₹75,000. Wages and overheads amounted to ₹79,800 and ₹21,285, respectively. Actual issue of material to production was ₹68,500. Finished stock was 2,500 units. There was no loss in process.

At the end of month, the work-in-progress inventory was 500 units, 60 per cent complete as to labour and overheads, and 80 per cent complete as to the material. Prepare a process account for recording the month's transactions and a process cost sheet showing the total unit costs.

RQ.14.21 A product passes through two processes, A and B. Output of process A is transferred to process B at cost plus 25 per cent and finished output of B is similarly transferred to finished stock at cost plus 25 per cent. There is no work-in-progress in any process on December 31. At this date, the following information is further available: LO 14.2

	Process A	*Process B*
Materials consumed	₹8,000	₹24,000
Wages	12,000	16,000
Closing stock (valued at prime cost)	4,000	12,000

Out of the finished stock, a portion remained at hand valued at ₹11,000 and the balance was sold for ₹58,000.

Prepare process accounts and the finished stock account. Question of overheads and opening stock is to be ignored. Also show how much reserves will be created for the unrealised profit.

RQ.14.22 Product Z yields by-products X and Y. The joint manufacturing expenses are ₹65,500. From the following information, show how you would apportion the joint expenses of manufacture. LO 14.2, 3

	X	*Y*	*Z*
(i) Sales	₹1,00,000	₹40,000	₹25,000
(ii) Manufacturing costs after separation	20,000	5,000	4,000
(iii) Estimated selling expenses on sales (%)	20	20	20
(iv) Estimated profit on sales (%)	20	25	30

RQ.14.23 The Assam Oil Company Ltd. processes crude oil in Department 1. During the current period, the following costs were incurred in Department 1 to obtain 20,000 barrels of product A and 30,000 barrels of product B: LO 14.3

Direct materials	₹50,000
Direct labour	1,50,000
Variable overheads	75,000
Fixed overheads	53,000
	3,28,000

Product A could be sold at the split-off point for ₹5 per barrel or processed in Department 2 at an additional cost of ₹4 per barrel and then sold for ₹10 per barrel. During the current period, all 20,000 barrels of A were processed in the Department. There was an ending inventory of 5,000 barrels of product A.

Product B must be processed further in Department 3. The following information from the current period is available about Department 3: Barrels processed, 31,000; Costs, ₹3,10,000.

The figure of 31,000 barrels includes 1000 barrels from the previous period's production of Department 1 processed in this period. There is an ending inventory of 1,000 barrels of B. The selling price of B is ₹20 per barrel.

You are required to determine to cost of ending finished inventories, using the net realisable value method to allocate the joint costs.

RQ.14.24 Calculate the estimated cost of production of by-products X and Y at the point of separation from the main product. LO 14.4, 5

	By-product X	By-product Y
Selling price per unit	₹12	₹24
Cost per unit after separation from the main product	3	5
Units produced	500	200

Selling expenses amount to 25 per cent of the total works cost, that is, including both pre-separation and post-separation works cost.

Selling prices are arrived at by adding 20 per cent of the total of all costs, that is, the sum of work costs and selling expenses.

RQ.14.25 Alfa Ltd. uses a chemical process to convert a single raw material into three separate products, A, B, and C which are separated at a single split-off point. A and B are ready for sale immediately after split-off point without further processing or any additional costs. Product C is processed further before being sold. During the year ending December 31, the quantities sold and the realisations were: **LO 14.4, 5**

Product	Quantity (M_t)	Sales value (₹lakh)
A	600	19.20
B	1,700	34.00
C	875	14.00

There were no opening inventories of A, B, and C. Total manufacturing costs for the year were ₹50.50 lakh. Costs after split-off point to process product C were ₹3 lakh. On December 31, the closing stocks were:

A	900 M_t
B	300 M_t
C	125 M_t

Prepare a statement of the 'cost' of inventories of A, B, and C. Your presentation should include a summary of the cost of goods sold by product-line and unit costs.

LOD: Difficult

RQ.14.26 An accountant has described cost allocations to joint products as a "necessary evil"? Comment. **LO 14.3**

RQ.14.27 When is the sales value method preferable to the quantity method as a means of allocating joint costs? In many manufacturing processes, waste products and by-products are produced. What problems do these present in costing the main product and how are they overcome? **LO 14.3, 4**

ANSWERS

RQ.14.7 Abnormal loss 1,000 units in process A; cost per unit of process A, ₹3.15; process B: cost per unit, ₹5.7; abnormal gain, 400 units.

RQ.14.8 Share of joint costs for products A, M^1 and M^2 is ₹1,16,800, ₹9,600, respectively; Net profit for these products is ₹1,45,600 (A), ₹6,400 (M^2) and ₹14,400 (M^2).

RQ.14.17 Process A: Cost of completed (36,000) units, ₹91,870, work-in-process (2,000 units), ₹4130; Process B: cost of completed (32,000) units, ₹1,19,860. Work-in-process (2,500 units), ₹8,010.

RQ.14.18 Equivalent units produced, 80,000 in terms of material, 64,000 in terms of labour and overhead; cost of finished output (56,000 units), ₹8,29,500; work-in-process (24,000 units), ₹2,60,500.

RQ.14.19 Cost of production transferred to next process, ₹2,27,640; work-in-process, ₹6,840; abnormal loss, ₹1,152.

RQ.14.20 Transfer to finished stock ₹1,56,095, work-in-process ₹21,485, Equivalent cost: materials ₹25, Labour ₹33,000, Overheads ₹8.06

RQ.14.21 Total profit, ₹21,413; Reserve for unrealised profit-finished stock, ₹2,787, Process B: ₹800.

RQ.14.22 Joint expenses should be apportioned among X, Y and Z is the ratio of 40 : 17 : 8.5. (₹40,000, ₹17,000, ₹8,500).

RQ.14.23 Share of joint costs: ₹93,714 (product A), ₹2,34,286 (product B): Closing inventories, ₹43,450 (product A), ₹17,810 (Product B).

RQ.14.24 Estimated cost of production at the point of separation: By-product X, ₹5 per unit (Total ₹2,500); By-product Y, ₹11 per unit (Total ₹2,200).

RQ.14.25 Cost of inventories: A, ₹14,40,000; B, ₹3,00,000; C, ₹1,18,750.

[Comprehensive solutions to all numerical review questions are available on the companion website: http://www.mhhe.com/khan_jain_ma7e]

15 Variable Costing and Absorption (Full) Costing

Learning Objectives

After reading this chapter you will be able to:

- **LO 15.1** Compare variable costing and full (absorption) costing from the view point of income determination
- **LO 15.2** Explain the reconciliation of differences in income between variable and absorption costing methods
- **LO 15.3** Review the merits and demerits of variable costing

Introduction

Variable costing is a technique in which only variable costs are taken into account for product costing, inventory valuation and other allied management decisions.

Absorption costing takes into account total costs.

Variable costing and absorption costing are not systems of costing such as process, operating, batch or job costing. Variable costing is a technique in which only variable costs are taken into account for purposes of product costing, inventory valuation and other allied important management decisions. In absorption costing, total costs are taken into account for these purposes. Thus, the variable costing technique is in marked contrast to the orthodox costing system known as 'full/absorption/traditional/conventional costing'. The material point of difference between the two techniques of costing is that the 'full' costing method 'absorbs' all costs necessary to produce the product and have it in a saleable form, while the variable costing technique recognises only variable costs as production costs. Thus, direct material, direct labour and variable overheads constitute the only relevant costs in variable costing whereas the full/absorption costing technique recognises fixed overheads also as a product cost in addition to material, labour and variable overheads. Hence, conceptually these two techniques differ in only one respect: fixed manufacturing overheads are included in product cost under absorption costing; they are excluded under variable costing.

The two techniques of costing are, however, not mutually exclusive and are complementary in character. Income statements for external reporting and for tax purposes are to be on a full costing basis.[1] The usefulness of variable costing is that, it helps management in arriving at profit-maximising decisions in certain situations. It is for this reason that variable costing becomes more useful for internal reporting purposes. Thus, both techniques are significant. Which costing technique is to be employed depends on the purpose.

A comparison of variable and absorption costing from the point of view of income determination is presented first. The merits and demerits of variable costing are listed subsequently. The chapter concludes with the main points.

VARIABLE AND ABSORPTION COSTING: A COMPARISON

LO 15.1 Compare variable costing and full (absorption) costing from the view point of income determination

Variable costing is employed under the assumption that a certain investment in facilities and other productive factors is required before products can be manufactured. For instance, a factory building is to be hired for which rent is to be paid, plant is to be installed on which there will be a depreciation charge, factory insurance payment, property taxes, salary of plant manager and such other expenses have to be initially and subsequently incurred each year in the manufacturing business. Hence, the fixed costs resulting from this investment are not product costs but period cost. These costs must be incurred in order to have a manufacturing establishment and they will recur each year. Logically, therefore, "the fixed costs of manufacturing should be expensed each year and not carried as part of the cost of an inventory."[2] In other words, the principle underlying variable costs is that fixed manufacturing overhead are not inventoriable costs; they are period costs and must be matched against the revenue of that year. In contrast to this, absorption costing indicates that the manufacturing fixed overheads are inventoriable costs; they are the product costs and must be matched against the revenue of the year in which sales are made. Format 15.2 shows the flow of costs in an absorption costing system. The cost flow pattern for variable costing in shown in Format 15.1.

FORMAT 15.1 Income Statement (Variable Costing)

		Amount
Sales revenue (Units sold × selling price)		
Less: Variable costs (production costs):		
Direct material cost	.....	.....
Direct labour cost	.....	
Variable manufacturing overheads	.....	
Total cost of good manufactured	.....	
Plus: Cost of inventory in the beginning of the year (Units × variable cost)	.....	
Less: Cost of inventory at the end of the year (Units × variable cost)	(.....)	
Cost of goods manufactured and sold		(.....)
Contribution (manufacturing)		.....
Less: Variable non-production costs:		
Selling and distribution costs		—
Administrative costs	.....	(.....)
Other costs (specify)	.....	.....
Contribution (final)	.....	—
Less: Fixed costs:		
Fixed production costs	.....	
Fixed non-production costs (specify individual items)	.....	(.....)
Net income before income taxes		
Less: Income taxes		(.....)
Net income after income taxes		

FORMAT 15.2 Income Statement (Absorption Costing)

		Amount
Sales revenue (Number of units sold × selling price)		—
Less: Total costs of manufacturing:		
Direct material cost	—	
Direct labour cost	—	
Variable manufacturing overhead	—	
Fixed manufacturing overhead	—	
Total cost of goods manufactured		—
Plus: Cost of inventory in the beginning of the year (Units × total cost)		—
Less: Cost of inventory at the end of the year (Units × total cost)	( )	
Cost of goods manufactured and sold		( )
Gross margin (manufacturing) (unadjusted)		
Adjustment for capacity variance (+Favourable –Unfavourable)		(±)
Gross margin (adjusted)		
Less: Non-production costs:		
Selling and distribution costs	—	
Administrative costs	—	
Other costs (specify)	—	
Net income before income taxes		( )
Less: Income taxes		( )
Net income after taxes		

Note: If the firm's operating capacity is different from the normal capacity, there will be capacity variance.

The adjustment for such a variance is to be made before determining the gross margin. If capacity variance is favourable, the amount is to be deducted from the total costs of goods manufactured and sold; the amount is added to the cost if capacity variance is unfavourable.

Everything is common in both the formats except that fixed manufacturing overheads form part of production costs with 'full' costing whereas it is non-production cost is the case of variable costing. It is also important to note that the treatment of overheads other than manufacturing, namely, selling and administrative, is the same under both the techniques, full or variable.

The justification of the use of variable costing *vis-à-vis* absorption costing is based on two important factors:

1. Fixed costs relate to a particular period of time and should, therefore, be charged to that period only and to no other.
2. There is no method which is capable of apportioning fixed manufacturing costs to products. In the full costing method, fixed overheads are recovered from production by some agreed recovery method. This recovery can never be accurate and may even sometimes be misleading. Further, fixed overheads (such as rates and insurance), are predominantly concerned with time rather than volume of output and so should be recovered during the current period and not carried forward to burden the next.[3]

The differences between the two costing techniques can be better highlighted by showing the procedure of income statement preparation under the two costing concepts/techniques.

In variable costing, as explained earlier, product costs should include only the variable factory costs, and the fixed (period) costs should be charged to the revenue of the accounting period. The excess of sales revenue (SR) over variable costs (VC) is known as contribution (C) utilised towards the recovery of *first* fixed expenses (FC/period costs) and, second, to contribute to profits. On the other hand, absorption costing is based on the principle that all the manufacturing costs (direct, variable, as well as non-variable costs) should be charged to the production of a given period and fixed manufacturing overheads are charged to the products by using a pre-determined rate, designated as the standard fixed overhead rate (SFOR) of recovery. This rate is elaborated in a later chapter in detail and is usually determined with reference to budgeted fixed manufacturing overheads and the hours of operation at a normal level of production. The SFOR is determined by dividing the former amount with the latter amount. The products are assigned a standard charge for fixed overheads. If the plant operates above or below its normal capacity, the fixed manufacturing overheads will be over/under-absorbed; the over/under-absorbed overhead amount is designated as the capacity variance and is written off to operations for the year.

From the above principles of absorption costing, it follows that profits are affected not only by the sales volume, selling price, cost of production, but also by the quantity of units produced during the period. Accordingly, a firm may produce goods regardless of sales, and still the profit and loss account may reflect profit earned, whereas in reality there is simply a piling up of stocks of inventory in the factory godowns. The hypothetical/typical case for such a situation is that a firm has produced more than its normal capacity and, therefore, over-absorbed its actual fixed overheads. The firm, in spite of not making sales of even a single unit, will show gross margin to the extent of over-absorption of the fixed manufacturing overheads. Example 15.1 illustrates this point.

◆ Example 15.1

Hypothetical Ltd furnishes the following information from its cost records for the first quarter of the current year:

Normal production (units)	1,000
Actual production (units)	1,100
Actual overheads per quarter at normal production	₹4,000
Other expenses per quarter	300
Standard fixed overhead rate per unit	4
Variable costs per unit	6
Sales volume (selling price is ₹14)	Nil

Prepare the income statement under absorption and variable costings.

Solution

The income statements are shown in Tables 15.1 and 15.2 respectively.

TABLE 15.1 Income Statement (Absorption Costing)

Particulars		*Amount*
Sales revenue		Nil
Less: Total cost of manufacturing:		
Variable costs (1,100 × ₹6)	₹6,600	
Fixed overheads (1,100 × ₹4)	4,400	
	11,000	
Less: Cost of inventory at the end of the year (1,100 × ₹10)	11,000	Nil
Cost of goods manufactured and sold		
Gross margin (unadjusted)		Nil
Capacity variance (favourable) (over-absorbed, 100 × ₹4)		₹400
Gross margin (adjusted)		400
Less: Other expenses		300
Net income before taxes		100

TABLE 15.2 Income Statement (Variable Costing)

Particulars		*Amount*
Sales revenue		Nil
Less: Variable costs (production costs) (1,100 × ₹6)	₹6,600	
Less: Cost of inventory at the end of the year (1,100 × ₹6)	6,600	
Cost of goods manufactured and sold		Nil
Contribution		Nil
Less: Fixed costs:		
Fixed overheads	4,000	
Other expenses	300	₹(4,300)
Net income before taxes (loss)		(4,300)

There is a marked difference in the profit results under the two methods: absorption costing shows net profit of ₹100, while a loss of ₹4,300 is reported under variable costing. This result is ascribed to the fact that under absorption costing, the fixed manufacturing overheads are inventoriable, whereas in variable costing inventory is valued only at variable costs. In Example 15.1, inventory is valued at ₹11,000 in absorption costing, while its valuation is ₹6,600 in variable costing. This is how the difference of ₹4,400 is accounted for.

From the above, it may be deduced that changes in inventory will influence reported income under the two costing techniques because under variable costing, fixed costs are deducted in the period in which they are incurred whereas under absorption costing, a portion of fixed costs is carried over with inventory. The reported net income, thus, differs under the two methods. When production exceeds sales, fixed cost absorption is more in full costing compared to variable costing and, therefore, to that extent, income/profits under absorption costing are more. The results are reversed when sales exceed production. Profits would be identical under the two methods, if production coincides with sales. Example 15.2 clearly brings out these differences.

◆ Example 15.2

Hypothetical Ltd furnishes the following information for its three different periods:

Particulars	*Year 1*	*Year 2*	*Year 3*
Production (units)	*10,000*	*10,000*	*10,000*
Sales (units)	10,000	5,000	15,000

Sales price per unit, ₹12
Variable cost per unit, ₹6
Fixed costs per year (at normal capacity of 10,000 units), ₹40,000
Standard fixed overhead rate: ₹4 per unit.
Show the profit under variable and absorption costing in different years.

Solution

The profit is shown in Table 15.3.

TABLE 15.3 Income Statements for the Years Ended 1, 2, 3

Particulars	*Absorption Costing*	*Variable Costing*
	Year 1 (Production = Sales)	
Sales (10,000 × ₹12)	₹1,20,000	₹1,20,000
Less: Cost of goods manufactured		
Variable costs (10,000 × ₹6)	60,000	60,000
Fixed costs (10,000 × ₹4)	40,000	

(Contd.)

(Contd.)

Cost of goods manufactured and sold	1,00,000	60,000
Gross margin	20,000	—
Contribution	—	60,000
Less: Fixed costs	—	40,000
Net income before taxes	20,000	20,000
	Year 2 (Production > Sales)	
Sales (5,000 × ₹12)	60,000	60,000
Less: Cost of goods manufactured		
Variable costs (10,000 × ₹6)	60,000	60,000
Fixed costs (10,000 × ₹4)	40,000	—
Total cost of goods manufactured	1,00,000	60,000
Less: Cost of inventory at the end of the year		
(5,000 × ₹10)	(50,000)	
(5,000 × ₹6)		(30,000)
Cost goods manufactured and sold	50,000	30,000
Gross margin	10,000	—
Contribution	—	30,000
Less: Fixed costs	—	40,000
Net income (loss)	10,000	(10,000)
	Year 3 (Sales > Production)	
Sales (15,000 × ₹12)	1,80,000	1,80,000
Less: Cost of goods manufactured:		
Variable costs (10,000 × ₹6)	60,000	60,000
Fixed costs (10,00 × ₹4)	40,000	—
Total cost of goods manufactured	1,00,000	60,000
Plus: Cost of inventory in the year's beginning		
(5,000 × ₹10)	50,000	
(5,000 × ₹6)		30,000
Cost of goods manufactured and sold	1,50,000	90,000
Gross margin	30,000	—
Contribution	—	90,000
Less: Fixed costs		40,000
Net income	30,000	50,000

Summary of Results

Year 1: Net income is identical in both the methods.
Year 2: Absorption costing shows more profit than variable costing.
Year 3: Variable costing shows more profit than absorption costing.
All Years Combined: The total net income will be the same under either costing method because the total production and sales are equal (30,000 units).

Reasons for the Differences In year 1, the results of net income are identical because the equality of production and sales does not affect the level of inventory on hand. All goods produced have been sold and, thus, all fixed costs of production are charged to the income statement under absorption costing as well as variable costing.

In year 2, when sales are less than production, there is an increase in the level of inventory on hand. Under absorption costing, the increase in inventory carries proportionate fixed costs (to be spent next year) which means that fixed costs charged to revenue are less under absorption costing than under variable costing. Thus, the net income reported under variable costing is less than under absorption costing. The amount of ₹20,000 is equivalent to 5,000 units of inventory multiplied by ₹4 (standard fixed overhead rate).

In year 3, when sales exceed production, there is a decrease in the level of inventory on hand. Under absorption costing, the inventory of year 2 would carry a part of fixed costs (₹20,000). Thus, under absorption costing fixed costs charged against the revenue of the current year will be higher by ₹20,000 compared to variable costing. Hence, the additional fixed costs of ₹20,000 under full costing makes the net income revealed by variable costing more by this amount.

The fact that fixed costs move along with inventory signifies that the fixed costs will be released as part of goods sold in a later year(s) when sales are in excess of production. Hence, profits will not necessarily increase with increase in sales revenue. In fact, the profits will decrease if the effect of shifting fixed costs from one year to another as a part of inventory cost is more than the increased contribution to be derived from increased sales.[4]

The situation visualised above is by no means imaginary. For obvious reasons, the management will be bewildered by the decrease in profits with increased sales volume when no change whatsoever has occurred in selling prices and costs. In general, profits are expected to increase with increase in sales volume. Consider Example 15.3.

◆ Example 15.3

Hypothetical Ltd had the following relevant information for years 1 and 2:

Standard variable costs per unit		₹6
Sales price per unit		10
Fixed manufacturing overhead (at normal capacity of 1,50,000 units)		3,00,000
Selling and administrative expenses		
Fixed		1,30,000
Variable (per cent of sales)		5
Production volume: units	Year 1	1,70,000
	2	1,40,000
Sales volume:	1	1,40,000
	2	1,60,000

There was no inventory at the beginning of year 1. Income tax rate is 35 per cent.

REQUIRED: **1.** Prepare income statements for the two years under absorption costing and variable costing.

2. Show a reconciliation of the difference in net income for the two years (1 and 2) taken together.

Solution

TABLE 15.4 Income Statement (Absorption Costing) for the Years 1 and 2

Particulars	*Year 1*	*Year 2*
Number of units produced	1,70,000	1,40,000
Number of units sold	1,40,000	1,60,000
Sales revenue	₹14,00,000	₹16,00,000
Less: Cost of manufacturing:		
Standard variable cost (₹6 per unit)	10,20,000	8,40,000
Fixed cost (₹2 per unit)	3,40,000	2,80,000
Total standard cost of manufacturing (₹8 per unit)	13,60,000	11,20,000
Plus: Cost of inventory (beginning)	—	2,40,000
Less: Cost of inventory (ending)	(2,40,000)	(80,000)
Cost of goods manufactured and sold (at standard absorption cost)	11,20,000	12,80,000

(Contd.)

(*Contd.*)

Gross margin manufacturing (unadjusted)	2,80,000	3,20,000
± Capacity variance	40,000 (F)	20,000 (A)
Gross margin (adjusted)	3,20,000	3,00,000
Less: Non-production costs:		
Selling and administrative expenses	2,00,000	2,10,000
Net income before taxes	1,20,000	90,000
Less: Income taxes (0.35)	42,000	31,500
Net income after taxes	78,000	58,500

F = Favourable, A = Adverse

TABLE 15.5 Income Statement (Variable Costing) for the Years 1 and 2

Particulars	*Year 1*	*Year 2*
Number of units produced	1,70,000	1,40,000
Number of units sold	1,40,000	1,60,000
Sales revenue	₹14,00,000	₹16,00,000
Less: Variable costs:		
Standard variable cost @ ₹6 per unit	10,20,000	8,40,000
+ Cost of inventory at standard cost (beginning)	Nil	1,80,000
– Cost of inventory at standard cost (ending)	(1,80,000)	(60,000)
Standard cost of goods manufactured and sold	8,40,000	9,60,000
@ of ₹6 per unit sold	8,40,000	9,60,000
Contribution (manufacturing)	5,60,000	6,40,000
Less: Variable non-production costs:		
Selling and administrative expenses	70,000	80,000
Contribution (final)	4,90,000	5,60,000
Less: Fixed costs:		
Fixed overheads	3,00,000	3,00,000
Selling and administrative expenses	1,30,000	1,30,000
Net income before taxes	60,000	1,30,000
Less: Taxes (0.35)	21,000	45,500
Net income after taxes	39,000	84,500

The income statement under absorption costing shows that the company earned less profit in year 2 compared to year 1 inspite of 20,000 more units sold in year 2 and there was no decrease either in selling price or increase in cost (both fixed and variable). Ordinarily, profits are expected to increase with increase in sales volume.

The income statement constructed on a variable costing basis shows, that the contribution has increased in year 2 as result of selling 20,000 more units. The profits are in tune with sales volume when the variable costing technique is adopted.

VARIABLE AND ABSORPTION COSTING: RECONCILIATION

LO 15.2 Explain the reconciliation of differences in income between variable and absorption costing methods

The difference in results given by the above two methods can be explained in terms of: (i) The standard fixed overhead rate (SFOR); and (ii) The change in the inventories that has taken place during the period under consideration. Table 15.6 provides a complete explanation of the differences in results.

TABLE 15.6 Reconciliation Statement of Net Income Before Taxes under Absorption Costing and Variable Costing

Particulars	*Year 1*	*Year 2*	*Combined*
Net income before taxes as per:			
Absorption costing	₹1,20,000	₹90,000	₹2,10,000
Variable costing	60,000	1,30,000	1,90,000
Difference (to be explained)	60,000	(40,000)	20,000
(a) Standard fixed overhead rate	2	2	2
Change in inventory units:			
Opening inventory	Nil	30,000	—
Ending inventory	30,000	10,000	10,000
(b) Change in inventory	30,000	(20,000)	10,000
(c) Increase (decrease) difference in net income is explained by the product of (a) × (b)	60,000	(40,000)	20,000

Likewise, an increase in net income before taxes under variable costing by ₹70,000 in year 2 compared to year 1 can be explained in the form of a reconciliation statement (Table 15.7 and Table 15.8).

TABLE 15.7 Reconciliation Statement (Variable Costing)

Particulars	*Amount*
Increase in sales revenue in year 2 (20,000 × ₹10)	₹2,00,000
Less: Increased manufacturing variable cost in year 2 (20,000 × ₹6)	1,20,000
Increased contribution (20,000 × ₹4)	80,000
Less: Increased selling and administrative costs (0.05 × ₹2,00,000)	10,000
Increased contribution (final)	70,000

TABLE 15.8 Reconciliation Statement (Absorption Costing)

Particulars	*Amount*
Increased contribution (already explained in variable costing reconciliation statement)	₹70,000
Less: Fixed costs of year 1 on 30,000 units at the rate of ₹2 per unit shifted to year 2 (decreases year 1 cost)	(60,000)
Fixed costs of year 1 shifted to year 2 (increases year 2 cost)	(60,000)
Add: Fixed cost of year 2 on 10,000 units at the rate of ₹2 per unit shifted to year 3 (decreases year 2 cost)	20,000
Increase in costs caused by shift in fixed cost	1,00,000
Net decrease in net income before income taxes	(30,000)

Emphasis on Production or Sales Example 15.3 shows that variable costing focuses on sales, while the emphasis of absorption costing is on production. In profit making organisations, sales are generally regarded more important than production because out of sales all expenses are to be met and profits earned. It is very difficult to believe that profits can increase with more production without being sold. Therefore, a variable costing report on profits earned by the firm is more logical than an absorption costing report based on production. "However differences attributable to a lack of balance between sales and production are not revealed by variable costing. Sales activity may be overemphasised at the expense of production. In reality, profits depend upon both sales and production."[5]

Still another noteworthy feature of income determination under the two costing methods relates to total profits across time periods. A reference to Example 15.2 shows that the total net income for three years is ₹60,000 under both the methods.

In most industries, production will tend to equal sales over a long period of time. Therefore, over the long run, the two methods will produce similar results. Any controversy between the advocates of absorption costing and variable costing, in terms of income determination, is a matter of timing in the matching of fixed costs with revenues.[6]

As a logical sequel to the above, if a company follows the practice of preparing interim income statements quarterly/half-yearly to take stock of the firm's profits and if the demand for inventories and internal financial statements for its product is seasonal, profits will tend to fluctuate widely. This aspect should be recognised by management while studying income statements constructed on the principle of variable costing.

As stated earlier, the controversy between the two methods is futile. The controversy can be examined from two perspectives: external financial statements prepared for investors and internal financial statements for the use of management. The absorption costing method is adopted for the first purpose. The second purpose is best served by variable costing. This conclusion will be further reinforced by the discussion that follows which overwhelmingly demonstrates that the marginal contribution approach of variable costing is an important tool of profit planning and cost control. Thus, the choice of either method of costing is based upon a particular situation rather than on the innate superiority of one over the other.

ADVANTAGES AND LIMITATIONS OF VARIABLE COSTING

LO 15.3 Review the merits and demerits of variable costing

Advantages

We now briefly outline the advantages of variable costing:

1. In contrast to absorption costing, there is no problem of allocating and absorbing fixed overheads in variable costing as all fixed costs are considered period costs and written off against the total contribution of that period.
2. There is no complication of over-absorption of factory overheads or even their under-absorption as in the case of absorption costing. It may be recalled that the income under absorption costing is to be adjusted upwards for favourable capacity variance (over-absorption is to be adjusted upwards when the actual production exceeds the normal capacity) and downwards for unfavourable capacity variance (under-absorption of factory overheads when the actual production is less than the normal capacity). This aspect makes the income statement under absorption costing more difficult to prepare and understand than the income statement based on variable costing.
3. Management usually finds it easier to understand a variable income statement than one prepared on the basis of absorption costing. This is so because the former statements show profit responding more to changing sales levels than the combination of sales and production levels inasmuch as income statements prepared on the basis of absorption costing may show less profits with increased sales volume, though the cost and selling prices remain unchanged. Thus, the variable costing technique provides a measure of income, which is more accurate than under absorption costing. In fact, in situations of favourable capacity variance, absorption costing with no sales will show profits.

4. The impact of fixed costs on profits is emphasised because the total amount of such cost for the period appears in the income statement.
5. The process of bifurcation of costs into fixed and variable is of immense practical utility in cost control. There is a close nexus between variable costs and the controllable costs classification. This relationship assists the control function. It is imperative for effective cost control that responsibility of cost control must be with those who make cost-incurring decisions. This is possible through variable costing as it recognises the diverse behaviour of costs in relation to volume and/or time; only variable costs are charged to production, while the period costs which the management decides upon are not charged to production and so the foreman is not accountable for depreciation, insurance, property taxes, rent and such other fixed costs over which he has no control. Fixed costs for this reason are controllable only at the highest level of management. On the other hand, variable costs are incurred by all levels of management and by operators. The responsibility for variable costs can be traced with a substantial degree of certainty and, thus, allow the necessary control to be exercised. Thus, variable costing delineates responsibility clearly and assists management in the control function.

   In marked contrast, variable and fixed costs are treated alike under absorption costing, though they require different types of treatment for facilitating control. In this system, variable costs are clubbed with fixed costs, which are not controllable at the departmental level. From the above, it follows that variable costing is in alignment with responsibility accounting and, thus, facilitates management by exception.
6. Variable costs are relevant inputs for correct decision-making in many situations. Without variable costs data, management is likely to take wrong decisions affecting the profitability of the company. In recent years, there is an increasing acceptance among industries to use variable costing as a tool of profit planning.
7. Variable costing ties on with such effective plans for cost control as standard costs and flexible budgets. In fact, the flexible budget is an aspect of variable costing and many companies, thus, use variable costing methods for this purpose without recognising them as much.[7]

Limitations

The users of variable costing should, however, guard against its limitations both as regards income measurement and as a tool of profit planning:

1. Segregation of total cost into fixed and variable elements is a difficult task, particularly in the case of semi-variable costs. In such situations, resort to arbitrary classification may have to be made.
2. Variable costing carries the potential danger of encouraging a short-sighted approach to profit planning at the cost of a long-term view. There is the danger of too many sales being made at a price slightly higher than variable costs, possibly resulting in losses or very low profits. Management should not lose sight of the fact that profits will not result unless all the costs have been recovered; it should recognise that in the ultimate analysis fixed costs are also to be recovered from the selling price only. Management is likely to gather a very wrong impression of recovering only variable costs from the selling price.
3. Variable costing carries the danger of misinterpretation particularly where products require high investment outlay and the variable cost may constitute a small proportion of total cost of a product. The total contribution yield may be insufficient to warrant such an outlay. "In a manufacturing plant that is highly automated, the amount of variable cost may be small and this situation magnifies the problem of applying the technique."[8]

4. Focusing attention on the contribution margin and the possible non-recognition of fixed cost by management may be dangerous.
5. There is a difficulty in applying the technique to industries where large stocks of work-in-progress are locked up, particularly in contracting firms. If overheads were not included in the closing value of work-in-progress for each year of the contract, there would be losses, while at the end of the contract, when revenue is received, there would be a large profit. The fluctuations in profits in partly evened out by valuing work-in-progress at the total cost plus some element of profit."[9]

To sum up, it can be said that in principle there is no conflict between variable costing and absorption costing as regards accounting of costs. Both are equally important–variable costing for internal reporting and absorption costing for external users. Being so, management should recognise the importance of variable costing in profit planning (in specific situations) and cost control in general. The most useful contribution of variable costing is that it helps management in vital decision-making, particularly in dealing with problems, which require short-term decisions where fixed costs do not count.

SUMMARY

- Variable costing is a technique in which only variable costs are considered for product costing, inventory valuation and other allied management decisions. It is, thus, in marked contrast to the orthodox costing system known as full costing, absorption costing, traditional costing, conventional costing and so on.
- The material point of difference between these two techniques is that the full costing method 'absorbs' all costs necessary to produce the product and have it in a saleable form, while variable costing recognises only variable cost as production and selling cost. In operational terms, the two techniques differ in one respect: fixed manufacturing overheads are excluded from product cost under variable costing but are included as a part of product cost under absorption costing.
- Nevertheless, they are not mutually exclusive; rather they are complementary in nature. Income statements for external reporting and for income-tax purposes are to be prepared on a full costing basis. The usefulness of variable costing is that it helps management to arrive at profit-maximising decisions in certain situations. It is for this reason that variable costing is more useful for internal reporting. Thus, both techniques are important and which technique is to be employed depends upon the purpose and the circumstances.

LO 15.1

- The principle underlying variable costing is that the fixed manufacturing overheads are not inventoriable costs; they are period costs and must be matched against the revenue for the period. In contrast, absorption costing indicates that the manufacturing overheads are inventoriable costs; they are product costs and must be matched against the revenue for the year in which sales are made. The preparation of the income statement, therefore, in the case of variable costing is different from absorption costing. The concept of variable costs (separation of fixed costs from variable costs) is, however, not only useful in income measurement but is also very significant in managerial decision-making.

LO 15.2

- The core of variable costing is the contribution margin. Contribution margin is the difference between sales revenue and variable costs. It is out of the contribution that the fixed costs are met and the excess of contribution over fixed costs represents the profit. The contribution approach is useful for decision-making.

LO 15.3

REFERENCES

1. C.T. Horngren, Introduction to Management Accounting, (Prentice-Hall, Englewood Cliffs, N.J., 1978), p. 455.
2. C.L. Moore and R.K. Jaedicke, Management Accounting, (South Western Publishing Company, Ohio, 1972), p. 401.
3. J.L. Brown and L.R. Howard, Principles and Practice of Management Accounting, (English Language Book Society, London, 1969), p. 270.
4. C.L. Moore and R.K. Jaedicke, *op. cit.*, p. 406.
5. *Ibid*, p. 408.
6. D.T. Decoster and E.L. Schafer, Management Accounting–A Decision Emphasis, (John Wiley and Sons, New York, 1976), p. 200.
7. National Association of Accountants, Research Series No. 23, New York, quoted in C.L. Moore and R.K. Jaedicke, *op. cit.*, p. 410.
8. Norman Thornton, Management Accounting, (Allied Publishers, Bombay, 1979), p. 259.
9. J.L. Brown and L.R. Howard, *op. cit.*, p. 287.

SOLVED PROBLEMS

P.15.1 The Hind General Corporation Ltd produces a product, which has the following costs: LO 15.1 LOD: E
Variable manufacturing costs: ₹4 per unit
Fixed manufacturing costs: ₹2,00,000 per year
The normal capacity is set at 2,00,000 units
There are no work-in-process inventories

Last year, the company produced 2,00,000 units and sold 90 per cent at a price of ₹7 per unit. In the current year, the company produced 2,10,000 units and sold 2,15,000 units at the same price.

Prepare income statement for both the years based on (a) absorption costing, and (b) variable costing.

Solution

Income Statement for the Previous Year and Current Year (Absorption Costing) of Hind General Corporation Ltd

Particulars	*Previous year*	*Current year*
Production (units)	2,00,000	2,10,000
Sales (units)	1,80,000	2,15,000
Opening inventory (units)	—	20,000
Closing inventory (units)	20,000	15,000
Sales revenue @ ₹7 per unit	₹12,60,000	₹15,05,000
Less production costs:		
Variable manufacturing costs @ ₹4 per unit	8,00,000	8,40,000
Fixed manufacturing costs @ ₹1 per unit (₹2,00,000 ÷ 2,00,000 normal capacity in units)	2,00,000	2,10,000
Total production cost of the current year	10,00,000	10,50,000
Add cost of inventory at the beginning of the year @ ₹5 per unit	—	1,00,000
Less cost of inventory at the end of the year @ ₹5 per unit	(1,00,000)	(75,000)
Cost of goods sold	9,00,000	10,75,000
Gross margin (unadjusted)	3,60,000	4,30,000
Add favourable capacity variance in the current year (10,000 × ₹1)	—	10,000
Gross margin (adjusted)/net income	3,60,000	4,40,000

Income Statements of the Previous Year and Current Year (Variable Costing)

Particulars	*Previous year*	*Current year*
Production (units)	2,00,000	2,10,000
Sales (units)	1,80,000	2,15,000
Opening inventory (units)	—	20,000
Closing inventory (units)	20,000	15,000
Sales revenue @ ₹7 per unit	₹12,60,000	₹15,05,000
Less production costs:		
Variable manufacturing costs @ ₹4 per unit	8,00,000	8,40,000
Add cost of inventory @ ₹4 per unit	—	80,000
Less cost of inventory @ ₹4 per unit at the end of the year	(80,000)	(60,000)
Cost of goods sold	7,20,000	8,60,000
Contribution (manufacturing and final)	5,40,000	6,45,000
Less non-production costs	(2,00,000)	(2,00,000)
Net income	3,40,000	4,45,000

P.15.2 Aggarwal Industries Ltd has a standard variable manufacturing cost of ₹8 per unit produced. Fixed production costs are ₹1,10,000 per month (for standard volume of 11,000 units per month) and fixed selling and administrative expenses are ₹70,000 per month. The firm begins January with no inventories and had the following activity in January, February and March: **LO 15.1** **LOD: M**

	January	*February*	*March*
Production (units)	12,000	10,000	11,000
Sales (units)	10,000	11,000	11,000

The selling price was ₹30 per unit in each month.

You are required to prepare monthly income statements using both variable and absorption costing methods. You are also required to account for the difference, if any, in the results reported under the two methods.

Solution

Comparative Income Statements (from January to March) of Aggarwal Industries Ltd Under Absorption and Variable Costing Methods

Particulars	*January*		*February*		*March*	
	Absorption	*Variable*	*Absorption*	*Variable*	*Absorption*	*Variable*
Production (units)	12,000	12,000	10,000	10,000	11,000	11,000
Sales (units)	10,000	10,000	11,000	11,000	11,000	11,000
Sales revenue	₹3,00,000	₹3,00,000	₹3,30,000	₹3,30,000	₹3,30,000	₹3,30,000
Less production costs:						
Variable manufacturing cost @ ₹8 per unit	96,000	96,000	80,000	80,000	88,000	88,000
Fixed manufacturing overheads @ ₹10 per unit (₹1,100,000 ÷ 11,000)	1,20,000	—	1,00,000	—	1,10,000	—
Plus cost of opening inventory	—	—	36,000	16,000	18,000	8,000
Less cost of closing inventory	(36,000)	(16,000)	(18,000)	(8,000)	(18,000)	(8,000)
Cost of goods produced and sold	1,80,000	80,000	1,98,000	88,000	1,98,000	88,000
Gross margin unadjusted/ Contribution	1,20,000	2,20,000	1,32,000	2,42,000	1,32,000	2,42,000

(Contd.)

(*Contd.*)

Add capacity variance favourable (less unfavourable) @ ₹10 per unit	10,000	—	(10,000)	—	—	—
Gross margin adjusted/ Contribution	1,30,000	2,20,000	1,22,000	2,42,000	1,32,000	2,42,000
Less non-production costs:						
Fixed manufacturing costs	—	(1,10,000)	—	(1,10,000)	—	(1,10,000)
Fixed selling and administrative expenses	(70,000)	(70,000)	(70,000)	(70,000)	(70,000)	(70,000)
Net income	60,000	40,000	52,000	62,000	62,000	62,000

Reconciliation Statement of Income (January - March)

Particulars	Net income January	February	March
Absorption costing	₹60,000	₹52,000	₹62,000
Variable costing	40,000	62,000	62,000
Difference to be explained: increase (decrease) in profits of absorption costing *vis-à-vis* variable costing	20,000	(10,000)	—
(a) Inventory units			
Opening inventory	—	2,000	1,000
Closing inventory	2,000	1,000	1,000
Increase (decrease) in inventory	2,000	(1,000)	—
(b) Standard fixed overhead rate per unit (₹)	10	10	—
(c) Change in net income [(a) × (b)]	20,000	(10,000)	—

P.15.3 S.K. Industries Ltd produced and sold 1,50,000 plastics buckets. Each bucket was sold at a price of ₹20. The variable costs were ₹14 per bucket and fixed manufacturing costs were ₹3,00,000 per annum. The company's normal production capacity is 1,50,000 plastic buckets. **LO 15.1** **LOD: M**

1. You are required to prepare income statements under absorption costing and variable costing methods and comment on the results.
2. What would be the effect on income under the two different costing methods in the following situations: **(a)** Buckets produced and sold, 1,40,000 and **(b)** Buckets produced and sold, 1,60,000.

Solution

Income Statement (Absorption and Variable Costing Methods)

Particulars	Absorption costing	Variable costing
Production and sales (units)	1,50,000	1,50,000
Sales revenue	₹30,00,000	₹30,00,000
Less production costs:		
Variable costs @ ₹14 per unit	21,00,000	21,00,000
Fixed overheads @ ₹2 per unit (₹3,00,000 ÷ 1,50,000 normal capacity)	3,00,000	—
Total cost of production/cost of goods sold	24,00,000	21,00,000
Income/Contribution	6,00,000	9,00,000
Less non-production costs:		
Fixed manufacturing costs	—	3,00,000
Income	6,00,000	6,00,000

Incomes are the same under both the costing methods, for production is equivalent to sales (1,50,000 units). Differences in net income arise only when production varies from sales.

Income Statements under Variable and Absorption Costing Systems, Assuming Production and Sales: **(a)** 1,40,000 units, **(b)** 1,60,000 units:

Particulars	*(a) 1,40,000 units*		*(b) 1,60,000 units*	
	Absorption	*Variable*	*Absorption*	*Variable*
Sales revenue @ ₹20 per unit	₹28,00,000	₹28,00,000	₹32,00,000	₹32,00,000
Less production costs:				
Variable costs @ ₹14 per unit	19,60,000	19,60,000	22,40,000	22,40,000
Fixed overheads @ ₹2 per unit	2,80,000	—	3,20,000	—
Cost of goods produced and sold	22,40,000	19,60,000	25,60,000	22,40,000
Gross margin (adjusted)/Contribution	5,60,000	8,40,000	6,40,000	9,60,000
Less capacity variance: Unfavourable and add capacity variance favourable @ ₹2 per unit (10,000 units)	(20,000)	—	20,000	—
Gross margin (adjusted)/Contribution	5,40,000	8,40,000	6,60,000	9,60,000
Less non-production costs:				
Fixed manufacturing costs	—	3,00,000	—	3,00,000
Net income	5,40,000	5,40,000	6,60,000	6,60,000

Net incomes again are the same under both costing systems, as production is equal to sales in both situations. The fact whether production is equal to normal capacity or not, does not have any impact whatsoever on the net income. Here, production of 1,40,000 units as well as 1,60,000 units is different from 1,50,000, the normal level of production.

P.15.4 The Seers Can Company Ltd has two plants, one in Mumbai, and the other in Kolkata. The physical characteristics of the plants are similar and the results of the operations of both plants are compared each month in order to judge the performance of the two managements. The April income statements of the two plants were as follows: **LO 15.1** **LOD: D**

Particulars	*Mumbai plant*	*Kolkata plant*
Sales	₹18,00,000	₹18,00,000
Less: Manufacturing cost of sales	12,60,000	13,60,000
Selling and administrative expenses	4,40,000	4,40,000
Net income	1,00,000	—

Each plant sells its product for the same price. During the month of April, each plant sold and shipped 3,00,000 cans. The production for the month at the two plants was as follows:

Particulars	*Mumbai plant*	*Kolkata plant*
Opening stock (number of cans)	1,00,000	1,00,000
Production during the month	4,00,00,000	3,00,00,000
	4,01,00,000	3,01,00,000
Cans shipped during the month	3,00,00,000	3,00,00,000
Closing stock	1,01,00,000	1,00,000

The Mumbai plant built up its stock in April in anticipation of the canning season, which begins in May on the West Coast. The East Coast canning season begins in the middle of June.

The standard cost sheet for the type of can sold in April discloses the following information for both plants:

	Cost per 1,000 cans
Direct material	₹25
Direct labour	5
Variable overheads	2
Fixed overheads	10
	42

For each plant, the manufacturing fixed costs budgeted for the month were ₹4,00,000. There were no spending or efficiency variances. All selling and administrative expenses were of a fixed nature.

Prepare revised income statements for the two plants, using variable costing. Explain the difference in income between the two plants.

Solution

Income Statement (Variable Costing) for the Month Ending April

Particulars	*Mumbai plant*	*Kolkata plant*
Production (cans)	4,00,00,000	3,00,00,000
Sales (cans)	3,00,00,000	3,00,00,000
Sales revenue	₹18,00,000	₹18,00,000
Less: production costs:		
Direct material	10,00,000	7,50,000
Direct labour	2,00,000	1,50,000
Variable overheads	80,000	60,000
Total cost of production	12,80,000	9,60,000
Add cost of opening inventory(at standard cost)	3,200	3,200
Less closing inventory (at standard cost)	(3,23,200)	(3,200)
Cost of cans produced and sold	9,60,000	9,60,000
Contribution	8,40,000	8,40,000
Less: non-production costs:		
Fixed overheads	4,00,000	4,00,000
Selling and administrative expenses	4,40,000	4,40,000
Net income	Nil	Nil

Difference in income statements of the two plants on the basis of variable costing is nil. There would be a difference when a comparison is made of income statements for the Bombay plant on the basis of variable costing and absorption costing. The following reconciliation statement will explain the difference.

Reconciliation Statement of Income for Mumbai Plant for the Month of April

Net income:	
Absorption costing	₹1,00,000
Variable costing	Nil
Difference to be explained:	1,00,000
(a) Standard fixed overhead rate ₹10 (per 1,000 cans)	
(b) Change in inventory units:	
Opening inventory	1,00,000
Closing inventory	1,01,00,000
Change in inventory (increase)	1,00,00,000
(c) Difference in net income [(a) × (b)]	1,00,000

The Bombay plant produced 4,00,00,000 cans and, therefore, could absorb the entire amount of fixed overheads of ₹4,00,000 @ ₹10 per 1,000 cans. The Calcutta plant operated at below its normal capacity, as only 3,00,00,000 cans were produced.

There is a capacity variance unfavourable to the extent of ₹1,00,000 (fixed overheads were under-absorbed by ₹1,00,000). This also explains the difference in the net income between the two plants even on an absorption costing basis.

P.15.5 For several months the top management of a company has been puzzled by fluctuations in the income as reported by the accountant. The results for February, March and April as reported are as follows: LO 15.1 LOD: M

Particulars	February	March	April
Sales	₹18,00,000	₹18,00,000	₹9,00,000
Less: Manufacturing cost of sales	16,60,000	13,60,000	4,30,000
Selling and administrative expenses	4,40,000	4,40,000	4,40,000
Total	21,00,000	18,00,000	8,70,000
Net income (loss)	(3,00,000)	—	30,000

There has been no change in sales price during the three month period. During the months of February and March, the plant sold 3,00,00,000 units. In April, it sold 1,50,00,000 units.

The production for the three months was as follows:

Particulars	February	March	April
Opening inventory (units)	3,01,00,000	1,00,000	1,00,000
Production during the month	—	3,00,00,000	6,00,00,000
	3,01,00,000	3,01,00,000	6,01,00,000
Units sold	3,00,00,000	3,00,00,000	1,50,00,000
Closing inventory	1,00,000	1,00,000	4,51,00,000

The standard cost for the type of the units sold discloses the following information:

	Cost per 1,000 units
Direct material and labour	30
Overheads: Variable	2
Fixed	10
	42

The fixed manufacturing costs budgeted for each of the months were ₹4,00,000. There were no spending or efficiency variances during the three months. All selling and administrative expenses were of a fixed nature.

You are required to prepare comparative income statements for the three months, using variable costing.

Solution

Income Statement for February, March and April (Variable Costing)

Particulars	February	March	April
Production (units)	Nil	3,00,00,000	6,00,00,000
Sales (units)	3,00,00,000	3,00,00,000	1,50,00,000
Sales revenue	₹18,00,000	₹18,00,000	₹9,00,000
Less: production costs:			
Standard variable cost (@) ₹32 per 1,000) Nil	9,60,000	19,20,000	
Add: opening inventory	9,63,200	3,200	3,200
Less: opening inventory	(3,200)	(3,200)	(14,43,200)
Cost of goods produced and sold	9,60,000	9,60,000	4,80,000
Contribution (manufacturing)	8,40,000	8,40,000	4,20,000
Less: non-production costs:			
Fixed overheads	4,00,000	4,00,000	4,00,000
Selling and administrative expenditure	4,40,000	4,40,000	4,40,000
Net income (loss)	Nil	Nil	(4,20,000)

P.15.6 As the chief financial analyst of a company, you have been asked by the chief executive to explain the differences between two income statements prepared for his consideration: one was prepared by the controller and the other by the sales manager. Both used the same data from operations. LO 15.1,2 LOD: D

Particulars	Statement A	Statement B
Sales (30,000 units)	₹30,00,000	₹30,00,000
Cost of goods sold:		
Opening inventory	—	—
Production costs	18,00,000	27,00,000
Less: closing inventory	(6,00,000)	(9,00,000)
Total	12,00,000	18,00,000
Gross profit	18,00,000	12,00,000
Less: other costs	(15,00,000)	(6,00,000)
Income	3,00,000	6,00,000

The only variable costs of production are ₹40 per unit.

(i) Determine which statement was prepared using variable costing and which using absorption costing. Explain how do you know it?

(ii) Determine: **(a)** fixed production costs; **(b)** selling and administrative costs; **(c)** production in units; and (d) cost per unit of inventory for both statements.

Solution

1. Statement A was prepared using variable costing and statement B using absorption costing. This can be determined in several ways: **(a)** Production costs are less in statement A because fixed costs are excluded, **(b)** Similarly, value of inventory is less in statement A because inventory is valued only at variable cost and fixed costs are excluded, **(c)** Other costs (non-production costs) are higher in statement A because of inclusion of fixed costs which are charged against the income of the same year.

2. (a) *Determination of fixed production costs:*

Production cost (absorption costing)	₹27,00,000
Production cost (variable costing)	18,00,000
Difference represents fixed production costs	9,00,000

(b) *Determination of selling and administrative costs*

Other costs	15,00,000
Less fixed production costs	9,00,000
Selling and administrative costs	6,00,000

(c) *Production (in units) Statement A*

1. Cost of goods sold (30,000 units)	₹12,00,000
2. Variable cost per unit (₹12,00,000 ÷ 30,000)	40
3. Total production cost (variable)	18,00,000
4. Production in units (₹18,00,000 ÷ ₹40)	45,000

(d) *Cost Per Unit of Inventory*

Particulars	Variable costing basis	Absorption costing basis
1. Closing inventory	₹6,00,000	₹9,00,000
2. Closing inventory (units) (45,000 — 30,000)	15,000	15,000
3. Cost per unit (1) ÷ (2)	40	60

P.15.7 Following is the income statement of Jain Tubes Company Ltd prepared on the basis of absorption costing: LO 15.1,2 LOD: M

Sales		₹4,70,000
Cost of goods sold:		
Opening inventory (variable costs, ₹42,000)	₹70,000	
Current production cost	2,56,000	
Less: closing inventory (variable costs, ₹31,200)	3,26,000	
	(52,000)	2,74,000
Gross margin (manufacturing) (unadjusted)		1,96,000
Less capacity variance (unfavourable)		32,000
Gross margin (adjusted)		1,64,000
Less: selling and distribution cost		20,000
Administrative cost		22,000
Net income before taxes		1,22,000

Additional Information

(a) The fixed manufacturing overheads are absorbed at a standard rate per unit of product.
(b) Total fixed cost of the current year (budgeted as well as actual) is ₹1,34,400.
(c) All units in inventory at the end of the year were manufactured during the year.
(d) Prepare an income statement on variable costing basis.

Solution

Income Statement (Variable Costing Basis)

Particulars	*Amount*
Sales revenue	₹4,70,000
Less cost of goods sold:	
Variable manufacturing cost (current production) (Working note)	1,53,600
Add cost of opening inventory	42,000
Less cost of closing inventory	(31,200)
Total	1,64,400
Contribution (manufacturing and final)	3,05,600
Less non-production costs:	
Fixed manufacturing costs	(1,34,400)
Selling and distribution costs	(20,000)
Administrative costs	(22,000)
Net income before taxes	1,29,200

Working Notes

Current production costs (absorption costing)		₹2,56,000
Less fixed overheads absorbed:		
Total fixed overheads	₹1,34,400	
Less unfavourable capacity variance (representing un-absorbed fixed overheads)	32,000	(1,02,400)
Current production costs (variable)		1,53,600

P.15.8 Mr Mukesh, The Chief Accountant of the Standard Glass Manufacturing Company Ltd has prepared the following income statement on traditional costing basis for three quarters of the current year. LO 15.1,2 LOD: M

Particulars	Quarter 1	Quarter 2	Quarter 3
Sales revenue	₹5,25,000	₹4,50,000	₹5,25,000
Less total current cost of manufacturing goods	4,55,000	5,20,000	3,90,000
Add cost of opening inventory	Nil	Nil	1,30,000
Less cost of closing inventory	Nil	(1,30,000)	(65,000)
Cost of goods produced and sold	4,55,000	3,90,000	4,55,000
Gross margin (unadjusted)	70,000	60,000	70,000
Less capacity variance	15,000	Nil	30,000
Gross margin (adjusted)	55,000	60,000	40,000
Selling and administrative expenses	20,000	20,000	20,000
Net income before taxes	35,000	40,000	20,000
Less income taxes (0.35)	12,250	14,000	7,000
Net income after taxes	22,750	26,000	10,000

(a) *Additional information:*

Units produced	35,000	40,000	30,000
Units sold	35,000	30,000	35,000

(b) Standard fixed manufacturing overhead rate is ₹3 per unit.

The management of the company is surprised at the results of the second quarter. It believes there must be some mistake in the income statement.

You are required to explain the income differences to the management by revising the statements on variable costing basis.

Solution

Income Statements for Three Quarters of Current Year on Variable Costing Basis

Particulars	Quarter 1	Quarter 2	Quarter 3
Units produced	35,000	40,000	30,000
Units sold	35,000	30,000	35,000
Opening inventory (units)	—	—	10,000
Closing inventory (units)		10,000	5,000
Sales revenue	₹5,25,000	₹4,50,000	₹5,25,000
Less: manufacturing variable costs of goods sold (see working note)	3,50,000	4,00,000	3,00,000
Add cost of opening inventory @ ₹10 per unit	—	—	1,00,000
Less cost of closing inventory	—	(1,00,000)	(50,000)
Cost of goods sold	3,50,000	3,00,000	3,50,000
Contribution (final)	1,75,000	1,50,000	1,75,000
Less non-production costs:			
Fixed manufacturing overheads	(1,20,000)	(1,20,000)	(1,20,000)
Fixed selling overheads	(20,000)	(20,000)	(20,000)
Net income before income taxes	35,000	10,000	35,000
Less income taxes (0.35)	(12,250)	(3,500)	(12,250)
Net income after taxes	22,750	6,500	22,750

WORKING NOTES

1. Determination of variable costs:

Total cost of goods manufactured (including fixed overheads)	4,55,000	5,20,000	3,90,000
Less fixed overheads @ ₹3 per unit	(1,05,000)	(1,20,000)	(90,000)
Variable costs	3,50,000	4,00,000	3,00,000

2. Fixed manufacturing overhead (Fixed costs absorbed + Capacity variance)= ₹1,05,000 + ₹15,000
= ₹1,20,000.

P.15.9 The Chief Executive of PS Ltd, is puzzled by the income statements of the two most recent months–April and May, because sales increased in May and yet profits declined. He asks you to explain the results: **LO 15.1** **LOD: M**

Income Statement

Particulars	*April*	*May*
Sales (₹20 per unit)	₹2,00,000	₹2,50,000
Standard cost of sales	1,20,000	1,50,000
Standard gross profit	80,000	1,00,000
Capacity variance favourable (unfavourable)	8,000	(16,000)
Selling and administrative expenses	20,000	20,000
Income	68,000	64,000

The standard fixed cost per unit is ₹8, based on normal production capacity of 12,000 units per month. You are required to

1. Determine production in each month.
2. Explain the results to the chief executive.
3. Prepare income statements based on variable costing.

Solution

1. *Determination of Volume of Production:*

Particulars	*April*	*May*
(a) Capacity variance representing actual production Production is more (less) than normal production	₹8,000	₹(16,000)
(b) Standard fixed cost per unit	8	8
(c) Production more (less) than normal [(a) ÷ (b)]	1,000	(2,000)
(d) Normal production	12,000	12,000
(e) Actual production [(d) ± (c)]	13,000	10,000

2. Explanation: The Chief Executive should be advised that the income statements have been prepared on the basis of absorption costing in which the size of profit is influenced, inter-alia, by the level of production. Since production was more in April, so were the profits. The true picture will emerge only when income statements are prepared on a variable costing basis.
3. Income Statement Based on Variable Costing

Particulars	*April*	*May*
Production (units)	13,000	10,000
Sales (units) [sales revenue ÷ ₹20]	10,000	12,500
Opening inventory (units)	—	3,000
Closing inventory (units)	3,000	500
Sales revenue	₹2,00,000	₹2,50,000
Less cost of goods sold:		
Variable manufacturing cost @ ₹4 per unit	52,000	40,000
Plus cost of opening inventory @ ₹4 per unit		12,000
Less cost of closing inventory	(12,000)	(2,000)
Total cost of goods sold	40,000	50,000
Contribution (final)	1,60,000	2,00,000
Less non-production costs:		
Fixed overheads (12,000 × ₹8)	(96,000)	(96,000)
Selling and administrative expenses	(20,000)	(20,000)
Profit	44,000	84,000

WORKING NOTE

Determination of variable costs	*April*	*May*
Total standard cost of sales	₹1,20,000	₹1,50,000
Less fixed overheads @ ₹8 per unit:		
April (10,000 × ₹8)	(80,000)	
May (12,500 × ₹8)	(1,00,000)	
Variable costs (balancing figure)	40,000	50,000

P.15.10 Aggarwal Industries Ltd has taken a loan from a large bank. Among the provisions of the loan agreement are that: **(a)** the current ratio must be at least 300 per cent and that **(b)** the ratio of total debt to shareholders' equity must not be higher than 75 per cent. The balance sheet of the firm for the current year is as follows: LO 15.1,2 LOD: D

Liabilities	*Amount*	*Assets*	*Amount*
Equity capital	₹15,20,000	Inventory (40,000 units at variable cost)	₹4,00,000
12 % Long term bank loan	6,00,000	Cash and debtors	9,20,000
Current liabilities	4,00,000	Fixed assets (net)	12,00,000
	25,20,000		25,20,000

The budgeted income statement for next year is as follows:

Sales (1,00,000 units)		₹20,00,000
Less variable production costs		10,00,000
Contribution (manufacturing)		10,00,000
Less other variable costs (variable with sales)		1,00,000
Contribution (final)		9,00,000
Less fixed costs		
Manufacturing	₹6,00,000	
Other costs	1,00,000	7,00,000
Profit		2,00,000

Budgeted production is 1,00,000 units. The chief accountant of the firm anticipates substantial expenditure for fixed assets and intends to obtain a new loan to help finance these expenditures. For the purpose, he is negotiating with a bank. To complete the requisite papers, he projects the following proforma balance sheet for March, next year:

Liabilities	*Amount*	*Assets*	*Amount*
Equity capital	₹15,20,000	Inventory and receivables	₹8,00,000
Profit and loss A/c	2,00,000	Inventory (40,000 units at variable cost)	4,00,000
12% Long-term bank loan	9,20,000		
Current liabilities	4,80,000	Fixed assets (net)	19,20,000
	31,20,000		31,20,000

He sees that the firm will be in default on both provisions of the loan agreement. To resolve the problem, he lists the following points:

1. To work at normal capacity of 1,50,000 units.
2. The firm could perhaps benefit if absorption costing were used.

You are required to do the following:

(a) Recast the income statement and balance sheet using absorption costing, taking the normal capacity of 1,50,000 units as the basis for absorption of fixed manufacturing overheads.

(b) Assume that all increased production costs are paid in cash. Is the firm safe within limits of the loan agreement?

(c) Is the firm better off using absorption costing?

Solution

(1) *Budgeted Income Statement for the Next Year (Absorption Costing Basis)*

Particulars	Amount
Sales (1,00,000 units)	₹20,00,000
Less production costs	
Variable cost of current production @ ₹10 per unit	15,00,000
Fixed overheads @ ₹4 per unit (₹6,00,000 ÷ 1,50,000)	6,00,000
Total current production cost	21,00,000
Add opening inventory @ ₹10 per unit	4,00,000
Less closing inventory @ ₹14 per unit	(12,60,000)
Cost of goods sold	12,40,000
Gross margin	7,60,000
Less non-production costs:	
Variable (with sales)	1,00,000
Fixed	1,00,000
Net income	5,60,000

Proforma Balance Sheet

Liabilities	Amount	Assets		Amount
Equity capital	₹15,20,000	Inventory (90,000 units @ ₹14 per unit)		₹12,60,000
Profit and loss A/c	5,60,000	Cash and receivables	₹8,00,000	
12% Long term bank loan	9,20,000	*Less* added variable cost of 50,000 units at ₹10 per unit	5,00,000	3,00,000
Current liabilities	4,80,000	Total current assets		15,60,000
		Fixed assets (net)		19,20,000
	34,80,000			34,80,000

2. Current ratio (₹15,60,000 ÷ ₹4,80,000) × 100 = 325 per cent; Debt-equity ratio (₹14,00,000 ÷ ₹20,80,000) × 100 = 67.3 per cent. Yes, the firm is within safe limits of the loan agreement.
3. The use of absorption costing enables the firm to get the loan and, therefore, is very useful. However, the firm's situation is not good economically. Cash is reduced by ₹5,00,000, which may have an adverse impact on its ability to meet its current liabilities as reflected in the acid-test ratio (62.5 per cent as against the standard form of 100 per cent). The firm is required to carry a large volume of inventory (90,000 units, 90 per cent of the budgeted sales) adding to the expenses of the firm as carrying of inventory involves cost.

REVIEW QUESTIONS

LOD: Easy

RQ.15.1 Indicate whether the following statements are 'true' or 'false'. **LO 15.1,2**

(i) Variable costing and absorption costing techniques are similar to job and process costing.

(ii) Direct materials, direct labour and variable overheads constitute the only relevant cost in variable costing.

(iii) While variable costing is useful for tax purposes, absorption costing is useful for internal reporting purposes.

(iv) Fixed manufacturing costs are considered product costs in absorption costing.
(v) Fixed manufacturing costs are period costs in the context of variable costing.
(vi) Like fixed manufacturing costs, selling and administrative costs are also treated differently in variable costing compared to absorption costing.
(vii) Fixed manufacturing costs form part of closing inventory both in variable costing and full costing methods.
(viii) Variable costing focuses on sales whereas the emphasis of full costing is on production.
(ix) Both variable costing and full costing methods provide the same results in terms of profit or loss when production (in units) is equal to sales (in units).
(x) Capacity variance concept is applicable in variable costing as well as in absorption costing.

[Answer: (i) False, (ii) True, (iii) False, (iv) True, (v) True, (vi) False, (vii) False, (viii) True, (ix) True, (x) False.]

RQ.15.2 If a company sells more units than it produces, would the profits reported by absorption costing tend to be higher or lower than the profits reported by variable costing? Why? **LO 15.1**

RQ.15.3 Standard unit costs are given for the production of a spray attachment manufactured by Carson Products Company Ltd: **LO 15.1**

Direct materials	₹16
Direct labour	15
Variable manufacturing overheads	12
Fixed manufacturing overheads	30

At normal operating capacity, 2,00,000 units of product should be manufactured. Variable selling and administrative expenses amount to ₹5 per unit, and the fixed selling and administrative expenses amount to ₹7,50,000 a year. Income taxes are estimated at 40 per cent of net income before taxes.

Production and sales data are as follows:

Inventory on hand, April 1, year 1	28,000
Number of units produced in year 1	2,00,000
Number of units sold in year 1	1,60,000
Number of units produced in year 2	1,50,000
Number of units sold in year 2	1,80,000

In both years, each spray attachment was sold for ₹105. Prepare income statements for the two years by the absorption costing method. Also, prepare income statement for the two years by the variable costing method.

LOD: Medium

RQ.15.4 Distinguish between variable costing and absorption costing. Also, examine their relative appropriateness. **LO 15.1,3**

RQ.15.5 "Direct costing produces income statements that are a more accurate reflection of the true profit fluctuations than the income statements produced by absorption costing." State briefly why you either agree or disagree with this statement. **LO 15.1**

RQ.15.6 "It is said that an income statement prepared by the variable costing procedure is more helpful to management than an income statement prepared by the absorption cost method." Do you agree? Discuss with the help of a suitable illustration. **LO 15.1,3**

RQ.15.7 The following data relate to Strong Company Limited for three years: **LO 15.1,2**

	Year 1	Year 2	Year 3
Units produced	1,00,000	80,000	70,000
Units sold	60,000	90,000	1,00,000
Unit selling price	₹5	₹5	₹5
Unit variable manufacturing cost	2	2	2
Unit variable selling and administrative cost	0.50	0.50	0.50
Total fixed manufacturing cost		₹1,00,000	
Total fixed selling and administrative expenses		50,000	
Normal capacity (units)		1,00,000	
Inventory at the beginning of year 1		Nil	

You are required to prepare income statements for three years individually and collectively under absorption costing and variable costing methods, assuming that actual costs are in conformity with budgeted costs. You are also required to account for difference, if any, in the result report under the two methods.

LOD: Difficult

RQ.15.8 What advantages are gained by separating fixed expenses from variable expenses? **LO 15.1,2** It has been said that the statement "fluctuating overheads are those which vary with output" is an unjustifiable simplification. How would you qualify the statement? How would your qualification affect your treatment of fluctuating overheads when compiling costs?

RQ.15.9 The manager of Royal Industries Ltd. is confused by the income statement he has **LO 15.1,2** received from his accountant. He is particularly concerned that his return on sales declined much more than sales in February as compared to January.

Income Statement

Particulars	*January*	*February*
Sales revenue	₹4,50,000	₹3,75,000
Cost of sales	1,80,000	1,50,000
Gross profit	2,70,000	2,25,000
Operating expenses:		
Rent	6,000	6,000
Salaries, wages, commissions	1,57,500	1,42,500
Property insurance, taxes, etc.	4,500	4,500
Supplies	9,000	7,500
Miscellaneous	29,500	29,500
Total	2,06,500	1,90,000
Operating profit	63,500	35,000
Return on sales (per cent)	14.11	9.33

The manager informs you that in salaries, wages, and commissions, the accountant included the salaries of several clerks and himself. All salesmen work on commissions @ 20 per cent of sales. Expenses on account of supplies vary directly with sales. For various reasons, sales in February were expected to decline by ₹75,000. But he had expected income of ₹52,912.50 on sales of ₹3,75,000 @ 14.11 per cent.

You are required to explain the income differences to the manager by using contribution based income statement.

ANSWERS

RQ15.3 Absorption costing profit: ₹21,42,000 (year 1), ₹15,66,000 (year 2); Variable costing profit: ₹14,22,000 (year 1), ₹21,06,000 (year 2).

RQ15.7 Absorption costing profit: ₹40,000 (year 1), ₹65,600 (year 2). ₹70,000 (year 3), ₹1,75,000 (years 1-3); Variable costing profit: Zero (year 1), ₹75,000 (year 2), ₹1,00,000 (years 3), ₹1,75,000 (years 1-3).

RQ15.9 Profit: ₹63,500, January; ₹35,000, February.

[Comprehensive solutions to all numerical review questions are available on the companion website: http://www.mhhe.com/khan_jain_ma7e]

PART 5

PROFIT PLANNING

Cost data are an important input in internal managerial planning. The most widely-used profit planning techniques are illustrated in this part. The volume-cost-profit analysis, as a tool of profit planning, is covered in Chapter 16. Budgeting, as a systematic approach to planning, is elaborated in Chapter 17.

16 Volume-Cost-Profit Analysis

LEARNING OBJECTIVES

After reading this chapter you will be able to:

LO 16.1 Explain break-even point as well as algebraic and graphical methods through which it is determined

LO 16.2 Discuss break-even analysis applications in profit planning

LO 16.3 Understand cash break-even point and its applications

INTRODUCTION

Profit planning is a function of the selling price of a unit of product, the variable cost of making and selling the product, the volume of product units sold, and, in the case of multi-product companies, sales-mix and, finally, the total fixed costs. The **volume-cost-profit (VCP) analysis** is a management accounting tool to show the relationship between these ingredients of profit planning. The entire gamut of profit planning is associated with VCP inter-relationships. A widely-used technique to study VCP relationships is break-even analysis.

Volume-cost-profit analysis shows the relationship among the various ingredients of profit planning, namely, unit sale price, variable cost, sales volume, sales mix and fixed cost.

A break-even analysis is concerned with the study of revenues and costs in relation to sales volume and, particularly, the determination of that volume of sales at which the firm's revenues and total costs will be exactly equal (or net income = zero). Thus, the break-even point (**BEP**) may be defined as a point at which the firm's total revenues are exactly equal to total costs, yielding zero income. The "no-profit, no-loss" point is a break-even point or a point at which losses cease and profits begin.

Break-even analysis, as a technique, seeks to provide answers to the following questions:

1. What sales volume is necessary to produce an X amount of operating profit?

2. What will the operating profit or loss at X sales volume be?

3. What profit will result from an X per cent increase in sales volume?

4. What is the additional sales volume required to make good an *X* per cent reduction in selling prices so as to maintain the current profit level?
5. What will the effect on operating profit be if the company's fixed costs have increased?
6. What will the effect on income be if the firm achieves a reduction in variable costs (say, material or direct labour)?
7. What is the required sales volume to cover the additional fixed charges from the proposed new project?
8. What will the effect on operating profit of the firm be if the sales mix is changed?
9. What will the effect on income be if there is an increase in fixed costs by an *X* amount due to new plant but will decrease the labour costs by *Y* amount per unit?
10. What sales volume is needed to achieve the budgeted profit?

BREAK-EVEN ANALYSIS

LO 16.1 Explain break-even point as well as algebraic and graphical methods through which it is determined

A break-even analysis shows the relationship between the costs and profits with sales volume. The sales volume which equates total revenue with related costs and results in neither profit nor loss is called the **break-even volume or point (BEP)**. If all costs are assumed to be variable with sales volume, the BEP would be at zero sales. If all costs were fixed, profits would vary disproportionately with sales and the BEP would be at a point where total sales revenue equalled fixed costs. However, both are purely hypothetical situations. In actual practice, costs consist of both fixed and variable elements.

The BEP can be determined by two methods:

1. Algebraic methods: **(a)** Contribution margin approach and **(b)** Equation technique, and
2. Graphic presentation: **(a)** Break-even chart and **(b)** Profit volume graph.

Algebraic Methods

Contribution margin is the excess of unit sale price over unit variable cost.

Contribution Margin Approach The logic underlying the determination of the BEP under this approach can be stated by answering the following question: "How many ice-creams, having a unit cost of ₹20 and a selling price of ₹30, must a vendor sell in a fair to recover the ₹8,000 fees paid by him for getting a selling stall and additional cost of ₹4,000 to install the stall?" The answer can be determined dividing the fixed cost by the difference between the selling price (₹30) and cost price (₹20). Thus,

$$\text{BEP (units)} = \frac{\text{Fixed cost (Entry fees + Stall expenses)}}{\text{(Sales price – Unit variable cost)}} \quad \textbf{(16.1)}$$

(₹8,000 + ₹4,000)/(₹30 – ₹20) = 1,200 units

Or,

$$\text{BEP (units)} = \frac{\text{Fixed costs}}{\text{Contribution margin } (CM) \text{ per unit}} \quad \textbf{(16.2)}$$

Or,

BEP (amount)/BEP (Sales revenue)/*BESR* = BEP (units) × Selling price (*SP*) per unit

= 1,200 × ₹30 = ₹36,000 **(16.3)**

Or,

$$\text{BEP (amount)} = \frac{\text{Fixed costs}}{\text{Profit volume ratio (P/V ratio)}} \tag{16.4}$$

$$\text{P/V ratio}^{1} = \frac{\text{Contribution margin per unit}}{\text{Selling price per unit}} \tag{16.5}$$

$$\frac{₹1}{₹3} = \text{or } 33.33 \text{ per cent}$$

$$\text{BEP (amount)} = ₹12{,}000 \div 0.3333 = ₹36{,}000$$

From the P/V ratio, the variable cost to volume ratio (*V/V* ratio) can be easily derived:

$$V/V \text{ ratio} = 1 - \text{P/V ratio} \tag{16.6}$$

In the vendor's case, it is = 1–1/3 = 2/3 = 66.67 per cent

The *V/V* ratio, as the name suggests, establishes the relationship between variable costs (VC) and sales volume in amount. The direct method of its computation is:

$$\frac{\text{Variable cost}}{\text{Sales revenue}} = ₹20 \div ₹30 = 66.67 \text{ per cent} \tag{16.7}$$

Thus, P/V ratio + *V/V* ratio = 1 or 100 per cent

$$(1/3 + 2/3) = 1 \text{ (33.33 per cent + 66.67 per cent)} = 100 \text{ per cent} \tag{16.8}$$

Margin of Safety The excess of the actual sales revenue (ASR) over the break-even sales revenue (*BESR*) is known as the **margin of safety**. Symbolically, margin of safety = (ASR – BESR) **(16.9)**

Margin of safety is the excess of actual sales revenue over the break-even sales revenue.

When the margin of safety (amount) is divided by the actual sales (amount), the margin of safety ratio (*M/S* ratio) is obtained. Symbolically,

$$M/S \text{ ratio} = \frac{\text{(ASR – BESR)}}{\text{ASR}} \tag{16.10}$$

The *M/S* ratio indicates the percentage by which the actual sales may be reduced before they fall below the break-even sales volume. It is important that there should be a reasonable margin of safety, lest a reduced level of activity should prove disastrous. The higher the margin of safety ratio, the better it is from the point of view of the company as it indicates that a "sizeable" sales volume can fall before the BEP is reached. This measure acquires special significance in depression/recession.

Assume in the vendor's case that sales is 2,000 units (₹60,000); margin of safety (₹60,000 – ₹36,000) = ₹24,000; and the *M/S* ratio is ₹24,000 ÷ ₹60,000 = 40 per cent.

The amount of profit can be directly determined with reference to the margin of safety and P/V ratio. Symbolically,

$$\text{Profit} = [\text{Margin of safety (amount)}] \times \text{P/V ratio} \tag{16.11}$$

$$\text{Or Profit} = [\text{Margin of safety (units)} \times CM \text{ per unit}] \tag{16.12}$$

In the vendor's case, profit = ₹24,000 × 0.3333 (33.33 per cent) = ₹8,000 or 800 × ₹10 = ₹8,000.

[1]A better term would be contribution to revenue ratio (*C/V*) as the numerator is the contribution margin (difference between the selling price and variable costs) and not profit. The *P/V* ratio in a strict sense of the term represents the relationship between profit and selling price only after the BEP, that is, when fixed costs have been recovered. Therefore, the *C/V* ratio is more appropriate term. In the text, both the terms have been used.

The reason is that once the total amount of fixed costs has been recovered, profits will increase by the difference of sales revenue and variable costs.

Equation Technique This is the most general form of analysis, which can be applied to any cost-volume-profit situation. It is based on an income equation: Sales revenue-Total costs = Net profit

Breaking up total costs into fixed and variable, Sales revenue – Fixed costs – Variable costs = Net profit. Or Sales revenue = Fixed costs + Variable costs + Net profit.

If *S* be the number of units required for break-even and sales revenue (*SP*) and variable costs (VC) are on per unit basis, the above equation can be written as follows:

$$SP\,(S) = \text{FC} + \text{VC}\,(S) + NI \qquad \textbf{(16.13)}$$

Where SP = Selling price per unit

S = Number of units required to be sold to break-even

FC = Total fixed costs

VC = Variable costs per unit

NI = Net income (zero)

$$SP\,(S) = \text{FC} + \text{VC}\,(S) + \text{zero}$$

$$SP\,(S) - \text{VC}\,(S) = \text{FC}$$

or

$$S\,(SP - \text{VC}) = \text{FC}$$

$$S = \frac{\text{FC}}{SP - \text{VC}} \qquad \textbf{(16.14)}$$

It can be seen that Eq. 16.14 is identical to Eq. 16.2 (contribution margin approach). Yet, it is *specially useful in situations in which unit price and unit variable costs are not clearly identifiable.*

◆ Example 16.1

SV Ltd, a multi-product company, furnishes you the following data relating to the current year:

Particulars	First half of the year	Second half of the year
Sales	₹45,000	₹50,000
Total costs	40,000	43,000

Assuming that there is no change in prices and variable costs and that the fixed expenses are incurred equally in the two half-year periods, calculate for the year: (i) The profit-volume ratio, (ii) Fixed expenses, (iii) Break-even sales, and (iv) Percentage margin of safety.

Solution

Sales revenue – Total costs = Net profit

₹45,000 – ₹40,000 = ₹5,000 (first half)

₹50,000 – ₹43,000 = ₹7,000 (second half)

On a differential basis: Δ Sales revenue, ₹5,000 – Δ Total costs, ₹3,000 = Δ Total profit, ₹2,000

We know that only VC changes with a change in sales volume and, hence, change in total costs are equivalent to VC (₹3,000). Accordingly, the additional sales of ₹5,000 has earned a contribution margin of ₹2,000 [₹5,000 (*S*) – ₹3,000 (VC)].

P/V ratio = ₹2,000 ÷ ₹5,000 = 40 per cent

V/V ratio = 100 per cent – 40 per cent = 60 per cent

Accordingly, 60 per cent of the total costs are made up of variable costs and the balance represents the total fixed costs (FC).

Sales revenue = Fixed costs + Variable costs + Net profit

₹95,000 = FC + 0.60 × (₹95,000) + ₹12,000

₹95,000 = FC + ₹57,000 + ₹12,000

₹95,000 – ₹69,000 = FC or ₹26,000 = FC

BEP (amount) = ₹26,000 ÷ 0.40 = ₹65,000

TABLE 16.1 Verification

Particulars	*Amount*	*Per cent*
Break-even sales	₹65,000	100
Variable costs	39,000	60
Contribution	26,000	40
Fixed costs	26,000	40
Net income	Nil	Nil

$$M/S \text{ ratio} = \frac{(₹95{,}000 - ₹65{,}000)}{₹95{,}000} = 31.58 \text{ per cent}$$

BREAK-EVEN ANALYSIS APPLICATIONS

The break-even applications are illustrated below.

LO 16.2 Discuss break-even analysis applications in profit planning

Sales Volume Required to Produce Desired Operating Profit

One application of a BE analysis is to determine the required sales volume to generate a budgeted amount of profit. The required sales are given by Eq. 16.15.

(Fixed expenses + Desired operating profit) ÷ P/V ratio **(16.15)**

In Example 16.1, if the desired operating profit of *SV* Ltd is ₹13,000, required sales volume = (₹26,000 + ₹13,000)/0.40 = ₹97,500

A variant of the above approach is that the management may be interested in knowing the required sales volume to produce the desired profit after taxes. In this case, the analysis must be expanded slightly. Assume that *SV* Ltd wants a net income after taxes of ₹13,000 and that its current tax rate is 35 per cent, the net income after taxes is 65 per cent of the net income before taxes.

$$\text{Required sales volume} = \frac{\text{Fixed costs} + \left[\dfrac{\text{Desired income after taxes}}{1 - \text{tax rate}}\right]}{P/V \text{ ratio}} \quad \textbf{(16.16)}$$

$$= \frac{₹\,26{,}000 + \left[\dfrac{₹\,13{,}000}{1 - 0.35}\right]}{0.40} = ₹\,1{,}15{,}000$$

TABLE 16.2 Verification

Sales volume	₹1,15,000
Less: Variable costs (0.60)	69,000
Contribution	46,000
Less: Fixed costs	26,000
Profits before taxes	20,000
Less: Taxes (0.35)	7,000
Profit after taxes	13,000

Operating Profit at a Given Level of Sales Volume

[Actual Sales Revenue (ASR) – Break-even Sales Revenue (BESR)] × P/V ratio **(16.17)**

Effect on Operating Profit of a Given Increase in Sales Volume

[Budgeted Sales Revenue(*BSR*) – BESR] × P/V ratio **(16.18)**

Suppose that *SV* Ltd forecasts 10 per cent increase in sales next year, the projected profit will be:

(₹1,04,500 – ₹65,000) × 0.40 = ₹15,800

Additional Sales Volume Required to Offset a Reduction in Selling Price

The sales manager on the basis of a market research/survey may report to the management that due to increased competition in the market and the liberal import policy of the government, the present price is relatively higher. He may advise reduction in prices to stay in competition.

Suppose that *SV* Ltd reduces its selling price from ₹10 a unit to ₹9. The sales volume needed to offset reduced selling price/maintain a present operating profit of ₹12,000 would be:

$$= \frac{\text{Desired profit } (P) + \text{Fixed expenses } (FC)}{\text{Revised } P/V \text{ ratio } (₹3/₹9)} = ₹(12{,}000 + ₹26{,}000) \div 0.3333 = ₹1{,}14{,}000$$

The required sales volume of ₹1,14,000 represents an increase of about 20 per cent over the present level. The management should explore new avenues of sales potential to maintain the existing amount of profit.

On the other hand, if the firm has the opportunity to increase the unit selling price of the product, the impact of increased sales price would be that the BEP will be reached sooner because an increase in the selling price will raise the contribution margin, assuming no change in the variable costs. An increased contribution margin will decrease the sales volume necessary to reach a desired goals.

Assume that the management of *SV* Ltd increases the selling price of its product from ₹10 to ₹12, the desired sales volume would be: $\frac{FC + P}{\text{Revised } P/V \text{ ratio}} = ₹38{,}000 \div 0.50\ (₹6 \div ₹12) = ₹76{,}000$

Effect of Changes in Fixed Costs

A firm may be confronted with the situation of increasing fixed costs. An increase in the total budgeted fixed costs of a firm may be necessitated either by external factors, such as, an increase in property taxes, insurance rates, factory rent, and so on, or by a managerial decision of an increase in salaries of executives. More important than this in the latter category are expansion of the present plant capacity so as to cope with additional demand. The increase in the requirements of fixed costs would imply the computation of the following:

(a) Relative break-even points
(b) Required sales volume to earn the present profits
(c) Required sales volume to earn the same rate of profit on the proposed expansion programme as on the existing ones.

The effect of the increased FCs will be to raise the BEP of the firm. Assume the management of *SV* Ltd decides a major expansion programme of its existing production capacity. It is estimated that it will result in extra fixed costs of ₹8,000 on advertisement to boost sales volume and another ₹16,000 on account of new plant facility.

(a) *The relative BEPs will be:*

Present facilities = Fixed costs ÷ P/V ratio = ₹26,000/0.40 = ₹65,000

Proposed facilities = (Present FC*s* + Additional FC*s*) ÷ *P/V* ratio **(16.19)**

= (₹26,000 + ₹24,000)/0.40 = ₹1,25,000

It may be noted that increase in FC*s* (from ₹26,000 to ₹50,000) has caused disproportionate increase in the BEP (from ₹65,000 to ₹1,25,000).

(b) *The required sales volume to earn the present profit:*

[Present FC*s* + Additional FC*s* + Present profit (*NI*)] ÷ *P/V* ratio **(16.20)**

= [₹26,000 + ₹24,000 + ₹12,000] ÷ 0.40 = ₹1,55,000

(c) *The required sales volume to earn the present rate of profit on investment:*

(Present FC*s* + Additional FC*s* + Present return on investment + Return on new investment) *P/V*ratio **(16.21)**

Let us assume that the present investment is ₹1,00,000 and the new investment will involve an additional financial outlay of ₹60,000. The required sales volume will be (₹26,000 + ₹24,000 + ₹12,000+ ₹7,200 (0.12 × ₹60,000)/0.40 = ₹1,73,000

These computations may be reported in a summary form to the management as follows (Table 16.3).

TABLE 16.3 Effect of Changes in Fixed Costs

Particulars	*Present facilities*	*Prospective facilities*	*Increase*
Fixed costs	₹26,000	₹50,000	₹24,000
BEP sales volume	65,000	1,25,000	60,000
BEP sales volume (units)	6,500	12,500	6,000
Sales volume to earn existing profit	95,000	1,55,000	60,000
Sales volume in units to earn existing profit	9,500	15,500	6,000
Sales volume to earn existing ROI	95,000	1,73,000	78,000
Sales volume to earn existing ROI (in units)	9,500	17,300	7,800

Effect of Changes in Variable Costs

Assuming an increase of VC by ₹1 a unit for *SV* Ltd, the new contribution margin will be: ₹3 (₹10 – ₹7) and the revised P/V ratio 0.30 that is, (₹3 ÷ ₹10).

Revised BEP = (₹26,000)/0.30 = ₹86,667

Desired sales volume to earn existing profit = ₹38,000/0.30 = ₹1,26,667

Assuming that variable costs of *SV* Ltd decline by ₹1 per unit, revised BEP = ₹26,000/0.50 = ₹52,000.

Desired sales volume to maintain existing profit = ₹38,000/0.50 = ₹76,000.

Effects of Multiple Changes

So far we have assumed that a change takes place in one of the three variable affecting profits—cost, price and sales volume. In cases where more than one factor is affected, the BEP *analysis* can be applied as shown below:

$$\frac{FC + FC\,(\text{new}) + \left[\dfrac{\text{Desired } EAT}{1 - \text{tax rate}}\right]}{[\text{Contribution margin per unit (New } SP - \text{New } VC)] \div \text{New selling price (New } SP)]} \qquad \textbf{(16.22)}$$

Assuming the following set of new Figures for *SV* Ltd:

Particulars	*Existing data*	*New data*
Selling price per unit	₹10	₹11
Fixed costs	26,000	40,000
Variable cost per unit	6	5.50
Contribution margin per unit	4	5.50
Desired earnings after taxes (to maintain the existing ROI)	12,000	25,000
Tax rate	35 per cent	

Solution

Desired sales volume (on the basis of new data) [₹26,000 + ₹14,000 + (₹25,000 ÷ 0.65)] ÷ 0.50, that is (₹5.5 ÷ ₹11) = (₹78,461.5) ÷ 0.50 = ₹1,56,923

Desired sales volume on the basis of existing data = [₹26,000 + (₹12,000 ÷ 0.65)] ÷ 0.40 (₹4 ÷ ₹10) = ₹44,462 ÷ 0.40 = ₹1,11,154.

VCP Analysis and a Segment of the Business

The fundamental approach of applying the VCP analysis to a segment of the business is the same as applying it to the business as a whole. The VCP approach "may be applied to problems relative to individual product lines, territories, methods of sale, channels of distribution or any particular segment of the business which is under scrutiny"[2]. In all these decisions, fixed costs and P/V ratio are the required inputs. Where fixed costs are inclusive of allocated costs also, in additional to direct costs, two BEPs may be determined.

◆ Example 16.2

SV Ltd has four sales divisions. The relevant data for its northern division is reproduced below:

Direct fixed costs, ₹10,000

P/V ratio, 0.40

Allocated fixed costs from head office, ₹5,000

The sales volume required to cover direct expenses would be: Direct fixed costs/ P/V ratio

= ₹10,000/0.40 = ₹25,000 **(16.23)**

The total sales volume required to cover all fixed costs would be higher as shown by equation 16.24:

$$\frac{\text{Direct FCs + Allocated FCs}}{\text{P/V ratio}} \qquad \textbf{(16.24)}$$

= (₹10,000 + ₹5,000) ÷ 0.40 = ₹37,500

Multi-product Firms (Sales-mix)

So far, we have confined our discussion to a one-product company. However, many manufacturers make more than one type of product. The relative proportion of each product sold in the aggregate sales is known as the sales-mix. A change in the mix of products sold usually affects the weighted average P/V ratio and, hence, the BEP. Thus, when the products have different P/V ratios, changes in the sales-mix/product-mix will affect the BEP and the results from operation.

◆ Example 16.3

The Garware Paints Ltd presents to you the following income statement in a condensed form for the first quarter ending March 31:

Particulars	Product X	Product Y	Product Z	Total
Sales	₹1,00,000	₹60,000	₹40,000	₹2,00,000
Variable costs	80,000	42,000	24,000	1,46,000
Contribution	20,000	18,000	16,000	54,000
Fixed costs				27,000
Net income				27,000
P/V ratio	0.20	0.30	0.40	0.27
Break-even sales				1,00,000
Sales-mix (per cent)	0.50	0.30	0.20	100

If ₹40,000 of the sales shown for Product *X* could be shifted equally to products *Y* and *Z*, the profit and the BEP would change as shown in Table 16.4.

TABLE 16.4 Break-even Point

Particulars	Product X	Product Y	Product Z	Total
Sales	₹60,000	₹80,000	₹60,000	₹2,00,000
Less: Variable costs	48,000	56,000	36,000	1,40,000
Contribution	12,000	24,000	24,000	60,000
Less: Fixed costs				27,000
Net income				33,000
P/V ratio	0.20	0.30	0.40	0.30
BE sales				90,000
Sales-mix (per cent)	0.30	0.40	0.30	100

Example 16.3 shows that by increasing the mix of high P/V products (*Y* from 30 to 40 per cent, *Z* from 20 to 30 per cent) and decreasing the mix of a low P/V product (*X* from 50 to 30 per cent), the company can increase its overall profitability. In fact, it can further augment its total profits, if it can make, and the market can absorb, more quantities of *Y* and *Z*, say ₹1 lakh each (Table 16.5).

TABLE 16.5

Particulars	Product Y	Product Z	Total
Sales	₹1,00,000	₹1,00,000	₹2,00,000
Less: Variable costs	70,000	60,000	1,30,000
Contribution	30,000	40,000	70,000
Less: Fixed costs			27,000
Net income			43,000
P/V ratio	0.30	0.40	0.35
BE sales			77,143
Sales-mix (per cent)	0.50	0.50	100

From the above, it can be generalised that, other things being equal, management should stress products with higher contribution margins. For individual product line income statements, fixed costs should not be allocated or apportioned.

Finally, it may be stressed that there is a need for a closer study of cost structures of individual product line/department within the same firm or of two different companies. It may be possible that the two departments/companies may have the same profits but very different cost structures. For instance, observe the Figures in Table 16.6 of two departments of *SV* Ltd.

TABLE 16.6

Particulars	Department X		Department Y	
	Amount	Per cent	Amount	Per cent
Sales revenue	₹1,00,000	(100)	₹1,00,000	(100)
Less: Variable costs	70,000	(70)	20,000	(20)
Contribution / P/V ratio	30,000	(30)	80,000	(80)
Less: Fixed costs	20,000		70,000	
Profit	10,000		10,000	
BEP (amount)	66,667		87,500	
Margin of safety (MS)	33,333		12,500	
Margin of safety ratio	0.3333		0.125	

Department *Y* is operating closer to the BEP than Department *X*. Department *Y* has a narrower margin of safety (12.5 per cent) compared to 33.33 per cent of *X*. The margin of safety ratio signifies that if the sales of *Y* decreases by more than 12.5 per cent, it will operate at a loss. In other words, the margin/cushion of safety is relatively smaller. *X* will not operate at a loss unless its sales volume drops by more than 33.33 per cent.

This type of profit analysis for two different companies is of special significance from the point of view of outside investor who want to invest in one of the two companies. Assuming companies *X* and *Y* in place of the departments *X* and *Y* in the above tabulation, Company *X* is certainly less risky than Company *Y*.

Graphic Presentation

Under the algebraic technique of break-even analysis, separate computations were needed to arrive at the above set of figures. The utility of the graphical technique is that such a set of figures can be determined without involving any separate calculations.

Break-Even Chart/Volume Cost Profit (VCP) Graph The **break even chart** is a graphic relationship between volume, costs and profits. It shows not only the BEP but also the effects of costs and revenue at varying levels of sales. The break-even chart can, therefore, be more appropriately called the volume-cost-profit graph (VCP graph).

Assumptions Regarding the VCP Graph are

1. Costs can be bifurcated into variable and fixed components.
2. Fixed costs will remain constant during the relevant volume range of graph.
3. Variable cost per unit will remain constant during the relevant volume range of graph.
4. Selling price per unit will remain constant irrespective of the quantity sold within the relevant range of the graph.
5. In the case of multi-product companies, in addition to the above four assumptions, it is assumed that the sales-mix remains constant.
6. Finally, production and sales volumes are equal.

The VCP graph may be prepared in a simple or elaborate manner. Figure 16.1 is an example of a simple and traditional form. In Figure 16.1, sales are shown on the horizontal axis; the vertical axis measures costs and revenues corresponding to varying volume of sales. Sales are expressed in terms of units, rupees and percentage level of activity. The VCP relationships portrayed in such a graph are valid only within the relevant range that underlies the construction of the graph. The importance of a relevant range should be recognised because in practice most firms will progressively reduce fixed costs as the volume tends to decrease towards zero activity. Similarly, fixed costs are to be increased beyond a certain volume. Accordingly, in Figure 16.1 the lower limit and upper limit of the VCP have been drawn.

The BEP lies at the point of intersection of the sales line and the total cost line. The vertical distance between the sales revenue and the total cost line measures the estimated net income (after the BEP) and the estimated net loss (before the BEP) at the related sales volume. The fixed cost line is parallel to the horizontal axis. The variable cost line is superimposed on the fixed cost line and moves upward uniformly with sales volume at the variable cost to volume ratio. This is the total cost line. The sales revenue line starts from the point of origin and moves upward uniformly with volume. The meeting point of the total cost line and sales line is the BEP. At this point, an angle is formed known as the angle of incidence. The management objective should be to have an angle of as large a size as possible because a high angle is a sign of a high rate of profit after the fixed costs have been covered; the narrower angle will signify that profits after the fixed costs have been covered; the narrower angle will signify that profits will increase at a lower rate after the BEP, showing that variable costs form a large part of cost of sales. Figure 16.1 is based on the following data relating to Hypothetical Ltd (Example 16.4).

◆ Example 16.4

Selling price per unit		₹10
Fixed costs		60,000
Variable costs per unit		5
Relevant range (units) : Lower limit		6,000
: Upper limit		20,000
Break-up of variable costs per unit:		
Direct material	₹2	
Direct labour	1.50	
Direct expenses	1	
Selling expenses	0.50	
Actual sales, 18,000 units (₹1,80,000)		
Plant capacity, 20,000 units (₹2,00,000)		
Tax rate, 50 per cent		

Figure 16.1 has been drawn by using a sales line and a total cost line (including both fixed and variable costs). The steps involved in drawing the VCP graph are enumerated as follows:

1. Select an appropriate scale for sales volume on the horizontal axis, say, 2,000 units (₹20,000) per square, and plot the point for total sales revenues at relevant volume: 6,000 units × ₹10 = ₹60,000. Draw the sales line from the origin to ₹2,00,000 (the upper limit of the relevant range). Ensure that *all the points*, 0, ₹60,000 and ₹2,00,000 *fall in the same line.* This should be ensured for the total cost line also.
2. Select an appropriate scale for costs and sales revenues on the vertical axis, say, ₹10,000 per square. Draw the line showing ₹60,000 fixed cost parallel to the horizontal axis.
3. Determine the variable portion of costs at two volumes of scales (beginning and ending): 6,000 units × ₹5 = ₹30,000; 20,000 units × ₹5 = ₹1,00,000.
4. Variable costs are to be added to fixed costs (₹30,000 + ₹60,000 = ₹90,000). Plot the point at 6,000 units sales volume and ₹1,00,000 + ₹60,000 = ₹1,60,000. Point is to be plotted at 20,000 units sales volume. This obviously is the total cost line.
5. The point of intersection of the total cost line and sales line is the BEP. To the right of BEP, there is a profit area and to the left of it, there is a loss area.
6. *Verification*: FC ÷ *CM* per unit = ₹60,000 ÷ ₹5 per unit = 12,000 units or ₹1,20,000

Figure 16.1 has been drawn using different scales for the horizontal and vertical axis. Figure 16.2 has been drawn on a uniform scale for both axes. Since the scales are the same, the 45° *line will always be the proxy of the sales line.* Any amount of sales revenue on the horizontal axis will correspond to costs and revenue on the vertical axis. Let us illustrate taking two sales levels.

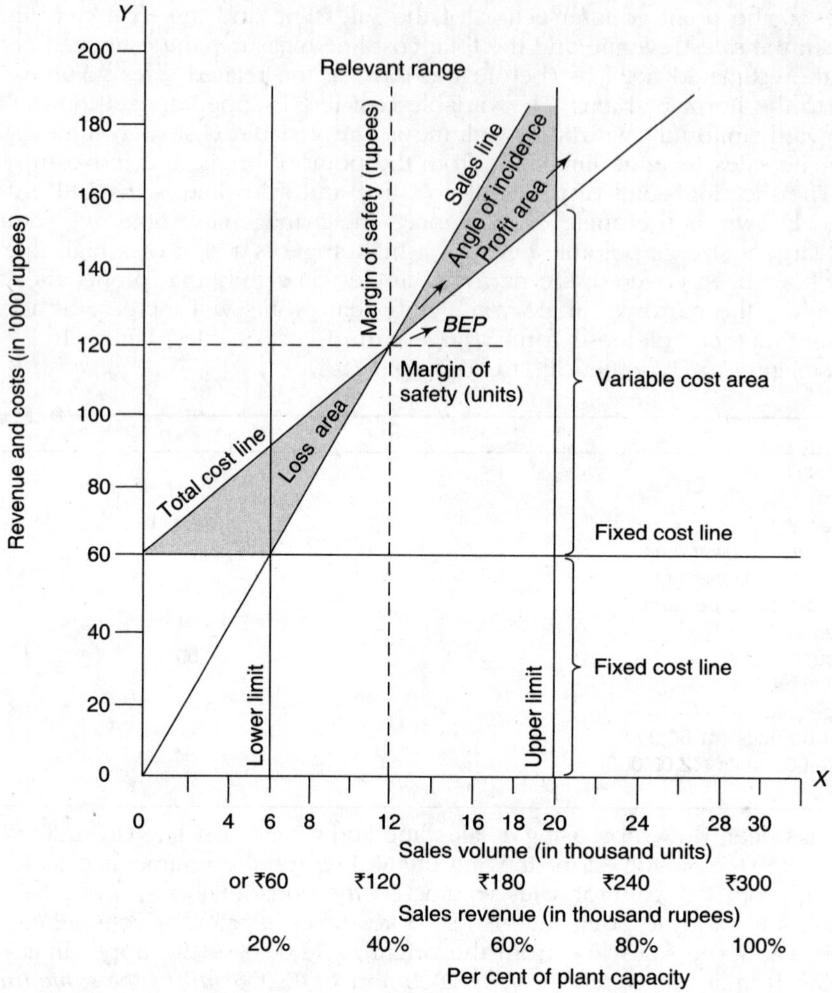

Fig. 16.1 *Volume-Cost-Profit Graph, Different Scale*

1. *₹60,000:* FC = ₹60,000
VC = 30,000 (50 per cent variable cost to volume ratio)
TC = 90,000
Loss = 30,000 (*TC*, ₹90,000 – ₹30,000, sales revenue)

Thus, ₹60,000 = ₹60,000 + ₹30,000 – ₹30,000. Point A in Figure 16.2 clearly shows these three relevant figures at the sales volume of ₹60,000.

2. *₹1,80,000:* FC = ₹ 60,000
VC = 90,000
TC = 1,50,000
Profit = 30,000

Thus, ₹1,80,000 = ₹60,000 (FC) + ₹90,000 (VC) + ₹30,000 (Profit). Point *B* in Figure 16.2 portrays these three relevant figures at the sales volume of ₹1,80,000.

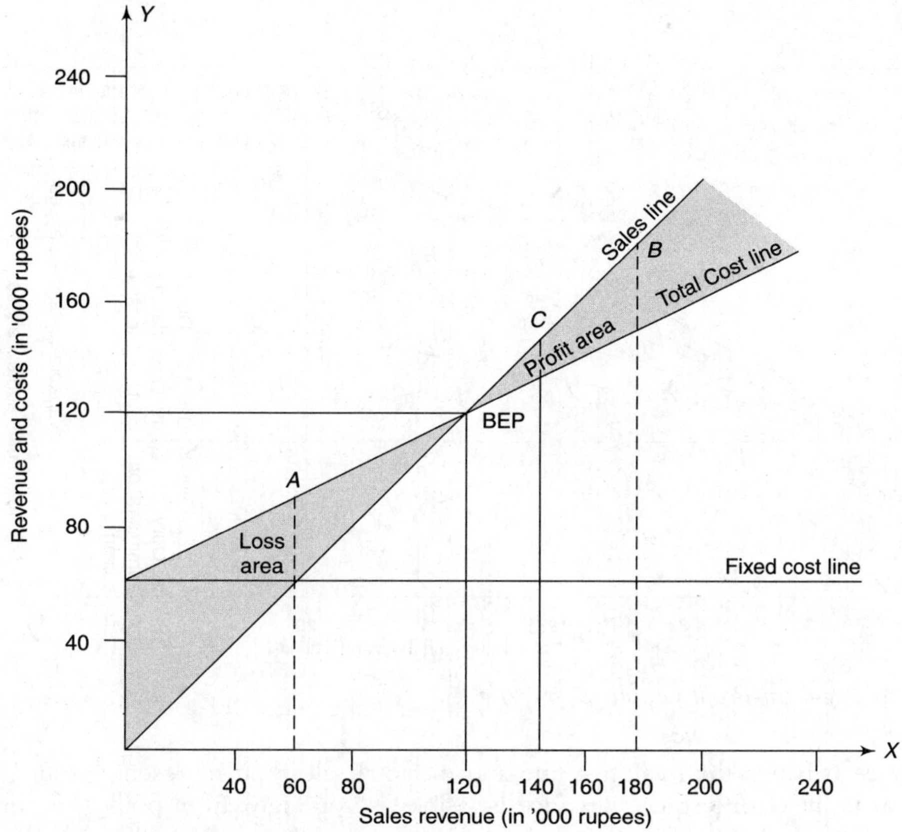

FIG. 16.2 *Volume-Cost-Profit Graph, Same Scale*

The VCP graph in Figure 16.3 is drawn with the details of the individual segment of variable cost and is more informative. The steps involved in drawing the graph include an additional step of adding variable costs to the fixed cost. This is to be repeated four times for four different components: material, labour, direct expenses and selling expenses. In fact, fixed costs can also be further split-up into parts. Such a graph provides a bird's-eye view of the entire cost structure to the management. By drawing a line perpendicular from any volume (horizontal axis), the corresponding cost and profit variables can be ascertained on the vertical axis. For instance, at 20,000 unit level, following are the various cost figures, as shown by the VCP graph (line *A*).

Fixed costs	₹60,000
Variable costs:	
Material	40,000
Labour	30,000
Direct expenses	20,000
Selling expenses	10,000
Profit before taxes	40,000

VCP Applications Like the algebraic break-even applications, the VCP graph can also be applied to analyse the VCP relationship/profit planning. To illustrate, the company's management wants to know the sales volume, which will yield an operating profit of ₹10,000. As explained earlier, the

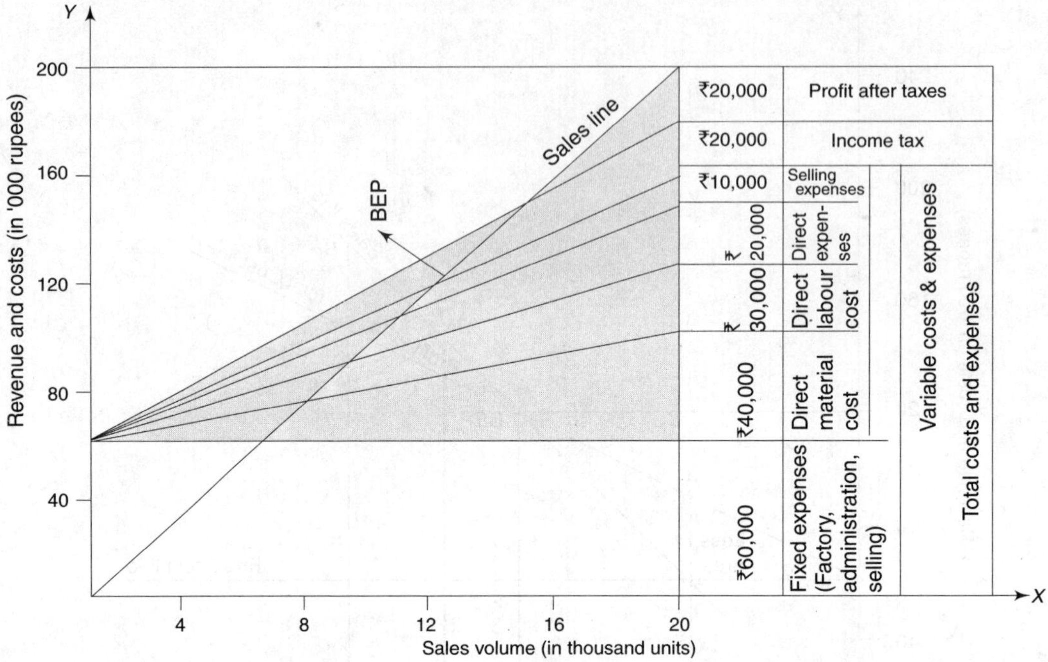

FIG. 16.3 *Volume-Cost-Profit Graph, Cost-Wise*

vertical distance between the total cost line and the total sales line represents profit (one square is ₹10,000). At point *C*, one square distance is visible. Accordingly, from point C a perpendicular drawn to the horizontal axis gives the desired sales volume, that is, ₹1,40,000. Likewise, answers to similar other questions are available in the VCP graph. The VCP graph can be modified to show the changes in the profitability factors of Example 16.4, such as,

1. Change in fixed costs (₹10,000 both ways)
2. Change in variable costs (20 per cent both ways)
3. Change in selling price (25 per cent both ways).

Table 16.7 provides a summary of the results due to the above changes. Only one change is taken at a point of time.

TABLE 16.7

Variable	*Effect on BEP*	*Margin of safety*	*Operating profit*
Fixed costs (₹10,000):			
Increase	Increase (₹20,000)	Decrease (₹20,000)	Decrease (₹10,000)
Decrease	Decrease (₹20,000)	Increase (₹20,000)	Increase (₹10,000)
(Figure 16.4)			
Variable costs:			
Increase (to 60 per cent)	Increase (₹30,000)	Decrease (₹30,000)	Decrease (₹18,000)
Decrease (to 40 per cent)	Decrease (₹20,000)	Increase (₹20,000)	Increase (₹18,000)
(Figure 16.5)			
Selling price (25 per cent):			
Increase	Decrease (₹20,000)	Increase (₹20,000)	Increase (₹18,000)
Decrease	Increase (₹60,000)	Increase (₹60,000)	Decrease (₹30,000)
(Figure 16.6)			

Important Points Regarding Figure 16.6 In Figures 16.4 and 16.5, there are two cost lines to show the increase and decrease. But Figure 16.6, which is designed to reveal the change due to the selling price, has only one sales line (45°). The impact of change in the sales price is reflected indirectly in the variable cost line (which is merged with FC line and is represented by the total cost line). This is due to the fact that the *V/V* ratio which is an essential input for drawing the chart gets changed when the selling price is changed. In other words, Figure 16.6 is like Figure 16.5. The new *V/V* ratio has been determined as follows.

(i) When there is *an increase in selling price* by 25 per cent
Sales price (revised)= ₹5.50 (₹10 + 25 per cent) or 125 per cent (₹12.5 per unit)
Variable costs= ₹5 or 50 per cent (existing)
V/V Ratio= (₹5 ÷ ₹12.50) or (50 ÷ 125) or 40 per cent

(ii) When *there is a decrease in sales price* by 25 per cent
Sales price= ₹7.50 (₹10 – ₹2.50) or 75 per cent (₹7.5 per unit)
Variable costs= ₹5 or 50 pr cent (existing)
V/V Ratio= (₹5 ÷ ₹7.50) or (50 ÷ 75) or 66.67 per cent
Total cost line= ₹60,000 + 66.67 per cent sales

Since the *V/V* ratio assumes a fractional form, care has been taken to plot points at sales levels of ₹1,50,000 and ₹2,40,000 so that corresponding variable cost figures can be whole numbers, that is, ₹1,00,000 and ₹1,60,000 respectively.

Figure 16.7 portrays VCP relationships of a sales-mix for multi-product firm (Example 16.3).

The steps regarding the plotting of a sales line and fixed cost line are identical with those of a simple VCP graph concerning one product. An additional step pertains to the drawing of a variable cost line. For the purpose, the required input is the weighted average variable cost. In Example 16.3, it is 73 per cent (in an original sales mix of 5:3:2 for products *X*, *Y* and *Z* respectively). The figure 73 per cent is arrived at by deducting weighted P/V ratio from 100 (100 per cent-27 per cent, P/V ratio). For the revised sales-mix, it is 70 per cent (100 per cent-30 per cent).

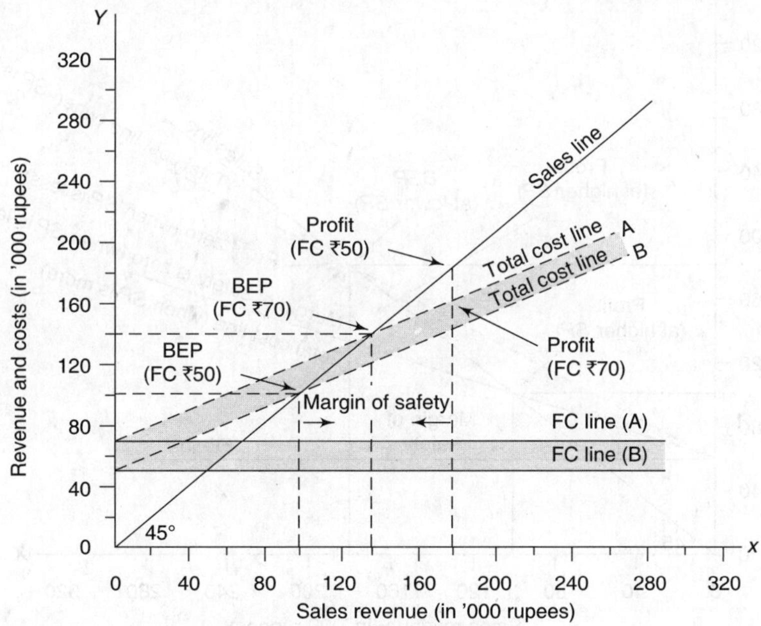

FIG. 16.4 *Volume-Cost-Profit Graph, Change in Fixed Cost*

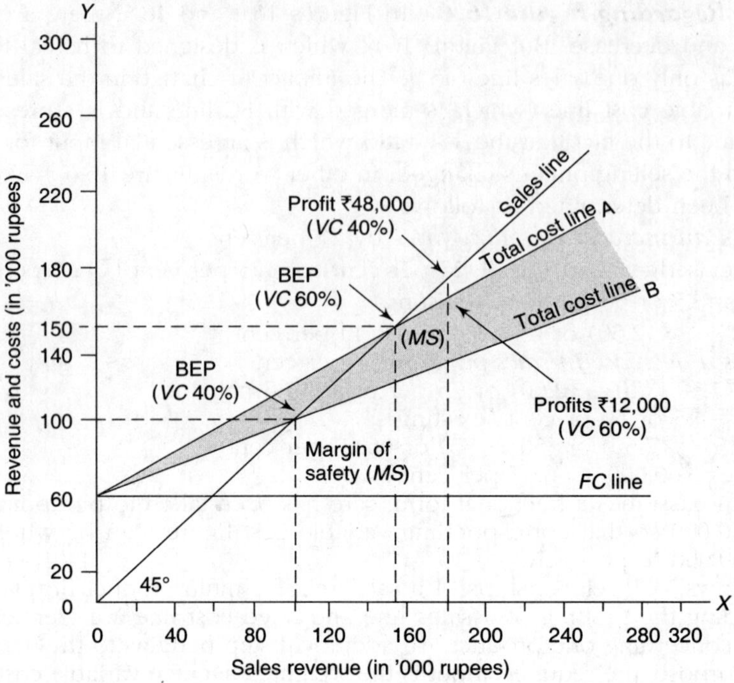

FIG. 16.5 *Volume-Cost-Profit Graph, Change in Variable Cost*

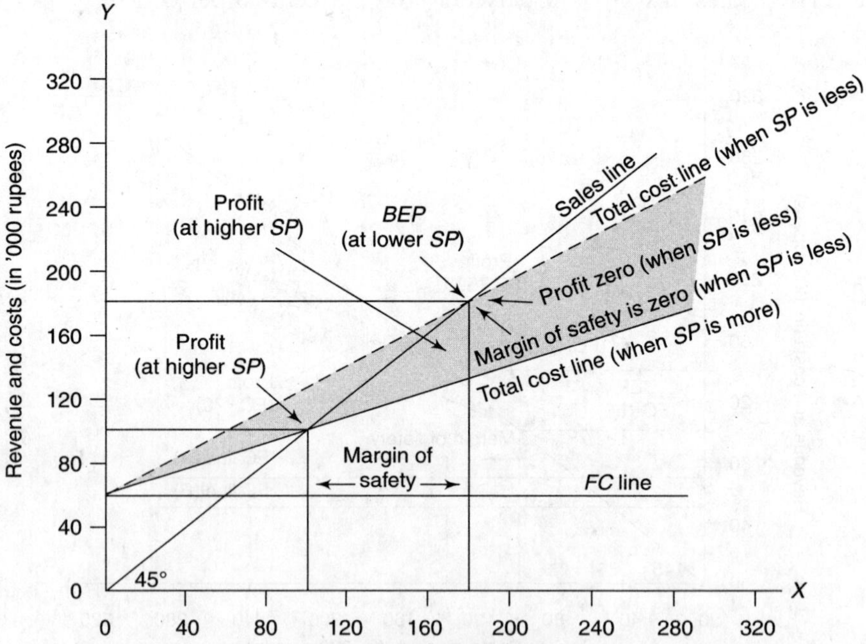

FIG. 16.6 *Volume-Cost-Profit Graph, Change in Selling Price*

However, the composite VCP graph is inadequate, it does not enable the management to know product-wise BEPs and profits. One way to overcome this difficulty is to have individual break-even analysis charts for each product.

V/P graph shows relationship between volume and profit.

The Volume-Profit (V/P) Graph/Chart The volume-profit graph portrays the relationship of profit to volume. The profit-volume analysis graph, sometimes called V/P chart, supplements the VCP graphs. The usefulness of V/P graphs is that they show a direct relationship between sales volume and profits. Separate lines for costs and revenues are eliminated from the V/P chart as only profit points are plotted. In a way, therefore, they are more easy to understand the profit-volume relationship. However, both are often used together to obtain the advantages peculiar to each construction of V/P graph/chart.

Steps in the Construction of V/P Graph are

1. Select an appropriate scale for sales volume on the horizontal axis as for the VCP chart. This horizontal axis itself forms the sales line. This line should be drawn in the middle region of the graph because losses are to be represented on the side below the sales line and profits on the side above the sales line.
2. Select an appropriate scale for profit and loss (fixed cost) on the vertical axis. Total fixed costs are represented below the sales line on the left hand side of the vertical axis and profits are shown on the right hand side above the sales line.
3. Points are plotted on the V/P graph for the required fixed costs and profit at two or three assumed sales levels. Profits should be selected in such a way that one point is plotted below the sales line and the other above the sales line.

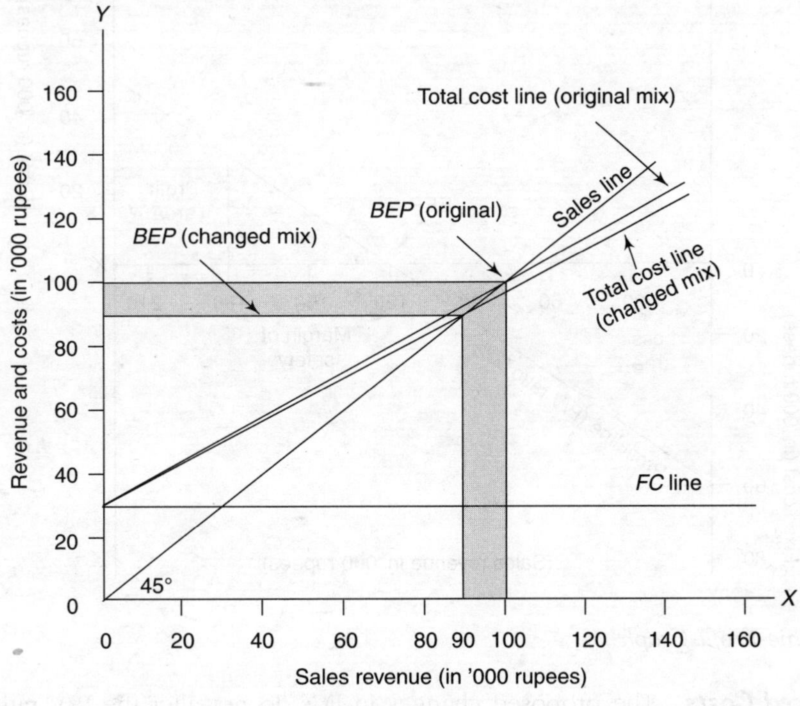

FIG. 16.7 *Volume-Cost-Profit Graph, Change in Sales Mix*

4. Like the VCP graph, the origin of the curve (profit line) would be a point of total fixed cost (showing the entire amount as loss) at zero sales level.
5. Join the point of origin with two points developed as per step 3 by a diagonal line which crosses the sales line at the BEP.

Like the VCP graph, the V/P chart does not aim at projecting only the BEP. It contains a set of points where each point measures the quantum of profit/loss in relation to the sales volume. Using the figures of Example 16.4 (except the upper limit increased to 21,000 units), the V/P graph has been drawn in Figure 16.8. The chart visualises what changes will take place in the profit and loss pattern with changes in sales revenue.

For instance, let us suppose that the management for the next year projects a sales revenue of ₹2,10,000 (with no increase in fixed costs). The V/P chart readily shows that the amount of profit is ₹45,000, whereas in the VCP graph, the amount is to be determined.

TABLE 16.8 *Determination of Two Points for Figure 16.8 as per Step 3*

Particulars	*Point I*	*Point II*
Sales revenue	₹60,000	₹2,10,000
Less variable costs (0.50)	30,000	1,05,000
	30,000	1,05,000
Less fixed costs	60,000	60,000
Profit/(loss)	(30,000)	45,000

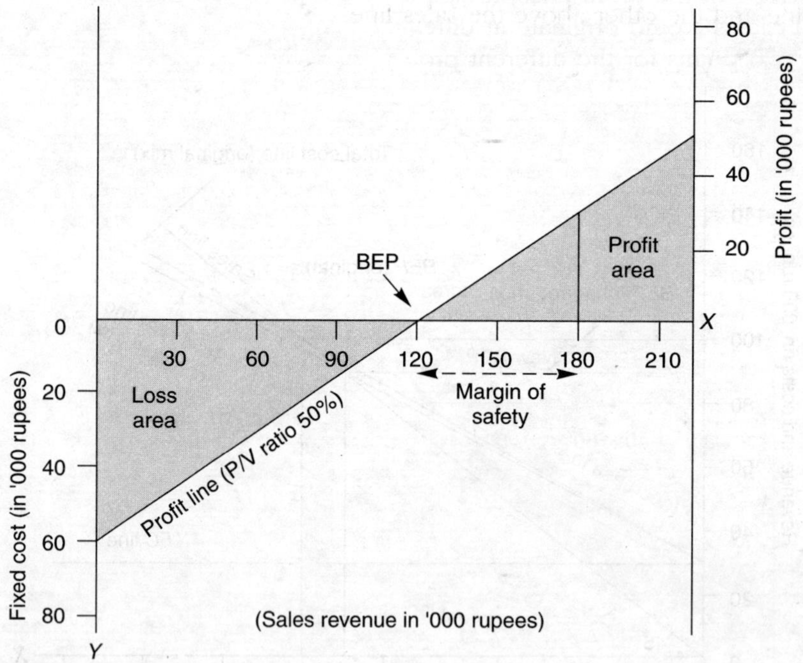

FIG. 16.8 *Volume-Profit Graph*

Changes in Fixed Costs The proposed changes in FCs do not alter the P/V ratio. But they do affect both BEP and profits. An increase in the amount of FCs decreases profits above the BEP and increases losses below BEP; while the reverse holds true when there is a decrease in the amount of FCs.

In Example 16.4, with the proposed change of ₹10,000 (both ways) in fixed costs, the changes are summarised in Table 16.9.

TABLE 16.9 *Impact of Change in Fixed Costs on BEP, and Profit*

Particulars	Fixed costs		
	Increase (₹10,000)	*Original amount*	*Decrease (₹10,000)*
Sales revenue	₹1,80,000	₹1,80,000	₹1,80,000
Less variable costs	90,000	90,000	90,000
Contribution	90,000	90,000	90,000
Less fixed costs	70,000	60,000	50,000
Net income	20,000	30,000	40,000
Change in net income	(10,000)	N.A.	+ 10,000
BEP	1,40,000	1,20,000	1,00,000
Change in BEP	+ 20,000	N.A.	(20,000)
Margin of safety	40,000	60,000	80,000
Change in margin of safety	(20,000)	N.A.	+20,000
P/V ratio (per cent)	50	50	50

All the changes in Table 16.9 are clearly portrayed in Figure 16.9. Since the P/V ratio remains unchanged, the slope of the profit lines in Figure 16.9 remains the same. The only point of difference is that profit lines would originate at different points on the vertical axis. The procedure for determining the two points for the different profit lines is shown for Figure 16.9 in Table 16.10.

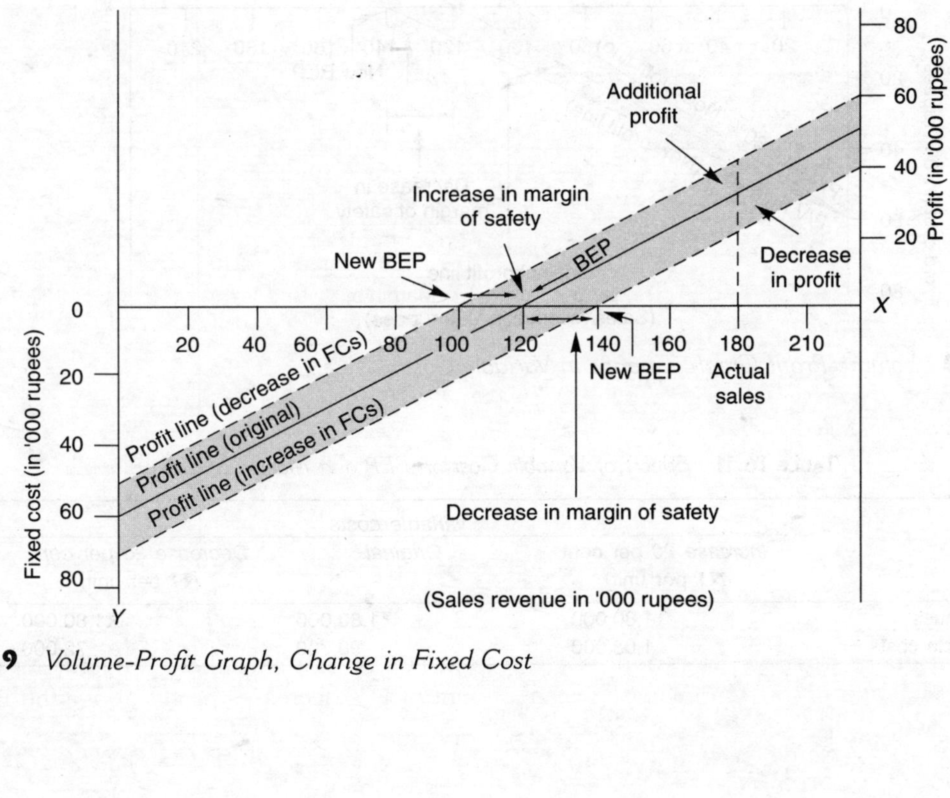

FIG. 16.9 *Volume-Profit Graph, Change in Fixed Cost*

TABLE 16.10

Particulars	Point I				Point II			
Sales revenue		₹60,000				₹2,10,000		
Less variable costs		30,000				1,05,000		
Contribution		30,000				1,05,000		
Less fixed costs	(i)	50,000	(ii)	₹70,000	(i)	50,000	(ii)	₹70,000
Profit/(loss)	(i)	(20,000)	(ii)	(40,000)	(i)	55,000	(ii)	35,000

Changes in Variable Costs The proposed changes in variable costs change the P/V ratio, the BEP and the net income at any sales volume. Figure 16.10 is based on changes in the VC of 20 per cent (both sides) for data included in Example 16.4 Table 16.11 incorporates the results due to the proposed change.

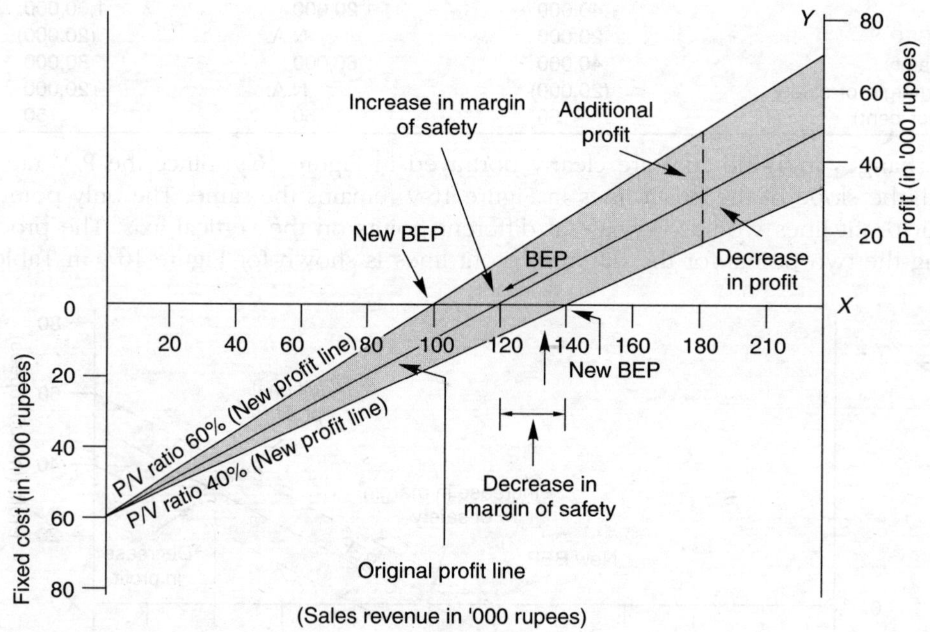

FIG. 16.10 *Volume-Profit Graph, Change in Variable Cost*

TABLE 16.11 *Effecrt of Variable Cost on BEP and Margin of Safety*

Particulars	Variable costs		
	Increase 20 per cent (₹1 per unit)	*Original*	*Decrease 20 per cent (₹1 per unit)*
Sales revenues	₹1,80,000	₹1,80,000	₹1,80,000
Less: variable costs	1,08,000	90,000	72,000

(*Contd.*)

(Contd.)

Contribution	72,000	60,000	1,08,000
Less: fixed costs	60,000	60,000	60,000
Net income	12,000	30,000	48,000
Changes in net income	(18,000)	—	+ 18,000
BEP	1,40,000	1,20,000	1,00,000
Change in BEP	+ 20,000	—	(20,000)
Margin of safety	40,000	60,000	80,000
Change in margin of safety	(20,000)	—	+ 20,000

V/P graph, product-wise shown in Fig. 16.11, is based on data used in Example 16.5.

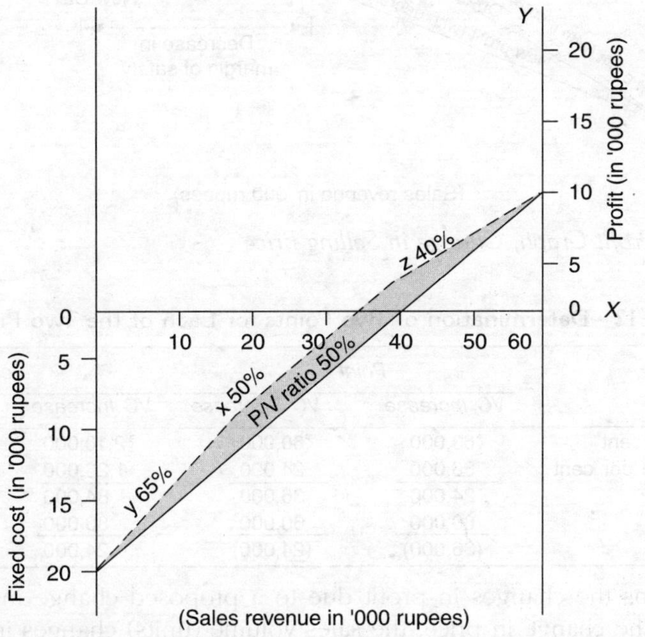

FIG. 16.11 *Volume-Profit Graph, Product-wise*

Changes in Selling Prices The proposed changes in selling prices affect the P/V ratio, the BEP and the net income/loss. To illustrate how well a profit-volume chart lends itself to portraying different profit lines, data used in Example 16.4 are revised so as to incorporate 25 per cent change in the price per unit from the original price and have been plotted in a V/P graph (Figure 16.12). The change pertains to both increase and decrease in the selling price.

The revised profit line lies above the original profit line in the case of increase in the selling price and lies below the original profit line when there is a decrease in the selling price per unit. The originating point of all the three profit lines remains unchanged.

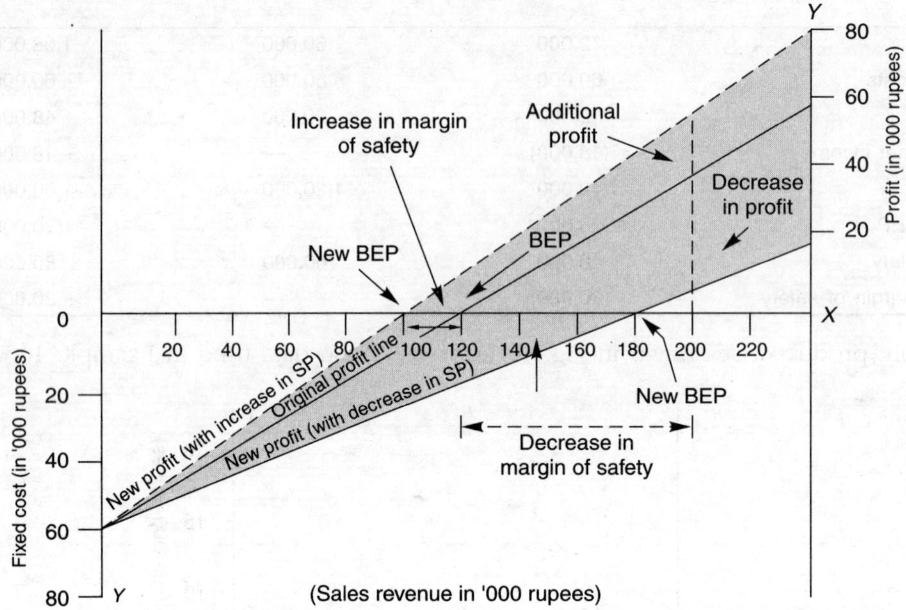

FIG. 16.12 *Volume-Profit Graph, Change in Selling Price*

TABLE 16.12 Determination of Two Points for Each of the Two Profit Lines

Particulars	Point I		Point II	
	VC Increase	*VC Decrease*	*VC Increase*	*VC Decrease*
Sales revenue (i) 60 per cent	₹60,000	₹60,000	₹2,10,000	₹2,10,000
Less: variable cost (ii) 40 per cent	36,000	24,000	1,26,000	84,000
Contribution	24,000	36,000	84,000	1,26,000
Less: fixed cost	60,000	60,000	80,000	60,000
Profit/(loss)	(36,000)	(24,000)	24,000	66,000

Table 16.13 contains the changes in profit due to a proposed change in the selling price. It is assumed that due to the change in price, the sales volume (units) changes in such a way that total sales revenue remains at ₹1,80,000 (original amount).

TABLE 16.13 Effect of Change in Selling Price on Profit, BEP and Margin of Safety

Particulars	Selling price		
	Increase 25 per cent *(₹2.5 a unit)*	*Original (₹10 a unit)*	Decrease 25 per cent *(₹2.5 a unit)*
Number of units	14,400	18,000	24,000
Unit selling price	₹12.5	₹10	₹7.5
Sales revenue	1,80,000	1,80,000	1,80,000
Less: variable costs (₹5 a unit)	72,000	90,000	1,20,000
Contribution	1,08,000	90,000	60,000
Less: fixed costs	60,000	60,000	60,000
Net profit/loss	48,000	30,000	—
Change in profit	+ 18,000	—	(– 30,000)

(Contd.)

(Contd.)

BEP	1,00,000	1,20,000	1,80,000
Change in BEP	(– 20,000)	—	+ 60,000
Margin of safety	80,000	60,000	—
Change in margin of safety	+ 20,000	—	(– 60,000)

The management may prepare the V/P chart showing the effect of various combinations of price increase/decrease, sales value decrease/increase and profit. There will be as many profit lines as there are profit plans. Such a chart certainly will be more fruitful to the management.

Assume a firm is dealing in a perfectly inelastic demand product. Therefore, it is assumed that sales volume in units (which was 18,000 in Example 15.4) remains unchanged. Figure 16.11 can be used to portray the changes. Table 16.15 provides the effects on profit factors which are clearly visible also on the volume-profit graph (Figure 16.11).

TABLE 16.14 Determination of Two Points for Each of the Two Profit Lines

Particulars	*Point I*		*Point II*	
	Selling price (SP)		*Selling price (SP)*	
	Increase	*Decrease*	*Increase*	*Decrease*
Sales revenues	₹60,000	₹60,000	₹2,10,000	₹2,10,000
Less: variable costs				
(i) SP increase (40 per cent)				
(₹5 ÷ ₹12.5)	24,000	40,000	84,000	1,40,000
(iii) SP decrease (66.67 per cent)				
(₹5 ÷ ₹7.5)				
Contribution	36,000	20,000	1,26,000	70,000
Less: fixed costs	60,000	60,000	60,000	60,000
Net profit (loss)	(24,000)	(40,000)	66,000	10,000

TABLE 16.15

Particulars	*Selling Price*		
	Increase 25% (₹2.5 a unit)	*Original (₹10 a unit)*	*Decrease 25% (₹2.5 a unit)*
Number of units	18,000	18,000	18,000
Unit selling price	₹12.5	₹10	₹7.5
Sales revenue	2,25,000	1,80,000	1,35,000
Less: variable costs (₹5 a unit)	90,000	90,000	90,000
Contribution	1,35,000	90,000	45,000
Less: fixed costs	60,000	60,000	60,000
Net profit/(loss)	75,000	30,000	(15,000)
Change in profit/(loss)	45,000	N.A.	(45,000)
BEP	1,00,000	1,20,000	1,80,000
Change in BEP	(-20,000)	N.A.	+60,000
Margin of safety	1,25,000	60,000	(45,000)
Change in margin of safety	(65,000)	N.A.	(1,05,000)

However, it may be noted that changes prominently shown relate to earlier data where sales volume remains at ₹1,80,000.

V/P Graph for Individual Products So far we have dealt with total sales and total profits for single-product firms. The virtue of the V/P graph is that it can be used to indicate the profit path of each product. It may be recalled here that the CVP chart fails to show such a relationship for individual products. The P/V chart portrays the cumulative effect of each product on the profit of the enterprise. The importance of such information is overwhelming from the point of view of the management because the management should know the figures showing not only the overall picture of P/V ratio but also the ratio for each product so that action can be taken to deal with any product(s) yielding a low P/V ratio. Low profit volume products can be replaced with more profit-yielding products.

◆ Example 16.5

Hypothetical Ltd company produces three products. The following are the results of one quarter.

Product	*Sales*	*Variable cost*
X	₹10,000	₹5,000
Y	20,000	7,000
Z	30,000	18,000

Fixed overheads: ₹20,000

Solution

These results can be analysed as follows (Table 16.16).

TABLE 16.16

Product	*Sales revenue*	*Variable cost*	*Contribution margin*	*P/V ratio(%)*
X	₹10,000	₹5,000	₹5,000	50
Y	20,000	7,000	13,000	65
Z	30,000	18,000	12,000	40
	60,000	30,000	30,000	50
Less: fixed costs			20,000	
Net income			10,000	

BEP = FC ÷ PV ratio = ₹20,000 ÷ 0.50 = ₹40,000

Margin of safety = ₹20,000

Procedure for Drawing a V/P Graph (Figure 16.11)

1. Construct the P/V graph in the normal way as has been done for Figure 16.8, taking the weighted P/V ratio (Example 16.5) as 50 per cent of the profit line.
2. Arrange the given data in such a way that products are in order of descending P/V ratios. In Example 16.5, the sequence of products is Y, X and Z.
3. The profit yielding the highest P/V ratio is plotted first (product Y, 65 per cent PV ratio) and the product giving the lowest P/V ratio (product Z, P/V ratio, 40 per cent) is plotted last. The profit line for product Y begins at total fixed cost point of ₹20,000 and is drawn to the ₹7,000 point in the loss area directly below the sales volume of ₹20,000.
4. The plotting shows that ₹13,000 of the ₹20,000 fixed costs have been recovered.

   The profit path of Product X starts at a point where Y's path ends. X's contribution is ₹5,000 at the sales volume of ₹10,000. It implies that out of ₹7,000 unrecovered fixed costs (step 3), ₹5,000 has been recovered. Therefore, the point is to be plotted at ₹2,000 in the loss area directly below the sales volume of ₹30,000 [₹20,000 (Y) + ₹10,000 (X)].
5. The profit line for Product Z (having the lowest P/V ratio) starts at a point where the profit path for X ends. Z's contribution is ₹12,000 and its sales volume is ₹30,000. This indicates that not only has the uncovered fixed cost of ₹2,000 been recovered but there is a net profit of ₹10,000. Accordingly, its line starts in the loss area and ends in the profit area, crossing the sales line. The point is plotted at the profit figures of ₹10,000 directly below the sales revenue of ₹60,000 (₹20,000 Y + ₹10,000 X + ₹30,000 Z).

The plotting of the profit line for an individual product is a useful pictorial presentation from the point of view of management. If any of the products result in a loss and yields no contribution margin, its slope will be downward.

From Figure 16.11, it can be inferred that the larger the P/V ratio, the steeper is the profit path. Therefore, the management's objective should be to increase the P/V ratio, whenever it is possible to do so; where it cannot be increased, its endeavour should be to maintain it. The P/V ratio can be improved by increasing the selling price and decreasing the variable costs in the case of single-product companies. In the case of multiple-product companies, the additional factor can be the change in product-mix, as explained earlier.

Application of the P/V (C/V) Ratio

1. Determination of BEP = FC ÷ P/V ratio
2. Determination of profit at given/budgeted sales volume = (Actual sales – *BE* sales) × *P/V*ratio.
3. Determination of sales volume to earn budgeted profit = (FC + *DP*) ÷ P/V ratio
4. Determination of change in sales volume to maintain the current level of profit if there is (a) a change in sales price, (b) change in variable cost = (FC + *DP*) ÷ Revised P/V ratio.
5. Determination of the percentage of net profit with the help of margin of safety ratio = (P/V ratio × *MS* ratio) **(16.25)**

CASH BREAK-EVEN POINT

LO 16.3 Understand cash break-even point and its applications

Cash break-even point is total cash fixed cost divided by contribution margin per unit.

The VCP relationship can also be used to show the liquidity position of the firm. This is done through the computation of **cash break-even point** or cash break-even sales revenue (CBEP/CBESR). Algebraically:

$$CBEP = \frac{\text{Total cash fixed cost } (CFC)}{\text{Contribution margin per unit}} \quad \textbf{(16.26)}$$

$$CBESR = \frac{\text{Total cash fixed cost}}{C/V \text{ ratio}} \quad \textbf{(16.27)}$$

Graphically, the CBEP is determined at the point of intersection of total cash cost line and total sales line. The area to the left of the curve signifies cash losses and the area on the right side is indicative of cash profits.

Assuming for Example 16.4, the cash fixed cost to be ₹15,000, the CBESR using Equation 16.27 would be ₹30,000 = ₹15,000 ÷ 0.50

Figure 16.13 portrays the graphic presentation of the cash break-even sales revenue.

To conclude, the uses of break-even analysis, as a technique for profit planning, have been discussed in detail in this chapter. In brief, break-even analysis shows the interplay of profit factors, that is, cost, revenue and volume in a way, which assists management in choosing the best feasible alternative now and in the future. "The break-even system is at once an *X*-ray, exploratory and planning tool intended for frequent use and a proper cost-volume-profit analysis supported by the break-even chart can eliminate many of the time-consuming reports now being prepared at the company."[3]

The graphs can be used to analyse the impact of various alternative proposals under consideration on the profit structure. Thus, the break-even system provides more readily understandable facts than conventional accounting or statistical data regarding the profit structure of the company.

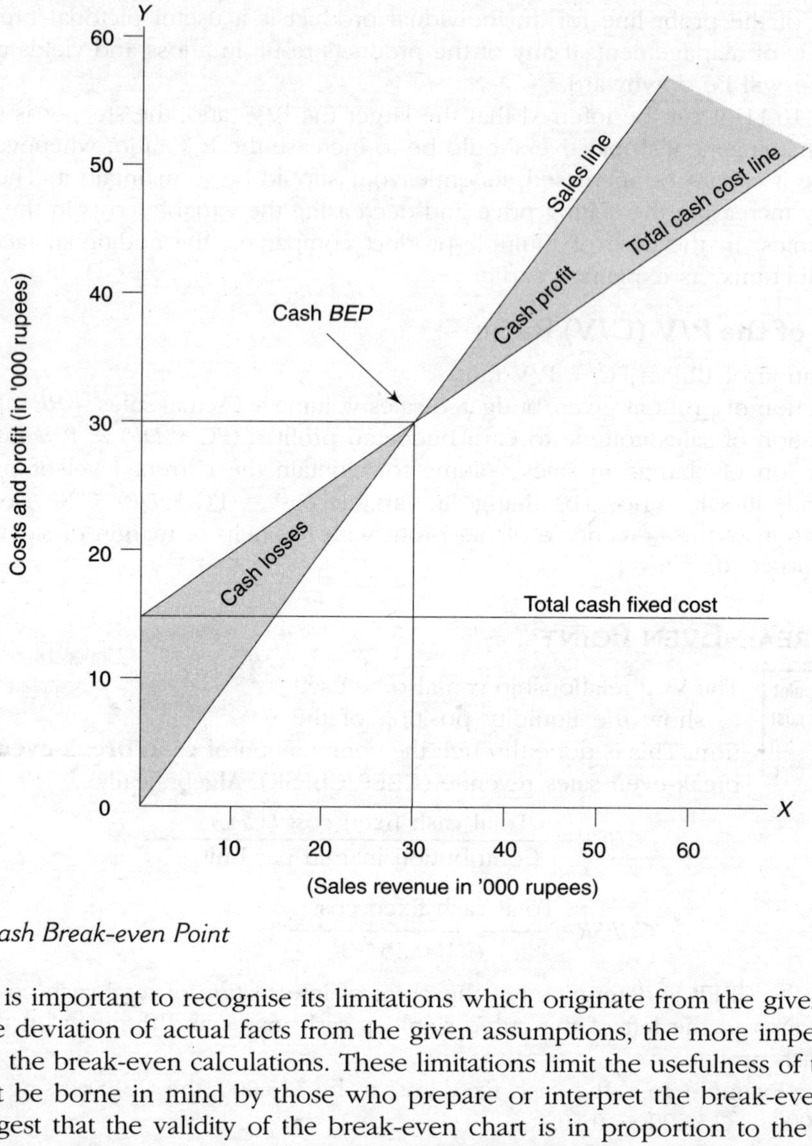

FIG. 16.13 *Cash Break-even Point*

However, it is important to recognise its limitations which originate from the given assumptions. The greater the deviation of actual facts from the given assumptions, the more imperfect, incorrect and invalid are the break-even calculations. These limitations limit the usefulness of the break-even chart and must be borne in mind by those who prepare or interpret the break-even chart. These limitations suggest that the validity of the break-even chart is in proportion to the validity of the assumptions. One of the assumptions of the break-even analysis is that an enterprise's cost are either perfectly variable or absolutely fixed over all ranges of operating volume. In other words, variable cost is a linear function of volume: fixed costs are assumed not to be affected by volume at all. In practice, these assumptions are not likely to be valid over all ranges of volume. Even within the relevant range of volume, there is a likelihood of some degree of imprecision and to that extent validity of the results is affected. For instance, variable costs are likely to increase as the firm approaches full capacity. The reason may be due to less efficient labour or costly overtime having been resorted to. This limitation can be overcome by studying the relationship between total costs and volume, non-linear, to correspond with economic reality.

Another assumption of the break-even analysis is that it is possible to classify total costs of an enterprise as either fixed or variable. Many costs defy clear division because they are partly fixed and partly variable. These costs are known as **semi-variable costs**.

Yet another assumption of the break-even analysis is that selling price per unit remains unchanged, irrespective of volume. In other words, total sales revenue is perfectly variable with its physical sales volume. For some firms, operating in the seller's market, this assumption may be perfectly valid. For most others, however, it is not a realistic assumption because price reductions may be necessary to increase the sales volume. Once again, this limitation can be remedied by studying the relationship between total sales revenue and costs.

SUMMARY

- The cost-volume-profit (*CVP*) analysis is a tool to show the relationship between various ingredients of profit planning, namely, unit sales price (*SP*), unit variable cost (*VC*), fixed costs (*FC*), sales volume, and sales-mix (in the case of multi-product firms).
- The *CVP* analysis shows the relationship between costs and profit, and sales volume. The crucial step in this analysis is the determination of break-even point (*BEP*), which is defined as the sales level at which the total revenues equal total costs. It is the level at which losses cease and beyond which profit starts. The break-even technique has many applications for purposes of the *CVP* analysis.
- *BEP* can be determined by the following two methods; (1) *Algebraic*, comprising (a) Contribution margin approach and (b) Equation technique. (2) *Graphic presentation*, comprising (a) Break-even chart and (b) Volume-profit graph.
- In the *contribution margin approach, BEP* is computed on the basis of the relationship between the fixed costs and the contribution margin (*CM*). The *CM* represents the difference between the sales revenue and the variable costs.
- The *equation technique* is particularly useful in situations where unit price and unit variable costs are not clearly defined. The excess of actual sales over the *BE* sales is the margin of safety. When margin of safety is divided by the actual sales, we get margin of safety ratio which indicates the percentage by which actual sales may decline without causing any loss to the firm.. The break-even analysis is summarised below:

Contribution Margin Approach

(1) $$BEP\text{ (units)} = \frac{\text{Fixed costs } (FC)}{\text{Unit sale price (SP)} - \text{Unit variable cost } (VC)}$$

(2) $$= \frac{\text{Total fixed costs}}{\text{Unit contribution margin } (CM)}$$

(3) $$BEP\text{ (amount)}/BESR = BEP\text{ (units)} \times SP$$

(4) $$= \frac{\text{Total fixed costs}}{\text{Contribution/Profit volume ratio } (C/V \text{ or } P/V \text{ ratio})}$$

(5) $$C/V\ (P/V)\text{ ratio} = \frac{CM}{SP} \times 100$$

(6) $$= \frac{\text{Total contribution } (TC)}{\text{Total sales revenue } (TSR)} \times 100$$

(7) $$\text{Variable cost to volume } (V/V)\text{ ratio} = \frac{VC}{SP} \times 100$$

(8) $$= \frac{\text{Total variable costs } (TVC)}{TSR} \times 100$$

(9) $$= 1 - C/V\ (P/V)\text{ ratio}$$

(10) In brief, $C/V(P/V)$ ratio + V/V ratio = 1 (100%)

(11) $$BESR \text{ (multi-product firm)} = \frac{FC}{\text{Weighted } C/V \text{ ratio}} \times 100$$

(12) $$\text{Weighted } C/V \text{ ratio} = \frac{TC \text{ from all products}}{TSR \text{ from all products}} \times 100$$

(13) $$\text{Margin of safety } (MS) = TSR - BESR$$

(14) $$\text{MS ratio} = \frac{TSR - BESR}{TSR} \times 100$$

(15) $$\text{Profit} = MS \text{ (rupees)} \times C/V(P/V) \text{ ratio}$$

(16) $$= MS \text{ (units)} \times CM$$

Equation Technique

(17) $$BESR = TFC + TVC + NI \text{ (zero profit)}$$

LO 16.1

- The break-even applications are summarised below:

1. (a) *Sales revenue required to earn desired operating profits (EBIT)*

$$= \frac{FC + \text{desired } EBIT}{C/V \text{ ratio}}$$

(b) *Sales revenue required to earn desired profits/earnings after taxes (EAT)*

$$= \frac{FC + (EAT/1 - \text{tax rate}, t)}{C/V \text{ ratio}}$$

2. *Operating profit at a given sales volume*

$$= (TSR - BESR) \times C/V \text{ ratio}$$

3. *Sales revenue to off-set reduction in sales price to maintain existing operating profits*

$$= \frac{FC + EBIT}{\text{Revised } C/V \text{ ratio}}$$

4. *Effect of changes in fixed costs*

(a) *The required sales revenue to maintain present operating profit*

$$= \frac{\text{Present } FC + \text{Additional } FC + \text{Present } EBIT}{C/V \text{ ratio}}$$

(b) *The required sales revenue to earn the present rate of return on investment*

Present F C + Additional FC + Present return on investment + Return on new investment

$$= \frac{\text{Present } FC + \text{Additional } FC + \text{Present return on investment} + \text{Return on new investment}}{C/V \text{ ratio}}$$

5. *Effect of changes in variable costs*

The required sales revenue to maintain existing operating profit

$$= \frac{FC + EBIT \text{ (Existing)}}{\text{Revised } C/V \text{ ratio}}$$

6. *Effect of multiple changes*
   The required sales revenue to earn desired *EAT*

$$= \frac{FC + \text{Additional } FC + [\text{Desired } EAT/(1-t)]}{\text{Revised } C/V \text{ ratio}}$$

7. *Effect of change in sales-mix*
   The desired sales revenue to maintain existing *EBIT*

$$= \frac{FC + EBIT}{\text{Revised Weighted } C/V \text{ ratio}}$$

$$\text{Revised weighted C/V ratio} = \frac{\text{Total contribution at revised mix}}{\text{Total sales revenue at revised mix}} \; 3\ 100$$

- The break-even chart is a graphic presentation of the relationship between costs, profits, and sales. It shows not only the break-even sales but also the estimated costs and profit at various levels of the sales revenue. It is, therefore, also referred to as volume-cost-profit (*VCP*) graph/chart.
- The volume-profit graph shows a direct relationship between sales revenue and profits.

LO 16.2

- The VCP relationship is also useful to assess the liquidity position of the firm. For the purpose, cash break-even point (CBEP) or cash break-even sales revenue is computed.

1. $\text{Cash BEP (in units)} = \frac{\text{Total cash Fixed cost}}{\text{Contribution margin per unit}}$

2. $\text{Cash BESR (in amount)} = \frac{\text{Total cash Fixed cost}}{C/V \text{ ratio}}$

LO 16.3

REFERENCES

1. Wilson, J.D., "Practical Application of Cost-Volume-Profit Analysis" quoted by Anderson, D.L and D.L. Raun, *Information Analysis in Management Accounting* (John Wiley, New York, 1978), p 162.
2. Tuckker, S.A., *Break-Even System: A Tool for Profit Planning*, (Prentice Hall, Englewood Cliffs, N.J. 1963).

SOLVED PROBLEMS

LO 16.1,2
LOD: E

P.16.1 From the following data, calculate the:

1. Break-even point expressed in terms of sale amount/revenue.
2. Number of units that must be sold to earn a profit of ₹60,000 per year.

Sales price (per unit)	₹20
Variable manufacturing cost per unit	11
Variable selling cost per unit	3
Fixed factory overheads (per year)	5,40,000
Fixed selling costs (per year)	2,52,000

Solution

1. BEP *(amount)* = (Fixed factory overheads + Fixed selling costs)/P/V ratio (Sales price – Variable manufacturing cost – Variable selling cost) ÷ Sales price = (₹5,40,000 + ₹2,52,000)/0.30 (₹6 ÷ ₹20) = ₹26,40,000
2. *Desired sales volume (in units) to earn a profit of* ₹60,000 = (₹7,92,000 + ₹60,000)/ ₹6 (CM per unit) = ₹1,42,000 units

P.16.2 On investigation it was found that variable cost in *XYZ* Ltd is 80 per cent of the selling price. If the fixed expenses are ₹10,000, calculate the break-even sales of the company. **LO 16.1** **LOD: M**

Another firm, IMN Company Ltd, having the same amount of fixed expenses, has its break-even point at a lower figure than that of *XYZ* Ltd. Comment on the causes.

Solution

BEP (amount) = ₹10,000/ P/V ratio (100 per cent-Variable cost to volume ratio = 0.80)
= ₹10,000/0.20 = ₹50,000 (*XYZ* Ltd)

The lower break-even point of IMN Ltd *vis-à-vis XYZ* Ltd is due to its lower variable expenses to volume ratio, which in turn may be either due to its lower VC per unit or higher *SP* per unit, eventually yielding higher contribution margin and, hence, higher P/V ratio and lower BEP.

P.16.3 Two businesses, AB Ltd and CD Ltd, sell the same type of product in the same type of market. Their budgeted profit and loss accounts for the current year ending March 31, are as follows: **LO 16.1** **LOD: E**

Particulars		*AB Ltd*		*CD Ltd*
Sales		₹150,000		₹1,50,000
Less: Variable costs	₹1,20,000		₹1,00,000	
Fixed costs	15,000	1,35,000	35,000	1,35,000
Net budgeted profit		15,000		15,000

You are required to:

1. Calculate the break-even points of each business; and
2. State which business is likely to earn greater profits in conditions of: (a) heavy demand for the product, (b) low demand for the product.

Solution

1. BEP (amount) = Fixed cost/ P/V ratio; P/V ratio = Contribution/Sales revenuee
   BEP (AB Ltd) = ₹15,000/0.20 = ₹75,000
   P/V ratio = ₹30,000/ ₹1,50,000 = 20 per cent
   BEP (CD Ltd) = ₹35,000/0.3333 = ₹1,05,000
   P/V ratio = ₹50,000/ ₹1,50,000 = 33.33 per cent
2. Projected profit (heavy demand for the products):
   (a) CD Ltd is likely to earn larger profits in conditions of heavy demand of the product because its P/V ratio is higher than that of AB Ltd.
   (b) AB Ltd is likely to earn larger profits in condition of low demand of the product because its burden of fixed costs is much smaller than that of CD Ltd.

P.16.4 During the current year, *AB* Ltd showed a profit of ₹1,80,000 on a sale of ₹30,00,000. The variable expenses were ₹21,00,000. **LO 16.1, 2** **LOD: E**

You are required to work out:

1. The break-even sales at present
2. The break-even sale if variable costs increase by 5 per cent
3. The break-even sale to maintain the profit as at present, if the selling price is reduced by 5 per cent.

Solution

₹30,00,000, Sales = ₹21,00,000, VC + FC + ₹1,80,000, profit or FC = ₹7,20,000

1. BEP = ₹7,20,000/ PV ratio = ₹7,20,000/0.30 = ₹24,00,000
P/V ratio = ₹9,00,000/30,00,000 = 0.30

2. BEP (revised) = ₹7,20,000/0.265 = ₹27,16,981
P/V ratio = ₹7,95,000/ ₹30,00,000 = 0.265
₹7,95,000 Contribution = (₹30,00,000 – ₹22,05,000, VC)

3. Revised P/V ratio with reduction in price

Sales revenue	₹28,50,000
Variable costs	21,00,000
Contribution	7,50,000

P/V ratio (₹7,50,000 ÷ ₹28,50,000) = 26.316 per cent
Desired sales volume = ₹9,00,000 (FC + *DP*)/0.26316 = ₹34,19,973

P.16.5 Calculate from the following data (i) the value of output at which the business breaks even; and (ii) the percentage of capacity at which it breaks even: **LO 16.1** **LOD: E**

Particulars	*Budget based on 100 per cent capacity*	*Shut down expenditure*
Direct wages	₹2,09,964	
Direct materials	2,44,552	
Works expenses	88,292	₹93,528
Selling and distribution expenses	21,000	40,188
Administrative expenses	9,492	20,508
Net sales	8,40,000	

Solution

P/V Ratio

(i) *Net sales*		₹8,40,000
Less: Variable costs:		
Direct wages	₹2,09,964	
Direct materials	2,44,552	
Works expenses	88,292	
Selling and distribution expenses	21,000	
Administrative expenses	9,492	5,73,300
Contribution (C)		2,66,700
P/V ratio (C ÷ Sales) (per cent)		31.75

BEP (amount) = Fixed costs (shut down expenditure)/P/V ratio = ₹1,54,224/0.3175 = ₹4,85,744.88
(ii) Break-even sales/Sales at 100 per cent capacity = ₹4,85,744.88/₹8,40,000 = 57.83 per cent

P.16.6 The Soft-Flow Ink Ltd's income statement for the preceding year is presented below. Except as noted, the cost/revenue relationship for the coming year is expected to follow the same pattern as in the preceding year. Income statement for the year ending March 31 is as follows: **LO 16.2** **LOD: M**

Sales (20,000 bottles @ ₹25 each)		₹5,00,000
Variable costs	₹3,00,000	
Fixed costs	1,00,000	4,00,000
Pre-tax profit		1,00,000
Less: Taxes (0.35)		35,000
Profit after tax		65,000

1. What is the break-even point in amount and units?
2. Suppose that a plant expansion will add ₹50,000 to fixed costs and increase capacity by 60 per cent. How many bottles would have to be sold after the addition to break-even?
3. At what level of sales will the company be able to maintain its present pre-tax profit position even after expansion?
4. The company's management feels that it should earn at least ₹10,000 (pre- tax per annum) on the new investment. What sales volume is required to enable the company to maintain existing profits and earn the minimum required return on new investments?
5. Suppose the plant operates at full capacity after the expansion, what profit after tax will be earned?

Solution

1. BEP (amount) = ₹1,00,000/0.40 (₹2,00,000 ÷ ₹5,00,000) = ₹2,50,000
   BEP (units) = ₹1,00,000/₹10 = 10,000 units; CMPU = ₹25 – ₹15 VC = ₹10
2. BEP (increase in FC) = [₹1,00,000 + ₹50,000 (Additional FC)] ÷ ₹10 per unit = 15,000 units
3. Desired sales volume to maintain a pre- tax profit of ₹1,00,000 = [₹1,50,000 (FC) + ₹1,00,000] ÷ 0.40 = ₹6,25,000 (or 25,000 units)
4. Desired sales volume to earn a pre-tax profit of ₹1,10,000 (₹1,00,000 + ₹10,000) = [₹1,50,000 + ₹1,10,000]/0.40 = ₹6,50,000 (or 26,000 units)
5. Present capacity (assumed operating at 100 per cent capacity) (bottles) and additional capacity:

Present capacity (assumed operating at 100 per cent capacity) (bottles)	20,000
Add: Additional capacity (60 per cent)	12,000
Total capacity (bottles)	32,000

Statement of Income (32,000 units)

Sales (32,000 bottles @ ₹25)	₹8,00,000
Less: Variable costs, 0.60 × (₹3,00,000 + ₹5,00,000)	4,80,000
Contribution	3,20,000
Less: Fixed costs	1,50,000
Pre-tax profits	1,70,000
Less: Income tax (0.35)	59,500
Profits after income tax	1,10,500

P.16.7 The following data are obtained from the records of a factory: **LO 16.2 LOD: M**

Sales (4,000 units @ ₹25 each)		₹1,00,000
Variable costs:		
Materials consumed	₹40,000	
Labour charges	20,000	
Variable overheads	10,000	
Fixed overheads	18,000	88,000
Net profit		12,000

Calculate:

1. Number of units by selling which the company will break-even.
2. Sales needed to earn a profit of 20 per cent on sales.
3. Extra units, which should be sold to obtain the present profit if it is proposed to reduce the selling price by 20 per cent and 25 per cent.
4. Selling price to be fixed to bring down its break-even point to 600 units under present conditions.

Solution

1. BEP (units), Fixed overheads = ₹18,000/CM per unit, ₹7.50 = 2,400 units

Determination of CM per Unit

Sales revenue (4,000 units)		₹1,00,000
Less: Variable costs		
Materials consumed	₹40,000	
Labour charges	20,000	
Variable overheads	10,000	70,000
Contribution (4,000 units)		30,000
CM per unit (₹30,000 ÷ 4,000)		7.5

2.(a) Sales revenue (SR) is a sum of total costs (TC) and total profits (TP) or (SR = TC + TP).

(b) TC can be split into FC and VC.

(c) VC will vary in direct proportion to SR.

(d) Accordingly, SR = FC + VC (SR) + TP (SR). Let us suppose, SR = 100 per cent; TC = 80 per cent; TP = 20 per cent; VC = 70 per cent (₹70,000/₹1,00,000); FC = ₹18,000

Substituting the values, we have,

100% SR = ₹18,000 + 0.70 SR + 0.20 SR

0.10 SR = ₹18,000

SR = ₹18,000/0.10 = ₹1,80,000

Verification

Sales revenue		₹1,80,000
Less: Variable cost (0.70)	₹1,26,000	
Less: Fixed overheads	18,000	1,44,000
Net profit		36,000
Net profit as percentage of sales revenue		20

3. Revised Contribution Margin per unit and Additional Units Required to maintain Profit of ₹12,000

Particulars	*Selling price reduced by*	
	20 per cent	*25 per cent*
Revised selling price	₹20.00	₹18.75
Less: Variable cost (0.70 × ₹25, original sales price)	17.50	17.50
Contribution	2.50	1.25
Desired sales volume (FC + NP) ÷ CM	30,000/2.50	30,000/1.25
Number of units required	12,000	24,000
Less: Existing number of units sold	4,000	4,000
Extra units to be sold to maintain a profit of ₹12,000	8,000	20,000

4. BEP = FC/CM per unit

CM per unit = FC/BEP = ₹18,000/600 units = ₹30

Sales price (per unit) = CM per unit + Variable cost per unit = ₹30 + ₹17.50 = ₹47.5

P.16.8 Calculate the break-even sales from the following data for a company producing three products: LO 16.1 LOD: E

Product	*Sales*	*Variable costs*
A	₹10,000	₹6,000
B	5,000	2,500
C	5,000	2,000
	20,000	10,500

Total fixed costs amount to ₹5,700.

Solution

Determination of Weighted P/V Ratio

Product	Sales	Variable costs	Contribution
A	₹10,000	₹6,000	4,000
B	5,000	2,500	2,500
C	5,000	2,000	3,000
	20,000	10,500	9,500

Weighted P/V ratio = (Total contribution/Total sales) × 100 = (₹9,500/ ₹20,000) × 100 = 47.5 per cent
BEP = FC/Weighted P/V ratio = ₹5,700/0.475 = ₹12,000

P.16.9 *ABC* Ltd manufactures and sells four types of products under the brand names of *A*, *B*, *C* and *D*. The sales-mix in value comprises 33.33, 41.67, 16.67 and 8.33 per cents for products *A*, *B*, *C* and *D* respectively. The total budgeted sales (100 per cent) are ₹60,000 per month. Operating costs are: **LO 16.1** **LOD: M**

Variable costs as per cent of selling price: Product *A*, 60, *B*, 68, *C*, 80, and *D* 40. Fixed costs, ₹14,700 per month.

Calculate the break-even point for the products on an over-all basis.

Solution

Determination of Weighted PV Ratio

Product	Sales revenue	(%)	Variable costs	(%)	Contribution	P/V ratio (%)
A	₹20,000	(33.33)	₹12,000	(60)	₹8,000	40
B	25,000	(41.67)	17,000	(68)	8,000	32
C	10,000	(16.67)	8,000	(80)	2,000	20
D	5,000	(8.33)	2,000	(40)	3,000	60
Total	60,000	(100)	39,000	(65)	21,000	35

BEP = Fixed costs/ Weighted P/V ratio = ₹14,700/0.35 = ₹42,000

Confirmation

Variable costs (0.65 × ₹42,000)	₹27,300
Fixed costs	14,700
Total costs	42,000
Total sales revenue	42,000

P.16.10 There are two similar plants under the same management. The management desires to merge these two plants. The following particulars are available: **LO 16.1** **LOD: M**

	Factory I	Factory II
Capacity (%)	100	60
Sales (₹lakh)	300	120
Variable costs	220	90
Fixed costs	40	20

You are required to calculate: (a) What the break- even capacity of the merged plant would be, and (b) What the profitability on working at 75 per cent of the merged capacity would be?

Solution

(a) Break-even Capacity

	Factory I (at 100% capacity)	Factory II (at 100% capacity)	Combined (at 100% capacity)
Sales (₹lakh)	300	200	500
Less: Variable costs	220	150	370
Contribution	80	50	130

Break-even (amount) = Fixed costs/Combined P/V ratio = ₹60 lakhs/0.26 = ₹230.769 lakh
0.26 = (₹130 lakh/₹500 lakh) × 100
Break-even point (per cent capacity) = (Break-even sales/Total capacity) × 100
= (₹230.8 lakh/ ₹500 lakh) × 100 = 46.15 per cent. The break-even capacity of the merged plant would be approximately 46.15 per cent.

(b) Income Statement at 75 per cent Merged Capacity

Sales (₹lakh)	375.00
Less: Variable costs (0.74 × ₹375)	277.50
Contribution	97.50
Less: Fixed costs	60.00
Net profit	37.50

Alternatively, (Actual sales – BE sales) × P/V ratio = (₹375 lakh – ₹230.769 lakh) × 0.26 = ₹37.50 lakh

P.16.11 The *XYZ* Ltd operates a chain of toy stores. The stores sell 10 different styles of toys with identical purchase costs and selling prices. The company is trying to determine the desirability of opening another store, which would have the following expense and revenue relationships per pair. LO 16.1, 2 LOD: M

Variable data:	
Selling price	₹30.00
Cost of toy	19.50
Salesmen's commission	1.50
Total variable expenses	21.00
Annual fixed expenses:	
Rent	60,000
Salaries	2,00,000
Advertising	80,000
Other fixed expenses	20,000
	3,60,000

Required (consider each question independently):

1. What is the annual break-even point in sales amount and in unit sales?
2. If 35,000 toys are sold, what would the store's net income be?
3. If the store manager was paid ₹0.30 per pair commission, what would the annual break-even point be in sales amount and in unit sales?
4. Refer to the original data. If the store manager were paid ₹0.30 per toy as commission on each toy sold in excess of the break-even point, what would be the store's net income if 50,000 toys were sold?
5. Refer to the original data. If sales commissions were discontinued in favour of ₹81,000 increase in fixed salaries, what would the annual break-even point be in amount and in unit sales?
6. If the store wants to build up stocks by the end of the accounting period, will your analysis still hold good?

Solution

1. Selling price ₹30
   Less: Variable costs 21
   CM per unit (pair) 9
   P/V ratio (%) 30
   BEP (amount) = ₹3,60,000/0.30 = ₹12,00,000
   BEP (units) = ₹3,60,000/ CM per unit = ₹3,60,000/₹9 = ₹40,000 units
2. Income if 35,000 pairs of shoes are sold

Contribution (35,000 × ₹9)	₹3,15,000
Less: Fixed cost	3,60,000
Loss	(45,000)

3. Contribution is ₹8.70 (*less* by 30 paise commission paid to store manager): (₹30 – ₹21.30)
   BEP (units) = ₹3,60,000/₹8.70 = 41,380 pairs
   BEP (amount) = ₹3,60,000/0.29 = ₹12,41,379.30
   P/V ratio = ₹8.70/₹30 = 29 per cent
4. CM per unit beyond the BEP × Margin of safety in units = Income
   ₹8.70 × 10,000 (50,000 – 40,000) = ₹87,000
5. Revised CM and P/V ratio
   Sales price ₹30.00
   Cost of shoes 19.50
   CM 10.50
   P/V ratio (%) 35
   Fixed costs = ₹3,60,000 + ₹81,000 = ₹4,41,000
   BEP (in units) = ₹4,41,000/₹10.50 = 42,000 units
   BEP (amount) = ₹4,41,000/0.35 = ₹12,60,000
   Alternatively, 42,000 × ₹30 = ₹12,60,000
6. No, the analysis will not hold true because in the volume-cost-profit relationship, it is assumed that production is equal to sales in the manufacturing firms or purchases are equal to sales in the case of trading firms.

P.16.12 Market Well Ltd manufactures filing cabinets. For the current year, the company expects to sell 4,000 cabinets involving a loss of ₹2,00,000. Only 40 per cent of the plant's normal capacity is being utilised during the current year. The fixed costs for the year are ₹10,00,000 and fully variable costs are 60 per cent of sales value. **LO 16.1, 2** **LOD: D**

You are required to

1. Calculate the break-even point;
2. Calculate the profit if the company operates at 70 per cent of its normal capacity;
3. Calculate the sales required to achieve a profit of ₹60,00,000;
4. Calculate the revised break-even point if the existing selling prices are decreased by 10 per cent, the total fixed and variable expenses remaining the same.

Solution

1. BEP (amount) = FC/ PV ratio = ₹10,00,000/0.40 = ₹25,00,000
2. Determination of the Existing Sales Volume and Sales Price per Cabinet

Sales revenue	*X*
Less: Variable cost (0.60)	0.6 *X*
Contribution	(*X* – 0.6*X*)
Less: Fixed costs	₹10,00,000
Loss (given)	2,00,000

0.4 X – ₹10,00,000 = (– ₹2,00,000)
0.4 X = ₹8,00,000
X = 20,00,000 (sales revenue)
Sales price per cabinet = ₹20,00,000/4,000 cabinets = ₹500
Number of cabinets sold at 70 per cent capacity = 7,000 = (4,000 × 70/40)

Projected Income Statement at 70 per cent Capacity

Sales revenue (7,000 × ₹500)	₹35,00,000
Less: Variable cost (0.60)	21,00,000
Contribution	14,00,000
Less: Fixed costs	10,00,000
Profit	4,00,000

Alternatively, (Expected sales revenue – Break-even sales revenue) × P/V ratio or (Margin of safety) × P/V ratio = (₹35,00,000 – ₹25,00,000) × 0.40 = ₹4,00,000

3. Desired sales volume to earn a profit of ₹60,00,000 = (FC + ₹60,00,000)/0.40 = (₹10,00,000 + ₹60,00,000)/0.40 = ₹1,75,00,000

4. Break-even Point (Revised) at Reduced Selling Price by 10 per cent

Sales price	₹450
Less: Variable cost (0.60 × ₹500)	300
CM	150
P/V ratio (₹150/₹450) (%)	33.33
BEP ₹(10,00,000/0.3333)	30,00,000

P.16.13 The question as to which products to stress in order to obtain the most profitable sales-mix has always been of prime importance to businessmen. The amount of profit contribution, or the difference between the selling price and the variable costs, tells how much each product is contributing to fixed costs and profit in the present sales-mix. This information assists management in forming an opinion as to which products will add to profits if sales of these units can be increased. LO 16.1, 2 LOD: M

Direct cost data can be utilised in this type of analysis when management seeks an answer to the question: "Which product shall we push"?

Data	*Product A*	*Product B*
Selling price	₹126.00	₹55.00
Variable cost	96.20	41.80
Fixed costs	20.70	6.50
Units per hour	45	70

1. What is the amount of net profit for each product?
2. What is the percentage of profit to selling price for each product?
3. What is the amount of profit contribution towards fixed cost and the profit for each product?
4. What is the profit contribution ratio?
5. What is the profit contribution per hour for each product?
6. If one allocates: (a) 200 hours to Product *A* and 100 hours to Product *B* or (b) 100 hours to Product *A* and 200 hours to Product B, which of the two courses is more profitable?

Solution

1. Net Profit for Products *A* and *B*

Particulars	A	B
Selling price	₹126.00	₹55.00
Less: Costs:		
Variable	96.20	41.80
Fixed	20.70	6.50
Net profit	9.10	6.70

	A	B
2. Percentage of profit to selling price = (Net profit × 100) ÷ Selling price	7.22	12.18
3. Profit contribution (Selling price-Variable costs)	29.80	13.20
4. P/V ratio (%)	23.65	24
5. (Profit contribution per unit × Units produced per hour)		
Product *A* : ₹29.8 × 45	1,341	
B : ₹13.2 × 70		924

6. Statement of Profit Contribution

Particulars	Alternative (a)	Alternative (b)
Product A (Profit contribution per hour × Hours)	₹1,341 × 200	₹1,341 × 100
	(a) 2,68,200	(a) 1,34,100
Product B (Profit contribution per hour × Hours)	924 × 100	924 × 200
	(b) 92,400	(b) 1,84,800
Total profit contribution [(a) + (b)]	3,60,600	3,18,900

Alternative (a) of allocating 200 hours to Product *A* and 100 hours to Product *B* is the more profitable course as it yields higher contribution.

P.16.14 A.T. Ltd operating at 80 per cent level of activity furnishes the following information: LO 16.1, 2 LOD: D

Particulars	Products		
	A	B	C
Selling price/units	₹10	₹12	₹20
Profit as percentage on selling price	25	33.33	20
Units produced and sold	10,000	15,000	5,000
Fixed costs	40,000	45,000	25,000

During the year, the variable costs are expected to increase by 10 per cent. There will, however, be no change in fixed costs, the selling prices and the units to be produced and sold. The sales potential for each of the products is unlimited.

(i) You are required to prepare a statement showing the P/V ratio, break-even point and margin of safety for each product and for the company as a whole.

(ii) The company intends to increase the production of only one of the three products to reach the full capacity level by utilising the spare capacity available. Assuming that all the three products take the same machine time, advise with reasons, which of the three products should be produced so that the overall profitability is the maximum.

Solution

(i) Statement showing BEP, Margin of Safety and P/V Ratio of A.T. Ltd for Year 1 and 2

Particulars	Year 1				Year 2			
	A	B	C	All combined	A	B	C	All combined
Units produced and sold	10,000	15,000	5,000	30,000	10,000	15,000	5,000	30,000
Selling price per unit	₹10	₹12	₹20	₹12.666	₹10	₹12	₹20	₹12.666
Sales revenue	1,00,000	1,80,000	1,00,000	3,80,000	1,00,000	1,80,000	1,00,000	3,80,000
Less: Variable costs (see working notes)	35,000	75,000	55,000	1,65,000	38,500	82,500	60,500	1,81,500
Contribution	65,000	1,05,000	45,000	2,15,000	61,500	97,500	39,500	1,98,500
Less: Fixed costs	40,000	45,000	25,000	1,10,000	40,000	45,000	25,000	1,10,000
Operating profit	25,000	60,000	20,000	1,05,000	21,500	52,500	14,500	88,500
P/V ratio (%)	65	58.33	45	56.58	61.5	54.17	39.5	52.24
BEP				1,94,419				2,10,580
Margin of safety				1,85,581				1,69,420

WORKING NOTES

A ₹1,00,000 = 40,000 FC + ₹25,000 profit (0.25 × ₹1,00,000) + VC, that is, ₹35,000.

B ₹1,80,000 = 45,000 FC + ₹60,000 profit (0.3333 × ₹1,80,000) + VC, that is, ₹75,000.

C ₹1,00,000 = 25,000 FC + ₹20,000 profit (0.20 × ₹1,00,000) + VC, that is, ₹55,000.

(ii) Product *C* should be produced to utilise the *SP* are capacity of 20 per cent as its marginal contribution per unit is maximum as shown below:

Particulars	A	B	C
Sales price	₹10	₹12	₹20
Less: Variable cost per unit	3.5	5.0	11
CM	6.5	7.0	9.0

P.16.15 Hansa Ltd manufacturing a single product is facing severe competition in selling it at ₹50 per unit. The company is operating at 60 per cent level of activity at which level sales are ₹12,00,000; variable costs are ₹30 per unit; semi-variable costs may be considered fixed at ₹90,000 when output is nil and the variable element is ₹250 for each additional 1 per cent level of activity; fixed costs are ₹1,50,000 at the present level of activity, but if a level of activity of 80 per cent or above is reached, these costs are expected to increase by ₹50,000. **LO 16.2** **LOD: M**

To cope with the competition, the management of the company is considering a proposal to reduce the selling price by 5 per cent. You are required to prepare a statement showing the operating profit at levels of activity of 60 per cent, 70 per cent and 82 per cent, assuming that:

1. The selling price remains at ₹50; and
2. The selling price is reduced by 5 per cent.

Show also the number of units, which will be required to be sold to maintain the present profits if the company decides to reduce the selling price of the product 5 by per cent.

Solution

Statement Showing Operating Profit (Flexible Budgets)

Particulars	Percentage of capacity					
	60		70		82	
	Old selling price	New selling price	Old selling price	New selling price	Old selling price	New selling price
Units	24,000	24,000	28,000	28,000	32,800	32,800
Sales price	₹50	₹47.50	₹50	₹47.50	₹50	₹47.50

(Contd.)

(Contd.)

Sales revenue	12,00,000	11,40,000	14,00,000	13,30,000	16,40,000	15,58,000
Less:	Costs:					
Variable costs	7,20,000	7,20,000	8,40,000	8,40,000	9,84,000	9,84,000
Semi-variable costs	1,05,000	1,05,000	1,07,500	1,07,500	1,10,500	1,10,500
Fixed costs	1,50,000	1,50,000	1,50,000	1,50,000	2,00,000	2,00,000
Total costs	9,75,000	9,75,000	10,97,500	10,97,500	12,94,500	12,94,500
Operating profit	2,25,000	1,65,000	3,02,500	2,32,500	3,45,500	2,63,500

Sales volume required to maintain present level of profit: (Fixed costs + Profit)/CM per unit = (₹1,50,000 + 90,000 + 2,25,000)/₹16.875 = 27,556 units

WORKING NOTE

Selling price		₹47.50
Less: Variable cost	₹30.00	
Semi variable cost (variable element)	0.625	30.625
CM per unit		16.875

P.16.16 From the cost records of a company for a specific period, for product X, the information given in the first column can be ignored since it is only one of the several projections of an assistant accountant, but it may be useful to you. LO 16.2 LOD: D

	This period actual	*One of the future projections*
Sales (units)	10,000	20,000
Profit (loss)	₹(10,000)	₹10,000
Fixed costs	30,000	30,000
Variable cost per unit	8	8

On the basis of the first column, determine

1. What increased sales volume is required to cover an additional attractive packaging cost of ₹0.50 per unit, to increase the sales, at the existing sales price, to yield zero profit?
2. What increased sales volume in required at the present sale price, to cover an additional publicity expense of ₹5,000 for that period, while yielding a profit of ₹5,000.
3. What increased sale volume is required to reach a profit of ₹4,000 while reducing the selling price by 3 per cent per unit?

Solution

1. *Sales volume required to yield zero profit*: = Fixed costs/CM per unit = ₹30,000/₹1.50 = 20,000 units
   Sales volume required = 20,000 units (₹2,00,000)
   Existing sales volume = 10,000 units (₹1,00,000)
   Difference represents increase in sales volume required to make zero profit = 10,000 units (₹1,00,000)
2. *Assuming situation (2) independent of (1)*: Sales volume required to earn a profit of ₹5,000 = [₹30,000 + ₹5,000 (publicity expenses) + ₹5,000 (profit)]/₹2 = 20,000 units (₹2,00,000); 10,000 units (₹1,00,000) is the increased sales volume required.
3. *Assuming (3) to be independent of situations (1) and (2)*: Desired sales volume to earn a profit of ₹4,000 = (₹30,000 + ₹4,000)/ (₹9.70 – 8) = 20,000 units (or ₹1,94,000). Increased sales volume required is 10,000 units.

WORKING NOTE

Determination of total sales revenue and selling price per unit:

Total sales revenue = Total costs – Loss

Total costs = FC + (VC per unit × Sales in units)

₹80,000 = ₹30,000 + (₹8 × 10,000)

Total sales revenue = ₹1,10,000 – ₹10,000 = ₹1,00,000

SP per unit = ₹1,00,000/10,000 = ₹10

P.16.17 The ABC Ltd operates a restaurant with recreational facilities. The manager of the complex having 100 rooms, has asked your assistance in planning the coming year's operations. He is particularly concerned about the level of profits the firm is likely to earn. LO 16.2 LOD: M

Your conversation with the manager shows that he expects occupancy to be 70 per cent during the 200-day season that it is open. All rooms would be rented for ₹500 per day for any number of persons. On an average, two persons occupy a room. This is the past experience, which the manager believes is an accurate guide to the future. He further informs you that each person staying in the hotel spends ₹125 per day in the shops (also owned by the company) and ₹250 in the restaurant. There are no charges for the use of recreational facilities.

Cost data are:

Particulars	*Variable cost to volume ratio*	
	Shop	*Restaurant*
Cost of goods sold	50	25
Supplies	5	15
Others	5	10

For the hotel, the variable costs are ₹100 per day per occupied room, for cleaning, laundry, and utilities. Total fixed costs for the complex are ₹60,00,000 per year.

You are required to do the following:

1. Prepare an income statement for the coming year based on the information given.
2. The manager believes that if room rent were reduced to ₹400 per day, the occupancy would increase to 90 per cent. Will you endorse his suggestion of reducing the rent rates?

Solution

1. *Income Statement*

Sales revenues:		
Hotel rooms (100 × 200 × 0.70 × ₹500)	₹70,00,000	
Shops (100 × 200 × 0.70 × 2 × ₹125)	35,00,000	
Restaurant (100 × 200 × 0.70 × 2 × ₹250)	70,00,000	
		₹1,75,00,000
Less: variable costs		
Hotel rooms (100 × 200 × 0.70 × ₹100)	14,00,000	
Shops (₹35,00,000 × 0.60, that is, 0.50 + 0.10)	21,00,000	
Restaurant (₹70,00,000 × 0.50 that is, 0.25 + 0.15 + 0.10)	35,00,000	70,00,000
Contribution		1,05,00,000
Less: fixed costs		60,00,000
Profit		45,00,000

2. *Income Statement (If Room Rents are Reduced)*

Sales revenue		
Hotel room (100 × 200 × 0.90 × ₹400)	₹72,00,000	
Shops (100 × 200 × 0.90 × 2 × ₹125)	45,00,000	
Restaurant (100 × 200 × 0.90 × 2 × ₹250)	90,00,000	₹2,07,00,000
Less: variable costs		
Hotel rooms (100 × 200 × 0.90 × ₹100)	18,00,000	
Shops (₹45,00,000 × 0.60)	27,00,000	
Restaurant (₹90,00,000 × 0.50)	45,00,000	90,00,000
Contribution		1,17,00,000
Less: fixed costs		60,00,000
Profit		57,00,000

Yes, we endorse the manager's suggestion to reduce the room rent as it augments profit.

P.16.18 After a study of cost-volume relationships, the Kaling Tubes Company Ltd concluded that its costs for any given volume of sales could be expressed as ₹1,00,000 for fixed costs plus variable costs equal to 60 per cent of sales. The company's range of volume was from zero to ₹8,00,000 of sales. LO 16.2 LOD: M

Prepare a graph, which will illustrate this cost-volume relationship. Also draw a proper sales line to the graph to form a break-even chart. Determine the break-even point.

A competitor operating a plant of the same size as Kaling also has fixed cost of approximately ₹1,00,000 per year, but his break-even point is ₹3,00,000 of sales. What may be the probable causes of the difference between the break- even points of the Kaling Company Ltd and its competitor?

Solution

Since selling price per unit is not given, it is necessary to draw the cost-volume graph on the same scale so that a 45° line can be the proxy of the sales line.

Determination of Two Points for Drawing the Total Cost Line

Sales revenue	FC	VC	TC
₹1,00,000	₹1,00,000	₹60,000	₹1,60,000
8,00,000	1,00,000	4,80,000	5,80,000

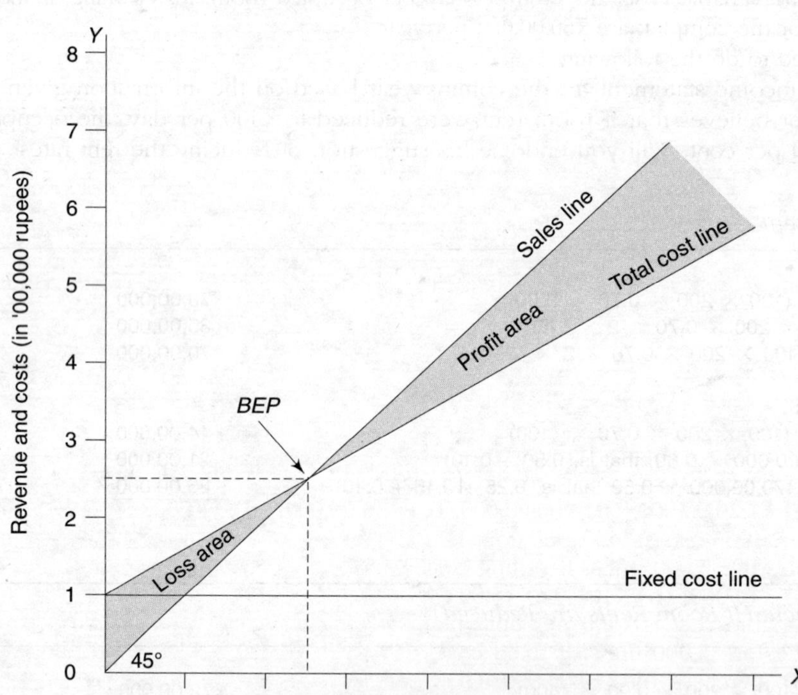

FIG. 16.14 *Volume-Cost-Profit Graph*

The point of intersection of the TC line and sales line is BEP (₹2,50,000).

Verification: FC/P/V ratio = ₹1,00,000/0.40 = ₹2,50,000

Possible causes for the differences in BEP:

1. The competitors are having a higher variable cost to volume ratio than the Kaling Tubes Ltd. It is 66.67 per cent for the competitors, assuming the selling price per unit for both the firms is same.

BEP = FC/ P/V ratio = ₹3,00,000 = ₹1,00,000 P/V ratio
P/V ratio = ₹1,00,000/ ₹3,00,000 = 33.33 per cent

2. The competitors are having lower sales price per unit. Their prices per units are 6.67 per cent lower than those of the Kaling Tubes Ltd as shown below:
BEP = ₹1,00,000/(0.9333-0.60) = ₹1,00,000/0.3333 = ₹3,00,000
3. Partly due to higher variable cost to volume ratio or partly due to lower selling price, the sum of the difference is 6.67 per cent.

REVIEW QUESTIONS

LOD: Easy

RQ.16.1 In the following multiple choice questions, select the correct answers. LO 16.1,2

(i) The margin of safety for a firm in a very volatile market is 5 per cent. Which of the following is true?
(a) The margin of safety is probably too high, **(b)** The margin of safety is probably too low, **(c)** The margin of safety is adequate, **(d)** We can't tell.

(ii) Contribution per unit is ₹100. Fixed costs are ₹6,00,000. Production and sales are 8,000 units. When sales rise
(a) total contribution rises by an amount greater than profit, **(b)** total contribution rises by an amount smaller than profit, **(c)** total contribution and profit rise by the same amount, **(d)** contribution margin drops.

(iii) Contribution per unit is ₹100. Fixed costs are ₹6,00,000. Production and sales are 8,000 units. Total contribution is
(a) ₹6,00,000, **(b)** ₹4,00,000, **(c)** ₹8,00,000, **(d)** None of the above.

(iv) Contribution per unit is ₹100. Fixed costs are ₹6,00,000. Production and sales are 8,000 units. Profit is
(a) ₹2,00,000, **(b)** ₹6,00,000, **(c)** ₹6,00,000, **(d)** None of the above.

(v) Break-even is not affected with changes in
(a) sales price per unit, **(b)** variable cost per unit, **(c)** total fixed costs, **(d)** number of units sold.

(vi) Contribution margin ratio (C/V ratio) is 25%. The fixed costs are ₹30,00,000. The break even point is
(a) ₹1,20,00,000, **(b)** ₹60,00,000, **(c)** ₹30,00,000, **(d)** ₹15,00,000.

(vii) Variable cost is ₹400 per unit, fixed costs are ₹80,00,000, selling price per unit is ₹900, sales are 5,000 units. If selling price increases by ₹100, contribution increases by
(a) ₹10,000, **(b)** ₹100, **(c)** ₹5,00,000, **(d)** ₹80,00,000.

(viii) Variable cost is ₹400 per unit, fixed costs are ₹80,00,000, selling price per unit is ₹900, sales are 5,000 units. If fixed costs increase by ₹10,00,000, contribution
(a) increases by ₹10,00,000, **(b)** decreases by ₹10,00,000, **(c)** remains unchanged, **(d)** can't say.

(ix) Variable cost is ₹400 per unit, fixed costs are ₹80,00,000, selling price per unit is ₹900, sales are 5,000 units. If sales decrease by 2,000 units, contribution margin
(a) increases by ₹10,00,000, **(b)** decreases by ₹10,00,000, **(c)** remains unchanged, **(d)** can't say.

(x) Variable cost is ₹400 per unit, fixed costs are ₹80,00,000, selling price per unit is ₹900, sales are 5,000 units. The target profit is ₹1,00,00,000. What must the sales revenue be?
(a) ₹3,24,00,000, **(b)** ₹2,00,00,000, **(c)** ₹1,60,00,000, **(d)** ₹3,53,00,000.

(xi) Company B sells two products:
Product A: [Contribution margin ratio = 20%, Sales = ₹100,000]

Product B: [Contribution margin ratio = 40%, Sales = ₹200,000]
If actual sales were (A) ₹200,000 and (B) ₹100,000, total contribution would:
(a) increase by ₹20,000, **(b)** decrease by ₹20,000, **(c)** increase by ₹40,000, **(d)** decrease by ₹40,000

(xii) Company B sells two products:
Product A: [Contribution margin ratio = 20%, Sales = ₹100,000]
Product B: [Contribution margin ratio = 40%, Sales = ₹200,000]
If actual sales were (A) ₹200,000 and (B) ₹100,000, fixed costs are ₹50,000. The break-even point in sales revenue would be
(a) ₹175,000, **(b)** ₹200,000, **(c)** ₹150,000, **(d)** ₹187,970.

(xiii) One of the following is not an assumption that underlies CVP analysis.
(a) Fixed costs per unit will remain the same throughout the relevant range. **(b)** Variable cost per unit will increase as sales increases. **(c)** Variable costs have a linear relationship with sales. **(d)** Selling price is constant throughout the relevant range.

(xiv) Which is the correct equation that calculates P (profit before tax)
Assume, Selling Price per unit = ₹S, Variable Cost per unit = ₹V, Number of units sold = U units and Total Fixed costs = ₹F.
(a) P = SV – F, **(b)** P = U (S – V) – F, **(c)** P = FS – V, **(d)** P = S (V – S).

(xv) The break-even point is 10,000 units, sales are 12,000 units. The margin of safety expressed in percentage is:
(a) 16.67%, **(b)** 80%, **(c)** 120%, **(d)** 20%.

[Answers: (i) b (ii) c (iii) c (iv) a (v) d (vi) a (vii) c (viii) c (ix) b (x) a (xi) b (xii) d (xiii) b (xiv) b (xv) a.]

RQ.16.2 Define break-even analysis and outline its uses and applications. LO 16.2

RQ.16.3 **(a)** Discus the importance of the following in relation to break-even analysis: LO 16.1,2
(1) Break-even point
(2) Margin of safety
(3) Contribution
(4) Profit volume ratio.
(b) Write a short note on the angle of incidence in a break-even chart.

RQ.16.4 Explain the limitations of a break-even analysis. LO 16.2

RQ.16.5 What is cash break-even point? Draw a cash break-even chart with hypothetical figures. LO 16.3

RQ.16.6 Asian Industries Ltd. specialises in the manufacture of small capacity motors. The cost structure of a motor is as under: Material, ₹50; Labour, ₹80; Variable over-heads, 75 per cent of labour cost. Fixed overheads of the company amount to ₹2.40 lakh per annum. The sale price of the motor is ₹230 each. LO 16.1,2
(a) Determine the number of motors that have to be manufactured and sold in a year in order to break-even.
(b) How many motors have to be made and sold to make a profit of ₹1 lakh per year?
(c) If the sale price is reduced by ₹15 each, how many motors have to be sold to break-even?

RQ.16.7 You are given the following information: LO 16.1,2

Output and sales (10,000 units)	₹2,00,000
Variable costs per unit	12
Fixed cost	40,000

It is proposed to reduce the selling price by 10 per cent.
(a) Calculate present and future profit–volume ratio

(b) Calculate present and future break–even points and

(c) Compute the sales volume to maintain the profit at the present level

RQ.16.8 **(a)** From the following data of a manufacturing unit, find out (i) sales to break-even and (ii) sales to earn a profit of ₹8,000. LO 16.1,2

Sales (8,000 units @ ₹10)	₹80,000
Variable expenses	64,000
Contribution	16,000
Fixed expenses	24,000
Loss	(8,000)

(b) The following information is available for companies A and B.

	Company A		Company B	
Units produced and sold		40,000		40,000
Revenue		₹80,000		₹80,000
Variable costs	₹20,000		₹60,000	
Fixed costs	50,000	70,000	10,000	70,000
Net operating income		10,000		10,000

(i) What is the break-even point for each company?

(ii) How would you explain the difference that you observe between these companies' break-even points?

LOD: Medium

RQ.16.9 Explain the significance and objective of a break-even chart and state the factors which would cause the break-even point to change. LO 16.2

RQ.16.10 A "break-even chart must be used with intelligent discrimination, with an adequate grasp of assumptions underlying the technique surrounding its practical application." Elucidate the statement giving illustrations. LO 16.2

RQ.16.11 Draw a break-even chart with a few illustrative figures. Explain the VCP relationship. How would a change in selling price affect the above? LO 16.2

RQ.16.12 The "volume-cost-profit relationships provide management with a simplified framework for organising its thinking on a number of problems." Discuss. LO 16.2

RQ.16.13 From the following information, find (a) BEP in rupees, and **(b)** number of units to be sold to earn a net income of 10% of sales: LO 16.1,2

Selling price	₹20 per unit
Variable cost	12 per unit
Fixed cost	₹2,40,000

RQ.16.14 For two periods sales and profits were as under LO 16.1,2

	Period I	Period II
Sales	₹4,00,000	₹5,00,000
Profit	1,00,000	1,40,000

Find **(a)** BESR, **(b)** Sales for a profit of ₹2,00,000, **(c)** Profit when sales are ₹6,00,000, and **(d)** Margin of safety when profit is ₹50,000.

RQ.16.15 Two companies P Ltd. and Q Ltd. producing and selling similar products forecasted their Profits and Loss a/c for the next year, which is as follows: LO 16.1,2

	P Ltd.		Q Ltd.	
Sales		₹3,00,000		₹3,00,000
Less: Variable Cost	₹2,00,000		₹2,25,000	
Fixed Expenses	50,000	2,50,000	25,000	2,50,000
Estimated Profit		50,000		50,000

Calculate:

(a) P/V ratio, break-even point, and margin of safety for both the companies. **(b)** Sales required to earn a profit of ₹30,000 for both companies. **(c)** Under the following situations, which company will show better results (i) Increase in sales (ii) Decrease in sales.

RQ.16.16 The Taylor Company Ltd. produces two products, A and B. Expected data for the first year of operations is: **LO 16.1,2**

	A	B
Expected sales (units)	8,000	12,000
Selling price	₹45	₹55
Variable costs	30	35

Total fixed costs are expected to be ₹3,60,000 for the year.

You are required to answer the following:

(i) If sales, prices, and costs are as expected, what will be the operating income and the break-even volume in sales revenue?

(ii) Assume that prices and costs were as expected, but Taylor sold 12,000 units of A and 8,000 units of B. Recalculate the operating income and the break-even volume in sales revenue.

RQ.16.17 The per tyre price structure of a cycle made by the Cycle Company Ltd. is as follows: **LO 16.2**

Material	₹60
Labour	20
Variable overheads	20
	100
Fixed overheads	50
Profit	50
Selling price	200

This is based on the manufacture of 1 lakh tyres per annum.

The company expects that due to competition, they will have to reduce selling price, but they want to keep the total profit intact. What level of production will have to be reached, that is, how many tyres will have to be made to get the same amount of profits, if: (a) the selling price is reduced by 10 per cent, (b) the selling price is reduced by 20 per cent?

RQ.16.18 Two manufacturing companies, having the following operating details, decide to merge: **LO 16.1,2**

	Company 1	Company 2
Capacity utilization (%)	90	60
Sales (₹lakh)	540	300
Variable costs (₹lakh)	396	225
Fixed costs (₹lakh)	80	50

Assuming that the merger goes through, calculate:

(i) Break-even sales of the merged plant and the capacity utilisation at that stage.

(ii) Profitability of the merged plant at 80 per cent capacity utilisation.

(iii) Sales turnover of the merged plant to earn a profit of ₹75 lakh.

(iv) When the merged plant is working at a capacity to earn a profit of ₹75 lakh, what percentage increase in selling price is required to sustain an increase of 5 per cent in fixed overheads?

RQ.16.19 A, B, and C are three similar plants under the same management who wants to merge them for better operation. The details are as under: **LO 16.1,2**

Plant	A	B	C
Capacity operated (%)	100	70	50
Turnover (₹lakh)	300	280	150
Variable costs	200	210	75
Fixed costs	70	50	62

You have to find out: (i) the capacity of the merged plant for breaking event, (ii) the profit at 75 per cent capacity of the merged plant, and (iii) the turnover from the merged plant to give a profit of ₹28 lakh.

RQ.16.20 Cookwell Ltd. manufactures pressure cookers with the selling price being ₹300 per unit. **LO 16.2** Currently the capacity utilisation is 60 per cent with a sales turnover of ₹18 lakh. The company proposes to reduce the selling price by 20 per cent but desires to maintain the same profit position by increasing the output. Assuming that all the increased output could be made and sold, determine the level at which the company should operate to achieve the desired objective.

The following data is further available:

(i) Variable costs per unit, ₹60.

(ii) Semi-variable costs (including a variable element of ₹10 per unit), ₹1,80,000.

(iii) Fixed costs, ₹3,00,000 will remain constant up to 80 per cent level. Beyond this an additional amount of ₹60,000 will be incurred.

RQ.16.21 Kalyan University conducts a special course on "Computer Applications" for a month during summer. For this, it invites applications from graduates. An entrance test is taken of the candidates and based on the same, a final selection of hundred candidates is made. The entrance test consists of four objective type examinations and is spread over four days with one examination per day. Each candidate is charged a fee of ₹50 for appearing in the entrance text. The following data relates to the past two years: **LO 16.1,2**

Statement of net revenue from the entrance text for the course on "Computer Applications"

	Year 1	*Year 2*
Gross revenue (fees collected)	₹1,00,000	₹1,50,000
Costs		
Valuation	40,000	60,000
Question booklets	20,000	30,000
Hall rent at ₹2,000 per day	8,000	8,000
Honorarium to chief administrator	6,000	6,000
Supervision charges (one supervisor for every 100 candidates at the rate of ₹50 per day)	4,000	6,000
General administration expenses	6,000	6,000
Total costs	84,000	1,16,000
Net revenue	16,000	34,000

You are required to compute **(a)** the budgeted net revenue if 4,000 candidates are expected to take up the entrance test next year, **(b)** the break-even number of candidates, and **(c)** the number of candidates to be enrolled if the net income desired is ₹20,000.

RQ.16.22 Bharat Company Ltd. is at present operating at 60 per cent capacity, producing at the rate of 10,000 units a month, a single product selling for ₹9 a unit. The current year's results are as follows: **LO 16.1,2**

Sales (1,20,000 units @ ₹9)		₹10,80,000
Cost of sales		
Direct material	₹1,80,000	
Direct labour	3,60,000	
Variable overheads	90,000	
Fixed overheads	1,35,000	7,65,000
Gross profit		3,15,000
Selling expenses		
Fixed	₹50,000	
Variable	36,000	22,000
Administration expenses: fixed		22,000
		2,07,000

Although this firm is operating at a relatively high net profit rate of almost 20 per cent on sales even at a plant capacity of 60 per cent; it is a fact that if the price per unit could be reduced by 20 per cent, the volume of sales would increase to 1,80,000 units per year with an increase in the fixed manufacturing overheads of ₹9,000 per year. If sales price could be reduced by $33^1/_3$ per cent, the volume of sales would increase to a full capacity of 2,00,000 units with increase in excess of the 60 per cent level as follows: fixed manufacturing overheads, ₹11,000; fixed selling expenses, ₹2,000; and fixed administrative expenses, ₹6,000.

You are required to prepare **(i)** a comparative statement showing the net income under the three alternative profit-volume relationships, and **(ii)** compute the break-even sales point in each case.

RQ.16.23 A company is considering expansion. Fixed costs amount to ₹4,20,000 and are expected to increase by 1,25,000 when plant expansion is completed. The present plant capacity is 80,000 units a year. Capacity will increase by 50 per cent with expansion. Variable costs are currently ₹6.80 per unit and are expected to go down by ₹0.40 per unit with the expansion. The current selling price is ₹16 per unit and is expected to remain the same under each alternative. What are the break-even points under each alternative? Which alternative is better, and why? **LO 16.1,2**

RQ.16.24 The sales of Forma Ltd. in the first half of the current year amounted to ₹2,70,000 and profit earned was ₹7,200. The sales in the second half year registered an increase and amounted to ₹3,42,000. The profit earned was ₹20,700 in that half year. Assuming no change in fixed cost, calculate **(i)** the *P/V* ratio, **(ii)** the amount of profit when sales are ₹2,16,000, and **(iii)** the amount of sales required to earn a profit of ₹36,000. **LO 16.2**

RQ.16.25 The following particulars are given: current unit price, ₹1,000; unit variable cost, ₹500; fixed costs, ₹30 lakh. **LO 16.2**

The following two suggestions are under the consideration of the management of an industrial company: **(a)** 10 per cent reduction in price to yield an increase in sales volume from 6,600 to 7,900 units **(b)** 10 per cent increase in price with decrease in volume of sales from 6,600 to 5,700 units.

Prepare a statement comparing gross revenue, profit contribution and *P/V* ratio of these two alternatives with the present results. Which suggestion would you recommend?

RQ.16.26 Reprographics Ltd. manufactures a document-reproducing machine which has a variable cost structure as follows: **LO 16.2**

Material	₹40
Labour	10
Overheads	4
Selling price	90

Sales during the current year are expected to be ₹13,50,000 and fixed overheads, ₹1,40,000.

Under a wage agreement, an increase of 10 per cent is payable to all direct workers from the beginning of the forthcoming year, while the material costs are expected to increase by 7.5 per cent, variable overhead costs by 5 percent, and fixed overhead costs by 3 per cent.

You are required to calculate: **(a)** the new selling price if the current profit/volume ratio is to be maintained, and **(b)** the quantity to be sold during the forthcoming year to yield the same amount of profit as the current year, assuming the selling price is to remain at ₹90.

RQ.16.27 The cost structure (%) of an article with a selling price of ₹45,000 is as follows: **LO 16.2**

Direct material	50
Direct labour	20
Overheads	30

An increase of 15 per cent in the cost of material and of 25 per cent in the cost of labour is anticipated. These increased costs in relation to the present selling price would cause a 25 per cent decrease in the amount of present profit per article.

You are required **(a)** to prepare a statement of profit per article at present and **(b)** the revised selling price to produce the same percentage of profit to sales as before.

LOD: Difficult

RQ.16.28 "The effect of a price increase is always to increase the P/V ratio, to bring down the break-even point and to widen the margin of safety." Discuss. **LO 16.2**

RQ.16.29 An analysis of costs of Sullivan Manufacturing Company gives the following information. You are required to determine **LO 16.1,2**

(a) Break-even sales volume

(b) Profit at the budgeted sales of ₹18,50,000.

Cost elements	*Variable costs (Percentage of sales)*	*Fixed costs*
Direct materials	32.8	
Director labour	28.4	
Factory overheads	12.6	₹1,89,900
Distribution overheads	4.1	58,400
Administrative overheads	1.1	66,700

RQ.16.30 PQR Ltd. has furnished the following data for the two years: **LO 16.1,2**

	Year I	*Year II*
Sales	₹8,00,000	?
Profit/volume ratio (P/V ratio) (%)	50	37.5
Margin of safety sales as a % of total sales	40	21.875

There has been substantial savings in the fixed cost in the year 2 due to the restructuring process. The company could maintain its sales quantity level of year 1 in year 2 by reducing selling price.

You are required to calculate the following:

(i) Sales for year 2

(ii) Fixed cost for year 2

(iii) Break-even sales for year 2

RQ.16.31 For two consecutive years, sales and losses were as follows: **LO 16.1**

Particulars	*Year 1*	*Year 2*
Sales revenue	₹10,00,000	₹15,00,000
Loss	2,00,000	50,000

Determine break-even sales.

RQ.16.32 A company has an opening stock of 6,000 units of output. The production planned for the current period is 24,000 units and expected sales for the current period amount to 28,000 units. The selling price per unit of output is ₹10. Variable cost per unit is expected to be ₹6 per unit while it was only ₹5 per unit during the previous period. What is the break-even volume for the current period if the total fixed costs for the current period are ₹86,000? Assume that the first-in first-out system is followed. **LO 16.1**

RQ.16.33 Small Ltd. has been offered a choice to buy one out of two machines, 'A' and 'B'. You are required to compute: **LO 16.1,2**

(a) Break-even point for each of the machines.

(b) The level of sales at which both machines would earn equal profit.

(c) The range of sales at which one is more profitable than the other.

The relevant data is given below:

	Machines	
	A	*B*
Annual output in units	10,000	10,000
Fixed costs	₹30,000	₹16,000
Profit at above level of production	30,000	24,000

The market price of the product is expected to be ₹10 per unit.

RQ.16.34 The following information is furnished to you with regard to a manufacturing concern for its operations during year 1. **LO 16.1,2**

Direct material	₹1,75,000
Direct labour	50,000
Fixed overheads	55,000
Semi-variable overheads	70,000
Variable overheads	65,000
Sales (at ₹800 per unit)	4,00,000

It was estimated that, at *the existing level of capacity utilisation,* half the semi-variable overheads were in the nature of fixed overheads, whereas variable overheads accounted for the other half.

You are required to make necessary calculations to answer the following queries:

(i) At what level of output is the break-even point likely to be reached during the year 2, if there is no change in the price level?

(ii) What price per unit should be quoted in respect of a tender to be executed during year 3 if fixed costs are likely to go up by 10 per cent, variable costs by 20 per cent, and a 12 per cent profit margin is sought to be attained on the total cost?

ANSWERS

RQ.16.6 **(a)** BEP 6,000 motors, **(b)** 8,500 motors, **(c)** 9,600 motors
RQ.16.7 **(a)** P/V ratio 40% and 33⅓, **(b)** BEP 5,000 and 6,667 units, **(c)** ₹2,40,000
RQ.16.8 **(a) (i)** BESR ₹1,20,000 **(ii)** ₹1,60,000
(b) (i) BSER ₹66,667 (Company A), ₹40,000 (Company B)
(ii) Fixed costs of Company A are higher than those of Company B
RQ.16.13 **(a)** BESR ₹6,00,000, **(b)** 40,000 units
RQ.16.14 **(a)** BESR ₹1,50,000, **(b)** ₹6,50,000, **(c)** ₹1,80,000, **(d)** ₹1,25,000
RQ.16.15 **(a)** P Ltd.: P/V ratio 33⅓%, BESR ₹1,50,000, Margin of safety ₹1,50,000; Q Ltd.: P/V ratio 25%, BESR ₹1,00,000, Margin of safety ₹2,00,000 **(b)** P (₹2,40,000), Q (₹2,20,000) **(c) (i)** Company P **(ii)** Company Q
RQ.16.16 **(i)** BESR ₹10,20,000, operating income is zero **(ii)** BESR ₹10,37,647, operating loss ₹20,000
RQ.16.17 **(a)** 1,25,000 cycles, **(b)** 1,66,667 cycles
RQ.16.18 **(i)** ₹25.9 lakh, **(ii)** ₹93 lakh, **(iii)** ₹791.23 lakh, **(iv)** 0.82%
RQ.16.19 **(i)** 52%, **(ii)** ₹80.5 lakh, **(iii)** ₹600 lakh
RQ.16.20 84.7% level of capacity
RQ.16.21 **(a)** ₹52,000 **(b)** 1,111 **(c)** 2,230
RQ.16.22 **(i)** Net income ₹2,07,000 (Existing), ₹81,000 (Reduction in price by 20%), loss ₹1,36,000 (Reduction in price by 33⅓%) **(ii)** BESR ₹5,40,000 (Existing), ₹9,42,546 (Reduction in price by 20%) ₹30,13,333 (Reduction in price by 33⅓%).
RQ.16.23 BEP 45,653 (Pre-expansion), BEP 56,771 (Post-expansion)
Net income ₹3,16,000 (Pre-expansion), ₹6,07,000 (Post-expansion)
RQ.16.24 **(i)** P/V ratio 18.75% **(ii)** Net loss ₹2,925 (6 months), ₹46,350 (12 months) **(iii)** ₹6,55,200
RQ.16.25 Increase in selling price is recommended.
RQ.16.26 **(a)** ₹97 **(b)** 17,114 units
RQ.16.27 **(a)** Profit ₹15,000 **(b)** ₹50,625
RQ.16.29 **(a)** BESR ₹15,00,000 **(b)** ₹73,500
RQ.16.30 **(i)** ₹6,40,000 **(ii)** ₹1,87,500 **(iii)** ₹5,00,000
RQ.16.31 BESR ₹16,66,667
RQ.16.32 BEP = 20,000 units
RQ.16.33 **(a)** BEP 5,000 units (Machine A), 4000 units (Machine B) **(b)** 7,000 units **(c)** 4,000 – 6,999 (B will be more profitable) for 7,000 units and above (A will be more profitable)
RQ.16.34 **(i)** 600 units **(ii)** ₹1,095.36

[Comprehensive solutions to all numerical review questions are available on the companion website: http://www.mhhe.com/khan_jain_ma7e]

CASES

16.C.1 Thandak Desert Coolers (VCP Analysis) Mr Coolguy of 'Thandak' desert coolers enjoys a monopoly in his local market catering to around 10,000 customers every year. His friend Mr Imandar Singh of 'Zordar' pumps supplies him good quality pumps at very reasonable rates (₹400 per pump). The year 2012 was not a good year for Mr. Coolguy. He lost his good friend Mr Imandar in a road accident. He also lost most of his savings in share market scam. The Sun God did not bless him with a hot summer and the sales were expected to fall by 20 per cent. To make the matter worse, the new head of 'Zordar' pumps, Mr Opportunist Singh increased the price of pumps by 30 per cent.

Mr Coolguy asked his chief accountant, Mr Calculator Singh, to show the current financial data and the projected financial data if the supply from Zordar pumps were to be maintained. Mr Calculator Singh came out with the following reports.

Cost Data

The cost data is divided into two parts: fixed cost and variable cost. The fixed and the variable components of the mixed costs are separated. The variable costs are divided into three major categories: direct material cost, direct labour costs and the variable overheads. The division of all the cost data is tabulated, for 10,000 units as well as 8,000 units, as follows:

(I) **Present Scenario (10,000 units)**

Item	*Fixed cost*	*Variable cost and expenses*		
		Direct material	*Direct labour*	*Variable overheads*
Labour	₹12,10,000		₹20,00,000	
Steel sheets		₹60,00,000		
Electricity	35,000			₹1,00,000
Depreciation	15,06,620			
Pumps (@ 400 per unit)		40,00,000		
Khus		9,00,000		
Tubes		5,00,000		
Wires		50,000		
Fan		14,50,000		
Telephone	4,580			4,60,000
Rent (office)	1,20,000			
Office expenses	22,000			3,46,000
Bank charges	18,000			
Insurance	35,000			
Repair and maintenance	25,000			2,40,000
Recruitment				64,000
Travel				3,80,000
Conveyance	16,800			1,90,000
Post, courier and parcel	7,000			1,70,000
Miscellaneous				1,50,000
Total	30,00,000	129,00,000	20,00,000	21,00,000

(II) **Future Scenario if Pumps are Bought from Zordar Pumps (8,000 units)**

Item	*Fixed cost*	*Variable cost and expenses*		
		Direct material	*Direct labour*	*Variable overheads*
Labour	₹12,10,000		₹16,00,000	
Steel sheets		₹48,00,000		
Electricity	35,000			₹80,000
Depreciation	15,06,620			
Pumps (@ 520 per unit)		41,60,000		
Khus		7,20,000		

(*Contd.*)

(*Contd.*)

Tubes		4,00,000		
Wires		40,000		
Fan		11,60,000		
Telephone	4,580			3,68,000
Rent (office)	1,20,000			
Office expenses	22,000			3,46,000
Bank charges	18,000			
Insurance	35,000			
Repair and maintenance	25,000			2,76,800
Recruitment				51,200
Travel				3,04,000
Conveyance	16,800			1,52,000
Post, courier and parcel	7,000			1,36,000
Miscellaneous				1,20,000
Total	30,00,000	112,80,000	16,00,000	18,34,000

(III) Comparative Analysis of Both Scenarios

Item	*10,000 units*	*8,000 units*
Sales revenue @ ₹2,500 per unit	₹250,00,000	₹200,00,000
Less: Variable costs		
Direct material	129,00,000	112,80,000
Direct labour	20,00,000	16,00,000
Variable overheads	21,00,000	18,34,000
Total contribution	80,00,000	52,86,000
Less: Total fixed costs	30,00,000	30,00,000
Operating profits	50,00,000	22,86,000

After going through the report Mr Coolguy realised that his profits would drop by ₹27.14 lakh if he continued to purchase pumps from Zordar pumps and sales drop to 8,000 units. Since there were no other pump manufacturers in the market, the only alternative for Mr Coolguy was to manufacture the pumps indigenously. But he had lost most of his money and for manufacturing pumps he needed to expand his factory and purchase a new machinery (overall ₹5 lakh more was needed). Raw material for pumps would be needed which would cost ₹300 per unit. Additional labour would be required to make the pumps, thus increasing the labour costs to ₹250 per unit. The making of pumps would also draw more electricity etc. thereby increasing the variable overhead costs. The banks were not willing to finance him. Mr Lalchi Singh, the loan shark, saw opportunity to make money and offered to loan money to Mr Coolguy for a period of one year at the rate of more than 20 per cent, the loan to be paid in two instalments of, ₹3 lakh each, the first one is to be made in the first six months and the second instalment at the end of the year. The interest would be paid at the end of the year. If Mr Coolguy fails to pay back the interest and the principal on the due date, Mr Lalchi would be entitled to auction off the factory and get back his sum. Mr Coolguy now has to decide whether to accept the offer or not.

Mr Coolguy asked Mr Calculator to find out the implications of the above mentioned factors on the profits and whether he would be able to satisfy Mr Lalchi's conditions. Mr Calculator came out with the following reports:

(IV) Cost if Loan is Taken for Production of Pumps

Item	*Fixed cost*	*Variable cost and expenses*		
		Direct material	*Direct labour*	*Variable overheads*
Labour	₹12,10,000		₹20,00,000	
Steel sheets		₹48,00,000		
Electricity	35,000			₹360,000
Depreciation	15,06,620			
Khus		7,20,000		
Tubes		4,00,000		
Wires		40,000		
Fan		11,60,000		
Telephone	4,580			3,68,000
Rent (office)	1,20,000			
Office expenses	22,000			3,46,000
Bank charges	18,000			
Insurance	35,000			
Repair and maintenance	25,000			2,76,800
Recruitment				51,200
Travel				3,04,000
Conveyance	16,800			1,52,000
Post, courier and parcel	7,000			1,36,000
Machinery	5,00,000			
Miscellaneous				1,20,000
Pump shaft		800,000		
Pump wires		400,000		
Pump cylinder		10,00,000		
Lubrication and insulation		200,000		
Total	3500,000	95,20,000	20,00,000	21,14,000

(V) Projected Profit when Pumps are Produced

Sales revenue @ ₹2,500 per unit (8,000 units)	₹200,00,000
Less: Variable costs	
Direct material	95,20,000
Direct labour	20,00,000
Variable overheads	21,14,000
Total contribution	63,66,000
Less: Fixed costs	35,00,000
Operating profit	28,66,000
Less: Interest + Principal	6,00,000
EBT	22,20,000

Contribution per unit = ₹63,66,000/8,000 = ₹795.75

BEP (units) = Total fixed cost/contribution margin per unit

= ₹41,00,000/795.75 = 5,152 units

Attributing no fixed cost in the first six months so as to pay the first instalment comfortably:

Number of units to be sold in the first six months = ₹300,000/contribution margin per unit

= ₹300,000/₹795.75 = 377 units

Number of units to be sold in the next six months = ₹38,00,000/₹795.75 = 4,775 units

Attributing half the fixed costs in the first six months:

Number of units to be sold in the first six months = ₹20,50,000/₹795.75 = 2,576 units

Number of units to be sold in the next six months = ₹20,50,000/₹795.75 = 2,576 units

Mr Calculator's Inference:

Manufacturing pumps indigenously would eat away the profits by another ₹66,000. There is also an inherent risk of default of the first instalment to Mr Lalchi as it would not be possible to sell even 377 units in the off season. There is no reason why Mr Coolguy should go ahead with the idea of indigenous pumps.

After seeing the income statement and break-even analysis, Mr Coolguy decided not to take the loan but since his son, Mr Cooldude (doing MBA from IIT Delhi) had come home for a few days. He thought it wise to take his opinion too.

Cooldude came up with a radically different opinion. He suggested that since the machinery was meant for long-term use, it would not be prudent to charge its cost in the current year itself. It would be better to amortise the cost over a period of five years. He suggested to amortise ₹1 lakh per year (assuming no sale value at the end of 5 years). This gave a different picture altogether.

(VI) **Cost Estimate (Revised)**

Item	Fixed cost	Variable cost and expenses for 8,000 units		
		Direct material	Direct labour	Variable overhead
Labour	₹12,10,000		₹20,00,000	
Steel sheets		₹48,00,000		
Electricity	35,000			₹360,000
Depreciation	15,06,620			
Khus		7,20,000		
Tubes		4,00,000		
Wires		40,000		
Fan		11,60,000		
Telephone	4,580			3,68,000
Rent (office)	1,20,000			
Office expenses	22,000			3,46,000
Bank charges	18,000			
Insurance	35,000			
Repair and maintenance	25,000			2,76,800
Recruitment				51,200
Travel				3,04,000
Conveyance	16,800			1,52,000
Post, courier and parcel	7,000			1,36,000
Miscellaneous				1,20,000
Depreciation on machinery	100,000			
Interest	1,00,000			
Pump shaft		800,000		
Pump wires		400,000		
Pump cylinder		10,00,000		
Lubrication and insulation		200,000		
Total	32,00,000	95,20,000	20,00,000	21,14,000

(VII) **Projected Profits (Revised)**

Sales revenue @ ₹2,500 per unit		₹200,00,000
Less: Variable costs		
Direct material		96,00,000
Direct labour		20,00,000
Variable overheads		20,34,000
Total contribution		63,66,000
Less: Fixed costs		32,00,000
EBIT		31,66,000

Cooldude then explained his father that charging the entire cost of the machine in the current year leads to the reduction in profits of the current year. Such purchases (capital expenditures) should be amortised over a period of time. Besides, payment of loan is not an expense. It is expense only to the extent of interest paid. Thus, what seemed to be a decrease in profit by ₹66,000 was actually an increase by ₹8,80,000.

At this juncture, Mr Coolguy became very enthusiastic about taking the loan. Cooldude then warned his father that Mr. Lalchi might have set up a trap for him as it was the beginning of February. Generally, desert coolers are not bought in these months. It would be difficult to sell even a modest target of 377 units (not taking the fixed costs into account in the first six months) in these months. However, by offering heavy off-season discount (up to 20 per cent) the sales can be pushed up significantly. Proper advertising should be done so as to inform the people that the discount would be available only for a short-term. As Thandak has a monopoly in the region, the people would like to cash on this opportunity, and the sales would go up. The discount should be discontinued as soon as the cash position (with respect to the first payment of instalment) is reached.

New selling price = ₹2,000

Revise contribution per unit = ₹295.75

₹3,00,000/₹295.75 = 1,014 units.

As soon as 1,014 units are sold the discount should be discontinued.

(VIII) **Projected Profits with Change in Selling Price**

Total contribution = 1,014* ₹295.75 + (8,000 – 1014)* ₹795.75	₹58,59,000
Less: Fixed costs	32,00,000
EBIT	26,59,000

Thus, the proposition of Mr Lalchi is not devoid of connivance. In order to pay the first instalment of ₹3 lakh to Mr Lalchi, Mr Coolguy would have to forego a substantial profit.

Recommendations

- Mr Coolguy should not take the loan this year.
- A mild summer one year is usually a harbinger of a scorching summer in the following year, in the city of Mr Coolguy. The demand for desert coolers is likely to shoot up the next year. It would not be prudent then to keep up purchasing pumps from Mr Opportunity Singh.
- Investment for making pumps should me made next year's winter from the profits of this year's summer.

16.C.2 (Break-even Point) Sybergrid Solutions is a Web Publishing firm involved in the design and hosting of websites for corporates and business houses. As the initial investment required to start web publishing is low, several new entrants have entered/are planning to enter this business. There are also some established players who are willing to operate at low margins. Website publishing is highly competitive coupled with low market demand.

A website consists of a number of web pages. On average, any website would be made up of 50 web pages. The costs, revenues and time are calculated on the basis of production of one web page, that is 1 unit = 1 web page (selling as ₹1,000).

Besides, Biplab Saha, the owner of Sybergrid Solutions, there are three permanent employees—a visualiser who does the conceptualising and designing the graphics, a DTP operator to enter data and make the design on the computer and an office boy. One contract programmer is also hired as and when Sybegrid gets an order for developing a website. The total hours available in a month are (7.5 × 25 × 3) 564 hours. The annual capacity is (564 × 12) 6,768 hours. The total man-hours per web page to make 1 web page are 8 hours consisting of 3 hours each taken by visualiser and owner/entrepreneur and 2 hours by the DTP operator.

The monthly man-power expenses are as follows: (i) Owner/entrepreneur, ₹12,000 (ii) Visualiser, ₹5,000, (iii) DTP operator, ₹4,000 and (iv) Office boy, ₹1,500.

The investments and operational expenses are summarised below:

Capital cost:		
Computers (2)	₹80,000	
Printer (1)	12,000	
Scanner (1)	35,000	
Internet connection per annum	15,000	₹1,42,500
Fixed cost per month:		
Rent	3,000	
Telephone	600	
Electricity	1,000	
Floppy disk, stationery and office expenses	500	
Books	250	
Magazines/newspapers	150	
Conveyance	1,000	6,500

The variable costs are given below:

Cost	*Rate*	*Time taken per web page*
Additional labour	₹30/hr	1 hour
Telephone	1.5/minute	10 minutes
Electricity	₹20 per web page	

These costs are classified into fixed and variable in Exhibit 1.

EXHIBIT 1 Fixed and Variable Costs

Cost element	*Fixed cost (annual)*	*Variable cost per 100 web page*		
		Direct labour	*Direct expenses*	*Selling expenses*
Labour:		₹3,000		
Owner/entrepreneur	₹1,44,000			
Visualiser	60,000			
DTP operator	48,000			
Office boy	18,000			
	2,70,000			
Rent	36,000			
Telephone	7,200		₹1,500	
Electricity	12,000		2,000	
Internet connection	15,000			
Floppy disks, stationery and office expenses	6,000		1,000	₹200

(*Contd.*)

(*Contd.*)

Depreciation (10%)*	12,700			
Interest (13%)**	16,500			
Conveyance	12,000			500
Magazine/newspapers	1,800			
Books	3,000			
Total	3,92,000	3,000	4,500	700

*₹1,27,000 (₹80,000 + ₹12,000 + ₹35,000) × 0.10

**₹1,27,000 × 0.13 (This is the opportunity cost of interest lost on owners funds used to buy computer, scanner and printer).

REQUIRED:

(a) Compute break-even sales revenue to establish viability of business.
(b) Compute number of orders to make operating profit of ₹15,000 per month.
(c) Determine sales volume required to offset reduction in sale price from ₹1,000 to ₹700 to maintain operating profit of ₹15,000 per month.
(d) Determine selling price at which Sybergrid would not suffer cash losses.

Solution

(a) Viability of business:

- Breakeven point (amount): Fixed cost ÷ CV ratio = ₹3,92,000 ÷ 0.918[@] = ₹4,27,015
  [@]Sales price, ₹1,000 – ₹82, variable cost per unit (₹8,200 ÷ 100) = ₹918 ÷ ₹1,000 = 91.8% = 0.981
- Break-even point (units) = ₹4,27,015 ÷ ₹1,000 = 427 pages
  Number of orders for website to break-even in one year = 427 pages ÷ 50 pages for an order on website = 8.54 (9) orders.

Man-hours required = 398 × 8 = 3,184
Total capacity = 6,278 man-hours
Capacity utilisation = 6,278 ÷ 3,184 = 50%

(b) Number of orders to get a desired profit of ₹15,000 per month (₹1,80,000 annual)
= [Fixed expenses + Desired profit] ÷ C/V ratio
= (₹3,92,000 + ₹1,80,000] ÷ 0.918 = ₹6,23,094 ÷ ₹1,000 = 623 pages
Number of website sale to make classified profit = 623 pages ÷ 50 pages = 12.46(13) orders per year to get the desired profit of ₹15,000 per month

(c) Additional sales volume required to offset a reduction in selling price from ₹1,000 to ₹700
Contribution (₹700 – ₹82) = ₹618 (revised)
C/V ratio = 88.29%
Sales volume to offset reduced selling price = [Desired profit + Fixed expenses] ÷ Revised C/V ratio
= ₹5,72,000 ÷ 0.8829 = ₹6,47,865 ÷ 100 = 648 web pages to be sold
Number of orders per year = 648 pages ÷ 50 pages = 13 orders

(d) Lowest selling price at which Sybergrid would not suffer cash losses.
Cash fixed cost = ₹3,92,000 – ₹12,700 Depreciation = ₹3,79,300
Desired Contribution per page = ₹3,79,300/427 BEP = ₹888.29
Desired selling price per page = Desired contribution (₹888.29) per page + Variable cost (₹82) per page = ₹970.29
Thus, the minimum price per web page should be ₹970.29 to avoid any cash losses.

16.C.3 (Break-even Analysis) Amit Behki is an automobile engineer. After graduating from the IIT-Delhi, he is planning to set up an automobile service station in NOIDA. The Amit Automobile Service Station (AASS) would carry out three activities: (i) free services of new vehicles under warranty, (ii) paid services including changing of parts and (ii) denting and painting of cars/vehicles.

The land on which the AASS would be set up, the estimated cost of which is ₹44,00,000 is owned by his family. A feasibility analysis conducted by Amit has revealed that the initial fixed cost of setting up of the AASS would be as detailed in Exhibit 1.

EXHIBIT 1 Initial Fixed Cost Estimates

Item/Description	*Amount*
Salary and wages	₹1,57,776
Staff welfare	6,852
Repair and maintenance	32,166
Conveyance	11,184
Printing/stationery	2,816
General expenses	1,539
Consumable stores (LUBES)	3,656
Postage/Telephone	8,948
Professional fee	15,000
Electricity	18,000
Local taxes	10,000
	2,67,937

The feasibility analysis also estimates the revenues and operating cost associated with the three workshop activities as detailed below:

Free Service of New Vehicles The service charges would be reimbursed by the Vehicle Dealer. The average reimbursement for the first, second and third services would be ₹233 per vehicle.

The variable costs related to the various service jobs performed by the cleaners/washers in servicing the vehicles are estimated as shown below.

• Detergents	₹20
• Diesel	18
• Cloth	20
• Polish	20
• Grease	30
• Stationery	5
• Customer hospitality (cold drink)	20
	133

Paid Services The variable costs would be the same as in the case of free servicing. An additional cost on parts changed would average ₹1,000 per vehicle.

The per vehicle average revenue would be ₹275. There would also be a 10 per cent margin on the parts changed.

Denting and Painting The lumpsum charged for full painting averages ₹8,000 per vehicle. The variable costs per vehicle are also shown below:

(i) Labour (painter) cost		₹1,500
(ii) Material costs:		
— Cleanser (4 litres × ₹26)	₹104	
— Additive solvent (8 litres × ₹126)	1,008	
— Putty	450	

(Contd.)

(Contd.)

— Paint (4 litres × ₹350)	1,400	
— Sheet metal	110	
— Sand paper	100	
— M-seal	350	
— Carbide for welding gas (8 × ₹32)	256	
— Welding rod	60	
— Files (2 × ₹375)	150	
— Rubbing and polish	200	
— Rubber seal compound	150	
— Nut bolts	100	4,438
		5,938

REQUIRED:

(a) If Amit wants the AASS to break-even in the first year, compute the breakeven (i) in units (number of cars) and (ii) in amount for all the three services offered?

(b) If Amit wants to earn a monthly surplus of ₹10,000, what would be the answer to (i) and (ii)?

Solution

(a) (i) Computation of break-even (in units) for free services, paid services and denting and painting

Free Service: Fixed cost ÷ Contribution margin per car = ₹2,67,937 ÷ ₹100 (₹233 – ₹133) = 2,680 vehicles ÷ 312 days (26 days in a month x 12 months) = 9 vehicles daily

Paid Services: ₹2,67,937 ÷ ₹242 [₹275 + ₹100(0.10 × ₹1,000) – ₹133 or ₹1,275 – ₹1,033] = 1,108 vehicles ÷ 312 days = 4 vehicles daily

Denting and Painting: ₹2,67,937 ÷ ₹2,062 [₹8,000 – ₹5,938] = 130 vehicles ÷ 12 = 11 vehicles per month

(a) (ii) Computation of break-even (amount)

Free Services: Fixed cost ÷ VC ratio = ₹2,67,937 ÷ 0.4292 (contribution margin, ₹100 ÷ ₹233, operating revenue) = ₹6,24,271

Paid Services: ₹2,67,937 ÷ 0.1898 (₹242 ÷ ₹1,275) = ₹14,11,681

Denting and Painting: ₹267,937 ÷ 0.25775 (₹2,067 ÷ ₹8,000) = ₹10,39,523

(b) (i) Computation of break (units) to earn a monthly surplus of ₹10,000 (annual surplus, ₹1,20,000)

Free Services: (Fixed cost, ₹2,67,937 + Desired surplus, ₹1,20,000) ÷ ₹100 = 3,880 vehicles per annum ÷ 312 days = 12 vehicles per day

Paid Services: (₹2,67,937 + ₹1,20,000) ÷ ₹242 = 1,603 vehicles ÷ 312 = 6 cars daily

Denting and Painting: (₹2,67,937 + ₹1,20,000) ÷ ₹2,062= 188 vehicles per year ÷ 12 = 16 vehicles monthly.

(b) (ii) Break-even (amount)

Free Services:(₹2,67,937 + ₹1,20,000) ÷ 0.4292 = ₹9,03,861

Paid Services:(₹2,67,937 + ₹1,20,000) ÷ 0.1898 = ₹20,43,925

Denting and Painting: (₹2,67,937 + ₹1,20,000) ÷ 0.25775 = ₹15,05,090.

16.C.4 (Break-even Analysis) Mr. Sharma has been manufacturing wooden table tops of sewing machines in Ajmer district of Rajasthan for the last 20 years. He supplies these wooden tables tops to various sewing machine table stand manufacturers and also sells them in the open market. Mr. Sharma had also started a foundry unit 20 years ago with one partner but this unit was closed and sold due to large losses and dispute with the partner after two years. Meanwhile, he earned good profit and reputation in manufacturing wooden table tops and visited various sewing machines table stand manufacturing units in the country. Based on his rich experience in this market, and in order to expand his business, he decided to manufacture sewing machine table stand himself under the 'GAUTAM' brand. For this, he decided to set up a new foundry unit to manufacture various table stand cast parts required in sewing machine table in addition to the existing wooden top manufacturing unit.

To fulfill his wish, Mr. Sharma purchased agricultural land 20 kilometers away from city in close proximity of Rajasthan Industrial Credit Corporation (RICCO) industrial area and later on converted it into industrial land for setting up the new casting unit. He designed the factory layout, cupola, heating furnace and also purchased required machinery and tools for casting within six months based on his experience. The unit started production in April, 2009.

Although Mr. Sharma is very sincere and hard working, he does not have any formal education in engineering and finance. His administrative staff is also not well educated. He is worried about his new casting unit because of his lack of formal knowledge in engineering and finance and due to his past failure.

Therefore, Mr. Sharma asked his son-in-law, Nitin Tiwari, who is faculty member in the Mechanical Engineering Department of Government Engineering College, Ajmer, to assist him. Nitin is an expert in design engineering and could not help much in this regard, but to maintain his rapport with his father-in-law, he decided to take help from one colleague, Mr. Devendra Choudhary, who has his post-graduation in Industrial Engineering and also has experience in financial management.

Mr. Choudhary readily agreed to help in order to get hands-on experience in this new and small casting unit. He visited Mr. Sharma and his company with Nitin in October, 2009 and gathered various cost data for break-even analysis.

Cost Data: Mr. Choudhary segregated cost data provided by Mr. Sharma into the following three categories:

Fixed Cost (at Normal Capacity of 60,000 Table Stands per Year)

Cupola	₹4,00,000
Expected life of cupola (years)	7
Temporary building shed	12,00,000
Expected life (years)	7
Heating furnace cost	2,00,000
Cost of Diesel Generator (DG) set	1,75,000
Cost of power connection	3,50,000
Monthly salary of permanent staff	35,000
Annual maintenance cost	2,00,000
Minimum monthly electricity bill	3,000
Minimum monthly telephone bill	3,000
Cost of patterns per year	30,000
Cost of machine block (air compressor sand blasting, lathe, grinding, drilling etc.)	13,25,000
Other annual costs which are fixed in nature (moulding boxes and crucibles)	14,429

The average economic life of plants in the casting industry is seven years. Annual fixed cost = (Cupola + Temporary building shed + Heating furnace cost + DG set + Cost of power connection + Cost of Machine block) = ₹36.4 lakh ÷ 7 = ₹5.2 lakh + (Annual maintenance cost + Cost of patterns + Others) + (Salaries of permanent staff per month + Minimum monthly electricity bill + Minimum monthly telephone bill) × 12 = ₹12,56,429.

VARIABLE COST

Direct material cost for charging cupola once:	
Coal	₹18,620
Cast iron scrap	45,000
Flux	150
Others	1,280
Less scrap @ 5%	2,250
Total	62,800
Direct labour cost for producing finished goods for above cupola discharge	20,000
Cost of machining, blasting, painting, heating, packaging for all other products produced during a charge of cupola	12,000
Other variable overheads	3,000
Total variable cost for charging cupola once	97,800
Number of table stands manufactured from above discharge of cupola	600
Variable cost per table stand (₹97,800 ÷ 600)	163

MIXED COST

Month	*Total units produced (X)*	*Total mixed cost (Y)*	*XY*	*X²*
April	1,134	7,90,890	89,68,69,260	12,85,956
May	1,584	9,61,488	152,29,96,992	25,09,056
June	2,171	12,18,672	264,57,36,912	47,13,241
July	2,353	13,13,455	309,05,59,615	55,36,609
August	1,672	10,50,232	175,59,87,904	27,95,584
September	3,458	20,91,612	723,27,94,296	1,19,57,764
October	4,856	29,13,600	1,414,84,41,600	2,35,80,736
	17228	1,03,39,949	3,129,33,86,579	5,23,78,946

Segregation of mixed cost into fixed and variable cost using method of least square.

The basic straight line regression equation is

$$Y = a + b X$$

Where Y = Total mixed cost

a = Fixed cost element of mixed cost

b = Variable cost element of mixed cost

X = Total units produced per month

Two linear equations are:

$$\Sigma Y = na + b\Sigma X$$

$$\Sigma XY = a\Sigma X + b\Sigma X^2$$

Substituting the values from table of mixed cost gives

$$1{,}03{,}39{,}949 = 7a + 17{,}228b \quad (1)$$

$$3{,}129{,}33{,}86{,}579 = 17{,}228a + 5{,}23{,}78{,}946b \quad (2)$$

Solving equations 1 and 2 gives

a = 35,408 (fixed cost)

b = 586 (variable cost)

Total annual fixed cost = ₹12,56,429 + (₹35,408 × 12) = ₹16,81,325

Total variable cost per table stand = ₹163 + ₹586 = ₹749.

Break-even Analysis

Sales price per unit = ₹850 (excluding 4% VAT and CST)

Contribution margin per unit (CMPU) =Sales price per unit – Variable cost per unit = ₹101

C/V Ratio = Contribution margin per unit (CMPU) ÷ Sales price per unit

= 11.88 per cent

V/V Ratio = 100 per cent – C/V Ratio = 88.12 per cent

BEP (in units) = Total annual fixed cost ÷ Contribution margin per unit (CMPU)

= 16,81,325 ÷ ₹101 = 16,647 units

BESR = Total annual fixed cost ÷ C/V Ratio

= 16,81,325 ÷ 0.1188 = ₹1,41,52,567

Cash Break-even Point (in units) = (Total annual fixed cost – Depreciation/Amortisation) ÷ CMPU

= (₹16,81,325 – ₹5,20,000) ÷ 101 = 11,498 units

CBESR = (Total cash annual fixed cost = ₹11,61,325) ÷ C/V ratio

= ₹97,75,463

Margin of Safety (in units) = Actual/estimated sales – BEP (in units) = 35,000 – 16,647 = 18,353

Projected EBT = Margin of safety (₹) =18,353 × ₹101 = ₹18,53,653

Margin of Safety Ratio = (Margin of Safety ÷ Actual/Estimated sales) x 100 = 52.44 per cent

Desired sales volume (in units) to earn EBT of ₹10,00,000

= (Total annual fixed cost + Desired EBT) ÷ CMPU

= (₹16,81,325 + ₹10,00,000) ÷ ₹101 = 26,548

CONFIRMATION

Total sales revenue (26,548 × ₹850)	2,25,65,800
Less variable cost (26,548 × ₹749)	1,98,84,452
Total contribution	26,81,348
Less total fixed cost	16,81,325
EBT/EAT	10,00,023

Sensitivity Analysis

(a) BEP (in units) if variable cost increase by 5 per cent due to inflation:

Revised variable cost = ₹749 × 1.05 = ₹787

Revised CMPU = ₹850 – ₹787 = ₹63

Revised BEP (in units) = Total annual fixed cost ÷ revised CMPU = ₹16,81,325 ÷ ₹63

= ₹26,688

(b) BEP (in units) if variable cost increases by 10 per cent due to inflation:

Revised variable cost = ₹749 × 1.10 = ₹824

Revised CMPU = ₹850 – ₹824 = ₹26

Revised BEP (in units) = Total annual fixed cost ÷ revised CMPU = ₹16,81,325 ÷ ₹26 = 64,666.

COMMENTS: The company will incur losses if variable cost increases by 10 per cent because of inflation even though it produces at its normal capacity, that is, 5,000 table stands per month.

16.C.5 (Break-even Analysis) Mr. Deepu Narayan is the proprietor of DoorStep Delivery Company (DDC) which deals in logistics transfer between two cities, Aravalibad and Nilgiribad. In each of these two cities, Deepu has opened a small warehouse cum-office which incurs him the following costs: (a) Office rent: ₹25,000 per month for each office, (b) Insurance: ₹40,000 per year for all the trucks, (c) Miscellaneous expenses: ₹5,000 per month and (d) Annual depreciation: ₹40,000 per truck.

He runs a fleet of 5 trucks, which run to and from the two cities covering a round the trip distance of 1,000 kms. He charges ₹11,000 per trip. The trucks cover the round trip in four days. A truck can do a maximum number of 80 trips a year and the following are the costs involved: (a) Fuel costs per km: ₹4, (b) Wear/tear cost per km: ₹0.2 and (c) Annual maintenance charges: ₹60,000. Every round trip involves paying ₹200 as toll tax at the border toll booth and ₹300 as food expenses to the truck staff. At both the cities loading and unloading of cargo is needed. This activity is outsourced to hired labourers who charge him ₹400 per loading/unloading of truck.

Deepu has also hired the following staff for operating his trucks and manning his warehouse/office(s): (1) Supervisor for each office @ ₹5,000 per month, (2) Driver for each truck @ ₹5,000 per month, and (3) Cleaner for each truck @ ₹2,000 per month.

Before the start of the financial year 2009-10, the economy went into recession. The company is not sure about the number of delivery orders that would be received in the coming financial year. But due to existing goodwill the company got proposals for annual contracts, at the current prices from two firms – Kaanch Manufacturers Limited (KML) dealing in glass products and Taj Mahal Marble (TM) dealing in different varieties of marble floorings. Both the companies agreed to provide DoorStep Delivery orders equivalent to 100 per cent (i.e. 400 round trips) of the company. However, the cost structure of the company has changesd due to the following factors:

- Accepting proposal from KML would lead to additional protective packaging cost of ₹2,00,000 per year which has been outsourced to Surakasha Packaging.
- Accepting proposal from TM would lead to rise in fuel costs by ₹0.6 per km because of additional freight weight. Also, wear and tear charges would be double.

REQUIRED:

(i) Compute the original BEP, BESR and EAT at 100 per cent capacity utilisation, assuming 35 per cent tax.

(ii) Due to uncertainty in future demand, the DoorStep Delivery Company is keen on accepting one of the above two proposals. Suggest which proposal the company should go for. Calculate BEP and BSER for the selected proposal.

(iii) After the first 6 month period, there is increase in the fuel prices by ₹0.80 per km. Also, the toll tax was abolished. Calculate the revised BEP, BESR and EAT.

Solution

(i) Computation of BEP/BESR/EAT

Sales revenue = (₹11,000/round trip × 400 round trips)	₹44,00,000
Less: Variable costs:	
Fuel costs: (₹4 × 1,000 × 400)	16,00,000
Wear and tear costs (₹0.2 × 1,000 × 400)	80,000
Toll tax (₹200 × 400)	80,000
Food expenses for truck staff (₹300 × 400)	1,20,000
Loading and unloading charges (2 × 400 Trips × ₹400)	3,20,000
	22,00,000

(Contd.)

(Contd.)

Fixed costs:	
Salaries for supervisors (2 × ₹5,000 × 12)	1,20,000
Salaries for truck drivers (5 × ₹5,000 × 12)	3,00,000
Salaries for cleaners (5 × ₹2,000 × 12)	1,20,000
Rent (2 × ₹25,000 × 12)	6,00,000
Annual maintenance charges	60,000
Insurance	40,000
Miscellaneous (electricity etc.)	60,000
Annual depreciation for 5 trucks (5 × ₹40,000)	2,00,000
	15,00,000
Earnings before taxes [₹44,00,000 – (₹22,00,000 + ₹15,00,000)]	7,00,000
EAT (at 35 per cent tax) = [₹7,00,000 (1 – 0.35)]	4,55,000
Selling price per unit (SP of one round trip)	11,000
Variable cost per unit for 400 trips (₹22,000 ÷ 400)	5,500
Contribution margin per unit [CMPU = SP – VCPU) = ₹11,000 – ₹5,500)	5,500
Contribution to volume ratio = ₹5,500 ÷ ₹11,000 = 50 per cent	
Break even point for the year 2009-2010 (Fixed cost ÷ CMPU = ₹15,00,00 ÷ ₹5,500) = 273 roundtrips	
Cash BEP (₹13,00,000 ÷ ₹5,500) = 236 roundtrips	
Break even sales revenue for the year 2008-2009 = Fixed Cost ÷ CV ratio (₹15,00,000 ÷ 0.05) = ₹30,00,000	
Cash BESR (₹13,00,000 ÷ 0.5) = ₹26,00,000	

(ii) Computation of BE and BESR

(a) Accepting Proposal From Kaanch Manufacturers Ltd:	
Sales revenue (₹11,000 × 400 roundtrips)	₹44,00,000
Less Variable costs:	
Fuel costs (₹4 × 1,000 × 400)	16,00,000
Wear and tear costs (₹0.2 × 1,000 × 400)	80,000
Toll tax (₹200 × 400)	80,000
Food expenses for truck staff (₹300 × 400)	1,20,000
Loading and unloading charges (2 × 400 × ₹400)	3,20,000
	22,00,000
Fixed costs:	
Salaries for supervisors (2 × ₹5,000 × 12)	1,20,000
Salaries for truck drivers (5 × ₹5,000 × 12)	3,00,000
Salaries for cleaners (5 × ₹2,000 × 12)	1,20,000
Rent (2 × ₹25,000 × 12)	6,00,000
Annual maintenance charges	60,000
Insurance	40,000
Miscellaneous (electricity etc)	60,000
Annual depreciation for 5 trucks (5 × ₹40,000)	2,00,000
Annual payment to Suraksha Packages	2,00,000
	17,00,000
Earnings before taxes [₹44,00,000 – (₹22,00,000 + ₹17,00,000)	5,00,000
EAT (at 35% tax) (₹5,00,000 (1 – 0.35)	3,25,000

(Contd.)

(*Contd.*)

(b) Accepting Proposal From Tajmahal Marbles	
Sales revenue (11000/round trip × 400 roundtrips	44,00,000
Less: Variable costs:	
Total fuel cost (₹4.6 × 1,000 × 400)	18,40,000
Wear and tear costs (₹0.4 × 1,000 × 400)	1,60,000
Toll tax (₹200 × 400)	80,000
Food expenses for truck staff (₹300 × 400)	1,20,000
Loading and unloading charges (2 × 400 × ₹400)	3,20,000
	25,20,000
Fixed costs:	
Salaries for supervisors (2 × ₹5,000 × 12)	1,20,000
Salaries for truck drivers (5 × ₹5,000 × 12)	3,00,000
Salaries for cleaners (5 × ₹2,000 × 12)	1,20,000
Rent (2 × ₹25,000 × 12)	6,00,000
Annual maintenance charges	60,000
Insurance	40,000
Miscellaneous (electricity etc)	60,000
Annual depreciation for 5 trucks (5 × ₹40,000)	2,00,000
	15,00,000
Earnings before taxes [₹44,00,000 – (₹25,20,000 + ₹15,00,000)	3,80,000
EAT (at 35% tax) ₹3,80,000 (1 – 0.35)	2,47,000
BEP = (₹17,00,000 ÷ ₹5,500) = 310 roundtrips	
BESR (17,00,000 ÷ 0.5) = ₹34,00,000	
Cash BEP (₹15,00,000 ÷ ₹5,500) = 273 units	
Cash BESR (₹15,00,000 ÷ 0.5) = ₹30,00,000	

Therefore, DoorStep Delivery Service should accept the proposal from Kaanch Manufacturers as the EAT is more.

(iii) Computation of Revised BEP/BESR/EAT

Total sales revenue for the first 6 months (200 × ₹11,000)	₹22,00,000
Total fixed cost recovered for the first 6 months (CMPU × No. of trips in 6 month) (₹5,500 × 200)	11,00,000
Total fixed costs left to be recovered (₹17,00,000 – ₹11,00,000)	6,00,000
Due to changes in variable costs, new CPMU would change:	
Existing variable cost per trip	5,500
Add, Petrol charges (₹0.8 × 1,000)	800
Less toll charges abolished	(200)
New variable cost per trip	6,100
New CMPU per trip (₹11,000 – ₹6,100)	4,900
New C/V ratio (₹4,900 ÷ ₹11,000) = 0.45	
Therefore, number of trips to recover fixed cost (₹6,00,000 ÷ ₹4,900) = 122	
Sales revenue to recover fixed cost (₹6,00,000 ÷ 0.45) = ₹13,33,333	
Therefore, new BEP (200 + 123) = 323 trips	
Number of trips to recover ₹4,00,000 (excluding depreciation) (₹4,00,000 ÷ 4,900) = 82	
Cash BEP (200 + 82) = 282 roundtrips	
New BESR (₹22,00,000 + ₹13,33,333)	35,33,000
Cash BESR	33,33,000

(*Contd.*)

(Contd.)

Total contribution margin for first six months	11,00,000
Total contribution margin for next six months	9,80,000
Total contribution margin for the year	20,80,000
Less fixed costs	17,00,000
Earnings before taxes (₹20.8 – ₹17)	3,80,000
Less corporate taxes (@ 35%)	1,33,000
Earnings After Taxes (EAT)	2,47,000
Depreciation charged	2,00,000
Therefore Cash profit after taxes	4,47,000

Summary

1. The original BEP, BESR and EAT at 35 per cent tax rate is 273 roundtrips, ₹30,00,000 and ₹4,55,000 respectively.
2. DoorStep Delviery Service should accept the proposal of Kaanch Manufacturers with a BEP of 310 roundtrips and a BESR of ₹34,00,000.
3. Revised BEP is 323 round trips and BESR is ₹35,33,000 and EAT ₹2,47,000.

Budgeting and Profit Planning

17

LEARNING OBJECTIVES

After reading this chapter you will be able to:

LO 17.1 Understand the planning process
LO 17.2 Explain the definition, meaning and purpose of a budget
LO 17.3 Discuss types of budgets and illustrate their preparation

INTRODUCTION

Budgets are an important tool of profit planning. The purpose of this chapter is to present a general view of budgeting as a device of planning and illustrate the preparation of various types of budgets. The chapter provides a brief account of the planning process *vis-à-vis* budgeting. It also elaborates on the meaning of a budget and the purpose of budgeting. The important types of budgets are discussed and illustrated subsequently. The major points are summarised by way of recapitulation.

PLANNING PROCESS

LO 17.1 Understand the planning process

Budgeting, as a tool of planning, is closely related to the broader system of planning in an organistion. **Planning** involves the specification of the basic objectives that the organisation will pursue and the fundamental policies that will guide it. In operational terms, it involves four stages: (i) Objectives (ii) Goals (iii) Strategies, and (iv) Plans/Budgets.

Planning involves specifications of basic objectives and fundamental policies.

Objectives

The first stage in the planning and control system is setting the **objectives** which are defined as the *broad and long-range desired state or position in the future.* They are motivational or directional in nature and are expressed in

Objectives are broad and long-range desired state or position in future.

qualitative terms. Examples of fundamental objectives are identification of the line of business, customer satisfaction, employee welfare, and so on. Thus, they are the basic policies.

Goals are quantitative targets to be achieved in specified period.

Goals

The second stage in the planning process is specifying the **goals**. The term goal, as an element in planning, represents targets, specific in quantitative terms, to be achieved in a specific period of time. The timing of introducing new products, purchase of new plant and machinery and expected rate of return are examples of time and quantity-oriented goals.

Strategies represent specific course of action to achieve goals.

Strategies

The next step involves laying down the strategies. **Strategies** denote specific methods/courses of action to achieve the goals, for instance, promotion of sales through price reduction or aggressive advertisement, financial alternatives, and so on.

Plans/Budgets

The final step is the preparation of budgets/profit plans. Basically, budgeting is the periodic planning to implement the alternatives during a particular fiscal period, usually one year. It converts, in other words, goals and strategies into annual operating plans.

BUDGET—DEFINITION, MEANING AND PURPOSE

LO 17.2 Explain the definition, meaning and purpose of a budget

A budget is defined as a 'comprehensive and coordinated plan, expressed in financial terms, for the operations and resources of an enterprise for some specified period in the future.'[1] According to this definition, the essential elements of a budget are: (i) Plan, (ii) Operations and resources, (iii) Financial terms, (iv) Specified future period, (v) Comprehensiveness, and (vi) Coordination.

Plan

The first ingredient of a budget is its plan. The term 'plan' with reference to budgeting has a *specific connotation.* It includes two aspects which have a bearing on the operations of an enterprise. One set of factors, which determine a firm's future operations are wholly external and beyond its control. Included in this category of factors are general business conditions, government policy and size and composition of population. The second set of factors affecting future activities are within the firm's control and discretion, that is, they are internal. The promotional programmes and manufacturing processes are illustration of these factors. Budgeting, as a plan, covers both these aspects. In other words, budgeting not only suggests what should happen but should also make things happen.[2] In brief, a budget (plan) is an expression partly of what the management expects to happen and partly of what the management intends to happen.

Operations and Resources

A budget is a mechanism to plan for the firm's operations and resources. The operations are reflected in revenues and expenses. This means that a budget should quantify the revenues to be realised from products/services and the expenses to be incurred on goods/services used in generating revenues.

The plan also covers the resources of the firm. The planning of resources means the planning of the various assets and the sources of capital to finance these assets. The assets could be fixed assets as well as current assets.

Financial Terms

Budgets are prepared in financial terms, that is, in terms of monetary value such as the rupee, dollar, and so on. The reason is that the monetary unit is a common denominator. The various activities and operations are expressed in different units, for example, material in terms of weight, labour in terms of number/man-hours, sales in terms of territories, advertisement in terms of magazine space, and so on. If they have to be integrated in a plan, they must be expressed in comparable units of measurement. Monetary units provide such a measure.

Specified Future Period

A budget relates to a specified period of time, usually one year. If it is not related to a time horizon, it will be meaningless. Planning merely for a given amount of, say, sales/profits will not constitute a budget unless a time dimension is added, that is, the budget sales/profit is planned to be achieved in a predetermined time framework.

Comprehensiveness

Master budget is the overall budget for the entire organisation.

A budget is comprehensive in that all the activities and operations of an organisation are included in it. It covers the organisation as a whole and not only some segments. The *modus operandi* is that budgets are prepared for each segment/facet/activity/division of an organisation. These are integrated into an overall budget for the entire organisation. The overall budget is referred to as the **master budget**.

Coordination

Budgets are prepared for the different components/segments/divisions/facets/activities of an organisation so as to take care of the situations and problems of each component. The budgets for each of the components are prepared in harmony with each another. This is called coordination.

Budgets—Purpose

As a tool, budgets serve as a guide to the conduct of operations and a basis for evaluating actual results. The main objectives of budgeting are: (i) Explicit statement of expectations, (ii) Communication, (iii) Coordination, and (iv) Expectations as a framework for judging performance.[3]

Explicit Statement of Expectations One purpose of budgeting is to state expectations in formal terms so that most of the underlying assumptions may be identified. A firm has the basic objective of optimising long-run profit. Its long-range goals also include survival, consumer satisfaction, employee welfare, personal power and prestige, and so on. These long-range objectives can be achieved in successive phases over a period of time. In other words, long-range objectives have to be split into short-term operational plans. Thus, a budget can be said to be a device to express goals which are sought to be achieved in a short period of time. In other words, it is a means to establish congruence between short-term goals and the long-term objectives of the firm. Therefore, budgets formulate targets of expected performance. The advantage is that by laying down targets, budgets contain an explicit statement of expectations. These targets help direct their operations, identify problems, help motivate lower-level employees and clarify the relationship between current activities and future policies.[4] Another implication is that budgets explicitly state the underlying assumptions and goal and/or the means of attaining it. To illustrate, if the sales target (projected sales) for any given period is ₹5,00,000, the budget will not only indicate this figure but will also give details about the assumed prices, quantity, sales efforts, and so on. This explicit statement of assumption is one of the most important contributions of budgeting for managerial planning and control.

However, a budget does not lay down a statement of expectations in rigid terms. Budgets, as observed earlier, are based on factors which are either uncertain or are beyond the control of management. Some of these are economic, social and business conditions; supply and demand; competition; consumer taste; technological innovations; and so on. A budget should be modified when necessary in the light of the changes in the factors/assumptions on which the original estimates were based.

Communication Another purpose of budgeting is to communicate or inform others of the goals and methods selected by top management. Since budgeting deals with fundamental policies and objectives, it is prepared by top management. A formal budget by itself will not ensure that a firm's operations will be automatically geared to the achievement of the goals set in the budget. For this to happen, the managers and lower-level employees have to understand the goals and support them and coordinate their efforts to attain them. In other words, the employees should be aware well in advance of the level of performance expected of them. It is for this reason that a budget is viewed as a means of communicating to the employees the level of performance expected of them so that the goals set out in the budget can be accomplished.

Coordination Yet another purpose of budgeting is coordination. The term 'coordination' refers to the operation of all departments of an organisation in such a way that there is no bottleneck or imbalance. In other words, coordination implies a harmonious relationship between various departments to ensure smooth and uninterrupted operation of each of them. If an organisation is to achieve its long-run goals, coordination in the activities of all its departments is necessary. If there is no coordination, imbalances will be created which will hinder smooth operation and stand in the way of the accomplishment of the goals of the budgets.

To illustrate, one type of imbalance may be between the manufacturing/production and sales departments. The manufacturing department may be producing goods, which the sales department may not be able to sell. Conversely, the sales department may like the production department to produce goods which the production department is incapable of producing. Another example of lack of coordination is the purchasing-manufacturing imbalance when the production schedule is not related to the raw material purchases. Further, the production schedule may not be based on the capability of employees and capacity of plant and machinery.

In view of the above, coordination is a major function of budgeting. Budgets should be drafted in such a way that the operations of the various departments are related to each other for the achievement of the overall goal. Apart from the interdepartmental reconciliation, budgets also provide for flexibility to accommodate plans and operations to unexpected situations.

Expectations as a Framework for Judging Performance Finally, a budget establishes expectations as a framework for judging employee performance. A budget, as observed earlier, defines the goals, the means of implementing them and the level of performance by the employees. The extent to which employees have succeeded in the task assigned to them, can be judged on the basis of a comparison of the actual performance/achievement with the budget. If the actual performance equals or exceeds the budgeted level, it may be termed satisfactory, otherwise not. Thus, a budget can serve as a yardstick to judge employee performance or as a control device.

To conclude, budgeting, as a tool of planning and control, serves as a guide to conduct operations and a basis for evaluating actual results. Actual results can be judged satisfactory or unsatisfactory in the light of the relevant budgeted data and also in the light of changes in conditions. However, a budget should not be regarded as a rigid requirement of performance. Many of the factors upon which a budget is based are beyond the control of management and all of them are uncertain. The budget should, therefore, be regarded as a plan, not an immutable commitment of performance; it is a means of control, but not a straitjacket on operations.[5] In view of its significance as a managerial tool, the preparation of a budget is illustrated in the pages that follows.

PREPARATION/TYPES OF BUDGETS

LO 17.3 Discuss types of budgets and illustrate their preparation

It may be recalled that a budget with reference to planning and control refers to a comprehensive and coordinated budget generally known as master budget. In operational terms, a comprehensive or overall budget has several components. A master budget normally consists of three types of budgets: **(i)** Operating budgets, **(ii)** Financial budgets, and **(iii)** Special decision budgets. Another classification of a master budget is: **(i)** Fixed/static budget and **(ii)** Flexible/variable/sliding budget. In the discussions that follow we illustrate the preparation of the various components of a master budget, namely, operating and financial budgets. The mechanics of the preparation of a flexible budget is also discussed.

Operating Budgets

Operating budgets relate to the physical activities/operations of a firm such as sales, production, purchasing, debtors collection and creditors payment schedules. In specific terms, an **operating budget** has the following components:

Operating budgets relate to physical activities/operations such as sales, production, and so on.

1. Sales budget,
2. Production budget,
3. Purchase budget,
4. Direct labour budget,
5. Manufacturing expenses budget, and
6. Administrative and selling expenses budget, and so on.

Financial Budgets

Financial budgets are concerned with expected cash receipts/disbursements, financial position and results of operations. In other words, a financial budget has the following components:

Financial budgets are concerned with expected cash flows, financial position and result of operations.

1. Budgeted income statement,
2. Budgeted statement of retained earnings,
3. Cash budget, and
4. Budgeted balance sheet.

Cash Budget The principal aim of the cash budget, as a tool of planning, is to ascertain whether, at any time, there is likely to be an excess or shortage of cash. The preparation of a cash budget involves various steps.

The *first* element of a cash budget is the selection of the period of time to be covered by the budget. Alternatively, it is referred to as the 'planning horizon'. The planning horizon means the *time span* and the sub-periods within that time span over which the cash flows are to be projected. There is no hard and fast rule. The period coverage of a cash budget will differ from firm to firm depending upon its nature and the degree of accuracy with which the estimates can be made. As a general rule, the period selected should be neither too long nor too short. If it is too long, it is likely that the estimates will be upset as we cannot visualise them at the time of the preparation of the budget. If on the other hand, the time span is too small, the disadvantage are: **(i)** Failure to take into account important events which lie just beyond the period covered by the budget; **(ii)** Heavy workload in preparation; and **(iii)** Abnormal factors that may be operative.

The planning horizon of a cash budget should be determined in the light of the circumstances and requirements of a particular case. For instance, if the flows are expected to be stable and dependable, such a firm may prepare a cash budget covering a long period, say, a year and divide it into quarterly intervals. In the case of a firm whose flows are uncertain, a quarterly budget divided into monthly intervals may be appropriate. Where flows are affected by seasonal variations, monthly sub-divided into weekly or even daily budgets may be necessary. If the flows are subject to extreme fluctuations, a daily budget may be called for. The idea behind sub-dividing the budget period into smaller intervals is to highlight the movement of cash from one sub-period to another. The sub-division will provide information on the fluctuations in the cash reservoir level during the time span covered by the budget.

The *second* element of the cash budget is the factors that have a bearing on cash flows. The items included in the cash budget are the cash items only, non-cash items such as *depreciation* are excluded.[6] The factors that generate cash flow are generally divided, for purposes of constructing a cash budget, into two broad categories: **(a)** Operating and **(b)** Financial. This two-fold classification of cash budget items is based on their 'nature'. While the former category includes cash flows generated by the operations of the firms and are known as the 'operating cash flows,' the latter consist of the 'financial cash flows.' The major components of the two types of cash flows are outlined below.

Operating Cash Flows The main operating factors/items which generate cash outlfows and inflows over the time span of a cash budget are tabulated in Exhibit 17.1.

EXHIBIT 17.1 Operating Cash Flow Items

Cash inflows/Receipts	*Cash outflows/Disbursements*
1. Cash sales	1. Accounts payable/Payable payments
2. Collection of accounts receivable	2. Purchase of raw materials
3. Disposal of fixed assets	3. Wages and salary (pay roll)
	4. Factory expenses
	5. Administrative and selling expenses
	6. Maintenance expenses
	7. Purchase of fixed assets

Among the operating factors affecting cash flows, the collection of accounts receivable (inflows) and accounts payable (outflows) are the most important. The terms of credit and the speed with which the customers pay would determine the lag between the creation of the accounts receivable and their collection. Also, discounts and allowances for early payments, return from customers and bad debts affect the cash inflows. Similarly, accounts payable relating to credit purchases are affected by the purchase terms.

Financial Cash Flows The major financial factors/items affecting generation of cash flows are depicted in Exhibit 17.2.

EXHIBIT 17.2 Financial Cash Flow Items

Cash inflows/Receipts	*Cash outflows/Payments*
1. Loans/borrowings	1. Income tax/tax payments
2. Sale of securities	2. Redemption of loan
3. Interest received	3. Re-purchase of shares
4. Dividend received	4. Interest paid
5. Rent received	5. Dividends paid
6. Refund of tax	
7. Issues of new shares and securities	

After the time span of the cash budget has been decided upon and pertinent operating and financial factors have been identified, the final step is the construction of the cash budget.

The preparation of the master budget is illustrated in Example 17.1.

◆ Example 17.1

The following data relate to Hypothetical Limited:

Balance Sheet as at March 31, Current Year

Liabilities	*Amount*	*Assets*		*Amount*
Accounts payable	₹40,000	Cash		₹3,00,000
(all for March purchases)		Accounts receivable		
Taxes payable	25,000	(all from March sales)		2,50,000
(all for March income)		Inventories:		
Share capital	11,00,000	Raw materials (9,600 kgs × ₹3)		28,800
Retained earnings	10,26,800	Finished goods		
		(1,800 units × ₹35)		63,000
		Fixed assets:		
		Cost	₹20,00,000	
		Less: Accumulated		
		depreciation	(4,50,000)	15,50,000
	21,91,800			21,91,800

2. *Sales forecasts:* Assume the marketing department has developed the following sales forecast for the first quarter of the next year and the selling price of ₹50 per unit.

Month	*Units sales*
April	9,000
May	12,000
June	16,000

3. The management desires closing inventory to equal 20 per cent of the following month's sales.
4. The manufacturing costs are as follows:

Direct materials: (5 kgs × ₹3) (per unit)	₹15
Direct labour	5
Variable overheads	9
Total fixed overheads (per annum)	7,20,000

5. Normal capacity is 1,20,000 units per annum. Assume absorption costing basis.
6. Each unit of final product requires 5 kgs of raw materials. Assume management desires closing raw material inventory to equal 20 per cent of the following month's requirements of production.
7. Assume fixed selling and administrative expenses are ₹20,000 per month and variable selling and administrative expenses are ₹5 per unit sold.
8. All sales are on account. Payment received within 10 days from the date of sale are subject to a 2 per cent cash discount. In the past, 60 per cent of the sales were collected during the month of sale and 40 per cent are collected during the following month. Of collections during the month of sale, 50 per cent are collected during the discount period. Accounts receivable are recorded at the gross amount and cash discounts are treated as a reduction in arriving at net sales during the month they are taken.
9. Tax rate is 35 per cent.

10. Additional information:
(a) All purchases are on account. Two-thirds are paid for in the month of purchase and one-third, in the following month.
(b) Fixed manufacturing costs include depreciation of ₹20,000 per month.
(c) Taxes are paid in the following month.
(d) All other costs and/or expenses are paid during the month in which incurred.
From the foregoing information prepare a master budget for the month of April only.

Solution

1. Production Budget

Particulars	April	May
Sales (units)	9,000	12,000
Add: Desired closing inventory (0.20 × next month's sales)	2,400	3,200
Total finished goods requirement	11,400	15,200
Less: Opening inventory	(1,800)	(2,400)
Required production (units)	9,600	12,800

2. Manufacturing Cost Budget

Particulars	April
Required production (units)	9,600
Direct material cost (5 kgs × ₹3 per kg)	× ₹15
Total direct material cost	₹1,44,000
Total direct labour cost (₹5 per unit)	48,000
Total variable overhead cost (₹9 per unit)	86,400
Total variable manufacturing costs	2,78,400
All fixed manufacturing overheads (₹7,20,000 ÷ 12 months)	60,000
Total manufacturing cost	3,38,400

3. Purchase Budget (Raw Materials)

Particulars	April	May
Production requirement (units)	9,600	12,800
Raw material required for production @ 5 kgs per unit (kgs)	48,000	64,000
Add: Desired closing inventory (0.20 × May requirements)	12,800	
Total requirements	60,800	
Less: Opening inventory	(9,600)	
Purchase requirement	51,200	
Purchase requirement (amount @ ₹3 per kg)	₹1,53,600	

4. Selling and Administrative Expenses Budget

Particulars	April
Units sales	9,000
Variable costs @ ₹5 per unit	₹45,000
Fixed costs	20,000
Total selling and administrative expenses	65,000

5. Cost of Goods Sold Budget

Particulars	April
Units sold	9,000

(Contd.)

(*Contd.*)

Cost per unit		
Variable	₹29	
Fixed (₹60,000 ÷ 10,000 units)	6	× ₹35
Total cost		3,15,000

6. Budgeted Income Statement for the Month of April

Gross sales (9,000 × ₹50)	₹4,50,000
Less: Cash discount (₹4,50,000 × 0.6 × 0.5 × 0.02)	2,700
Net sales	4,47,300
Less: Cost of goods sold	3,15,000
Gross margin (unadjusted)	1,32,300
Less: Capacity variance unfavourable (400 units × ₹6)	2,400
Gross margin (adjusted)	1,29,900
Less: Selling and administrative expenses	65,000
Earnings before taxes	64,900
Less: Taxes (0.35)	22,715
Earning after taxes	42,185

7. Budgeted Statement of Retained Earnings

Opening balance	₹10,26,800
Add: Earnings after taxes	42,185
Closing balance	10,68,985

8. Cash Budget (April)

Opening balance			₹3,00,000	
Cash inflows:				
Collection from debtors:				
March sales		₹2,50,000		
April sales (gross) (₹4,50,000 × 0.60)	₹2,70,000			
Less: Cash discount (₹2,70,000 × 0.5 × 0.02)	2,700	2,67,300	5,17,300	₹8,17,300
Cash outflows:				
Payment to creditors:				
For March purchases		40,000		
For April purchases (₹1,53,600 × 2/3)		1,02,400	1,42,400	
Direct labour			48,000	
Variable manufacturing overhead			86,400	
Fixed manufacturing overhead		60,000		
Less: Depreciation		(20,000)	40,000	
Variable selling and administrative overheads			45,000	
Fixed selling and administrative overheads			20,000	
Taxes			25,000	4,06,800
Closing balance				4,10,500

9. Proforma Balance Sheet as at March 31, Next Year

Liabilities	*Amount*	*Assets*	*Amount*
Accounts payable (₹40,000 + ₹1,53,600 – ₹1,42,400)	₹51,200	Cash	₹4,10,500
		Accounts receivable (₹4,50,000 × 0.40)	1,80,000

(*Contd.*)

(*Contd.*)

Taxes payable (₹25,000 + ₹22,715 – ₹25,000)	22,715	Inventories:		
Share capital	11,00,000	Raw material (12,800 × ₹3)	₹38,400	
Retained earnings	10,68,985	Finished goods (2,400 × ₹35)	84,000	1,22,400
		Fixed assets:		
		Cost	20,00,000	
		Less: Accumulated depreciation	(4,70,000)	15,30,000
	22,42,900			22,42,900

Special Decision Budgets

The third category of budgets are special decision budgets. They relate to inventory levels, break-even analysis, and so on. These are discussed comprehensively in other chapters of this volume.[7] The long-term capital budgets are covered in detail in chapter 24.

Flexible Budgets

The discussion of the **master budget** and its components in the preceding section was based on the assumption of fixed level of activity. In other words, the budgets were related to a specific level of operation implying thereby that a firm can accurately and precisely forecast the level of its behaviour/operations in a given period of time. If the business environment is capable of accurate prediction, this approach to budgeting is likely to yield dependable results. If, however, changes take place during the budget period, the budget will serve no useful purpose. Such a budget is technically referred to as a fixed/static budget. In other words, budgets prepared at a single level of activity, with no prospect of modification in the light of the changed circumstances, are fixed or static budgets. The alternative to fixed budgets are **flexible/variable/sliding budgets**. The term 'flexible' is the most apt description of the essential features/characteristics of these budgets and is used here to refer to such budgets.

Flexible budget estimates costs at several levels of activity.

A **flexible budget** estimates costs at several levels of activity. The merit of a flexible budget is that instead of one estimate it contains several estimates/plans in different assumed circumstances. Since business activities cannot be accurately predicted as the business conditions/environment are uncertain, it is a useful tool in real business situations, that is, an unpredictable environment. In view of its significance as a more realistic basis of budgeting, the setting up of a flexible budget is demonstrated in the discussions that follow.

It may at the outset be noted that the construction of a flexible budget is similar to that of a fixed budget except in one respect. While the fixed budget is based on costs and other business operations/activities at one level, the flexible budget considers several alternatives/levels/volumes of activity. The term 'volume/level' of activity refers to the usage of capacity. In other words, volume/level of activity signifies the percentage use of capacity. The term 'capacity' means the *installed capacity* of plant and personnel, that is, the fixed amount invested in these. For instance, if a plant when fully operated can produce 5,000 units, its capacity is 5,000 units of production. Assuming 2,500 units of production in a given period, the volume/level of activity is 50 per cent.

Thus, the essence of a flexible budget is the presentation of estimated cost data in a manner that permits their determination at various levels of volume. This means that all costs must be identified as to how they behave with a change in volume—whether they vary or remain fixed.

The conceptual framework of flexible budgeting, therefore, relates to: **(i)** Measure of volume and **(ii)** Cost behaviour identified with change in volume.

Measure of Volume The volume measure selected for any given department/firm should be that quantity which displays the greatest degree of correlation with those costs that vary with the level of operating activity. Different departments may use different measures of volume. In the first place, the measure of volume may be expressed in terms of the activity or factor that causes costs to vary, for example, labour costs vary on the basis of number of hours worked, material costs vary due to quantity of materials consumed. Secondly, the volume measure should be related to factors controllable by management, that is, number of hours worked, the quantity of materials consumed and number of machine hours operated. Further, the activity chosen as a unit of measure should be one that is not greatly affected by factors other than volume, that is, quantity more useful than cost as indicator of volume. In brief, volume should be expressed in terms of some unit of input, such as direct labour hours, direct labour cost or machine hours. The measure applied in any particular case will depend on the peculiarities. For instance, in the light machinery department, direct labour hours may be an appropriate measure. But for the heavy machinery department, machine hours may be the best indicator of cost behaviour.

Cost Behaviour with Change in Volume Three different types of cost behaviour can be visualised with changes in volume/level of activity: **(i)** Fixed costs, **(ii)** Variable costs, and **(iii)** Mixed costs.

Fixed Costs The fixed costs are associated with inputs that do not fluctuate in response to changes in the total activity or output of the firm, within relevant range for a given budget period. They may also be called *non-variable costs.* They are normally fixed for a relevant range of volume but fluctuate beyond that range. Moreover, fixed costs are to be analysed in relation to a given period of time; they are subject to change over a period of time.

> **Fixed costs** are fixed for a relevant range of volume for a given budget period.

Fixed costs may be: **(i)** Committed and **(ii)** Discretionary. Fixed costs that are associated with the acquisition of capacity-producing assets are known as the committed fixed costs. The identifying characteristic of a committed cost is that its occurrence as well as amount are predetermined and can be altered only by another major decision to reverse or amend the earlier commitment. Also known as *managed costs,* discretionary costs result from management decisions. They are incurred as well as reduced at the discretion of the management.

Each of the two types of fixed costs has a different implication for the budgetary process. Committed fixed costs can be budgeted on the basis of past commitment. Discretionary fixed cost, on the other hand, can be budgeted on the basis of inquiry from the decision-makers/management.

Variable Costs The variable costs are costs that are assumed to fluctuate in direct proportion to production activity/sales activity/some other measure of volume within relevant range for a given budget period. The level of variable costs at any volume can be estimated easily if the relationship between costs and volume is shown.

> **Variable costs** fluctuate in direct proportion to activity/volume within relevant range for a given budget period.

Mixed Costs The mixed costs are composed of both fixed and variable elements. The fixed part of mixed costs often represents a cost of capacity, while the variable element is influenced by changed in activity. For budgeting purposes, mixed costs must be broken down into their fixed and variable components/segments. Once this is done, the amount of fixed costs and the rate at which total variable costs change in proportion to total changes in output/volume can be worked out. That is, the fixed costs remain constant regardless of activity, but the variable portion is

> **Mixed costs** are composed of both fixed and variable elements.

assumed to change in direct proportion to change in labour hours, labour costs, machine hours, material costs/material quantity, and so on.

The main elements in the construction of a flexible budget have been outlined above. To summarise, a flexible budget, in a sense, is a series of fixed budgets and an increase or decrease (any change) in the level/volume of activity must be reflected in it. Each expense in each department/segment is to be categorised into fixed, variable and mixed components. A budget may be first prepared at the expected level of activity, say, 100 per cent of capacity. Additional columns may then be added for costs below and above 100 per cent, say, 90 per cent and 110 per cent.

Hypothetical flexible budgets corresponding to the procedure described above for two departments of a firm: Maintenance and Manufacture, are illustrated in Tables 17.1 and 17.2.

TABLE 17.1 Hypothetical Ltd—Flexible Budget (Maintenance Department)

Volume (labour-hours)	*400*	*450*	*500*	*550*	*600*
Variable costs:					
Labour	₹6,000	₹6,750	₹7,500	₹8,250	₹9,000
Material	2,400	2,700	3,000	3,300	3,600
Others	800	900	1,000	1,100	1,200
Mixed costs:					
Labour	2,300	2,400	2,500	2,600	2,700
Maintenance	1,400	1,450	1,500	1,550	1,600
Other supplies	2,500	2,750	3,000	3,250	3,500
Discretionary fixed costs:					
Training	1,500	2,000	2,000	2,000	2,500
Experimental methods	3,500	4,000	4,000	4,000	4,500
Committed fixed costs:					
Depreciation	5,000	5,000	5,000	5,000	5,000
Rent, lease cost	3,500	3,500	3,500	3,500	3,500
Total	28,900	31,450	33,000	34,550	37,100

TABLE 17.2 Hypothetical Ltd—Flexible Budget (Manufacturing Department)

Volume(machine-hours)	*50*	*60*	*70*	*80*	*90*
Variable costs:					
Power	₹500	₹600	₹700	₹800	₹900
Helpers	250	300	350	400	450
Discretionary fixed costs:					
Training	800	900	900	900	1,000
Tools	200	200	200	300	300
Committed fixed costs:					
Depreciation	1,200	1,200	1,200	1,200	1,200
Rent	1,000	1,000	1,000	1,000	1,000
Total	3,950	4,200	4,350	4,600	4,850

Modified Flexible Budgets From the preceding discussion it should be clear that flexible budgets, as a tool of planning and control, are superior to fixed budgets. The major weaknesses of static budgets are their inability to: **(i)** Disclose the potential variability of various estimates used in preparing the budget and **(ii)** Indicate the range within which costs can be expected to fall. They are not useful, therefore, in an uncertain and unpredictable environment. Flexible budgets are better in that they present estimates of costs at different level/volume of activity. But their one limitation is that they do not explicitly consider the relative probability that any particular volume or cost will be achieved.[8] This limitation can be overcome by using a modified flexible budget, which will include columns for different levels of estimates—most likely, optimistic and pessimistic. The hypothetical modified flexible budget is shown in Table 17.3.

TABLE 17.3 Hypothetical Ltd—Modified Flexible Budget (Manufacturing Department)

	Pessimistic	*Most likely*	*Optimistic*
Volume (labour-hours)	*425*	*500*	*585*
Variable costs:			
Labour	₹6,375	₹7,500	₹8,775
Materials	2,650	3,000	3,510
Others	850	1,000	1,170
Mixed costs:			
Labour	2,350	2,500	3,425
Maintenance	1,425	1,500	1,585
Other supplies	2,625	3,000	2,670
Discretionary fixed costs:			
Training	1,750	2,000	2,250
Experimental methods	3,750	4,000	4,250
Committed fixed costs:			
Depreciation	5,000	5,000	5,000
Rent, etc.	3,500	3,500	3,500
Total	30,275	33,000	36,135

SUMMARY

- Budgeting is a tool of planning. Planning involves specification of the basic objectives that the organisation will pursue and the fundamental policies that will guide it. In operational terms, it involves four steps: **(i)** Objectives defined as the broad and long-range desired state/position of the firm, **(ii)** Specified goals-targets in quantitative terms to be achieved in a specified period of time, **(iii)** Strategies or specific methods/course of action to achieve these goals, and **(iv)** Budgets to convert goals and strategies into annual operating plans.

LO 17.1

- A budget is defined as a comprehensive and coordinated plan, expressed in financial terms, for the operations and resources of an enterprise for some specified period in the future. The essential elements of a budget are: **(i)** Plan, **(ii)** Financial terms, **(iii)** Operations and resources, **(iv)** Specific future period, **(v)** Comprehensive coverage, and **(vi)** Coordination. As a tool, a budget serves as a guide to conduct operations and a basis for evaluating actual results. The main objectives of budgeting are: **(i)** Explicit statement of expectations, **(ii)** Communication, **(iii)** Coordination, and **(iv)** Expectations as a framework for judging performance.
- The overall budget is known as the master budget. It has the following components: **(i)** Sales budget, **(ii)** Production budget, **(iii)** Purchase budget, **(iv)** Direct labour budget, **(v)** Manufacturing expenses budget, **(vi)** Administrative and selling expenses budget, **(vii)** Budgeted income statement, **(viii)** Cash budget, and **(ix)** Budgeted balance sheet.

- The cash budget is a device to help a firm to plan for and control the use of cash. It is a statement showing the estimated cash inflows and cash outflows over the planning period. The principal aim of the cash budget, as a tool to predict cash flows over a period of time, is to ascertain whether there is likely to be excess/shortage of cash at any time.

LO 17.2

- The preparation of a cash budget involves several steps. The first element of a cash budget is the selection of the period of the budget, that is, the planning horizon. The planning horizon of a cash budget should be determined in the light of the circumstances and requirements of a particular case. The second element of the cash budget is the selection/identification of the factors that have a bearing on cash flows. The factors that generate cash are generally divided into two broad categories: **(i)** Operating and **(ii)** Financial. The first category includes cash flows from the operations of the firm, for example, sales, collections of receivables and so on. The second category of cash flows comprise collections and payment of financial nature, for example, borrowings, dividends paid, taxes paid and so on.
- Budgets prepared at a single level of activity, with no prospect of modification in the light of changed circumstances, are referred to as fixed budgets.
- The alternative to fixed budgets are flexible/variable/sliding budgets. The term 'flexible' is an apt description of the essential features of these budgets. A flexible budget estimates costs at several levels of activity. Its merit is that instead of one estimate, it contains several estimates/plans in different assumed circumstances. It is a useful tool in real world situations, that is, unpredictable environment. A flexible budget, in a sense, is a series of fixed budgets and any increase/decrease in the level/volume of activity must be reflected in it. The conceptual framework of flexible budgeting relates to: **(i)** Measure of volume and **(ii)** Cost behaviour with change in volume. Each expense in each department/segment is to be categorised into fixed, variable and mixed components. A budget may first be prepared at the expected level of activity, say, 100 per cent capacity. Additional columns may then be added for costs below and above, 90 per cent and 110 per cent capacity and so on.
- Flexible budgets, as a tool of planning and control, are superior to fixed budgets. The major weaknesses of fixed budgets are their inability to: **(i)** Show the potential variability of various estimates used in the preparation of the budget, and **(ii)** Indicate the range within which costs may be expected to vary. They are, therefore, not useful in an uncertain and unpredictable environment. Flexible budgets present estimates at different levels of activity, and are more useful.
- Flexible budgets suffer from one limitation in that they do not explicitly consider the relative probability of a particular volume/cost being achieved. This limitation can be overcome by using a modified flexible budget which will include columns for different levels of estimates: most likely, optimistic and pessimistic.

LO 17.3

REFERENCES

1. J M Fremgen, *Accounting for Managerial Analysis,* (Richard D. Irwin, Homewood, Illinois, 1976), p 150.
2. *Ibid.*, p. 151.
3. R M Copeland and P E Dascher, *Managerial Accounting,* (John Wiley and Sons, New York, 1978), p. 35.
4. *Ibid.*, p. 34.
5. Fremgen, *op cit.*, p. 153.
6. It should, however, be noted that depreciation will be relevant to the computation of taxes.
7. Break-even analysis is discussed in Chapter 16 and inventory in Chapter 8.
8. Copeland and Dascher, *op cit.*, p. 86.

SOLVED PROBLEMS

P.17.1 Your company manufacturers two products, A and B. A forecast of the units to be sold in the first seven months of the year is given below: **LO 17.3** **LOD: E**

Month	*Product A*	*Product B*
January	1,000	2,800
February	1,200	2,800
March	1,600	2,400
April	2,000	2,000
May	2,400	1,600
June	2,400	1,600
July	2,000	1,800

It is anticipated that (a) there will be no work-in-process at the end of any month, and (b) finished units equal to half the sale for the next month will be in stock at the end of each month (including the previous December).

Budgeted production and production costs for the whole year are as follows:

Particulars	*Product A*	*Product B*
Product (units)	22,000	24,000
Per unit direct material	₹12.50	₹19.00
Per unit direct labour	4.50	7.00
Total factory overhead (apportioned)	66,000	96,000

Prepare for the six months period ending June 30 (i) (a) production budget for each month, and (ii) a summarised production cost budget.

Solution

(i) Production Budget of Products A and B (units) for six months (January to June)

Month	*Sales*		*Planned inventory*				*Budget production*	
			closing		*opening*		*(Col. 2 + 4 − 6)*	*(Col. 3 + 5 − 7)*
	A	*B*	*A*	*B*	*A*	*B*	*A*	*B*
1	2	3	4	5	6	7	8	9
January	1,000	2,800	600	1,400	500	1,400	1,100	2,800
February	1,200	2,800	800	1,200	600	1,400	1,400	2,600
March	1,600	2,400	1,000	1,000	800	1,200	1,800	2,200
April	2,000	2,000	1,200	800	1,000	1,000	2,200	1,800
May	2,400	1,600	1,200	800	1,200	800	2,400	1,600
June	2,400	1,600	1,000	900	1,200	800	2,200	1,700

(ii) Cost of Production Budget for six months from January to June of Products A and B

Particulars	*Product A*			*Product B*			*Total cost (A + B)*
	Cost per Particulars	*Number of units unit*	*Total cost produced*	*Cost per*	*Number of units unit*	*Total produced*	
Variable costs:							
Direct material	₹12.50	11,100	₹1,38,750	₹19	12,700	₹2,41,300	₹3,80,050
Direct labour	4.50	11,100	49,950	7	12,700	88,900	1,38,850

(Contd.)

(Contd.)

Fixed costs:							
Factory overheads apportioned at the rate of ₹3 (A) and ₹4 (B)	3.00	11,100	33,300	4	12,700	50,800	84,100
	20.00	11,100	2,22,000	30	12,700	3,81,000	6,03,000

P.17.2 The Delhi Electrical Supply Company Ltd has a business of supplying electrical goods to various government and non-government companies. The controller, in collaboration with the economist, has developed the following equation that, he says, will forecast sales quite well, based on past pattern of behaviour: monthly sales (amount) = ₹1,00,000 + (₹2,000 x orders received in prior month). **LO 17.3 LOD: M**

The sales manager is confused and seeks your advice. He presents you with the following data regarding actual and forecast numbers of orders. The forecasts have generally been quite accurate.

August (actual)	200
September (forecast)	300
October	450
November	700
December	650

It is the first week of September, the sales manager would like the forecasts of sales and income for as many months as you can prepare. The cost accountant informs you that costs of goods sold, which are all fixed costs, amount to ₹2,00,000 per month.

You are required to prepare the budgeted income statement for as many months as you can.

Solution

Budgeted Income Statement of Delhi Electric Supply Company Ltd

Particulars	*September*	*October*	*November*	*December*	*January*
Sales:					
Fixed component	₹1,00,000	₹1,00,000	₹1,00,000	₹1,00,000	₹1,00,000
Variable component (₹2,000 × orders received in previous months)	4,00,000	6,00,000	9,00,000	14,00,000	13,00,000
Total sales	5,00,000	7,00,000	10,00,000	15,00,000	14,00,000
Less: Cost of goods sold (0.50 × of sales)	2,50,000	3,50,000	5,00,000	7,50,000	7,00,000
Contribution (manufacturing)	2,50,000	3,50,000	5,00,000	7,50,000	7,00,000
Less: Other variable costs (0.20 × sales)	50,000	70,000	1,00,000	1,50,000	1,40,000
Contribution (final)	2,00,000	2,80,000	4,00,000	6,00,000	5,60,000
Less: Fixed costs	2,00,000	2,00,000	2,00,000	2,00,000	2,00,000
Income	—	80,000	2,00,000	4,00,000	3,60,000

P.17.3 The administrator of Delhi Nursing Home has sought your assistance in preparing the budget for the next year. The nursing home obtains its revenues through charges for use of a hospital room and charges for use of the operating theatre. The use of basic room depends on whether the patient undergoes surgery during the stay in the nursing home. The following estimated data is provided for your guidance: **LO 17.3 LOD: M**

Patients requiring	*Number of patients expected*	*Average stay (days)*	*Percentage occupancy of rooms*		
			Private	*Semi-private*	*Ward*
Medical attention only	1,000	6	10	50	40
Surgical attention	1,200	12	20	70	10

The basic room charges are ₹1,000, ₹600 and ₹200 for private, semi-private and wards respectively.

Charges for use of the operating theatre depend on the length of the operation and the number of persons required to perform it. The charges are ₹50 per man-minute. (A 'man-minute' is one person for one minute). If an operation requires 4 persons for 60 minutes, the charges would be 240 minutes at ₹50 per minute = ₹12,000). Based on past experience, the following is a breakdown of the types of operations to be performed:

Type of operation	Number	Minutes per operation	Number of persons required
Minor	600	60	3
Major	500	120	6

You are required to do the following:

1. Prepare a budgeted revenue statement of room charges by type of patient and type of room;
2. Prepare of budgeted revenue statement of operating theatre charges by type of operation.

Solution

1. Budgeted Revenue Statement (Room Charges)

Type of patient	Total patient-days	Type of room Private	Semi-private	Ward	Total (₹)
Medical attention (1,000 × 6)	6,000	600 (0.10)	3,000 (0.50)	2,400 (0.40)	
Multiplied by room rate		₹1,000	₹600	₹200	
Revenues (a)		6,00,000	18,00,000	4,80,000	28,80,000
Surgical (1,200 × 12)	14,400	2,880 (0.20)	10,080 (0.70)	1,440 (0.10)	
Multiplied by room rates		× ₹1,000	× ₹600	× ₹200	
Revenues (b)		28,80,000	60,48,000	2,88,000	92,16,000
Total revenue (a + b)		34,80,000	78,48,000	7,68,000	1,20,96,000

2. Budgeted revenue statement (Operating Theatre Charges)

Type of operation	Man-minutes (Average number of minutes × persons)	Number of operations	Total man-minutes (Col. 2 × 3)	Total revenue (Col. 4 × ₹50)
1	2	3	4	5
Minor	60 × 3 = 180	600	1,08,000	₹54,00,000
Major	120 × 6 = 720	500	3,60,000	1,80,00,000
Total revenue				2,34,00,000

P.17.4 The GEC Ltd manufacturers pumps used in coolers. The firm has developed a forecasting tool that has been successful in predicting sales for the company: Sales = 10,000 + (0.25 × coolers sold). The coming year's cooler sales are expected to be 2,00,000. **LO 17.3** **LOD: M**

The pump contains material costing ₹50. Direct labour is ₹60 per unit and variable manufacturing overhead is ₹40 per pump. Besides the variable manufacturing costs, there are commissions to sales people of 10 per cent of sales amount. The pump sells for ₹250 per unit. Fixed costs of manufacturing are ₹10,00,000 per year and fixed selling and administrative expenses are ₹5,00,000 per year. Both are incurred evenly over the year.

Sales are seasonal, and about 75 per cent are in the April-September period which begins from April 1. The sales forecast by months, as percentages of yearly sales, are given below:

April	10
May	15
June	20
July	15
August	8
September	7
October	5
November	3

The company has a policy of keeping inventory of finished product equal to the budgeted sales for the following two months. Materials are purchased and delivered daily and no inventory is kept. The inventory of finished product on March 31 is expected to be 15,500 units.

You are required to prepare a:

(i) Budgeted income statement for the coming year

(ii) Budgeted income statement for the first six months of the year.

(iii) Production budget by months for the first six months, in unit.

Solution

(i) and **(ii)** Budgeted Income Statement

Particulars	*Six months*	*Year*
Sales (units)	45,000	60,000
Sales price per unit	₹250	₹250
Total sales revenue	1,12,50,000	1,50,00,000
Less: Variable costs:		
Materials (₹60 per unit)	22,50,000	30,00,000
Labour (₹50 per unit)	27,00,000	36,00,000
Overheads (₹40 per unit)	18,00,000	24,00,000
Contribution (manufacturing)	45,00,000	60,00,000
Less: Sales commission (0.10 × sales)	11,25,000	15,00,000
Contribution (final)	33,75,000	45,00,000
Less: Fixed costs		
Manufacturing	5,00,000	10,00,000
Selling and administrative	2,50,000	5,00,000
Income	26,25,000	30,00,000

(iii) Production Budget (units)

Month	*Sales*	*Planned inventory*		*Required production*
		Closing	*Opening*	*(Col. 2 + 3 – 4)*
1	2	3	4	5
April	6,000	21,000	15,500	11,500
May	9,000	21,000	21,000	9,000
June	12,000	13,800	21,000	4,800
July	9,000	9,000	13,800	4,200
August	4,800	7,200	9,000	3,000
September	4,200	4,800	7,200	1,800

WORKING NOTES

(i) Sales forecasts for the coming year = 10,000 + (0.25 × 2,00,000) = 60,000 units

Sales forecasts by month (units):

April (0.10)	6,000	
May (0.15)	9,000	
June (0.20)	12,000	
July (0.15)	9,000	
August (0.08)	4,800	
September (0.07)	4,200 =	45,000 units (75 per cent)
October (0.05)	3,000	
November (0.03)	1,800	

P. 17.5 The cost of an article at the capacity level of 5,000 units is given under A below. For a variation of 25 per cent in capacity above or below this level, the individual expenses vary as indicated under B below: LO 17.3 LOD: M

Particulars	*A*	*B (per cent)*
Material cost	₹2,50,000	100 (variable)
Labour cost	1,50,000	100 (variable)
Power	12,500	80 (semi-variable)
Repairs and maintenance	20,000	75 (semi-variable)
Stores	10,000	100 (variable)
Inspection	5,000	20 (semi-variable)
Administration overheads	50,000	25 (semi-variable)
Selling overheads	30,000	50 (semi-variable)
Depreciation	1,00,000	100 (fixed)
Total	6,27,500	
Cost per unit	125.50	

Prepare the production cost budget at 4,000 units and 6,000 units.

Solution

Production Cost (Flexible) Budget

Particulars	*4,000 units*	*6,000 units*
Material cost (variable)	₹2,00,000	₹3,00,000
Labour cost (variable)	1,20,000	1,80,000
Stores (variable)	8,000	12,000
Power (semi-variable)	10,500	14,500
Repairs and maintenance (semi-variable)	17,000	23,000
Inspection (semi-variable)	4,800	5,200
Administration overheads (semi-variable)	47,500	52,500
Selling overheads (semi-variable)	27,000	33,000
Depreciation (fixed)	1,00,000	1,00,000
Total	5,34,800	7,20,200
Cost per unit	133.70	120.00

P.17.6 The following data relate to the working of a small factory at Wardha for the current quarter: LO 17.3 LOD: M

Capacity worked, 50 per cent		
Fixed costs:		
Salaries	₹84,000	
Rent and rates	56,000	
Depreciation	70,000	
Other administrative expenses	80,000	₹2,90,000
Variable costs:		
Materials	2,40,000	
Labour	2,56,000	
Other expenses	38,000	5,34,000

(Contd.)

(Contd.)

Possible sales at various levels of working are:

Capacity (per cent)	Sales
60	₹9,50,000
75	11,50,000
90	13,75,000
100	15,25,000

Prepare a flexible budget and show the forecast of profit at 60, 75, 90, and 100 per cent capacity operations.

Solution

Flexible Budget

Percentage of capacity worked	*60*	*75*	*90*	*100*
Sales revenue	₹9,50,000	₹11,50,000	₹13,75,000	₹15,25,000
Less: Costs:				
Variable costs:				
Materials	2,88,000	3,60,000	4,32,000	4,80,000
Labour	3,07,200	3,84,000	4,60,800	5,12,000
Other expenses	45,600	57,000	68,400	76,000
(A) Total variable cost	6,40,800	8,01,000	9,61,200	10,68,000
Fixed costs:				
Salaries	84,000	84,000	84,000	84,000
Rent and rates	56,000	56,000	56,000	56,000
Depreciation	70,000	70,000	70,000	70,000
Other administrative expenses	80,000	80,000	80,000	80,000
(B) Total fixed cost	2,90,000	2,90,000	2,90,000	2,90,000
Total cost (**A** + **B**)	9,30,800	10,91,000	12,51,200	13,58,000
Forecast profits	19,200	59,000	1,23,800	1,67,000

P.17.7 A company is drawing its production plan for the next year in respect of two of its products 'Gamma' and 'Delta'. The company's policy is not to carry any closing work-in-process (WIP) at the end of any month. However, its policy is to hold a closing stock of finished goods at 50 per cent of the anticipated quantity of sales of the succeeding month. For the next year, the company's budgeted production is 20,000 units of 'Gamma' and 25,000 units of 'Delta'. The following is the estimated cost data: **LO 17.3** **LOD: M**

Particulars	*Gamma*	*Delta*
Direct material per unit	₹50	₹80
Direct labour per unit	20	80
Other manufacturing expenses apportionable to each type of product based on production	2,00,000	3,75,000

The estimated units to be sold in the first 7 months of the next year are as under:

Particulars	*April*	*May*	*June*	*July*	*August*	*September*	*October*
Gamma	900	1100	1400	1800	2200	2200	1800
Delta	2900	2900	2500	2100	1700	1700	1900

You are required to

(a) Prepare a production budget showing month-wise number of units to be manufactured:

(b) Present a summarised production cost budget for the half-year ending September 30.

Solution

(a) Production Budget (Units) for the half year ending September 30

Particulars	*April*	*May*	*June*	*July*	*August*	*September*	*Total*
Product—Gamma:							
Budgeted sales	900	1,100	1,400	1,800	2,200	2,200	9,600
Add: Closing stock	550	700	900	1,100	1,100	900	900
	1,450	1,800	2,300	2,900	3,300	3,100	10,500
Less: Opening stock	450	550	700	900	1,100	1,100	450
Budgeted production	1,000	1,250	1,600	2,000	2,200	2,000	10,050
Product—Delta:							
Budgeted sales	2,900	2,900	2,500	2,100	1,700	1,700	13,800
Add: Closing stock	1,450	1,250	1,050	850	850	950	950
	4,350	4,150	3,550	2,950	2,550	2,650	14,750
Less: Opening stock	1,450	1,450	1,250	1,050	850	850	1,450
Budgeted production	2,900	2,700	2,300	1,900	1,700	1,800	13,300

(b) Cost Budget for the half year ending September 30

Particulars (units)	*Gamma (10,050 units)*		*Delta (13,300 units)*	
	Total	*Per unit*	*Total*	*Per unit*
Direct material	₹5,02,500	₹50	₹10,64,000	₹80
Direct labour	2,01,000	20	3,99,000	30
Other manufacturing expenses[1]	1,00,500	10	1,99,500	15
	8,04,000	80	16,62,500	125

[1]Other manufacturing expenses are apportioned on the basis of production.

	Gamma	*Delta*
1. Units to be produced	20,000	25,000
2. Other manufacturing expenses	₹2,00,000	₹3,75,000
3. Per unit (2 ÷ 1)	10	15

LO 17.3 LOD: M

P.17.8 From the following particulars of Hypothetical Ltd, prepare a cash budget (₹in lakh):

	May	*June*	*July*	*August*	*Sept-ember*	*Octo-ber*	*Nov-ember*	*Dece-mber*	*Janu-ary*
1. Sales (net of cash discounts)	10	10	20	30	40	20	20	10	10
2. Purchases	7	14	21	28	14	14	7	7	—
3. Wages and salaries	—	—	1.50	2	2.50	1.50	1.50	1	—
4. Rent	—	—	0.50	0.50	0.50	0.50	0.50	0.50	—
5. Other expenses	—	—	0.20	0.30	0.40	0.20	0.20	0.10	—
6. Taxes	—	—	—	—	—	4	—	4	—
7. Payment for plant construction	—	—	—	—	—	10	—	—	—

All sales are made on terms that allow a cash discount for payment within 20 days; if the discount is not taken, full payment may be made in 40 days. However, the experience has been that on 20 per cent of sales, payment is made during the month in which sales are made; on 70 per cent of the sales, payment is made during the second month and on the balance 10 per cent of sales, payment is made during the third month.

Materials amount to 70 per cent of sales and are bought in the month before the firm expects to sell the finished goods. Its purchase terms permit the company to delay payment for one month. The firm has to pay tax of ₹4 lakh on September 15 and on December 15.

Assume the firm needs to keep a minimum cash balance of ₹5 lakh in hand at all times. It is assumed to have an opening cash balance of ₹6 lakh on July 1.

Estimate the firm's requirements of cash for the period from July to December.

Solution

Cash Budget (₹ *in lakh*)

Particulars	July	August	September	October	November	December
1. Cash inflows:						
Collections						
(a) during month of sales (0.20)	4	6	8	4	4	2
(b) during second month (0.70)	7	14	21	28	14	14
(c) during third month (0.10)	1	1	2	3	4	2
Total	12	21	31	35	22	18
2. Cash outflows:						
(a) Purchases (one month lag)	14	21	28	14	14	7
(b) Wages and salary	1.5	2	2.5	1.5	1.5	1
(c) Rent	0.5	0.5	0.5	0.5	0.5	0.5
(d) Other expenses	0.2	0.3	0.4	0.2	0.2	0.1
(e) Taxes	—	—	4	—	—	4
(f) Payment for plant construction	—	—	—	10	—	—
Total	16.2	23.8	35.4	26.2	16.2	12.6
(C) Net cash receipt/outflow (A – B)	(4.2)	(2.8)	(4.4)	8.8	5.8	5.4
Cash at start of month*	6	5	5	5	5	9.2
Less desired level of cash	(5)	(5)	(5)	(5)	(5)	(5)
Borrowings (cumulative)	3.2	6	10.4	1.6	—	—
Surplus cash (cumulative)	—	—	—	—	4.2	9.6

*Cash at the beginning plus net receipts/less payments. It is equal to the cash at the end.

P. 17.9 From the following particulars of a firm, prepare a cash budget fort the six months, January-June: **LO 17.3** **LOD: M**

1. *Balance Sheet as on December 31*

Liabilities		*Assets*		
Share capital	₹40,00,000	Cash		₹16,00,000
Reserves	60,00,000	Accounts receivables		10,00,000
		Inventory		49,00,000
		Fixed assets	₹30,00,000	
		Less depreciation	5,00,000	25,00,000
	1,00,00,000			1,00,00,000

2. *Sales Forecast*

January	₹20,00,000	April	₹60,00,000
February	40,00,000	May	90,00,000
March	50,00,000	June	50,00,000
		July	10,00,000

3. *Salary Expenses*

January	₹3,00,000	April	₹9,00,000
February	5,00,000	May	11,00,000
March	7,00,000	June	6,00,000

4. Monthly selling and distribution expenses are expected to be 10 per cent of sales. Depreciation charges are 1 per cent per month.

5. The firm operates on the following terms:

(a) Sales are on a 30-day basis. But payments are not received until the following month.

(b) All purchases of the firm are in cash.

(c) The firm purchases enough inventory each month to cover 125 per cent of the following month's sales. The firm has a policy of maintaining 20 per cent gross profit margin on sales.
(d) A minimum cash balance of ₹10 lakh is maintained.

6. Additional information: New equipment purchased for ₹5 lakh is scheduled for delivery on March 1 against payment.

Solution

Cash Budget (₹ lakh)

Particulars	January	February	March	April	May	June
1. Cash inflows:						
Collections:						
During month following sale	₹10	₹20	₹40	₹50	₹60	₹90
2. Cash outflows:						
1. Purchases	40	50	60	90	50	10
2. Selling and distribution expenses	2	4	5	6	9	5
3. Salary expenses	3	5	7	9	11	6
4. Payment for new equipment	—	—	5	—	—	—
Total	45	59	77	105	70	21
3. *Net cash receipts or (payments)*	(35)	(39)	(37)	(55)	(10)	69
Cash at the start of month	10	10	10	10	10	10
Less: desired level of cash	(10)	(10)	(10)	(10)	(10)	(10)
Borrowings (cumulative)	35	74	111	166	176	107

LO 17.3 LOD: D

P.17.10 The following information is available in respect of a firm:

1. *Balance Sheet as on August 1* (₹ thousand)

Liabilities	Amount	Assets		Amount
Accrued wages	₹600	Cash		₹5,100
Capital	59,200	Accounts receivable		14,700
Other liabilities	2,000	Inventory		26,000
		Fixed assets	₹20,000	
		Less depreciation	4,000	16,000
	61,800			61,800

2. *Assume:*

(a) Sales are 40 per cent against cash, 60 per cent on credit.
(b) Of the credit sales, 75 per cent are collected in the first month following sales and 25 per cent in the second month following sales.
(c) All inventory purchases are paid for during the month in which they are made.
(d) A basic inventory of ₹1 crore (cost) is constantly maintained and the firm follows a policy of purchasing enough additional inventory each month to cover 1.25 times the following month's sales. Its gross profit margin is 20 per cent on sales.
(e) A minimum cash balance of ₹20 lakh is to be maintained by the firm.
(f) "Accrued wages" and "other current liabilities" remain unchanged.

3. *Past Sales:* (₹ thousand)

June	₹18,000
July	20,000

4. *Sales Budget:*

(₹ *thousand*)

August	₹20,000	November	₹40,000
September	26,000	December	50,000
October	24,000	January	18,000
	February	16,000	

5. *Monthly Expenses:*

(a) Wages and Salaries:

(₹ *thousand*)

August	₹1,400	November	₹2,000
September	1,600	December	3,000
October	1,600	January	1,400

(b) Rent: ₹4 lakh per month

(c) Depreciation: ₹1.5 lakh per month

(d) Other expenses: 1 per cent of sales

Required: Indicate the maximum amount of necessary borrowings.

Solution

Cash Budget

(*Amount in* ₹ *thousand*)

Particulars	August	September	October	November	December	January
(A) Cash inflows (collections):						
(i) Cash sales	₹8,000	₹10,400	₹9,600	₹16,000	₹20,000	₹7,200
(ii) Collection from debtors (2nd month of sales)	9,000	9,000	11,700	10,800	18,000	22,500
(iii) Collection from debtors (3rd month of sales)	2,700	3,000	3,000	3,900	3,900	6,000
Total	19,700	22,400	24,300	30,700	41,900	35,700
(B) *Cash outflows*:						
(i) Wages and salaries	1,400	1,600	1,600	2,000	3,000	1,400
(ii) Rent	400	400	400	400	400	400
(iii) Other expenses	200	260	240	400	500	180
(iv) Payment for purchases	26,000	24,000	40,000	50,000	18,000	16,000
Total	28,000	26,260	42,240	52,800	21,900	17,980
(C) Net cash receipts (deficit) (A-B)	(8,300)	(3,860)	(17,940)	(22,100)	20,000	17,720
Cash at start of month	5,100	2,000	2,000	2,000	2,000	2,000
Less: desired level of cash	(2,000)	(2,000)	(2,000)	(2,000)	(2,000)	(2,000)
Borrowings (cumulative)	(5,200)	(9,060)	(27,000)	(49,100)	(29,100)	(11,380)

P.17.11 The following quarterly results are expected by XYZ Ltd next year (₹in thousands) LO 17.3 LOD: D

	Quarter 1	2	3	4
Sales	7,500	10,500	18,000	10,500
Cash payments:				
Production costs	7,000	10,000	8,000	8,500
Selling, administrative and other costs	1,000	2,000	2,900	1,600
Purchases of plant and other fixed assets	100	1,100	2,100	2,100

Debtors at the end of a quarter are one-third of sales for the quarter. The opening balance of debtors is ₹30,00,000. Cash in hand at the beginning of the year is ₹6,50,000 and the desired minimum balance is

₹5,00,000. Borrowings are made in multiples of ₹10,000 at the beginning of the quarter in which need will occur and are repaid at the end of the quarter. Interest charges may be ignored..

You are required to prepare:

(i) Cash budget by quarters for the year, and

(ii) State the amount of loan outstanding at he end of the year.

Solution

(i) *Cash Budget, Next Year (Quarter-wise)* *(Amount in '000 ₹)*

Particulars	Quarter 1	2	3	4	Total
(A) Cash inflows					
Collection from debtors					
(i) From prior quarter (1/3 of sales)	₹3,000	₹2,500	₹3,500	₹6,000	₹15,000
(ii) From current quarter (2/3 of sales)	5,000	7,000	12,000	7,000	31,000
Total cash receipts	8,000	9,500	15,500	13,000	46,000
(B) Cash outflows					
Production costs	7,000	10,000	8,000	8,500	33,500
Selling, administrative and other costs	1,000	2,000	2,900	1,600	7,500
Plant and other fixed assets purchase	100	1,100	2,100	2,100	5,400
Total cash payments	8,100	13,100	13,000	12,200	46,400
(C) Surplus/(deficit)	(100)	(3,600)	2,500	800	(400)
Opening balance	650	550	500	500	650
Closing balance (indicated)	550	3,050	3,000	1,300	250
Borrowings required (deficit minimum cash required)	—	3,550	—	—	3,550
(Repayments) made (balance minimum cash required)	—	—	(2,500)	(800)	(3,300)
Closing balance (actually now estimated)	550	500	500	500	500

(ii) Loan outstanding is ₹35,50,000 – ₹33,00,000 = ₹2,50,000

P.17.12 The following data pertain to a shop. The owner has made the following sales forecasts for the first five months of the coming year. LO 17.3 LOD: M

January	₹40,00,000
February	45,00,000
March	55,00,000
April	60,00,000
May	50,00,000

Other data are as follows:

1. Debtors' and creditors' balances at the beginning of the year are ₹30 lakh and ₹14 lakh, respectively. The balances of other relevant assets and liabilities are: Cash balance, ₹7.5 lakh; Stock, ₹51 lakh; Accrued sales commission, ₹3.5 lakh.
2. 40 per cent sales are on cash basis. Credit sales are collected in the following month.
3. Cost of sales is 60 per cent of sales.
4. The only other variable cost is a 5 per cent commission to sales agents. Sales commission is paid in the month after it is earned, that is, the time-lag is one month.
5. Inventory (stock) is kept equal to sales requirements for the next two months' budgeted sales.
6. Trade creditors are paid in the month following purchases.
7. Fixed costs are ₹5 lakh per month, including ₹2 lakh depreciation.

You are required to prepare a cash budget for each of the first three months of the coming year.

Solution

Cash Budget for Coming Year (Month-wise)

Particulars	*Month*		
	January	*February*	*March*
(A) Cash inflows			
Cash sales (0.40 × total sales)	₹16,00,000	₹18,00,000	₹22,00,000
Collection from debtors (one month after sale)	30,00,000	24,00,000	27,00,000
Total cash receipts	46,00,000	42,00,000	49,00,000
(B) Cash outflows			
Paid to trade creditors for purchase (working notes)	14,00,000	33,00,000	36,00,000
Sales commission (0.05 × previous month's sales)	3,50,000	2,00,000	2,25,000
Fixed costs (₹5,000 – ₹2,000 depreciation)	3,00,000	3,00,000	3,00,000
Total cash payments	20,50,000	38,00,000	41,25,000
(C) Surplus/(deficit) (A) – (B)	25,50,000	4,00,000	7,75,000
Opening balance	7,50,000	33,00,000	37,00,000
Closing balance (indicated)	33,00,000	37,00,000	44,75,000

WORKING NOTES

Purchase Budget

Desired closing inventory (at cost price)	₹60,00,000	₹69,00,000	₹66,00,000
Plus cost of goods sold (current month)	24,00,000	27,00,000	33,00,000
Total requirements	84,00,000	96,00,000	99,00,000
Less opening inventory	51,00,000	60,00,000	69,00,000
Purchases	33,00,000	36,00,000	30,00,000

REVIEW QUESTIONS

LOD: Easy

RQ.17.1 Fill in the following blanks: LO 17.1,2,3

(i) Overall budget is also known as ________.

(ii) Budgets prepared at the single level of activity are referred to as ________.

(iii) ** estimates costs at several levels of activity.

(iv) For most of the business firms, ________ is key budget.

(v) Budgets are an important tool of ________.

(vi) Minimum desired cash balance concept is useful in the preparation of ________ budget.

(vii) Cash budget is a tool of ________ financial planning.

(viii) Factors generating cash are categorised into two broad categories, namely, ________.

(ix) The primary objective of cash budget is to ascertain whether there is likely to be ________ of cash at any time.

(x) Sales and production budgets are ________ budgets.

[Answers: (i) master budget, (ii) fixed budgets, (iii) flexible budget, (iv) sales budget, (v) profit planning, (vi) cash budget, (vii) short-term, (viii) operating and financial, (ix) excess/shortage, (x) operating]

RQ.17.2 Are you in agreement with the view that budgeting should better be called 'profit planning and control'? LO 17.1,2

RQ.17.3 In what respects does the production budget contribute to managerial (I) planning, (ii) coordination, and (iii) control. LO 17.2,3

RQ.17.4 Write a note on the advantages and limitations of budgeting. LO 17.2

RQ.17.5 Define budgetary control and discuss the objectives of introducing a budgetary control system in your own organisation. LO 17.1,2

RQ.17.6 What do you understand by the terms budget and budgetary control? What are the advantages of budgetary control? LO 17.2

RQ.17.7 ABC Company Ltd. expects the following sales by months in units for the first six months of next year. LO 17.3

January	5,400	April	5,700
February	5,700	May	6,000
March	7,500	June	4,500

The company has a policy of maintaining an inventory equal to budgeted sales for the following two months. The beginning inventory reflects this policy. Each unit costs ₹10.

You are required to prepare purchases budget for as many months as you can both in units and rupees. Also explain why you had to stop where you did.

RQ.17.8 The Royal Industries Ltd. has prepared its annual sales forecast, expecting to achieve sales of ₹30,00,000 next year. The controller is uncertain about the pattern of sales to be expected by month and asks you to prepare a monthly budget of sales. The following sales data pertain to the year, which is considered to be representative of a normal year. LO 17.3

Month	*Sales*	*Month*	*Sales*
January	₹1,10,000	July	₹2,60,000
February	1,15,000	August	3,30,000
March	1,00,000	September	3,40,000
April	1,40,000	October	3,50,000
May	1,80,000	November	2,00,000
June	2,25,000	December	1,50,000

Prepare a monthly sales budget for the coming year on the basis of the above data.

RQ.17.9 Prepare a flexible budget at 60, 80, and 100 per cent capacities from the following information: LO 17.3

(a) Fixed expenses	₹1,49,500
(b) Semi-variable expenses at 50% capacity	89,500
(c) Variable expenses at 50% capacity	2,67,000

Semi-variable expenses remained constant between 40 and 70 per cent capacity, increase by 10 per cent between 70 and 85 per cent capacity and by 15 per cent between 85 and 100 per cent capacity. Sales at 60 per cent capacity are ₹5,10,000, at 80 per cent capacity ₹6,80,000, and at 100 per cent capacity ₹8,50,000 (Assume that all products are sold).

LOD: Medium

RQ.17.10 'If sales forecast is subject to error, then, there is no purpose of budgeting.' Do you agree? Also explain how a flexible budget can be used by management to help control costs. LO 17.3

RQ.17.11 Why do responsible people in an organisation tend to accept budgetary control in theory but resist in practice? Explain. LO 17.1,2

RQ.17.12 A manufacturing company operating a system of budgetary control finds that their production capacity during the year varies between 75 per cent and 90 per cent as against the budgeted capacity of 80 per cent for the year. It has been suggested that a system LO 17.3

of flexible budgets should be introduced to effectively control costs. Outline the steps you would take to implement this suggestion keeping in mind that the management would still require periodic comparison with their overall budget during the year.

RQ.17.13 Readymade Textiles Ltd. makes and sells baby suits. It has brisk sales in the October-December period as shown by the following sales budget (in units): **LO 17.3**

July	5,000	October	8,000
August	5,000	November	10,000
September	5,500	December	12,500

The firm's normal inventory policy has been to have a two months' supply of finished product on hand. The production manager has criticised the policy because it requires wide swings in production, which adds to costs. He estimates that unit-variable manufacturing cost is ₹2 higher than normal for each unit produced in excess of 9,000 units per month. The finance manager also supports the production manager on this. He estimates that it costs the firm ₹1 per unit in ending inventory, consisting of insurance, financing, and handling costs. He stresses that these costs are variable.

All the managers agree that the firm should have 22,500 units on hand by the end of October. The production manager wants to spread the required production equally over the four months.

(i) Prepare a production budget for July-October following the firm's current policy. Inventory on July 1 is 10,000 units.

(ii) Prepare a production budget using the production manager's preference.

(iii) Determine which budget gives lower costs.

RQ.17.14 Lookahead Ltd. produces and sells a single product. Sales budget for the current calendar year by quarter is as under: **LO 17.3**

Quarter	Units to be sold
I	12,000
II	15,000
III	16,500
IV	18,000

The year is expected to open with an inventory of 4,000 units of finished product and close with an inventory of 6,500 units. Production is customarily scheduled to provide for two-thirds of the current quarter's sales demand plus one-third of the following quarter's demand. The standard cost details for one unit of the product is as follows:

Direct material, 1 lb @ ₹5 paise per lb
Direct labour, 12 minutes @ ₹30 per hour
Variable overheads, 12 minutes @ ₹7.5 per hour
Fixed overheads, ₹1,80,000 are to be shared equally among 4 quarters.

(i) Prepare a production budget, by quarters, showing the number of units to be produced and the total costs of direct material, direct labour, variable overheads, and fixed overheads.

(ii) If the budgeted selling price per unit is ₹17, what would be the budgeted profit for the year as a whole?

(iii) In which quarter of the year is the company expected to break-even?

RQ.17.15 The demand for output of a certain company is very elastic and a modern plant recently installed is capable of greatly increased production. Output at present is 80,000 units per year, and 5 lakh units are estimated to be within the capacity of the new plant. The present selling price per unit is ₹15. **LO 17.3**

The need for flexible budgeting is recognised and six alternative levels of output, in addition to the present level, are contemplated. Six equal increments in annual output level, up to a maximum of 5,00,000 units, would involve corresponding reductions of ₹1 each in unit price to ₹9 per unit at the maximum output.

The present variable costs amount to ₹4,00,000. Fixed costs which at present amount to ₹2,00,000 are not expected to increase for any of the six alternative output levels contemplated. Semi-fixed cost are expected to vary from the present annual figure of ₹2,30,000 to ₹3,20,000, the upward steps being to ₹2,60,000 at 2,20,000 units, ₹2,80,000 at 3,60,000 units, and ₹3,20,000 at 5,00,000 units. The costs classified as variable at the six projected levels of output are calculated to be as follows:

₹7,50,000	₹11,00,000	₹15,00,000
17,50,000	20,50,000	25,00,000

Prepare the flexible budget and identify the volume which should be set for the budgeted output.

RQ.17.16 Prepare a flexible budget from the following data made available in respect of a half-yearly period and forecast the working results at 70, 85, and 100 per cents of capacity when the respective sales are ₹50 lakh, ₹60 lakh, and ₹85 lakh. While fixed expenses remain constant, semi-variable expenses are constant between 55 and 75 per cent of capacity, increasing by 10 per cent between 75 and 90 per cent of capacity and by 20 per cent between 90 and 100 per cent of capacity. The expenses at 60 per cent capacity are as follows: *(Amount in lakh of rupees)* LO 17.3

Semi-variable:	Maintenance and repairs	1.25
	Indirect labour	5.00
	Sales department expenses	1.50
	Sundry overheads	1.25
Variable:	Material	12.00
	Labour	13.00
	Other expenses	2.00
Fixed:	Wages and salaries	4.20
	Rent, rates and taxes	2.80
	Depreciation	3.50
	Sundry overheads	4.50
		51.00

LOD: Difficult

RQ.17.17 'Budgeting is profit planning.' Elaborate this statement. What accounting devices would you use where output varies? LO 17.2

RQ.17.18 ABC Ltd. manufactures cakes in three varieties—A, B, and C—each requiring similar material, labour, and production facilities. The trading results of the firm for current year ending March are as under: LO 17.3

Particulars	A	B	C	*Total*
Sales	₹21,44,000	₹17,20,000	₹10,40,000	₹49,04,000
Variable costs:				
Material	5,36,000	5,16,000	4,16,000	14,68,000
Wages	4,28,800	2,58,000	3,36,000	10,22,800
Overheads	4,28,800	2,58,000	3,36,000	10,22,800
Total	13,93,600	10,32,000	10,88,000	35,13,600
contribution	7,50,400	6,88,000	(48,000)	13,90,400
Fixed overheads				8,70,400
Profit				5,20,000

The cake of variety C, despite best efforts, does not yield the desirable margin and thus the firm has decided to discontinue its production. However, the other two varieties, A and B, have good potential to grow and the market can easily absorb the increased production. The firm has, therefore, decided to raise the production of these varieties by diverting the labour and production facilities engaged in production of variety C.

In accordance with this, it is decided, effective April 1, to transfer two-thirds of the labour engaged in variety C to variety A and the remaining one-third to variety B, thus totally discontinuing production of variety C.

The following data for the next year beginning April is also available:

(a) Total direct wage bill for the next year would be at the same level as for the last year ending March.

(b) Similarly, the variable costs per unit of production and the selling price are to be assumed unchanged in the forthcoming year beginning April.

(c) Fixed overheads would increase by ₹55,200.

You are required:

(a) To prepare the budget for next year beginning April in the same format as given above

(b) To analyse and compare the budget for the year beginning April with that of the previous year and highlight main features, and

(c) To advise the management on comparative profitability if two-thirds of the workers engaged in C are transferred to B instead of A and the remaining one-third are engaged in A instead of B. Give detailed reasoning for your advice.

RQ.17.19 Messers Up-to-date Ltd. has instructed you to prepare a cash budget for October to December from the following particulars: **LO 17.3**

(i) *Cash and bank balance as on October* 1, ₹20,000.

(ii) *Actual and budgeted sales*:

June (actual)	₹60,000	October (budgeted)	₹80,000
July	65,000	November	82,000
August	70,000	December	89,000
September	75,000		

(iii) *Purchases: actual and budgeted*:

June	₹36,000	October	₹48,000
July	40,000	November	40,000
August	48,000	December	50,000
September	45,000		

(iv) *Salaries and other expenses: actual and budgeted*:

Month	*Wages*	*Expenses*
August (actual)	₹15,000	₹5,000
September	15,000	6,000
October (budgeted)	18,000	6,000
November	18,000	8,000
December	20,000	8,000

(v) Special points:

(a) Advance income tax, ₹5,000 in November.

(b) Plant, ₹10,000 in October.

(vi) ₹300 rent payable in advance.

(vii) 10 per cent of purchases and sales are on cash terms.

(viii) Time lag:

(a) Credit sales, 2 months

(b) Credit purchases, 1 month

(c) Salaries, two weeks
(d) Expenses, one week

RQ.17.20 ABC Ltd. produces a single product that sells for ₹75 per unit. Cost data are: LO 17.3

(a) Variable manufacturing costs, ₹35 per unit.
(b) Variable selling and administrative expenses, ₹5 per unit.
(c) Fixed manufacturing costs requiring cash, ₹2,50,000 per month. Fixed selling and administrative expenses, ₹2,00,000 per month, all requiring cash. Depreciation, ₹60,000 per month.
Other relevant data are:
(d) The firm has a policy of maintaining a two-month's supply of finished products. The opening inventory (January 1) is 42,000 units.
(e) The firm does not hold raw materials inventory and purchases raw materials as needed. The cost of raw materials is included in the variable manufacturing cost of ₹35.
(f) The firm has a practice of making all sales on credit, collecting 30 per cent in the month of sale and the balance in the following month. There are no bad debts and overdue accounts. The opening debtors' balance is ₹7,00,000.
(g) The firm pays all manufacturing costs in the month of production.
(h) The firm pays four-fifths of selling and administrative expenses in the month of incurrence and the balance one-fifth is paid in the following month. On January 1, the firm owed ₹30,000 for December expenses.
(i) The minimum desired cash balance is ₹80,000, which is also the amount the firm has on January 1. Borrowings are possible and can be made in multiples of ₹10,000. It must borrow at the beginning of a month and repay at the end if sufficient cash is available. The interest rate is 10 per cent and the firm pays interest when it repays loans or portions of them.
(j) The sales budget for the first six months in units is: January, 20,000; February, 26,000; March, 30,000; April, 32,000; May, 30,000; June, 28,000.

You are required to prepare an individual monthly cash budget for the first three months of the year, and also a consolidated budget for the same period.

ANSWERS

RQ.17.7 Purchase budget: January ₹75,000 (7,500 units), February ₹57,000 (5,700 units), March ₹60,000 (6,000 units), April ₹45,000 (4,500 units).
Budgeting beyond April is not possible as the data for July and August is not available.

RQ.17.8 January (₹1,32,000), Feb. (₹1,38,000), March (₹1,20,000), April (₹1,68,000), May (₹2,16,000), June (₹2,70,000), July (₹3,12,000), August (₹3,96,000), September (₹4,08,000), October (₹4,20,000), November (₹2,40,000), December (₹1,80,000)

RQ.17.9 Flexible budget: At 60% (Loss ₹49,400), At 80% (Profit ₹4,850), At 100% (₹63,575).

RQ.17.13 **(i)** Product budget: July 5,500 units, August 8,000 units, September 10,000 units, October 12,500 units
(ii) Monthly production of 9,000 units
(iii) Current budget provides lower costs.

RQ.17.14 **(i)** Production budget: Quarter I (13,000 units), Quarter II (15,500 units), Quarter III (17,000 units), Quarter IV (18,500 units)
Total cost: Quarter I (₹2,07,500), Quarter II (₹2,38,750), Quarter III (₹2,57,500), Quarter IV (₹2,76,250)
(ii) Budgeted profit ₹96,750
(iii) Quarter III.

RQ.17.15 4,30,000 units is the desired volume; at this volume the company has maximum budgeted income, ₹17,70,000.

RQ.17.16 Budgeted loss at ₹5.5 lakh (at 70%), loss ₹3.15 lakh (at 85%), profit ₹14.20 lakh (at 100%).

RQ.17.18 **(a)** Budgeted profit ₹12,03,467

(b) There is a significant increase in the important financial parameters. Profits ₹12,03,467 (next year).

(c) Profits would be higher at ₹13,06,133.

RQ.17.19 Cash balance: October-end ₹12,900, November-end ₹10,600, December-end ₹23,200.

RQ.17.20 Borrowings: January ₹6,00,000, February ₹60,000; Repayments: March ₹3,80,000 plus interest ₹9,500; March-end balance ₹85,500.

[Comprehensive solutions to all numerical review questions are available on the companion website: http://www.mhhe.com/khan_jain_ma7e]

CASE

C.17.1 (Profit Planning) Sound Future Communications Limited (SFCL) is planning profit for the current year. The Chairman and Managing Director of the Company, Mr Wise has asked the Accounts and Finance Department to prepare the budget outlining the implications of achieving the profit goal of ₹7 lakh. The Budgeting Department has compiled the information related to its operating and financing activities as detailed in schedules I to VIII.

I. **Balance Sheet as at March 31 of the Current Year**

Liabilities	*Amount*	*Assets*		*Amount*
Share capital	₹31,77,428	Fixed assets	₹48,00,000	
Retained earnings	18,96,400	*Less:* Accumulated		
Creditors	44,000	depreciation	(12,00,000)	₹36,00,000
Taxes payable	74,000	Inventories:		
		Direct materials	1,35,828	
		Finished goods	1,60,000	2,95,828
		Debtors	11,20,000	
		Less: Provision for		
		bad debts	(64,000)	10,56,000
		Cash		2,40,000
	51,91,828			51,91,828

Notes: (i) Debtors include ₹1,60,000 from the third quarter sales of ₹20,00,000 and ₹9,60,000 from fourth quarter sales of ₹12,00,000; (ii) Direct materials include 6,300 kgs of material A @ ₹5.88 per kg and 12,600 kgs of material B @ ₹7.84 per kg; and (iii) Finished goods include 4,000 units @ ₹40 per unit.

II. *Budget assumptions*

(i) Selling price, ₹60 per unit

(ii) Quarterly sales forecast (units)

Quarter	*Next year*	*Year following next year*
First	20,000	30,000
Second	30,000	
Third	40,000	
Fourth	20,000	

III. *Inventory policy*

- Finished goods: 20 per cent of the following quarter's requirements at the end of each quarter.
- Raw materials: 30 per cent of the following quarter's requirements at the end of each quarter.
- The firm wishes to have 9,200 kgs of each type of direct material on hand at March 31 of the next year.

IV. *Manufacturing cost per unit*

Direct materials:		
1 kg of A @ ₹5.88	₹5.88	
2 kgs of B @ ₹7.84	15.68	₹21.56
Direct labour: 0.5 × direct labour-hour @ ₹8		4.00
Overheads:		
Variable (0.5 × direct labour-hour @ ₹12)	6.00	
Fixed (₹8,44,000 per year/Normal level of activity, 1,00,000 units)	8.44	14.44
Total		40.00

The quarterly fixed manufacturing costs of ₹2,11,000 include depreciation totaling ₹50,000. All production variances are written off as an adjustment to the cost of goods sold in the period in which they occurred. The firm follows absorption costing method for income determination.

V. *Selling and administrative costs*:

Commission and distribution, ₹6 per unit sold
Advertising, ₹10,000 per quarter
Administrative, ₹20,000 per quarter.

VI. *Cash disbursement policy*: Raw materials are purchased on terms of 2/10, net/30. Discount is always taken and purchases are recorded at net; 90 per cent of the purchases are paid for in the quarter of purchase and remainder are paid for in the following quarter. The list prices of materials A and B are ₹6 per kg and ₹8 per kg respectively. With the exception of income taxes, which are paid during the following quarter, all other payments are made when incurred.

VII. *Cash collection experience*: 20 per cent sales are for cash and 80 per cent are on credit. The terms of sales are 2/10, net/60 days. However, for payments, the sales are billed to customers on the first day of the following quarter; 50 per cent of the credit sales are collected during the discount period and another 40 per cent are received after the discount period but during the quarter in which the billing is done; 7.5 per cent are received during the following quarter and 2.5 per cent are bad debts. These accounts are written off at the end of the 2nd quarter following the sales. A provision of 2 per cent of sales is made for bad debts at the time of sales. Sales discounts are recorded as a deduction from sales in the quarter the discounts are taken. Based on prior experience, this deduction equals 0.8 per cent of the previous quarter's sales (0.8 × 0.5 × 0.02).

VIII. *Other information:*

- Income tax rate is 50 per cent.
- Cash dividends amount to ₹80,000 at the end of quarter 2 and quarter 4.
- At the end of the 4th quarter, equipment costing ₹6,00,000 was purchased.

Prepare a comprehensive, quarter-wise, budget to show the projected income of SFCL for the year.

Solution

Quarter-wise Sales Forecast Schedule

Quarter	*First*	*Second*	*Third*	*Fourth*	*Total*
Units sales	20,000	30,000	40,000	20,000	1,10,000
Unit sale price	× ₹60	× ₹60	× ₹60	× ₹60	× ₹60
Sales revenue	12,00,000	18,00,000	24,00,000	12,00,000	66,00,000

PRODUCTION BUDGET (UNITS)

Quarter	*First*	*Second*	*Third*	*Fourth*	*Total*
Sales	20,000	30,000	40,000	20,000	1,10,000
Add: Desired closing inventory (0.20 × next quarter)	6,000	8,000	4,000	6,000	6,000
Total finished goods requirement	26,000	38,000	44,000	26,000	1,16,000
Less: Opening Inventory	4,000	6,000	8,000	4,000	4,000
Required production	22,000	32,000	36,000	22,000	1,12,000

QUARTERLY MANUFACTURING COST BUDGET

Quarter	*First*	*Second*	*Third*	*Fourth*	*Total*
Required production (units)	22,000	32,000	36,000	22,000	1,12,000
Variable costs:					
A (₹5.88 per unit)	₹1,29,360	₹1,88,160	₹2,11,680	₹1,29,360	₹6,58,560
B (₹15.68 per unit)	3,44,960	5,01,760	5,64,480	3,44,960	17,56,160
Direct labour (₹4 per unit)	88,000	1,28,000	1,44,000	88,000	4,48,000
Overheads (₹6 per unit)	1,32,000	1,92,000	2,16,000	1,32,000	6,72,000
	6,94,320	10,09,920	11,36,160	6,94,320	35,34,720
Fixed costs:					
Depreciation	50,000	50,000	50,000	50,000	2,00,000
Other overheads	1,61,000	1,61,000	1,61,000	1,61,000	6,44,000
	2,11,000	2,11,000	2,11,000	2,11,000	8,44,000
Total costs	9,05,000	12,20,920	13,47,160	9,05,320	43,78,720
Budgeted fixed costs	2,11,000	2,11,000	2,11,000	2,11,000	8,44,000
Less: Fixed costs charged (@₹8.44 per unit)	1,85,680	2,70,080	3,03,840	1,85,680	9,45,280
Capacity variance	25,320 (Unfavourable)*	59,080 (Favourable)**	92,840 (Favourable)	25,320 (Unfavourable)	1,01,280 (Favourable)

*Under-recovery/under-absorption of fixed costs;
**Over-recovery/over-absorption of fixed costs.

QUARTERLY PURCHASE BUDGET OF RAW MATERIALS

Quarter	*First*	*Second*	*Third*	*Fourth*	*Total*
Material (A):					
Production requirement (in units)	22,000	32,000	36,000	22,000	1,12,000
Raw material required @ 1 kg per unit	22,000	32,000	36,000	22,000	1,12,000
Add: Desired ending inventory (30 per cent of the next quarter's requirement)	9,600	10,800	6,600	9,200	9,200
Total requirement	31,600	42,800	42,600	31,200	1,21,200
Less: Opening inventory	6,300	9,600	10,800	6,600	6,300
Purchase requirement (kgs)	25,300	33,200	31,800	24,600	1,14,900
Purchase cost (@ ₹5.88 per kg)	₹1,48,764	₹1,95,216	₹1,86,984	₹1,44,648	₹6,75,612
Material (B):					
Raw material required @	44,000	64,000	72,000	44,000	2,24,000

(Contd.)

(*Contd.*)

2 kg per unit)					
Add: Desired ending inventory (30 per cent of the next quarter's requirement)	19,200	21,600	13,200	9,200	9,200
Total requirements	63,200	85,600	85,200	53,200	2,33,200
Less: Opening inventory	12,600	19,200	21,600	13,200	12,600
Purchase requirement (kgs)	50,600	66,400	63,600	40,000	2,20,600
Purchase cost (@ ₹7.84 per kg)	₹3,96,704	₹5,20,576	₹4,98,624	₹3,13,600	₹17,29,504
Total purchase cost **(A + B)**	5,45,468	7,15,792	6,85,608	4,58,248	24,05,116

Quarterly Selling and Administrative Expenses Budget

Quarter	*First*	*Second*	*Third*	*Fourth*	*Total*
Units sales	20,000	30,000	40,000	20,000	1,10,000
Variable costs:					
Commission and distribution (₹6 per unit)	₹1,20,000	₹1,80,000	₹2,40,000	₹1,20,000	₹6,60,000
Fixed costs:					
Advertising	10,000	10,000	10,000	10,000	40,000
Administrative	20,000	20,000	20,000	20,000	80,000
	30,000	30,000	30,000	30,000	1,20,000
Total	1,50,000	2,10,000	2,70,000	1,50,000	7,80,000

Qarterly Budgeted Income Statement (Absorption Costing)

Quarter	*First*	*Second*	*Third*	*Fourth*	*Total*
Sales revenue	₹12,00,000	₹18,00,000	₹24,00,000	₹12,00,000	₹66,00,000
Less: Provision for bad and doubtful debts (0.02 × sales)	24,000	36,000	48,000	24,000	1,32,000
Less: Sales discount (0.8 × previous quarter's sales)	9,600	9,600	14,400	19,200	52,800
Net sales	11,66,400	17,54,400	23,37,600	11,56,800	64,15,200
Less: Cost of goods sold (@ ₹40 per unit)	8,00,000	12,00,000	16,00,000	8,00,000	44,00,000
Gross margin (unadjusted)	3,66,400	5,54,400	7,37,600	3,56,800	20,15,200
Add: Capacity variance favourable					
Less: Unfavourable	(25,320)	59,080	92,840	(25,320)	1,01,280
Gross margin (adjusted)	3,41,080	6,13,480	8,30,440	3,31,480	21,16,480
Less: Selling and administrative costs	1,50,000	2,10,000	2,70,000	1,50,000	7,80,000
Earnings before taxes	1,91,080	4,03,480	5,60,440	1,81,480	13,36,480
Less: Taxes (0.50)	95,540	2,01,740	2,80,220	90,740	6,68,240
Earnings after taxes	95,540	2,01,740	2,80,220	90,740	6,68,240

QUARTERLY BUDGETED STATEMENT OF RETAINED EARNINGS

Quarter	First	Second	Third	Fourth	Total
Opening balance	₹18,96,400	₹19,91,940	₹21,13,680	₹23,93,900	₹18,96,400
Add: Earnings after taxes	95,540	2,01,740	2,80,220	90,740	6,68,240
Closing balance	19,91,940	21,93,680	23,93,900	24,84,640	25,64,640
Less: Dividends paid		80,000	—	80,000	1,60,640
Closing balance	19,91,940	21,13,680	23,93,900	24,04,640	24,04,640

QUARTERLY SCHEDULE RELATING TO COLLECTION FROM DEBTORS

Quarter	First	Second	Third	Fourth	Total
Opening balance	₹11,20,000	₹10,56,000	₹15,36,000	₹20,64,000	₹11,20,000
Add: Credit sales	9,60,000	14,40,000	19,20,000	9,60,000	52,80,000
Total amount due	20,80,000	24,96,000	34,56,000	30,24,000	64,00,000
Less: Collection:					
(i) During discount period (0.50 × prior quarter credit sales)	4,80,000	4,80,000	7,20,000	9,60,000	26,40,000
(ii) After discount period (0.40 × prior quarter credit sales)	3,84,000	3,84,000	5,76,000	7,68,000	21,12,000
(0.075 × 2nd prior quarter credit sales)	1,20,000	72,000	72,000	1,08,000	3,72,000
Written-off bad debts (0.025 × credit sales of 2nd prior quarter credit sales)	40,000	24,000	24,000	36,000	1,24,000
Closing balance	10,56,000	15,36,000	20,64,000	11,52,000	11,52,000

QUARTERLY SCHEDULE RELATING TO PAYMENT TO CREDITORS

Particulars	First	Second	Third	Fourth	Total
Opening balance	₹44,000	₹54,546.80	₹71,579.20	₹68,560.80	₹44,000
Add: Credit purchases (net of discount)	5,45,468	7,15,792.00	6,85,608.00	4,58,248	24,05,116
Total amount payable	5,89,468	7,70,338.80	7,57,187.20	5,26,808,80	24,49,116
Less: Payments:					
(i) During the same quarter (0.90)	4,90,921.20	6,44,212.80	6,17,047.20	4,12,423.20	21,64,604.4
(ii) For the prior quarter (0.10)	44,000.00	54,546.80	71,579.20	68,560.80	2,38,686.8
Closing balance	54,546.80	71,579.20	68,560.80	45,824.80	45,824.8

QUARTERLY CASH BUDGET

Particulars	First	Second	Third	Fourth	Total
Cash inflows:					
Cash sales (0.20)	₹2,40,000	₹3,60,000	₹4,80,000	₹2,40,000	₹13,20,000
Collection from debtors:					
Credit sales subject to discount (0.50)	4,80,000	4,80,000	7,20,000	9,60,000	26,40,000
Less: Discount (0.02)	9,600	9,600	14,400	19,200	52,800

(Contd.)

Net amount	4,70,400	4,70,400	7,05,600	9,40,800	25,87,200
0.40 × prior quarter credit sales	3,84,000	3,84,000	5,76,000	7,68,000	21,12,000
0.075 × 2nd prior quarter sales	1,20,000	72,000	72,000	1,08,000	3,72,000
Total collections from debtors	9,74,400	9,26,400	13,53,600	18,16,800	50,71,200
Total cash inflows	12,14,400	12,86,400	18,33,600	20,56,800	63,91,200
Cash outflows:					
Payment to creditors	₹5,34,921.20	₹6,98,759.60	₹6,88,626.40	₹4,80,984.00	₹24,03,291.20
Direct labour	88,000	1,28,000.00	1,44,000	88,000	4,48,000.00
Variable overheads	1,32,000	1,92,000	2,16,000	1,32,000	6,72,000.00
Fixed overheads	1,61,000	1,61,000	1,61,000	1,61,000	6,44,000.00
Selling and administrative overheads	1,50,000	2,10,000	2,70,000	1,50,000	7,80,000.00
Income taxes	74,000	95,540	2,01,740	2,80,220	6,51,500.00
Dividends	—	80,000	—	80,000	1,60,000.00
Equipment	—	—	—	6,00,000	6,00,000.00
Total cash outflows	11,39,921.20	15,65,299.60	16,81,366.40	19,72,204	63,58,791.20
Net cash inflows	74,478.80	(2,78,899.60)	1,52,233.6	84,596.00	32,408.8
Opening balance	2,40,000.00	3,14,478.80	35,579.2	1,87,812.80	2,40,000.0
Closing balance	3,14,478.80	35,579.20	1,87,812.80	2,72,408.80	2,72,408.8

Budgeted Balance Sheet as at March 31, Next Year

Liabilities	*Amount*	*Assets*		*Amount*
Share capital	₹31,77,428	Fixed assets	₹54,00,000	
Retained earnings	24,04,640	*Less:* Accumulated		
Creditors	45,824.80	depreciation	14,00,000	₹40,00,000
Taxes payable	90,740	Inventories:		
		Direct material	1,26,224	
		(Material A, 9,200 × ₹5.88)		
		(Material B, 9,200 × ₹7.84)		
		Finished goods		
		(6,000 × ₹40)	2,40,000	3,66,224
		Debtors	11,52,000	
		Less: Allowances for bad debts		
		(₹64,000 + ₹1,32,000 –		
		₹1,24,000)	72,000	10,80,000
		Cash		2,72,408.80
	57,18,632.8			57,18,632.8

PART 6

COST CONTROL

Cost data are an important input for managerial control. The most widely-used cost control techniques are illustrated in this part. The discussions in Chapter 18 relate to standard and quality costs as a setting for the subject matter of other chapters in this part. Chapters 19 and 20 relate to cost efficiency through standard costs in terms of variance analysis (Chapter 19 deals with cost variance and Chapter 20 with revenue/profit variances). Responsibility accounting as a measure of divisional performance is examined in Chapter 21. Balanced score card as a measure of firm's performance has been explained in Chapter 22.

18

Standard Costs and Quality Costs

Learning Objectives

After reading this chapter you will be able to:

LO 18.1 Understand the meaning of standard costs
LO 18.2 Discuss the ways to establish cost standards
LO 18.3 Explain the main components of standard costs
LO 18.4 Examine and illustrate quality costs

Introduction

As observed earlier, management accounting is concerned with financial information for the use of management. It enables decision-making about the firm on behalf of the outside parties as well as *for* the firm for purposes of internal management. In particular, the availability of relevant information is a prerequisite for effective planning and control. The term "planning" refers to what a firm wishes to achieve and the actions to be taken to achieve the desired objectives. Control is the process of ensuring that action conform to plans. In other words, control as a management function, means that once a course of action has been decided, operational decisions and activities of management should coincide with the plans. This implies that management needs some criterion for judging the results of operating decisions. Cost data constitute an important element of the financial information to accomplish it. One approach to ensure that operations are in conformity with plans is to compare the actual performance with some standard. A widely-used technique is "standard cost" and variance analysis. The objective of this chapter is to discuss this control concept. In other words, standard cost is considered here as a criterion to measure performance. It covers meaning of standards, their establishment and components, and quality costs. The main points are summarised by way of recapitulation.

Meaning of Standards

LO 18.1 Understand the meaning of standard costs

Standards are performance expectations.[1] In other words, standards may be defined as measured quantities which

Standard is a precise measure of what should occur if performance is efficient.

should be attained in connection with some particular operation or activity. Stated in terms of a test of efficiency, a standard is a precise measure of what should occur if the performance is efficient. For example, a certain number of words per minute is a standard for an efficient steno-typist; a certain percentage of marks may be a standard to qualify in a certain examination or to obtain a certain grade, say A, or a division, say first, and so on. In other words, when we say that the standard for a typist is, say, 80 words per minute, what is meant is that a particular typist is considered efficient depending on his typing speed per minute *vis-à-vis* 80 words per minute. If he attains, or exceeds this level, his performance will be rated satisfactory, if not, he has to improve if the goals of the organisation are to be achieved. Thus, in a sense, a standard describes an approach to implement and achieve the goals of the firm. The standards are generally set by management in accordance with the best judgement. However, standards can be set only for repetitive tasks, that is, for work which is repeated again and again; standards cannot be set for tasks which are not performed regularly and continuously.

Thus defined, standards are different from another criterion to evaluate performance, namely, budgets. Budgets, as a tool of planning and control, have already been discussed in an earlier chapter of this book. One difference between standards and budgets is to be found in their scope of activity. While a budget relates to an entire activity or operation, the standard presents the same information on a per unit basis. For instance, the cost of material to produce 1,000 units is ₹5,000. In terms of budget, the cost of materials is expected to be ₹5,000. The standard would express it as ₹5 per unit. Secondly, budgets and standards are set by different persons. Usually, a budget committee prepares the budgets; the standards are generally established by management accountants in consultation with engineers, management, and so on. Moreover, functionally, budgets are used for planning and coordination purposes, whereas standards are primarily used as a control device.

Standard cost is a criterion/ meas™ure of acceptable cost performance.

Standard cost may, therefore, be defined as a criterion or measure of acceptable cost performance. That is to say, whether the cost incurred by a firm is reasonable or not, can be judged in relation to the standard costs. Standard costs may be: **(i)** Ideal, **(ii)** Expected, and **(iii)** Normal/attainable. The ideal standard cost refers to estimates of costs under ideal or perfect conditions. The assumption would be that there would be no waste, no scrap, no idle items, no machine breakdown, and so on. Such a standard, obviously, cannot be achieved in real world situations.

The expected standard cost is based upon the most likely attainable result. Technically, it means what *can* happen and not what *should* happen. It is really not a standard in the real sense of the term as there is no inherent element of efficiency, which is the basic consideration underlying standard costs.

Normal standard costs are costs which are attainable if operations/activities are efficient.

Normal standards or currently attainable standards assume normal conditions as opposed to perfect conditions in the sense that normal wastage, normal breakdown and normal mistakes are visualised as part of the operations. Therefore, such standard costs may be defined as costs which are attainable but their achievement requires that operations and activities are efficient.[2] *For our purpose, standard costs invariably refer to the normal standard costs.*

ESTABLISHING COST STANDARDS

LO 18.2 Discuss the ways to establish cost standards

The effectiveness of standard cost, as a tool, will ultimately depend upon how the standards themselves have been established. Care, therefore, must be taken to set up standards which consider all relevant facts such as the employees, their abilities and aspirations and their degree of control over operations, and so on. There are several ways to devise standards: **(i)** Engineering estimates, **(ii)** Observed behaviour, **(iii)** Predicted behaviour, and **(iv)** Desired behaviour. The standard cost in a particular situation may be based on two or more of these techniques.

Engineering Estimates

One basis of setting up cost standards is engineering estimates. Technically, a standardised relationship between, say, a given unit of output and given units of input (say, raw materials) can be estimated fairly accurately depending upon the specifications of the machinery. On the basis of such technical specifications, cost standards can be set. Thus, cost standards according to the engineering estimates are based on what can be accomplished.

Observed Behaviour

Another technique to establish cost standards is past experience. Here, the approach is to treat the achievements of the past as standards for the future. If the processes and procedures of the past have not changed and are likely to operate in future also, this can provide a reliable guide for the future. If, however, changes occur in the processes and procedures, observed behaviour (what happened in the past) can certainly not provide a reliable basis for setting cost standards.

Predicted Behaviour

It is also likely that certain changes, such as technological, may be in the offing. These are likely to have a bearing on the cost estimates. In such cases, what is most likely to happen, that is, predicted behaviour in terms of adjustment to the historical standard cost, can be used to set cost standards.

Desired Behaviour

Desired behaviour can also affect standard cost. The term "desired behaviour" means what management desires. The desire of the management may be based on the experience of similar concerns or the industry as a whole. This basis will bring the cost standards of the company in line with those of the industry as a whole.

In brief, while several techniques are available to establish cost standards, it is basically based on management's judgement. In setting up of standards, management should be careful. Standards should be set at a level at which they are attainable with reasonable efforts. If they are too strict and too high, they may be difficult to achieve, leading to all-round demoralisation. If, on the other hand, cost standards are set low, there may not be sufficient motivation to achieve them.

Components of Standard Cost

LO 18.3 Explain the main components of standard costs

From the preceding discussion standard costs may be defined as costs that should be reasonably incurred in the manufacturer of a product.[3] The main components of standard costs are: **(i)** Standard direct material cost, **(ii)** Standard direct labour cost, and **(iii)** Manufacturing overheads.

Standard costs are costs that should be reasonably incurred in the manufacture of a product.

Standard Direct Material Cost

The standard direct material cost of a product is based upon price and quantity standards. In operational terms,

Standard direct material cost = Price standards of direct material
× Quantity standard of direct material **(18.1)**

Direct Materials Price Standard

One of the most important items of cost is the cost of direct materials used in the manufacture of goods. To exercise control over the cost, therefore, an important element of cost control is the price paid for the purchase of materials. In other words, one important dimension of materials cost control is that the price paid should be reasonable. Hence, the need for a materials price standard which is defined as the price which should be paid for particular direct raw material under the most favourable possible conditions. What is the most *favourbale possible condition* will differ from firm to firm depending upon the circumstances of each case. Therefore, material price standards should be set for each firm and not for the industry as a whole.

The standard material price should include all the components of the amount which is to be spent to acquire a particular material. To illustrate, in the first place, assuming the same quality of goods, the standard should be set on the basis of the lowest price. If, however, the supplier who is prepared to sell the material at the lowest cost, is not able to deliver them when needed, or he is not dependable, there will be no real saving to the firm. In such cases, differences in quality and/or in service may justify the setting up of the price standard on the basis of the higher price to be charged by the more reliable suppliers. Secondly, a firm has to incur freight charges on the purchase of raw materials which affect the cost of the materials. Since freight charges normally vary with the distance between the buyer and the supplier, while setting a material price standard, the firm should consider purchasing from the closest possible supplier, other things being equal. A related aspect is that in the case of purchase through imports, additional cost is involved in the form of import duties. These have to be taken into account while fixing standard price. Thirdly, discounts available on the purchase of materials are also relevant to the fixation of price standards. The discounts fall into two categories: **(i)** Quantity discounts which are granted for purchase in relatively large doses; **(ii)** Cash discounts which are granted for prompt payment. The effect of discounts is lower costs and, hence, lower price standards. The setting up of a materials price standard is illustrated in Example 18.1.

◆ Example 18.1

Hypothetical Ltd, on the basis of investigation of alternative sources of supply, decides to purchase raw materials from the most advantageous supplier—ABC Ltd which quotes a list price of ₹1,820 per tonne, exclusive of freight charges. It also offers a quantity discount @ ₹70 per tonne for orders exceeding 20 tonnes. It also allows 2 per cent cash discount for payment within 15 days. Moreover, freight charges are likely to be ₹1,700 per carload (20 tonnes of materials) and payable directly to the carrier. Compute the standard materials price for Hypothetical Ltd.

Solution

Computation of Standard Materials Price

1. List price (per tonne)	₹1,820
2. *Less* quantity discount (per tonne)	70
Car load price	1,750
3. *Less* cash discount (0.02)	35
	1,715
4. *Add* freight charges (₹1,700 ÷ 20 tonnes)	85
Standard price per tonne	1,800

This standard price provides a basis for planning future material costs and for controlling current costs by providing a criterion against which actual prices paid may be evaluated.

Materials Quantity (Usage) Standard The quantity of the materials used is the second factor affecting cost of material. In order to standardise cost of materials, therefore, the quantity of materials used for the production of a particular product should also be standardised. The standards of the quantity of consumption of raw materials is referred to as materials quantity standards or materials usage standards. Such standards can be determined on the basis of two factors: **(i)** The necessary input-output relationship between materials and products and also upon observation of actual experience, **(ii)** The inherent loss of materials in the production processes owing to factors such as weight losses due to scrapping and smoothing, shrinkage and evaporation, and so on. Consider Example 18.2.

◆ Example 18.2

Hypothetical Ltd of Example 18.1 produces a single product by using steel. Each finished product weighs 380 kgs. Past experience coupled with careful engineering studies show that a loss of 5 per cent occurs in the weight of the input material in the production process. What is the standard material usage per unit?

Solution

Computation of Standard Materials Usage Per Unit

Weight of finished product (kgs)	380
Allowance for normal loss in the production process (0.05)	20
Standard material usage	400

Two points in this connection are notable. First, there will be different quantity standards for different materials; and different standards may apply to the usage of a single material in different products/departments. Second, the material quantity standard does not provide for loss of materials due to: **(1)** Careless handling, **(2)** Damage to units in process, and **(3)** Other undesirable circumstances. In fact, the material usage standard is intended to eliminate such types of material losses.

Total Material Cost Standard The total material cost standard is computed by multiplying price standards by quantity standards. This is illustrated in Example 18.3.

◆ Example 18.3

Continuing the case of Hypothetical Ltd of **Examples 18.1** and **18.2**, the standard price is ₹1,800 per tonne; the standard quantity is 420 kgs per finished units of product. Compute the total standard material cost.

Solution

Standard material cost = (Standard usage × Standard price per kg)
Standard price per kg = ₹1,800/ 2,000 = ₹0.9
Standard material cost = ₹0.9 × 400 = ₹360

Standard Direct Labour Cost

The second component of total standard cost is direct standard labour cost. It is calculated by multiplying Labour rate standards by Labour time standards.

Labour Rate/Price Standards The payment to labour for carrying on production is wages, which is paid either on a time basis (monthly, weekly, daily) or on a piece basis (per piece of production). The use of the term "labour rate/ price standard" is conventionally limited to wage rates standard only, that is, in case of time wage payment only. The wage rate standards are normally either a matter of company policy, or more often, the result of negotiations between management and union. Moreover, in most cases, there will be several different wage rates depending upon the degree of skill, the element of danger, seniority of workers, and so on. Thus, labour rate standards are quite different from material price standards. They are not entirely under the control of management. To illustrate, assume that Hypothetical Ltd has two production departments. In the first, the current standard wage rate is ₹48 per hour. In the second, the standard wage rate is ₹50 per hour. This has to be related to the labour time standard to work out the total labour standard.

Labour time standards is the amount of time which a particular operation should take.

Labour Time Standards The quantity (amount) of labour is measured in terms of time devoted to the completion of a particular operation. Therefore, labour time standards may be defined as the amount of time which a particular operation should take. They are normally established on the basis of observation of actual operations and a critical evaluation of whether or not those operations are being performed as efficiently as is feasible.[4] A fairly familiar and popular example are time and motion studies. It is on the basis of these that labour time standards are generally set. They should, of course, include provision for a reasonable amount of time lost simply because human beings are not mechanical devices and cannot utilise every single moment on the job for actual production. However, no allowance is made while setting standards for prolonged periods of illness or for incompetence.

Assuming that engineering studies in Hypothetical Ltd show that in one of its departments one unit of output should be produced in one-fourth of an hour, whereas in the other department it is one-half of an hour, the total labour time standard is three quarter-hour.

Total Labour Cost Standard The total labour cost standard is equal to labour rate standard multiplied by labour time standard. For Hypothetical Ltd the total labour cost standard would be:

(a) For Department 1 : ₹48 × 1/4 hour =	₹12
(b) For Department 2 : ₹50 × 1/2 hour =	25
(c) Total = (a + b)	37

Overheads Standards

The third component of cost standard is overheads. There is a basic difference between overheads standard and material and labour standards. It has been shown in the preceding sections that the standard material and labour costs are based upon price and quantity standards. The logic underlying this is that a functional relationship exists between the number of units of a product and the quantities of material and labour required as also the fact that each material has its standard price and each worker his standard wage rate. In sharp contrast, no such functional relationships exists between the units produced and total overheads cost. Even that portion of manufacturing overhead which varies with the volume of production cannot be directly related to production in the same way as direct material and direct labour. Therefore, the determination of overhead standard is different from that of direct materials and labour.

For these reasons, standard costs for overheads are generally based on budget and not upon standards. Operationally, they are determined essentially in the same way as normal manufacturing overhead rates which are covered in another chapter of this book. The overheads are, for purposes of planning and control, classified into: **(i)** Variable, and **(ii)** Fixed. The standard variable rate is set directly per unit of volume just as a normal variable rate. The volume measure is some measure of input, such as direct labour cost or hours. The determination of the standard fixed overhead is slightly different from that of the normal fixed overhead. This difference lies in the volume at which they are set. Normal fixed rates, illustrated in an earlier chapter in this book, are set at the budgeted volume for the budget period. Standard fixed rates, on the other hand, are usually set at some volume representative of the firm's operations over a longer period than a single budget period.

The volume level most commonly selected for setting standard manufacturing overheads rates is normal volume. The more logical and feasible concept of normal volume is the preferred rate of operating capacity. Each firm identifies a particular rate, or level of capacity/activity at which it would most like to operate its plants. Logically, this is the level at which the mix of productive inputs is optimal and the total manufacturing cost per unit is minimum. Such a concept of normal volume is consistent with the notion of standard cost—cost that should be incurred under efficient operating conditions. It is estimated that the preferred level of operating capacity is at or near 90 per cent of full capacity.[5]

◆ Example 18.4

Assume that Hypothetical Ltd uses direct labour-hours as the basis to allocate overheads to production. The variable overhead is budgeted at ₹160 per direct labour-hour in Department 1. The fixed manufacturing overhead is budgeted at a total of ₹16,00,000 per year and normal production volume has been established at 40,000 direct labour-hour per year. In Department 2, variable manufacturing overhead is budgeted at ₹100 per direct labour-hour and fixed overhead at ₹12,00,000 per year. Normal production volume is 80,000 labour-hours per year. Compute the standard overhead rates.

Solution

Computation of Standard Overhead Rates

	Department 1	*Department 2*
1. Standard fixed overhead rate per Labour-hour (Fixed overheads ÷ Normal production volume)	₹40 (₹16,00,000/40,000)	₹15 (₹12,00,000/80,000)
2. Variable overhead per unit (Standard labour time × Variable overhead)	40 (1/4 hour × ₹160)	50 (1/2 hour × ₹100)
3. Fixed overhead per unit (Standard labour time × Standard fixed overhead rate)	10 (1/4 hour × ₹40)	7.5 (1/2 hour × ₹15)

Standard Cost Sheet

A summarised view of total standard cost is presented in the form of a standard cost sheet or standard cost card. The information about Hypothetical Ltd is presented in Table 18.1.

TABLE 18.1 Hypothetical Limited—Standard Cost Sheet

(a) Direct materials (400 kgs × ₹0.9)		₹360.00
(b) Direct labour:		
Department 1	₹12	
Department 2	25	37.00
(c) Variable manufacturing overhead:		
Department 1	40	
Department 2	50	90.00
(d) Fixed manufacturing overhead:		
Department 1	10	
Department 2	7.5	17.50
		504.50

Quality Costs

Quality is the total features and characteristics of a product/service made/performed according to specifications to satisfy customers at the time of purchase and during use.

LO 18.4 Examine and illustrate quality costs

To satisfy the customers needs for good quality products and short delivery times, it is necessary to find cost effective ways to continuously improve the quality of products and to shorten delivery times. **Quality is the total features and characteristics of a product/service made/performed according to specifications to satisfy customers at the time of purchase and during use.** Focussing on the quality of a product will generally build expertise in producing it, lower costs of making it, create higher satisfaction for using it and generate higher future revenues for the company selling it[6]. There are two basic aspects of quality: First, quality of design in terms of how closely the characteristics of a product/service meet the needs/wants of customers. Failure of a bank to provide online services is an example of a quality-of-design failure. Second, conformance quality in the sense of the performance of a product/service relative to its design/specifications. Deposit of a customer's cheque into the wrong account by a bank is an example of failure on conformance quality. To ensure that performance will achieve customer satisfaction, companies must first design products to satisfy customers through quality of design. They must then meet design specifications through conformance quality.

Costs of Quality/Quality Costs

Cost of Quality are the costs incurred to prevent, or the cost arising as a result of, producing a low-quality product.

The costs of quality are the costs incurred to prevent, or the cost arising as a result of, producing a low-quality product. These include any costs in excess of those that would have been incurred if goods were manufactured/service provided exactly right at the first time.[7] These costs typically are categorised into four groups, described below.

Prevention costs are incurred to prevent defects and other quality problems/ to preclude the production of goods that do not conform to specifications.

Prevention Costs Such costs *are incurred to prevent defects and other quality problems/* to preclude the production of goods that do not conform to specifications. Examples of these costs are: design engineering, process engineering, supplier evaluation, preventive equipment maintenance, quality training, new materials used to manufacture products and so on. In a sense, they are "good quality" costs in the sense that they represent activities that often significantly reduce costs in the other three categories of quality costs.[8]

Quality appraisal costs are incurred to detect which individual unit of a product does not conform to specifications

Quality Appraisal (Detection) Costs Such costs are incurred to detect which individual unit of a product does not conform to specifications. Examples of these costs are inspection, testing and other activities designed to find problems before goods are delivered to customers.

Internal Failure Costs These costs are incurred as a result of the appraisal activities. These are incurred on a defective product before it is despatched to customers. Examples of such costs are spoilage, rework, scrap, breakdown maintenance, manufacturing/process engineering on internal failure and other activities to "make things better" before a product is delivered.

External failure costs are costs of making things right when a quality problem has occurred after the product has been delivered to the customer

External Failure Costs These are costs of making things right when a quality problem has occurred after the product has been delivered to the customer. Examples of this category of quality cost are refunds, warranty costs in terms of both repairs and replacements, product liability costs and the costs of repeating a service that was not performed properly at first time. Included in this category of costs is also the cost of lost future business resulting from dissatisfied customers.

Unlike product costs, the quality costs often are estimates based on special studies rather than the output of routine accounting system. Such costs are charged to the specific product that caused them to be incurred.

Quality Costs Illustrated

The cost of quality of design is mainly in the form of the opportunity cost of sales lost from not producing a product that consumers want. It is very difficult to measure the financial cost of design quality objectively.

We illustrate below the computation of quality costs in terms of cost of conformance quality. We use step-wise activity-based costing approach **(discussed in Chapter 12)** here to determine the cost of quality.

Step 1: Identify the Chosen Product Assume the product is 20,000 photocopying machines of Modi Xerox Ltd. The revenues and operating income from the sale of 20,000 machines are ₹70 crore and ₹6 crore respectively in 2007.

Step 2: Select Cost-Allocation Base for Allocating Indirect Costs of Quality The activities that result in quality costs are listed in Exhibit 18.1 (Column 1).

Step 3: Identify Indirect Costs Associated with Each Cost-Allocation Base These are the total costs computed by multiplying the rate per hour **(Column 2 for Exhibit 18.1)** and quantity **(Column 3 of Exhibit 18.1)** on each of the cost-of-quality activities.

Step 4: Compute the Rate Per Unit of Each Cost Allocation Base Used to Allocate Indirect Costs of Quality to Product For each activity, the total costs **(computed in Step 3)** are divided by the total quantity of the cost allocation base (calculated in Step 2) to compute the rate per unit of each cost allocation base. **Column 2 of Exhibit 18.1 shows these rates.**

Step 5: Compute the Indirect Costs of Quality Allocated to the Product These are shown in Column 4 of Exhibit 18.1.

Step 6: Compute the Total Costs of Quality by Adding All Costs of Quality Assigned to the Product This is **shown in Column 5** of Exhibit 18.1.

EXHIBIT 18.1 Analysis of Activity-based Cost of Quality of Photocopying Machines of Modi Xerox Ltd.

Cost of Quality Activities	*Allocation Base/Cost Driver*			*Percentage of revenue*
	Rate	*Quantity*	*Total costs [(2) × (3)]*	*[(4) ÷ ₹70 crore] %*
(1)	*(2)*	*(3)*	*(4)*	*(5)*
Prevention Costs:				
Design Engineering	₹400 per hour	20,000 hours	₹80,00,000	1.1%
Process Engineering	300 per hour	22,500 hours	67,50,000	1.0
Total			1,47,50,000	2.1
Appraisal Costs:				
Inspection	200 per hour	1,20,000 hours	2,40,00,000	3.4
Total			2,40,00,000	3.4

(Contd.)

(Contd.)

Internal Failure Costs:				
Rework	500 per hour	50,000 hours	2,50,00,000	3.6
Total			2,50,00,000	3.6
External Failure Costs:				
Customer support	250 per hour	6,000 hours	15,00,000	0.2
Transportation	1,200 per hour	1,500 hours	18,00,000	0.3
Warranty repair	550 per hour	60,000 hours	3,30,00,000	4.7
Total			3,63,00,000	5.2
Total Cost of Quality			10,00,50,000	14.3

Non-Financial Measures of Quality and Customer Satisfaction

Financial measures of quality, discussed earlier, focus on the start-run. To evaluate how well their actual performance satisfies customer needs, companies supplement financial measures with non-financial measures of quality of design and conformance quality. Non-financial measures indicate the future needs and preferences of customer as well as specific areas that need improvement. They are, in a sense, indicator of future long-term performance. The non-financial measures of customer satisfaction, *inter-alia,* include the following:[9]

- Market research information on customer preferences/satisfaction with specific product features.
- Number of defective units delivered to customers as percentage of total units delivered.
- Number of customer complaints.
- Percentage of products that fail soon/often.
- Delivery delays in terms of differences between the scheduled delivery date and the date requested by the customers.
- On-time delivery rate (i.e. percentage of delivery made on/before the scheduled delivery date).
- Surveys to measure customer satisfaction.

Management should monitor whether there is improvement or deterioration over time. Any improvement may be indicative of strong operating income in future whereas deterioration may indicate weak operating income.

SUMMARY

- Standard costs represent a control technique. In a sense, they are a target, which the management attempts to achieve. The control process involves a comparison of the actual performance with the standards set by management. The extent of success would be revealed by the relationship between the actual and the standard. If the actual performance coincides with the target, the performance can be said to be satisfactory. In case of divergence or deviations, management would have to analyse the causes. These deviations are technically referred to as "variance". Therefore, variance analysis is an important control concept related to standard costs. In other words, the variances which basically represent performance deviations are a significant element of the information base of an effective control system. The next two chapters discuss cost and revenue variances.

LO 18.1,2,3

- Costs of quality are costs incurred to prevent or the cost arising as a result of, producing a low quality product. Such costs are categorised into prevention costs, quality appraisal (detection) costs, internal failure costs and external failure costs.
- Prevention costs are incurred to prevent defects and other quality problems/to preclude the production of goods that do not conform to specifications. Quality appraisal costs are incurred to detect which individual unit of a product does not conform to specifications. Internal failure costs are incurred on defective products before they are delivered to customers. External failure costs are costs of making things right when a quality problem has occurred after the product has been delivered to the customer.
- Financial measures of quality focus on the short-run. Non-financial measures indicate the future needs and preferences of customers as well as the specific areas that need improvement.

LO 18.4

REFERENCES

1. R.M. Copeland and P.E. Dashcher, *Management Accounting,* (John Wiley and Sons, New York, 1978), p. 382.
2. D.T. Decoster and E.L. Schafer, *Management Accounting,* (John Wiley and Sons, New York, 1979), p. 204
3. J.M. Fremgen, *Accounting for Managerial Analysis,* (Richard D. Irwin, Homewood, Illinois, 1976), p. 237.
4. *Ibid.*, p. 233.
5. *Ibid.*, p. 239.
6. Horngren, C. T., *Cost Accounting,* Pearson (2004), p. 654.
7. *Ibid,* p. 655.
8. Anthony, R. N., *Accounting: Text and Cases,* TMH (2005), p. 560.
9. Horngren, *op. cit,* p. 661.

REVIEW QUESTIONS

LOD: Easy

RQ.18.1 Indicate whether the following statements are 'true' or 'false'. LO 18.1, 2, 3

(i) Standard costs are the measures of acceptable cost performance.
(ii) Standards should be tight to be an effective tool of cost control
(iii) Standards are used for planning and coordination purposes.
(iv) Standards should be current and attainable with reasonable efforts.
(v) Standard material price is based only on the cost price at which materials can be procured by the purchase manager.
(vi) Material quantity standard should also provide for normal loss of materials in the production process.
(vii) Labour time standards are generally set on the basis of motion and time studies.
(viii) Standard fixed overhead rate is based on budgeted output.
(ix) Overhead standards are set like material and labour standards.
(x) Standard direct labour cost is summation of labour rate standard and labour time standard.

[Answers: (i) True, (ii) False, (iii) False, (iv) True, (v) False, (vi) True, (vii) True, (viii) False, (ix) False, (x) False.]

RQ.18.2 What is "standard costing" and how would you distinguish it from "budgetary control?" **LO 18.1, 2**

RQ.18.3 Write short notes on the following: **LO 18.1, 2**
(a) Standard costing as tool of management control.
(b) Control through standard costs.

RQ.18.4 How do standards and standard costs facilitate managerial planning and control? **LO 18.2**

RQ.18.5 What factors should be considered in setting a: **(a)** Materials price standard; **(b)** Materials usage standard; **(c)** Labour rate standard; and **(d)** Labour time standard? **LO 18.3**

RQ.18.6 Define quality and explain the two aspects of quality. **LO 18.4**

RQ.18.7 Define quality costs. Explain the main categories of these costs. **LO 18.4**

LOD: Medium

RQ.18.8 (a) What are the points of similarity and points of difference between budgets and standard costs? **LO 18.1, 2**
(b) What are the several types of standards and what are the assumptions on which these standards are based?

RQ.18.9 What is the nature of the fundamental difference between standard costs for direct materials and labour and standard manufacturing overhead costs? **LO 18.3**

RQ.18.10 Explain briefly the non-financial measures of quality and customer satisfaction. **LO 18.4**

19

Cost Variances Analysis

LEARNING OBJECTIVES

After reading this chapter you will be able to:

- **LO 19.1** Explain the nature of cost variances
- **LO 19.2** Discuss material variances and the factors responsible for various types of material variances
- **LO 19.3** Illustrate the various types of labour variances and the reasons for such variances
- **LO 19.4** Understand variable and fixed manufacturing overhead costs separately as well as jointly
- **LO 19.5** Review the methods of analysing overhead variances jointly
- **LO 19.6** Show how to incorporate standard costs in the accounting records

INTRODUCTION

Chapter 18 introduced an important control concept-standard costs. The object of this chapter is to illustrate the use of standard costs for purposes of planning and control of costs in a manufacturing concern.

NATURE OF COST VARIANCES

LO 19.1 Explain the nature of cost variances

This objective is achieved by the process of comparison of actual costs (AC) incurred with the pre-determined standard costs (SC) and then seeking the reasons for the variances, if any. *Variance represents the difference between AC and SC.* If AC is less than SC, this is a sign of efficiency and the difference is termed as "favourable" variance (F). If the AC is more than SC, this is a sign of inefficiency and the difference is designated as "unfavourable"/"adverse" variance (U/A). Favourable variance is also sometimes referred to as "positive variance" while unfavourable variance is called "negative variance". The words favourable/positive and unfavourable/negative are merely indicative of the direction of variance from the SC. They need not necessarily be good or bad from the point of view of the firm. Such a

Variance is the difference between actual cost and standard cost.

qualitative evaluation can be made only after the underlying cause of the variance has been determined. And, above all, the answer will depend on the type of standards set by the firm. If standards are properly set in that they are reasonable and accurate and are revised from time to time in the light of changed circumstances, deviations would be true deviations. However, if standards are not properly set, conclusions drawn—favourable or unfavourable—will be distorted. A still more serious situation would occur, when guided by such a wrong conclusion, futile efforts would be initiated by the management to correct the "not - incorrect operation."

Given the fact that standards are properly set (currently attainable), variances would serve as useful tool in the implementation of the concept of "management by exception" in that variances keep the management informed about the erratic and out-of-line behaviour of the business. The basic rule of management by exception is to concentrate on operations and segments of an enterprise that deviate from target performance and not to spend much time reviewing satisfactory performances. Further, both favourable and unfavourable variances deserve attention. An unfavourable variance suggests a condition that may require correction. A favourable variance may suggest an opportunity that management can exploit.[1]

Variances, as a control device, are calculated to assign/fix responsibility for deviations from the SC and, thus, to control the cost. For purposes of control, variances are classified as controllable and uncontrollable cost variances.

If a variance can be traced with the responsibility of a particular individual, it is said to be a "controllable" variance. If variance stems from causes beyond the control of responsible individuals, it is said to be "uncontrollable". Thus, uncontrollable variance arises when the responsibility for the variance cannot be attributed to any individual in an organisation. For instance, the increase in the price of materials and increase in the wage rates are commonly referred to as un/non-controllable variances, whereas excessive usage of materials in production, more than standard hours taken by labourers in production, are examples of controllable variances. This distinction of variances into controllable and uncontrollable is extremely important. Controllable variances are carefully analysed and reported to the management to enable it to pursue corrective action, and, thus, facilitate the implementation of the principle of management by exception.

As already observed, variances relate to costs of manufacturing enterprises. The three elements of the costs of such enterprises are: (i) Material, (ii) Labour and (iii) Overheads. A complete list of the different types of variances is given in Figures 19.1 and 19.2.

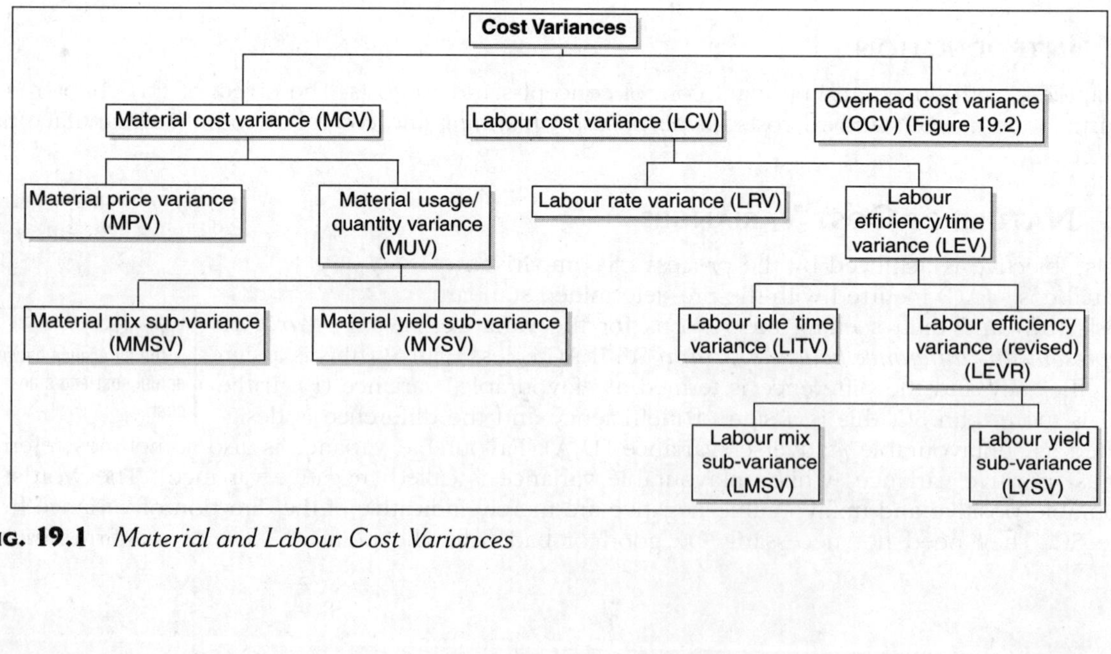

FIG. 19.1 *Material and Labour Cost Variances*

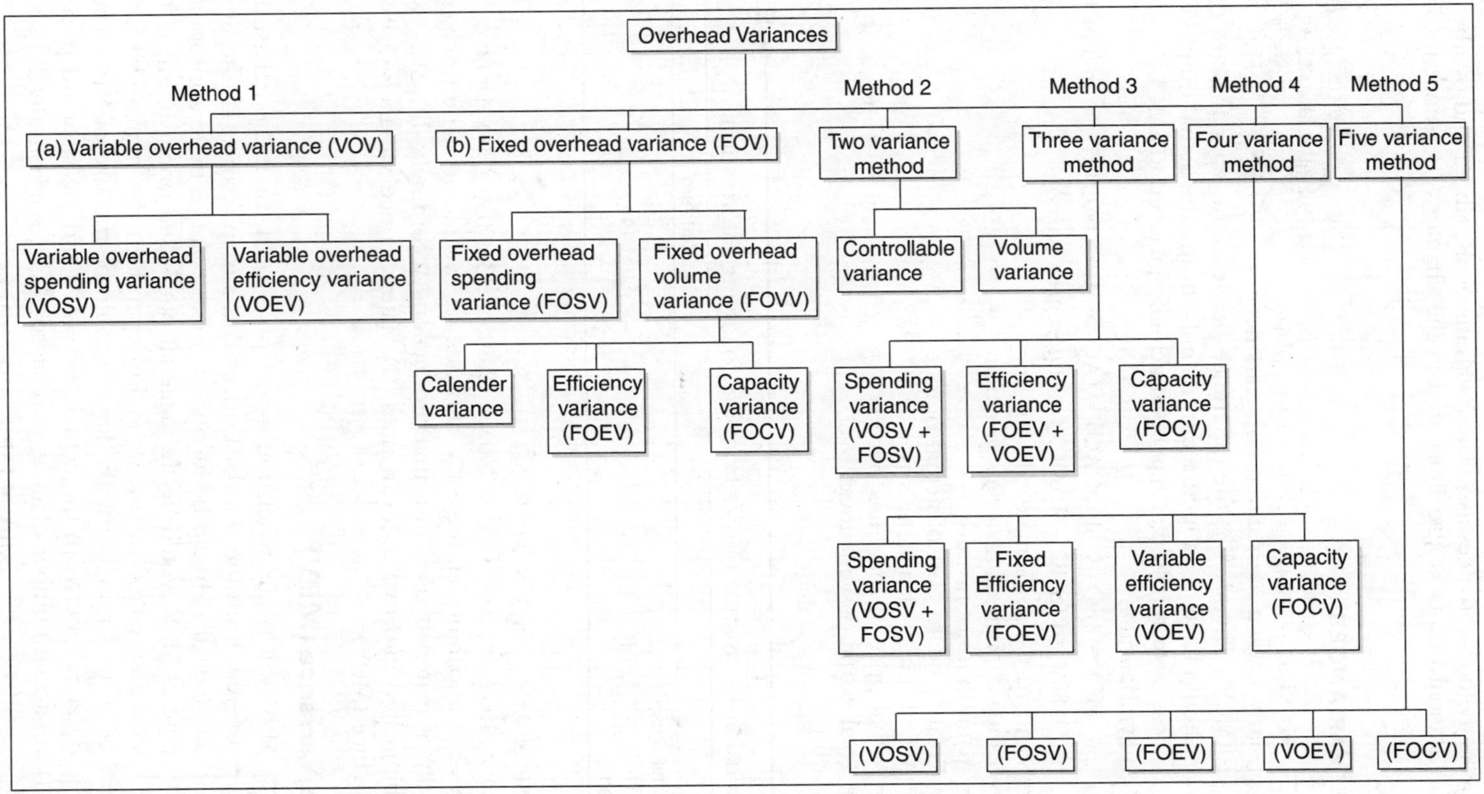

FIG. 19.2 *Overhead Variances*

The chapter covers the cost variances associated with materials, labour and overheads respectively. The accounting for standard costs is also illustrated in the chapter. The summary is given by way of recapitulation.

MATERIAL VARIANCES

LO 19.2 Discuss material variances and the factors responsible for various types of material variances

Material cost variance is the difference between the standard cost of materials and the cost of materials actually incurred.

Material variances are more popularly known as material cost variances (MCV). The MCV is the difference between the standard cost of materials that should have been incurred in manufacturing the actual output (TSMC) and the cost of materials that has been actually incurred (TAMC).

Symbolically,

$$MCV = (SQ \times SP \times AO) - (AQ \times AP \times AO) \text{ (on per unit basis)} \quad \textbf{(19.1)}$$

$$MCV = (TSMC - TAMC) \text{ (on aggregate basis)} \quad \textbf{(19.2)}$$

Where,
SQ = Standard usage of materials per unit
SP = Standard price of materials per unit
AO = Actual output in units
TSMC = Total standard cost of actual output
AQ = Actual usage of materials per unit
AP = Actual price of materials per unit
TAMC = Total actual cost incurred

Consider Example 19.1.

◆ Example 19.1

Compute the material cost variance (MCV) from the following information.

Particulars	*Standard*	*Actual*
Material usage per unit (kgs)	2	2.2
Price per kilogram (₹)	14	15
Actual units produced		100

Solution

MCV = (SQ × SP × AO) – (AQ × AP × AO)
= (2 × ₹14 × 100) – (2.2 × ₹15 × 100) = ₹2,800 – ₹3,300 = ₹500 (Unfavourable/Adverse)

From the above, it is apparent that the MCV depends on two factors—the price paid for materials, and the quantity of materials used in actual production. Accordingly, the MCV which is a total variance can be bifurcated into two sub-variances: (i) Material price variance (MPV); (ii) Material usage/quantity variance (MUV).

Material Price Variance (MPV)

Material price variance is the difference between the actual price paid for purchase of materials and the standard price.

MPV will occur when the actual price paid for the purchase of materials is different from the standard price. This variance arises at the time of purchase and logically should be identified at that point. A more appropriate title for this type of MPV would be the material purchased price variance.[2] Obviously, the total amount of variance should depend on the number of units purchased; the greater the number of units purchased, the larger should be the size of MPV. Thus, the MPV is a function of (i) the difference between the actual price (AP) and the standard price (SP) per unit of material; and (ii) the actual number of units purchased (AQ). Symbolically,

$$MPV = (SP - AP) \times AQ \quad \textbf{(19.3)}$$

When actual price exceeds standard price, the variance is unfavourable (U/A); favourable variance (F) results when standard price is greater than actual price. There will be no variance if both the prices are equal. For the facts, in Example 19.1, the MPV would be: (₹15 – ₹14) × 220 kgs = ₹220 (unfavourable/A)

Factors Responsible for MPV There may be many causal factors for the MPV. Some of them may be acting favourably while others unfavourably. An illustrative list of the factors having a bearing on MPV is given below:

1. Changes in the basic price of materials due to inflation.
2. Excess transport charges, that is, freight on goods purchased which are normally considered as part of the cost of purchases.
3. Change in the pattern of amount of taxes and customs duties.
4. Increased excise duty on goods purchased and, hence, a higher price charged by the suppliers of their products.
5. In situations of material shortages, the price charged by, and paid to, the suppliers may be higher than the normal price.
6. Purchases may not have been made from the most desirable supplier or favourable market.
7. Not availing of cash discounts due to inadequate cash resources, while such discounts were well taken into account while determining the standard price.
8. Failure to take advantage of off-season low price.
9. Sudden change in the production volume, forcing the purchase manager to buy uneconomic quantities.
10. Change in standard quality or specifications of materials resulting in different prices being paid.
11. Use of substitute material having a different unit price from the standard.
12. Failure to purchase in the pre-estimated lot size resulting in a loss of trade discount.

Responsibility for MPV Material price variance is mainly the responsibility of the purchase officers who are in charge of making the entire purchases of the firm. Normally, they are required to prepare a statement which analyses the reasons for the variances. From the factors enumerated above, it is very clear that the purchase department may not be always held responsible for paying higher or lower than the standard price; the responsibility for some of the factors may rest with persons other than purchasing officers. For instance, the responsibility of a sudden change in production schedule rests with the production manager. Likewise, a general price increase falls beyond the jurisdiction of purchase officers. The purchases of smaller quantities depriving the benefit of trade discount and making late payment resulting in foregoing cash discount on account of lack of finances with the firm are not factors for which they are accountable. For example, the average market price of the materials purchased by a firm has increased by 10 per cent (on account of additional excise duty imposed on the manufacturer supplying the material to the firm) from the firm's standard price, and the MPV is unfavourable by 7 per cent. The situation implies efficient purchasing practices whereas simple computation would yield the opposite conclusion of ineffective/inefficient purchasing practices. On the contrary, the purchase manager might succeed in achieving a favourable material price variance by purchasing from an unreliable supplier, but consequent delivery delays may be fatal to the firm in that it may cause partial shutdown of production facilities, having an adverse impact on meeting customer's orders in time. Such a variance is favourable only in name and clearly not in effect.

Obviously, it would be naive to automatically assign all results directly to the purchasing department without a detailed analysis. It is logical, therefore, to attribute a segment of material price variance to a department(s) other than purchasing. For example, if a foreman of a production department fails to notify purchase requisitions of materials in time, an emergency order may become imperative to make available the required supplies so as to avert a production stoppage, entailing higher price being paid and perhaps also higher freight charges. Clearly, the production department is responsible for the creation of such a variance. From the *operational* viewpoint, however, it can be said that the causes rest with the purchase officer and it is his responsibility to explain unusual circumstances.

Material Usage/Quantity Variance (MUV)

Material usage variance occurs when actual usage of materials differs from standard usage.

The second component of MCV, material quantity/usage variance (MUV), measures how well the materials in production are utilised. This variance occurs when actual usage of material differs from standard usage. The data for actual usage of materials is collected from a summary of materials issue reports during the relevant period, while the standard quantity of materials in production would simply be the product of standard quantity of materials required for each unit of product and the number of units produced during the period. Since the MPV has already taken into account price differences, the MUV ignores such differences and the difference of quantities is multiplied by the standard price per unit. Symbolically

$$MUV = [(SQ \times AO) - (AQ \times AO)] \times SP \qquad \textbf{(19.4)}$$

For Example 19.1, the MUV would be: = [(2 × 100) – (2.2 × 100)] × ₹14 = ₹280 (unvarouable).

Since the actual consumption of materials is more than the standard quantity required for producing 100 units of output, the MUV is unfavourable.

Factors Responsible for MUV There may be several reasons for a material quantity variance. The important ones are listed below:

1. Carelessness in the use of materials handled by workers and other production personnel.
2. Poor or improper machine adjustment.
3. Substitution of sub-standard or defective materials causing excessive materials consumption.
4. Change in product specification or design requiring usage different from the standard.
5. Inefficient and inadequate inspection of raw materials.
6. Theft of the materials due to poor janitorial services.
7. Wastage due to inefficient production methods or unskilled/untrained employees.
8. Substitution of higher quality materials than the standard leading to lower usage of materials.
9. Improvement in the production process and extra care taken by the workers in carrying out their jobs.
10. Pilferage, wastage and spoilage due to poor stock-keeping function.
11. Defective tools, machines, plant and equipment coupled with their improper maintenance leading to frequent breakdowns and more usage of raw materials.
12. Actual mix of materials being different from the standard mix.
13. Actual yield being different from the standard yield.

Responsibility for MUV The overall responsibility for this variance lies with the production personnel. However, this should not be allowed to become a general premise as in the case of MPV. For instance, the principal cause of a favourable MUV should be the substitution of above-standard materials which result in less waste than what was anticipated when the standard quantity was set. But the purchase of above-standard materials is certainly likely to contribute to an unfavourable material price variance as the higher quality materials would cost more. "Both variances would have been unavoidable, if the materials specified in developing the standard costs were not available, and the purchasing agent bought what he could".[3] From a practical viewpoint, for such a variance, production personnel do not deserve any appreciation and purchasing personnel any criticism. Likewise, the changes in product specifications may cause either favourable or unfavourable usage variances for which the only solution is to change the material usage standard. These examples tend to show that mere arithmetical computation of MUV or for that matter of any variance is not enough. It is the investigation into the causes of variances, which is more fruitful/useful from the point of control.

Graphical Presentation of Material Variances

In Figure 19.3, total MCV (unfavourable) or ₹500 is partly the result of the high material prices and partly the result of more quantities used.

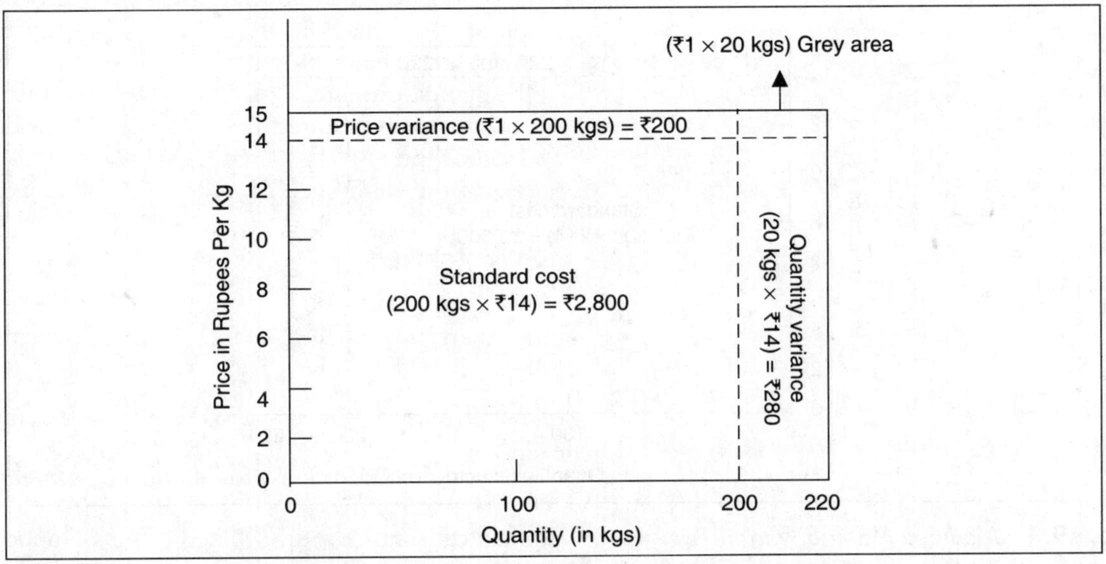

FIG. 19.3 *Material Variances*

Clearly, at least ₹200 of the variance is a material price variance and ₹280 is the material usage variance. But the remaining ₹20 is what is called as a "grey area"[4]. It is an inextricable combination of the influence of both a high rate and more material used. But it will be just logical if ₹20 variance is clubbed with material price variance because the production personnel cannot be held responsible for the high prices paid by the purchase department. Moreover, it is the responsibility of the purchase manager to make the materials available at standard rates to the production department and, therefore, Figure 19.3 needs modification in terms of clubbing the grey area with price variance. The modification is shown in Figure 19.4.

It is in this context that the conventional variance analysis, which includes the joint price-efficiency variance as a part of an overall price variance, is said to be logically deficient. Further, the efficiency variance is considered more important than the price variance as the manager can exert more direct influence over the efficiency variance. It is also felt that joint-price efficiency variance is less likely to cause arguments if it is buried in the price variance.[5]

The MUV can be further subdivided into **(i)** Material mix sub-variance and **(ii)** Material yield sub-variance.

Material Mix Sub-Variance (MMSV) It is possible that a product may use more than one type/grade of raw materials or combination of materials. This

Material mix sub-variance is the difference between the standard mix and the actual mix input/ quantities of all grades of material actually used and their corresponding standard price.

combination is called the material mix. In such a situation, it may be possible to alter the mix of materials used from the pre-determined standard mix (ratio) set, the reasons being non-availability or inadequate supply of one or more types of raw material, or the price of a particular type of material may have gone up making it uneconomical in the given price situations of its finished product: the availability of a new substitute for one or more types of raw materials already being used either because they are cheaper and/or better in quality.

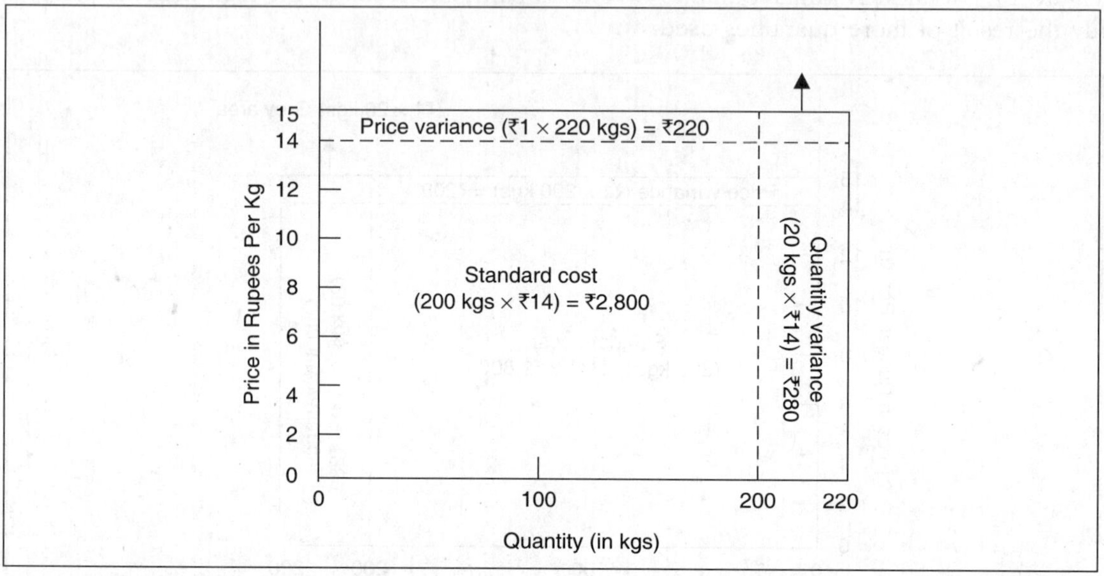

FIG. 19.4 *Modified Material Variances*

Thus, substituting one raw material for another, even though the total input quantity of all materials does not exceed the standard amount, merits a separate computation. This is determined by a material mix variance. It may be stressed that the material mix variance is not an additional variance; it is a sub-variance of material usage/quantity variance and, therefore, it is more appropriately designated as material mix sub-variance (MMSV). Thus, the MMSV is a function of the difference between the standard mix and the actual mix input/quantities of all grades of materials actually used and their corresponding standard prices. Such a variance is to be calculated for each type of material. Symbolically,

MMSV = (Standard mix of actual total quantity of material used) – (Actual mix of actual quantity of material used) × SR

For the sake of abbreviation, standard mix may be referred to as revised standard quantity (RSQ) and actual mix (AM). Accordingly,

$$\text{MMSV} = (\text{RSQ} - \text{AQ}) \times \text{SR} \quad \textbf{(19.5)}$$

◆ Example 19.2

A manufacturing company uses the following standard mix of their compound in one batch of its production line:

50 kgs of material X at the standard price of ₹20.
30 kgs of material Y at the standard price of ₹30.
20 kgs of material Z at the standard price of ₹40.

The actual mix was as follows:

60 kgs of material X
40 kgs of material Y
10 kgs of material Z.

Determine the MMSV.

Solution

The determination of MMSV involves the following steps:

1. Standard proportion (mix) of materials X, Y and Z (5:3:2) or (50:30:20).
2. Actual total quantity used, 110.
3. Standard mix of actual quantity used (RSQ) by using the following criterion:

(Total actual quantity used) × (Standard proportion of each type of material) **(19.6)**

Where

X = 110 kgs × 5/10 = 55 kgs
Y = 110 kgs × 3/10 = 33 kgs
Z = 110 kgs × 2/10 = 22 kgs

MMSV = (RSQ – AQ) × SP

X (55 – 60) × ₹20 = ₹100 (unfavourable)
Y (33 – 40) × ₹30 = ₹210 (unfavourable)
Z (22 – 10) × ₹40 = ₹480 (favourable)
Net MMSV = ₹170 (favourable)

Example 19.2 demonstrates that MUV is unfavourable as the total usage (110 kgs) exceeds the actual usage (100 kgs) but the MMSV is favourable. This may be indicative of general production inefficiencies.

MMSV will occur only when there is a difference between standard material mix ratio and actual material mix ratio. It has no relation with actual material consumption. There may be a higher or lower amount of material usage from the standard but there will be no MMSV if standard mix matches with actual mix. This is illustrated in Table 19.1.

TABLE 19.1 Material Mix Sub-variance

Type of materials	*Combination of materials (kgs)*			
	Standard	*Actuals (in different situations)*		
		(1)	*(2)*	*(3)*
X	50	45	55	45
Y	30	27	33	36
Z	20	18	22	19
	100	90	110	100

In situations (1) and (2), there will be no MMSV as the proportion of the AQ used is in tune with standard proportion or RSQ and AQ are the same. To take situation (1) for illustration purposes:

(RSQ – AQ) × SR

X = 90 × 5/10 = (45 – 45) × ₹20 = Nil
Y = 90 × 3/10 = (27 – 27) × ₹30 = Nil
Z = 90 × 2/10 = (18 – 18) × ₹40 = Nil

In situation (3), though there is no material usage variance, there is MMSV:

X = (50 – 45) × ₹20 = ₹100 (favourable)
Y = (30 – 36) × ₹30 = ₹180 (unfavourable)
Z = (20 – 19) × ₹40 = ₹ 40 (favourable)
Net MMSV = ₹ 40 (unfavourable)

Thus, the MMSV is a consequence of relative rather than absolute differentials in materials usage.

The computation of the MMSV is a useful exercise in that it reveals information that might otherwise be concealed. It shows separately the effect of varying the mix of materials on the material cost variance. Above all, the substantial deviations from the standard product mix may adversely affect the quality of the product.

In Example 19.2, the unfavourable MUV is ₹100, as shown by the following calculations:

MUV = (SQ – AQ) × SR

X = (50 kgs – 60 kgs) × ₹20 = ₹200 (unfavourable)
Y = (30 kgs – 40 kgs) × ₹30 = ₹300 (unfavourable)
Z = (20 kgs – 10 kgs) × ₹40 = ₹400 (favourable)
Net MUV = ₹100 (unfavourable)

Taking away the MMSV (₹170 favourable), there is a balance of ₹270 (unfavourable) to be explained. Obviously, this figure represents excess usage. The materials usage variance (revised) should reveal the excess usage (₹270), as shown in Table 19.2.

TABLE 19.2 Material usage Variance

Material	*SQ*	*AQ*	*SP*	*Total SC*
A	50	60	₹20	₹1,000
B	30	40	30	900
C	20	10	40	800
	100	110	27	2,700

MUV (revised) = (AQ – SQ) × Weighted average SP = (110 – 100) × ₹27 = ₹270 (unfavourable)
Weighted average standard price = Total SC/Total SQ = ₹2,700/100 = ₹27. Thus,

MUV = MMSV + MUV (revised) **(19.7)**

Material Yield Sub-Variance (MYSV) The material usage variance (revised) can be more appropriately designated as material yield sub-variance (MYSV). Excess or under material usage from the standard clearly reflects that actual production (yield) is more or less than standard production (yield) expected out of the actual materials input. "The world 'yield' denotes 'output', but this facts is not always directly recognised in the calculations used to ascertain the sub-variance. Often inputs of materials for a specific output are considered."[6] In other words, if the actual material usage is more than the standard, the yield variance would be negative or unfavourable. On the other hand, if standard material quantity exceeds the actual usage, the yield is favourable in that actual production is more than standard production.

In Example 19.2, on the basis of inputs, the yield sub-variance would be given by the following formula: (Actual input-Standard input) × Weighted average standard input price = (110 – 100) × ₹2.7 = ₹27 (unfavourable)

Keeping in view the meaning of yield as production, it will be more logical to determine MYSY on the basis of ouputs, that is, standard and actual production (yield). It is determined as follows:

MYSV = (Standard yield – Actual yield) × Standard material cost per unit of finished output **(19.8)**

Alternatively, MYSV = (Standard loss of final product in units – Actual loss of final product of units) × Standard material cost unit of finished output **(19.9)**

The concept of MYSV is particularly useful in the case of process industries like sugar, chemicals, and so on where a certain specified yield is expected from a given input of materials.

◆ **Example 19.3**

In a chemical manufacturing company, 80 per cent is the standard yield expected of actual inputs; 50 units of inputs are introduced in the process and actual final production achieved is 38 units. The standard price per unit of input is ₹8. Determine the material yield sub-variance by various methods.

Solution

(a) *Output basis:*

(i) (Standard yield – Actual yield) × Standard material cost per unit of finished output

= [40 (0.80 × 50) – 38] × ₹10 (₹8 × 100/80) = ₹20 (unfavourable)

(ii) (Standard loss – Actual loss) × (Standard material per unit of finished output)

= (10 – 12) × ₹10 = ₹20 (unfavourable).

(b) *Input basis:*

(Actual input – Standard input) × Standard input price = [50 – 47.5 (38 × 10)/8] × ₹8 = ₹20 (unfavourable)

It is important to note that in the case of the output basis of determining the MYSV, the multiplying factor is standard yield price which is higher than standard input price. This is because the actual input required to produce one unit of final output would be higher. Therefore, loss or gain in the actual output from the standard should be at the standard yield price.

In the case of the input basis, the excess or lower consumption of materials for obvious reasons should be valued at the standard input price. In the case of products making use of more than one type of raw material, the multiplying factor should be the weighted average standard input price. Both the methods would give identical results.

LABOUR VARIANCES

LO 19.3 Illustrate the various types of labour variances and the reasons for such variances

Labour variance is popularly known as labour cost variance. Labour, unlike materials, cannot be stored. Therefore, the purchase and usage of labour services go hand in hand. However, labour cost variance (LCV) is computed like material cost variance. It is the difference between the standard labour costs and the actual labour costs of the period. Symbolically,

Labour cost variance is the difference between the standard labour costs and the actual labour costs.

LCV = (SH × SR × AO) – (AH × AR × AO) (on per unit basis) **(19.10)**

LCV = (TSLC – TALC) (on aggregative basis) **(19.11)**

Where

SH = Standard labour hours required per unit

SR = Standard wage rate per hour

AO = Actual output achieved during the period

AH = Actual labour hours spent per unit

AR = Actual wage rate per hour

TSLC = Total standard labour cost of actual output

TALC = Total actual labour cost of actual output

◆ **Example 19.4**

From the following information, compute the labour cost variance (LCV).

Particulars	Standard	Actual
Labour-hours per unit	4	5
Wage rate (₹)	25	30
Units produced		100

Solution

LCV = [(SH × SR × AO) – (AH × AR × AO)]

= (4 × ₹25 × 100) – (5 × ₹30 × 100) = ₹5,000 (₹10,000 – ₹15,000) (unfavourable/A)

It is useful to mention here that the treatment of labour variances, in large measure, parallels material variances. The LCV can be divided into: **(i)** Labour rate variance and **(ii)** Labour efficiency variance.

Labour/Wage Rate Variance (LRV)

Labour rate variance is the difference between the actual wage rate and the standard wage rate.

This arises when there is a difference between the actual wage rate paid and the pre-determined standard wage rate. The LRV ignores the question of whether the actual labour-hours worked during the period were more or less than the standard labour-hours required to complete the work; it is concerned only with actual worked hours. Thus, the LRV is a function of the difference between the actual wage rate (AR) and the standard wage rate (SR) and the actual total labour-hours worked. Symbolically,

$$LRV = (SR - AR) \times AH \times AO \quad \textbf{(19.12)}$$

In Example 19.4, LRV = (₹25 – ₹30) × 5 × 100 = ₹2,500 (unfavourable)

It is important to note here that if the mode of wage payment is on a product basis, the LRV would be equal to the difference between the standard piece wage rate and the actual piece wage rate multiplied by the actual units produced during a period. The LRV should be determined for each grade of labour, namely, skilled, semi-skilled and unskilled separately.

Factors Responsible for LRV The labour rate variance can be traced to a variety of causes. The important of these are enumerated below:

1. Change in the basic wage structure or in piece work rate not yet reflected in the standard wage rage.
2. Employing a worker-mix (explained later) different from the standard-mix which was originally planned. For instance, less skilled workers may be employed in place of skilled workers planned in the standard wage rate. Conversely, work which used to be performed by lower paid employees may have been assigned to the more skilled workers. In either case, a wage rate which is different from the standard wage rate will be paid.
3. To meet the demand of urgent orders, workers may have been asked to work overtime. The overtime rates may be higher than the standard wage rate, causing a variance to result.
4. During a recession period of lower demand and output, the lower paid unskilled labourers may have been laid off and their task assigned to higher paid skilled labourers. Skilled labourers are to be paid at a higher wage rate as compared to unskilled labourers.
5. Casual and temporary workers employed to meet seasonal demands or some special urgent job orders, are paid at the rates different from the standard.

Responsibility for LRV From the reasons outlined above, it is very clear that the LRV, often, will be an uncontrollable variance for rates are usually determined by supply and demand conditions in the labour market, wage awards by Wage Tribunals/Boards, and so on. The departmental executives may be held responsible only for that portion of the LRV which arises due to employment of wrong grades of labour. It does not mean that the LRV is of no significance to the management. Being largely uncontrollable in nature, the management should revise the wage rate standard for future periods.

Labour Efficiency Variance (LEV)

This is similar to the material usage variance. The time required by the labour force is an index of its efficiency. Accordingly, the variance which seeks to isolate the impact of working greater or lesser number of hours than the standard hours in production is called the labour efficiency variance (LEV) or labour time variance. Like material usage variance, LEV is concerned only with the standard wage rate. Thus, LEV is a function of the difference between the hours workers should have consumed in actual production and the actual hours worked and the standard wage rate. Symbolically,

Labour efficiency variance is a function of the difference between the hours workers should have consumed in actual production and the actual hours worked and the standard wage rate.

$$LEV = [(SH \times AO) - (AH \times AO)] \times SR \quad \textbf{(19.13)}$$

In Example 19.4, LEV will be: [(4 × 100) – (5 × 100)] × ₹25 = ₹2,500 (unfavourable)

However, if the method of piece wages payment is followed in the organisation, there will be no labour efficiency variance.

Reasons for LEV The chief causes giving rise to LEV are outlined as follows:

1. Lack of congenial working conditions adversely affecting the efficient working of the labour force. Examples of poor working conditions are inadequate or excessive heating, lighting and ventilation.
2. Failure to maintain machinery, equipment and tools in proper working condition or workers having to work with old and defective machines and tools which have frequent breakdowns.
3. Use of sub-standard raw materials, or higher standard raw materials requiring more or less time than the standard.
4. Inefficient organisation leading to delays in routing work, materials, tools and instructions.
5. Incompetent supervision or more strict supervision than required.
6. Work on new machines, equipment or tools in a factory requiring less time than provided for, but the standard remains unrevised.
7. Basic inefficiency of workers due to inadequate training, incorrect instructions and worker's dissatisfaction owing to low morale and lack of motivation.
8. Change in the quality control standards.
9. Increase in labour turnover.
10. Gang composition (labour-mix) being different from the standard.

This variance is of prime significance to the production managers. It is the best indication of labour efficiency. Hence, its causes should be carefully thought over and reported so that prompt action can be initiated to overcome the cause. This variance, unlike LRV, is largely controllable in nature, is more amenable to managerial action and management's prompt action can lead to large savings. To overcome an unfavourable LEV, management's endeavour should be to provide a conducive environment in terms of the introduction of new equipment or tools and their proper maintenance, proper lighting and ventilation facilities, and so on. These measures will help in improving the general efficiency of the workers.

The labour efficiency variance can be sub-divided into **(a)** Idle time variance; **(b)** Labour revised efficiency variance consisting of **(i)** Labour mix sub-variance and **(ii)** Labour yield sub-variance.

Idle Time Variance This variance represents that segment of the LEV which arises due to the standard cost of those actual hours for which the workers have been paid but during which they remain idle due to non-availability of raw materials, breakdown of machines, failure of power and such other abnormal circumstances. This variance, by definition, is unfavourable and is calculated as follows:

$$(\text{Idle time in hours} \times \text{Standard wage rate}) \quad \textbf{(19.14)}$$

Therefore, it will be more coherent to compute the true labour efficiency variance after making an adjustment for this factor. In the absence of that, the LEV is likely to be misunderstood. The management may regard the labour force inefficient which in fact may not be the case. In other words, employees will be blamed for inefficiency when the true cause may have been beyond their control, such as breakdown in power supply, and so on. To demonstrate the point, assume in Example19.4 that the number of idle time hours during the period was 110. The idle time variance would be unfavourable by ₹2,750 (110 hours × ₹25). The workers, in fact, actually worked only for 390 hours, the standard hours allowed for which were 400. Clearly, the workers are more efficient and not inefficient. The earlier conclusion has just got reversed. The revised LEV is ₹250 favourable [(390 hours – 400 hours) × ₹25]. Thus, it is useful to segregate idle time variance from the total LEV:

Idle time variance	₹2,750 (unfavourable)
Labour efficiency variance (revised)	250 (favourable)
Total labour efficiency variance	2,500 (unfavourable)

This form of presentation of reporting LEV is certainly more useful to the management for controlling future costs and initiating control action compared to the single figure of the total LEV of ₹2,500.

Labour revised efficiency variance is a function of the difference between the actual labour mix and the standard labour mix and the standard wage rate.

Labour Revised Efficiency Variance Sometimes a change in the grade of labour employed on an operation has to be made from the standard labour-mix due to shortage of one grade of labour during a certain period. The variance which isolates the impact of such a change in gang composition (labour-mix) on the labour cost variance is designated as the labour-mix variance or gang composition variance. Like the material mix sub-variance (MMSV), this variance is a function of the difference between the actual labour-mix and standard labour-mix and the standard wage rate. Symbolically,

LEV = [Standard mix of actual labour hours worked (RSH) – Actual mix of actual hours worked (AH)] × SR **(19.15)**

◆ Example 19.5

The standard labour – mix for producing 100 units a of product is:

4 skilled men @ ₹30 per hour for 20 hours

6 unskilled men @ ₹20 per hour for 20 hours

But due to shortage of skilled men, more unskilled men were employed to produce 100 units. Actual hours paid for were:

2 skilled men @ ₹40 per hour for 25 hours

10 unskilled men @ ₹25 per hour for 25 hours.

Compute the labour mix variance.

Solution

The data can be presented as follows:

Category of workers	*Standard*					*Actual*				
	Number	*Hours*	*Total hours*	*SR (₹)*	*TSLC (₹)*	*Number*	*Hours*	*Total hours*	*AR (₹)*	*TALC (₹)*
Skilled	4	20	80	30	2,400	2	25	50	40	2,000
Unskilled	6	20	120	20	2,400	10	25	250	25	6,250
Total			200	24	4,800			300	27.50	8,250

LCV = TSLC – TALC = ₹4,800 – ₹8,250 = ₹3,450 (unfavourable)

(a) LRV = (SR – AR) × AH)

(i) Skilled = (₹30 – ₹40) × 50 = ₹500 (unfavourable)

(ii) Unskilled = (₹20 – ₹25) × 250 = ₹1,250 (unfavourable)

Total LRV = ₹1,750 (unfavourable)

(b) LEV = (SH – AH) × SR

(i) Skilled = (80 – 50) × ₹30 = ₹900 (favourable)

(ii) Unskilled = (120 – 250) × ₹20 = ₹2,600 (unfavourble)

Total LEV = ₹1,700 (unfavourable)

Total LEV can be split into: **(a)** Labour mix sub-variance, and **(b)** Labour yield sub-varinace

Labour Mix Sub-Variance To determine the labour mix sub-variance (LMSV), we are required to calculate the values of revised standard hours for two grades of labour. The revised standard hours for skilled and unskilled labourers respectively would be: Actual total hours × Proportion of skilled hours to the total standard hours.

$$= \frac{300 \times 80}{200} = 120 \text{ hours (skilled)}$$

$$= \frac{300 \times 120}{200} = 180 \text{ hours (unskilled)}$$

LMSV = (RSH – AH) × SR

(i) Skilled = (120 – 50) × ₹30 = ₹2,100 (favourble)

(ii) Unskilled = (180 – 250) × ₹20 = ₹1,400 (unfavourble)

Total LMSV = ₹ 700 (favourable)

The residual LEV should be ₹2,400 (unfavourable).

Labour Yield Sub-Variance Like the material yield sub-variance, it is determined after taking away the materials mix sub-variance. The basis of computation of labour yield sub-variance (LYSV) would be to find out how many more or less than the total absolute standard hours (and not their break-up) are used in making the actual production (here 100 units). Here, the number of standard hours required are 200; the actual hours worked are 300. The difference is to be multiplied by the weighted average standard rate. Symbolically.

LYSV = (TSHs – TAHs) × Weighted average SR = (200 – 300) × ₹24 = ₹2,400 (unfavourable)

The above method of determining the LYSV is based on the input basis. The LYSV like the MYSV can be determined on the output basis also. The formula is:

(Standard yield in units expected from the actual hours worked-Actual yield) × Standard labour cost per unit **(19.16)**

= (150 – 100) × ₹48 = ₹2,400 (unfavourable)

In 300 hours, the standard yield should be 150 units because in 200 hours, the expected yield is 100 units.

LEV = LMSV = ₹ 700 (favourable)
LYSV = ₹2,400 (unfavourble)
= ₹1,700 (unfavourable)

This information indicates to the management that on account of employing more unskilled labourers, the LMSV turned out to be favourable. But it had an adverse bearing on the overall efficiency as the actual hours used were considerably larger than standard hours required to complete the work.

It is important to note that the two labour sub-variances—LMSV and LYSV—are parts of LEV adjusted for idle time variance. Total LEV has three sub-variances. To illustrate, assume idle time hours are 30. The revised values of various labour variances would be as follows:

LCV = (As in Example 19.5) = ₹3,450 (unfavourable)
LRV = ₹1,750 (unfavourable)
TLEV = ₹1,700 (unfavourable)

Labour idle time variance:
Skilled: (5 hours × ₹30) = ₹150
Unskilled:(25 hours × ₹20)= ₹500
₹650 (unfavourable)

The other two sub-variances will be based on the remaining working hours (300 – 30) = 270 hours.

$$\text{RSH: Skilled} = 270 \times \frac{80}{200} = 108 \text{ hours}$$

$$\text{Unskilled} = 270 \times \frac{120}{200} = 162 \text{ hours}$$

LMSV = (RSHs – AHs) × SR
Skilled = (108 – 45) × ₹30 = ₹1,890 (favourable)
Unskilled = (162 – 225) × ₹20 = ₹1,260 (unfavourable)
Total LMSV = ₹ 630 (favourable)

Note It is assumed that actual idle hours were in the ratio of 1:5 (50 : 250, actual hours worked).
LYSV = (200 – 270) × ₹24 = ₹1,680 (unfavourable)

Overhead Variances

LO 19.4 Understand variable and fixed manufacturing overhead costs separately as well as jointly

At the outset, it may be noted that unlike direct materials and labour, the manufacturing overhead is not entirely variable with the level of production. Therefore, standard costs for factory overheads are based upon budgets and not on standards. Being so, the analysis concerning manufacturing overhead variances is materially different from that of variances relating to materials and labour. However, like material and labour variances, manufacturing overhead/factory overhead/overhead/variance is the difference between the actual overhead cost incurred and standard overhead cost charged to production. For the purpose of determining the latter amount, the distinction between variable and fixed manufacturing overhead costs is very significant. In fact, one method of analysing factory overhead variance is to study separately variable overhead variances and fixed overhead variances. Alternatively, they can be analysed jointly. Both types of analyses are presented in this Section.

Variable Overhead Variances (VOV)

These are also called variable overhead cost variances (VOCV). In fact, the VOCV parallels the material and labour cost variances. The reason is that variable overheads by definition should change with production volume. Therefore, the standard variable overhead cost (SVOC) per unit will be uniform, production volume notwithstanding. Thus, the VOCV is the difference between the actual and standard variable overhead costs for actual output. Symbolically,

Variable overhead cost variance is the difference between the actual and standard variable overhead costs for actual output.

$$VOCV = (SVOC \times AO) - (AVOC \times AO) \text{ (on unit basis)} \quad \textbf{(19.17)}$$

$$VOCV = TSVOC - TAVOC \text{ (on aggregative basis)} \quad \textbf{(19.18)}$$

Where

SVOC = Standard variable overhead cost per unit

AVOC = Actual variable overhead cost per unit (Total variable overheads incurred ÷ Actual output in units)

TAVOC = Total standard variable overhead costs to achieve actual production.

TAVOC = Total actual variable overhead costs incurred

◆ Example 19.6

The following is an extract of some relevant data of Hypothetical Ltd relating to its variable factory overheads.

Standard hours allowed (per unit)	2
Standard variable overhead costs allowed per direct labour-hour	₹30
Actual production (units)	80
Actual direct labour-hours	165
Actual variable overheads incurred	₹5,180

Determine the VOCV.

Solution

VOCV = (₹60* × 80) – ₹5,180 = ₹4,800 – ₹5,180 = ₹380 (unfavourable)

*₹60 = (SHs × SVOC per hour) = 2 × ₹30

₹38 (unfavourable) VOCV can be either due to overspending over the standard budget or due to more hours taken by the workers from the standard hours allowed. Accordingly, VOCV can be split up into two sub-variances: (a) Variable factory overhead efficiency variance (VFOEV); **(b)** Variable factory overhead spending variance (VFOSV).

Variable Factory Overhead Efficinecy Variance (VFOEV) The VFOEV is the function of the difference between the standard hours and actual hours and the standard variable factory overhead rate per hour (SVFOR). Symbolically,

$$VFOEV = [(AO \times SHs \text{ per unit}) - AHs] \times SVFOR \quad \textbf{(19.19)}$$

$$= (80 \times 2 - 165) \times ₹30 = ₹150 \text{ (unfavourable)}$$

The variance is adverse because the actual hours (AHs) have exceeded the standard hours (SHs). The company wasted ₹150 on overheads because the workers were not efficient. It may be recalled that VFOEV is like the labour efficiency variance inasmuch as the formula is the same with the obvious difference of the multiplying factor. Therefore, *the actual factors for the variable factory overheads efficiency would be identical with the causes for labour efficiency variance.* For this reason, some firms club together the labour efficiency

Variable factory overhead efficiency variance is the function of the difference between the standard hours and actual hours and the standard variable factory overhead rate per hour.

and variable factory overhead efficiency variances.[7] The formula for this variance would require modification only in terms of the multiplying factor as shown below:

[(AO × SHs per unit) – AHs] × [SVFOR + Standard wage rate per hour] **(19.20)**

The above formula will be valid only if the company employs direct labour-hours as the basis of measuring cost variability. In the case of machine-hours, the formula would be:

VFOEA = [(Actual output × Standard machine-hours per unit) – (Actual machine hours × Standard variable factor overhead rate)] **(19.21)**

The causes for such variances include lack of repairs and maintenance of tools, plant, machinery and equipment, causing more frequent break-down.

Variable factory overhead spending variance is the difference between the actual and budgeted overhead costs for actual production

Variable Factory Overhead Spending Variance (VFOSV) The VFOSV is the difference between the actual overhead costs incurred and the amount that the flexible budget indicates should have been incurred for the actual production volume. To determine the standard costs, actual hours should be taken into account because the actual amount spent would be in relation to the actual hours worked. Thus, the standard hours are irrelevant. Symbolically,

VFOSV = (Actual hours worked) × (Standard variable overhead rate per hour) – (Actual variable factory overhead costs) **(19.22)**

= (165 × ₹30) – ₹5,180 = ₹230 (unfavourable)

Thus VFOV = VFOEV + VFOSV: ₹380 = ₹150 + ₹230 (all unfavourable) **(19.23)**

Fixed Factory Overhead Variances (FFOV)

The treatment of FFOV is significantly different from that of VFOV. The reason is that fixed factory overheads do not vary with production volume. A proper understanding of the FFOV requires prior understanding of various concepts of production volume. The concept of under-absorption or over-absorption of fixed overheads is already explained in an earlier chapter. In brief, it can be stated here that fixed overheads are absorbed (charged to the production) at a pre-determined standard fixed overhead rate (SFOR). This SFOR is determined by dividing the budgeted fixed overheads by some production volume. So far as the amount of budgeted fixed overheads is concerned, it does not pose any problem whatsoever as the relevant figure can be seen from the budget. However, production volume is subject to different interpretations, that is, whether it should be normal volume, budgeted volume or actual volume. Normal volume refers to that level of production which can be achieved on the basis of the available plant capacity and other facilities in the factory. Budgeted volume signifies the level of production envisaged for the current budget period. Actual volume indicates actual production. It is rare, if ever, when all these three production volumes will be identical. Obviously, the amount of SFOR per unit (per hour, if production volume is expressed in hours), will depend on what production volume constitutes the denominator for the purpose.

◆ **Example 19.7**

The budgeted fixed overheads of a company for a period are ₹4,00,000 and the normal production volume, budgeted volume and actual volume are 20,000, 16,000 and 10,000 units respectively. Compute the SFOR for different volumes.

Solution

The SFOR will be ₹20 per unit, (₹4,00,000 ÷ 20,000 units) on a normal volume basis; ₹25 (on a budgeted volume basis); and ₹40 (on the actual production basis).

Clearly, there will be different value of FFOV under the three different situations. The National Association of Accountants, USA, has advocated normal volume as the basis of determining SFOR. The interpretation of the term "normal level" should be determined in advance and should be applied consistently. Normal level should be related to the basis of normal capacity, that is, ability to produce, ability to sell or both along with the number of years, for example, 3, 4, 5 and 6 years to be taken as normal period.[8] Where normal volume is not shown, budgeted volume should be used.

The standard fixed overheads charged to production (absorbed overheads) will be given by the following formula: (Number of units produced × SFOR) **(19.24)**

SFOR = Budgeted fixed overheads/Normal level of activity

In Example 19.7, the standard fixed overhead cost is: 10,000 × ₹20 = ₹2,00,000

The costs unabsorbed are ₹2,00,000 = (₹4,00,000 actual fixed overheads – ₹2,00,000 charged to production). From the above the following may be deduced:

1. If the actual level of activity corresponds to the normal level of activity (referred to above as normal volume), there will be no unabsorbed fixed overhead costs. There will be no volume variances, as actual production corresponds to normal production. But the occurrence of such a case is only a theoretical possibility.
2. When the actual level of activity is less that the normal activity, the volume variance is unfavourable in that the entire amount of fixed overheads cannot be charged to production.
3. When the actual level of activity exceeds the normal activity, the volume variance is favourable as it amounts to better than expected utilisation of facilities.

There is no such volume variance for variable overheads. Thus, volume variance is the unique or special feature of fixed overhead variances which distinguishes it from other variances.

Fixed Overhead Cost Variance (FOCV) This variance represents the difference between the actual fixed overhead cost incurred and the standard fixed overheads charged to production. Symbolically,

FOCV = TAFOC – (SFOR per unit × AO) **(19.25)**

In the case of hours basis: FOSV = TAFOC – (SFOR per hour × SHs per unit × AO) **(19.26)**

Where

TAFOC = Total actual factory overhead cost incurred

SFOR = Standard fixed overhead rate

◆ Example 19.8

The following data relate to the fixed overheads of a company for a week:

1. Actual fixed overheads incurred, ₹5,300.
2. Budgeted fixed overheads, ₹5,000
3. Normal level of activity for the period, 100 units or 200 hours
4. Standard hours allowed, 2 hours per unit
5. Actual production, 90 units
6. Actual hours worked, 190 hours

Determine the fixed overhead variances.

Solution

FOCV = ₹5,300 – (₹50 × 90) = ₹800 (unfavourable)

SFOR = ₹5,000 ÷ 100 units = ₹50 per unit

Alternatively (on hourly basis): FOCV = ₹5,300 – (₹25 × 2 × 90) = ₹800 (unfavourable)

SFOR = ₹5,000 ÷ 200 hours = ₹25 per hour

The FOCV (₹800) can be split into three sub-variances: **(i)** Fixed factory overhead spending variance, **(ii)** Fixed factory overhead efficiency variance and **(iii)** Volume variance.

Fixed Factory Overhead Spending Variance (FOSV) This variance is the difference between the planned level of fixed overheads expenditure and the actual level of fixed overheads incurred. Symbolically.

FOSV = (Actual fixed overhead costs) – (Budgeted fixed costs) **(19.27)**
= ₹5,300 – ₹5,000 = ₹300 (unfavourable)

The causal factors for the FOSV are at least as many as there are distinct cost items. The budget provides a certain amount per period for each fixed cost item. These budgeted amounts are based upon expected prices, consumption rates of various fixed items and a variety of other operating conditions. Any one or combination of these budget expectations may prove to be inaccurate. For instance, indirect materials may be more costly than budgeted; rise in property tax rates, power charges, insurance, factory rent and such other fixed items. To have a meaningful analysis of spending variance (as also variable overheads), we must take into account individual cost items. It is likely to be a non-controllable variance.

Fixed Overhead Efficiency Variance (FOEV) Like other efficiency variances, this variance is based on the actual hours and standard hours. Symbolically,

FOEV = [(AO × SHs per unit) – AHs] × SFOR (per hour) **(19.28)**
= (90 × 2 – 190) × ₹25 = ₹250 (unfavourable)

Volume Variance As mentioned earlier, volume variance pertains only to the fixed overheads and is not applicable to variable overheads. Therefore, the volume variance is not pre-fixed with "fixed-overheads".

The volume variance is concerned with the difference between normal hours and actual hours multiplied by the SFOR. In Example, 19.8,

Volume variance = (SHs – AHs) × SFOR = (200 – 190) × ₹25 = ₹250 (unfavourable)

It may be noted that the actual hours worked is less than the standard hours and still the variance is unfavourable, while in the case of efficiency variance such a variance is considered favourable. The reason for this difference is that in the case of efficiency variance the interest is to determine the standards hours required to achieve actual production and then to compare with actual hours. But the volume variance is concerned with the hours worked irrespective of the output achieved. In operational terms, volume variance, here, indicates that the plant has not been used up to its full capacity: In brief,

FOCV = FOSV + FOEV + Volume variance **(19.29)**
= ₹800 (unfavourable) = ₹300 (unfavourable) + ₹250 (unfavourable) + ₹250 (unfavourable)

It is important to mention here that volume variance should be determined on the basis of hours, otherwise it will not be a true indicator of excess or under-utilisation of plant's capacity. Moreover, if computed, on a units basis, it will submerge in it the fixed overhead efficiency variance. Management will not be supplied with the figure of the FOEV—a variance figure of utmost interest to management from the point of view of controlling future costs. Therefore, it will be another serious shortcoming of measuring volume variance on a unit basis. Thus, an hourly approach is recommended for determining FOCV[9].

In Example 19.8, volume variance on a unit basis will be ₹500 (unfavourable) as follows:

(Normal produciton – Actual produciton) × SFOR per unit **(19.30)**
= (100 units – 90 units) × ₹50 = ₹500 (unfavourable)

Causes Volume variance is attributed solely to the fact that the SFOR is computed at the normal level of activity and is then applied to production at some other volume. The fundamental nature of fixed costs, of course, is that they are some specified amount per period of time, regardless of operating volume. Thus, while a fixed manufacturing overhead rate per unit of volume may be required for cost accounting purposes, it detracts from the true nature of fixed costs. The volume variance, in other words, is a "man-made" variance.[10] As such, it is of no significance to management for purposes of planning and control. If budgeted production volume were not equal to normal volume (and it often would not be), a volume variance would be anticipated at the start of the period. Hence, it would signal no exception requiring management's attention.

What is of more significance to the management is the difference between the budgeted output and the actual output. This variance may be caused by shifts in demand for products, labour problems, strikes and lockouts, material shortages, poor product quality due to high labour turnover affecting sales and, therefore, production, and so on. Some of these factors are controllable by management while others are not.

Volume variance (output basis) in order to be used to the management should be split up into sub-variances. The important sub-variances are: **(i)** Fixed overhead efficiency variance (explained above); **(ii)** Calendar variance; **(iii)** Capacity variance.

Calendar Variance This variance should be calculated only when the actual number of working days are more or less than the standard number of working days scheduled for that period. This may be the result of unexpected public holidays being declared. If working days worked are more, the plant capacity will be greater in the sense that there is an increase in the number of hours (volume). The calendar variance will be favourable. Likewise, if the work is done for a lesser number of working days, the plant capacity will be reduced and so also the number of hours actually available for production. Obviously, the calendar variance will be unfavourable. Therefore, in order to compute the correct capacity variance, it will be necessary to adjust the budgeted hours available for production.

The calendar variance can be computed by the following formula:
[Number of standard working days (SD) – Number of actual working days (AD)] × Standard fixed overheads per day (SFOD)
Standard fixed overheads per day = Total budgeted fixed overheads ÷ Standard number of working days Symbolically,

$$(SD - AD) \times SFOD \quad \textbf{(19.31)}$$

Capacity Variance The terms "capacity" and "volume variances" are indiscriminately used in common practice. But in view of the fact that we are calculating efficiency and calendar variances separately, capacity variance here would be sub-variance of volume variance.

Since the difference between actual and standard hours has already been taken care of by the overhead efficiency variance, the capacity variance will not be concerned with this difference. The capacity variance will be the function of the difference between the budgeted hours available on the basis of actual working days (budgeted hours per day × actual days worked) and the actual hours worked multiplied by the standard fixed overhead rate per hour:

(Budgeted hours on the basis of actual days worked – Actual hours worked) × SFOR per hour **(19.32)**

We now take a comprehensive example to calculate all overhead variances — variable and fixed (Example 19.9).

◆ Example 19.9

The following figures are extracted from the books of a company:

Particulars	*Budget*	*Actual*
Output (units)	6,000	6,500
Hours	3,000	3,300
Overhead cost—fixed	₹1,20,000	₹1,25,000
Variable overheads	60,000	66,500
Number of days	25	27

Compute and analyse the overhead variances.

Solution

Total overhead variance (TOV) = [Actual overheads costs – Standard costs charged to production (standard hours for actual production) × TSOR per hour] = ₹1,91,500 – ₹1,95,000 or (3,250 × ₹60) = ₹3,500 (favourable)

Standard fixed overhead rate (SFOR) = ₹1,20,000 ÷ 3,000 = ₹40 per hour

SFOR (per unit) = ₹1,20,000 ÷ 6,000 = ₹20 per unit

Standard hours per unit = 3,000 hours ÷ 60,000 hours = 30 minutes

Standard variable overhead (SVOR) rate = ₹60,000 ÷ 3,000 = ₹20 per hour

SVOR (per unit) = ₹60,000/6,000 = ₹10 per unit

Total standard overhead rate (TSOR) = ₹1,80,000 ÷ 3,000 = ₹60 per hour

TSOR (per unit) = ₹1,80,000 ÷ 6,000 = ₹30 per unit

TOV can be split into (A) Variable overhead cost variance (VOV), and (B) Fixed overhead cost variance (FOV):

(A) VOV = Actual variable overhead costs – Standard variable costs charged to production = ₹66,500 – (3,250 standard hours × ₹20) = ₹65,000 = ₹1,500 (adverse)

There are two sub-variances of VOV:

(i) *Variable overhead spending variance: Actual variable overhead costs incurred – Standard variable overhead costs at actual hours* = ₹66,500 – (3,300 hours × ₹20) – ₹66,000 = ₹500 (adverse)

(ii) *Variable overhead efficiency variance: (Standard hours required for actual output – Actual hours worked for actual output) × Standard variable overhead rate per hour* = (3,250 – 3,300) × ₹20 = ₹1,000 (adverse)

(B) *Fixed overhead cost variance (FOV): (Actual fixed overhead costs incurred – Standard fixed overhead charged to production)* = ₹1,25,000 – (3,250 standard hours × ₹40 = ₹1,30,000) = ₹5,000 (favourable)

There are two sub-variances of FOV:

(i) *Fixed overhead budget/spending variance:* (Actual fixed overhead costs incurred – Budgeted fixed overhead) = ₹1,25,000 – ₹1,20,000 = ₹5,000 (adverse)

(ii) *Volume variance:* [3,000 – (6,500 × 1/2 hour)] × ₹40 = 250 hours × ₹40 = ₹10,000 (favourable) Volume variance has three sub-parts:

(a) *Calendar variance:* (Number of scheduled working days – Number of actual working days) × Standard fixed overhead rate per day = (25-27) × ₹4,800 = ₹9,600 (favourable)

(b) *Fixed overhead efficiency variance:* (Standard hours allowed for actual production – Actual hours worked) × SFOR per hour = (3,250 – 3,300) × ₹40 = ₹2,000 (adverse)

(c) *Capacity variance*: (Budgeted hours on the basis of actual days worked – Actual hours worked) × Standard fixed overhead per hour or [Budgeted hours per day × Actual days worked] – (Actual hours worked) × SFOR = [(120 × 27) = 3,240 – 3,300] × ₹40 = ₹2,400 (favourable)

CONFIRMATION: Figure 19.5 provides a confirmation of the above calculations.

Figure 19.5 indicates that spending and efficiency variances relate to both variable and fixed overheads. The volume variance is entirely for fixed overheads. Instead of showing the first two variances separately, they are clubbed together. For instance, there can be one overhead spending variance (fixed overhead spending variance + variable overhead spending variance). Likewise, there can be only one overhead efficiency variance.

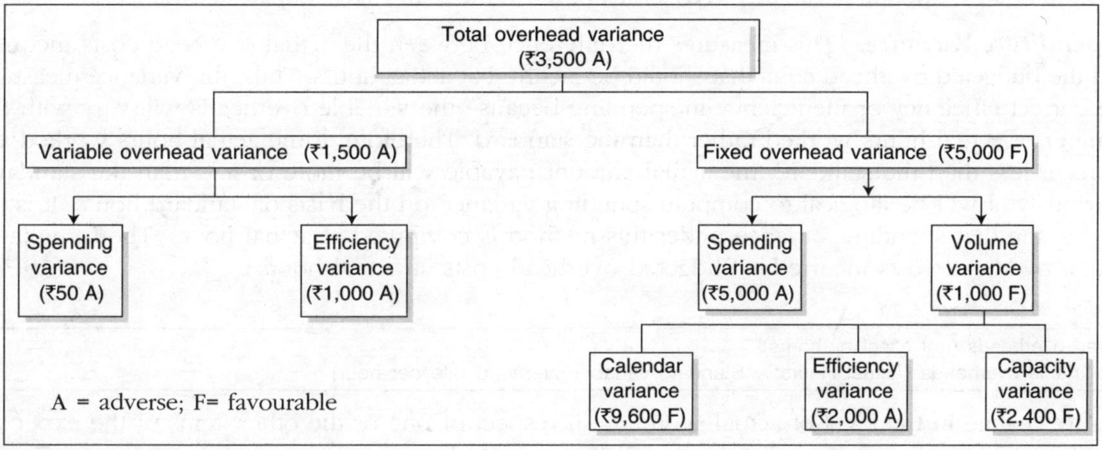

FIG. 19.5 *Overhead Variances*

JOINT BASIS OF OVERHEAD ANALYSIS

LO 19.5 Review the methods of analysing overhead variances jointly

On the basis of the number of variances calculated, there are four methods of analysing overhead variances:

1. Two-variance method;
2. Three-variance method;
3. Four-variance method;
4. Five-variance method.

Two-Variance Method When production volume is measured in units of output and not in units of input (hours), the two separate manufacturing overhead variances can be calculated, viz. **(i)** controllable variance, and **(ii)** volume variance.

Controllable Variance is the difference between the actual expenditure and the budgeted expenditure at the actual level of production. Budgeted expenditure is determined as follows:

Budgeted fixed overheads (not affected by production volume) + Variable overheads (Actual units produced × Standard variable overhead cost per unit).

Volume Variance is the difference between the standard fixed manufacturing overhead cost charged to production and the budgeted fixed manufacturing overhead cost. In other words, volume variance indicates the unabsorbed or over-absorbed amount of fixed cost. It is the function of the difference between the normal capacity and the actual capacity and the standard fixed overhead rate per unit of output. It is computed as follows:

(Normal capacity in units – Actual production in units) × Standard fixed overhead rate per unit **(19.33)**

The two-variance method has a serious shortcoming, in that it does not reveal the efficiency variance. It identifies only spending and volume variances.

Three-Variance Method The limitation of the two-variance method is overcome by the three-variance method which identifies efficiency variance separately. Under this method, production volume is expressed in units of hours. There are three sub-variances of total overhead cost variance: **(i)** Expenditure/Spending variance; **(ii)** Efficiency variance; and **(iii)** Capacity variance.

Expenditure Variance This measures the difference between the actual overhead costs incurred and the budgeted overhead costs that should be incurred at actual hours. Thus, this variance measures the correct efficiency or inefficiency in spending because the variable overheads will vary with the number of actual hours worked rather than the standard. Therefore, if the actual hours worked are more or less than the standard, the actual amount payable will be more or less than the standard. Obviously, it will be illogical to compute spending variance on the basis of standard hours. It is for this reason that spending variance under this method is computed at actual hours. The formula is:
Actual overhead costs incurred – Budgeted overhead costs at actual hours **(19.34)**

Budgeted Overhead Cost

Fixed overheads (not affect by hours)	....
+ Variable overheads (Actual Hours × Standard variable overhead rate per hour)	....

Any change in the level of actual spending in respect of one or the other items of the expenses which constitute the total overhead cost results in expenditure variance.

Overhead Efficiency Variance This is that portion of the overhead variance which is due to the difference between actual hours used for the output achieved and the standard hours allowed multiplied by standard overhead rate. The formula is:

$$(SHs - AHs) \times SOR \qquad \textbf{(19.35)}$$

Capacity Variance This is that segment of overhead variance which arises due to the difference between the normal capacity available in hours, and the actual hours worked multiplied by the standard fixed overhead rate. The formula is:

$$[\text{Normal capacity in hours, NHs} - \text{AHs}] \times \text{SFOR} \qquad \textbf{(19.36)}$$

Four-Variance Method Under this method four sub-variances are computed: **(i)** Spending variance, **(ii)** Capacity variance, **(iii)** Fixed efficiency variance, and **(iv)** Variable efficiency variance.

Five-Variance Method The *modus operandi* of determining efficiency and capacity variances is the same as in the three-variance method. A notable feature is that, spending variance is bifurcated into two sub-parts: fixed overhead spending variance and variable overhead spending variance. These variances have already been discussed when we discussed fixed and variable overheads separately.

Example 19.10 illustrates the computation of overhead variance under all the above methods.

◆ Example 19.10

SK Industries Ltd uses a standard cost system. The budget relating to overheads for the month of January of the current year is as follows:

Normal capacity: 22,000 direct labour-hours, or 11,000 production units

Budgeted overheads at normal (100%) capacity:
- Fixed expenses, ₹3,30,000 or ₹15 per hour
- Variable expenses, ₹2,20,000 or ₹10 per hour
- Standard overhead rate, ₹25 per hour
- Standard overhead rate, ₹50 per unit

For the month of January, actual facts were:
- Actual hours worked, 21,000
- Standard hours allowed for actual production of 10,900 units, 21,800
- Actual overheads incurred, ₹5,47,000 (Fixed ₹3,34,900 + Variable ₹2,12,100)

Compute the overhead variances under the various methods.

Solution

Total overhead variance = (Actual overheads incurred – Standard overhead cost charged to production) = ₹5,47,000 – (21,800 SHs × ₹25, SOR per hour = ₹5,45,000) = ₹2,000 (unfavourable)

1. *Two-variance method*

(a) Controllable variance: Actual overheads incurred – Budgeted overheads at actual production = ₹5,47,000 – ₹5,48,000* = ₹1,000 (favourable)

* Fixed overheads	₹3,30,000
+ Variable overheads (10,900 × ₹20)	2,18,000
	5,48,000

(b) Volume variance: (Normal capacity in units – Actual production) × SFOR per unit = (11,000 – 10,900) × ₹30 = ₹3,000 (unfavourable)

Alternatively, (Normal capacity in hours – Standard hours allowed for actual production) × SFOR per unit = (22,000 – 21,800) × ₹15 = ₹3,000 (unfavourable)

Summary:

(a) Controllable variance	= ₹1,000 (favourable)
(b) Volume variance	3,000 (unfavourable)
Total overhead variance	2,000 (unfavourable)

2. *Three-variance method*

(a) Spending variance = Actual overheads incurred – Budgeted overheads at AHs = (₹5,47,000 – ₹5,40,000*) = ₹7,000 (unfavourable)

*Budgeted overheads costs – Fixed overheads	₹3,30,000
+ Variable overheads (AHs × SVOR per hour)	2,10,000
	5,40,000

(b) Efficiency variance = (SHs – AHs) × SOR per hour (21,800 – 21,000) × ₹25 = ₹20,000 (favourable)

(c) Capacity variance = (SHs – AHs) × SFOR per hour = (22,000 – 21,000) × ₹15 = ₹15,000 (unfavourable)

Summary:

(a) Spending variance	₹7,000 (unfavourable)
(b) Efficiency variance	20,000 (favourable)
(c) Capacity variance	15,000 (unfavourable)
Total overhead variance	2,000 (unfavourable)

3. *Four-variance method:*

(a) Spending variance	₹7,000 (unfavourble)
Efficiency variance:	
(b) Fixed = (SHs – AHs) × SFOR	
= (21,800 – 21,000) × ₹15	12,000 (favourable)
(c) Variable = (21,800 – 21,000) × ₹10	8,000 (favourable)
(d) Capacity variance	15,000 (unfavourable)
Total overhead variance	2,000 (unfavourable)

4. *Five-variance method:*

(a) Fixed spending variance (₹3,34,900 – ₹3,30,000)	₹4,900 (unfavourble)
(b) Variable spending variance ($AVOR_{PH}$ – $SVOR_{PH}$) × AH (₹10.10 – ₹10.00) × 21,000	2,100 (unfavourable)
(c) Fixed efficiency variance	12,000 (favourable)
(d) Variable efficiency variance	8,000 (favourable)
(e) Capacity variance	15,000 (unfavourable)
Total overhead variance	2,000 (unfavourable)

STANDARD COST ACCOUNTING

LO 19.6 Show how to incorporate standard costs in the accounting records

The preceding discussions have shown that variance analysis is based on a comparison of standard and actual data. The availability of standard data is, therefore, a prerequisite of variance analysis. This section dwells on the methods of incorporating standard costs in the accounting records.

Standard costs should be considered as costs which pass through the cost accumulation procedure into financial statements. There are three methods of incorporating standard costs in the costs accounting cycle: **(i)** single plan (full standard costing plan), **(ii)** partial plan, and **(iii)** dual plan. Of these, the first, namely, full standard costing plan is more appropriate for purposes of variance analysis, because debits and credits to the work-in-process account under this plan are made at standard costs only.

Under the single plan, the difference between standard and actual costs are debited or credited to the related variance account. Favourable variances are represented by credit balances as they reflect cost reductions or savings as compared with standard costs. Conversely, debit balances imply unfavourable variances as they represent excess costs.

The accounting procedure is similar to that of the actual cost system, the only difference being that there is an additional variance account that appears on the debit side in the case of excess actual cost, and on credit side in the case of lower actual costs, compared with standard costs. The accounting procedure of recording variances is illustrated below:

1. (a) (i) *Purchase of materials* (AP > SP):	
Materials Inventory A/c	Dr
Materials Price Variance A/c	Dr
To Suppliers/Cash	
(ii) (AP < SP)	
Materials Inventory A/c	Dr
To Materials Price Variance A/c	
To *Suppliers/Cash*	

The materials inventory account is debited, in all the cases, at the standard price of the units purchased. The liability in terms of the amount payable to the suppliers (in the case of credit purchases) is always at the actual cost, the difference being in the balance to be transferred to the materials price variance account.

(b) (i) *Usage of materials:* (AQ > SQ)

Work-in-process A/c	Dr
Materials Usage Variance A/c	Dr
To Materials Inventory A/c	

(ii) (SQ < AQ)

Work-in-process A/c	Dr
To Materials Inventory A/c	
To Materials Usage Variance A/c	

(iii) (SQ = AQ)

Work-in-process A/c	Dr
To Materials Inventory A/c	

The work-in-process account is debited for the standard quantity of materials to be consumed in producing the actual output at standard price. Materials inventory account, as already appearing at the standard price, will be credited by the product of actual quantities used and the standard price.

2. (a) (i) *Accruals of direct labour* (AR > SR)

Direct labour payroll	Dr
Labour rate variance	Dr
To Accrued payroll	

(ii) (SR < AR)

Direct labour payroll	Dr
To Accrued payroll	
To Labour rate variance	

(iii) (SR = AR)

Direct labour payroll	Dr
To Accrued payroll	

The direct labour payroll account is debited in all the cases at the standard wage rate (SR). The total amount debited would be equal to actual hours worked, multiplied by the SR per hour. The accrued payroll account will be credited with the actual amount payable to the workers. The labour rate variance accounts for this difference.

(b) (i) *Actual hours used:* (AH > SH)

Work-in-process A/c	Dr
Labour efficiency variance A/c	Dr
To Direct labour payroll	

(ii) (AH < SH)

Work-in-process A/c	Dr
To Direct labour payroll	
To Labour efficiency variance	

(iii) (AH = SH)

Work-in-process A/c	Dr
To Direct labour payroll	

The work-in-process account is debited for the standard hours in production at the standard wage rate. The direct labour payroll amount is determined by multiplying actual hours worked with standard wages rate. The difference between the two represents favourable or unfavourable labour efficiency variance.

3. *Manufacturing Overhead*

As outlined in the previous section, the treatment of manufacturing overhead is different and more typical compared to material and labour costs. Accordingly, the standard cost accounting procedure pertaining to overheads differs from that of material and labour. In fact, there is more than one way of determining overhead variances. (Details regarding the computation of variances have already been discussed).

◆ Example 19.11

Hypothetical Ltd furnishes you the following information

— Normal capacity: 12,000 hours
— Fixed expenses: ₹1,00,000
— Variable expenses (at normal capacity): ₹1,40,000
— Actual hours worked: 11,280
— Standard hours allowed for the work done: 11,400
— Actual factory overhead expenses: ₹2,31,750 (including variable overheads of ₹1,30,000)

Compute the factory overhead variances.

Solution

The factory overhead variances can be computed by using the two-variance, three-variance, or four-variance methods. Accordingly, the entries have been framed under various methods.

(a) *Two-Variance Method*

(i) Actual factory overhead cost incurred:			
Factory overhead control A/c	Dr	₹2,31,750	
To Various accounts (details for each head is to be given separately)			₹2,31,750

It may be noted that the actual factory overhead costs are recorded under the standard costing system in the same way as under the actual cost system.

(ii) When overhead is applied to work-in-process:			
Work-in-process A/c	Dr	₹2,28,000	
To Factory overhead control A/c			₹2,28,000

The amount to be transferred to the work-in-process account is determined by the product of standard hours (SHs) required for actual output and standard overhead rate (SOR) per hour. Here, the standard overhead rate is ₹20, or [(₹1,00,000 + ₹1,40,000) ÷ 12,000 hours]. Accordingly, the amount is 11,400 hours × ₹20 = ₹2,28,000.

(iii) The factory overhead control account now has a debit balance of ₹3,750 which can be analysed and closed as follows:			
Volume variance A/c	Dr	₹5,000@	
To Controllable variance A/c			₹1,250
To Factory overhead control A/c			3,750

@ Volume variance = (NHs – SHs) × SOR = (12,000 – 11,400) × ₹100/12 = ₹5,000 (adverse)

Controllable variance = (AOC – Budgeted overhead cost at SH) = ₹2,31,750 – [₹1,00,000 (fixed) + (11,400 × 140/12) (variable) = ₹1,33,000 = ₹2,33,000] = ₹1,250 (favourable).

(b) *Three-Variance Method*

(i) For actual factory overhead:			
Factory overhead control A/c	Dr	₹2,31,750	
To Various accounts			₹2,31,750
(ii) When overhead is applied to work-in-process			
Work-in-process A/c	Dr	₹2,28,000	
To Factory overhead control A/c			₹2,28,000
(iii) The factory overhead control A/c now has a debit balance of ₹3,750, which can be broken up into the following three variance:			
Factory overhead spending variance A/c	Dr	₹150	
Idle capacity variance A/c		6,000	
To Factory overhead efficiency variance A/c			₹2,400
To Factory overhead control A/c			3,750

(c) *Four-Variance Method:* The first two entries for actual factory overhead, and the amount applied to work-in-process would be the same as under the three-variance method. There will be minor difference only in the last entry. The point of difference pertains to factory overhead efficiency variance. The amount will be bifurcated into fixed overhead efficiency variance and variable overhead efficiency variance. The fixed overhead efficiency variance would be: (120 hours) × SFOR, i.e. ₹100/12 = ₹1,000 (favourable)

The variable overhead efficiency variance would be: (120 hours) × SVOR, i.e. ₹140/12 = ₹1,400 (favourable)

The last entry for closing the factory overhead control account which has a debit balance of ₹375 would be:

Factory overhead spending variance A/c	Dr	₹150	
Idle capacity variance A/c	Dr	6,000	
To Variable factory overhead efficiency variance A/c			₹1,400
To Fixed factory overhead efficiency variance A/c			1,000
To Factory overhead control A/c			3,750

(d) *Five-Variance Method:* The distinguishing feature would pertain to spending variance. It will be sub-divided into two parts, fixed and variable. Fixed spending variance = ₹1,00,000 – ₹1,01,750 = ₹1750 (adverse).

Variable spending variance = ₹1,31,600 – ₹1,30,000 = ₹1,600 (favourable). The entry would be,

Fixed overhead spending variance A/c	Dr	₹1,750	
Idle capacity variance A/c	Dr	6,000	
To Variable overhead spending variance A/c			₹1,600
To Variable overhead efficiency variance A/c			1,400
To Fixed overhead efficiency variance A/c			1,000
To Factory overhead control A/c			3,750

Standard Accounting Procedure for Completed Products

Under the single plan system, the work-in-process account is debited at standard costs only. Consequently, it will be standard costs of the completed units that will be transferred from that account to the finished product account. The required entry for the purpose is:

Finished product (at standard cost)	Dr
To Work-in-process (at standard costs)	
When goods are sold to customers the following two entries will be required:	
1. Debtors A/c	Dr
To Sales (at selling price)	
2. Cost of goods sold (at standard cost)	
To Finished cost inventory (at standard cost)	Dr

SUMMARY

- Variance analysis is a control technique. The control process involves comparison of actual costs *(AC)* with the standard costs *(SC)*. Variances represent the difference between *AC* and *SC*. They basically relate to performance deviations. If *AC* is less than *SC*, it is a sign of efficiency and the difference is termed 'favourable'/'positive'. If it is more than *SC*, it is a sign of inefficiency and the difference is referred to as 'unfavourable'/'negative'.
- As controlling devices, variances help to assign responsibility for deviations and, thus, to control cost. For this purpose, they are classified as controllable and uncontrollable. If a variance can be traced with the responsibility of a particular segment, it is said to be controllable. If a variance arises from causes beyond the control of responsible individuals, it is said to be *uncontrollable*. This distinction is extremely important for managerial control.
- The cost variances relate to the costs of a manufacturing enterprise. The three elements of the costs of such an enterprise are: material, labour, and overheads.

LO 19.1

- Material variances are summarised below:

Variance	*Formula*
(A) Material cost variance (*MCV*) (unit basis)	(*AQ* × *AO* × *AP*) – (*SQ* × *SP* × *AO*)
or MCV (aggregate basis)	*TAMC* – *TSMC*
(B) (i) Material purchase price variance	(*AP* – *SP*) × *AQ* purchased
(ii) Material price variance (*MPV*)	(*AP* – *SP*) × *AQ* issued
(C) Material usage/quality variance (*MUV*)	[(*AQ* × *AO*) – (*SQ* × *AO*)] × *SP*
(unit basis) *or MUV* (aggregate basis)	or (*TAMQ* – *TSMQ*) × *SP*
(i) Material-mix sub-variance (*MMSV*) and	(*RSQ* – *AQ*) × *SP*
(ii) Material-yield sub-variance (*MYSV*)	(*AY* – *SY*) × *SMC* per finished unit
(output basis) *or MYSV* (input basis)	(*TAMQ* – *TSMQ*) × Weighted average standard price per unit of material

Where,

AQ	Actual usage of material per unit
AO	Actual output in units
AP	Actual price of material per unit
SQ	Standard usage of material per unit
SP	Standard price of material per unit
TAMC	Total actual material costs incurred
TSMC	Total standard costs of actual output
TAMQ	Total actual quantity of material used
TSMQ	Total standard quantity of material required

RSQ	Revised standard quantity, i.e. standard mix/proportion of actual total quantity of material used
AY	Actual yield (actual finished output)
SY	Standard yield (expected output, given the actual input).

LO 19.2

- Labour variances are summarised below:

Variance	*Formula*
(A) Labour cost variance (*LCV*), (unit basis)	[(*AH* × *AO* × *AR*) – (*SH* × *SR* × *AO*)]
or LCV (aggregate basis)	(*TALC* – *TSLC*)
(B) Labour/Wage rate variance (*LRV*)	(*AR* – *SR*) × *TAH* paid for
(C) Labour efficiency variance (*LEV*)	(*TAH* – *TSH*) × *SR* per hour
or	
(i) Labour idle time variance (*LIV*) *and*	(*IH*) × *SR* per hour
(ii) Labour efficiency variance revised (*LEV* revised)	(*TAHW* – *TSH*) × *SR* per hour
or	
Labour-mix sub-variance (*LMSV*)	(*RSH* – *AH*) × *SR* per hour
Labour-yield sub-variance (*LYSV*) (output basis)	(*AY* – *SY*) × Standard labour cost per finished unit
or LYSV (input basis)	(*TAH* – *TSH*) × Weighted average standard rate per hour

Where,

AH	Actual labour-hours spent per unit
AO	Actual output achieved in units
AR	Actual wage rate per hour
SH	Standard labour-hours required per unit
SR	Standard wage rate per hour
TALC	Total actual labour cost of actual output
TSLC	Total standard labour cost of actual output
TAH	Total actual labour-hours paid for
TSH	Total standard hours allowed for actual output
IH	Idle hours
TSHW	Total actual hours worked for production *(TAH – IH)*
RSH	Revised standard hours, i.e. standard proportion of actual hours used.

LO 19.3

- Manufacturing Overheads Variances are summarised below:

Variance	*Formula*
(A) Variable overheads	
Variable overheads cost variance (*VOCV*)	[(*AH* × *AO* × *AVOR*) – (*SH* × *AO* × *SVOR*)
(unit basis) *or VOCV* (aggregate basis)	*TAVOC* – *TSVOC*
(a) Variable overheads spending variance (*VOSV*)	[*TAVOC* – (*TAH* × *SVOR*)]
(b) Variable overheads efficiency variance (*VOEV*)	(*TAH* – *TSH*) × *SVOR* per hour
For confirmation, *VOCV*	*VOEV* + *VOSV*
(B) *Fixed overheads*	
Fixed overheads cost variance (*FOCV*)	[*TAFOC* – (*SFOR* per unit × *AO*)]
(output basis) *or FOCV* (times basis)	[*TAFOC* – (*SFOR* per hour × *SH* × *AO*)]
(a) Fixed overheads spending variance (*FOSV*)	*TAFOC* – *BFOC*
(b) Volume variance (output basis) (*VV*)	[(*NO* – *AO*) × *SFOR* per unit]

or	
(i) Fixed overheads efficiency (*FOEV*)	[(*TAH* – *TSH*) × *SFOR* per hour]
(ii) Calender variance	(*AD* – *SD*) × SFOD
(iii) Capacity variance (*CV*)	[(*TAH* – *TNH*) × *SFOR* per hour]
For confirmation, *FOCY*	*FOSV* + *VV*
	or
	FOSV + *FOEV* + Calender variance + *CV*

The following may be used as an alternative to the above.

Overheads cost variance (*OCV*)	[*TAOC* – (*SOR* per unit × *AO*)]
or *OCV* (hours basis)	[*TAOC* – (*SOR* per hour × *SH* per unit × *AO*)]
(A) *Two-variance method*	
(i) Controllable expenditure variance	[*TAOC* – (*BFOC* + *SVOC* per unit × *AO*)]
(ii) Volume variance	(*NO* – *AO*) × *SFOR* per unit
(B) *Three-variance method*	
(i) Spending variance	[*TAOC* – (*BFOC* + *SVOC* per hour × TAH)]
(ii) Efficiency variance	[*TAH* – *TSH*) × *SOR* per hour]
(iii) Capacity variance	(*NH* – *TAH*) × *SFOR* per hour
(C) *Four-variance method*	
(i) Spending variance	As B(i) above
(ii) Variable efficiency variance	(*TAH* – *TSH*) × *SVOR* per hour
(iii) Fixed efficiency variance	(*TAH* – *TSH*) × *SFOR* per hour
(iv) Capacity variance	As B(iii) above
(D) *Five-variance method*	
(i) Fixed spending variance	*TAFOC* – *TBFOC*
(ii) Variable spending variance	$(AVOR_{PH} - SVOR_{PH}) \times TAH$
(iii) Variance efficiency variance	As C (ii) above
(iv) Fixed efficiency variance	As C (iii) above
(v) Capacity variance	As C (iv) above

Where,

AVOR	Actual variable overheads (per hour or per unit, as the case may be)
SVOR	Standard variable overheads (per hour or per unit, as the case may be)
TAVOC	Total actual variable overheads incurred
TSVOC	Total standard variable overhead costs
SFOR	Standard fixed overheads rate (per unit or per hour, as the case may be)
TAFOC	Total actual fixed overheads cost
BFOC	Budgeted fixed overheads cost
NO	Normal output in units
AD	Actual days
SD	Standard/budgeted days for which production was scheduled
SFOD	Standard fixed overheads cost per day
TNH	Total normal hours capacity
TAOC	Total actual overheads cost (*TAVOC* + *TAFOC*)
SOR	Standard overheads rate (per unit or per hour, as the case may be)

LO 19.4,5

REFERENCES

1. J.M. Fremgen, *Accounting for Managerial Analysis*, (Richard D. Irwin, Homewood, Illinois, 1976), p. 250.
2. The assumption regarding this variance of MPV is that the quantity of raw material consumed is equal to the quantity of raw material purchased.
3. D.T. Decoster and E.L. Schafer, *Management Accounting—A Decision Empahsis*, (John Wiley, New York, 1976), p. 480.
4. R.N. Anthony, *Management Accounting, Text and Cases*, (Irwin, Georgetown, 1970), pp. 534-53.
5. C.T. Horngren, *Introduction to Management Accounting, (Prentice-Hall*, Englewood Cliffs, N.J., 1978), p. 193.
6. J. Batty, *Standard Costing*, (Macdonald and Evans, London, 1970), p. 68.
7. Decoster and Schaffer, *op. cit.* p. 484.
8. National Association of Accountants, "Accounting for Costing of Capacity" *N.A.A. Research Report No. 39* (New York, 1963), p. 64.
9. While the term 'volume' variance is sometimes used interchangeably with 'capacity variance, it is more appropriate to consider capacity variance, as a part of volume variance. The latter approach is adopted by us.
10. Fremgen, *op. cit.*, p. 265

SOLVED PROBLEMS

P.19.1 In a manufacturing process the following standards apply

LO 19.2
LOD: E

Standard price : Raw material X @ ₹10 per kg
Raw material Y @ ₹50 per kg

Standard mix (by weight) : 75% X, 25% Y

Standard yield : (Weight of product as percentage of weight of raw material, 90%)

In a period, the actual costs, usages and output were as follows:

Used: 4,400 kgs, X costing ₹46,500
1,600 kgs, Y costing ₹78,500

Output: 5,670 kgs of products

The budget output for the period was 7,200 kgs.

Prepare a statement, showing how the material cost variance is built up, and give activity and yield percentages.

Solution

Total input requirement = 5,670 kgs × 100/90 = 6,300 kgs

Raw material X = 4,725 kgs (0.75 × 6,300 kgs)
Y = 1,575 kgs (0.25 × 6,300 kgs)

	Standard			Actual		
Raw material	*(SQ)(kgs)*	*(SR)*	*(SC)*	*(AQ) (kgs)*	*(AR)*	*(AC)*
X	4,725	₹10	₹47,250	4,400	₹4,650/440	₹46,500
Y	1,575	50	78,750	1,600	7,850/160	78,500
Total	6,300	20	1,26,000	6,000	1,250/60	1,25,000

Material cost variance: (SC – AC) = (₹1,26,000 – ₹1,25,000) = ₹1,000 (favourable)

Material cost variance is built up of the following three sub-variances:

1. *Material price variance:* (SR – AR) × AQ = (SR × AQ) – (AR × AQ)
   Raw material X = (₹10 × 4,400) – ₹46,500 = ₹2,500 (adverse)
   Y = (₹50 × 1,600) – ₹78,500 = 1,500 (adverse)
   4,000 (adverse)
2. *Material mix variance* = (Standard mix of actual quantity used – Actual mix of actual quantity used) × SR
   Raw material X (0.75 × 6,000 = 4,500 – 4,400) × ₹10 = ₹1,000 (favourable)
   Y (0.25 × 6,000 = 1,500 – 1,600) × ₹50 5,000 (adverse)
   Total material mix variance 4,000 (adverse)
3. *Material yield variance:* (Standard yield – Actual yield) × SC per unit = (5,400 – 5,670) × ₹1,26,000/5,670 = ₹6,000 (favourable)
   Standard yield = 0.90 × 6,000 kgs = 5,400 kgs
   Alternatively, material yield variance, can be calculated on an input basis also: (Standard quantity of raw materials required to produce actual output – Actual quantity used for actual production) × Standard weighted average cost per kg = (6,300 – 6,000) × ₹20 = ₹6,000 (favourable).
   The material cost variance is built up of MPV, ₹1,000 (A), MMV, ₹4,000 (A), and MYV, ₹6,000 (F) = 1,000 (favourable).

$$\text{Activity percentage} = \frac{\text{Standard yield for actual input}}{\text{Budgeted output}} \times 100 = \frac{5{,}400}{7{,}200} \times 100 = 75 \text{ per cent}$$

$$\text{Yield percentage} = \frac{\text{Actual yield}}{\text{Standard yield}} \times 100 = \frac{5{,}670}{5{,}400} \times 100 = 105 \text{ per cent}$$

P.19.2 The standard material cost for 100 kgs of chemical D is made up of **LO 19.2 LOD: M**

Chemical A—30 kgs @ ₹40 per kg
Chemical B—40 kgs @ ₹50 per kg
Chemical C—80 kgs @ ₹60 per kg

In a batch, 500 kgs of chemical D were produced from a mix of:

Chemical A—140 kgs at a cost of ₹5,880
Chemical B—220 kgs at a cost of ₹10,560
Chemical C—440 kgs at a cost of ₹28,600

How do the yield, mix and the price factors contribute to the variance in the actual cost per 100 kgs of chemical D over the standard cost?

Solution

Table Containing Actual Input Used for 100 kgs (500 kgs ÷ 5 = 100 kgs)

Chemical	*SQ (kgs)*	*SR*	*SC*	*AQ (kgs)*	*AR*	*AC*
A	30	₹40	₹1,200	28	₹42	₹1,176
B	40	50	2,000	44	48	2,112
C	80	60	4,800	88	65	5,720
	150	53.33	8,000	160	56.30	9,008

Material cost variance: (TSC – TAC) = (₹8,000 – ₹9,008) = ₹1,008 (adverse)

1. *Material price variance:* (SR – AR) × AQ
   A: (₹40 – ₹42) × 28 kgs = ₹56 (adverse)
   B: (₹50 – ₹48) × 44 kgs = 88 (favourable)
   C: (₹60 – ₹65) × 88 kgs = 440 (adverse)
   408 (adverse)

2. *Material mix variance:* (RSQ – AQ) × SR
A: 160 × 30/150 = (32 kgs – 28 kgs) × ₹40 = ₹160 (favourable)
B: 160 × 40/150 = (42.67 kgs – 44 kgs) × ₹50 = 66.67 (adverse)
C: 160 × 80/150 = (85.33 kgs – 88 kgs) × ₹60 = 160 (adverse)
66.70 (adverse)

3. *Material yield variance:* [Standard yield (SY) – Actual yield (AY) × SC per unit] = (106.667 – 100) × ₹80 = ₹533.30 A
Standard yield = Standard production expected from actual quantity used, that is, (160 kgs × 100)/150 kgs = 106.67 kgs
SC per unit = Total standard cost/Total standard output = ₹8,000/100 kgs = ₹80 per kg

Alternatively, material yield variance can be calculated on input basis also: (Total standard quality of raw material required to produce actual output – Actual quantity used for actual production) × Standard weighted average cost per kg = (150 kgs – 160 kgs) × ₹53.33 = ₹533.30 (adverse).

P.19.3 A foundry producing castings of a standard alloy uses standard costs. The standard mixture is as follows: **LO 19.2** **LOD: D**

40 per cent material A at ₹3,000 per tonne
30 per cent material B at ₹1,000 per tonne
10 per cent material C at ₹4,200 per tonne
20 per cent scrap metal of this alloy.

It is expected that from each charge, there will be a 5 per cent loss in melt, 35 per cent will be returned to scrap stock (runners, heads, etc.) and 60 per cent will be good castings. Scrap is credited and charged at the standard average cost of the metal mixture. Scrap is credited and charged at the standard average cost of the metal mixture. In a certain period, the following materials are purchased and used:

380 tonnes material A at ₹3,100 per tonne
330 tonnes material B at ₹1,100 per tonne
90 tonnes material C at ₹4,200 per tonne
200 tonnes scrap metal at standard price.

From this material, 608 tonnes of good castings are produced and 340 tonnes of scrap metal are returned to scrap metal stock.

Prepare information for management showing standard metal costs, and variances from standard in respect of this period.

Solution

The standard mixture of 608 tonnes of good casting will be as follows:

Since 60 tonnes of good castings require a standard mixture of 100 tonnes, 608 tonnes require = (608 × 100)/60 = 6,080/6 tonnes, the standard inputs of materials A, B, C and scrap would be 40 per cent, 30 per cent, 10 per cent, and 20 per cent of 6,080/6 tonnes, respectively.

The following table presents the above information:

Materials	Standard			Actual		
	SQ (tonnes)	SR	SC	AQ (tonnes)	AR	AC
Material A	1,216/3	₹3,000	₹12,16,000	380	₹3,100	₹11,78,000
B	304	1,000	3,04,000	330	1,100	3,63,000
C	608/6	4,200	4,25,600	90	4,200	3,78,000
Scrap metal	608/3	2,400	4,86,400	200	2,400	4,80,000
Total	6,080/6	2,400	24,32,000	1,000	2,399	23,99,000

Standard average price of scrap metal: Total standard cost of material A + B + C/Total quantity of material A, B, C = ₹19,45,600 ÷ 4,864/6 = ₹2,400

Total quantity of material A, B, C 4,864/6

Standard metal cost per tonne (₹24,32,000 ÷ 608) = ₹4,000

Material cost variance: (₹24,32,000 – ₹23,99,000) = ₹33,000 (favourable)

(A) *Material price variance:* (SR – AR) × AQ

Material	A (₹3,000 – ₹3,100) × 380 =	₹38,000 (adverse)
	B (₹1,000 – ₹1,100) × 330 =	33,000 (adverse)
	C (₹4,200 – ₹4,200) × 90 =	Nil
		71,000 (adverse)

(B) *Material usage variance:* (SQ – AQ) × SR

Material	A (1,216/3 tonnes – 380 tonnes) × ₹3,000	=	₹76,000 (favourable)
	B (304 tonnes – 330 tonnes) × ₹1,000	=	26,000 (adverse)
	C (608/6 tonnes – 90 tonnes) × ₹4,200	=	47,600 (favourable)
Scrap metal	(608/3 tonnes – 200 tonnes) × ₹2,400	=	6,400 (favourable)
			1,04,000 (favourable)

Material usage variance has two components:

(a) *Material mix variance:* (Standard mix of actual quantity used – Actual mix of actual quantity) × SR

Material	A (0.40 × 1,000 = 400 tonnes – 380 tonnes) × ₹3,000	=	₹60,000(favourable)
	B (0.30 × 1,000 = 300 tonnes – 330 tonnes) × ₹1,000	=	30,000 (adverse)
	C (0.10 × 1,000 = 100 tonnes – 90 tonnes) × ₹4,200	=	42,000 (favourable)
Scrap metal	(0.20 × 1,000 = 200 tonnes – 200 tonnes) × ₹2,400		Nil
			72,000 (favourable)

(b) *Material yield variance:* (Standard yield – Actual yield) × SC per tonne

(600 tonnes – 608 tonnes) × ₹4,000 = ₹32,000 (favourable)

Total material cost variance = ₹71,000 (adverse) + ₹72,000 (favourable) + ₹32,000 (favourable)
= ₹33,000 (favourable).

P.19.4 Standard material for 100 kgs Chemical 456 is given below

LO 19.2
LOD: D

Kgs		Total
45	of material A @ ₹20 per kg	₹900
40	of material B @ ₹40 per kg	1,600
25	of material C @ ₹60 per kg	1,500
110		
10	standard loss	
100		4,000

Actual production 2,000 units of Chemical 456 and actual material usage is as follows:

Material A	1,000 kgs @ ₹19 per kg	₹19,000
Material B	850 kgs @ ₹42 per kg	35,700
Material C	450 kgs @ ₹65 per kg	29,250
	2,300 kgs	83,950

Calculate the following: **(i)** Material cost variance, **(ii)** Material price variance, **(iii)** Material mixture variance, **(iv)** Material yield variance, and **(v)** Material usage variance.

Solution

Standard material input required to produce 2,000 units of chemical 456

Material A: (45/100 × 2,000) = 900 kgs

B: (40/100 × 2,000) = 800 kgs

C: (25/100 × 2,000) = 500 kgs

Material	Standard SQ (kgs)	SR	SC	Actual AQ (kgs)	AR	AC
A	900	₹20	₹18,000	1,000	₹19	₹19,000
B	800	40	32,000	850	42	35,700
C	500	60	30,000	450	65	29,250
	2,200	36.30	80,000	2,300	36.5	83,950
	200 (standard loss)					
	2,000 (standard output)					
	₹40 SC per unit					

1. *Material cost variance:* (SC – AC): (₹80,000 – ₹83,950) = ₹3,950 (adverse)
2. *Material price variance:* (SR – AR) × AQ
   Material A: (₹20 – ₹19) × 1,000 kgs = ₹1,000 (favourable)
   B: (₹40 – ₹42) × 850 kgs = 1,700 (adverse)
   C: (₹60 – ₹65) × 450 kgs = 2,250 (adverse)
   2,950 (adverse)
3. *Material mix variance:* (RSQ – AQ) × SR
   Material A: [(2,300 × 45) ÷ 110) – 1,000 kgs] × ₹20 = ₹1,181.80 (adverse)
   B: [(2,300 × 40) ÷ 110) – 850 kgs] × ₹40 = 545.50 (adverse)
   C: [(2,300 × 25) ÷ 110) – 450 kgs] × ₹60 = 4,363.60 (favourable)
   2,636.30 (favourable)
4. *Material yield variance:* (SY – AY) × SC per kg = [(2,300 × 100) ÷ 110) – 2,000 units] × ₹40
   = ₹3636.30 (adverse)
5. *Material usage variance:* (SQ – AQ) × SR
   Material A: (900 kgs – 1,000 kgs) × ₹20 = ₹2,000 (adverse)
   B: (800 kgs – 850 kgs) × ₹40 = 2,000 (adverse)
   C: (500 kgs – 450 kgs) × ₹60 = 3,000 (favourable)
   1,000 (adverse)

Alternatively,

Material mix variance ₹2,636.30 (favourable)
Plus, material yield variance 3,636.30 (adverse)
1,000 (adverse)

P.19.5 From the data given below, calculate: LO 19.2 LOD: D

(a) Individual material price variance for the two materials, X and Y, assuming that the variances are calculated at the time of purchase;

(b) Individual material usage variances for material X and Y assuming that there was no work-in-progress, either at the commencement or at the end of the period.

Particulars	Material X Quantity (kg)	Value	Material Y Quantity (kg)	Value
Raw material purchases	2,000	₹40,000	5,000	₹62,500
Issued to work	2,150		3,950	
Work stock of material				
Opening	300		1,000	
Closing	200		1,250	
Standard price				
Material X – ₹19 per kg				
Material Y – ₹13 per kg				
Standard usage:				

	Material X	Material Y
Product A	1 kg	1 kg
Product B	0.5 kg	1 kg
Output during the period		
Product A—1,130 units		
Product B—2,550 units		

Solution

(a) *Material purchase price variance* = [Actual rate (AR) – Standard rate (SR)] × Actual quantity (AQ) purchased

Material X : [(AR × AQ) – (SR × AQ)] = [₹40,000 – (₹19 × 2,000)] = ₹40,000 – ₹38,000 = ₹2,000 (unfavourable)

Material Y = [₹62,500 – (₹13 × 5,000)] = ₹62,500 – ₹65,000 = ₹2,500 (unfavourable)

(b) *Material usage variance* = (Actual quantity used – Standard quantity) × SR

	Material X	Material Y
Actual quantity used:		
Opening stock (kgs)	300	1,000
Add issues to work	2,150	3,950
Less closing stock	(200)	(1,250)
	2,250	3,700
Standard usage:		
Product A	1,130	1,130
Product B	1,275	2,550
	2,405	3,680

Material X: (2,250 kgs – 2,405 kgs) × ₹19 = ₹2,945 (favourable)
Material Y: (3,700 kgs – 3,680 kgs) × ₹13 = ₹260 (favourable)

P.19.6 One kg of the product K requires two chemicals, A and B. The following are the details of the product K for the month of June. **LO 19.2** **LOD: D**

(a) Standard mix of chemical A, 50 per cent and chemical B, 50 per cent
(b) Standard price per kg of chemical A, ₹120 and chemical B, ₹150
(c) Actual input of chemical B, 70 kgs
(d) Actual price per kg of chemical A, ₹150
(e) Standard normal loss,10 per cent of total output
(f) Material cost variance, total, ₹6,500 adverse
(g) Material yield variance, total, ₹1,350 adverse
(h) Actual output, 90 kgs

You are required to calculate: **(i)** Material mix variance(total), **(ii)** Material usage variance(total), **(iii)** Material price variance(total), **(iv)** Actual loss of actual input, **(v)** Actual input of chemical A, and **(vi)** Actual price per kg of chemical B.

Solution

(i) *Material mix variance* = (Standard mix of actual quantity used – Actual mix) × Standard rate

A: [(110 kgs × 0.50 = 55 kgs – 40 kgs)] × ₹120 = ₹1,800 (favourable)
B: [(110 kgs × 0.50 = 55 kgs – 70 kgs)] × ₹150 = 2,250 (unfavourable)
450 (unfavourable)

(ii) *Material usage variance* = Material mix variance + Material yield variance = ₹450 (unfavourable) + ₹1,350 (unfavourable) = ₹1,800 (unfavourable)

(iii) *Material price variance* = (SR – AR) × AQ

A: (₹120 – ₹150) × 40 kgs = ₹1,200 (unfavourable)

B: (₹150 – ₹200) × 70 kgs = 3,500 (unfavourable)

4,700 (unfavourable)

(iv) *Actual loss of actual input* = (Actual input – Actual output) = 110 kgs – 90 kgs = 20 kgs

(v) *Actual input of chemical A,* = 40 kgs

(vi) *Actual price per kg of chemical B* = ₹200

WORKING NOTES

Standard material input and cost required to produce 90 kgs of product K

(a)	Chemical A	50 kgs @ ₹120 per kg	₹6,000
	Chemical B	50 kgs @ ₹150 per kg	7,500
		100 kgs	13,500
	Less standard normal loss	10 kgs	
	Actual output	90 kgs	

(b) Standard rate per kg of product K = ₹13,500/90 kgs = ₹150

(c) Material yield variance = (SY – AY) × SR per kg of final product

₹1,350 U = (SY – 90 kgs) × ₹150

₹1,350 U = 150 SY – ₹13,500

₹1,350 U + ₹13,500 = 150 SY

₹14,850 = 150 SY or SY = ₹14,850/150 = 99 kgs

(d) Actual total input of A and B chemicals = 99 kgs × 100/90 = 110 kgs

(e) Actual inputs of chemical being 70 kgs, input of chemical A would be 40 kgs

(f) Actual costs of material used = Standard cost (₹13,500) + (unfavourable) material cost variance (₹6,500) = ₹20,000

(g)

Total cost of chemicals A and B	₹20,000
Less cost of chemical A (40 kgs × ₹150)	6,000
Costs of chemical B (70 kgs)	14,000
Cost of chemical B per kg (₹14,000/70 kgs)	200

P.19.7 From the data given below, calculate each of the three wage variances for the two departments: **LO 19.3** **LOD: E**

Particulars	*Department A*	*Department B*
Actual gross wages	₹2,00,000	₹1,80,000
Standard hours produced	8,000	6,000
Standard rate per hour	₹30	₹35
Actual hours worked	8,200	5,800

Solution

Labour cost variance: Actual wages paid – Standard wages charged to production (SH × SR)

Department A: ₹2,00,000 – (8,000 × ₹30) = ₹40,000 (favourable)

B: ₹1,80,000 – (6,000 × ₹35) = ₹30,000 (favourable)

Labour rate variance: (SR – AR) × Actual hours (AH) worked) or : (SR × AH) – (AR × AH)

Department A: (₹30 × 8,200) – ₹2,00,000 = ₹46,000 (favourable)

B: (₹35 × 5,800) – ₹1,80,000 = ₹23,000 (favourable)

Labour efficiency variance: (Standard hours produced – Actual hours worked) × Standard rate per hour

Department A: (8,000 – 8,200) × ₹30 = ₹6,000 (adverse)
B: (6,000 – 5,800) × ₹35 = ₹7,000 (favourable)

Confirmation

Particulars	Department A	Department B
Labour rate variance	₹46,000 (favourable)	₹23,000 (favourable)
Labour efficiency variance	6,000 (adverse)	7,000 (favourable)
Labour cost variance	40,000 (favourable)	30,000 (favourable)

P.19.8 The standard output of product EXE is 25 units per hour in the manufacturing department of a company, employing 100 workers. The standard wage rate per labour-hour is ₹60. In a 42-hour week, the department produced 1,040 units of EXE despite loss of 5 per cent of time paid due to abnormal reasons. The hourly wage rates actually paid were ₹62, ₹60, and ₹57, respectively, to 10,30 and 60 of the workers. **LO 19.4** **LOD: M**

Compute relevant variances.

Solution

Basic data:

1. *Standard man-hour per unit* Since 25 units are standard output when 100 workers are engaged for 1 hour, the standard man-hours per unit is 4.

2. *Standard data*

Standard man-hours for actual output	*Rate per hour*	*Amount*	*Number of workers*	*Actual hours Col. 4 (×) 42*	*Idle time paid for*	*Effective hours*	*Rate per hour*	*Amount paid*
(1)	*(2)*	*(3)*	*(4)*	*(5)*	*(6)*	*(7)*	*(8)*	*(9) = (5× 8)*
4,160*	₹60	₹2,49,600	10	4,200	21	399	₹62	₹26,040
			30	12,600	63	1,197	60	75,600
			60	25,200	126	2,394	57	1,43,640
		2,49,600		42,000	210	3,990		2,45,280

*1,040 units × 4 hours

Computation of variances:

Labour cost variance = (Standard labour cost – Actual labour cost) = (₹2,49,600 – ₹2,45,280)
= ₹4,320 (favourable)

Labour rate variance = (Standard rate per hour – Actual rate per hour) × Actual hours
(₹60 – ₹62) × 420 hours = ₹840 (adverse)
(₹60 – ₹60) × 1,260 hours = Nil
(₹60 – ₹57) × 2,520 hours = 7,560 (favourable)
6,720 (favourable)

Labour efficiency variance = (Standard man-hours – Actual production hours) × Standard rate per hour
= (4,160 hours – 3,990 hours) × ₹60 = ₹10,200 (favourable)

Labour idle variance = Standard rate per hour × Idle time = ₹60 × 210 hours = ₹12,600 (adverse)

Verification:

Labour cost variance = Labour rate variance + Labour efficiency variance + Labour idle time variance
₹4,320 (favourable) = ₹6,720 (favourable) + ₹10,200 (favourable) – ₹12,600 (adverse)

P.19.9 The standard labour, and the actual labour employment in a week for a job are as under: LO 19.3 LOD: M

Particulars	Skilled workers	Semi-skilled workers	Unskilled workers
(A) Standard number of workers in the gang	32	12	6
(B) Standard wage rate per hour	₹30	₹20	₹10
(C) Actual number of workers employed in the gang during the week	28	18	4
(D) Actual wage rate per hour	40	30	20

During the 40-hours working week, the gang produced 1,800 standard labour-hours of work. Calculate the: (1) Labour efficiency variance; (2) Labour mix variance; (3) Rate of wages variance; and (4) Total labour cost variance.

Solution

Category of workers	Number of workers	Number of hours	Total hours	Wage rate	Total wages
			Standard		
Skilled	32	40	1,280	₹30	₹38,400
Semi-skilled	12	40	480	20	9,600
Unskilled	6	40	240	10	2,400
			2,000	25.20	50,400
			Actual		
Skilled	28	40	1,120	40	44,800
Semi-skilled	18	40	720	30	21,600
Unskilled	4	40	160	20	3,200
			2,000	34.80	69,600

1. *Labour efficiency variance:* (Standard labour-hours – Actual labour-hours) × Standard weighted average wage rate = (1,800 – 2,000) × ₹25.20 = ₹5,040 (adverse)
2. *Labour mix variance:* (Standard mix of actual hours worked – Actual mix of actual hours) × Standard wage rate

   Since standard total hours and actual total hours are the same (2,000 hours), there is no need to calculate a revised standard mix of actual hours.

   Accordingly,

   Skilled workers: (1,280 – 1,120) × ₹30 = ₹4,800 (favourable)
   Semi-skilled workers: (480 – 720) × ₹20 = 4,800 (adverse)
   Unskilled workers: (240 – 160) × ₹10 = 800 (favourable)
   Total labour mix variance 800 (favourable)
3. *Rate of wages variance:* (SR – AR) × AH

   Skilled workers: (₹30 – ₹40) × 1,120 = ₹11,200 (adverse)
   Semi-skilled workers: (₹20 – ₹30) × 720 = 7,200 (adverse)
   Unskilled workers: (₹10 – ₹20) × 160 = 1,600 (adverse)
   Total labour rate variance 20,000 (adverse)
4. *Total labour cost variance:* (Total standard labour cost at standard hours – Actual labour cost at actual hours)

   Standard labour cost = (Standard hours × Standard weighted average wage rate)
   = (1,800 × ₹25.20) = ₹45,360 – ₹69,600 = ₹24,240 (adverse)

P.19.10 A gang of workers normally consists of 30 highly skilled, 15 skilled, and 10 semi-skilled. They are paid standard hourly rates as under: LO 19.3 LOD: D

Highly skilled	₹80
Skilled	60
Semi-skilled	40

In a normal working week of 40 hours, the gang is expected to produce 2,000 units of output.

During the week ended December 31, the gang consisted of 40 highly skilled, 10 skilled, and 5 semi-skilled. The actual wages paid were at the rate of ₹70, ₹65 and ₹30, respectively. Four hours were lost due to abnormal idle time and 1,600 units were produced.

Calculate: **(i)** Wage variance; **(ii)** Wage rate variance; **(iii)** Labour efficiency variance; **(iv)** Gang composition variance (labour mix variance); and **(v)** Labour idle time variance.

Solution

1. *Wage variance:* (Standard labour cost of actual output – Actual labour cost) = ₹1,18,400 – ₹1,44,000 or (40 × ₹3,600) = ₹25,600 (adverse)

Standard cost = (Standard cost per gang-hour × Standard gang-hours required for actual output) = (₹3,700 × 32) = ₹1,18,400

Standard Labour Cost (SLC) per Gang-hour

Composition of gang	*Number*	*Rate*	*TSC*
Highly skilled	30	₹80	₹2,400
Skilled	15	60	900
Semi-skilled	10	40	400
Total SLC per gang hour			3,700

Standard gang-hours required: (Actual output ÷ Standard output per gang-hour) = 1,600/50 (2000 ÷ 40) = 32

Actual Labour Cost (ALC) per Gang-hour

Particulars	*Number*	*AR*	*Total AC*
Highly skilled	40	₹70	₹2,800
Skilled	10	65	650
Semi-skilled	5	30	150
Total ALC per gang hour			3,600

2. *Wage rate variance:* (Standard rate – Actual rate) × Actual hours paid for

Highly skilled:	(₹80 – ₹70) × 40 × 40=	₹16,000 (favourable)
Skilled:	(₹60 – ₹65) × 10 × 40=	2,000 (adverse)
Semi-skilled:	(₹40 – ₹30) × 5 × 40 =	2,000 (favourable)
		16,000 (favourable)

3. *Labour Efficiency Variance*

	Standard composition of gang		*Standard gang hours for actual production*		*Total standard hours required*		*Actual hours paid for*		*Standard wage rate per hour*		*Labour efficiency variance*
Highly skilled	(30	×	32	=	960	–	1,600)	×	₹80	=	51,200 (adverse)
Skilled	(15	×	32	=	480	–	400)	×	₹60	=	4,800 (favourable)
Semi-skilled	(10	×	32	=	320	–	200)	×	₹40	=	4,800 (favourable)
											41,600 (adverse)

4. *Labour idle time variance:* (Idle hours × Standard rate)

Highly skilled: (40 × 4) × ₹80 = ₹12,800 (adverse)

Skilled:	(10 × 4) × ₹60 =	2,400 (adverse)
Semi-skilled	(5 × 4) × ₹40 =	800 (adverse)
		16,000 (adverse)

5. *Labour mix variances* (Gang composition variance): (Standard mix used for actual hours used in the production – Actual mix of actual hours) × SWR

Actual hours used = (Total actual hours – Idle time)

Highly skilled	(40 × 40)	1,600
Skilled	(10 × 40)	400
Semi-skilled	(5 × 40)	200
		2,200
Less: Idle time	(55 × 4)	220
Total actual hours		1,980

[Standard mix of actual hours		–	*Actual mix]*	×	*SWR*	=	*Labour mix variance*
Highly skilled:	(6/11 × 1,980) = 1,080	–	1,440 (40 × 36)	×	₹80	=	₹28,800 (adverse)
Skilled:	(3/11 × 1,980) = 540	–	360 (10 × 36)	×	₹60	=	10,800 (favourable)
Semi-skilled:	(2/11 × 1,980) = 360	–	180 (5 × 36)	×	₹40	=	7,200 (favourable)
	1,980		1,980				10,800 (adverse)

Labour efficiency variance (revised): (Standard gang-hours required for actual production – Actual gang hours used in production) × Standard wage rate per gang-hour = (32 – 36) × ₹3,700 = ₹14,800 (adverse).

Summary:

- Wage variance (₹25,600, adverse)
  - Wage rate variance (₹16,000 favourable)
  - Labour efficiency variance (₹41,600 adverse)
    - Labour mix variance (₹10,800 adverse)
    - Idle time variance (₹16,000 adverse)
    - Revised efficiency variance (₹14,800 adverse)

P.19.11 The Standard Supply Company Ltd produces a single article which goes through two operating departments. The standard cost card for this article indicated the following data: **LO 19.3** **LOD: M**

	Standard time (hours)	*Standard rate*	*Total*
Department A	2.2	₹54	₹118.80
Department B	1.6	60	96.0

The production for the month of August is 1,000 units. The actual labour costs in the two departments were:

	Hours	*Cost*
Department A	2,000	₹1,29,080
Department B	1,800	1,02,000

Compute the labour cost, rate and efficiency variances.

Solution

Department	Standard time required to produce 1,000 units	Standard wage rate	Total standard wage bill	Actual time taken (hours)	Actual cost
A	2,200 (1,000 × 2.2)	₹54	₹1,18,800	2,000	₹1,29,080
B	1,600 (1,000 × 1.6)	60	96,000	1,800	1,02,000
	3,800 (1,000 × 3.8)	56.5	2,14,800	3,800	2,31,080

Labour cost variance: (Total standard labour cost – Total actual labour cost) = (₹2,14,800 – ₹2,31,080) = ₹16,280 (adverse)

1. Labour rate variance

Department A : (₹54 × 2,000) – ₹1,29,080 = ₹21,080 (adverse)
Department B : (₹60 × 1,800) – ₹1,02,000 = 6,000 (favourable)
15,080 (adverse)

Labour efficiency variance

Department A : (2,200 hours – 2,000 hours) × ₹54= ₹10,800 (favourable)
Department B : (1,600 hours – 1,800 hours) × ₹60= 12,000 (adverse)
1,200 adverse

P.19.12 From the following data of ABC Ltd relating to the budgeted and actual performance for the month of March, compute direct material and direct labour cost variances. LO 19.2,3 LOD: M

Budgeted data for March:	
Units to be manufactured	1,50,000
Units of direct material required (based on standard rates)	4,95,000
Planned purchase for raw material (units)	5,40,000
Average unit cost of direct material (₹)	8
Direct labour-hours per unit of finished goods	0.75
Total direct labour costs (₹)	29,92,500
Actual data at the end of March:	
Units actually manufactured	1,60,000
Direct material costs(purchase costs based on units actually issued)	43,41,900
Direct material costs (purchase costs based on units actually issued)	45,10,000
Average unit costs of direct material (₹)	8.20
Total direct labour-hours for March	1,25,000
Total direct labour costs for March (₹)	33,75,000

Solution

(i) *Material Cost Variance*

Actual material costs		₹43,41,900
Less standard material costs:		
Units actually manufactured	1,60,000	
(×) Direct raw material per unit (₹4,95,000/₹1,50,000)	× 3.3	
Total units of raw material	5,28,000	
(×) Standard unit cost of direct material	× ₹8	42,24,000
		1,17,900 (unfavourable)

(a) Material price variance (SR – AR) × AQ = (₹8 – ₹8.20) × 5,29,500 units* = ₹1,05,900 (unfavourable)
*5,29,500 units = ₹43,41,900/₹8.20 per unit

(b) Material usage variance (SQ – AQ) × AR = (5,28,000 – 5,29,500) × ₹8 = ₹12,000 (unfavourable)

(ii) *Labour Cost Variance*

Actual labour costs		₹33,75,000
Less standard labour costs:		
Units actually manufactured	1,60,000	
(x) Direct labour cost per unit	× ₹19.95	31,92,000
		1,83,000 (unfavourable)

(a) Labour rate variance: (SR – AR) × AH = (₹26.60@ × 1,25,000) – ₹33,75,000 = ₹50,000 (unfavourable) [@ ₹19.95 per unit/0.75 hour = ₹26.60 per hour]

(b) Labour efficiency variance: (SH – AH) × SR per hour = (1,60,000 × 0.75 = ₹1,20,000 hours – 1,25,000) × ₹26.6 = ₹1,33,000 (unfavourable)

P.19.13 A company manufacturing two products operates a standard costing system. The standard overhead content of each production in cost centre 101 is: LO 19.4 LOD: M

Product A, ₹240 (8 direct labour-hours @ ₹30 per hour)
Product B, ₹180 (6 direct labour-hours @ ₹30 per hour)

The rate of ₹30 per hour is arrived at as follows

Budgeted overheads, ₹57,000
Budgeted direct labour-hours, 1,900

For the month of October, the following data was recorded for cost centre 101:

Output of product A, 100 units
Output of product B, 200 units
No opening or closing stock
Actual direct labour-hours worked, 2,320
Actual overheads incurred, ₹64,000

1. You are required to calculate total overhead variance for the month of October.
2. Show its division into (a) Overhead expenditure variance, **(b)** Overhead capacity variance, (c) Overhead efficiency variance.

Solution

1. *Total overhead variance:* (Actual overhead incurred – Standard overheads charged to production) = (₹64,000 – ₹60,000) = ₹4,000A

   Standard overheads charged to production:

   Product A: (₹240 × 100)= ₹24,000
   B: (₹180 × 200)= 36,000
   60,000

2. (a) *Overhead expenditure variance:* (Actual overheads – Budgeted overheads) = (₹64,000 – ₹57,000) = ₹7,000(A)

   (b) Overhead capacity variance: (NH – AH) × SOR = (1,900 – 2,320) × ₹30 = ₹12,600 (favourable)

   (c) Overhead efficiency variance: (Standard hours allowed for actual production – Actual hours used in production) × SOR = (2,000 hours* – 2,320 hours) × ₹30 = ₹9,600 (adverse)

   * Standard hours: Product A (100 units × 8) = 800
   B (200 units × 6) = 1,200
   2,000

P.19.14 The following data is given for Hypothetical Ltd. LO 19.4 LOD: M

Particulars	*Budget*	*Actuals*
Production (in units)	400	360
Man-hours to produce above	8000	7000
Variable overheads	₹1,00,000	₹91,500

The standard time to produce one unit of the product is 20 hours.

Calculate variable overhead variances, and give necessary journal entries to record the transactions.

Solution

Basic data

1. Standard variable overhead rate (SVOR) per unit = ₹1,00,000/400 units = ₹250
2. Standard variable overhead rate (SVOR) per hour = ₹1,00,000/8,000 hours = ₹12.50
3. Variable overheads recovered = Actual output × SVOR per unit = 360 units × ₹250 = ₹90,000
4. Budgeted variable overhead = Actual hours worked × SVOR per hour = 7,000 hours × ₹12.50 = ₹87,500
5. Standard hours for actual output = Actual output × SH per unit = 360 units × 20 hours = 7,200 hours

Variances:

(i) *Variable overhead cost variance* = (Standard variable overheads – Actual variable overheads)
= ₹90,000 – ₹91,500 = ₹1,500 (adverse)

(ii) *Variable overhead expenditure variance*
= (Budgeted variable overheads at AH – Actual variable overheads)
= ₹87,500 – ₹91,500 = ₹4,000 (adverse)

(iii) *Variable overhead efficiency variance*
= (Standard hours for actual output – Actual hours) × SVOR per hour
= (7,200 – 7,000) × ₹12.50 = ₹2,500 (favourable)

Verification:

Variable overhead cost variance = ₹1,500 (adverse = Variable overhead efficiency variance + Variable overhead expenditure variance = ₹4,000 (adverse) + ₹2,500 (favourable)

Journal Entries

Variable overhead A/c	Dr	₹87,500	
Variable overhead expenditure variance	Dr	4,000	
To Creditors for expenses			₹91,500
Work-in-progress A/c	Dr	90,000	
To Variable overheads A/c			87,500
To Variable overhead efficiency variance A/c			2,500

P.19.15 Determine the various overhead variances from the following information **LO 19.5** **LOD: M**

Actual hours worked, 6,200
Fixed overhead (8,00 hours normal capacity), ₹3,20,000
Actual production, 50 units
Standard man-hours per unit, 120
Standard overhead rate per standard man-hour, ₹100
Actual overheads incurred, ₹6,50,000

Solution

Total overhead variance: (Actual overheads incurred – Standard overheads charged to production) = (₹6,50,000 – ₹6,00,000) = ₹50,000 (A)

Standard overheads = Units produced × Hours per unit × Standard overhead rate per hour)
= 50 × 120 × ₹100 = ₹6,00,000

1. *Two variance method*

(a) Expenditure variance = (Actual overheads – Budgeted overheads at standard hours)
= (₹6,50,000 – ₹6,80,000) = ₹30,000 (favourable)

Budgeted overheads:

Fixed overheads	₹3,20,000
Add variance overheads [6,000 standard hours (x) ₹60 standard variable overhead rate (₹100 TSOR – ₹40 SFOR, that is, ₹3,20,000 ÷ 8,000)]	3,60,000
	6,80,000

(b) Volume variance: (NH – SH) × SFOR per hour = (8,000 hours – 6,000 hours) × ₹40 = ₹80,000 (adverse)

2. *Three-variance method*

(a) Spending variance: (Actual overheads incurred – Budgeted overheads at actual hours) = (₹6,50,000 – ₹6,92,000) = ₹42,000 (favourable)

Budgeted overheads:

Fixed overheads	₹3,20,000
Plus variable overheads (6,200 hours × ₹60)	3,72,000
	6,92,000

(b) Efficiency variance: (SH – AH) × SOR per hour = (6,000 hours – 6,200 hours) × ₹100 = ₹20,000 (adverse)

(c) Capacity variance: (NH – AH) × SFOR per hour = (8,000 hours – 6,200 hours) × ₹40 = ₹72,000 (adverse).

3. *Four-variance method:*

(i) and **(iii)** are the same as in the three-variance method. Efficiency variance will be split up into two sub-parts:

(a) Fixed overhead efficiency variance = (SH – AH) × SFOR = (6,000 hours – 6,200 hours) × ₹40 = ₹8,000 (adverse)

(b) Variable overhead efficiency variance = (SH – AH) × SVOR = (6,000 hours – 6,200 hours) × ₹60 = ₹12,000 (adverse)

P.19.16 XYZ Ltd forecasts its overhead expenditure for a period as under. **LO 19.5** **LOD: D**

₹3,00,000 for 10,000 hours
₹2,75,000 for 9,000 hours
₹2,50,000 for 8,000 hours

The normal volume of activity is 10,000 hours. During a period, 8,750 hours were utilised for a total overhead expenditure of ₹2,87,500, of which fixed overheads totalled ₹52,500.

The utilisation of labour-hours should have been less by 5 per cent. How will you analyse the overhead variance?

Solution

1. Determination of variable overhead rate per hour (SVOR) = Change in overhead expenditure ÷ Change in hours = [₹50,000 (₹3,00,000 – ₹2,50,000)] ÷ 2,000 hours (10,000 – 8,000)] = ₹25 per hour
2. Fixed overheads

Total overheads at 10,000 hours	₹3,00,000
Less variable overheads (10,000 × ₹2.50)	2,50,000
Fixed overheads at normal capacity	50,000

3. Fixed overhead rate per hour (SFOR) = (₹50,000 ÷ 10,000 hours) = ₹5
4. Total overhead rate per hour (TSOR) = ₹30 (₹25 + ₹5)

Total overhead variance = Actual overheads incurred – Standard overheads charged to production = ₹2,87,500 – ₹2,49,375 = ₹38,125 (adverse)

Standard overheads:

Actual hours	8,750
Less 5% (more hours taken)	437.50
Standard hours	8,312.50
(x) TSOR per hour	₹30
	2,49,375

Four-variance method:

1. *Spending variance:* (Actual overheads incurred – Budgeted overheads at actual hours)
= (₹2,87,500 – ₹2,68,750) = ₹18,750 (adverse)

Budgeted overheads:

Fixed overheads	₹50,000
Plus variable overheads (8,750 hours × ₹25)	2,18,750
	2,68,750

2. *Fixed overhead efficiency variance:* (SH – AH) × SFOR = (8,312.5 hours – 8,750 hours) × ₹5 = ₹2,187.50 (adverse)
3. *Variable overhead efficiency variance:* (SH – AH) × SVOR = (8,312.5 hours – 8,750 hours) × ₹25 = ₹10,937.50 (adverse)
4. *Capacity variance:* (NH – AH) × SFOR = (10,000 hours – 8,750 hours) × ₹5 = ₹6,250 (adverse)

The spending variance can be bifurcated into two sub-variances:

1. **(a)** *Fixed overhead spending variance:* (₹52,500 – ₹50,000) = ₹2,500 (adverse)
   (b) *Variable overhead spending variance:* (₹2,35,000 – ₹2,18,750) = ₹16,250 (adverse)

P.19.17 Bharat Manufacturing Ltd manufactures the product DRYDRAP in standard batches of 100 units. A standard cost system is used. The standard costs for a batch are: LO 19.5 LOD: M

Raw materials, 60 kgs @ ₹5	₹300
Direct labour, 40 hours @ ₹25 per hour	1,000
Factory overhead, 40 hours @ ₹20 per hour	800
Total standard cost per batch for 100 units	2,100

Production for March amounted to 210 batches.

Relevant data are:

Normal capacity per month: 24,000 units
Direct labour cost (8,600 hours): ₹2,10,700
Actual factory overhead: ₹1,73,250
Fixed overhead for standard output: ₹72,000

The management has noted that actual costs per batch deviate from standard costs. Make a variance analysis of the factory overheads by using the two-variance, three-variance and four-variance methods for overheads.

Solution

Factory overhead variance: (Actual overheads costs – Standard overhead costs charged to production) = (₹1,73,250 – ₹1,68,000) = ₹5,250 (adverse)

Standard overhead costs charged to production: (Actual batches produced × Standard overhead cost per batch) = (210 × ₹800) = ₹1,68,000

Two-variance method:

1. *Controllable variance:* (Actual overhead costs – Budgeted overhead costs at actual production) = (₹1,73,250 – ₹1,77,000) = ₹3,750 (favourable)

Budgeted overhead costs:	Fixed overhead	₹72,000
	+ Variable overhead	1,05,000*
		1,77,000

(Actual batches produced × Standard variable overhead cost per batch: 210 × ₹500)

*Factory overhead rate per batch	₹800
Less fixed factory overhead rate (₹72,000 ÷ 240)	300
Variable factory overhead rate	500

2. *Volume variance:* (Normal capacity in batches – Actual production in batches) = (240 – 210) × ₹300 = ₹9,000 (A)

Controllable variance + Volume variance = Total variance = ₹3,750F + ₹9,000 A = ₹5,250 (adverse)

Three-variance method:

1. *Spending variance:* (Actual overhead costs – Budgeted overhead costs at actual hours) = (₹1,73,250 – ₹1,79,500) = ₹6,250 (favourable)

   Budgeted overhead costs:

Fixed overhead	₹72,000
+ Variable overhead	1,07,500*
	1,79,500

   *(Actual hours used × Standard variable overhead rate per hour) = (8,600 × ₹12.50) = ₹1,07,500

2. *Efficiency variance:* (Actual batch production × Standard hours per batch) – (Actual hours worked × (Standard overhead rater per hours) = [(210 × 40) – 8,600] × ₹20 = 200 × ₹20 = ₹4,000 (adverse)
3. *Capacity variance:* (Normal capacity in hours – Actual hours worked) × Fixed standard overhead rate per hour = [9,600 (240 batches × 40) – 8,600] × ₹7.5 = 1,000 × ₹7.5 = ₹7,500 (adverse)

Confirmation: ₹6,250F + ₹4,000A + ₹7,500A = ₹5,250 (adverse)

Four-variance method:

Spending variance and capacity variance remain unchanged. Efficiency variance will be broken up into two parts: Fixed factory overhead efficiency variance, and Variable factory overhead efficiency variance.

1. *Fixed factory overhead efficiency variance:* (Actual batch production × Standard hours per batch) – (Actual hours worked × Fixed standard overhead rate per hour) = (210 × 40 – 8,600) × ₹7.5 = ₹1,500 (adverse)
2. *Variable factory overhead efficiency variance:* 200 × ₹12.5 = ₹2,500 (adverse)

   ₹6,250F + ₹1,500A + ₹2,500A + ₹7,500A = ₹5,250 A

P.19.18 From the following information compute: (i) Spending variance, (ii) Idle capacity variance, (iii) Efficiency variance. **LO 19.5** **LOD: M**

Normal capacity, 12,000 hours

Fixed expenses, ₹10,00,000

Variable expenses (at normal capacity), ₹14,00,000

The plant worked for 11,280 actual hours, executing work for which 11,400 hours were allowed. Actual factory overhead expenses amounted to ₹23,17,500.

Solution

(i) *Spending variance:* (Actual overhead costs – Budgeted overhead costs at actual hours) = (₹23,17,500 – ₹23,16,000) = ₹1,500 (adverse)

Budgeted overhead costs:

Fixed expenses	₹10,00,000
+ Variable expenses (11,280 hours × ₹1,400/12)	13,16,000
	23,16,000

(ii) *Idle capacity variance:* (Normal capacity in hours – Actual hours worked) × Standard fixed overhead rate per hour = (12,000 – 11,280) × ₹1,000/12 = ₹60,000 (adverse)

(iii) *Efficiency variance:* (SH_s – AH_s) × SOR = (11,400 – 11,280) × ₹200 = ₹24,000 F

Total overhead variance = ₹1,500A + ₹60,000 A + ₹24,000 F = ₹37,500 (adverse)

Confirmation:

Factory overhead variance = (Actual overhead costs – Standard overhead cost charged to production)
= [₹23,17,500 – ₹22,80,000 or (11,400 standard hours × ₹200)]
= ₹37,500 (adverse).

P.19.19 For the month of April, you are given the following figures for a manufacturing firm: **LO 19.5** **LOD: M**

Particulars	Standard	Actual
Number of units produced	15,000	8,000
Capacity (hours)	30,000	17,500
Variable overheads	₹30,00,000	₹15,00,000
Fixed overheads	45,00,000	46,30,000

Calculate expenditure variance and volume variance.

Solution

SOR (per unit) = Total overheads/Units produced = ₹75,00,000/15,000 = ₹500
SOR (per hour) = Total overheads/Capacity hours = ₹75,00,000/30,000 = ₹250
Fixed SOR per unit = ₹45,00,000 ÷ 15,000 units = ₹300
Fixed SOR per hour = ₹45,00,000 ÷ 30,000 hours = 150
Variable SOR per unit = ₹30,00,000 ÷ 15,000 units = 200
Variable SOR per hour = ₹30,00,000 ÷ 30,000 hours = 100

Expenditure variance: (Actual overhead costs – Budgeted overhead costs at SH) = (₹61,30,000 – ₹61,00,000) = ₹30,000 (adverse)

Budgeted overhead costs:

Fixed overheads	₹45,00,000
Variable overheads (16,000 standard hours × ₹100)	16,00,000
	61,00,000

Volume variance: (Normal capacity in hours – Standard hours allowed for actual production) × Standard fixed overhead rate per hour = (30,000 – 16,000) × ₹150 = ₹21,00,000 (adverse)

Total overhead variance: ₹30,000 A + ₹21,00,000 A = ₹21,30,000 (adverse)

Confirmation: (Actual overhead costs – Standard overhead costs charged to production) = ₹61,30,000 – ₹40,00,000 = ₹21,30,000 (adverse)

Alternatively, the problem can be solved taking units produced as the basis for standard cost. For instance, *Expenditure variance:* (Actual overhead costs – Budgeted overhead costs, at actual production) = ₹61,30,000 – ₹61,00,000 = ₹30,000 (adverse).

Likewise, Volume variance would be, [normal capacity (in units) – Actual production] × Standard fixed overhead rate per unit = (15,000 – 8,000) × ₹300 = ₹21,00,000 (adverse).

P.19.20 A company's annual expenditure budget for the year was set at ₹48,00,000. Accordingly, monthly budget was taken at ₹4,00,000. Standard output for the year, on a 300 working days basis, was 3,00,000 units, and standard overhead recovery rate was fixed on this basis. **LO 19.4,5** **LOD: D**

In February, there were 24 working days (28 days, less 4 Sunday). During this month production achieved was 23,000 units. Actual expenses in February totalled ₹4,10,000.

Calculate total overhead variance, budget, efficiency, volume and calendar variances.

Solution

Summary of Overhead Expenditure for February (Budgeted and Actual)

	Budgeted	Actual
Overhead expenditure	₹4,00,000	₹4,10,000
Working days	25	24
Production	25,000	23,000

Overhead recovery rate = ₹16 per unit = ₹48,00,000/3,00,000 units

Total overhead variance: (Actual overhead cost incurred – Standard overhead charged to production) = ₹4,10,000 – (23,000 × ₹16) = ₹42,000 (adverse)

Budget variance: (Actual overhead cost – Budgeted overhead costs) = ₹4,10,000 – ₹4,00,000 = ₹10,000 (adverse)

Volume variance: (Budgeted output – Actual output) × SOR per unit = (25,000 – 23,000) × ₹16 = ₹32,000 (adverse)

Volume variance has two components:

Efficiency variance: [(Budgeted output per day × Actual working days) – Actual output] × SOR per unit (1,000 × 24 = 24,000 – 23,000) × ₹16 = ₹16,000 (adverse)

Calendar variance: (Number of scheduled working days – Actual working days) × SOR per day = (25 – 24) × ₹16,000 = ₹16,000 (adverse)

P.19.21 Eastern Manufacturers Ltd operates a standard costing system. In connection with the weekly cost report for the process X, you have been informed that: **LO 19.3,4,5** **LOD: M**

1. The standard costs per hour of the process, based on a normal week of 40 hours work, are:

Wages	₹90
Variable expenses	25
Fixed expenses	125
	240

Standard output in units per hour, 20.

2. The following information has been recorded in respect of the process for one week:

Hours worked	36
Non-productive hours (awaiting work)	4
Total hours paid for	40
Output (units)	850
Actual wages paid	₹3,700
Actual variable expenses	1,200
Actual fixed expenses	5,000

You are required to compute the variances relating to process X for the week.

Solution

1. *Labour cost variance:* (Actual labour costs – Standard labour costs charged to production) = (₹3,700 – ₹3,825) = ₹125 F

Standard labour cost: (Standard hours required for actual production × Standard wages rate per hour) = (42.5 hours) or (850 units/20) × ₹90 = ₹3,825

(a) Labour rate variance: (Standard wage rate per hour – Actual wage rate per hour) × Actual hours worked = (₹90 – ₹92.50) × 40 hours = ₹100 (adverse)

(b) Idle time variance: (Idle hours/non-productive hours) × Standard wage rate per hour) = 4 hours × ₹90 = ₹360 (adverse)

(c) Labour efficiency variance: [(Actual units produced × Standard hours per unit) – Actual hours worked] × Standard wage rate = [(850 × 1/20) – 36] × ₹90 = ₹585 F

Total labour cost variance: ₹100 A + ₹360 A + ₹585 F = ₹125 F

2. *Factory overhead variance:* (Actual overhead costs – Standard overhead costs charged to production) = [₹6,200 – ₹6,375 (₹7.5 × 850 units)] = ₹175 (favourable)

Two-variance method:

(a) Controllable variance: (Actual overhead costs – Budgeted overhead costs at standard hours) = (₹6,200 – ₹6,062.50) = ₹137.50 (adverse)

Budgeted overhead costs:

Fixed expenses (40 hours × ₹125)	=	₹5,000
Variable expenses (42.5 hours × ₹25)	=	1,062.50
		6,062.50

(b) Volume variance: (Normal capacity in hours – Standard hours) × Fixed overhead rate per hour (40 – 42.5) × ₹125 = ₹312.50 F

Total overhead variance = ₹137.50 A + ₹312.50 F = ₹175 (favourable)

P.19.22 From the following data, compute the following: (1) Total overhead variance, (2) Overhead expenditure variance, (3) Overhead volume variance, (4) Overhead calendar variance, (5) Overhead capacity variance, and (6) Overhead efficiency variance. **LO 19.4,5** **LOD: M**

Particulars		*Budgeted*		*Actual*
Production (units)		10,000		12,000
Production (hours)		5,000		6,100
Number of days		25		27
Overhead expenses:				
Fixed	₹3,00,000		₹3,70,000	
Variable	1,00,000	₹4,00,000	1,20,000	₹4,90,000

Solution

1. *Total overhead variance:* (Actual overheads incurred – Standard overheads charged to production) = (₹4,90,000 – ₹4,80,000) = ₹10,000 (adverse)

   SOR:

Standard fixed overhead rate (₹3,00,000 ÷ 10,000 units)	₹30
+ Standard variable overhead rate (₹1,00,000 ÷ 10,000 units)	10
Standard overhead rate per unit	40
Standard overheads (12,000 units)	₹4,80,000
Standard overhead rate per hour (₹60 + ₹20)	80

2. *Overhead expenditure variance:* (Actual overheads incurred – Budgeted overheads at standard hours) = (₹4,90,000 – 4,20,000) = ₹70,000 (adverse)

   Budgeted overheads:

Fixed overheads	₹3,00,000
Plus variable overheads (6,000 standard hours × ₹20, SVOR per hour)	1,20,000
	4,20,000

3. *Overhead volume variance:* (Normal capacity in hours – Standard hours) × SFOR per hour = (5,000 hours – 6,000 hours) × ₹60 = ₹60,000 (favourable)
4. *Overhead calendar variance:* (Budgeted working days – Actual working days) × SFOR per day = (25-27) × ₹12,000, that is, (₹3,00,000 ÷ 25 days) = ₹24,000 (favourable)
5. *Overhead capacity variance:* (Normal capacity in hours on the basis of actual working days – Actual hours used) × SFOR per hour = (200 hours per day × 27 = 5,400 hours – 6,100 hours) × ₹60 = ₹42,000 (favourable)

6. *Overhead efficiency variance:* (SH – AH) × SOR per hour = (6,000 hours – 6,100 hours) × ₹60 = ₹6,000 (adverse)

P. 19.23 A chemical company produces a chemical which has a standard cost per 50 litres as follows: LO 19.2,3,4 LOD: D

Material	
15 litres of A @ ₹20	₹300
35 litres of B @ ₹2.5	87.50
Labour	
2 hours @ ₹20	40
Factory overhead	
Variable, 2 hours @ ₹75	150
Fixed, 2 hours @ ₹50	100
	677.50

Actual results for the current year are as follows:

Production completed : 5,00,000 litres
Direct labour-hours : 21,000 @ ₹22 per hour
Material usage : 1,60,000 litres of A @ ₹20 per litre and 3,60,000 litres of B @ ₹2.5 per litre
Variable factory overhead : ₹16,50,000
Fixed factory overhead : ₹13,00,000
Normal capacity 25,000 direct labour-hours

Inventory data:

Opening: 25,000 litres, 100 per cent complete as to materials and 50 per cent complete as to labour and overheads.

Closing: 40,000 litres, 100 per cent complete as to materials, and 50 per cent complete as to labour and overheads.

Determine and analyse the following: (1) Material cost variances (2) Labour cost variances (3) Overhead cost variances.

Solution

1. *Materials cost variances:* (Standard cost of 5,15,000 litres – Actual cost of 5,15,000 litres) = (₹39,91,250 – ₹41,00,000) = ₹1,08,750 (adverse)

Standard cost: (₹387.50 ÷ 50 litres = ₹7.75) × 5,15,000 litres	₹39,91,250
Actual cost:	
1,60,000 litres of A (×) ₹20	32,00,000
3,60,000 litres of B (×) ₹2.50	9,00,000
	41,00,000

5,15,000 litres = Production completed + Closing stock – Opening stock = 5,00,000 litres + 40,000 litres – 25,000 litres

(a) Materials price variance: = Nil

(b) Materials mix variance: (RSQ – AQ) × SR

Material A:	1,56,000 litres – 1,60,000] × ₹20 =	₹80,000 (adverse)
B:	3,64,000 litres – 3,60,000] × ₹2.50 =	10,000 (favourable)
		70,000 (adverse)

(c) Material yield variance: (SY – AY) × SMC per unit = (5,20,000 litres – 5,15,000) × ₹7.75 = ₹38,750 (adverse)

2. *Labour cost variance:* (Standard labour cost of 5,07,500 litres – Actual labour cost of 5,07,500 litres) = (₹4,06,000 – ₹4,62,000) = ₹56,000 (adverse)

Standard labour cost: (₹40 ÷ 50) × 5,07,500 litres = ₹4,06,000

(a) Labour rate variance: (SR – AR) × AH = (₹20 – ₹22) × 21,000 = ₹42,000 (adverse)

(b) Labour efficiency variance: (SH – AH) × SR = (20,300 hours – 21,000 hours) × ₹20 = ₹14,000 (adverse)

Standard hours = (5,07,500 ÷ 25) × 2 = 20,300 hours; 5,07,500 litres = 5,00,000 litres + 20,000 litres Closing, (0.50 × 40,000) – 12,500 litres, opening (0.50 × 25,000)

3. *Overhead cost variance:* (Actual overheads incurred – Standard overheads of 5,07,500 litres) = (₹29,50,000 – ₹25,37,500) = ₹4,12,500 (adverse)

Standard overheads: (₹250 ÷ 50) × 5,07,500 = ₹25,37,500

(a) Spending variance: (Actual overheads – Budgeted overhead at AH) = ₹29,50,000 – ₹28,25,000 = ₹1,25,000 (adverse)

Budgeted overheads:

Fixed overheads (25,000 hours × ₹50) (Assuming normal capacity as the basis of absorption of fixed overheads)	₹12,50,000
Plus variable overheads (21,000 hours × ₹75)	15,75,000
	28,25,000

(b) Variable overheads efficiency variance: (SH – AH) × SVOR = (20,300 hours – 21,000 hours) × ₹75 = ₹52,500 (adverse)

(c) Fixed overheads efficiency variance: (SH – AH) × SFOR = (20,300 hours – 21,000 hours) × ₹50 = ₹35,000 (adverse)

(d) Capacity variance: (NH – AH) × SFOR = (25,000 hours – 21,000 hours) × ₹50 = ₹2,00,000 (adverse)

P. 19.24 The Amindon Company Ltd produces a product with the following standard cost per unit: **LO 19.2,3,4** **LOD: D**

Material	2 kgs at ₹50	₹100
Labour	5 hours at ₹20	100
Overheads	5 hours at ₹40	200
		400

The overhead rate for the year was determined on the basis of the following data:

Fixed overheads	₹25,00,000
Variable overheads	75,00,000
Expected output (units)	5,00,000

Actual data for the year was as follows:

1. Purchases 1,00,000 kgs of material at ₹49 per kg.
2. Labour was obtained at a price of ₹31 per hour.
3. Production completed, 37,500 units.
4. Labour-hours, 1,90,000.
5. Material used, 90,000 kgs.
6. Fixed overheads, ₹25,00,000.
7. Variable overheads, ₹58,90,000.

Inventories data: Opening, 1,000 units, 50 per cent complete as to material, labour and overhead.
Closing, 4,000 units, 75 per cent complete as to material, labour and overhead.

REQUIRED

1. Calculate material price variance at the point of purchase and issue,
2. Calculate labour variances,
3. Calculate fixed factory overhead variances, and
4. Calculate variable factory overheads variances.

Solution

1.(a) *Material purchase price variance:* (SR – AR) × AQ purchased = (₹50 – ₹49) × 1,00,000 kgs = ₹1,00,000 (favourable)

(b) *Material price variance* (at the time of issue): (SR – AR) × AQ used = (₹50 – ₹49) × 90,000 kgs = ₹90,000 (favourable)

2. *Labour variance:*

Labour cost variance = (Standard labour cost of 40,000 units* – Actual labour cost) = [₹40,00,000 – 58,90,000] = ₹18,90,000 (adverse)

*Units produced during the year:

Production completed	37,500
Plus closing inventory (4,000 × 0.75)	3,000
Less opening (1,000 × 0.50)	500
	40,000

(a) Labour rate variance: (SR – AR) × AH = (₹20 – ₹31) × 1,90,000 = ₹20,90,000 (adverse)

(b) Labour efficiency variance: (SH – AH) × SR = [2,00,000 hours or (40,000 × 5) – 1,90,000 hours] × ₹20 = ₹2,00,000 (favourable)

3. *Fixed factory overhead variance:* (Actual fixed overhead incurred – Standard fixed overhead charged to production) = [₹25,00,000 – (40,000 units × ₹50, SFOR)] = ₹5,00,000 (adverse)

SFOR = Fixed overheads/Expected output = ₹25,00,000/50,000 units = ₹50 per unit

SFOR = ₹25,00,000/2,50,000 hours (50,000 × 5) = ₹10 per hour

(a) Spending variance: (Actual overheads – Budgeted overheads) = (₹25,00,000 – ₹25,00,000) = Nil

(b) Efficiency variance (SH – AH) × SOFR per hour = (2,00,000 hours – 1,90,000 hours) × ₹10 = ₹1,00,000 (favourable)

(c) Capacity variance: (NH – AH) × SFOR per hour = (2,50,000 hours – 1,90,000 hours) × ₹10 = ₹6,00,000 (adverse)

4. *Variable factory overheads variance:* (Actual variable overheads incurred – Standard variable overheads charged to production of 40,000 units) = ₹58,90,000 – (40,000 × ₹150, SVOR) = ₹1,10,000 (favourable)

SVOR = ₹75,00,000 ÷ 50,000 units = ₹150 per unit

SVOR = ₹75,00,000 ÷ 2,50,000 hours = ₹30 per hour

(i) Spending variance: (Actual variable overheads – Budgeted variable overheads at actual hours) = ₹58,90,000 – 57,00,000 = ₹1,90,000 (adverse)

(ii) Efficiency variance: (SH – AH) × SVOR (2,00,000 hours – 1,90,000 hours) × ₹30 = ₹3,00,000 (favourable)

REVIEW QUESTIONS

LOD: Easy

RQ.19.1 Indicate whether the following statements are true or false. **LO 19.2,3,4**

(i) Material price variance is an uncontrollable variance.

(ii) The purchase manager is held accountable for unfavourable material usage variance.

(iii) Material mix variance measures whether the proportion of total actual quantity of materials used is in conformity with the standard proportion specified.

(iv) Material mix variance is controllable variance.

(v) Labour efficiency variance is favourable when actual hours used are higher than standard hours-allowed.

(vi) Labour rate variance is the product of difference in wage rates (standard and actual) and total standard hours.

(vii) Normal loss of materials is considered while setting standard related to material quantity to be used in producing a product.

(viii) A product requires use of materials X, Y and Z in making a product (to be used in a standard proportion). Assume material quantity various is favourable, it implies material mix sub-variance for each material X, Y and Z will also be favourable.

(ix) Unfavourable fixed overhead spending variance implies that the firm is not working upto its full capacity.

(x) Variable overhead efficiency variance is the product of difference in hours (actual and standard) and standard variable overhead rate per hour.

[Answers: (i) True, (ii) False, (iii) True, (iv) False, (v) False, (vi) False, (vii) True, (viii) False, (ix) False, (x) True.]

RQ.19.2 Fill in the following blanks (in same cases choices are provided). **LO 19.2,3,4**

(i) Idle time variance is always ______________ variance (favourable/unfavourable).

(ii) For unfavourable material mix variance ______________ manager is held accountable.

(iii) Management should focus more on ______________ variances (efficiency/rate).

(iv) Efficiency variances by and large are ______________ variances (controllable/uncontrollable).

(v) If variable overhead efficiency is favourable, it also implies that ______________ will also be favourable.

(vi) Volume variance is sub-divided into fixed overhead efficiency variance and ______________.

(vii) Difference in quantity of material used is multiplied by ______________ to determine material quantity variance (actual price/standard price).

(viii) Rate variances, by and large, are ______________ variances (controllable/uncontrollable).

(ix) If actual labour hours used are more than normal capacity hours, capacity variance is said to be ______________. (favourable/unfavourable).

(x) Material yield variance is ______________ when standard yield is higher than actual yield (favourable/unfavouralbe).

[Answers: (i) unfavourable, (ii) production, (iii) efficiency, (iv) controllable, (v) labour efficiency and fixed overhead efficiency variances, (vi) capacity variance, (vii) standard price, (viii) uncontrollable, (ix) favourable, (x) unfavourable.]

RQ.19.3 What is the significance of the term "variance" relating to standard costing? What types of variances are computed for **(a)** materials, **(b)** labour, and **(c)** factory overheads? **LO 19.1**

RQ.19.4 Distinguish between:

1. Labour rate variance and Labour efficiency variance. **LO 19.3**
2. Variable overheads and Fixed overheads. **LO 19.4**
3. Materials price variance and Materials usage variance. **LO 19.2**

RQ.19.5 State the significance and the method of computing the following:

1. Materials mix variance. **LO 19.2**
2. Variable overhead efficiency variance. **LO 19.4**
3. Fixed overhead efficiency variance. **LO 19.4**

RQ.19.6 From the following figures given to you, calculate material variances: LO 19.2

Particulars	*Material X*	*Material Y*
Standard price per kg.	₹240	₹320
Actual price paid per kg.	227.50	308
Actual quantity (kgs.)	16	13

The standard production for the period is 400 units, for which the standard quantity allowances for material are 30 kgs. of X and 25 kgs. of Y. Actual production for the period is 192 units.

RQ.19.7 The Standard Supply Company Ltd. produces a single article, which goes through two operating departments. The standard card for this article indicated the following data: LO 19.3

	Standard time (hours)	*Standard rate*	*Total*
Department A	2.2	₹54	₹118.80
Department B	1.6	60	96

The production for the month of August is 1,000 units. The actual labour costs in the two departments were:

	Hours	*Cost*
Department A	2,000	₹1,29,080
Department B	1,800	1,02,000

What are the labour cost and labour efficiency variances?

LOD: Medium

RQ.19.8 What are the differences between two-variance and three-variance analysis of indirect manufacturing costs? What are the variances computed in each case, and how are they calculated? LO 19.5

RQ.19.9 "The presence of under-absorbed overheads reflects operating inefficiency." Discuss. LO 19.4

RQ.19.10 A company produces a certain chemical, the standard material cost being: LO 19.2

40 per cent of material *X* at ₹20 per kg.

60 per cent of material *Y* at ₹30 per kg.

A standard loss of 10 per cent is expected in production. During one month, 171 kgs. of chemical was produced from the use of 90 kgs. of material *X* at ₹18 per kg. and 110 kgs. of material *Y* at ₹34 per kg. Calculate the following variances for the month: (i) materials price variance, (ii) materials mix variance, and (iii) materials yield variance.

RQ.19.11 Using the following information, calculate each of the three labour variances for each department: LO 19.3

	Department X	*Department Y*
Gross wages (direct)	₹2,80,800	₹1,93,700
Standard hours worked	8,640	6,015
Standard rate per hour	30	34
Actual hours worked	8,200	6,395

RQ.19.12 A gang of workers normally consists of 10 skilled, 5 semi-skilled and 5 unskilled, paid at standard hourly rates of ₹40, ₹30 and ₹20, respectively. In a normal working week of 40 hours, the gang is expected to produce 1,000 units of output. LO 19.3

In a certain week, the gang consisted of 13 skilled, 4 semi-skilled and 3 unskilled, 72 hours were worked, actual wages paid amounted to ₹25,000, and 1,000 units of output were produced.

Present the information in respect of labour cost variance arising during this period.

RQ.19.13 The standard overhead rate per unit of product is as follows: Variable, ₹20 + Fixed (₹30,000 ÷ 3,000), ₹100 = ₹120. **LO 19.4**

Standard time for producing each unit of output is 10 hours. During a period, the following actual data is available:

Hours worked, 27,000; Output, 2,600 units.

Overheads = Variable, ₹50,000 + Fixed, ₹2,80,000 = ₹3,30,000.

Calculate different overheads variances, including efficiency variance and capacity variance.

RQ.19.14 From the following information, compute the various variances: **LO 19.2,3,4**

Standard:	
Materials quantity	1 kg per unit
Materials price	₹14 per kg
Direct labour-hours	1.5 hours per unit
Labour rate	₹30 per unit
Overheads	₹10 per standard direct labour-hour
Capacity	5,000 units
Actual:	
Materials purchased	10,000 kgs
Material price	₹15 per kg
Materials used	5,400 kgs
Direct labour hours	8,000
Labour rate	₹3,150 per hour
Overheads	₹88,000
Units produced	5,000

RQ.19.15 Calculate overhead variances for the following data. **LO 19.5**

Items	*Budgeted*	*Actual*
Number of working days	20	22
Man-hours per day	8,000	8,400
Output per man-hour (units)	1	0.9
Overhead cost	₹16,00,000	₹16,80,000

RQ.19.16 In Department X, the following data is submitted for the week ended February 20: **LO 19.4**

Standard output for 40 hours per week (units)	1,400
Standard fixed overhead	₹14,000
Actual output (units)	1,200
Actual hours worked	32
Actual fixed overhead	₹15,000

Calculate the relevant overhead variances.

RQ.19.17 From the following data for a factory for the month of January, compute overhead variances under the four-way analysis: **LO 19.5**

	Standard	*Actual*
Number of units produced	15,000	8,000
Capacity (hours)	30,000	17,000
Variable overheads	₹3,00,000	₹1,55,000
Fixed overheads	4,50,000	4,60,000

LOD: Difficult

RQ.19.18 A chemical company produces a petro-product, using the following proportion of material: LO 19.2

Particulars	(kgs.)	Cost per kg.	Amount
Material A	50	₹50	₹2,500
Material B	40	60	2,400
Material C	60	30	1,800
	150		6,700
Standard shrinkage ($33\frac{1}{3}$%)	50	—	—
Net weight and costs	100	67	6,700

A recent production-run yielding 100 kgs. output required an input of:

Particulars	(kgs.)	Per kgs.	Amount
Material A	40	₹52	₹2,080
Material B	55	60	3,300
Material C	65	26	1,690
	160		7,070

Calculate materials price, mix, and yield variances.

ANSWERS

19.6 MCV, ₹348 U, MPV, ₹356 F, MUV, ₹718.55 U, MMV, ₹14.54 F.
19.7 LCV, ₹16,280 U, LRV, ₹15,080 U, LEV, ₹1,200.
19.10 **(a)** ₹260 U,
(b) ₹100 F,
(c) ₹260 U,
19.11 Department X (Labour variances): Cost, ₹21,600 U, Rate, ₹34,800 U, Efficiency, ₹13,200 F. Department Y: Cost, ₹10,810 F, Rate, ₹23,730 F, Efficiency, ₹12,920 U.
19.12 TLCV = ₹1,000 F, LEV = ₹24,400 U (LMSV ₹3,600 U + LESV ₹20,800 U), LRV = ₹25,400 F.
19.13 **(a)** TOCV = ₹18,000 U;
(b) VOSV = ₹4,000 F,
VOEV = ₹2,000 U, and
TVOCV = ₹2,000 F
(c) FOSV = ₹20,000 F,
FOEV = ₹10,000 U, CV ₹ 30,000 U = TFOCV ₹20,000 U
19.14 Material: Cost variance, ₹11,000 U, MPV, ₹5,400 U, MUV, ₹5,600 U; Labour: Cost variance, ₹27,000 U, LRV, ₹12,000 U, LEV, ₹15,000 U; Overhead: Cost variance, ₹13,000 U, Spending variance, ₹8,000 U, Efficiency variance, ₹5,000 U.
19.15 Total overhead variance, ₹16,800 U, spending, ₹80,000 U, volume, ₹63,200 F (Calendar ₹16,000 F, Efficiency, ₹1,84,800 U, Capacity, ₹88,000 F).
19.16 Total fixed overhead variance, ₹3,000 U: Spending, ₹1,000 U, Efficiency, ₹800 F, Capacity, ₹2800 U.
19.17 Total overhead variance, ₹2,15,000 U: Spending, ₹5,000 F, Variance efficiency, ₹10,000 U, Fixed efficiency, ₹15,000 U, Capacity, ₹1,95,000 U.
19.18 MPV, ₹180 F, MMV, ₹103.30 U, MYV, ₹446.90 U.

[Comprehensive solutions to all numerical review questions are available on the companion website: http://www.mhhe.com/khan_jain_ma7e]

CASE

C.19.1 (Material Cost Variance): *Concrete cement Ltd* manufactured 15,000 bags of cement during the month of October of current year. Consumption of raw material during the period was as follows:

Table showing consumption and of raw material (actual and standard)

Material	*Quantity Used (tons)*	*Standard Mix per bag (kg)*	*Actual Price (₹/ton)*	*Standard Price (₹/ton)*
Gypsum	110	8	780	780
Limestone	155	11	754	750
Clay	200	12	268	270
Sand	350	22	153	150

The company uses variance analysis as a tool of cost control. Variances are computed with reference to standard cost; the company ensures that standards set are reliable and attainable given the working milieu of the firm. Also, standards are revised from time-to-time in the light of changed circumstances.

The Management Accountant of the firm calculates the relevant material cost variances as follows:

He prepares a table that indicates total standard material cost (TSMC) and total actual material cost (TAMC) of actual units produced.

Table showing TAMC and TSMC of 15,000 units

Materials	*Actual Material Cost(TAMC)*			*Standard Material Cost (TSMC)*		
	TAQ (tons)	*AP (₹)*	*TAMC (₹)*	*TSQ (tons)*	*SP (₹)*	*TSMC (₹)*
Gypsum	110	780	85,800	120	780	93,600
Limestone	155	754	1,16,870	165	750	1,23,750
Clay	200	268	53,600	180	270	48,600
Sand	350	153	53,550	330	150	49,500
	815		3,09,820	795		3,15,450

1. TMCV = TAMC — TSMC
   = (₹3,09,820 — ₹3,15,450)
   = ₹5,630 (Favourable)

   (i) Material Price variance(MPV): (AP-SP) * AQ
   Gypsum = (₹780 — ₹780) * 110 tons = Nil
   Limestone = (₹754 — ₹750) * 155 tons = ₹620 (Unfavourable)
   Clay = (₹268 — ₹270) * 200 tons = ₹400 (Favourable)
   Sand = (₹153 — ₹150) * 350 tons = ₹1,050 (Unfavourable)
   ₹1,270 (Unfavourable)

   (ii) Material Quantity Variance(MQV): (AQ — SQ) * SP
   Gypsum = (110 — 120) * ₹780 = ₹7,800 (Favourable)
   Limestone = (155 — 165) * ₹750 = ₹7,500 (Favourable)
   Clay = (200 — 180) * ₹270 = ₹5,400 (Unfavourable)
   Sand = (350 — 330) * ₹150 = ₹3,000 (Unfavourable)
   ₹6,900 (Favourable)

TMCV shows positive variance implying firm's actual cost to purchase raw material is less than the standard cost. It results in lower cost of production and eventually to higher profits.

MPV comes out to be adverse. Since purchase manager is responsible for making purchases at a price higher than standard price, management held him accountable for deviating from standards.

On the other hand, the organisation appreciates the efforts of the production manager, as MQV is favorable and rewards him adequately in recognition of his efficient performance.

Despite the best practices (of cost control) being followed by the company, there has been a continuous decline in sales and as a result the company is rapidly losing its market share. In view of these developments, in recent past, the management of the company is much tensed.

The purchase manager has been held accountable for higher price paid to purchase materials compared to the standard price. On the other hand, the management is very much satisfied with the efficient production system & so with the production manager. But the management could not identify the actual reason of declining sales being faced by the firm.

Even Management Accountant is perplexed to see what is happening and is unable to understand the reason of substantial reduction in sales.

On finding Management Accountant incapable of coming out with an appropriate course of action and eventually of taking a corrective measure, the firm hires the services of a financial consultant, Mr. Eloquent, to help the firm regain its lost market share. Mr. Eloquent analyses the whole situation and submits the following report:

TMCV = TAMC — TSMC
= (TAQ * AP) — (TSQ * SP)
= (₹3,09,820 — ₹3,15,450)
= ₹5,630 (Favourable)

Since TAMC is lower than TSMC allowed, TMCV is evidently favourable. It is apparent that difference in price paid for materials purchased in relation to standards and difference in quantity of materials used are the two factors causing this variance. Accordingly, TMCV can be bifurcated into two sub-variances:

(i) Material price variance: (AP — SP) * AQ (at ₹1,270 unfavourable)
Strike at the supplier's factory forced the firm to make purchases at a higher rate from others resulting in unfavourable price variance. MPV (adverse) is caused due to factors beyond the control of purchase manager as well as of the organisation as a whole.
Mr. Eloquent, therefore, suggested that purchase manager should not be held liable and there is no immediate need of any remedial measures. Hence, there is no need to revise the standard price at this very moment.

(ii) Material quantity variance: (₹6,900 favourable)
Prima facie, MQV appears favourable on account of the following reasons:
1. There is no careless handling in use of materials.
2. No use of sub-standard/defective material in the production process.
3. Company employs adequately trained workers.
4. Training programs are conducted on regular basis for existing workforce.
5. Machines are well maintained causing negligible break-down of machines.
6. Workers are well motivated.
7. Working environment of the organisation is very pleasant.

But a close look at the situation reveals that the production manager has used more of cheaper inputs (sand and clay) and less of expensive materials (Gypsum and limestone). As a result, he could achieve favorable variance at the cost of low quality of the product. If such a mix were possible, the management itself would have set such a standard mix.

By altering the product mix production manager has successfully reduced the material quantity variance but resulted in poor quality of the product. It has an adverse bearing on the brand/image of the company's product. It is, primarily, the reason for reduction in sales and consequent pruning of market share. Therefore, there is a need to isolate the impact of material mix sub-variance (from MQV).

Determination of MMSV involves two steps:

Step 1:

Table showing calculation of standard Mix of 815 tons of Materials used

Material	*Standard Mix*
Gypsum	815 * 120/795 = 123
Limestone	815 * 165/795 = 169
Clay	815 * 180/795 = 185
Sand	815 * 330/795 = 338

Step 2:

MMSV = (Actual mix — Standard mix) * Standard price

Table showing computation of MMSV

Material	*Actual Mix*	*Standard Mix*	*SP*	*MMSV*
Gypsum	110	123	780	₹10,140 (Favourable)
Limestone	155	169	750	₹10,500 (Favourable)
Clay	200	185	270	₹4,050 (Unfavourable)
Sand	350	338	150	₹1,800 (Unfavourable)
				₹14,790 (Favourable)

Table showing computation of Material Quantity Variance (Revised)

MQV	₹6,900 (Favourable)
Less: MMSV	₹14,790 (Favourable)
MQV (Revised)	₹7,890 (Unfavourable)

It is important to emphasize that earlier pseudo conclusion of the management (based on MQV) of the better performance of the production manager gets reversed. In contrast, he has actually used more of raw materials (815 tons) than was allowed (795 tons) which gets reflected in MQV (revised).

Conclusion:

Therefore, production manager should be held accountable for loss in sales and not the purchase manager. Purchase manager is not even responsible for negative/adverse MPV as it resulted due to factors beyond his control.

Mr. Eloquent further mentions that the words favourable/positive and unfavourable/adverse are merely indicative of the direction of variance from the SC. They need not be necessarily good or bad from the point of view of the firm. Such a qualitative analysis can be made only after the underlying cause of the variance has been determined.

Therefore, the firm should not be guided by quantitative facts only. The firm should also look into the qualitative aspects of variance analysis as numbers alone can distort the true picture and, therefore, may cause distortion in assigning responsibilities to various managers.

20

Revenue and Profit Variance Analysis

Learning Objectives

After reading this chapter you will be able to:

LO 20.1 Discuss sales variances and their causes
LO 20.2 Illustrate the various profit variances
LO 20.3 Understand reconciliation of actual profit and budgeted profit
LO 20.4 Explain the method of reporting variances
LO 20.5 Examine the methods for disposing off variances

Introduction

The preceding chapter has dealt with the determination and analysis of variances relating to three major elements of manufacturing cost, namely, materials, labour and factory overheads. Outside the manufacturing areas, standard costs and variances are usually not incorporated in the accounts, but are determined by supplemental analysis.[1] For this reason, variances relating to selling and administrative costs were not discussed in the preceding chapter. In this chapter, attention is directed to the determination and analysis of revenue variances. The chapter first deals with sales variances, followed by profit variances. A comprehensive illustration has been attempted to cover all revenue and expenses variances, to provide a summary to management, of all variances responsible for deviations in actual profit as compared to budgeted profit. To be more specific, effort will be made to reconcile actual profit with budgeted profit. The chapter subsequently deals with variance reporting and disposition of variances respectively. The main points are also summarised by way of recapitulation.

Sales Variances

LO 20.1 Discuss sales variances and their causes

The principal sales variances are sales revenue variances. They are divided into **(a)** Sales price variance, **(b)** Sale volume variance sub-divided into **(i)** Sales mix sub-variance, and **(ii)** Sale volume sub-variance.

Sales Revenue Variance

Sales revenue variance is the difference between the standard sale value and the actual sale value

Like material cost variance, sales revenue variance (SRV) is the aggregate variance or net variance. It is determined by the difference between the standard sales value (SSV) and actual sales value (ASV). The formula may be abbreviated as follows:

$$SRV = SSV - ASV \text{ (unfavourable)} \quad (20.1)$$

$$SRV = ASV - SSV \text{ (favourable)} \quad (20.2)$$

The chief causes responsible for SRV may be one or more of the following:

1. Actual sales prices are more or less than budgeted sales price (Sales price variance).
2. Actual sales volume is larger or smaller than budgeted sales volume (Sales volume variance).
3. Actual sales-mix is different from the standard sales-mix originally envisaged in the budget (Sales-mix variance). Such a variance will result only in the case of multi-product manufacturing and selling companies.
4. Actual sales allowance is more or less than the budgeted/standard allowance.

Sales Price Variance The sales price variance (SPV) is a sub-variance of SRV. This variance, like material price variance, is obtained by the difference between actual selling price (ASP) and standard selling price (SSP) multiplied by actual units (AQ) sold. Like the SRV, the SPV formula can be abbreviated as follows:

$$SPV = (ASP - SSP) \times AQ \text{ (favourable)} \quad (20.3)$$

$$SPV = (SSP - ASP) \times AQ \text{ (unfavourable)} \quad (20.4)$$

The possible reasons for unfavourable sales price variance are as follows:

1. Unforeseen market competitive conditions forcing the organisation to cut its planned sales price.
2. Management decisions to try new marketing strategies in terms of changing the channel of distribution from retailers followed hitherto to wholesalers.
3. Management decisions to tap new markets, and decisions to offer products at lower than standard prices. This may particularly hold true for export markets, and large tenders from reputed business units, or government departments having prospects of a perpetual source of demand in the future.
4. Latitude allowed to individual sales managers or sales people in quoting prices.[2]

In the case of multi-product firms, the SPV is to be determined for each line of the product sold.

Sales Volume Variance Sales volume variance (SVV) emanates from the difference in the actual product units sold and the planned sales of product units. The formula for determining SVV can be stated as follows:

$$SVV = [(\text{Actual volume (AQ)} - \text{Standard volume (SQ)}] \times \text{Standard selling price (favourable)} \quad (20.5)$$

$$SVV = (SQ - AQ) \times \text{Standard selling price (unfavourable)} \quad (20.6)$$

The following reasons[3] can contribute to SVV:

1. Unexpected competition,
2. Ineffective sales promotion,
3. Ineffective advertising,
4. Customers meeting adverse business conditions, thus, unable to take their usual order, and
5. Lack of proper supervision and control of salesmen.

To have a complete picture, sales volume variance should be determined for each line of the product sold.

In the case of a single-product firm, SPV and SVV together will account for total SRV. However, in the case of multi-product firms, it is necessary to have a break-up of sales volume variance into two sub-variances: **(1)** Sales mix sub-variance, and **(2)** Sales volume sub-variance.

Sales Mix Sub-Variance Sales mix sub-variance, or sales-mix variance (SMV) originates when the actual sales-mix deviates from the standard sales-mix. SMV will be present only when the proportion of actual units sold differs from the standard proportion. Therefore, this variance does not bear any relationship whatsoever with the sales volume variance. It may be quite possible that actual total quantity sold varies very significantly from the planned sales quantity. Yet, there is no SMV. Likewise, there is a possibility of a reverse situation also. Consider Examples 20.1 and 20.2.

◆ Example 20.1

(No Sales Mix Variance)
The following is a summary statement of budgeted and actual sales (for January) of ABC Ltd:

Products	*Budgeted (units)*	*Actual (units)*	*Budgeted selling price*
A	5,000	4,000	₹40
B	4,000	3,200	50
C	1,000	800	100
	10,000	8,000	

Determine sales-mix variance.

Solution

Sales mix variance (SMV) = [Standard mix of actual quantity sold (RSQ) – Actual mix of actual quantity sold (AQ)] × Standard selling price **(20.7)**

The respective standard proportion of products, A, B, and C is 5:4:1 [5,000 (A), 4,000 (B), 1,000 (C)]. The RSQ of products A, B and C would be:

A : 8,000 × 5/10 = 4,000 units
B : 8,000 × 4/10 = 3,200 units
C : 8,000 × 1/10 = 800 units

Incorporating the calculated values in Equation (20.7), we have

SMV = (RSQ – AQ) × Standard selling price
A : (4,000 – 4,000) × ₹40 = Nil
B : (3,200 – 3,200) × ₹50 = Nil
C : (800 – 800) × ₹100 = Nil

The entire variance pertains to sales volume sub-variance.

◆ Example 20.2

(No Sales Volume Sub-Variance)
The following is a summarised sales report of XYZ Ltd:

Products	*Budgeted sales (units)*	*Actual sales (units)*	*Budgeted selling price*
X	5,000	4,200	₹40
Y	4,000	4,500	50
Z	1,000	1,300	100
	10,000	10,000	

Determine the sales-mix variance.

Solution

Sales mix variance SMV = (RSQ – AQ) × Selling price

X : (5,000 – 4,200) × ₹40 = ₹32,000 (unfavourable)
Y : (4,000 – 4,500) × ₹50 = 25,000 (favourable)
Z : (1,000 – 1,300) × ₹100= 30,000 (favourable)
Net SMV 23,000 (favourable)

There is no sales volume sub-variance as total units sold are identical with the total budgeted sales units. Thus, the sales-mix variance alone accounts for the entire sales volume variance.

The net SMV is likely to be favourable, when in actual sales there is a larger proportion of such products which have higher selling prices, as compared to their corresponding standard proportions. When there is a larger proportion of lower selling price products in the actual units sold, the emerging net SMV is likely to be unfavourable. However, it is important to note that in net SMV some product(s) will have favourable SMV, while other(s) will have unfavourable SMV. For instance, in Example 20.2, sales-mix variances for products Y and Z are favourable while, for product X, are unfavourable. For products, X, Y, and Z individually all SMV cannot be either favourable or unfavourable. Some of them will be favourable, while other(s) will be unfavourable.

Sales Volume Sub-Variance Sales volume sub-variance (SVSV) is the second part of sales volume variance. Like material yield variance, it is based on the *aggregate* figures of budgeted sales and actual sales, the difference so obtained being multiplied by average selling price. The following are the formulae for determining sales volume sub-variance:

SVSV (favourable) = [Total actual units sold – Total budgeted unit sales] × Average standard selling price **(20.8)**

SVSV (unfavourable) = [Total budgeted unit sales – Total actual units sold] × Average standard selling price **(20.9)**

Consider Example 20.3.

◆ Example 20.3

Hypothetical Ltd budgets to sell in the first quarter of the current year, 500 units of product X at ₹30 per unit, 400 units of product Y at ₹20 per unit, and 100 units of product Z at ₹50 per unit. During the quarter, actual sales were as follows:

— 400 units of product X at ₹40 per unit.
— 500 units of product Y at ₹10 per unit.
— 50 units of product Z at ₹40 per unit.

You are required to determine all sales variances.

Solution

Determination of Sales Variances (SRV)

Product	*Standard*			*Actual*		
	Quantity (SQ) (units)	*Price (SSP)*	*Total sales*	*Quantity (AQ) (units)*	*Price (ASP)*	*Total sales*
X	500	₹30	₹15,000	400	₹40	₹16,000
Y	400	20	8,000	500	10	5,000
Z	100	50	5,000	50	40	2,000
	1,000	28	28,000	950		23,000

SRV = (TSV – ASV) = ₹28,000 – ₹23,000 = ₹5,000 (unfavourable)

SPV = (ASP – SSP) × AQ

X: (₹40 – ₹30) × 400 units = ₹4,000 (favourable)

Y: (₹10 – ₹20) × 500 units = 5,000 (unfavourable)

Z: (₹40 – ₹50) × 50 units = 500 (unfavourable)

Total SVP = 1,500 (unfavourable)

SVV = (AQ – SQ) × Standard selling price

X: (400 – 500) × ₹30 = ₹3,000 (unfavourable)

Y: (500 – 400) × ₹20 = 2,000 (favourable)

Z: (50 – 100) × ₹50 = 2,500 (unfavourable)

Total SVV = 3,500 (unfavourable)

There are two sub-parts of SVV:

(i) *Sales-mix variance:* (SMV) = (RSQ – AQ) × Standard selling price

X: [475 (950 × 5/10) – 400] × ₹30 = ₹2,250 (unfavourable)

Y: [380 (950 × 4/10) – 500] × ₹20 = 2,400 (favourable)

Z: [95 (950 × 1/10) – 50] × ₹50 = 2,250 (unfavourable)

= 2,100 (unfavourable)

(ii) *Sales volume sub-variance:* SVSV = [Total budgeted sales of all products – Total actual units sold] × Average standard selling price = (1,000 – 950) × ₹28 = ₹1,400 (unfavourable)

Confirmation: SRV = ₹5,000 (unfavourable) consisting of:

(i) SPV = ₹1,500 (unfavourable)

(ii) SMV = 2,100 (unfavourable)

(iii) SVSV = 1,400 (unfavourable)

PROFIT VARIANCES

LO 20.2 Illustrate the various profit variances

Sales variances are significant as they have a direct bearing on profits earned by the organisation. In fact, sales variances can be used as the basis of determining profit variance.

Profit variance = Sales revenue variance – Standard cost of sales of products not sold (The formula will hold true when there are no cost variances).

The importance of the determination of profit variance lies in the fact that it helps management to take the necessary remedial actions to achieve its profit target. It enables management to assign responsibility to the heads of various responsibility *centres.* In fact, it may provoke management to probe into the matter by looking into the sales performance territory-wise, or market-channel-wise. Above all, it permits scrutiny of the performance of individual sales managers.

The principal profit variance is *overall profit variance.* It is divided into: **(a)** Sales price variance, **(b)** Sales volume variance sub-divided in to **(i)** Sales mix sub-variance, **(ii)** Sales volume sub-variance, and **(c)** Cost variance.

Except cost variance, there is no difference between the various sales variances and profit variances as, their names as well as break-up are identical. Such variances have, therefore, not been discussed here. Nevertheless, it is important to note the changes in the formulae in respect of those profit variances which differ from selling variances.

Overall Profit Variance

Standard/budgeted profit – Actual profit (unfavourable)
Actual profit – Standard/budgeted profit (favourable)
Standard profit can be determined in either of the following ways:

(i) *Profit Basis:* Number of budgeted units sold for each product × Standard profit per unit of the concerned product **(20.10)**

(ii) *Cost Basis:* Under both the methods = [Standard sales revenue of budgeted sales of each product – Standard cost of budgeted sales of each product] **(20.11)**

In the case of multi-product firms, a product-wise break-up should be made.

The calculation of actual profit is simple, that is, (Actual quantity sold × Actual profit per unit) or (Actual sales revenue – Actual costs incurred).

Sales Price Variance The formula is the same (20.3) as the difference in selling prices directly affects the profits or losses of the firm.

Sales Volume Variance The formula, from the point of view of determining profit variance, needs minor modification. The amended formula is:

(AQ – SQ) × Standard profit per unit (favourable) **(20.12)**
(SQ – AQ) × Standard profit per unit (unfavourable) **(20.13)**

Sales Mix Variance and Sales Volume Sub-Variances The expression, standard price, would be substituted for standard profit and average standard profit respectively.

Sales mix variance = (RSQ – AQ) × Standard profit per unit **(20.14)**
Sales volume sub-variance = [Total budgeted sales – Total actual sales] × Average standard profit **(20.15)**

Cost Variances As the name suggests, the cost variance will result when actual costs differ from standard costs. Since the previous chapter has already enumerated the various cost variances in detail, reference to their calculations can be made from that chapter. In brief, cost variances can be determined by the following formula:

(Standard cost – Actual cost) × Actual quantity sold (favourable) **(20.16)**
(Actual cost – Standard cost) × Actual quantity sold (unfavourable) **(20.17)**

The computation of profit variances is illustrated in Example 20.4.

◆ Example 20.4

In Example 20.3 of Hypothetical Ltd, assume that standard costs of products X, Y, and Z respectively are ₹20, ₹10 and ₹30. Further, assume that actual costs are in line with budgeted costs.

You are required to determine the profit variances.

Solution

Computation of Profit

Products	*Standard*			*Actual*		
	SQ (units)	*Profit per unit (SP)*	*Total profit*	*AQ (units)*	*Profit per unit (AP)*	*Total profit*
X	500	₹10	₹5,000	400	₹20	₹8000
Y	400	10	4,000	500	0	Nil
Z	100	20	2,000	50	10	500
	1,000	11	11,000	950		8,500

Standard selling price – Standard costs = Standard profit

X: (₹30 – ₹20) = ₹10 per unit
Y: (₹20 – ₹10) = ₹10 per unit
Z: (₹50 – ₹30) = ₹20 per unit

Overall profit variance: Budgeted profit – Actual profit = ₹11,000 – ₹8,500 = ₹2,500 (unfavourable)

(i) Sales price variance: ₹1,500 (unfavourable) (See solution to Example 20.3)

(ii) Sales volume variance: (SQ – AQ) × SP per unit

X (500 – 400) × ₹10	=	₹1,000 (unfavourable)
Y (400 – 500) × ₹10	=	1,000 (favourable)
Z (100 – 50) × ₹20	=	1,000 (unfavourable)
Total	=	1,000 (unfavourable)

(a) Sales mix sub-variance: (RS Q – AQ) × SP per unit

X (475 – 400) × ₹10	=	₹750 (unfavourable)
Y (380 – 500) × ₹10	=	1,200 (favourable)
Z (95 – 50) × ₹20	=	900 (unfavourable)
Total	=	450 (unfavourable)

(b) *Sales volume sub-variance:* [Total budgeted sales of all production - Total actual units sold] × Average standard profit per unit = (1,000 – 950) × ₹11 = ₹550 (unfavourable)

Confirmation: Overall profit variance = ₹2,500 (unfavourable). It consists of (i) Sales price variance, ₹1,500 (unfavourable), (ii) Sales mix variance, ₹450 (unfavourable), and (iii) Sales volume sub-variance, ₹550 (unfavourable)

Alternatively, overall profit variance:

Sales revenue variance	₹5,000 (unfavourable)
Less standard cost of sales of products not sold:	
100 units of X at ₹20	2,000 (unfavourable)
100 units of Y at ₹10	1,000 (favourable)
50 units of Z at ₹30	1,500 (unfavourable)
Profit variance	2,500 (unfavourable)

So far, we have assumed that there are no cost variances. Let us now incorporate cost variances also to complete the discussion on profit variance.

Assuming that the actual cost per unit of products X, Y and Z are ₹22, ₹8 and ₹28 respectively as against ₹20, ₹10 and ₹30 assumed earlier, the effects of cost variances on profit variances are shown below:

Determination of actual profit: (AP – AC) = AP × AQ = Total profit

X (₹40 – ₹22) = ₹18 × 400	=	₹7,200
Y (₹10 – ₹8) = ₹2 × 500	=	1,000
Z (₹40 – ₹28) = ₹12 × 50	=	600
Total		8,800

Overall profit variance:

Standard profit =	₹11,000
Actual profit	8,800
	2,200 (unfavourable)

Cost variance: (SC – AC) × AQ

X (₹20 – ₹22) × 400	=	₹800 (unfavourable)
Y (₹10 – ₹8) × 500	=	1,000 (favourable)
Z (₹30 – ₹28) × 50	=	100 (favourable)
Total		300 (favourable)

Confirmation: Overall variance given in solution to Example 20.4 =	₹2,500 (unfavourable)
Less cost variance	300 (favourable)
Total profit variance	2,200 (unfavourable)

ACTUAL PROFIT AND BUDGETED PROFIT: RECONCILIATION

LO 20.3 Understand reconciliation of actual profit and budgeted profit

As stated earlier, the primary objective of variance analysis is to enable management to know the responsibility centres which can be held accountable for various variances. In operational terms, management should be informed about various cost and revenue variances so that it may know the various reasons why actual profits have differed from the budgeted profits. For control purposes, the information regarding the profit earned by the firm on the basis of historical cost recording will not be as relevant as the information on the basis of standard cost. For this reason, an income statement depicting actual costs and standard costs and variances along with their causes is of greater value to management *vis-à-vis* a historical income statement. Such a statement, as can be seen from the following proforma income statement (**Format 20.1**) and subsequent example, clearly highlights inefficiencies causing lower profits, and also efficient factors (like labour efficiency) adding to more profits. In brief, such information will be of immense practical utility to management in controlling cost.

FORMAT 20.1 Proforma Income Statement (Reconciliation)

	Favourable	Unfavourable	
Budgeted sales revenue:			
Sales variance adjustment (Product-wise details may be given):			
Sales price variance			
Sales mix variance			
Sales volume sub-variance			(+) or (–) as the case may be
Actual sales revenue:			
Less: standard cost in units sold:			
Material (direct)	....		
Labour (direct)	....		
Other direct expenses (if any)	....		
Variable overheads (main details may be given)			
Fixed overhead (main details may be given.	....	....	
Budgeted profit			
Cost variances:			
Material			
Price variance			
Yield variance			
Mix variance			

(*Contd.*)

(Contd.)

Labour variances:		
Rate variance		
Mix variance		
Efficiency variance		
Idle time variance		
Variable overhead variances:		
Spending variance		
Efficiency variance		
Fixed overhead variances:		
Spending variance		
Efficiency variance		
Capacity variance		
Calendar variance		
		(+) or (–) as the case may be
Actual profit	______	______

It may be noted that transactions relating to taxation, interest and dividends do not form a part of this income statement because these items are non-controllable costs.

Consider Example 20.5.

◆ Example 20.5

The income statement of Modern Electricals Ltd for the first quarter of the current year is given as follows:

Sales revenue (18,000 units)		₹ 72,00,000
Less: cost of goods sold:		
Direct materials	₹43,28,000	
Direct labour	11,66,000	
Other direct expenses	3,04,000	
Factory overheads	4,40,000	
Administrative and selling expenses	3,20,000	65,58,000
Net profit		6,42,000

The standard output and sales for the period was 20,000 units and the standard cost and profit per unit is as under:

Direct material (3 units at the rate of ₹75)	₹225
Direct labour (3 hours at the rate of ₹20)	60
Other direct expenses	15
Factory overheads:	
Fixed overheads	15
Variable	10
Administrative and selling charges (fixed)	15
Total standard cost	340
Standard profit	40
Selling price (standard)/(budgeted)	380

Labour was paid at the rate of ₹22 per hour and material prices were ₹80 per unit. Factory overheads (actual) include ₹2,80,000, fixed, and the balance amount represents variable. There was no inventory at the beginning or at the end of the year. The company employs labour-hour rate as the basis of absorption of fixed overheads.

You are required to:

1. Calculate, cost, sales, and profit variances.
2. Prepare a reconciliation statement of profit variances with as many details as possible.

Solution

Elements of cost	Standard			Actual		
	Input (units/hours)	Rate	Total cost	Input (units/hours)	Rate	Total cost
Direct materials	54,000	₹75	₹40,50,000	54,100	₹80	₹43,28,000
Direct labour	54,000	20	10,80,000	53,000	22	11,66,000
Other direct expenses	18,000	15	2,70,000	N.A.	N.A.	3,04,000
Factory overheads:						
Fixed	54,000	5.0	2,70,000	53,000	Not required	2,80,000
Variable	54,000	₹10/3	1,80,000	53,000	Not required	1,60,000
Administrative and selling charges	18,000	15	2,70,000	18,000	Not required	3,20,000
			61,20,000			65,58,000

(A) *Total cost variance:* TSC – TAC = (₹61,20,000 – ₹65,58,000) = ₹4,38,000 (unfavourable)

1. Material cost variance: SMC – AMC = (₹40,50,000 – ₹43,28,000) = ₹2,78,000 (unfavourable)
   (a) *Material price variance:* (SR – AR) × AQ = (₹75 – ₹80) × 54,100 = ₹2,70,500 (unfavourable)
   (b) *Material usage variance:* (AQ – SQ) × SR = (54,100 – 54,000) × ₹75 = ₹7,500 (unfavourable)
2. Labour cost variance: SLC – ALC = ₹10,80,000 – ₹11,66,000 = ₹86,000 (unfavourable)
   (a) *Labour rate variance*: (SR – AR) × AH = (₹20 – ₹22) × 53,000 = ₹1,06,000 (unfavourable)
   (b) *Labour efficiency variance*: (SH – AH) × SR = (54,000 – 53,000) × ₹20 = ₹20,000 (favourable)
3. Direct expense variance: Standard expenses – Actual expenses = ₹2,70,000 – ₹3,04,000 = ₹34,000 (unfavourable)
4. Fixed overhead variance: (Actual fixed overheads incurred – Standard fixed overheads charged to production) = (₹2,80,000 – ₹2,70,000) = ₹10,000 (unfavourable)
   (a) *Fixed overhead spending variance*: Budgeted overheads – Actual overheads = [₹3,00,000 or (20,000 × ₹15) = ₹2,80,000] = ₹20,000 (favourable)
   (b) *Fixed overhead efficiency variance*:(SH – AH) × Standard fixed overhead rate per hour = (54,000 – 53,000) × ₹5 = ₹5,000 (favourable)
   (c) *Capacity variance*: (Normal capacity in hours – Actual hours utilised) × Standard fixed overhead rate per hour = (60,000 – 53,000) × ₹5 = ₹35,000 (unfavourable)
5. Variable overhead variance: SOC – AOC = (₹1,80,000 – ₹1,60,000) = ₹20,000 (favourable)
   (a) *Variable overhead spending variance*: Actual overheads-Standard overhead cost at actual hours = (₹1,60,000 – ₹1,76,666.67) = ₹16,666.67 (favourable)
   (b) *Variable overhead efficiency variance*: (SH – AH) × Standard variable overhead rate per hour = (54,000 – 53,000) × ₹10/3 = ₹3333.33 (favourable)
6. **(A)** Administrative and selling charges: Standard cost – Actual cost = (₹2,70,000 – ₹3,20,000) = ₹50,000 (unfavourable)
   (a) *Administrative overhead spending variance*: Budgeted overheads–Actual overheads = (₹3,00,000 – ₹3,20,000) = ₹20,000 (unfavourable)

(b) *Capacity variance:* (Normal output and sales – Actual output and sales) × Standard overhead rate per unit = (20,000 – 18,000) × ₹15 = ₹30,000 (unfavourable)

(B) *Sales revenue variance (SRV):* Budgeted sales – Actual sales
₹76,00,000 – ₹72,00,000 = ₹4,00,000 (unfavourable)

(a) *Sales price variance (SPV):* (ASP – SSP) × AQ = (₹400 – ₹380) × 18,000 = ₹3,60,000 (favourable)

(b) *Sales volume variance (SVV):* (SQ – AQ) × SSP = (20,000 – 18,000) × ₹380 = ₹7,60,000 (unfavourable)

(C) *Profit Variance:*
Standard profit – Actual profit (₹8,00,000 – ₹6,42,000) = ₹1,58,000 (unfavourable)

(a) *Sales price variance:* ₹3,60,000 (favourable) (calculated above)

(b) *Sales volume variance:* = (SQ – AQ) × Standard profit per unit
= (20,000–18,000) × ₹40 = ₹80,000 (unfavourable)

(c) *Cost variance* already calculated = ₹4,38,000 (unfavourable)

Profit Reconciliation Statement (taking sales as basis)

Particulars			Amount
Budgeted sales revenue (20,000 × ₹380)			₹76,00,000
Sales revenue variance:	*Favourable*	*Unfavourable*	
Sales price variance	₹3,60,000		
Sales volume variance		(₹7,60,000)	(4,00,000)
Actual sales revenue			72,00,000
Less: standard cost of 18,000 units sold:			
Direct materials		40,50,000	
Direct labour		10,80,000	
Other direct expenses		2,70,000	
Factory overheads: Fixed		2,70,000	
Variable		1,80,000	
Administrative and selling charges		2,70,000	61,20,000
Budgeted net profit			10,80,000
Cost variances:			
Material price variance		2,70,500	
Material usage variance		7,500	
Labour rate variance		1,06,000	
Labour efficiency variance	20,000		
Direct expenses variance		34,000	
Fixed overhead spending variance	20,000		
Fixed overhead efficiency variance	5,000		
Capacity variance		35,000	
Variable overhead spending variance	16,666.67		
Variable overhead efficiency variance	3333.33		
Administrative overhead spending variance		20,000	
Capacity variance		30,000	4,38,000
Actual profit			6,42,000

The profit reconciliation statement shows that cost variances are primarily responsible for distorting the profit picture. Within cost variances, efficiency variances, in general, are favourable. Price variance pertaining to material and labour account for a substantial portion of unfavourable cost variance. It may be possible that material prices may have gone up in the market and so the labour rate, warranting upward revision of their standard rates. The favourable sales price variance further confirms the necessity for the same. The fact that whatever is produced is sold indicates that idle capacity variance is a reflection of the inefficiency of the production department. The production manager should be called for explanation, and efforts should be made to overcome all production hurdles in future to ensure normal production.

VARIANCE REPORTING

LO 20.4 Explain the method of reporting variances

Basically, variances can be favourable or unfavourable. While it is true that unfavourable variances call for management attention, favourable variances should not be completely ignored, the reason being that favourable variances do not always necessarily mean efficient performance. For instance, a favourable labour efficiency variance may result not merely from more efficient means of producing output, but may also be at the cost of the quality of the product. Similarly, material price variance may arise due to the use of sub-standard material acquired at a lower price although, the fact that the variance is favourable may *prima facie* be indicative of economical procurement at lower prices.

The unfavourable variances also are not necessarily due to inefficient performance. To illustrate, an unfavourable material price variance may have been caused by the purchase of better quality than the budgeted ones. The recruitment of better skilled and trained workers may lead to an unfavourable labour rate variance.

In view of these possibilities, favourable and unfavourable variances should not be taken at their face value; there is rather a need for indepth analysis and investigation by management. The degree of investigation will depend upon: **(i)** The nature of variance—controllable or uncontrollable and **(ii)** The significance in terms of its magnitude and frequency of occurrence.

Controllable variances are variances that are controllable at the level of various responsibility centres.

The controllable variances are those that are controllable at the level of the various responsibility centres. Examples of such variances are material usage variance, labour efficiency, and overhead efficiency variances. The variances that are generally not controllable include material price variance, labour rate variance, and fixed and variable spending variances. The solution to uncontrollable variances in most situations is a revision of the relevant standards. Controllable variances merit management attention and should be properly reported.

The second factor having a bearing on the degree of investigation is the amount and frequency of occurrence of the variances. The larger the amount of variance, the more significant it is to the management. Moreover, the likelihood of a variance recurring is of still greater significance to management. Thus, if the variance is both large and persistent, management should analyse it in detail to identify the probable causes. Whether a variance is large enough will vary from firm to firm, and within the same firm from one operation to another. One possible approach to determine whether the size of the variance is significant, is the establishment of arbitrary limits based on managerial judgement. A better alternative would be to look at the trend of past variances. If, for example, in the past, a particular operation has frequently generated variances of say, 10 per cent, this 10 percent can be used to determine whether the size of a variance in that operation is significant or not. This 10 per cent variance represents the cut-off or tolerance limit for purposes of determining the significance of a variance of a particular size. Moreover, the variance should also be viewed in the light of the *tightness* of the underlying standards. If the standards are tight, a higher tolerance limit may be set. If the standards are attainable, a lower tolerance limit may be more appropriate.

The variances can be expressed either in absolute figures or in relative figures. The relative figures are usually shown in the form of ratios. The key ratios relating to the variances are listed below:

$$\text{Material price variance ratio} = \frac{\text{Actual price}}{\text{Standard price}} \quad (20.18)$$

$$\text{Material usage variance ratio} = \frac{\text{Actual quantity}}{\text{Standard quantity required for actual output}} \quad (20.19)$$

$$\text{Material yield ratio} = \frac{\text{Actual output (yield)}}{\text{Standard yield from actual output}} \quad (20.20)$$

$$\text{Material cost variance ratio} = [\text{Material price variance ratio} \times \text{Material usage variance ratio}] \quad (20.21)$$

$$\text{Labour rate variance ratio} = \frac{\text{Actual wage rate}}{\text{Standard wage rate}} \quad (20.22)$$

$$\text{Labour efficiency variance ratio} = \frac{\text{Actual hours}}{\text{Standard hours required for actual production}} \quad (20.23)$$

$$\text{Labour cost variance ratio} = \text{Labour rate variance ratio} \times \text{Labour efficiency variance ratio} \quad (20.24)$$

$$\text{Overhead expenditure variance ratio} = \frac{\text{Actual overheads incurred}}{\text{Budgeted overheads required for actual output, that is, Fixed overheads} + [\text{Actual output} \times \text{Variable overhead rate per unit}]} \quad (20.25)$$

$$\text{Volume (capacity) variance ratio or overhead utilisation ratio} = \frac{\text{Actual production}}{\text{Normal production}} \quad (20.26)$$

A good management reporting system requires that top management should be furnished with such other ratios also which gauge the overall performance of the business firm from the point of view of assessing its utilisation of capacity, labour, material and other resources. Some significant ratios for the purpose are enumerated below:

$$\text{Efficiency ratio} = \frac{\text{Standard hours required for actual production}}{\text{Actual hours worked}} \times 100 \quad (20.27)$$

$$\text{Activity ratio} = \frac{\text{Standard hours required for actual output}}{\text{Budgeted standard hours}} \times 100 \quad (20.28)$$

$$\text{Capacity usage ratio} = \frac{\text{Budgeted hours}}{\text{Normal capacity hours}} \times 100 \quad (20.29)$$

$$\text{Capacity utilisation ratio} = \frac{\text{Actual hours worked}}{\text{Budgeted hours}} \times 100 \quad (20.30)$$

The capacity utilisation, activity and efficiency of ratios are illustrated in Example 20.6.

◆ Example 20.6

Product X takes 5 hours to make and Y requires 10 hours. In a month of 25 effective days of 8 hours a day, 1,000 units of X and 600 units of Y were produced. ABC Ltd employs 50 workers in the production department. The budgeted hours are 1,02,000 for the year. Calculate capacity utilisation ratio, activity ratio and efficiency ratio.

Solution

Computation of Ratios

$$\text{Capacity utilisation ratio} = \frac{\text{Actual hours worked*}}{\text{Budgeted hours}} \times 100 = \frac{1,20,000}{1,02,000} \times 100 = 117.65 \text{ per cent}$$

*Actual hours worked in a year = Working hours per day × Number of workers × Number of effective days in a year × 12 months = (8 × 50 × 25 × 12) = 1,20,000 hours

$$\text{Activity ratio} = \frac{\text{Standard hours required for actual production}}{\text{Budgeted standard hours}} \times 100 = \frac{1,32,000}{1,02,000} \times 100 = 129.41 \text{ per cent}$$

Standard hours required (yearly basis) = Standard hours required to produce a unit × Number of units produced per year

Product X = (5 × 1,000 × 12) =	60,000
Product Y = (10 × 600 × 12) =	72,000
	1,32,000

$$\text{Efficiency ratio} = \frac{\text{Standard hours required for actual production}}{\text{Actual hours worked}} \times 100 = \frac{1,32,000}{1,20,000} \times 100 = 110 \text{ per cent}$$

Once the tolerance limits, namely, upper control limit and lower control limit, have been determined, significant variance can be reported in two forms: **(i)** In graphic form and **(ii)** In a tabular format.

The graphic method/control chart is the effective method of reporting significant variances. Figure 20.1 presents the control chart.

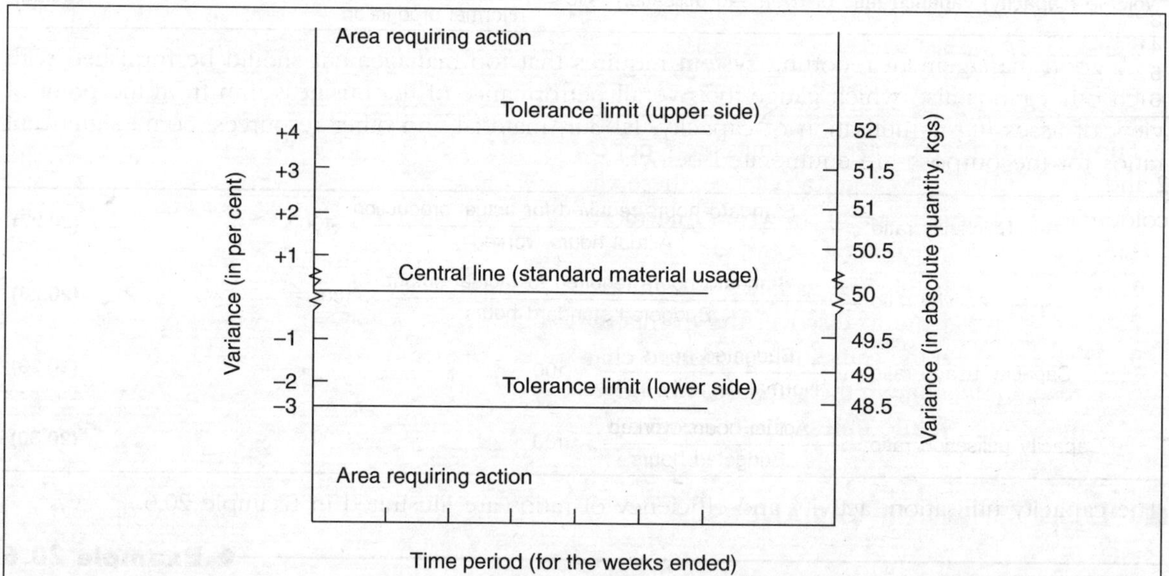

FIG. 20.1 *Control Chart*

It is a graphic report of the materials usage variance in a production department over a period of about 1.5 months. It exhibits variances as percentages of standard quantity required. The central line represents standard material usage required per unit. On both sides of this line, there are tolerance limits: 4 per cent on the upper side and 3 per cent on the lower side. It is significant to observe that tolerance excess usage (4 per cent of standard) is greater than the tolerance variance below standard (3 per cent). It may be needed to maintain the product quality, in the sense that, if material consumption falls below the minimum, it may so adversely effect the product quality that the products may be rejected when put to a quality test. From Figure 20.1, it is apparent that management is not required to initiate any control action as the actual observations at different times are within control limits.

The immense utility of graphs, for the purpose of understanding broad relationships and trends notwithstanding, they tend to be less precise and informative than tabulations. Therefore, to fill up the gap and to provide the full information to the top management, the tabulation method of variance reporting is appropriate. Under this method, there are four columns: **(i)** Standard cost, **(ii)** Actual cost, **(iii)** Variance, and **(iv)** Those variances that exceed the required cut-off point. The last column would require management attention. Example 20.7 presents information on a tabular basis of the production department of a company for six weeks.

Example 20.7

Week	*Standard cost of material allowed for actual output*	*Actual cost*	*Variance: Favourable (F)/ Adverse (A)*	*Relative amount (per cent)*
1	₹3,000	₹3,015	₹15 A	0.5
2	2,400	2,496	96 A	4.0
3	2,400	2,280	120 F	5.0
4	3,300	3,311	11 A	0.3
5	3,000	3,030	30 A	1.0
6	2,400	2,424	24 A	1.0

Suppose further that tolerance limits are 3 per cent of standard; the variance for consecutive weeks, 2 and 3 require investigation. In practice, these variances may either be circled or written in different colours or may be separately shown in one more column added to the above presentation.

Steps involved in variance reporting

1. Determine whether the variance is significant.
2. If it is, investigate to discover the events, which caused the variance.
3. Depending on the cause, take action to change future operating conditions, or to re-plan with a resulting change in the standard, or budget so that this variance will not recur from the same cause in the future unless the corrective action was ineffective.

DISPOSITION OF VARIANCES

LO 20.5 Examine the methods for disposing off variances

Cost variances may be disposed off by following either of the following two methods: (i) They may be transferred to the current year's income statement; or (ii) They may be considered as cost of the product and, thus, can be allocated to work-in-process, finished goods and cost of goods sold. In fact, the scientific procedure is to judge each variance individually and then to make a decision based on the nature of the cause of the variance. Therefore, there is no question of exclusive adoption of one or another. Both are complementary in character. For instance, unfavourable material price variance caused by a permanent increase in the prices of raw materials should be considered as a part of the cost of the product, and accordingly should be allocated to product cost. On the other hand, idle capacity variance caused by operating 1,000 direct labour-hours instead of 2,000 normal direct labour-hours per fortnight should be written off against the current year's revenues, as they represent losses caused by inactivity; these are cost of inefficiencies and it would be illogical to consider them as a part of the cost of product. We now illustrate the methods of disposition of variance.

Transfer to Current Period's Income Statement

Under this method, the profit and loss account of the concerned period is debited for unfavourable variances and credited for favourable variances. In the profit and loss account, the net effect of all variances is adjusted to the gross profit figure. If the net variance is favourable, it is added to the gross profit computed at standard costs. The structure of the income statement is illustrated in Format 20.2:

FORMAT 20.2 Variance-adjusted Income Statement

Sales revenue			
Less cost of goods sold (at standard cost)			
Gross profit (at standard cost)			
Adjustment for various variances:			
	Debit balances (unfavourable)	*Credit balances (favourable)*	
Material usage variance			
Labour rate variance			
Spending variance			
Capacity variance			
Material price variance			
Labour efficiency variance			
Fixed overhead efficiency variance			
Variable overhead efficiency variance			
Net variance			
Gross profit (adjusted)			
Less other expenses			....
Net profit			

This method is theoretically sound and practically satisfactory for disposing of variances if standards are *current and attainable* because, variances are valid indicators of departures from cost levels that should have been attained otherwise.

Allocating Variance as Part of the Cost of Goods Sold and Inventories

If standards are tight or loose and do not reflect *currently attainable cost levels*, the standards are not reasonably representative of what costs ought to be. The treatment of charging off net variances to current revenues may result in an overstatement or understatement of the current period's net income. In other words, inventories and cost of goods sold would tend to be incorrectly overvalued or undervalued. In such a case, it is appropriate to adjust work-in-process, finished goods inventory and cost of goods sold figures to actual costs by allocating the manufacturing variances among them. The amount allocated to each of these accounts (work-in-process, finished goods inventory and cost of goods sold inventory), would be determined by the relative proportion of standard cost in each amount, to the total amount of that standard cost charged to production during the period as illustrated in Example 20.8.

◆ **Example 20.8**

Accounts	Materials		Labour		Factory overhead	
	Amount	Per cent	Amount	Per cent	Amount	Per cent
Work-in-process	₹2,000	20	₹1,000	20	₹6,000	40
Finished goods inventory	3,000	30	1,000	20	1,500	10
Cost of goods sold	5,000	50	3,000	60	7,500	50
Total standard cost	10,000	100	5,000	100	15,000	100
Total actual cost	11,000		6,000		17,000	

Material price variance	₹1,000 (unfavourable)
Labour efficiency variance	1,000 (unfavourable)
Controllable variance	500 (favourable)
Volume variance	2,500 (unfavourable)

Show the allocation of the variances.

Solution

Allocation of Variances

Name of the variance	Total amount	Work-in-process	Finished goods inventory	Cost of goods sold
Materials price variance	₹1,000 (U)	₹200	₹300	₹500
Labour efficiency variance	1,000 (U)	200	200	600
Controllable variance	1,500 (F)	(200)	(50)	(250)
Volume variance	2,500 (U)	1,000	250	1,250
Total	4,000	1,200	700	2,100

Further, supposing that sales revenue is ₹25,000, the income statement of hypothetical company would appear as follows:

Income Statement (Method I)

Sales revenue	₹25,000
Cost of goods sold [standard adjusted to actual (₹15,500 + ₹2,100)]	17,600
Gross profit (actual)	7,400
Less other expenses (assumed)	1,900
Net profit	5,500

Income Statement (Method II)

	Debit balances	Credit balances	
Sales revenue			₹ 25,000
Cost of goods sold (standard cost)			15,500
Gross profit (standard)			9,500
Adjusted for variances:			
Material price variance	₹1,000		
Labour efficiency variance	1,000		
Controllable variance:		₹500	
Volume variance	2,500		
Net debit variance	(4,500)	500	(4,000)
Gross profit (adjusted)			5,500
Less other expenses			1,900
Net profit			3,600

The net profit under the second method is more by ₹1,900 (₹5,500 – ₹3,600). The difference is attributable to the following:

Cost added to:

Work-in-process	₹1,200
Finished goods inventory	700
	1,900

In Example 20.8, it is assumed that there is no material inventory. In practice, the situation is not likely to be so. In such a situation, the material price variance would partly be allocated to materials inventory, and the balance in the three accounts in the manner shown above.

SUMMARY

- The second major category of variances consists of (i) Sales variances and (ii) Profit variances.
- Sales Variances are summarised below:

Variance	*Formula*
Sales revenue variance (*SRV*) (unit basis)	[(*AQ* × *ASP*) – (*BQ* × SSP)]
or *SRV* (aggregate basis)	*TASR* – *TBSR/TSSR*
(a) Sales price variance (*SPV*)	(*ASP* – *SSP*) × *AQ* sold
(b) Sales volume variance (*SVV*)	(*TAQ* – *TBQ*) × *SSP* per unit
or	
(i) Sales mixture sub-variance (*SMSV*)	(*RSQ* – *AQ*) × *SSP*
and	
(ii) Sales quantity sub-variance (*SQSV*)	(*TAQ* – *TBQ*) × Weighted average *SSP*

Where,

AQ	Actual units sold
ASP	Actual selling price per unit
BQ	Budgeted sales in units
SSP	Standard (budgeted) selling price per unit
TASR	Total actual sales revenue
TBSR	Total budgeted/standard sales revenue
TAQ	Total actual sales in units
TBQ	Total budgeted sales in units
RSQ	Revised standard quantity, i.e. standard mix of actual units sold

LO 20.1

- Profit variances are summarised below:

Variance	*Formula*
Profit variance (unit basis)	[(*AP* × *AO*) – (*BP* × *AO*)]
or Profit variance (aggregate basis)	*TAP* – *TBP*
or	
(A) Sales price variance	(*ASP* – *SSP*) × *AQ* sold
(B) Sales volume variance	(*TAQ* – *TBQ*) × BP per unit
or	
(i) Sales mixture sub-variance	(*RSQ* – *AQ*) × *BP* per unit
(ii) Sales quantity sub-variance	(*TAQ* – *TBQ*) × Weighted average budgeted profit per unit
(C) Cost variance	(*AC* – *SC*) × *AQ* sold

Where,

AP	Actual profit per unit
BP	Budgeted/standard profit per unit
TAP	Total actual profit
TBP	Total budgeted profit
TAQ	Total actual units sold
TBQ	Total budgeted sales in units
AC	Actual cost per unit
SC	Standing/budgeted cost per unit

LO 20.2

- The primary aim of variance analysis is to enable the management to assign responsibility for the deviations. For purposes of managerial control, an income statement depicting actual costs and standard costs and variances along with their causes is prepared. This is referred to as proforma income statement (reconciliation) to reconcile the actual profits and budgeted profits.

LO 20.3

- Another aspect of variance analysis is variance reporting. The variances can be reported either in absolute figures or in relative figures in terms of ratios. The key ratios relating to variances are: **(i)** Material price variance ratio, **(ii)** Material usage variance ratio, **(iii)** Material yield variance ratio, **(iv)** Material cost variance ratio, **(v)** Labour rate variance ratio, **(vi)** Labour efficiency variance ratio, **(vii)** Labour cost variance ratio, **(viii)** Overhead expenditure variance ratio, **(x)** Efficiency ratio, **(xi)** Activity ratio, and **(xii)** Capacity usage/Utilisation ratio.

LO 20.4

- Finally, cost variances may be disposed of in either of two ways: **(i)** They may be transferred to the current year's income statement, or **(ii)** They may be considered as cost of the product, and allocated as part of cost of goods sold and inventory.

LO 20.5

REFERENCES

1. C.L. Moore and Robert K., Jaedicke, *Managerial Accounting*, (South West Publishing Co, Ohio, 1972), p. 378.
2. Jack Gray and Kenneth S. Johnston, Accounting and Management Action, (McGraw Hill, New York, 1977), p. 653.
3. J. Batty, *Standard Costing*, (Macdonald and Evans Ltd, London, 1970), p. 263.

SOLVED PROBLEMS

P.20.1 The budgeted and the actual sales for a month in respect of three products are given below: LO 20.1 LOD: M

Budgeted sales:

Product	*Quantity*	*Price*	*Value*
A	1,000	₹5	₹5,000
B	750	10	7,500
C	500	15	7,500
	2,250		20,000

(Contd.)

(Contd.)

Actuals sales:

Product	Quantity	Price	Value
A	1,200	₹6	₹7,200
B	700	9	6,300
C	600	14	8,400
	2,500		21,900

Calculate sales variances.

Solution

Budgeted Sales

Product	Budgeted Quantity	Budgeted Price	Budgeted Value	Actual Quantity	Actual Price	Actual Value	Actual quantity × Budgeted price
A	1,000	₹5	₹5,000	1,200	₹6	₹7,200	₹6,000
B	750	10	7,500	700	9	6,300	7,000
C	500	15	7,500	600	14	8,400	9,000
	2,250		20,000	2,500		21,900	22,000

Sales variances:

1. *Sales revenue variances* = Actual sales – Budgeted sales = ₹(21,900 – 20,000) = 1,900 (favourable)
2. *Sales volume variances* = (Actual quantity – Budgeted quantity) × Budgeted selling price per unit
   A : (1,200 – 1,000) × ₹5 = ₹1,000 (favourable)
   B : (700 – 750) × ₹10 = 500 (adverse)
   C : (600 – 500) × ₹15 = 1,500 (favourable)
   2,000 (favourable)
3. *Sales price variance* = (Actual price – Budgeted price) × Actual quantity
   A : (₹6 – ₹5) × 1,200 = 1,200 (favourable)
   B : (₹9 – ₹10) × 700 = 700 (adverse)
   C : (₹14 – ₹15) × 600 = 600 (adverse)
   100 (adverse)

   Sales volume variance has the following two components:
4. *Sales mix variance* = (Standard mix of AQ sold – Actual mix) × Budgeted selling price per unit
   A : (2,500 × 4/9 = 1111.11 – 1,200) × ₹5 = ₹444 (favourable)
   B : (2,500 × 3/0 = 833.33 – 700) × ₹10 = 1,333 (unfavourable)
   C : (2,500 × 2/9 = 555.56 – 600) × ₹15 = 667 (favourable)
   222 (unfavourable)
5. *Sales volume sub-variance* = (Total budgeted unit sales – Total actual units sold) × Average budgeted selling price
   = (2,250 – 2,500) × ₹20,000/2,250 = ₹2,222 (favourable)

P.20.2 Royal Industries Ltd provides the following data regarding actual and budgeted sales, costs and profit for a month of the current year: **LO 20.2** **LOD: M**

Budgeted data

Product	Quantity (units)	Selling price per unit	Sales value	Cost per unit	Total cost	Standard profit (SP) per unit	Total profit
A	4,000	₹15	₹60,000	₹7.50	₹30,000	₹7.50	₹30,000
B	4,800	25	1,20,000	12.50	60,000	12.50	60,000
C	7,200	40	2,88,000	20.00	1,44,000	20.00	1,44,000
	16,000	29.25	4,68,000		2,34,000		2,34,000

Actual data

A	3,600	15	54,000	7.50	27,000	7.50	27,000
B	4,000	26	1,04,000	13.00	52,000	13.00	52,000
C	6,400	37.50	2,40,000	20.00	1,28,000	17.50	1,12,000
	14,000		3,98,000		2,07,000		1,91,000

Compute sales and profit variances.

Solution

(A) Sales variances (*SRV*): (Budgeted sales-Actual sales)=(₹4,68,000–₹3,98,000) = ₹70,000 (adverse/unfavourable)

1. *Sales price variance* (SPV) : (SSP – ASP) × AQ

   Product A: (₹15 – ₹15) × 3,600 units = Nil
   B: (₹25 – ₹26) × 4,000 units = ₹4,000 (favourable)
   C: (₹40 – ₹37.50) × 6,400 units = 16,000 (adverse)
   12,000 (adverse)

2. *Sale mix sub-variance* (SMSV): (RSQ – AQ) × SSP

   Product A: (3,500 units – 3,600 units) × ₹15 = ₹1,500 (favourable)
   B: (4,200 units – 4,000 units) × ₹25 = 5,000 (adverse)
   C: (6,300 units – 6,400 units) × ₹40 = 4,000 (favourable)
   500 (favourable)

   *Standard proportion is 4,000: 4,800: 7,200 for products A, B and C, that is, ₹5: 6: 9 or 5/20, 6/20, 9/20 (of 14,000 units sold) respectively.

3. *Sales volume sub-variance (SVSV):* [Total budgeted sales of all products – Total actual sales of all products] × Weighted standard selling price = (16,000 units – 14,000 units) × ₹29.25 = ₹58,500 (adverse)

4. *Sales volume variance (overall):* (SQ – AQ) × SSP

   Product A: (4,000 units – 3,600 units) × ₹15 = ₹6,000 (adverse)
   B: (4,800 units – 4,000 units) × ₹25 20,000 (adverse)
   C: (7,200 units – 6,400 units) × ₹40 32,000 (adverse)
   58,000 (adverse)

Confirmation: SPV, ₹12,000 (A) + SMSV, ₹500 (F) + SVSV, ₹58,500 (A) = ₹70,000 (adverse)

(B) *Profit variance (overall):* (Budgeted profit–Actual profit) = (₹2,34,000 – ₹1,91,000) = ₹43,000 (adverse)

1. *Sales price variance:* ₹12,000 (adverse) (calculated above)

2. *Sales mix sub–variance (SMSV):* (RS Q – AQ) × SP per unit

   Product A (3,500 units – 3,600 units) × ₹7.50 = ₹750 (favourable)
   B (4,200 units – 4,000 units) × ₹12.50 = 2,500 (adverse)
   C (6,300 units – 6,400 units) × ₹20.00 = 2,000 (favourable)
   250 (favourable)

3. *Sales volume sub-variance (SVSV):* [Total budgeted sales of all products-Total actual sales of all products] × Weighted standard profit per unit = (16,000 units-14,000 units) × ₹14,625=₹29,250 (adverse)

4. *Cost variance:* (SC –AC) × AQ sold

   Product A : (₹7.50 – ₹7.50) × 3,600 units = Nil
   B : (₹12.50 – ₹13) × 4,000 units = ₹2,000 (adverse)
   C : (₹20 – ₹20) × 6,400 units = Nil
   2,000 (adverse)

Confirmation: (i) ₹12,000 (A) + (ii) ₹250 (F) + (iii) ₹29,250 (A) + (iv) ₹2,000 (A) = ₹43,000 (A)

P.20.3 The accounting department of SIL Ltd, has furnished the following information to its management for the first quarter of the current year: LO 20.2,3 LOD: M

Standard cost and profit sheet per unit:	
Materials cost (2 kgs @ ₹50)	₹100
Wages (direct, 1 hour @ ₹20 per hour)	20
Variable overhead (1 hour @ ₹20 per hour)	20
Fixed overheads (normal capacity 10,000 buckets per quarter): 1 hour @ ₹40 per hour	40
Total standard cost	180
Standard profit per unit	20
Standard price per unit	200
Budgeted sales: 10,000 units per quarter.	
Actual cost, production and sales data:	
Materials purchased and consumed, 16,500 kgs @ ₹48 per kg	7,92,000
Wages: 9,000 hours @ ₹16 per hour	1,44,000
Variable overheads	1,62,000
Fixed overheads	3,80,000
Actual sales (₹210 per unit)	16,80,000
Actual production (units)	8,000

You are required to:

1. Calculate cost, sales and profit variances.
2. Prepare a reconciliation statement of profit variances with as many details as possible.

Solution

Elements of cost	*Standard*			*Actual*		
	Input (kgs/hours)	*Rate*	*Total cost*	*Input (kgs/hours)*	*Rate*	*Total cost*
Material	16,000	₹50	₹8,00,000	16,500	₹48	₹7,92,000
Wages	8,000	20	1,60,000	9,000	16	1,44,000
Variable overheads	8,000	20	1,60,000	9,000	18	1,62,000
Fixed overheads	8,000	40	3,20,000*	9,000	Not required	3,80,000
			14,40,000			14,78,000

*₹3,20,000 is the standard cost of fixed overheads charged to production.

(A) *Total cost variance:* (Actual cost of 8,000 units – Standard cost of 8,000 units) = (₹14,78,000 – ₹14,40,000) = ₹38,000 (adverse).

1. Material cost variance: (SMC – AMC) = (₹8,00,000 – ₹7,92,000) = ₹8,000 (favourable)
   (a) Material price variance: (SR – AR) × AQ = (₹50 – ₹48) × 16,500 kgs = ₹33,000 (favourable)
   (b) Material usage variance: (SQ – AQ) × SR = (16,000 – 16,500) × ₹50 = ₹25,000 (adverse)
2. Labour cost variance: (SLC – ALC) = (₹1,60,000 – 1,44,000) = ₹16,000 (favourable)
   (a) Labour rate variance: (SR – AR) × AH = (₹20 – ₹16) × 9,000 = ₹36,000 (favourable)
   (b) Labour efficiency variance: (SH – AH) × SR per hour = (8,000 – 9,000) × ₹20 = ₹20,000 (adverse)
3. Variable overhead variance: (SVOC – AVOC) = (₹1,60,000 – 1,62,000) = ₹2,000 (adverse)
   (a) Variable overhead spending variance: (Actual overhead cost incurred – Standard overhead cost at actual hours) = (₹1,62,000 – ₹1,80,000) = ₹18,000 (favourable)
   (b) Variable overhead efficiency: (SH – AH) × Standard VOR per hour = (8,000 – 9,000) × ₹20 = ₹20,000 (adverse)
4. Fixed overhead variance: (Actual fixed overhead spent – Standard fixed overhead charged to production)

   = [₹3,80,000 – ₹3,20,000] = ₹60,000 (adverse)

(a) Fixed overhead spending variance: (Budgeted overhead–Actual overhead)
= [₹4,00,000 – ₹3,80,000]
= ₹20,000 (favourable)

(b) Fixed overhead efficiency variance: (SH–AH) × Standard FOR per hour = (8,000 – 9,000) × ₹40
= ₹40,000 (adverse)

(c) Capacity variance:(Normal capacity in hours–Actual hours utilised) × Standard FOR per hour
= (10,000 – 9,000) × ₹40 = ₹40,000 (adverse)

(B) *Sales variance (sales revenue variance):* (Budgeted sales – Actual sales) = [₹20,00,000 – ₹16,80,000]
= ₹3,20,000 (adverse)

(a) Sales price variance (SPV): (ASP – SSP) × AQ = (₹210 – ₹200) × 8,000 = ₹80,000 (favourable)

(b) Sales volume variance: (SQ – AQ) × SSP = (10,000 – 8,000) × ₹200 = ₹4,00,000 (adverse)

(c) Profit variance: (Standard profit – Actual profit) = ₹2,00,000 – ₹2,02,000* = ₹2,000 (favourable)

*Statement Showing Actual Profit

Actual sales revenue		₹16,80,000
Less: actual costs:		
Materials	₹7,92,000	
Wages	1,44,000	
Variable overheads	1,62,000	
Fixed overheads	3,80,000	14,78,000
Actual profit		2,02,000

1. *Sales price variance* = ₹80,000 (favourable: already calculated)
2. *Sales volume variance* =(SQ–AQ) × Standard profit per bucket = (10,000–8,000) × ₹20
= ₹40,000 (adverse)
3. *Cost variance* = (SC – AC) = ₹14,40,000 – ₹14,78,000 = ₹38,000 (adverse)

(C) *Statement of Reconciliation of Actual Profit with Budgeted Profit*

	Favourable	Adverse	
Budgeted profit			₹2,00,000
(a) Sales variances:			
Sales price	₹80,000		
Sales volume		₹40,000	
(b) Cost variances:			
Material price	33,000		
Material usage		25,000	
Labour rate	36,000		
Labour efficiency		20,000	
Variable overhead spending	18,000		
Variable overhead efficiency		20,000	
Fixed overhead spending	20,000		
Fixed overhead efficiency		40,000	
Capacity		40,000	
	1,87,000	(1,85,000)	2,000
Actual net profit			2,02,000

Alternatively: Profit Reconciliation Statement (taking Sales as Basis)

	Favourable	Adverse	
Budgeted sales revenue (10,000 × ₹200)			₹20,00,000
Sales revenue variance:			
Sales price	₹80,000		
Sales volume		(₹4,00,000)	(3,20,000)
Actual sales revenue			16,80,000

(*Contd.*)

(Contd.)

Less: standard cost of 8,000 buckets sold:			
Material	8,00,000		
Labour	1,60,000		
Variable overheads	1,60,000		
Fixed overheads	3,20,000		14,40,000
Standard net profit			2,40,000
Cost variance:			
Material price	33,000		
Material usage		25,000	
Labour rate	36,000		
Labour efficiency		20,000	
Variable overhead spending	18,000		
Variable overhead efficiency		20,000	
Spending fixed overhead	20,000		
Fixed overhead efficiency		40,000	
Capacity variance		40,000	
	1,07,000	(1,45,000)	(38,000)
Actual net profit			2,02,000

P.20.4 At the end of the current year, the cost accounting department of SK Industries Ltd has furnished the following summary of labour and material variances to its management: **LO 20.2** **LOD: D**

Materials price variance	₹15,68,000 (Dr)
Materials usage variance	49,600 (Dr)
Labour rate variance (skilled labour)	3,84,000 (Dr)
Labour efficiency variance (skilled labour)	13,32,000 (Dr)

Mr Harishanker, the managing director of the company, finds it difficult to understand why the variances are so large. During the year, the company operated at 96,000 direct labour-hours and produced 4,80,000 units.

The standard cost sheet per unit is as follows:

Direct materials (2 units @ ₹12.4)	₹24.80
Direct labour (7.5 minutes @ ₹74 per hour)	9.25

The management is informed that materials can now be purchased only at ₹14 a unit. The material consumed during the period is 9,64,000 units.

The new wage rates of skilled labourers as per the new agreement with their trade union is ₹82. It is also brought to the notice of the management that only 5 units of product can be produced per labour–hour.

You are required to (i) Set up a more realistic schedule of standard unit costs for materials and labour, and (ii) Recompute the variances according to the new schedule.

Solution

(A) Statement showing standard cost per unit	
Material cost (2 units @ ₹14 a unit)	₹28
Direct labour cost (12 minutes @ ₹82 per hour)	16.40
Standard cost per unit (total)	44.40
(B) 1. *Material price variance (revised)*. It would be less by ₹1.6 per unit of raw materials consumed.	
(a) Material price (standard revised)	14
Less material price (existing standard)	12.40
	1.60

(Contd.)

(*Contd.*)

(b) × units produced	9,64,000
	15,42,400
(c) Existing MPV (adverse)	15,68,000
(d) Material price variance (unfavourable)	25,600
2. *Material usage variance (revised)*	
(Standard usage – Actual usage) × ₹1.6 = (9,60,000 units – 9,64,000) × ₹1.6	6,400
Existing MUV (adverse)	49,600
MUV (adverse)	56,000
3. *Labour rate variance (revised)*	
Direct labour rate per hour (revised standard)	82
Less direct labour rate per hour (existing standard)	74
	8
(×) Direct labour hours used	96,000
	7,68,000
Existing labour rate variance (adverse)	3,84,000
Labour rate variance (favourable)	3,84,000
4. *Labour efficiency variance (revised)* = (SH – AH) × SR per hour = (96,000 – 96,000) × ₹82 = Nil	

P.20.5 ABC Ltd follows standard costing system. The standard output for a period is 20,000 units and the standard cost and profit per unit are as under: **LO 20.2,3** **LOD: D**

Direct material (3 units @ ₹15)	₹45
Direct labour, unskilled (3 hours @ ₹10)	30
Direct expenses	5
Factory overheads: Variable	2.5
Fixed	3.0
Administrative overheads	3.0
Total cost	88.50
Profit	11.50
Selling price (fixed by the Government)	100.00

The actual production and sales for a period was 14,400 units. There has been no price revision by the government during the period.

The following are the variances worked out at the end of the period:

	Favourable	*Adverse*
Direct material:		
Price		₹42,500
Usage	₹10,500	
Direct labour:		
Rate		40,000
Efficiency	32,000	
Factory overheads:		
Variable expenditure	4,000	
Fixed expenditure	4,000	
Fixed volume		16,800
Administrative overheads:		
Expenditure		4,000
Volume		16,800

You are required to: (i) Ascertain the details of actual costs and prepare a profit and loss statement for the period showing the actual profit/loss (show workings clearly), (ii) Reconcile the actual profit with the standard profit.

Solution

(i) *Statement Showing Determination of Actual Cost*

Type of cost	*Standard cost (14,400 units)*	*Variances (F)*	*Variances (A)*	*Actual cost [Add (A) Less(F)]*
Direct material	₹6,48,000	₹10,500	₹42,500	₹6,80,000
Direct labour	4,32,000	32,000	40,000	4,40,000
Factory overhead:				
Variable expenditure	36,000	4,000		32,000
Fixed expenditure and volume	43,200	4,000	16,800	56,000
Administrative overheads:				
Expenditure and volume	43,200		4,000 16,800	64,000

Profit and Loss Statement

Sales revenue (14,400 units × ₹100)			₹14,40,000
Less costs			
Direct material		₹6,80,000	
Direct labour		4,40,000	
Direct expenses (assumed to have no variance)		72,000	
Factory overheads:			
Variable	₹32,000		
Fixed	56,000	88,000	
Administrative overheads		64,000	13,44,000
Actual profit			96,000
Standard profit (20,000 units × ₹11.50)			2,30,000

Sales variances:

Sales price variance: (SR – AR) × AQ = (₹100 – ₹100) × 14,400 = Nil

Sales volume variance: (SQ – AQ) × SP per unit = (5,600 units × ₹11.50) = ₹64,400 (adverse)

Statement of Reconciliation of Actual Profit with Budgeted Profit

Budgeted profit			₹2,30,000
	Favourable	*Adverse*	
Sales volume		₹64,400	
Material price variance		42,500	
Material usage variance	₹10,500		
Labour rate variance		40,000	
Labour efficiency variance	32,000		
Factory overheads			
Expenditure variance (variable)	4,000		
Expenditure variance (fixed)	4,000		
Volume (fixed)		16,800	
Administrative overheads:			
Expenditure		4,000	
Volume		16,800	
	50,500	(1,84,500)	(1,34,000)
Actual profit			96,000

P.20.6 You are appointed cost accountant of Zed Ltd. Given below is the company's operating report for the month of March: LO 20.3,4 LOD: D

	Standard and variances	Actual
Sales (budgeted)	₹18,000	
Variance due to		
Volume of orders	1,000	
Selling prices	400	₹19,400
Profit (budgeted)	3,800	
Variance due to		
Sales volume	240	
Sales price	400	4,440
Production cost variances		
Labour —rate	(250)	
—efficiency	(100)	(350)
Material —price	150	
—usage	(60)	90
Overhead—expenditure (fixed)	100	
—variable	(250)	
—efficiency	200	
—capacity	100	150
Operating profit		4,330

Your assistant provides the following information about sales and costs for the month of April:

Product	Budgeted units	Sales value	Actual units	Sales value
A	250	₹10,000	280	₹10,800
B	200	6,000	190	5,500
C	150	3,000	180	3,500
		19,000		19,800

Product	Standard selling prices per unit	Standard product costs per unit
A	₹40	₹31
B	30	25
C	20	15

Labour:	
Standard labour cost per hour	₹ 0.90
Budgeted hours	4,000
Actual clocked hours	4,400
Standard hours produced	4,500
Actual labour costs	4,260
Material:	
Standard costs of material actually used	5,230
Standard costs of material allowed	5,330
Actual costs of material used	5,430
Overheads:	
Budgeted rates of overheads recovery per Labour-hour	
Fixed	0.50
Variable	1.00
Total	1.50

(Contd.)

(Contd.)

Actual overhead costs	
Fixed	2,000
Variable	4,300
Total	6,300

Prepare the operating statement for the month of April in the same form as for the month of March.

Solution

Operating Statement for the Month of April

Particulars				*Standard and variance*	*Actual*
Sales (budgeted)				₹19,000	
Add favourable (F) variances and					
Less unfavourable (U) variances					
Volume of orders (1) (i)				1,500 (F)	
Selling prices 1 (ii)				700 (U)	₹19,800
Profit (budgeted)					
(BQ × Standard profit per unit)					
(250 × ₹9)			₹2,250		
(200 × ₹5)			1,000		
(150 × ₹5)			750	4,000	
Variance due to					
Sales volume	(2) (i)			370 (F)	
Sales price	(2) (ii)			700 (U)	3,670
Production cost variances					
Labour-rate (3) (i)				300 (U)	
—efficiency	(3) (ii)			90 (F)	210 (U)
Material —price	(4) (i)			200 (U)	
—usage	(4) (ii)			100 (F)	100 (U)
Overhead —expenditure (fixed)		(5) (i)		Nil	
—variable	(5) (ii)			100 (F)	
—efficiency	(5) (iii)			150 (F)	
—capacity	(5) (iv)			200 (F)	450 (F)
Operating profit					3,810

Working Notes

Determination of variances

1. *Sales variances* due to

   (i) Volume of orders measured by sales quantity variance = (Budgeted sales in units – Actual sales in units) × Budgeted selling price per unit

   A : (250 – 280) × ₹40 = ₹1,200 (favourable)
   B : (200 – 190) × ₹30 = 300 (unfavourable)
   C : (150 – 180) × ₹20 = 600 (favourable)
   1,500 (favourable)

   Selling prices measured by sales price variance = (Budgeted selling price – Actual selling price) × actual quantity

   or, [(Budgeted selling price × AQ) – (Actual selling price × AQ)]

   A : (₹40 × 280 = ₹11,200) – ₹10,800 = ₹400 (unfavourable)
   B : (₹30 × 190 = ₹5,700) – ₹5,500 = 200 (unfavourable)
   C : (₹20 × 180 = ₹3,600) – ₹3,500 = 100 (unfavourable)
   700 (unfavourable)

2. *Profit variance* due to
   (i) Sales volume = (Budgeted sales in units – Actual sales in units) × Budgeted profit per unit
   A : (250 – 280) × ₹9 = ₹270 (favourable)
   B : (200 – 190) × ₹5 = 50 (unfavourable)
   C : (150 – 180) × ₹5 = 150 (favaourable)
   370 (favourable)

   (ii)Sales price = ₹700 (unfavourable) (calculated in part 1)
3. *Labour cost variance*
   (i) Labour rates variances (Standard wage rate – Actual wage rate) × Actual hours or,
   [(Standard wage rate × AH) – (Actual wage rate × AH)] = [(₹0.90 × 4,400 = ₹3,960) – (₹4,260)]
   = ₹300 (unfavourable)

   (ii) Labour efficiency variance = (SH – AH) × SR = (4,500 – 4,400) × 0.90 = ₹90 (favourable)
4. *Material cost variance*
   (i) Material price variance = (SR – AR) × AQ or [(SR × AQ) – (AR × AQ)]
   = ₹5,230 – ₹5,430 = ₹200 (unfavourable)

   (ii) Material usage variance = (SQ – AQ) 3 SR or [(SQ × SR) – (AQ × SR)]
   = ₹5,330 – ₹5,230 = ₹100 (favourable)
5. *Overhead costs variance*
   (i) Fixed expenditure variance = Budgeted fixed overheads – Actual fixed overheads
   = (₹0.50 × 4,000 = ₹2,000 – ₹2,000) = Nil

   (ii) Variable expenditure variance = (Budgeted variable overheads at AH – Actual variable overheads)
   = (₹1 × 4,400 = ₹4,400 – ₹4,300) = ₹100 (favourable)

   (iii) Efficiency variance = (SH – AH) × Standard overheads rate per hour
   = (4,500 – 4,400) × ₹1.50 = ₹150 (favourable)

   (iv) Capacity variance = (Budgeted/normal capacity hours–Actual hours) × Standard fixed overhead rate per hour
   = (4,000 – 4,400) × ₹0.50 = ₹200 (favourable)

P.20.7 The managers of Garware Company Ltd, which manufactures paints, were disappointed at the shortfall in profits for the current year as shown below: LO 20.2,3 LOD: M

Income Statement for the Current Year *(₹ in lakh)*

Particulars	*Budgeted*	*Actual*
Units sales (in lakh of litres)	5	5.4
Sales revenue	60.00	61.02
Variable manufacturing costs:		
Materials	10.00	10.90
Direct labour	7.50	8.50
Variable overheads	2.50	2.60
Total variable costs	20.00	22.00
Contribution	40.00	39.02
Fixed costs:		
Manufacturing	25.00	25.40
Selling and administrative	10.00	9.95
Total fixed costs	35.00	35.35
Profit before tax	5.00	3.67

The President of the company asks you to make an analysis in detail showing why the results fell short of the budgeted profits. Production equalled sales during the period under reference.

Solution

Profit variance (overall): (Budgeted profit–Actual profit) = (₹5 lakh–₹3.67 lakh) = ₹1.33 lakh (adverse)

1. *Sales price variances:* (SSP–ASP) × AQ sold = (₹12–₹11.30) × ₹5.4 lakh = ₹3.78 lakh (adverse)
2. *Sales volume variance:* (SQ – AQ) × SP per unit = (5 lakh – 5.4 lakh) × ₹1 = ₹0.4 lakh (favourable)
3. *Cost variances:*
   (a) Materials (SMC – AMC) × AQ or (SMC × AQ) – (AMC × AQ) = (₹2 per unit × 5.4 lakh) – ₹10.9 lakh
   = ₹0.1 lakh (adverse)
   (b) Direct labour (SLC – ALC) × AQ or [(SLC × AQ) – (ALC × AQ)] = (₹1.50 per unit × 5.4 lakh) – ₹5.4 lakh) – ₹8.5 lakh = ₹0.4 lakh (adverse)
   (c) Variable overheads (SVOR – AVOR) × AQ or (AVOR × AQ) – (AVOR × AQ) = (₹0.50 per unit × 5.4 lakh) – ₹2.6 lakh = ₹0.1 lakh (favourable)
   (d) Fixed overheads variance: (Actual overheads – Standard overheads charged to production) = [(₹35.35 lakh (5.4 lakh units × ₹7 SFOR per unit)] = ₹2.45 lakh (favourable)
   (i) Spending variance: (Actual overheads–Budgeted overheads) = (₹35.35 lakh – ₹35.0 lakh) = ₹0.35 lakh (adverse)
   (ii) Capacity variance: (Budgeted capacity – Actual capacity) × SFOR = (5 lakh units – 5.4 lakh) × ₹7 = ₹2.8 lakh (favourable)

Reconciliation Statement of Budgeted Profits with Actual Profits (*₹ in lakh*)

Particulars	Variances: Favourable	Variances: Adverse	Amount
Budgeted profit			5.00
Sales price variance		3.78	
Sales volume variance	0.4		
Material variance		0.10	
Direct labour variance		0.40	
Variable overheads variance	0.1		
Fixed overheads variances:			
Spending variance		0.35	
Capacity variance	2.8		
Total	3.3	(4.63)	(1.33)
Actual profit			3.67

P.20.8 A department in a factory working 40-hours a week can employ upto maximum of 30 employees. In a budget period of 4 weeks, it is expected that 4,000 labour-hours will be worked and that production will equal 5,000 standard hours. **LO 20.4** **LOD: M**

At the end of the period, it is found that 3,600 labour-hours have actually been used and production amounts to 4,000 standard hours.

Present figures to management to illustrate the efficiency, activity and capacity usage. Show where there is scope for improvement and how improvement may be effected.

Solution

Efficiency ratio = (Standard hours for actual production/Actual hours) × 100 = (4,000/3,600) × 100 = 111.11 per cent

Activity ratio = (Standard hour for actual output/Budgeted standard hours) × 100 = (4,000/5,000) × 100 = 80 per cent

Capacity usage ratio = (Actual hours worked/Budgeted hours) × 100 = 3,600/4,000) × 100 = 90 per cent

There is need for increasing the use of idle capacity (represented by less then 100 per cent activity and capacity utilisation ratios). This can be effected by increasing production.

REVIEW QUESTIONS

LOD: Easy

RQ.20.1 Indicate whether the following statements are 'True' or 'False'. LO 20.1,2,3,4,5

(i) Profit variance is explained by total cost variance and total sales variance.
(ii) Profit variance is explained by total cost variance, sales price variance and sales volume variance.
(iii) Sales mix variance originates when the proportion of actual units sold differs from the standard proportion.
(iv) The basis of determining sales volume variance is the same whether it is a part of profit variance or sales variance.
(v) The basis of determining sales volume variance differs when it is a part of profit variance and when it is a part of sales variance.
(vi) If profit variance is unfavourable, it implies that its all sub-variances are also unfavourable.
(vii) A good management reporting system requires that significant variances only should be reported.
(viii) Tabular format is the more effective method of reporting variances than control chart.
(ix) Cost variances can be disposed off by following either of the two methods. The firm has an option of exclusive adoption of one or another.
(x) Variances can be disposed off by transferring to profit and loss account. This method is appropriate if standards are current and attainable.

[Answers: (i) False, (ii) True, (iii) True, (iv) False, (v) True, (vi) False, (vii) True, (viii) True, (ix) False, (x) True]

RQ.20.2 Fill in the following blanks. LO 20.4,5

(i) ________ chart is an effective method of reporting significant variances.
(ii) There are two methods of disposing off cost variances: first is they may be transferred to profit and loss account and the second method requires them to be considered as ________.
(iii) Efficiency ratio is determined dividing ________ by actual hours worked.
(iv) Capacity utilisation ratio is determined dividing actual hours worked by ________.
(v) Material yield ratios is based on actual yield and ________.
(vi) Volume variance ratio shows the relationship between actual production and ________.
(vii) Material cost variance ratio is the product of material price variance ratio and ________.
(viii) Control chart is primarily based on ________.
(ix) ________ is prepared to reconcile actual profit and budgeted profits.
(x) Profit variance is difference between actual profit and ________.

[Answers: (i) Control, (ii) cost of product, (iii) standard hours required for actual production, (iv) budgeted hours, (v) standard yield, (vi) Normal production, (vii) material usage variance ratio, (viii) tolerance limits, (ix) Profit reconciliation statement, (x) budgeted profit]

RQ.20.3 In what ways is variance analysis helpful to management? LO 20.4

RQ.20.4 Certain ratios are very important in connection with budgetary control and standard costing. What are these ratios? State the application of such ratios. LO 20.4

RQ.20.5 What are the two approaches to disposing off variances? Which will be preferred, when, and why? Take suitable examples to support your viewpoint. LO 20.5

RQ.20.6 Write short notes on:
1. Tolerance limits LO 20.5
2. Significant and non-significant variances LO 20.5

3. Graphic and tabular presentation of variances LO 20.4
4. Disposal of variances. LO 20.5

RQ.20.7 From the following data for a particular period, compute sales and profit variances: LO 20.1,2

Budgeted sales: X, 3,000 units @ ₹20 (standard cost ₹12)
Y, 2,000 units @ ₹10 (standard cost ₹6)

Actual sales: X, 4,000 units @ ₹18 each
Y, 2,500 units @ ₹11 each

LOD: Medium

RQ.20.8 Describe the procedure of determining sales and profit variances. Are they similar in certain respects? LO 20.2,3

RQ.20.9 "Variances are not an end in themselves." In the light of the above statement, explain briefly what do you understand by variances control and responsibility? LO 20.4

RQ.20.10 Comment on the following statements:

1. "Variances should not be viewed in isolation." LO 20.4
2. "Profit reconciliation statement is an important statement from the point of view of management." LO 20.3
3. "Management should not be guided by the designated variances—favourable or unfavourable." LO 20.4

RQ.20.11 From the following details, reconcile the budgeted sales with actual sales and standard profit with actual profit in terms of variances: LO 20.1,2,3

Products	*Budgeted*			*Actual*		
	Quantity (units)	*Selling price*	*Cost*	*Quantity (units)*	*Selling price*	*Cost*
Product A	4,000	₹24	₹14	4,500	₹22	₹15
Product B	6,000	18	12	3,000	20	11

RQ.20.12 PH Ltd. furnishes the following information relating to budgeted sales and actual sales for April. LO 20.1

	Product	*Sales quantity (units)*	*Selling price per unit*
Budgeted	A	1,200	₹15
	B	800	20
	C	2,000	40
Actual sales	A	880	18
	B	880	20
	C	2,640	38

Calculate the following variances:

(1) Sales quantity variance,
(2) Sales mix variance,
(3) Sales price variance, and
(4) Total sales variance.

RQ.20.13 From the following information, calculate the various sales variances. LO 20.1

Product	*Standard*		*Actual*	
	Quantity	*Price*	*Quantity*	*Price*
X	15,000	₹5.00	18,000	₹5.10
Y	9,000	8.00	10,000	7.00
Z	6,000	10.00	5,000	9.50

LOD: Difficult

RQ.20.14 From the following budgeted and actual figures, calculate and present the variances in respect of profit on sales and cost of sales. LO 20.1,2

Budget:	Sales, 2,000 units @ ₹15 each	₹30,000
	Cost of sales @ ₹12 each	24,000
	Profit	6,000
Actual:	Sales, 1,900 units @ ₹14 each	26,000
	Cost of sales @ ₹10 each	19,000
	Profit	7,600

ANSWERS

RQ.20.7 Total sales variance, ₹19,500 (F): SPV, ₹5,500 (A); SMV, ₹1,000 (F); SVV, ₹24,000 (F)
Total profit variance, ₹4,500 (F): SPV, ₹5,500 (A); SMV, ₹400 (F); SVV, ₹9,600 (F).

RQ.20.11 SPV, ₹3,000 (A); SMV, ₹9,000 (F); SVSV, ₹51,000 (A); Total sales variance, ₹45,000 (A). Profit variance, ₹17,500 (A); SPV, ₹3,000 (A); SMV, ₹6,000 (F); SVSV, ₹19,000 (A); Cost variance, ₹1,500 (A).

RQ.20.12 **(i)** SQV, ₹11,400 (F);
(ii) SMV, ₹11,000 (F);
(iii) SPV, ₹2,640 (A);
(iv) Total sales variance, ₹19,760 (F).

RQ.20.13 Total sales variance, ₹2,300 (F): SPV, ₹10,700 A; SMV, ₹7,700 A; SVV, ₹20,700 (F).

RQ.20.14 **(a)** Total sales variance ₹3,400 (A); SPV, ₹1,900 (A); SVV, ₹1,500 (A)
(c) Cost of sales variance, ₹3,800 (F).
(d) Overall profit variance, ₹1,600 (F): SPV, ₹1,900 (A), SVV, ₹3,000 (A), Cost variance, ₹3,800 (F).

[Comprehensive solutions to all numerical review questions are available on the companion website: http://www.mhhe.com/khan_jain_ma7e]

CASES

20.C.1 (Profit Variance Analysis) Supreme Ltd. is an auto-parts manufacturing company. Supreme has shown consistently profitable performance over the last 8 years. However, in the last quarter of the current year, Supreme's net profits and net sales dipped by 20 per cent and 25 per cent respectively.

The CEO of Supreme, Saurabh Bharat, directed the Controller, Sumantra Chatterjee, to present an account of the budgeted and actual performance of the company for the current month. Sumantra Chatterjee, with the help of the Chief Cost Accountant, presented the relevant cost/profit data summarised in Exhibit 1.

Exhibit 1 Cost/Profit Data for October

Standard Data:		
1. Material cost (per unit):		
Material A (5 kgs @ ₹50/kg)	₹250	
B (3 kgs @ ₹70/kg)	210	
C (2 kgs @ ₹105/kg)	210	₹670
2. Labour cost (per unit):		
Department X (6 hours × ₹20/hr)	120	
Department Y (4 hours × ₹25/hr)	100	220

3. Variable overheads per unit (10 hours × ₹10/hr)		100
4. Fixed overheads per unit (10 hours × ₹8/hr)		80
	1,070	
5. Unit sale price		1,400
6. Budgeted sales (units)		4,000
7. Normal capacity (units)		5,000
8. Budgeted fixed overheads (₹)		4,00,000
Actual Data:		
1. Material cost (total):		
Material A (24,500 kgs @ ₹48/kg)	11,76,000	
B (10,500 kgs @ ₹72/kg)	7,56,000	
C (3,500 kgs @ ₹105/kg)	3,67,500	22,99,500
2. Labour cost (total):		
Department X (28,000 hours @ ₹18/hr)	5,04,000	
Y (10,500 hours @ ₹27/hr)	2,83,500	7,87,500
3. Vehicles overheads (38,500 hours @ ₹11/hr)		4,23,500
4. Fixed overheads		4,20,000
5. Sales (units)		3,500
6. Unit sale price (₹)		1,350

Based on the above, the Controller prepared a comparative profit statement to present to the CEO (Exhibit 2)

EXHIBIT 2 Profit Calculations—Budgeted and Actual

Budgeted Profit:			
Budgeted profit per unit, ₹330 × Budged sales, 4,000 units			₹13,20,000
Actual Profit:			
Sales (₹1,350 × 3,500 units)			47,25,000
Less costs:			
Material costs:			
Material A	₹11,76,000		
B	7,56,000		
C	3,67,500	22,99,500	
Labour costs:			
Department X	5,04,000		
Y	2,83,500	7,87,500	
Variable overheads		4,23,500	
Fixed overheads		4,20,000	39,30,500
Profit			7,94,500

REQUIRED:

Prepare a detailed variance analysis and highlight the remedial measures that Supreme should take to remedy the situation arising out of declining profitability and sales in recent months and fix responsibility for the variances.

Solution

Total Profit Variance = ₹(13,20,000 budgeted – ₹7,94,500 actual) = ₹5,25,500 (unfavourable)

(A) Sales Price Variance = (₹1,350 budgeted – ₹1,400 actual) × 3,500 = ₹1,75,000 (unfavourable)

(B) Sales Quantity Variance (3,500 actual – 4,000 budgeted) × ₹330 = ₹1,65,000 (unfavourable)

(C) Total Cost Variance (₹39,30,500 actual – ₹37,45,000 budgeted) = ₹1,85,500 (unfavourable)

(a) Total Actual Material Cost and Total Standard Material Cost of 3,500 Units

Raw Material	Actual			Standard		
	AQ (kgs)	AP	TAMC	SQ (kgs)	SP	TSMC
A	24,500	₹48	₹11,76,000	17,500	₹50	₹8,75,000
B	10,500	72	7,56,000	10,500	70	7,35,000
C	3,500	105	3,67,500	7,000	105	7,35,000
Total	38,500		22,99,500	35,000		23,45,000

AQ = actual quantity SP = standard price
AP = actual price TAMC = total actual material cost
SQ = standard quantity TSMC = total standard material cost

Total Material Cost Variance (TMCV) = (₹22,99,500 – ₹23,45,000) = ₹45,500 (favourable)

TMCV is sub-divided into the following 3 sub-variances:

- Material Price Variance

Material A (₹48 – ₹50) × 24,500 kgs = ₹49,000 (favourable)
B (₹72 – ₹70) × 10,500 kgs = 21,000 (unfavourable)
C (₹105 – ₹105) × 3,500 kgs = Nil
28,000 (favourable)

- Material Mix Sub Variance

Material A (24,500 – 19,250) kgs × ₹50 = ₹2,62,500 (unfavourable)
B (10,500 – 11,550) kgs × ₹70 = 73,500 (favourable)
C (3,500 – 77,000) kgs × ₹105 = 4,41,000 (favourable)
2,52,000 (favourable)

- Material Yield Sub Variance (MYSV)

Standard yield = 38,500/(5 + 3 + 2) = 3,850 units

Standard material cost per kg of finished production = (5 kgs × ₹50 + 3kgs × ₹70 + 2 kgs × 105)
= ₹670

MYSV = (3,500 – 3,850) kgs × ₹670 = ₹2,34,500 (unfavourable)

(b) Labour Cost Variance

Total Actual Labour Cost and Total Standard Labour Cost of 3,500 Units Department-wise

Department	Actual			Standard		
	TAH	AR	TALC	TSH	SR	TSLC
X	28,000	₹18	₹5,04,000	21,000	₹20	₹4,20,000
Y	10,500	27	2,83,500	14,000	25	3,50,000
Total	38,500		7,87,500	35,000		7,70,000

TAH = total actual hour SR = standard rate
AR = actual rate TALC = total actual labour cost
TSH total standard hours TSLC = total standard labour cost

Total Labour Cost Variance (TLCV) = (₹7,87,500 – ₹7,70,000) = ₹17,500 (unfavourable)

TLCV is sub divided into 2 sub-variances:

- Labour Rate Variance

Department X (₹18 – ₹20) × 28,000 hours = ₹56,000 (favourable)
Y (₹27 – ₹25) × 10,500 hours = 21,000 (unfavourable)
₹35,000 (favourable)

- Labour Efficiency Variance (LEV)

Department	X (28,000 hrs – 21,000 hrs) × ₹20	=	₹1,40,000 (unfavourable)
	Y (10,500 hrs – 14,000 hrs) × 25	=	87,500 (favourable)
			52,500 (unfavourable)

LEV can be further subdivided into two sub-variances:

(1) Labour Mix Sub Variance

Department	X (28,000 hrs – 23,100 hrs) × ₹20	=	₹98,000 (unfavourable)
	Y (10,500 hrs – 15,500 hrs) × 25	=	1,22,500 (favourable)
			24,500 (unfavourable)

(2) Labour Yield Sub Variance (LYSV)

Standard yield = 38,500/(6 + 4)	=	3,850 units
Standard rate per unit = (₹6 × 20 + 4 × ₹25)	=	₹220
LYSV = (3,500 – 3,850) × ₹220	=	₹77,000 (unfavourable)

(c) Total Variable Overhead Cost Variance (TVOCV) = (₹4,23,500 – ₹3,50,000) = ₹73,500 (unfavourable)

TVOCV is further subdivided into the following 2 sub-variances:

- Variable Overhead Spending Variance
  (₹11 – ₹10) × 38,500 = ₹38,500 (unfavourable)
- Variable Overhead Efficiency Variance
  (38,500 – 35,000) × ₹10 = ₹35,000 (unfavourable)

(d) Total Fixed Overhead Cost Variance (TFOCV) = (₹4,20,000 – ₹2,80,000) = ₹1,40,000 (unfavourable)

TFOCV is further subdivided into the following 3 sub-variances:

- Fixed Overhead Spending Variance = (₹4,20,000 – ₹4,00,000) = ₹20,000 (unfavourable)
- Fixed Overhead Efficiency Variance = (38,500 – 35,000) × ₹8 = ₹28,000 (unfavourable)
- Capacity Variance = (38,500 hrs – 50,000 hrs) × ₹8 = ₹92,000 (unfavourable)

Statement of Reconciliation of Actual Profit with Budgeted Total Profit

Budgeted Profits		₹13,20,000
Add Favourable Variances:		
Material Price Variance	₹28,000	
Material Mix Sub Variance	2,52,000	
Labour Rate Variance	35,000	
Labour Mix Sub Variance	24,500	3,39,500
Less Unfavourable Variance:		
Sales Price Variance	₹1,75,000	
Sales Quantity Variance	1,65,000	
Material Yield Sub Variance	2,34,500	
Labour shield Sub Variance	77,000	
Variable Overhead Spending Variance	38,500	
Variable Overhead Efficiency Variance	35,000	
Fixed Overhead Spending Variance	20,000	
Fixed Overhead Efficiency Variance	28,000	
Capacity Variance	92,000	(8,65,000)
Actual Profit		7,94,500

Summary: Unfavourable Variance

Controllable	*Responsibility*
Sales Quantity Variance	Sales manager
Material Yield Sub Variance	Production manager
Labour Yield Sub Variance	Production manager
Variable Overhead Efficiency Variance	Production manager
Fixed Overhead Efficiency Variance	Production manager

20.C.2 (Profit Variance Analysis) Mughal Pharmaceuticals manufactures and sells prickly heat powder under the brand Shower to Towel. The standard cost sheet per carton (100 packs of 200 grams each) of Shower to Towel powder is given in Exhibit 1.

EXHIBIT 1 COST AND PRICE DATA

Standard Cost:		
1. Materials:		
Boric acid (1 kg @ ₹250 per kg)	₹250	
Zinc oxide (3 kgs @ ₹200 per kg)	600	
Perfumed talc base (16 kgs @ ₹75 per kg)	1,200	₹2,050
2. Labour cost (5 hours @ ₹20 per hour)		100
3. Variable overheads (5 hours @ ₹40 per hour)		200
4. Fixed overheads (5 hours @ ₹100 per hour)		500
		2,850
Standard price per carton		4,000
Budgeted sales volume (cartons in the current quarter)		6,000
Normal capacity (cartons per quarter)		6,000
Actual Cost for First Quarter, Current Year:		
1. Materials purchased/consumed:		
Boric acid (4,730 kgs @ ₹240 per kg)	₹11,35,200	
Zinc oxide (14,450 kgs @ ₹210 per kg)	30,34,500	
Perfumed talc base (81,350 kgs @ ₹78 per kg)	63,45,300	1,05,15,000
2. Labour cost (25,000 hours @ ₹22)		5,61,000
3. Variable overheads (25,500 hours @ ₹42)		10,71,000
4. Fixed overheads (30,000 hours @ ₹101)		30,60,000
		1,52,07,000
Actual production/sales (5,000 cartons @ ₹4,000 per carton)		2,00,00,000
Idle hours		850

The profit statement for the quarter is given in Exhibit 2.

EXHIBIT 2 Profit Statement for the Quarter

Budgeted Profit:			
6,000 cartons × ₹1,150 (sales price ₹4,000 – ₹2,850, cost)			₹69,00,000
Actual Profit:			
Sales (₹4,000 × 5,000 cartons)		₹2,00,00,000	
Less costs:			
Material cost	₹1,05,15,000		
Labour cost	5,61,000		
Variable overheads	10,71,000		
Fixed overheads	30,60,000	1,52,07,000	47,93,000
(Budgeted profit – Actual profit)			21,07,000

Mr Akbar, the CEO of Mughal Pharmaceuticals is unable to make out where the problem was in the business that could account for the reduction in profits in the current quarter.

REQUIRED

Prepare a detailed variance analysis to identify the causes for the decline in profit for the consideration of the CEO.

Solution

Total Profit Variance = Total Actual Profit – Total Budgeted Profit
= ₹47,93,000 – ₹69,00,000 = ₹21,07,000 (unfavourable). This variance is caused due to the following three sub-variances:

(1) Total Quantity Variance: [Actual Quantity (AQ) – Budgeted Quantity (BQ) × Standard profit per unit
= (5,000 AQ – 6,000 BQ) × ₹1,150 = ₹11,50,00 (unfavourable)

(2) Sales Price Variance= [Actual Price (AP) – Budgeted Price (BP) × AQ sold
= (₹4,000 – ₹4,000) × 5,000 = 0.

(3) Total Cost Variance = [Total Actual Cost (AC) – Total Standard Cost (SC)]
= (₹1,52,07,000 – ₹1,42,50,000) = ₹9,57,000 (unfavourable)

Total cost variance is further sub-divided into various sub-cost variances (material, labour and overheads):

(A) Total Material Cost Variance = Total actual material cost – Total standard material cost = ₹1,05,15,000 – 1,02,50,000 = ₹2,65,000 (unfavourable)

(a) Material Price Variance = (Actual price – standard price) × Actual quantity

Boric acid (₹240 – ₹250) ×	4,730 kgs	₹47,300 (favourable)
Zinc oxide (₹210 – ₹200) ×	14,450 kgs	1,44,500 (unfavourable)
Perfumed talc base (₹78 – ₹75) ×	81,350 kgs	2,44,050 (unfavourable)
Total	1,00,530 kgs	3,41,250 (unfavourable)

(b) Mix Variance = (Standard mix of actual quantity – actual mix) × Standard price

Boric acid [(1,00,530 × 1/20) – 4,730] × ₹250	=	₹74,125 (favourable)
Zinc oxide [(1,00,530 × 3/20) – 14,450] × ₹200	=	1,25,900 (favourable)
Perfumed talc base [(1,00,530 × 16/20) – 81,350] × ₹75	=	69,450 (unfavourable)
Total		1,30,575 (favourable)

(c) Material Yield Variance = (Standard Yield – Actual Yield) × Standard material cost per unit
= (5,026.5* – 5,000) × ₹2,050 = ₹54,325 (unfavourable)

*(1,00,530 kg mix should yield 1,00,530/20 = 5,026.5 cartons)

(B) Total Labour Cost Variance = Total actual labour cost – Total standard labour cost = ₹5,61,000 – ₹5,00,000 = ₹61,000 (unfavourable)

(a) Labour efficiency variance = (Actual hours – Standard hours) × Standard rate per hour) = (25,500 – 25,000) × ₹20 = ₹10,000 (favourable)

(i) Idle time variance = (Idle hours × Standard cost per hour) = 850 × ₹20 = ₹17,000 (unfavourable)

(ii) Revised labour efficiency variance = (Actual hours worked – Standard hours) × Standard rate per hour = (24,650 – 25,000) × ₹20 = ₹7,000 (favourable)

(b) Labour rate variance = (Actual rate – Standard rate) × Actual hours paid = (₹22 – ₹20) × 25,500 = ₹51,000 (unfavourable)

(C) Total variable overhead cost variance = Total actual variable cost – Total Standard variable overhead cost = ₹10,71,000 – ₹10,00,000 = ₹71,000 (unfavourable)

(a) Variable overhead efficiency variance = (Actual hours – Standard hours) × Standard variable overhead rate per hour = (25,500 – 25,000) × ₹40 = ₹20,000 (unfavourable)

(b) Variable overhead rate variance = (Actual rate – Standard rate) × Actual hours = (Total actual variable overheads – (Standard rate × Actual hours) = ₹10,71,000 – (₹40 × 25,500) = ₹51,000 (unfavourable)

(D) Total fixed overhead cost variance = Total actual fixed overhead cost – Total standard fixed overhead cost = ₹30,60,000 – ₹25,00,000 = ₹5,60,000 (unfavourable)

(a) Fixed overhead efficiency variance = (Actual hours – Standard hours) × Standard overhead rate per hour = (25,500 – 25,000) × ₹100 = ₹50,000 (unfavourable)

(b) Fixed overhead spending variance = (Total actual fixed overhead cost – Total budgeted fixed overhead cost) = ₹30,60,000 – ₹30,00,000 = ₹60,000 (unfavourable)

(c) Capacity variance = (Normal hours – Actual hours) × Standard overhead rate per hour = (30,000 – 25,500) × ₹100 = 4,50,000 (unfavourable).

Causes for Variances

1. The significant reduction in profit was mainly due to the discrepancies caused by the maintenance and the production departments.
2. Maintenance department should be attributed the major share of reduction in the profits. The capacity variance is ₹5,60,000 and could be due to breakdown in the machinery last month. The idle labour hours might also have been due to the same factor for the efficiency variance of the labour is favourable. An explanation is required from the manager of the department.
3. Production manager has much more digressed from the normal course of his business by not only purchasing materials at the higher rate (causing material cost variance unfavourable) but also by changing the product-mix to get positive mix variance. He has used more quantity of cheaper talc base material and less of costlier Boric acid material. This can bring hazard to the future sales of the powder for it is a mix sensitive product. An explanation should be called from him.

20.C.3 (Cost Variance Analysis) HydeSign Leathers Ltd. manufactures leather jackets in Ludhiana. The company has witnessed steady increase in business and profits. Hyde Sign sells jackets to exporters and design houses. It makes leather jackets in three sizes: small, medium and large, medium being the most popular size in terms of demand followed by large and small. Each size of leather jacket takes the same amount of labour-hours and has the same variable and fixed overheads. The material cost and quality is also the same for each jacket size. The only difference is in the amount of material (i.e. leather, lining cloth and accessories) each size of jacket takes. The standard cost sheet for the three sizes of leather jackets is given in Exhibit 1.

Exhibit 1 Standard Cost Sheet For Jackets (Capacity: 20,000 jackets)

Particulars	*Small Jackets (Budgeted Sales 4,000 jackets)*	*Medium jackets (Budgeted Sales 10,000 jackets)*	*Large jackets (Budgeted Sales 6,000 jackets)*
1. Materials:			
Leather: (4 meters × ₹400)	₹1,600		
(5 meters × ₹400)		₹2,000	
(6.5 meters × ₹400)			₹2,600
Lining cloth: (4 meters × ₹50)	200		
(5 meters × ₹50)		250	
(7 meters × ₹50)			350
Accessories	100	100	100
Total	1,900	2,350	3,050
2. Labour cost (5 hours × ₹30)	150	150	150
3. Variable overheads (5 hours × ₹40)	200	200	200
4. Fixed overheads (5 hours × ₹60)	300	300	300
Total cost	2,550	3,000	3,700
5. Unit sales price	3,000	3,500	4,200
6. Profit per unit	450	500	500

The actual cost sheet for the most current year is given in Exhibit 2.

EXHIBIT 2 Actual Total Cost Sheet (Production: 20,000 jackets)

	Small jackets (4,000 units)	Medium jackets (10,000 units)	Large jackets (6,000 units)
1. Material cost:			
Leather: (4 meters × ₹390 × 4,000)	₹62,40,000		
(5 meters × ₹390 × 10,000)		₹1,95,00,000	
(6.5 meters × ₹390 × 6,000)			₹1,52,10,000
Lining cloth: (4 meters × ₹55 × 4,000)	8,80,000		
(5 meters × ₹55 × 10,000)		27,50,000	
(6.5 meters × ₹55 × 6,000)			23,10,000
Accessories	4,80,000	12,00,000	7,20,000
	76,00,000	2,34,50,000	1,82,40,000
2. Labour cost: (22,000 hours × ₹30.50)	6,71,000		
(55,000 hours × ₹30.50)		16,77,500	
(33,000 hours × ₹30.50			10,06,500
3. Variable overheads	9,90,000	24,75,000	14,85,000
4. Fixed overheads (5 hours × ₹60)	13,20,000	33,00,000	19,80,000
	1,05,81,000	3,09,02,500	2,27,11,500

The total budget profit and actual profit are shown in Exhibit 3.

EXHIBIT 3 Budgeted and Actual Profits

Budgeted Profit:			
Small jackets	(4,000 × ₹450)	₹18,00,000	
Medium	(10,000 × ₹500)	50,00,000	
Large	(6,000 × ₹50)	30,00,000	₹98,00,000
Actual Profit:			
Sales:			
Small	(4,000 × ₹3,000)	₹1,20,00,000	
Medium	(10,000 × ₹3,500)	3,50,00,000	
Large	(6,000 × ₹4,200)	2,52,00,000	₹7,22,00,000
Less Costs:			
Material (₹76,00,000 + ₹2,34,50,000 + ₹1,82,40,000)		₹4,92,90,000	
Labour (₹6,71,000 + ₹16,77,500 + ₹10,06,500)		33,55,000	
Variable overheads (₹9,90,000 + ₹24,75,000 + ₹14,85,000)		49,50,000	
Fixed overheads (₹13,20,000 + ₹33,00,000 + ₹19,90,000)		66,00,000	6,41,95,000
Profit			80,05,000

The CEO of Hyde Sign, Kalpana Singh, is unable to figure out why profits have declined. She asks the CFO, Tarun Soneja, to carry out a detail analysis of the reasons for drop in profit.

REQUIRED

Compute the various cost variances to identify the causes and suggest remedial measures.

Solution

Total Profit Variance = Total Actual Profit – Total Budgeted Profit

= ₹80,05,000 – ₹98,00,000 = ₹17,95,000 (unfavourable)

Sales price variance = Nil

Sales Quantity Variance = (Actual Quantity 20,000 – Budgeted Quantity 20,000) × Standard Profit per Unit = Nil

Total cost variance = Total actual costs – Total budgeted costs
= ₹6,41,95,000 – ₹6,24,00,000 = ₹17,95,000 (unfavourable)

Total Cost Sub-Variance is further sub-divided into various sub-cost variances:

Total Material Cost Variance = Total Actual Material Cost – Total Standard Material Cost
= ₹4,92,90,000 - ₹4,94,00,000 = ₹1,10,000 (favourable)

Material Price Variance = (Actual Price – Standard Price) × Actual Quantity

Leather (₹390 – ₹400) × 3,10,000 meters	₹31,00,000 (favourable)
Lining Cloth (₹55 – ₹50) × 3,20,000 meters	16,00,000 (unfavourable)
Accessories (₹120 – ₹100) × 20,000 jackets	4,00,000 (unfavourable)
	11,00,000 (favourable)

Total Labour Cost Variance = Total Actual Labour Cost – Total Labour Cost
= ₹33,55,000 – 30,00,000 = ₹3,55,000 (unfavourable)

Labour Efficiency Variance = (Actual Hours – Standard Hours) × Standard Rate Per Hour
= (1,10,000 – 1,00,000) × ₹30 = ₹3,00,000 (unfavourable)

Labour Rate Variance = (Actual Rate – Standard Rate) × Actual Hours Paid
= (₹30.5 – ₹30) × 1,10,000 = ₹55,000 (unfavourable)

Total Variable Overhead Cost Variance
= Total Actual Variable Overhead Cost – Total Standard Variable Overhead Cost
= ₹49,50,000 – ₹40,00,000 = ₹9,50,000 (unfavourable)

Variable Overhead Efficiency Variance
= (Actual Hours – Standard Hours) × Standard Overhead Variable Overhead Rate Per Hour
= (1,10,000 – 1,00,000) × ₹40 = ₹4,00,000 (unfavourable)

Variable Overhead Rate Variance = (Actual Rate – Standard Rate) × Actual Hours
= (₹45 – ₹40) × 1,10,000 = ₹5,50,000 (unfavourable)

Total Fixed Overhead Variance = Total Actual Fixed Overhead – Total Standard Fixed Overhead
= ₹66,00,000 – ₹60,00,000 = ₹6,00,000 (unfavourable)

Fixed Overhead Efficiency Variance = (Actual hours – Standard hours) × Standard overhead rate per hour
= (1,10,000 – 1,00,000) × ₹60 = ₹6,00,000 (unfavourable)

Fixed Overhead Spending Variance = Total Actual Fixed Overhead Cost – Total Budgeted Fixed Overhead Cost
= ₹66,00,000 – ₹60,00,000 = ₹6,00,000 (unfavourable)

Capacity Variance = (Normal Hours – Actual Hours) × Standard Fixed Overhead Rate Per Hour
= (1,00,000 – 1,10,000) × ₹60 = ₹6,00,000 (favourable).

Reasons for Drop in Profits: The dip in profits (₹17,95,000) is mainly due to increase in production costs as sales variance is nil. An important contributory factor in substantially higher production cost is the increase in labour cost as reflected in labour efficiency variance. The unfavourable labour efficiency variance is the result of increase in number of hours taken to produce each jacket by half-hour as well as increase in labour costs by ₹0.50 per hour. The variable overheads have also increased due to increase in the number of hours of production.

The responsibility for these variance should rest with the heads of the production and personnel departments. The sales department should be commended for achieving the budgeted sales volume and revenue.

21

Responsibility Accounting

Learning Objectives

After reading this chapter you will be able to:

LO 21.1 Understand responsibility accounting as divisional performance measurement
LO 21.2 Review cost centre as a responsibility centre
LO 21.3 Analyse profit centre as a responsibility centre
LO 21.4 Evaluate investment centre as a responsibility centre

Introduction

As observed earlier, one of the uses of management accounting is managerial control. Among the control techniques, "responsibility accounting" occupies considerable significance. While the other control devices are applicable to the organisation as a whole, responsibility accounting represents a method of measuring the performance of various divisions of an organisation. The term "division" with reference to responsibility accounting is used in a general sense to **include any logical segment/component/sub-component of an organisation**. Defined in this way, it includes a division, a department, a branch office, a service centre, a product-line, a channel of distribution, a class of customers, and so on. The test to identify a division is that the operating performance is separately identifiable and measurable in some way that is of practical significance to management[1]. The purpose of the present chapter is to describe the organisational structure in which the management control process through responsibility accounting takes place. The chapter briefly discusses the meaning and structure of responsibility accounting as divisional performance measurement followed by its objectives. It also provides an in-depth analysis of the structure-responsibility centres. The coverage includes illustration as well as evaluation of the three centres, namely, cost, profit, and investment. The main points are also summarised by way of recapitulation.

Division includes any logical segment/component/sub-component of an organisation.

MEANING AND OBJECTIVES

Responsibility accounting is a device to measure divisional performance.

Meaning

LO 21.1 Understand responsibility accounting as divisional performance measurement

"Responsibility accounting collects and reports planned and actual accounting information about the inputs and outputs of responsibility centres."[2] From this description one may deduce the following features of responsibility accounting: (i) Inputs and outputs (ii) Planned and actual and (iii) Responsibility centres.

Inputs and Outputs Responsibility accounting is based on information relating to inputs and outputs. The resources used are called inputs. The resources used by an organisation are essentially physical in nature, such as quantity of materials consumed, hours of labour, and so on. For managerial control, these heterogeneous physical resources are converted into a common denominator—monetary measure. When physical resources are expressed in monetary terms, they are called "cost". Thus, inputs are expressed as cost. Similarly, outputs are measured in monetary terms as "revenues". In other words, responsibility accounting is *based on cost and revenue data for financial information.*

Planned and Actual The financial information included is both actual and planned. For planning and control, it not only contains historical information about cost/revenues, but also estimated future cost angd revenue data.

Responsibility centre is the unit of an organisation that is separable and identifiable for operating purposes and its performance measurement should be possible

Responsibility Centres Responsibility accounting focuses on responsibility centres. A responsibility centre is a sub-unit of an organisation under the control of a manager who is responsible for the activities of that responsibility centre. A small firm can possibly be managed by an individual or a small group of individuals. However, for effective control, a large firm is divided into meaningful segments/departments. Each sub-unit has certain activities to perform and its manager is assigned the responsibility/authority to carry out those activities. These sub-units of an enterprise, for the purpose of control, are called responsibility centres/divisions. The responsibility centre can be a big unit, such as a production department or division, or a small unit such as the cash section of the accounting department. The important criterion for creating a responsibility centre is that the *unit of the organisation should be separable and identifiable for operating purposes and its performances measurement should be possible.*

For control purposes, responsibility centres are generally categorised into: **(i)** Cost centres, **(ii)** Profit centres, and **(iii)** Investment centres. While these are discussed in detail in the next section of this chapter, a simplified view of responsibility centres (based on cost) in illustrated in Example 21.1.

◆ Example 21.1

The following information is available relating to the cost of production of the Hypothetical Ltd:

(₹ in lakh)

Cost item	*Amount*
Direct material	₹400
Direct labour	260
Overheads	280
Total	940

It may be assumed that the firm has four departments—two production and two service. Assuming an imaginary division of the cost between the four departments (responsibility centres), show the cost allocation.

Solution

The allocation of the costs to the four responsibility centres is illustrated in Table 21.1.

TABLE 21.1 Allocation of Costs to Responsibility Centres

		Responsibility Centres (Departments) (₹ in lakh)			
	Total	*A*	*B*	*C*	*D*
Direct material	₹400	₹360	₹40	₹—	₹—
Direct labour	260	80	180	—	—
	660	440	220	—	—
Overheads:					
Supervision	76	14	18	16	28
Indirect labour	132	12	16	42	62
Supplies	24	10	8	2	4
Other costs	48	6	16	10	16
	280	42	58	70	110
Total	940	482	278	70	110

Thus, responsibility accounting is a method for dividing the organisation structure into various responsibility centres to measure the performance of each of the responsibility centres. In other words, *responsibility accounting is a device to measure divisional performance.*

Objectives

The objective of divisional performance measurement may be classified into three basic categories: (i) To determine the contribution of a division to the total organisation, (ii) To provide basis for evaluation of quality of performance, and (iii) To motivate, consistent with the basic goals of the organisation.

Determination of Contribution of a Division The performance of a responsibility centre can be measured in terms of its *efficiency* and/or in terms of its *effectiveness.* Efficiency measures the relationship of inputs to outputs; and the relationship between output and the goals of the organisation is called effectiveness. Efficiency is a relative term: the lower the consumption of resources (input) to turn out a given amount of output, the greater is the efficiency. A particular responsibility centre may be found more/less efficient if the cost of production in a month is lower/higher than in one preceding/following month. Similarly, in comparison to another centre, it may be more/less efficient. In brief, an efficient responsibility centre is one that does whatever it does with the lowest consumption of resources[3].

Efficient responsibility centre is one which does what it does with the lowest consumption of resources.

Effectiveness is related to the goals of the organisation. Applied to responsibility accounting, it implies how well a responsibility centre contributes to the goals of the organisation. If a centre is not able to contribute what is expected of it, it is not effective. In determining the contribution of each responsibility centre to the organisation as a whole, both efficiency and effectiveness are relevant, that is, a responsibility centre should be both efficient and effective.

Evaluation of Quality of Performance Responsibility accounting is used to measure the performance of managers and it, therefore, influences the way the managers behave. In discussing responsibility accounting, we must take behavioural considerations into account. It is for this reason that responsibility accounting contains a discussion of how managers are influenced by the nature of accounting information they receive.

Could a valid distinction be made between the performance of a division as an entity and the personal performance of a divisional manager? The two may not be distinguishable in the long run. In the short term, however, a very useful and necessary distinction may be made. It is conceivable that a division may not have made a satisfactory contribution to the goals of the organisation. Yet the manager may be judged to have discharged his responsibility very well.

Motivation Consistent with Organisational Goals As observed earlier, any performance measurement system can be expected to influence the behaviour of the managers affected by it. Divisional performance measurement (responsibility accounting) should be designed in such a way that, in seeking to achieve their own goals, divisional managers will simultaneously work to achieve the goals of the firm. This is called "goal congruence."[4] This can be ensured through a system of incentives, for example, bonus for good performance, and so on.

In brief, responsibility accounting as a control device aims at measuring the performance of the various responsibility centres or divisions of an organisation. It may be noted that *it is measurement and not evaluation of performance*. In other words, responsibility accounting focuses on *what and not how well the performance is.*

For purposes of measuring financial performance, the divisions of a firm may be classified according to the type of financial data used in the measurement of performance. Three basic classes of divisions can be identified on these grounds: Expense/cost centre, Profit centre, and Investment centre.

EXPENSE/COST CENTRES

LO 21.2 Review cost centre as a responsibility centre

Expense/cost centre is a segment of an organisation whose financial performance is measured in terms of cost.

An expense centre is a responsibility centre in which inputs, but not outputs, are measured in monetary terms.[5] It has been pointed out earlier that responsibility accounting is based on financial information relating to inputs (cost) and outputs (revenues). In an expense centre of responsibility, the accounting system records only the cost incurred in/by the centre/division/unit but the revenues earned (output) are excluded. Stated differently, an expense centre is a segment whose financial performance is measured in terms of cost. Since the performance of an expense centre is measured by the financial measure of input (cost) only, an essential requirements is that the cost of operating the division be directly traceable to it. This means that the relevant costs are the *incremental or avoidable* cost of operating that division.[6] The incremental cost would include both variable and fixed costs but would exclude costs common to several divisions and allocated among them on some arbitrary basis.

From the viewpoint of the measurement of performance of the divisional manager, the implication of the expense centre is that his performance will be judged on the basis of the cost incurred in his department/division; what is done in the division (output/revenue) will be of no consequence. The analysis of performance is restricted to the consumption of resources in the division, and there is no reference to what the division has achieved as a consequence of consuming those resources. In other words, the performance measure in an expense centre is the efficiency of operation in that centre in terms of the quantity of inputs used in producing some given output. The *modus operandi* is to compare actual inputs to some pre-determined level that represents efficient utilisation (planned/budgeted/standard). The variance between the actual and the budget/standard/plan would be indicative of the efficiency of the division/divisional manager.

Suitability What is the suitability of cost as an index of performance? The expense centre can be employed in three situations.

In the first place, in several cases, the output (revenue) of a responsibility centre cannot be reliably measured in financial terms. Included in this category are centres such as legal departments, accounting departments, public relations departments and the personnel departments. Each of these centres/divisions has a conceptually identifiable output—legal advice (legal department), good public relations (public relations department), reliable accounting reports (accounting department), and better qualified personnel (personnel department). Their outputs cannot obviously be expressed in monetary terms. The only measurable performance measure is their efficiency in the use of inputs. Thus, such divisions can be evaluated only as expense centres. In brief, *cost is a suitable measure of performance in staff units/divisions.*

Secondly, if a production centre/unit/segment is producing one single product, its performance can be measured as expense centre in terms of *efficiency* and *effectiveness.* Although, the output cannot be expressed in monetary terms, the number of units produced can reasonably represent output. The cost per unit of the product would be indicative of the efficiency of department. A comparison of the actual number of units produced of a single product with the units produced in some previous period would measure divisional effectiveness.

Thirdly, an expense centre can also be suitably employed to measure performance if the responsibility of the departmental manager is to produce a stated quantity of outputs at the lowest feasible cost.[7]

Limitations However, in general, an expense centre is not a useful basis of measuring performance of responsibility centres. This is mainly because it ignores output (revenues) measured in financial terms. A common feature of production departments is that they are multi-product units. There must be some common basis to aggregate the dissimilar products to arrive at the overall output of the department/responsibility centre. If this is not done, the efficiency and effectiveness of the responsibility centre cannot be measured. Monetary measure represents the common denominator to measure the overall output of the responsibility centre producing multi-products. The implication is, that to arrive at the overall output, the different products have to be expressed in financial terms. This is a limitation of the expense centre. The profit centre provides a solution to this problem.

Cost Centre Evaluation Cost centre evaluation techniques include variance analysis, job order system, process costing system. These methods can be applied directly to the particular manufacturing department, product-line, marketing function, or other segments. These cost control techniques have already been discussed extensively earlier in this book. These techniques can, however, be used in profit centre/investment centre evaluation also.

PROFIT CENTRES

LO 21.3 Analyse profit centre as a responsibility centre

Profit centre is a segment of an organisation in which financial performance is measured on the basis of profit.

"A profit centre is a responsibility centre in which inputs are measured in terms of expenses and outputs are measured in terms of revenues."[8] Both the elements of accounting information—cost (input) and revenues (output) are considered. In other words, in a profit centre, the measure of performance is broader than in an expense centre because in an expense centre the accounting system measures only one element (cost), whereas in a profit centre both the elements (cost as well as revenue) are measured in monetary terms. The difference between revenues and costs is profit. Stated operationally, the profit centre is a division/sub-unit of an organisation in which financial performance is measured on the basis of profit, that is, revenues less costs. While the cost figures are the same as used in expense centres, the term "revenue" with reference to responsibility accounting is used in a different sense. It may be recalled that the generally accepted principle of accounting is to recognise revenue only when sales are made to outside customers. For purposes of profit centre performance, revenue represents a monetary measure of the output of a profit centre in a given accounting period whether or not the firm actually realises the revenue in that period. *The test is that a department has output (goods and services) which are amenable to monetary measurement.*

Since in a profit centre there are financial measures of the output as well as of the input, it is possible to measure the effectiveness and efficiency of performance in financial terms. Profit analysis can be used as a basis for evaluating the performance of a division as an entity and/or for evaluating the performance of a divisional manager. A profit centre requires all of the data needed in an expense centre as well as additional data regarding revenues. Therefore, management can determine whether the division was efficient in the utilisation of resources and, whether the division was effective in attaining its objectives. This objective is presumably to earn a *satisfactory* "profit". The criterion for a satisfactory profit may be budgeted profit/past profit in the division/profits of other similar divisions/some combination of two or more of these. "Profit", as a performance measure, is based on revenues and expenses directly traceable to the division and avoidable if the division were closed down. This concept of divisional profit is referred to as "profit contribution," as it is the amount of profit contributed directly by the division. It might also be described as "incremental profit" or the additional profit earned solely as a result of operations of the division. Further, divisional profits are before taxes, the reason being that taxes are assessed on the basis of the income of the entire company and they may be regarded as similar to common costs and excluded from the calculation of the divisional profit.

Divisional profit/profit contribution is the amount of profit contributed by the division.

There is the yet another element in the computation of profit as performance measurement for a profit centre. This relates to the types of profit centres. A profit centre, for example, a product division, uses inputs (cost) and produces output (revenues). Such a profit centre is very like an independent firm. It is called a "natural profit centre". The alternative to the natural profit centre is the "constructive profit centre."[9] It is not a natural profit centre but it may be made to appear as one. An example is the computer centre or data processing department. It makes use of inputs (cost) but it produces no revenues (output) as it renders computer services to other departments and does not sell its products/services. This is logically an expense centre. However, the management has an alternative to owning and operating a computer: to purchase computer time from a data processing service. The management will compare the two alternatives and select one which involves a lower cost. *The cost avoided is the revenue to the firm by owing a computer. This is constructive profit. Divisional profit data can be used to evaluate the performance of the division/divisional manager in the case of natural profit centres alone.*

Natural profit centre is a division which uses costs and produces revenues like an independent firm.

In brief, the relevant profit to form the basis of performance measurement of a profit centre is the *before-tax incremental/contribution profit/margin of a natural profit centre.* The profits of all the divisions thus calculated will not necessarily be equal to the profit of the entire firm. The divergence would arise from the fact that costs not attributable to any single division are excluded from the computation of the profit of the organisation as a whole. It may, therefore, be concluded *that divisional profit is a unique concept, designed to serve specific managerial needs.*

Advantages A profit centre, as a responsibility centre, is of considerable significance in measuring the performance of divisions/divisional managers. Three aspects deserve special mention.

In the first place, profit, defined as the differences between revenues and costs/expenses, is a combined measure of both effectiveness and efficiency. It provides a powerful tool for measuring how well the profit centre/manager of the profit centre has performed.

Secondly, a profit centre resembles a business in miniature. Like a separate firm, its profits are calculated. The performance of the managers is measured by profit. Therefore, they will be motivated to take decisions about inputs and outputs in such a way that the profit of a profit centre is maximised. In other words, managers can be expected to behave as if they were running their own business. For this reason, the profit centre is a good training ground for general management responsibility.

Thirdly, the profit centre is closely related to the organisational principle of decentralisation; profit centres make decentralised organisation possible. Top management can safely delegate the authority to the divisional managers because the profit centre reports provide adequate information about how well the operating managers are doing their jobs.[10]

In brief, profit centres provide a broader and more inclusive measurement of performance than the expense centres. If managers are responsible for both revenue and expense aspects of performance (profit centre), the contribution of each manager to the goal of the entire organisation is easier to measure than when no single manager is responsible for both revenues and expenses (expense centres).

Limitations The profit centre approach also encounters certain problems. These relate to: **(i)** Criterion for profit centres, **(ii)** Measurement of expenses, and **(iii)** Transfer prices.

Criteria for Profit Centres One problem with profit centre is that it cannot be used for all responsibility centres. The criteria to use profit centre as a responsibility centre includes the consideration of the following points: **(i)** Extra record-keeping is involved to measure input and output in monetary terms; **(ii)** When a responsibility centre is required by management to provide service to other responsibility centres, the service department (for example, internal audit) should not be a profit department; **(iii)** Unless the divisional managers of responsibility centres have reasonable authority to decide on the quality/quantity of outputs or on the relations of output to costs, a profit centre will be of little use as a control device; **(iv)** If the output of a product/division is fairly homogeneous (for example, cement), a profit centre may not offer substantial advantage, however, an expense centre may do so; **(v)** There may be friction between profit centres due to the spirit of intense competition. Moreover, it may generate too much interest in short run profit to the detriment of long-term results. The operational implication is that unless these problems are overcome, the profit centre technique would not serve its purpose and should, therefore, not be used.

Measurement of Expenses Another problem with profit centres may relate to the measurement of certain types of expenses which have to be included in the computation of profit centres. There is a scope for difference of opinion relating to the treatment of those expenses which relate to the organisation as a whole. In view of the special nature of divisional profits, such expenses should not be considered since, they are not the responsibility of the division/divisional manager. That such expenses are not the responsibility of the division is another way of saying that they cannot be traceable/attributable to it and should be ignored in working out the profit of the division as a profit centre.

Transfer Prices The measurement of profit in a profit centre type of responsibility accounting is also complicated by the problem of transfer prices. A transfer price is a price used to measure the value of goods/services furnished by a profit centre to other responsibility centres within a company.[11] In other words, when internal exchange of goods and services take place between the different divisions of a firm, they have to be expressed in monetary terms. The monetary amount for these inter-divisional exchanges/transfers is called the transfer price. The determination of an appropriate transfer price is one of the major problems of profit centres. The implication of the transfer price is that for the selling division (the division whose goods/services are being transferred) it is a source of revenue, whereas, for the buying division (the division which is receiving/acquiring the goods/services) it is an element of cost. It will, therefore, have a significant bearing on the revenues, costs, and profits of responsibility centres. Hence, the need for correct determination of transfer prices. The determination is, however, complicated because a wide variety of alternative methods are available. We, therefore, first discuss the basic types of transfer prices. Transfer price policies to indicate the circumstances in which different types of transfer prices are suitable are also examined.

Transfer price is the monetary amount of inter-divisional exchanges/transfer of goods and services.

In order to assess the validity and acceptability of different transfer pricing methods, three criteria are generally used. In the first place, the transfer price should be objectively determinable. Secondly, it should be equal to the value of the intermediate products being transferred, that is, the transfer price should reward/compensate the transferring division and charge the buying/acquiring division in keeping with the value of the functions performed and/or the value of the product exchanged. Finally, it should be compatible with the policy that maximises attainment of company goals and evaluation of segment performance.

Types of Transfer Prices There are two general approaches to the determination of a transfer price: **(i)** Cost-based; and **(ii)** Market-based. Based on these, there are six basic types of transfer prices: **(a)** Cost, **(b)** Cost plus a normal mark-up, **(c)** Incremental cost, **(d)** Market price, **(e)** Negotiated price, and **(f)** Dual (two-way) prices.

Cost Price According to this, transfer price is equal to the cost price. This means the goods/services transferred will be priced on the basis of the selling division's unit cost of production. The cost could be either actual cost of production or, where available, standard cost of production.

The merit of this method is simplicity and convenience because all the required information is available in the cost accounting records. But it is inappropriate for profit centre analysis. The reason is that transfer prices based on cost would distort the profit figures. For the selling division, the profit figures would be an underestimate as it will not earn any profit on goods/services sold to the sister divisions. The profit figures for the purchasing department would be inflated to the extent the cost of purchases of goods would be lower because there is no element of profit for the selling divisions. If profit figures are distorted, the profit centre analysis would not be of much value.

Cost Plus a Normal Mark-up This type of transfer price is an improvement over the first category. It includes, besides unit cost of production, some profit margin or normal mark-up. Thus, the price received/paid by the selling and the purchasing departments respectively will contain an element of profit. There are two ways in which the normal mark-up/profit margin is determined. First, the management of the firm may set a target profit. Alternatively, the normal mark-up may be equivalent to the profit margin that a competing firm might reasonably be expected to realise. If the second basis is adopted, the transfer price will approximate a market value. Depending upon its closeness to the real market value, it may be useful for profit centre analysis. But if the basis is the managerial pre-determined target, the mark-up is an artificial margin dictated by policy.[12] Therefore, its validity as performance measurement of a division/divisional manager, is open to question. On the whole, therefore, this type of transfer price has no unique value of its own for profit centre analysis.

Incremental Cost Yet another basis of transfer prices is the incremental cost in the selling division. Depending upon the circumstances, incremental cost can be computed in two ways. The first situation may be such that the entire production of the selling division is transferred to the sister divisions, and there are no independent outside customers for the goods. In that case, incremental cost includes all variable costs plus any fixed costs directly and exclusively attributable to the internal transfer/internal divisional transfer. Transfer pricing at incremental cost defined in this sense is inconsistent with the objectives of measuring divisional profit as performance measurement.

An alternative market situation arises when there may be outside customers for the goods and the division is unable to produce the full demand (from the outside customers as well as sister divisions). The incremental cost to the selling division in that case would be the revenue lost on sales to outside customers that must be foregone to make the internal transfer to a sister division. Then, the incremental cost would equal the market price for those goods/services. This version of the incremental cost data could be useful for profit centre analysis. The incremental cost data related to the internal production costs is not of much analytical value.

Market Price Another approach to transfer pricing is the market price based approach. There are three ways to arrive at the market price.

First, through the prevailing market price if there is an active market for the goods/services transferred between divisions. The prevailing price would require adjustment for discounts as well as for certain selling costs that are not involved in inter-divisional exchange. The merits of this basis of transfer price are: **(i)** Market prices represent the alternatives to the divisions. That is to say, if the selling division sells the goods to outside customers, or if the buying division purchases the goods from outside suppliers, the market price will be the basis. **(ii)** They are neither arbitrary nor artificial, rather they reflect the collective values of several buyers/sellers. In operational terms, a market price-based approach implies that the selling division will receive equal to what it would get by selling the goods to outside customers, while the purchasing division will pay what it would pay to outside suppliers. Yet, both the selling and the buying divisions would derive some special benefits. The advantages to the selling division include: **(a)** No risk of bad debt on sales to sister divisions, and **(b)** No direct promotional expenses on sale to a sister division. The special benefit to the buying department will be in the form of assured delivery schedules and full customer service. Therefore, where divisions have the alternative to buy/sell to/from the open market, they would prefer to buy from/sell to the sister division.

Secondly, in cases where easily identified market prices are not available, costs plus a normal profit margin can be a reasonable approximation of the market price.

Finally, in situations in which market price is not readily available, bids from several different manufactures can form the basis. The low bid may be taken as the market price and used for internal transfer pricing. This alternative of market price suffers from two limitations: either spurious bids would be submitted by the bidders, or bids will not be submitted. This is likely because the bidders would come to know that the firm does not intend buying the goods but, will only use the bid for internal pricing.

Negotiated Price The inter-divisional exchange pricing can also be based on a price mutually agreed upon by the buying as well as the selling departments, through negotiation. The advantage of this approach is that it will lead to a transfer price mutually advantageous to both, the divisions as well as the entire organisation. The limitation is that it can be applied only in situations in which the selling division has a choice of customers and the purchasing division has a choice of suppliers.

Dual (Two-Way) Prices According to this method of transfer pricing for segment performance evaluation, the transferring division is credited with one price but the acquiring division is charged at different price. The merit of this method is that it eliminates the possibility of conflict caused by a single transfer price, in which case one segment receives relatively less contribution of profit because the price setting process entitles the segment to receive relatively more.

The price to be charged to the acquiring division should be based on what it costs the firm as a whole to produce and distribute the intermediate product internally under normal conditions. The appropriate transfer prices are *incremental costs* in non-recurring situations, and *full standard costs* for long-run continuous situations. These prices reflect the effective cost of the resources consumed by the firm and by the segment. For this reason, this is an appropriate basis for evaluating the performance of the user of those resources. The transferring division, on the other hand, should receive the market price for the intermediate product. If no market price exists, a negotiated price based on the market price of the final product should be used to approximate the net realisable value of intermediate product. This price represents the best possible assessment of the exchange value of the intermediate product.[13]

The use of dual prices would lead to a divergence between the segment profits and the total profits of the company. But it should not stand in the way of the use of this method because, the transfer price is intended only for purposes of segment performance evaluation and not for decision-making.

Transfer Price Policies Transfer price policies refer to the selection of policies/methods that would govern the calculations of such prices under various circumstances. The concern of transfer price policies is with developing a transfer pricing system that allows: **(i)** A measure of performance to reflect the use of resources by a division and **(ii)** The optimal allocation of the firms' resources.[14] In other words, suitable transfer prices should be related to: **(a)** Management performance assessment and **(b)** Decision-optimisation.

Management Performance The best transfer price for measuring management performance is the one that reflects the price in an open, competitive market. These market prices are the best measure of revenue for the selling division, and of cost for the purchasing division. For market prices to have maximum effectiveness in management performance measurement, both the buying and the selling divisions must be able to act independently, that is, the selling division must have a choice of customer and the purchasing department must have a choice of suppliers.

If, however, a market price for the goods/services is not readily available, negotiated prices may be used to determine the transfer price. This price is negotiated between the buying and the selling units.

In circumstances where there are no competitive market prices and a negotiated transfer price cannot be established, the firm cannot set up profit centres. It can use cost centres for management performance measurement. By using standard cost as the transfer prices for cost centres, the selling divisions are encouraged to have good control.

Decision-Optimisation The ideal transfer price for management decision-making is the price that would be used by a firm if it were not divided into units/divisions. In other words, for decision-making purposes, the transfer price should reflect the opportunity cost of the goods/services transferred between divisons.[15] This is so, because an optimal allocation of resources takes place only if the goods/services are priced on transfer at the opportunity cost that would be incurred to obtain the goods/services elsewhere, when they are needed. The best measure of opportunity cost is the open market price, if available. In case, market prices are not readily available, the top management may prescribe a transfer price. Alternatively, a negotiated price between divisions with arbitration, if necessary, by top management, reflecting the corporate objectives, and coordination of the activities of all the divisions, may be taken to be the opportunity cost. One widely-used approach treats the incremental costs of the selling division as the transfer price. The advantage of this is that if price/standard costs are used, the inefficiency of the selling division will not be *ipso facto* passed on to the buying division.

To conclude, the question of appropriate transfer prices for the two functions of management—performance measurement, and decision-optimisation does not have any easy answer. There is no single measure of transfer price that can fit all circumstances. The firm must give serious consideration to its goals and objectives in using transfer prices before adopting a particular measure. Another possibility is to use a dual pricing system. Such a basis of transfer pricing removes some of the deficiencies and conflicts that would, otherwise, be present in segment performance evaluation. It also permits a more objective assessment of segments as individual entities.

Profit Centre Evaluation[16] Profit centre evaluation requires an income statement approach. The conventional income statement format can be recast to highlight the various sub-categories. These sub-categories are arranged according to the criteria of **(i)** variability, **(ii)** controllability, and

(iii) attributability. The controllable concept implies that the performance attributes should be controllable by the division/responsibility centre. The attributability concept refers to the outcomes/performance characteristics that are directly associated with, or directly traceable to the existence and operations of a segment. According to the variability attribute, costs that are neither directly controllable by a particular segment, nor attributable to it, are excluded from the measurement of divisional performance. Included in this category of costs are administrative salaries, property taxes, depreciation, and so on. The main sub-categories that might be included in a typical segmented income statements are: **(1)** Sales and other major revenues, **(2)** Controllable variable costs, **(3)** Controllable contribution margin, **(4)** Controllable fixed costs, **(5)** Controllable segment margin, **(6)** Attributable segment costs, **(7)** Segment profit contribution, **(8)** Common firm-wide cost, and **(9)** Segment net income.

Sales and Other Major Revenues Sales earned by a particular segment are usually easy to identify and measure when these are made to outside customers only, or, market transactions determine the amount of sales or the products/services sold by one division as distinct from those of other divisions. However, there may be some difficulty in estimating the revenue of a segment due to the problems associated with transfer pricing.

To evaluate a segment's sales revenues, they must be compared with other performance measures such as: **(i)** Prior period sales of the same segment, **(ii)** Sales volumes of a comparable department of the same firm, **(iii)** Sales of other companies in the same industry, and **(iv)** The division's predetermined budgeted sales volume. These comparisons may be made in terms of total amount, physical volume, rates of change, or deviations from budgeted amounts. Only short-run sales data should not be used as a basis for divisional performance measurement. Trend and comparative measures are more useful for this purpose.

Controllable Variable Costs All the costs in this group are directly controllable by the divisional managers and vary according to the division's activity levels, namely, the division's variable cost of goods sold, and variable administrative and marketing costs. These can be usually measured objectively except when transfer prices for individual acquisitions are involved. These costs should be evaluated using variance analysis, trend analysis, variable cost to sales ratio analysis, comparison with other segments of the same firm and with similar segments of other companies in the same industry.

> **Controllable variable costs**
> are costs directly controllable by the divisional managers at a given activity level.

Controllable Contribution Margin Sales revenue minus controllable variable cost equals the division's controllable contribution margin. It measures the profitability of the sales of a department. It can be used to evaluate the ability of a division to sustain itself, to make a contribution to costs of other divisions, common costs of the firm and profits of the organisation. The evaluation would primarily be based on variance analysis.

Controllable Fixed Costs The controllable fixed costs are those fixed costs of a period that are directly and exclusively related to the decisions of the management of a division. Such costs are, for example, divisional rental charges for equipment and property, executives' salaries, advertising costs, and so on. Such costs should be compared with budgeted fixed costs to evaluate performance.

Controllable Segment Margin The excess of controllable contribution margin over controllable fixed costs is the controllable segment margin. This should be compared with the previous period's results and pre-determined budgeted amounts.

> **Attributable segment costs**
> include all costs uncontrollable by a divisional manager.

Attributable Segment Costs Included in such costs are all those costs which are not controllable by a divisional manager and which could have been avoided had the decision been withdrawn. Examples of such costs are the divisional manager's salary, depreciation, rent, insurance on facilities used exclusively by the division but acquired as a results of decision made at higher management levels, and interest charges on debt that was incurred specifically to support the operations of a division but which was decided upon outside the division. Obviously, these costs are not directly controllable by the divisional manager. Yet, they should be considered in overall segment performance through comparison with the budgeted amounts and with the division's results for the prior period.

Segment Profit Contribution The segment profit contribution is the difference between the controllable segment margin and the attributable segment costs. Variance analysis, percentage analysis of individual costs and revenues, and trend and time period analysis can be used to evaluate the various components of segment profit contribution. Comparison can also be made with industry or product line standards.

Common firm-wide costs are costs incurred for the firm as a whole which should be proportionately recovered from the revenues of the segments.

Common Firm-Wide Costs The common firm-wide costs are incurred for the firm as a whole. Such costs do not relate to any specific segment. Nevertheless, they have to be proportionately recovered from the revenues of these segments to calculate the profit of the firm. The share of each segment will naturally depend on the method applied to allocate these common costs to various segments. If the allocation method is inappropriate, it may distort the profitability of a segment. Hence, the need for a proper objective and scientific method of apportioning common costs. In the short-run, however, such allocated cost may not be relevant for performance evaluation of a segment as the division may have a positive controllable contribution margin, but may show losses due to the share of allocated common costs. In the long run, segments must collectively generate sufficient contribution to the total profit to allow the recovery of the firm-wide costs and the achievement of corporate profit goals. It is, however, difficult to decide how much of the common costs of the firm should be borne by each division to justify its long-term existence.

Segment Net Income The last sub-category of the segment income statement is the segment net income, which is equal to the difference between the segment profit contribution minus the allocated common firm-wide cost. However, this measure should be used with caution as a criterion for evaluation in view of the problems associated with apportionment of the firm's common costs.

We now illustrate the profit centre evaluation in Example 21.2.

◆ Example 21.2

The Hypothetical Ltd employs a budgetary control system and measures performance on segmented basis of its product line divisions, A and B. The budgeted and actual sales figures for the month of March are as follows:

Division	*Unit sales*		*Sales revenue*	
	Budgeted	*Actual*	*Budgeted*	*Actual*
A	20,000	24,000	₹2,00,000	₹2,40,000
B	40,000	40,000	2,00,000	2,40,000

The standard unit controllable variable costs are ₹4 for product line A and ₹2 for product line B. The company's budgeted controllable fixed costs for the month are ₹20,000 each for products A and B, whereas the actuals amounted to ₹22,000 for product A and ₹26,000 for product B. The attributable segment costs are: For product A, ₹40,000 (budgeted) and ₹44,000 (actual), and for product B, ₹60,000 (budgeted) and ₹64,000 (actual).

Assume that these costs represent all manufacturing costs and no opening and closing inventories. Actual variable manufacturing costs during March were ₹84,000 and ₹96,000 for divisions A and B respectively. The common firm-wide costs are assumed to be ₹48,000 to be apportioned on the basis of segment sales revenue.

From the above, prepare a performance evaluation report, if the Hypothetical Ltd employs profit centre basis of divisional performance measurement.

Solution

Since, the basis of divisional performance measurement is the profit centre, the performance evaluation report should be compiled in the form of a segment income statement. These are illustrated sequence-wise in Table 21.2.

TABLE 21.2 Performance Evaluation Report

(Figures in '000)

Particulars	Product Line A			Product Line B			Total		
	Budget	*Actual*	*Variance*	*Budget*	*Actual*	*Variance*	*Budget*	*Actual*	*Variance*
Sales revenue	₹200	₹240	₹40F	₹200	₹240	₹40F	₹400	₹480	₹80F
Less controllable variable costs	80	84	4A	80	96	16A	160	180	20A
Controllable contribution margins	120	156	36F	120	144	24F	240	300	60F
Less controllable fixed costs	20	22	2A	20	26	6A	40	48	8A
Controllable segment margin	100	134	34F	100	118	18F	200	252	52F
Less attributable segment costs	40	44	4A	60	64	4A	100	108	8A
Segment profit contribution	60	90	30F	40	54	14F	100	144	44F
Less common firm-wide costs	24	24	—	24	24	—	48	48	—
Net income	36	66	30F	16	30	14F	52	96	44F

*F = Favourable, A = Adverse.

Uses of Profit Centre The profit centre, as a measurement of performance, can be used: **(i)** For evaluation and ranking of profit centres and **(ii)** As a basis for decisions to modify operations of profit centres.

Evaluation and Ranking of Profit Centres Profit centres may be evaluated on the basis of their performance in relation to the various types of profit goals. As observed in the preceding discussion, the various profits goals with reference to profit centre performance are, controllable contribution margin, controllable segment margin, segment profit contribution, contribution margin ratio, segment profit contribution rate, and so on. In evaluating profit centres, it has to be seen whether individual segments have achieved their objectives and ranking given to the comparative performance of segments. Table 21.3 exhibits comparative performance based on segment profit contribution.

TABLE 21.3 Income Statement for the Quarter Ended March 31

Particulars	Divisions			Total
	A	B	C	
Sales	₹6,00,000	₹8,00,000	₹10,00,000	₹24,00,000
Less controllable variable costs	2,00,000	4,00,000	6,00,000	12,00,000
Controllable contribution margin	4,00,000	4,00,000	4,00,000	12,00,000
Less direct fixed costs	1,00,000	2,00,000	1,00,000	4,00,000
Controllable segment margin	3,00,000	2,00,000	3,00,000	8,00,000
Less attributable segment costs	1,40,000	2,40,000	80,000	4,60,000
Segment Profit contribution	1,60,000	(40,000)	2,20,000	3,40,000
Less firm-wide cost	—	—	—	1,40,000
Corporate net income	—	—	—	2,00,000

Based on their segment profit contribution, the three divisions would be ranked (1) C, (2) A, and (3) B. The negative segment profit contribution for division B shows its inability to recover all of its fixed and attributable costs. However, it does not follow automatically that it should be closed down. In order to decide whether to continue or discontinue division B, it is necessary to know whether all these fixed and attributable costs are avoidable. If not, the division should continue as its closure would cause a larger deficit than ₹40,000.

Further, since the three divisions show significant differences in sales value, contribution margin ratios, fixed costs, and attributable costs, ranking them on the basis of segment profit contribution would seem to be unfair. A better alternative would be a comparison between actual and budgeted segment profit contribution.

Performance evaluation in terms of other variables such as product lines, sales territories, wholesale and retail distribution channel, and so on is an alternative to segment reporting based on division. Assume for Table 21.3 that the sales of the three divisions, territory-wise, are as follows:

Division	*Northern territory*	*Southern territory*	*Total*
A	₹2,40,000	₹3,60,000	₹6,00,000
B	4,00,000	4,00,000	8,00,000
C	6,00,000	4,00,000	10,00,000
	12,40,000	11,60,000	24,00,000

Costs were directly identified with sales territories as follows:

	Northern territory	*Southern territory*	*Total*
Direct fixed costs	₹1,00,000	₹2,00,000	₹3,00,000
Attributable costs	1,40,000	2,40,000	3,80,000

Due to re-classification of the basis from divisions to territory, the remaining costs totalling ₹3,20,000 must be classified as common firm-wide costs. The income statement segmented on a sales-territory basis is presented in Table 21.4.

TABLE 21.4 Territory-wise Segmented Income Statement for the Quarter Ended March 31

Particulars	*Northern Sales Territory*	*Southern Sales Territory*	*Total*
Sales₹12,40,000	₹11,60,000	₹24,00,000	
Less controllable costs	6,40,000	5,60,000	12,00,000
Controllable segment margin	6,00,000	6,00,000	12,00,000
Less direct fixed costs	1,00,000	2,00,000	3,00,000
Controllable segment margin	5,00,000	4,00,000	9,00,000
Less attributable segment costs	1,40,000	2,40,000	3,80,000
Segment Profit contribution	3,60,000	1,60,000	5,20,000
Less firm-wide costs			3,20,000
Corporate net income			2,00,000

To summarise the discussion relating to alternative measures of profit centre performance, various indicators are appropriate depending on the purpose of analysis and the time period involved. For short-run evaluation, for instance, assuming that direct fixed costs and attributable costs do not vary with changes in segment activity level, *controllable contribution margin* is an appropriate measure. *Controllable segment margin* is a suitable measure of the long-run use of resources by segment managers. *Segment profit contribution* is the preferable long-term measure of a segment's ability to sustain itself as a separate company sub-unit. Profit centres should not be judged solely on the basis of their ability to maximise their sales revenues; to do so may lead to production and sale of products that generate higher sales revenues but a smaller profit contribution.

Decisions to Modify Operations of Profit Centres Apart from evaluation for ranking of profit centres, another use of profit centre performance assessment is that it guides decisions to modify operations of the profit centres. The modification in operations of profit centres comprises expansion, contraction, addition, or closure. The decision criterion in such cases would be the incremental effect on the overall profits of the company. In the short-run, assuming all attributable segment costs as constant, expansion or contraction in a profit centre's operations will affect the controllable contribution margin. In the long run, account will also have to be taken of changes in direct fixed costs and/or attributable segment costs. The decision whether to add or discontinue the entire segment will depend on the effect this may have on the segment profit contribution provided the decision does not affect the common firm-wide costs or the profit performance of other segments.

INVESTMENT CENTRES

LO 21.4 Evaluate investment centre as a responsibility centre

The third type of responsibility centre is an investment centre. It is defined as a responsibility centre in which inputs are measured in terms of cost/expenses and outputs are measured in terms of revenues and in which assets employed are also measured[17]. In other words, investment centres consider not only cost and revenues but also the assets used in the division. As a responsibility centre, the performance of a unit would be measured in relation to the revenues/profits and the assets employed in a division. The essence of investment centre analysis is the relationship between the profits and the assets that are used to generate those profits. It may, therefore, be said to be an extension of the profit centre in that it covers all the elements relevant to the measurement of the overall performance of a firm/its various divisions. In point of fact, an investment centre is essentially a profit centre. It is for this reason that it is sometimes said that there is no distinction between investment centres and profit centres, and the term "profit centre" is used to apply to both. Since, however, the investment centre is one step above a profit centre in terms of the additional financial data (assets), it should best be treated as a separate responsibility centre.

Investment centre is a responsibility centre whose performance is measured in relation to revenues/profits and the assets employed in the division.

The investment centre analysis can be used as a basis for evaluating the contribution of a division as an entity as also the performance of a divisional manager. The measure of performance in an investment centre is based on the relationship between the profits/income, and the amount of assets employed in generating the profits. There are two ways to relate income to assets: **(i)** Return on investment and **(ii)** Residual income.

Segment return on investment is the segment profit contribution divided by the segment assets/resources.

Return on Investment (ROI) Analysis The determination of ROI has already been shown in Chapter 6. With reference to responsibility accounting, the ROI will be the segment return on investment (SROI). Symbolically,

$$\text{SROI} = \text{Segment profit contribution (SPC)} \div \text{Segment resources/assets (SR/SA)} \quad \textbf{(21.1)}$$

The SROI can be used both for operating performance measurement, and managerial evaluation. Accordingly, there are two variations of segment return on investments, namely,

$$\text{SROI} = \text{SPC before interest} \div \text{Segment total assets} \quad \textbf{(21.2)}$$

$$\text{SROI (net)} = \text{SPC after interest} \div \text{Segment net assets} \quad \textbf{(21.3)}$$

The SROI is useful in evaluating the total earning power of all assets directly employed by a segment regardless of how they are financed. The net SROI is a better indicator of a division's ability to generate profit contributions in excess of the direct cost of financing its operations.

Alternatively, the SROI can be viewed as the product of two components, namely, segment profit contribution margin, and segment assets turnover. Symbolically,

$$\text{SROI} = \frac{\text{Segment profit contribution (SPC)}}{\text{Segment salts revenue}} \times \frac{\text{Segment salts revenue}}{\text{Segment assets}} \quad \textbf{(21.4)}$$

Advantages There are several advantages in using ROI to measure divisional performance. In the first place, ROI is the generally accepted measure of overall performance. As a measure of divisional performance, it is consistent with a firm-wise rate of return analysis. It is also compatible with the common sense view that investments are made to achieve the goal of a desired rate of return.

Secondly, ROI analysis is a relative, and not absolute measure. It is, in fact, a ratio/percentage. It, therefore, serves as a common denominator so that a comparison can be made between the performance of different divisions. By enabling an interdivisional comparison, ROI is of great practical significance.

Thirdly, ROI is conceptually easy to understand and interpret.

Finally, ROI analysis can provide incentive for optimum utilisation of the assets of a firm. In operational terms, it encourages divisional managers to obtain/retain assets that provide satisfactory return on investment and to discard/dispose off assets that are not giving acceptable returns.

Limitations The ROI analysis is conceptually sound and appealing, as a performance measure. Nevertheless, it suffers from certain operational limitations: **(i)** Determination of investment base and **(ii)** Determination of net income.

Investment base is the measurement of the value of divisional investment.

Investment Base One operational problem with the ROI analysis relates to the determination of the investment base. One significant element in the ROI analysis is the assets/investment employed in the generation of net income/ profits. The determination/measurement of the value of investments is referred to as "investment base". The measurement of the divisional investment base requires: **(i)** A precise definition of all elements that should be included and **(ii)** The value that should be assigned to them. There are, however, operational problems in respect of each of these aspects in that there are alternatives available which imply different practices. This is so because the measurement of investments/assets is not standardised. The problems of measuring investment in assets in connection with the investment centre analysis fall into two categories: **(i)** Problems of allocation/apportionment and **(ii)** Problems of valuation.

Allocation Problems These arise out of the possibility of different treatment of assets that are pooled/shared among the different divisions. The most common of such assets are cash, receivables, and inventories. How should such assets be allocated among different divisions? One alternative is to ignore them while working out the investment base of a division, the underlying principle being that only those assets which are exclusively used/directly traceable to a division should be included. Alternatively, the common/jointly shared assets should be allocated to the benefiting divisions for the proper measurement of their individual investments. Apart from the theoretical differences as to whether such assets should be allocated or not, there is a more difficult problem of identification of assets with separate divisions and reasonable allocation.

The second aspect of the allocational problem relates to the treatment of assets that are currently idle. If such assets are excluded as they presumably do not generate income, the ROI would be actually a return on capital employed rather than on the total investments/assets/available invested capital. This approach would tend to raise the ROI. This will not, however, reveal how efficiently assets have been used, the basic objective of ROI analysis. The presence of idle assets is suggestive of inefficient utilisation of resources. Its inclusion/exclusion would affect the ROI.

Valuation Problems Apart from the problem allocation/traceability of items of assets, the measurement of investment base is complicated by the difficulty of assigning values to the assets of a division. There are variety of methods to value assets for purpose of ROI analysis. They include: **(i)** Book value, **(ii)** Gross book value (original costs), and **(iii)** Current replacement cost.

Book Value The most readily available method of valuation of assets, defined as the original cost less accumulated depreciation, is probably the least useful measure owing to an inherent weakness. Due to the declining investment base as a result of depreciation charge, the carrying value of assets declines. If the net income of the division remains constant, or does not decline as rapidly as the book value of the division's assets, the divisional ROI would show improving performance as the assets become more worn-out and obsolete. Since continued use of obsolete resources due to a low investment base would inflate ROI, the division's productive capacity would ultimately decline.

Gross Book Value Which is the original cost without any deduction for depreciation, provides a partial solution to the defect in ROI analysis based on book values. If earnings are constant, this approach will give a constant ROI over the years. A variation of this approach is to use a method of depreciation with increasing charges over the life of the assets. It will result in a constant ROI, as each year a lower income is related to a smaller asset base. While this approach thus avoids the problem of meaningless rise in the ROI as time passes, it is not a measure of the current economic value of the assets involved.

Replacement Cost Basis Provides the best measure of current performance. Its weakness, however, is that replacement cost is difficult to determine and may require subjective assessment.

In brief, in arriving at the value of the assets that generate income for ROI analysis, several alternative approaches/practices are available/possible. That several approaches can be adopted is another way of saying that the measurement of the investment base is problematic.

Net Income The second element in the computation of ROI is the net income/profit of a responsibility centre. The determination of divisional net income also involves some problems.

First, as an extension of the profit centre, *the investment centre analysis encounters all the problems of the profit centre analysis.*

In addition, there are some special problems of income measurement as a rate of return is to be calculated. These relate to the treatment of **(a)** tax **(b)** interest. These items are outside the control of the divisional managers. Should they be considered in calculating the divisional income? According to the incremental approach, since these items do not fall in the areas of responsibility of a division, that is, they are not controllable by the division, they are to be excluded. Further, should depreciation be based on historical cost or replacement cost? If replacement cost is the basis of asset valuation, depreciation should also be based upon replacement cost. Moreover, since the ROI measures current operating performance, non-recurring items such as extraordinary gains and losses should be excluded. Thus, items having a bearing on net income can be treated in different ways. This creates problems in the measurement of net income for ROI analysis.

Segment residual income is the difference betwen the actual operating income of a division and the required expected income.

Segment Residual Income An alternative measure of financial performance in an investment centre is segment *residual income.* The preceding discussion clearly shows that the SROI suffers from serious limitations. Essentially, it is a relative measure, that is, a ratio or rate of return. This is so because net profit is related to investments which encounter several problems. The segment residual income alternative to measure divisional performance avoids some of the problems associated with the SROI analysis.

Residual income is the amount that remains after deducting an "implied" interest charge from operating income. The implied interest charge reflects an opportunity cost. The basis of the interest charge is the amount of assets in each investment centre. The rate of interest charge is equal to the minimum rate on investment specified by top management as part of the corporate strategic plan. Operationally, the management of the firm lays down an amount of interest charge as a compensation for providing the original investment to a division. The difference between the actual operating income of a division and the required/expected income is segment residual income.

Symbolically,

$$SRI = SPC - (SROI \times SR) \quad \textbf{(21.5)}$$

where,

SRI = Segment residual income
SPC = Segment profit contribution
SROI = Desired segment ROI
SR = Segment resources

To illustrate, assume the budgeted investment of a firm is ₹10 lakh. Assume further, a budgeted net income of ₹2 lakh. The required rate of return (cost of capital) may be assumed to be 15 per cent. The residual income of the division would be:

Divisional income	₹2,00,000
Required income (0.15 × ₹10 lakh)	(1,50,000)
Segment residual income	50,000

Merits The residual income approach has some merits.

A principal advantage is that it encourages capital investment any time a divisional manager can earn more than the required/cut-off rate. The amount of the residual income indicates the investment centre's ability to earn more than a normal profit on the amount of capital that it uses. Any new investment will increase the residual income if it yields an income higher than the required/cut-off percentage.

A second advantage is that it allows different rates of return for different divisions/assets, for example, higher rates for risky and lower for less risky/certain.

Limitations Residual income as performance measure overcomes some of the shortcomings of ROI analysis. But it is not a perfect measure. It has certain limitations. First, most of the problems in measuring the divisional income and divisional investment base are also present in the measurement of residual income. There is an additional problem of selecting/specifying a fair and equitable measure of the required/cut-off percentage (that is, the cost of capital).

SUMMARY

- Segment profit contribution is the best direct measure of profit performance attributable to, and controllable by a segment. Segment net income may also be a useful measure as it emphasises the long-run ability of a segment to contribute to the profits of an organisation. Segment profit contribution and segment net income may be used for **(i)** evaluating segment performance in relation to pre-determined objectives, **(ii)** competitive ranking of segments, **(iii)** decisions relating to the expansion, contractions, additions or discontinuation of segments.
- Responsibility accounting, as a control device, is relevant to divisional performance measurement, whereas the other control devices are applicable to the organisation as a whole. The objectives of divisional performance measurement are: 1. To determine the contribution that a division makes to the organisation as a whole. 2. To provide a basis for evaluating the quality of the divisional managers' performance. 3. To motivate the divisional manager to operate his division in line with the basic goals of the organisation.
- Responsibility accounting focuses on responsibility centres. A responsibility centre is a sub-unit of an organisation under the control of a manager, who is responsible for the activities of that responsibility centre. The important criterion for creating responsibility centres is that the unit of the organisation should be separable and identifiable for operating purposes and evaluation of its performance. For the purpose of measuring divisional performance, the responsibility centres are divided into: **(1)** Expense centres,

(2) Profit centres, and (3) Investment centres. The *modus operandi* of responsibility accounting is the comparison of budgeted and actual performance.

LO 21.1

- An expense centre is a segment whose financial performance is measured in terms of cost. The analysis of performance is restricted to the use of resources in the division; what has been achieved as a consequence of consuming those resources is not considered. The suitability of cost, as an index of performance, and, therefore, of expense centres as divisional performance measure, is relevant in situations in which the revenue of a responsibility centre cannot be reliably measured, or the segment produces one single product, or, if the divisional manager is to produce a stated quantity of output at the lowest feasible cost. The cost centres evaluation techniques include variance analysis and job and process costing systems. However, in general, an expense centre is not a useful basis for measuring the performance of responsibility centres.

LO 21.2

- The profit centre is that division of an organisation in which financial performance is measured on the basis of profit (revenue-expenses). With reference to responsibility accounting, a profit related performance criterion must be developed to suit the requirements of the divisional performance measurement. The traditional income statement format can be modified to provide a criterion for profit centre performance. The key categories in the revised income statement are: **(i)** Controllable contribution margin, **(ii)** Segment contribution margin, **(iii)** Segment profit contribution, and **(iv)** Segment net income.
- Although the profit centre basis is superior to expense centre, as a criterion for divisional performance measurement, this approach suffers from certain operational problems. These relate to criteria for profit centres, measurement of expenses and transfer prices. Of the three, transfer price is a critical aspect of profit centre performance evaluation. The choice of transfer pricing system has to reconcile the requirements of managerial decision-making, on the one hand, and performance evaluation, on the other. Alternative transfer prices for performance evaluation include market-based prices, cost-based prices, cost plus normal mark-up, incremental cost, negotiated prices and dual prices. All of these lack one or more of the desired transfer pricing criteria of **(i)** objectivity, **(ii)** equivalence to the value of change, and **(iii)** compatibility of decision-making with the goals of the segment and those of the organisation as a whole.

  The market price of a product, that is, equivalent to the intermediate product, being transferred between segments, is by and large, the most suitable for segment performance evaluation although it has limited value for decision-making purposes.

LO 21.3

- The investment centre approach is an extension of the profit centre approach. The measure of performance in an investment centre is based on the relationship between the segment profit contribution and segment assets. There are two ways to relate segment profit contribution to segment resources: segment rate of return on investment and segment residual income.

  The computation of segment rate of return on investment (*SROI*) is summarised below:

(1) $$SROI = \frac{\text{Segment profit contribution } (SPC)}{\text{Segment resources/assets } (SR/SA)} \times 100$$

(2) $$SROI = \frac{(SPC)}{\text{Segment sales revenue}} \times \frac{\text{Segment sales revenue}}{\text{Segment assets}}$$

(3) $$SROI \text{ (operating)} = \frac{SPC \text{ before interest}}{\text{Segment total assets}} \times 100$$

(4) $$SROI \text{ (net)} = \frac{SPC \text{ After interest}}{\text{Segment net assets}} \times 100$$

(5) Segment residual income (*SRI*) is = $SRI = SPC - (SROI \times SR)$

- The segment *ROI*, as a measure of divisional performance, has the merit of being a generally accepted measure consistent with firm-wise rate of return analysis. It is, moreover, a relative measure. It is conceptually easy to understand and interpret, and it can provide incentive for optimal utilisation of the resources of the firm. In spite of its conceptual soundness and appeal, it suffers from certain operational problems. These are: **(i)** determination of the segment investment base, and **(ii)** determination of the segment contribution. The problem of measuring segment resources are basically problems of allocation and valuation. The determination of contribution margin is associated with the problem of transfer pricing and the treatment of tax and interest.
- An alternative measure of financial performance in an investment centre is the segment residual income. The main advantage of this approach is that it encourages capital investment any time a divisional manager can earn more than a required rate of return. It also allows different rates of return for different divisions and, thus, is consistent with the decision-criterion in capital budgeting. Thus, it overcomes some of the shortcomings of the *SROI* analysis.
- In brief, among the approaches to measure performance in investment centre analysis, segment residual income is conceptually superior but segment *ROI* is more widely-used.

LO 21.4

REFERENCES

1. J.M. Fremgen, *Accounting for Managerial Analysis,* (Richard D. Irwin, Homewood, Illinois, 1976), p. 328.
2. R.N. Anthony and G.A. Welsch, *Management Accounting,* (Richard D. Irwin, Homewood, Illinois, 1977), p. 403.
3. *Ibid.*, p. 406.
4. Fremgen, *op. cit.*, p. 329.
5. Anthony and Welsch, *op. cit.*, p. 407.
6. Fremgen, *op. cit.*, p. 331.
7. Anthony and Welsh, *op. cit.*, p. 407.
8. *Ibid.*, p. 408
9. Fremgen, *op. cit.*, p. 334.
10. Anthony and Welsch, *op. cit.*, p. 411
11. *Ibid.*, p. 413
12. Fremgen, *op. cit.*, p. 343.
13. Chartfield, M. and Neilson, Denis, Cost Accounting, (Harcourt Brace Jovanovich, New York), 1983, p. 987.
14. D.T. Decoster and E.L. Schafer, Management Accounting, (John Wiley and Sons, New York, 1979), p. 426.
15. *Ibid.*, p. 427.
16. Based on Chatfield, M. Neilson, D., *Cost Accounting,* Harcourt Braces Jovanoich, Inc., New York), 1983.
17. Anthony and Welsch, *op. cit.*, p. 417.

SOLVED PROBLEMS

P.21.1 ABC Ltd operates a number of divisions located in different regions. Division A incurred losses in the first quarter of the current year. Relevant revenue and cost data pertaining to this division are as follows: LO 21.3 LOD: E

Sales revenue	₹6,50,000
Controllable variable costs	3,50,000
Controllable fixed costs	2,00,000
Attributable segment costs	50,000
Common firm-wide costs allocated to division A	60,000
Loss	(10,000)

You are required: **(i)** To prepare a performance evaluation report of division A in the proper format and **(ii)** Advise the management whether its operations should be continued or shut down.

Solution

(i) *Performance Evaluation Report of Division A*

Particulars	*Amount*
Sales revenue	₹6,50,000
Less controllable variable costs	3,50,000
Controllable contribution margin	3,00,000
Less controllable fixed costs	2,00,000
Controllable segment margin	1,00,000
Less attributable segment costs	50,000
Segment profit contribution	50,000
Less common firm-wide costs	60,000
Loss	(10,000)

(ii) In the short-run, division A justifies its existence as it generates a positive segment profit contribution (₹50,000), regardless of its share of firm-wide costs. Of course, in the long-run, division A must collectively generate sufficient total profit contribution to allow the recovery of all firm-wide costs and the achievement of corporate profit goals.

P.21.2 The Hypothetical Ltd has the following total operating results for the first half of current year: LO 21.3 LOD: M

Sales revenue	₹56,00,000
Less variable costs	37,20,000
Contribution	18,80,000
Less fixed costs	10,00,000
Net income	8,80,000

The following additional information concerning the performance of each of the firm's three operating departments has been provided:

	Departments		
	A	*B*	*C*
Sales revenue	₹24,00,000	₹20,00,000	₹12,00,000
Variable costs	16,80,000	12,00,000	8,40,000
Direct fixed costs	3,20,000	2,80,000	2,00,000

1. Rank the three departments on the basis of their proportionate measure of relative profitability.
2. A proposal to increase advertising expenses by ₹1,23,200 is expected to generate a 10 per cent increase in sales in all three departments. Analyse the effect of this proposal on the firm as a whole and on

each department. Assume that the cost of advertising will be allocated to divisions according to each division's percentage to sales, and is to be considered as an attributable fixed cost of each department.

Solution

1. *Performance Evaluation Report*

Particulars	*Departments* A	B	C	*Total*
Sales revenue	₹24,00,000	₹20,00,000	₹12,00,000	₹56,00,000
Less controllable variable costs	16,80,000	12,00,000	8,40,000	37,20,000
Controllable contribution margin	7,20,000	8,00,000	3,60,000	18,80,000
Less controllable/direct fixed costs	3,20,000	2,80,000	2,00,000	8,00,000
Segment profit contribution	4,00,000	5,20,000	1,60,000	10,80,000
Less common firm-wide costs				2,00,000
Net income				8,80,000
Segment profit contribution as per cent of sales revenue	16.67	26	13.33	
Ranking	2	1	3	

2. *Performance Evaluation Report (Impact of Advertisement Cost Analysed)*

Particulars	*Departments* A	B	C	*Total*
0				
Sales revenue	₹26,40,000	₹22,00,000	₹13,20,000	₹61,60,000
Less controllable variable cost	18,48,000	13,20,000	9,24,000	40,92,000
Controllable contribution margin	7,92,000	8,80,000	3,96,000	20,68,000
Less direct fixed costs (existing)	3,20,000	2,80,000	2,00,000	8,00,000
Less advertising costs (allocated on the basis of sales ratio, additional)	52,800	44,000	26,400	1,23,200
Segment profit contribution	4,19,200	5,56,000	1,69,600	11,44,800
Less common firm-wide costs				2,00,000
Net income				9,44,800
Segment profit contribution as per cent of sales	15.88	25.27	12.85	
Ranking	2	1	3	

Although there has been a decline in segment profit contribution as percentages of sales for all the three departments, total segment profit contribution as a sequel to advertisement campaign, has shown a rise. As a result, the firm's net income has increased from ₹8,80,000 to ₹9,44,800.

P. 21.3 The current year's operating results of the three divisions (A, B, and C) of Hypothetical Ltd are given below: LO 21.4 LOD: M

(Amount in '000 ₹)

	Divisions A	B	C
Sales revenue	400	400	2,000
Less expenses	360	200	1,800
Segment profit contribution	40	200	200
Segment assets	200	800	4,000

Determine the rate of return for the three divisions and rank these divisions assuming that the firm follows investment centre basis of performance evaluation.

Solution

Segment Rates of Return of A, B and C Divisions of Hypothetical Ltd (Amount in '000' ₹)

Particulars	Divisions A	B	C
1. Sales revenue	400	400	2,000
2. *Less* expenses	360	200	1,800
3. Segment profit contribution	40	200	200
4. Segment assets	200	800	4,000
5. Return on sales [(3) ÷ (1)] (per cent)	10	50	10
6. Asset turnover rate [(1) ÷ (4)] (times)	2	0.5	0.5
7. Segment rate of return (per cent)	20	25	5

In absolute terms, segment profit contributions are similar (₹2,00,000) for divisions B and C. However, in relative terms, B's performance is far better than that of division C, the respective figures for return on sales being 50 and 10 per cents. Segment rate of return of division B is also much higher (25 per cent) than that of C (5 per cent).

Although A and C both have 10 per cent rate of return on sales, A earned a 20 per cent return on investment compared to C's 5 per cent because asset turnover rate of A is 2 whereas that of C is only 0.5.

Based on their segment rate of return, the three divisions would be ranked B (1), A (2) and C (3).

P. 21.4 A.N. Vinod, the chief accounts officer of XYZ Ltd, has set a number of transfer prices to be used by service departments within the firm, all of which used to be cost centres. One is for typing services. The charge is ₹100 per hour which is based on total budgeted hours of available service and total budgeted costs for the typing service pool. The manager of one of the operating departments, a profit centre, has obtained a price of ₹70 per hour of typists' time from an outside agency. The task will take about 100 hours. The manager informs A.N. Vinod and B.C. Mehta, the manager of the typing service cost centre, of the outside price. In turn, he was informed that he could avail of the outside facility if he so desired, but the price set internally would not be lowered from the existing rate of ₹100 per hour. LO 21.2 LOD: M

Comment on the position taken by the managers. Budgeted costs for a pool are about 75 per cent fixed. Make your recommendations.

Solution

The outside typing facility should be availed of by the operating department to improve its performance.

Judging the problem from the point of view of the manager of typing cost centre, it does not really matter for him if the operating manager seeks typing facilities from outside. This is so because efficiency of cost centre is to be evaluated by reference to budgeted costs which remain unaffected by the operating manager seeking outside services.

Looking at the problem from the angle of the firm as a whole, the operating managers' suggestion may not be a profitable proposition as the variable cost saved is ₹25 per hour and incremental variable costs will be ₹70 per hour, entailing a loss of ₹45 per hour (total loss being ₹4,500 for 100 hours). However, such a conclusion would not hold good if typists were overburdened and working at full capacity. If that were the case, *in the short run,* it would pay the firm if the operating manager makes use of 'outside' typing facilities. If the typing cost centre is operating below capacity, it would be in the interest of the firm to set the transfer price equal/below the outside market to discourage managers to go outside for typing facilities.

P.21.5 Hypothetical Ltd, a large-sized well established manufacturing enterprise has set up most of its service departments as artificial profit centres. The firm rents a computer for a fixed fee of ₹15,000 per month which is charged to the manager of the computer centre. The manager, in turn, charges operating units for use of the computer at ₹200 per hour. One of the operating managers, has an acquaintance in a data processing service company that charges only ₹150 per hour for *similar* type of computer services that the manager rents. LO 21.3 LOD: M

The managers in the firm are free to buy services inside or outside the firm. The operating manager told the manager of the computer centre either to reduce his price to ₹150 per hour or he would use the outside firm.

REQUIRED:

(i) Suppose that the operating department uses 20 hours of computer time per month and the firm has idle capacity. What would your recommendation be regarding lowering price from the point of view of the firm?

(ii) If the firm's computer is overloaded and demand exceeds the total time available in a month, what would your recommendation be regarding lowering price?

Solution

(i) It would be profitable for the firm to lower the transfer price to ₹150 because the computer costs are fixed and there is idle capacity. The firm will lose ₹3,000 (20 hours × ₹150) if the operating department opts for outside computer services.

(ii) If the computer is overloaded at ₹200 per hour, it might be completely swamped at ₹150, with an increased in turnaround time, leading to possible dissatisfaction on the part of the users. Moreover, if the time is a critical factor for information desired, the company may suffer on account of delayed decisions.

Apart from *qualitative* factors, in monetary terms also, when business can be obtained at ₹200 per hour, there is no need of lowering the transfer price to ₹150. The department will lose 20 hours at ₹200 and gain them back at ₹150. However, it should be ensured that it does not lead to mass following from other departments rendering the capacity of the computer centre idle in future.

P.21.6 The sales manager of Bombay Textiles Ltd is judged by the total sales. Exceeding the sales budget is considered good performance. The sales budget and cost data for the current quarter are shown below: LO 21.3 LOD: M

Particulars	*Products*			*Total*
	Sarees	*Long-cloth*	*Bedsheets*	
Sales budget	₹4,50,000	₹9,00,000	₹16,50,000	₹30,00,000
Variable costs	(2,25,000)	(4,05,000)	(4,95,000)	(11,25,000)
Contribution	2,25,000	4,95,000	11,55,000	18,75,000
Actual sales	15,00,000	12,00,000	6,00,000	33,00,000

Actual prices were equal to budgeted prices and variable costs incurred were as budgeted per unit.

REQUIRED:

(i) Did the sales manager perform well? Support your answer with calculations.

(ii) Suggest better performance measurement criterion to be used by the firm.

Solution

Performance Evaluation Report

Particulars	*Products*			*Total*
	Sarees	*Long-cloth*	*Bedsheets*	
Sales	₹15,00,000	₹12,00,000	₹6,00,000	₹33,00,000
Less variable costs:				
(50 per cent of sarees)	(7,50,000)			
(45 per cent of long cloth)		(5,40,000)		
(30 per cent of bedsheets)			(1,80,000)	
(44.54 per cent of total sales)				(14,70,000)
Contribution	7,50,000	6,60,000	4,20,000	18,30,000
Contribution margin ratio (per cent)	50	55	70	55.45

(i) Apparently, the sales manager seems to have performed well as the actual sales exceeded budgeted sales by ₹3,00,000, but the actual contribution is ₹45,000 lower than budgeted. This has happened because of the unfavourable change in the sales-mix, the most profitable product (bedsheets) has the least sales volume and the relatively less profitable products have much higher sales volume.

As a sequel to such a change, the weighted average contribution margin based on planned mix which was 62.5 per cent (₹18,75,000 ÷ ₹30,00,000) has decreased to 55.45 per cent. In real terms, the sales manager did not perform better than planned.

(ii) The use of total sales, without reference to relative profitability of sales of different products, is unwise. It may not be possible to sell high-profit yielding products in budgeted volumes. If it is so, the sales manager could concentrate on low-profit yielding products, which may be more easily sold.

The performance of the sales manager should better be judged by the following criterion: Sales revenue less *(i) budgeted variable costs of production and (ii) actual selling costs.*

In the present system of transferring product at actual costs, the production department passes on its inefficiencies to the sales department, which should not be responsible for such costs. The sales manager should be charged with actual selling costs as he is responsible for incurrence of such costs and, above all, such costs are controllable at his level.

P.21.7 The following is the profit plan prepared for ABC Ltd for the current year ending March 31 (₹ in lakh): **LO 21.3** **LOD: D**

Particulars	*Product line*			*Total*
	X	Y	Z	
Sales revenue	1,000	600	400	2,000
Controllable variable cost to make and sell	500	360	280	1,140
Controllable contribution margin	500	240	120	860
Common firm-wide costs (fixed)	—	—	—	660
				200

The income statement for the current year ended March 31 showed the following (₹ in lakh):

Particulars	*Product line*			*Total*
	X	Y	Z	
Sales	660	660	880	2,200
Less special discounts	20	—	—	20
	640	660	880	2,180
Controllable variable costs to make and sell	332	400	620	1,352
Controllable contribution margin	308	260	260	828
Common firm-wide costs (fixed)				670
Profit				158

Two steps were taken to increase the sales of product line X: **(a)** Special discounts were granted on large orders and **(b)** An additional appropriation of ₹6 lakh was approved for advertising and sales promotion. Selling prices did not change in the current year.

You are required to prepare an analysis of the changes in net income that would be helpful in fixing responsibility, using the contribution approach.

Solution

Statement Showing Analysis of Changes in Income (₹in lakh)

Particulars				*Decrease*	*Increase*
Increase in contribution [(₹200 lakh sales revenue × 0.43, per cent weighted contribution to volume ratio, that is, ₹860 ÷ ₹2,000)]					86
Decrease in contribution due to special discounts				20	
Decrease in contribution due to unfavourable sales-mix:					
Budgeted contribution (₹2,200 × 0.43)			946		
Less actual contribution (See working note)					
Product	X: (₹660 × 0.50)	330			
	Y: (₹660 × 0.40)	264			
	Z: (₹880 × 0.30)	264	858		
Total				88	

(Contd.)

(Contd.)

Decrease in contribution due to increase in variable cost:				
Actual variable costs		1,352		
Less budgeted variable costs				
Product X: (₹660 × 0.50)	330			
Y: (₹660 × 0.60)	396			
Z: (₹880 × 0.70)	616	1,342	10	
			118	86
Decrease in contribution (net)				32
Increase in advertisement cost				6
Increase in other common firm-wide costs (fixed)				4
Decrease in income (net)				42

WORKING NOTES

	Contribution ratio (per cent)		Variable cost ratio (per cent)
Product	X: (₹500 ÷ ₹1,000)	= 50	50
	Y: (₹240 ÷ ₹600)	= 40	60
	Z: (₹120 ÷ ₹400)	= 30	70

P.21.8 Home Comforts Ltd deals in three products, Ace, Nice, and Grace and these are sold directly through salesmen in three zones, Prime, Extension, and Outreach. The responsibility for sales promotion rests with the headquarters and so does the overall control of distribution and sales. Cost of sales as per cent of sales are: Ace, 85; Nice, 80; Grace, 75. Details of sales and selling and distribution expenses for the year are as follows: LO 21.3 LOD: M

Zones	*Products*	*Sales*	*Selling and distribution expenses allocated direct*
Prime zone	Ace	₹9,00,000	₹63,990
	Nice	9,00,000	84,465
	Grace	4,50,000	47,160
		22,50,000	1,95,615
Extension zone	Ace	6,75,000	46,710
	Nice	4,50,000	47,700
	Grace	2,25,000	23,940
		13,50,000	1,18,350
Outreach zone	Ace	2,25,000	18,900
	Nice	1,80,000	15,165
	Grace	4,95,000	66,375
		9,00,000	1,00,440

Selling and distribution expenses at headquarters are as follows:

Office expenses	₹94,500
Advertisement	1,35,000
Other expenses	1,21,500

Advertisement costs are allocated to zones and products on the basis of sales. Office expenses and other expenses are apportioned equally to the zones or the products, while computing the profit or loss for the zones or the products, as the case may be.

Prepare a comparative profit and loss statement, presenting zonal performance as distinct from product performance.

Solution

Comparative Profit and Loss Statement (Evaluating Zonal Performance)

Particulars	*Zones*			*Total*
	Prime	*Extension*	*Outreach*	
Sales revenue	₹22,50,000	₹13,50,000	₹9,00,000	₹45,00,000
Less cost of sales:				
Ace (0.85)	7,65,000	5,73,750	1,91,250	15,30,000
Nice (0.80)	7,20,000	3,60,000	1,44,000	12,24,000
Grace (0.75)	3,37,500	1,68,750	3,71,250	8,77,500
Total	18,22,500	11,02,500	7,06,500	36,31,500
Gross profit/margin	4,27,500	2,47,500	1,93,500	8,68,500
Less selling and distribution expenses:				
Direct costs (allocated)	1,95,615	1,18,350	1,00,440	4,14,405
Advertisement (apportioned in sales ratio: 225: 135: 90)	67,500	40,500	27,000	1,35,000
Office expenses (apportioned equally)	31,500	31,500	31,500	94,500
Other expenses (equally)	40,500	40,500	40,500	1,21,500
Total selling and distribution costs	3,35,115	2,30,850	1,99,440	7,65,405
Net profit (loss)	92,385	16,650	(5,940)	1,03,095

P.21.9 Alfa Ltd has two divisions, A and B. A division is currently operating at full capacity. It has been asked to supply its product to division B. Division A sells its product to its regular customers for ₹30 each. Division B (currently operating at 50 per cent capacity) is willing to pay ₹20 each for the component produced by division A (this represents the full absorption cost per component at division A). The components will be used by division B in supplementing its main product to conform to the need of special order. As per the contract terms of sale, the buyer calls for reimbursement of full cost to division B, plus 10 per cent. LO 21.3 LOD: M

Division A has a variable cost of ₹17 per component. The cost per unit of division B subsequent to the buying part from division A is estimated as follows:

Purchased parts—outside vendors	₹90
Purchased part—division A	20
Other variable costs	50
Fixed overheads and administration	40
	200

The company uses return on investment in the measurement of divisional and division manager's performance.

REQUIRED:

(a) As manager of division A, would you recommend sales of your output to division B at the stipulated price of ₹20?

(b) Would it be in the over-all interest of the company for division A to sell its output to division B?

(c) Suggest an alternative transfer price and show how could it lead to goal congruence?

Solution

(a) As manager of division A, I would not recommend sales at ₹20 per unit to division B. The division is already operating at its full capacity and the market is presumably absorbing all its output at ₹30 per unit. The internal transfer made to division B, hence, would reduce its profit (by ₹10 per unit) as well as the ROI.

(b) *Decision Analysis (Whether to Transfer Part from Division A to Division B at ₹20 per unit or Not).*

Particulars	Sold externally	Transferred to division B
Sale price (division A)	₹30	
Sale price (division B) (₹200 + 10 per cent)		₹220
Less relevant/incremental cost:		
For part of division A	17	17
Purchased parts from outside	—	90
Other variable costs	—	50
Profit per unit	13	63

Yes, it will be the over-all interest of the company that the transfer takes place as it would augment the firm's profit by ₹50 per unit.

(c) Dual price basis of effecting transfer is the most appropriate. In this case, the relevant transfer price will be ₹30 (sale) so far as division A is concerned, and ₹20 (purchase) so far as division B is concerned. It will keep the profits of division A unaffected and will facilitate the utilisation of the idle capacity of division B, as also increase its profit:

Sale price (₹200 + 10 per cent)	₹220
Less costs (₹90 + ₹20 + ₹50)	160
	60

P.21.10 Royal Industries Ltd has two divisions, A and B. Division A manufactures product X which it sells in an outside market as well as to division B, which processes it to manufacture Z. The manager of division B has expressed the opinion that the transfer price is too high. LO 21.3,4 LOD: D

The two divisional managers are about to enter into discussions to resolve the conflict, and the manager of division A wants you to supply him with some information prior to the discussions.

Division A has been selling 40,000 units to outsiders and 10,000 units to division B, all at ₹20 per unit. It is not anticipated that these demands will change. The variable cost is ₹12 per unit and the fixed costs are ₹2 lakh.

The manager of division A anticipates that division B will want a transfer price of ₹18. If he does not sell to division B, ₹30,000 of fixed costs and ₹1,75,000 of assets can be avoided. The manager of division A would have no control over the proceeds from the sale of the assets and is judged primarily on his rate of return. The firm's existing assets are of ₹8 lakh.

(a) Should the manager of division A transfer its products at ₹18 to division B?

(b) What is the lowest price that the division A should accept? Support your decision with detailed calculations.

Solution

(a) *Comparative Statement of Profit of Division A*

Particulars	*Alternative situations*		
	Sell at ₹20	*Transfer at ₹18*	*Do not transfer*
Sales revenue:			
Market sales (40,000 units × ₹20)	₹8,00,000	₹8,00,000	₹8,00,000
Transfer to division B (10,000 units)	2,00,000	1,80,000	—
Total (a)	10,00,000	9,80,000	8,00,000
Variable costs (₹12 per unit)	6,00,000	6,00,000	4,80,000
Fixed costs	2,00,000	2,00,000	1,70,000
Total (b)	8,00,000	8,00,000	6,50,000
Total profit (a – b)	2,00,000	1,80,000	1,50,000
Total assets	8,00,000	8,00,000	6,25,000
SROI (per cent)	25	22.5	24

The manager of division A should not agree to sell at ₹18 per unit as it lowers down its rate of return—the index of his evaluation.

(b) The lowest transfer price acceptable to division A is one which maintains its rate of return of 24 per cent (the possible SROI without selling to division B):

$$\frac{\text{Toal sales revenue} - \text{Total cost}}{\text{Total assets}} = \frac{₹8,00,000 + 10,000X - ₹8,00,000}{₹8,00,000} = 0.24$$

Where X = transfer price per unit

10,000 X = ₹1,92,000

X = ₹19.20

The lowest transfer price acceptable to division A is ₹19.20 per unit.

P.21.11 The AB Ltd has two divisions, X and Y. One of the parts produced by division X is used in the manufacture of a product that is assembled at division Y. The part is not unique and there is a readily defined market such that X can sell outside the firm and Y can buy from outside. The following information is descriptive of the normal expectations of division X: LO 21.3 LOD: D

Capacity to produce the part (units)	1,25,000
External sales at ₹100 per unit (units)	1,00,000
Transfer to division Y (units)	25,000
Costs:	
Variable manufacturing cost per unit	₹84
Variable selling costs (on external sales only but not incurred on internal transfers)	2
Fixed manufacturing cost (based on 1,25,000 units)	6
Fixed selling cost (based on 1,00,000 units)	1

The division Y presents the following data on the assumption of a volume of 25,000 units (one part is needed for each unit of its own production):

Variable manufacturing cost per unit (exclusive of transfer price or outside purchase price)	₹100
Variable selling expenses per unit	6
Fixed manufacturing cost	10
Fixed selling expenses	4
Selling price of finished product	240

REQUIRED:

(i) If division X could sell 1,25,000 units at ₹100 each in the outside market, what transfer price would the company management prefer in order to provide proper motivation to division Y?

(ii) As management accountant, would you advise division Y to buy at the transfer price determined in part (i)?

(iii) Assume the situation and the transfer price determined in part (i). If the selling price dropped to ₹200, should Y buy at that price? Would this be desirable from the point of the firm? Why?

(iv) Assume that division X's product did not have an outside demand in excess of 1,00,000 units and its total fixed manufacturing cost could be reduced by 10 per cent, if the volume of production were reduced by 10 per cent, if the volume of production were reduced to 1,00,000 units, what is the appropriate transfer price?

(v) Suppose that X division's maximum outside demand is 1,10,000 units at ₹100, and there is no other usage for the capacity. What transfer price(s) should the company management prefer?

(vi) Suppose the unit selling price of Y's product is ₹180; one of its customers is also a customer of division X; division Y refuses to buy the part from the outside market at ₹100 since the selling price of ₹180 would not be high enough to even cover the variable costs. If division X does not lower the transfer price, division Y will not sell to this customer who, in turn, will probably cancel the usual order of 50,000 units to division X; there is no other demand for the product and no other usage of X's capacity; fixed costs would not change at either division. What is the lowest transfer price that the division X would be well advised to accept? Support your recommendation with computations.

Solution

(i) *Determination of Transfer Price*

(a) Variable manufacturing cost of division X		₹84
(b) Opportunity cost (in terms of contribution foregone by transfer to division Y):		
Selling price	₹100	
Less total variable costs to make and sell (₹84 + ₹2)	86	14
Transfer price		98

(ii) *Statement of Contribution Per Unit—Division Y*

Selling price		₹240
Less variable costs:		
Manufacturing cost (division Y)	₹100	
Transfer price from division X	98	
Variable selling expenses	6	204
Contribution margin per unit		36

Yes, division Y is advised to buy from division X.

(iii) At ₹200 selling price per unit, division Y will not be able to earn a positive contribution:

Selling price	₹200
Less variable costs (part ii)	204
Negative contribution	(4)

No, division Y should not buy at that price. Yes, it would be desirable from the standpoint of the firm also due to higher contribution on external sales:

Comparative Income Statement of the Firm

	Sell externally	*Transfer to Y*
Selling price per unit	₹100	₹200
Out-of-pocket-costs:		
Division X	86	84
Division Y	—	106
Contribution margin	14	10

(iv) *Appropriate Transfer Price Per Unit*

Variable cost	₹84
Plus opportunity cost (in terms of reduction of fixed manufacturing cost by 10 per cent) (see working note 1)	3
	87

(v) Transfer Price

Units	*Transfers price*
15,000 units (working note 2)	₹84
10,000 units (part ii)	98

(vi) Determination of Transfer Price

Variable cost of production of 25,000 units (25,000 units × ₹84)	₹21,00,000
Less opportunity cost of lost sales (working note 3)	7,00,000
Lowest transfer price of 25,000 units	14,00,000
Transfer price per unit (₹14,00,000 ÷ 25,000 units)	56

WORKING NOTES

1. Present cost of manufacturing (1,25,000 × ₹6) ₹7,50,000
   Less budgeted costs (0.90 × ₹7,50,000) 6,75,000
   Fixed cost of manufacturing 25,000 units 75,000
   Opportunity cost per unit (₹75,000 ÷ 25,000 units) 3
2. For 15,000 units [1,25,000 units capacity (1,10,000 units market can absorb)], the opportunity cost is zero. The transfer price should, therefore, be equal to the variable cost, that is, ₹84.
3. *Opportunity cost of losing sale of 50,000 units*

Sales revenues (50,000 units × ₹100)	₹50,00,000
Less variable manufacturing and selling costs (50,000 units × ₹86)	43,00,000
	7,00,000

REVIEW QUESTIONS

LOD: Easy

RQ.21.1 Fill in the following blanks. In some cases choices are provided. LO 21.2,3,4

(i) Responsibility accounting focuses on ________.

(ii) ________ is a sub-unit of an organisation under the control of a manager who is responsible for its activities.

(iii) Responsibility centres are: ________.

(iv) A sub unit of an organisation whose financial performance is measured in terms of cost is referred to as ________.

(v) Division of an organisation in which financial performance is measured on the basis of revenues-expenses is known as ________.

(vi) ________ is a price used to measure the value of goods/services furnished by a profit centre to other responsibility centres within a firm.

(vii) Controllable segment margin = Sales revenue (–) Controllable variable costs (–) ________.

(viii) Segment profit contribution = Controllable segment margin (–) ________.

(ix) That method of transfer pricing in which the transferring division is credited with one price and acquiring division is charged with different price is known as ________.

(x) ________ considers not only costs and revenues but also the assets used in the division.

(xi) Segment ROI = Segment profit contribution/________.

(xii) Segment residual income = Segment profit contribution - (Segment assets × ________).

(xiii) Corporate/firm's net income = S segment profit contribution from all divisions of a firm (–) ________.

(xiv) Fixed costs that are directly and exclusively related to the decisions of the management of a division are referred to as ________

(xv) Sales revenue (–) controllable variable costs = ________.

[Answers: (i) responsibility centres, (ii) responsibility centre, (iii) (a) expenses, (b) profit and (c) investment, (iv) expense centre, (v) profit centre, (vi) transfer price, (vii) controllable fixed costs, (viii) attributable segment costs, (ix) dual prices, (x) investment centre, (xi) segment assets, (xii) desired segment ROI, (xiii) firm-wide costs, (xiv) controllable fixed costs, (xv) controllable contribution margin.]

RQ.21.2 What is responsibility accounting? Discuss its significance in divisional performance measurement. LO 21.1

RQ.21.3 Define an expense centre. What is the suitability of the measure of performance in an expense centre? LO 21.2

RQ.21.4 Define residual profit. Discuss its suitability as a performance measure. LO 21.3

RQ.21.5 "ROI is the best measure of overall performance." Do you agree? LO 21.4

RQ.21.6 Briefly differentiate expense centres, profit centres and investment centres. Identify the basic characteristics of each. LO 21.2,3,4

RQ.21.7 Explain briefly the elements of profits centre performance. LO 21.3

RQ.21.8 Alfa Ltd. has two decentralised divisions, D_1 and D_2. D_1 has always purchased certain units from D_2 at ₹300 per unit. As D_2 plans to raise the price to ₹400 per unit, D_1 desires to purchase these units from outside suppliers for ₹300 per unit. The costs of D_2 are as follows: LO 21.2

Variable cost per unit	₹250
Annual fixed costs	50,000
Annual production for D_1 (units)	1,000

If D_1 buys from an outside supplier, the facilities D_2 uses to manufacture these units would remain idle.

From the viewpoint of the company as a whole, should D_1 purchase from D_2 at ₹400 per unit, or from outside at ₹300 per unit?

LOD: Medium

RQ.21.9 What kind of performance is measured in profit centres? What are the criteria for evaluating that performance? LO 21.3

RQ.21.10 What is transfer prices? What are the different types of transfer prices? Under what circumstances is each type of transfer price appropriate and useful? LO 21.3

RQ.21.11 Why is ROI classified as a composite performance measure? Explain its significance. LO 21.4

RQ.21.12 "Responsibility accounting consists in accumulation and reporting of costs by levels of responsibility within an organisation." Offer your observations on the above statement. LO 21.1

RQ.21.13 "In addition to full cost accounting and differential accounting, a third type of accounting information is used in the management control process." (Anthony and Reece). What is this third type of accounting information called? What are its functions and how is it useful to management? LO 21.1

RQ.21.14 "What management does, or at least what it attempts to do, is to control the action of the people who are responsible for incurring costs." Comment. LO 21.1,2

RQ.21.15 "An important management function is that of assuring that activities of members of the organisation help to accomplish the organisation's goals." LO 21.1

RQ.21.16 "The management control process involves human beings, from those in the lowest responsibility centres of the organisational hierarchy up to and including each member of top management." Discuss. LO 21.1

RQ.21.17 Explain why a decision centre should be treated as a profit centre rather than as a cost centre. LO 21.2,3

RQ.21.18 What problems exist with regard to firm-wide common costs when segments are treated and evaluated as profit centres? What are the alternative treatments available? LO 21.3

RQ.21.19 Why must profit centres be evaluated and/or ranked? What problems arise when undue emphasis is placed on the comparison of segment profit performance? LO 21.3,4

RQ.21.20 Explain why an incremental approach is most useful in making decisions that involve possible modifications to the operations of segments of the profit centres. LO 21.3

RQ.21.21 What are the potential merits of a dual (two-way) transfer pricing system? What are its limitations? LO 21.3

RQ.21.22 The ABC Ltd. has three divisions, A, B, and C. For the current year, the following data were reported: LO 21.3,4

Particulars	*Divisions*		
	A	*B*	*C*
Sales revenue	₹4,00,000	?	?
Profit	40,000	₹3,20,000	?
Investment	2,00,000	?	₹10,00,000
Investment turnover	?	4	?
Margin of profit on sales	?	?	0.15
SROI	?	0.2	?
Segment profits using 10 per cent cost of capital	?	?	1,01,000

(a) Complete the table.
(b) Rank the divisions in terms of their effective use of resources in capturing the market.

RQ.21.23 The home appliances division of Benjamin Industries Ltd. now shows a profit of 5 per cent on sales of ₹12 lakh. An investment of ₹4,00,000 is needed to finance these sales. The management of the firm in considering the following two alternative plans for improving operations submitted by two employees, E_1 and E_2: LO 21.4

(a) E_1 believes that the sales volume can be doubled by greater promotional effort. It would lower the profit rate to 4 per cent of sales and require an additional investment of ₹1,00,000.

(b) E_2 favours eliminating some unprofitable appliances and improving efficiency by adding ₹2,00,000 in capital equipment. This alternative would decrease sales volume by 10 per cent but improve the profit rate to 7 per cent of sales.

You are required to determine: **(a)** The company's current rate of return on investment in the division, **(b)** The anticipated rates of return under the alternatives suggested by E_1 and E_2, and **(c)** Which plan, if any, will you recommend?

RQ.21.24 Hypothetical Ltd. has two divisions, A and B, which are operated as profit centres. Division A has been selling a part of its production to division B at ₹200 per unit. Annual output of division A is 10,000 units; sales are made as follows: LO 21.2,3

Division B	4,000 units
Outside companies	6,000 units
Units costs in division A are as follows:	
Fixed	₹75
Variable	100
	175

Division B has found that it can negotiate a contract to buy from an outside supplier at ₹150 per unit. Should division B be allowed to purchase from outside? In the light of its implications, can you suggest an alternative?

RQ.21.25 Avon Ltd. with two manufacturing divisions is organised on profit centre basis. Division A is the only source for the supply of a component that is used in division B in the manufacture of a product, KLIM. One such part is used in each unit of the product, KLIM. As the demand for the product is not steady, division B can obtain orders for increased quantities only by spending more on sales promotion and by reducing the selling prices. The manager of division B has accordingly prepared the following forecast of sales quantities and selling prices: LO 21.3

Sales units per day	*Average selling price per unit*
1,000	₹52.50
2,000	39.80
3,000	33.00
4,000	27.80
5,000	24.00
6,000	20.10

The manufacturing cost of KLIM in division B is ₹37,500 for the first 1,000 units and ₹7,500 per 1,000 units in excess of 1,000 units.

Division A incurs total cost of ₹15,000 per day for an output upto 1,000 components, and the total costs will increase by ₹9,000 per day for every additional 1,000 components manufactured. The manager of division A states that the operating results of his division will be optimised if the transfer price of component is set at ₹12 per unit, and he has accordingly set the aforesaid transfer price for his supplies of the component to division A.

Required:

(a) Prepare a schedule showing the profitability at each level of output for division A and division B.

(b) Find the profitability of the company as a whole at the output level at which

(i) Division A's net profit is maximum

(ii) Division B's net profit is maximum.

(c) If the company is not organised on profit centre basis, what level of output will be chosen to yield the maximum profit?

LOD: Difficult

RQ.21.26 "Transfer prices must always be equal to externally determined market prices of comparative products or services." Comment fully. **LO 21.3**

RQ.21.27 The installed capacity of XYZ Ltd. is 50,000 units per month. Sales normally permit operations at 80 per cent of this capacity. At normal capacity, indirect manufacturing overheads total ₹3,60,000. **LO 21.3**

During the month of April of the current year, sales demand was above normal and 45,000 units were manufactured and sold. Indirect manufacturing costs of the order of ₹3,87,000 were recorded.

An argument has ensued between the plant superintendent and the production supervisor. The supervisor claims credit for reducing unit cost. The superintendent contends that waste and inefficiency have crept into the plant, as reflected in cost increases.

The chief executive of the company cannot follow the superintendent's reasoning and has called you to settle the argument.

The analysis of the company's costs shows that fixed indirect manufacturing costs are ₹2,00,000 per month. The company has the practice of recovering these costs from the normal capacity.

You are required to prepare a report for the chief executive of the company to help him in rewarding the right man/or assigning responsibility for poor performance.

ANSWERS

RQ.21.8 Should buy from D_2.

RQ.21.22 **(i)** Sales revenue: B, ₹8,00,000; C, ₹13,40,000

(ii) Profit: C, ₹2,01,000

(iii) Investment: B, ₹2,00,000

(iv) Investment turnover: A, 2; C, 1.34
(v) Margin of profit on sales: A, 0.1; B, 0.05
(vi) SROI: A, 0.20; C. 0.201
(vii) Segment profit: A, ₹20,000; B, ₹3,00,000.

RQ.21.23 **(a)** 15 per cent
(b) (i) 19.2 per cent
(ii) 12.6 per cent
(c) E_1 plan.

RQ.21.24 Division B should continue to buy form division A. Dual (two-way) price could be an alternative.

RQ.21.25 **(a)** (i) ₹(3,000), Nil, ₹3,000, ₹6,000, ₹9,000, and ₹10,000
(ii) ₹3,000, ₹10,600, ₹10,500, ₹3,200, (₹7,500) and (₹26,400)
(b) (i) ₹(14,400) loss
(ii) ₹10,600.
Maximum profit (₹13,500) at the level of 3,000 units produced and sold.

RQ.21.27 The contention of the superintendent in correct.

[Comprehensive solutions to all numerical review questions are available on the companion website: http://www.mhhe.com/khan_jain_ma7e]

22

Balanced Scorecard

LEARNING OBJECTIVES

After reading this chapter you will be able to:

LO 22.1 Understand the factors contributing to the emergence of balanced scorecard
LO 22.2 Explain the elements of the balanced scorecard framework and the four perspectives of balanced scorecard as a measurement system
LO 22.3 Discuss the advantages and pitfalls of balanced scorecard system

INTRODUCTION

Balanced scorecard is a new framework for tracking organisational performance. It is a carefully selected set of quantifiable measures derived from an organisation's strategy. The measures represent a tool to communicate to employees/shareholders the outcomes and performance drivers by which to achieve missions/strategic objectives of an organisation. The balanced scorecard evaluates key performance measures and helps companies/managers to know how well they are doing and how they score against the measures they strive to meet.

CONTRIBUTORY FACTORS

LO 22.1 Understand the factors contributing to the emergence of balanced scorecard

The two factors that have contributed to the emergence of balanced scorecard, as a framework for improved performance measurement/reporting, are: **(i)** limitations of financial measures of performance as the true way to gauge success and **(ii)** inability of organisations to successfully execute their strategies.

Limitations of Financial Measures

Traditionally, summary financial measures such as operating profits and return on capital employed have been used to evaluate the effectiveness and efficiency by which operating divisions use financial and physical capital to evaluate value for shareholders. However, almost exclusive reliance on financial measures of performance has several serious limitations:

- Financial measures are inconsistent with contemporary business realities of a competitive environment. They facilitate and monitor efficient allocation of tangible physical and financial capital. But difficulties in placing a reliable financial value on intangible assets such as new product lines, process, capabilities, employee skills, motivations, flexibility, customer loyalties, data base and systems preclude them from being recognised in performance evaluation. Such assets/capabilities are critical in a competitive environment.

Tangible assets are not the primary driver of enterprise value. Intangible assets now provide the bulk of value of corporate. They enable an organisation to:

(i) Develop customer relationship that retain the loyalty of the existing customers and enable new customer segments and market areas to be served effectively/efficiently;
(ii) Introduce innovative products/services desired by targeted customer segments;
(iii) Produce customised high quality products/services at low cost and with short lead time;
(iv) Mobilise employee skills and motivations for continuous improvements in process capabilities, quality and response times; and
(v) Deploy information technology, data and system.

- Financial results on their own are not indicative of future performance.
- Financial measures do not capture the cross-functional dependency.
- Financial measures are not relevant to many (specially low) levels of an organisation.

Balanced scorecard provides balance specifically related to three areas: **(i)** financial and non-financial indicators of success, **(ii)** internal (employees and other internal resources) and external (shareholders and customers) constituents of the organisation in terms of the contradictory needs of these groups in effectively implementing strategy, and **(iii)** lag and lead indicators of performance.

Barriers to Strategy Execution

The execution of a strategy is more valuable than its formulation. The barriers to strategy execution include: **(i) Vision barriers** in terms of the inability to communicate vision/strategy to employees; **(ii) People barrier** in terms of the inability to link incentives to strategy; **(iii) Resource barrier** in terms of the inability to link budgets with strategy; and **(iv) Management barrier** in terms of the inability of executives to discuss strategy.

What is needed is a system that provides real insight into operations of an organisation, balances the historical accuracy of financial numbers with the drivers of future performance and assists in implementing strategy. The **balanced scorecard** is the tool that answers all these challenges. As a tool, it provides balance specifically related to three areas: **(i)** financial and non-financial indicators of success, **(ii)** internal (employees and other internal resources) and external (shareholders and customers) constituents of the organisation in terms of the contradictory needs of these groups in effectively implementing strategy, and **(iii)** lag and lead indicators of performance. **Lag** indicators generally represent past performance such as customer satisfaction, revenues and so on. While such measures are objective/accessible, they lack predictive power. **Lead** indicators are performance drivers that lead to the achievement of lag indicators and include the measurement of processes/activities. Response time may represent an indicator of lagging measure of customer satisfaction. Predictive in nature, the correlation may be subjective and data difficult to collect. A balanced scorecard is a mix of lag and lead indicators.

Lag indicators represent past performance such as customer satisfaction.

Lead indicators are performance drivers that lead to the achievement of lag indicators.

The balanced scorecard, as a tool to measure corporate performance, has three elements: **(i)** Measurement system, **(ii)** Strategic management system and **(iii)** Communication tool. These are elaborated subsequently. Features of good balanced scorecard and its implementation including pitfalls in implementation are also discussed. The main points are summarised by way of recapitulation.

ELEMENTS OF BALANCED SCORECARD

LO 22.2 Explain the elements of the balanced scorecard framework and the four perspectives of balanced scorecard as a measurement system

The three elements of balanced scorecard are measurement, strategic management and communication tool.

Balanced Scorecard as a Measurement System

Financial performance measures provide, as mentioned earlier, an excellent review of what has happened in the past but they are inadequate in addressing the real value-creating mechanism, namely, intangible assets such as knowledge and network of relationships. As outcomes of action previously taken, financial measures are **lag** indicators. The **balanced scorecard** compliments the lag indicators with the drivers of future economic performance, that is, **lead** indicators. Both the lag and the lead performance measures are derived from the strategy of the organisation. All the measures on the balanced scorecard serve as the translation of the strategy of the organisation. The balanced scorecard enables an organisation to translate its mission/strategies into objectives and measures organised into four perspectives/dimensions: **(i)** financial, **(ii)** customer, **(iii)** internal business process and **(iv)** learning and growth.

Balanced scorecard enables an organisation to translate its mission/ strategies into objectives/measures.

Financial Perspective Despite their limitations as a performance measure, financial measures are retained in the balanced scorecard framework as a valuable tool in summarising the readily measureable economic consequences of action already taken. Financial performance measures indicate whether the strategy implementation/execution contribute to the bottom-line improvement of the organisation. They are typically related to profitability. The balanced scorecard measures in the financial perspective included: **(i)** Income measures in terms of operating income, gross margin, **(ii)** Revenue and cost measures, namely, revenue growth, revenue from new products, cost reductions in key areas, and **(iii)** Income and investment measures in terms of return on investment.

Customers Perspective In the customers perspective, two questions are critical: **(i)** who are target customers, and **(ii)** what is value proposition in serving them?

Customer/Market Segments The organisation/managers should identify the customers and market segments in which the business unit will compete and the measures of performance in these targeted segments. Organisations should have a target customer audience and not "**all things to all customers**" strategy. The lack of focus on customers will prevent an organisation from differentiating itself from competitors. This perspective typically includes several core/generic measures of the successful outcomes from a well formulated/implemented strategy. Included in the core outcome measures are: **(i)** customers satisfaction, **(ii)** customer retention, **(iii)** acquisition of new customers, **(iv)** customer profitability and **(v)** market share in targeted segments. These generic measures should be customised to the targeted group whom the business unit expects its greatest growth and profitability to be derived from.

Value Proposition Value proposition perspective is delivered to attract/retain customers in the targeted segments. While value propositions vary among industries/market segments within industries, a common set of attributes to organise value propositions fall into three categories, namely, **(i)** Product and service attributes/operational excellence with focus on the functionality of the product/service, its

Value proposition is delivered to attract/ retain customers.

price and quality, **(ii)** Customer relationship/convenience, trust, responsiveness dimension includes the delivery of the product/service to the customer including response delivery time and how the customer feels about the experience of purchasing from the company, and **(iii)** Image and reputation (brand equity) dimension enables a company to proactively define itself for its customers.

In brief, the customers perspective enables managers to articulate their unique customer/market-based strategy for producing superior financial results. The balanced scorecard measures in respect of customer perspectives are: market share, customer satisfaction, customer-retention percentage, time taken to fulfill customer requests and number of customer complaints. A practical approach is to choose one dimension in which the organisation possesses strong attributes and maintain at least threshold standard of performance in other dimensions.

Internal business process perspective identifies the key / critical processes in which the organisation should excel.

Internal Business Process Perspective The third balanced scorecard perspective, internal business process (IBP), identifies the key/critical processes in which the organisation should excel. The focus should be on IBPs which would have the greatest impact on customer satisfaction and achieving the financial objectives of the business unit. They would enable the business units to **(a)** deliver the value proposition that will retain/attract customers in the targeted market segments, and **(b)** satisfy shareholders expectation of excellent financial results. While each business has its unique set of processes for creating value for customers and producing financial results, companies can customise for their own objectives and measures in their IBP perspective from a generic value chain model. The model covers three principal processes: **(i)** innovation process/cycle, **(ii)** operation process/cycle and **(iii)** post-sales service process.

Innovation Process/Cycle This process has two components: First, managers perform market research to identify the market size and the nature of the customers preferences and the price points for the targeted products/services. Accurate/valid information on market size and customer preferences is vital to the process to meet specific customer needs. Second, the cycle should, in addition to the survey of existing potential customers, visualise entirely new opportunities/markets for products/services that the organisation could supply. The balanced scorecard measures pertaining to the innovation process, in brief, include: operating capabilities, number of new products/services, new product development times and number of new patents.

Operation process relates to the production and delivery of the existing products/ services that will meet the needs of the customers.

Operation Process/Cycle It relates to the production and delivery of the existing products/services that will meet the needs of the customers. The stress should be on efficient, consistent and timely delivery of existing products/services to existing customers.

Traditionally, the operating processes have been monitored and controlled by financial measures such as standard costs, budgets and variances. However, excessive focus on narrow financial measures such as labour efficiency, machine efficiency and price variance may result in highly dysfunctional actions, namely: **(i)** keeping labour/machine busy, **(ii)** building inventory unrelated to customer orders, **(iii)** switching from supplier to supplier to chase cheaper prices, and **(iv)** ignoring costs of large volume order, poor quality, uncertain delivery times and disconnected ordering/receiving/invoicing and collection processes between lower-priced suppliers and customers. The traditional costs and financial measurements are supplemented by the balanced scorecard framework with additional measures in terms of strategic initiatives, that is, **(i)** improving manufacturing quality, **(ii)** reducing delivery time to customers, **(iii)** meeting specified delivery dates to measure yield, order-delivery time and on-time deliveries and **(iv)** defect rates, setup time and manufacturing downtime.

Post-sales Services Process The final stage in the internal value chain/business process is service to the customer after the original sale/delivery of products/services. Included in post-sales services in the balanced scorecard framework are: **(i)** warranty/repair activities, **(ii)** treatment of defects/returns/replacements, **(iii)** processing/administration of payments such as credit card administration. The organisations can adopt explicit strategies to offer superior post-sales services to add value to the use of the products/services offerings to the customers. These activities may include the following:

- Offer of **(i)** training programmes by companies to employees of customers to help them to use the equipment/system more effectively/efficiently and **(ii)** rapid response to actual/potential failures and down time;
- Cost, quality and cycle-time measurement to billing/collection and dispute resolution processes by companies with sales on credit or company-specific credit cards;
- Generous terms for exchange/return of merchandise;
- Introduction of critical performance measures associated with the safe disposal of waste and byproducts from the product process by companies dealing with hazardous/environmentally sensitive chemicals/materials.

Internal Business Process Perspective: Traditional Vs Balanced Scorecard Approaches to Performance Measurement There are two fundamental differences in the two approaches to performance measurement:

First, the traditional approach focuses on monitoring and improving existing business processes although it may incorporate, in addition to financial measures, quality and time-based matrices. The balanced scorecard approach, in contrast, highlights the processes several of which may not be currently performed by the organisation but are critical for the strategy to excel to meet anticipated customer needs and financial objectives.

Second, the focus of the traditional performance measurement system is on the process of delivering existing products to existing customers. The balanced scorecard framework incorporates innovation processes into the internal business process perspective. The drivers for long-term financial success may necessitate creation of entirely new products to meet the emerging needs of the existing/future customers. The innovation process is a more powerful driver for future financial performance than the short-term operation cycle. The ability to manage successfully a multi-year product development process or to develop a capacity to reach an entirely new category of customers may be more critical for some companies for future financial performance than managing existing operations effectively, consistently and responsibly. The balanced scorecard approach to internal business process incorporates objectives and measures both for long-wave innovation cycle and the short-term operation cycle.

Learning and Growth Perspective This fourth perspective identifies the capabilities the organisation must excel so as to achieve superior internal processes that, in turn, create value for customers and shareholders. The measures in this perspective are really the **enablers** of the other perspectives. In essence, they are the foundation upon which the balanced scorecard is built. In other words, the learning and growth perspective identifies/focuses on the infrastructure that the organisation must build to create long term growth and improvement. Businesses are unlikely to be able to meet their long-term targets for their customers and internal processes without using technologies and capabilities. Also, intense global competition requires that companies improve their capabilities for delivering value to customers and shareholders. The three principal sources of organisational learning and growth are: **(i)** people, **(ii)** systems and **(iii)** procedures.

Learning and growth perspective identifies the capabilities the organisation must excel so as to achieve superior internal processes that, in turn, create value for customers and shareholders.

The financial, customer and internal business process objectives on balanced scorecard will typically reveal large gaps between existing capabilities of people, systems and procedures and what will be required to achieve targets for breakthrough performance. To close these gaps, businesses must invest in re-skilling employees, enhancing information technology/systems and aligning organisational procedures and routines. These objectives are articulated in the learning and growth perspective of the balanced scorecard.

People The employee/people-based balanced scorecard measures include several generic outcome measures, namely, **(i)** employee education and skill levels, **(ii)** employee-satisfaction ratings, **(iii)** employee turnover rates, **(iv)** percentage of suggestions of employees implemented, and **(v)** percentage of compensation based on individual and team incentives.

Systems The information/technology system capabilities can be measured by real-time availability of accurate, critical customer and internal process information to employees on the front-line decision-making and action.

Procedures The organisational procedures may examine alignment of employee incentives with overall organisational success factors and measured rates of improvement in critical customer-based and internal processes.

Balanced Scorecard As a Strategic Management System

The second element of balanced scorecard, as a performance evaluation measure, is strategy management. As a strategic management system, the balanced scorecard framework acts as a critical tool in aligning short-term actions with their strategy. It alleviates many of the issues associated with effective strategy implementation, namely, **(i)** Vision barrier, **(ii)** People barrier, **(iii)** Resource barrier, and **(iv)** Management barrier.

Overcoming Vision Barrier Through Translation of Strategy The balanced scorecard approach overcomes the vision barrier among employees through translation of strategy/vision into objectives, measures, targets and initiatives in each of the respective perspectives. This is done through a precise/quantifiable meaning of vague and nebulous terms contained in the vision/strategy statements, such as **targeted customers, superior service** and so on. For instance, **superior service** may be taken to mean responding to inquiries within 24 hours. Accordingly, all employees would understand the requirement and focus on response accordingly. This would facilitate strict implementation of the mission of superior service.

Vision barrier is the inability to communicate mission/strategy to employees.

Overcoming People Barrier through Cascading the Balanced Scorecard Cascading the balanced scorecard means driving the scorecard down into the organisation and giving employees at all levels the opportunity to demonstrate how their day-to-day activities contribute to the strategy of the organisation. In operational terms, all levels of the organisation would distinguish their value-creating activities by developing scorecards linked to the objectives of the organisation at the highest level. All employees would focus on performance drivers of the future value and which actions/decisions are necessary to achieve those outcomes.

People barrier is the inability to link incentives to strategy.

Overcoming Resource Barrier through Strategic Resource Allocation The balanced scorecard framework enables tieing of resources allocation to the strategy of the organisation. The human and financial resources necessary to achieve the scorecard targets should form the basis for the development of the annual budgeting process. The costs/profits associated with these targets are clearly articulated in

Resource barrier is the inability to link budgets with strategy.

the budget documents of the respective departments. This enhances executive learning about the strategy as the group is forced to make tough choices and trade-offs regarding which initiatives to fund and which to defer.

Overcoming Management Barrier through Strategic Learning The balanced scorecard approach provides the necessary elements of a model in which the scorecard results become the starting point for reviewing/questioning and learning about strategy. A strategy is a hypothesis/best guess of how to achieve success. For instance, investment in employee training or improving employee access to key information would help in achieving targets needs date verification and choice accordingly made.

Management barrier is the inability of executives to discuss strategy.

Balanced Scorecard As a Communication Tool

Sharing scorecard results throughout the organisation gives the employees the opportunity to discuss the assumptions underlying the strategy, learn from the unexpected results and discuss future modifications as necessary. Understanding the strategy can unlock many hidden capacities of the organisation as employees know how they can contribute in the process. The dissemination of information to the employees is the best tool for open-book management of the organisation.

Merits and Pitfalls of Balanced Scorecard

LO 22.3 Discuss the advantages and pitfalls of balanced scorecard system

The features of a good balanced scorecard and pitfalls in implementing a balanced scorecard are briefly outlined below.

Features/Merits of a Good Balanced Scorecard

A well-designed balanced scorecard has several features/merits. These are:

- It tells the story of the strategy of an organisation and articulates the sequence of cause and effect relationship in terms of the link among the various perspectives that align implementation of the strategy. Each measure in the scorecard is part of a cause-and-effect chain resulting into financial results. A major benefit of balanced scorecard is that it promotes **causal thinking.**[1] It is, in a way, a linked scorecard or a casual scorecard. Managers must look for empirical evidence to test the validity and strength of the various connections. It enables a company to focus on the key drivers that steer the implementation of the strategy. Without convincing links, the scorecard would lack much value.
- It helps to communicate the strategy of the organisation to all its members. This is done by translating the strategy into a coherent and linked set of understandable and operational targets. Managers and employees would take action and make decisions according to the scorecard to achieve the strategy of the organisation.
- It motivates managers to take actions that result in improved financial performance. When financial and non-financial performance measures are properly linked, the latter serve as leading indicators of lagging future financial performance.
- It limits the number of measures to the most critical ones. Limiting the number of measures enables managers to focus on those that most affect strategy implementation. Too many measures make processing of relevant information difficult.
- It highlights less-than-optimal trade-offs caused by the failure of managers to consider operational and financial measures together. For instance, a company whose strategy is innovation and product differentiation can achieve superior financial performance by reduced

spending on research and development. A good balanced scorecard would signal that such action would hurt future financial performance due to decline in a leading indicator of that performance, namely, research and development.

Pitfalls in Implementation of a Balanced Scorecard

Pitfalls in implementing a balanced scorecard include the following:

- The cause-and-effect linkages among the financial and non-financial measures are not precise. They are merely hypotheses/best guesses. The strength and timing of these linkages should be reviewed over time. Understanding that the scorecard should evolve would help managers to avoid unproductively spending time and money in designing a "**perfect**" scorecard at the outset.[2] Moreover, the measures in the scorecard should change with changes in business environment and strategy.
- Cost-benefit considerations should be central element in designing a balanced scorecard.
- Both objectives such as operating income and subjective such as customer and employee satisfaction ratings measures should be used in the balanced scorecard. While using the subjective measures, it should be ensured that they are accurate and not amenable to easy manipulation.
- Managers tend to focus on what their performance is measured by. Non-financial measures should not be ignored when evaluating managers/employees. Non-inclusion of non-financial measures in performance evaluation of employees would reduce their significance/importance to managers/employees.

SUMMARY

- Balanced scorecard is a new framework for tracking organisational performance. Two factors have contributed to its emergence as a framework for improved performance measurement/reporting: **(i)** limitations of financial measures of performance and **(ii)** inability of organisations to successfully execute their strategies.
- Traditionally, financial measures such as operating income and return on capital employed have been used to evaluate corporate performance. But exclusive reliance on them has several limitations. They are inconsistent with contemporary business realities of a competitive environment. They monitor physical and financial capital but are incapable of evaluation of intangible assets which now provide the bulk of value of corporate. Moreover, financial results on their own are not indicative of future performance. Moreover, they do not capture the cross-functional dependency. They are also not relevant to the low levels of the organisation.
- The barriers to strategy execution are: **(i)** vision barrier in terms of inability to communicate to employees, **(ii)** people barrier in terms of inability to link incentives to strategy, **(iii)** resource barrier in terms of inability to link budgets with strategy and **(iv)** management barrier in terms of inability of executives to discuss strategy.

LO 22.1

- The balanced scorecard system provides real insight into the operations of an organisation, balances the historical accuracy of financial numbers with the drivers of future performance and assists in implementing strategy. As a tool, it provides balances specifically related to three areas: **(i)** financial and non-financial indicators of success, **(ii)** internal (employee and other internal resources) and external (shareholders and customers) constituents of the organisation in terms of the contradictory needs of these groups and effectively implementing strategy and **(iii)** lag and lead indicators of performance. While lag indicators represent past performance, lead indicators are future performance drivers.

- As a tool to measure corporate performance, balanced scorecard has three elements: **(i)** a measurement system, **(ii)** strategy management system and **(iii)** communication tool.
- A balanced scorecard enables an organisation to translate its strategy into objectives and measures organised into four dimensions/perspectives: **(i)** financial, **(ii)** customer, **(iii)** internal business process and **(iv)** learning and growth.
- The balanced scorecard measures pertaining to financial perspective include: **(i)** Income measures in terms of operating income and gross margin percentage, **(ii)** Revenue and cost measures in terms of revenue growth, revenues from new products, cost reductions in key areas, and **(iii)** Investment measure in terms of return on investment.
- The customer perspective balanced scorecard measures include market share, customer satisfaction, customer retention percentage, time taken to fulfill customer requests, number of customers complaints.
- The balanced scorecard measures relating to internal business perspective are:
  (a) **Innovation process**: Operating capabilities, number of new products/services, new product development times and number of new patents;
  (b) **Operations process**: Yield, defect rates, time taken to deliver product to customers, percentage of on-time deliveries, average time taken to respond to orders, setup time, manufacturing down time.
  (c) **Post-sale service**: Time taken to replace/repair defective products, hours of customer training for using the product.
- The scorecard measures for learning and growth perspective relate to **(i)** employee measures and **(ii)** technology measures. The employee measures include education/skills levels, satisfaction level/rating, turnover rates, percentage of suggestions implemented, percentage of compensation based on individual and team incentives.
- As strategic management system, the balanced scorecard framework acts as a critical tool in aligning short-term actions with their strategy. It alleviates the issues associated with effective strategy implementation. It overcomes **(i)** vision barrier through translation of strategy into objectives/targets/initiatives in each of the perspectives, **(ii)** people barrier through cascading the balanced scorecard, **(iii)** resource barrier through strategic resource allocation, and **(iv)** overcomes management barrier through strategic learning.
- Finally, balanced scorecard is a communication tool in terms of dissemination of information to the employees.

LO 22.2

- Balanced scorecard focuses on measures that affect strategy implementation most. Its other advantages are **(i)** it helps to communicate the strategy of the organisation to all its members, **(ii)** it motivates managers to take actions that result in improved financial performance and, **(iii)** it limits the number of measures to the most critical ones.
- The major pitfalls of balance scorecard include the following: first, the cause and effect linkages among the financial and non-financial measures tend to reduce their significance to managers as well as employees. This may not be in the interest of an organisation.

LO 22.3

REFERENCES

1. Horngren, C.T. *et. al.*, *Cost Accounting: Managerial Emphasis* (Perason, 2010), pp. 539-48.
2. Ibid.

REVIEW QUESTIONS

LOD: Easy

RQ.22.1 Discuss the factors that have contributed to the emergence of balanced scorecard as a framework for performance measurement/reporting. LO 22.1

RQ.22.2 Define balanced scorecard. What are the three areas it specifically balances? LO 22.2

RQ.22.3 Describe the features of a good balanced scorecard. LO 22.3

LOD: Medium

RQ.22.4 Describe the three broad elements of the balanced scorecard approach to measure corporate performance. LO 22.2

RQ.22.5 What are the four key perspectives in balanced scorecard as a measurement system? LO 22.2

RQ.22.6 Explain briefly the elements of balanced scorecard as a strategic management system. LO 22.2

RQ.22.7 What are the pitfalls to avoid when implementing a balanced scorecard? LO 22.3

PART 7

DECISION-MAKING

This part is devoted to a discussion of the use of cost analysis in decision-making. Decision-making essentially involves choosing one or more of several available alternatives. The main task is to determine how costs and profits would be affected if a particular alternative is chosen. The process is called differential/incremental analysis. Differential analysis is the process of estimating the consequences of alternative actions that a decision-maker may take. It is used both for short-term and long-term decisions. The short-term decision refers to a decision-horizon usually not exceeding one year over which the capacity of the organisation would remain unchanged. The main distinction between short-term and long-term decisions arises from the need to incorporate time value of money in the latter, while in the short-run analysis the amount of costs and profits is important but their timing is assumed to be unimportant. Short-term decisions relating basically to pricing and product have been discussed in Chapter 23. The long-term capital budgeting decisions are covered in Chapter 24.

23

Short-run Decision Analysis

LEARNING OBJECTIVES

After reading this chapter you will be able to:

- **LO 23.1** Describe the analytical framework for short-term decisions in terms of relevant data
- **LO 23.2** Illustrate the application of differential costs/revenues in various decision situations
- **LO 23.3** Explain target costing.

INTRODUCTION

The main purpose of this chapter is two-fold: **(i)** To describe the framework of analysis for short-term decisions, and **(ii)** Its application for such decision-making. First, the chapter sets out the analytical framework in terms of the data requirement, that is, the differential/incremental costs and revenues. It subsequently deals with the application of the framework in different situations. Target costing is also explained. The main points are summarised by way of recapitulation.

ANALYTICAL FRAMEWORK

LO 23.1 Describe the analytical framework for short-term decisions in terms of relevant data

Decision-making involves the act of selecting one course of action from among various feasible alternatives available. Short-term decisions are of a special nature. The type of information required for decision-making depends on the decision situation under consideration. The information required for such decisions is called '*relevant data.*' The relevant data refers to decision-making elements required to meet the needs of specific situations. The conventional accounting data would not serve the purpose. They have to be altered/modified in terms of addition/deletion to tailor the historical costs to the requirements of decision-making.

Relevant data are decision-making elements required to meet the needs of specific situations.

Future costs are costs expected to happen under an assumed set of conditions.

The first element of the relevant data is that it is future-oriented, that is, it relates to a future period. The underlying consideration is that these decisions imply some future activity. In other words, while historical cost represents what has happened under existing conditions, the future costs refer to what is expected to happen under an assumed set of conditions. They are special purpose costs that are applicable only to the situations for which they are constructed. They do not have universal applicability.

The second component of the analytical framework of short-term decision-making is that is is primarily quantitative (tangible). Factors having a bearing on decision-making can be either qualitative (intangible)—defined as factors which are not amenable to precise and direct measurement, or quantitative—which can be expressed in numerical terms. It is true that quantitative factors do influence decision-making, for example, the management of a company may decide to manufacture certain components even though it costs less to buy them from outside, in view of a long-term policy of avoiding dependence on outside suppliers. Yet, these are not of operational significance because they cannot be included in accounting information.

Thus, short-term decision-making is based on quantifiable, future accounting information. This is derived from the alteration of the historical cost data. The modification is based on the following cost concepts. A detailed discussion of these concepts was made in an earlier chapter. They are briefly recapitulated here.

Relevant Costs

Relevant costs are costs which would change as a result of the decision.

These are the costs which would change as a result of the decision under consideration, whereas *irrelevant costs* are those which would remain unaffected by the decision. Therefore, only relevant costs would be included in the analytical framework.

Opportunity Costs

Opportunity costs are monetary benefits foregone for not pursuing the alternative course.

Another costs concept relevant to the short-term decision-making is the opportunity/imputed costs. When a decision to follow one course of action is made, the opportunity to pursue some other course is foregone. The monetary benefits that would accrue from taking the alternative course are sacrificed and these benefits, if measurable, should be added to the costs of the decision.

Sunk Costs (Committed Costs)

Sunk costs are costs already incurred.

Such costs are historical costs that are irrevocable in a given situation. They are the costs that have been incurred by a decision that was made in the past and cannot be changed by any decision that would be made in the future. They are, therefore, irrelevant in decision-making and have to be deleted from the historical costs.

Avoidable/Escapable/Discretionary Costs

Avoidable costs are costs that can be avoided in future as a result of managerial choice.

These costs can be avoided in the future as a result of managerial choices because management can choose not to incur them. Avoidable costs are relevant costs when particulars decision-alternatives are compared.

Incremental/Differential Costs

Differential costs include variable costs and additional fixed costs resulting from particular decision.

These costs are also useful in planning and decision-making. They provide a device for testing the profitability of increased output, and give a better measure than the average cost. Defined in this sense, incremental costs differ from variable costs. The former is a comprehensive term, which includes, besides variable costs, additional fixed costs resulting from a particulars decision, whereas, the latter is comprised of variable costs only. The difference between incremental/differential costs and revenues is the incremental/

differential contribution. Format 23.1 shows the procedure of computing incremental contribution. The incremental contribution so computed is the basis of short-term decision-making.

FORMAT 23.1 Incremental Contribution

Incremental revenues (product-wise)	___
Add cost savings (specify items)	___
Total incremental revenues	___
Less lost contribution (product-wise)	___
Less incremental costs (specify items)	___
Incremental contribution	___

DECISION-SITUATIONS

LO 23.2 Illustrate the application of differential costs/revenues in various decision situations

This Section demonstrates the application of incremental/differential costs and revenue data for decision-making in the following situations:

1. Sales volume related
2. Sell or further process
3. Make or buy
4. Product lines/divisions/departments
5. Short-term use of scarce resources
6. Joint outputs of common processing operations
7. Operate or shut-down

Sales Volume Related Decisions

Such decisions cover: **(i)** Acceptance of special/extra sales orders, **(ii)** Disposing of inventories, and **(iii)** Loss leaders.

Special Orders One decision-situation relates to increase in sales volume outside the normal marketing pattern. Typical examples of such types of sales are acceptance of special orders, one-time quantity sale, and sales to foreign customers. If such special sales do not affect the normal sales, the accept-reject decision would be based on the incremental contribution. In case, the special sale would affect the future sales volume and/or selling price, the opportunity cost in terms of lost revenue will also be relevant to the decision-making. This is illustrated in Example 23.1

◆ Example 23.1

(Pricing Special Orders)

Assume that Royal Industries Ltd has excess capacity. The normal plant capacity is 3,00,000 units per year and current production is 2,00,000 units. There is no alternative use for the idle facilities. The company receives an offer from a foreign customer to buy 1,00,000 units at ₹10 a unit. The regular market price is ₹14 a unit. The current manufacturing and selling costs are:

Particulars	*Per unit*	*Total*
Total variable cost:		
Direct labour	₹2	₹4,00,000
Direct material	3	6,00,000
Variable overheads	2	4,00,000
Manufacturing cost	7	14,00,000
Variable selling cost	1	2,00,000
	8	16,00,000
Fixed overheads:		
Manufacturing	2.50	5,00,000
Selling	0.50	1,00,000
Total cost	11.00	22,00,000

(a) Should the offer be accepted assuming that shipment charges of ₹50,000 are to be borne by the seller? There will be a special packing of the products which will involve packing cost of ₹0.25 per unit. Being an export order, the management is convinced of the fact that the regular market price of ₹14 a unit will not be affected;

(b) Assume that the order is from a local supplier and, therefore, should the order be accepted, all products in future are to be offered at the special order price.

Solution

The decision analysis in situations (a) and (b) is depicted in Tables 23.1 and 23.2.

TABLE 23.1 (a) Decision Analysis

Particulars	*Without special order*	*Amount*	*With special order*	*Amount*
Sales	(2,00,000 × ₹14)	₹28,00,000	(2,00,000 × ₹14)	₹28,00,000
			(1,00,000 × ₹10)	10,00,000
		28,00,000		38,00,000
Less incremental costs:				
Direct labour	(2,00,000 × ₹2)	4,00,000	(3,00,000 × ₹2)	6,00,000
Direct material	(2,00,000 × ₹3)	6,00,000	(3,00,000 × ₹3)	9,00,000
Variable overheads	(2,00,000 × ₹2)	4,00,000	(3,00,000 × ₹2)	6,00,000
Packing costs	—	—	(1,00,000 × ₹0.25)	25,000
Selling costs	(2,00,000 × ₹1)	2,00,000	(2,00,000 × ₹1)	2,00,000
Shipment costs	—	—		50,000
Contribution		12,00,000		14,25,000

The incremental contribution is 2,25,000 and, therefore, the order should be accepted.

TABLE 23.2 (b) Decision Analysis

Particulars		*Amount*
Sales (3,00,000 × ₹10)		₹30,00,000
Less relevant costs:		
Manufacturing variable costs (3,00,000 × ₹7)	₹21,00,000	
Packing costs (1,00,000 × ₹0.25)	25,000	
Variable selling costs (2,00,000 × ₹1)	2,00,000	
Shipment costs	50,000	23,75,000
Contribution		6,25,000

Since the contribution has declined, the order from the local supplier should not be accepted.

Disposing of Inventories Pricing decisions must consider the relative marketability of inventories. Due to damage/obsolescence or lack of demand, inventory may not be saleable through normal marketing channels or under normal operating conditions. In such cases, incremental analysis is appropriate for decision-making as all prior costs of producing/acquiring inventory are sunk costs and, therefore, irrelevant to the decisions. Example 23.2 illustrates the point.

◆ Example 23.2

(Disposal of Inventories)

ABC Ltd has on hand 5,000 units of a product that cannot be sold through regular sales. These were produced at a total cost of ₹1,50,000, and would normally have been sold for ₹40 per unit. Three alternatives are being considered:

(i) Sell the items as scrap for ₹2 per unit.

(ii) Repackage at a cost of ₹20,000, and sell them at ₹8 per unit.

(iii) Dispose them off at the city dump at removal cost of ₹2,500.

Which alternative should be accepted?

Solution

Table 23.3 exhibits the decision analysis.

TABLE 23.3 Decision Analysis

Particulars	Alternatives (I) Sell as scrap	(II) Repackage and sell	(III) Disposal
Sales revenue	₹10,000	₹40,000	—
Less costs:			
Repackage cost	—	20,000	—
Removal cost	—	—	2,500
Contribution (Loss)	10,000	20,000	(2,500)

Alternative II should be accepted.

Loss leaders are sales deliberately priced to suffer loss to be offset by additional sales in future.

Loss Leaders Sometimes an item may be deliberately priced so low that the firm has to suffer loss in the expectation that additional sales will be generated which will offset the loss. Such sales are referred to as loss leaders.[1] Consider Example 23.3.

◆ Example 23.3

The contribution margin of Hypothetical Ltd is 50 per cent. Its regular monthly gross sales average ₹4,00,000. Monthly fixed costs are ₹1,00,000. To increase the sales, the firm plans to sell a special product at ₹8 each. If 10,000 units of this item can be purchased for ₹12 per unit, determine the increase in the sales revenue of the normally priced items to make the promotion worthwhile.

Solution

TABLE 23.4 Decision Analysis

Particulars	*Amount*
Incremental revenue	₹80,000
Less incremental costs	1,20,000
(Incremental loss)	(40,000)
Desired increase in sales revenue = Loss (₹40,000)/ C/V ratio (0.50)	80,000

The interpretation of ₹80,000 is that the increase in the sales revenue exceeding this amount will justify the promotional campaign.

Sell Now or Process Further Decisions

Short-term incremental analysis also applies to *sell or process further* decision-situations. As already discussed in an earlier chapter, when an item of production passes through various processes, it is saleable at different stages/points, that is, at various physical stages of production. In deciding at what stage to sell the product, the two critical variables are: (i) Identification of sunk costs and (ii) Calculation of incremental returns at various sales alternatives. All costs, whether fixed or variable, incurred before the sell or process further point, should be treated as sunk, and therefore, irrelevant costs. The incremental return relevant to the decision is the difference between the costs that are incurred beyond the decision point and the revenues. If, however, the fixed resources would remain idle as a result of not processing the product further, and if they could be diverted to some other use, *opportunity cost* would also become relevant to the decision analysis. Such decisions are illustrated in Examples 23.4 and 23.5.

Example 23.4

(Additional Processing-Single Product)

Avon Ltd manufactures a single product, which it sells to firms which process it further before sale. The normal quarterly operating volume for the company is 50,000 units produced and sold. The relevant cost data are as follows:

Selling price		₹100
Standard costs:		
Direct materials	₹30	
Direct labour	15	
Variable manufacturing overheads	10	
Fixed manufacturing overheads (₹2,50,000 per quarter)	5	
Variable selling overheads	10	
Fixed selling expenses (₹1,25,000 per quarter)	2.5	72.50
Standard profit per unit		27.50

The company management is considering the possibility of further processing it itself, necessary for the operation to sell directly to the customers. The management estimates that the product can be sold @ ₹140 per unit after further processing. The following are the estimates of the additional costs of processing 50,000 units:

Direct labour (per unit)	₹10
Variable manufacturing overheads (per unit)	5
Variable selling costs (per unit)	2
Additional fixed manufacturing overheads per quarter	1,00,000
Additional sales expenses per quarter	50,000

You are required to decide whether further processing should be done or not.

Solution

Table 23.5 presents the decision analysis.

TABLE 23.5 Decision Analysis

Particulars	*Without further processing*		*With further processing*		*Incremental revenues and costs*	
	Per unit	*Total*	*Per unit*	*Total*	*Per unit*	*Total*
Sales	₹100	₹50,00,000	₹140	₹70,00,000	₹40	₹20,00,000
Less incremental costs:						
Direct material	30	15,00,000	30	15,00,000	0.0	—
Direct labour	15	7,50,000	25	12,50,000	10	5,00,000
Manufacturing overheads	10	5,00,000	17*	8,50,000	7*	3,50,000
Selling overheads	10	5,00,000	13*	6,50,000	3*	1,50,000
Contribution	35	17,50,000	55	27,50,000	20	10,00,000

* including additional fixed overheads.

Since further processing would result in a greater contribution, the new proposal would be more profitable and should be accepted.

Example 23.5

(Sell or Process Further—Multiple Products)

Hypothetical Ltd produces three products, A, B and C. One type of raw material is used for all these products. The raw material enters the process in Department 1 of the factory. Department 1 separates materials for products A, B and C. During the quarter, material worth ₹4,00,000 was issued to Department 1. Other direct costs of operating Department 1 were ₹2,00,000. The output of products from Department 1 was: A, 10,000 units; B, 5,000 units; and C, 2,000 units.

Products A, B and C can be sold after being processed from Department 1 (split-off point) at prices of ₹60, ₹30 and ₹20, respectively. After the split-off, product A could be processed further in Department 2. With additional processing cost of ₹50,000, this product can be sold for ₹70 per unit. After the split-off, product B could be processed further in Department 3 for ₹30,000 additional cost, and will then fetch ₹35 per unit. Product C is not suitable for further processing and has to be sold at the point of split-off. What action should the management take?

Solution

Table 23.6 presents the decision analysis.

TABLE 23.6 Decision Analysis

Particulars	*Product A*			*Product B*		
	Sell now	*Process further*	*Incremental revenues and costs*	*Sell now*	*Process further*	*Incremental revenues and costs*
Sales	₹6,00,000	₹7,00,000	₹1,00,000	₹1,50,000	₹1,75,000	₹25,000
Less separable costs	—	50,000	50,000	—	30,000	30,000
Contribution	6,00,000	6,50,000	50,000	1,50,000	1,45000	(5,000)

Table 23.6 shows that it is profitable to process product A further because it yields an incremental contribution of ₹50,000. The decision is based on the assumption that there is no other opportunity cost for using the facilities of Departments 2 and 3. The management is advised to process product A further and sell product B as it is.

Make or Buy Decisions

Committed costs are costs if a firm has idle capacity.

Many firms have to choose between manufacturing certain components themselves or acquiring them from outside suppliers. Incremental analysis provides solution to this kind of decision-problems too. The relevant input information is the committed/avoidable costs if the firm has adequate idle capacity to make the components, because the firm would not be required to incur fixed costs to produce the components. If, however, there is need to enlarge the capacity of existing plant, or the existing capacity of the plant is diverted for the production of the components, opportunity cost in terms of lost contribution will be relevant to the decision analysis. Examples 23.6 and 23.7 illustrate the make or buy decision involving avoidable committed costs and opportunity cost.

◆ Example 23.6

(Make or Buy Decision)

The Philips Company Ltd produces most of its tube parts in its own plant. The company is at present considering the feasibility of buying a part from an outside supplier for ₹4.5 per part. If this were done, monthly costs would increase by ₹5,000.

The part under consideration is manufactured in Department 1 along with numerous other parts. On account of discontinuing the production of this part, Department 1 would have somewhat reduced operations. The average monthly usage production of this part is 20,000 units. The costs of producing this part on per unit basis are as follows:

Material	₹1.80
Labour (half-hour)	2.40
Fixed overheads	0.80
Total costs	5.00

The company follows the practice of applying manufacturing overheads on the basis of direct labour-hours. Normal production volume in Department 1 is 1,50,000 hours per month, and current actual production is at about the same level. Discontinuation of production of this part would cause an unfavourable volume variance of ₹16,000 per month in this department.

How would you advise the management in this regard?

Solution

Table 23.7 presents the decision analysis.

TABLE 23.7 Decision Analysis

Particulars	Make costs		Buy cost	
	Total	*Per unit*	*Total*	*Per unit*
Relevant costs:				
Materials	₹36,000	₹1.80	—	—
Labour	48,000	2.40	—	—
Purchasing cost	—	—	₹90,000	₹4.50
Additional cost of purchasing from outside	—	—	5,000	0.25
	84,000	4.20	95,000	4.75
Differential costs favouring making of the parts	11,000 per month	0.55 per unit		

The company should continue the practice of producing the part in Department 1.

WORKING NOTES

(i) Unfavourable volume variance of ₹16,000 (10,000 hours required in producing 20,000 parts @ ₹1.60 per hours) indicates that there is no alternative use of the facilities, and they would remain idle if part production is discontinued. Therefore, they are irrelevant costs.

◆ Example 23.7

(Make or Buy Decision)

The ABC Company Ltd produces most of its own parts and components. The standard wage rate in the parts department is ₹30 per hour. Variable manufacturing overheads is applied at a standard rate of ₹20 per labour-hour and fixed manufacturing overheads are charged at a standard rate of ₹25 per hour.

For its current years's output, the company will require a new part. This part can be made in the parts department without any expansion of existing facilities. Nevertheless, it would be necessary to increase the cost of product testing and inspection by ₹50,000 per month. Estimated labour time for the new part is half an hour per unit. Raw materials cost has been estimated at ₹60 per unit.

The alternative choice before the company is to purchase part from an outside supplier at ₹90 per unit. The company has estimated that it will need 2,00,000 new parts during the current years.

Advise the company whether it would be more economical to buy or make the new parts. Would your answer be different if the requirement of new parts was only 1,00,000 parts?

Solution

The decision analysis is presented in Table 23.8.

TABLE 23.8 (i) Decision Analysis: 2,00,000 units

Particulars	Make costs Total	Make costs Per unit	Buy costs Total	Buy costs Per unit
Raw material	₹1,20,00,000	₹60	—	—
Direct wages	30,00,000	15	—	—
Variable overheads	20,00,000	10	—	—
Additional fixed costs:				
Product testing and inspection (₹50,000 × 12)	6,00,000	3	—	—
Purchase costs	—	—	₹1,80,00,000	₹90
Total costs	1,76,00,000	88	1,80,00,000	90
Differential costs favouring the decision of making the component ₹4,00,000 total, ₹2 per component				

The company is advised to make the new part.

(ii) Decision Analysis: 1,00,000 units:

Particulars	Make costs Total	Make costs Per unit	Buy costs Total	Buy costs Per unit
Raw material	₹60,00,000	₹60	—	—
Direct wages	15,00,000	15	—	—
Variable overheads	10,00,000	10	—	—
Fixed costs	6,00,000	6	—	—
Purchase costs	—	—	₹90,00,000	₹90
Total costs	91,00,000	91	90,00,000	90

If the requirement of the new part is 1,00,000 units, the company would be well advised to buy from an outside supplier. Buy costs are ₹90 per unit, compared to make costs of ₹91 per unit.

Addition/Elimination of Product Lines/Divisions/Shifts/Departments

When a firm is divided into multiple sales outlets, product lines, divisions, departments (segments), it may have to evaluate their individual performances to decide whether or not to continue operations of each of these segments or add a new segment. The decision criterion would be the *segment margin.* The segment margin equals segment's contribution margin less fixed costs that are directly traceable to that segment. Examples 23.8 and 23.9 illustrate such decisions.

Segment margin equals segments contribution margin less fixed costs directly traceable to the segment.

◆ Example 23.8

(Addition of Second Shift)

Ulfa Ltd produces a single product in its plant. This product sells for ₹100 per unit. The standard production cost per unit is as follows:

Raw materials (0.5 kg @ ₹80 per kg)	₹40
Direct labour (0.2 hour @ ₹50 per kg)	10
Variable manufacturing overheads	10
Fixed manufacturing overheads	20
	80

The plant is currently operating at full capacity of 1,00,000 units per years on a single shift. This output is inadequate to meet the projected sales demand, and the sales manager has estimated that the firm will lose sales of 40,000 units next years if the capacity is not expanded

Plant capacity could be doubled by adding a second shift. This would require additional out-of-pocket fixed manufacturing overhead costs of ₹10,00,000 annually. Also, a night work wage premium equal to 25 per cent of the standard wage would have to be paid during the second shift. However, if annual production volume were 1,30,000 units or more, the company could take advantage of 2 per cent quantity discount on its raw material purchases.

You are required to advise whether it would be profitable to add the second shift in order to obtain the sales volume of 40,000 units per year?

Solution

Table 23.9 presents the decision analysis.

TABLE 23.9 Decision Analysis

Particulars	*Profit without expansion*	*Profits with expansion*
Sales revenue	₹1,00,00,000	₹1,40,00,000
Less variable costs:		
Raw materials	40,00,000	54,88,000@
Direct labour	10,00,000	15,00,000@@
Variable manufacturing overhead	10,00,000	14,00,000
Contribution	40,00,000	56,12,000
Less fixed costs (₹1,00,000 × 20)	20,00,000	30,00,000
Net income	20,00,000	26,12,000

@(₹39.20 × 1,40,000 units)

@@ (₹10,00,000 + (40,000 units × 0.2 hour × ₹62.50 per hour = ₹5,00,000) = ₹15,00,000

Yes, it would be profitable to add the second shift as it would increase profits by ₹6,12,000.

◆ Example 23.9

(Elimination of a Product Line)

Avon Garments Ltd manufactures readymade garments and uses its cut-pieces of cloth to manufacture dolls. The following statement of cost has been prepared:

Particulars	*Readymade garments*	*Dolls*	*Total*
Direct material	₹80,000	₹6,000	₹86,000
Direct labour	13,000	1,200	14,200
Variable overheads	17,000	2,800	19,800
Fixed overheads	24,000	3,000	27,000
Total cost	1,34,000	13,000	1,47,000
Sales	1,70,000	12,000	1,82,000
Profit (loss)	36,000	(1,000)	35,000

The cut-pieces used in dolls have a scrap value of ₹1,000 if sold in the market. As there is a loss of ₹1,000 in the manufacturing of dolls, it is suggested to discontinue their manufacture. Advise the management.

Solution

Table 23.10 presents the decision analysis.

TABLE 23.10 Decision Analysis

Particulars	*Production of dolls*	*Non-production of dolls*
Sales revenue	₹12,000	
Scrap value of cut-pieces	—	₹1,000
Less avoidable costs		
Direct material	6,000	
Direct labour	1,200	
Variable overheads	2,800	
Differential revenue	2,000	1,000

The management is advised that the differential revenue favours continuation of production of dolls.

Short-term Use of Scarce Resources

Incremental analysis can also be used to allocate resources that are limited in quantity (key factors). The key factor refers to scarce resource which may be raw material, skilled labour or machine capacity. If the machine capacity is inadequate to permit manufacture of all products, the most profitable course of action is to use the available machine capacity/hours to make the products which contribute the maximum contribution margin per machine hour. If materials are in short supply, the management should produce according to the largest contribution margin per input of material. Thus, the contribution per unit of the key factor of production is to be determined and the products ranked according to the descending order of contribution per unit of key factor. This will maximise the total contribution of the firm. Consider Example 23.10.

◆ Example 23.10

(Use of Scarce Resources)

Precision Engineers Pvt. Ltd are producing to specific orders. Their factory capacity is limited by one major machine forming a critical cost centre through which all products pass. The factory normally works for 250 days in a year on 24 hours, 3 shifts a day, and 5 days a week basis. The maximum achievable capacity is 80 per cent, corresponding to the average level of activity in the critical cost centre. The operating results summarised for management in previous year are as follows (₹in lakh):

Sales		₹48
Less costs:		
Materials	₹18.00	
Labour-variable costs	5.75	
Factory-variable costs	6.25	
Factory-fixed costs	3.00	
Selling and administration costs	10.00	43
Profit		5

The average profitability experienced during the previous years is being maintained during the current year also.

The company has an opportunity of taking any one of two large contracts either of which will substitute for a large amount of current production without affecting the hourly variable production costs. Details of the contracts are:

Particulars	*Contract X*	*Contract Y*
Material cost per unit	₹375	₹1,750
Machine-hours (critical cost centre) per unit	2	3
Contract price per unit	1,500	3,750
Extra selling expenses per unit	25	50

Prepare a report for the managing director making your recommendations as to which of the two contracts should be preferred.

Solution

TABLE 23.11 Decision Analysis

Particulars	*Contract X* 2,400 units (4,800 ÷ 2)		*Contract Y* 1,600 units (4,800 ÷ 3)	
	Per unit	*Total*	*Per unit*	*Total*
Contract price	₹1,500	₹36,00,000	₹3,750	₹60,00,000
Less incremental costs:				
Material costs	375	9,00,000	1,750	28,00,000
Other variable production cost	500	12,00,000	750	12,00,000
Additional selling expenses	25	60,000	50	80,000
Contribution	600	14,40,000	1,200	19,20,000
Contribution per machine-hour (key factor)	300*		400**	
Less fixed costs:				
Factory overheads		3,00,000		3,00,000
Selling and administration (assumed)		10,00,000		10,00,000
Profit		1,40,000		6,20,000
Present profit			5,00,000	

*(₹600 ÷ 2); **(₹1,200 ÷ 3)

The managing director is advised to accept contract Y, as its contribution margin per machine-hour as well as profit is higher.

WORKING NOTES

1. Machine-hours available = (Working days × 24 hours) = 250 × 24 = 6,000 hours
   Operating capacity available = 0.80 × 6,000 hours = 4,800 hours
2. Variable production costs (other than materials) per hour: (₹5,75,000 + ₹6,25,000) ÷ 4,800 hours = ₹250 per hour.
3. It is assumed that the company, at present, is operating at its maximum achievable capacity, that is, 4,800 hours. In operational terms, the variable production costs (labour and other variable costs) are at the level of 4,800 hours.
4. The company would be in a position to sell all the units of Y contract.
5. Selling and administration overheads are assumed to be fixed.

Joint Outputs of Common Processing Operations

A decision-situation faced by the management is whether to sell joint outputs at the split-off point or process them further. The decision-criterion should be to choose the alternative, which will maximise the total contribution of the various joint products to the common processing costs. As the common processing costs before the split-off point are sunk costs, that have already been incurred to create the joint products, they are irrelevant and will not be considered in decision-making. The only relevant costs will be the additional common processing costs. Example 23.11 illustrates the point. A related short-term decision involves selecting an alternative processing plan for joint products when the proportions of the outputs (sales-mix) from the common processing costs can be varied (Example 23.12).

Example 23.11

(Sell at Split-off Point or Beyond)

The Premier Chemicals Ltd manufactures two chemical solvents, A and B, in fixed proportions of 1: 2 respectively. During one month, 60,000 litres were produced and common processing costs of ₹2,40,000 were incurred. A and B solvents could be sold in their present form for ₹6 and ₹8 per litre respectively. However, solvent A can be sold as A-Plus for ₹8 per litre by adding an extra ingredient costing ₹1.50 per litre. Solvent B can be sold as Super-B for ₹12 per litre if it is reprocessed at an additional cost for ₹4 per litre plus an additional ₹40,000 per month for hiring a special filtering machine with a capacity of 40,000 litres per month.

Should the solvents be sold at the split-off point or be processed further?

Solution

TABLE 23.12 Decision Analysis

Particulars	*Solvents*	
	A	*B*
Incremental revenue	₹40,000	₹1,60,000
Less incremental cost:		
Manufacturing costs	30,000	1,60,000
Less hiring costs	—	40,000
Contribution (loss)	10,000	(40,000)

Therefore, solvent A should be processed further and solvent B should be sold at the split-off point.

Example 23.12

(Different Mix of Joint Outputs)

Royal Industries Ltd manufactures three different plastic products from a single raw material and by a common process.

Budgeted data for the coming years are presented below. The production costs identified with the individual products are only the separate processing costs incurred after the split-off point.

Particulars	*Products*			*Joint cost*
	A	*B*	*C*	
Output (units)	45,000	30,000	15,000	
Selling price per unit	₹6	₹12	₹18	
Production units:				
Direct material	—	—		3,00,000
Direct labour	24,000	36,000	30,000	1,50,000
Variable manufacturing overheads	12,000	18,000	12,000	48,000
Fixed manufacturing overheads	18,000	30,000	24,000	96,000

The sales manager has suggested the following sales-mix of products A, 30,000; B, 40,000; and C, 20,000 involving additional joint processing costs of ₹1,00,000.

Comment on the economic feasibility of the proposed mix.

Solution

TABLE 23.13 Decision Analysis

Particulars		*Present sales mix*	*Proposed sales mix*	*Incremental revenues and cost*
Sales revenue	A	₹2,70,000	₹1,80,000	₹(90,000)
	B	3,60,000	4,80,000	1,20,000
	C	2,70,000	3,60,000	90,000
Total		9,00,000	10,20,000	1,20,000
Less incremental costs:				
Joint processing cost		4,98,000	5,98,000	(1,00,000)
Direct labour		90,000	90,000	—
Manufacturing overheads		42,000	42,000	—
Contribution		2,70,000	2,90,000	20,000

The proposed mix is economically desirable.

Operate or Shut Down

> **Shut-down point** is a point at which losses from continued operations are equal to the shut-down costs.

The decision criterion in such a situation will be based on the comparison of the shut-down losses and the losses associated with continuing operations. In case, shut-down losses are more than the losses from continuing operations, it would be beneficial for the firm to continue its business operations. In case, shut down losses are less than the losses from continued operations, it would be profitable for the firm to shut-down its operations. Thus, the shut-down point may be defined as a point at which losses from continued operations are equal to the shutdown costs. The concept is illustrated in Example 23.13.

◆ Example 23.13

(Operate or Shut Down)

The annual budget of ABC Ltd at 60 per cent and 80 per cent level of performance is as under (₹in thousands):

Particulars	*60 per cent*	*80 per cent*
Direct material	360	480
Direct labour	480	640
Production overheads	252	276
Administrative overheads	124	132
Selling and distribution overheads	136	148
Total	1,352	1,676

The company is experiencing difficulties in selling its products and is at present operating at 50 per cent capacity level.

The sales revenue for the year is estimated at ₹9,90,000. The directors are seriously considering suspending operations till the market picks up.

Market research undertaken by the company reveals that in about 12 months, the sales will pick up and the company can comfortably operate at 75 per cent level of performance and earn a sales income of ₹18 lakh in that year.

The sales personnel of the company do not want to suspend operations for fear of adverse reactions in the market, but the directors want to decide the issue purely on financial considerations.

If the manufacturing and other operations of the company are suspended for a year, it is estimated that:

1. The present fixed cost could be reduced to ₹2,20,000 per annum.
2. The settlement cost of personnel not required would amount to ₹1,50,000.
3. The maintenance of plant has to go on and that would cost ₹20,000 per annum.
4. On resuming operations, the expenditure connected with reopening after shut down would amount to ₹80,000.

Submit a report to the directors, and indicate therein, based on purely financial considerations, whether it would be advisable to suspend the company's operation in the current year.

Solution

TABLE 23.14 Decision Analysis

Particulars			*Operate the factory*	*Shut-down the factory*
Sales revenue			₹9,90,000	—
Less variable costs				
Direct material			3,00,000	—
Direct labour			4,00,000	—
Variable overheads: (see working notes)				
Production	(₹72,000 ÷ 60) × 50		60,000	—
Administration	(₹24,000 ÷ 60) × 50		20,000	—
Selling and distribution	(₹36,000 ÷ 60) × 50		30,000	—
Contribution			1,80,000	—
Less fixed costs:				
Production		₹1,80,000		
Administration		1,00,000		
Selling and distribution		1,00,000	3,80,000	₹2,20,000
Settlement costs (personnel)			—	1,50,000
Maintenance of plant			—	20,000
Overhauling costs			—	80,000
Net income (loss)			(2,00,000)	(4,70,000)

It is not advisable for the company to suspend operations as shut-down loss is higher than the loss associated with continued operation of the plant.

WORKING NOTES

Segregation of various total overheads costs into fixed and variable components

Nature of overhead cost	*Budgeted expenditure at various capacity levels*		*Difference at 20 per cent capacity level showing variable expenses*	*1 per cent capacity difference*	*Total*	
	60 per cent	*80 per cent*			*Variable overheads (60 per cent)*	*Fixed overheads*
Production	₹2,52,000	₹2,76,000	₹24,000	₹1,200	₹72,000	₹1,80,000
Administration	1,24,000	1,32,000	8,000	400	24,000	1,00,000
Selling and distribution	1,36,000	1,48,000	12,000	600	36,000	1,00,000

TARGET COSTING

LO 23.3 Explain target costing

Manufacturing companies are always searching for ways to cut costs. Unfortunately, once a product is designed, that is, its features are specified, detailed engineering plans are made and manufacturing of the product is ready to commence, it is very difficult to make changes that will reduce costs. It is estimated that 80 per cent of the production-related expenses are committed once the process begins.[2] These committed resources cannot be changed later without great cost to the company. The primary reason for this state of affairs is that product features drive costs. Consider the case of Maharaja Home Appliance Ltd. (MHA). The MHA is considering bringing a new coffeemaker to the market designed with an automatic grinder, a water filter and a stainless steel carafe that keeps coffee warm for five hours. The cost of manufacturing the coffee pot will be largely determined by these features. It will be very difficult to reduce the cost once the production of the coffee pot starts. In fact, costs related to purchase of equipment to produce the grinders, the filters and the carafes are sunk costs/investments and cannot be changed.

Target costing provides a solution to the above problem/difficulty. It is **an integrated approach to determining product features, product price, product cost and product design that helps ensure a company will earn reasonable profit on new products.**[3]

Target costing is an integrated approach to determine product features, product price, product costs and product design that helps ensure a company will earn reasonable profit on new products.

Target Costing Process

Target costing is a business process aimed at the earliest stages of new product and service development before creation and design of production methods. It is a process driven by the customer, focused on design and encompassing the entire life of the product. The objective is to create for the company a production process that provides adequate profits.

The target costing process begins with the customer. The desire of customers about functionality, quality and price drive the analysis. Having a clear understanding of customer need is critical. There are likely to be functional requirements to meet customer needs. Moreover, the customer may be unwilling to trade off functional requirements for lower price/quality. Knowing customer requirements also means understanding competitor offerings. Consumers do not operate in a vacuum. They demand product characteristic based on what is available in the market. If a competitor offers a higher-quality product with a similar functionality at a lower price, then companies attempt to re-engineer their processes to meet that competition.[4]

Components of Target Costing Process The *desired target cost* is the cost of the resources that should be consumed to create a product that can be sold at a target price. **A target price is the estimated price for a product/service that potential customers will pay.** This estimate is based on an understanding of customers' perceived value for a product and how competitors will price competing products. A company's sales and marketing organisation, through close contact and interaction with customers, is usually in the best position to identify customer's needs and their perceived value for a product. Companies also conduct market research studies about product features that customer want and the prices they are willing to pay for these features. Understanding what customers value is a key aspect of being customer focussed.

Target cost is the cost of the resources that should be consumed to create a product that can be sold at a target price.

Target price is the estimated price for a product/service that potential customers will pay.

Target price, calculated using information from customers and competitors, forms the basis for target cost. Target cost per unit is the target price minus target operating income per unit. Target operating income per unit is the

Target operating income per unit is the operating income that a company aims to earn per unit of a product/service sold.

Target cost per unit is the estimated long-run cost per unit of a product/service that enables the company to achieve its target operating income per unit when selling at the target price.

operating income that a company aims to earn per unit of a product/service sold. Target cost per unit is the estimated long-run cost per unit of a product/service that enables the company to achieve its target operating income per unit when selling at the target price. Target cost per unit is often lower than the existing full cost per unit of the product. It is only a target that the company must aim for. To achieve target cost per unit and target operating cost per unit, the company must reduce the cost of making its products. The basic target cost formula is as follows:

Target Cost = Target price – Profit margin.

To illustrate, assume that Maharaja Home Appliances, given the features of its new coffee maker, can sell 50,000 units per year for ₹2,000 each. Assume further that Maharaja wants a profit margin of 30 per cent or, alternatively, a profit of ₹600. The target cost is ₹1,400 (₹2,000 – ₹600). Maharaja Home Appliances should design a product that can be produced at ₹1,400 or less. If it cannot be produced for ₹1,400 per unit, Maharaja will reconsider features and price. For example, it may decide to slightly lower its price and go with a plastic carafe as opposed to more expensive stainless steel carafe.

The components of the target costing process are exhibited in Figure 23.1.[5] There are four components of target costing process: (i) planning and market analysis, (ii) development, (iii) production design and (iv) production and continuous improvement. The first two components lead to an expected target price. The latter two stages are where the achievement of the target cost occurs.

Planning and Market Analysis Significant resources are consumed in planning and market analysis. At this stage, the customer **niche** is identified and thoroughly documented.

Concept Development This stage focuses on product feasibility studies. Development involves a cycle of testing and reformulating the product to understand customer requirements.

Production Design and Value Engineering This phase follows the establishment of the product concept in the development phase engineering and experienced production personnel use **value engineering** to determine the least costly combination of resources to create a product desired by the customers.

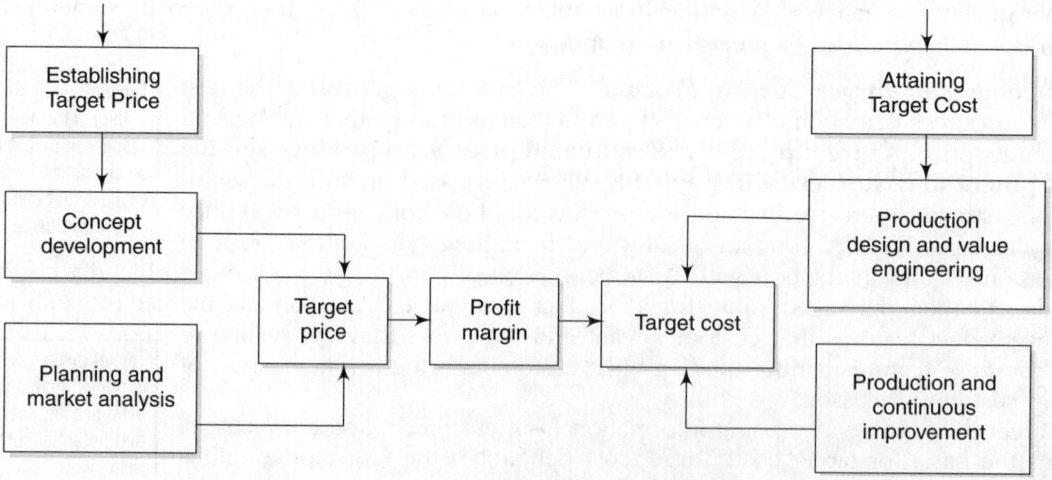

FIG. 23.1 *Target Costing Process*

Production and Continuous Improvement Finally, production begins and a continuous process is used to attain the target costs.

Target Costing Illustrated

We illustrate the step-wise target pricing and target costing below.

Assume HCL Ltd. manufactures two brands of personnel computers (PCs): Deskpoint and Provalue. Deskpoint is HLL's top-of-the-line product, a Pentium 4 chip-based PC. Provalue is a less powerful Pentium chip-based machine. The HLL currently produces 1,50,000 units of Provalue. The per unit sale price of Provalue is ₹10,000. The full cost of Provalue is ₹1,35,00,00,000 consisting of manufacturing cost of ₹102,00,00,000 and operating cost of ₹33,00,00,000.

Step 1: Develop a Product That Satisfies Needs of Potential Customers Marketing research indicates that customers do not value Provalue's extra features such as special audio features and designs that accommodate upgrades that can make the PC run faster and perform calculations more quickly. They want HLL to redesign Provalue into a no-frills PC and sell it at a much lower price. The HLL is, accordingly, planning design modification for Provalue.

Step 2: Choose a Target Price The HLL expects its competitors to lower the price of PCs that compete against Provalue by 15 per cent. The management of HLL wants to respond aggressively by reducing Provalue's price by 20 per cent from ₹10,000 to ₹8,000 per unit. At this lower price, marketing manager of HLL forecasts an increase in annual sales from 1,50,000 to 2,00,000 units.

Step 3: Derive a Target Cost Per Unit (Target Price – Target Operating Income) The management of HLL wants a 10 per cent target operating income on sales revenues.

Total target revenues = ₹8,000 per unit × 2,00,000 units = ₹1,60,00,00,000.

Total target operating income = 0.10 × ₹1,60,00,00,000 = ₹16,00,00,000

Target operating income per unit = ₹16,00,00,000 × 2,00,000 units = ₹800 per unit

Target cost per unit = Target price per unit – Target operating income per unit = ₹8,000 – ₹800 = ₹7,200

Total full costs of Provalue = ₹1,35,00,00,000

Current full per unit cost of Provalue = ₹1,35,00,00,000 ÷ 1,50,000 units = ₹9,000 per unit

The target cost value of Provalue of ₹7,200 is well below its existing ₹9,000 unit cost. The HLL's goal is to reduce its unit cost by ₹1,800. The cost reduction efforts should be extended to all parts of the chain value – from R&D to customer service including seeking lower prices from suppliers of materials and components.

Step 4: Perform Value Engineering to Achieve Target Cost Value engineering is a systematic evaluation of all aspects of value chain business functions with the objective of reducing costs while satisfying customer needs. It can result in improvements in product design, changes in materials specifications and modification in process methods. **A detailed account of value engineering is, however, beyond the scope of our discussion.**

SUMMARY

- Cost data collected under conventional accounting principles do not serve the purpose for short-term decision-making. They have to be specially tailored to the requirements of specific decisions. Which costs are relevant depends on the decision under consideration. Decision-making involves choosing between different courses of action. The tailoring of the data in line with the decision-situations requires the application of different concepts, which are not in consonance with the generally accepted accounting principles for external reporting purposes. All costs must, of course, be covered in the long-run, otherwise a firm will not survive. Nevertheless, in the short-run, some costs can be ignored.

- The cost concepts which are relevant to short-term decision-making are opportunity cost, sunk costs, avoidable costs, and incremental/differential costs. Only costs that have a bearing on the decision are applicable to the choice between alternatives. ***Decision-making costs are the relevant costs***, defined as the future costs that will change with the decision.

LO 23.1

- The major short-term choices relate to: Sales volume related decisions, Sell or further process decisions, Make or buy decisions, Addition/elimination of product lines/decisions/departments, Short-term use of scarce resources, Joint outputs of common processing operations, and Operate or shut-down decisions.
- The general format of differential contribution, as a framework for short-term decision-making is summarised below:

Particulars		*Amount*
(I) Incremental revenues (product-wise)		—
Add cost savings (specify items)		—
Total incremental revenues		—
(II) *Less incremental costs*		
Increase in existing fixed costs	—	
Increase in variable costs	—	—
Less decrease in contribution of existing products (specify each product) due to reduction in sales		—
Less opportunity cost foregone (say, by using equipment/space which was earlier leased/rented out)		—
Incremental (decrease in) contribution/profits		—

- Incremental analysis for acceptance of special order is summarised below

Particulars		*Amount*
Increase in sales revenue		—
Less incremental costs of executing sales order		
Direct material	—	
Direct labour	—	
Variable manufacturing overheads	—	
Freight costs (if to be incurred by seller)	—	
Production set-up costs	—	
Additional fixed costs (if any)	—	—
Incremental profits		—

- Decision analysis for further processing is summarised below:

Particulars	*Without further processing*		*With further processing*		*Incremental revenues/costs*	
	Per unit	*Total*	*Per unit*	*Total*	*Per unit*	*Total*
Sales revenue						
Less costs						
Direct material						
Direct labour						
Variable overheads						
Manufacturing						
Administrative						
Selling						
Fixed overheads (if incremental)						
Income (loss)						

- Make or buy Decision is summarised below:

Particulars	*Make costs*	*Buy costs*
Direct material	—	
Direct labour	—	
Power	—	
Other variable overheads	—	
Avoidable fixed overheads	—	
Buying costs		—
Freight costs		—
Indirect labour (receiving, inspecting and handling of the purchased parts)		—

- Decision analysis (operate or shut-down plant) is summarised below:

Particulars	*Operate plant*	*Shut down plant*
Sales revenue	—	
Less variable costs		
Direct material	—	
Direct Labour	—	
Variable overheads		
Manufacturing	—	
Administration	—	
Selling	—	
Contribution		
Less fixed costs		
Manufacturing	—	—
Administration	—	—
Selling	—	—
Other costs		
Settlement cost (personnel)		—
Other closing down costs		—
Maintenance of plant		—
Overhauling costs		—
Net profit (loss)		

LO 23.2

- Target costing is an integrated approach to determining product features, product price, product cost and product design that helps ensure a company will earn reasonable profit on new products.
- Target cost is the cost of resources that should be consumed to create a product that can be sold at a target price.
- Target price is the estimated price for a product/service that potential customers will pay.
- There are four components of target costing process: planning and market analysis, development, production design and production and continuous improvement.

LO 23.3

REFERENCES

1. Chartifield, M. and Neilson, Denis, Cost Accounting (New York, Harcourt Brace Jovanovich, Inc.), 1983, p. 389.
2. William, J. R., *Financial and Managerial Accounting,* TMH, 2004, p. 783.
3. Jiambaloo, J., *Managerial Accounting,* John Wiley, NY, 2004, p. 278.
4. William, J. R., *op. cit,* p.783.
5. *Ibid,* p 784.

SOLVED PROBLEMS

P.23.1 (a) Standard Sports Ltd produces high quality balls. It has received an offer from a sports store to buy 10,000 balls at ₹10 per ball. The store would sell the ball for ₹13 each which is ₹5 less than is normally charged by dealers selling the company's product. It is promised by the owner of the store that he would not disclose the maker's name. LO 23.2 LOD: E

The company can produce 1,00,000 balls per year. Planned results for the coming years without considering the order from the store are as follows:

Sales (80,000 balls @ 12 per ball)	₹9,60,000
Cost of goods sold (80,000 balls @ 7 per ball)	5,60,000
Gross profit	4,00,000
Selling and administrative expenses (all fixed)	2,50,000
Income	1,50,000

Cost of goods sold contains variable cost of ₹5 per ball. It is estimated that variable cost of printing the name on the ball is ₹0.25 per ball.

You are required to advise whether the company should accept the offer or not. Will your answer change if the seller's name is to appear on the ball to be sold by the store?

Solution

Incremental Analysis (Accept Special Offer or Not)

Particulars	*Amount*
Increase in sales revenue (10,000 × ₹10)	₹1,00,000
Less variable costs (₹4.75 × 10,000)	47,500
Incremental profit	52,500

The offer should be accepted. The firm has enough capacity to make the balls and the incremental revenues exceed the incremental cost.

The answer *may* or *may not* change, but the factors that must be considered is whether regular sales would be affected if customers come to know that they could buy the balls at ₹13 instead of ₹18 per ball. It may be contended that the maximum loss might be 10,000 balls, the number that the store would sell, as a result of which planned sales would decrease by 10,000 balls to 70,000. In that case, the firm would suffer a loss of ₹20,000 by accepting the offer. Sales revenue of 10,000 balls @ 12 per ball was 1,20,000. Instead of selling to the store, the company would get ₹1,00,000 (10,000 × ₹10). Moreover, there could be some ill will among customers affecting, thus, future sales

(b) The Vittetaw Company Ltd, a maker of a variety of metal and plastic products, is in the midst of a business downturn and is saddled with many idle facilities. The National Hospital Supply Company Ltd has approached Vittetaw Ltd to produce 3,00,000 nonslide serving trays. National will pay ₹12 for each. LO 23.2 LOD: E

Vittetaw predicts that its variable costs will be ₹13 each. However, its fixed cost, which has been averaging ₹10 per unit on a variety of other products, will now be spread over twice as much volume. The managing director commented, "Sure, we will lose ₹1 each on the variable costs, but we will gain ₹5 per unit by spreading our fixed costs. Therefore, we should take the offer because it represents an advantage of ₹4 per unit."

Do you agree with the managing director? Why? Suppose the regular business had a current volume of 3,00,000 units, sales of ₹60,00,000, variable costs of ₹39,00,000 and fixed costs of ₹30,00,000. Show your workings of operating income or loss without acceptance of the bid and with acceptance of the bid.

Solution

We do not agree with the managing director's comment. As a result of accepting the bid, the firm would be incurring an additional loss of ₹3,00,000 because incremental revenue is ₹12 per unit while additional variable costs will be ₹13 per unit. The managing director's comment is based on the wrong premise of spreading of fixed costs. Fixed costs (₹30,00,000) in absolute figures will remain unchanged whether the order is accepted or not. Therefore, consideration of fixed costs is an irrelevant factor here, as shown in the following operating income statement:

Contribution Based Income Statement With and Without Acceptance of the Bid of Vittetaw Company

Particulars	*Income (loss) if*	
	bid is accepted	*bid is not accepted*
Sales revenue		
Regular sales (3,00,000 × ₹20)	₹60,00,000	₹60,00,000
Bid sales (3,00,000 × ₹12)	36,00,000	—
Total	96,00,000	60,00,000
Less: variable costs @ ₹13 per unit	78,00,000	39,00,000
Contribution	18,00,000	21,00,000
Less: fixed costs	30,00,000	30,00,000
Operating loss	(12,00,000)	(9,00,000)

P.23.2 The Sick Instruments Company Ltd (SICL) manufacturers calculators under the brand 'PURANA', using old technology. It was selling them at ₹500 each. The normal capacity of SICL is 10,000 calculators. Due to the availability of calculators based on new technologies, the SICL's sales are adversely affected. There is a pile-up of inventories of 1,000 units of PURANA calculators at a cost of ₹250 each and 2,000 units of raw materials at ₹100 per unit, production of one calculator requiring one unit of raw materials. The calculators can now fetch only 10 per cent of cost as salvage value and the raw materials which have become obsolete could be sold as a scrap for ₹20,000. **LO 23.2** **LOD: M**

Meanwhile, the SICL receives an offer from Sellwell Marketing Company Ltd (SWML) to buy 5,000 PURANA calculators at ₹200 each with a 20 per cent commission on sales. The cost associated with the production of 5,000 units is estimated as shown below:

- Existing total labour cost, ₹1,20,000
- Fixed cost, ₹4,50,000
- Additional labour cost, ₹40,000
- Current price of materials, ₹125
- Additional overheads, ₹50,000

The chief accountant computes the cost per calculator for the offer as given below:

Raw material cost:		
Existing raw material cost @ ₹100 × 2,000 units	₹2,00,000	
Additional new raw material cost @ ₹125 × 2,000 units	2,50,000	₹4,50,000
Labour cost:		
Existing total labour cost	1,20,000	
Additional labour cost	40,000	1,60,000
Overhead cost:		
Fixed overhead costs	4,50,000	
Additional overhead charges	50,000	5,00,000
Finished goods:		
'PURANA' Calculators (@ ₹250 × 1000 units)		2,50,000
Commission: (@ 0.20 × ₹200 × 5,000)		2,00,000
Total costs		15,60,000
Cost per calculator (₹15,60,000 ÷ 5,000)		312

With the above calculations, the chief accountant suggests the Managing Director not to accept the offer as it would result in a loss of ₹112 per calculator and pushing the cumulative losses further. Should the SWML's offer be accepted?

Solution

Incremental Analysis (whether to Accept the Offer of Selling PURANA Calculators or Not)

Incremental sales revenue: (5,000 units of PURANA calculators × ₹200)		₹10,00,000
Incremental costs:		
Incremental raw materials (new) (2,000 units @ ₹125 per unit)	₹2,50,000	
Incremental labour cost	40,000	
Incremental overheads	50,000	
Commission (0.20 × 5,000 units × ₹200)	2,00,000	
Opportunity cost of raw material scrap value	20,000	
Calculator salvage value (0.10 × 1,000 × ₹250)	25,000	5,85,000
Incremental profit		4,15,000

Recommendation SICL should accept the offer of SWML as it reduces losses.

P.23.3 Snowhite Ltd makes readymade shirts (of one male size). Revenue and cost data relating to the coming years are given below: LO 23.2 LOD: D

Sales (9,000 shirts @ ₹1,000 per shirt)	₹90,00,000
Cost of sales	64,00,000
Gross profit	26,00,000
Selling and administrative expenses	15,00,000
Income	11,00,000

The firm has a capacity to make 10,000 shirts per year. The fixed costs included in the cost of goods sold are ₹10,00,000. The only variable selling, general and administrative expenses are: 4 per cent sales commission, and ₹20 per shirt paid to the designer.

A chain store manager has approached the sales manager of Snowhite Ltd offering to by 1,000 shirts at ₹700 per shirt. The sales manager believes that accepting this offer would result in a loss because the average cost of a shirt is higher than ₹700. He feels that a loss would still result, even if sales commission would not be paid on the sales order. The designer has agreed to waive 50 per cent of his fee on any number of shirts sold to such a store.

(i) Tender you advice to the sales manager of Snowhite Ltd.
(ii) Suppose that the order was for 2,500 instead of 1,000 shirts, what would be your advice?
(iii) Assuming the same facts as in part (ii), what is the lowest price that the firm would accept and still earn ₹11,00,000?

Solution

(i) *Incremental Analysis Approach (Accept Special Offer or Not : 1,000 shirts)*

Particulars		*Amount*
Increase in sales revenue (1,000 × ₹700)		₹7,00,000
Less incremental costs:		
Variable cost (1,000 × ₹600)*	₹6,00,000	
Designer's fees (1,000 × ₹10)	10,000	6,10,000
Incremental profit		90,000

*(₹64,00,000 – ₹10,00,000) ÷ 9,000

The sales manager is advised to accept the offer as it yields additional income of 90,000.

(ii) Special offer: 2,500 shirts

Additional contribution (2,500 × ₹90)	₹2,25,000
Less lost profit contribution (1,500 × ₹340) on regular sales of 1,500 units (regular sales would be 9,000 – 1,500 = 7,500 shirts) @ 340 per unit arrived as follows:	5,10,000
Decrease in contribution	(2,85,000)

Selling price	₹1,000
Less: variable making cost	600
Sales commission	40
Designer's fees	20
	340

The firm's income would be less by ₹2,85,000. The sales manager should not accept this offer.

(iii) Computation of the lowest price

Sales price (offered)	₹700
Add additional contribution required to be earned so that profit level is maintained:	
₹2,85,000 from 2,500 units to be sold: increase in sales price per shirt is (₹2,85,000 ÷ 2,500)	114
The lowest price for accepting the offer of 2,500 shirts	814

P.23.4 Sound Well Music Company Ltd (SMC) manufactures cassette record players. It is operating at full capacity of 10,000 units annually with a sales price of ₹3,000 per unit. The cost data are: **(i)** Raw materials, ₹900 per unit, **(ii)** Direct labour, ₹400 per unit, **(iii)** Variable overheads, ₹300 per unit, and **(iv)** Fixed cost, ₹60,00,000. LO 23.2 LOD: M

While the SMC was planning to expand its operations, Audiocon Ltd launched a new competitive product: HiFi CD player at ₹3,500 per unit. To meet the competition from this new product, the SMC has under consideration two alternatives: **(i)** Reduce the price of the cassette player to ₹2,499 **(ii)** Add new features to the product by further processing and sell for ₹3,700.

The further processing of the product would involve the following.

— Raw materials cost, ₹600 per unit;
— Labour charges, ₹300 per unit;
— Additional variable overheads, ₹300 per unit; and
— Additional fixed costs, ₹40,00,000.

As a consultant, what course of action would you recommend the SMC to follow?

Solution

Decision Analysis (Whether to Sell cassette record players as they are, or Process them Further) (₹in lakh)

Particulars	*Sell now*	*Process further*
Sales revenue	₹249.90	₹370
Less variable costs:		
Raw material	90.00	150
Direct labour	40.00	70
Variable overheads	30.00	60
Contribution	89.90	90
Less fixed overheads	60.00	100
Net profit (loss)	29.90	(10)

Recommendation The SMC is advised to sell cassette record players at ₹2,499 (without undergoing any further processing)

P.23.5 A cycle tyre manufacturing company (engaged in producing tyres for cycles of kids) has been approached by a large shopkeeper to buy 10,000 tyres at ₹32 each. Delivery must be made within 30 days. The production capacity of the company is 64,000 units per month and there is inventory of 2,000 tyres on hand. Expected sales at regular prices for the coming month are 60,000 tyres. It is estimated by the sales manager that about 50 per cent of sales lost during the month would be made up in later months. Price and cost data per unit are as follows: LO 23.2 LOD: M

Selling price		₹48
Variable costs:		
Production	₹24	
Selling	6	30
Profit contribution		18

The variable selling costs on the special order would be ₹1 per unit.

(i) Determine whether the offer should be accepted by the firm or not.

(ii) Determine the lowest price that the company could charge on the special order and not reduce its income.

(iii) Suppose now that the shopkeeper offers to buy 8,000 tyres per month at ₹32 per tyre. The offer would be for an entire year. Expected sales are 60,000 tyres per month without accepting the special order. Assuming further that there is no beginning inventory and that sales lost during the year would not be made up in the following year, determine whether the offer should be accepted, and determine the lowest price that the company could accept.

Solution

(i) *Decision Analysis (Acceptance of Special Offer or Not: 10,000 Tyres)*

Particulars	*Special order*	*Loss in regular sales*	*Effect*
Units sold (loss in regular sales)	10,000	(2,000)*	
(x) Contribution margin per tyre: Special order (₹32 – ₹24 – ₹1)	7	18	
Total contribution	₹70,000	₹(36,000)	+ ₹34,000

The company is advised to accept the offer.

WORKING NOTES

**Regular Unit Sales Lost*:

Inventory	2,000
Production	64,000
Available production	66,000
Special order	10,000
Available for regular sales	56,000
Expected regular sales	60,000
Sales lost	4,000
Less 50 per cent recovery in the following month	2,000
Net lost sale	(2,000)

(ii) *Statement Showing the Determination of the Lowest Price*

Profit contribution lost on regular sales	₹36,000
÷ Units of special order	10,000
Required contribution margin per tyre	3.60
Add variable cost @ ₹25 per unit	25.00
Lowest price	28.60

(iii) *Decision-making (new terms)*

Particulars	*Contribution margin per month*		
	Special order	*Regular sales*	*Effect*
Units sold (loss in regular sales)	8,000	(4,000) @	
(x) Contribution margin per unit	₹7	₹18	
Total contribution gained (lost)	56,000	(72,000)	(16,000)

@ (60,000 units – 56,000 units)

The special order would reduce income by ₹16,000 per month.

Lowest Price Per Unit

Profit contribution lost on regular sales	₹72,000
(÷) Number of units of special order	8,000
Required contribution per tyre	9
Add variable costs @ 25 per unit	25
	34

P.23.6 Young Orchids Ltd (YOL) is a shoe manufacturing company that started business two years back. Their target group of customers are kids below the age of five. Its production capacity is 6,500 pairs of shoes per month and there is inventory of 200 pairs of shoes on hand. Expected sales at regular prices for the coming month are 6,000 pairs of shoes. Price and cost data per unit are as follows: **LO 23.2** **LOD: M**

Selling price		₹500
Variable costs:		
Production	₹240	
Selling	60	300
Profit contribution		200

The OYL has received an order from a store to buy 1,000 pairs at ₹350 each. The variable selling costs on the special order would be ₹10 per unit. The delivery is to be made within 30 days.

(i) Should young Orchids go for the offer or reject it straight away?

(ii) What should be the lowest price that the YOL should charge on the special order and not reduce its income?

(iii) Suppose now that the shopkeeper offers to buy 800 pairs per month at ₹350 per pair. The offer would be for an entire year. Expected sales are 6,000 pairs per month without accepting the special order. Assuming further that there is no beginning inventory, determine whether the offer should be accepted by YOL.

Solution

(i) *Analysis Whether to Accept Store Order of Supplying 1,000 Pairs of Shoes or Not*

Contribution earned (₹350 – ₹240 – ₹10) × 1,000 units	₹1,00,000
Less contribution foregone on lost sales (₹200 × 300 units*)	60,000
Increase in contribution	40,000

*(Inventory, 200 units + Production, 6,500 units – Present offer, 1,000 units = 5,700 units available for regular sales; Existing sales, 6,000 units – 5,700 units available for sale = 300 units)

Recommendation As contribution is positive, the company is advised to accept the store order.

(ii) *Statement Showing the Lowest Price*

Contribution lost on regular sales	₹60,000
Divided by number of units of store order	(÷) 1,000
Desired contribution to be recovered per unit	60
Add variable cost (₹240 + ₹10)	250
Lowest price	310

(iii) *Analysis Whether to Accept Store Order of Supplying 800 Pairs of Shoes Per Month or Not*

Contribution earned (₹100 × 800 units)	₹80,000
Less contribution foregone on lost sales (₹200 × 300 units)**	60,000
Increase in contribution	20,000

**6,500 units produced – Present offer, 800 units = 5,700 units available for regular sales; Existing sales 6,000 units – 5,700 units available for sale = 300 units.

Recommendation Offer should be accepted as it augments contribution by ₹20,000 per month. Between the two, this offer is better as it augments profit by ₹2,40,000 in a year (₹20,000 × 12 months), vis-avis, ₹40,000 one time increase in earlier offer.

P.23.7 Baluja Shoes Ltd which has a chain of shoe shops throughout the country has two shops in Madras of which Shop I makes a profit and Shop II makes a loss. The following is the summarised profit and loss account of shop II for the current month ended March 31: **LO 23.2** **LOD: M**

Sales	₹6,00,000
Cost of sales	4,92,000
Gross profit	1,08,000

(*Contd.*)

(Contd.)		
Expenses:		
Commission to salesmen	₹6,000	
Manager's salary	12,000	
Head office expenses	10,500	
Motor van expenses:		
Fixed (allocated)	6,900	
Variable (allocated)	2,400	
Other items (like rent, insurance, salesmen's salaries)	1,09,950	1,47,750
Loss for the year		(39,750)

The commission to salesmen is a fixed percentage on turnover. There is a common manager for the two shops and his salary is equally shared by the two shops. The motor van is also common to the two shops. Its fixed expenses are shared equally by the two shops but the running expenses are apportioned on the basis of the turnover.

Prepare a report explaining the financial implication of the closing down Shop II, assuming that 20 per cent of its turnover will be gained by Shop I without that shop needing any additional staff.

Solution

Differential Cost and Revenue Statement (Operate or Shut-down Shop II)

Particulars	Operate Shop II	Shut down Shop II	Differential costs and revenues (decrease)
Sales revenue	₹6,00,000	₹1,20,000	₹(4,80,000)
Less variable costs:			
Cost of sales	4,92,000	98,400	(3,93,600)
Salesmen's commission	6,000	1,200	(4,800)
Motor van expenses	2,400	480	(1,920)
Contribution	99,600	19,920	(79,680)
Less common fixed costs:			
Manager's salary	12,000	12,000	—
Head office expenses	10,500	10,500	—
Motor van expenses	6,900	6,900	—
Less avoidable fixed costs:			
Other items (like rent, insurance, salary of salesman, etc. which no longer will be incurred)	1,09,650	—	(1,09,650)
Loss	(39,450)	(9,480)	(29,970)

Shop II should be shut down as it will lead to cost savings of ₹29,970 per month.

P. 23.8 A company manufactures three products. The respective details are: LO 23.2 LOD: M

Particulars	A	B	C
Capacity engaged (per cent)	20	40	40
Units produced	2,000	5,000	6,000
Cost per unit:			
Material cost	20	32	36
Wages	10	12	16
Variable overheads	7	9	11
Fixed overheads	6	9	10
Total	43	62	73
Selling price per unit	40	75	85
Profit (loss) per unit	(3)	13	12

The management proposes to discontinue line A as for the last few years it has been showing losses. Future prospects of the other two lines being good, it is intended to utilise the disengaged capacity in line A, in line B and, C equally. Expected per cent rise in prices and costs are:

	B	*C*
Material	10	10
Wages	5	5
Selling price	2	5

Fixed overheads shall remain the same. You are required to prepare a statement of projected profitability and advise the management as to whether the scheme may be adopted.

Solution

Statement of Projected Profitability with Products B and C only

Particulars		*Products*		*Combined*
		B	*C*	
Capacity engaged (per cent)		50	50	100
Units produced		6,250	7,500	
Selling price		₹76.50	₹89.25	—
Sales revenue		4,78,125	6,69,375	₹11,47,500
Less variable costs:				
Material cost:				
B: ₹35.20 per unit		2,20,000		2,20,000
C: ₹39.60 per unit			2,97,000	2,97,000
Wages:				
B: ₹12.60		78,750		78,750
C: ₹16.80			1,26,000	1,26,000
Variable overheads:				
B: ₹9		56,250		56,250
C: ₹11			82,500	82,500
Total		3,55,000	5,05,500	8,60,500
Contribution		1,23,125	1,63,875	2,87,000
Less: fixed overheads:				
A: 2,000 × ₹6 =	₹12,000			
B: 5,000 × ₹9 =	45,000			
C: 6,000 × ₹10 =	60,000			1,17,000
Net profit				1,70,000

Statement of Profitability with Products A, B and C (summary form)

Particulars		*Products*		*Combined*
	A	*B*	*C*	
Capacity engaged (%)	20	40	40	100
Units produced	2,000	5,000	6,000	—
Sales revenue	₹80,000	₹3,82,500	₹5,35,500	₹9,98,000
Less variable costs (new)	74,000	2,84,000	4,04,400	7,62,400
Contribution	6,000	98,500	1,31,100	2,35,600
Less fixed costs				1,17,000
Net profit				1,18,600

Assumptions

(i) Selling price per unit as well as variable cost per unit pertaining to product A does not increase.

(ii) Profitability statement with products A, B and C taken together is prepared on the basis of revised cost data, as variable costs as well as selling prices in respect of products B and C will increase, irrespective of the fact whether product A is dropped or not. The only point of difference is the number of units produced.

P.23.9 The following costs and other data apply to two component parts used by Bajaj Electricals Ltd: LO 23.2 LOD: D

Particulars	*Part X*	*Part Y*
Direct material	₹8.0	₹160.0
Direct labour	20.0	94.0
Overheads	80.0	40.0
Unit cost	108.0	294.0
Units needed per year	6,000	8,000
Machine-hours per unit	2	1
Unit cost, if purchased	100	300

The company hitherto has been manufacturing all its required components. However, in the current years, only 14,000 hours of otherwise idle machine time can be devoted to the production of components. Accordingly, some of the parts must be purchased from outside suppliers. In producing parts, overhead is applied at ₹40 per machine-hour. Fixed capacity costs, which will not be affected by any make or buy decision, represent 70 per cent of the applied overhead.

REQUIRED

1. Assuming that the 14,000 hours of available machine time are to be scheduled so that the company realises maximum potential cost savings, determine the relevant production cost that should be considered in the decision to schedule machine time.
2. Compute the number of units that Bajaj Electricals Ltd should produce if it allocates the machine time on the basis of the potential cost savings per machine-hour.

Solution

The relevant production costs are: direct material, direct labour, overheads (to the extent of 30 per cent), and buying costs. Scheduling of machine time will be governed by cost savings per machine-hour. This is shown in the following calculations.

Particulars	*Part X*		*Part Y*	
	Total	*Per unit*	*Total*	*Per unit*
(A) Buying cost	₹6,00,000	₹100	₹24,00,000	₹300
(B) Making cost:				
Direct material	48,000	8	12,80,000	160
Direct labour	1,20,000	20	7,52,000	94
Overheads (30 per cent assumed variable)	1,44,000	24	96,000	12
Total (making)	3,12,000	52	21,28,000	266
Cost savings@	2,88,000	48	2,72,000	34
Machine-hour per unit		2		1
Cost savings per machine-hour		24		34

@Excess buy costs payable are equal to cost savings.

Since cost savings per machine-hour are more in the case of product Y, the company should allocate 8,000 hours in producing 8,000 parts of Y and the remaining 6,000 hours should be utilised for producing 3,000 parts of X.

P.23.10 Perfect Product Ltd is currently buying a component from a local supplier at 15 each. The supply is tending to be irregular. Two proposals are under consideration: LO 23.2 LOD: M

(i) Buy and instal a semi-automatic machine for manufacturing this component, which would involve an annual fixed cost of ₹9 lakh and a variable cost of ₹6 per manufactured component.

(ii) Buy and instal an automatic machine for manufacturing this component, incurring an annual fixed cost of ₹15 lakh and a variable cost of ₹5 per manufactured component. Determine with necessary computation:

1. The annual volume required in each case to justify the switchover from "outside purchase" to "own manufacture."

2. The annual volume required to justify selection of the automatic machine instead of semi-automatic machine.
3. If the annual requirement for the coming year is expected to be 5,00,000 units and the volume is expected to increase rapidly thereafter, would you recommended the automatic or semi-automatic machine? Justify your recommendation.

Solution

1. Volume required to justify own manufacture of a component = Fixed costs (incremental)/(Buying cost per unit – Variable cost per unit):
   (a) Semi-automatic machine = ₹9,00,000 ÷ (₹15 – ₹6) = 1,00,000 units
   (b) Automatic machine = ₹15,00,000 ÷ (₹15 – ₹5) = 1,50,000 units
2. 1,50,000 units as shown in (1) b.
3. *Production Cost Statement*

Particulars	Automatic machine	Semi-automatic machine
Number of units	5,00,000	5,00,000
Variable cost per unit	₹5	₹6
Total variable cost	25,00,000	30,00,000
Plus fixed cost	15,00,000	9,00,000
Total cost	40,00,000	39,00,000
Per unit cost	8	7.8

At the expected volume of 5,00,000 units, calculations suggest that the semi-automatic machine should be bought. However, as the demand is expected to increase rapidly after one year, from the long-term point of view, purchase of the automatic machine is recommended as cost per unit would be equal to 6,00,000 units as shown below:

Production Cost Statement (6,00,000 units)

Particulars	Automatic machine	Semi-automatic machine
Total variable cost	₹30,00,000	₹36,00,000
Plus fixed cost	15,00,000	9,00,000
Total cost	45,00,000	45,00,000
Cost per unit	7.50	7.50

Clearly, at the production volume of greater than 6,00,000 units, total cost per unit would be lower with the automatic machine compared to the semi-automatic machine.

P.23.11 Farishta Company Ltd's old equipment for making sub-assemblies is worn-out. The company is considering two courses of action: (a) Completely replacing the old equipment with a new equipment, (b) Buying sub-assemblies from a reliable outside supplier who has quoted a unit price of ₹10 on a 7-year contract for a minimum of 50,000 units per year. **LO 23.2** **LOD: D**

Production was 60,000 units in each of the past two years. Future needs for the next 7 years are not expected to fluctuate beyond 50,000 to 70,000 units per year. Cost records for the past 2 years reveal the following unit costs of manufacturing the sub-assemblies:

Direct material	₹2.50
Direct labour	4.00
Variable overheads	1.00
Fixed overheads (including ₹1.0 for depreciation and ₹1.0 for supervision and other direct departmental fixed overhead)	2.50
	10.00

The new equipment will cost ₹18,80,000, will last 7 years, and will have a disposal value of ₹2,00,000. The current disposal value of the old equipment is ₹1,00,000. The salesman for the new equipment has summarised his position as follows: The increase in machine speed will reduce direct labour and variable overhead by ₹3.50 per unit. Consider last year's experience of one of our major competitors with identical equipment. They produced 1,00,000 units under operating conditions very comparable to us and showed the following unit costs:

Direct material	₹2.50
Direct labour	1.00
Variable overheads	0.50
Fixed overhead, including ₹2.40, depreciation	4.00
	8.00

You are required to compare the alternative on a: **(i)** Total cost basis **(ii)** Per unit basis for annual needs of 60,000 units. Which alternative seems more attractive? (Assume that any idle facilities cannot be put to alternative use, and also assume that ₹0.5 of the old Farishta unit cost is allocated fixed overhead that will be unaffected by the decision). Ignore interest and tax cost.

Solution

Differential Cost Statement Regarding Making or Buying a Component (60,000 units)

	Make with a machine		*Buying from outside supplier*	
Particulars	*Per unit*	*Total*	*Per unit*	*Total*
Direct material	₹2.50	1,50,000	—	—
Direct labour	1.00	60,000	—	—
Variable overheads	0.50	30,000	—	—
Relevant fixed overheads:				
Depreciation (₹2,40,000[@] ÷ 60,000 units)	4.00	2,40,000	—	—
Supervision cost	1.00	60,000	—	—
Irrelevant fixed overheads:				
Allocated costs	N.A.	N.A.	—	—
Purchase costs	—	—	10	6,00,000
	9.00	5,40,000	10	6,00,000
Differential costs (favourable for making)			1.0	60,000

[@](₹18,80,000 – ₹2,00,000)/7 years = ₹2,40,000

P.23.12 Hypothetical Ltd produces two products, X and Y. As per the existing operations, raw materials are processed in Department 1, and the two products are separated at the end of this processing. For every unit of product X, 3 units of Y are obtained. X is then finished in Department 2 and Y in Department 3. Budgeted operating data for year 1 are as follows: **LO 23.2** **LOD: M**

	Departments		
Particulars	*1*	*2*	*3*
Units produced and sold:			
Product X	1,00,000	1,00,000	
Y	3,00,000		3,00,000
Costs incurred:			
Direct materials	₹6,00,000		
Direct labour	3,20,000	₹1,20,000	₹1,60,000
Variable manufacturing overheads	80,000	40,000	80,000
Fixed manufacturing overheads	3,60,000	1,00,000	1,40,000

All costs are directly traceable to the individual departments. At present, X is sold for ₹10 per unit and Y for ₹5 per unit. Both products are also readily saleable at the completion of processing in Department 1—product X for ₹8 per unit and product Y for ₹3 per unit.

You are required to advise the company whether each product should be sold after final completion or at the split-off point.

Solution

Incremental Profit Analysis (Sell Now or Process Further)

Particulars	Product X			Product Y		
	Sell now	Process in Department 2	Differential (costs) and revenue	Sell now	Process in Department 2	Differential (costs) and revenue
Sales revenue	₹8,00,000	₹10,00,000	₹2,00,000	₹9,00,000	₹15,00,000	₹6,00,000
Less: costs:						
Departments 2 and 3						
Direct labour	—	1,20,000	(1,20,000)	—	1,60,000	(1,60,000)
Variable manufacturing overheads	—	40,000	(40,000)	—	80,000	(80,000)
Contribution (incremental)			40,000			3,60,000
Less: fixed costs: (direct/avoidable)	—	1,00,000	(1,00,000)	—	1,40,000	(1,40,000)
Production margin (incremental) (Profit/loss)		(60,000)			2,20,000	

Product X should be sold after the split-off point (that is after processing in Department 1). Product Y should be sold after final completion (that is after processing in Department 3).

Note

(i) Costs of Department 1 are joint costs and, therefore, irrelevant for the decision-making.
(ii) Fixed costs are avoidable costs and, therefore, relevant costs.

P.23.13 The XYZ Ltd produces a single product which passes through three successive departments, X, Y and Z. Following are the budgeted annual production costs for an output of 30,000 units which is considered to be the normal volume. **LO 23.2** **LOD: M**

Particulars	Departments X	Y	Z
Direct materials	₹66,000	₹23,000	—
Direct labour	42,000	54,000	₹25,000
Variable manufacturing overheads	21,000	27,000	13,500
Fixed manufacturing overheads (15 per cent of direct labour)	63,000	81,000	37,500
	1,92,000	1,85,000	76,000

The marketing manager of the company has informed the management that it can purchase a semi-finished product at a price of ₹5, delivered. Department Y can directly use this product instead of the basic raw material processed in Department X. However, direct labour and variable manufacturing overhead costs in Department Y would be 5 per cent more because of changes in operations necessitated by the introduction of the semi-finished product into the departments.

You are required to advise the company on the basis of short-run profitability whether it should purchase the semi-finished product or continue its existing practice of producing in Department X.

Solution

Decision Analysis (Make or Buy Semi-finished Product, 30,000 units)

Particulars	Make costs (Department X)		Costs if purchased from outside supplier	
	Total	Per unit	Total	Per unit
Direct materials	₹66,000	₹2.20	—	—
Direct labour	42,000	1.40	—	—
Variable manufacturing overheads	21,000	0.70	—	—
Purchasing costs	—	—	₹1,50,000	₹5.00

(Contd.)

(Contd.)

Additional out-of-pocket costs if semi-finished *product is processed in Department Y*:				
Direct labour (₹54,000 × 0.05)	—	—	2,700	0.09
Variable manufacturing overheads (₹27,000 × 0.05)	—	—	1,350	0.045
Total cost	1,29,000	4.30	1,54,050	5.135

Differential costs favouring making of the product in Department X, ₹25,050, total and ₹0.835 per unit. The company should continue its existing practice of producing it in Department X.

Assumptions **1.** There is no alternative use of facilities released from Department X.

2. Fixed costs are committed costs and unavoidable.

P.23.14 A company produces three products on the same plant. Fixed costs are applied to products based on the number of direct labour-hours required to make the product. The rate of application is based on budgeted fixed costs of ₹60,00,000 and budgeted direct labour-hours of 1,00,000. Per unit data for the three products are as follows. LO 23.2 LOD: D

Particulars	*P*	*R*	*S*
Selling price	₹800	₹340	₹450
Production costs, including applied fixed costs based on predetermined rate	750	280	400
Direct labour-hours required per unit of product	5	2.5	1

You are required to do the following:

1. Determine variable production costs per unit for each product.
2. Assuming that variable costs of production are the only variably costs, determine which product yields: (a) the highest contribution margin per unit, (b) the highest contribution margin percentage, and (c) the highest contribution margin per direct labour-hour.
3. If the firm asks you which product should be given more emphasis, what will be your answer?

Solution

1. *Determination of Variable Costs*

Particulars	*P*	*R*	*S*
Total costs per unit	₹750	₹280	₹400
Less fixed costs included @ ₹6 per labour-hour (₹60,00,000 ÷ 1,00,000)			
P: (₹60 × 5)	300		
R: (₹60 × 2.5)		150	
S: (₹60 × 1)			60
Variable costs per unit	450	130	340
2. Selling price per unit	800	340	450
Less variable costs per unit	450	130	340
(a) Contribution margin per unit	350	210	110
(b) Contribution margin percentage	43.75	61.76	24.44
(c) Direct labour hours	5	2.5	1.0
(d) Contribution margin per direct labour-hour [(a) ÷ labour hours]	70	84	110

3. The answer depends on the purpose for which the firm wants the information. Product P has the highest marginal contribution on a unit basis, product R on percentage basis and product S on labour-hour basis. Thus, if labour force is a scarce (key) factor and sales is no problem, product S should be given the maximum emphasis. If labour is not a key factor and promotion is expected to increase unit sales (of any product by the same amount), the per rupee spent emphasis should go to product P. Product R is the best if sales are expected to increase equally from the promotion campaign.

P.23.15 In a factory producing two different kinds of articles, the limiting factor is availability of material but the same material is used in both articles. LO 23.2 LOD: M

Particulars	Product A	Product B
Cost per unit		
Materials	₹15	₹10.00
Labour	6	4.50
Overheads: Variable	2	1.00
Fixed	6	4.50
Total	29	20.00
Selling price per unit (net)	35	24.50

The demand during each period for the two products is 10,000 units of A and 8,000 units of B. It is also considered desirable that, should demand be there, the firm should be willing to meet at least half the demand stated above in all circumstances. The total availability of materials for some time will be restricted to the quantity available for ₹1,20,000 only.

State how the available raw materials should be utilised.

Solution

Statement Showing Utilisation of Raw Materials (Key Factor) With Given Constraints of Producing Minimum Number of Products, A and B.

Particulars	Product A	Product B
Selling price unit	₹35.00	₹24.50
Less variable costs		
Materials	15.00	10.00
Labour	6.00	4.50
Variable overheads	2.00	1.00
Total variable costs	23.00	15.50
Contribution margin	12.00	9.00
Contribution margin per rupee of material used		
(₹12 ÷ ₹15)	0.80	
(₹9 ÷ ₹10)		0.90
Value of raw material consumed		
(5,000 × ₹15)	75,000	
(4,000 × ₹10)		40,000
Units produced	5,000	4,000
Raw material left (₹1,20,000 – ₹75,000 – ₹40,000) = ₹5,000 to be used in producing product B as its contribution margin is higher. Number of units of B produced (₹5,000 ÷ ₹10, consumption of raw material per unit)	—	500
Desired production (units)	5,000	4,500
Utilisation of raw material (₹)	75,000	45,000

P.23.16 During a year, a manufacturing company has produced and sold 3 products: Product A—20,000 units, Product B—14,000 units and Product C—10,000 units. LO 23.2 LOD: E

The following further information is per unit also available:

Particulars	A	B	C
Variable costs	₹100	₹180	₹160
Time taken (hours)	2.5	3.0	2.5
List price	200	300	400
Fixed cost (total)		₹20,00,000	

The list prices of the products are subject to a uniform trade discount of 10 per cent. Due to labour shortage, the available working hours for the next year are estimated to be only 90,000. Suggest a suitable sales-mix for the next year:

1. When there is enough demand for all the products.
2. When the potential demand is 18,000 units for product A, 10,000 units for product B and 12,000 units for product C.

Solution

1. *Optimal Sales-mix (No Demand Constraint)*

Particulars	Product		
	A	B	C
Effective selling price (list price-trade discount)	₹180	₹270	₹360
Less: Variable cost	100	180	160
Contribution margin (per unit)	80	90	200
Time (key factor) per unit (hours)	2.5	3.0	2.5
Contribution margin per hour	32	30	80

Given no market constraint, the manufacturing company should concentrate on production of C because its contribution margin per hour is maximum, (₹80 per hour); 36,000 units of product C can be produced = Estimated working hours ÷ Hours required per unit = 90,000 ÷ 2.5 = 36,000 units

2. *Optimal Sales-mix (With Demand Constraints)*

Particulars	Products		
	C	A	B
Contribution margin per hour	₹80	₹32	₹30

Optimal sales-mix with demand constraint should be decided on the basis of descending contribution margin per hour of the various products. Accordingly, as many units of product C should be produced as can be sold, followed by A and B: Time taken per unit × Demand (units) = Total time consumed (hours)

Product C (2.5 hours × 12,000) = 30,000
A (2.5 hours × 18,000) = 45,000
B (3 hours × 5,000) = 15,000

Note: After producing C and A, only 15,000 hours are available for product B. Thus, the suitable sales-mix for the next year is C: 12,000 units; A: 18,000 units; and B: 5,000 units.

LO 23.2
LOD: E

P.23.17 The following particulars are extracted from the records of a company:

Particulars	Product A	Product B
Sales	₹1,000	₹1,200
Material cost	100	150
Direct wage cost	150	100
Direct expenses	50	60
Overhead expenses:		
Fixed	50	100
Variable	150	200
Machine-hours used	3	2
Consumption of materials (kgs)	2	3
Direct wages per hour	₹50	

Comment on the profitability of each product when:

(i) Total sales potential in units is limited.

(ii) Total sales potential in value is limited.

(iii) Raw material is in short supply.

(iv) Production capacity (in terms of machine hours) is the limiting factor.

2. Assuming raw material as the key factor, the availability of which is 10,000 kgs., and the maximum sales potential of each product is 3,500 units, find out the product-mix which will yield the maximum profit.

Solution

1. (i) *Statement of Profitability for Products A and B:*

Particulars	Product A	Product B
Sales price per unit	₹1,000	₹1,200
Less: Variable costs:		
Material cost	100	150
Direct wage cost	150	100
Direct expenses	50	60
Overheads	150	200
Total	450	510
Contribution margin	550	690

Product B will be more profitable because its contribution margin is higher.

(ii) Total sales potential in value is limited: P/V ratio = (Contribution margin/sales) × 100

A = (₹550/₹100) × 100 = 55 per cent

B = (₹690/₹120) × 100 = 57.5 per cent

Product B is more profitable because it has a higher P/V ratio.

(iii) Raw material is the key factor: Contribution margin per kg of raw material used = Contribution margin per unit/Consumption of materials (kgs)

A = ₹550/2 kgs = ₹275

B = ₹690/3 kgs = ₹230

Product A is more profitable.

(iv) Machine hour is the key factor: Contribution margin per machine hour:

A = ₹550/3 = ₹183.33

B = ₹690/2 = ₹345.00

Product B is more profitable.

2. The optimal product-mix with raw materials and sales as key factors should be on the basis of descending contribution margin per kg. Accordingly, the company should produce 3,500 units of product A and the unused materials should be used to produce B.

Materials consumed per unit × Demand of units = Total consumed used

Product A (2 kgs × 3,500) = 7,000 kgs

Product B (3 kgs × 1,000) = 3,000 kgs

Statement of Profit

Particulars	Product A	Product B	Combined
Sales revenue	₹35,00,000	₹12,00,000	₹47,00,000
Less: Variable costs	15,75,000	5,10,000	20,85,000
Contribution	19,25,000	6,90,000	26,15,000
Less: Fixed costs	1,75,000	1,00,000	2,75,000
Net income	17,50,000	5,90,000	23,40,000

It is assumed that actual fixed costs are equivalent to the amount absorbed.

P.23.18 The Managing Director of XYZ Ltd, which manufactures three products, X, Y and Z, wants your advice on the production-mix of the company. He has furnished you the following data: **LO 23.2** **LOD: M**

	Product X	Product Y	Product Z
Direct materials	₹400	₹300	₹200
Variable overheads	20	50	30

Direct labour:

Department	Rate per hour	Hours	Hours	Hours
1	₹10	6	10	5
2	20	6	15	11

Data from current budget:			
Production (number of units per year)	5,000	6,000	10,000
Selling price per unit	₹780	₹1,000	₹600
Fixed overheads		₹20,00,000	
Forecast by the sales department of the maximum possible sales during the next year (number of units)	6,000	8,000	12,000

Note: The type of labour required by Department 1 is in short supply and it is not possible to increase the manpower of this department beyond its present level.

You are required to present a statement to the managing director of the company, showing the most profitable mix of the products to be made and sold. The statement should give the following formation:

1. The profit expected on the current budgeted production, and
2. The profit which could be expected if the most profitable mixture was produced.

Solution

1. *Statement Showing Profit on the Current Budgeted Production*

Particulars	Products			Total
	X	Y	Z	
Sale revenue	₹39,00,000	₹60,00,000	₹60,00,000	₹1,59,00,000
Less: Variable costs:				
Direct materials	20,00,000	18,00,000	20,00,000	58,00,000
Direct labour:				
Department 1	3,00,000	6,00,000	5,00,000	14,00,000
Department 2	6,00,000	18,00,000	22,00,000	46,00,000
Variable overheads	1,00,000	3,00,000	3,00,000	7,00,000
Total	30,00,000	45,00,000	50,00,000	1,25,00,000
Contribution	9,00,000	15,00,000	10,00,000	34,00,000
Less: Fixed costs				20,00,000
Net profit				14,00,000

2. Optimal product-mix is to be decided by determining contribution margin per hour of Department 1 (key factor).

Product X = ₹9 lakh/5,000 = ₹180/6 hours = ₹30 per hour
Product Y = ₹15 lakh/6,000 = ₹250/10 hours = ₹25 per hour
Product Z = ₹10 lakh/10,000 = ₹100/5 hours = ₹20 per hour

Optimal Product-mix:

Product	Time taken of Department 1 per unit	× Expected sales in units	= Total hours spent
X	(6 hours	× 6,000)	= 36,000
Y	(10 hours	× 8,000)	= 80,000
Z@	(5 hours	× 4,800)	= 24,000
			1,40,000

@ Total existing capacity (in hours) product:			
X	(6 hours	× 5,000 units)	30,000
Y	(10 hours	× 6,000 units)	60,000
Z	(5 hours	× 10,000 units)	50,000
			1,40,000

Statement of Profit at Optimal Product-mix:

Particulars	Products			Total
	X	Y	Z	
Sales revenue	₹46,80,000	₹80,00,000	₹28,80,000	₹1,55,60,000
Less: Variable costs:				
Direct materials	24,00,000	24,00,000	9,60,000	57,60,000
Direct labour:				
Department 1	3,60,000	8,00,000	2,40,000	14,00,000
2	7,20,000	24,00,000	10,56,000	41,76,000
Variable overheads	1,20,000	4,00,000	1,44,000	6,64,000
Total	36,00,000	60,00,000	24,00,000	1,20,00,000
Contribution	10,80,000	20,00,000	4,80,000	35,60,000
Less: Fixed cost				20,00,000
Net profit				15,60,000

P. 23.19 On the basis of following information, determine the product-mix to give the highest attainable profit rate: **LO 23.2** **LOD: M**

Material per unit (kgs)	20	12	30
Machine-hours per unit	3	5	4
Selling price per unit	₹2,500	₹2,000	₹4,000
Maximum possible sales (units)	1,500	1,000	750

Machine-hours for production are available up to 9,200 maximum at a cost of ₹100 per hour and 50,000 kgs of raw material @ ₹100 per kg can be obtained.

Solution

Determination of Contribution Margin Per Key Factor

Particulars	Products		
	A	B	C
Selling price per unit	₹2,500	₹2,000	₹4,000
Less relevant costs:			
Material	2,000	1,200	3,000
Machine charges	300	500	400
Contribution margin (CM)	200	300	600
Key factors: Material (kgs)	20	12	30
CM per kg	10	25	20
Key factor: Machine-hours	3	5	4
CM per kg per hour	₹3.33	5.0	5.0

Since contribution margin per key factor is the same for products B and C, the priority in determining product-mix would be maximum possible production of B and C and the left-over inputs used in product A.

Statement Indicating Product-mix

Product	Maximum production possible	Use of inputs Materials (kgs)	Machine-hours	Inputs left Materials (kgs)	Machine-hours	Actual product mix
B	1,000	12,000	5,000	38,000	4,200	1,000
C	750	22,500	3,000	15,500	1,200	750
A	1,500	8,000	1,200	7,500	—	400

Product-mix as shown in the last column would give the highest profit

P.23.20 XY Ltd. is manufacturing three household products A, B and C, and selling them in a competitive market. Details of current demand, selling price and cost structure are given below: **LO 23.2 LOD: M**

Particulars	A	B	C
Expected demand (units)	10,000	12,000	20,000
Selling price per unit (₹)	20	16	10
Variable cost per unit (₹)			
Direct materials (₹10/kg.)	6	4	2
Direct labour (₹15/hr.)	3	3	1.50
Variable overheads	2	1	1
Fixed overhead per unit (₹)	5	4	2

The company is frequently affected by acute scarcity of raw material and high labour turnover. During the next period, it is expected to have one of the following situations:

(a) Raw materials available will be only 12,100 kgs.

(b) Direct labour-hours available will be only 5,000 hours.

(c) It may be possible to increase sales of any one product by 25 per cent without any additional fixed costs but by spending ₹20,000 on advertisement. There will be no shortage of materials or labour.

Suggest the best production plan in each case and the resultant profit that the company would earn according to your suggestion.

Solution

Determination of Profitability Ranking in Various Situations

Particulars	Products A	B	C
Selling price per unit	₹20	₹16	₹10
Less variable costs per unit:			
Direct material	6	4	2.00
Direct labour	3	3	1.50
Variable overheads	2	1	1.00
Total variable cost per unit	11	8	4.5
Contribution per unit	9	8	5.5
C/V ratio	45% (rank 3)	50% (Rank 2)	55% (Rank 1)
Ranking with raw material as key factor:			
Raw material used per unit			
(Raw material cost)/(Price per kg)	0.6 kg	0.4 kg	0.2 kg
Contribution per kg of raw material	₹15 (Rank 3)	₹20 (Rank 2)	₹27.50 (Rank 1)
Ranking with labour as key factor	111	11	1
Labour hours required per unit			
(Labour cost/Wages per hour)	1/5	1/5	1/10
Contribution per labour-hour	₹45 (Rank 2)	₹40 (Rank 3)	₹55 (Rank 1)

Situation (a): Optimal Production Plan when Raw Material Available is 12,100 kgs

Product	Number of units	Raw material required (kgs)	Contribution per unit	Total contribution
C	20,000	4,000	₹5.50	₹1,10,000
B	12,000	4,800	8.00	96,000
A	5,500@	3,300	9.00	49,500
		12,100		2,55,500
Less fixed costs				1,38,000@@
Net profit				1,17,500

@3300 ÷ 0.06 kg = 5500 units

@@ *Determination of fixed costs:*

A 10,000 × ₹5 =	50,000
B 12,000 × ₹4 =	48,000
C 20,000 × ₹2 =	40,000
	1,38,000

Situation (b): Optimal Production Plan when Labour-Hours Available is 5,000 Hours

Product	Number of units	Labour-hours required	Contribution per unit	Total contribution
C	20,000	2,000	₹5.50	₹1,10,000
A	12,000	2,000	9.00	90,000
B	5,000@	1,000	8.00	40,000
		5,000		2,40,000
Less, fixed costs				1,38,000
Net profit				1,02,000

@ 1,000 hours ÷ 1/5 = 5,000 units

Situation (C): Since there is no shortage of material and labour, ranking will be based on C/V ratio. Accordingly, production of C product with highest C/V ratio will be increased by 5,000 units (0.25 × 20,000).

Statement of Profit at Optimal Production Plan

Product	Number of units		Contribution per unit	Total contribution
A	10,000		₹9.00	₹90,000
B	12,000		8.00	96,000
C	25,000		5.50	1,37,500
				3,23,500
Less fixed cost		₹1,38,000		
Additional advertisement expenditure		20,000		1,58,000
Net profit				1,65,500

P.23.21 The following particulars are taken from the records of a company engaged in manufacturing two products, A and B, from a certain material: **LO 23.2** **LOD: M**

Particulars	Product A (Per unit)	Product B (Per unit)
Sales	₹2,500	₹5,000
Material cost (₹50 per kg)	500	1,250
Direct labour (₹30 per hour)	750	1,500
Variable overhead	250	500
Total fixed overheads:		₹10,00,000

Comment on the profitability of each product when:

(i) Total sales in value is limited.

(ii) Raw materials is in short supply.

(iii) Production capacity (in terms of direct labour hours) is the limiting factor.

(iv) Total availability of raw materials is 20,000 kgs. and maximum sales potential of each product is 1,000 units. Find the product mix to yield maximum profits.

Solution

(i) *Contribution Per Unit*

Particulars		*Product A*		*Product B*
Sales		₹2,500		₹5,000
Less variable costs				
Material	₹500		₹1,250	
Labour	750		1,500	
Overheads	250	1,500	500	3,250
Contribution per unit		1,000		1,750
P/V ratio/C/V ratio (%)		40		35
Raw material required per unit (kgs).		10@		25@@
Contribution per kg of raw material		100		70
Labour-hours per unit		25(x)		50(xx)
Contribution per hour of labour		40		35

@₹500/₹50 = 10 kgs; @@ ₹1,250/₹50 = 25 kgs

(x) ₹750/₹30 = 25 hours (xx) ₹1,500/₹30 = 50 hours

(i) *Profitability when total sales in value is limited*

Since P/V ratio of product A (40 per cent) is more than that of product B (35 per cent) producing and selling of product A will be more profitable.

(ii) *Profitability when raw material is in short supply*

Since contribution per kg of raw material is higher is case of product A (₹100) than product B (₹70), producing and selling of product A will be more profitable in the case of short supply of raw material.

(iii) *Profitability when production capacity is limited*

Since contribution per direct labour hour is higher in case of product A (₹40) than that of product B (₹35), producing and selling of product A will be more profitable.

(iv) Statement of Product Mix to Yield Maximum Profit when Raw Material Supply is Limited to 20,000 kgs

Product	*Units*	*Raw material consumed*	*Contribution per unit*	*Total contribution*	*Fixed cost*	*Profit*
A	1,000	10,000*	₹1,000	₹10,00,000	—	
B	400**	10,000	1,750	7,00,000	—	
				17,00,000	₹10,00,000	₹7,00,000

* 1,000 × 10 = 10,000 kgs; ** 10,000 ÷ 25 kgs = 400 units

P.23.22 When Alps Ltd operates at normal capacity, it manufactures 2,00,000 units of product per year. The unit cost of manufacturing at normal capacity is as follows: **LO 23.2** **LOD: M**

Direct materials	₹7.80
Direct labour	2.10
Variable overheads	2.50
Fixed overheads	4.00
Product cost (per unit)	16.40
Selling price	21.00

During the next 3 months, only 10,000 units can be purchased and sold. Management plans to shut down the plant, estimating that the fixed manufacturing overheads can be reduced to ₹74,000 for the quarter when the plant is not operating; the fixed overhead costs are incurred at a uniform rate throughout the year. Additional costs of plant shutdown for the 3 months are estimated at ₹14,000.

You are required to answer:

(a) Should the plant be shut down for 3 months? Show computations?

(b) What is the shutdown point for the 3 months in units of product?

Solution

(a) *Decision Analysis (Shut-down Plant)*

Particulars		Operate plant	Shutdown plant
(i) *Estimated revenue* (10,000 × ₹21)		₹2,10,000	—
(ii) *Estimated variable cost:*			
Direct materials	₹7.80		
Direct labour	2.10		
Variable overheads	2.50		
	12.40	(1,24,000)	—
(iii) Estimated contribution		86,000	—
Less fixed costs		(2,00,000)	(74,000)
Shut-down costs		—	(14,000)
Net profit (loss)		(1,14,000)	(88,000)

The plant should be shut down for 3 months as the loss is ₹88,000 only, while operating the plant would entail a greater loss (₹1,14,000).

(b) The shut-down point = [Fixed cost when plant is operating – Shut-down costs when plant is not operating] ÷ Contribution margin per unit = (₹2,00,000 – ₹88,000) ÷ ₹8.60 = 13,023 units

P.23.23 Alfa Engineering Works Ltd had the following annual budget for the current year ending March 31: LO 23.2 LOD: M

Product capacity	60 per cent	80 per cent
Costs: (₹in lakh)		
Direct material	9.60	12.80
Direct labour	7.20	9.60
Factory expenses	7.56	8.04
Administrative expenses	3.72	3.88
Selling and distribution expenses	4.08	4.32
Total	32.16	38.64
Profit	4.86	10.72
Sales	37.02	49.36

Owing to adverse trading conditions, the company has been operating during April-June of this years at 40 per cent capacity realising budgeted selling prices.

Owing to acute competition, it has become inevitable to reduce prices by 25 per cent even to maintain the sales at the existing level. The directors are considering whether or not their factory should be closed down until the trade recession has passed. A market research consultant has advised that in about a years' time there is every indication that sales will increase to 75 per cent of normal capacity and that the revenues to be produced for a full year at that volume could be expected to be ₹40 lakh.

If the directors decide to close down the factory for a year it is estimated that

(a) The present fixed costs would be reduced to ₹6 lakh per annum;
(b) Closing down costs (redundancy payments, etc.) would amount to ₹2 lakh;
(c) Necessary maintenance of plant would cost ₹50,000 per annum; and
(d) On re-operating the factory, the cost of overhauling the plant, training and engagement of new personnel would amount to ₹80,000.

Prepare a report for the directors, making you recommendations.

Solution

Decision Analysis (continue or shut-down the factory) (₹in lakh)

Particulars	Operate	Shut-down	Differential revenues and costs
Sales revenue	18.51	—	18.51
Costs:			
Direct material	6.40	—	(6.40)
Direct labour	4.80	—	(4.80)

(Contd.)

(Contd.)

Factory expenses (variable)	0.96	—	(0.96)
Factory expenses (fixed)	6.12	6.00	(0.12)
Administrative expenses (variable)	0.32	—	(0.32)
Administrative expenses (fixed)	3.24	—	(3.24)
Selling and distribution expenses (variable)	0.48	—	(0.48)
Selling and distribution expenses (fixed)	3.36	—	(3.36)
Closing down costs:			
Redundancy payments	—	2.00	2.00
Maintenance of plant	—	0.50	0.50
Overhauling costs	—	0.80	0.80
Total costs	25.68	9.30	(16.38)
Differential revenues favouring the decision to operate the plant			2.13

The directors are advised to operate the plant.

P.23.24 Infotech Ltd is a leading software company with clientele overseas. It received an order from Double Standard Railway Network Inc of America to develop software for their railway networks on payment of ₹35,00,000. The software was to consist of 100 programmes and was to be done in four stages. The stage-wise expenditures as calculated by Infotech Ltd is detailed below; **LO 23.2** **LOD: D**

Stage	*Expenditure per programme*	*Duration (months)*
Preparation of high level design	₹5,000	2
Preparation of low level design	4,000	1
Coding (programming)	3,000	2
Testing	1,000	1
Total	13,000	6

The project was started in a rented place, the monthly rent being ₹1,00,000. Infotech Ltd acquired 10 new terminals at a cost of ₹50,000 each, besides a server for ₹1,00,000. Other fixed costs for the project were estimated at ₹1,00,000.

At the completion stage of coding, Double Standard Railway Network cancelled the order in the aftermath of the American sanctions following the nuclear test—Pokharan II.

According to information available with Infotech's office in Paris, Opportunist Consultants are ready to buy the software for ₹10,00,000 if the testing stage is completed. The office also reports that Anglesent Railway Company (ARC) in France wants the software for their operations for ₹34,00,000. The cost and other parameters of the alternative proposal are:

- The required software will consist of 150 programmes.
- The project will take 4 months to complete.
- The ARC will send 2 managers to assist Infotech to modify the 100 programmes already written to suit their requirements. They will stay for 5 days in India and the daily cost of their stay would be ₹20,000. Their air fare will be borne by ARC.
- The modification of softwares will involved additional cost of ₹500 per programme and a fixed cost of ₹50,000.
- The ARC has agreed to give 2 years maintenance contract to Infotech for ₹2,00,000. The maintenance cost worked out by Infotech is ₹1,00,000.
- The cost incurred in connection with the visit of a manager of Infotech to negotiate the deal is ₹1,00,000.

Should Infotech Ltd accept the offer to sell the software to ARC? Why?

Solution

Incremental Analysis (whether to accept the offer from ARC or not)

Incremental revenue:		
From software	₹34,00,000	
From maintenance	2,00,000	₹36,00,000

(Contd.)

(*Contd.*)

Less incremental costs:		
Preparation of high level design (₹5,000 × 50)	2,50,000	
Preparation of low level design (₹4,000 × 50)	2,00,000	
Coding/Programming (₹3,000 × 50)	1,50,000	
Testing (₹1,000 × 150)	1,50,000	
Office rent (₹1,00,000 × 4)	4,00,000	
Additional fixed cost	50,000	
Cost of modification of existing programmes	50,000	
Expenditure on managers from ARC (₹20,000 × 5)	1,00,000	
Maintenance cost	1,00,000	
Opportunity cost/Net selling cost to Opportunist		
Consultants (₹10,00,000 – ₹1,00,000, cost of testing)	9,00,000	23,50,000
Incremental profit		12,50,000

Recommendation The offer should be accepted as it yields incremental profit of ₹12,50,000.

Working Notes

The following costs since already incurred have been ignored:

Preparation of high level design (₹5,000 × 100 programmes)	₹5,00,000
Preparation of low level design (₹4,000 × 100)	4,00,000
Coding (₹3,000 × 100)	3,00,000
Office rent (₹1,00,000 × 5 months)	5,00,000
Hardware cost:	
Terminals (10 × ₹50,000)	5,00,000
Server	1,00,000
Other fixed costs	1,00,000
Cost incurred on manager's visit	1,00,000
	25,00,000

P.23.25 Uttam Computers Ltd (UCL) provides assembled computers to retail outlets as well as network support to small/medium business organisations. Anticipating boom in demand after the reduced import duty, UCL assembled 50 computers in advance to meet demand. The specifications of the computer were as follows: **LO 23.2** **LOD: D**

Parts	*Specifications*	*Cost*
(a) Computer Kit		
• Mother board	Universal serial bus	₹5,000
• Microprocessor chip	133 MHz chip XL of Megahurts	5,000
• Floppy drive	1.44 MB	1,500
• Hard disk	1.2 GB Ultra	4,000
• VGA card	1 MB VRAM	1,500
• RAM	16 MB SDRAM	2,500
(b) Multimedia Kit		
• CD Rom	32 X Drive	3,500
• Sound Card	Surround sound wave blaster	1,700
• Speaker	100 W PMPO (< 1% distortion)	800
(c) Cabinet With digital display and SMPS	1,500	
(d) Keyboard	105 keys membrane	500
(e) Monitor 1024 × 768 pixels	8,000	
(f) Mouse 3 Button mouse	500	
(g) Cables	—	200
(h) Labour and packaging	—	500
(i) Software	OEM pack "Khirki 98"	500
		37,200

The current market price is ₹40,000 per computer. Pending the sales of the computers, Megahurts, the microprocessor chip manufacturing company, introduced a new upgraded version of its existing chip XL. The new chip—Chip XXL (266 MHz)—is 100 per cent faster than chip XL and also includes enhanced multimedia technology. Costing ₹7,000, it is compatible with all other parts except that it needs a new kind of mother board priced at ₹5,000. The price of computers with new chip and motherboard is quoted at ₹42,000.

The introduction of the new chip XXL has led to a decrease in demand for computers fitted with old chip and mother board as a result of which quoted market price declined to ₹35,000.

The UCM was contemplating to replace the old chips/mother board by new ones. The replacement would involve additional labour and packing cost of ₹5,000. It can sell the old chip/mother board in the grey market which is ready to absorb them for ₹5,000.

It was about this time that another alternative emerged. The Bright Futures School (BFS) has agreed to buy 45 Uttam computers with old chip/mother board for its computer lab. Aware as it is of the new chips, the BFS stipulates as follows:

- It will buy 45 computers at ₹1,000 less than the quoted price of ₹40,000.
- It will like to receive free of cost network support for its lab and installation. For network support, each of the 45 computers will require a LAN (Local Area Network) card which are priced at ₹2,000 each. In addition, the network would require about 50 feet of cables @ ₹20 per foot as well as 3 signal boosters/hubs with price of ₹3,000 per piece. Also, the installation cost of the network and server software and accessories will amount to ₹15,000.

If the BFS's offer is accepted, the remaining 5 computers can be sold for ₹35,000 each.

The UCL seeks your advice as to which course of action to choose: **(i)** Replace old chip/mother board with new ones or **(ii)** Accept BFS's offer. Give your recommendations together with the reasons.

Solution

Incremental Analysis (whether to Replace Old Chip and Mother Board with New Ones)

Incremental sales revenues:		
(a) Sale of 50 computers @ ₹42,000 per computer	₹21,00,000	
(b) Salvage value of 50 old chips and motherboard @ ₹5,000 combined	2,50,000	₹23,50,000
Incremental costs:		
(a) Cost of 50 Chip XXL @ ₹7,000 per chip	3,50,000	
(b) Cost of 50 new motherboards @ ₹5,000 per unit	2,50,000	
(c) Additional labour and packaging cost	5,000	
(d) Opportunity cost of selling at reduced price of ₹35,000	17,50,000	23,55,000
Incremental loss		(5,000)

Incremental Analysis (whether to Accept Bright Futures Offer)

Incremental sales revenue:		
Sale of 45 computers @ ₹39,000 per computer	₹17,55,000	
Sale of 5 computers @ ₹35,000 per computer	1,75,000	₹19,30,000
Incremental costs		
Network additions		
3 network signal boosters/hubs @ ₹3,000 per piece	9,000	
45 LAN cards @ ₹2,000 per card	90,000	
Cabling 50 feet @ ₹20 per foot	1,000	
Server accessories and software	15,000	
Opportunity cost of selling at reduced price (₹35,000 × 50)	17,50,000	18,65,000
Profits		65,000

Recommendations The UCL is advised to accept the offer of BFS. It is financially profitable. Also, the company would be increasing its clientele domain from business organisation to educational institutions. In addition, it would also generate some revenues from after sales service/maintenance contracts with the school.

REVIEW QUESTIONS

LOD: Easy

RQ.23.1 Indicate whether the following statements are true or false. LO 23.1,2

(i) Costs incurred in selecting a site for construction of a factory are sunk costs.
(ii) Existing fixed costs are relevant costs for decision-making.
(iii) A firm is engaged in production of multiple products. One of its products incurs losses. Without any further cost analysis, the production of the said product should be discontinued.
(iv) Avoidable costs are irrelevant costs for decision-making.
(v) Incremental costs consist of variable costs only.
(vi) Committed costs are like sunk costs and therefore irrelevant costs for decision-making.
(vii) All future costs are relevant costs.
(viii) A branch of business segment that shows negative operating income should be shut-down.
(ix) Variable costs are always relevant and fixed costs are always irrelevant.
(x) Opportunity costs are out-of-pocket cash costs.

[Answers: (i) True, (ii) False, (iii) False, (iv) False, (v) False, (vi) True, (vii) True, (viii) False, (ix) False, (x) False.]

RQ.23.2 Fill in the following blanks (in some cases choices are provided). LO 23.1,2

(i) __________ analysis is appropriate technique for short-term decisions.
(ii) Sales made at loss in expectation of additional sales in future are referred to as __________.
(iii) Resources that are limited in quantity are known as __________.
(iv) Maximising __________ should be the basis for determining optimal product mix when input resources are scarce.
(v) Common processing costs in the case of joint products are __________.
(vi) All those costs which affect the decision are known as __________.
(vii) Sunk costs are __________ costs.
(viii) Only __________ fixed costs are reckoned in decision-making.
(ix) In the case of analysing special order decisions, it is assumed that the existing sale price charged by the firm is __________.

[Answers: (i) incremental, (ii) loss leaders, (iii) key factors, (iv) contribution margin per unit of key factor, (v) sunk costs, (vi) relevant costs, (vii) committed, (viii) incremental, (ix) not affected.]

RQ.23.3 What decision criteria are appropriate for short-run decisions? Outline the format used for such decisions. LO 23.1

RQ.23.4 What comparisons should be made in deciding whether or not to accept a one-time order at a price different from the regular sales price? LO 23.2

RQ.23.5 Briefly explain the target costing process. LO 23.3

RQ.23.6 Write brief note on the components of target costing process. LO 23.3

RQ.23.7 Explain: **(i)** Target costing, **(ii)** Target pricing. LO 23.3

RQ.23.8 Uniform Product Company Ltd. produces a single product. Its maximum annual production capacity is 4,80,000 labour-hours. Currently, it is producing at an annual rate of 3,75,000 labour-hours. Normal volume (the basis of absorption of fixed overhead) is 4,50,000 hours. LO 23.2

The company has received an offer of 70,000 such units at a special price of ₹120 per unit. The regular selling price is ₹150 per unit. The standard cost sheet for one unit of the product is as follows:

Direct materials (2 kgs @ ₹25)	₹50
Direct labour (1.5 hours @ ₹20)	30
Variable overheads (1.5 hours @ ₹20)	30
Fixed overheads (1.5 hours @ ₹10)	15
	125

In the short run, would it be profitable to accept the offer?

RQ.23.9 Three different product lines are sold by M/s Mercury Mills Ltd. Product A contributes 20 per cent of its revenue to fixed costs and profits. Product B contributes 10 per cent, and Product C contributes 50 per cent. The products sell for the following prices: Product A, ₹80; Product B, ₹20; Product C, ₹30. **LO 23.2**

The company earned a net profit of ₹5,00,000 before income tax last year by selling 50,000 units of Product A, 1,50,000 units of Product B, and 60,000 units of Product C. The sales manager believes that the profit picture can be improved by eliminating product B and concentrating the sales efforts on products A and C. He sees an opportunity to increase the sales of products A to 70,000 units, but admits that product C will probably sell at the same amount next year.

Prepare a projected profit and loss statement using sales manager's assumption. Do you agree with him? Explain what would cause the profit to increase or decrease, as the case may be.

LOD: Medium

RQ.23.10 Differentiate between 'sunk' and 'avoidable' costs. What is the relevance of such a distinction for short-run decisions? **LO 23.1**

RQ.23.11 What is an opportunity cost? When do opportunity costs affect short-run decisions? What accounting problems do opportunity costs involve? **LO 23.1**

RQ.23.12 In disposing of inventory that has already been manufactured, what costs should be considered when the product is: **(i)** Still marketable in a normal way and **(ii)** Obsolete, damaged or out of fashion? **LO 23.2**

RQ.23.13 Explain the role of **(i)** Committed, **(ii)** Sunk, **(iii)** Avoidable, and **(iv)** Opportunity costs in make-or-buy decisions? **LO 23.1**

RQ.23.14 Explain the role of: **(i)** Incremental revenues and **(ii)** Subsequent processing cost in sell-or- process-further decisions. **LO 23.2**

RQ.23.15 Electric Manufacturing Company Ltd. is engaged in producing a variety of precision instruments and other specialised electric components. The company is presently following a policy of pricing all of its products at 150 per cent of the total variable costs to produce and sell them. Because of the specialised nature of these products, this has proved to be a useful pricing policy. **LO 23.2**

Recently, the Government invited tender for 1,000 electric components to be used at the TV station. The company's management is exploring the possibility of the firm entering into a Government contract. The management accountant has prepared the following cost estimates for the purpose:

Direct materials	₹8,00,000
Direct labour	5,50,000
Variable overheads	2,25,000
Fixed manufacturing overheads	3,00,000
Production set-up costs	1,25,000
Special tools and dyes (no salvage value after use)	3,00,000
Total costs	23,00,000
Unit cost (₹23,00,000 ÷ 1,000 units):	2,300

The Government requires delivery of all 1,000 units within one year. In order to meet that schedule, the company would have to forego a regular sales order of value of ₹22,50,000.

You are required to state the lowest price the company could bid on the contract for the components without sacrificing short-run profit. State your assumptions, if any.

RQ.23.16 X Ltd., having an installed capacity of 1,00,000 units of a product, is currently operating at 70 per cent utilisation. At current levels of input prices, the FOB unit cost (after taking credit for applicable export incentives) works out as follows: **LO 23.2**

Capacity utilisation (per cent)	*FOB unit costs*
70	₹97
80	92
90	87
100	82

The company has received 3 foreign offers from different sources: A, 5,000 units at ₹55 per unit FOB; B, 10,000 units at ₹52 per unit FOB; and C, 10,000 units at ₹51 per unit FOB. Advise the company as to whether any, or all, export orders should be accepted or not.

RQ.23.17 Kerala Engineering Ltd., manufactures and markets three products: X, Y, and Z in varying proportions during a year. Based upon past experience and future market expectations, the management accountant of the company provides the followed information for the current year: LO 23.2

Product	*Price per unit*	*Variable cost per unit*	*Possible sale*	
			Mix 1	*Mix 2*
X	30	12	6,00,000	3,00,000
Y	40	20	3,00,000	2,00,000
Z	25	15	1,00,000	5,00,000

The fixed costs during the year are estimated at ₹2,64,000. Which product-mix would you adopt?

RQ.23.18 Vinak Ltd., which produces three products, furnishes you the following data for the current year. LO 23.2

Particulars	*Products*		
	A	*B*	*C*
Selling price per unit	₹100	₹75	₹50
Profit volume ratio (per cent)	10	20	40
Maximum sales potential (units)	40,000	25,000	10,000
Raw material content as percentage of variable costs (per cent)	50	50	50

The fixed expenses are estimated at ₹6,80,000. The company uses a single raw material in all the three products. Raw material is in short supply and the company has a quota for the supply of raw materials of the value of ₹18,00,000 for the current year for the manufacture of its products to meet its sales demand.

You are required to:

1. Set a product-mix which will give a maximum overall profit keeping the short supply of raw materials in view.
2. Compute the maximum profit.

RQ.23.19 You are the cost accountant of a manufacturing company. The top management seeks your assistance in arriving at a decision whether to continue manufacturing a part or to buy it from an outside supplier. The part is a component used in several of the company's finished products. LO 23.2

The following data have been arrived at on the basis of cost records and further investigation:

1. The annual requirement is 40,000 units.
2. The lowest list price quotation from a supplier was ₹27.50 per unit.
3. Following are the total costs incurred last year, when 40,000 parts were produced in Department A of the company:

Materials	₹12,00,000
Labour	15,00,000
Indirect labour	4,00,000
Light and heat	80,000
Power	1,20,000
Depreciation	7,00,000
Property taxes and insurance	70,000
Miscellaneous	1,50,000

4. The following proportions (percentages) of the variable costs in Department A could be avoided if production of parts was discontinued: Materials, 35; Direct labour, 40; Power, 25.

5. If parts are purchased from an outside supplier, average freight cost is ₹0.50 per unit. Also, indirect labour in Department A would increase by ₹30,000 annually because of receiving, inspecting and handling of the purchased parts.

On the basis of the above information, advise management on the commercial feasibility of the proposed plan.

RQ.23.20 XYZ Company Ltd. buys crude vegetable oil. The refining of this oil results in four products, A, B, C, and D. The cost of oil refined in the current year was ₹2,76,000, and the refining department has total processing costs of ₹7,00,000. The output and sales for the four products were as follows: **LO 23.2**

Product	*Output (gallons)*	*Sales*	*Additional processing cost after split-off*
A	5,00,000	₹11,50,000	₹3,00,000
B	10,000	1,00,000	60,000
C	5,000	40,000	—
D	9,000	3,00,000	10,000

REQUIRED

(i) Assume that the net realisable value at split-off is used for allocating joint costs. What is the net income for products, A, B, C, and D? Joint costs total ₹9,76,000.

(ii) The company had been tempted to sell out at split-off directly to other processors. If that alternative had been selected, sales per galloon would have been: A, ₹150; B, ₹5; C, ₹8 and D, ₹30. The company expects to operate at the same level of output and sales in the forthcoming year. Could the company increase net income by altering processing decisions? If so, what would the expected overall net income be? Which products should be processed further and which should be sold at split-off? Assume that all costs incurred after split-off are variable.

RQ.23.21 The management of a company considers that product Y, one of its three main lines, is not as profitable as the other two, with the result that no particular efforts are being made to push its sales. The selling prices and costs of the products are: **LO 23.2**

Product	*Selling price*	*Direct material*	*Direct labour*		
			Department A	*Department B*	*Department C*
X	₹68	₹10	₹8	₹2	₹2
Y	58	6	2	8	2
Z	64	8	2	2	8

Overhead rates on each department per rupee of direct labour are as follows:

	Department A	*Department B*	*Department C*
Variable overhead	1.20	0.40	1.00
Fixed overhead	1.20	2.00	1.40
	2.40	2.40	2.40

What advice would you give to the management about the profitability of product Y? Give reasons.

LOD: Difficult

RQ.23.22 When the discontinuation of a product line, division, or department is being considered, what relevant data are useful in short-run situations? **LO 23.2**

RQ.23.23 A factory is divided into three departments, D1, D2 and D3, in each of which the capacity available during the 3 months (January 1 to March 31) is 2,000 hours. The fixed and variable overhead expenses budgeted for each department for this period are as follows: **LO 23.2**

Department	Fixed	Variable per hour
D1	₹20,000	₹35
D2	25,000	25
D3	70,000	30

On January 1, 2 orders (O_1 and O_2) were received for each of which a selling price of ₹6,00,000 can be charged and on each of which prime costs are expected to be ₹2,50,000. The use which the two orders would make of factory capacity differs and is expected to be as follows:

Department	O_1 (hours)	O_2 (hours)
D1	1,000	2,000
D2	400	600
D3	2,000	1,000

You are required to state which of the two orders (if any) should be accepted, and to show the calculations on which your opinion is based.

RQ.23.24 A confectioner markets three products all of which require sugar. His average monthly sales, cost of sales and sugar consumption are as follows: **LO 23.2**

	Products			Total
	X	Y	Z	
Sales	₹1,00,000	₹1,20,000	₹80,000	₹3,00,000
Cost of sales (variable)	60,000	80,000	56,000	1,96,000
Sugar requirement (kgs)	500	800	240	1,540

Due to the Government restrictions, his sugar quota has been reduced to 1,405 kgs per month. Suggest a suitable sales mix which would give the company maximum profit under the given circumstances.

RQ.23.25 A company has asked for your assistance in determining the most profitable sales and product mix of its products for current year. The company manufactures a line of toys. The sales department has provided you with the following budget data: **LO 23.2**

Toy	Estimated demand (units)	Selling price per toy
A	60,000	₹14.50
B	1,00,000	7.90
C	70,000	16.60
D	45,000	25.20
E	2,20,000	6.00

The cost account has developed the following additional data from the accounting files.

1. Standard direct production cost per unit are as follows:

Toy	Materials	Labour
A	₹4.10	₹5.00
B	2.10	2.50
C	5.50	6.00
D	10.00	8.00
E	1.90	1.50

2. The standard wage rate of ₹10 per hour is expected to continue unchanged throughout the year. The plant has an effective production capacity of 1,51,000 labour-hours per year on a single shift. The current equipment can be used to produce any and all of the toys.

3. Variable manufacturing overhead is budgeted at ₹3 per direct labour-hour. Total fixed manufacturing overhead is planned at ₹7,20,000.
You are required to:
(i) Prepare a schedule that will be most useful to management in planning the product-mix. Determine the amount of net income at such a product-mix.
(ii) Is the present effective capacity on a single shift adequate to meet the estimated sales demand in current year? If not, what will the optimal product-mix be to keep producing within the limits of a single shift?

ANSWERS

RQ.23.8 Yes, profitable to accept the order; increase in profits by ₹7,00,000.
RQ.23.9 Profit, ₹5,20,000. Yes.
RQ.23.15 ₹27,50,000 lowest price; no sales value of special tools after their use, interest costs are ignored.
RQ.23.16 Accept all export orders; increase in profits by ₹3,05,000.
RQ.23.17 Net income, ₹2,86,000 (sales-mix 1), ₹2,16,000 (sales-mix 2).
RQ.23.18 **(i)** Product A, 20,000 units; Product B, 25,000 units; Product C, 10,000 units.
(ii) ₹95,000.
RQ.23.19 Continue to make the parts; purchases from outside supplier will increase costs by ₹1,00,000.
RQ.23.20 **(i)** Net income for product A is ₹1,70,000; product B, ₹8,000; product C, ₹8,000; and product D, ₹58,000.
(ii) Net income would decrease by altering processing decisions by ₹1,10,000 (from ₹2,44,000 to ₹1,34,000). Products A and D should be processed further; incremental profits are ₹1,00,000 and ₹20,000 respectively; unprofitable to process product B as it decreases profits by ₹10,000.
RQ.23.21 Product Y is profitable; contribution margin per unit is ₹32.40; continue its production.
RQ.23.23 Accept both the order; order O_1 will increase profits by ₹2,45,000 and O_2 by ₹2,35,000.
RQ.23.24 Sales mix for products Z, X and Y is ₹80,000, ₹1,00,000 and ₹99,750 respectively. It is assumed that sales of individual products cannot be increased beyond ₹1,00,000 (product X), ₹1,20,000 (product Y) and ₹80,000 (product Z).
RQ.23.25 **(i)** Contribution margin per hour (key factor) is ₹7.8 (A); ₹10.20 (B), ₹5.50; (C), ₹6.00 (D); and ₹14.33 (E). Net income is ₹6,06,500.
(ii) No.

[Comprehensive solutions to all numerical review questions are available on the companion website: http://www.mhhe.com/khan_jain_ma7e]

CASES

23.C.1 (Acceptance of Special Orders) M/s Precision Company Ltd (PCL) is in the business of making **Fingertrips'** brand calculators. Fingertrips brand of calculators has a good reputation among students, office staff and college faculty for its quality and price. Its current market price is ₹310 per calculator. Its unit cost structure is given in Exhibit 1.

Exhibit 1 Cost Structure of Fingertrips Calculators

Direct material cost	₹150
Direct labour cost	40
Variable overheads (including printing cost, ₹2 and packaging cost, ₹5)	40
Allocated fixed overheads	50
Total	280

The PCL was started three years ago. A market research had estimated a demand for 1,80,000 calculator annually. The PCL was set up with an installed capacity of 2,00,000 calculators. But even after 3 years the annual demand for Fingertrip calculators stood at 1,50,000 units. The CEO of PCL, Bharm Dharan, was concerned about its future prospects. Meanwhile, he got an export order from Dutch Exim Ltd (DEL), Netherlands, for 1,00,000 calculators at ₹260 per calculator.

DEL is in the business of marketing stationery to schools and offices and has planned to start selling calculators as well. It would import the Fingetrip brand calculators but put its own brand name and would also take care of packaging to suit the local market requirements. Initially, it is one-year contract renewable depending on market conditions.

The CEO of PCL is interested in the order as it would help in utilising the spare capacity of 50,000 units. The marketing manager of PCL, Sonal Agarwal, supports the proposal because the calculator would be sold in Netherlands under a different brand name, and the sale of Fingertrip calculators in the local market would not be adversely affected.

According to John Mathew, production manager, to increase the production capacity by 50,000 units, a new machine, similar to the one being currently used, would have to be acquired. Two alternative machines are available in the market. The first machine could be leased at an annual cost of ₹25 lakh. The maintenance cost per year is estimated to be ₹2 lakh. The second machine uses a new technology. It can be leased for an yearly rental of ₹30 lakh. However, the maintenance cost would be ₹1.5 lakh per year. The new technology-based machine would also reduce the labour cost and variable overhead cost by ₹5 and ₹2 per calculator respectively.

The CEO asks the finance manager to carry out a financial analysis of the alternatives.

REQUIRED

Based on the financial analysis, what recommendation would you, as the finance manger, make to the CEO of PCL?

Solution

Financial (Incremental) Analysis of Export Order with Old Technology Machine

Increment revenues (₹260 × 1,00,000 calculators)		₹2,60,00,000
Less:		
• Direct material cost (₹150 × 1,00,000)	₹150,00,000	
• Direct labour cost (₹40 × 1,00,000)	40,00,000	
• Variable overheads (₹33@ × 1,00,000)	33,00,000	
• Lease rent	25,00,000	
• Maintenance cost	2,00,000	2,50,00,000
Incremental profits		10,00,000

@[₹40 – (₹2 printing cost – ₹5 packaging cost)]

Financial Analysis of Export Order With New Technology Machine

Increment revenues (₹260 × 1,00,000)		₹2,60,00,000
Less:		
• Direct material cost (₹150 × 1,00,000)	₹1,50,00,000	
• Direct labour cost [(₹40 × 50,000) + (₹35 × 50,000)]	37,50,000	
• Variable overheads [(₹33 × 50,000) + (₹31 × 50,000)]	32,00,000	
• Lease rent	30,00,000	
• Maintenance cost	1,50,000	2,51,00,000
Incremental profits		9,00,000

RECOMMENDATION The CEO should accept the export order. To increase the production capacity to meet the order, he should lease the old-technology machine as the incremental profits are higher.

23.C.2 (Shut-down Decision) M/S Janta Watch Company (JWC) manufacturers electronic watches in its manufacturing plant at Noida. It has not been doing well recently due to old technology and lack of effort in research and development. Moreover, due to the recent Free Trade Agreement between India and Thailand, chip electronic watches manufactured in Thailand and China are flooding the Indian market. As a result, the JWC is currently running only at its 50 per cent capacity. When the market conditions were good, JWC used to operate at full capacity of 4,00,000 watches per annum. The cost structure of JWC per watch is given in Exhibit 1.

EXHIBIT 1 Cost Structure of Janta Watches Per Watch

Direct material cost	₹30
Direct labour cost	8
Variable manufacturing overheads	12
Variable administrative overheads	10
	60

The unit sale price of Janta Watches is ₹100. The imported watches are available at a much lower price. JWC is consequently incurring huge losses. Meanwhile, a Japanese firm, Citizen Watch Company (CWC) has offered a new technology to JWC to compete with the imported watches. But due to some contractual obligations, the CWC would be able to handover the technology to JWC after one year.

The Chief Operating Officer of JWC, Sheshadri Chatterjee, has proposed a shutdown of operations for one year and its reopening after the new technology would be available. The CFO, Yogendra Dhabi, is not in favour of the one-year shutdown. The shutdown costs estimated by him are given in Exhibit 2.

EXHIBIT 2 One-year Shutdown Costs of JWC

Fixed costs (present, ₹90,00,000)	₹24,00,000
Settlement costs of personnel laid-off	6,00,000
Shut-down cost of plant	1,00,000
Reopening cost after 1 year	2,00,000
Total	33,00,000

REQUIRED In view of the conflicting opinion of the COO and the CFO, what course of action should the CEO of JWC take?

Solution

Financial Analysis of CFO's proposal (Operate Plant)

Sales revenue [₹100 × 2,00,000 units (4,00,000 × 0.50)		₹2,00,00,000
Less Variable costs:		
Direct material costs (₹30 × 2,00,000)	₹60,00,000	
Direct labour cost (₹8 × 2,00,000)	16,00,000	
Manufacturing overheads (₹12 × 2,00,000)	24,00,000	
Administrative overheads (₹10 × 2,00,000)	20,00,000	1,20,00,000
Total contribution		80,00,000
Less fixed costs		90,00,000
Loss		(10,00,000)

Decision: As against a loss of ₹10,00,000 when the plant is operated, the shutdown cost (Exhibit 2) is ₹33,00,000. So the incremental cost of shutdown is ₹23,00,000. The CEO of JWC would be well advised to continue operating the Noida plant for one year, pending the introduction of new Japanese technology. In addition to the financial loss, the shutdown would also have implications in terms of adverse effect on reputation/distribution system, hampering of production line, theft of spare parts, unauthorised encroachment and so on.

23.C.3 (Shut-down Decision) Monte Carlo (MC) manufactures winter wear. For the coming season MC is planning to expand its product line by adding a new jacket as a follow-up to a market research conducted on its behalf involving an expenditure of ₹20,000. A committee comprising the finance manager, production manager, marketing manager and human resources manager has, after proper analysis, concluded as follows:

- The demand in the coming season would be for 10,000 jackets.
- The requirement of a special material which would have no other use would cost ₹100 per meter.
- There would be need for additional skilled and unskilled labour. Since there is a shortage of skilled labour, MC would have to reduce the production of one of its products, namely, pullovers, by 10,000 units, the unit contribution of pullovers being ₹10. The skilled labour will also require special training of 15 days in tune with the requirement of the new product at an estimated cost of ₹50,000.
- A new machine would have to be purchased at an estimated cost of ₹1,00,000, with a salvage value of ₹10,000 after producing 10,000 jackets.
- The cost, sales and profit data are developed by the cost accountants are summarised in Exhibit 1.

EXHIBIT 1 Cost Sheet

Material cost (2 meteres × ₹50)	₹100
Skilled labour (₹75 × 1 hour)	75
Market research (₹20,000 ÷ 10,000)	2
Training expenses (₹50,000 ÷ 10,000)	5
Unskilled labour (1 hour × ₹45)	45
Allocated fixed overheads	30
Additional allocated fixed costs	10
Salary of sales personnel	5
Sales commission	5
Advertisement	5
Total cost per unit	282
Profit per unit	8
Sales price per unit	290

- The skilled labour will require compensation @ 50 per cent of their regular wages for the entire remaining units if the production of jackets is discontinued at any stage.
- Raw material would be purchased in advance to avoid price rises and avail of purchase discounts.
- Advertising before launching the product will cost ₹50,000. The existing sales force would be used on commission basis to sell the new product.

To cope with the seasonal demand of jackets, production started immediately after a green signal from the CEO, Alok Dixit. After producing 5,000 jackets, the marketing department advertised the product. While collecting orders, the sales force found that other players have also entered the market. It was not possible to sell the jackets at the ₹290 quoted price. The marketing manager was able to find 5 wholesalers in different cities, each of whom was ready to purchase a lot of 2,000 jackets each for ₹260 per jacket. They were ready to acquire jackets in two equal lots, one right now and another after one month. The production system of MC is capable of producing 5,000 jackets every month.

If, however, production is stopped after producing the first 5,000 jackets, the machine purchased for the purpose can be sold for ₹15,000.

REQUIRED

The CEO of MC is confronted with the situation whether to discontinue further production of 5,000 jackets. What advise would you give him?

23.C.4 (Product Decision) Amrita Agro Ltd. (AAL) has since 1990 been manufacturing and marketing *vanaspati ghee*, cheese and chips under the brand names Gagan Vanastpai Ghee, Gagan Cheese and Gagan Chips. The AAL's performance has been satisfactory and it had consolidated its position in the market over the years. However, in recent months, Gagan Chips has been incurring losses. The product-wise income statement of AAL for the most recent month is summarised in Exhibit 1.

EXHIBIT 1 Product-wise Income Statement of AAL for Most Recent Month

Particulars	*Gagan Vanaspati*	*Gagan Cheese*	*Gagan Chips*	*Total*
Sales revenues	₹2,00,000	₹80,000	₹12,000	₹2,92,000
Less variable costs	80,000	50,000	5,000	1,35,000
Contribution margin	1,20,000	30,000	7,000	1,57,000
Less fixed costs for product line	10,000	5,000	4,000	19,000
Segment/product margin	1,10,000	25,000	3,000	1,38,000
Less firm-related fixed costs	10,000	8,000	4,000	22,000
Net income	1,00,000	17,000	(1,000)	1,16,000

The CEO of AAL, Komila Punia, and the Joint CEO, Annapurna Alladi, are concerned about the profitability of Gagan Chips.

REQUIRED:

Should Gagan Chips be dropped?

Solution

Financial Analysis (Income Statement of AAL Without Gagan Chips)

Sales (₹2,00,000 + ₹80,000)	₹2,80,000
Less variable costs (₹80,000 + ₹50,000)	1,30,000
Contribution margin	1,50,000
Less product-line fixed costs	15,000
Product margin	1,35,000
Less firm-related fixed costs	22,000
Net income	1,13,000

Decision: Dropping of product line Gagan Chips would result in decline in profits of AAL. Its production should continue.

23.C.5 (Product-Mix) Assume for **22.C.4** the price and cost data per unit summarised in Exhibit 1.

EXHIBIT 1 Unit Sale Price and Cost of AAL

	Gagan Ghee	*Gagan Cheese*	*Gagan Chips*
Sales price per unit	₹40	₹25	₹15
Direct material cost per unit	6	3	3
Direct labour cost per unit	20	16	8
Variable overheads per unit	4	2	1

The projected output for a month is *ghee* 7,000 units, cheese 4,000 units and chips 10,000 units.

Due to employee turnover in recent months, AAL is now left with only 350 workers. They work 24 days in a month and 8 hours per day. The direct wage rate is ₹4 per hour.

REQUIRED:

Determine the optimal product mix for AAL.

Solution

Ranking In Order of Profitability of Products of AAL

		Gagan Ghee		Gagan Cheese		Gagan Chips
1. Sales price per unit		₹40		₹25		₹15
2. Less variable cost per unit:						
• Direct material	₹6		₹3		₹3	
• Direct labour	20		16		8	
• Variable overheads	4	30	2	21	1	12
3. Contribution margin per unit		10		4		3
4. Direct labour hours (DLH) [Direct labour cost ÷ ₹4]		5		4		2
5. Contribution margin per DL hour (3 ÷ 4)		2		1		1.5
6. Rank (in order of profitability)		1		3		2

Statement Showing Utilisation of DLH Yielding Optimal Product-mix

Total direct labour-hours available: (350 workers × 25 days × 8 hours)		70,000
Direct labour-hours required to produce:		
• Gagan Ghee (7,000 × 5)	35,000	
• Gagan Chips (10,000 × 2)	20,000	55,000
DLHs available for Gagan Cheese		15,000
Units of cheese that can be produced (15,000 ÷ 4)		3,750

Income Statement for the Most Current Month of AAL

Particulars	*Gagan Ghee*	*Gagan Cheese*	*Gagan Chips*	*Total*
1. Units sold	7,000	3,750	10,000	
2. Unit sale price	₹40	₹25	₹15	
3. Sales revenue (1 × 2)	2,80,000	93,750	1,50,000	₹5,23,750
4. Variable costs per unit	30	21	12	
5. Total variable costs (1 × 4)	2,10,000	78,750	1,20,000	4,08,750
6. Contribution (3 – 5)	70,000	15,000	30,000	1,15,000
7. Total fixed costs				50,000
8. Net income				65,000

Decision: The optimal product-mix is: Gagan Ghee, 7,000; Gagan Cheese, 3,750; and Gagan Chips 10,000.

23.C.6 (Product Decisin) Apeksha Jain is the CEO of Nanak Milk Company Ltd. (NMCL). The NMCL has been in milk supply business over 20 years and has developed a good distribution channel for its business. Apeksha has invested in new technologies for pasteurising milk as a result of which milk stays fresh for 60 hours even after packaging. The milk is sold in special **PET** bottles which are bought from Avon Bottling Company Ltd for ₹0.50 per 500 ml (0.50 litre) bottle. The bottle are "take home" type, that is, the buyer takes away the bottle and need not return after consumption of milk. Keeping the brand reputation and Government regulations in view, NMCL has standing instructions to distributors to crush the unsold bottles after 2 days. The monthly production of milk by NMCL is 20,00,000 bottles and on average 80,000 bottles have to be crushed.

The cost (all variable) of a milk bottle is ₹9 comprising of procurement cost, ₹5.50, other variable cost, ₹3, and bottling cost ₹0.50. Total fixed costs amount to ₹1,20,00,000. The sale price of a bottle of milk is ₹12.

Due to competition from Mother Dairy, the sales of NMCL are declining having an adverse effect on its profitability. The CEO directs Adheer Upadhayay, CFO, to seek the opinion of Smart Consultants about the course of action to meet the situation. Smart Consultants have suggested the following alternatives:

Alternative I: Reduce production/supply by 50,000 bottles.

Alternative II: Make *paneer* from the unsold milk. The recalling costs of unsold (80,000) bottles to the factory would be ₹3 per bottle. The recalled bottles can be reused after washing. Milk from 4 bottles can be used to make 1 packet (200 gms) of *paneer* which can be sold at ₹35 per packet. All the *paneer* packets can be sold. The monthly incremental costs of manufacturing and selling *paneer* packets are as follows: **(a)** Labour cost, 20,000; **(b)** Overheads, ₹40,000; and **(c)** Selling costs, ₹30,000. The technology and machinery needed to make *paneer* is available with the NMCL.

REQUIRED: What course of actions should Apeksha Jain choose?

Solution

Financial (Cost Savings) Analysis (To Decrease Production/Sale of Milk by 50,000 Bottles)

Total savings in variable cost (50,000 bottles × ₹9)	₹4,50,000
Loss of incremental profits (₹3 x 50,000 bottles)	1,50,000
	3,00,000

Financial Analysis (To Enter into *Paneer* Production)

Incremental sales (80,000 × 0.25 × ₹35)	₹7,00,000	
Savings in bottling cost (80,000 × 0.50)	40,000	₹7,40,000
Less incremental costs:		
• Labour costs	20,000	
• Overheads	40,000	
• Selling costs	30,000	
• Recalling costs (80,000 × ₹3)	2,40,000	3,30,000
		4,10,000

Decision: Apeksha Jain, the CEO of Nanak Milk Company should go for making *paneer.*

23.C.7 Supreme Construction Company (SCC) Ltd (Acceptance of Special Order) The SCC, a reputed construction firm, has won a contract for constructing 1,000 three-bedroom flats for a real estate firm, Dream Homes Limited. It has quoted a very competitive rate which is ₹17,00,000 per flat. The flats are to be completed in one year. The work is in progress at site. The SCC has submitted the bid price of ₹17,00,000 per flat on the basis of following analysis:

COST STATEMENT

Fixed Costs:\		
Office cost		₹10,00,000
Cost of concrete batching plant, tower crane and other equipments		20,00,00,000
Cost of shuttering		6,00,000
Cost of sample flat		9,00,000
Salary of permanent staff:		
Junior engineers (6 × ₹20,000 per month)	₹14,40,000	
Sr. engineers (3 × ₹40,000 per month)	14,40,000	
Project manager (₹90,000 per month)	10,80,000	
Clerks (2 × ₹10,000 each per month)	2,40,000	42,00,000
Total fixed cost		20,67,00,000
Variable Cost per flat:		
Raw material	8,50,000	
Labour cost	4,00,000	
Other variable costs	2,00,000	14,50,000
Total variable cost (1,000 flats × ₹14,50,000)		145,00,00,000

INCOME STATEMENT

Sales revenue	₹170,00,00,000
Less: Total cost	165,67,00,000
Profit before taxes	4,33,00,000
Tax @ 35 per cent	1,51,55,000
Earnings after taxes (EAT)	2,81,45,000

The Dream Homes Limited (DHL) is selling the flats at ₹23,00,000 per flat which it has already booked fully through pre-launch. The cost of land incurred by Dream Homes is ₹2,00,000 per flat. It is earning a profit of ₹4,00,000 after paying ₹17,00,000 per flat to the SCC.

The DHL has another adjacent site where it wants to launch phase-II of its scheme consisting of 600 three-bedroom flats. However, due to recession in the market and demand for affordable housing, DHL is not able to sell its flats at its previous price of ₹23,00,000. The DHL's marketing team has assessed that they can get a maximum price of ₹21,00,000 per flat now. Therefore, it has given an offer of constructing 600 flats to the SCC at ₹16,00,000 per flat.

The technical team of the SCC has informed the CEO of the SCC, Himanshu Pandey, that they can complete the additional requirement of 600 flats in remaining six months with the same batching and equipments. However, they will require three more junior engineers and additional shuttering material costing ₹2,00,000. The CEO is contemplating whether to reject this offer as cost per flat is already ₹16,56,700 and the technical team has additional requirement of ₹5,60,000. He has asked his finance manager, Neeraj Bodra, to give his opinion.

REQUIRED: What advice should the finance manager give to the CEO of the SCC? Why?

Solution

The finance manager after going through the costs involved presented the following incremental analysis to the CEO:

Sales revenue (₹16,00,000 × 600)	₹96,00,00,000
Incremental cost: Total variable cost (₹14,50,000 × 600)	87,00,00,000
Additional cost salary of 3 junior engineers (3 × ₹20,000 × 6)	3,60,000
Additional shuttering material	2,00,000
Incremental profit	8,94,40,000

As the SCC is expected to earn incremental profit of ₹8,94,40,000, the CEO should accept the offer.

23.C.8 (Special Order) Mr. Bharat Bhushan is the owner of a small manufacturing firm, Twinkle Light, which is into manufacturing of night lamps. Predicting a great demand for Diwali lights, he started producing the same as he had a confirmed order of 1,000 units from a buyer at ₹70 per unit; and who has paid a non-refundable advance of ₹5,000. To produce these lamps, he has to employ two additional workers, each at ₹300 per day. Also, he has to take on rent a machine which is used to make covers for fancy lights for ₹15,000 per month. He has also to purchase some consumables like lubricant oil, etc., for ₹2,000.

He started producing 50 units per day. Eight days after starting production, he received a call from the buyer expressing his inability to buy all the 1,000 units since the market price of Diwali lights had fallen due to unexpectedly high import of cheaper Chinese lights. However, he was wiling to buy the units made up to that time at ₹40 per unit. If Mr. Bharat decides to sell the units produced during the eight days, he would have to pay to each labour ₹1,000 as compensation charges. The scrap value of the remaining raw material is ₹2,000. He also has an offer from a buyer who is ready to buy completed 1,000 units at ₹30 per unit. The buyer would accept the complete order or nothing at all. What should Mr. Bharat Bhushan do now?

Solution

(1) Determination of Incremental Sale Revenue if Units Made in 8 days are Sold @ ₹40

Sales (400 units × ₹40)	₹16,000
Less advance payment	(5,000)
Payment to be received from the buyer	11,000
Scrap value of raw materials	2,000
Total	13,000
Less incremental costs: Compensation to labour (₹1,000 × 2)	2,000
Incremental profit (decrease in loss)	11,000

INCOME STATEMENT

Costs already incurred:	
Machine rent	₹15,000
Consumables	2,000
Material cost	30,000
Labour cost (2 workers × ₹300 × 8 days)	4,800
Labour compensation (2 workers × ₹1,000)	2,000
Total cost	53,800
Sales revenue	11,000
Advanced payment received	5,000
Sale of raw material	2,000
Total revenues	18,000
Loss	(35,800)

(2) Determination of Incremental Profit if an Offer to Supply 1,000 units @ ₹30 is Accepted

Sale (1,000 units x ₹30)	₹30,000
Labour compensation saved	2,000
Less incremental costs:	
Wages of labour (₹300 × 2 × 12)	(7,200)
Raw material opportunity cost	(2,000)
Incremental profit/Decrease in loss	22,800

Income Statement

Machine rent	₹15,000
Consumables	2,000
Material cost	30,000
Labour cost (2 workers × ₹300 × 20 days)	12,000
Total cost	59,000
Sales revenue (1,000 units × ₹30)	30,000
Advanced payment received	5,000
Total revenues	35,000
Loss	(24,000)

RECOMMENDATION There is a decrease in loss of ₹11,800 (₹35,800 – ₹24,000) when the decision to sell the complete order at ₹30 is taken. Therefore, Mr. Bharat Bhushan should accept the offer from the second buyer.

23.C.9 (Special Order) Telshodan Ltd (TL) is in the business of refining and marketing of petroleum products. The company imports crude oil and refines in its refinery situated at Panvel near Mumbai. There are three finished products after refining, namely, petrol, diesel and lube oil. It sells the finished product to registered dealers in India. As the dealers take delivery of the finished products from the refinery, there is no transportation cost for Telshodhan Limited.

Presently, TL has capacity of 15 MMTPA (million metric ton per annum) crude refining. It is operating presently at a capacity of 11.5 MMTPA crude refining. Normally, 5 per cent of the input is lost during the process of refining. The normal mix of the total finished product contains 38 per cent of petrol, 50 per cent of diesel and 12 per cent lube oil.

The crude oil currently costs ₹290 crore per MMT, the labour cost is ₹30 crore per MMT and other variable cost (including maintenance cost) is ₹40 crore per MMT for crude oil processing. The current selling price of finished products are ₹540 crore, ₹310 crore and ₹680 crore per MMT for petrol, diesel and lube oil, respectively. It is expected that the cost of crude oil is not going to vary in the coming year and the price of finished products are also likely to remain constant.

Telshodhan Limited got a fresh order of 1.9 MMT of petrol, 2.5 MMT of diesel and 0.6 MTM of lube oil for ₹510 crore, ₹290 crore and ₹630 crore per MMT for petrol, diesel and lube oil, respectively, from Telvikreta Limited. If the TL buys the finished products from another refining company, Telzone Limited, it will have to pay ₹508 crore, ₹287 crore and ₹628 crore per MMT for petrol, diesel and lube oil, respectively. It will also involve an additional safe packaging (because petroleum products are highly inflammable and require proper safety precautions in packaging) and transportation cost (to deliver up to the tankers of Telshodhan Ltd in specially designed safe transporting tankers) of ₹35 crore per MMT of finished products.

Mr. Sanjay Khanna, the MD of Telshodhan Limited, convened a meeting of managers from the finance, production, marketing and technical departments of the company to discuss the proposal so as to take a final decision on the new order by Televikreta Ltd. The following additional facts emerged in the meeting:

- As the machines are working at a capacity of 11.5 MMTPA, the unused capacity of 3.5 MMTPA is available for further production.
- As it is an opportunity to expand the market, the company should not lose the order. However, the production department is not ready to refine more than their maximum capacity, that is, 15 MMTPA.
- The technical department is agreeable to increase the capacity by 2 MMTPA. It will require setting up an additional vessel in whole volume capacity like 1, 2, 3 MMTPA and not in fraction like 1.5, 2.3 and so on to meet additional demand of Televikreta Ltd. This will require an additional fixed cost of ₹50 crore.
- The labour cost and other variable cost for crude oil processing will remain the same, that is, ₹30 crore and ₹40 crore per MMT, respectively.

On the basis of above information and other relevant financial aspects, the finance manager, Virendra Rathi, was then asked to submit a report on the alternatives available to carry out the offer/proposal, namely:

1. Increase the processing capacity of crude oil by 2 MMTPA to 17 MMTPA
2. Utilise the full capacity of existing refinery and outsource the additional volume of finished products from Telzone Ltd.

The data compiled by Virendra Rathi, in consultation with Bikrant Singh, the Controller of Accounts, for the purpose of the analysis of the two alternatives is summarised below.

Alternative 1: Increase the Processing Capacity of Crude Oil from 15 MMTPA to 17 MMTPA

COMPUTATION OF INCREMENTAL PROFIT

Particulars	*Amount (₹crore)*	*Total Amount (₹crore)*
Increase in Sales Revenue:		
1.9 MMTPA of petrol (1.9 × ₹510)	969.0	
2.5 MMTPA of diesel (2.5 × ₹290)	725.0	
0.6 MMTPA of petrol (0.6 × ₹630)	378.0	2,072.0
Less Incremental Cost:		
Additional material cost (5.263[@] × ₹290)	1,526.27	
Additional labour cost (5.263 × ₹30)	157.89	
Additional variable overheads (5.263 × ₹40)	210.52	
Additional fixed cost for setting up of an additional vessel	50.00	1,944.68
Incremental Profit (₹2,072.0 – ₹1,944.68)		127.32

[@]The volume crude oil required for 5.0 MMTPA finished product (as 5 per cent crude is lost in processing) = (5.0/0.95) MMTPA = 5.263 MMTPA.

Alternative 2: Buy Additional Requirement of Finished Products From Telzone Limited.

COMPUTATION OF INCREMENTAL PROFIT (₹CRORE)

Increase in Sales Revenue:		
1.9 MMTPA of petrol (1.9 × ₹510)	₹969.0	
2.5 MMTPA of diesel (2.5 × ₹290)	725.0	
0.6 MMTPA of petrol (0.6 × ₹630)	378.0	₹2,072.0
Less Incremental Cost:		
Additional material cost (3.5 × ₹290)	1,015.0	
Additional labour cost (3.5 × ₹30)	105.0	
Additional variable overheads (3.5 × ₹40)	140.0	
Additional cost of purchase of finished petrol (0.636 × ₹508)	323.09	
Additional cost of purchase of finished diesel (0.837 × ₹287)	240.22	
Additional cost of purchase of finished lube oil (0.202 × ₹628)	126.9	
Additional cost of packaging and transporting of finished products (1.675 × ₹35)	58.62	2,008.83
Incremental Profit (₹2072.0 – ₹2008.79)		63.17

Summary: The report of the finance manager shows that alternative 1 is better than alternative 2 as the incremental profit is more but in the second alternative the capacity of refining crude oil of Telshodhan Limited will increase from 15 MMTPA to 17 MMTPA and the dependence on another supplier to execute additional order will be avoided. So, it is better for Telshodhan Ltd to go for expansion to meet the order of Telvikreta Ltd.

WORKING NOTES

1. By processing 3.5 MMTPA crude in own refinery, 3.325 MMTPA finished products will be manufactured in the following quantities:

Quantity of petrol produced (0.38 × 3.325) MTTPA	= 1.264 MMTPA
Quantity of diesel produced (0.50 × 3.325) MTTPA	= 1.663 MMTPA
Quantity of lube oil produced (0.12 × 3.325) MTTPA	= 0.399 MMTPA

2. Quantity of finished products required purchasing from Telzone Limited

Quantity of petrol to be purchased (1.900 – 1.264) MMTPA	= 0.636 MMTPA
Quantity of diesel to be purchased (2.500 – 1.663) MMTPA	= 0.837 MMTPA
Quantity of petrol to be purchased (0.600 – 0.398) MMTPA	= 0.202 MMTPA

Total finished product volume to be purchased from Telzone Limited = (0.636 + 0.837 + 0.202) = 1.675 MMTPA. The packaging and transportation cost will be applicable on this volume.

23.C.10 (Product Mix) BASF is planning to introduce three new products in the market, namely, Relugan RE, Relugan RF and Relugan FS. The budgeted annual production of the three chemicals agreed upon by the top management comprising of Sachin Wasuja and Nikhil Pathak in discussion with the production manager, Malay Khasnavis, is 12,000, 16,000 and 20,000 kg, respectively. The sale price of each of the products as decided by the top management is ₹90, ₹120 and ₹60 per kg of the respective products. The fixed overheads associated with the manufacturing of these three products are found to be ₹5,00,000 per annum. The sales department, however, is very enthusiastic about the products and is predicting the sales to be at least 25 per cent higher than the budgeted production level. The BASF has a policy of pricing their products three times of the direct material consumed. It has observed that in manufacturing a product, the major costs incurred are the direct material and the direct labour costs which account for 80 per cent of the total variable costs. There are two departments within the company, namely, (i) the production department and (ii) the spray drying department, through which the products are manufactured into its final form. The cost of labour in the production department is ₹2 per hour and in the spray department is ₹1 per hour. One kg of Relugan RE takes 8 and 4 hours in the production and spray drying departments, respectively. Corresponding time taken by Relugan RF is 10 hours in each department and by Relugan FS are 4 and 6 hours in each of the departments, respectively. The spray drying department employs skilled labour set which is in short supply. So, the spray drying department is not in a position to enhance its capacity.

REQUIRED: The BASF management has furnished the above information to its financial advisor, Mr. Rajeev Khandelwal, and has sought his advice on the product-mix profitability of the project.

Solution

Statement Showing Profit on Current Budgeted Production

Particulars	*Products*							
	Relugan RE		*Relugan RF*		*Relugan FS*		*Total*	
Sales revenue		₹10,80,000		₹19,20,000		₹,12,00,000		₹,42,00,000
Less: Variable costs:								
Direct materials	₹3,60,000		₹6,40,000		₹4,00,000		₹14,00,000	
Direct labour:								
Production Department	1,92,000		3,20,000		1,60,000		6,72,000	
Spray Drying Department	48,000		1,60,000		1,20,000		3,28,000	
Overheads	1,50,000	7,50,000	2,80,000	14,00,000	1,70,000	8,50,000	6,00,000	30,00,000
Contribution		3,30,000		5,20,000		3,50,000		12,00,000
Less: Fixed Costs								5,00,000
Operating profit								7,00,000

STATEMENT SHOWING PROFIT ON PRODUCTION OF OPTIMAL PRODUCT MIX

Particulars	*Products*							
	Relugan RE		*Relugan RF*		*Relugan FS*		*Total*	
Sales revenue		₹13,50,000		₹24,00,000		₹, 6,80,000		₹, 44,30,000
Less: Variable costs:								
Direct materials	₹, 4,50,000		₹, 8,00,000		₹2,26,700		₹14,76,700	
Direct labour:								
Production Department	2,40,000		4,00,000		90,600		7,30,600	
Spray Drying Department	60,000		2,00,000		68,000		3,28,000	
Overheads	1,87,500	9,37,500	3,50,000	17,50,000	96,300	4,81,600	6,33,800	31,69,100
Contribution		4,12,500		6,50,000		1,98,400		12,60,900
Less: Fixed Costs								5,00,000
Operating profit								7,60,900

WORKING NOTES

The labour hours in the Spray Drying Department are limited because we are not in a position to hire additional workforce to increase the labour hours to maximise our profit. So, we need to alter our product mix in such a manner so that there is a maximum contribution margin per hour used of Spray Drying Department. This, in turn, would maximise operating profits of the firm.

Total labour hours available in the Spray Drying Department = (4 × 12,000) + (10 × 16,000) + (6 × 20,000) = 3,28,000

Contribution margin per hour of the Spray Drying Department:

Relugan RE = ₹3,30,000 ÷ (12,000 × 4) = ₹6.875
Relugan RF = ₹5,20,000 ÷ (16,000 × 10) = 3.250
Relugan FS = ₹3,50,000 ÷ (20,000 × 6) = 2.917

Relugan RE having the highest contribution margin amongst all the three products should be given the highest priority in production followed by Relugan RF and Relugan FS, respectively. So, Relugan RE needs to be produced as per the full requirement of 15,000 kg, and in the same way Relugan RF needs to be produced 20,000 kgs.

Total labour hour consumed in production of the required quantity of Relugan RE and Relugan RF = (4 × 15,000) + (10 × 20,000) = 2,60,000

Remaining labour hours in the Treatment Department = 3,28,000 – 2.60,000 = 68,000.

Number of units of Relugan FS that can be produced = 68,000 ÷ 6 = 11,333.

23.C.11 (Shutdown Vs Operate Plant) ABJ Computer Services Private Limited was established in 1998 on the Build-Market-Retail Model of HP Inc of the USA. Its founder Managing Director is Mr. Ankur Sood who is conservative in his approach in dealing with financial details of his company. Mr. Ankur Sood has worked very hard for establishing the ABJ Computers and since the company was doing well he was satisfied with his efforts. ABJ's crown jewel is its manufacturing plant which is renowned for its efficiency in India and abroad. It manufactures various models of computers catering to the needs of the modern consumer. India being a low penetration market, the MD of the ABJ Computers, focussed on the US for its growth and has since enjoyed a large share of the market in the US It has established itself as a household brand image/equity.

Markets in the US have been under serious strain in recent times due to the Subprime crisis and the orders for computers are drying up fast. The situation is tense for Mr. Ankur Sood whose company is in throes due to this financial crisis. Like a silver lining to the cloud, Mr. Ankur Sood received an order for 15,800 computers for four different models of computers for the month of October 2009. Mr Sood who is a big supplier and usually deals with order size greater than 2,00,000 and above is reasonably disappointed and rejects the order on the following grounds:

- His company is a big company and will not supply such a small order.
- This order size would entail considerable costs on the machines and labour used since Mr. Sood feels that the marginal costs for large orders keep on reducing as the order size grows larger than 2,00,000.
- His company would not be able to recover the additional expenses entailed in processing such a small order.
- The crisis would lead to a further drop in the rates of computers and since the company is not hedging the price of the order it doesn't make sense to accept such a small order.

Mr. Ankur Sood discusses the order with his finance director, Balamurgan, and the marketing director, Jitendra Kumar. He also tells them about his decision of not taking the order and asks them about his opinion. He asks the finance director to examine the order more closely and advise him in regard to the acceptance of the order. In the light of the order schedule for October 2009 and the costing for the four computers, the following facts emerge.

(i) Break-up of Fixed Costs

Administration Cost:	
Office expenses	₹55,00,000
Electricity	18,00,000
Salary	3,09,00,000
Manufacturing Cost:	
Factory insurance	24,00,000
Factory rent	1,50,00,000
Indirect labour cost	53,00,000
Workflow standardisation	1,40,00,000
Selling Cost:	
Warehousing and storage	2,60,00,000
Transportation	56,00,000
Distribution and logistics	1,70,00,000
Total	12,35,00,000

The finance director estimates that approximately ₹1,00,00,000 would be incurred as additional fixed costs on account of maintenance of machines and production set-up costs in case the company decides to accept the order.

(ii) Estimated Variable Costs Per Unit Produced

Part Name	*Destktop*	*Server*	*Laptop*	*Tablet*
Hard disk	₹2,500	₹50,000	₹4,000	₹6,000
RAM	3,000	10,000	5,000	7,000
Graphics card	500	N/A	1,500	2,500
TFT screen	10,000	N/A	15,000	30,000
Motherboard	4,000	15,000	8,000	10,000
Keyboard	1,000	N/A	3,000	4,000
Mouse	250	N/A	N/A	N/A
Processor	6,000	25,000	15,000	20,000
Touchpad	N/A	N/A	2,000	2,000
Battery	N/A	N/A	1,000	2,000
UPS	2,000	5,000	N/A	N/A
Direct labour	300	500	800	1,000
Variable Overheads:				
Manufacturing	80	160	260	320
Administration	40	40	90	90
Selling	60	100	130	190
Total Variable Cost Per Unit	29,730	1,05,800	55,780	85,100

(iii) Order Schedules for October as Detailed Out in Purchase Books

Product	Number of Units	Selling Price/Unit
Desktop	6,500	₹35,000
Server	1,800	1,25,000
Laptop	5,000	64,000
Tablet	2,500	92,000

The finance director then performs an incremental analysis to analyse the situation and judge whether to accept the order or shut down the plant in the month of October.

Decision Analysis Whether to Accept the Order or Not

Product	Number of units	Selling price per unit	Total revenue
Incremental sales revenue:			
Desktop	6,500	₹35,000	22,75,00,000
Server	1,800	1,25,000	22,50,00,000
Laptop	5,000	64,000	32,00,00,000
Tablet	2,500	92,000	23,00,00,000
Total	15,800		100,25,00,000
Incremental cost:			
Desktop	6,500	₹29,730	₹19,32,45,000
Server	1,800	1,05,800	19,04,40,000
Laptop	5,000	55,780	27,89,00,000
Tablet	2,500	85,100	21,27,50,000
Additional fixed cost			1,00,00,000
Total			88,53,35,000
Incremental profit (₹10,025,00,000 – ₹88,53,35,000)			11,71,65,000

Decision Analysis: Shut Down or Operate Plant

Particulars	Operate	Shutdown
Estimated Revenue	₹100,25,00,000	
Less Variable Cost	87,53,35,000	
Contribution	12,71,65,000	
Less Fixed Cost	12,35,00,000	₹12,35,00,000
Less Additional fixed cost	1,00,00,000	
Net profit (loss)	(63,35,000)	(12,35,00,000)

RECOMMENDATION After carrying all the analyses, the finance director submits his report to the MD which is as under:

- ABJ Computers should accept the order in October as the incremental profit (which is the decrease in loss) is ₹11,58,65,000.
- By operating the plant the company is reducing the losses from ₹12,35,00,000 (if plant is shut down in October) to ₹63,35,000 if the company continues with the small order in hand.

24

Capital Budgeting

Learning Objectives

After reading this chapter you will be able to:

LO 24.1 Discuss the nature of capital budgeting
LO 24.2 Explain the relevant data requirement for capital budgeting
LO 24.3 Describe capital budgeting evaluating techniques, namely, ARR, PB method, NPV and IRR

Introduction

This Chapter is devoted to a discussion of the principles and techniques of capital budgeting. The nature of capital budgeting in terms of meaning, importance, difficulties, rationale and types is discussed first. The identification of relevant data for capital budgeting decisions is explained subsequently. The chapter also examines the evaluation techniques. The main points are summarised by way of recapitulation.

Nature of Capital Budgeting

LO 24.1 Discuss the nature of capital budgeting

Meaning

Capital budgeting decisions pertain to fixed/long-term assets which by definition refer to assets which are in operation, and yield a return, over a period of time, usually, exceeding one year. They, therefore, involve a current outlay or series of outlays of cash resources in return for an anticipated flow of future benefits.[1] In other words, the system of capital budgeting is employed to evaluate expenditure decisions which involve current outlays but are likely to produce benefits over a period of time longer than one year. These benefits may be either in the form of increased revenues or reduced costs. **Capital expenditure** management, therefore, includes addition,

> **Capital budgeting** is the process of evaluating and selecting long-term investments that are consistent with the goal of shareholders (owners) wealth maximisation.

Capital expenditure is an outlay of funds that is expected to produce benefits over a period of time exceeding one year.

disposition, modification and replacement of fixed assets. From the preceding discussion may be deduced the following basic features of capital budgeting[2]: **(i)** potentially large anticipated benefits; **(ii)** a relatively high degree of risk; and **(iii)** a relatively long time period between the initial outlay and the anticipated returns. The term capital budgeting is used interchangeably with capital expenditure decision, capital expenditure management, long-term investment decision, management of fixed assets and so on.

Importance

Capital budgeting decisions are of paramount importance in financial decision making. In the first place, such decisions affect the profitability of a firm. They also have a bearing on the competitive position of the enterprise mainly because of the fact that they relate to fixed assets. The fixed assets represent, in a sense, the true earning assets of the firm. They enable the firm to generate finished goods that can ultimately be sold for profit. The current assets are not generally earning assets. Rather, they provide a buffer that allows the firms to make sales and extend credit. True, current assets are important to operations, but without fixed assets to generate finished products that can be converted into current assets, the firm would not be able to operate. Further, they are 'strategic' investment decisions as against 'tactical'—which involve a relatively small amount of funds. Therefore, such capital investment decisions may result in a major departure from what the company has been doing in the past. Acceptance of a strategic investment will involve a significant change in the company's expected profits and in the risks to which these profits will be subject. These changes are likely to lead stockholders and creditors to revise their evaluation of the company.[3] Thus, capital budgeting decisions determine the future destiny of the company. An opportune investment decision can yield spectacular returns. On the other hand, an ill-advised and incorrect decision can endanger the very survival even of the large firms. A few wrong decisions and the firm may be forced into bankruptcy.

Secondly, a capital expenditure decision has its effect over a long time span and inevitably affects the company's future cost structure. To illustrate, if a particular plant has been purchased by a company to start a new product, the company commits itself to a sizable amount of fixed costs, in terms of labour, supervisors' salary, insurance, rent of building, and so on. If the investment turns out to be unsuccessful in future or yields less profit than anticipated, the firm will have to bear the burden of fixed costs unless it writes off the investment completely. In short, future costs, break-even point, sales and profits will all be determined by the selection of assets.

Thirdly, capital investment decisions, once made, are not easily reversible without much financial loss to the firm because there may be no market for second-hand plant and equipment and their conversion to other uses may not be financially viable.

Finally, capital investment involves costs and the majority of the firms have scarce capital resources. This underlines the need for thoughtful, wise and correct investment decisions, as an incorrect decision would not only result in losses but also prevent the firm from earning profits from other investments which could not be undertaken for want of funds.

Difficulties

Capital expenditure decisions are of considerable significance as the future success and growth of the firm depends heavily on them. But, they are beset with a number of difficulties.

Firstly, the benefits from investments are received in some future period. The future is uncertain. Therefore, an element of risk is involved. For instance, a decision to acquire an asset that is going to last for 15 years requires a 15-year forecast. A failure to forecast correctly will lead to serious errors which can be corrected only at a considerable expense. Future revenue involves estimating the size of the market for a product and the expected share of the firm in that. These estimates depend on a variety of factors, including price, advertising and promotion, and sales effort and so on. Adding to the uncertainties are the possibilities of shifts in consumer preferences, the actions of competitors, technological developments and changes in the economic or political environment.

Secondly, costs incurred and benefits received from the capital budgeting decisions occur in different time periods. They are not logically comparable because of the time value of money.

Thirdly, it is not often possible to calculate in strict quantitative terms all the benefits or the costs relating to a particular investment decision.

Rationale

The rationale underlying the capital budgeting decision is efficiency. Thus, a firm must replace worn and obsolete plants and machinery, acquire fixed assets for current and new products and make strategic investment decisions. This will enable the firm to achieve its objective of maximising profits either by way of increased revenues or cost reductions. The quality of these decisions is improved by capital budgeting. Capital budgeting decision can be of two types: **(i)** those which expand revenues, and **(ii)** those which reduce costs.

Investment Decisions Affecting Revenues Such investment decisions are expected to bring in additional revenue, thereby raising the size of the firm's total revenue. They can be the result of either expansion of present operations or the development of new product lines. Both types of investment decisions involve acquisition of new fixed assets and are income-expansionary in nature in the case of manufacturing firms.

Investment Decisions Reducing Costs Such decisions, by reducing costs, add to the total earnings of the firm. A classic example of such investment decisions are the replacement proposals when an asset wears out or becomes outdated. The firm must decide whether to continue with the existing assets or replace them. The firm evaluates the benefits from the new machine in terms of lower operating cost and the outlay that would be needed to replace the machine. An expenditure on a new machine may be quite justifiable in the light of the total cost savings that result.

A fundamental difference between the above two categories of investment decision lies in the fact that cost-reduction investment decisions are subject to less uncertainty in comparison to the revenue-affecting investment decisions. This is so because the firm has a better 'feel' for potential cost savings as it can examine past production and cost data. However, it is difficult to precisely estimate the revenues and costs resulting from a new product line, particularly when the firm knows relatively little about the same.

Capital budgeting process includes four distinct but interrelated steps used to evaluate and select long-term proposals: proposal generation, evaluation, selection and follow up.

Kinds

Capital budgeting process refers to the total process of generating, evaluating, selecting and following up on capital expenditure alternatives.[4] The firm allocates or budgets financial resources to new investment proposals. Basically, the firm may be confronted with three types of capital budgeting decisions: **(i)** the accept-reject decision; **(ii)** the mutually exclusive choice decision; and **(iii)** the capital rationing decision.

Accept reject decision/ approval is the evaluation of capital expenditure proposal to determine whether they meet the minimum acceptance criterion.

Accept-reject Decision This is a fundamental decision in capital budgeting. If the project is accepted, the firm would invest in it; if the proposal is rejected, the firm does not invest in it. In general, all those proposals which yield a rate

Independent projects are projects whose cash flows are unrelated/independent of one another; the acceptance of one does not eliminate the others from further consideration.

of return greater than a certain required rate of return or cost of capital are accepted and the rest are rejected. By applying this criterion, all **independent projects** are accepted. Independent projects are projects that do not compete with one another in such a way that the acceptance of one precludes the possibility of acceptance of another. Under the accept-reject decision, all independent projects that satisfy the minimum investment criterion should be implemented.

Mutually exclusive projects (decisions) are projects that compete with one another; the acceptance of one eliminates the others from further consideration.

Mutually Exclusive Project Decisions **Mutually exclusive projects** are those which compete with other projects in such a way that the acceptance of one will exclude the acceptance of the other projects. The alternatives are mutually exclusive and only one may be chosen. Suppose, a company is intending to buy a new folding machine. There are three competing brands, each with a different initial investment and operating costs. The three machines represent mutually exclusive alternatives, as only one of these can be selected. It may be noted here that the mutually exclusive project decisions are not independent of the accept-reject decisions. The project(s) should also be acceptable under the latter decision. In brief, in our example, if all the machines are rejected under the accept-reject decision, the firm should not buy a new machine. Mutually exclusive investment decisions acquire significance when more than one proposal is acceptable under the accept-reject decision. Then, some technique has to be used to determine the 'best' one. The acceptance of this 'best' alternative automatically eliminates the other alternatives.

Capital rationing is the financial situation in which a firm has only fixed amount to allocate among competing capital expenditures.

Unlimited funds is the financial situation in which a firm is able to accept all independent projects that provide an acceptable return.

Capital Rationing Decision In a situation where the firm has **unlimited funds**, all independent investment proposals yielding return greater than some predetermined level are accepted. However, this situation does not prevail in most of the business firms in actual practice. They have a fixed *capital budget.* A large number of investment proposals compete for these limited funds. The firm must, therefore, ration them. The firm allocates funds to projects in a manner that it maximises long-run returns. Thus, **capital rationing** refers to a situation in which a firm has more acceptable investments than it can finance. It is concerned with the selection of a group of investment proposals out of many investment proposals acceptable under the accept-reject decision. Capital rationing employs ranking of the acceptable investment projects. The projects can be ranked on the basis of a predetermined criterion such as the rate of return. The projects are ranked in the descending order of the rate of return.

DATA REQUIREMENT: IDENTIFYING RELEVANT CASH FLOWS

LO 24.2 Explain the relevant data requirement for capital budgeting

Cash Flows Vs Accounting Profit

Capital budgeting is concerned with investment decisions which yield return over a period of time in future. The foremost requirement for evaluation of any capital investment proposal is to estimate the future benefits accruing from the investment proposal. Theoretically, two alternative criteria are available to quantify the benefits: **(i)** accounting profit, and **(ii)** cash flows. The basic difference between them is primarily due to the inclusion of certain non-cash expenses in the profit and loss account, for instance, depreciation. Therefore, the accounting profit is to be adjusted for non-cash expenditures to determine the actual cash inflow. The cash flow approach of measuring future benefits of a project is superior to the accounting approach as cash flows are theoretically better measures of the net economic benefits of costs associated with a proposed project.

In the first place, while considering an investment proposal, a firm is interested in estimating its economic value. This *economic value* is determined by the economic outflows (costs) and inflows (benefits) related with the investment project. Only cash flows represent the cash transactions. The firm must pay for the purchase of an asset with cash. This cash outlay represents a foregone opportunity to use cash in some other productive alternatives. Consequently, the firm should measure the future net benefits in cash terms. On the other hand, under the accounting practices, the cost of the investment is allocated over its economic useful life in the nature of depreciation rather than at the time when costs are actually incurred. The accounting treatment clearly does not reflect the original need for cash at the time of inflows and outflows in later years. Only cash flows reflect the actual cash transactions associated with the project. Since investment analysis is concerned with finding out whether future economic inflows are sufficiently large to warrant the initial investment, only the cash flow method is appropriate for investment decision analysis.[5]

Secondly, the use of cash flows avoids accounting ambiguities. There are various ways to value inventory, allocate costs, calculate depreciation and amortise various other expenses. Obviously, different net incomes will be arrived at under different accounting procedures. But there is only one set of cash flows associated with the project. Clearly, the cash flow approach to project evaluation is better than the net income flow approach (accounting approach).

Thirdly, the cash flow approach takes cognisance of the time value of money whereas the accounting approach ignores it. Under the usual accounting practice, revenue is recognised as being generated when the product is sold, not when the cash is collected from the sale; revenue may remain a paper figure for months or years before payment of the invoice is received. Expenditure, too, is recognised as being made when incurred and not when the actual payment is made. Depreciation is deducted from the gross revenues to determine the before-tax earnings. Such a procedure ignores the increased flow of funds potentially available for other uses. In other words, accounting profits which are quite useful as *performance measures* often are less useful as *decision criteria*. Therefore, from the viewpoint of capital expenditure management, the cash flow approach can be said to be the basis of estimating future benefits from investment proposals. The data required for the purpose would be cash revenues and cash expenses. The difference between the cash flow approach and the accounting profit approach is depicted in Table 24.1.

TABLE 24.1 A Comparison of Cash Flow and Accounting Profit Approaches (Amount in '000 ₹)

Accounting Approach Towards 'Benefits'			*Cash Flow Approach Towards 'Benefits'*	
Revenues	₹1,000		₹1,000	
Less: Expenses:				
Cash expenses	₹500		₹500	
Depreciation	300	800		
Earnings before tax		200		
Taxes (0.35)		70	70	570
Net earnings after taxes/Cash flow		130		430

Table 24.1 shows that the accounting profits amounting to ₹1.3 lakh are less than the cash flow (₹4.3 lakh). This difference can be attributed to the depreciation charge of ₹3 lakh. The cash available with the firm is ₹4.3 lakh. This can be utilised for further investment. The accounting approach indicates that only ₹1.3 lakh is available and hence gives only a partial picture of the tangible benefits available. Clearly, such an approach does not bring out the total benefits of the project available for reinvesting. Therefore, in place of earnings, the cash flow information is employed in evaluating capital expenditure alternatives.

Incremental Cash Flow

Relevant cash flow is the incremental after-tax cash outflow (investment) and resulting subsequent inflows associated with a proposed capital expenditure.

Incremental cash flows are the additional cash flows (outflows as well as inflows) expected to result from a proposed capital expenditure.

The second aspect of the data required for capital budgeting relates to the basis on which the **relevant cash outflows** and inflows associated with proposed capital expenditure are to be estimated. The widely prevalent practice is to adopt incremental analysis. According to incremental analysis, only differences due to the decision need be considered. Other factors may be important but not to the decision at hand.[6] For purposes of estimating cash flows in the analysis of investments, **incremental cash flows**, that is, those cash flows (and only those cash flows) which are directly attributable to the investment are taken into account. It is for this reason that fixed overhead costs, which remain the same whether the proposal is accepted or rejected, are not considered. However, if there is an increase in them due to the new proposal, they must be considered.

Effect of Taxes

Finally, the incremental cash flows are adjusted for tax liability. In other words, taxes paid are deducted from the cash flows to estimate the benefits arising out of the investment decision.

To conclude the above discussion relating to the data required for the capital budgeting decision, the expenses/costs to be considered are '*incremental after-tax cash flows*'. Table 24.2 summarises the relevant and irrelevant information in relation to asset selection decisions.

TABLE 24.2 Relevant and Irrelevant Outflows

Relevant Cash Outflows	*Irrelevant Cash Outflows*
1. Variable labour expenses	1. Fixed overhead expense (existing)
2. Variable material expenses	2. Sunk costs
3. Additional fixed overhead expenses	
4. Cost of the investment	
5. Marginal taxes	
6. Opportunity costs	

Sunk costs are cash outflows that have already been made (i.e., past outlays) and therefore have no effect on the cash flows relevant to a current decision.

Conventional cash flow pattern is an initial outflow followed by a series of inflows.

Cash Flow Pattern

Cash flow pattern associated with capital investment projects can be classified as conventional or non-conventional.

Conventional Cash Flows They consist of an initial cash outlay followed by a series of cash inflows. Most of the capital expenditure decisions display this pattern of cash flow. To illustrate, the firm may spend ₹150 lakh in time period zero and as a result may expect to receive a ₹30 lakh cash inflow at the end of each year for the next 8 years.

Non-conventional cash flow pattern is a pattern in which an initial outflow is not followed by a series of inflows.

Non-Conventional Cash Flows They refer to the cash flow pattern in which an initial cash outlay is not followed by a series of inflows. Alternating inflows and outflows and an inflow followed by outflows are examples of non-conventional cash flow patterns. A classic example of such cash flow patterns is that of the purchase of an asset that generates cash inflows for a period of years, is overhauled, and again generates a stream of cash inflows for a number of years. To illustrate, a machine purchased for ₹10 lakh generates cash inflows of ₹2.5 lakh each for five years. In the sixth year, an outlay of ₹4 lakh is required to overhaul the machine, after which it generates cash inflows of ₹2.5 lakh for four years.

Cash Flow Estimates

For capital budgeting cash flows have to be estimated. There are certain ingredients of cash flow streams.

Tax Effect It has been already observed that cash flows to be considered for purposes of capital budgeting are net of taxes. Special consideration needs to be given to tax effects on cash flows if the firm is incurring losses and, therefore, paying no taxes. The tax laws permit carrying losses forward to be set off against future income. In such cases, therefore, the benefits of tax savings would accrue in future years.

Effect on Other Projects Cash flow effects of the project under consideration, if it is not economically independent, on other existing projects of the firm must be taken into consideration. For instance, if a company is considering the production of a new product which competes with the existing products in the product line, it is likely that as a result of the new proposal, the cash flows related to the old product will be affected. Assume that there is a decline of ₹5 lakh in the actual flow from the existing product. This should be taken into consideration while estimating the cash streams from the new proposal. In operational terms, the cash flow from the new product should be reduced by ₹5 lakh. This is in conformity with the general rule of the incremental cash flows which involves identifying changes in cash flows as a result of undertaking the project being evaluated. Clearly, the cash flow effects of the project should not be evaluated in isolation, if it affects other project(s) in any way.

Effect of Indirect Expenses Another factor which merits special consideration in estimating cash flows is the effect of overheads. The indirect expenses/overheads are allocated to the different products on the basis of wages paid, materials used, floor space occupied or some other similar common factor. The question that arises is: should such allocation of overheads be taken into account in the cash flows? The answer hinges upon whether the amount of overheads will change as a result of the investment decision. If yes, it should be taken into account. If, however, overheads will not change as a result of the investment decision, they are not relevant.

A company allocates overheads on the basis of the floor space used. Assume it intends to replace an old machine by a new one. Further assume that the new machine would occupy less space so that there would be a reduction in the overhead charged to it. Since there is no effect on cash flows, a change in the overhead is not relevant to the cash flow streams of the machine being acquired. But if the surplus space is used for an alternative use, and if any cash flow is generated, it will be relevant to the calculations. Thus, the deciding factor is whether there is any alternative use. The alternative use rule is a corollary of the incremental cash flow rule.[7]

Depreciation is a non-cash expense that affects the taxes paid in cash.

Effect of Depreciation **Depreciation**, although a non-cash item of cost, is deductible expenditure in determining taxable income. Depreciation provisions are prescribed by the Companies Act for accounting purposes and by the Income Tax Act for taxation purposes.

The purpose of the provisions of depreciation contained in the Companies Act is the computation of managerial remuneration, dividend payment and disclosure in financial statements. Since companies in India are regulated by the Companies Act, they should provide depreciation in the books of accounts in accordance with Schedule XIV of the Act which prescribes the rate of depreciation for various types of depreciable assets on written down value (WDV) basis as well as straight line basis. It also permits companies to charge depreciation on any other basis provided it has the effect of writing off 95 per cent of the original cost of the asset on the expiry of the specified period and has the approval of the government. In actual practice, however, companies follow the provisions of the Income Tax Act with the basic objectives of its tax deductibility.

The provisions of Income Tax Act relating to depreciation are contained in Section 32. The section envisages three important conditions for following depreciation, namely, **(i)** the asset is owned by the assessee, **(ii)** the asset is used by the assessee for the purpose of business and **(iii)** the asset is in the form of buildings, furniture, machinery and plants including ships, vehicles, books, scientific apparatus, surgical equipments and so on.

The amount of annual depreciation on an asset is determined by **(a)** the actual cost of the asset and **(b)** its classification in the relevant block of assets. The actual cost means the cost of acquisition of the asset and the expenses incidental thereto which are necessary to put the asset in a usable state, for instance, freight and carriage inwards, installation charges and expenses incurred to facilitate the use of the asset like expenses on the training of the operator or on essential construction work.

Block of assets are assets which fall in the same class and in respect of which the same depreciation rate is applicable irrespective of their nature.

Depreciation is charged, with a view to simplify computation, not on an individual asset but on a block of assets. A **block of assets** defined as a group of assets falling within a class of assets, being building, machinery, plant or furniture in respect of which the same rate of depreciation is prescribed. Thus, assets which fall within the same class of assets and in respect of which the same percentage/rate of depreciation has been prescribed irrespective of their nature form one block of assets. For example, all assets under the category of plant and machinery which qualify for depreciation at 15 per cent will form one block and depreciation is computed with reference to the actual cost of the block. Similarly, assets depreciable at 40 per cent will constitute another block; a third block consists of assets depreciable at 50 per cent, and the fourth block comprises assets subject to a 100 per cent write-off.

Depreciation is computed at block-wise rates on the basis of written down value (WDV) method only. Presently, the block-wise rates for plant and machinery are at 25 per cent, 40 per cent and 100 per cent. The depreciation allowance on office buildings and furniture and fittings is 10 per cent. Where the actual cost of plant and machinery does not exceed ₹5,000, the entire cost is allowed to be written off in the first year of its use. If an asset acquired during a year has been used for a period of less than 180 days during the year, depreciation on such assets is allowed only at 50 per cent of the computed depreciation according to the relevant rate.

Apart from the simplification of the computation of the amount of depreciation, a significant implication of categorising assets into blocks is that if an asset falling in a block is sold out, there is no capital gain or terminal depreciation or balancing charge. The sale proceeds of the asset are reduced from the WDV of the block. Capital gain/loss can arise in these situations:

(i) When the sale proceeds exceeds the WDV of the whole block;
(ii) When the entire block is sold out; and
(iii) In case of 100 per cent depreciable assets.

The terminal loss is not allowed in the relevant assessment year but is spread over a number of years to be allowed by way of depreciation.

In case of insufficiency/absence of profit, unabsorbed depreciation can be set off against income under any head against business income as in the case of unabsorbed loss. Effective 1996-97, it can be carried forward for a maximum period of eight years.

The mechanics of computation of depreciation is illustrated in Example 24.1.

◆ Example 24.1

ASSUME THE FOLLOWING FACTS RELATING TO AVON LTD (AL):

Block of Assets	Depreciation Rate (percentage)	WDV as on 1.4.20X4 (₹ lakh)	Addition During 20X4–5 (₹ lakh)
A	25	500	250
B	40	300	150

Assets sold during 20X4–5 amounted to ₹35 lakh (Block A) and ₹50 lakh (Block B). It is expected that fresh investments in assets during 20X5–6 will be: Block A (₹160 lakh) and Block B (₹80 lakh). It is also projected by the AL that disinvestment proceeds from the assets will amount to ₹45 lakh in case of Block A and ₹25 lakh in case of Block B. Assume that about 50 per cent of additional investment during 20X5–6 will be made after September 20X5.

Compute the relevant depreciation charge for 20X4–5 and the projected depreciation charge for 20X5–6.

Solution

The relevant depreciation charge for 20X4–5 and the projected depreciation charge for 20X5–6 is calculated in Tables 24.3 and 24.4 respectively.

TABLE 24.3 Computation of Depreciation Charge During 20X4–5 (₹ lakh)

Particulars	Blocks A	Blocks B
1. WDV as on 1.4.20X4	500	300
2. *Add:* Cost of assets acquired during 20X4–5	250	150
	750	450
3. *Less:* Sales during 20X4–5	35	50
4. WDV (for depreciation)	715	400
5. Depreciation allowance	179	160
6. WDV as on 1.4.20X5	536	240

TABLE 24.4 Computation of Depreciation Charge During 20X5–6 (₹ lakh)

Particulars	Blocks A	Blocks B
1. WDV as on 1.4.20X5	536	240
2. *Add:* Cost of assets acquired during 20X5–6	160	80
	696	320
3. *Less:* Expected proceeds of sales during 20X5–6	45	25
4. WDV (for depreciation)	651	295
5. Depreciation allowance@	153	110
6. WDV as on 1.4. 20X6	498	185

	A	B
@Normal depreciation allowance	163	118
Less: Depreciation allowance inadmissible in respect of assets acquired after 30.9.20X5	10 (80 × 0.25 × 0.5)	8 (40 × 0.4 × 0.5)
	153	110

Note If the entire block of assets is sold during a year for an amount exceeding (1 + 2) or the sale proceeds of the block sold is higher than (1 + 2), the difference represents short-term capital gains subject to tax. Where the sale proceeds are lower than (1 + 2), the difference is short-term capital loss and the AL is entitled to tax shield.

In case block consists of a single asset (e.g. plant and machinery), **no depreciation is to be charged in the terminal year in which it is sold**. The difference between the written down value (WDV) of the machine at the beginning of the year and its sale proceeds represents short-term capital gain (when sale proceeds exceeds written down value/book vale of the machine) and short-term capital loss (in case the book value exceeds sale proceeds/salvage value). Such short-term capital gains (STCG) and losses (STCL) have been accorded **special tax treatment**. The STCL can be set-off only against STCG or long-term capital gains. In the case of inadequate/no profits, the STCL can be carried forward upto eight assessment years.

To illustrate the implication of the tax provisions for capital budgeting, let us assume, a company buys a new machine for ₹10 lakh (forming a separate block). The machine is subject to 20 per cent depreciation on WDV basis. It is expected to have economic useful life of 5 years at the end of which its expected salvage value is ₹1 lakh.

The depreciation in the first four years would be ₹2 lakh, ₹1.6 lakh, ₹1.28 lakh and ₹1.024 lakh respectively. The accumulated depreciation would be ₹5.90 lakh. As a result, the WDV/book value of the machine at the beginning of year-5 would be ₹4.10 lakh. With no depreciation charged in year-5 and sale proceeds of ₹1 lakh, there would be short-term capital loss of ₹3.10 lakh. This loss, in turn, would yield tax shield. Assuming 30 per cent tax rate, the tax shield is (₹3.10 lakh × 0.30) ₹92,880. This amount would be reckoned as **cash inflow in year 5**.

The tax shield would be ₹92,880 in financial accounting also. It would consist of two components: (i) depreciation in year 5, ₹81,920 (0.20 × ₹4,09,600) and (ii) loss on sale of machine ₹2,27,680 (₹4,09,600 – ₹1,00,000 – ₹81,920). The tax advantage on depreciation would be ₹24,576 (0.30 × ₹81,920) and on loss ₹68,304 (0.30 × ₹2,27,680). The total (₹24,576 + ₹68,304) is ₹92,880. Thus, the firm does not suffer any loss by not charging depreciation in the terminal year (as per income-tax requirement).

In case block consists of several assets (plants/machinery/equipments), depreciation is charged in the terminal year in which the machine is sold on its **closing balance** (written down value at the beginning of year of sales – sale value). The terminal loss is allowed to be carried forward to be charged as depreciation in subsequent years (though the asset does not exist). This tax provision implies that the terminal loss would provide tax shield in the subsequent years.

To illustrate, continuing with the present example, assuming the machine purchased for ₹10 lakh is one of several machines, depreciation charged in year 5 would be on ₹3,09,600 (₹4,09,600 – ₹1,00,000, sale value) at 20 per cent, that is, ₹61,920. The terminal loss due to sale of machine is (₹3,09,600 – ₹61,920) ₹2,47,680. This loss in terms of unabsorbed depreciation would provide tax advantage in future years.

In practice, as the block is likely to consist of several machines for manufacturing firms, the tax provision puts business firms at disadvantage as the tax advantage on terminal loss is available in a number of years and not in single year.

Net working capital change is the difference between change in current assets and change in current liabilities.

Working Capital Effect Working capital constitutes another important ingredient of the cash flow stream which is directly related to an investment proposal. The term **working capital** is used here in net sense, that is, current assets minus current liabilities (net working capital). If an investment is expected to increase sales, it is likely that there will be an increase in current assets in the form of accounts receivable, inventory and cash. But part of this increase in current assets will be offset by an increase in current liabilities in the form of increased accounts and notes payable. Obviously, the sum equivalent to the difference between these additional current assets and current liabilities will be needed to carry out the investment proposal. Sometimes, it may constitute a significant part of the total investment in a project. The increased working capital forms part of the initial cash outlay. The additional net working capital will, however, be returned to the firm at the end of the project's life. Therefore, the recovery of working capital becomes part of the cash inflow stream in the terminal year. The initial investment in, and the subsequent recovery of, working capital do not balance out each other due to the time value of money.

Almost all revenue-expansion capital investment proposals require additional working capital. Likewise, almost all cost-reduction capital investment projects release the existing amount of working capital. Such projects enhance the firm's efficiency in such a way that the amount of inventory on hand or accounts receivable can be reduced. Improved inventory control systems or improved billing and collection systems are some classic examples. From the point of view of evaluating an investment project, the amount of working capital so released should be seen as a cash inflow in the zero time period (when the investment proposal is being considered), reducing the net cash investment required for the project. In the terminating year of the project, it should be treated as a cash outflow and adjusted against the cash inflow of that year.

Determination of Relevant Cashflows

The data requirement for capital budgeting are cash flows, that is, outflows and inflows. Their computation depends on the nature of the proposal. Capital projects can be categorised into: **(i)** single proposal, **(ii)** replacement situations and **(iii)** mutually exclusive.

Single Proposal The cash outflows, comprising cash outlays required to carry out the proposed capital expenditure are depicted in Format 24.1, while the computation of the cash inflows after taxes (CFAT) is shown in Format 24.2. The computation is illustrated in Example 24.2 and Example 24.3.

FORMAT 24.1 Cash Outflows of New Project [Beginning of the Period at Zero Time (t = 0)]

1. Cost of new project
2. + Installation cost of plant and equipments
3. ± Working capital requirements

FORMAT 24.2 Determination of Cash Inflows: Single Investment Proposal (t = 1 – N)

Particulars	*Years*					
	1	*2*	*3*	*4*	....	*N*
Cash sales revenues						
Less: Cash operating cost						
Cash inflows before taxes (CFBT)						
Less: Depreciation						
Taxable income						
Less: Tax						
Earning after taxes						
Plus: Depreciation						
Cash inflows after tax (CFAT)						
Plus: Salvage value (in nth year)						
Plus: Recovery of working capital (in *n*th year)						

Example 24.2

An iron ore company is considering investing in a new processing facility. The company extracts ore from an open pit mine. During a year, 1,00,000 tonnes of ore is extracted. If the output from the extraction process is sold immediately upon removal of dirt, rocks and other impurities, a price of ₹1,000 per ton of ore can be obtained. The company has estimated that its extraction costs amount to 70 per cent of the net realisable value of the ore.

As an alternative to selling all the ore at ₹1,000 per tonne, it is possible to process further 25 per cent of the output. The additional cash cost of further processing would be ₹100 per ton. The proposed ore would yield 80 per cent final output, and can be sold at ₹1,600 per ton.

For additional processing, the company would have to instal equipment costing ₹100 lakh. The equipment is subject to 25 per cent depreciation per annum on reducing balance (WDV) basis/method. It is expected to have useful life of 5 years. Additional working capital requirement is estimated at ₹10 lakh. The company's cut-off rate for such investments is 15 per cent. Corporate tax rate is 35 per cent and so of the short-term capital gains.

Assuming there is no other plant and machinery subject to 25 per cent depreciation, should the company instal the equipment if **(a)** the expected salvage is ₹10 lakh, **(b)** there would be no salvage value at the end of year 5 and (c) for tax purposes, the firm would have sufficient short-term capital gains in year 5.

Solution

Financial Evaluation Whether to Instal Equipment for Further Processing of Iron Ore

(A) Cash Outflows

Cost of equipment	₹ 1,00,00,000
Plus: Additional working capital	10,00,000
	1,10,00,000

(B) Cash Inflows (CFAT)

Particulars	*Year* 1	2	3	4	5
Revenue from processing [(₹1,600 × 20,000) – ₹1,000 × 25,000)]	₹70,00,000	₹70,00,000	₹70,00,000	₹70,00,000	₹70,00,000
Less: Processing costs: Cash costs (₹100 × 25,000 tons)	25,00,000	25,00,000	25,00,000	25,00,000	25,00,000
Depreciation (*working note* 1)	25,00,000	18,75,000	14,06,250	10,54,688	—
Earnings before taxes	20,00,000	26,25,000	30,93,750	34,45,312	45,00,000
Less: Taxes (0.35)	7,00,000	9,18,750	10,82,813	12,05,859	15,75,000
Earnings after taxes (EAT)	13,00,000	17,06,250	20,10,937	22,39,453	29,25,000
Add: Depreciation	25,00,000	18,75,000	14,06,250	10,54,688	
CFAT	38,00,000	35,81,250	34,17,187	32,94,141	29,25,000

WORKING NOTES

1 Depreciation Schedule

Year	Depreciation base of equipment	Depreciation @ 25% on WDV
1	₹ 1,00,00,000	₹ 25,00,000
2	75,00,000	18,75,000
3	56,25,000	14,06,250
4	42,18,750	10,54,688
5	31,64,062	Nil[@]

[@]As the block consists of a single asset, no depreciation is to be charged in the terminal year of the project.

(C) (a) Determination of NPV (Salvage Value = ₹10 lakh)

Year	CFAT	PV factor (0.15)	Total PV
1	₹ 38,00,000	0.870	₹ 33,06,000
2	35,81,250	0.756	27,07,425
3	34,17,187	0.658	22,48,509
4	32,94,141	0.572	18,84,249
5	29,25,000	0.497	14,53,725
Salvage value	10,00,000	0.497	4,97,000
Tax benefit on short-term capital loss	7,57,422[b]	0.497	3,76,439
Recovery of working capital	10,00,000	0.497	4,97,000
Gross present value			1,29,70,347
Less: Cash outflows			1,10,00,000
Net present value (NPV)			19,70,347

(b) 0.35 × (₹31,64,062 – ₹10,00,000) = ₹7,57,422.

Recommendation: The company is advised to instal the equipment as it promises a positive NPV.

(D) Determination of NPV (Salvage Value = Zero)

PV of operating CFAT (1 – 5 years)	₹ 1,15,78,421
Add: PV of tax benefit on short term capital loss (₹31,64,062 × 0.35 = ₹11,07,4,22 × 0.497, PV factor)	5,50,389
Add: PV of recovery of working capital	4,97,000
Total present value	1,26,25,810
Less: Cash outflows	1,10,00,000
NPV	16,25,810

Since the NPV is still positive, the company is advised to instal the equipment.

◆ Example 24.3

For the company in Example 24.2, assume there are other plants and machinery subject to 25 per cent depreciation (i.e. in the same block of assets). What course of action should the company choose?

Solution

(a) Cash outflows would remain unchanged.

(b) The annual depreciation will also remain the same for the first 4 yeas: In year 5, the depreciation = ₹21,64,062 (opening WDV of equipment, ₹31,64,062 – ₹10,00,000, salvage value) × 0.25 = ₹5,41,016.

(c) The CFAT (operating) for years, 1-4 will not change. In year 5, it will be shown as below:

Particulars	*CFAT (t = 5)*
Revenue from processing	₹ 70,00,000
Less: Processing costs:	
Cash costs	25,00,000
Depreciation	5,41,016
Earning before taxes	39,58,984
Less: Taxes (0.35)	13,85,644
EAT	25,73,340
CFAT	31,14,356

Determination of NPV (Salvage Value = ₹10 lakh)

Year	*CFAT*	*PV factor*	*Total PV*
1	₹38,00,000	0.870	₹33,06,000
2	35,81,250	0.756	27,07,425
3	34,17,187	0.658	22,48,509
4	32,94,141	0.572	18,84,249
5	31,14,356	0.497	15,47,835
Salvage value	10,00,000	0.497	4,97,000
Recovery of working capital	10,00,000	0.497	4,97,000
Gross present value			1,26,88,018
Less: Cash outflows			1,10,00,000
Net present value (NPV)			16,88,018@

@In fact, the NPV of the equipment is likely to be higher as tax advantage will accrue on the eligible depreciation of ₹16,23,046, i.e. (₹21,64,062 – ₹5,41,016) in future years.

Recommendation: The company should instal the equipment.

Determination of NPV (Salvage Value = 0)

(i) For the first 4 years, depreciation amount will remain unchanged. In the fifth year, depreciation = ₹31,64,062 (₹31,64,062, opening WDV less zero salvage value) × 0.25 = ₹7,91,015.

(ii) Operating CFAT for years 1–4 will remain unchanged. The CFAT for 5th year would be ₹32,01,855 as shown below:

Revenues from processing	₹70,00,000
Less: Processing costs (₹25,00,000 + ₹7,91,015)	32,91,015
EBIT	37,08,985
Less: Taxes (0.35)	12,98,145
EAT	24,10,840
Add: Depreciation	7,91,015
CFAT	32,01,855

(iii) PV of operating CFAT (1–4 years)	1,01,24,696
Add: PV of operating CFAT (5th year) (₹32,01,855 × 0.497)	15,91,322
Add: PV of recovery of working capital	4,97,000
Total PV	1,22,13,018
Less: Cash outflows	1,10,00,000@
NPV	12,13,018

@In effect, NPV would be higher as tax advantage will accrue on depreciation of ₹23,73,047 in future years.

Recommendation: The decision does not change, as NPV is positive.

Replacement Situation In the case of replacement of an existing machine (asset) by a new one, the relevant cash outflows are *after-tax incremental cash flows.* If a new machine is intended to replace an existing machine, the proceeds so obtained from its sale reduce cash outflows required to purchase the new machine and, hence, part of relevant cash flows. The calculation of after-tax incremental cash outflows is illustrated in Format 24.3 and Format 24.4 which provide depreciation base in the case of replacement situations.

FORMAT 24.3 Cash Outflows in a Replacement Situation

1. Cost of the new machine
2. + Installation Cost
3. ± Working Capital
4. — Sale proceeds of existing machine

FORMAT 24.4 Depreciation Base of New Machine in a Replacement Situation

1. WDV of the existing machine
2. + Cost of the acquisition of new machine (including installation costs)
3. — Sale proceeds of existing machine

The computation is illustrated in Example 24.4.

◆ Example 24.4

Royal Industries Ltd is considering the replacement of one of its moulding machines. The existing machine is in good operating condition, but is smaller than required if the firm is to expand its operations. It is 4 years old, has a current salvage value of ₹2,00,000 and a remaining life of 6 years. The machine was initially purchased for ₹10 lakh and is being depreciated at 25 per cent on the basis of written down value method.

The new machine will cost ₹15 lakh and will be subject to the same method as well as the same rate of depreciation. It is expected to have a useful life of 6 years, salvage value of ₹1,50,000 at the sixth year end. The management anticipates that with the expanded operations, there will be a need of an additional net working capital of ₹1 lakh. The new machine will allow the firm to expand current operations and thereby increase annual revenues by ₹5,00,000; variable cost to volume ratio is 30 per cent. Fixed costs (excluding depreciation) are likely to remain unchanged.

The corporate tax rate is 35 per cent. Its cost of capital is 10 per cent. The company has several machines in the block of 25 per cent depreciation.

Should the company replace its existing machine? What course of action would you suggest, if there is no salvage value?

Solution

Financial Evaluation Whether to Replace Existing Machine

(A) Cash Outflows (Incremental)

Cost of the new machine	₹ 15,00,000
Add: Additional working capital	1,00,000
Less: Sale value of existing machine	2,00,000
	14,00,000

(B) Determination of Incremental CFAT (Operating)

Year	Incremental contribution[a]	Incremental depreciation[b]	Taxable income	Taxes (0.35)	EAT [Col.4 – Col.5]	CFAT [Col.6 + Col.3]
1	2	3	4	5	6	7
1	₹ 3,50,000	₹ 3,25,000	₹ 25,000	₹ 8,750	₹ 16,250	₹ 3,41,250
2	3,50,000	2,43,750	1,06,250	37,188	69,062	3,12,812
3	3,50,000	1,82,813	1,67,187	58,515	1,08,672	2,91,485
4	3,50,000	1,37,109	2,12,891	74,512	1,38,379	2,75,488
5	3,50,000	1,02,832	2,47,168	86,509	1,60,659	2,63,491
6	3,50,000	39,624	3,10,376	1,08,632	2,01,744	2,41,368

[a]₹5,00,000 – [₹5,00,000 × 0.30, variable cost to value (V/V) ratio] = ₹3,50,000
[b](Working note)

WORKING NOTE

1. Incremental Depreciation (t = 1 – 6)

Year	Incremental asset cost base	Depreciation (25% on WDV)
1	₹13,00,000	₹3,25,000
2	9,75,000	2,43,750
3	7,31,250	1,82,813
4	5,48,437	1,37,109
5	4,11,328	1,02,832
6	3,08,496	39,624[c]

[c]0.25 × (₹3,08,496 – ₹1,50,000, salvage value) = ₹39,624

2. (i) Written Down Value (WDV) of Existing Machine at the Beginning of the Year 5

Initial cost of machine	₹ 10,00,000
Less: Depreciation @ 25% in year 1	2,50,000
WDV at beginning of year 2	7,50,000
Less: Depreciation @ 25% on WDV	1,87,500
WDV at beginning of year 3	5,62,500
Less: Depreciation @ 25% on WDV	1,40,625
WDV at beginning of year 4	4,21,875
Less: Depreciation @ 25% on WDV	1,05,469
WDV at beginning of year 5	3,16,406

(ii) Depreciation Base of New Machine

WDV of existing machine	3,16,406
Add: Cost of the new machine	15,00,000
Less: Sale proceeds of existing machine	2,00,000
	16,16,406

(iii) Base for Incremental Depreciation

Depreciation base of a new machine	16,16,406
Less: Depreciation base of an existing machine	3,16,406
	13,00,000

(C) Determination of NPV (Salvage Value = ₹1.50 lakh)

Year	CFAT	PV factor (0.10)	Total PV
1	₹ 3,41,250	0.909	₹3,10,196
2	3,12,812	0.826	2,58,383
3	2,91,485	0.751	2,18,905
4	2,75,488	0.683	1,88,158
5	2,63,491	0.621	1,63,628
6	2,41,368	0.564	1,36,132
6 Salvage value	1,50,000	0.564	84,600
6 Recovery of working capital	1,00,000	0.564	56,400
Gross present value			14,16,402
Less: Cash outflows			14,00,000
Net present value			16,402

Recommendation: Since the NPV is positive, the company is advised to replace the existing machine. The NPV is likely to be higher as tax advantage will accrue on the eligible depreciation of ₹1,18,872 (₹3,08,496 – ₹1,50,000 – ₹39,624) in the future years.

Determination of NPV (Salvage Value = Zero)

(i) For the first 5 years, depreciation will remain unchanged. In the sixth year, it will be = ₹3,08,496 × 0.25 = ₹77,124.

(ii) Operating CFAT for years 1–5 will remain unchanged.

CFAT for year 6 would be:

Incremental contribution	₹ 3,50,000
Less: Incremental depreciation	77,124
Taxable income	2,72,876
Less: Taxes (0.35)	95,507
EAT	1,77,369
Add: Depreciation	77,124
CFAT	2,54,493

(iii)

PV of operating CFAT (1 – 5 years)	11,39,270
Add: PV of operating CFAT (6th year) (₹2,54,493 × 0.564)	1,43,534
Add: PV of working capital	56,400
Total present value	13,39,204
Less: Cash outflows	14,00,000
NPV	(66,796)

Recommendation: Since the NPV is negative, the existing machine should not be replaced.

Mutually Exclusive Situations In the case of mutually exclusive proposals, the selection of one proposal precludes the choice of other(s). The calculation of the cash outflows and inflows are on lines similar to the replacement situations. This is illustrated in Example 24.5.

◆ Example 24.5

A company is considering two mutually exclusive proposals, X and Y. Proposal X will require the purchase of machine X, for ₹1,50,000 with no salvage value but an increase in the level of working capital to the tune of ₹50,000 over its life. The project will generate additional sales of ₹1,30,000 and require cash expenses of ₹30,000 in each of the 5 years of its life. Proposal Y will require the purchase of machine Y for ₹2,50,000 with no salvage value and additional working capital of ₹70,000. The project is expected to generate additional sales of ₹2,00,000 with cash expenses aggregating ₹50,000.

Both the machines are subject to written down value method of depreciation at the rate of 25 per cent. Assuming the company does not have any other asset in the block of 25 per cent; has 12 per cent cost of capital and is subject to 35 per cent tax, advise which machine it should purchase? What course of action would you suggest if Machine X and Machine Y have salvage values of ₹10,000 and ₹25,000 respectively?

Solution

Financial Evaluation of Proposals, X and Y

Proposal X

Cash outflows	
Cost price of machine	₹ 1,50,000
Additional working capital	50,000
Initial investment	2,00,000
CFAT and NPV	
(i) Incremental sales revenue	1,30,000
Less: Cash expenses	30,000
Incremental cash profit before taxes	1,00,000
Less: Taxes (0.35)	35,000
CFAT (*t* = 1 – 5)	65,000
(×) PV factor of annuity for 5 years (0.12)	× 3.605
Present value	2,34,325

(ii) PV of Tax Savings Due to Depreciation

Year	*Depreciation*	*Tax savings*	*PVF*	*Present value*	
1	₹ 37,500	₹ 13,125	0.893	₹ 11,721	
2	28,125	9,844	0.797	7,846	
3	21,094	7,383	0.712	5,257	
4	15,820	5,537	0.636	3,522	28,346

(iii) PV of tax savings on short-term capital loss (STCL): (₹47,461 STCL × 0.35 × 0.567)	9,419
(iv) Release of working capital (₹50,000 × 0.567)	28,350
Total present value	3,00,440
Less: Cash outflows	2,00,000
NPV	1,00,440

Proposal Y

Cash outflows	
Cost price of machine	2,50,000
Additional working capital	70,000
Initial investment	3,20,000
CFAT and NPV	
(i) Incremental sales revenue	2,00,000
Less: Cash expenses	50,000
Incremental cash profits before taxes	1,50,000
Less: Taxes (0.35)	52,500
CFAT (t = 1 – 5)	97,500
(×) PV factor of annuity for 5 years (0.12)	× 3.605
Present value	3,51,488

(ii) PV of Tax Savings Due to Depreciation

Year	Depreciation	Tax savings	PVF	Present value	
1	₹62,500	₹21,875	0.893	₹19,534	
2	46,875	16,406	0.797	13,076	
3	35,156	12,305	0.712	8,761	
4	26,367	9,229	0.636	5,869	47,240

(iii) PV of tax savings on short term capital loss (₹79,102 × 0.35 × 0.567)	15,698
(iv) Release of working capital (₹70,000 × 0.567)	39,690
Total present value	4,54,116
Less: Cash outflows	3,20,000
NPV	1,34,116

Advice: Proposal **Y** is recommended in view of its higher NPV.

Alternatively (Incremental Cashflow Approach)

Incremental Cash Outflows	
Investment required in Proposal **Y**	₹ 3,20,000
Less: Investment required in Proposal **X**	2,00,000
	1,20,000
Incremental CFAT and NPV	
(i) Incremental sales revenue (**Y** – **X**)	70,000
Less: Incremental cash expenses (**Y** – **X**)	20,000
Incremental cash profit before taxes	50,000
Less: Taxes (0.35)	17,500
Incremental CFAT (t = 1 – 5)	32,500
(×) PV of annuity for 5 years (0.12)	×3.605
Incremental present value	1,17,162

(ii) PV of Tax Savings Due to Incremental Depreciation

Year	Incremental depreciation	Tax savings	PVF	Present value	
1	₹ 25,000	₹ 8,750	0.893	₹ 7,814	
2	18,750	6,562	0.797	5,230	
3	14,062	4,922	0.712	3,504	
4	10,547	3,691	0.636	2,348	18,896

(iii) PV of tax savings on incremental (**Y** – **X**) short term capital loss (STCL): (₹79,102 – ₹47,461) × 0.35 × 0.567	6,279
(iv) Incremental (**Y** – **X**) *working capital* (₹70,000 – ₹50,000) × 0.567	11,340
Incremental present value	1,53,677
Less: Incremental cash outflows	1,20,000
Incremental NPV	33,677

Recommendation: Proposal **Y** is better.

Financial Evaluation of Proposals, Assuming Salvage Value of Machines X and Y (Incremental Approach)

(a) Sum of PV of items (i), (ii) and (iv) (₹1,17,162 + ₹18,896 + ₹11,340)@	₹ 1,47,398
(b) PV of incremental salvage value (₹15,000 × 0.567)	8,505
(c) PV of tax savings on incremental STCL@@ (₹54,102 – ₹37,461) × 0.35 × 0.567	3,302
Incremental present value	1,59,205
Less: Incremental cash outflows	1,20,000
Incremental NPV	39,205

Decision: Decision (superiority of proposal Y) remains unchanged.

@Items (i), (ii) and (iv) when there is no salvage will not change due to salvage value.

@@As a result of salvage value, the amount of short-term capital loss (STCL) will change.

EVALUATION TECHNIQUES

LO 24.3 Describe capital budgeting evaluating techniques, namely, ARR, PB method, NPV and IRR

This section discusses the important evaluation techniques for capital budgeting. Included in the methods of appraising an investment proposal are those which are objective, quantified and based on economic costs and benefits.

The methods of appraising capital expenditure proposals can be classified into two broad categories: **(i)** traditional, and **(ii)** time-adjusted. The latter are more popularly known as discounted cash flow (DCF) techniques as they take the time factor into account. The first category includes **(i)** average rate of return method and **(ii)** pay back period method. The second category includes **(i)** net present value method, **(ii)** internal rate of return method, and **(iii)** profitability index.

Traditional Techniques

Average Rate of Return **Computation** The average rate of return (ARR) method of evaluating proposed capital expenditure is also known as the accounting rate of return method. It is based upon accounting information rather than cash flows. There is no unanimity regarding the definition of the rate of return. There are a number of alternative methods for calculating the ARR. The most common usage of the average rate of return (ARR) expresses it as follows:

$$\text{ARR} = \frac{\text{Average annual profits after taxes}}{\text{Average investment over the life of the project}} \times 100 \qquad \textbf{(24.1)}$$

The average profits after taxes are determined by adding up the after-tax profits expected for each year of the project's life and dividing the result by the number of years. In the case of annuity, the average after-tax profits are equal to any year's profits.

The average investment is determined by dividing the net investment by two. This averaging process assumes that the firm is using straight line depreciation, in which case the book value of the asset declines at a constant rate from its purchase price to zero at the end of its depreciable life. This means that, on the average, firms will have one-half of their initial purchase price in the books.[8] Consequently, if the machine has salvage value, then only the depreciable cost (cost-salvage value) of the machine should be divided by two in order to ascertain the average net investment, as the salvage money will be recovered only at the end of the life of the project. Therefore, an amount equivalent to the salvage value remains tied up in the project throughout its life time. Hence, no adjustment is required to the sum of salvage value to determine the average investment.[9] Likewise, if any additional net working capital is required in the initial year which is likely to be released only at the end of the project's life, the full amount of working capital should be taken in determining relevant investment for the purpose of calculating ARR. Thus,

$$\begin{aligned}\text{Average investment} &= \text{Net working capital} + \text{Salvage value} \\ &\quad + 1/2\ (\text{Initial cost of machine} - \text{Salvage value})\end{aligned} \qquad \textbf{(24.2)}$$

For instance, given the information: initial investment (purchase of machine), ₹11,000, salvage value, ₹1,000, working capital, ₹2,000, service life (years) 5 and that the straight line method of depreciation is adopted, the average investment is: ₹1,000 + ₹2,000 + 1/2 (₹11,000 – ₹1,000) = ₹8,000.

◆ **Example 24.6**

Determine the average rate of return from the following data of two machines, A and B.

Particulars	*Machine A*	*Machine B*
Cost	₹ 56,125	₹ 56,125
Annual estimated income after depreciation and income tax:		
Year 1	3,375	11,375
2	5,375	9,375
3	7,375	7,375
4	9,375	5,375
5	11,375	3,375
	36,875	36,875
Estimated life (years)	5	5
Estimated salvage value	3,000	3,000

Depreciation has been charged on straight line basis.

Solution

$$\text{ARR} = (\text{Average income/Average investment}) \times 100$$

$$\text{Average income of Machines A and B} = \frac{₹36{,}875}{5} = ₹7{,}375$$

Average investment= Salvage value + 1/2 (Cost of machine – Salvage value)
= ₹3,000 + 1/2 (₹56,125 – ₹3,000) = ₹29,562.50

ARR (for machines A and B) = (₹7,375/₹29,562.50) × 100 = 24.9 per cent

In addition to the above, there are other approaches to calculate the average rate of return (ARR). One approach, which is a variation of the above, involves using original rather than the average cost of the project. In the case of this alternative approach, the ARR for both the machines would be 13.1 per cent (₹7,375 ÷ ₹56,125).

Accept-reject Rule With the help of the ARR, the financial decision maker can decide whether to accept or reject the investment proposal. As an accept-reject criterion, the actual ARR would be compared with a predetermined or a minimum required rate of return or cut-off rate. A project would qualify to be accepted if the actual ARR is higher than the minimum desired ARR. Otherwise, it is liable to be rejected. Alternatively, the ranking method can be used to select or reject proposals. Thus, the alternative proposals under consideration may be arranged in the descending order of magnitude, starting with the proposal with the highest ARR and ending with the proposal having the lowest ARR. Obviously, projects having higher ARR would be preferred to projects with lower ARR.

Evaluation of ARR In evaluating the ARR, as a criterion to select/reject investment projects, its merits and drawbacks need to be considered. The most favourable attribute of the ARR method is its easy calculation. What is required is only the figure of accounting profits after taxes which should be easily obtainable. Moreover, it is simple to understand and use. In contrast to this, the discounted flow techniques involve tedious calculations and are difficult to understand. Finally, the total benefits associated with the project are taken into account while calculating the ARR. Some methods, pay back for instance, do not use the entire stream of incomes.

However, this method of evaluating investment proposals suffers from serious deficiencies. The principal shortcoming of the ARR approach aries from the use of accounting income instead of cash flows. The cash flow approach is markedly superior to accounting earnings for project evaluation. The earnings calculations ignore the reinvestment potential of a project's benefits while the cash flow takes into account this potential and, hence, the total benefits of the project.

The second principal shortcoming of ARR is that it does not take into account the time value of money. The timing of cash inflows and outflows is a major decision variable in financial decision making. Accordingly, benefits in the earlier years and later years cannot be valued at par. To the extent the ARR method treats these benefits at par and fails to take account of the differences in the time value of money, it suffers from a serious deficiency. Thus, in Example 24.6, the ARR in case of both machines, A and B is the same, although machine B should be preferred since its returns in the early years of its life are greater. Clearly, the ARR method of evaluating investment proposals fails to consider this.

Thirdly, the ARR criterion of measuring the worth of investment does not differentiate between the size of the investment required for each project. Competing investment proposals may have the same ARR, but may require different average investments, as shown in Table 24.5. The ARR method, in such a situation, will leave the firm in an indeterminate position.

TABLE 24.5

Machines	*Average Annual Earnings*	*Average Investment*	*ARR (per cent)*
1	2	3	4
A	₹ 6,00,000	₹ 30,00,000	20
B	2,00,000	10,00,000	20
C	4,00,000	20,00,000	20

Finally, this method does not take into consideration any benefits which can accrue to the firm from the sale or abandonment of equipment which is replaced by the new investment. The 'new' investment, from the point of view of correct financial decision making, should be measured in terms of incremental cash outflows due to new investments, that is, new investment minus sale proceeds of the existing equipment ± tax adjustment. But the ARR method does not make any adjustment in this regard to determine the level of average investments. Investments in fixed assets are determined at their acquisition cost.

For these reason, the ARR leaves much to be desired as a method for project selection.

> **Payback (period) method** is the exact amount of time required for a firm to recover its initial investment in a project as calculated from cash inflows.

Pay Back Method Computation The **pay back method** (PB) is the second traditional method of capital budgeting. It is the simplest and, perhaps, the most widely employed, quantitative method for appraising capital expenditure decisions. This method answers the question: How many years will it take for the cash benefits to pay the original cost of an investment, normally disregarding salvage value? Cash benefits here represent CFAT ignoring interest payment. Thus, the pay back method (PB) measures the number of years required for the CFAT to pay back the **original outlay** required in an investment proposal.

> **Original/initial investment (outlay)** is the relevant cash outflow for a proposed project at time zero (t = 0).

There are two ways of calculating the PB period. The first method can be applied when the cash flow stream is in the nature of **annuity** for each year of the project's life, that is, CFAT are uniform. In such a situation, the initial cost of the investment is divided by the constant annual cash flow:

> **Annuity** is a stream of equal cash inflows.

$$PB = \text{Investment/Constant annual cash flow} \qquad \textbf{(24.3)}$$

For example, an investment of ₹40,00,000 in a machine is expected to produce CFAT of ₹8,00,000 for 10 years,

$$PB = ₹40,00,000/₹8,00,000 = 5 \text{ years}$$

The second method is used when a project's cash flows are not uniform **(mixed stream)** but vary from year to year. In such a situation, PB is calculated by the process of cumulating cash flows till the time when cumulative cash flows become equal to the original investment outlay. Table 24.6 presents the calculations of pay back period for Example 24.6.

Mixed stream is a series of cash inflows exhibiting any pattern other than that of an annuity.

TABLE 24.6

Year	*Annual CFAT*		*Cumulative CFAT*	
	A	*B*	*A*	*B*
1	₹ 14,000	₹ 22,000	₹ 14,000	₹ 22,000
2	16,000	20,000	30,000	42,000
3	18,000	18,000	48,000	60,000
4	20,000	16,000	68,000	76,000
5	25,000*	17,000*	93,000	93,000

* CFAT in the fifth year includes ₹3,000 salvage value also.

The initial investment of ₹56,125 on machine A will be recovered between years 3 and 4. The pay back period would be a fraction more than 3 years. The sum of ₹48,000 is recovered by the end of the third year. The balance ₹8,125 is needed to be recovered in the fourth year. In the fourth year CFAT is ₹20,000. The pay back fraction is, therefore, 0.406 (₹8,125/₹20,000). The pay back period for machine A is 3.406 years. Similarly, for machine B the pay back period would be 2 years and a fraction of a year. As ₹42,000 is recovered by the end of the second year, the balance of ₹14,125 needs to be recovered in the third year. In the third year CFAT is ₹18,000. The pay back fraction is 0.785 (₹14,125/₹18,000). Thus, the PB period for machine B is 2.785 years.

Accept-Reject Criterion The pay back period can be used as a decision criterion to accept or reject investment proposals. One application of this technique is to compare the actual pay back with a predetermined pay back, that is, the pay back set up by the management in terms of the maximum period during which the initial investment must be recovered. If the actual pay back period is less than the predetermined pay back, the project would be accepted; if not, it would be rejected. Alternatively, the pay back can be used as a ranking method. When mutually exclusive projects are under consideration, they may be ranked according to the length of the pay back period. Thus, the project having the shortest pay back may be assigned rank one, followed in that order so that the project with the longest pay back would be ranked last. Obviously, projects with shorter pay back period will be selected.

Evaluation The pay back method has certain merits. It is easy to calculate and simple to understand. Moreover, the pay back method is an improvement over the ARR approach. Its superiority arises due to the fact that it is based on cash flow analysis. The results of Example 24.6 illustrated in Table 24.9 can be cited in support of this. Thus, though the average cash flows for both the machines under the ARR method were the same, the pay back method shows that the pay back period for machine B is shorter than for machine A. The pay back period approach shows that machine B should be preferred as it refunds the capital outlay earlier than machine A.

The pay back approach, however, suffers from serious limitations. Its major shortcomings are as follows:

The first major shortcoming of the pay back method is that it completely ignores all cash inflows after the pay back period. This can be very misleading in capital budgeting evaluations. Table 24.7 reveals alternative projects with the same pay back period (3 years).

TABLE 24.7

Particulars	Project X	Project Y
Total cost of the project	₹ 15,00,000	₹ 15,00,000
Cash inflows (CFAT)		
Year 1	5,00,000	4,00,000
2	6,00,000	5,00,000
3	4,00,000	6,00,000
4	0	6,00,000
5	0	3,00,000
6	0	3,00,000
Pay back period (years)	3	3

In fact, the projects differs widely in respect of cash inflows generated after the pay back period. The cash flow for project X stops at the end of the third year, while that of Y continues up to the sixth year. Obviously, the firm would prefer project Y because it makes available to the firm cash inflows of ₹12,00,000, in years 4 through 6, whereas project X does not yield any cash inflow after the third year. Under the pay back method, however, both the projects would be given equal ranking, which is apparently incorrect. Therefore, it cannot be regarded as a measure of profitability. Its failure lies in the fact that it does not consider the total benefits accruing from the project.

Another deficiency of the pay back method is that it does not measure correctly even the cash flows expected to be received within the pay back period as it does not differentiate between projects in terms of the timing or the magnitude of cash flows. It considers only the recovery period as a whole. This happens because it does not discount the future cash inflows but rather treats a rupee received in the second or third year as valuable as a rupee received in the first year. In other words, to the extent the pay back method fails to consider the pattern of cash inflows, it ignores the time value of money.

Table 24.8 shows that both the projects A and B have (i) the same cash outlays in the zero time period; (ii) the same total cash inflows of ₹15,00,000; and (iii) the same pay back period of 3 years. But project A would be acceptable to the firm because it returns cash earlier than project B, enabling A to repay a loan or reinvest it and earn a return. A possible solution to this problem is provided by determining the pay back period of discounted cash flows. This is illustrated in the subsequent section of this chapter.

TABLE 24.8 Cashflows of Projects

Particulars	Project A	Project B
Total cost of the project	₹ 15,00,000	₹ 15,00,000
Cash inflows (CFAT)		
Year 1	10,00,000	1,00,000
2	4,00,000	4,00,000
3	1,00,000	10,00,000

Another flaw of the pay back method is that it does not take into consideration the entire life of the project during which cash flows are generated. As a result, projects with large cash inflows in the latter part of their lives may be rejected in favour of less profitable projects which happen to generate a larger proportion of their cash inflows in the earlier part of their lives. Table 24.9 presents the comparison of two such projects. On the basis of the pay back criterion, project A will be adjudged superior to project B.

TABLE 24.9

Particulars	Project A	Project B
Total cost of the project	₹ 40,00,000	₹ 40,00,000
Cash inflows (CFAT)		
Year 1	14,00,000	10,00,000
2	16,00,000	10,00,000
3	10,00,000	10,00,000
4	4,00,000	10,00,000
5	2,00,000	12,00,000
6	1,00,000	16,00,000
7	Nil	17,00,000
Pay back period (years)	3	4

It is quite evident just from a casual inspection that project B is more profitable than project A, since the cash inflows of the former amount to ₹45,00,000 after the expiry of the pay back period and the cash flows of the latter beyond the pay back period are only ₹7,00,000.

The above weaknesses notwithstanding, the pay back method can be gainfully employed under certain circumstances.[10] In the first place, where the long-term outlook, say in excess of three years, is extremely hazy, the pay back method may be useful. In a politically unstable country, for instance, a quick return to recover the investment is the primary goal, and subsequent profits are almost unexpected surprises. Likewise, this method may be very appropriate for firms suffering from liquidity crisis. A firm with limited liquid assets and no ability to raise additional funds, which nevertheless wishes to undertake capital projects in the hope of easing the crisis, might use pay back as a selection criterion because it emphasises quick recovery of the firm's original outlay and little impairment of the already critical liquidity situation. Thirdly, the pay back method may also be beneficial in taking capital budgeting decisions for firms which lay more emphasis on short-run earning performance rather than its long-term growth. The pay back period is a measure of liquidity of investments rather than their profitability. Thus, the pay back period should more appropriately be treated as a constraint to be *satisfied* than as a profitability measure to be *maximised.*[11] Finally, the pay back period is useful, apart from measuring liquidity, in making calculations in certain situations. For instance, the internal rate of return can be computed easily from the pay back period. The pay back method is a good approximation of the internal rate of return which otherwise requires a trial and error approach.

To conclude the discussion of the traditional methods of appraising capital investment decisions, there are two major drawbacks of these techniques. They do not consider the total benefits in terms of **(i)** the magnitude and **(ii)** the timing of cash flows. For these reasons,the traditional methods are unsatisfactory as capital budgeting decision criteria. The two essential ingredients of a theoretically sound appraisal method, therefore, are that **(i)** it should be based on a consideration of the total cash stream, and **(ii)** it should consider the time value of money as reflected in both the magnitude and the timing of expected cash flows in each period of a project's life. The time-adjusted (also known as discounted cash flow) techniques satisfy these requirements and, to that extent, provide a more objective basis for selecting and evaluating investment projects.

Discounted Cashflow (DCF)/Time-Adjusted (TA) Techniques

The distinguishing characteristics of the DCF capital budgeting techniques is that they take into consideration the time value of money while evaluating the costs and benefits of a project. In one form or another, all these methods require cash flows to be discounted at a certain rate, that is, the cost of capital. The cost of capital (K) is the minimum discount rate earned on a project that leaves the market value unchanged.

The second commendable feature of these techniques is that they take into account all benefits and costs occurring during the entire life of the project.

In the discussions that follow, we have attempted to discuss the DCF evaluation methods. First, we have explained the general procedure behind DCF. This is followed by a discussion of the first DCF technique, namely, net present value (NPV). We have then covered the internal rate of return (IRR) method and profitability index (PI) or benefit-cost ratio.

Present Value (PV)/Discounted Cash Flow (DCF) General Procedure The present value or the discounted cash flow procedure recognises that cash flow streams at different time periods differ in value and can be compared only when they are expressed in terms of a common denominator, that is, present values. It, thus, takes into account the time value of money. In this method, all cash flows are expressed in terms of their present values.

The present value of the cash flows in Example 24.6 are illustrated in Table 24.10.

TABLE 24.10 Calculations of Present Value of CFAT

	Machine A			Machine B		
Year	*CFAT*	*PV factor (0.10)*	*Present value*	*CFAT*	*PV factor (0.10)*	*Present value*
1	2	3	4	5	6	7
1	₹ 14,000	0.909	₹ 12,726	₹ 22,000	0.909	₹ 19,998
2	16,000	0.826	13,216	20,000	0.826	16,520
3	18,000	0.751	13,518	18,000	0.751	13,518
4	20,000	0.683	14,660	16,000	0.683	10,928
5	25,000*	0.621	15,525	17,000*	0.621	10,557
			69,645			71,521

*includes salvage value.

The PV so determined is compared with the PV of cash outflows. The present values of cash inflows of both the machines are higher than cash outflows, and, therefore both are acceptable.

The PV of CFAT (Col. 4 and Col. 7 of Table 24.10) now can be used to determine the 'discounted' pay back period. It is determined on the basis of discounted present value of CFAT *vis-a-vis* unadjusted cash flows (Col. 2 and Col. 5 of Table 24.10) used in the 'simple' pay back method. The relevant values of the 'discounted' pay back period are 4.2 and 3.66 years for Machines A and B respectively in Example 24.6.

Net present value (NPV) is found by subtracting a projects initial investment from the present value of its cash inflows discounted at the firm's cost of capital.

Net Present Value (NPV) Method The first DCF/PV technique is the NPV. **NPV** may be described as the summation of the present values of cash proceeds (CFAT) in each year minus the summation of present values of the net cash outflows in each year. Symbolically, the NPV for projects having conventional cash flows would be:

$$\text{NPV} = \sum_{t=1}^{n} \frac{CF_t}{(1+K)^t} + \frac{S_n + W_n}{(1+K)^n} - CO_0 \qquad \textbf{(24.4)}$$

If cash outflow is also expected to occur at some time other than at initial investment (non-conventional cash flows) the formula would be:

$$\text{NPV} = \sum_{t=1}^{n} \frac{CF_t}{(1+K)^t} + \frac{S_n + W_n}{(1+K)^n} - \sum_{t=0}^{n} \frac{CO_t}{(1+K)^t} \qquad \textbf{(24.5)}$$

The decision rule for a project under NPV is to accept the project if the NPV is positive and reject if it is negative. Symbolically,

(i) NPV > zero, *accept*, (ii) NPV < zero, reject **(24.6)**

Zero NPV implies that the firm is indifferent to accepting or rejecting the project. However, in practice it is rare if ever such a project will be accepted, as such a situation simply implies that only the original investment has been recovered.

In Example 24.6 we would accept the proposals of purchasing machines A and B as their net present values are positive. The positive NPV of machine A is ₹13,520 (₹69,645 – ₹56,125) and that of B is ₹15,396 (₹71,521 – ₹56,125).

In Example 24.6, if we incorporate cash outflows of ₹25,000 at the end of the third year in respect of overhauling of the machine, we shall find the proposals to purchase either of the machines are unacceptable as their net present values are negative. The negative NPV of machine A is ₹6,255 (₹68,645 – ₹74,900) and of machine B is ₹3,379 (₹71,521 – ₹74,900).

As a decision criterion, this method can also be used to make a choice between mutually exclusive projects. On the basis of the NPV method, the various proposals would be ranked in order of the net present values. The project with the highest NPV would be assigned the first rank, followed by others in the descending order. If, in our example, a choice is to be made between machine A and machine B on the basis of the NPV method, machine B having larger NPV (₹15,396) would be preferred to machine A (NPV being ₹12,520).

Evaluation The present value method including the NPV variation possesses several merits. The first, and probably the most significant, advantage is that it explicitly recognises the time value of money. In Example 24.6, for instance (Table 24.10), the total cash inflows (CFAT) pertaining to the two machines (A and B) are equal. But the present value as well as the NPV is different. As can be seen from Table 24.11, this is primarily because of the differences in the pattern of the cash streams. The magnitude of CFAT in the case of machine A is lower in the earlier years as compared to the machine B while it is greater in the latter years. Because of larger inflows in the first two years, the NPV of machine B is larger than that of machine A. The need for recognising the time value of money is, thus, satisfied by this method.

Secondly, it also fulfills the second attribute of a sound method of appraisal in that it considers the total benefits arising out of the proposal over its lifetime.

Thirdly, a changing discount rate can be built into the NPV calculations by altering the denominator. This feature becomes important as this rate normally changes because the longer the time span, the lower is the value of money and the higher is the discount rate.

Fourthly, this method is particularly useful for the selection of mutually exclusive projects. This aspect will be discussed in detail in the latter part of the chapter, where it is shown that for mutually exclusive choice problems, the NPV method is the best decision-criterion.

Finally, this method of asset selection is instrumental in achieving the objective of financial management which is the maximisation of the shareholders' wealth. The rationale behind this contention is the effect on the market price of shares as a result of the acceptance of a proposal having present value exceeding the initial outlay or, as a variation having NPV greater than zero. The market price of the shares will be affected by the relative force of what the investors expect and what actual return is earned on the funds. The discount rate that is used to convert benefits into present values is the minimum rate or the rate of interest is that when the present values of cash inflows is equal to the initial outlay or when the NPV = 0, the return on investment just equals the expected or required rate by investors. There would, therefore, be no change in the market price of shares. When the present value exceeds the outlay or the NPV > 0, the return would be higher than expected by the investors. It would, therefore, lead to an increase in share prices. The present value method is, thus, logically consistent with the goal of maximising shareholders' wealth in terms of maximising the market price of the shares.

In brief, the present value method is a theoretically correct technique for the selection of investment projects. Nevertheless, it has certain limitations also.

In the first place, it is difficult to calculate as well as understand and use in comparison with the pay back method or even the ARR method. This, of course, is a minor flaw.

The second, and a more serious problem associated with the present value method, involves the calculation of the required rate of return to discount the cash flows. The discount rate is the most important element used in the calculation of the present values because different discount rates will give different present values. The relative desirability of a proposal will change with a change in the discount rate. For instance, for a proposal involving an initial outlay of ₹9,000, having annuity of ₹2,800 for 5 years, the net present values for different required rates of return are given in Table 24.11.

TABLE 24.11 Net Present Value With Different Discount Rates

Discount rate (per cent)	*Net present value*
Zero	₹ 5,000.00
4	3,465.00
8	2,179.50
10	1,614.00
12	1,093.50
16	168.00
20	(626.50)

The importance of the discount rate is, thus, obvious. But the calculation of the required rate of return presents serious problems. The cost of capital is generally the basis of the discount rate. The calculation of the cost of capital is very complicated. In fact, there is a difference of opinion even regarding the exact method of calculating it.

Another shortcoming of the present value method is that it is an absolute measure. *Prima facie* between two projects, this method will favour the project which has higher present value (or NPV). But it is likely that this project may also involve a larger initial outlay. Thus, in case of projects involving different outlays, the present value method may not give dependable results.

Finally, the present value method may also not give satisfactory results in the case of two projects having different effective lives. In general, the project with a shorter economic life would be preferable, other things being equal. A project which has a higher present value may also have a larger economic life so that the funds will remain invested for a longer period, while the alternative proposal may have shorter life but smaller present value. In such situations, the present value method may not reflect the true worth of the alternative proposals.

Internal rate of return (IRR) is the discount rate that equates the present values of cash inflows with the initial investment associated with a project, thereby causing NPV = 0.

Internal Rate of Return (IRR) Method The second discounted cash flow (DCF) or time-adjusted method for appraising capital investment decisions is the internal rate of return (IRR) method. This technique is also known as *yield on investment, marginal efficiency of capital, marginal productivity of capital, rate of return, time-adjusted rate of return* and so on. Like the present value method, the IRR method also considers the time value of money by discounting the cash streams. The basis of the discount factor, however, is different in both cases. In the case of the net present value method, the discount rate is the required rate of return and being a predetermined rate, usually the cost of capital, its determinants are external to the proposal under consideration. The IRR, on the other hand, is based on facts which are internal to the proposal. In other words, while arriving at the required rate of return for finding out present values the cash flows—inflows as well as outflows—are not considered. But the IRR depends entirely on the initial outlay and the cash proceeds of the project which is being evaluated for acceptance or rejection. It is, therefore, appropriately referred to as internal rate of return.

The **internal rate of return** is usually the rate of return that a project earns. It is defined as *the discount rate (r) which equates the aggregate present value of the net cash inflows (CFAT) with the aggregate present value of cash outflows of a project.* In other words, it is that rate which gives the project NPV of zero.

Assuming conventional cash flows, mathematically, the IRR is represented by the rate, *r*, such that

$$CO_0 = \sum_{t=1}^{n} \frac{CF_t}{(1+r)^t} + \frac{S_n + W_n}{(1+r)^n} \quad \textbf{(24.7)}$$

$$\text{Zero} = \sum_{t=1}^{n} \frac{CF_t}{(1+r)^t} + \frac{S_n + W_n}{(1+r)^n} - CO_0 \quad \textbf{(24.8)}$$

For unconventional cash flows, the equation would be:

$$\sum_{t=0}^{n} \frac{CF_t}{(1+r)^t} + \frac{S_n + W_n}{(1+r)^n} = \sum_{t=1}^{n} \frac{CO_0}{(1+r)^t} \quad \textbf{(24.9)}$$

$$\text{Zero} = \sum_{t=1}^{n} \frac{CF_t}{(1+r)^t} + \frac{S_n + W_n}{(1+r)^n} - \sum_{t=0}^{n} \frac{CO_t}{(1+r)^t} \quad \textbf{(24.10)}$$

where r = The internal rate of return
CF_t = Cash inflows at different time periods
S_n = Salvage value
W_n = Working capital adjustments
CO_t = Cash outlay at different time periods

Accept-Reject Decision The use of the IRR, as a criterion to accept capital investment decisions, involves a comparison of the actual IRR with the required rate of return also known as the cut-off rate or hurdle rate. The project would qualify to be accepted if the IRR (*r*) exceeds the cut-off rate (*k*). If the IRR and the required rate of return are equal, the firm is indifferent as to whether to accept or reject the project.

Computation Unlike the NPV method, calculating the value of IRR is more difficult. The procedure will depend on whether the cash flows are annuity or mixed stream.

Annuities The following steps are taken in determining IRR for an annuity:

- Determine the pay back period of the proposed investment.
- In Table A-4 (present value of an annuity) look for the pay back period that is equal to or closest to the life of the project.
- In the year row, find two PV values or discount factor (DF_r) closest to PB period but one bigger and other smaller than it.
- From the top row of the table, note interest rate (*r*) corresponding to these PV values (DF_r).
- Determine actual IRR by interpolation. This can be done either directly using Equation 24.11 or indirectly by finding present values of annuity (Equation 24.12).

$$IRR = r - \left(\frac{PB - DF_r}{DF_{rL} - DF_{rH}}\right) \quad (24.11)$$

where PB = Pay back period

DF_r = Discount factor for interest rate r.

DF_{rL} = Discount factor for lower interest rate

DF_{rH} = Discount factor for higher interest rate.

r = Either of the two interest rates used in the formula

Alternatively,

$$IRR = r - \left(\frac{PV_{CO} - PV_{CFAT}}{\Delta PV}\right) \times \Delta r \quad (24.12)$$

where PV_{CO} = Present value of cash outlay

PV_{CFAT} = Present value of cash inflows (DF_r x annuity)

r = Either of the two interest rates used in the formula

Δr = Difference in interest rates

ΔPV = Difference in calculated present values of inflows

The computations are shown in Example 24.7.

Example 24.7

A project costs ₹36,000 and is expected to generate cash inflows of ₹11,200 annually for 5 years. Calculate the IRR of the project.

Solution

(1) The pay back period is 3.214 (₹36,000/₹11,200)

(2) According to Table A-2, discount factors closest to 3.214 for 5 years are 3.274 (16 per cent rate of interest) and 3.199 (17 per cent rate of interest). The actual value of IRR which lies between 16 per cent and 17 per cent can, now, be determined using Equations 24.11 and 24.12.

Substituting the values in Equation 24.11 we get: $IRR = 16 + \left(\frac{3.274 - 3.214}{3.274 - 3.199}\right) = 16.8$ per cent

Alternatively (starting with the higher rate), $IRR = 17 - \left(\frac{3.214 - 3.199}{3.274 - 3.199}\right) = 16.8$ per cent

Instead of using the direct method, we may find the actual IRR by applying the interpolation formula to the present values of cash inflows and outflows (Equation 24.12). Here, again, it is immaterial whether we start with the lower or the higher rate.

$$PV_{CFAT}\ (0.16) = ₹11{,}200 \times 3.274 = ₹36{,}668.8$$

$$PV_{CFAT}\ (0.17) = ₹11{,}200 \times 3.199 = ₹35{,}828.8$$

$$IRR = 16 + \left(\frac{36{,}668.8 - 36{,}000}{36{,}668.8 - 35{,}828.8}\right) \times 1 = 16.8 \text{ per cent}$$

Alternatively (starting with the higher rate), $IRR = r - \frac{(PV_{CO} - PV_{CFAT})}{\Delta PV} \times \Delta r$

$$IRR = 17 - \left(\frac{36,000 - 35,828.8}{840}\right) \times 1 = 16.8 \text{ per cent}$$

For a Mixed Stream of Cash Flows Calculating the IRR for a mixed stream of cash flows is more tedious. In a mixed stream of cash flows, the inflows in various years are uneven or unequal. One way to simplify the process is to use 'fake annuity' as a starting point.[12] The following procedure is a useful guide to calculating IRR:

1. Calculate the average annual cash inflow to get a 'fake annuity'.
2. Determine 'fake pay back period' dividing the initial outlay by the average annual CFAT determined in step 1.
3. Look for the factor, in Table A-2, closest to the fake pay back value in the same manner as in the case of annuity. The result will be a rough approximation of the IRR, based on the assumption that the mixed stream is an annuity (fake annuity).
4. Adjust subjectively the IRR obtained in step 3 by comparing the pattern of average annual cash inflows (as per step 1) to the actual mixed stream of cash flows. If the actual cash flows stream happens to be higher in the initial years of the project's life than the average stream, adjust the IRR a few percentage points upward. The reason is obvious as the greater recovery of funds in the earlier years is likely to give a higher yield rate (IRR). Conversely, if in the early years the actual cash inflows are below the average, adjust the IRR a few percentage points downward. If the average cash flows pattern seems fairly close to the actual pattern, no adjustment is to be made.
5. Find out the present value (using Table A-1) of the mixed cash flows, taking the IRR as the discount rate as estimated in step 4.
6. Calculate the PV, using the discount rate. If the PV of CFAT equals the initial outlay, that is, NPV is zero, it is the IRR. Otherwise, repeat step 5. Stop, once two consecutive discount rates that cause the NPV to be positive and negative, respectively have been calculated. Whichever of these two rates causes the NPV to be closest to zero is the IRR to the nearest 1 per cent.
7. The actual value can be ascertained by the method of interpolation as in the case of an annuity.

◆ Example 24.8

Let us apply this procedure for determining the IRR of Example 24.6 of a mixed stream of CFAT for machines A and B. The cash flows associated with the machines are given in Table 24.6.

Solution

1. The sum of cash inflows of both the machines is ₹93,000 which when divided by the economic life of the machine (5 years), results in a 'fake annuity' of ₹18,600.
2. Dividing the initial outlay of ₹56,125 by ₹18,600, we have 'fake average pay back period' of 3.017 years.
3. In Table A-2, the factor closest to 3.017 for 5 years is 2.991 for a rate of 20 per cent.
4. Since the actual cash flows in the earlier years are greater than the average cash flows of ₹18,600 in machine B, a subjective increase of, say, 1 per cent is made. This makes an estimated rate of IRR 21 per cent for machine B. In the case of machine A, since cash inflows in the initial years are smaller than the average cash flows, a subjective decrease of, say, 2 per cent is made. This makes the estimated IRR rate 18 per cent for machine A.
5. Using the PV factors for 21 per cent (Machine B) and 18 per cent (Machine A) from Table A-1 for years 1-5, the PVs are calculated in Table 24.12.

TABLE 24.12

Year	Machine A			Machine B		
	CFAT	PV factor (0.18)	Total PV	CFAT	PV factor (0.21)	Total PV
1	₹ 14,000	0.847	₹ 11,858	₹ 22,000	0.826	₹ 18,172
2	16,000	0.718	11,488	20,000	0.683	13,660
3	18,000	0.609	10,962	18,000	0.564	10,152
4	20,000	0.516	10,320	16,000	0.467	7,472
5	25,000	0.437	10,925	17,000	0.386	6,562
Total present value			55,553			56,018
Less: Initial investment		56,125			56,125	
NPV			(572)			(107)

6. Since the NPV is negative for both the machines, the discount rate should be subsequently lowered. In the case of machine A the difference is of ₹572 whereas in machine B the difference is ₹107. Therefore, in the former case the discount rate is lowered by 1 per cent in both the cases. As a result, the new discount rate would be 17 per cent for A and 20 per cent for B.

The calculations given in Table 24.13 shows that the NPV at discount rate of 17 per cent is ₹853 (Machine A) and ₹1,049 for Machine B at 20 per cent discount.

TABLE 24.13

Year	Machine A			Machine B		
	CFAT	PV factor (0.17)	Total PV	CFAT	PV factor (0.20)	Total PV
1	₹ 14,000	0.855	₹ 11,970	₹ 22,000	0.833	₹ 18,326
2	16,000	0.731	11,696	20,000	0.694	13,880
3	18,000	0.624	10,232	18,000	0.579	10,422
4	20,000	0.534	10,680	16,000	0.484	7,712
5	25,000	0.456	11,400	17,000	0.442	6,834
PV of cash inflows			56,978			57,174
Less: Initial outlay			56,125			56,125
Net present value			853			1,049

(a) For machine A: Since 17 per cent and 18 per cent are consecutive discount rates that give positive and negative net present values, interpolation method can be applied to find the actual IRR which will be between 17 and 18 per cent.

$$\text{IRR} = 17 + \left[\frac{₹56,978 - ₹56,125}{₹56,978 - ₹55,553}\right] \times 1 = 17.6 \text{ per cent}$$

(b) For machine B: $\text{IRR} = 20 + \left[\frac{₹57,174 - ₹56\ 125}{₹57,174 - ₹56,018}\right] \times 1 = 20.9 \text{ per cent}$

Evaluation of IRR The IRR method is a theoretically correct technique to evaluate capital expenditure decisions. It has the advantages which are offered by the NPV criterion such as: **(i)** it considers the time value of money, and **(ii)** it takes into account the total cash inflows and outflows.

In addition, the IRR is easier to understand. Business executives and non-technical people understand the concept of IRR much more readily than they understand the concept of NPV. They may not be following the definition of IRR in terms of the equation but they are well aware of its usual meaning in terms of the rate of return on investment. For instance, business executives will understand the investment proposal in a better way if told that IRR of machine B is 21 per cent and *k* is 10 per cent instead of saying that the NPV of machine B is ₹15,396.

Another merit of IRR is that it does not use the concept of the required rate of return/the cost of capital. It itself provides a rate of return which is indicative of the profitability of the proposal. The cost of capital, of course, enters the calculations later on.

Finally, it is consistent with the overall objective of maximising shareholders' wealth. According to IRR, as a decision-criterion, the acceptance or otherwise of a project is based on a comparison of the IRR with the required rate of return. The required rate of return is, by definition, the minimum rate which investors expect on their investment. In other words, if the actual IRR of an investment proposal is equal to the rate expected by the investors, the share prices will remain unchanged. Since, with IRR, only such projects are accepted as have IRR > required rate, the share prices will tend to rise. This will naturally lead to the maximisation of shareholders' wealth.

Its theoretical soundness notwithstanding, the IRR suffers from serious limitations.

First, it involves tedious calculations. As shown above, it generally involves complicated computational problems. *Secondly,* it produces multiple rates which can be confusing. This aspect is further developed later in this chapter. *Thirdly,* in evaluating mutually exclusive proposals, the project with the highest IRR would be picked up to the exclusion of all others. However, in practice, it may not turn out to be the one which is the most profitable and consistent with the objectives of the firm, that is, maximisation of the shareholders' wealth. This aspect also has been discussed in detail later in this chapter. *Finally,* under the IRR method, it is assumed that all intermediate cash flows are reinvested at the IRR. In our example, the IRR rates for machines A and B are 17.6 per cent and 20.9 per cent respectively. In operational terms, 17.6 per cent IRR signifies that all cash inflows of machine A can be reinvested at 17.6 per cent whereas that of B at 20.9 per cent. It is rather ridiculous to think that the same firm has the ability to reinvest the cash flows at different rates.

There is no difference in the 'quality of cash' received either from project A or B. The reinvestment rate assumption under the IRR method is, therefore, very unrealistic. Moreover, it is not safe to assume always that intermediate cash flows from the project will be reinvested at all. A portion of cash inflows may be paid out as dividends. Likewise, a portion of it may be tied up in current assets such as stocks, debtors or cash. Clearly, the firm will get a wrong picture of the capital project if it assumes that it invests the entire intermediate cash proceeds. Further, it is not safe to assume, as is often done, that they will be reinvested at the same rate of return as the company is currently earning on its capital (IRR) or at the current cost of capital, *k*. In order to have correct and reliable results it is obvious, therefore, that they should be based on realistic estimates of the interest rate (if any) at which income will be reinvested. Terminal value takes care of this aspect.

Profitability Index (PI) or Benefit-Cost Ratio (B/C Ratio) Yet another time-adjusted capital budgeting technique is profitability index (PI) or benefit-cost ratio (B/C). It is similar to the NPV approach. The **profitability index** approach measures the present value of returns per rupee invested, while the NPV is based on the difference between the present value of future cash inflows and the present value of cash outlays. A major shortcoming of the NPV method is that, being an absolute measure, it is not a reliable method to evaluate projects requiring different initial investments. The PI method provides a solution to this kind of problem. It is, in other words, a relative measure. It may be defined as the ratio which is obtained dividing the present value of future cash inflows by the present value of cash outlays. Symbolically,

Profitability index measures the present value of returns per rupee invested.

$$\text{PI} = \frac{\text{Present value cash inflows}}{\text{Present value of cash outflows}} \quad \textbf{(24.13)}$$

This method is also known as the B/C ratio because the numerator measures benefits and the denominator costs. A more appropriate description would be *present value index.*

Accept-Reject Rule Using the B/C ratio or the PI, a project will qualify for acceptance if its PI exceeds one. When PI equals 1, the firm is indifferent to the project.

When PI is greater than, equal to or less than 1, the net present value is greater than, equal to or less than zero respectively. In other words, the NPV will be positive when the PI is greater than 1; will be negative when the PI is less than one. Thus, the NPV and PI approaches give the same results regarding the investment proposals.

The selection of projects with the PI method can also be done on the basis of ranking. The highest rank will be given to the project with the highest PI, followed by others in the same order.

In Example 24.6 (Table 24.10) of machine A and B, the PI would be 1.22 for machine A and 1.27 for machine B:

$$\text{PI (Machine A)} = \frac{₹69{,}645}{₹56{,}125} = 1.24$$

$$\text{PI (Machine B)} = \frac{₹71{,}521}{₹56{,}125} = 1.27$$

Since the PI for both the machines is greater than 1, both the machines are acceptable.

Though it is common to define PI as the ratio of the PV of the cash inflows divided by the PV of cash outflows, the PI may also be measured on the basis of the net benefits of a project against its current cash outlay rather than measure its gross benefits against its total cost over the life of the project. This aspect becomes very important in situations of capital rationing.[13] In such a situation,the decision rule would be to accept the project if the PI is positive and reject the project it it is negative.

Evaluation Like the other discounted cash flow techniques, the PI satisfies almost all the requirements of a sound investment criterion. It considers all the elements of capital budgeting, such as the time value of money, totality of benefits and so on. Conceptually, it is a sound method of capital budgeting. Although based on the NPV, it is a better evaluation technique than NPV in a situation of capital rationing. For instance, two projects may have the same NPV of ₹10,000 but project A requires an initial investment of ₹50,000 whereas B only of ₹25,000. Project B should be preferred as will be suggested by the PI method. The NPV method, however, will give identical rankings of both the projects. Thus, the PI method is superior to the NPV method as the former evaluates the worth of projects in terms of their relative rather than absolute magnitudes. However, in some problems of a mutually exclusive nature, the NPV method would be superior to the PI method.

SUMMARY

- Capital budgeting decisions relate to long-term assets which are in operation and yield a return over a period of time. They, therefore, involve current outlays in return for series of anticipated flow of future benefits.
- Such decisions are of paramount importance as they affect the profitability of a firm, and are the major determinants of its efficiency and competing power. While an opportune investment decision can yield spectacular returns, an ill-advised/incorrect decision can endanger the very survival of a firm. A few wrong decisions and the firm may be forced into bankruptcy.

- Capital expenditure decisions are beset with a number of difficulties. The two major difficulties are: **(i)** The benefits from long-term investments are received in some future period which is uncertain. Therefore, an element of risk is involved in forecasting future sales revenues as well as the associated costs of production and sales; **(ii)** It is not often possible to calculate in strict quantitative terms all the benefits or the costs relating to a specific investment decision.
- Such decisions are of two types, namely, revenue expanding investment decisions and cost reducing investment decisions. The latter types of decisions are subject to less risk as the potential cash saving can be estimated better from the past production and cost data. It is more difficult to estimate revenues and costs of a new product line.
- The capital outlays and revenue benefits associated with such decisions are measured in terms of cash flows after taxes. The cash flow approach for measuring benefits is theoretically superior to the accounting profit approach as it **(i)** avoids the ambiguities of the accounting profits concept, **(ii)** measures the total benefits and **(iii)** takes into account the time value of money.
- The major difference between the cash flow and the accounting profit approaches relates to the treatment of depreciation. While the accounting approach considers depreciation in cost computation, it is recognised, on the contrary, as a source of cash to the extent of tax advantage in the cash flow approach.
- For taxation purposes, depreciation is charged (on the basis of written down value method) on a block of assets and not on an individual asset. A block of assets is a group of assets (say, of plant and machinery) in respect of which the same rate of depreciation is prescribed by the Income-Tax Act.

  Depreciation is charged on the year-end balance of the block which is equal to the opening balance plus purchases made during the year (in the block considered) minus sale proceeds of the assets during the year.

  In case the entire block of assets is sold during the year (the block ceases to exist at year-end), no depreciation is charged at the year-end. If the sale proceeds of the block sold is higher than the opening balance, the difference represents short-term capital gain which is subject to tax. Where the sale proceeds are less than the opening balance, the firm is entitled to tax shield on short-term capital loss. The adjustment related to the payment of taxes/tax shield is made in terminal cash inflows of the project.

LO 24.1

- The data requirement for capital budgeting are after tax cash outflows and cash inflows. Besides, they should be incremental in that they are directly attributable to the proposed investment project. The existing fixed costs, therefore, are ignored. In brief, incremental after-tax cash flows are the only relevant cash flows in the analysis of new investment projects.
- The investment in new capital projects can be categorised into **(i)** a single proposal, **(ii)** a re-placement proposal and **(iii)** mutually exclusive proposals.
- In the case of single/independent investment proposal, cash outflows primarily consist of **(i)** purchase cost of the new plant and machinery, **(ii)** its installation costs and **(iii)** working capital requirement to support production and sales (in the case of revenue expanding proposals/release of working capital in cost reduction proposals.

  The cash inflows after taxes (CFAT) are computed by adding depreciation (D) to the projected earnings after taxes (EAT) from the proposal. In the terminal year of the project, apart from operating CFAT, the cash inflows include salvage value (if any, net of removal costs), recovery of working capital and tax advantage\taxes paid on short-term capital loss\gain on sale of machine (if the block ceases to exist).
- In the case of replacement situation, the sale proceeds from the existing machine reduce the cash outflows required to purchase the new machine. The relevant CFAT are *incremental* after-tax cash inflows.
- In the case of mutually exclusive proposals, the selection of one proposal precludes the sele-ction of the other(s). The computation of the cash outflows and cash inflows are on lines similar to the replacement situation.

LO 24.2

- The capital budgeting evaluation techniques are: **(i)** traditional, comprising **(a)** average/accounting rate of return (ARR) and **(b)** pay back (PB) period; **(ii)** discounted cash flow (DCF), primarily consisting of **(a)** net present value (NPV), **(b)** internal rate of return (IRR) and **(iii)** profitability/present value index (PI).
- The ARR is obtained dividing annual average profits after taxes by average investments. Average investment = 1/2 (Initial cost of machine – Salvage value) + Salvage value + net working capital. Annual average profits after taxes = Total expected after tax profits/Number of years

  The ARR is unsatisfactory method as it is based on accounting profits and ignores time value of money.
- The pay back method measures the number of years required for the CFAT to pay back the initial capital investment outlay, ignoring interest payment. It is determined as follows:
  (i) In the case of annuity CFAT: Initial investment/Annual CFAT.
  (ii) In the case of mixed CFAT: It is obtained by cumulating CFAT till the cumulative CFAT equal the initial investment.

  Although the pay back method is superior to the ARR method in that it is based on cash flows, it also ignores time value of money and disregards the total benefits associated with the investment proposal.
- The DCF methods satisfy all the attributes of a good measure of appraisal as they consider the total benefits (CFAT) as well as the timing of benefits.
- The NPV may be described as the summation of the present values of **(i)** operating CFAT (CF) in each year and **(ii)** salvages value(S) and working capital(W) in the terminal year(n) minus the summation of present values of the cash outflows(CO) in each year. The net present value is computed using cost of capital (k) as a discount rate. Symbolically,

$$NPV = \sum_{t=1}^{n} \frac{CF_t}{(1+k)^t} + \frac{S_n + W_n}{(1+k)^n} - \sum_{t=0}^{n} \frac{CO_t}{(1+k)^t}$$

  The project will be accepted in case the NPV is positive.
- The IRR is defined as the discount rate (r) which equates the aggregate present value of the operating CFTA received each year and terminal cash flows (working capital recovery and salvage value) with aggregate present value of cash outflows of an investment proposal. Symbolically,

$$IRR = \sum_{t=1}^{n} \frac{CF_t}{(1+r)^t} + \frac{S_n + W_n}{(1+r)^n} = \sum_{t=0}^{n} \frac{CO_t}{(1+r)^t}$$

  The project will be accepted when IRR exceeds the required rate of return.
- The profitability index/present value index measures the present value of returns per rupee invested. It is obtained dividing the present value of future cash inflows (bot operating CFAT and terminal) by the present value of capital cash outflows. The proposal will be worth accepting if the PI exceeds one.

LO 24.3

REFERENCES

1. Quirin, G D, The Capital Expenditure Decision, Richard D. Irwin, Homewood Ill., 1967, p 2.
2. Osteryoung, J, *Capital Budgeting: Long-term Asset Selection*, Grid, Columbus, Ohio, 1992, p 4.
3. Bierman, H., and S. Smidt, *The Capital Budgeting Decision*, Macmillan, New York, 1974, p 4. Reprinted by permission from Macmillan Publishing Co. Inc. New York, USA.
4. Gitman, Lawrence, J, *Principles of Managerial Finance*, Harper and Row, New York, 1997, p 239.
5. Joy, O M, *Introduction to Financial Management*, Richard Irwin, Homewood, Ill, 1991, p 126.
6. Solomn, Ezra and J J Pringle. *An Introduction to Financial Management,* Goodyear Publishing Company,Santa Monica Calif. 1977, p 282.
7. For further details, refer to Solomon, and JJ Pringle, *op cit*., pp 282-92.

8. Gitman, L J, *op cit.* p 287.
9. Osteryoung, *op cit.*, p 55.
10. Bolten, S E, *Managerial Finance-Principles and Practices,* Houghton Mifflin Comapny, Boston, 1976, p 162.
11. Weingartner, H M, 'Some new views on the pay back period and capital budgeting decisions', *Management Science*, August 1969, pp 594-607.
12. Gitman, L J, *op cit.*, pp 295-96.
13. Osteryoung, J S, *op cit.*, p 114.

SOLVED PROBLEMS

P.24.1 A company is considering an investment proposal to instal new milling controls at a cost of ₹50,000. The facility has a life expectancy of 5 years and no salvage value. The tax rate is 35 per cent. Assume the firm uses straight line depreciation and the same is allowed for tax purposes. The estimated cash flows before depreciation and tax (CFBT) from the investment proposal are as follows: LO 24.3 LOD: E

Year	*CFBT*
1	₹10,000
2	10,692
3	12,769
4	13,462
5	20,385

Compute the following:

(i) Pay back period.
(ii) Average rate of return.
(iii) Internal rate of return.
(iv) Net present value at 10 per cent discount rate.

Solution

Determination of Cashflows after Taxes (CFAT)

Year	*CFBT*	*Depreciation*[a] *(₹50,000/5)*	*Profits before tax (Col.2 – Col.3)*	*Taxes (0.35)*	*EAT (Col.4 – Col.5)*	*CFAT (Col.6 + Col.3)*
1	2	3	4	5	6	7
1	₹10,000	₹10,000	Nil	Nil	Nil	₹10,000
2	10,692	10,000	₹692	₹242	₹450	10,450
3	12,769	10,000	2,769	969	1,800	11,800
4	13,462	10,000	3,462	1,212	2,250	12,250
5	20,385	10,000	10,385	3,635	6,750	16,750
					11,250	61,250

(i) *Pay Back (PB) Period:*

Year	*CFAT*	*Cumulative CFAT*
1	₹10,000	₹10,000
2	10,450	20,450
3	11,800	32,250
4	12,250	44,500
5	16,750	61,250

The recovery of the investment falls between the fourth and fifth years. Therefore, the PB is 4 years plus a fraction of the 5th year. The fractional value = ₹5,500 ÷ ₹16,750 = 0.328. Thus, the PB is 4.328 years.

(ii) *Average rate of return (ARR)* = $\frac{\text{Average income}}{\text{Average investment}} \times 100 = \frac{₹2,250\ (₹11,250 \div 5)}{₹25,000\ (₹50,000 \div 2)} \times 100 = 9$ per cent

(iii) *Internal rate of return (IRR)*:

$$₹50,000 = \frac{₹10,000}{(1+r)^1} + \frac{₹10,450}{(1+r)^2} + \frac{₹11,800}{(1+r)^3} + \frac{₹12,250}{(1+r)^4} + \frac{₹16,750}{(1+r)^5}$$

The fake pay back period = 4.0816 (₹50,000/₹12,250). From Table A-4, the value closest to the fake pay back period of 4.0816 against 5 years is 4.100 against 7 per cent. Since the actual cash flow stream is the initial years is slightly below the average cash flow stream, the IRR is likely to be lower than 7 per cent. Let us try with 6 per cent.

Year	*CFAT*	*PV factor*		*Total PV*[a]	
		0.06	*0.07*	*0.06*	*0.07*
1	₹10,000	0.943	0.935	₹9,430	₹9,350
2	10,450	0.890	0.873	9,300	9,123
3	11,800	0.840	0.816	9,912	9,629
4	12,250	0.792	0.763	9,702	9,347
5	16,750	0.747	0.713	12,512	11,942
Total				50,856	49,391
Less initial outlay				50,000	50,000
NPV				856	(609)

The IRR is between 6 and 7 per cent. By interpolation, IRR = 6.6 per cent.

(iv) *Net Present Value (NPV)*

Year	*CFAT*	*PV factor (0.10)*	*Total PV*[a]
1	₹10,000	0.909	₹9,090
2	10,450	0.826	8,632
3	11,800	0.751	8,862
4	12,250	0.683	8,367
5	16,750	0.621	10,401
Total			45,352
Less initial outlay			50,000
NPV			(4,648)

P.24.2 A project costing ₹5,60,000 is expected to produce annual net cash benefits (CFAT) of ₹80,000 over a period of 15 years. Estimate the internal rate of return (IRR). Also, find the pay back period and obtain the IRR from it. How do you compare this IRR with the one directly estimated? **LO 24.3** **LOD: E**

Solution

$$\text{PB value} = \frac{₹5,60,000}{₹80,000} = 7.000$$

The present value interest factors closet to 7.000 are 7.191 at 11 per cent rate of discount and 6.811 at 12 per cent rate of discount against 15 years (Table A-4). The actual IRR would be between 11 and 12 per cent.

Using interpolation, the IRR would be 0.11 + 0.05 (0.19 ÷ 0.38) = 11.5 per cent.

IRR determination through PB period: The reciprocal of the PB period is good approximation of the IRR if: (i) The life of the project is at least twice the PB period and (ii) The project generates annuity cash inflows. Accordingly, IRR would be the reciprocal of the PB period, that is, 1/7 = 0.1428 = 14.28 per cent.

Comparison: The two IRRs are different. But the IRR which is directly estimated is correct as at this rate of discount, NPV of cash flow stream of the project would be zero. The NPV cannot be zero at 14.28 per cent. The IRR through the PB period is only an approximate measure.

P.24.3 Modern Enterprises Ltd is considering the purchase of a new computer system for its Research and Development Division, which would cost ₹35 lakh. The operation and maintenance costs (excluding depreciation) are expected to be ₹7 lakh per annum. It is estimated that the useful life of the system would be 6 years, at the end of which the disposal value is expected to be ₹1 lakh. LO 24.3 LOD: M

The tangible benefits expected from the system in the form of reduction in design and draftsmanship costs would be ₹12 lakh per annum. The disposal of used drawing office equipment and furniture initially is anticipated to net ₹9 lakh.

As capital expenditure in research and development, the proposal would attract 100 per cent write-off for tax purposes. The gains arising from disposal of used assets may be considered tax free. The effective tax rate is 35 per cent. The average cost of capital of the company is 12 per cent.

After appropriate analysis of cash flows, advise the company of the financial viability of the proposal.

Solution

Assessment of Financial Viability of Proposal: (₹ in lakh)

Incremental cash outflows	
Cost of new computer system	35
Less sale proceeds from drawing office equipment and furniture	9
	26
Incremental CFAT and NPV:	
(a) *Cost savings (years 1 - 6)*	
Reduction in design and draftsmanship costs	12
Less operation and maintenance costs	7
Cost savings (earnings) before taxes	5
Less taxes (0.35)	1.75
Earnings after taxes (CFAT)	3.25
(×) PV factor of annuity for 6 years (0.12)	× 4.111
Total PV of cost savings	13.36
(b) *Tax savings on account of depreciation*	
Cost of new computer system (₹35 lakh × 0.35)	12.25
(×) PV factor for year 1	× 0.892
Total PV	10.93
(c) *Terminal salvage value at the end of year, 6* (₹1 lakh × 0.507)	0.507
(d) Gross PV of CFAT [(a) + (b) + (c)]	24.797
Less cash outflows	26.000
NPV	(1.203)

Recommendation Since NPV is negative, the proposal is not financially viable.

P.24.4 A plastic manufacturer has under consideration the proposal of production of high quality plastic glasses. The necessary equipment to manufacture the glasses would cost ₹1 lakh and would last 5 years. The tax relevant rate of depreciation is 25 per cent on written down value. There is LO 24.3 LOD: M no other asset in this block. The expected salvage value is ₹10,000. The glasses can be sold at ₹4 each. Regardless of the level of production, the manufacturer will incur cash cost of ₹25,000 each year if the project is undertaken. The overhead costs allocated to this new line would be ₹5,000. The variable costs are estimated at ₹2 per glass. The manufacturer estimates it will sell about 75,000 glasses per year; the tax rate is 35 per cent. Should the proposed equipment be purchased? Assume 20 per cent cost of capital and additional working requirement, ₹50,000.

Solution

Cash outflows	
Cost of production equipment	₹1,00,000
Additional working capital requirement	50,000
	1,50,000

Determination of CFAT and NPV

Particulars	Years				
	1	*2*	*3*	*4*	*5*
Sales revenue (75,000 × 4)	₹3,00,000	₹3,00,000	₹3,00,000	₹3,00,000	₹3,00,000
Less costs:					
Variable costs (75,000 × 2)	1,50,000	1,50,000	1,50,000	1,50,000	1,50,000
Additional fixed costs	25,000	25,000	25,000	25,000	25,000
Depreciation (D)	25,000	18,750	14,062	10,547	Nil@
Earning before taxes	1,00,000	1,06,250	1,10,938	1,14,453	1,25,000
Less taxes	35,000	37,187	38,838	40,059	43,750
Earnings after taxes (EAT)	65,000	69,063	72,110	74,394	81,250
CFAT (EAT + D)	90,000	87,813	86,172	84,941	81,250
Add recovery of WC					50,000
Add salvage value (SV)					10,000
Add tax benefit on short term capital loss@@					7,574
					1,48,824
Multiplied by PV factor (0.20)	0.833	0.694	0.579	0.482	0.402
PV (CFAT × PV factor)	74,970	60,942	49,894	40,942	59,827
Total PV (t = 1 – 5)					2,86,575
Less cash outflows					1,50,000
NPV					1,36,575

@As the block consists of single asset, no depreciation is to be charged in the terminating year as the asset has been sold in the year.

@@(₹1,00,000 – ₹68,359 accumulated depreciation – ₹10,000, SV) × 0.35

Recommendation The company is advised to buy the proposed equipment to produce high quality plastic glasses.

P.24.5 BS Electronics Ltd is considering a proposal to replace one of its machines. In this connection, the following information is available. LO 24.3 LOD:M

The existing machine was bought 3 years ago for ₹10 lakh. It was depreciated at 25 per cent per annum on reducing balance basis. It has remaining useful life of 5 years, but its annual maintenance cost is expected to increase by ₹50,000 from the 6th year of its installation. Its present realisable value is ₹6 lakh.

The new machine costs ₹15 lakh and is subject to the same rate of depreciation. On sale after 5 years, it is expected to net ₹9 lakh. With the new machine, the annual operating costs (excluding depreciation)

are expected to decrease by ₹1 lakh. In addition, the new machine would increase productivity on account of which net revenues would increase by ₹1.5 lakh annually.

The tax rate applicable to the firm is 35 per cent and the cost of capital is 10 per cent.

Is the proposal financially viable? Advise the firm on the basis of NPV of the proposal.

Solution

Financial Evaluation Whether to Replace an Existing Machine (Using NPV Method)

(a) *Incremental Cash Outflows*

Cost of new machine	₹15,00,000
Less sale value of existing machine	6,00,000
	9,00,000

(b) *Determination of CFAT (Operating)*

Year	Incremental cash profits before taxes	Incremental depreciation	Taxable income (col. 2 – col. 3)	Taxes (0.35)	EAT (col. 4 – col. 5)	CFAT (col. 6 + col. 3)
1	₹2,50,000	₹2,25,000	₹25,000	₹8,750	₹16,250	₹2,41,250
2	2,50,000	1,68,750	81,250	28,438	52,812	2,21,562
3	3,00,000	1,26,563	1,73,437	60,703	1,12,734	2,39,297
4	3,00,000	94,922	2,05,078	71,777	1,33,301	2,28,223
5	3,00,000	71,191	2,28,809	8,0083	1,48,726	2,19,917

(c) *Determination of Net Present Value*

Year	CFAT	PV factor (0.10)	Total present value
1	₹2,41,250	0.909	₹2,19,296
2	2,21,562	0.826	1,83,010
3	2,39,297	0.751	1,79,712
4	2,28,223	0.683	1,55,876
5	2,19,917	0.620	1,36,349
5 (Net salvage value)	9,00,000*	0.620	5,58,000
Total present value			14,32,243
Less incremental cash outflows			9,00,000
Net present value			5,32,243

*at the beginning of year 6.

Recommendation Since NPV is positive, the company is advised to replace the existing machine.

Working Notes

(i) *WDV of existing machine in the beginning of year 4*

Initial cost of machine	₹10,00,000
Less depreciation @ 25% in year 1	2,50,000
WDV at beginning of year 2	7,50,000
Less depreciation @ 25% on WDV	1,87,500
WDV at beginning of year 3	5,62,500
Less depreciation @ 25% on WDV	1,40,625
WDV at beginning of year 4	4,21,875

(ii) *Depreciation base of new machine*

WDV of existing machine	4,21,875
Plus cost of the new machine	15,00,000
Less sale proceeds of existing machine	(6,00,000)
	13,21,875

(iii) *Base for incremental depreciation*

Depreciation base of new machine	13,21,875
Less depreciation base of existing machine	4,21,875
	9,00,000

(iv) *Incremental Depreciation (t = 1 – 5)*

Year	Incremental asset cost base	Depreciation @ 25% on WDVs
1	₹9,00,000	2,25,000
2	6,75,000	1,68,750
3	5,06,250	1,26,563
4	3,79,687	94,922
5	2,84,765	71,191

(v) *Incremental Cash Profits Before Taxes (in terms of* decrease in operating costs and increase in revenues) *Owing to the New Machine*

Year	Savings in operating costs	Increase in revenue before taxes	Incremental cash profit before taxes
1	₹1,00,000	₹1,50,000	₹2,50,000
2	1,00,000	1,50,000	2,50,000
3	1,50,000@	1,50,000	3,00,000
4	1,50,000	1,50,000	3,00,000
5	1,50,000	1,50,000	3,00,000

@Maintenance expenses of existing machine are expected to increase by ₹50,000 from 6th year of installation.

P.24.6 XYZ Company manufactures several different products. One of the principal products sells for ₹20 per unit. The sales manager of XYZ has stated repeatedly that he could sell more units of this product if they were available. To substantiate his claim, he conducted a market research study last year at a cost of ₹35,000. The study indicated that XYZ could sell 18,000 units of this product annually for the next five years. **LO 24.3** **LOD: D**

The equipment currently in use has the capacity to produce 11,000 units annually. The variable production costs are ₹9 per unit. The equipment has a value of ₹60,000 for tax purposes and a remaining useful life of five years. The salvage value of the equipment is negligible now and will be zero in five years.

A maximum of 20,000 units could be produced annually on the new machinery which can be purchased. The new equipment costs ₹2,50,000 and has an estimated useful life of five years with no salvage value. The production manager estimates that the new equipment would provide increased production efficiencies that would reduce the variable production costs to ₹7 per unit.

XYZ Company uses written down value method of depreciation on all of its equipments. The firm is subject to a 35 per cent tax and its after-tax cost of capital is 15 per cent.

The sales manager felt so strongly about the need for additional capacity that he attempted to prepare an economic justification for the equipment although this was not one of his responsibilities. His analysis, presented below, disappointed him because it did not justify acquiring the equipment.

Purchase price of new equipment		₹2,50,000
Disposal of existing equipment:		
Loss on disposal	₹60,000	
Less tax benefit (0.35)	21,000	39,000
Cost of market research study		35,000
Total investment		3,24,000

(*Contd.*)

(Contd.)

Contribution margin from product:	
Using the new equipment [18,000 × (₹20 – 7)]	2,34,000
Using the existing equipment [11,000 × (₹20 – 9)]	1,21,000
Increase in contribution	1,13,000
Less depreciation	50,000
Increase in before-tax income	63,000
Income tax (0.35)	22,050
Increase in income	40,950
Less cost of capital on the additional investment required (0.15 × ₹3,24,000)	48,600
Net annual return of proposed investment in new equipment	(7,650)

The controller of XYZ Company plans to prepare a discounted cash flow analysis for this investment proposal. He has asked you to prepare corrected calculations of: **(a)** the required investment in new equipment, **(b)** the recurring annual cash flows. Give your recommendation on the basis of above information and assuming 25 per cent depreciation on the block of assets to which the machine belongs.

Solution

Financial Evaluation Whether to Replace Existing Equipment

(a) *Required investment in new equipment:*	
Purchase price of new equipment	₹2,50,000
(b) *Recurring annual cash flows:*	
(i) Depreciation base of new machine:	
Book value of existing machine	60,000
Add cost of new machine	2,50,000
	3,10,000
(ii) Base for incremental depreciation:	
Depreciation base of new machine	3,10,000
Less book value of existing machine	60,000
	2,50,000

(iii) *Incremental depreciation (t = 1 – 5):*

Year	*Incremental WDV base*	*Depreciation*
1	₹2,50,000	₹62,500
2	1,87,500	46,875
3	1,40,625	35,156
4	1,05,469	26,367
5	79,102	19,775

Note Unabsorbed depreciation is ₹59,327 (₹79,102 – ₹19,775); tax advantage on this will be available in future years.

(ii) *Determination of CFAT and NPV*

Particulars	*Years*				
	1	*2*	*3*	*4*	*5*
Incremental contribution	₹1,13,000	₹1,13,000	₹1,13,000	₹1,13,000	₹1,13,000
Less incremental depreciation	62,500	46,875	35,156	26,367	19,775
Incremental taxable income	50,500	66,125	77,844	86,633	93,225

(Contd.)

(Contd.)

Less taxes	17,675	23,144	27,245	30,322	32,629
Earnings after taxes	32,825	42,981	50,599	56,311	60,596
CFAT (EAT + Depreciation)	95,325	89,856	85,755	82,678	80,371
(x) PV factor (0.15)	0.870	0.756	0.658	0.572	0.497
Present value	82,933	67,931	56,427	47,292	39,944
Total present value					2,94,527
Less purchase price of new equipment					2,50,000
Net present value					44,527

Recommendation The company is advised to replace the existing equipment.

REVIEW QUESTIONS

LOD: Easy

RQ.24.1(a) Indicate whether the following statements are true or false.

LO 24.2,3

(i) Two mutually exclusive projects (A and B) have been evaluated. Project A has an NPV of ₹8 lakh and an IRR of 16 per cent; Project B has NPV of ₹7 lakh but has IRR or 18 per cent. Since Project B has higher IRR, it should be selected.

(ii) The cost of capital for new projects is 15 per cent. Two competing projects (X and Y) respectively have IRRs of 14 per cent and 12 per cent respectively; since IRR of project X is higher, it should be selected.

(iii) Two competing projects have the following NPVs: Project X, + ₹5 lakh (with initial outlay of ₹25 lakh) and Project Y, + ₹4,20,000 (with initial outlay of ₹20,00,000). The company should opt for project X as it has higher NPV.

(iv) A project requires an initial investment of ₹10,00,000. The estimated cash inflows from the project are as follows: ₹3 lakh (year 1), ₹1 lakh (year 2), ₹3 lakh (year 3), ₹6 lakh (Year 4) and ₹4 lakh (year 5). The pay back of the project is 4 years.

(v) A project requires an investment of ₹20 lakh. The estimated profit after tax for years 1–5 are: ₹3 lakh, ₹3 lakh, ₹3 lakh, ₹6 lakh and ₹8 lakh. The accounting rate of return is 21 per cent

(vi) In the case of independent investment projects, if the NPV of the project is zero, IRR is equal to cost of capital.

(vii) A company has evaluated 3 investment proposals under IRR method, yielding different rates of return. Though the IRR values are varying, reinvestment rate of intermediate cash inflows is assumed to be the same for all these 3 proposals.

(viii) Since IRR is expressed in percentage figure, it is the best method for evaluating capital budgeting projects.

(ix) The more distant the CFAT, the higher is the present value of such cash flows.

(x) NPV is the best method of evaluating long-term investment proposals.

(b) Fill in the following blanks:

(xi) ____________ present value tables can be used only when cashflows are uniform to determine NPV.

(xii) In the case of mixed stream of cash flows, __________ present value tables are used to determine NPV.

(xiii) ____________ determines the number of years required to recover initial investment outlay.

(xiv) In the case of __________ investment proposals, IRR and NPV method provides the same result.

(xv) In the case of conflict in ranking. ________ method provides better result than ________ method.

[Answers: (i) False, (ii) False, (iii) True, (iv) False, (v) False, (vi) True, (vii) False, (viii) False, (ix) False, (x) True, (xi) Annuity, (xii) simple, (xiii) Payback method, (xiv) independent, (xv) NPV, IRR.]

RQ.24.2 Why is it important to evaluate capital budgeting projects on the basis of after-tax cash incremental flows? Why not use accounting data instead of cash flow? LO 24.2

RQ.24.3 What are the components of net cash outlay in the capital budgeting decision? At what time is such an outlay incurred in the case of conventional cash flows? LO 24.2

RQ.24.4 What is pay back period? Also, discuss the utility of the pay back period in determining the internal rate of return. LO 24.3

RQ.24.5 What does the profitability index signify? What is the criterion for judging the worth of investments in the capital budgeting technique based on the profitability index? LO 24.3

RQ.24.6 A large-sized chemical company is considering investing in a project that costs ₹5,00,000. The estimated salvage value is zero; tax rate is 35 per cent. The company uses straight line method of depreciation for tax purposes and the proposed project has cash flows before tax (CFBT) as follows: LO 24.3

Year	*CFBT*
1	₹1,00,000
2	1,00,000
3	1,50,000
4	1,50,000
5	2,50,000

Determine the following: (i) Payback period and (ii) Average rate of return.

RQ.24.7 XYZ Ltd., whose cost of capital is 10 per cent, is considering two mutually exclusive projects, X and Y, the details of which are: LO 24.3

		Project X	*Project Y*
Investment		₹70,000	₹70,000
Cash inflow:	year 1	10,000	50,000
	2	20,000	40,000
	3	30,000	20,000
	4	45,000	10,000
	5	60,000	10,000
		1,65,000	1,30,000

Compute the NPV, profitability index and IRR for the two projects.

RQ.24.8 A company wants to purchase a plant for its expanding operations. The desired plant is available at ₹3,00,000 in cash or ₹4,50,000 to be paid in 5 equal annual instalments due at the end of each year. Assuming the required rate of return of 15 per cent, which option should the company exercise? Ignore taxes. LO 24.3

LOD: Medium

RQ.24.9 How should working capital and sunk costs be treated in analysing investment opportunities? Explain with suitable examples. LO 24.2

RQ.24.10 Explain clearly the concept of block of assets *vis-a-vis* depreciation in the context of replacement situations of capital budgeting. LO 24.2

RQ.24.11 It is said that only cash costs are relevant for capital budgeting decision. However, depreciation which is a non-cash cost is a prominent part of cash flow analysis for such an investment decision. How do you explain this paradox? **LO 24.2**

RQ.24.12 What are the critical factors to be observed while making replacement investment decision? **LO 24.2,3**

RQ.24.13 Do the profitability index and the NPV criterion of evaluating investment proposals lead to the same acceptance-rejection and ranking decisions? **LO 24.3**

RQ.24.14 One of three projects of a company is doing poorly and is being considered for replacement. The projects are expected to require ₹2,00,000 each, have an estimated life of 5 years, 4 years, and 3 years respectively, and have no salvage value. The required rate of return is 10 per cent. The anticipated cash flows after taxes (CFAT) for the three projects are as follows: **LO 24.3**

Year	CFAT		
	A	B	C
1	₹50,000	₹80,000	₹1,00,000
2	50,000	80,000	1,00,000
3	50,000	80,000	10,000
4	50,000	30,000	—
5	1,90,000	—	—

(i) Rank each project applying the methods of payback, average rate of return, net present value, and internal rate of return.

(ii) Recommend the project to be adopted and give reasons.

RQ.24.15 A company is planning to purchase a machine to meet the increased demand for its products in the market. The machine costs ₹50,000 and has no salvage value. The expected life of the machine is 5 years, and the company employs straight-line method of depreciation for tax purposes. The estimated earnings after taxes are ₹5,000 each year for 5 years. The after-tax required rate of return of the company is 12 per cent. **LO 24.3**

Determine the IRR. Also, find the payback period and obtain the IRR from it. How do you compare this IRR with the one directly estimated? What are the reasons for the differences between the two IRRs so estimated?

RQ.24.16 A textile company is considering two mutually exclusive investment proposals for its expansion programme. Proposal A requires an initial investment of ₹7,50,000 and yearly operating costs of ₹50,000. Proposal B requires an initial investment of ₹5,00,000 and yearly operating costs of ₹1,00,000. The life of the equipment used in both the investment proposals will be 12 years with no salvage value; depreciation is on straight-line basis for tax purposes. The anticipated increase in revenues is ₹1,50,000 per year in both the investment proposals. The tax rate is 35 per cent and cost of capital, 15 per cent. **LO 24.3**

Which investment proposal should be undertaken by the company?

LOD: Difficult

RQ.24.17 Suppose a firm is considering replacing an old machine with a new one. The firm does not anticipate that any new revenues will be created by the replacement since demand for the product generation by both the machines is the same. However, in the CFAT work sheet used in evaluating the proposal, the analyst shows positive CFBT in the operating cash flow section. What creates operating CFBT in this situation? **LO 24.2,3**

RQ.24.18 Royal Industries Ltd. is considering the replacement of one of its moulding machines. The existing machine is in good operating condition but is smaller than required if the firm is to expand its operations. The machine is 5 years old, has a current salvage value of ₹30,000 and a remaining depreciable life of 10 years. The machine was originally purchased for ₹75,000 and is being depreciated at ₹5,000 per year for tax purposes. **LO 24.3**

The new machine will cost ₹1,50,000 and will be depreciated on a straight-line basis for tax purposes over 10 years, with no salvage value. The management anticipates that with the expanded operations, there will be a need of additional net working capital of ₹30,000. The new machine will allow the firm to expand current operations and thereby, increase annual sales from ₹4,00,000 to ₹4,40,000; annual operating costs from ₹2,00,000 to ₹2,10,000. The company's tax rate is 35 per cent and its cost of capital is 10 per cent. Should the company replace its existing machine? Assume that the loss on sale of existing machine can be claimed as short-term capital loss in the current year itself.

ANSWERS

24.6 **(i)** 4.18 years, **(ii)** 13% (accounting basis) **(iii)** 14.66%, **(iv)** – ₹3,477.50.

24.7 NPV: ₹46,135 (Project X), ₹36,550 (Project Y); Profitability index: 1.659 (X), 1.522 (Y); IRR: 27.2% (X), 37% (Y).

24.8 Cash option.

24.14 **(i)** Ranking on the basis of PB method: Projects C,B,A (Rank 1,2,3); ARR: Projects A,C,B (Rank 1,2,3); NPV:Projects A,B (Rank 1,2); IRR: projects A,B (Rank 1,2) **(iii)** 1.0, NPV is negative, **(iv)** Project A.

24.15 PB period 3.333 years, IRR 15.4%, IRR with the help of PB period, 30%. The life of the project is not twice that of the PB period.

24.16 Proposal B, PV of savings in proposal A is ₹2,15,805 as against the additional cost of ₹2,50,000.

24.18 Yes. (NPV – ₹9,915).

[Comprehensive solutions to all numerical review questions are available on the companion website: http://www.mhhe.com/khan_jain_ma7e]

CASES

24.C.1 (Hiring Vs Buying) Tel Samrat is a large Indian conglomerate with interest in petroleum, petroleum products, textiles, telecom and life sciences. It has a refinery in Ankleshwar in Gujarat. The refinery has a peak capacity for producing 27 lakh tons of finished petroleum products. Ankaleshwar is a major oil terminal with sophisticated state of art facility for docking of very large crude carrier (VLCC) and ultra large crude carrier (VLCC). Tel Samrat imports crude oil from the Middle East for its refinery operations and has its own fleet of oil tankers for this purpose.

Tel Samrat has been availing of the services of rented oil barges from the British Company, MAR-OIL for loading fuel oil for running its tankers in Ankaleshwar. MAR-OIL has an Indian subsidy–MAR OIL INDIA (MOI) which provides the barge services in India. Tel Samrat pays MOI for its services at the rate of ₹40,000 per hour to cover running and maintenance costs. On an average, Tel Samrat has been hiring barges for 90 hours per month for its fleet of 15 tankers. However, the contract with MOI stipulates payment for at least 100 hours.

An alternative to hiring the barges from MOI is to acquire oil barges. A Japanese firm Ichikawa Harima Heavy Industries (IHI) is offering two oil barges for 40 million Yen with a service life of 10 years. The barges would have a salvage value of 4 million Yens. [Exchange rate: Current, ₹2.5/Yen; After 10 years, ₹5/Yen).

The insurance cost for the barges would be 1 per cent per year for 1—5 years and 2 per cent for years 6—10 as per the Loyd Registrar of Shipping (LRS) regulations. The running and maintenance costs for the two barges would be ₹20,00,000 per year for the first 5 years and ₹40,00,000 annually for the next 5 years.

The yearly employee/staff/crew cost for the first 5 years would be as given below:

Rank	*Number*	*Monthly salary*
Captain	1	₹80,000
Chief Engineer	1	80,000
Chief Officer	1	60,000
Duty Engineer	1	60,000
Oil man	1	15,000
Seaman	1	15,000
Shore staff	2	14,000
		3,24,000

After 5 years, the salary of employees/crew/staff would increase by 10 per cent.

REQUIRED

Should Tel Smart acquire the two barges from IHI? Or should it continue availing of the services of MOI? Assume 12 per cent required rate of return.

Solution

Financial Evaluation of Hiring Vs Buying of Barges

	Years	
Incremental Cash Outflows:	*1–5*	*6–10*
Present scenario (Hiring of barges)	₹4,80,00,000	₹4,80,00,000
Proposed scenario (Buying of barges)	1,48,80,000[1]	1,82,80,000[1]
Cost savings (EBT)	3,31,20,000	2,97,20,000
Less tax (0.375)	1,24,20,000	1,11,45,000
EAT	2,07,00,000	1,85,75,000
Add back depreciation	80,00,000	80,00,000
Savings in Cost (CFAT)	2,87,00,000	2,65,75,000

Determination of NPV:

Year	*CFAT*	*PV factor (0.12)*	*Total PV*
1–5	₹2,87,00,000	3.605	₹10,34,63,500
6–10	2,65,75,000	2.045@	5,43,45,875
10 salvage value	(–20,00,000) (4 million Yen × ₹5)	0.322	(–6,44,000)
Total			15,71,65,375
Less cash outflow (cost of barges) (40 million Yen × ₹2.5)			10,00,00,000
NPV			5,71,65,375

@PV annuity for 6–0 years = PV for annuity for 10 years – PV of annuity for 5 years = 5.65 – 3.605 = 2.045

1 Cost estimates

	Year 1–5	Year 6–10
Running and maintenance cost	₹20,00,000	₹40,00,000
Employee cost (₹3,24,000 × 12)	38,80,000	42,80,000*
Insurance cost	10,00,000	20,00,000
Depreciation (₹10,00,00,000 ÷ 20,00,000) ÷10	80,00,000	80,00,000
Total	1,48,80,000	1,82,80,000

*(₹3,24,000 × 1.10 × 12)

Decision: Since the NPV is positive (₹5,71,65,375), Tel Samrat should buy the two barges from IHI. It should stop hiring them from MOI.

24.C.2 (Net Present Value) Choolah Chimney Ltd (CCL) is a leading manufacturer of items used in kitchens such as gas stoves, electric chimneys, ovens and so on. It has grown significantly under the CEO Vivek Razdan's dynamic leadership. In line with his belief to enhance competitiveness by using research and development for launching innovative products in the market, the CCL has recently developed a zero Maintenance Electric Chimney (known as Zimney) which is ideally suited for Indian cooking. The research and development cost of Zimney amounts to ₹20,00,000.

To gauge the market prospects for Zimney, a market survey was conducted by Bazar Gyani, the V.P., Marketing, at an estimated cost of ₹5,00,000. The results of the survey were very positive showing a significant demand for Zimney. The survey report also indicated that Zimney could capture 8 per cent of the current market size of 1,00,000 units of gas electric chimney. Considering the growth of satellite towns/cities and residential colonies, the market is expected to grow at 2 per cent annually. The VP, Marketing suggested to the CEO that a market penetration pricing strategy would be most suitable and Zimney should be priced at ₹5,000 per unit in the initial year of the launch. The price could be raised in subsequent years by 5 per cent annually. The marketing and administrative costs are expected to be ₹4,00,000 per year.

The CCL is presently using 6 machines acquired 3 years ago at a cost of ₹10,00,000 each, having a useful life of 7 years, with no salvage value. These machines are currently being used for manufacturing other types of chimneys. They could be sold for ₹2,00,000 per machine with a removal cost of ₹30,000 for each.

The machine to manufacture Zimney is available in that market for ₹1,00,00,000 with a useful life of 4 years and salvage value of ₹10,00,000. It can produce other types of chimneys also.

The new machine, being state of the art technology would improve the productivity of the workers by 5 per cent annually as well reduce the unit variable cost of manufacture to ₹600. Exhibit 1 summarises the labour cost with the existing machine and the new equipment.

Category	Existing		New Machine/Equipment	
	Number	Monthly salary	Number	Monthly salary
Skilled labour	20	₹4,000	15	₹4,000
Maintenance men	2	6,000	1	6,000
Floor managers	3	8,000	2	8,000

The maintenance costs currently amount to 1,00,000 per year (existing machine). They would total ₹70,000 with the new equipment. The net working capital required to start production of Zimney would be ₹60,00,000.

The policy of CCL is to pay five months salary as compensation in case of lay-off of employees.

REQUIRED

Should the CCL launch the Zimney. Assume the following: (i) Tax, 35 per cent (ii) Required rate of return, 14 per cent and (iii) Straight line depreciation for the tax purposes.

Solution

Financial Evaluation of Proposal to launch Zimney

(A) Incremental Cash Outflow (t = 0):

1. Cost of new machine	₹1,00,00,000
2. Less sale proceeds of existing machines[a]	(10,20,000)
3. Less tax benefits on loss of sale of existing machines[b]	(8,42,999)
4. Cost of laying-off workers[c]	1,70,000
5. Additional working capital	60,00,000
	1,43,07,001

[a]Sale proceeds of existing machines [(6 × ₹2,00,000, sale price – (6 × ₹30,000, removal cost)] = ₹10,20,000

[b]Tax benefits on loss of existing machine

1. Book value of existing machine [(6 × ₹10,00,000) – (3 × ₹8,57142, annual depreciation i.e. ₹60,00,000 ÷ 7)] = ₹60,00,000 – ₹25,71,428 = ₹34,28,571.
2. Loss on sale of existing machine [book value, ₹34,28,571 – ₹10,20,000, sale proceeds] = ₹24,08,571.
3. Tax benefit (₹24,08,571 x 0.35) = ₹8,42,999.

[c]Cost of lay-off:

1. Skilled labour 5 × ₹4,000 × 5 (months)	=	₹1,00,000
2. Floor manager = 1 × ₹8,000 × 5	=	40,000
3. Maintenance person = 1 × ₹6,000 × 5	=	30,000
		1,70,000

(B) Incremental Cash Inflows: (t = 1 — 4):

Particulars	*Year* 1	2	3	4
1. Sales revenue[a]	₹4,00,00,000	₹4,28,40,000	₹4,58,81,640	₹4,91,34,408
2. Add savings in maintenance cost[b]	30,000	30,000	30,000	30,000
3. Add savings in labour cost[c]	4,08,000	4,08,000	4,08,000	4,08,000
4. Less variable cost[d]	(52,00,000)	(55,40,800)	(59,05,796)	(62,96,663)
5. Less incremental depreciation[e]	(13,92,858)	(13,92,858)	(13,92,858)	(13,92,858)
6. EBT	3,38,45142	3,63,44,342	3,90,20,986	4,18,82,887
7. Less tax (0.35)	(1,18,45,799)	(1,27,20,519)	(1,36,57,346)	(1,46,59,010)
8. EAT	2,19,99,342	2,36,23,822	2,53,63,640	2,72,23,876
9. Add incremental depreciation	13,92,858	13,92,858	13,92,858	13,92,858
10. CFAT	2,33,92,200	2,50,16,680	2,67,56,498	2,86,16,734
11. Release of working capital	—	—	—	60,00,000
12. Total	2,33,92,200	2,50,16,680	2,67,56,498	3,46,16,734

[a]Sales revenue : Year	1 (0.08 × 1,00,000 × ₹5,000)	=	₹4,00,00,000
	2 (0.08 × 1,02,000 × ₹5,250)	=	4,28,40,000
	3 (0.08 × 1,04,040 × ₹5,512)	=	4,58,81,640
	4 (0.08 × 1,06,120 × ₹5,787)	=	4,91,34,408

[b]Savings in maintenance cost (₹1,00,000, existing – ₹70,000 proposed) = ₹30,000

[c]Savings in labour cost:

1	Existing:	Skilled labour (20 × ₹4,000 × 12 months)	₹9,60,000	
		Floor manager (3 × ₹8,000 × 12)	2,88,000	
		Maintenance (2 × ₹6,000 × 12)	1,44,000	₹13,92,000
2	New:	Skilled labour (15 × ₹4,000 × 12)	7,20,000	
		Floor manager (2 × ₹8,000 × 12)	1,92,000	
		Maintenance (1 × ₹6,000 × 12)	72,000	9,84,000
				4,08,000

[d]Variable cost and general administrative costs:

Year			
1	[(0.08 × 1,00,000 × ₹600) + ₹4,00,000]	=	₹52,00,000
2	[(0.08 × 1,02,000 × ₹630) + ₹4,00,000]	=	55,40,000
3	[(0.08 × 1,04,040 × ₹661) + ₹4,00,000]	=	59,05,796
4	[(0.08 × 1,06,120 × ₹694) + ₹4,00,000]	=	62,96,663

[e]Incremental depreciation:

1. New equipment (₹1,00,00,000 – ₹10,00,000) ÷ 4	₹22,50,000
2. Existing (Book value, ₹34,28,571 – 0) ÷ 4	8,57,142
	13,92,858

(C) Computation of NPV

Year	*Incremental cash inflows*	*PV factor (0.14)*	*Total PV*
1	₹2,33,92,200	0.877	₹2,05,14,959
2	2,50,16,680	0.769	1,92,37,826
3	2,67,56,498	0.675	1,80,60,636
4	3,46,16,734	0.592	2,04,93,106
Total			7,83,06,527
Less Incremental cash outflow			1,43,07,001
NPV			6,39,99,526

Decision: The Chola Chimney should launch the Zimney

NOTE:

The research and development cost of Zimney (₹20,00,000) and expenses incurred on market survey (₹5,00,000) are sunk cost and, therefore, irrelevant for analysis.

24.C.3 (Opening of Show Room Vs Online Shopping on Website) Shobhit Kaushik is proprietor of a small firm SaiDiamond.com dealing in manufacturing and retailing of certified diamond jewellry handcrafted in 18 K hallmarked gold. Presently, she operates her business from home. Most of the customers are ladies who are referred through word of mouth from existing clients. The website is a media to explore prospective customers and interaction between customers and view jewellry designs at their homes, and exchange of information.

In spite of recession in the economy, there is good demand for diamond jewellry, from working ladies and housewives who like ornaments and purchase it as an asset to hedge inflation, since there is an upward trend in the price of gold in the recent years. The customers are attracted due to superior diamond quality and excellent designs, making and finishing of jewellry articles and at a very reasonable prices as compared to showrooms in the local market due to negligible selling and administrative expenses, fixed cost, other overheads and lower inventory cost, operating from home. Her income statement for the current year is summarised in Schedule I.

SCHEDULE I Income Statement of Shobhit Kaushik for the current year

Sales revenue, 150 articles, ₹16,000 per article		₹24,00,000
Cost of goods sold:		
Diamond, 120 carat, (₹9,000 per carat)	₹10,80,000	
Gold 480 grams, (₹13,500 per 10 gram)	6,48,000	
Labour, (₹150 per gram of gold)	72,000	
Hallmarking, (₹25 per gram of gold)	12,000	
Certification charges, (₹300 per carat of diamond)	36,000	18,48,000
Gross profit		5,52,000
Selling expenses and other overheads	60,000	
Insurance premium	84,000	
Registration fee for BIS approved lab for Hallmarking license	18,000	1,62,000
EBIT (earnings before interest and taxes)		3,90,000
Less Interest		72,000
EBT (earnings before taxes)		3,18,000
Taxes (0.30)		95,400
EAT(earnings after taxes)		2,22,600

There are unfulfilled orders due to small infrastructure and lack of funds for maintaining sufficient inventory. Most of the work of manufacturing jewellry is outsourced manually through artisans. There is negligible machinery required for manufacturing. Most of the capital is required for purchasing raw material like gold and diamonds. Banks are reluctant to give loans for working capital and inventory.

Because of the potential in the market and growing demand, Shobhit suggested to her husband, Sanjeev Agarwal, to help her open a diamond jewellry showroom in the market. The following costs would need to be incurred, for which she can get loan from the Prime Minister Employment Guaranty Scheme (PMEGS), which offers a subsidy of ₹5,00,000 after five years. The associated revenues and cost forecasts are listed in Schedule II.

SCHEDULE II Revenue and Cost Forecasts

Renovation of showroom	₹5,00,000
Additional working capital	25,00,000
Car	4,00,000
Sales revenue	54,00,000
Variable cost (Cost of gold, diamond, labour, HM, certification)	33,00,000
Fixed cost (Lease rent, salary of staff, insurance, electricity, registration fee for BIS approved lab for Hallmarking license)	7,25,000

Assume 15 per cent growth in sales revenue every year, annual increase in variable cost, 8 per cent every year and increase in fixed cost 6 per cent every year. The car would be depreciated using straight line depreciation over its 5-year useful life. It would have a salvage value of ₹45,000. Assume 12 per cent cost of capital.

However, Mr Agarwal is not willing to take risk of opening a showroom since he has to leave his job where he is earning ₹40,000 per month with 15 per cent hike every year. He suggests instead the alternative of developing a website for online shopping. He thinks that sales revenue can be increased by 15 per cent in one year and 20 per cent in every subsequent year. The annual increase in variable and fixed costs would be 8 per cent and 6 per cent respectively by developing the web site for online shopping at a cost of ₹50,000 and annual maintenance cost of ₹18,000.

Required: Shobhit Kaushik submits two alternatives to a financial consultant, Vijay Kumar, for advise, whether they should open a showroom in market or expand business and increase the sale by further developing website for online shopping. The financial consultant carries out a detailed financial analysis and makes his recommendations for their consideration (Schedule III).

Solution

SCHEDULE III Evaluation of Alternative Proposals Using NPV Method

Option 1: *Open Showroom*

(A) Cash Outflow (t = 0):

Renovation and lease charges of showroom	₹5,00,000
Additional working capital	25,00,000
Car	4,00,000
Total	34,00,000

(B) Cash Inflow After Taxes (CFAT) (t = 1 — 5)

	Year-end				
	1	*2*	*3*	*4*	*5*
Sales revenue	₹54,00,000	₹62,10,000	₹71,41,500	₹82,12,725	₹94,44,634
Less costs:					
Variable cost	33,00,000	35,64,000	38,49,120	41,57,050	44,89,614
Fixed cost	7,25,000	7,68,500	8,14,610	8,63,486	9,15,296
Loss of opportunity of leaving job for Mr Agarwal	4,80,000	5,52,000	6,34,800	7,30,020	8,39,523
Depreciation of car	80,000	80,000	80,000	80,000	80,000
Total cost	45,85,000	49,64,500	53,78,530	58,30,556	63,24,433
EBT	8,15,000	12,45,500	17,62,970	23,82,169	31,20,201
Less Taxes (0.30)	2,44,500	3,73,650	5,28,891	7,14,651	9,36,060
EAT	5,70,500	8,71,850	12,34,079	16,67,518	21,84,141
Add Depreciation	80,000	80,000	80,000	80,000	80,000
CFAT (EAT + Depreciation	6,50,500	9,51,850	13,14,079	17,47,518	22,64,141
Subsidy at end of year – 5					5,00,000
Release of working capital					25,00,000
Salvage value of car					45,000
					53,09,141

DETERMINATION OF NET PRESENT VALUE

Year-end	*CFAT*	*PV Factor (0.12)*	*Total PV*
1	₹6,50,500	0.893	₹5,80,897
2	9,51,850	0.797	7,58,624
3	13,14,079	0.712	9,35,624
4	17,47,518	0.636	11,11,422
5	53,09,141	0.567	30,10,283

Gross present value	63,96,850
Less Cash outflow	34,00,000
NPV	29,96,850

Option 2: *Develop Website for Online Shopping*

Cash Outflow (t = 0):	
Development of website	50,000
Total	50,000

Cash Inflow After Taxes (CFAT) (t = 1 — 5)

	Year-end				
	1	*2*	*3*	*4*	*5*
Sales revenue	₹27,60,000	₹33,12,000	₹39,74,400	₹47,69,280	₹57,23,136
Less costs:					
Variable cost	19,95,840	21,55,507	23,27,947	25,14,184	27,15,318
Fixed cost	1,71,720	1,82,023	1,92,945	2,04,521	2,16,793
Annual maintenance contract	18,000	18,000	18,000	18,000	18,000
Total cost	21,85,560	23,55,530	25,38,892	27,36,705	29,50,111
EBT	5,74,440	9,56,470	14,35,508	20,32,575	27,73,025
Less Taxes (0.30)	1,72,332	2,86,941	4,30,652	6,09,773	8,31,908
EAT/CFAT	4,02,108	6,69,529	10,04,8556	14,22,802	19,41,117

Determination of NPV

Year-end	*CFAT*	*PV Factor (0.12)*	*Total PV*
1	₹4,02,108	0.893	₹3,59,082
2	6,69,529	0.797	5,33,615
3	10,04,856	0.712	7,15,457
4	14,22,802	0.636	9,04,902
5	19,41,117	0.567	11,00,613
Gross present value			36,13,669
Less Cash outflow			50,000
Net Present Value			35,63,669

Recommendation: As NPV in both the options is positive, both the options are financially viable. However, the alternative proposals are mutually exclusive. The NPV in Option 2 is higher than in option 1, in spite of higher sales in Option 1, mainly due to higher fixed cost. Other qualitative aspects also merits consideration. Mr Agarwal need not leave his respectable job in the times of economic slowdown. There could be risk of investing capital in showroom, due to recession in the economy and slowdown in the market, as the project is to be financed through PMEGS. For these reasons, the proposal to open a showroom in market should be rejected. The proposal of Mr Agawral to expand business and increase sales revenue by developing the website for online shopping is commendable.

23.C.4 (Acquisition of Insta Coffee) The Coco Express Ltd is a leading manufacturer of items such as coffee maker, tea maker, and so on. It has recently developed a electric coffee maker "Insta Coffee" with an all-inclusive cost of ₹20,00,000.

A market survey was conducted by the marketing manager, Kaushik Dey, with a budget of ₹5,00,000 to gauge the interest of the buyers in "Insta Coffee". The report estimated that "Insta Coffee" could have a market share of 8 per cent considering the fast growth of satellite cities and residential societies. The domestic market size for electric coffee maker machines, which is 1,00,000 units at present, is expected to grow at 2 per cent annually. It was suggested that "Insta Coffee" should not be priced more than ₹5,000 per unit in the initial year of its launch. The price could be raised by 5 per cent annually in subsequent years. The annual marketing and administrative costs are expected to be ₹4,00,000.

The production manager, Shashank Bajpai, worked out that Coco Express Ltd is presently using six machines acquired three years ago at the cost of ₹10,00,000 each having a useful life of seven years each, with no salvage value. These machines were currently being used for manufacturing conventional types of coffee maker. They can be sold for ₹2,00,000 each with an estimated removal cost of ₹30,000 each.

Shashank Bajpai suggested that there is mention about a new machine in a popular magazine "Future-Machines", which would be required for the production of "Insta Coffee". They estimated that Coco Express Ltd would have to invest additional ₹1,00,00,000 in equipment to make "Insta Coffee". It is capable of producing other types of coffee maker also. It is expected to have useful life of four years and salvage value of ₹10,00,000. Shashank, being an experienced person, sensed that the new machine would not only require fewer people to operate but the variable cost to produce Insta Coffee would also decline to ₹600 per unit. There will be reduction/lay offs in labour in this case. The company would have to pay five months salary as compensation in case any employee had to be laid off. The variable costs, however, are unexpected to rise 5 per cent annually. The production manager furnished the following additional data:

	Existing machine	*New machine*	*Savings (annual)*	*Lay off costs*
Direct labour (₹4,000 per month)	20	15	₹2,40,000	₹1,00,000
Floor manager (₹8,000 per month)	3	2	96,000	40,000
Maintenance person (₹6,000 per month)	2	1	72,000	30,000
Maintenance cost	₹1,00,000	₹70,000	30,000	

The CEO of Coco Express has desired the finance manager, Sandeep Kumar, to prepare a detailed financial report for the proposal of the production manger. The financial report prepared by him is summarised below:

➢ Forecasted market capacity (units)	:	1,00,000
➢ Forecasted sales of Insta Coffee (units)	:	8,000
➢ Annual sales growth rate (%)	:	2
➢ Variable cost per unit (₹)	:	600
➢ Annual variable cost rise per unit (%)	:	5
➢ Selling price per unit (₹)	:	5,000
➢ Annual price rise (%)		5

REQUIRED: The CEO of Coco Express Ltd seeks your opinion as a financial consultant on the viability of the proposal. Should, in your opinion, the Coco Express Ltd acquire the Insta Coffee? The Coco Express is in 35 per cent tax bracket and uses straight line method of depreciation and the same is accepted for tax purposes. Its required rate of return is 14 per cent.

Solution

Incremental Cash Outflow (t = 0)

Cost of new machine	₹1,00,00,000
Additional working capital	60,00,000
Sales proceeds of existing machines	(10,20,000)
Tax benefits on loss on sale of existing machines (working note 3)	(8,43,000)
Cost of lay off (after tax)	1,10,500
Total	1,42,47,500

Computation of CFAT (t = 1 — 4)

Year	*1*	*2*	*3*	*4*
Sales revenue(Working note 1)	₹4,00,00,000	₹4,28,40,000	₹4,58,84,699	₹4,91,40,120
Savings in maintenance cost	30,000	30,000	30,000	30,000
Savings in labour costs	4,08,000	4,08,000	4,08,000	4,08,000
Total income (a)	4,04,38,000	4,32,78,000	4,63,22,699	4,95,78,120
Variable costs (1)	48,00,000	51,40,800	55,09,826	59,00,550
Administrative and marketing costs	4,00,000	4,00,000	4,00,000	4,00,000
Incremental depreciation (Working note 2)	13,92,857	13,92,8587	13,92,857	13,92,857
Total costs (b)	65,92,857	69,33,657	73,02,683	76,93,407
EBIT (a – b)	3,38,45,143	3,63,44,343	3,90,20,016	4,18,84,713
Tax (0.35)	1,18,45,800	1,27,20,520	1,36,57,006	1,46,59,650
EAT	2,19,99,343	2,36,23,823	2,53,63,010	2,72,25,063
CFAT (EAT + Depreciation)	2,33,92,200	2,50,16,680	2,67,55,867	2,86,17,920

COMPUTATION OF NPV:

	CFAT	*PVT (0.14)*	*PV*
Year 1	₹2,33,92,200	0.877	₹2,05,14,959
2	2,50,16,680	0.769	1,92,37,827
3	2,67,55,867	0.675	1,80,60,210
4	2,86,17,920	0.592	1,69,41,809
Working capital released 4	60,00,000	0.592	35,52,000
Salvage value	10,00,000	0.592	5,92,000
Gross PV			7,88,98,805
Cash outflows			1,42,47,500
NPV			6,46,51,305

RECOMMENDATION The proposal is financially viable. The Coco Express Ltd should "accept the proposal" to acquire Insta Coffee as the NPV of the project under consideration is positive and quite substantial.

WORKING NOTES

1. Forecasted Sales and Costs:

Years	*1*	*2*	*3*	*4*
1. Sales (units)	8,000	8,160	8,323	8,490
2. Selling price	₹5,000	₹5,250	₹5,513	₹5,788
3. Total sales (1 × 2)	4,00,00,000	4,28,40,000	4,58,84,699	4,91,40,120
4. Variable cost per unit	600	630	662	695
5. Total variable cost (1 × 4)	48,00,000	51,40,800	55,09,826	59,00,550
6. Fixed administrative cost	4,00,000	4,00,000	4,00,000	4,00,000

2. Computation of Incremental Depreciation:

Depreciation of Existing Machine:	
Cost of existing machine (6 x ₹10,00,000)	₹60,00,000
Economic useful life (years)	7
Depreciation per year (₹60,00,000 ÷ 7)	8,57,143
Accumulated depreciation (₹8,57,143 × 3)	25,71,429
Depreciation on New Machines:	
Price of new machine	₹1,00,00,000
Useful life (years)	4
Salvage value	10,00,000
Depreciation (₹90,00,000 ÷ 4)	22,50,000
Incremental depreciation (₹22,50,000 – ₹8,57,143)	13,92,857

3. Tax Benefit Due to Loss on Sale of Existing Equipments:

Book value of existing machine ₹(60,00,000 – 25,71,429)	₹34,28,571
Less Proceeds from sale of existing machine ₹(2,00,000 – 30,000) × 6	10,20,000
Short term capital loss	(24,08,571)
Tax benefit (loss × 0.35)	8,43,000

24.C.5s (Owning Versus Hiring Decision) The 'Flagship' Exploration and Production Company Ltd (FEPC) has been hiring 'Pawan Hans' helicopters for its oil field, about 100 miles off the coast of Bombay, a collection of about 50 oil platforms, divided roughly into two groups: Bombay High North and Bombay High South. The movement of personnel between the platforms in each of these groups is managed by a radio operator who is centrally located. But three of these platforms are unmanned. The people who work on these platforms have to be flown out at the end of the day. After doing its rounds for the morning, the helicopter would return to the main platform. At lunch time, the helicopter it would fly lunch boxes to the crews working at the unmanned platforms. For the final sortie of the day, the radio operator would send instructions that would ensure that all the crews are returned safely to their home platforms before the chopper was released to return to the base for the night stay.

The hiring charges, including operation and maintenance charges, are ₹50,000 per hour. The records for the past two years show that, on an average, helicopters have been hired 30 hours a month. As per terms of the contract entered with '**Pawan Hans**', the company is required to pay for a minimum of 40 hours a month.

During a recent world summit, Mr Rajesh Dohare, the CEO of the FEPC had interaction with Mr Wealth Creator, the CEO of 'Global Helicorp', one of the leading helicopter companies of US which recently implemented an ERP package. 'Mr Wealth Creator' expressed his interest in offering helicopters to the FEPC for 2 million dollars. The salvage value will be 0.30 million dollars and they will buy back for that value at the end of its 8-year useful life. The foreign exchange rates as applicable are as follows: (i) Current rate, ₹45/$; (ii) Projected Rate (8 years later), ₹50/$. The insurance cost would be 1 per cent per annum while the annual operation and maintenance cost will be ₹30,00,000 during the first four years and ₹50,00,000 during the next four years.

The manpower requirement would be two pilots and two ground staff members. A pilot will be paid ₹50,000 per month while a ground staff will be paid ₹20,000 per month during the initial four years. After four years, there will be an increase of 10 per cent in the salary of all the four employees.

The CEO of the FEPC, Rajesh Dahare, has asked the CFO, A. Shantram to carry out a financial analysis of the two alternatives: (i) buy a helicopter and operate it in-house or (ii) continue hiring the helicopter from Pawan Hans and make a recommendation for his consideration. The result of the financial analysis carried out by the CFO are summarised below:

(A) Existing Arrangement (Hiring of Helicopter from Pawan Hans):
Total hiring charges: (₹50,000 per hour × 40 hours × 12 months) = ₹2,40,00,000.

(B) Proposed Scenario (Buy the Helicopter and Operate In-House):
Cost of helicopter: USD 2 million × ₹45 = ₹9,00,00,000
Salvage value at the end of 8-year life (USD 0.30 million × ₹50) = ₹1,50,00,000
Annual depreciation: (₹9,00,00,000 — ₹1,50,00,000) ÷ 8 = ₹93,75,000
Annual insurance cost (0.01 × ₹9,00,00,000) = ₹9,00,000
Running and Maintenance Cost: Year 1 — 4, ₹30,00,000 per year; Year 5 — 8 ₹50,00,000 per year.
Manpower Costs: (i) Year 1 — 4 [(2 pilots × ₹50,000) + (2 ground staff × ₹20,000)] × 12 months = ₹16,80,000 per year; (ii) Year 5 — 8 [(2 pilots × ₹55,000) + (2 ground staff × ₹22,000)] × 12 months = ₹18,48,000
Cost of capital: 15 per cent.

Summary of Costs

Particulars	*Year 1 – 4*	*Year 5 – 8*
Running and maintenance cost	₹30,00,000	₹50,00,000
Insurance cost	9,00,000	9,00,000
Manpower cost	16,80,000	18,48,000
Depreciation	93,75,000	93,75,000
	1,49,55,000	1,71,23,000

Determination of Net Cash Inflows

Particulars	*Year 1 – 4*	*Year 5 – 8*
Expenditure in existing arrangement (hiring of helicopter)	₹2,40,00,000	₹2,40,00,000
Less expenditure in alternative arrangement (buying of helicopter)	1,49,55,000	1,71,23,000
Savings (earnings before taxes)	90,45,000	68,77,000
Taxes (0.35)	31,65,750	24,06,950
Net savings (earnings after taxes)	58,79,250	44,70,050
Add depreciation	93,75,000	93,75,000
Net incremental ash inflows	1,52,54,250	1,38,45,050

Determination of Net Present Value (NPV)

Year	*CFAT*	*PV Factor (0.15)*	*Total PV*
1 – 4	₹1,52,54,250	2.855 (Table A-2)	₹4,35,50,884
5 – 8	1,38,45,050	1.632* (Table A-2)	2,25,95,122
8	1,50,00,000	0.327	49,05,000
Total present value			7,10,51,006
Less cash outflows			9,00,00,000
Net Present Value			(1,89,48,994)

*(PV of Annuity for 8 years — PV of annuity of 4 years, i.e., 4.487 — 2.855).

RECOMMENDATION Since the NPV of the proposal for buying a helicopter and operating it in-house is negative, it should not be acquired.

24.C.6 (Outsourcing) Sachin Yadav is working as a Senior Executive Vice President in the global telecom giant Kyunkia. Sachin heads the IPR (Intellectual Property Rights) division of the legal department of Kyunkia. The IPR division is responsible for creating and managing the intellectual properties of Kyunkia. Functionally, just like any other corporate department, the IPR division provides services to units of work. Sachin has his office in New York, the global headquarters of Kyunkia. Around 60 employees (mostly lawyers and attorneys) spread across the United States report directly/indirectly to Sachin. The CEO of Kyunkia, Haito Qian, trusts Sachin's capabilities in making smart moves.

Due to economic slowdown, there is huge pressure on the CEO to control costs and prevent possible losses. The CEO has passed the buck to Sachin to make a plan on how he can reduce costs of the entire corporate department starting from his own IPR division. After meeting with the CEO, Sachin goes deep in tizzy. He was planning an expansion of his department since the last several years. Over the years, Sachin has observed an increase in the work load on his subordinates. Recent attrition caused some work (320 workunits) to pile up and hiring (expansion) was inevitable. After a sleepless night, Sachin breaks open in front of his top team and communicates the CEO's message. Sachin delegates the job to Pankul Varma, a young employee who recently completed his executive MBA from a top business school. Sachin briefed Pankul on the situation and gave him directions to explore and study the financial aspects of the various proposals.

Proposal 1: Hire two attorneys in one of the regional offices in San Diego, US; 320 units of work are queued in the IPR division of Kyunkia. According to a conservative estimate, an attorney can finish around 60 units of work in a year. Sachin believes that due to economic slowdown the business units of Kyunkia would cut down their expenditures, and thus, the IPR division would be needed to provide lesser units of work/services in coming years. In line with this thought, Sachin believes that after hiring two attorneys, the work queue would become empty in three years. Some additional information available is: (1) labour cost (salary of an attorney), $120,000 per year, and (2) other costs, $25,000 per year.

Proposal 2: Outsource the piled up work to a well-established law firm, **Intellecta**, based in New York. The local law firm charges money on hourly basis. An attorney at Intellecta on an average spends 25 hours to finish one unit of work. After several rounds of negotiations, the local law firm has agreed to charge $275 per hour for the work-units outsourced from Kyunkia.

Proposal 3: Outsource the piled up work to a new and growing knowledge process outsourcing (KPO) firm, Lexolex in India. Sachin learnt about the cost advantage in outsourcing work to India after studying the success stories of the BPO's, KPO's and the LPO's in India. Considering Sachin as an attractive client, the management of Lexolex has agreed to charge $2,200 per unit of work.

Proposal 4: Opening a new regional office of Kyunkia in the NCR region of India and hiring 10 fresh engineers from top colleges in Northern India, training the engineers on IPR issues and getting the work output from the India team. It is estimated that an engineer would turn 7 work-units in the first year and 12 work-units in the second year. It is also estimated that from the third year the work-output per engineer would stabilise at around 15 work-units per year. Some additional information available is as follows:

1. Cost of new office (3,000 sq ft of space in an IT park)	₹2,10,00,000
2. Other fixed costs	20,00,000
3. Working capital requirement	5,00,000
4. Labour costs (salary of an engineer)	4,00,000
5. Variable costs per-unit work (IT resources needed for work, stationary items, etc.	2,000
6. Exchange rate for $:	
Present rate: ₹47	
One Year later: 48	
Two years later: 49	
Three years later: 50	

Pankul analysed all the proposals and submitted a financial report to Sachin in a week. Pankul's financial report is summarised below.

Analysis of Proposal 1 (Hiring Attorneys in the US)

Incremental labour costs per year ($ 120,000 × 2)	$ 240,000
Other annual incremental costs	25,000
Total	2,65,000
Total cost over a period of three years ($2,65,000 × 3)	7,95,000

Analysis of Proposal 2 (Outsourcing to a Local Law Firm in US)

Time taken to finish one unit of work (hours)	25
Time taken (hours) to finish 320 units of work (25 × 320)	8,000
Outsourcing cost per unit hour	$ 275
Total outsourcing cost (8,000 × $ 275)	2,200,000

Analysis of Proposal 3 (Outsourcing to a KPO in India)

Cost of per unit work	$2,200
Total outsourcing cost for 320 units of work (320 × $ 2,200)	7,04,000

Analysis of Proposal 4 (Setting Up Office in India)

1. Cash Outflows: (T = 0)	
(a) Cost of new office	₹2,10,00,000
(b) Office setup costs (other fixed costs)	20,00,000
(C) Working capital requirements	5,00,000
Total	2,35,00,000
2. During first year (T = 1)	41,40,000
Variable costs: [(₹4,00,000 × 10 engineers) + (₹2,000 × 7 work units × 10 engineers)]	
3. During second year (T = 2)	42,40,000
Variable costs: [(₹4,00,000 × 10 engineers) + (₹2,000 × 12 work units × 10 engineers)]	
4. During third year (T = 3)	43,00,000

Variable costs: [(₹4,00,000 × 10 engineers) + (₹2,000 × 15 work units × 10 engineers)]	43,00,000
Release of working capital	(5,00,000)
	38,00,000

Calculation of Present Value of Cash Outflows:

Time	*Cash Outflows*	*PV Factor at (0.14)*	*Present Value*
T = 0	₹2,35,00,000	1.000	₹2,35,00,000
Year 1	41,40,000	0.877	36,30,780
Year 2	42,40,000	0.769	32,60,560
Year 3	38,00,000	0.675	25,65,000
Total present value of cash outflows in $: [(2,35,00,000 + ₹47) + (36,30,780 ÷ 48) + (32,60,560 ÷ 49) + (25,65,000 ÷ 50)]			$6,93,483

RECOMMENDATION Proposal 4 is the best proposal. Haito Qian would be well advised to outsource the work by opening an office in India.

APPENDIX 24A

TIME VALUE OF MONEY

The objective of this appendix is to provide a synoptic profile of time value of money/mathematics of finance so that you can comprehend DCF methods of capital budgeting decisions better. For easy understanding, the subject-matter has been explained with the help of simple examples/ illustrations.

Suppose an investor is offered a choice to have ₹1,00,000 today (technically referred to as time (t) zero period) or ₹1,00,000 after one year (year-end 1), which choice will you exercise? Obviously, the investor would opt for the first choice of receiving ₹1,00,000 today. The reason is very simple; ₹1,00,000 today will compound to more than ₹1,00,000 after one year on account of reinvestment opportunity for funds. Let us suppose, that he can deposit this sum of ₹1,00,000 with commercial bank for one year at 10 per cent rate of interest. ₹1,00,000 sum will compound to ₹1,10,000 at the year-end 1 [₹1,00,000 (1 + 0.1)].

As a logical corollary of the above follows that there is a time value of money, i.e. a rupee received ***today*** is worth more than a rupee received in ***future***. In other words, value of a rupee received in **future** is less than a value of a rupee received **today**. For this reason, ***there is a preference for current receipts to future receipts***. Viewed from the business perspective, the future cash inflows are less valuable than the present cash inflows.

Given 10 per cent as a compound rate of interest, an investor will be indifferent if the choice is to receive ₹1,00,000 (at $t = 0$) or ₹1,10,000 at year-end 1 (at $t = 1$). Let us extend this example further. Investor is now given an option to have ₹1,00,000 at $t = 0$ or to have ₹1,20,000 at year-end 2. Is he indifferent between the two options? No, he will prefer to receive ₹1,00,000 today as this sum can be compounded to ₹1,21,000 at year-end 2 as shown by Equation 24A.1.

$$P(1 + i)^n = A \qquad (24A.1)$$

Where P is the principal sum invested today;

i = Interest rate;

n = Number of years;

₹1,00,000 $(1 + 0.1)^2$ = ₹1,21,000

Suppose, investor was having a choice to receive ₹1,25,000 at year-end 2 or ₹1,00,000 at $t = 0$. Obviously, he should prefer the option of receiving money at year-end 2 (as ₹1,00,000 will compound to ₹1,21,000 only at year-end 2 @ 10 per cent compound rate of interest as shown above). In operational terms, the present value (at $t = 0$) of ₹1,25,000 received at year-end 2 is more than ₹1,00,000.

It is useful to know how present value of the future sum is determined. The process is simple. The present value (PV) is simply the reverse of compounding. Being so, the equation 24A.1 ($P(1 + i)^n = A$) which is used for compounding the sum can be readily transformed into a PV formula. Now P is the sum to be determined given other values, value of P is given by equation 24A.2.

$$P = \frac{A}{(1+i)^n} \qquad (24A.2)$$

where P = Present value of the future sum (say CFAT) to be received
A = Future sum (say CFAT) to be received.
i = Interest rate
n = Number of years

Accordingly,

$$P = \frac{₹1,25,000}{(1+0.1)^2} = \frac{₹1,25,000}{1.21} = ₹1,03,305.79$$

In simple terms, the PV (at t = 0) of ₹1,25,000 (received at year-end 2) is ₹1,03,305.79. Evidently, it is greater than ₹1,00,000.

It is important for you to note that the PV is just the reciprocal of compounding value. Let us illustrate, ₹1 compounds (at the interest rate of 10 per cent to ₹1.10 at year-end 1, ₹1.21 at year-end 2, ₹1.331 at year-end 3 and so on. The PV of these compounded sums (in terms of ₹ one) is shown in Table 24A-1.

TABLE 24A-1 Present value of one ₹ received in years 1, 2, 3

Year-end	*Compounded sum of one ₹*	*Present value of one ₹*
1	₹1.10	1/1.10 = ₹0.909
2	1.21	1/1.21 = 0.826
3	1.331	1/1.31 = 0.751

The value ₹0.909 implies that the PV of one ₹ received at year-end 1 is ₹0.909 (at t = 0); likewise, the PV of 1 ₹ received at year-end 2 and year-end 3 are ₹0.826 and ₹0.751 respectively.

The present values (more popularly known as the present value interest factor, PVIF) are readily available for various ranges of interest rates (i) and time period (n). Table A-1 (provided in Appendix at the end of book) contains the PVIF for interest rates (also known as discount rates) upto 20 per cent for a period upto 50 years.

Since Table A-1 enumerates the PVIF for the various combination of i and n, the PV of the future sums (CFAT) can be readily determined multiplying future sum with the appropriate PVIF. Symbolically,

$$\text{PV} = \text{Future sum, A } (\times) \text{ PVIF} \tag{24A.3}$$

There is an immense use of the PVIF (as shown by the present value table A-1) in the capital budgeting decisions as such decisions involve the current cash outflows in expectations of future benefits (measured in terms of CFAT) during its useful life. Since, CFAT are available to the firm in several future years (1, 2, 3, ... n), they certainly cannot be added as they have different values (₹1,00,000 received at year-end 3 has not the same value as ₹1,00,000 received at year-end 1). There is a need to determine the PV of all these future cash flows (CFAT) at time zero period so that the benefits can then be compared with cash outflows (investment outlays) made at time zero period. Consider Example 24A-1.

◆ Example 24A-1

A firm is contemplating to buy a machine for ₹25,00,000; it is expected to generate cash inflows after taxes (CFAT) in subsequent 5 years as follows:

Year 1	₹6,00,000
Year 2	8,00,000
Year 3	11,00,000
Year 4	9,00,000
Year 5	8,00,000

(i) Determine the present value, assume 10 per cent as cost of capital (ii) determine the NPV.

Solution

TABLE 24A-2 Determination of present value and net present value

Year-end	*CFAT*	*PVIF at 10 per cent as per Table A-1*	*Total PV (CFAT × PVIF)*
1	₹6,00,000	0.909	₹5,45,400
2	8,00,000	0.826	6,60,800
3	11,00,000	0.751	8,26,100
4	9,00,000	0.683	6,14,700
5	8,00,000	0.621	4,96,800
(i) Total present value (GPV)			31,43,800
Less cost of machine/cash outflows			25,00,000
(ii) Net present value (NPV)			6,43,800

Will the GPV / NPV decrease / increase if the cost of capital is higher than 10 per cent (say 12 per cent)? Obviously, it will decrease. It is apparent that the higher interest/discount rate will obviously cause the lower PV. It is very apparent from the perusal of equation 24A.2; the discount rate is denominator; higher is the denominator, lower is the PV. As a result, the PVIFs (at 12 per cent) are lower than the PVIFs (at 10 per cent) as shown in Table 24A-3.

TABLE 24A-3 PVIF at 12 per cent and 10 per cent (for t = 1 – 5 years)

Year-end	*1*	*2*	*3*	*4*	*5*
PVIF (at 0.12)	0.893	0.797	0.712	0.636	0.567
PVIF (at 0.10)	0.909	0.826	0.751	0.683	0.621

It may be noted that higher is the interest rate/discount rate/cost of capital, lower is the PVIF. Likewise, cash inflows received in more distant years will have the lower PVIF than the cash inflows received relatively in earlier years (due to reinvestment opportunity of existing funds). This is very apparent from the various PVIFs contained in Table 24A-3. For these simple reasons, the PVIFs shown in Table 24A-1 (present value of Re 1) are in decreasing order both row-wise and column-wise.

In the case of equal cash inflows (known as annuity) to be received in future, the determination of PV/NPV becomes a very simple exercise. Consider Example 24A-2.

◆ Example 24A-2

A company is contemplating to invest ₹25,00,000 in buying a new machine. It is expected to provide CFAT of ₹8,00,000 per year for next 5 years Assuming cost of capital of 13%, determine the NPV.

TABLE 24A-4 NPV at 13 per cent cost of capital/discount rate

Year-end	*CFAT*	*PVIF at 0.13*	*Total PV*
1	₹8,00,000	0.885	₹7,08,000
2	8,00,000	0.783	6,26,400
3	8,00,000	0.693	5,54,400
4	8,00,000	0.613	4,90,400
5	8,00,000	0.543	4,34,400
Gross present value (GPV)		3.517	28,13,600
Less cash outflows			25,00,000
Net present value (NPV)			3,13,600

Table 24A-4 contains the long way of determining the PV of annuity cash flows. There is a potential of reducing calculations to a marked extent; ₹8,00,000 is a common factor; each time PVIF is to be multiplied by the uniform sum of ₹8,00,000. Instead of this exercise of multiplication repeated each time (5 times in Table 24.4); only one multiplication exercise can be adequate enough to provide PV of annuity of ₹8,00,000 (for a period of 5 years). The following paragraph provides explanation for the same.

The sum of PVIFs at 0.13 for 5 years is 3.517. It implies that one rupee received at the end of each of next 5 years will have PV of 3.517. Therefore, total present value of ₹8,00,000 received at the end of each year for next 5 years will be ₹28,13,600 (₹8,00,000 x 3.517 PVIF of annuity of ₹1 for 5 years at 0.13). The answer is the same.

It is useful to note that ready-made calculations are available in Table A-2 (Appendix) in this regard (present value of annuity of ₹1, given at the end of book). This table presents the sum of the present values of an annuity (PVIFA) for the wide range of interest rate, *i* (from 1 per cent to 20 per cent) and the number of years, *n* (from year 1 to 50). In view of the function PVIFA serves, it can also be referred to as annuity discount factor (ADF); let us interpret 3.517 in the sense of ADF. It implies the discounted value (present value) of one rupee received at the end of each year for the next 5 years is ₹3.517.

Since, such calculations are readily available in Table A-2 (please find on your own ADF of ₹1 for 5 years at 13% from Table A-2; it will be 3.517), the NPV of future annuity CFAT can be more easily computed. Let us determine PV/NPV of Example 24A-2 as per Table A-2.

TABLE 24A-5 Determination of NPV (as per annuity table)

Year-end	*CFAT*	*PVIF at 0.13*	*Total PV*
1-5	₹8,00,000	3.517	₹28,13,600
	Less cash outflows		25,00,000
	Net present value (NPV)		3,13,600

Note: Annuity table can be used only when cash inflows are uniform in all the years.

Appendices

TABLE A-1 The Present Value of One Rupee

Year	*1%*	*2%*	*3%*	*4%*	*5%*	*6%*	*7%*	*8%*	*9%*	*10%*
1	.990	.980	.971	.962	.952	.943	.935	.926	.917	.909
2	.980	.961	.943	.925	.907	.890	.873	.857	.842	.826
3	.971	.942	.915	.889	.864	.840	.816	.794	.772	.751
4	.961	.924	.888	.855	.823	.792	.763	.735	.708	.683
5	.951	.906	.863	.822	.784	.747	.713	.681	.650	.621
6	.942	.888	.837	.790	.746	.705	.666	.630	.596	.564
7	.933	.871	.813	.760	.711	.665	.623	.583	.547	.513
8	.923	.853	.789	.731	.677	.627	.582	.540	.502	.467
9	.914	.837	.766	.703	.645	.592	.544	.500	.460	.424
10	.905	.820	.744	.676	.614	.558	.508	.463	.422	.386
11	.896	.804	.722	.650	.585	.527	.475	.429	.388	.350
12	.887	.789	.701	.625	.557	.497	.444	.397	.356	.319
13	.879	.773	.681	.601	.530	.469	.415	.368	.326	.290
14	.870	.758	.661	.577	.505	.442	.388	.340	.299	.263
15	.861	.743	.642	.555	.481	.417	.362	.315	.275	.239
16	.853	.728	.623	.534	.458	.394	.339	.292	.252	.218
17	.844	.714	.605	.513	.436	.371	.317	.270	.231	.198
18	.836	.700	.587	.494	.416	.350	.296	.250	.212	.180
19	.828	.686	.570	.475	.396	.331	.227	.232	.194	.164
20	.820	.673	.554	.456	.377	.312	.258	.215	.178	.149
21	.811	.660	.538	.439	.359	.294	.242	.199	.164	.135
22	.803	.647	.522	.422	.342	.278	.226	.184	.150	.123
23	.795	.634	.507	.406	.326	.262	.211	.170	.138	.112
24	.788	.622	.492	.390	.310	.247	.197	.158	.126	.102
25	.780	.610	.478	.375	.295	.233	.184	.146	.116	.092
30	.742	.552	.412	.308	.231	.174	.131	.099	.075	.057
35	.706	.500	.355	.253	.181	.130	.094	.068	.049	.036
40	.672	.453	.307	.208	.142	.097	.067	.046	.032	.022
45	.639	.410	.264	.171	.111	.073	.048	.031	.021	.014
50	.806	.372	.228	.141	.087	.054	.034	.021	.013	.009

(Contd.)

TABLE A-1 The Present Value of One Rupee *(Contd.)*

Year	*11%*	*12%*	*13%*	*14%*	*15%*	*16%*	*17%*	*18%*	*19%*	*20%*
1	.901	.893	.885	.877	.870	.862	.855	.847	.840	.833
2	.812	.797	.783	.769	.756	.743	.731	.718	.706	.694
3	.731	.712	.693	.675	.658	.641	.624	.609	.593	.579
4	.659	.636	.613	.592	.572	.552	.534	.516	.499	.482
5	.593	.567	.543	.519	.497	.476	.456	.437	.419	.402
6	.535	.507	.480	.456	.432	.410	.390	.370	.352	.335
7	.482	.452	.425	.400	.376	.354	.333	.314	.296	.279
8	.434	.404	.376	.351	.327	.305	.285	.266	.249	.233
9	.391	.361	.333	.308	.284	.263	.243	.225	.209	.194
10	.352	.322	.295	.270	.247	.227	.208	.191	.176	.162
11	.317	.287	.261	.237	.215	.195	.178	.162	.148	.135
12	.286	.257	.231	.208	.187	.168	.152	.137	.124	.112
13	.258	.229	.204	.182	.163	.145	.130	.116	.104	.093
14	.232	.205	.181	.160	.141	.125	.111	.099	.088	.078
15	.209	.183	.160	.140	.123	.108	.095	.084	.074	.065
16	.188	.163	.141	.123	.107	.093	.081	.071	.062	.054
17	.170	.146	.125	.108	.093	.080	.069	.060	.052	.045
18	.153	.130	.111	.095	.081	.069	.059	.051	.044	.038
19	.138	.116	.098	.083	.070	.060	.051	.043	.037	.031
20	.124	.104	.087	.073	.061	.051	.043	.037	.031	.026
21	.112	.093	.077	.064	.053	.044	.037	.031	.026	.022
22	.101	.083	.068	.056	.046	.038	.032	.026	.022	.018
23	.091	.074	.060	.049	.040	.033	.027	.022	.018	.015
24	.082	.066	.053	.043	.035	.028	.023	.019	.015	.013
25	.074	.059	.047	.038	.030	.024	.020	.016	.013	.010
30	.044	.033	.026	.020	.015	.012	.009	.007	.005	.004
35	.026	.019	.014	.010	.008	.006	.004	.003	.002	.002
40	.015	.011	.008	.005	.004	.003	.002	.001	.001	.001
45	.009	.006	.004	.003	.002	.001	.001	.001	.000	.000
50	.005	.003	.002	.001	.001	.001	.000	.000	.000	.000

Table A-2 The Present Value of an Annuity of One Rupee

Year	1%	2%	3%	4%	5%	6%	7%	8%	9%	10%
1	.990	.980	.971	.962	.952	.943	.935	.926	.917	.909
2	1.970	1.942	1.913	1.886	1.859	1.833	1.808	1.783	1.759	1.736
3	2.941	2.884	2.829	2.775	2.723	2.673	2.624	2.577	2.531	2.487
4	3.902	3.808	3.717	3.630	3.546	3.465	3.387	3.312	3.240	3.170
5	4.853	4.713	4.580	4.452	4.329	4.212	4.100	3.993	3.890	3.791
6	5.795	5.601	5.417	5.242	5.076	4.917	4.767	4.623	4.486	4.355
7	6.728	6.472	6.230	6.002	5.786	5.582	5.389	5.206	5.033	4.868
8	7.652	7.326	7.020	6.733	6.463	6.210	5.971	5.747	5.535	5.335
9	8.566	8.162	7.786	7.435	7.108	6.802	6.515	6.247	5.995	5.759
10	9.471	8.983	8.530	8.111	7.722	7.360	7.024	6.710	6.418	6.145
11	10.368	9.787	9.253	8.760	8.306	7.887	7.499	7.139	6.805	6.495
12	11.255	10.575	9.954	9.385	8.863	8.384	7.943	7.536	7.161	6.814
13	12.134	11.348	10.635	9.986	9.394	8.853	8.358	7.904	7.487	7.103
14	13.004	12.106	11.296	10.563	9.899	9.295	8.746	8.244	7.786	7.367
15	13.865	12.849	11.938	11.118	10.380	9.712	9.108	8.560	8.061	7.606
16	14.718	13.578	12.561	11.652	10.838	10.106	9.447	8.851	8.313	7.824
17	15.562	14.292	13.166	12.166	11.274	10.477	9.763	9.122	8.544	8.022
18	16.398	14.992	13.754	12.659	11.690	10.828	10.059	9.372	8.756	8.201
19	17.226	15.679	14.324	13.134	12.085	11.158	10.336	9.604	8.950	8.365
20	18.046	16.352	14.878	13.590	12.462	11.470	10.594	9.818	9.129	8.514
21	18.857	17.011	15.415	14.029	12.821	11.764	10.836	10.017	9.292	8.649
22	19.661	17.658	15.937	14.451	13.163	12.042	11.061	10.201	9.442	8.772
23	20.456	18.292	16.444	14.857	13.489	12.303	11.272	10.371	9.580	8.883
24	21.244	18.914	16.936	15.247	13.799	12.550	11.469	10.529	9.707	8.985
25	22.023	19.524	17.413	15.622	14.094	12.783	11.654	10.675	9.823	9.077
30	25.808	22.397	19.601	17.292	15.373	13.765	12.409	11.258	10.274	9.427
35	29.409	24.999	21.487	18.665	16.374	14.498	12.948	11.655	10.567	9.644
40	32.835	27.356	23.115	19.793	17.159	15.046	12.332	11.925	10.757	9.779
45	36.095	29.490	24.519	20.720	17.774	15.456	13.606	12.108	10.881	9.863
50	39.197	31.424	25.730	21.482	18.256	15.762	13.801	12.234	10.962	9.915

(Contd.)

TABLE A-2 The Present Value of an Annuity of One Rupee *(Contd.)*

Year	11%	12%	13%	14%	15%	16%	17%	18%	19%	20%
1	.901	.893	.885	.877	.870	.862	.855	.847	.850	.833
2	1.713	1.690	1.668	1.647	1.626	1.605	1.585	1.566	1.547	1.528
3	2.444	2.402	2.361	2.322	2.283	2.246	2.210	2.174	2.140	2.106
4	3.102	3.037	2.974	2.914	2.855	2.798	2.743	2.690	2.639	2.589
5	3.696	3.605	3.517	3.433	3.352	3.274	3.199	3.127	3.058	2.991
6	4.231	4.111	3.998	3.889	3.784	3.685	3.589	3.498	3.410	3.326
7	4.712	4.564	4.423	4.288	4.160	4.039	3.922	3.812	3.706	3.605
8	5.146	4.968	4.799	4.639	4.487	4.344	4.207	4.078	3.954	3.837
9	5.537	5.328	5.132	4.946	4.772	4.607	4.451	4.303	4.163	4.031
10	5.889	5.650	5.426	5.216	5.019	4.833	4.659	4.494	4.339	4.192
11	6.207	5.938	5.687	5.453	5.234	5.029	4.836	4.656	4.487	4.327
12	6.492	6.194	5.918	5.660	5.421	5.197	4.988	4.793	4.611	4.439
13	6.750	6.424	6.122	5.842	5.583	5.342	5.118	4.910	4.715	4.533
14	6.982	6.628	5.303	6.002	5.724	5.468	5.229	5.008	4.802	4.611
15	7.191	6.811	6.462	6.142	5.847	5.575	5.324	5.092	4.876	4.675
16	7.379	6.974	6.604	6.265	5.954	5.669	5.405	5.162	4.938	4.730
17	7.549	7.120	6.729	6.373	6.047	5.749	5.475	5.222	4.990	4.775
18	7.702	7.250	6.840	6.467	6.128	5.818	5.534	5.273	5.033	4.812
19	7.839	7.366	6.938	6.550	6.198	5.877	5.585	5.316	5.070	4.843
20	7.963	7.469	7.024	6.623	6.259	5.929	5.628	5.353	5.101	4.870
21	8.075	7.562	7.102	6.687	6.312	5.973	5.665	5.384	5.127	4.891
22	8.176	7.645	7.170	6.743	6.359	6.011	5.696	5.410	5.149	4.909
23	8.266	7.718	7.230	6.792	6.399	6.044	6.723	5.432	5.167	4.925
24	8.348	7.784	7.283	6.835	6.434	6.073	5.747	5.451	5.182	4.937
25	8.422	7.843	7.330	6.873	6.464	6.097	5.766	5.467	5.195	4.948
30	8.694	8.055	7.496	7.003	6.566	6.177	5.829	5.517	5.235	4.979
35	8.855	8.176	7.586	7.070	6.617	6.215	5.858	5.539	5.251	4.992
40	8.951	8.244	7.634	7.105	6.642	6.233	5.871	5.548	5.258	4.997
45	9.008	8.283	7.661	7.123	6.654	6.242	5.877	5.552	5.261	4.999
50	9.042	8.305	7.675	7.133	6.661	6.246	5.880	5.554	5.262	4.999

Select Bibliography

Anderson, D.L. and D.L. Raun, *Information Analysis in Management Accounting* (Santa Barbara, John Wiley), 1978.

Anderson, W.T., C.A. Moyer and A.R. Wyatt, (Ed.), *Accounting: Basic Financial, Cost and Control Concepts* (New York John Wiley), 1965.

Anthony, R.N., *Management Accounting—Text and Cases* (Illinois, Irwin), 1970.

—, *Accounting: Text and Cases* (New Delhi, Tata McGraw-Hill), 1995

— and J. Dearden, *Management Control Systems: Text and Cases* (Illinois, Irwin), 1980.

— and V. Govindarajan, *Management Control Systems,* (New Delhi, Tata McGraw-Hill), 1998.

— and J.S. Reece, *Management Accounting Principles,* (Delhi, A.I.T.B.S. Publishers & Distributors), 2005.

— and R.E. Herzlinger, *Management Control in Non-Profit Organisations* (Illinois, Irwin), 1980.

— and G.A. Welsch, *Fundamentals of Management Accounting,* (Illinois, Irwin), 1981.

Anthony, R.N., Hawkins, D.F. and Merchant, K., *Accounting: Text and Cases* (New Delhi, Tata McGraw-Hill Publishing Co.), 2005.

Baxter, W.T. and S. Davidson (Eds.), *Studies in Accounting, (London, England Institute of Chartered Accountants),* 1977.

Bierman, H., Jr. and A.R. Drebin, *Management Accounting,* (New York, Macmillan), 1976.

Bierman, H., Jr and S. Smidt, *The Capital Budgeting Decision,* (London, Macmillan), 1975.

Boer, G., *Direct Cost and Contribution Accounting,* (London, John Wiley), 1974.

Brown, J.L., and L.R. Howard, *Principles and Practice of Management Accountancy,* (London, English Language Book Society), 1975.

Brown, R.G., *Decision Rules for Inventory Management,* (New York, Holt, Rinehart and Winston), 1963.

Bruns, W.J. and D.T. Decoster, *Accounting and Its Behavioural Implications,* (New York, McGraw-Hill), 1969.

Bull, R.J., *Accounting in Business,* (London, Butterworths), 1980.

Chatfield, M. and D. Neilson, *Cost Accounting,* (New York, Harcourt Brace Jovanovich, Inc.) 1983.

Copeland, R.M. and P.E. Dascher, *Management Accounting,* (New York, John Wiley), 1978.

Crowningshield, G.R. and K.A. Gorman, *Cost Accounting: Principles and Managerial Applications,* (Boston, Houghton Mifflin Company), 1979.

Cushing, B.E., *Accounting Information Systems and Business Organisation*, (London, Addison Wesley), 1978.

Davidson, S. and R.L. Weil (Eds.) *Handbook of Modern Accounting*, (New York, McGraw-Hill), 1977.

—, *Handbook of Cost Accounting*, (New York, McGraw-Hill), 1978.

Dearden, J., *Cost Accounting and Financial Control Systems*, (California, Addison-Wesley Pub. Co.), 1976.

Dearden, J. and J. Shank, *Financial Accounting and Reporting*, (New Jersey, Prentice-Hall), 1975.

Decoster, D.T. and E.L. Schafer, *Management Accounting: A Decision Emphasis*, (New York, John Wiley), 1979.

Fertig, P. and Others, *Using Accounting Information: An Introduction*, (New York, Harcourt), 1971.

Foulke, R.A., *Practical Financial Statement Analysis*, (Illinois, Irwin), 1976.

Garrison, R.H. *Management Accounting, Concepts for Planning, Control, and Decision Making*, (Business Publishers, Texas), 1976.

Garrison, R.H. and Eric Noreen, *Managerial Accounting*, (New York, McGraw-Hill), 1997.

Gibbs, G., *Accounting for Management Decisions*, (Scranton, International Textbook), 1968.

Gordon, M.J. and G. Shillinglow, *Accounting: A Management Approach*, (Illinois, Irwin), 1974.

Greener, M., *Between the Lines of the Balance Sheet*, (London, Pergamon Press), 1968.

Hartley, R.V., *Cost and Managerial Accounting*, (Boston, Allyn and Bacon, Inc.), 1983.

Helfert, E.H., *Techniques for Financial Analysis*, (Illinois, Irwin), 1997.

Horngren, C.T., *Accounting for Management Control*, (New Jersey, Prentice-Hall), 1978.

—, *Cost Accounting: A Managerial Emphasis*, (New Delhi, Prentice-Hall), 1997.

Horngren, C.T., Datar, S.M. and Foster, G. *Cost Accounting—A Managerial Emphasis* (New Delhi, Pearson Education), 2013.

Horngren, C.T. and G.L. Sundlem, *Introduction to Management Accounting*, (New Delhi, Prentice-Hall), 1990.

Institute of Chartered Accountants, *Standard Costing: An Introduction to the Accounting Processes*, (London), 1956.

Institute of Chartered Accountants in England and Wales, *Recommendations on Accounting Principles*, 1975.

James, J., *Managerial Accounting* (Singapore, John Wiley & Sons), 2004.

Kaplan, R.S., *Advanced Management Accounting*, (New Delhi, Prentice-Hall), 1988.

Keith, L., *Accountancy: A Management Perspective*, (Englewood Cliffs, Prentice-Hall), 1980.

Khan M.Y. and P.K. Jain, *Financial Management, Fourth Edition*, (New Delhi, Tata McGraw-Hill), 2004.

Laidler, E., *Variance Accounting*, (London, Mcmillan), 1976.

Matz, A. and M.F. Usry, *Cost Accounting: Planning and Control*, (Ohio, South Western Publishing Company), 1976.

Maner, M.W., *Cost Accounting*, (New York, McGraw-Hill), 1997.

Meigs, R.F., *Accounting: The Basis for Business Decisions*, (McGraw-Hill, New York), 1996.

Metcalf, R.W. and P.L. Titard, *Principles of Accounting*, (Philadelphia, W.B. Saunder), 1976.

Moore, C.L. and R.K., Jaedicke, *Managerial Accounting*, (New York, South Western Publishing Company), 1976.

Morse, D., Managerial Accounting, (New York, McGraw-Hill), 1997.

Moscove, S.A. *et. al.*, *Cost Accounting-with Managerial Applications* (Boston, Houghton Mifflin Company), 1985.

Mariarity, S. and C.P. Allen, *Cost Accounting* (New York, Haper and Row), 1984.

Mayer, J.N., *Financial Statement Analysis*, (New Jersey, Prentice-Hall), 1969.

National Association of Accountants, *Statement on Management Accounting Practices*, (New York, NAA), 1971.

—, *Managing the Cash Flow*, 1974.

—, *Developing and Reporting of Variances,* 1962.
—, *Direct Costing,* 1953.
—, *Separating and Using Costs as Fixed and Variable, 1960.*
—, *Applications of Direct Costing,* 1961.
—, *Cost-Volume-Profit Relationships,* 1962.
—, *Accounting for Costs of Capacity,* 1963.
—, *Product Costs for Pricing Purposes,* 1953.
—, *Analysis of Non-manufacturing Costs for Managerial Decisions,* 1951.
Osteryoung, J.S., *Capital Budgeting: Long-term Asset Selection,* (Columbus, Ohio, Grid), 1979.
Pierce, G.J., *Measurement of Capital Employed* (London, Business Books), 1972.
Rayburn, L.G., *Principles of Cost Accounting: Managerial Applications,* (Homewood, Illinois, Irwin), 1983.
Shillinglow, G., *Managerial Cost Accounting,* (Illinois, Irwin), 1977.
—, *Cost Accounting: Analysis and Control,* (Illinois, Irwin), 1967.
Stice, E.K., Stice J.D. and Diamond, M.A., *Financial Accounting* (South-Western, Thomson), 2003.
Thacker, R.J., *Introduction to Modern Accounting,* (New Jersey, Prentice-Hall), 1977.
— and R.L. Smith, *Modern Management Accounting,* (Reston, Reston Publishing Company), 1977.
Tracy, J.F., *Fundamentals of Management Accounting,* (New York, John Wiley), 1976.
Weygandt, J.J., Kieso, D.E. and Kimmel, P.D., *Financial Accounting* (Singapore, John Wiley & Sons), 2003.
Willsmore, A.W., *Accounting for Management Control,* (London, Pitman), 1971.
Williams, J.R., Haka, S.F., Bettner, M.S. and Meigs, R.F., *Financial and Managerial Accounting,* (New Delhi, Tata McGraw-Hill Publishing Co. Ltd.), 2004.
Woelfel, C.J., *Accounting: An Introduction,* (California, Goodyear Publishing Company), 1977.
Wood, F., *Business Accounting,* (London, English Language Book Society and Longman Group), 1979.
Zimmerman, J., *Accounting for Decision Making and Control,* (New York, McGraw-Hill), 1997.

Index